THE ONTARIO HISTORICAL STUDIES SERIES

The Ontario Historical Studies Series is a comprehensive history of Ontario from 1791 to the present, which will include several biographies of former premiers, numerous volumes on the economic, social, political, and cultural development of the province, and a general history incorporating the insights and conclusions of the other works in the series. The purpose of the series is to enable general readers and scholars to understand better the distinctive features of Ontario as one of the principal regions within Canada.

Researchers, teachers, and students will welcome this comprehensive new bibliography of printed materials relating to the history of Ontario since 1867. The work is a revised, updated, and greatly expanded version of *Ontario since 1867: A Bibliography,* published in 1973 by the Ministry of Colleges and Universities. It lists some 15,000 bibliographies, monographs, pamphlets, periodical articles, and theses dealing with the history of the province, including library locations for each. The items are arranged in four broad categories: economic, social, political, and cultural and intellectual history. An index of authors, titles, and subjects is included.

This massive and important reference provides a new starting point for the study of most aspects of Ontario's history as a province.

OLGA B. BISHOP is Professor Emeritus in the Faculty of Library Science at the University of Toronto. She has published two bibliographies of government documents.

BARBARA I. IRWIN is a reference librarian in the Science and Technology Division of the Metropolitan Central Library, Toronto.

CLARA G. MILLER, now retired, was formerly chief librarian of Imperial Oil Limited in Toronto.

OLGA B. BISHOP

assisted by
BARBARA I. IRWIN
CLARA G. MILLER

Bibliography of Ontario History 1867-1976 Cultural, Economic, Political, Social

VOLUME I

A project of the Ontario Historical Studies Series
for the Government of Ontario
Published by University of Toronto Press
Toronto Buffalo London

Canadian Cataloguing in Publication Data

Bishop, Olga B., 1911-
    Bibliography of Ontario history, 1867-1976
    (Ontario historical studies series ISSN 0380-9188)
    Second, enlarged and updated, edition of Ontario
    since 1867 : a bibliography.
    Includes index.
    ISBN 0-8020-2359-2 (set)

    1. Ontario - History - Bibliography.   I. Irwin, Barbara I. II. Miller, Clara G. III.
Title. IV. Title: Ontario since 1867 : a bibliography. V. Series.

Z1392.06B57   016.9713   c80-094196-9

Contents

The Ontario Historical Studies Series

When discussions about this series of books first arose, it was immediately apparent that very little work had been done on the history of Ontario. Ontario has many fine historians, but much of their work has been focused on national themes, despite the fact that the locus of many of the important developments in the history of Canada – as recent events remind us – was, and is, in the provinces. While other provinces have recognized this reality and have recorded their histories in permanent form, Ontario is singularly lacking in definitive works about its own distinctive history.

Thus, when the Ontario Historical Studies Series was formally established by Order-in-Council on 14 April 1971, the Board of Trustees was instructed not only to produce authoritative and readable biographies of Ontario premiers but also 'to ensure that a comprehensive program of research and writing in Ontario history is carried out.'

From the outset the Board has included both professional historians and interested and knowledgeable citizens. The present members are: Margaret Angus, Kingston; J.M.S. Careless, Toronto; Floyd S. Chalmers, Toronto; R.E.G. Davis, Toronto; Gaetan Gervais, Sudbury; D.F. McOuat, Toronto; Jacqueline Neatby, Ottawa; J. Keith Reynolds, Toronto; and J.J. Talman, London. E.E. Stewart and Raymond Labarge served as valued members of the Board in its formative period. The combination of varied interests and skills of Board members has proven useful. A consensus was soon reached on the need for research in neglected areas of Ontario history and for scholarly and well-written works that would be of interest and value to the people of Ontario. We trust our work will satisfy these criteria.

After much careful deliberation the Board settled on six major areas in which to pursue its objectives: biographies of premiers; a bibliography; a historical atlas; a group of theme studies on major developments (social, economic, and cultural as well as political) in the province; the recording on tape of the attitudes, opinions, and memories of many important leaders in Ontario; and, as a culmination of these studies, a definitive history of Ontario.

The first edition of the bibliography was published in [1974]. Our first major publication was the biography of G. Howard Ferguson by Peter Oliver (1977). This was followed in 1978 by *Ontario since 1867*, a general history of the province by Joseph Schull. The *Bibliography of Ontario History, 1867-1976*, by Olga Bishop, is a revised and enlarged version of the original bibliography. We believe that it will be a valuable guide to the study of all aspects of the history of the province.

The Board has been heavily dependent upon its two editors, Goldwin S. French, Editor-in-Chief, and Peter N. Oliver, Associate Editor. Both men have served the Board with diligence and devotion and we are greatly indebted to

them for the refinement of topics and the selection of authors for the many
projects we have undertaken.

Murray G. Ross
Chairman, Board of Trustees
Ontario Historical Studies Series

Toronto
1 December 1979

For many years the principal theme in English-Canadian historical writing has
been the emergence and the consolidation of the Canadian nation. This theme
has been developed in uneasy awareness of the persistence and importance of
regional interests and identities, but because of the central role of Ontario in the
growth of Canada, Ontario has not been seen as a region. Almost
unconsciously, historians have equated the history of the province with that of
the nation and have depicted the interests of other regions as obstacles to the
unity and welfare of Canada.

The creation of the province of Ontario in 1867 was the visible embodiment
of a formidable reality, the existence at the core of the new nation of a powerful
if disjointed society whose traditions and characteristics differed in many
respects from those of the other British North American colonies. The
intervening century has not witnessed the assimilation of Ontario to the other
regions in Canada; on the contrary it has become a more clearly articulated
entity. Within the formal geographical and institutional framework defined so
assiduously by Ontario's political leaders, an increasingly intricate web of
economic and social interests has been woven and shaped by the dynamic
interplay between Toronto and its hinterland. The character of this regional
community has been formed in the tension between a rapid adaptation to the
processes of modernization and industrialization in modern Western society
and a reluctance to modify or discard traditional attitudes and values. Not
surprisingly, the Ontario outlook is a compound of aggressiveness,
conservatism, and the conviction that its values should be the model for the rest
of Canada.

The purpose of the Ontario Historical Studies Series is to describe and
analyse the historical development of Ontario as a distinct region within
Canada. The Series as planned will include approximately thirty-four volumes
covering many aspects of the life and work of the province from its original
establishment in 1791 as Upper Canada to our own time. Among these will be
biographies of several prominent political figures, a three-volume economic
history, numerous works on such topics as social structure, education, minority
groups, labour, political and administrative institutions, literature, theatre, and
the arts, and a comprehensive synthesis of the history of Ontario, based upon
the detailed contributions of the biographies and thematic studies.

In planning this project, the Editors have encouraged the Board to maintain a reasonable balance between different kinds and areas of historical research, and to appoint authors ready to ask new kinds of questions about the past and to answer them in accordance with the canons of contemporary scholarship. Ten biographical studies have been included, if only because through biography the past comes alive most readily for the general reader as well as the historian. The historian must be sensitive to today's concerns and standards as he engages in the imaginative recreation of the interplay between human beings and circumstances in time. He should seek to be the mediator between all the dead and the living, but in the end the humanity and the artistry of his account will determine the extent of its usefulness.

One of the first steps taken by the Board of Trustees of the Ontario Historical Studies Series was to initiate the preparation of a bibliography of works dealing with the history of Ontario. This was published in [1974] as *Ontario since 1867: a bibliography*, by the Ministry of Colleges and Universities, and has been distributed by the Ontario Government Bookstore.

Although the first edition contained only some three thousand entries and had no index, it proved useful to many university teachers and students. On the advice of the Series' Editors, the Board approved the preparation of a second edition. Dr. Olga Bishop, a noted bibliographer, who was engaged actively in bibliographical research on Ontario government publications, was appointed as senior editor for this project.

The Editors asked Dr. Bishop and her collaborators to prepare a comprehensive bibliography of the printed materials relating to the history of Ontario since 1867. It was agreed at the outset that general works on Canadian history would be excluded and that, wherever possible, duplication of existing bibliographies would be avoided. Second, it was decided that, in order to complement the volumes to be published in the Series, entries should be grouped largely under four broad categories of economic, social, political, and cultural and intellectual history. Third, 1976 was selected as the terminal date, thereby extending significantly the period covered in the first edition. Finally, it was understood that, if possible, the entire collection would be incorporated in a data bank in a form that would facilitate later revision and the publication of supplementary editions.

Dr. Bishop and her assistants have searched assiduously and efficiently through the collections in many libraries and have consulted all relevant bibliographies. They have compiled and verified some fifteen thousand items; to our knowledge this is the most extensive bibliography of Ontario history in existence. Doubtless they have missed some entries; similarly there will be some which seem of marginal importance. Nevertheless, we believe that this work will be invaluable to senior scholars, to research students, and more broadly to all those interested in some aspect of the history of the province. It will provide a comprehensive view of what has been written and of the areas in which little research or writing has been done.

The Board and the Editors are deeply grateful to Dr. Bishop and her colleagues for making this publication possible.

Goldwin S. French
Editor-in-Chief
Peter N. Oliver
Associate Editor

Toronto
1 December 1979

Preface

This book is a second, enlarged and updated, edition of *Ontario since 1867: a bibliography*. Work began on it on 1 November 1974, when Barbara Irwin began the task of checking periodicals for articles on Ontario. A second research assistant, Clara Miller, was appointed in January 1975. While her main work has been to check theses at the University of Toronto and Queen's University, she has also assisted in locating and checking a number of monographs.

The bibliography lists monographs, pamphlets, periodical articles, and theses dealing with the history of Ontario, arranged by the major areas indicated by the chapter titles and subdivided into the specific subjects shown on the list of contents. The subjects have been subdivided into (1) bibliography; (2) monographs and pamphlets; (3) periodical articles; and (4) theses. Within these sections the works have been arranged alphabetically by author, with one exception: publications that concern a royal commission or a committee have been listed with the commission or committee report. Manuscripts and maps have been excluded. If a work contains maps this has been noted in the collation. The valuable historical atlases published in the last quarter of the nineteenth century and the recent reprints of these atlases have been listed.

Chapters 1, 2, and 3 include works that cover several subjects: bibliographies that deal with Ontario history or Canadian history generally are in chapter 1; general histories of Ontario or Canada in chapter 2; collective biographical works in chapter 3. Bibliographies, histories, and biographies on specific subjects are listed under those subjects.

At least one library location has been given for monographs and pamphlets; the locations of periodicals appear in the appendix listing rather than with the individual articles. Theses are normally available at the university granting the degree, and that is the location shown for theses from Ontario universities, and also for some theses from universities in other provinces and in the United States. Theses which were not listed in *Canadiana* or *Dissertation Abstracts* were verified for us by the library of the university. However, *Canadiana* was the source of bibliographical information for most theses from other provinces, and *Dissertation Abstracts* for most American theses, and are shown as the location in those listings, along with the microform number for ease of ordering. Any work which has the location symbol OTAR may be used only in the Ontario Archives.

Bibliographies of Ontario government publications being already available, we have limited our listing of such publications to those which have resulted from royal commissions, advisory and select committees, task forces, and conservation reports. We have, however, included publications of the federal government or other provincial governments that deal with Ontario history.

Histories of individual churches and schools have been excluded. A history of a diocese or presbytery or a group of schools has been listed. Local histories which give valuable insight into the life and culture of a community have been included regardless of the size of the community. Reports on urban and rural planning and on the settlement and utilization of land which are generally available in libraries have been included. Directories of cities and counties published between 1867 and 1912, which contain valuable histories of the city or county, have been listed.

An author, title, and subject index has been arranged in alphabetical order. Government corporate authors generally have been listed under the subject. To bring works on a given topic together the work has been listed under the subject. All individuals whose names appear in the bibliography have been listed.

No bibliography can ever claim to be completely definitive. We have, however, searched the holdings of the many libraries listed, and we can claim to have covered more material available in print than any previous bibliography on Ontario History.

Olga B. Bishop

London
15 November 1979

Acknowledgments

The resources of many libraries in Canada, particularly in Ontario, a number in the United States, and several in Great Britain were used. Grateful acknowledgment is made to the chief librarian of all libraries cited in the List of Location Symbols. Personal visits were made to many libraries and letters were sent to other libraries which could not be visited. Grateful acknowledgment must be made to the following persons who not only supplied the information requested, but suggested further sources of material: Sylvia Osterbind, Brock University; Hilda Gifford, Carleton University; Marion Cameron, Patricia Grenier, The University of Guelph; Grace Schmidt, Kitchener Public Library; Shirley Hagdu, Lakehead University; Eileen Glotz, Laurentian University; Mary Faulkner, Ontario Legislative Library; Barbara Brown, Pamela Hardisty, Library of Parliament; Elizabeth Silvester, McGill University; Marilyn McDermott, Narender Passi, McMaster University; Catharine MacKenzie, Midland Public Library; Beryl Anderson, Betty Deavy, Gwynneth Evans, Joan Honeywell, Patricia Madaire, Dorothy Ryder, Marion Wilson, National Library of Canada; Carol Brégaint, Office of the Secretary of State; Ethelyn Harlow, Dorothy Kealey, Susan Watt, Ontario Archives; M. Doreen Taylor, Ontario Hydro; Jeannette Schmidt, Ontario Institute for Studies in Education; Dawn Munro, Public Archives of Canada; George F. Henderson, William F.E. Morley, Elizabeth Skeath, Queen's University; Mary C. Shantz, Sudbury Public Library; Jean Bohne, Cecily Blackstock, Eileen Bradley, Jack Cain, Barbara Gallivan, Peter Hajnal, Diane Henderson, Catharine Matthews, Pamela Manson-Smith, Dorothy Service, Mary Shortt, Joan Winearls, University of Toronto; Susan Bellingham, Carolynne Presser, University of Waterloo; John Lutman, Edward Phelps, The University of Western Ontario; Jerry Malone, University of Windsor; Lynette Skulj, Welland Public Library; Lillian Montour, Woodland Indian Cultural Educational Centre; and Mary Stevens, York University.

Many items would have been missed out but for the generosity of John Coutts, Niagara Falls, who allowed the undersigned to search his Canadiana file for items relating to Ontario history, and of Leslie Straus who made it possible to make weekly visits to John Coutts Library Services Limited. In order not to miss any of their recent titles, Clarke, Irwin & Company Limited very kindly presented me with a copy of recent works to peruse at leisure.

Grateful acknowledgment also has to be made to: Edith Jarvi, Faculty of Library Science, and Isabel K. McLean who checked library catalogues for holdings of items already identified in bibliographies; Catharine Czuma, Barbara England, and Rosemary Wallace who typed the manuscript from handwritten cards; Wendy Kennedy who assisted in compiling the index; Philip Bellamy, Howarth & Smith Limited, who not only managed the text application of the computer programme but saw the work through the page proof stage; John Ecclestone, University of Toronto Press, for his technical assistance and advice; Goldwin French and Peter Oliver who made valuable suggestions on the scope of the work.

Any errors or omissions are the sole responsibility of the authors.

Olga B. Bishop

List of Location Symbols

ONTARIO LIBRARIES

OBA	Barrie Public Library
OBRT	Brantford Public Library
OBRWI	The Woodland Indian Cultural Education Centre, Brantford
OCHA	Chatham Public Library
OG	Guelph Public Library
OGAL	Cambridge Public Library
OGU	University of Guelph
OH	Hamilton Public Library
OHC	Le College Université de Hearst, Hearst
OHM	McMaster University, Hamilton
OI	Ingersoll Public Library
OK	Kingston Public Library
OKIT	Kitchener Public Library
OKQ	Queen's University, Kingston
OKQL	Law Library, Queen's University, Kingston
OL	London Public Library and Art Museum
OLSSJ	Sisters of St. Joseph, London
OLU	University of Western Ontario, London
OLUL	Law Library, University of Western Ontario, London
OLUM	Health Science Centre, University of Western Ontario, London
OLUS	School of Library and Information Science, University of Western Ontario, London
OMI	Midland Public Library
OOA	Public Archives/Archives publiques, Ottawa
OOAG	Main Library, Department of Agriculture/Bibliothèque centrale, Ministère de l'agriculture, Ottawa
OOC	Ottawa Public Library/Bibliothèque publique d'Ottawa
OOCC	Carleton University, Ottawa
OOCW	Canadian Council on Social Development/Conseil canadien de développement social, Ottawa
OOL	Department of Labour/Ministère du travail, Ottawa
OON	Canada Institute for Scientific and Technical Information, National Research Council/Institut canadien de l'information scientifique et technique, Conseil national des recherches, Ottawa
OONG	National Gallery/Galerie nationale, Ottawa
OONL	National Library/Bibliothèque nationale, Ottawa
OOP	Library of Parliament/Bibliothèque du Parlement, Ottawa
OORD	Department of Indian Affairs and Northern Development

OORI	Orillia Public Library
OOS	Statistics Canada/Statistique Canada, Ottawa
OOSH	Oshawa Public Library
OOSS	Department of the Secretary of State/Secrétariat d'état, Ottawa
OOU	University of Ottawa/Université d'Ottawa
OPAL	Lakehead University, Thunder Bay
OPET	Trent University, Peterborough
OPETP	Peterborough Public Library
OSTC	St. Catharines Public Library
OSTCB	Brock University, St. Catharines
OSTR	Streetsville Public Library
OSTT	St. Thomas Public Library
OSU	Sudbury Public Library
OSUL	Laurentian University/Université Laurentienne, Sudbury
OTAR	Archives of Ontario, Toronto
OTBS	Bishop Strachan School Archives
OTC	Faculty of Education, University of Toronto
OTCA	Ontario College of Art, Toronto
OTCC	United Church of Canada Archives, Toronto
OTCH	Anglican Church House, Toronto
OTCJCA	Canadian Jewish Congress Central Region Archives, Toronto
OTDRE	Ontario Ministry of Treasury, Economics and Inter-governmental Affairs, Toronto
OTDT	Ontario Ministry of Transportation and Communications, Toronto
OTDU	Ontario Ministry of Colleges and Universities, Toronto
OTE	Emmanuel College, Victoria University, Toronto
OTER	Ontario Institute for Studies in Education, Toronto
OTH	Hydro-Electric Power Commission, Toronto
OTHOP	Ontario Paper, Thorold
OTK	Knox College, University of Toronto
OTL	Legislative Library, Toronto
OTLS	Law Society of Upper Canada, Toronto
OTMCL	Metropolitan Toronto Central Library
OTOWC	Ontario Welfare Council, Toronto
OTOTF	Ontario Teachers Federation
OTP	Toronto Public Libraries
OTREC	Regis College, Toronto
OTRM	Royal Ontario Museum, Toronto
OTSTM	University of St. Michael's College, Toronto
OTTC	University of Trinity College, Toronto
OTU	University of Toronto
OTUAR	University of Toronto Archives
OTUCR	Centre of Criminology, University of Toronto
OTUDP	Clarke Institute of Psychiatry, University of Toronto
OTUFM	Faculty of Music, University of Toronto

OTUFP	Faculty of Pharmacy, University of Toronto
OTUH	School of Hygiene, University of Toronto
OTUL	Faculty of Law, University of Toronto
OTULS	Faculty of Library Science, University of Toronto
OTUMA	Map Library, University of Toronto
OTUP	Department of Physics, University of Toronto
OTURS	Department of Rare Books & Special Collections, University of Toronto
OTUSA	School of Architecture, University of Toronto
OTV	Victoria University, Toronto
OTY	York University, Toronto
OW	Windsor Public Library
OWA	University of Windsor
OWO	Woodstock Public Library
OWTL	Wilfrid Laurier University [formerly/anciennement Waterloo Lutheran University] Waterloo
OWTU	University of Waterloo

OTHER LIBRARIES

AEU	University of Alberta, Edmonton
BM	British Museum
BVAU	University of British Columbia, Vancouver
BVIP	Provincial Library, Victoria
MWU	University of Manitoba, Winnipeg
QMCN	Canadian National Railway
QMM	McGill University, Montreal
QMU	Université de Montréal
QQLA	Université Laval, Québec
SSU	University of Saskatchewan, Saskatoon
Clark U.	Clark University, Worcester, Massachusetts
Columbia	Columbia University, City of New York
Harvard	Harvard University Library, Cambridge, Massachusetts
Michigan State	Michigan State University, East Lansing, Michigan
Ohio State	Ohio State University, Columbus, Ohio
U. Buffalo	State University of New York at Buffalo
U. Edinburgh	Edinburgh University Library
U. Kansas	University of Kansas, Lawrence, Kansas
U. London	University of London
U. Maryland	University of Maryland, College Park, Maryland
U. Minnesota	University of Minnesota, Saint Paul, Minnesota
U. Paris	University of Paris, Paris, France
U. Rochester	Eastman School of Music, The University of Rochester, Rochester, New York

U. Wisconsin   University of Wisconsin, Madison, Wisconsin
Yale   Yale University, New Haven, Connecticut

BIBLIOGRAPHICAL SOURCES

Can   Canadiana, National Library of Canada, Ottawa
DA   Dissertation Abstracts, Ann Arbor, Michigan
MA   Masters Abstracts, Ann Arbor, Michigan

OTHER SOURCES

City Clerk's Office, Barrie
The Society   Geographical Society of Philadelphia, Philadelphia

BIBLIOGRAPHY OF ONTARIO HISTORY 1867-1976
VOLUME I

1

Bibliographical Works: General

Avison, Margaret Kirkland, 1918–
  The research compendium: review and abstracts of graduate research
  1942–1962. [Toronto] University of Toronto Press [1964]
  viii, 276 p.
  Published in celebration of the fiftieth anniversary of the School of Social
  Work, University of Toronto.   OTU OONL
Bellingham, Susan.
  Bowlby family papers. Waterloo Historical Society. Annual Volume 64:
  70–73, 1976.
Bishop, Olga.
  Checklist of historical works on western Ontario in the libraries of the
  University of Western Ontario. Western Ontario Historical Notes 14(no. 1):
  24–30, 1957; 14(no. 2): 30–37, 1958; 14(no. 3): 42–47, 1958; 14(no. 4):
  31–39, 1958; 14(no. 5): 39–49, 1958; 15(no. 2): 19–27, 1959; 15(no. 3):
  11–24, 1959; 15(no. 4): 59–63, 1959; 16: 32–39, 85–93, 1960; 17: 53–66,
  1961; 18: 37–51, 1962.
  Checklists for 14 counties of western Ontario.
Brock University.
  A guide to research resources for the Niagara region. Compiled by Brock
  University. Final report: September 1, 1971. Randy Olling, project leader.
  St. Catharines, Ontario [1971]
  299 leaves.   OTU
Bucksar, R   G   (comp.).
  Bibliography of socio-economic development of northern Ontario
  (northwestern and northeastern regions). Ottawa: The Canadian Research
  Centre for Anthropology; Toronto: Regional Development Branch,
  Department of Treasury and Economics, 1968.
  112 leaves. map.   OONL

— Supplement, 1969.
    64 leaves.   OONL
— Supplement, 1972. Compiled for the Regional Development Branch,
    Ministry of Treasury, Economics and Intergovernmental Affairs. Toronto:
    1972.
    86, v leaves. map.   OONL
Burpee, Lawrence Johnstone, 1873–1946 (ed.).
    Index and dictionary of Canadian history, edited by Lawrence J. Burpee
    and Arthur G. Doughty. Toronto: Morang & Co., Limited, 1911.
    xii, 446 p. fold. front., fold. map. (Makers of Canada v. 21).   OLU
Canada. Geological Survey.
    A list of recently published memoirs, preliminary papers and maps of
    Ontario. Ottawa: 1954.
    28 p.   OTUMA
Canada. National Library.
    Canadiana. January 15, 1951–   Ottawa: 1951–
    monthly   OTULS
Canada. Public Archives.
    Catalogue of pamphlets in the Public Archives of Canada. Prepared by
    Magdalen Casey. Ottawa: F.A. Acland, printer to the King's Most Excellent
    Majesty, 1931–1932.
    2 v.
    Contents: v.1, 1493–1877; v.2, 1878–1931.   OTULS
— Parish registers for the province of Ontario. Compiled by John E. Coderre
    and Paul A. Lavoie. Ottawa: Ottawa Branch, Ontario Genealogical Society,
    1975.
    1 v. (unpaged). Computer print-out.   OOA
Canadian graduate theses in the humanities and social sciences 1921–1946.
    Thèses des gradués Canadiens dans les humanitiés et les sciences sociales.
    Ottawa: Edmond Cloutier, printer to the King's Most Excellent Majesty,
    1951.
    194 p.   OTC
Canadian Historical Association.
    Index to the annual report, 1922–51. Ottawa: The Association, 1952.
    ix, 43 p.   OTU
Canadian Historical Review.
    Index v. I–X, 1920–1929, by Julia Jarvis and Alison Ewart. [Toronto] The
    University of Toronto Press, 1930.
    284 p.   OLU
— v. XI–XX, 1930–1939, compiled by the Editorial Department of the
    University of Toronto Press under the direction of Alison Hewitt. Toronto:
    The University of Toronto Press, 1944.
    vi, 432 p.   OLU
— v. 21–30, 1940–1949, compiled by the Editorial Department of the
    University of Toronto Press. [Toronto] University of Toronto Press [c1959]
    404 p.   OLU

— 1950–1964. Index des articles et des comptes rendus de volumes. Quebec: Centre de Documentation, Université Laval, 1969.

   1 v. (various pagings).   OLU

— v. XXXI–LI, 1950–1970.[Toronto] University of Toronto Press [c1974]

   219 p.   OLU

Clark, Mary Jane, 1945–   (comp.).

   Reference aids in Canadian history in the University of Toronto Library. Toronto: Reference Department, University of Toronto Library, 1972.

   75 p. (University of Toronto Library, Reference series, 14).   OTU

Cole, Arthur Harrison, 1889–   (ed.).

   A finding-list of Royal Commission reports in the British Dominions. Cambridge, Massachusetts: Harvard University Press, 1939.

   134 p.

   Ontario: pp. 102–104.   OTU

Emard, Michel, 1942–

   Inventaire sommaire des sources manuscrites et imprimées concernant Prescott – Russell, Ontario. Présentation by Lucien Brault. Rockland, Ontario: The Author, 1976.

   172 p. cartes.   OTU

Erie access catalogue, extending regional information to everyone. n.p.: 1974.

   108 p. illus.

   Haldimand – Norfolk history.   OONL

Garbutt, Lorne H

   In days of yore. York Pioneer and Historical Society. Annual Report 81–86, 1964.

   Old records and papers of the society.

Granatstein, Jack Lawrence, 1939–   (ed.).

   Canada since 1867: a bibliographical guide, by J.L. Granatstein and Paul Stevens. Toronto: Hakkert, 1974.

   x, 179 p.

   Contents: pp. 109–137, Ontario by Peter Oliver.   OTU

Harrison, Cynthia.

   Women in Canada, 1965 to 1972: a bibliography. Hamilton, Ontario: McMaster University Library Press, 1972 [i.e. 1973]   OTU

Herrington, Walter S   (comp. and ed.).

   The Canniff Collection: being a number of papers and documents presented to the Society by the late Dr. William Canniff. Lennox and Addington Historical Society. Papers and Addresses 9: 5–63, 1917.

   iv, 51p.   OTU

Jones, Richard C

   Annotated bibliography of the Sudbury area. 2d ed. Sudbury, Ontario: Sudbury Public Library, 1972.

   55 p.   OTU

— Bibliography of the Sudbury area. Sudbury, Ontario: Laurentian University Press, 1970.

   ii leaves, 50 p. form, map.   OTU

Kingsford, William, 1819–1898.
   The early bibliography of the province of Ontario, Dominion of Canada,
   with other information. A supplemental chapter of Canadian archaeology.
   Toronto: Rowsell & Hutchison, 1892.
   140 p.
   Chiefly pre-Confederation.   OTU
Kuehl, Warren F   1924–
   Dissertations in history: an index to dissertations completed in history
   departments of United States and Canadian Universities [Lexington,
   Kentucky] University of Kentucky Press, 1965 [1972]
   2 v.
   Contents: v.1, 1873–1960; v.2, 1961–June 1970.   OLU
Leverette, Clarke Edward, 1936–
   Index to little magazines of Ontario, 1967–1973. London, Ontario: Killaly
   Press, 1971–1973.
   6 v. for the years: 1971, 1972, 1973, 1975 (3 parts).
   Contents: 1967–1970 (3 parts: part 1, A–F; part 2, G–M; part 3, N–Z), 1971,
   1972, 1973.   OLU
Lochhead, Douglas Grant, 1922–   (comp.).
   Bibliography of Canadian bibliographies/Bibliographie des bibliographies
   canadiennes, 2d ed. rev. and enl. Compiled by Douglas Lochhead. Index
   compiled by Peter E. Greig. Toronto: Published in association with the
   Bibliographical Society of Canada by University of Toronto Press [1972]
   xiv, 312 p.
   1st edition 1960. See Tanghe.   OTU
London, Ontario. University of Western Ontario. Lawson Memorial Library.
   A list of theses accepted by the University of Western Ontario in partial
   fulfilment of the requirements for the degrees of Master of Arts, Master of
   Science, Bachelor of Laws, 1909–1947. London, Ontario: Lawson Memorial
   Library, University of Western Ontario, 1948.
   25 leaves.   OLU
London, Ontario. University of Western Ontario. Libraries. Special Collections
   Department.
   List of historical articles published 1942–1972 in *Western Ontario Historical
   Notes* and *Western Ontario History Nuggets*. London, Ontario: Library,
   University of Western Ontario, 1972.
   16, 2 leaves.   OLU
McGill University thesis directory. Prepared for the Faculty of Graduate Studies
   and Research by Frank Spitzer and Elizabeth Silvester, editors. Montreal:
   Faculty of Graduate Studies and Research, c1975–1976.
   2 v.
   Contents: v.1, 1881–1959; v.2, 1960–1973.   OLU
MacKerracher, Christina.
   Bibliography of imprints in London, Ontario. London, Ontario: 1939.
   28 leaves.   OLU

Maddaugh, Peter D   1942–
  Bibliography of Canadian legal history. Toronto: York University Law
  Library, 1972.
  xii, 77 leaves.   OTU
Metropolitan Toronto. Borough of York.
  Township of York: historical sources [1840–1900. Toronto: Borough of York,
  1974]
  224 p.
  "A continuation of Heritage of York: an historical bibliography 1793–1840".
                                                                     OTAR
Mills, Judy Eileen, 1943–   (comp.).
  University of Toronto doctoral theses, 1897–1967; a bibliography compiled
  by Judy Mills and Irene Dombra. [Toronto] Published for University of
  Toronto Library, by University of Toronto Press [c1968]
  xi, 186 p.   OTU
Ontario Historical Society.
  Index to the publications of the Ontario Historical Society 1899–1972
  [compiled by Hilary Bates and Robert Sherman]. Toronto: Ontario
  Historical Society, 1974.
  x, 175 p.   OTAR
Ontario Historical Studies Series.
  Ontario since 1867: a bibliography. Toronto [Ontario Ministry of Colleges
  and Universities] 1973.
  2, 2, 330 p.   OTU
Ottawa. University. Information Retrieval Center.
  Repertoire des thèses présenteés à l'Université d'Ottawa dans le domaine des
  sciences social et des humanities. Catalogue of social sciences and humanities
  thesis [sic] presented at the University of Ottawa. [Ottawa] 1972.
  v, 219 p.   OTU
Ottawa. University. Libraries.
  Reference works for the historians; a list of reference works of interest to
  historians in the libraries of the University of Ottawa by Julian Gwyn.
  [Ottawa] Printed and distributed by the Central Library, University of
  Ottawa, 1971.
  iv, 131 leaves.   OTU
Phelps, Edward.
  The Fairbank Collection at the University of Western Ontario. Western
  Ontario Historical Notes 17: 89–91, 1961.
Preston, R   A   and Leopold Lamontagne.
  Comments on "The Sources of Local History". Ontario History 49: 120–124,
  1957.
Queen's University. Library.
  Canadiana, 1698–1900, in the possession of the Douglas Library, Queen's
  University, Kingston, Ontario. Kingston, Ontario: 1932.
  86 p.   OTU

Ryder, Dorothy E   (ed.).
    Canadian reference sources: a selective guide. Ottawa: Canadian Library
    Association, 1973.
    x, 185 p.   OTU
— Supplement. Ottawa: Canadian Library Association, 1973.
    xi, 121 p.   OTU
Spencer, Loraine Margaret Inglis, 1937–   (comp.).
    Northern Ontario; a bibliography, compiled by Loraine Spencer and Susan
    Holland. [Toronto] University of Toronto Press [c1968]
    x, 120 p. map.   OTU
Stevenson, Hugh.
    The Coyne Papers; an addition to the University Library. Western Ontario
    Historical Notes 16: 72–74, 1960.
Tanghe, Raymond.
    Bibliography of Canadian bibliographies. Toronto: Published in association
    with the Bibliographical Society of Canada by University of Toronto Press,
    1960.
    206 p.   OTU
— Supplement, 1960 & 1961. Toronto: Bibliographical Society of Canada,
    1962.
    24 p.   OTU
— Supplement, 1962 & 1963, compiled by Madeleine Pellerin. Toronto:
    Bibliographical Society of Canada, 1964.
    27 p.   OTU
— Supplement, 1964 & 1965, compiled by Madeleine Pellerin. Toronto:
    Bibliographical Society of Canada, 1966.
    32 p.   OTU
Thibault, Claude.
    Bibliographia Canadiana. [Don Mills, Ontario] Longman Canada Limited
    [c1973]
    lxiv, 795 p.
    A bibliographical guide to Canadian historical literature.   OTU
Toronto Area Archivists Group.
    Guide to archives in the Toronto area. Toronto: The Group, 1975.
    vi, 46 p.   OTU
Trotter, Reginald George, 1888–1951.
    Canadian history: a syllabus and guide to reading. Toronto: The Macmillan
    Company of Canada Limited, 1926.
    162 p.   OLU
— New and enl. ed. Toronto: Macmillan Company of Canada Limited, 1934.
    xiv, 193 p.   OLU
Tudor, Dean Frederick, 1943–   (comp.).
    Sources of statistical data for Ontario. Ottawa: Canadian Library
    Association, 1972.
    iv, 33 p.
    A guide to local and regional sources of statistical information.   OTRM

Wallace, William Stewart, 1884–1970 (comp.).
   The Ryerson imprint; a check-list of the books and pamphlets published by
   the Ryerson Press since the foundation of the house in 1829. Toronto: The
   Ryerson Press [1954]
   141 p.   OTU
Wilmot, Blair C
   The John Buchan Collection at Queen's. Ontario Library Review 42:
   18–20, 1958.
Wong, Chuck.
   A checklist of university theses on northeastern Ontario. Sudbury, Ontario:
   Laurentian University Library, 1975.
   45 leaves.   OTU
Wood, William Donald, 1920–
   Canadian graduate theses 1919–1967: an annotated bibliography (covering
   economics, business and industrial relations) by W.D. Wood, L.A. Kelly and
   P. Kumar. Kingston, Ontario: Industrial Relations Centre, Queen's
   University, 1970.
   xiv, 483 p. (Industrial Relations Centre, Queen's University. Bibliography
   series, no.4).   OTU

2

General Works

Monographs and Pamphlets

Armstrong, Frederick Henry, 1926–
  Aspects of nineteenth-century Ontario. Essays presented to James J.
  Talman, edited by F.H. Armstrong, H.A. Stevenson, and J.D. Wilson.
  [Toronto] Published in association with the University of Western Ontario
  by University of Toronto Press [c1974]
  xiii, 355 p. illus., port., maps, tables.
  Contents: James John Talman: historian and librarian, by Hugh A.
  Stevenson; The settlement of the Western district 1749–1850, by Leo A.
  Johnson; The origins of local government, by G.P.de T. Glazebrook; Robert
  Baldwin and decentralization 1841–9, by C.F.J. Whebell; Some aspects of
  urbanization in nineteenth-century Ontario, by J.M.S. Careless; The rise of
  London: a study of urban evolution in nineteenth-century southwestern
  Ontario, by Frederick H. Armstrong & Daniel J. Brock; William Allan: a
  pioneer business executive, by M.A. Magill; Construction materials in
  colonial Ontario 1831–61, by W.R. Wightman; The security of land:
  mortgaging in Toronto Gore township 1835–95, by David P. Gagan; The
  common man in the era of the rebellion in Upper Canada, by Fred Landon;
  Pioneer drinking habits and the rise of the temperance agitation in Upper
  Canada prior to 1840, by M.A. Garland & J.J. Talman; Old Ontario and
  the emergence of a national frame of mind, by Allan Smith; The teacher in
  early Ontario, by J. Donald Wilson; The English public school tradition in
  nineteenth-century Ontario, by J.D. Purdy; Myths in some nineteenth-
  century Ontario newspapers, by James Reaney; The illustrated historical
  atlases of Ontario with special reference to H. Belden & Co., by Lillian Rea
  Benson; The frontier politician, by M. Elizabeth Arthur; Edward Barnes

Borron, 1820–1915: northern pioneer, and public servant extraordinary, by
Morris Zaslow; Ontario denied: the Methodist Church on the Prairies
1896–1914, by George N. Emery; Bookmen and scholars, by Carl F. Klinck;
Bibliography of academic and journalistic writings by James J. Talman, by
Hilary Bates.   OTU
Auer, Harry Anton.
The north country. Cincinnati, Ohio: Robert Clarke Company, 1906.
viii, 208 p. front., plates.   OKQ
Avison, Margaret Kirkland, 1918–
History of Ontario. Toronto: W.J. Gage & Company Limited [c1951]
v, 138 p. illus., maps.   OTURS
Braithwaite, John Victor Maxwell, 1911–
Max Braithwaite's Ontario. Vancouver: J.J. Douglas, 1974.
215 p. 16 leaves of plates, illus., map.   OTU
Broadfoot, S   Rupert.
Holidaying in Canada on the Ottawa River. Ottawa: The Author [1942]
203 p. illus., port.   OTU
Brown, Robert Craig.
Canada, 1896–1921: a nation transformed, by Robert Craig Brown and
Ramsay Cook. [Toronto] McClelland & Stewart [c1974]
xiv, 412 p. illus.   OTU
Burkholder, Mabel Grace (Clare), 1881–1973.
History of central Ontario (southwestern). Montreal: Historical Foundation,
1951–2.
679 p. illus., ports. (Canada and her people; Encyclopedia, v. 2).   OLU
Campbell, Marjorie Elliot (Wilkins), 1901–
Ontario. Toronto: The Ryerson Press [1953]
x, 219 p. illus., map.   OTU
Canniff, William, 1830–1910.
— History of the province of Ontario (Upper Canada). Containing a sketch of
Franco–Canadian history – the bloody battle of the French and Indians, –
the American revolution... including biographies of prominent first settlers.
And the census of 1871. Toronto: A.H. Hovey, 1872.
xxxi, 670 p.
The 1871 census is not bound with the copy examined. The preface date is
March 27, 1869.   OTU
— The settlement of Upper Canada; with a new introduction by Donald
Swainson and a full index. Belleville, Ontario: Mika Silk Screening, 1971.
v, xxi, 671, 27 p. (Canadian reprint series, no. 1)
1869 edition of History of the settlement of Upper Canada (Ontario) with special
reference to the Bay of Quinte.   OTU
Charlesworth, Hector Willoughby, 1872–1945.
The Canadian scene: sketches; political and historical. Toronto: The
Macmillan Company of Canada Limited, 1927.
235 p.   OTU

Conant, Thomas, 1842–1905.
  Life in Canada. Toronto: William Briggs, 1903.
  xi, 290 p. front., illus., ports.
  Chiefly pre-Confederation.   OKQ
— Upper Canada sketches. Toronto: William Briggs, 1898.
  viii, 243 p. facsim., map, port.
  Chiefly pre-Confederation   OTAR
Creighton, Donald Grant, 1902–
  Canada: the heroic beginnings. Toronto: Macmillan of Canada, in co-
  operation with Indian and Northern Affairs and Parks Canada [c1974]
  255 p. illus.   OTU
— Canada's first century, 1867–1967. Toronto: Macmillan of Canada [c1970]
  372 p. illus.   OTU
— Ontario, by D.G. Creighton and Helen Marsh. Ottawa: King's Printer,
  1944.
  19 p.
  Also published in *Canadian Affairs* v.1, no.16, September 1, 1944.   OONL
— The story of Canada. Toronto: Macmillan Company of Canada Limited,
  1959.
  291 p. illus., ports., maps.   OTU
Crysler, John M
  A short history of the township of Niagara touching upon transportation,
  education and municipal affairs from 1793 to 1893. [Niagara, Ontario] The
  Niagara Advance, 1943.
  79 p. facsims., tables.   OKQ
Denis, Keith, 1909–
  Canoe trails through Quetico. Drawings by Selwyn Dewdney. [Toronto]
  Quetico Foundation [c1959]
  ix, 84 p. illus., fold. col. map.   OTU
Dent, John Charles, 1841–1888.
  The last forty years: Canada since the Union of 1841. Toronto: George
  Virtue [1881]
  2 v. illus., ports.   OTU
Edgar, James David, 1841–1899.
  Canada and its capital: with sketches of political and social life at Ottawa.
  Toronto: George N. Morang, 1898.
  217 p. illus., ports.   OTU
Encyclopedia of Canada: general editor, W. Stewart Wallace. Toronto:
  University Associates of Canada, 1935–37.
  6 v. illus.
  Ontario: v. 5, pp. 49–57.   OTU
Encyclopedia of Ontario. v. 1–   Belleville, Ontario: Mika Publishing Co.,
  1974–
  7 v. illus.
  Contents: v. 1, Historic sites of Ontario; v. 2, Places in Ontario; v. 3, People

of Ontario; v. 4, Cultural life in Ontario; v. 5, Transportation in Ontario;
v. 6, Sports in Ontario; v. 7, Chronology of Ontario.
v.1 only published by November 2, 1976.   OKQ
Fraser, Alexander, 1860–1936.
  A history of Ontario: its resources and development. Toronto: Canada
  History Company, 1907.
  2 v. plates, ports.   OTU
Garvin, Amelia Beers (Warnock), 1878–1956.
  Canadian cities of romance. Drawings by Dorothy Stevens, Toronto:
  McClelland & Stewart [c1922]
  191 p. illus.
  Ontario: pp. 45–55, 95–132.   OTU
— This is Ontario, by Katherine Hale [*pseud.*] with photographic illustrations
  by "Jay" and an end paper by Stanley Turner. Toronto: The Ryerson Press
  [c1937]
  ix, 241 p. front., plates, maps.   OTU OKQ
— This is Ontario, by Katharine Hale. Photographs by Sir Ellsworth Flavelle.
  [2d ed.] Toronto: The Ryerson Press [1947, c1946]
  xi, 245 p. front., plates, maps.   OKQ
Gentilcore, Rocco Louis, 1924–   (ed.).
  Ontario. [Toronto] University of Toronto Press [c1972]
  x, 126 p. illus. (Studies in Canadian geography).
  Published for the 22nd International Geographical Congress.   OTU
Grant, George Monro, 1835–1902.
  Ocean to ocean: Sandford Fleming's expedition through Canada in 1872.
  Toronto: Campbell, 1873.
  371 p. illus.   OLU
— Enlarged and rev. London: Sampson Low, Marston, Searle, & Rivington,
  1877.
  394, 32 p. illus.   OLU OTAR
— Enlarged and rev. ed. Toronto: Rose Belford, 1879.
  vi, 394 p. front., plates.   OLU
— Revised ed. containing the best features of the two former editions published
  in 1873 and 1879. Toronto: Radisson Society of Canada Limited, 1925.
  xxi, 412 p. illus., port.   OLU OTAR
— Being a diary kept during a journey from the Atlantic to the Pacific, with the
  expedition of the engineer-in-chief of the Canadian Pacific and Intercolonial
  railways. Toronto: J. Campbell & Son; London: Sampson Low, Marston
  Low & Searle, 1873. [Toronto: Coles Publishing Company, c1970]
  xiv, 371 p. illus., maps. (Coles Canadiana collection).
  Facsimile reprint.   OTAR
— Picturesque Canada: the country as it was and is. Illustrated under the
  supervision of L.R. O'Brien. Toronto: James Clarke [c1882]
  2 v. front., illus., plates.
  Ontario: pp. 343–674.   OTAR

— Picturesque spots of the north: historical and descriptive sketches of the
scenery and life in the vicinity of Georgian Bay, the Muskoka lakes, the
upper lakes in central and eastern Ontario, and in the Niagara district.
Chicago: Alexander Belford, 1899.
205 p. illus.   OLU OTAR

Gundy, Henry Pearson, 1905–
Canada. Amsterdam: Vangendt & Co., 1972.
86 p. facsims. (The spread of printing).
Chiefly pre-Confederation for Ontario.   OTU

Hammond, Melvin Ormond, 1876–1934.
Simpson's confederation jubilee series, 1867–1927. Toronto: The Robert
Simpson Company Limited [c1927]
61 p.   OTAR

Henderson, John, 1905–1931.
Ontario, the story of a great province of Canada, by John Henderson
assisted by Frank Fairbrother, with an introduction by the Hon. G. Howard
Ferguson. Toronto: Macmillan Company of Canada Limited, 1931.
[x] 213 p. illus.   OTU

Hopkins, John Castell, 1864–1923.
The province of Ontario in the war: a record of government and people.
Toronto: Warwick Bros. & Rutter, Limited, 1919.
vii, 126 p. illus., ports.   OTU

Ingolfsrud, Elizabeth Thompson.
All about Ontario beds. Toronto: House of Grant (Canada) Ltd. [c1975]
63 p. illus.   OLU

— All about Ontario chairs. Photos by Rob Gordon. Toronto: House of Grant
(Canada) Ltd. [c1974]
64 p. illus.   OLU OTU

— All about Ontario chests. Photos by Rob Gordon. Toronto: House of Grant
(Canada) Ltd. [c1973]
48 p. illus.   OLU OTU

— All about Ontario tables. Toronto: House of Grant (Canada) Ltd. [c1976]
63 p. illus.   OLU OONL

Kerr, Donald Gordon Grady, 1913–1976.
Canada: a visual history, by D.G.G. Kerr and R.I.K. Davidson. Toronto:
Thomas Nelson & Sons (Canada) Limited [c1966]
170 p. chiefly illus., maps.   OTULS

Kilbourn, William Morley, 1926–   (ed.).
Canada: a guide to the peaceable kingdom. Toronto: Macmillan of Canada
[c1970]
xviii, 345 p.   OTU

Lacroix, Henry Olivier, 1826–1897.
Lacroix' Canadian guide and book of reference with descriptions and
statistics of all places along the lines of railway in the province of Ontario,
including a description of the city of Quebec. 1st. ed. Montreal: Witness
Printing House, 1873.
xi, 116 p. fold. map.   OTURS

Lamb, William Kaye, 1904–
   Canada's five centuries: from discovery to present day. Toronto:
   McGraw–Hill Company of Canada Limited [c1971]
   326 p. illus. (part col.), facsims., ports., maps (part col.).   OTU
Landon, Fred, 1880–1969.
   Western Ontario and the American frontier. Toronto: The Ryerson Press for
   the Carnegie Endowment for International Peace, Division of Economics
   and History, 1941.
   xvi, 305 p. maps.   OLU
— Reprinted. New York: Russell & Russell [1970, c1967]
   xxiii, 295 p. maps.   OLU
— Reprinted. [Toronto] McClelland and Stewart [c1967]
   xxi, 298 p. (The Carleton library, no.34).   OLU
London and Middlesex Historical Society, London, Ontario.
   Centennial review 1967. [London, Ontario: 1966?]
   152 p. illus. (*Its* Publication 16).   OTU
Lonn, George.
   Faces of Canada. Introduction by Marshall McLuhan. [Toronto] Pitt
   Publishing Company Limited [c1976]
   383 p. ports.   OONL
McDougall, Robert L   (ed.).
   Canada's past and present: a dialogue. [Toronto] Published in association
   with Carleton University by University of Toronto Press [c1965]
   xii, 179 p. (Our living tradition, fifth series).
   Contains sketch of O.D. Skelton.   OTU
McInnis, Edgar Wardwell, 1899–
   Canada: a political and social history, rev. and enl. Toronto: Clarke, Irwin
   & Company Limited [c1959]
   xvi, 619 p. illus., ports., maps.   OONL
Mackenzie, John.
   Ontario in your car, by John and Marjorie Mackenzie. Toronto: Clarke,
   Irwin & Company Limited, 1950.
   xvii, 291 p. illus.   OKQ
Mallory, Enid L
   Ontario calls you camping. Toronto: Macmillan of Canada, 1969.
   xii, 180 p. illus., maps.   OTU
Middleton, Jesse Edgar, 1872–1960.
   The province of Ontario: a history, 1615–1927 by Jesse Edgar Middleton...
   and Fred Landon... Toronto: The Dominion Publishing Company, Ltd.
   [c1927–28]
   5 v. fronts., illus. (facsim.), plates, ports., map.   OTU
— The romance of Ontario. Toronto: W.J. Gage & Co., Limited, 1931.
   x, 267 p. illus., ports., map.   OKQ
— Toronto: W.J. Gage & Co., Limited, 1944.
   x, 267 p. illus., ports., map.   OTU

Mika, Nick, 1912–
  Ontario of yesterday, by Nick and Helma Mika. Belleville, Ontario: Mika
  Silk Screening Ltd. [c1971]
    192 p. 88 col. plates.   OTU
Nickels, Nick (ed.).
  Southern Ontario/Quebec canoe routes. [Lakefield, Ontario: Trent
  Publishing Associates, 1971]
    119 p. illus.   OTU
Norfolk Historical Society, Simcoe, Ontario.
  Collections of the Norfolk Historical Society; preliminary inventory.
  [Ottawa] Public Archives of Canada, in co-operation with the Norfolk
  Historical Society, 1958.
    94 p.   OTU
O'Gorman, P   T
  Magnificent Ontario. Ilfracombe, England: Arthur H. Stockwell Ltd. [1952]
    175 p. illus.   OTU
Ontario Historical Society.
  First Canadian historical exhibition, held at Victoria college, Queen's Park,
  Toronto, June, 1899; report of secretary and treasurer. Toronto: [The
  Society] 1900.
    11 p.   OTV
— Pioneer and historical association of the province of Ontario, Canada.
  Organized at Toronto September 4th, 1888. n.p. [1895?]
    32 p.   OKQ
— Profiles of a province: studies in the history of Ontario; a collection of essays
  commissioned by the Ontario Historical Society to commemorate the
  centennial of Ontario. Toronto: Ontario Historical Society, 1967.
  xiii, 233 p. illus., maps.
  Contents: Part I, The making of a province. The United Empire Loyalists,
  by J.J. Talman; The reform movement in Upper Canada, by Fred Coyne
  Hamil; Upper Canada and the conservative tradition, by S.F. Wise; The
  districts of Upper Canada, 1788–1849, by George W. Spragge; The
  Anglo–American Magazine looks at urban Upper Canada on the eve of the
  railway era, by Frederick H. Armstrong and Neil C. Hultin; The genesis of
  Ontario politics in the Province of Canada (1838–1871), by Paul G. Cornell;
  Confederation: the atmosphere of crisis by C.P. Stacey; Part II, The political
  scene. Democracy and the Ontario fathers of Confederation, by Bruce W.
  Hodgins; Edward Blake: a portrait of his childhood, by Catherine Hume
  Blake, ed. by Margaret A. Banks; The Mowat era, 1872–1896: stability and
  progress, by A. Margaret Evans; The Ontario boundary question, by Morris
  Zaslow; James P. Whitney and the University of Toronto, by Charles W.
  Humphries; The evolution of a Victorian liberal: N.W. Rowell, by
  Margaret Prang; the Tory Hepburn, by Neil McKenty; Part III, Aspects of
  Ontario's economy. An introduction to the economic history of Ontario from
  outpost to empire, by H.A. Innis; Foundations of the Canadian oil industry,

1850–1866, by Edward Phelps; The impact of hydro on Ontario, by R.N.
Beattie; The changing patterns of tourism in Ontario, by R.I. Wolfe;
Agricultural settlement on the Canadian Shield: Ottawa river to Georgian
Bay, by Florence B. Murray; Part IV, The Ontario outlook. The Upper
Canada religious tradition, by John S. Moir; Educational leadership in
Ontario, 1867–1967, by Robert M. Stamp; Captain Charles Stuart,
abolitionist, by Fred Landon; The old buildings of Ontario, by W.S.
Goulding; Landscape painting in Upper Canada, by J. Russell Harper; The
pallid picture: the image of Ontario in modern literature, by William H.
Magee.   OTU

Ontario in colour. Don Mills, Ontario: J.M. Dent & Sons (Canada) Limited,
1975.
[48]p. chiefly col. illus.   OONL

Pearce, Bruce Murdock, 1900–
An outline of the seventy-five year history of the Norfolk Historical Society.
This historical sketch prepared by Bruce M. Pearce and Mrs. Dorothy A.
Packard. Simcoe, Ontario: Second Avenue Printing, 1975.
16 p. illus., ports.   OTU

Pictorial Ontario, the premier province of the Dominion as pourtrayed with pen
and pencil. Toronto: C.B. Robinson [188–]
viii, 138 p. illus., tables.   OTAR

Pierce, Edith Chown.
Canadian glass: a footnote to history. [Toronto] The Ryerson Press, 1954.
11 p.   OTAR

Prentice, Alison Leeds, 1934–
Family, school and society in nineteenth-century Canada. Edited by Alison
L. Prentice and Susan E. Houston. Toronto: Oxford University Press, 1975.
x, 294 p.   OONL

Pullen–Burry, Bessie.
From Halifax to Vancouver. Toronto: Bell and Cockburn [1912]
xvi, 352 p. illus.
Ontario: pp. 105–190.   OTU

Red Cross (Canada). Ontario Division.
The story of Hurricane Hazel and the part played by the Red Cross.
[Toronto: 1954]
18 p.   OTURS

Reid, Raymond A
Footprints in time: a source book in the history of Ontario. [Don Mills,
Ontario] J.M. Dent & Sons (Canada) Limited [c1967]
xvi, 141 p. illus., facsims. (Dent's Canadian texts)   OLU

Richmond, John Russell, 1926 –
Discover Ontario: originally published as a regular feature in *Toronto
Calendar Magazine*. [Don Mills, Ontario] Fitzhenry & Whiteside [c1974]
90 p. col. illus., maps.   OONL

— Discover Toronto: John Richmond's illustrated notebook. Toronto:
Doubleday Canada Limited, 1976.
122 p. chiefly illus.   OONL

St. John, Frederick Edward Molyneux, 1838–1904.

Ontario old and new. A pamphlet showing the progress that the settled portion of the province of Ontario has made up to date, with a description of the several districts of new Ontario recently surveyed and otherwise opened up for settlement. Winnipeg, Manitoba: Manitoba Free Press Company, 1901.

63 p. illus., map (col. fold.). OTU

St. Lawrence Parks Commission.

Upper Canada Village: "Ontario's living heritage", n.p. [1964?]
[36] p. illus. OTAR

— Upper Canada Village. Ontario's living heritage, 1784–1867 [Morrisburg, Ontario: 1975?]

7 v. (unpaged). illus. OTMCL

Schoonover, Frank Earle, 1877–1972.

The edge of the wilderness; a portrait of the Canadian north by Frank E. Schoonover; Edited by Cortlandt Schoonover. Toronto: Methuen, c1974.

166 p. illus. (some col.).

Travels in the Hudson Bay & James Bay areas between 1900 & 1915. OTU

The Scotsmen in Canada. Toronto: Musson Book Co. [1911]

2 v. ports.

Contents: v.1, Eastern Canada, including Nova Scotia, Prince Edward Island, New Brunswick, Quebec and Ontario, by Wilfred Campbell; v. 2, Western Canada, including Manitoba, Saskatchewan, Alberta, British Columbia, and portions of old Rupert's Land and the Indian Territories, by George Bryce. OTAR

Scott, James, 1916–

Ontario scene. Toronto: The Ryerson Press [c1969]

viii, 262 p. illus. OTU

Sears, Dennis T   Patrick, 1925–

Fair days along the Talbert. Don Mills, Ontario: Musson Book Company [c1976]

x, 199 p.

Life in Ontario during the thirties and forties. OONL

Shackleton, Philip.

The furniture of old Ontario. Toronto: Macmillan of Canada, c1973, 1974.

399 p. illus. (part col.).

Chiefly pre-Confederation. OTAR

Shantz, Stan.

Philately in London, Ontario 1825–1967: a brief history by Stan Shantz and Don Demaray. London, Ontario: London Philatelic Society [1967]

ix, 77 p. illus., facsims. OLU

Shortt, Adam, 1859–1931 (ed.).

Canada and its provinces, a history of the Canadian people and their institutions, by one hundred associates. Adam Shortt, Arthur G. Doughty, general editors. Toronto: Printed by T. & A. Constable at the Edinburgh University Press for the Publishers' Association of Canada, 1914.

23 v. illus., ports., maps, facsims.

Ontario: v. 17–18. OTU

Stevens, Gerald.
   Early Ontario furniture. [Toronto] Royal Ontario Museum, University of
   Toronto [c1966]
   [1] 16 [1] p. illus. (Royal Ontario Museum series, What? why? when? how?
   where? who? no. 13).   OTU
— Early Ontario glass. [Toronto] Royal Ontario Museum, University of
   Toronto, [c1965]
   [1] 16 [1] p. illus. (Royal Ontario Museum series. What? why? when? how?
   where? who? no. 2). 1962.   OTU
Symons, Harry, 1893–1962.
   Fences. Illustrations by C.W. Jeffreys. Toronto: The Ryerson Press [c1958]
   xliv, 155 p. illus.   OTAR
Toronto. Royal Ontario Museum.
   Modesty to mod: dress and underdress in Canada 1780–1967. Toronto
   [Governors of the University of Toronto, c1967]
   71 p. illus.
   In English and French.
   Chiefly dress in Ontario.   OTU
Turnbull, Robert.
   Canada: the story of Ontario. Toronto: McGraw–Hill Company of Canada
   Limited, c1966.
   128 p. illus. (part col.).   OKQ
Unitt, Doris Joyce, 1909–
   Canadian silver, silver plate and related glass by Doris and Peter Unitt.
   [Peterborough, Ontario] Clock House [c1970]
   256 p. illus., ports, facsims. (Collectable Canadiana series, 2).   OOA
— Collect in the Kawartha. [Peterborough, Ontario: Clock House
   Publications: 1966?]
   83 p. illus. (part col.), map, port.   OONL
University Editions Ltd., Montreal.
   Traveller's guides for Canada. Vol. II. Ontario. Toronto: Collins [c1950]
   252 p. maps.
   No volume I located.   OTU
Wallace, William Stewart, 1884–1970.
   A sketch of the history of the Champlain Society. Rev. ed. Toronto:
   Champlain Society, 1957.
   15 p.
   First published 1937. No copy located.   OKQ
Warkentin, Germaine (ed.).
   Stories from Ontario: a selection. [Toronto] Macmillan of Canada [c1974]
   xv, 272 p.   OTU
Weaver, Emily Poynton, 1865–1943.
   The story of the counties of Ontario. With 16 illustrations and a map.
   Toronto: Bell and Cockburn, 1913.
   x, 318 p. plates, map (fold.).
   Map missing.   OTU

Webster, Donald Blake, 1933– (ed.).
  The book of Canadian antiques. Toronto: McGraw–Hill Ryerson Limited
  [c1974]
  352 p. illus.
  Ontario: pp. 110–142.   OMI
Wilson, Barbara M   1931– (ed.).
  Ontario and the first World War 1914–1918: a collection of documents.
  Toronto: The Champlain Society, 1977.
  cxix, 201 p. illus., facsims. (Champlain Society, Toronto. Publications.
  Ontario series, 10).   OTAR

Periodical Articles

Armstrong, J   S   P
  Ontario, province of progress: its enterprise and resources. Commonwealth
  and Empire Review 82(1): 33–38, 1948.
Boylen, J   C
  Progressive Ontario. Canadian Magazine of Politics, Science, Art and
  Literature 40: 25–35, 1913.
Breithaupt, W   H
  The Waterloo Historical Society. Mer Douce 3 (2): 63–64, 1924.
Brief histories of the Society and its chapters. Canadian-German Folklore 4:
  7–13, 1971.
  Pennsylvania Folklore Society of Ontario.
Brown, Andrew H
  Ontario, pivot of Canada's power. National Geographic Magazine 104:
  822–852, 1953.
Canoe routes and geological features of Kowkash district, Ontario. Canadian
  Mining Journal 36: 556–560, 1915.
Carrière, Gaston.
  Nos archives et la Société canadienne d'histoire de l'Eglise catholique.
  Revue de l'Université d'Ottawa 34: 73–96, 1964.
Clay, Charles.
  This is Ontario. Atlantic Guardian 7(3): 37, 39, 42–44, 47–48, 51–52, 55–56,
  59–60, 62–63, 1950.
Courteau, Guy.
  Les origines de la Société Historique du Nouvel-Ontario. Société Historique
  du Nouvel-Ontario. Documents Historiques 1: 15–25, 1942.
Cross, Austin.
  Ontario is lucky. Canadian Business 16(9): 28–32, 162, 164–166, 1943.
Damm, Terry.
  The Kesagami experience. Canadian Geographical Journal 83: 52–59, 1971.
Duff, Louis Blake.
  The problems and opportunities of Canadian historical societies. Canadian
  Historical Review 13: 251–257, 1932.
  Primarily Ontario societies.

Fisher, Claude Laing.
  Ontario, the banner province. Empire Digest 3(12): 54–67, 1946.
Flynn, Louis J
  The early years of the Kingston Historical Society 1893–1906. Historic
  Kingston 11: 35–46, 1963.
— In retrospect; the Kingston Historical Society since 1906. Historic Kingston
  12: 19–26, 1964.
Fraser, Alexander.
  The Ontario Archives: scope of its operation. Paper read at the twenty-
  seventh annual meeting of the American Historical Society held at Buffalo,
  N.Y., December 27–30, 1911. American Historical Society. Annual report
  27: 353–362, 1911.
Harrington, Lyn.
  Canoe country. Canadian Geographical Journal. 33: 72–87, 1946.
Heathcote, A   P
  Guardians of Ontario's past. Ontario Library Review 53: 192–199, 1969.
  Ontario archives.
Hodgkinson, (Mrs.) W   D
  The Wellington County Historical Research Society. Western Ontario
  Historical Notes 2: 56–57, 1944.
Houston, M   Jean.
  Regional history. Ontario History 57: 165–168, 1965.
Howland, O   A
  The Canadian Historical Exhibition, 1897. Canadian Magazine of Politics,
  Science, Art and Literature 7: 165–170, 1897.
Ireland, Willard E
  The provincial archival scene. Canadian Historical Association. Historical
  Papers 69–76, 1953.
Johnson, William F
  The Head-of-the-Lake Historical Society. Western Ontario Historical Notes
  2: 29–31, 1944.
  Hamilton, Ontario.
Jones, Lottie M
  Early American and Canadian glass. Wentworth Bygones 11: 54–58, 1975.
  Chiefly Ontario.
Killan, Gerald.
  The good, the bad, and the occasional touch of the ugly: the Ontario
  Historical Society Papers and Records. Ontario History 67: 57–67, 1975.
Laberge, Joseph Alfred. Société Historique du Nouvel-Ontario. Documents
  Historiques 7: 22–30, 1945.
Lower, Arthur R   M
  Ontario–does it exist? Ontario History 60: 65–69, 1968.
McArthur Duncan.
  The Ontario Archives and the historical societies. Ontario Historical
  Society. Papers and Records 31: 5–10, 1936.

McFall, A   David.
   The York Pioneer and Historical Society–100 years.
   The York Pioneer and Historical Society. Annual Report 2–11, 1969.
McKellar, Peter.
   The decennary anniversary. Thunder Bay Historical Society. Papers 9:
   9–12, 1918.
McOuat, D   F
   Functions and operations of the Historical Branch, Department of Travel
   and Publicity. Ontario History 51: 280–288, 1959.
— Our provincial archives. Ontario History 45: 31–36, 1953.
— Report of the Historical Branch, Department of Travel and Industry.
   Ontario History 53: 137–145, 1961; 54: 107–114, 1962; 55: 164–172, 1963.
Milner, E   M
   The Kent Historical Society. Western Ontario Historical Notes 2: 58–59,
   1944.
Murray, J   McE
   The Ontario Historical Society. Ontario Library Review 16: 54–55, 1931.
Newbery, J   W   E
   Kasabonika–a story of Canadian neglect. Laurentian University Review
   5(no. 4): 51–59, 1973.
Oates, Mercedes.
   Richard H. Oates. York Pioneer and Historical Society. Annual Report,
   12–13, 1927.
Oberholtzer, R   S
   Fences in Waterloo county. Waterloo Historical Society. Annual Volume
   46: 42–45, 1958.
Ontario historical plaques. Ontario History 57: 53–56, 1965; 58: 195–198, 1966;
   59: 209–214, 1967; 60: 162–167, 1968.
The Ontario Historical Society and the preservation of the historic values of the
   St. Lawrence Seaway area. Ontario History 48: 81–85, 1956.
Outline of Wellington County Historical Research Society. Western Ontario
   Historical Notes 14(no. 2): 15–17, 1958.
Parker, John; first president of the Historical Society, Grey county. Mer Douce
   2(2): 28–29, 1922.
Pearce, Bruce M
   Fifty-year review of the Norfolk Historical Society. Western Ontario
   Historical Notes 8: 58–64, 1950.
   Reprinted from Simcoe Reformer February 16, 1950.
Phillips, W   E
   Historical research in Lambton county. Western Ontario Historical Notes 1:
   32–34, 1943.
Schmidt, M   Grace.
   Half-a-century with the Waterloo Historical Society. Waterloo Historical
   Society. Annual Volume 50: 12–16, 1962.
Simpich, Frederick.
   Ontario, next door. National Geographic Magazine 62: 131–184, 1932.

Subjects commemorated by the Archaeological and Historic Sites Board of the
   Province of Ontario in 1963. Ontario History 56: 146–149, 1956.
Talman, James J
   The Ontario Archives. Ontario Library Review 19: 64–66, 1935.
Thomas, Lewis H
   Archival legislation in Canada. Canadian Historical Association. Historical
   Papers 101–115, 1962.
Toronto Historical Board and Scadding Cabin. York Pioneer and Historical
   Society. Annual Report 4–5, 1963.
Warner, Clarance M
   A home for the Ontario Historical Society. Queen's Quarterly 20: 214–220,
   1912/1913.
Weaver, W   F
   Ontario surveys and the land surveyor. Canadian Geographical Journal 32:
   180–191, 1946.
Whitaker, J   R
   Peninsular Ontario: a primary regional division of Canada. Scottish
   Geographical Magazine 54: 263–284, 1938.
Wilson, Ian E
   Archives, the future of the past. Historic Kingston 18: 3–14, 1970.
Woodhouse, T   Roy.
   Twenty-five years. Wentworth Bygones 10: 4–5, 1973.
   Brief history of Head-of-the-Lake Historical Society.
Zaslow, Morris.
   Does northern Ontario possess a regional identity? Laurentian University
   Review 5(no. 4): 9–20, 1973.

Theses

Archer, John Hall, 1914–
   A study of archival institutions in Canada. Kingston, Ontario: 1969.
   2 v. [ix, 688 leaves]
   Ph.D. thesis, Queen's University (microfilm 3423).   OKQ
Clark, Cameron D
   The Algonquin canoeist: a preliminary study of his characteristics,
   motivation, use and attitudes. [Waterloo, Ontario] 1975.
   xvii, 172 leaves. diagrs., maps (part fold. part col.), tables.
   M.A. thesis, University of Waterloo.   OWTU
Cornies, Edward John, 1945–
   Architectural and historical preservation in Ontario. London, Ontario;
   1971.
   vii, 110 leaves.
   M.A. thesis, The University of Western Ontario (microfilm 7844).   OLU
Killan, Gerald.
   Preserving Ontario's heritage: a history of the Ontario Historical Society.
   Hamilton, Ontario: 1973.
   xi, 578 leaves.
   Ph.D. thesis, McMaster University (microfilm 19416).   OHM

Singer, Catharine Lynn.
  An analysis of the components of growth of three Canadian cities: Montreal,
  Toronto, Vancouver. [Toronto] 1975.
  v, 93 leaves, maps, tables.
  B.A. thesis, University of Toronto.   OTU
Staple, Marilyn Grace.
  The extent and intensity of metropolitan influence in eastern Ontario.
  Waterloo, Ontario: 1975.
  x, 187 leaves. diagrs., maps.
  M.A. thesis, University of Waterloo.   OWTU
Taylor, Matthew Craig, 1944–
  Modelling flows of canoeists in Algonquin provincial park. London,
  Ontario: 1972.
  xi, 141 leaves. graphs, tables, maps.
  M.A. thesis, The University of Western Ontario.   OLU
Vipond, Mary Jean, 1943–
  National consciousness in English–speaking Canada in the 1920's: seven
  studies. [Toronto] c1974.
  2 v. [iv, 558 leaves]
  Ph.D. thesis, University of Toronto (microfilm 27521).   OTU

3

Biographical Works: General

Monographs and Pamphlets

Adam, Graeme Mercer, 1839–1912 (ed.).
  Prominent men of Canada. A collection of persons distinguished in
  professional and political life, and in the commerce and industry of Canada.
  Toronto: Canadian Biographical Publishing Company, 1892.
  476 p. illus., ports.   OTAR
Advertiser Job Printing Company, limited, London, Ontario.
  London and its men of affairs. London, Canada: Advertiser Job Printing
  Company, limited [1915?]
  206 p. illus., ports.   OTU
Bannerman, Jean (MacKay), 1904–
  Leading ladies, Canada, 1639–1967. Dundas, Ontario: Carrswood [c1967]
  xxiii, 332 p. ports.   OTAR

Index to Bannerman
Watt, Susan (comp.).
  An alphabetical index to Jean Bannerman's *Leading ladies Canada, 1639–1967*.
  Toronto: 1976.
  vii, 37 p.   OTAR

Bell, Lily M
  Women of action: St. Catharines and area 1876–1976, by Lily M. Bell and
  Kathleen E. Bray. Foreward [sic] by The Honorable Robert Welch.
  Published for The Local Council of Women, for International Women's
  Year, 1975 and St. Catharines Centennial, 1976. [St. Catharines, Ontario:
  Advance Printing Limited, 1976]
  vi, 134 p.   OTAR

Biographical sketches of some residents of Elgin county. Toronto: Art Publishing
  Co. [1885]
  xxxiv p.   OLU
— Reprinted. [St. Thomas, Ontario] Elgin County Library System, 1972.
  xxxix leaves.
  Chiefly pre-Confederation.   OLU
Bissell, Claude Thomas, 1916–   (ed.).
  Seven Canadians. [Toronto] Published in association with Carleton
  University by University of Toronto Press [c1957]
  x, 149 p. (Our living tradition).
  E. Blake, G. Smith, J.A. Macdonald, A. Lampman, S. Leacock, W. Laurier,
  F.P. Grove.   OTU
The Canadian album. Men of Canada; or, Success by example, in religion,
  patriotism, business, law, medicine, education and agriculture. Edited by
  Wm. Cochrane. Brantford, Ontario: Bradley, Garretson & Co., 1891–96.
  5 v. fronts., illus., ports.
  v. 5 was edited by J. Castell Hopkins with title *The Canadian album Encyclopedic
  Canada, or The progress of a nation.*   OOA
Canadian biographical dictionary and portrait gallery of eminent and self-made
  men. Toronto: American Biographical Publishing Co., 1880–81.
  2 v. ports.
  Contents: [v.1] Ontario; [v.2] Quebec and the Maritime provinces.   OTU
Canadian Federation of University Women.
  The clear spirit: twenty Canadian women and their times. Edited by Mary
  Quayle Innis. [Toronto] University of Toronto Press [c1966]
  xvi, 304 p. ports.   OTU
Careless, James Murray Stockford, 1919–
  The Canadians 1867–1967, edited by J.M.S. Careless and R. Craig Brown.
  Toronto: Macmillan Company of Canada Limited, 1967.
  xix, 856 p. plates (part col.).   OTU
Carleton University.
  Our living tradition: second and third series. Edited by Robert L.
  McDougall. [Toronto] Published in association with Carleton University by
  University of Toronto Press [c1959]
  xvi, 288 p.
  Included are lives of: George Brown, Duncan Campbell Scott, A.J.M.
  Smith, E.J. Pratt, F.H. Varley, Egerton Ryerson.   OTURS
Chadwick, Edward Marion, 1840–1921.
  Ontarian families: geneologies of United Empire Loyalists and other pioneer
  families of Upper Canada. Toronto: Rolph, Smith & Co. 1894–1898.
  2 v. plates (part col.).   OKQ OTU
— Lambertville, New Jersey: Hunterdon House [1970]
  203, xii, 194, xii p.
  Reprint of the 1894 edition.   OTULS
— With a new introduction by William F.E. Morley. Belleville, Ontario: Mika
  Silk Screening, 1972.
  v.1 (Canadiana reprint series, no. 23).
  Facsimile reprint of the 1894 Toronto edition.   OTU

Charlesworth, Hector Willoughby, 1872–1945.
    A cyclopedia of Canadian biography: brief biographies of persons
    distinguished in the professional and political life and of commerce and
    industry of Canada in the twentieth century. Toronto: Hunter–Rose
    Company, Limited, 1919.
    xii, 303 p. illus., ports.   OTU
Commemorative biographical record of the county of Essex, Ontario ,
    containing biographical sketches of prominent and representative citizens
    and many of the early settled families... Toronto: J.H. Beers & Co., 1905.
    ix, 676 p. ports.   OTAR
Commemorative biographical record of the county of Kent, Ontario, containing
    biographical sketches of prominent and representative citizens and of many
    of the early settled families... Toronto: J.H. Beers & Co., 1904.
    xii, 874 p. ports.   OTAR
Commemorative biographical record of the county of Lambton, Ontario.
    Compiled by J.H. Beers & Co., Toronto, containing biographical sketches of
    prominent and representative citizens and many of the early settled families
    ... [Toronto] The Hill Binding Co., 1906.
    viii, 840 p. ports.   OKQ
Commemorative biographical record of the county of York, Ontario, containing
    biographical sketches of prominent and representative citizens and many of
    the early settled families... Toronto: J.H. Beers & Co., 1907.
    xiii, 673 p. ports.   OTU
Corbett, Gail (ed.).
    Portraits: Peterborough area women past and present. [Peterborough,
    Ontario: Portraits Group, c1975]
    206 p. illus., ports.   OTU
Dictionary of Canadian biography. Toronto: University of Toronto Press, 1966–
    v.
    Contents: v. 1, 1000–1700; v. 2, 1701–1740; v. 3, 1741–1770; v. 9,
    1861–1870; v. 10, 1871–1880.   OTU
Eby, Ezra E   1850–1901.
    A biographical history of early settlers and their descendants in Waterloo
    township, 1895 and 1896. Supplement by Joseph B. Snyder, 1931. Index,
    notes, maps and other documents by Eldin D. Weber. Kitchener, Ontario:
    Weber, 1971.
    1 v. (various pagings). illus., facsims., maps, port.   OTU
— A biographical history of the Eby family, being a history of their movements
    in Europe, during the Reformation and of their early settlement in America;
    as also much other unpublished historical information belonging to the
    family. Berlin, Ontario: Hett and Eby, 1889.
    144 p. illus.   OTURS
— A biographical history of Waterloo township and other townships of the
    county, being a history of the early settlers and their descendants, mostly all
    of Pennsylvania Dutch origin as also much other unpublished historical
    information, chiefly of a local character. Berlin, Ontario: 1895–96.
    2 v.   OTU

Gagan, David Paul, 1940–
  The Denison family of Toronto, 1792–1925. [Toronto] University of Toronto
  Press [1973]
  xii, 113 p. illus. (Canadian biographical studies, 5).   OTU
Gartshore, William Moir, 1853–1931.
  Leaves from a lifetime; being a brief history of the Gartshore family in
  Scotland; of the Gartshore and Moir families, as pioneers in early days in
  Ontario; and of the life and reminiscences to date of William Moir
  Gartshore. Edited by Margaret Wade. London, Ontario: A. Talbot & Co.
  [1929]
  165 p. ports.   OLU
The Globe, Toronto.
  Builders of Greater Toronto. Toronto, Wednesday, February 21, 1934.
  24 p. illus., ports.
  Special issue: v.91, no.26, 258.   OTU
Greater Toronto and the men who made it. Toronto: Inter–Provincial
  Publishing Co., 1911.
  237 p. chiefly illus., ports.
  With the signature of James L. Baillie.   OTURS
Hamilton, Ross (ed.).
  Prominent men of Canada, 1931–32. Montreal: National Publishing Co. of
  Canada [1932?]
  640 p.   OTU
Her own woman: profiles of ten Canadian women, by Myrna Kostash, Melinda
  McCracken, Valerie Miner, Erna Paris, Heather Robertson. Toronto:
  Macmillan of Canada [c1975]
  ix, 212 p. ports.   OTU
Holdaway, Dora, 1922–
  Famous Canadians of the Great Pine Ridge. Bewdley, Ontario: Pine Ridge
  Publications [1967]
  47 p. chiefly ports.   OTAR
Kincade, Winifred, 1888–
  The torch: Ontario monuments to great names. Regina, Saskatchewan:
  School Aids & Text Book Publishing Co. Ltd. [1962]
  298 p. illus.   OTAR OKQ
Leading financial and business men of Toronto; a work of artistic color plates
  designed to portray one hundred leading men of Toronto, both financially
  and socially... Toronto: E. McCormick, 1912.
  [204] p. col. ports.   OTU
Macdonald, Adrian, 1889–
  Canadian portraits. Toronto: The Ryerson Press [c1925]
  230 p.
  Includes Egerton Ryerson, Paul Peel, Archibald Lampman.   OTER
McFarlane, Alice (comp.).
  Some women in London's past. [London, Ontario: 1973]
  1 v. (unpaged).   OL

McLaren, John W
Our great ones: twelve caricatures cut in linoleum. With footnotes by
Merrill Denison and a foreword by E.J. Pratt. [1st ed.] Toronto: The
Ryerson Press, 1932.
[28] p. 12 plates.
Contents: Includes Colonel Talbot, John Strachan, George Brown, Egerton
Ryerson. OTURS

Matheson, Gwen Marion (ed.).
Women in the Canadian mosaic. Toronto: Peter Martin Associates, Limited
[c1976]
x, 353 p. ports., tables. OTU

Metropolitan Toronto. Central Library.
Index to biographical scrapbooks. [Toronto] Metropolitan Toronto Library
Board, 1973.
263 p.
The Biographical scrapbooks consist of 89 volumes, on 32 reels of microfilm,
of clippings from Toronto newspapers from 1911 to 1967, with a few earlier
clippings and pamphlets. OTMCL

Morgan, Henry James, 1842–1913.
The Canadian men and women of the time: a handbook of Canadian
biography. 1st ed. Toronto: William Briggs, 1898.
xii, 1117 p. OTU

— The Canadian men and women of the time: a handbook of Canadian
biography of living characters. 2d ed. Toronto: William Briggs, 1912.
xx, 1218 p. ports. OTU

— Types of Canadian women and of women who are or have been connected
with Canada. Toronto: William Briggs, 1903.
x, 382 p. ports.
A second volume was projected but never published. OTAR

Morris, Audrey Yvonne, 1930–
Gentle pioneers: five nineteenth-century Canadians. Toronto: Hodder and
Stoughton [1968]
xv, 253 p. facsims.
Chiefly pre-Confederation. OTAR

National encyclopedia of Canadian biography; Jesse Edgar Middleton and W.
Scott Downs, directing editors. Toronto: The Dominion Publishing
Company, Limited, 1935–37.
2 v. front., ports. OTU

Prominent people of the province of Ontario. Ottawa: Canadian Biographies,
1925.
273 p. illus., ports. OTU

Roberts, Leslie, 1896–
These be your gods... illustrated by A. G. Racey. Toronto: The Musson
Book Company Ltd. [c1929]
319 p. illus., ports.
Includes: Hon. G. Howard Ferguson, Sir Robert Falconer, Hon. Vincent
Massey. OLU

[Roebuck, Arthur Wentworth, 1878–1971]
  Sketches of early New Liskeard settlers. [New Liskeard, Ontario:
  Temiskaming Herald] 1904.
  1 v. (unpaged). illus.
  "Drawings by J.W. Bengough."   OTAR
Rose, George Maclean, 1829–1898 (ed.).
  A cyclopaedia of Canadian biography: being chiefly men of the time. A
  collection of persons distinguished in professional and political life; leaders in
  the commerce and industry of Canada, and successful pioneers. Toronto:
  Rose Publishing Company, 1886–1888.
  2 v.   OTU
St. Thomas and its men of affairs. St. Thomas, Ontario: Journal Printing
  Company, Limited, 1914.
  110 p. ports., illus.   OLU
— Reprinted, with an introduction to this edition by Donald L. Cosens. St.
  Thomas: Richard Cochrill Limited, 1976.
  110 p. illus., ports.   OLU
Stiles, H   M   (comp.).
  Who's who: a complete compendium containing facts and figures, in story
  and illustration, of the town of Smiths Falls and its inhabitants . . . The
  railway metropolis of the Ottawa valley. [Smiths Falls, Ontario:
  Record–News Press Ltd., 1924]
  94 p. illus., ports.   OKQ
Taché, Louis Joseph Charles Hyppolyte, 1859–1927 (comp.).
  Men of the day, a Canadian portrait gallery. [Popular ed.] Montreal:
  Montreal Paper Mills Co. [1890]
  507 p. facsims., ports.   OTU
Wallace, William Stewart, 1884–1970.
  The dictionary of Canadian biography. Toronto: Macmillan Company of
  Canada, 1926.
  iv, 433 p.   OTU
— [2d ed. rev. & enl.] Toronto: Macmillan Company of Canada, 1945.
  2 v.   OTU
— The Macmillan dictionary of Canadian biography. 3d ed. rev. and enl.
  Toronto: Macmillan, 1963.
  822 p.   OTU

Periodical Articles
Collingwood "old boys". Huron Institute. Papers and Records 2(part 1): 5–130,
  1914.
  Short biographical sketches of former Collingwood residents.

4

Climate and Physiography of Ontario

Bibliography
Donkin, Kate (comp.).
Union list of atlases in Ontario universities. Compiled by Kate Donkin and
Rita Finch. Toronto: Council of Ontario Universities, 1976.
253 p. diagrs.   OTU
May, Betty.
County atlases of Canada: a descriptive catalogue, compiled by Betty May,
assisted by Frank McGuire and Heather Maddick. [Ottawa] National Map
Collection Division, Public Archives of Canada, 1970.
xii, 192 p. illus., maps.   OTAR
Scollie, Frederick Brent.
Fort William, Port Arthur, Ontario, and vicinity, 1857–1969: an annotated
list of maps in Toronto libraries, compiled and with an introduction by
Frederick Brent Scollie. Thunder Bay, Ontario: 1971.
67 leaves. maps (part fold.).   OTUMA
Taylor, David Ruxton Fraser, 1937–
A computer atlas of Ottawa – Hull, with a bibliography of computer-
mapping, by D.R.F. Taylor and D.H. Douglas. 2d ed. Ottawa: Department
of Geography, Carleton University, 1970.
71 p. maps.   OTU
Thomas, Morley K   (comp.).
A bibliography of Canadian climate 1763–1957. Ottawa: Meteorological
Branch, Department of Transport, 1961.
114 p.   OTU
— A bibliography of Canadian climate 1958–1971/Bibliographie du climat
Canadien. Ottawa: Atmospheric Environment, Environment Canada, 1973.
170 p.   OTU

Monographs and Pamphlets
Brown, D   M
>The climate of southern Ontario, by D.M. Brown, G.A. McKay and L.J.
>Chapman. Toronto: Meteorological Branch, Canada Department of
>Transport, 1968.
>vii, 50 p. graphs, maps, tables. (Climatological studies, no. 5).   OTU
Canada. Commission of Conservation. Committee on Forests.
>Trent watershed survey. A reconnaissance by C.D. Howe and J.H. White,
>with an introductory discussion by B.E. Fernow. Ottawa: Bryant Press, 1913.
>[viii] 156 p. plates, maps, diagrs., tables.   OTAR OONL
Cannon, K
>Province of Ontario; geographical aspects. [Ottawa: The Canadian
>Geographical Society, 1948]
>1 v. (unpaged). illus., maps.   OOA
Chapman, Lyman John, 1908–
>The physiography of eastern Ontario, by L.J. Chapman and D.F. Putnam.
>n.p.: Scientific Agriculture, 1943.
>[18] p. illus., diagr., table.
>Reprinted from *Scientific Agriculture* 20: 424–441, 7 March, 1940.   OTU
— The physiography of southern Ontario, by L.J. Chapman and D.F. Putnam.
>[Toronto] Published for Ontario Research Foundation by the University of
>Toronto Press, 1951.
>284 p. illus., maps (part fold.).   OTU
— 2d ed. [Toronto] Published for the Ontario Research Foundation by
>University of Toronto Press, 1966.
>xiv, 386 p. illus., maps.   OTER
— The physiography of southwestern Ontario, by L.J. Chapman and D.F.
>Putnam. n.p.: Scientific Agriculture, 1943.
>[25] p. illus., diagrs.
>Reprinted from *Scientific Agriculture* 24: 101–125, November, 1943.   OTU
Dean, William George, 1921–
>Toronto into Muskoka; a geographic traverse [by] W.G. Dean and E.B.
>MacDougall. [Toronto: 1966]
>[2] 68 leaves. maps.
>"Prepared for field trip A, American Association of Geographers, annual
>meeting, August 29, 1966".   OTU
Fieguth, Wolfgang Wilfrid, 1925–
>The personality of North Simcoe county, a study in historical geography.
>Cartography by Sally B. Lyon. London, Ontario: Department of
>Geography, University of Western Ontario, 1968.
>53 leaves. maps. (Department of Geography, University of Western Ontario.
>Occasional paper, no. 2).   OMI OTU
Fernow, Bernhard Edward, 1851–1923.
>Conditions in the clay belt of new Ontario. [Ottawa] Commission of
>Conservation, 1913.
>36 p. map.   OOA

Findlay, B   F
  Climatography of Pukaskwa National Park, Ontario: a climatological
  inventory prepared for the National and Historic Parks Branch, Department
  of Indian Affairs and Northern Development. Toronto: Applications and
  Consultation Division, Atmospheric Environment Service, 1973.
  iii, 46 [7] 56 leaves. diagrs., maps, tables.   OTU
Gad, Günter Helmut Karl, 1939–
  A cartographic summary of the growth and structure of the cities of central
  Canada, by Günter Gad and Alan Baker. [Toronto] Department of
  Geography, University of Toronto, 1969.
  41 leaves. fold. maps. (Environment study. Research report no. 11).   OTU
Gage's county atlas, containing county maps of the province of Ontario, maps of
  the provinces of Manitoba and Quebec and railway maps of Ontario and
  Quebec, and map of the Eastern townships. Compiled from the most reliable
  sources and carefully revised to date. Toronto: W.J. Gage and Company,
  1886.
  1 v. (unpaged). maps.   OOA
Goad, Charles Edward,   –1910.
  Atlas of the city of Toronto and suburbs from special survey and registered
  plans showing all buildings and lot numbers. Toronto: The Author, 1884.
  163 p. col. maps.   OLU
— Atlas of the city of Toronto and suburbs; founded on registered plans and
  special surveys showing plan numbers, lots & buildings. 3d ed. Toronto:
  Goad's Atlas and Plan Co., 1910.
  3 v.   OTY
— Atlas of the city of Toronto and vicinity; from special survey founded on
  registered plans and showing all buildings and lot numbers. 2d ed.
  Montreal: C.E. Goad, 1890.
  50 fold. plans.   OTY
— [Rev.] 2d ed. Montreal [1891]
  50 fold. plans.   OTY
Hamilton – Wentworth Planning Area Board
  Atlas of the county of Wentworth. Hamilton, Ontario: The Board, 1959–60.
  38 maps.   OH
Hare, Frederick Kenneth, 1910–
  Climate Canada, by F. Kenneth Hare and Morley K. Thomas. Toronto:
  Wiley Publishers of Canada Limited [c1974]
  256 p. illus., diagrs., maps, tables.   OTMCL
Harrison, Philip Wyman, 1931–   (ed.).
  Credit River valley report: geology, hazard designations, and zoning of
  valley–wall materials between Port Credit and Glen Williams. [Toronto]
  Erindale College, University of Toronto, 1973.
  2 v. diagrs., maps, tables.   OTU

Higgins, Frank G
  A physical and cultural atlas of Lambton county, by Frank G. Higgins and
  Michael R. Kanouse. [Sarnia, Ontario] Lambton County Historical Society,
  c1969.
  ii, 65 leaves. diagrs., maps.   OTU
Kerr, Donald Gordon Grady, 1913–1976 (ed.).
  A historical atlas of Canada. Cartography preparation by C.C.J. Bond,
  drawing by Ellsworth M. Walsh assisted by Edward Banks and Ray
  Petticrew. Toronto: Thomas Nelson & Sons (Canada) Limited [c1960]
  ix, 120 p. illus., col. maps, col. diagrs.   OTUMA
— 2d ed. Don Mills, Ontario: Thomas Nelson & Sons (Canada) Limited
  [1966]
  ix, 120 p. illus. (part col.), col. maps.   OTULS
— 3d ed. rev. [Don Mills, Ontario] Thomas Nelson & Sons (Canada) Limited,
  1975.
  iii, 100 p. graphs (part col.), col. maps.   OTULS
Maddick, Heather (comp.).
  County maps; land ownership maps of Canada in the 19th century.
  Introduction by Joan Winearls. Ottawa: National Map Collection, Public
  Archives of Canada, 1976.
  vi, 94 p. maps, port.
  Text in English and French.   OTAR
Miles & Co., publishers.
  The new topographical atlas of the province of Ontario, Canada. Compiled
  from the latest official and general maps and surveys and corrected to date
  from the most reliable public and private sources of information, comprising
  an official railway, postal, and distance map of the whole province, and a
  correct and complete series of separate county maps on a large scale,
  showing lots and concessions, railways, post offices, opened and closed roads,
  churches, school-houses, main travelled roads, county statistics, division
  court boundaries, etc., together with maps of the chief cities and county
  towns, and a brief sketch of the history and geology of the province. Also a
  series of recently issued maps showing the whole Dominion of Canada and
  the United States. Toronto: Miles & Co., 1879.
  130 p. chiefly part. col. maps.   OKQ OLU
Nagy, Thomas L
  Ottawa in maps: a brief cartographical history of Ottawa. Ottawa par les
  cartes: brève histoire cartographie de la ville d'Ottawa, 1825–1973. Ottawa:
  National Map Collection, Public Archives Canada, 1974.
  li, 87 p. col. maps.   OTU
North York, Ontario. Public Works Department.
  Metropolitan Toronto Mapping Authority proposal. [J.H. Bleyney,
  chairman, Study Group Committee, Central Mapping Authority, North
  York, Ontario] 1973.
  1 v. (various pagings). maps.   OTUMA
Perly, Allan Morris, 1913–
  Bluemap atlas of greater Toronto, Malton, Port Credit, Cooksville,
  Clarkson, Streetsville, etc. Executive ed. [Toronto] Variprint Services, 1956.
  51 maps.   OTU

— Detail atlas, province of Ontario; counties, townships, municipalities and hamlets, populations, roads, forests, waterways, etc. Executive [1st] ed. Toronto: Variprint Service [c1957]
92 p. chiefly col. maps, coats of arms.   OTU
— Rev. Executive edition. Toronto: Variprint service, 1965.
1 v. (unpaged).   OTU

Putnam, Donald Fulton, 1903–   (ed.).
Canadian regions: a geography of Canada. Toronto: J.M. Dent & Sons (Canada) Limited [c1952]
ix, 601 p. illus., graphs., maps, tables.
Ontario: pp. 213–339.   OTU
— [2d ed.] Toronto: J.M. Dent & Sons (Canada) Limited [c1954]
No copy located.
— [3d. ed. rev.] Toronto: J.M. Dent & Sons (Canada) Limited [1957]
ix, 601 p. illus., graphs, maps, tables.   OTU
— [4th ed.] Toronto: J.M. Dent & Sons (Canada) Limited [1960]
No copy located.
— [5th ed.] Toronto: J.M. Dent & Sons (Canada) Limited [1961]
ix, 601 p. illus., graphs, maps, tables.   OLU
— [6th ed.] Toronto: J.M. Dent & Sons (Canada) Limited [1963]
ix, 601 p. illus., graphs., maps, tables.   OTU
— [7th ed.] Toronto: J.M. Dent & Sons (Canada) Limited [1965]
ix, 601 p. illus., graphs, maps, tables.   OLU
— A regional geography of Canada, by Donald F. Putnam and Donald P. Kerr. [rev. ed.] Toronto: J.M. Dent & Sons (Canada) Limited [c1964]
vii, 520 p. illus., graphs, maps.
Ontario: pp. 185–304.   OTU

Shenfeld, Louis.
The climate of Toronto, by Louis Shenfeld and D.F.A. Slater. n.p.: 1960.
52 p. diagrs., map.
At head of title: Meteorological Branch, Department of Transport, Canada.
                                                                           OTU

Vandall, Paul Ernest, 1920–   (ed.).
Atlas of Essex county: its cultural, economic and physical characteristics graphically presented. [Windsor, Ontario] Published under the sponsorship of the Essex County Historical Association [1965]
51 leaves. chiefly illus., maps.   OTU

Whebell, Charles Frederick John, 1930–
The cultural geography of the Norfolk sand plain: a field trip introduction to some landscapes of southwestern Ontario. London, Ontario: Department of Geography, University of Western Ontario, 1966.
iv, 38 leaves. maps. (Department of Geography, University of Western Ontario. Occasional papers, no. 1).   OTU

Periodical Articles
Bishop, J   M
    Aerial surveys in Ontario. Canadian Geographical Journal 32: 214–225,
    1946.
— A second look at aerial surveys in Ontario. Canadian Geographical Journal
    54: 78–89, 1957.
Chapman, Lyman J
    Climate of southern Ontario. Canadian Geographical Journal 18: 136–141,
    1938.
Classen, H   George.
    Georgian Bay survey; cradle of Canadian hydrography. Canadian
    Geographical Journal 66: 158–163, 1963.
Coates, Donald F
    Mapping the North; establishing the land control for aerial survey on James
    Bay. Canadian Geographical Journal 43: 58–69, 1951.
Coombs, Donald B
    The physiographic subdivisions of the Hudson Bay lowlands south of 60
    degrees north. Geographical Bulletin 6: 1–16, 1954.
McKenzie, Thomas H
    Topographical sketch of Hamilton as it was in 1830 and 1881. Wentworth
    Historical Society. Journal and Transactions 1: 178–181, 1892.
Magnetic survey of Albany River. Natural Resources, Canada, 9(no. 2): 2,
    1930.
Nichols, D   A
    The geographic setting of northern Ontario. Canadian Geographical
    Journal 18: 146–151, 1939.
Packer, R   W
    The geographical basis of the regions of southwestern Ontario. Canadian
    Historical Association. Historical Papers 45–52, 1953.
Richardson, A   II
    The Ganaraska watershed survey. Canadian Geographical Journal 28:
    188–197, 1944.
Riddell, William Renwick.
    Toronto in cartography. Ontario Historical Society. Papers & Records 28:
    143–145, 1932.
Robinson, J   Lewis.
    Windsor, Ontario: a study in urban geography. Canadian Geographical
    Journal 27: 106–121, 1943.
Taylor, Griffith.
    Climate and crop isopleths for southern Ontario. Economic Geography 14:
    89–97, 1938.

Watson, J   W
    Mapping a hundred years of change in the Niagara peninsula. Canadian
    Geographical Journal 32: 266–283, 1946.
Williams, W   R
    Georgian Bay gales. Inland Seas 9: 145–146, 1953.

Theses
Anderson, John C
    Climatonomic experiments in southern Ontario. [Toronto] 1971.
    ix, 139 leaves. figs., tables.
    M.A. research paper, University of Toronto.   OTU
Archer, Paula E
    The urban snow hazard. A case study of the perception of, adjustments to,
    and wage and salary losses suffered from snowfall in the city of Toronto
    during the winter of 1967–1968. [Toronto] 1970.
    vi, 43 [1] 5 leaves.
    M.A. research paper, University of Toronto.   OTU
Bradley, George Elmer.
    The snowbelt in western Ontario. [Toronto] 1962.
    v, 34 leaves. tables, figs.
    B.A. thesis, University of Toronto.   OTU
Didier, Louis M
    The Highland Creek watershed: a geographical appreciation. [Toronto]
    1955.
    45 leaves. illus., maps (part col.).
    B.A. thesis, University of Toronto.   OTU
Elliott, Flavia.
    Topographic control in Prince Edward county. [Toronto] 1948.
    52 leaves. illus. (part col.), maps (part col. part fold.).
    B.A. thesis, University of Toronto.   OTU
Fremlin, Gerald, 1924–
    Geomorphology of the Niagara escarpment, Niagara River – Georgian Bay.
    London, Ontario: 1958.
    xi, 163 leaves. illus., diagrs., map.
    M.A. thesis, The University of Western Ontario.   OLU
Geiger, Marjorie Jane.
    An analysis of the snowbelt phenomenon of southwestern Ontario. Waterloo,
    Ontario: 1971.
    vii, 87 leaves. graphs, maps, tables.
    M.A. thesis, University of Waterloo.   OWTU
Johnson, Ronald C   A   1944–
    Drought in the St. Clair region. Windsor, Ontario: 1969.
    vii, 82 leaves. diagrs., maps, tables.
    M.A. thesis, University of Windsor.   OWA

Laurence, Richard.
   On the potential for rainfall enhancement in southwestern Ontario.
   [Toronto] 1976.
   xii, 164 leaves. illus., maps.
   M.Sc. thesis, University of Toronto.   OTU
McClellan, John Burton.
   The physical and agricultural geography of Pelham township. [Hamilton,
   Ontario] 1955.
   vi, 79 leaves. plates, maps, graphs.
   B.A. thesis, McMaster University.   OHM
Martin, Barry G
   The historical geography of the Upper York River watershed up to 1930.
   Waterloo, Ontario: 1965.
   43 leaves. illus., maps, tables.
   B.A. thesis, Waterloo University College.   OWTL
Merrill, Curtis Leroy, 1917–
   The variability of precipitation in southwestern Ontario. [London, Ontario]
   1951.
   vii, 108 leaves. illus., graphs, tables, maps.
   M.Sc. thesis, The University of Western Ontario.   OLU
Midgley, Edward Ernest.
   Patterns of drought in southern Ontario. [Toronto] 1965.
   v, 30 leaves. diagrs., fold. maps.
   B.A. thesis, University of Toronto.   OTU
Ramasastry, C   V   1946–
   The probability of climatically derived seasonal surface runoff in southern
   Ontario. [Windsor, Ontario] 1976.
   vii, 90 leaves. diagrs., maps, tables.
   M.A. thesis, University of Windsor.   OWA
Roberts, Michael Charles.
   Aspects of the physiography of the Humber River basin. [Toronto] 1963.
   xii, 162 leaves. illus., figs. (1 fold.), maps (1 fold.).
   M.A. thesis, University of Toronto (accepted 1965).   OTU
Rouse, Wayne Robert.
   A physical and agricultural geography of Cavan township. [Hamilton,
   Ontario] 1961.
   v, 95 leaves. illus., maps.
   B.A. thesis, McMaster University.   OHM
Sangal, Beni Prasad, 1929–
   Estimation of evaporation and evapotranspiration: a comparative study of
   the Budyko approach with special reference to southern Ontario. London,
   Ontario: 1972.
   xvi, 214 leaves. graphs, tables, maps.
   Ph.D. thesis, The University of Western Ontario.   8LU

Saunders, Joan Stuart.
  Geographical distribution of precipitation in southern Ontario. [Toronto]
  1972.
  vii, 84 leaves. tables, figs., maps.
  B.A. thesis, University of Toronto.   OTU
Seifried, Neil Robert Michael, 1936–
  A study of summer precipitation at Windsor airport, London airport, and
  Toronto. [Toronto] 1960.
  iv, 55 leaves. illus., maps.
  B.A. thesis, University of Toronto.   OTU

5

Economic History

GENERAL

Bibliography
Brown, Barbara E   1927–   (ed.).
    Canadian business and economics: a guide to sources of information /sources
    d'informations economiques et commerciales Canadienne. [Ottawa:
    Canadian Library Association, 1976]
    xviii, 636 p.   OTULS

Monographs and Pamphlets
Brockville illustrated 1894: its growth, resources, commerce, manufacturing
    interests, educational advantages; also sketches of the leading business
    concerns which contribute to the city's progress and prosperity. Brockville,
    Ontario: J.H. Godkin and A.G. Davie [1894?]
    40 p. illus., ports.   OKQ
CCH Canadian Limited.
    Ontario portable pension plan legislation. Don Mills, Ontario [c1963]
    37 p. tables.   OONL
  — [2d ed.] Don Mills, Ontario [1963]
    37 p. tables.   OONL
  — 3d ed. Don Mills, Ontario [c1964]
    45 p. tables.   OONL
Campbell, William C
    Commercial gazetteer and atlas; containing commercial maps of the world,
    North America, Dominion of Canada, Ontario, Quebec, Maritime provinces
    and the United States, with sectional maps of all the counties of Ontario.
    Toronto: Oxford Publishing Co., 1885.
    1 v. (unpaged). col. maps   OTU

Canada. Bureau of Statistics.
>   Estimates of employees by province and industry 1961–1964. Ottawa:
>   Research and Analysis Section, Labour Division, Bureau of Statistics, 1965.
>   24 p. graph, tables.   OONL

Canada. Department of Agriculture.
>   Eastern Canada, comprising the Maritime provinces and the provinces of
>   Ontario and Quebec. Information respecting physical features, climate,
>   agricultural productions, fisheries, and manufacturing industries, 1897.
>   Ottawa: Government Printing Bureau, 1898.
>   63 p. illus., fold. col. map, table.   OTU

Canadian Institute of International Affairs.
>   The Canadian economy and its problems. Papers and proceedings of study
>   groups of members of the Canadian Institute of International Affairs,
>   1933–1934. Edited by H.A. Innis and A.F.W. Plumptre. Toronto: Canadian
>   Institute of International Affairs, 1934.
>   356 p. illus., diagrs., tables.   OTV

Collins, Lyndhurst, 1941–
>   Industrial migration in Ontario: forecasting aspects of industrial activity
>   through Markov chain analysis. Ottawa: Regional Statistics Research and
>   Integration Staff, Statistics Canada, 1972.
>   154 p. illus., map.   OTMCL

Colloquium on Regional Economic Development, Memorial University of
Newfoundland, 1969 .
>   Collected papers. St. John's, Newfoundland [1972]
>   176 p. illus., maps.
>   Contents: pp. 39–55, Thoman, Richard: Regional development in Ontario.
>   "Canadian Association of Geographers Annual conference".   OTER

Connor, Desmond Maurice, 1929–
>   Strategics for development. Ottawa: Development Press, 1968.
>   48 p. illus., forms.   OTER

Coward, Laurence E   1914–   (ed.).
>   Pensions in Canada, a compendium of fact and opinion. Don Mills,
>   Ontario: C.C.H. Canadian Limited [c1964]
>   ix, 226 p. tables.
>   Ontario: pp. 1–5, 27–44.   OTU

Crispo, John Herbert Gillespie, 1933–
>   The management gap in Ontario: a study commissioned by the Ontario
>   government, by John Crispo and John Wettlaufer. [Toronto] 1973.
>   79 leaves. illus.   OTU

Cross, Michael Sean, 1938–
>   The workingman in the 19th century. Toronto: Oxford University Press,
>   1974.
>   xii, 316 p. tables.   OTU

Currie, Archibald William, 1908–
>   Canadian economic development. Toronto: Thomas Nelson & Sons Limited
>   [c1942]
>   v, 386 p.   OTU

— Economic geography of Canada. Toronto: Macmillan Company of Canada
 Limited, 1945.
  xiv, 455 p. illus. maps.
  Ontario: pp. 313–387.   OTU
Dean, William George, 1921–
  Economic atlas of Ontario. By W.G. Dean and G.J. Matthews. [1st ed.
  Toronto] Published for the government of Ontario by University of Toronto
  Press [1969]
  1 v. (unpaged). 113 col. maps.   OTUMA
Erie Economic Council.
  Significant economic information. London, Ontario: Economic Council –
  Erie area, 1970.
  14 p. chiefly tables.   OTU
Farr, Charles Cobbold, 1851–1914.
  The Lake Temiscamingue district, province of Ontario, Canada. A
  description of its soil, climate, products, area, agricultural capabilities and
  other resources, together with information pertaining to the sale of public
  lands. Toronto: Warwick & Sons, 1893.
  16 p. map.   OTURS
Firestone, Otto Jack, 1913–
  Industry and education: a century of Canadian development. Ottawa:
  University of Ottawa Press, 1969.
  xviii, 295 p. tables. (Ottawa. University. Social science studies, no.5)   OTU
— Regional economic development. Ottawa: University of Ottawa Press, 1974.
  xi, 274 p. diagrs., tables. (Ottawa. University. Social science studies, no.9).
                                                                             OTU
Fraser, R   D
  A research agenda in health care economics. Toronto: Ontario Economic
  Council, 1975.
  1 v. (various pagings). diagrs. (Ontario Economic Council. Working paper
  2/75).   OTER
Gardner, H   W   (comp.).
  London, Ontario, Canada: a presentation of her resources, achievements
  and possibilities: an authentic compilation of the city's industrial, financial
  and civic activities. [London, Ontario] London Free Press, 1914.
  92 p. illus. (part col.), map, ports.   OLU
Hamilton, James Cleland, 1836–1907.
  The Georgian Bay, an account of its position, inhabitants, mineral interests,
  fish, timber and other resources with map and illustrations... Toronto:
  James Bain & Son, 1893.
  vii, 170 p. illus.
  Map missing from copy examined.   OTURS
Hard times in Ontario: a pretty story, certainly. Kingston: Daily News Office,
  1872.
  36 p.   OTAR

Heaton, Ernest (comp.).
    Opportunities in Ontario, 1919. [Toronto: Heaton's Agency, 1919]
    96 p. illus., map. (The Canadian provincial booklets).   OTAR
Innis, Harold Adams, 1894–1952 (ed.).
    Select documents in Canadian economic history, 1783–1885, edited by H.A.
    Innis and A.R.M. Lower. Toronto: University of Toronto Press, 1933.
    viii, 846 p. tables.   OTU
Innis, Mary Quayle, 1899–1972.
    An economic history of Canada. Toronto: The Ryerson Press [c1935]
    ix, 302 p. illus.   OTU
— [2d ed., enl.] Toronto: The Ryerson Press [1943]
    ix, 363 p. illus.   OTU
— [New ed.] Toronto: The Ryerson Press [1954]
    ix, 384 p. illus.   OTU
Jackson, Eric (ed.).
    The great Canadian debate: foreign ownership. Toronto: McClelland and
    Stewart Limited [c1975]
    64 p. illus. (Foundations of Contemporary Canada series, no.3).   OTER
Jackson, John Nicholas, 1925–
    Priority issues in south Ontario: a study by the South Ontario Economic
    Development Council. Grimsby, Ontario: South Ontario Economic
    Development Council, 1972.
    [16] p.   OOP
Judek, Stanislaw.
    Canada's seasonal variations in employment and unemployment 1953–73.
    Ottawa: Faculty of Social Sciences, University of Ottawa, 1975.
    i, 118 [9] leaves. tables.   OTY
Keirstead, Burton Seeley, 1907–1973 (ed.).
    Economics Canada: selected readings. Toronto: Macmillan of Canada,
    1974.
    495 p.   OTU
Kitchen, Harry M
    Some preliminary evidence on family income. [Toronto] Ontario Economic
    Council, 1975.
    41 leaves. tables. (Ontario Economic Council. Working paper, no.1/75).
                                                                              OTER
Kubursi, A   A
    Sectoral characteristics of the Ontario structure of production, by A.A.
    Kubursi and R.H. Frank. Hamilton, Ontario: Department of Economics,
    McMaster University, 1972.
    55 [4] leaves. (McMaster University. Department of Economics. Working
    paper series, no. 72–05).   OTU
— Sectoral performance indices of the Ontario structure of production , by A.A.
    Kubursi and R.H. Frank. Hamilton, Ontario: Department of Economics,
    McMaster University, 1973.

39 [5] leaves. (McMaster University. Department of Economics. Working
paper series, no.73–09).   OTU

— Sub-provincial regional income multipliers in the Ontario economy: an
input-output approach by A.A. Kubursi, J.R. Williams and P.J. George.
Hamilton, Ontario: McMaster University, Department of Economics, 1973.
27 [5] leaves. (McMaster University. Department of Economics. Working
paper series, no.73–04).   OTU

Lake Erie Regional Development Association.
An atlas of economic growth of Elgin, Middlesex, Norfolk and Oxford
counties (Lake Erie economic region). [Maps prepared by the Department
of Geography, University of Western Ontario, under the direction of R.W.
Packer] London, Ontario [1965?]
iv leaves. 43 maps.   OTUMA

Lawson, Matthew B   M
Jobs and the economy: a study of employment and employment generating
activities [Toronto] Municipality of Metropolitan Toronto Planning
Department, 1975.
xi, 428 p. illus., col. maps (part fold.), graphs, tables. (Background studies in
the metropolitan plan preparation programme, no.7).   OTUSA

— The maintenance of property – a program for Ontario. [Toronto: 1970?]
61 p. illus.   OTU

Lithwick, Norman Harvey.
Economic growth in Canada: a quantitative analysis. [Toronto] University
of Toronto Press [c1967]
xiv, 128 p. tables.   OTMCL

— 2d ed. [Toronto] University of Toronto Press [c1970]
xiv, 145 p. tables.   OTMCL

Metropolitan Toronto. Planning Board.
A brief, prepared by the Planning Board, heads of departments, and officials
of the municipality of Metropolitan Toronto, presented to the Royal
Commission on Canada's Economic Prospects by Frederick G. Gardiner,
January 23rd, 1956. [Toronto: 1956]
209 p. plans (part fold.).   OTUSA

Mid-Western Ontario Regional Development Association.
Economic research and feasibility study: report. Dryden and Smith,
planning consultants. [Stratford, Ontario: 1961]
4 v. fold. maps, tables.
Contents: Report 1, Population; Report 2, Land use and agriculture; Report
3, Forest resources; Report 4, Industry and manufacturing.   OTUSA

Morton, Desmond Paul Dillon, 1937–
Automation and employment. [Toronto: New Democratic Party of Ontario,
1965?]
[1] 18 p. illus., port.   OTURS

Nininger, J   R
A survey of changing employment patterns at the Lakehead cities of Port

Arthur and Fort William. Prepared for the Ontario Economic Council by
J.R. Nininger under the direction of F.W.P. Jones. London, Ontario:
University of Western Ontario [1964]
 xii, 65 leaves. diagrs., tables.   OTU
Northeastern Ontario Development Association.
— Economic survey of the district of Cochrane. North Bay, Ontario: 1963.
 iii, 186 p. maps, tables.   OTU
— Economic survey of the district of Temiskaming. North Bay, Ontario: 1964.
 iii, 119 p. diagr., map (part col.), tables.   OTU
— Municipal and industrial manual of northeastern Ontario, treasure chest of
 Canada: a directory of manufacturing and mining companies and products,
 municipal data sheets, communication, financial, fuel, power and
 transportation services, general information. 2d ed. North Bay, Ontario:
 1965.
 vi, 170 p. illus., maps, ports.
 First edition 1962. No copy located.   OONL
Northwestern Ontario Commission on Employment.
 Report. Port Arthur, Ontario: The Commission [1961?]
 9 p.   OTU
Officer, Lawrence H   (ed.).
— Issues in Canadian economics. Edited by Lawrence J. Officer and Lawrence
 B. Smith. Toronto: McGraw–Hill Ryerson Limited [1974]
 vi, 418 p. illus.   OTU
Ontario.
 The structure and aims of the Ontario Economic Council and its associated
 organizations. [Toronto?] 1962.
 21 p. fold. table.   OTU
— Submission of Ontario to the Royal Commission on Canada's Economic
 Prospects, January 26, 1956. [Toronto: 1956]
 x, 202 p. diagrs. (part fold.), tables.   OTU
Ontario. Commission on Unemployment.
 Interim report. Printed by order of the Legislative Assembly. Toronto: L.K.
 Cameron, printer to the King's Most Excellent Majesty, 1915.
 11 p.
 Chairman: John Willison.   OTU
— Report. 1916.
 viii, 334 p. fold. chart. tables.   OTU
Ontario. Committee on Portable Pensions.
 A summary report. [Toronto?] 1961.
 23 leaves.
 Joint Chairmen: D.C. MacGregor, G.E. Gathercole.   OTAR OTU
— Second report. [Toronto] 1961.
 vii, 146 p. tables.   OTAR OTU
— Public hearings, September 24, 1962.
 131 leaves.   OTU
— Public hearings, September 20–25, 1962.
 4 v.
 OTU unable to locate.   OTU

Ontario. International Conference on Regional Development and Economic
    Change, Toronto, 1965.
    [Papers] Toronto: Department of Economics and Development, 1965.
    212 p.   OTU
— Regional development: selected background papers. Toronto: Department
    of Economics and Development, 1965.
    1 v. (unpaged).   OTU
Ontario. Legislative Assembly. Special Committee of the Whole House on
    Portable Pensions.
    [Minutes] February 15, 1961.
    127 leaves:
    Chairman: R.J. Boyer.   OTU
Ontario. Office of the Prime Minister. Joint Committee on Economic Policy.
    Directions for economic and social policy in Ontario: report. Toronto: 1974.
    vii 37 p.
    Chairman Steering Committee: H.I. Macdonald.   OONL
Ontario. Royal Commission inquiry into the Grand River Flood 1974.
    Report. [Toronto: Ministry of the Attorney General, 1975]
    93 p. illus. (part col.), graphs, maps (part fold.).
    Commissioner: W.W. Leach.   OTAR
— Proceedings, July 9–November 14, 1974.
    37 v. [i.e. 8057 typewritten pages]   OTAR
— Minutes, July 9–November 14, 1974.
    42 leaves.   OTAR
— Proceedings, June 17, 1974.
    17 leaves.
    Commissioner: Andrew D. Booth.
    Dr. Booth conducted the proceedings prior to Judge Leach's appointment on
    June 26, 1974.   OTAR
Ontario Association of Architects.
    Economics of building. [Editors: W. Gerald Raymore and Stanley R. Kent]
    Toronto [1971]
    115 p. illus.   OTU
Ontario Economic Council. Windsor Economic Committee.
    Report on the Windsor Community. [Toronto? 1963]
    58 [4] leaves. tables.
    Chairman: Leroy D. Smithers.   OTU
Ontario Welfare Council. Committee on Public Welfare Policy.
    Economic needs and resources of older people in Ontario: report. Toronto:
    1959.
    xii, 50 p. tables.   OTU
Opportunities in Ontario. Land settlement, industrial opportunities. Toronto:
    Heaton's Agency, 1920.
    96 p. illus., map. (Heaton's Canadian provincial booklet series).   OOA

Payette, Joseph.
  Decouvrons le nord-Ontario: ses possibilites agricoles, commerciales,
  industrielles. Montreal: Bureau des Missionnaires-Colonisateurs, 1939.
  34 p. illus., carte, portr.   OOU
Porter, Glenn (ed.).
  Enterprise and national development; essays on Canadian business and
  economic history. Edited by Glenn Porter and Robert D. Cuff. Toronto:
  Hakkert, 1973.
  138 p. tables.   OTU
Queen's University Conference on Areas of Economic Stress in Canada, 1965.
  Areas of economic stress in Canada; proceedings. Editors: W.D. Wood and
  R.S. Thoman. Kingston, Ontario: Industrial Relations Centre, Queen's
  University, 1965.
  ix, 221 p. maps (part fold.), tables.   OTU
Richmond, D   R
  Poverty and institutional reform: a report. [Toronto] Ontario Economic
  Council [1969?]
  xi, 33 p.   OTER
Rodd, Robert Stephen, 1928–
  An economic analysis of the Manitoulin district. Guelph, Ontario:
  Department of Agricultural Economics, Ontario Agricultural College,
  University of Guelph, 1965.
  iii, 37 leaves. tables.   OTAR
— Economic growth and transition. [Cooperating Agencies: Department of
  Agricultural Economics, Ontario Agricultural College and others. Guelph,
  Ontario] University of Guelph, 1966.
  v, 48 p. (Background studies for resource development in the Tweed forest
  district, Ontario, no.9).   OTU
Sawyer, John Arthur, 1924–
  Macroeconomics, theory and policy in the Canadian economy. Rev
  Toronto: Macmillan of Canada [c1975]
  406 p. graphs, tables.   OTU
Sudbury, Ontario. City Corporation.
  1964, year of dilemma. Sudbury, Ontario: The Corporation, 1964.
  15 p. maps, photos.
  Brief submitted by the Mayor's Committee on Sudbury's financial problems
  to the Honourable John Robarts, prime minister.   OSUL
Temiskaming and Northern Ontario Railway Commission.
  Greater Ontario. The poor man's hope: what men who started bare-handed
  have accomplished. Toronto: Temiskaming and Northern Ontario Railway
  Commission, 1916.
  [26] p. illus. (*Its* pamphlet no. 13).
  Chairman: J.L. Englehart.
  Reproduced from *The Toronto Globe* of August, 1916.   OTU

Toronto. City Planning Board.
   A submission to the Royal Commission on Canada's Economic Prospects .
   Presented by His Worship Mayor Nathan Phillips, January, 1956. [Toronto:
   1956]
   78 [3] leaves.   OTU

Periodical Articles
Bell, William H   and Donald W   Stevenson.
   An index of economic health for Ontario counties and districts. Ontario
   Economic Review 2: no.5, 1964.
Bryant, C   R   and A   G   McLellan.
   Towards effective planning and control of the aggregate industry in Ontario.
   Plan Canada 15: 176–182, 1975.
Burkus, John
   Portable pensions – the Ontario approach. Ontario Economic Review 1:
   no.2, 1963.
Callender, D   M
   The Niagara economic region; present characteristics and prospects for the
   future. Ontario Economic Review 2: no.3, 1964.
Campbell, B   A
   Economic land classification as applied to eastern Canada. Economic
   Annalist 16: 12–17, 1946.
   Mainly Durham county, Ontario.
Chari, M   V   and R   H   Frank.
   The development of Ontario economic accounts. Ontario Economic Review
   8(no. 6): 5–17, 1970.
Chisholm, Paul
   1962 year of expansion for northeastern Ontario. Monetary Times 130(11):
   44, 46, 1962.
Clark, Philip T
   Ontario corporations tax. Canadian Chartered Accountant 37: 246–259,
   306–314, 1940.
Collins, F   W
   Canadian cities and towns. Agricultural and Industrial Progress in Canada
   26, 27, 28: 1944, 1945, 1946.
   Short articles on cities & towns, primarily in Ontario. Appeared almost
   every issue.
Cross, L   Doreen.
   Locating selected occupations: Ottawa, 1870. Urban History Review [3](2):
   5–14, 1974.
Dean, W   G
   A progress report on the Economic atlas of Ontario. Ontario Economic
   Review 3(no. 5): 7–8, 1965.

Dear, Michael and Andrew F   Burghardt.
    How is Hamilton coping with growth. Canadian Geographical Journal
    93(no. 2): 22–31, 1976.
Derry, Kathleen and Paul H   Douglas.
    The minimum wage in Canada. Journal of Political Economy 30: 155–188,
    1922.
Dolgoy, Sidney.
    The economy in 1967. Ontario Economic Review 6(no. 1): 1–13, 1968.
The economy: a look back at 1966. Ontario Economic Review 5(no. 1–2): 1–16,
    1967.
Eggleston, Wilfrid.
    The nuclear age in Canada. Canadian Geographical Journal 71: 182–191,
    1965.
Expansion of tourism salvation of northeast. Monetary Times 129(10): 89–90,
    1961.
Extra provincial companies. Canada Law Journal 33: 707, 1897.
Ferik, Enedina and J   P   Warner.
    The future structure of Ontario's economy. Ontario Economic Review
    11(no. 6): 1–3, 1973.
Frank, Robert H
    The distribution of personal income in Ontario and the ten economic
    regions. Ontario Economic Review 4(no. 10–11): 3–17, 1966.
— Ontario's demand for industrial and agricultural machinery to 1976.
    Ontario Economic Review 5(no. 11–12): 5–17, 1967.
— A pilot study on regional labour income in Ontario. Ontario Economic
    Review 2: no. 7, 1964.
Frank, Robert H   [et al.]
    The input-output structure of the Ontario economy. Ontario Economic
    Review 8(no. 1): 3–33, 1970.
Gillen, W   J   and A   Guccione.
    The estimation of postwar regional consumption in Canada. Canadian
    Journal of Economics 3: 276–290, 1970.
Gray, R   A
    A pension fund for teachers in the province of Ontario. Canada Educational
    Monthly 27: 128–132, 1905.
Innis, H   A
    An introduction to the economic history of Ontario from outpost to empire.
    Ontario Historical Society. Papers & Records 30: 111–123, 1934.
Jutlah, Clifford B
    A long-term economic forecast for Canada and Ontario. Ontario Economic
    Review 11(no. 4): 1–18, 1973.
Kaliski, S   F
    Structural unemployment in Canada: towards a definition of the geographic
    dimension. Canadian Journal of Economics 1: 551–565, 1968.

Keenleyside, Hugh L
   American economic penetration of Canada. Canadian Historical Review 8: 31–40, 1927.
Kindle, E   M
   The James Bay coastal plain: notes on a journey. Geographical Review 15: 226–236, 1925.
Kubursi, A   A   , J   R   Williams and P   J   George.
   Sub-provincial regional income multipliers in the Ontario economy: an input-output approach. Canadian Journal of Economics 8: 67–92, 1975.
Langman, R   C
   Northeastern Ontario "under the microscope". Canadian Geographical Journal 93(no. 1): 70–72, 1976.
Lemelin, Charles.
   Comment on Professor McInnis' paper. Canadian Journal of Economics 1: 471–473, 1968.
   Income differentiation in Canada.
Macdonald, H   Ian.
   "The new economics" and the province of Ontario. Ontario Economic Review 4(no. 4): 4–9, 1966.
McInnis, Marvin.
   The trend of regional income differentials in Canada. Canadian Journal of Economics 1: 440–470, 1968.
MacIntosh, W   A
   The Laurentian Plateau in Canadian economic development. Economic Geography 2: 537–549, 1926.
Madge, Helen L
   Ontario labour markets 1953–1963. Ontario Economic Review 2: no.1, 1964.
Marshall, John U
   City size, economic diversity, and functional type: the Canadian case. Economic Geography 51: 37–49, 1975.
The Monetary Times northeastern Ontario regional economic survey.
   Monetary Times 129(10): 54–55, 1961; 130(11): 48–49, 1962.
Morrison, Neil F
   The windfall tornado. Western Ontario Historical Notes 10: 19–20, 1952.
   From: Wheatley Journal, July 19, 1951.
The Ontario economy; annual review. Ontario Economic Review 1; no.1, no.9, 1963; 3(no. 8): 1–10, 1965.
The Ontario economy in 1968. Ontario Economic Review 7(no. 1): 1–3, 1969.
Ostry, Sylvia W
   Inter-establishment dispersion of occupational wage rates, Ontario and Quebec, 1957. Canadian Journal of Economics and Political Science 26: 277–288, 1960.
Palda, Kristian S
   A comparison of consumer expenditures in Quebec and Ontario. Canadian Journal of Economics and Political Science 33: 16–26, 1967.

Philbrick, Allen K
    The Erie Research Project: its relevance for regional development. Ontario
    Geography 4: 35–44, 1969.
Ray, D   Michael and Brian J   L   Berry.
    Multivariate socio-economic regionalization: a pilot study in central
    Canada. Canadian Political Science Association. Conference on Statistics,
    75–130, 1964.
Reuber, G   L
    Tillman Merritt Brown, 1913–73. Canadian Journal of Economics 7:
    290–294, 1974.
Shaw, Lillian M
    The Baker family of Hamilton. Wentworth Bygones 3: 30–34, 1962.
— Two Hamilton families. Western Ontario Historical Notes 16: 1–18, 1960.
    Baker & Stinson families.
Spencer, Byron G
    Determinants of the labour force participation of married women: a micro-
    study of Toronto households. Canadian Journal of Economics 6: 222–238,
    1973.
Studness, Charles M
    Economic opportunity and the westward migration of Canadians during the
    late nineteenth century. Canadian Journal of Economics and Political
    Science 30: 570–584, 1964.
Swan, N   M
    Differences in the response of the demand for labour to variations in output
    among Canadian regions. Canadian Journal of Economics 5: 373–385, 1972.
— The response of labour supply to demand in Canadian regions. Canadian
    Journal of Economics 7: 418–433, 1974.
Treadwell, William.
    The pellet makers. Canadian Geographical Journal 62: 186–205, 1966.
de Vos, Antoon and Alexander T   Cringan.
    Fur management in Ontario. Canadian Geographical Journal 55: 62–69,
    1957.
Weber, Jon N
    Ontario underground. Canadian Geographical Journal 61: 42–51, 1960.
Williamson, O   T   G
    The potentialities of Moosonee. Monetary Times 128(5): 78, 80–81, 1960.
Wolfe, Roy I
    Summer cottagers in Ontario. Economic Geography 27: 10–32, 1951.

Theses
Bannister, Geoffrey, 1945 –
    Modes of change in the Ontario economy. [Toronto] c1974.
    [14] 297 [8] leaves. diagr.
    Ph.D. thesis, University of Toronto (microfilm 27468).   OTU

Barnett, Robert Francis John.
A study of price movements and the cost of living in Kingston, Ontario for the years 1865 to 1900. Kingston, Ontario: 1963.
v, 71 leaves. tables (part fold), fold. charts.
M.A. thesis, Queen's University. OKQ
Dodge, David Allison.
Economic returns to investment in education in Ontario. Kingston, Ontario: 1965.
vi, 128 leaves. graphs, tables (part fold.).
B.A. thesis, Queen's University. OKQ
Dolgoy, Sidney.
Potential output in the Ontario economy to 1977. Winnipeg, Manitoba: 1972.
ix, 147 leaves. illus.
M.A. thesis, University of Manitoba (microfilm 12803). Can
Fisher, Paul.
Hornepayne: changing economic factors on an isolated northern Ontario community. Waterloo, Ontario: 1967.
x, 116 leaves. illus., maps, diagrs., tables.
B.A. thesis, Waterloo University College. OWTL
Hall, David John, 1946 –
Economic development in Elgin county, 1850–1880. [Guelph, Ontario] 1971.
ix, 228 leaves. illus., maps, tables.
M.A. thesis, The University of Guelph. OGU
— Petrolia, Ontario: Western District Publishing Company, 1972.
ix, 228 p. illus., facsims., maps, ports. OTAR
Hindle, Colin James, 1940 –
Negative income taxation and poverty in Ontario. Toronto: c1970.
xiii, 179 leaves. tables, figs.
Ph.D. thesis, University of Toronto (microfilm 27878). OTU
House, William James, 1939 –
Per capita income differentials in the provinces of Canada. Providence, Rhode Island: 1970.
ix, 124 leaves. illus.
Ph.D. thesis, Brown University (microfilm 71-13,882). DA
John, C   T
Differential wage rates in southern Ontario. Windsor, Ontario: 1968.
vi, 45 leaves. graphs, maps, tables.
Geography thesis, University of Windsor. OWA
Keys, C
An analysis of the central place system of southeastern Ontario. [Toronto] 1975.
125 leaves. tables, figs.
B.A. thesis, University of Toronto. OTU

Kostich, Radmila, 1938 –
  Economic returns to an investment in education for professional engineers in
  Ontario. Kingston, Ontario: 1966.
  xiii, 161 leaves. tables, charts.
  M.A. thesis, Queen's University.   OKQ
Lawson, Margaret Ruth.
  Some economic phases of minimum wage legislation in Ontario. [Toronto]
  1926.
  141, 3 leaves. graphs, tables.
  M.A. thesis, University of Toronto.   OTU
McQueen, David A
  Some determinants of economic developments in north western Ontario.
  [Toronto] 1975.
  3, 44 leaves.
  B.A. research paper, University of Toronto.   OTU
Mennill, David Charles, 1939 –
  Residence and employment locations in London, Ontario. London, Ontario:
  1966.
  viii, 75 leaves. graphs, tables, maps.
  M.A. thesis, The University of Western Ontario.   OLU
Plewes, Melvyn Edward.
  Regional open space as a resource. Waterloo, Ontario: 1970.
  viii, 174 leaves.
  M.A. thesis, University of Waterloo (microfiche 18120).   Can
Sauve, R   C
  Economic growth of eastern Ontario: trend and structural analysis. Ottawa:
  1969.
  vi, 189 leaves. tables.
  M.A. thesis, University of Ottawa.   OOU
Schier, Lewis, 1929 –
  A study of the occupational mobility of the managerial elite of the province
  of Ontario, Canada. New York: 1971.
  vi, 221 leaves. illus.
  Ph.D. thesis, New York University (microfilm 71-25,519).   DA
Schmieder, Allen Arthur.
  The historical geography of the Erie triangle. Columbus, Ohio: 1963.
  267 p.
  Ph.D. thesis, Ohio State University. (microfilm 64-07049)   DA
Silva, Wanniaratchige Percy Terrence, 1930 –
  The southern Georgian Bay region, 1855–1961; a study in economic
  geography. [Toronto] c1966.
  xiv, 330 leaves. tables, maps.
  Ph.D. thesis, University of Toronto (microfilm 1065).   OTU
Stankovic, Dan.
  Spatial and temporal patterns in short term employment change within the
  southern Ontario urban system. Hamilton, Ontario: 1974.
  xii, 165 leaves. graphs, maps, tables.
  M.A. research paper, McMaster University.   OHM

Watson, Denis McLean, 1939 –
    Frontier movement and economic development in northeastern Ontario,
    1850–1914. Vancouver, British Columbia: 1971.
    viii, 359 leaves. illus., maps.
    M.A. thesis, University of British Columbia.   BVaU
Williams, Keith Graham.
    Income changes and urban economic growth in selected Canadian cities
    1941 and 1961. Toronto: 1966.
    vi, 136 leaves. tables, figs., maps.
    M.A. thesis, University of Toronto.   OTU

DEMOGRAPHY

Bibliography
Canada. Public Archives.
    Checklist of Ontario census returns, 1842–1871. [Ottawa: Roger Duhamel,
    Queen's Printer, 1963]
    46 p.   OTER

Monographs and Pamphlets
Algonquin College. Planning Department.
    Part 1 (population profile) of the Algonquin College region demographic
    study. Researched, compiled and edited by Lorne V. McCool. [Ottawa]
    Algonquin College, 1975.
    257 leaves. illus., map, graphs, tables.   OONL
Barber, Gerald Maurice, 1947–
    Occupational structure and population growth in the Ontario – Quebec
    urban system 1941–1966, by G.M. Barber and John N.H. Britton. [Toronto]
    Centre for Urban and Community Studies, University of Toronto [1971]
    23 [2] p. (Environment study. Research paper no.49).   OTU
Bladen, Vincent Wheeler, 1900–   (ed.).
    Canadian population and northern colonization. Toronto: University of
    Toronto Press, 1962.
    x, 158 p. map, diagrs.
    "Symposium presented to the Royal Society of Canada... 1961"   OTER
Canada. Bureau of Statistics.
    Population and housing characteristics by census tracts: Toronto.
    Caractéristiques de la population et du logement: par secteur de
    recensement: Toronto. [Ottawa] 1963.
    69 p. fold. map. (Bulletin CT–15).   OONL
— Population characteristics by census tracts: Toronto. Caractéristiques par
    secteur de recensement: Toronto. [Ottawa] 1968.
    27 p. fold. map. (Bulletin C.20).   OONL

Canada. Census Division.
Population and housing characteristics by census tracts: Hamilton.
Caractéristiques de la population et du logement par secteur de
recensement: Hamilton. [Ottawa] 1973.
[14] p. fold. map. (*Its* Census tract bulletin. CT–9A).   OONL
Canada. Census 10th, 1961.
Population and housing characteristics by census tracts, Sudbury, 1961.
Ottawa: Bureau of Statistics, 1963.
9 p. tables. (Census of Canada. Bulletin CT–14).   OONL
— Population and housing characteristics by census tracts. London, 1961.
[Ottawa] Bureau of Statistics, 1961.
15 p. tables, map. (Bulletin CT11).   OL
Canada. Census 11th, 1966.
Population characteristics/caractéristiques: London. [Ottawa] Bureau of
Statistics 1968.
7 p. map, tables. (Bulletin C13).   OL
Canada. Census 12th, 1971.
Population and housing characteristics/Caractéristiques de la population et
du logement: London. [Ottawa] Statistics Canada, 1973.
1 v. (unpaged). map, tables. (Bulletin CT12A).   OL
— [Ottawa] Statistics Canada, 1974.
19 p. map, tables. (CT–12B).   OL
Conference on Implications of Demographic Factors for Educational Planning
and Research, Ontario Institute for Studies in Education, 1969.
Demography and educational planning: papers from a conference... June
9–10 1969. Edited by Betty Macleod. [Toronto] Ontario Institute for Studies
in Education [c1970]
xiv, 274 p. illus., maps, tables. (Ontario Institute for Studies in Education.
Monograph series no.7).   OTU
Denton, Frank Trevor, 1930
Demographic changes and the costs of education, by Frank T. Denton and
Byron G. Spencer. Hamilton, Ontario: Department of Economics,
McMaster University, 1973.
17 leaves. (Department of Economics, McMaster University. Working
paper, no.73/25).   OTU
DuWors, Richard Edward, 1914–
Studies in the dynamics of the residential populations of thirteen Canadian
cities. Phase 1: Dimensions and significance of turnover in community
residential populations by Richard E. DuWors, Jay Beaman and Allan
Olmsted. Winnipeg: Center for Settlement Studies, University of Manitoba,
1972.
xi, 41 leaves. (Series 5: Occasional paper no.3).   OTV
Erie Economic Council.
Erie economic area: population growth and distribution, past 20 years,
1951–71. London, Ontario: Erie Economic Council [1971]
10 p. map, tables.   OONL

— Population comparison southwestern Ontario with central Ontario area. London, Ontario: Erie Economic Council, 1972.
4 p. maps, tables.   OONL
— Population projections for 4 county Erie economic area, year 1971 to year 2001. London, Ontario: Erie Economic Council [1971?]
6 p. map, tables.   OONL
George, M   V
Internal migration in Canada: demographic analyses. Ottawa: Bureau of Statistics, 1970.
xv, 251 p. tables, graphs, maps.   OKQL
Grey/Owen Sound. Planning Board.
Demographic research report of the Grey/Owen Sound planning area. Burlington, Ontario [1970?]
75 p. diagrs., map, tables (part fold.).   OLU
Hamilton, Ontario. Planning Department.
Population and housing; characteristics. [Hamilton, Ontario: 1966]
[28] leaves. diagrs., maps. (Hamilton Planning Department. Special report 6a).   OTUSA
Hamilton – Wentworth Planning Area Board.
Metro Hamilton population growth and distribution. Hamilton, Ontario: City of Hamilton Planning Department [1966]
[41] leaves. diagrs., maps. (Hamilton Planning Department. Special report 10).   OTUSA
— Population and related statistics covering the metropolitan Hamilton area, the county of Wentworth and the Hamilton – Wentworth planning area. [Hamilton, Ontario] 1960.
1 v. (unpaged). tables.   OH
Helling, Rudolf Anton, 1929–
A demographic study of Essex county and metropolitan Windsor; presentation in map and chart form of the community of Essex county and metropolitan Windsor, Ontario, Canada, by Rudolf A. Helling and Edward Boyce. Issued on the authority and under the patronage of Most Rev. G. Emmett Carter. [London, Ontario] 1965.
15 [128] p. diagrs., maps.   OTU
— A demographic study of Middlesex county and metropolitan London: presentation in map and chart form of the community of Middlesex county and metropolitan London. Prepared by the Department of Sociology, University of Windsor and the Renewal Centre by Rudolf Helling and Edward Boyce. Issued on the authority and under the patronage of Most Rev. G. Emmett Carter. [London, Ontario] 1968.
vii, 159 p. diagrs., maps.   OTU
Hill, Frederick Irvin, 1947–
Spatio-temporal trends in population density: Toronto, 1932–1966 . [Toronto] Centre for Urban and Community Studies, University of Toronto, 1970.
[1] iii, 43, 3 leaves. illus. (Environment study. Research paper, no.34).   OTU

Hodge, Gerald.
    The identification of "growth poles" in eastern Ontario. Research assistant:
    Graham Murchie. n.p.: 1966.
    48 p. diagrs., maps.
    "A report to the Ontario Department of Economics and Development."
                                                          OTUSA
Kingston, Ontario. Planning Board.
    A population forecast for the Kingston area and the city of Kingston.
    Kingston, Ontario: 1954.
    17 leaves. tables. (*Its* Report, no.1, March 12, 1954).   OTMCL
Kubat, Daniel, 1928–
    A statistical profile of Canadian society by Daniel Kubat and David
    Thornton. Toronto: McGraw–Hill Ryerson Limited [c1974]
    xv, 200 p. illus., charts, map, tables.   OTU
Lackey, Alvin S
— Population changes in the Blue Water region 1901–1956. Guelph, Ontario:
    Ontario Agricultural College [1956?]
    42 p. graphs, tables.   OLU
LePage, (A.E.) Limited. Research & Planning Division.
    Population growth and planning: province of Ontario. [Toronto] c1975.
    100 p. graphs, maps, tables.   OONL
Letellier de Saint-Just, Charles.
    Situation demographique de l'élément français au Canada. Montreal: Les
    Éditions Bellarmin, 1951.
    31 p. tables. (Institut social populaire. Publication, no.444).   OTY
MacDougall, Edward Bruce, 1939–
    Farm numbers in Ontario and Quebec: analyses and preliminary forecasts.
    [Toronto] Department of Geography, University of Toronto, 1968.
    41 leaves. graphs, tables.   OTU
Macleod, Betty Belle Robinson, 1923–
    Enrollments, fertility and migration in Ontario. [Toronto] Ontario Institute
    for Studies in Education, 1969.
    16 leaves. tables, maps. (Ontario Institute for Studies in Education.
    Department of Educational Planning. Educational planning occasional
    papers, no.9).   OTER
— Patterns and trends in Ontario population; an Ontario population report by
    Betty Macleod, Carol Ivison and Nirmala Bidani. Toronto: Department of
    Educational Planning, Ontario Institute for Studies in Education, 1972.
    xiii, 308 p. graphs, illus., tables, maps.   OTU
Metropolitan Toronto. Planning Board. Research Division.
    Labour force and employment projections 1966–2001, Metropolitan
    Toronto planning area, Ontario and Canada. [Toronto] 1969.
    [22] p. graphs, tables.   OTUSA
— Population projections 1966–2001; Metropolitan Toronto planning area,
    Ontario and Canada. [Toronto] 1968.
    1 v. (various pagings). graphs, tables.   OTU

Mississauga, Ontario. Planning Board.
   Population and housing study, 1972. [Mississauga, Ontario] Mississauga
   Planning Board, 1973.
   v, 47 leaves. graphs (part col.).   OTU
Rodd, Robert Stephen, 1928–
   Small-area migration experience in southern Ontario, 1951–1961. Guelph,
   Ontario: School of Agricultural Economics and Extension, University of
   Guelph, 1971.
   34 p. maps, tables.   OONL
Rosenberg, Louis, 1893–
   A gazetteer of Jewish communities in Canada showing the Jewish
   population in each of the cities, towns & villages in Canada in the census
   years 1851–1951. Montreal: Bureau of Social and Economic Research,
   Canadian Jewish Congress [1957]
   xv, 46 p. diagrs., tables. (Canadian Jewish population studies. Canadian
   Jewish communities series no.7).   OTU
— The Jewish population of Canada: a statistical summary from 1851 to 1941.
   Montreal: Bureau of Social and Economic Research, Canadian Jewish
   Congress, 1947.
   32 p. tables. (Canadian Jewish population studies no.2)
   "Reprinted from the *American Jewish Year Book*, v.48, 1946/47."   OTU
— Population characteristics of the Jewish community of Toronto. Montreal:
   Bureau of Social and Economic Research, Canadian Jewish Congress, 1955.
   x, 58 p. diagrs., maps, tables. (Canadian Jewish population studies.
   Canadian Jewish community series, no.3).   OTU
— A study of the changes in the geographic distribution of the Jewish
   population in the metropolitan area of Toronto, 1851–1951. Montreal:
   Bureau of Social and Economic Research, Canadian Jewish Congress, 1954.
   25 leaves. maps, tables. (Canadian Jewish population studies. Canadian
   Jewish community series, no.2).   OTU
— A study of the changes in the population characteristics in Canada
   1931–1961. Montreal: Bureau of Social and Economic Research, Canadian
   Jewish Congress [1965]
   vii, 14 p. tables. (Canadian Jewish population studies. Canadian Jewish
   community series v.2, no.2).   OTU
Sanford Evans Statistical Service, Winnipeg.
   Ontario place guide, 1961 census. Ontario population maps. Winnipeg: The
   Author [1963]
   7 col. maps on 3 sheets, tables.   OTU
Social Planning Council of Hamilton and District. Research Department.
   The old age population in Hamilton; a report. [Hamilton, Ontario] 1964.
   12 leaves. tables.   OTU
Toronto. Board of Education. Research Department.
   Study of achievement; report on population study of junior and senior
   kindergarten pupils, 1960-61 and 1961-62. [Toronto] 1965.
   74 leaves. tables.   OONL

Town Planning Institute of Canada. Central Ontario Chapter. Census
Committee.
    Proposals for improvement of census information for planning purposes.
    Toronto: 1966.
    34 leaves.   OTU

Periodical Articles
Barratt, T   R
    An analysis of fertility trends in Ontario. Ontario Economic Review 9(no.
    3): 2–15, 1971.
Charles, Enid.
    Differential fertility in Canada, 1931. Canadian Journal of Economics and
    Political Science 9: 175–218, 1943.
Dallimore, D   C   and B   Lampert.
    Demographic trends in Ontario: some policy considerations. Ontario
    Economic Review 11(no. 4): 1–12, 1973.
Gagan, David and Herbert Mays.
    Historical demography and Canadian social history: families and land in
    Peel county, Ontario. Canadian Historical Review 54: 27–47, 1973.
Hunter, A   F
    The ethnographical elements of Ontario. Ontario Historical Society. Papers
    & Records 3: 180–199, 1901.
Hurd, W   Burton and Jean C   Cameron.
    Population movements in Canada, 1921–31: some further considerations.
    Canadian Journal of Economics and Political Science 1: 222–245, 1935.
Husain, H
    Components of population change in metropolitan area of Toronto,
    1951–1961. Plan Canada 5: 16–21, 1964.
Kelly, C   A
    Rural population changes in Dawn township (Lambton county). Western
    Ontario Historical Notes 12: 62–71, 1954.
Kogler, R
    An analysis of population growth trends in Ontario. Ontario Economic
    Review 7(no. 6): 4–17, 1969.
— Preliminary population projections for Ontario, 1971–1991. Ontario
    Economic Review 7(no. 1): 4–9, 1969.
Lemieux, O   A   [et al.]
    Factors in the growth of rural population in eastern Canada. Canadian
    Political Science Association. Proceedings 6: 198–219, 1934.
LeNeveu, A   H   and Y   Kasahara.
    Demographic trends in Canada, 1941–56, and their implications. Canadian
    Journal of Economics and Political Science 24: 9–20, 1958.
Lower, Arthur R   M
    Growth of the French population of Canada. Canadian Political Science
    Association. Papers and Proceedings 2: 35–47, 1930.

Madge, Helen L
    Ontario regional population projections 1961 to 1986. Ontario Economic
    Review 2: no.10, 1965.
— Population growth in Ontario. Ontario Economic Review 1: no.3, 1963.
Montagnes, James.
    Population 8,527. Canadian Business 13(10): 22–27, 76, 78, 1940.
Richards, J   Howard.
    Population and the economic base in northern Hastings county, Ontario.
    Canadian Geographer 3: 23–33, 1958.
Rumney, George R
    Population trends in the Sudbury area. Royal Canadian Institute.
    Transactions 29: 3–21, 1951.
Samuel, T   J
    Fertility and population growth in Ontario. Ontario Economic Review 5(no.
    3–4): 5–15, 1967.
Talman, James J
    Migration from Ontario to Manitoba in 1871. Ontario History 43: 35–41,
    1951.
Taylor, Iain C
    Population migration to and from Ontario 1870–1940. Ontario Economic
    Review 5(no. 7–8): 3–15, 1967.
Vining, R   L
    Rural depopulation. Ontario Agricultural College Review 26: 459–475,
    1914.
Watson, J   W
    Rural depopulation in southwestern Ontario. Association of American
    Geographers. Annals 37: 145–154, 1947.
Whebell, C   F   J
    Net migration patterns 1956–61 in southern Ontario. Ontario Geography 2:
    67–81, 1968.

Theses

Barrett, Nancy Helen.
    Study of concentrations of French population in southern Ontario, 1861 and
    1881. Ottawa: 1975.
    v, 58 leaves. illus., maps.
    B.A. research essay, Carleton University.   OOCC
Blair, James William.
    Components of population change in the Toronto region 1951–1971.
    Toronto: 1974.
    ix, 168 leaves. maps, tables.
    M.A. research paper, York University.   OTY
Brozowski, Roman Steve, 1946–
    Population changes in Ontario towns and villages, 1941–1966. [Windsor,
    Ontario] 1971.
    xiii, 137, xiv leaves. maps, tables.
    M.A. thesis, University of Windsor.   OWA

Cameron, Christina M
    Population growth in the Toronto centered region. Part one: Growth
    patterns: the Toronto centered region, 1961–1971. Part two: Growth
    processes: a case study. [Toronto] 1973.
    vii, 67 leaves. tables, graphs, maps (part col.).
    B.A. research paper, University of Toronto.   OTU
Cronyn, Lesley Brock Verschoyle, 1946–
    Population growth in Ontario by county and region 1951 to 1961. [Toronto]
    1969.
    60 leaves. diagrs., col. maps.
    B.A. thesis, University of Toronto.   OTU
Dawes, William Gordon.
    Changing population patterns in eastern Ontario, 1931–1961. Ottawa: 1968.
    x, 84 leaves. graphs, maps, tables.
    B.A. research essay, Carleton University.   OOCC
Ellwood, Wayne Franklin.
    Comparison of locations for the dispersal of projected population growth:
    Toronto centered region. Ottawa: 1972.
    ix, 308 leaves. maps, tables.
    M.A. thesis, Carleton University.   OOCC
Fraser, Frank Alexander.
    Computer mapping census data in the city of Toronto. [Toronto: 1966]
    v, 34 leaves. diagrs., 7 fold. maps (in pocket).
    B.A. thesis, University of Toronto.   OTU
Freedman, Harry, 1942–
    Daytime population; its use and potential with special reference to
    Metropolitan Toronto. [Toronto] 1965.
    iv, 47 leaves. maps (part fold., part col., 1 in pocket).
    B.A. thesis, University of Toronto.   OTU
Hughes, David Richard, 1942–
    Migration of young adults from Frontenac county, Ontario, 1961–1971.
    London, Ontario: 1971.
    xiv, 116 leaves. graphs, tables, maps.
    M.A. thesis, The University of Western Ontario (microfilm 8945).   OLU
Hymmen, E   Bruce.
    Net migration patterns in southern Ontario, 1966–1971. Waterloo, Ontario:
    1974.
    x, 124 leaves. diagrs., maps, tables.
    B.A. thesis, Wilfrid Laurier University.   OWTL
Kennedy, Ronald Alan.
    The population geography of the Niagara peninsula. [Hamilton, Ontario]
    1955.
    vi, 101 leaves. illus., diagrs., maps.
    B.A. thesis, McMaster University.   OHM

Kokich, George John Vjekoslav, 1940–
Interprovincial migration in Canada 1931 and 1941 with special reference to Ontario. London, Ontario: 1966.
xv, 99 [32] leaves. tables, maps.
M.A. thesis, The University of Western Ontario.   OLU
Koop, Rudolf Herbert.
Urban and rural migration flows in southern Ontario, 1951–61.
[Guelph, Ontario] 1967.
viii, 135 leaves. graphs, maps, tables.
M.Sc. thesis, The University of Guelph.   OGU
Latham, Robert Frederic, 1942–
Urban population densities and growth; with special reference to Toronto.
Kingston, Ontario: 1967.
ix, 115 leaves. tables, figs.
M.A. thesis, Queen's University.   OKQ
Lavis, Donald Reginald, 1944–
Ontario: the pill and the birth rate, 1960–1967. London, Ontario: 1970.
xii, 86 leaves. graphs, tables.
M.A. thesis, The University of Western Ontario (microfilm 6678).   OLU
Lawrence, William A   1938–
A geographical study of the elderly population of southwestern Ontario.
London, Ontario: 1966.
xv, 98 leaves. graphs, tables, maps (part col.).
M.A. thesis, The University of Western Ontario.   OLU
Lindsay, Colin.
Long-term forecasting: Ontario's population growth and electrical energy requirements to the year 2000. [Toronto] 1964.
49 leaves. tables, charts, graphs (part col.).
M.B.A. thesis, University of Toronto.   OTU
Lithwick, Irwin, 1944–
The growth of urban population in Canada to 1976; an economic model.
London, Ontario: 1974.
xii, 164 leaves. tables.
Ph.D. thesis, The University of Western Ontario (microfilm 23307).   OLU
Marshall, Peggy A
Rural-urban migration in Grey county. [Toronto] 1970.
vii, 70 leaves. tables, chart, map (fold.).
B.A. research paper, University of Toronto.   OTU
Morrison, Burton Angus, 1927–
Migration patterns of Grey county youth, 1961–1971. London, Ontario: 1972.
xvi, 118 leaves. graphs, tables, maps.
M.A. thesis, The University of Western Ontario.   OLU
Njau, Gilbert Japhlet, 1936–
The change in population distribution in Metropolitan Toronto: 1941–1961.
[Toronto] 1967.
vi, 80 leaves. diagrs., maps.
M.A. research paper, University of Toronto.   OTU

Orton, Larry James, 1946–
    An exploratory study of rural to urban migration, adjustment, and adult
    education: the case of Newfoundlanders in Toronto. [Toronto] c1970.
    iv, 149 leaves. tables.
    M.A. thesis, University of Toronto.   OTU
Plewman, G   W
    Rural depopulation in western Ontario. [Hamilton, Ontario] 1934.
    ii, 59, 9, 7 leaves. maps, tables.
    B.A. thesis, McMaster University.   OHM
Ray, David Michael, 1935–
    Settlement and rural out migration in easternmost Ontario, 1783–1956.
    Ottawa: 1961.
    242 leaves. diagrs., maps, tables.
    M.A. thesis, University of Ottawa.   OOU
Rego, Assumpta Belinda, 1939 –
    Some aspects of the migration of young working adults in southwestern
    Ontario with special reference to London. London, Ontario: 1969.
    xi, 136 leaves. graphs, tables, maps.
    M.A. thesis, The University of Western Ontario (microfilm 5780).   OLU
Saunders, Jeanne Mary, 1934–
    Population changes in Ontario 1951–1956 with special reference to the
    London region. London, Ontario: 1959.
    viii, 104 leaves. graphs, tables, maps.
    M.Sc. thesis, The University of Western Ontario.   OLU
Skinner, James Gordon, 1934–
    Demographic aspects of the Huron upland of southwestern Ontario.
    London, Ontario: 1964.
    xv, 95 [69] leaves. tables, maps (part fold.).
    M.A. thesis, The University of Western Ontario.   OLU
Steeves, Allan Daniel.
    An analysis of internal migration with specific reference to the flow of peopie
    from the Atlantic provinces to Guelph, Ontario. [Toronto] 1964.
    x, 130 leaves. tables.
    M.S.A. thesis, University of Toronto.   OTU
Taylor, Iain Cooper.
    Components of population change, Ontario, 1850–1940. [Toronto] 1967.
    viii, 292 leaves. illus., maps (part fold.), tables.
    M.A. thesis, University of Toronto.   OTU
Williamson, Terry Sewell.
    The population age patterns of southern Ontario towns and cities, 1966.
    [Toronto] 1971.
    80 leaves. "no pages numbered 47–49". illus., maps.
    B.A. research paper, University of Toronto.   OTU

AGRICULTURE

Monographs and Pamphlets

Agricultural Development Conference, Ontario Agricultural College, University of Guelph, 1972.
> A development program for Canadian agriculture: proceedings of the Agricultural Development Conference held in conjunction with Ontario Agricultural College annual conference on agriculture "Challenges for agriculture", January 4, 1972. [Guelph, Ontario] School of Agricultural Economics and Extension Education, 1972.
> 29 leaves. (Publication AE/72/3). OTU

Agriculture in the whirlpool of change: papers presented at the Centennial Symposium, Ontario Agricultural College, University of Guelph, October 17, 18, 1974. [Guelph, Ontario] Ontario Agricultural College [c1975]
> viii, 232 p. graphs. OTU

Algoma Central & Hudson Bay Railway Company.
> Farm lands in the clay belt of new Ontario. [Ottawa: The Mortimer Press, 1913?]
> 10 p. illus., map. OTAR
— [1914]
> 11 p. illus., map. OTAR

Algoma! The new Ontario! The new northwest! Algoma farmers testify. 1st ed. Sault Ste. Marie, Ontario: The Algoma Land and Colonization Company, Limited, 1892.
> 64 p. map. OTAR
— 2d ed. compiled by Frederick Rogers. 1894.
> 32 p. OTAR

Barg, Abram.
> My life, my story. Leamington, Ontario: The Author, 1975.
> 250 leaves. OOAG

Barnett, John.
> A relic of old decency: the 144 year history of this farmstead and the life-story of its builder Warren Clarkson, by John and Blanche E. Barnett, owners since 1936. [Clarkson, Ontario: MacNair Printing] 1963.
> 16 p. illus. OTU

Barry, P   J
> Financial analysis of expansion alternatives for cash grain farms in Ontario. Guelph, Ontario: School of Agricultural Economics and Extension Education, University of Guelph, 1971.
> ii, 67 p. tables. OONL

Blackburn, Donald J
> The educational and occupational aspirations of youth in midnorthern Ontario, by Donald J. Blackburn, Patricia A. Molnar and Duane C. Tulloch. Guelph, Ontario: School of Agricultural Economics and Extension Education, Ontario Agricultural College, University of Guelph, 1975.
> iv, 28 p. tables. OTU

Bridgman, Howard O
  Niagara Peninsula Fruit and Vegetable Growers' Association, 1896–1967.
  [Beamsville, Ontario: Rannie Publications Limited, 1967]
  60 p. illus., facsims., ports.   OTU
Brown, Walter James.
  Fortunes for farmers in new Ontario. [Sault Ste. Marie] Published for the
  Temiscaming and Northern Ontario Railway, 1910.
  [18] p. illus.   OTAR
Brownell, Evelyn.
  A study of Holland Marsh: its reclamation and development, by Evelyn
  Brownell and S. Gordon Scott. Ottawa: Immigration Branch, Department
  of Planning and Development, 1949.
  23 p. maps.   OOC
Canada. Census, 7th, 1931.
  Ontario census of agriculture. Ottawa: J.O. Patenaude, printer to the King's
  Most Excellent Majesty, 1935.
  cxii, 169 p. diagrs., map, tables.   OONL
Canada. Census, 8th, 1941.
  Ontario. Census of agriculture 1941. Ottawa: Edmond Cloutier, printer to
  the King's Most Excellent Majesty, 1946.
  xx, 318 p. map, tables.
  Text in English and French.   OONL
Canada. Department of Agriculture. Research Branch.
  Report of the Ontario soil survey no. 1–39. Prepared jointly by The
  Research Branch of Canada Department of Agriculture and the Ontario
  Agricultural College. Ottawa: Canada Department of Agriculture; Toronto:
  Ontario Department of Agriculture, 1944–1966.
  39 v. illus., maps.
  Contents: v. 1–6, maps only; v. 7, Soil survey of Carleton county, by G.A.
  Hills, N.R. Richards and F.F. Morwick; no. 8, Reconnaissance soil survey of
  parts of northwestern Ontario, by G.A. Hills and F.F. Morwick; no. 9, Soil
  survey of Durham county by L.R. Webber, F.F. Morwick and N.R.
  Richards; no. 10, Soil survey of Prince Edward county, by N.R. Richards
  and F.F. Morwick; no. 11, Soil survey of Essex county, by N.R. Richards,
  A.G. Caldwell and F.F. Morwick; no. 12, Soil survey of Grenville county, by
  N.R. Richards, B.C. Matthews and F.F. Morwick; no. 13, Soil survey of
  Huron county, by D.W. Hoffman, N.R. Richards and F.F. Morwick; no. 14,
  Soil survey of Dundas county, by B.C. Matthews and N.R. Richards; no. 15,
  Soil survey of Perth county, by D.W. Hoffman and N.R. Richards; no. 16;
  Soil survey of Bruce county, by D.W. Hoffman and N.R. Richards; no. 17,
  Soil survey of Grey county, by T.E. Gillespie and N.R. Richards; no. 18, Soil

survey of Peel county, by D.W. Hoffman and N.R. Richards; no. 19, Soil
survey of York county, by D.W. Hoffman and N.R. Richards; no. 20, Soil
survey of Stormont county, by B.C. Matthews and N.R. Richards; no. 21,
Soil survey of New Liskeard – Englehart area, Temiskaming district, by
D.W. Hoffman, R.E. Wicklund and N.R. Richards; no. 22, Soil survey of
Lambton county, by B.C. Matthews, N.R. Richards and R.E. Wicklund; no.
23, Soil survey of Ontario county, by A.B. Olding, R.E. Wicklund and N.R.
Richards; no. 24, Soil survey of Glengarry county, by B.C. Matthews, N.R.
Richards and R.E. Wicklund; no. 25, The soil survey of Victoria county, by
J.E. Gillespie and N.R. Richards; no. 26, Soil survey of Manitoulin Island,
by D.W. Hoffman, R.E. Wicklund and N.R. Richards; no. 27, Soil survey of
Hastings county, by J.E. Gillespie, R.E. Wicklund and N.R. Richards; no.
28, The soil survey of Oxford county, by R.E. Wicklund and N.R. Richards;
no. 29, Soil survey of Simcoe county, by D.W. Hoffman, R.E. Wicklund and
N.R. Richards; no. 30, Soil associations of southern Ontario, by D.W.
Hoffman, B.C. Matthews and R.E. Wicklund; no. 31, Soil survey of Parry
Sound district, by D.W. Hoffman, R.E. Wicklund and N.R. Richards; no.
32, The soils of Wentworth county, by E.W. Presant, R.E. Wicklund and
B.C. Matthews; no. 33, Soil survey of Russell and Prescott counties, by R.E.
Wicklund and N.R. Richards; no. 34, The soil survey of Lincoln county, by
R.E. Wicklund and B.C. Matthews; no. 35, Soil survey of Wellington
county, by D.W. Hoffman, B.C. Matthews and R.E. Wicklund; no. 36, The
soil survey of Lennox and Addington county, by J.E. Gillespie, R.E.
Wicklund and B.C. Matthews; no. 37, Soil survey of Renfrew county, by J.E.
Gillespie, R.E. Wicklund and B.C. Matthews; no. 38, Soil survey of Dufferin
county by D.W. Hoffman, B.C. Matthews and R.E. Wicklund; no. 39, The
soils of Frontenac county, by J.E. Gillespie, R.E. Wicklund and B.C.
Matthews.   OLU
Canada. Department of the Interior.
Canada: improved Ontario farms for old country farmers, by Arthur E.
Copping. Ottawa [King's Printer] 1912.
64 p. illus., col. fold. map.   OTU
— Handbook of information relating to the district of Algoma in the province
of Ontario. Letters from settlers and others, and information as to land
regulations. Issued under the authority of the Government of Canada
(Minister of the Interior). [London: McCorquodale & Co., Limited, 1893?]
32 p.   OKQ
Canadian Facts Limited.
A study of the Ontario farm market and the audience of *Farmer's Advocate*
and *Canadian Countryman*, June 1954. Based on interviews made in
November–December 1953. Conducted for *Farmer's Advocate* and *Canadian
Countryman*. n.p. [Farmer's Advocate and Canadian Countryman, 1954?]
56 p. col. map, tables.   OONL
Cartwright Agricultural Society.
Centennial fair 1865–1965, [Blackstock, Ontario: 1965?]
1 v. (unpaged). illus.   OTMCL

Clement, Frederick Moore, 1885–1974.
   My thoughts were on the land: autobiography of Fred Clement, Virgil,
   Ontario. White Rock, British Columbia: 1969.
   43 p. illus., ports.   OONL
Commercial Union Club of Toronto.
   What commercial union will do for the farmer in Ontario. [Toronto]
   Hunter, Rose & Co., 1888.
   4 p. illus. (Commercial Union Club leaflets, 1).   OOA
Dawson, J   A
   Changes in agriculture in Dundas county, Ontario. Ottawa: Department of
   Agriculture Marketing Service, Agricultural Economics Division, 1952.
   16 p. tables.   OONL
Day, Samuel Phillips, 1833–1916.
   Ontario, Canada: its present position, resources, and prospects as a field for
   settlement. London: "Labour News" Publishing Office, 1874.
   10 p. table.   OKQ
Edwards, William, 1810–1881.
   Correspondence and papers on various subjects by the late William
   Edwards, of Clarence, Ontario together with a sketch of his life. Compiled
   and arranged by his brother, James Edwards. Peterborough, Ontario: J.R.
   Stratton, 1882.
   iv, 170 p.   OTAR OKQ
Elgin County. Board of Trade.
   The best agricultural district in the Dominion of Canada. [St. Thomas,
   Ontario: Elgin Board of Trade and Publicity Association, 1914?]
   32 p. illus., map.   OSTT
Entomological Society of Ontario. London Branch.
   Accounts and minutes of the London Branch of the Entomological Society of
   Ontario, 1864–1881. Edited and with appendices by William W. Judd.
   London, Ontario: London Public Library and Art Museum, 1975.
   ii, 97 p. (London Public Library and Art Museum. Occasional paper no.
   20).   OTAR
— Minutes of the Entomological Society of Ontario while headquartered in
   London, Ontario, 1872–1906. Edited and with appendices by W.W. Judd.
   [London, Ontario] London Public Libraries, Galleries, Museums, 1976.
   ii, 75 p. (London Public Library and Art Museum. Occasional paper no.
   21).   OTAR
Epp, Henry.
   Agriculture in southern Ontario. [Don Mills, Ontario] J.M. Dent & Sons
   (Canada) Limited [c1972]
   33 p. illus. (part col.), maps (part col.).   OTAR
Essex County. Agricultural Committee.
   The county of Essex, sun parlour of Canada. n.p. [1966]
   [24] p. illus. (part col.).   OTAR

Finlayson, Isabella C
  Pioneer history of the Moore Agricultural Society commemorating 100 years
  of Brigden fall fairs, 1850–1950. [Brigden? Ontario: Moore Agricultural
  Society, 1950]
  17 p.   OLU
French, Michael.
  A Thornhill farm. [Toronto: D.M. Press] 1970.
  18 p. illus.   OONL
Funk, Thomas F
  Farmer buying behavior: an integrated review of literature. [Guelph,
  Ontario: Ontario Agricultural College, University of Guelph, 1972]
  34 leaves.   OTU
Gosselin, A
  ... Settlement problems in northwestern Quebec and northeastern Ontario,
  by A. Gosselin and G.P. Boucher. Ottawa [E. Cloutier] 1944.
  54 p. map, tables. (Canada. Department of Agriculture. Technical bulletin,
  no. 49).
  "Results of a land settlement study on the clay belt during the summer of
  1937."   OLU
Guelph, Ontario. University. Centre for Resources Development.
  Planning for agriculture in southern Ontario. Prepared for the A.R.D.A.
  Directorate of Ontario under A.R.D.A. project no. 85057 by the Centre for
  Resources Development, University of Guelph. Guelph, Ontario: 1972.
  xv, 331 p. illus. diagrs., maps, tables. (ARDA report, no. 7).   OTU
Guillet, Edwin Clarence, 1898–1975.
  The pioneer farmer and backwoodsman. Toronto: Ontario Publishing Co.
  Ltd., distributed by University of Toronto Press [c1963]
  2 v. illus.   OMI OTU
Haythorne, George Vickers, 1909–
  Agriculture and the farm population: a handbook of selected statistics
  grouped by counties and regions, for Ontario and Quebec. Toronto: Oxford
  University Press, 1938.
  143 p. charts. (McGill Social Research Bulletin no. 1).   QMM
— Land and labour, a social survey of agriculture and the farm labour market
  in central Canada by George V. Haythorne, in collaboration with Leonard
  C. Marsh. [Toronto] Published for McGill University by the Oxford
  University Press, 1941.
  xxviii [2] 568 p. map, tables, charts. (McGill Social Research series no. 11).
                                                                       OTU
High, N   H
  Population in process: a study of social change affecting selected farm
  operators and their descendants, 1918–1949, Dundas county, Ontario, by
  N.H. High and M.B. Blackwood. [Guelph, Ontario: Department of
  Agricultural Economics, Ontario Agricultural College, 1952]
  vi, 37 p. tables.   OLU

Hopkins, John Castell, 1864–1923.
    Historical sketch of the Ontario Department of Agriculture. n.p.: 1912.
    8 p.
    "Reprinted from Special supplement in *The Canadian Annual Review of Public
    Affairs* 1910."   OTU
Hudson, Samuel Claude, 1908–
    Taxation in rural Ontario. Ottawa: Department of Agriculture, 1936.
    32 p. graphs, tables.   OONL
Huff, Harry Bruce.
    Capital gains in Canadian agriculture, 1946–66, by H.B. Huff and T.J.
    Cusack. [Guelph, Ontario] School of Agriculture, Economics and Extension
    Education, University of Guelph, 1972.
    vii, 65 p. tables.   OTU
Hunt, Anson M   1863–1926 (comp.).
    Western Fair history, London, Ontario, Canada 1867–1910. London,
    Ontario [Henry & Colerick] 1910.
    59 p. illus., port.   OLU
James, Charles Canniff, 1863–1916.
    Agricultural work in Ontario, by C.C. James;
    Unsanitary housing, by Chas. A. Hodgetts. n.p. [1911?]
    59 p. illus. (Commission of Conservation Canada).   OTAR
Kennedy, H   A
    The heart of Canada; orchard and dairy region of Lake Ontario. Ottawa:
    Issued by direction of Hon. Frank Oliver, minister of the interior [1910?]
    32 p.   OKQ
Kirkwood, Alexander, 1823–1901.
    The undeveloped lands of northern and western Ontario, by A. Kirkwood
    and J.J. Murphy. Toronto: Hunter, Rose and Co., 1878.
    281 p. map.   OTU
Lane, S   H
    Farm labour in Ontario, by S.H. Lane and D.R. Campbell. Department of
    Agricultural Economics, Ontario Agricultural College, Guelph, Canada;
    Ontario Department of Agriculture. n.p. [1952?]
    91 p. illus., tables.   OTU
Langdon, Eustella.
    Pioneer gardens at Black Creek Pioneer Village. Toronto: Holt, Rinehart
    and Winston of Canada [c1972]
    62 [2] p. col. illus., facsims.   OTU
Lanoue, Al.
    The funny side of farming: as I remember it. [Ottawa: Dollco, 1972]
    120 p. illus.
    Recollections of Ottawa valley farming near Winchester more than fifty
    years ago.   OONL
Latzer, Beth Good, 1911–
    Myrtleville – a Canadian farm and family, 1837–1967. Carbondale, Illinois:
    Southern Illinois University Press [c1976]
    xiii, 312 p. illus., ports.   OTU

Leatherbarrow, Margaret F
> Gold in the grass. Toronto: The Ryerson Press [c1954]
> 278 p. illus., ports.
> Agriculture in Ontario.   OTU

Leeds County Committee.
> A very fair comparison of the relative condition of farmers in New York state
> and the province of Ontario. n.p. [1893?]
> 15 p.   OKQ

Leeson, Bruce.
> An organic soil capability classification for agriculture and a study of the
> organic soils of Simcoe county. Conducted under the Federal – Provincial
> Rural Development Agreement A.R.D.A. by Bruce Leeson and the Soil
> Science Department, Ontario Agricultural College, University of Guelph.
> Guelph, Ontario: 1969.
> v, 82 p. illus., diagrs., map.   OTU

Lu, W   F
> A demand analysis for fluid milk in Ontario, by W.F. Lu and R.G.
> Marshall. [Guelph, Ontario] School of Agricultural Economics and
> Extension Education, Ontario Agricultural College, University of Guelph,
> 1973.
> vi, 46 p. graphs, tables. (Publication AE/73/11).   OTU

McArthur, Ian S
> Production of sugar beets in southwestern Ontario: an economic study.
> Ottawa [Department of Agriculture] 1941.
> 71 p. tables.   OONL

Macdonald, Norman.
> Canada: immigration and colonization 1841–1903. [Aberdeen: The
> University Press, c1966]
> xi, 381 p. facsims., maps.   OTU

MacIntyre, Donalda.
> Once upon a farm. [San Francisco: D. von Poellnitz, c1974]
> 68 p. map.
> Farm life in Stormont county, Ontario.   OTAR

McLean, (Mrs.) Irven (comp.).
> Greenwood through the years. Compiled by Mrs. Irven McLean and
> Beatrice R. McLean for the Greenwood Farm Forum. [Greenwood,
> Ontario: 1960]
> 88 p. illus.   OTAR
> — [Greenwood, Ontario] c1963.
> 90 p. illus., ports.   OTU

McMurray, Thomas.
    The free grant lands of Canada, from practical experience of bush farming
    in the free grant districts of Muskoka and Parry Sound. Bracebridge,
    Ontario: Office of the "Northern advocate", 1871.
    xi, 146 [2] p. illus., fold. map, port.
    Map missing from copy examined.   OTURS
MacNaughton, M   A
    Farm family living in Lanark, Ontario 1947–48, by M.A. MacNaughton,
    J.M. Mann and M.B. Blackwood. [Ottawa: Department of Agriculture,
    1950]
    31 p. maps.   OONL
Magnuson, Bruce.
    Ontario's green gold. Introduction by B.F. Avery. [Toronto: Eveready
    Printers Limited, 1944]
    36 p. illus., map.   OTU
Marshall, John Ewing.
    Half century of farming in Dufferin. n.p. [1976]
    52 p. illus.   OTAR
Marshall, R   G
    Fluid milk pricing and producer quota policies in Ontario, 1965–1969. by
    R.G. Marshall and S.H. Lane. [Guelph, Ontario] Department of
    Agricultural Economics, University of Guelph, 1971.
    x, 97 p. map, tables.   OTU
Mason, Thomas Henry, 1858–
    My first 77 years. London, Ontario: London Advertiser, 1935.
    55 chapters.
    Clippings from London Advertiser.   OLU
Michell, Humfrey, 1883–1970.
    The Grange in Canada. Kingston, Ontario: Jackson Press, 1914.
    20 p. (Queen's University. Department of history and political and economic
    science. Bulletin, no. 13).   OTV
Middlesex Federation of Agriculture.
    Turn back the pages: 25 anniversary. [Compiled by Mrs. Tuckey. London,
    Ontario: 1964]
    1 v. (unpaged).   OLU
Mowat, Ruth Diane Pitman, 1940–
    All's fair: the story of Ontario's oldest fair and its home, Williamstown.
    Gananoque, Ontario: 1000 Islands Publishers Ltd. [1976]
    111 p. illus. (part col.), facsims., map, ports (part col.).   OONL
Muldrew, William Hawthorne, 1867–1904.
    Sylvan, Ontario: a guide to our native trees and shrubs. Toronto: William
    Briggs, 1901.
    67 p. illus.   OTU
Nightingale, Thomas   –1921.
    The diary of Thomas Nightingale, farmer & miner, 1867–1871. Picton,
    Ontario: Malcolm Wallbridge, 1967.
    138 p. illus., ports.
    Prince Edward county.   OTAR

Nowland, John L
  The agricultural productivity of the soils of Ontario and Quebec. Ottawa:
  Soil Research Institute, Research Branch, Agriculture Canada, 1975.
    19 p. 2 fold. col. maps.   OTU
100 years of Dundalk District Agricultural Society, 1855–1955. [Dundalk,
  Ontario: Dundalk Herald, 1955?]
    15 p. illus., ports.   OTAR
Ontario. Agricultural Commission, 1880.
  Canadian farming: an encyclopedia of agriculture. Toronto: C. Blackett
  Robinson, 1881.
    432 p. illus.   OTMCL OOA
— Toronto: Williamson & Co., 1889.
    432 p. illus.   OOA
— Report. Toronto: C. Blackett Robinson, 1881.
    4 v.   OTL
— Report. 3d ed. Toronto: C. Blackett Robinson, 1881.
    568, xxxiii, 23 p. fold. map, col. plates.   OTAF
Ontario. Agricultural Enquiry Commission.
  Report. Printed by order of the Legislative Assembly of Ontario. Toronto:
  Clarkson W. James, printer to the King's Most Excellent Majesty, 1925.
    93 p. tables.
    Chairman: D. Jamieson.   OTAR
Ontario. Commission of enquiry concerning the operation of the San José Scale
  Act.
  Report. Printed by order of the Legislative Assembly. Toronto: Warwick
  Bros. & Rutter, 1899.
    8 p.
    Chairman: James Mills.   OTL
Ontario. Commission to enquire into the practice of dehorning cattle.
  Report. Printed by order of the Legislative Assembly. Toronto: Warwick &
  Sons, 1892.
    127 p. illus.
    Chairman: Charles Drury.   OTL
Ontario. Commission to inquire into the working of the drainage laws of the
  province of Ontario.
  Report. Printed by order of the Legislative Assembly. Toronto: Warwick &
  Sons, 1893.
    135 p.
    Chairman: John B. Rankin.   OTL
— [Papers] Toronto: Warwick & Sons, 1891.
    118 p.   OTAR
Ontario. Committee on Farm Assessment and Taxation.
  Report. [Toronto: 1969]
    69 p. tables.
    Chairman: A.N. MacKay.   OTU

Ontario. Legislative Assembly. Select Committee on Butter and Cheese.
    Report. 1888.
    4 handwritten pages.
    Chairman: A.F. Wood.   OTAR
— Proceedings, February 14–March 19, 1888.
    1 v. (unpaged). handwritten.   OTAR
Ontario. Legislative Assembly. Select Committee on Crop Insurance.
    Interim report. [Toronto: 1961]
    34 leaves. tables.
    Chairman: Wm. A. Stewart.   OTAR
— Final report. [Toronto] 1962.
    48 p. tables.   OTAR
Ontario. Legislative Assembly. Select Committee on Farm Drainage.
    Report. [Toronto] 1948.
    11, 15 leaves.
    Chairman: George W. Perry.   OTAR
Ontario. Legislative Assembly. Select Committee on Land Drainage.
    Interim report. [Toronto] 1972.
    13, xvi p. port.
    Chairman: Lorne C. Henderson.   OTMCL OTAR
— Final report. [Toronto] 1974.
    xviii, 104 p. illus.   OTAR
— Minutes, July 12, 1972–March 19, 1973.
    6 v. (various pagings).   OTAR
— Minutes, January 8–February 26, 1974.
    1 v. (various pagings).   OTAR
— Hearings, June 27, 1973–September 19, 1973.
    24 v. (various pagings).   OTAR
— Briefs.
    116 v.   OTAR
Ontario. Legislative Assembly. Select Committee on the Land Improvement
    Fund.
    Report. Toronto: Hunter, Rose & Co., 1869.
    45 p.
    Chairman: T.B. Pardee.   OTAR
Ontario. Milk Commission.
    Report. Printed by order of the Legislative Assembly of Ontario. Toronto:
    L.K. Cameron, printer to the King's Most Excellent Majesty, 1910.
    142 p. illus., tables.
    Chairman: A.R. Pyne.   OTAR
Ontario. Milk Industry Inquiry Committee.
    Report. [Toronto?] 1965.
    330 p. maps, tables.
    Chairman: S.G. Hennessey.   OTU

Ontario. Provincial Farm Commission.
> Report. [Printed by order of the Legislative Assembly. Toronto: Hunter,
> Rose & Co., 1874]
> [8] p.
> Chairman: David Christie. OTL

Ontario. Relief Land Settlement Committee.
> First report. Toronto: Herbert H. Ball, printer to the King's Most Excellent
> Majesty, 1934.
> 29 p.
> No final report located. OTU

Ontario. Royal Commission on Milk.
> Report, 1947. Toronto: Baptist Johnston, printer to the King's Most
> Excellent Majesty, 1947.
> xv, 205 p. tables.
> Chairman: Dalton C. Wells. OTUL
> — Briefs.
> 67 v. OTAR

Ontario. Special Committee on Farm Income.
> The challenge of abundance being the report of the Special Committee on
> Farm Income. [Toronto] 1969.
> lx, 193 p. illus. (part col.), ports.
> Chairman: Everett Biggs. OTU
> — The fertilizer industry in Ontario (Appendix B to the corn industry in
> Ontario). Prepared by the Farm Economics Co-operatives and Statistics
> Branch, Ontario Department of Agriculture and Food for the Special
> Committee on Farm Income in Ontario. [Toronto] 1970.
> 102 p. diagrs., tables. OTU
> — Research report. [Toronto: 1969]
> 15 v. diagrs., tables.
> Contents: no. 1, Farm supply industries in Ontario; no. 2, Capital and credit
> in Ontario agriculture; no. 3, Land use in Ontario agriculture; no. 4, Farm
> management in Ontario; no. 5, Farm people in Ontario; no. 6, Resource
> requirements for specified incomes on Ontario farms; no. 7, Organization of
> the agricultural industry in Ontario; no. 8, Agricultural demand and supply
> relationships in Ontario; no. 9, Marketing of cereal crops in Ontario; no. 10,
> Marketing of dairy products in Ontario; no. 11, Marketing of beef and pork
> in Ontario; no. 12, Marketing of poultry and eggs in Ontario; no. 13,
> Marketing of fresh and processed fruits and vegetables in Ontario; no. 14,
> Wholesaling and retailing of food in Ontario; no. 15, Values, goals and
> means in agricultural policies.
> Letter dated April 2, 1970 enclosed in report no. 14 states: "Due to
> constraints of time and budget the following reports will not be published,
> nos. 7, 8, 9, 10, 15." OTU
> — Support paper: Supply management for agricultural products. [Toronto:
> 1969]
> v, 90 p. diagrs. OTU

Ontario Agricultural College and Experimental Farm. Department of
    Agricultural Economics.
    Tobacco farming in south western Ontario; a survey of 230 tobacco farms in
    Essex and Elgin counties for 1925, by G.W. Michael. Guelph, Ontario: 1926.
    26 leaves. tables.   OTU
Ontario Agricultural Commission of inquiry.
    Interim report. Toronto: 1945.
    74 typewritten pages.
    Chairman: A. Leitch.
    No final report appears to have been issued.   OTAR
Ontario Association of Agricultural Societies.
    The story of Ontario agricultural fairs and exhibitions 1792–1967, and their
    contribution to the advancement of agriculture and betterment of
    community life. [Picton, Ontario: Picton Gazette Publishing Co., Ltd., 1967]
    ix, 212 p. illus., ports.   OTAR
Ontario Economic Council.
    People and land in transition; opportunities for resource development on
    rural Ontario's marginal and abandoned acres. [Toronto: 1966]
    36 p. illus., diagrs.   OTUSA
Ontario Horticultural Association.
    The story of Ontario horticultural societies, and their contribution to making
    the province a more beautiful and better place in which to live, 1854–1973:
    a project of Ontario Horticultural Association. Compiled by Philip F. Dodds
    and H.E. Markle. Picton, Ontario: Picton Gazette Publishing Company,
    1973.
    268 p. illus., ports.   OTAR OTU
Ontario Institute of Agrologists.
    Energy and agriculture. Proceedings of the Ontario Institute of Agrologists
    fifteenth annual conference. Guelph, Ontario [1974]
    102 leaves. tables.   OONL
— Foodland: preservation or starvation. [Hillsburgh, Ontario] The Institute,
    1975.
    28 p.   OTU
Ontario Institute of Agrologists. Committee on Energy and Agriculture.
    Energy and agriculture in Ontario. [Hillsborough, Ontario] The Institute,
    1975.
    16 p.   OONL
Ontario Soil and Crop Improvement Association. Land use conference.
    Proceedings. Rexdale, 1972. Sponsored by the Ontario Soil and Crop
    Improvement Association in cooperation with the Ontario Ministry of
    Agriculture and Food. Planning for the future. Skyline Hotel, Rexdale,
    Ontario, December 12, 13, 1972. [Toronto: 1972?]
    1 v. (various pagings).   OTU

Perkins, Brian Banbury, 1934–
  Multiple jobholding among farm operators: a study of agricultural
  adjustment in Ontario. [Guelph, Ontario] School of Agricultural Economics
  and Extension Education, Ontario Agricultural College, University of
  Guelph, 1972.
  vii, 56 p. tables.   OTU
Pomeroy, Elsie May, 1886–
  William Saunders and his five sons. The story of the Marquis wheat family.
  Foreword by W. Sherwood Fox. Toronto: The Ryerson Press [c1956]
  xiii, 192 p. illus.   OTU
Purvis, James M
  A socio-economic study of new farm operators in eastern Ontario, by James
  M. Purvis and Henry F. Noble. [Toronto] Ontario Ministry of Agriculture
  and Food, 1973.
  43 p. illus., map.   OTV
Rannie, William Fraser, 1915–
  Cave Springs Farm: fact and fancy about one of the historic places of the
  Niagara peninsula. [2d ed. Beamsville, Ontario: Beamsville Express, 1960]
  35 p.   OTU
— [3rd ed. Beamsville, Ontario: Rannie Publications, 1968]
  35 p.
  First edition, 1932. No copy located.   OTU
Reaman, George Elmore, 1889–1969.
  A history of agriculture in Ontario [1615–1967]. With a foreword by
  William A. Stewart and J.A.C. Auld. [Toronto: Saunders, c1970]
  2 v. illus., ports.   OTU
Richards, N   R
  Report of the study of the organization of the Ontario Ministry of
  Agriculture and Food [to Hon. Wm. A. Stewart] Toronto: [J.C. Thatcher,
  Queen's Printer] 1973.
  107 p. map.   OTU
Rohmer, Richard H   1924–
  The green north. Toronto: Maclean Hunter [c1970]
  iv, 152 p. illus., maps, ports.   OTU
Rural Geography Symposium, Guelph, first, 1975.
  Part-time farming: problem or resources in rural development: proceedings
  of the first Rural Geography Symposium, Department of Geography,
  University of Guelph, June 18, 19, and 20th, 1975. Edited by Anthony M.
  Fuller and Julius A. Mage. [Guelph, Ontario: Department of Geography,
  University of Guelph, 1976]
  vi, 291 p. illus., maps, diagrs.   OLU
Ryerson, Adolphus Egerton, 1803–1882.
  First lessons on agriculture for Canadian farmers and their families. 2d ed.
  Toronto; Copp–Clarke & Co., 1871.
  xi, 216 p.
  No copy of first edition located.   OONL

Seymour – Campbellford Agricultural Society.
    A century of footprints. [Warkworth, Ontario: Warkworth Journal, 1967?]
    88 p.   OTU
Smallfield, Albert.
    Lands and resources of Renfrew county, province of Ontario: a handbook
    for the information of immigrant farmers desirous of obtaining cheap farms
    in an already settled district. Renfrew, Ontario: The Mercury Office, 1881.
    17 p.   OOA
Stiles, Harlow M
    Official history of the Cornwall Cheese and Butter Board. [Cornwall?
    Ontario] Published by authorization of the Cornwall Cheese and Butter
    Board [1919]
    306 p. illus., ports.   OTU
Sylvestre, Paul Emile.
    Producing beef on the farm: an analysis of light weight beef production in
    southwestern Ontario. Ottawa: Department of Agriculture, Experimental
    Farms Service, 1942.
    28 p. illus.   OOAG
Temiskaming and Northern Ontario Railway Commission.
    Homes for farmers in northern Ontario. Toronto: n.d.
    24 p. illus.
    Chairman: J.L. Englehart.   OTU
— The northland Temiskaming opinions of expert agriculturists and delegates
    from Toronto Board of Trade. Toronto: Temiskaming and Northern
    Ontario Railway Commission, 1911.
    64 p. illus. (*Its* pamphlet no. 9).
    Chairman: J.L. Englehart.   OTU
Tossell, W   E   1926–
— Agriculture and regional planning. [Guelph, Ontario] Centre for Resources
    Development, University of Guelph, 1972.
    6 leaves. (Guelph. University. Centre for Resources Development.
    Publication no. 61).   OONL
Walker, Henry James William, 1892–
    Renfrew and its fair through 100 years; Agricultural Society's centennial
    year 1953. Renfrew, Ontario: South Renfrew Agricultural Society [1953]
    104 p. illus., ports.   OTU
Waterston, Elizabeth, 1922–
    Canadian portraits: Massey, McIntosh, Saunders, pioneers in agriculture.
    Toronto: Clarke, Irwin & Company Limited, 1957.
    136 p. illus., ports.   OTAR
Watson, W   P   1902–
    The Royal: a history of the Royal Agricultural Winter Fair. Toronto:
    McClelland and Stewart Limited [c1968]
    192 p. illus., ports.   OTAR

Periodical Articles

Agricultural settlement by refugees in Ontario. Ontario Research Foundation Bulletin 7(8): 1–5, 8, 1940.

A.R.D.A. in Ontario. Ontario Economic Review 3(no. 4): 4–6, 1965.

Batrik, S   N
The input-output structure of the Niagara region. Ontario Economic Review 10(no. 1): 5–39, 1972.

Baxter, Isobel.
The Baxters of Cataraqui Grange. Historic Kingston 18: 45–53, 1970.

The beginning of agricultural extension in Waterloo county. Waterloo Historical Society. Annual Volume 48: 72–76, 1960.

Bélanger, Roger.
Région agricole Sudbury – Nipissing. Société Historique du Nouvel-Ontario. Documents Historiques 18: 4–37, 1949.

Bergey, Lorna L
Wilmot family farms. Waterloo Historical Society. Annual Volume 50: 62–64, 1962; 51: 70–73, 1963.

Blezard valley; paroisse agricole. Société Historique du Nouvel-Ontario. Documents Historiques 24: 29 41, 1953.

Bodnar, Laszlo.
Agricultural workers in Ontario. Ontario Economic Review 12(no. 4): 4–9, 1974.

— Soybeans in Ontario: production, utilization and prospects. Ontario Economic Review 5(no. 5–6): 3–13, 1967.

Bogue, Allan G
The fight farmer, William Weld. Western Ontario Historical Notes 3: 75–78, 1945.

Bolduc, N   G
The Waterloo Horticultural Society. Waterloo Historical Society. Annual Report 26: 12–16, 1938.

Bosanquet, Mary.
Life on an Ontario bush farm. Geographical Magazine 16: 492–501, 1944.

Boswell, A   M
Beef feeding in eastern Ontario, 1964-65. Canadian Farm Economics 2(no. 3): 23–31, 1967.

Boucher, G   P
Consumption of cream in Canada. Economic Annalist 7: 20–21, 1937. Ontario statistics.

Braithwaite, Max.
White hybrid corn in Ontario. Canadian Geographical Journal 35: 189–195, 1947.

Brown, Grant.
The greater production campaign of 1918. Industrial Canada 19(no. 6): 54–57, 1918.
Company gardens in Ontario.

Brown, Harry W
    History of the Kitchener Horticultural Society. Waterloo Historical Society.
    Annual Report 26: 6–12, 1938.
Brown, (Mrs.) P   J
    Dairying farming in Bruce county. Ontario Agricultural College Review 3:
    97–98, 1892.
Bryant, C   R
    Some new perspectives on agricultural land use in the rural-urban fringe.
    Ontario Geography 10: 64–78, 1976.
    Primarily in southern Ontario.
Buchanan, J
    Organized experimental work with field crops in Ontario. Ontario
    Agricultural College Review 22: 131–137, 1909.
Burns, J   R
    Tomatoes – carlot unloads – Toronto. Canadian Farm Economics 3(no. 1):
    6–7, 1968.
Cameron, Agnes Deans.
    The orchards of Ontario. Canadian Magazine of Politics, Science, Art and
    Literature 33: 449–456, 1909.
Campbell, D   R
    The economics of production control: the example of tobacco. Canadian
    Journal of Economics 2: 115–124, 1969.
Carpenter, J   Fred.
    Horticulture: a lesson from Norfolk county. Ontario Agricultural College
    Review 22: 308–312, 1910.
Carroll, J   A
    The activities of the Ontario Marketing Board. Canadian Society of
    Agricultural Economics. Proceedings 4: 47–49, 1932.
Cartwright, D   G
    Changes in the distribution of cheese factories in southwestern Ontario.
    Canadian Geographer 10: 225–233, 1966.
Chapman, Lyman J
    Adaptation of crops in Ontario. Canadian Geographical Journal 24:
    248–254, 1942.
— Farming in Ontario. Canadian Geographical Journal 51: 132–145, 1955.
Christie, George I
    Changing conditions in Ontario agriculture. Industrial Canada 30(no. 11):
    87–89, 100, 1930.
Cockshutt, Harry.
    Protection and the Ontario farmer. Ontario Agricultural College Review 20:
    291–295, 1908.
Coke, J
    The development of agricultural economics in Canada. Economic Annalist
    1(no. 8): 1-3; 1(no. 9): 3–6, 1931.
— A preliminary analysis of the organization of 148 Ontario farms. Economic
    Annalist 1(no. 6): 1–3, 1931.

— Sources of receipts on 380 farms in Nova Scotia, Quebec and Ontario 1929. Economic Annalist 2: 17–18, 1932.

Coke, J   and A   Gosselin.
An analysis of the incomes of apple growers in 1929-30. Economic Annalist 2: 47–51, 1932.

— Post war trends in farm machinery purchases in eastern Canada. Economic Annalist 16: 20–23, 1946.

The Colborne Agricultural Society. Huron Historical Notes 6: 13–14, 1970.

Colquette, R   D
The case of Robert John: a brief sketch of the affairs of an Ontario farmer. Ontario Agricultural College Review 27: 83–86, 1914.

Cooley, R   B
The Winter Fair. Ontario Agricultural College Review 22: 204–206, 1910. Ontario Provincial Winter Fair – Guelph.

Cost of milk production study. Economic Annalist 6: 74–75, 1936.

Couston, J   W
Number, production and location of dairy manufacturing dry skim milk and evaporated whole milk in Canada, 1953–58. Economic Annalist 30: 40–47, 1960.

Cowan, H   B
The agricultural societies of Ontario. Ontario Agricultural College Review 17: 381–384, 1905.

— The future of Ontario's agricultural societies. Ontario Agricultural College Review 20: 1–7, 1907.

Cowan, Jennie F
History at the International Plowing Match. Waterloo Historical Society. Annual Report 42: 34–42, 1954.

Crawford, M   Gail.
Patterson: family firm and village. York Pioneer 71(1): 2–10. 1976. Ontario agricultural history.

Creelman, G   C
Have Farmers' Institutes come to stay? Ontario Agricultural College Review 17(1): 1–5, 1904.

Cressman, Ella M
The sugar beet industry. Waterloo Historical Society. Annual Volume 60: 91–93, 1972.

Crow, J   W
Ontario and the apple. Ontario Agricultural College Review 23: 21–24, 77–80, 1910.

Curran, Howard.
The potato industry in Ontario. Ontario Agricultural College Review 27: 250–251, 1915.

Dairy products. Industrial Canada 5: 742–743, 1905.

Darling, E   H
Recent developments in the use of cold storage in Ontario. Canadian Geographical Journal 17: 122–125, 1938.

Dawson, J   A
    Changes on eastern Ontario dairy farms between 1937 and 1947. Economic
    Annalist 20: 45–46, 1950.
— Economic aspects of tractor use in Ontario and Quebec. Economic Annalist
    22: 60–63, 1952.
Day, W   H
    Electric power and the Ontario farmer. Ontario Agricultural College
    Review 20: 473–476, 1908.
Dix, Ernest.
    United States influence on the agriculture of Prince Edward county,
    Ontario. Economic Geography 26: 179–182, 1950.
Drayton, L   E
    Consumer demand for cheese in Ottawa, Toronto and Vancouver.
    Economic Annalist 22: 46–47, 1952.
Drummond, W   M
    The impact of the post-war industrial expansion in Ontario's agriculture.
    Canadian Journal of Economics and Political Science 24: 84–92, 1958.
Dryden, John.
    The future of sheep husbandry in Canada. Ontario Agriculture College
    Review 3: 65–68, 1892.
Elgie, R   H
    Agriculture in Algoma. Ontario Agricultural College Review 27: 301–304,
    1915.
Evans, A   Margaret and R   W   Irwin.
    Government tractors in Ontario, 1917 and 1918. Ontario History 61:
    99–109, 1969.
Farmer solidarity.[editorial] Canadian Forum 31: 28, 1951.
Fitzpatrick, J   M
    Labour requirements for dairy barn chores. Economic Annalist 24: 62–69,
    1954.
Forsyth, R   A
    The Agricultural Representative Service in Waterloo county (1907–1957).
    Waterloo Historical Society. Annual Report 44: 55–62, 1956.
Gagan, David P
    The indivisibility of land: a microanalysis of the system of inheritance in
    nineteenth century Ontario. Journal of Economic History 36: 126–141,
    1976.
Grant, J   Fergus.
    Implementing agriculture. Canadian Geographical Journal 18: 170–207,
    1939.
Grape culture in Ontario. Ontario Agricultural College Review 3: 6–7, 1891.
Greelman, G   C
    The new movement in Ontario agriculture. Ontario Agricultural College
    Review 20: 368–371, 1908.
Hamilton farm history, Perth county. Western Ontario Historical Notes 16:
    28–31, 1960.

Harcourt, R
  History of sugar beet industry in Canada. Ontario Agricultural College
  Review 16(7): 20–25, 1904.
Hare, H   R
  Farm management factors affecting labour earnings on Ontario dairy farms.
  Economic Annalist 8: 89–90, 1938.
Harkness, W   J   K
  Fish and wildlife management in Ontario. Canadian Geographical Journal
  48: 46–63, 1954.
Hart, S
  Experimental plots. Ontario Agricultural College Review 23: 108–112,
  1910.
Haviland, William E
  Ontario tobacco farm organization and selected new belt production
  problems. Economic Annalist 20: 127–133, 1950.
— Some economic aspects of tobacco farming in Ontario. Economic Annalist
  20: 107–113, 1950.
Heighton, V   A
  The grain corn enterprise in eastern Ontario, 1967. Canadian Farm
  Economics 3(no. 2): 4–8, 1968.
Henderson, I   B
  An investigation into the conditions of the poultry industry in Peterboro
  county. Ontario Agricultural College Review 23: 499–504, 1911.
Herniman, Charles.
  Development of artificial drainage systems in Kent and Essex counties,
  Ontario. Ontario Geography 2: 13–24, 1968.
Hills, G   A
  Pedology, 'the dirt science', and agricultural settlement in Ontario.
  Canadian Geographical Journal 29: 106–127, 1944.
Hodgetts, P   W
  Co-operation in Ontario. Ontario Agricultural College Review 20: 322–330,
  1908.
Hodson, F   W
  Live stock in Ontario. Ontario Agricultural College Review 18: 171–172,
  1906.
Hopper, W   C
  Consumption of eggs in farm homes in certain districts of Canada. Economic
  Annalist 8: 46, 1938.
Hudgins, Bert.
  Tobacco growing in southern Ontario. Economic Geography 14: 223–232,
  1938.
Hudson, S   C
  Assessment of farm property in Ontario. Economic Annalist 4: 24–29, 1934.
— A comparison in farm efficiency. Economic Annalist 5: 62–63, 1935.
— Farm taxes on selected groups of farms in Ontario, Quebec and Nova Scotia.
  Economic Annalist 3: 68–69, 1933.

Hudson, S   C   and J   G   Carson.
    The sheep enterprise on Ontario farms. Economic Annalist 22: 101–108,
    1952.
Hunsberger, Wilson A
    Threshing days in the twenties. Waterloo Historical Society. Annual
    Volume 64: 4–10, 1976.
Irwin, Ross W
    One hundred years of agricultural development in York county. York
    Pioneer and Historical Society. Annual Report 48–53, 1970.
James, C   C
    Agriculture in its relation to manufactures. Ontario Agricultural College
    Review 20: 413–418, 1908.
— The agriculture of Canada. Industrial Canada 5: 700–702, 1905.
Johnson, D
    What Ontario offers the young man in horticulture: fruit growing in
    Lambton county. Ontario Agricultural College Review 22: 68–70, 1909.
Johnston, S   C
    What the Motion Picture Bureau hopes to do in Ontario agriculture.
    Ontario Agricultural College Review 30: 260–262, 1918.
Jones, Robert Leslie.
    History of agriculture in Ontario, 1613–1880. University of Toronto Studies.
    History and Economics 12: xvi, 1–420, 1946.
Kent, Jon.
    Agriculture in the clay belt of northern Ontario. Canadian Geographer 10:
    117–126, 1966.
[Kidner, F] F   K
    Hamilton's Crystal Palace. Wentworth Historical Society. Journal and
    Transactions 3: 38–43, 1902.
King, Vernon.
    A summer in the Niagara peninsula. Ontario Agricultural College Review
    23: 136–140, 1910.
Kirk, D   W
    Settlement pattern of the Listowel region, southwestern Ontario. Economic
    Geography 23: 67–71, 1947.
Krueger, Ralph Ray.
    The disappearing Niagara fruit belt. Canadian Geographical Journal 38:
    102–113, 1959.
— The geography of the orchard industry of Canada. Geographical Bulletin 7:
    27–71, 1965.
    Ontario: pp. 46–56.
Kummer, O   A
    Preston Horticultural Society. Waterloo Historical Society. Annual Volume
    59: 64–70, 1971.
Kutas, F
    Tobacco – Ontario's major cash crop. Ontario Economic Review 1: no. 10,
    1964.

Langston, W   M
  The tobacco industry in Norfolk county. Journal of the Canadian Bankers'
  Association 37: 294–298, 1930.
Lawr, D   A
  The development of Ontario farming, 1870–1914: patterns of growth and
  change. Ontario History 64: 239–251, 1972.
Lawrence, Frank.
  Changes in costs and investment in machinery on dairy farms in eastern
  Ontario. Economic Annalist 30: 130–136, 1960.
— Optimum profits on eggs from small flocks in eastern Ontario. Economic
  Annalist 33: 127–133, 1963.
Leckie, H   K
  Farm receipts in three areas of Ontario. Economic Annalist 10: 94–95, 1940.
Leroux, M   Roméo.
  Le Sol et l'agriculture du comté de Sudbury. Société Historique du Nouvel-
  Ontario. Documents Historiques 1: 29–32, 1942.
Linfield, F   B
  Ontario and the west: "Go west young man". Ontario Agricultural College
  Review 20: 259–261, 1908.
Logsdail, A   J
  The Horticultural Experimental Station, Jordan Harbor. Ontario
  Agricultural College Review 21: 25–29, 1908.
Lovering, J   H
  Possibilities for farm development in southeastern Renfrew county, Ontario.
  Canadian Farm Economics 3(no. 1): 8–19, 1968.
MacArthur, Ian.
  Farm organization in southern Ontario. Economic Annalist 8: 55–57, 1938.
— Financial summary of sugar beet farms in southwestern Ontario. Economic
  Annalist 10: 88–90, 1940.
— Ontario hog-feed ratio. Economic Annalist 8: 90–93, 1939.
— Operating expenses on Ontario farms. Economic Annalist 10: 51–53, 1940.
— Relation of Ontario hog-feed ratio to changes in hog numbers. Economic
  Annalist 10: 5–7, 1940.
McCalla, W   C
  What Ontario offers the young man in horticulture: life and profits in the
  peach belt. Ontario Agricultural College Review 22: 259–262, 1910.
McCallum, J   M
  The Ontario Provincial Winter Fair. Ontario Agricultural College Review
  12(4): 8–11, 1901.
McDermott, George L
  Frontiers of settlement in the great clay belt, Ontario and Quebec.
  Association of American Geographers. Annals 51: 261–273, 1961.
McElroy, H   W
  Co-operation in the Rainy River valley. Ontario Agricultural College
  Review 26: 185–187, 1914.
  Potatogrowers' Co-operative Association.

McGill University. Social Sciences Research Committee.
Agriculture and the farm population: a handbook of selected statistics grouped by counties and regions, for Ontario and Quebec. Social Research Bulletin 1: 1–143, 1938.

McInnis, R   Marvin.
Farms and farm families in the St. Lawrence townships. Historic Kingston 24: 6–17, 1976.

McKenzie, Ruth I
Community action through Farm Forum. Canadian Forum 28: 59–60, 1948. Renfrew county.

McLarty, Duncan A
A century of development of agricultural science in western Ontario. Western Ontario Historical Notes 5: 48–54, 1947.

MacLennan, A   H
The Ontario Horticultural Exhibition. Ontario Agricultural College Review 20: 209–211, 1908.

McLennan, D   M
The Ontario provincial plowing match. Ontario Agricultural College Review 28: 144–147, 1915.

McLoughry, E   I
Agricultural progress in Waterloo county. Waterloo Historical Society. Annual Volume 50: 36–40, 1962.

Mann, Jean M.
Farming in Peterborough county, 1818–1900. Economic Annalist 17: 55–58, 1947.

Mills, Jason.
Notes on the recent progress of agriculture in the Dominion of Canada. Ontario Agricultural College Review 16(3): 4–6, 1903.

Mitchell, H
The Grange in Canada. Queen's Quarterly 001 161 188, 1914/1915.

Morley, E   Lillian.
The Mornington Fall Fair, 1859–1963. Western Ontario Historical Notes 19: 51–59, 1963.
Reprint from: *The Milverton Sun*, August 23, 1963.

Muskoka and Algoma. Ontario Agricultural College Review 2: 84–86, 1891.

Neale, J   C
Mixed farming in Ontario. Ontario Agricultural College Review 28: 40–44, 1915.

Nixon, W   G
Temiskaming and agriculture. Ontario Agricultural College Review 28: 268–269, 1916.

A note on Thomas Shaw. Western Ontario Historical Notes 7: 48–50, 1949.

Olaskey, Terry M
The history of threshing machinery in Waterloo county as seen at Doon Pioneer Village. Waterloo Historical Society. Annual Volume 62: 64–70, 1974.

Ontario Agriculture College. Farm Department.
Results of farm management survey: in Caledon township, Peel county.
Ontario Agricultural College Review 30: 456–461, 1918.
The Ontario Provincial Winter Fair. Ontario Agricultural College Review 23:
194–196, 1911.
Orchard, Joseph.
Experimenting in Ontario's northland. Ontario Agricultural College Review
27: 409–410, 1915.
Packman, D   J
Brief notes on trends in farm tenancy in Ontario. Economic Annalist 24:
134–136, 1954.
— Changes on dairy farms in Dundas county, Ontario, between 1918 and 1948.
Economic Annalist 19: 38–40, 1949.
— Farm forestry in Ontario. Economic Annalist 23: 5–10, 1953.
— The landlord–tenant situation on 200 southern Ontario farms, 1953.
Economic Annalist 25: 20–23, 1955.
— The production of maple syrup on Ontario farms. Economic Annalist 22:
65–69, 1952.
— Soybean production in Ontario. Economic Annalist 22: 131–137, 1952.
Pando, J   L
Factors affecting the production of tomatoes for processing. Canadian Farm
Economics 4(no. 2): 8–14, 1969.
Patterson, H   L
Significant economic changes in agriculture. Ontario Economic Review 2:
no. 11, 1965.
Pemberton, R   E   K
Tobacco road – Ontario version. Canadian Forum 21: 368–370, 1942.
— What promise for agriculture? Canadian Forum 21: 171–173, 1941.
Pettypiece, H   J
The farmer and the railway. Ontario Agricultural College Review 17:
327–333, 1905.
Philpotts, L   E   and V   R   Wallen.
The use of color infrared aerial photography in estimating loss in white bean
production in Huron county, Ontario, 1968. Canadian Farm Economics
5(no. 4): 25–30, 1970.
Pomfret, Richard.
The mechanization of reaping in nineteenth-century Ontario; a case study
of the pace and causes of the diffusion of embodied technical change. Journal
of Economic History 36: 399–415, 1976.
Porter, W   H
Lambton county as a fruit district. Ontario Agricultural College Review 25:
125–128, 1912.
Rachlis, M
Premiums received by growers for varieties and grades of western Ontario
apples. Economic Annalist 17: 52–54, 1947.

Randall, John R
    Settlement of the great clay belt of northern Ontario and Quebec. Bulletin of
    the Geographical Society of Philadelphia 35: 53–66, 1937.
[Raynor, M]
    The Ontario breeder's future. Ontario Agricultural College Review 10(6):
    4–5, 1899.
Reeds, Lloyd G
    Agricultural regions of southern Ontario: 1880 and 1951. Economic
    Geography 35: 219–227, 1959.
Reek, W   R
    New Ontario. Ontario Agricultural College Review 24: 61–64, 1911.
Reid, Ewart P.
    Ottawa produce market. Canadian Agricultural Economics Society.
    Proceedings 10: 129–134, 1938.
Rennie, John.
    Life of William Rennie. York Pioneer and Historical Society. Annual
    Report, 9–15, 1936.
Reynolds, J   B
    East and west. Ontario Agricultural College Review 23: 535–539, 1911.
— The O.A.C. and Ontario farming. Ontario Agricultural College Review 24:
    389–391, 1912.
— Temiskaming. Ontario Agricultural College Review 18: 358–362, 1906.
Riddell, Walter.
    Farming in Northumberland county: 1833 to 1895. Ontario Historical
    Society. Papers & Records 30: 143–149, 1934.
Robb, O   J
    The Vineland Experimental Farm. Ontario Agricultural College Review
    27: 201–203, 1915.
Rodd, R   Stephen.
    The crisis of agricultural land in the Ontario countryside. Plan Canada 16:
    160–170, 1976.
Roy, Bob.
    Large profits in farming in Ontario. Industrial Canada 19(no. 11): 120,
    1919. Reprinted from *Toronto Sunday World*.
Schierholtz, C   W
    The Elmira monthly fair. Waterloo Historical Society. Annual Report 35:
    32–33, 1947.
Schmidt, John T
    International Plowing Match, 1954; it took a hurricane to stop Waterloo
    county's largest agricultural event! Waterloo Historical Society. Annual
    Report 42: 28–33, 1954.
Schneller, W   J
    Waterloo county arboretum. Waterloo Historical Society. Annual Volume
    60: 75–77, 1972.

Sellers, Harry.
   The early history of the handling and transportation of grain in the district
   of Thunder Bay. Thunder Bay Historical Society. Papers 2: 21–26,
   1909/1910.
Shaw, Thomas.
   The future of the live stock industry of Ontario. Ontario Agricultural
   College Review 2: 52–56, 1891.
Shefrin, F
   Community wartime agricultural committees. Economic Annalist 13: 74–77,
   1943.
Slater, Jonathan.
   Markham Farmer's Club. York Pioneer and Historical Society. Annual
   Report 24–26, 1906.
Smith, E   D
   Niagara district fruit report. Ontario Agricultural College Review 24:
   139–141, 1911.
Smith, R   M
   Northern Ontario; limits of land settlement for the good citizen. Canadian
   Geographical Journal 23: 182–211, 1941.
Smith, W   L
   The farmers; transportation problem. Ontario Agricultural College Review
   16(4): 9–13, 1904.
— The tariff and the Ontario farmer. Ontario Agricultural College Review 20:
   239–241, 1908.
Spafford, Earle.
   Tobacco growing in Canada. Quarterly Review of Commerce 9: 261–269,
   1942.
Stewart, Alex. and H   K   Leckie.
   Some comparisons of Kent county, Ontario, farms in 1921 and 1938.
   Economic Annalist 8: 84–88, 1939; 10: 19–25, 1940.
Stutt, R   A
   Farm management in Canada. Canadian Farm Economics 2(no. 3): 12–22,
   1967.
— Policy and administration of public lands in Ontario with particular
   reference to agriculture. Canadian Farm Economics 1 (no.4): 14–18, 1966.
— Some highlights of a survey of incorporated family farms in Ontario.
   Canadian Farm Economics 4(no. 4): 9–13, 1969.
Sugar beet production costs in Ontario and Michigan. Economic Annalist 11:
   30–31, 1941.
Taylor, K   W
   Wilbur Francis Chown (1896–1950). Canadian Journal of Economics and
   Political Science 16: 422, 1950.
Toole, W
   Ontario and the sheep industry. Ontario Agricultural College Review 23:
   546–550, 1911.

Trevor, H   W
    Farm practices in beef production in five selected counties of Ontario, 1956.
    Economic Annalist 29: 83–90, 1959.
— Farming in the Rainy River and Dryden districts of northwestern Ontario.
    Economic Annalist 22: 140–144, 1952.
— Farming in the Rainy River district of Ontario. Economic Annalist 22:
    108–111, 1952.
— Pasture costs in five counties of southwestern Ontario, 1959. Economic
    Annalist 29: 70–71, 1959.
Turney, A   G
    The victory at Chicago. Ontario Agricultural College Review 20: 179–183,
    1908.
    Ontario Agricultural College at the International Stock Show.
Van Steen, Marcus.
    Niagara: vineyard of Canada. Canadian Geographical Journal 67: 128–133,
    1963.
— Tobacco: another Canadian achievement. Canadian Geographical Journal
    61: 10–17, 1960.
Walker, Gerald.
    How the Holland Marsh community developed. Canadian Geographical
    Journal 93(no. 1): 42–49, 1976.
Ward, Clifton.
    The progress of motor farming in Canada; International Ploughing Match
    near Brockville, Ontario, bring out modern machinery. Industrial Canada
    26(no. 7): 49, 82, 1925.
Way, W   C
    Rail distribution of Ontario fruits and vegetables. Economic Annalist 24:
    81–84, 1954.
Whitaker, J   R
    Agricultural gradients in southern Ontario. Economic Geography 14:
    109–120, 1938.
— Distribution of dairy farming in peninsular Ontario. Economic Geography
    16: 69–78, 1940.
White, E   W
    The Ontario Horticultural Exhibition. Ontario Agricultural College Review
    24: 205–208, 1912.
Wiancko, A   T
    Farming in Muskoka. Ontario Agricultural College Review 4(6): 7–8, 1893.
Wilman, M
    Changes in farm size and numbers in Canada to 1966. Canadian Farm
    Economics 2(no. 4): 21–28, 1967.
Wilson, Lois.
    Gardens and plantings at Wymilwood. Royal Architectural Institute of
    Canada. Journal 31: 55–57, 1954.

Worrall, Robert J
Farm abandonment in Bruce county. Bruce County Historical Society.
Yearbook 10–12, 1973.
Yang, W   Y
Changes in production and gross returns of twenty sheep enterprises in
southern Ontario, 1964 to 1967. Canadian Farm Economics 3(no. 3): 11–14,
1968.
Zavitz, C   A
Ontario's co-operative experiments in agriculture for a quarter of a century.
Ontario Agricultural College Review 23: 199–205, 1911.

Theses

Ackerman, Gerald Edward.
An examination of the crop and livestock practices associated with soil
conservation farming in Ontario with a view to determining their economic
significance. [Toronto] 1955.
ix, 100 leaves. tables, forms, map.
M.S.A. thesis, University of Toronto.   OTU
Attridge, Walter Ewing.
The dairy farm in eastern Ontario: a study in rural change. Ottawa: 1968.
95 leaves. tables.
M.A. research essay, Carleton University.   OOCC
Baker, Harold Reid.
An opinion survey of agricultural extension work in Ontario. Ithaca, New
York: 1959.
viii, 169 leaves. map, tables.
Ph.D. thesis, Cornell University (microfilm 59-02690).   DA
Bausenhart, Werner Albert, 1937–
The terminology of agronomy of the Pennsylvania German dialect of
Waterloo county, Ontario. Waterloo, Ontario: 1966 [c1971]
3, viii, 135 leaves. illus., maps.
M.A. thesis, University of Waterloo (microfilm 7561).   Can
Bogue, Allan George.
Ontario agriculture between 1880 and 1890 with special reference to
southwestern Ontario. [London, Ontario] 1946.
266 leaves. tables..
M.A. thesis, The University of Western Ontario.   OLU
Bodnar, Laszlo.
Some economic aspects of materials handling on dairy farms. [Toronto]
1963.
viii, 148 leaves. diagrs., tables (part fold.).
M.S.A. thesis, University of Toronto.   OTU
Bostwick, Wilda Bernice.
An examination of an agricultural boundary zone: the Kent – Lambton area
of southwestern Ontario. London, Ontario: 1967.
viii, 58 leaves. illus., graphs, maps, tables.
B.A. thesis, The University of Western Ontario.   OLU

Boyko, Maria, 1948–
    European impact on the vegetation around Crawford Lake in southern
    Ontario. [Toronto] c1973.
    viii, 115 leaves. col. illus., tables, figs., maps.
    M.Sc. thesis, University of Toronto.   OTU
Brent, David Gordon, 1944–
    The place of the horse in Ontario today, with special reference to London
    township. London, Ontario: 1974.
    xii, 93 leaves. illus., maps.
    M.A. thesis, The University of Western Ontario (microfilm 23263).   OLU
Brooksbank, Robert Dennis.
    Agricultural land resources and land use change in an urbanizing region.
    [Guelph, Ontario] 1976.
    xi, 173 leaves. tables.
    M.Sc. thesis, The University of Guelph (microfilm 28049).   OGU
Brookstone, Mildred.
    Correlation of oat yields with temperature and precipitation in southern
    Ontario. [Toronto] 1940.
    iv, 155 leaves. illus., maps (1 fold.).
    M.A. thesis, University of Toronto.   OTU
Brown, Jacqueline Larkin.
    Ontario's Farm Radio Forum. [Ottawa] 1968.
    57 leaves.
    M.A. research essay, Carleton University.   OOCC
Burkholder, Arthur Ronald.
    An inquiry into the spatial distribution of hogs in southern Ontario.
    [Toronto] 1969.
    v, 71 leaves. illus., maps (part col.).
    M.A. research paper, University of Toronto.   OTU
Byers, Marcia Lorraine.
    Effects of contract farming on agriculture in the London area. London,
    Ontario: 1972.
    x, 77 leaves. illus., graphs, tables.
    B.A. thesis, The University of Western Ontario.   OLU
Campbell, Neil MacDougall.
    An evaluation and policy proposal: Ontario farm enlargement and
    consolidation program. [Waterloo, Ontario] 1972.
    xi, 316 leaves. tables.
    Ph.D. thesis, University of Waterloo (microfilm 12902).   OWTU
Clark, Jack H
    Some economic aspects of the production and feeding of grass silage in the
    counties of Oxford and Middlesex in the province of Ontario. [Toronto]
    1953.
    112 leaves. tables.
    M.S.A. thesis, University of Toronto.   OTU

Clark, John Winder.
    Tobacco production in Ontario. [Hamilton, Ontario] 1949.
    vii, 86 p. diagrs., maps.
    B.A. thesis, McMaster University.   OHM
Cooper, James Carl, 1946–
    The factors behind the restructuring of Ontario agriculture by region,
    1882–1911. Kingston, Ontario: c1972.
    iv, 113 leaves. tables.
    M.A. thesis, Queen's University (accepted 1973) (microfilm 13695).   OKQ
Corder, Raymond Glen.
    Changing white bean acreage patterns in southwestern Ontario. [Waterloo,
    Ontario] 1971.
    130 leaves. graphs, maps, tables.
    M.A. thesis, University of Waterloo.   OWTU
Cringan, Alexander Thom, 1926–
    Some factors in selecting units for managing wildlife in Ontario. Ann Arbor,
    Michigan: 1965.
    xi, 154 leaves. illus., map.
    Ph.D. thesis, The University of Michigan. (microfilm 66-6589).   DA
Crothall, William Robert.
    French Canadian agriculture in Ontario, 1861–1871; a study of cultural
    transfer. [Toronto] 1968 [c1974]
    x, 139 leaves. tables (1 fold.), maps (part col.).
    M.A. thesis, University of Toronto (microfilm 18492).   OTU
Crown, Robert W
    Forecasting farm labour employment in Ontario to 1981. [Guelph, Ontario]
    1968.
    v, 62 leaves. tables.
    M.Sc. thesis, The University of Guelph.   OGU
Cummings, Francis Harry.
    Alternatives in farm decision making: a case study of dairy farms in Huron
    county. London, Ontario: 1970.
    ix, 94 leaves. illus., graphs, maps, tables.
    B.A. thesis, The University of Western Ontario.   OLU
Darnel, Benard Wolfram.
    Agricultural underdevelopment in Caistor township. [Hamilton, Ontario]
    1967.
    vi, 103 leaves. illus., fold. maps, tables.
    B.A. thesis, McMaster University.   OHM
— Socio-economic parameters in farm performance: a study of selected farms
    in Seneca township. [Hamilton, Ontario] 1969.
    viii, 214 leaves. maps, tables.
    M.A. thesis, McMaster University.   OHM
Da Silva, Wanda Maria, 1950–
    A comparison of soil capability and agricultural productivity in southern
    Ontario. London, Ontario: 1975.
    xv, 142 leaves. fold. graphs, fold. maps.
    M.A. thesis, The University of Western Ontario (microfilm 28197).   OLU

De Lisle, David de Garis.
  An analysis of the layout of the agricultural holdings in four townships of
  eastern Ontario. [Toronto] 1968.
  74 p. illus., figs., map.
  M.A. thesis, University of Toronto.   OTU
De Mille, Mary Susan, 1945–
  Ethnohistory of farming, Cape Croker: 1820–1930. [Toronto] c1971.
  vi, 372 leaves. tables, maps.
  Phil.M. thesis, University of Toronto.   OTU
Farrell, Marvin William, 1920–
  Land tenure in Canadian agriculture. Cambridge, Massachusetts: 1949.
  168 p.
  Ph.D. thesis, Harvard University.   DA
Fitzsimons, John Graham.
  Agricultural labour input allocation and efficiency in North Grimsby
  township. [Hamilton, Ontario] 1969.
  vii, 167 leaves. diagrs., maps.
  M.A. thesis, McMaster University.   OHM
Forester, Joseph Elwood, 1927–
  Fur farming in Ontario. London, Ontario: 1968.
  xv, 188 leaves. graphs, photos (part col.), tables, maps.
  M.A. thesis, The University of Western Ontario (microfilm 2719).   OLU
Forrester, James.
  The agricultural geography of Wentworth county. [Hamilton, Ontario]
  1954.
  [iv] 146 leaves. plates, maps (part fold.).
  M.A. thesis, McMaster University.   OHM
Gilman, Christopher Richard, 1945–
  Attitudes and problems associated with private woodlot ownership in
  southwestern Ontario. London, Ontario: 1975.
  xi, 127 leaves. charts, maps, tables.
  M.A. thesis, The University of Western Ontario (microfilm 24542).   OLU
Gossling, William Frank.
  Techniques and costs of production of milk in Ontario with special reference
  to the short run supply curve. [Toronto] 1961.
  xv, 362 leaves. tables, figs.
  M.S.A. thesis, University of Toronto (accepted 1962).   OTU
Greaves, Suzanne.
  Farm numbers and sizes, Albion township 1819–1971. [Toronto] 1972.
  vii, 138 leaves. illus., maps (part col., part fold.).
  B.A. research paper, University of Toronto.   OTU
Greaves, Suzanne Margaret.
  Severance development: a micro study of Albion township. [Waterloo,
  Ontario] 1975.
  xiii, 207 leaves. graphs, tables.
  M.A. thesis, University of Waterloo.   OWTU

Hale, Philip Richard.
   An examination of the distribution of "Hobby Farm" properties in the six
   townships surrounding London Ontario. London, Ontario: 1973.
   ix, 81 leaves. illus., graphs, maps, tables.
   B.A. thesis, The University of Western Ontario.   OLU
Hallman, Donald E
   Orchard resources in the Toronto – Hamilton area, 1931–1965. [Waterloo,
   Ontario] 1967.
   v, 95 leaves. graphs, maps, tables.
   M.A. thesis, University of Waterloo.   OWTU
Hancock, Richard Froude.
   Some economic aspects of beef production methods in three areas of Ontario.
   [Toronto] 1957.
   iv, 85 leaves. tables (part fold.).
   M.S.A. thesis, University of Toronto.   OTU
Haviland, William Edward.
   The economics of tobacco farming in Ontario. Cambridge, Massachusetts:
   1951.
   349 leaves.
   Ph.D. thesis, Harvard University.   Harvard
Hayward, Frederick Robert.
   The optimum allocation of capital for dairy farming in western Ontario.
   [Toronto] 1953.
   66 leaves.
   M.S.A. thesis, University of Toronto.   OTU
Helleiner, Frederick Maria, 1933–
   Changing orchard distributions in the London region since 1920. London,
   Ontario: 1966.
   xiii, 297 leaves. graphs, tables, maps.
   M.A. thesis, The University of Western Ontario.   OLU
Horner, John Henry Robert.
   Changing spatial patterns in the production and utilization of milk in
   southern Ontario, 1910–1961. Toronto: 1967.
   x, 148 leaves. tables, figs., maps.
   M.A. thesis, University of Toronto.   OTU
Howard, John F
   The impact of urbanization on the prime agricultural lands of southern
   Ontario. Waterloo, Ontario: 1972.
   v, 93 leaves. maps.
   M.A. thesis, University of Waterloo (microfilm 18119).   OWTU
Hubert, Judith L
   Agricultural productivity of the Pelee Marsh; an assessment of individual
   farmer's response to the physical and cultural environment. Waterloo,
   Ontario: 1973.
   v, 87, 7 leaves. diagrs., tables.
   B.A. thesis, Waterloo Lutheran University.   OWTL

Hunt, Earl Charles.
    The costs of producing eggs from four types of poultry on fifty-seven farms in
    south western Ontario: 1956–1957. [Toronto] 1958.
    v, 48 leaves. tables, forms, map.
    M.S.A. thesis, University of Toronto.   OTU
Irving, Robert McCardle.
    Agricultural land use in the Beatty – South Saugeen watershed. [Toronto]
    1956.
    xi, 144 leaves. illus., diagrs., maps (part col., part fold.).
    M.A. thesis, University of Toronto.   OTU
Jacobson, Muriel Winnifred.
    The effect of the American tariff on the agriculture of Ontario and Quebec,
    1867–1936. [Hamilton, Ontario] 1935.
    ii, 68 leaves. tables.
    M.A. thesis, McMaster University.   OHM
Joynt, Carey Bonthron, 1924–
    Agriculture in Huron county (1880–1945). London, Ontario: 1948.
    vii, 135, 118 leaves. graphs, tables.
    M.A. thesis, The University of Western Ontario.   OLU
Joynt, Marsha Isabell.
    Agricultural land use relationships along Twenty Mile Creek. Ottawa: 1971.
    viii, 40 leaves. maps (part fold.), tables.
    B.A. research essay, Carleton University.   OOCC
Keddie, Philip Desmond.
    The expansion of corn for grain in southern Ontario and its effects on the
    farm enterprise with specific reference to the mid-western Ontario region.
    [Waterloo, Ontario] 1975.
    xxv, 533 leaves. graphs, tables.
    Ph.D. thesis, University of Waterloo (microfilm 27051).   OWTU
Kelly, Kenneth, 1937–
    The agricultural geography of Simcoe county, Ontario, 1820–1880.
    [Toronto] c1968.
    vii, 220 leaves. figs., maps.
    Ph.D. thesis, University of Toronto (microfilm 2439).   OTU
Kent, Jon.
    Agriculture in the Cochrane clay belt. [Toronto] 1970.
    22 [2] leaves. map (part col.).
    M.A. research paper, University of Toronto.   OTU
Khan, Jafar Reza.
    Changing patterns of agricultural land use in Renfrew county, 1951–1971.
    Ottawa: 1977.
    x, 195 leaves. graphs, maps, tables.
    M.A. thesis, Carleton University.   OOCC
Khare, Brij Behari.
    A study of the capital needs of the low-income family farms in southwestern
    Ontario. [Toronto] 1959.
    vii, 146 leaves. tables, figs., map.
    M.S.A. thesis, University of Toronto.   OTU

Klosler, George.
 Opportunity costs of resources used in tobacco production in Norfolk county.
 [Guelph, Ontario] 1965.
 137 leaves. tables.
 M.Sc. thesis, The University of Guelph.   OGU
Kozumplik, Vera.
 Relative farming advantages in two regions of southern Ontario. [Guelph,
 Ontario] 1972.
 vii, 114 leaves. maps, tables.
 M.Sc. thesis, The University of Guelph.   OGU
Lawr, Douglas Archie, 1938–
 Agriculture in Oxford county, 1919–1939: survey of agricultural production
 improvement campaigns. London, Ontario: 1964.
 126 leaves. graphs, tables.
 M.A. thesis, The University of Western Ontario.   OLU
Layton, Ronald Leslie, 1951–
 Hobby farming: a characterisation: a case study of the rural-urban fringe of
 London, Ontario. London, Ontario: 1976.
 xvi, 240 leaves. diagrs., maps.
 M.A. thesis, The University of Western Ontario (microfilm 28269).   OLU
Lovering, James Herbert .
 Agricultural development possibilities, southeastern Renfrew county,
 Ontario. Ithaca, New York: 1967.
 236 p.
 Ph.D. thesis, Cornell University (microfilm 68-03509).   DA
McArthur, Donald Alexander.
 An analysis of the financial structure of a sample of Ontario farms. [Toronto]
 1963.
 viii, 124 leaves. tables, figs.
 M.S.A. thesis, University of Toronto.   OTU
McBean, Aston Bradford.
 An analysis of the factors associated with low income, with special reference
 to the Tweed forest district. [Toronto] 1963.
 ix, 154 leaves. tables, map (col. fold. in back pocket).
 M.S.A. thesis, University of Toronto.   OTU
McBride, William Allan.
 An application of activity analysis to selected farm enterprises in Ontario.
 [Toronto] 1964.
 viii, 145 leaves. tables, figs.
 M.S.A. thesis, University of Toronto.   OTU
McCardell, Nora E
 Agricultural success: an exploratory study of man, land and
 interrelationships. Waterloo, Ontario: 1975.
 xi, 291 leaves. illus., maps.
 Ph.D. thesis, University of Waterloo (microfilm 23411).   Can

McCauley, Ann Eloise.
  Farm vacation enterprises in Ontario. [Guelph, Ontario] 1975.
  viii, 153 leaves. tables.
  M.Sc. thesis, The University of Guelph (microfilm 24738).   OGU
MacDermaid, Darryl F
  Agricultural bargaining structures and contemporary farm organizations in
  Ontario. [Kingston, Ontario] 1972 [c1973]
  v, 184 leaves. tables, figs.
  M.B.A. thesis, Queen's University (microfilm 13701).   OKQ
McDonald, Geoffrey Thomas.
  Trend surface analysis of farm size patterns in Ontario and Quebec
  1951–1961. [Toronto] 1968.
  52 [20] leaves. figs., tables.
  M.A. research paper, University of Toronto.   OTU
McDonald, Geoffrey Thomas, 1945–
  Agricultural land use forecasting; an example of field crops in Ontario,
  1960–1968. [Toronto] c1972.
  203 [42] leaves. tables, figs., maps.
  Ph.D. thesis, University of Toronto (microfilm 18508).   OTU
MacDougall, Edward Bruce, 1939–
  Farm number changes in relation to land capability and alternative
  employment opportunity in the north part of central Ontario. [Toronto]
  c1967.
  129 leaves. figs., map.
  Ph.D. thesis, University of Toronto (microfilm 1870).   OTU
McWha, Albert Earl Morris.
  The evolution of agriculture in Huron county: a chapter in provincial
  economy. [Toronto] 1940.
  x, 406 leaves. tables, diagrs., maps.
  M.A. thesis, University of Toronto.   OTU
Mage, Julius Arnold.
  Part-time farming in southern Ontario with specific reference to Waterloo
  county. [Waterloo, Ontario] 1974.
  xix, 348 leaves. diagrs., maps, tables.
  Ph.D. thesis, University of Waterloo (microfilm 21615).   OWTU
Marcher, George Bernhard.
  An analysis of economic opportunities for farm adjustments on selected dairy
  farms shipping farm-separated cream and industrial milk in cans. [Guelph,
  Ontario] 1976.
  iv, 137 leaves. tables.
  M.Sc. thesis, The University of Guelph (microfilm 28102).   OGU
May, Joseph Austin, 1927–
  An analysis of some aspects of the A.R.D.A. (Agricultural Rehabilitation
  and Development Act) Program. London, Ontario: 1963.
  x, 215 leaves. charts, maps, tables.
  M.A. thesis, The University of Western Ontario.   OLU

Maynard, David George, 1943–
    An evaluation of small pond assistance programs in Ontario. London,
    Ontario: 1970.
    xiv, 131, xv [i.e.1] leaves. illus., maps.
    M.A. thesis, The University of Western Ontario (microfilm 6679).   OLU
Merritt, Donald.
    Agricultural co-operation in Ontario. [Hamilton, Ontario] 1942.
    111 leaves. map, tables.
    B.A. thesis, McMaster University.   OHM
Muller, Paul Gallus, 1923–
    A basic approach to the appraisal of farm real estate in the province of
    Ontario. [Toronto] 1951.
    165 leaves.
    M.S.A. thesis, University of Toronto.   OTU
Parsons, Diana Lee.
    The influence of type of owner on farm management in Chinguacousy
    township. Toronto: 1975.
    xiv, 142 leaves. maps, tables.
    M.A. thesis, York University (microfilm 25740).   OTY
Pierce, John T
    Variation of farm productivity in the rural-urban fringe. [Toronto] 1971.
    ii, 73 leaves. illus., maps.
    B.A. thesis, University of Toronto.   OTU
Prosser, David G
    The development of dairying in eastern Ontario. [Toronto] 1976.
    62 leaves. illus., maps (part col.).
    B.A. thesis, University of Toronto.
    Covers the years: 1851, 1861, 1871 and 1881.   OTU
Read, John A
    Spatial and temporal variations in crop production in Hastings and Prince
    Edward counties during the last half of the nineteenth century. [Toronto]
    1976.
    viii, 115 leaves. maps (part col.).
    B.A. thesis, University of Toronto.   OTU
Reeds, Lloyd George, 1917–
    The agricultural geography of southern Ontario. [Toronto] 1955.
    xiii, 448 leaves. figs., maps (3 fold. in rear pocket).
    Ph.D. thesis, University of Toronto (microfilm 19731).   OTU
— Agricultural geography of the Lindsay – Peterborough region. [Toronto]
    1942.
    iii 175 leaves illus., maps.
    M.A. thesis, University of Toronto (microfilm 22351).   OTU
Retallack, Joan Elizabeth.
    The changing distribution of wheat in southern Ontario, 1850–1890.
    [Toronto] 1966.
    iii, [4], 127 leaves. illus., maps (part col.).
    M.A. thesis, University of Toronto.   OTU

Riley, Charles Wilson.
An economic study of farm operations based upon data taken in Oxford
county. [Toronto: 1929]
118 [1] leaves.
M.S.A. thesis, University of Toronto.   OTU
Rose, Karl E
Factors influencing agricultural development in the counties of Bruce, Grey
and Huron, 1850 to 1880. Waterloo, Ontario: 1966.
v, 119 leaves. graphs (part fold.), maps, tables.
B.A. thesis, Waterloo Lutheran University.   OWTL
Rowlandson, Cynthia Ethel.
A study of the distribution and production of flue-cured tobacco in Ontario.
[Toronto] 1965.
ix, 57 leaves. illus., maps (part fold., part col.).
B.A. thesis, University of Toronto.   OTU
Sample, Katherine Ann.
Changes in agriculture on the Six Nations Indian Reserve. [Hamilton,
Ontario] 1968.
vi, 131 leaves. diagrs., maps, tables.
M.A. thesis, McMaster University.   OHM
Schoonhoven, Willem Smith.
A statistical analysis of the character and pattern of agriculture in northern
Ontario. [Toronto] 1963.
iii, 94 [52] leaves. illus., maps (part col., part fold.).
B.A. thesis, University of Toronto.   OTU
Scorgie, Edward Kim, 1947–
The diffusion of harvestore structures in southwestern Ontario, 1962–1970.
London, Ontario: 1973.
viii, 172 leaves. graphs, tables, maps.
M.A. thesis, The University of Western Ontario (microfilm 16449).   OLU
Seager, Joni K
Fruit farming in southern Ontario from 1850. [Toronto] 1976.
v, 56 leaves. tables, maps (part col.).
B.A. thesis, University of Toronto.   OTU
Seyfried, Jan A
The effect of bulk milk handling on farms and hauling costs in Ontario.
[Toronto] 1956.
91 [xii, 5] leaves. tables, figs.
M.S.A. thesis, University of Toronto.   OTU
Shapiro, Stanley Jack.
Decision making survival and the organized behavior system: a case study of
the Ontario hog producer organizations. Philadelphia, Pennsylvania: 1961.
208 p.
Ph.D. thesis, University of Pennsylvania (microfilm 62-02848).   DA

Skey, Boris Peter.
    A study of some important co-operative associations in Ontario agriculture.
    Toronto: 1931.
    327 leaves. tables.
    M.S.A. thesis, University of Toronto.   OTU
Skimson, Thomas Chute, 1943–
    Effectiveness of fur-bearer management in southwestern Ontario. London,
    Ontario: 1970.
    xiii, 199 leaves. graphs, tables, maps (part fold.).
    M.A. thesis, The University of Western Ontario (microfilm 6683).   OLU
Smith, Herbert Alfred.
    The Holland Marsh. [Toronto] 1962.
    iv, 144 leaves. illus., figs. (part col., 11 fold. in pocket), maps.
    M.A. thesis, University of Toronto (accepted 1963).   OTU
Sterrett, David James.
    A factorial typology of Ontario agriculture. [Waterloo, Ontario] 1969.
    xii, 144 leaves. graphs, maps, tables.
    M.A. thesis, University of Waterloo.   OWTU
Stock, George Elwood.
    The geography of small scale farming in Ontario. [Guelph, Ontario] 1975.
    xii, 230 leaves. graphs, maps.
    M.A. thesis, The University of Guelph (microfilm 22724).   OGU
Sundstrom, Marvin Thomas.
    Regional and farm level adjustments in southern Ontario's dairy industry,
    1968–1974. [Hamilton, Ontario] 1975.
    xiii, 211 leaves. graphs, maps, tables.
    Ph.D. thesis, McMaster University (microfilm 29748).   OHM
Taylor, John Stewart.
    Social and economic changes in Ontario's agriculture. [Toronto] 1971.
    82 leaves. illus., maps (fold., part col.).
    B.A. research paper, University of Toronto.   OTU
Teskey, Alan George.
    Some aspects of the input-output structure of Ontario agriculture. [Toronto]
    1963.
    vi, 198 leaves. tables, maps.
    M.S.A. thesis, University of Toronto.   OTU
Tessier, Maurice F
    Use of information sources by French speaking farmers in Ontario. [Guelph,
    Ontario] 1972.
    vi, 95, 8 leaves. tables.
    M.Sc. thesis, The University of Guelph.   OGU
Timothy, Earl Errol.
    The agricultural representative, in Ontario – his role in the changing
    agricultural scene and problems of impact on the total farming population.
    Guelph, Ontario: 1962.
    219 leaves.
    M.S.A. thesis, University of Toronto.   OTU

Toon, Charles C
  Some aspects of the history of agriculture in Canada West and Ontario
  between 1850 and 1870. London, Ontario: 1938.
  vi, 291 leaves. tables.
  M.A. thesis, The University of Western Ontario.   OLU
Vanden Heuval, Christina.
  A concentrated settlement of Dutch immigrant farmers in Huron county,
  Ontario since 1950. Waterloo, Ontario: 1975.
  x, 80 leaves. maps, tables.
  B.A. thesis, Wilfrid Laurier University.   OWTL
von Cube, Hans Gunther.
  Some aspects of the relationship of cost and use as a basis of predicting
  hourly costs of operating farm machinery in Ontario. [Toronto] 1955.
  vi, 124 leaves. tables, figs.
  M.S.A. thesis, University of Toronto.   OTU
Waddell, Donald James.
  Agricultural changes in Carleton county, 1940–1970. Ottawa: 1972.
  vi, 62 leaves. illus.
  B.A. research essay, Carleton University.   OOCC
Walter, William Howard.
  The development of agricultural productivity in the province of Ontario.
  [Toronto] 1916.
  x, 103 leaves.
  M.A. thesis, University of Toronto.   OTU
Worrall, Robert John.
  Farm abandonment in Bruce county. Waterloo, Ontario; 1973.
  vi, 117 leaves. diagrs., maps.
  B.A. thesis, Waterloo University College.   OWTL
— Non-resident ownership in the countryside of Bruce county: a case study of
  rural resettlement. Waterloo, Ontario: 1974.
  xv, 243 leaves. graphs, maps.
  M.A. thesis, Wilfrid Laurier University.   OWTL
Wright, Philip Alan.
  An economic analysis of potato yields on certain Ontario mineral soils in
  controlled fertilizer experiments, 1954–1956. Lansing, Michigan: 1962.
  137 p.
  Ph.D. thesis, Michigan State University. (microfilm 63-03750).   DA
Young, William Robert, 1947–
  The countryside on the defensive: agricultural Ontario's views of rural
  depopulation, 1900–1914. Vancouver, British Columbia: 1971.
  [8] 241 leaves.
  M.A. thesis, University of British Columbia (microfilm 22273).   Can
Zimmer, Bruce Edward.
  Socio-economic variables affecting A.R.D.A. proposals for eastern Ontario
  farms. [Guelph, Ontario] 1968.
  ix, 466 leaves. diagrs., map, tables.
  M.Sc. thesis, The University of Guelph.   OGU

RESOURCE INDUSTRIES

Bibliography
Bray, M   Phyllis.
Geco Mining Collection. Manitouwadge Public Library. Ontario Library Review 47: 177–179, 1963.
Guelph, Ontario. University. Centre for Resources Development.
Resources development graduate theses, M.A. and M.Sc., 1963–1971 . [Guelph] 1971.
3 leaves. (*Its* Publication, no. 37).   OTU
Papers, Orders-in-Council and correspondence on the mining and treatment of nickel and copper ore in the province of Ontario. Toronto: Warwick Bros. & Rutter, 1899.
15 p.   OTAR

Monographs and Pamphlets
Adams, Joseph.
Ten thousand miles through Canada: the natural resources, commercial industries, fish and game, sports and pastimes of the great Dominion, 2d.ed. London: Methuen & Co., Ltd. [1912]
xx, 310, 31 p. illus., map.
Ontario: pp. 28–121.
No copy of the first edition was located.   OTU
Agterberg, Frederick Pieter.
Geomathematical evaluation of copper and zinc potential of the Abitibi area, Ontario and Quebec, by F.P. Agterberg [et al.]. Ottawa: Department of Energy, Mines and Resources [1971]
55 p. maps. (Geological Survey of Canada. Paper no. 71–41).   OONL
Algoma and western Ontario: an account of lands, timber and mineral resources along the lines of the C.P.R. between Ottawa and Lake Superior. Montreal: Canadian Pacific Railway, 1888.
20 p.
Cover title: Wooded lands in Ontario.   OTAR
Anders, G
The impact of taxation and environmental controls on the Ontario mining industry: a pilot study, by A. Anders, W.P. Gramm and S.C. Maurice. Toronto: Mineral Resources Branch, Ministry of Natural Resources [1975?]
v, 197 p. graphs, tables. (Mineral Policy. Background paper no. 1).   OTU
Anderson, J   W   1893–
Fur trader's story. Foreword by Lord Tweedsmuir. Toronto: The Ryerson Press [c1961]
xv, 245 p. front. illus., maps.
Moose Factory.   OTAR
Atikokan, Ontario. Chamber of Commerce.
Atikokan, home of Canada's largest iron mine. [Atikokan, Ontario: 1950]
1 v. (unpaged). illus., map, plan.   OOP

Barlow, Alfred Ernest, 1861–1914.
    Report on the origin, geological relations and composition of the nickel and
    copper deposits of the Sudbury mining district Ontario, Canada. Ottawa:
    S.E. Dawson, printer to the King's Most Excellent Majesty, 1904.
    236 p. illus., tables. (Canada. Geological Survey. Annual report, new series
    v. 14, 1901, report H).   OLU
Barnes, Michael, 1934–
    Gold camp pioneer: Roza Brown of Kirkland Lake. Illustrated by John
    Slater. [Cobalt, Ontario] Highway Book Shop, 1973.
    [28] p. illus.   OTU
—— Gold in the porcupine. Cobalt, Ontario: Highway Book Shop [c1975]
    86 p. illus., map, ports.   OTU
—— Jake Englehart. Illustrated by John Slater. Cobalt, Ontario: Highway Book
    Shop, c1974.
    50 p. illus., ports.
    Cover title: Imperial Oil. Ontario's Northland Railroad, a clay belt town...
    join in the story of Jake Englehart.   OTU
Barrett, Robert John.
    Canada's century: progress and resources of the great Dominion; notes with
    snapshots and other illustrations of an intensive tour of British North
    America. London: Financier and Bullionist Limited, 1907.
    xiv, 538, xxx p. illus., ports., diagrs., tables.   OTAR
Bedore, Bernard Vance, 1923–
    The big pine: a story from the Ottawa valley of Canada. [Arnprior, Ontario:
    Mufferaw Enterprises, 1975, c1963]
    3 v. illus., facsims.
    Contents: Part 1, The shanty: Part 2, The drive; Part 3, Sawmill town.
    Only Part 1 published to date (May, 1977).   OOA
Bell, Robert, 1841–1917.
    The geology of Ontario, with special reference to economic minerals.
    Toronto: Warwick & Sons, 1889.
    56 p.   OONL
—— Report on the Sudbury mining district 1888–1890. Ottawa: S.E. Dawson,
    printer to the Queen's Most Excellent Majesty, 1891.
    95 p. illus., fold. col. map.   OTL
Benoist, Emile, 1895–
    L'Abitibi pays de l'or. Montreal: Editions du Zodiaque [1938?]
    199 p. illus., map.   OTU
Biggar, Emerson Bristol, 1853–1921 (ed.).
    Canada: a memorial volume. General reference book of Canada: describing
    the Dominion at large, and its various provinces and territories; with
    statistics relating to its commerce and the development of its resources.
    Montreal: E.B. Biggar, 1889.
    1 v. (various pagings). illus., maps, (part fold.), facsims.
    Ontario: Section VI.   OTAR

Black, Robson.
    The truth about Ontario's forest protection system. [Ottawa: Canadian
    Forestry Association, 1916?]
    [4] p.   OTAR
A brief history of the gold mines of the Kirkland Lake and Larder Lake mining
    districts of Ontario with statistics. [Kirkland Lake, Ontario: 1951]
    [6] p.   OKQ
Brown, C   K
    An analysis of the potential for wind energy production in northwestern
    Ontario, by C.K. Brown and D.F. Warne. Mississauga, Ontario: Ontario
    Research Foundation, 1975.
    172 p. charts, maps, tables.   OTU
Bruce, Everend Lester, 1884–
    Mineral deposits of the Canadian Shield. Toronto: Macmillan Company of
    Canada Limited, 1933.
    xxiv, 428 p. front., illus., diagrs., maps, tables.   OONL
Brumell, H   Peareth H
    Report on natural gas and petroleum in Ontario prior to 1891. Ottawa: S.E.
    Dawson, printer to the Queen's Most Excellent Majesty, 1892.
    94 p. fold. maps. (Canada. Geological Survey. Annual report new series v. 5,
    part II, 1890–1891, report Q).   OONL
Bullock, William Starr.
    Cobalt and its silver mines. A brief review of the geology, mineralogy,
    discovery, present development and future possibilities of the marvelously
    rich silver, cobalt and nickel and deposits in the wilderness of northern
    Ontario, Canada. New York [1906]
    87 p. illus., map, table.   OOA
Caley, John Fletcher, 1905–
    Natural gas in Brantford area, Ontario. Ottawa: 1940.
    31 p. (Canada. Department of Mines and Resources. Mines and Geology
    Branch. Geological Survey. Paper 4022).   BVIP
Canada. Bureau of Statistics.
    Canadian mineral statistics, 1886–1956; mining events, 1604–1956. Ottawa:
    Edmond Cloutier, Queen's Printer, 1957.
    120 p. diagrs., tables (*Its* Reference papers, no. 68).   OOP
Canada. Department of Mines.
    Economic minerals and mining industries of Canada. Ottawa: Government
    Printing Bureau, 1913.
    77 p. illus., tables.   OONL
Canada. Department of the Interior. National Development Bureau.
    Lennox and Addington county, Ontario, with special reference to its
    resources and industries. Ottawa: The Bureau [1930?]
    32 leaves. fold. maps.   OHM
Canada. Inland Waters Directorate.
    Northern Ontario water resources studies; summary report on engineering

feasibility and cost investigations. Ottawa: Inland Waters Directorate,
Water Resources Branch, 1973.
xiii, 39 p. illus., maps (part fold.).   OTU
Canada. National Committee on Forest Land. Sub-Committee on Multiple
Use.
Towards integrated resource management; report. Principaux commentaires
et recommandations. [Ottawa: Queen's Printer, 1970]
xxiii, 47 p. chart.
Chairman: W.W. Jeffrey.   OTUMA
Canadian Council of Resource Ministers.
An inventory of joint programs and agreements affecting Canada's
renewable resources to March 31, 1964. [Montreal: 1964]
181, 182 p.
Text in English and French.   OTU
Canadian Mining Journal.
Porcupine mining district. A series of illustrated articles, accompanied by a
complete geological map and claim maps of the various townships. Toronto:
Canadian Mining Journal, 1911.
86 p. illus., maps (part fold.).   OTU
Cartwright, Cosmo T
The production of copper, gold, lead, nickel, silver, zinc and other metals in
Canada during the year 1912-1913. Ottawa: Government Printing Bureau,
1913–1914.
2 v. tables. (Canada. Department of Mines).   OONL
Clergue, Francis Hector.
An instance of industrial evolution in northern Ontario. An address
delivered at a general meeting of the Board of Trade of the city of Toronto,
April 2nd, 1900. n.p.: 1900.
20 p.   OTU
Cobalt Daily Nugget, Limited.
Silver and gold: a pictorial souvenir of the mines of northern Ontario.
[Cobalt, Ontario] The Author, 1916.
64 p. chiefly illus.   OTAR
Cobalt Lake controversy. To all who value the honour of Ontario and the
public credit. n.p. [1908]
16 p.   OOA
Cole, Arthur A
Mineral wealth along the Temiskaming & Northern Ontario Railway.
[Toronto: 1917]
15 p. illus. (part col.).   OTAR
Coleman, Arthur Philemon, 1852–1939.
The nickel industry with special reference to the Sudbury region, Ontario.
Ottawa: Government Printing Bureau, 1913.
viii, 206 p. illus., tables.   OONL

Crerar, Thomas Alexander, 1876–
   The future of Canadian mining: a series of twelve radio addresses delivered
   over the national network of the Canadian Radio Commission January 31 to
   April 24, 1936. Ottawa: J.G. Patenaude, printer to the King's Most
   Excellent Majesty, 1936.
   vii, 83 p. illus., maps.   OONL
Cressman, David R
   The productive capacity of the natural resources of Manitoulin Island, a
   working document for the Canada Land Inventory. [Ottawa: R. Duhamel,
   Queen's Printer] 1968.
   viii, 195 p. col. maps (part fold.).   OTU
Davis, Harold Palmer.
   The Davis handbook of the Cobalt silver district with a manual of
   incorporated companies. [Toronto?] Canadian Mining Journal, 1910.
   108 p. illus., map, tables.   OTU
Davis, William Grenville, 1929–
   Statement on energy to the Legislature, Thursday, June 7, 1973. [Toronto:
   1973]
   24 leaves.   OTAR
Deverell, John.
   Falconbridge: portrait of a Canadian mining multi-national, by John
   Deverell and the Latin American Working Group. Toronto: James Lorimer
   & Company, 1975.
   184 p.   OTU
Dominion Management Associates Limited.
   Economic survey of the town of Timmins, Ontario, Canada: including a
   survey of economic development of the Ontario northland. Toronto: 1960.
   1 v. (various pagings). maps, tables.   OOREX
Dubnie, A
   Transportation and the competitive positions of selected Canadian minerals.
   [Ottawa: Roger Duhamel, Queen's Printer] 1962.
   140 p. maps (part fold.), tables. (Canada. Department of Mines and
   Techical Surveys. Mineral Resources Division. Mineral survey 2).   OONL
Eldorado Mining and Refining Limited.
   Uranium in Canada. Ottawa: Eldorado Mining and Refining Ltd. [1964]
   vii, 134 p. illus., maps, port.   OLU
Field, Frederick William, 1884–
   Resources and trade prospects of northern Ontario: a special report made on
   behalf of the Toronto Board of Trade. Toronto: Board of Trade [1912]
   111 p. tables.   OTL
Gard, Anson Albert, 1849–ca.1915.
   The real Cobalt: the story of Canada's marvellous silver mining camp.
   Toronto: The Emerson Press, 1908.
   iv, 128 p. illus., ports.   OTU
— The real Cobalt: the story of Canada's marvellous silver mining camp.
   Toronto: The Emerson Press, 1908.
   iv, 98 p. illus.
   Cover title: The silverland of Canada.   OTU

— Silverland and its stories. Toronto: Emerson Press, 1909.
iv, 104 p. illus., plates, map.   OTU
— 2d. ed. Toronto: Emerson Press, 1909.
iv, 140 p. illus., ports., fold. map.
Cover title: The silverland of Canada.   OTAR
Gillies Silver Mining Co. Limited.
Non personal liability. Haileybury, Ontario [1906]
12 p. map.
A Cobalt company.   OTAR
Goessmann, Charles Anthony, 1827–1901.
Report on the salt resources of Goderich, province of Ontario (Canada
West). Syracuse, New York [1868]
18 p.   OLU
Grand Trunk Railway System. General Passenger Department.
Cobalt the Eldorado of new Ontario: the rich new silver district recently
discovered. [Toronto: The Mail Job Print, 1906]
16 p. illus., maps.   OTAR
Great Lakes Water Resources Conference, Toronto, 1968.
Proceedings, June 24–26, 1968, Toronto, Canada. Sponsored by the
Engineering Institute of Canada, American Society of Civil Engineers.
[Toronto: 1968?]
viii, 489 p. graphs, maps, tables.
Co-chairmen: D.S. Caverly and E.W. Weber.   OTAR
Green, Marvin W
The charcoal industry in Ontario; a technical and economic appraisal of
additional production potential. [Toronto] Department of Field Service,
Ontario Research Foundation, 1961.
32 map, tables.   OTU
Griffin, J   W
A survey of the uranium industry in Canada. [Ottawa: Queen's Printer]
1959.
vii, 94 p. charts, maps, tables. (Canada. Department of Mines and Technical
Surveys. Mineral Resources Division. Mineral information bulletin MR34).
                                                                                   OONL
Harris, Edward William, 1832–1925.
Our great lake fisheries, a vanishing heritage. Toronto: William Briggs,
1906.
31 p.   OTU
— The Ontario commercial fisheries; how and why destroyed. [Toronto] 1906.
30 p.   OTU
Hawley, J   E
The Sudbury ores: their mineralogy and origin. [Ottawa] Mineralogical
Association of Canada, 1962.
xiv, 207 p. illus., map, diagrs., tables. (Canadian Mineralogist, v. 7, part 1,
1962).   OLU

Hedlin, Menzies & Associates, Ltd.
   The Ontario forest industry; its direct and indirect contribution to the
   economy. Prepared by Hedlin, Menzies and Associates Ltd. [Toronto]
   Department of Lands and Forests, 1969.
      x, 74 p. diagrs., map, tables.   OTU
Helling, Rudolf Anton, 1929–
   Elliot Lake, Ontario. Windsor, Ontario: Assumption University of Windsor,
   1960.
      iii, 80 p. maps (part fold.), table.   OTU
Hodge, Gerald.
   Prospects for an expanded non-ferrous metals industrial complex for
   northern Ontario, by Gerald Hodge and Cheuk C. Wong. Toronto:
   Department of Urban & Regional Planning, University of Toronto, 1970.
      viii, 101 p. illus., map, graphs.   OTUSA
Hoffman, Arnold David, 1903–
   Free gold: the story of Canadian mining. With illustrations by Irwin D.
   Hoffman. Toronto: Rinehart and Company Inc. [c1947]
      420 p. illus.   OTU
Hollinger Consolidated Gold Mines. Timmins, Ontario.
   Fifty years of progress, by Norman E. Greene. Timmins Ontario: Hollinger
   Consolidated Gold Mines [1960]
      11 leaves. illus.   OTAR
Hollinger Miner.
   Anniversary issue v. 15, nos. 6 and 7, July, 1960. Timmins, Ontario:
   Hollinger Consolidated Gold Mines Ltd., 1960.
      19 p. illus., ports.   OTAR
Hottenroth, Helmut.
   The great clay belts in Ontario and Quebec; Stuktur und Genese eines
   Pionierraumes an der nördlichen siedlungs-grenze Ost. Kanadas.
   Marburg/Lahn, Geographischen Institutes der Universität Marburg, 1968.
      167 p. maps (part fold.). (Marburger geographische Schriften heft 39).   OTU
Howard–White, F   B   1895–
   Nickel, an historical review. London, Ontario: Methuen & Co. Ltd. [c1963]
      xiii, 350 p. illus., graphs, maps, ports., tables.   OTU
Hughson, John W
   Hurling down the pine; the story of the Wright, Gilmour and Hughson
   families, timber and lumber manufacturers in the Hull and Ottawa region
   and on the Gatineau River, 1800–1920, by John W. Hughson and Courtney
   C.J. Bond. Old Chelsea, Quebec: Historical Society of the Gatineau, 1964.
      119 p. illus., maps, ports.   OTU
— 2d. ed. rev. Old Chelsea, Quebec: Historical Society of the Gatineau, 1965.
      vi, 130 p. illus., fold. maps, port.   OTU
A hundred years a-fellin. Some passages from the timber saga of the Ottawa in
   the century in which the Gillies have been cutting in the Valley 1842–1942.
   [Braeside, Ontario: Printed for Gillies Brothers, Limited by The Runge
   Press, Limited, 1943]
      xiv, 172 p. illus., maps. ports.   OKQ

Hutton, C   L   A
   Ontario Arctic watershed, by C.L.A. Hutton and W.A. Black. [Ottawa:
   Information Canada c1975]
   ix, 107 p. illus., fold. col. maps.   OTUMA
Ingall, Elfric Drew.
   Report on mines and mining on Lake Superior. Part 1; A, History and
   general conditions of the region; B, Silver mining. Published by authority of
   Parliament. Montreal: Dawson Brothers, 1888.
   1 v. (various pagings). illus., maps.   OTAR
Innis, Harold Adams, 1894–1952.
   Settlement and the mining frontier. Toronto: Macmillan, 1936.
   xiv, 424 p. illus., tables. (Canadian frontiers of settlement, v. 9, part 2).   OTU
International Nickel Company of Canada Limited.
   The land above and the ore below. [Toronto: The Company, 1971]
   [32] p. chiefly illus.   OONL
— A review of institutional advertising which has appeared in Canadian
   publications from 1932 to 1955, presenting important facts about the history
   and development of the nickel industry in Canada and its economic benefits
   to the Canadian people. [Toronto] The Company [1956]
   1 v. (unpaged). chiefly illus.   OLU
— The romance of nickel. [Sudbury, Ontario] The Company [1946]
   56 p. illus.   OTAR
Johnston, Arthur B
   Recollection of oil drilling at Oil Springs, Ontario, with notes of the Shaw
   gusher, the Drake well in Pennsylvania, the first flowing well and a
   description of the different operating systems to the present time.
   Tillsonburg, Ontario: Harvey F. Johnston [1938]
   20 p.   OTL
Killin, A   F
   The Canadian copper Industry in 1962. Ottawa: Mineral Resources
   Division, Department of Mines and Technical Surveys, 1963.
   vi, 108 p. illus., diagrs., maps, tables. (Canada. Department of Mines and
   Technical Surveys. Mineral Resources Division. Information bulletin MR68).
                                                                          OONL
Kimberly–Clark Pulp and Paper Company Limited.
   Terrance Bay: scenic centre of the north shore. [Terrance Bay, Ontario] The
   Author [1967?]
   1 v. (unpaged). illus.   OKQ
King, Alan John Campbell, 1933–
   The exciting story of nickel. Toronto: International Nickel Company of
   Canada, Limited, 1957.
   29 p. illus. (part. col.).   OTMCL
Krueger, Ralph Ray, 1927–   (ed.).
   Regional and resource planning in Canada. Edited by Ralph R. Krueger [et
   al.] Toronto: Holt, Rinehart and Winston [c1963]
   vi, 218 p. illus., maps, tables, diagrs.   OTU

— Rev. ed. Toronto: Holt Rinehart and Winston [c1970]
vi, 249 p. illus., diagrs., maps, tables.
Several papers on Ontario.
"A book of reading based primarily upon the *Resources for Tomorrow*
Conference background papers."   OTUO
— Regional patterns: disparities and development, by Ralph R. Krueger,
Robert M. Irving, Colin Vincent. [Toronto?] Canadian Association of
Geographers, Canadian Studies Foundation, 1975.
iii, 87 p. maps.   OONL
Lambert, Richard Stanton, 1894–
Renewing nature's wealth; a centennial history of the public management of
lands, forests & wildlife in Ontario, 1763–1967, by Richard S. Lambert, with
Paul Pross. Foreword by John P. Robarts. [Toronto?] Ontario Department
of Lands and Forests, 1967.
xvi, 630 p. illus. (part col.), maps, diagrs.   OTU
Laugharne, Grace.
Canada looks ahead. London: Royal Institute of International Affairs [1956]
158 p. illus.
Natural resources in Canada.   OTU
LeBourdais, Donat Marc, 1887–1964.
Canada's century. Toronto: Methuen Company of Canada Limited [1951]
ix, 214 p. illus., maps.
Natural resources, Ontario: pp. 52–66.   OTU
— Metals and men: the story of Canadian mining. Toronto: McClelland and
Stewart, Limited, 1957.
416 p. illus. (part col.), ports., maps.   OTU
— Sudbury basin: the story of nickel. Toronto: The Ryerson Press [c1953]
xiv, 210 p. illus., ports., maps (part col.).   OTU
Leith, J   Clark.
Exploitation of Ontario mineral resources: an economic policy analysis.
Toronto: Ontario Economic Council, c1976.
iii, 93 p. (Working paper. Ontario Economic Council: no. 2/76).   OTU
Livingstone, Janey C
Historic Silver Islet: the story of a drowned mine. Fort William, Ontario:
Times Journal Presses [1919?]
24 p. illus., ports.   OTAR
Longo, Roy M
Historical highlights of Canadian mining including Canadian personalities.
Research and documentation: Lawrence F. Jones and George Lonn. Editor
and consultant: Roy M. Longo. Toronto: Pitt Publishing Company Limited
[c1973]
xiii, 274 p. illus., ports.   OONL
Lougheed, (William) Associates, Toronto.
The gold-mining community a study of the problems of economic growth.
[Timmins, Ontario: Town of Timmins, Industrial Commission] 1958.
ix, 100 p. illus., charts, maps, tables.   OTAR

Lower, Arthur Reginald Marsden, 1889–
  The North American assault on the Canadian forest, a history of the lumber
  trade between Canada and the United States. Toronto: The Ryerson Press,
  1938.
  xxvii, 377 p. illus., maps, tables.   OTU
— Settlement and the forest frontier of eastern Canada. Toronto: Macmillan,
  1936.
  xiv, 424 p. illus., tables. (Canadian Frontiers of Settlement, v. 9, part 1).
                                                                               OTU
Macdonald, James Earl, 1908–
  Shantymen and sodbusters: an account of logging and settlement in
  Kirkwood township, 1869–1928. Sault Ste. Marie, Ontario: Sault Star
  Printing, 1966.
  vii, 134 p. illus., ports., map.   OTU
MacDougall, James Brown, 1871–1950.
  Two thousand miles of gold, from Val d'Or to Yellowknife. Toronto:
  McClelland and Stewart Limited [c1946]
  xvi, 234 p. plates, ports., maps.   OLU
MacEwan, John Walter Grant, 1902–
  Entrusted to my care. Saskatoon: Modern Press [1966]
  269 p. illus.
  Natural resources.   OTU
McFarlane, Leslie, 1902–
  A kid in Haileybury. Cobalt, Ontario: Highway Books [c1975]
  79 p. port.
  Gold strike days in northern Ontario.   OONL
McKellar, Peter.
  Mining on the north shore, Lake Superior. n.p.: 1874.
  26 p. illus., tables.   OTAR
Mackenzie, B   W
  Nickel – Canada and the world. [Ottawa: Roger Duhamel, Queen's Printer]
  1968.
  xi, 176 p. illus., graphs, maps, tables. (Canada. Department of Energy,
  Mines and Resources. Mineral Resources Division. Mineral report 16).
                                                                             OONL
MacLaren, (James F.) Limited.
  Report on water supply in Metropolitan Toronto. Toronto: 1970.
  47 p. illus., graphs, maps (part fold.).   OTU
MacPherson, William Batten.
  Summary of laws of the province of Ontario pertaining to mining. Toronto:
  The Author [c1925]
  74 p.   OTU
McPherson, William David, 1863–1929.
  The law of mines in Canada. Toronto: Carswell Company, Limited, 1898.
  lxi, 1294 p.
  Ontario: pp. 265–313.   OTU

Main, Oscar Warren, 1916–
  The Canadian nickel industry: a study in market control and public policy.
  [Toronto] University of Toronto Press, 1955.
  ix, 168 p. tables.   OTU
Mayall, Kenneth M
  The natural resources of King township, Ontario, 1938. Toronto [University
  of Toronto Press] 1938.
  54 p. illus., maps (part fold.), tables.   OTU
Mines Contract and Investigation Co. of Toronto Ltd.
  Special circular on the gold fields of Ontario and the mining of the province.
  [Toronto] The Author, 1899.
  58 p. fold. map.   OTAR
Mitchell, J   Murray.
  [Ottawa county, its resources and capabilities. Ottawa: 1882]
  40 p.   OTURS
Moore, Elwood S   1878–
  The American influence on Canadian Mining. With a foreword by H.A.
  Innis. Toronto: University of Toronto Press, 1941.
  xx, 144 p. illus., tables.
  Ontario: pp. 24–59.   OTU
— Canada's mineral resources. Toronto: Irwin & Gordon, Limited [c1929]
  xv, 301 p. tables, fold. maps.   OTV
— The mineral resources of Canada. Toronto: The Ryerson Press [c1933]
  xv, 301 p. fold. maps (part col.), tables.   OONL
Mutch, Douglas A
  Brief on taxation on the Ontario metal mining industry, 1907–1941.
  Prepared for the Ontario Mining Association by Douglas A. Mutch in
  collaboration with Balmer Neilly. Toronto: 1943.
  69, 9, 5 leaves.   OONL
— Schedules to accompany brief. Toronto: 1943.
  1 v. (various pagings). tables.   OONL
Natural resource development in Canada: multi-disciplinary seminar. Edited
  by Phillipe Crabbé and Irene M. Spry. Ottawa: University of Ottawa Press,
  1973.
  xii, 344 p. diagrs. (Cahiers des sciences sociales, no. 8).   OTU
Nelles, Henry Vivian, 1942–
  The politics of development: forests, mines and hydro-electric power in
  Ontario, 1849–1941. Toronto: Macmillan of Canada [1974]
  xiii, 514 p. illus., port.   OTU
Newton–White, Ernest, 1892–
  Canadian restoration. Toronto: The Ryerson Press [c1944]
  x, 227 p.
  Natural resources.   OTU
— Hurt not the earth. Drawings by Thoreau MacDonald. Toronto: The
  Ryerson Press [1958]
  xvi, 188 p. illus.   OTU

O'Meara, Michael.
    Oil Springs: the birthplace of the oil industry of North America, 1858–1958.
    [Oil Springs, Ontario: Centennial Historical Committee, 1958]
    49 p. illus., map, ports.   OTAR
Ontario. Commission to enquire upon the game and fish of the province of
    Ontario and the laws relating to their protection.
    Report. Printed by order of the Legislative Assembly. Toronto: Warwick
    and Sons, 1892.
    483 [i.e. 484 p.].
    Chairman: G.A. MacCallum.   OTL
Ontario. Commission to inquire into the causes of the fire which occurred in the
    Hollinger Mine in the town of Timmins.
    Report. [Toronto: 1928]
    2 v. typewritten.
    Commissioner: Thomas E. Godson.   OTAR
— Proceedings, February 27–April 14, 1928.
    3 v. [i.e. 1544 typewritten pages].   OTAR
— Newspaper clippings.
    1 v.   OTAR
Ontario. Iron Ore Committee.
    Report with appendix, 1923. Printed by order of the Legislative Assembly.
    Toronto: Clarkson W. James, printer to the King's Most Excellent Majesty,
    1924.
    vi, 306 p. illus., map, tables.
    Chairman: Lloyd Harris.   OTU
Ontario. Legislative Assembly. Committee of inquiry into the economics of the
    gold mining industry.
    Gold mining in Ontario. Report. Toronto: Baptist Johnston, printer to the
    Queen's Most Excellent Majesty, 1955.
    [xvii] 117 p. diagrs., illus., tables, maps.
    Chairman: F.A. Knox.   OTU
Ontario. Legislative Assembly. Select Committee appointed to inquire into the
    administration of the Department of Lands and Forests.
    Majority and minority reports. Toronto: T.E. Bowman, printer to the King's
    Most Excellent Majesty, 1941.
    64 p.
    Chairman: J.M. Cooper.   OTAR
— Minutes, December 1, 1939–May 3, 1940.
    1 v. (unpaged).   OTAR
— Proceedings, January 12–May 7, 1940.
    30 v. [i.e. 2164 typewritten pages]   OTAR
Ontario. Legislative Assembly. Select Committee on Mining.
    Report. [Toronto: Queen's Printer, 1966]
    v, 103 p. charts, map, tables, graphs.
    Chairman: Rene Brunelle.   OTAR OTUL
— Interim report. [Toronto] 1965.
    14 p. map, tables.   OTAR

— Proceedings, June 15, 1964–January 6, 1966.
   25 v. (various pagings).   OTAR
— Briefs.
   95 v. [i.e. 94]   OTAR

Submissions to Ontario Legislative Assembly Select Committee on Mining
Northern Ontario Natural Gas Company, Ltd.
   Memorandum submitted in connection with the hearings of the Ontario
   Legislative Assembly Select Committee on Mining. Prepared by Northern
   Ontario Natural Gas Company Limited and Twin City Gas Company
   Limited. [Toronto: 1964]
   17 leaves. fold. map, fold. table.   OTU

Ontario. Legislative Assembly. Special Committee on the Game Situation,
   1931–1933.
   Report. Printed by order of the Legislative Assembly of Ontario. Toronto:
   Herbert M. Ball, printer to the King's Most Excellent Majesty, 1933.
   152 p. illus., tables.
   Chairman: W.D. Black.   OTAR
Ontario. Legislative Assembly. Special Committee appointed to inquire into the
   socio-economic problems of the gold mining industry in Ontario.
   Interim report. [Toronto] 1955.
   51 leaves. charts, tables.
   Chairman: F.A. Knox.   OTU OTAR
— Gold mining in Ontario: report of the Committee. Toronto: Baptist
   Johnston, printer to the Queen's Most Excellent Majesty, 1955.
   117 p. illus., charts, tables, maps.   OTAR

Submission to Ontario Legislative Assembly Special Committee on Gold Mining in Ontario
United Steelworkers of America.
   A submission to the Special Committee appointed by the Ontario
   Legislature to inquire into the socio-economic problems of the gold mining
   industry in Ontario. Toronto: 1954.
   96, 25 leaves. diagrs.   OTU

Ontario. Royal Commission inquiring into the affairs of Abitibi Power and
   Paper Company Limited.
   Report. n.p.: 1918.
   20 p.
   Chairman: C.R. McTague.   OTAR
— Proceedings, November 4, 1940–January 8, 1941.
   14 v. [i.e. 1556 typewritten pages].   OTAR

Ontario. Royal Commission on Forest Reservation and National Park.
   Report. Printed by order of the Legislative Assembly. Toronto: Warwick &
   Sons, 1893.
   40 p. map.
   Chairman: Alexander Kirkwood.   OTL
— Papers and reports upon forestry, forest schools, forest administration and
   management in Europe, America and the British Possessions and upon
   forests as public parks and sanitary resorts. Printed by order of the
   Legislative Assembly. Toronto: Warwick & Sons, 1893.
   278 p.   OTL
Ontario. Royal Commission on Forestry.
   Report, 1947. Toronto: Baptist Johnston, printer to the King's Most
   Excellent Majesty, 1947.
   196 p. illus., fold. maps (part col.).
   Commissioner: Howard Kennedy.   OTAR OTU
— Proceedings, October 28, 1946–January 16, 1947.
   20 v. [i.e. 1411 typewritten pages]   OTAR
— Submissions.
   132 v.   OTAR
Ontario. Royal Commission on Forestry Protection and Perpetuation in
   Ontario.
   Preliminary report. Printed by order of the Legislative Assembly. Toronto:
   L.K. Cameron, printer to the Queen's Most Excellent Majesty, 1898.
   14 p.
   Chairman: E.W. Rathbun.   OTL
— Report. Printed by order of the Legislative Assembly. Toronto: L.K.
   Cameron, printer to the Queen's Most Excellent Majesty, 1899.
   29 p. map.   OTL
Ontario. Royal Commission on the Health and Safety of Workers in Mines.
   Report. [Toronto: Ministry of the Attorney General, 1976]
   329 p. tables.
   Commissioner: James M. Ham.   OTAR
— Proceedings, January 14–June 6, 1975.
   5662 typewritten pages.   OTAR
— Briefs.
   145 v.   OTAR

Background papers to Ontario Royal Commission on the Health and Safety of Workers in
   Mines
Liddell, F   D   K
   Health and safety in mines: a review of the literature with bibliography.
   Montreal: 1975.
   viii, 78 p. graphs., tables.   OTAR

Reimers, (Jan H.) and Associates.
Study of health and safety in metallurgical plants. Oakville, Ontario: Jan H.
Reimers and Associates Limited, 1975.
57 p. illus. OTAR

Ontario. Royal Commission on the Mineral Resources and Measures for their
Development.
Report. Printed by order of the Legislative Assembly. Toronto: Warwick &
Sons, 1890.
xxiv, 566 p. illus., fold. map.
Chairman: John Charlton. OTL
Ontario. Royal Ontario Mining Commission.
Report, 1944. [Toronto: King's Printer, 1945]
8 parts in 1 v.
Chairman: Norman C. Urquhart. OTRM
Ontario. Royal Ontario Nickel Commission.
Report with appendix. Printed by order of the Legislative Assembly of
Ontario. Toronto: A.T. Wilgress, printer to the King's Most Excellent
Majesty, 1917.
xlviii, 584, v, 219, 62 p. illus., charts, tables.
Chairman: George T. Holloway.
Appendix has own title page. OTAR
Ontario. Timber Commission.
Interim reports (First, Second, Third). Printed by order of the Legislative
Assembly of Ontario. Toronto: Clarkson W. James, printer to the King's
Most Excellent Majesty, 1921.
8 p.
Commissioners: William Renwick Riddell, Francis Robert Latchford. OTAR
— Report. Printed by order of the Legislative Assembly of Ontario. Toronto:
Clarkson W. James, printer to the King's Most Excellent Majesty, 1922.
65 p. tables. OTAR
— Proceedings, April 12, 1920–February 4, 1922.
12, 545 typewritten pages. OTAR
— Press clippings from various Toronto newspapers; October 12,
1920–February 15, 1921.
1 v. (unpaged). OTAR
Ontario. Water Resources Commission.
Grand valley watershed water resources and conservation management.
[Toronto: c1964]
18 p. tables. OTAR
— Industrial pollution control in municipalities, water management in
Ontario. [Toronto: 1972?]
18 p. OTU
— Report on a water resources survey of the county of Peel. [Toronto] 1963.
iv, 204 p. maps (part fold.), tables. OTUSA

Submission to Ontario Water Resources Commission
Kingston Area Planning Board.
 Water supply and water pollution in the Kingston planning area: a brief
 submitted to the Ontario Water Resources Commission, Kingston, Ontario,
 28th June, 1956. [Kingston, Ontario] 1956.
 6 leaves. fold. col. map.   OKQ

Ontario. Water Resources Commission. Division of Research.
 Water resources of the Upper Nottawasaga River drainage basin, by U.
 Sibul and A V. Choo–Ying, Toronto; 1971.
 xiii, 128 p. illus., diagrs., maps (part fold. part col.). (*Its* Division of Research.
 Report 3).   OTU
Ontario Economic Council.
 A forest policy for Ontario. [Toronto: 1970]
 38 [2] p. illus.   OTV
Ontario Game and Fisheries Commission appointed to inquire into and report
 on all matters appertaining to the game, fish, the fisheries and the game of the
 province of Ontario.
 Interim report. Printed by order of the Legislature Assembly of Ontario.
 Toronto: L.K. Cameron, printer to the King's Most Excellent Majesty,
 1910.
 58 p. fold. illus.
 Commissioner: Kelly Evans.   OTAR
— Final report. 1912.
 ii, 304 p. illus., maps.   OTAR
Ontario Mining Association.
 The miner at home: a story of northern Ontario. [Toronto: The Ontario
 Mining Association, 1948]
 [31] p. illus.   OTU
Pain, Sidney Albert, 1896–
 Three miles of gold: the story of Kirkland Lake. Toronto: The Ryerson Press
 [c1960]
 viii, 109 p. maps (1 fold.).   OTU
— The way north: men, mines and minerals, being some account of the curious
 history of the ancient route between North Bay and Hudson Bay in Ontario
 as collected and recollected by S.A. Pain. Toronto: The Ryerson Press
 [c1964]
 249 p. illus., map.   OTU
Parker, Victor J
 The planned non-permanent community; an approach to development of
 new towns based on mining activity. Ottawa: Northern Co-ordinating and
 Resource Centre, 1963.
 iv, 106 p.
 "Based on his M.Sc. thesis at The University of British Columbia".   OTU

Parrott, Donald Fleming, 1916–
    The Red Lake gold rush. n.p. [c1964]
    144 p. illus., maps.   OTU
— 2d ed. n.p.: 1967 [c1968]
    164 p. illus., maps.   OTU
— 3d ed. n.p.: 1970.
    167 p. illus., maps.   OTU
Pattullo, George Robson, 1845–1922.
    North western Ontario (now known as "the disputed territory"), the districts
    of Thunder Bay and Algoma, a brief description, together with the opinions
    of prominent residents, old pioneers, eminent scientists, explorers, special
    correspondents, travellers and others, upon the territory's varied resources,
    cereal, mineral and timber, and also of its matchless scenery. Port Arthur,
    Ontario: Evening Herald Printing and Publishing Company, 1883.
    24 p.   OTURS
Pearson, Norman, 1928–
    The Great Lakes basin: alternative institutional arrangements for multiple-
    purpose resources management [Guelph, Ontario] Centre for Resources
    Development, University of Guelph, 1972.
    27 leaves. (University of Guelph. Centre for Resources Development.
    Publication no. 55).   OTU
— The Great Lakes basin: prospects and problems. [Guelph, Ontario:
    University of Guelph. Centre for Resources Development] 1971.
    20 leaves. (University of Guelph. Centre for Resources Development.
    Publication no. 33).   OTU
Peat Committee (Canada and Ontario) 1918–1923.
    Final report of the Peat Committee appointed jointly by the governments of
    the Dominion of Canada and the province of Ontario. Peat: its manufacture
    and uses, by B.F. Haanel. Published jointly by the Mines Branch,
    Department of Mines, Canada and the Department of Mines, Ontario.
    Ottawa [F.A. Acland, printer to the King, 1926]
    xviii, 298 p. illus., figs., tables. (Mines Branch publication no. 64).
    Chairman: Arthur A. Cole.   OONL
Porcupine, Ontario. Golden Anniversary Committee.
    Souvenir booklet celebrating the golden anniversary of the Porcupine gold
    rush, July 1–5, 1959. [Timmins, Ontario: Northern Stationary & Printing
    Company, 1959]
    100 p. illus., map, ports.   OTU
Resources for Tomorrow Conference, Montreal, 1961.
    Resources for tomorrow. [Ottawa: Queen's Printer] 1961–62.
    4 v. illus., maps, diagrs., tables.

Contents: v. 1–2, Conference background papers (July 1961); v. 3,
Proceedings of the conference; Supplementary volume, Conference
background papers (Feb. 1962): Guide to benefit-cost analysis by W.R.D.
Sewell [et al].   OTUSA

Submission to Resources for Tomorrow Conference
Community Planning Association of Canada. Ontario Division.
Submission to the "resources for tomorrow conferences," prepared by a
committee... Dec. 15, 1960. Toronto: 1960.
iii, 12 leaves.   OTUSA

Richardson, Arthur Herbert, 1890–1971.
Forestry in Ontario, [compiled and written by Arthur Herbert Richardson.
Toronto: Southam Press, 1928?]
73 p. plates, fold. col. map.
Prepared for the Ontario Department of Forestry.   OTU
Richardson, W   George.
A survey of Canadian mining history. Montreal: Canadian Institute of
Mining & Metallurgy, 1974.
iii, 115 p. (Special volume 14).   OTU
Roberts, Leslie, 1896–
The Algoma story; the birth of a billion dollar uranium camp. n.p. [1955?]
24 [1] p. illus. (part col.), map, port.   OTU
— Noranda. Toronto: Clarke, Irwin & Company Limited [c1956]
xiii, 223 p. illus., ports., maps.   OTU
Robinson, A   H   A
The mineral industries of Canada. British Empire Exhibition edition.
Ottawa: Department of Mines, 1924.
128 p. illus., fold. map, tables.   OONL
Robinson, Ira M
New industrial towns on Canada's resource frontier. Chicago [Department
of Geography, University of Chicago] 1962.
ix, 190 p. illus., maps, tables.   OTU
Robinson, John Lewis, 1918–
Resources of the Canadian Shield. [Toronto] Methuen [c1969]
viii, 136 p. illus., maps.   OTU
Roland, Walpole   –1931.
Algoma West; its mines, scenery and industrial resources. Toronto: Warwick
& Sons, 1887.
217 p. illus., map (fold.).
Business directory of Port Arthur: pp. 191–217.
Royal Society of Canada.
Water resources of Canada symposia presented to the Royal Society of
Canada in 1966; Resources hydrauliques du Canada; colloques presented à

la Société royal du Canada en 1966, edited by Claude E. Doleman.
[Toronto] Published for the Society by the University of Toronto Press, 1967.
xviii, 251 p. illus., graphs, facsims., maps, ports., tables. (*Its* Studia varia, 11).
OTU

Sault Express.
East Algoma: facts about a wonderfully rich country that is open to the
homeseekers of the world. Sault Ste. Marie, Ontario: Sault Express, 1895.
56 p.   OTAR

Sault to Sudbury Press Ltd.
Elliot Lake, Ontario, Canada: a city born into the atomic age. [Elliot Lake,
Ontario] 1957.
1 v. (unpaged). illus., 2 fold. maps.   OTAR

A short history of the Porcupine gold mining area with statistics . n.p. [1961?]
10 leaves. tables.   OTU

Small, Henry Beaumont, 1831–1919.
Canadian forests: forest trees, timber and forest products. Montreal: Dawson
Brothers, 1884.
66 p. tables.   OTURS
— The mineral resources of the new Dominion, especially those of the Ottawa
valley. Ottawa: G.E. Desbarats, 1868.
28 p.   OTURS
— The resources of the Ottawa district. Ottawa: Times Printing Company,
1872.
39 p.   OTURS

Smithies, Walter R
The protection and use of natural resources in Ontario. Prepared for the
Ontario Economic Council. [Toronto] Ontario Economic Council, 1974.
89 p. (Evolution of policy in contemporary Ontario, no. 2).   OTAR

Snell, Rendol.
Mines and mining in eastern Ontario. Toronto: Murray Printing Company,
1901.
48 p. illus.   OOA

Spang, Edward.
"Cobalt" the mascot of Cobalt silver camp and other stories. Sudbury,
Ontario: Sudbury News Limited [1922]
134 p.   OTAR

Spruce Falls Power and Paper Company.
Kapuskasing, the model town of the north. [Kapuskasing, Ontario] The
Author [1967?]
15 p. illus., map.   OKQ

Stanley, Robert Crooke, 1876–1951.
The nickel industry in 1935. Copper Cliff, Ontario: International Nickel
Company of Canada [1935]
35 p.   OTU

Tassé, Joseph, 1848–1895.
  Lá vallée de l'Outaouaois: sa condition geographique; ses resources agricoles
  et industrielles; ses exploitations, forestieres; ses richesses minérales; ses
  advantages pour la colonisation et l'immigration ses canaux et ses chemins
  de fer. Montreal: Eusèbe Senécal, 1873.
  58 p.   OLU
Temiskaming and Northern Ontario Railway Commission.
  The great clay belt of northern Ontario. Toronto: Temiskaming and
  Northern Ontario Railway Commission [1913?]
  24 p. illus. (*Its* pamphlet no. 11).
  Chairman: J.L. Englehart.   OTU
Thompson, George S
  Up to date: or, The life of a lumberman. [Peterborough, Ontario: Times
  Printing Co., 1895]
  126 p. plates.   OTV
Thompson, John Fairfield, 1881–
  For the years to come: a story of International Nickel of Canada, by John F.
  Thompson, and Norman Beasley. Toronto: Longmans, Green & Company
  [1960]
  x, 374 p.   OTU
Toronto and York Planning Board.
  Report on water supply and sewage disposal for the city of Toronto and
  related areas. [Toronto] 1949.
  122 leaves. fold. maps, tables.
  At head of title: Gore & Storrie, consulting engineers.   OTUSA
Townsley, Benjamin Franklin, 1890–1939.
  Minefinders: the history and romance of Canadian mineral discoveries.
  Illustrations by Evan Macdonald. Toronto: Saturday Night Press [c1935]
  246 p. illus., maps, tables.
  Ontario: pp. 43–128.   OTAR
Wood quality; proceedings of symposia sponsored by the Advisory Committee
  on Forestry and Forest Products, Ontario Research Foundation. [Toronto]
  Research Branch, Ontario Department of Lands and Forests [1962]
  32, 27, 28 p. illus., graphs.
  Chairman: J.W.B. Sisam.   OTL
Zaslow, Morris, 1918–
  The opening of the Canadian north 1870–1914. Toronto: McClelland &
  Stewart [c1971]
  xii, 339 p. illus., maps.
  Ontario and Quebec: pp. 147–198.   OTU

Periodical Articles
Activity in Ontario goldfields. Canadian Mining Journal 37: 441, 1916.
Adams Mine officially opened March 10, 1965. Canadian Mining Journal 86
  (no. 5): 98–99, 1965.

Algoma Ore Properties Limited. Canadian Mining Journal 77(no. 11): 76–130, 1956.

Amendments to Ontario Mining Act. Canadian Mining Journal 76(no. 6): 65, 1955.

Annual report Beaver Consolidated Mines, Ltd. Canadian Mining Journal 37: 253–255, 1916.

Annual reports Nipissing Mines Co. and Nipissing Mining Co., 1915. Canadian Mining Journal 37: 187–192, 1916.

Armbrust, Duncan.
The trail beyond Cobalt. Canadian Magazine of Politics, Science, Art and Literature 38: 311–319, 1912.

Armstrong, H   S
Gold ores of the Little Long Lac area, Ontario. Economic Geology 38: 204–252, 1943.

Arsenic refining in Ontario. Canadian Mining Review 20: 240, 1901.

Ayres, L   D   , G   Bennett and R   A   Riley.
Geology and mineral possibilities of northwestern Patricia district, Ontario. Canadian Mining Journal 90(no. 4): 62–65, 1969.

Baelz, Walter.
The gold fields of new Ontario. Canadian Mining Journal 33: 299–304, 1912.

Bailey, Leslie and W   F   Morgan.
Mine rescue advanced training at Porcupine. Canadian Mining Journal 72(no. 11): 70–73, 1951.

Baker, T   J
Free fall testing of mine hoisting conveyances in Ontario mines in the interests of safety. Canadian mining Journal 79(no. 11): 84–90, 1958.
— Revised regulations promote safer hoisting for Ontario mines. Canadian Mining Journal 92(no. 9): 70–80, 84–88, 1971.

Barlow, Alfred Ernest.
Corundum mining in Ontario. Canadian Mining Journal 36: 379–382, 1915.

Barr, Elinor.
Lumbering in the Pigeon River watershed. Thunder Bay Historical Museum Society. Papers and Records 4: 3–9, 1976.

Barrett, C   M
Hoisting accidents in Ontario mines – 1958–1962. Canadian Mining Journal 84(no. 9): 67–73, 1963.

Bateman, G   C
The Cobalt silver district. Canadian Mining Journal 45: 595–597, 1924.
— The importance of the mining industry to old Ontario. Canadian Mining Journal 42: 401–404, 1921.
— Mines of the future. Canadian Mining Journal 38: 98, 1917.
Development of mines in northern Ontario.

Bayly, G   H
    Reforestation in Ontario – 1955. Canadian Geographical Journal 50: 44–61,
    1955.
Beach, Noel.
    Nickel capital: Sudbury and the nickel industry 1905–1925. Laurentian
    University Review 6(no. 3): 55–74, 1974.
Beard, W   J
    Regional forecasts for 1974. Canadian Mining Journal 95(no. 2): 50–53,
    1974.
Belknap, John.
    Vignettes of mining; the Ontario Prospectors and Developers Association.
    Canadian Mining Journal 57: 647–648, 1936.
Bell, J   Mackintosh.
    The influence of Cobalt on Canadian mining. Canadian Mining Journal 44:
    633–635, 1923.
Bell, Robert.
    The Cobalt mining district. Canadian Mining Journal 28(no. 10): 246–248,
    1907.
— The Cobalt mining district. Canadian Mining Review 27: 116–124, 1906.
— The nickel and copper deposits of Sudbury district, Canada. With an
    appendix on the silicified glass-Breccia of Vermilion River, Sudbury district
    by George H. Williams. Geological Society of America. Bulletin 2: 125–140,
    1891.
Beyond the clearings. Canadian Mining Review 27: 41–44, 1906.
    Mining districts in Ontario and Quebec.
The Big Ben Cobalt Mines, Limited. Canadian Mining Journal 28(no. 15):
    390–393, 1907.
The Black Donald graphite mine. Canadian Mining Journal 49: 482–486, 1928.
Blair, W   J
    Cobalt mines. Canadian Mining Review 27: 182 184, 1906.
Blind River; centre industriel. Société Historique du Nouvel-Ontario.
    Documents Historiques 24: 4–28, 1952.
Bonham, W   M
    Iron mines of Ontario. Canadian Mining Journal 69(no. 3): 75–78, 1948.
Breidenbach, Theodore.
    Bird's eye of the Bag Bay Lake of the Woods. Canadian Mining Review 19:
    36–37, 1900.
Brent, Charles.
    Algoma mining freaks. Canadian Mining Review 20: 80–81, 1901.
— Notes on the gold ores of western Ontario. Canadian Mining Review 22:
    33–35, 1903.
Brian, A
    The Lake Shore Mine; the story of its development and a description of
    some of its present equipment. Canadian Mining Journal 52: 89–92, 1931.

Brodie, J   D
  The forest-based industries of the northeastern Ontario economic region.
  Ontario Economic Review 1: no. 7, 1963.
— Timber management in Ontario. Canadian Geographical Journal 42:
  100–117, 1951.
Brokunier, Sam Hugh.
  The Kenora gold district, Ontario. Canadian Mining Journal 48: 302–303,
  1927.
— Those western Ontario ore deposits. Canadian Mining Journal 47: 977–978,
  1926.
Brouillette, Benoît.
  Le nickel et le cuivre de Sudbury. L'Actualité Économique 13(part 1): 1–17,
  1937.
— La region miniére de Sudbury. L'Actualité Économique 12(part 2):
  227–252, 1937.
Brown, L   Carson.
  Ontario. Canadian Mining Journal 81(no. 2): 120–123, 1960.
  Mineral industries for 1959.
— Ontario's mineral heritage. Canadian Geographical Journal 50: 84–103,
  1955; 76: 80–101, 1968.
— The Red Lake gold field. Canadian Geographical Journal 70: 114–125,
  1965.
Browne, D   F
  Canadian Copper Company. Canadian Mining Journal 30: 42–46, 1909.
Browne, David H
  Coal-dust fired reverberatory furnaces of Canadian Copper Co., Copper
  Cliff, Ontario. Canadian Mining Journal 36: 47–51, 1915.
— The mining and smelting equipment of the Canadian Copper Company .
  Canadian Mining Journal 28(no. 12): 305–312, 1907.
Browning, Harry.
  Mining in Ontario. Canadian Mining Journal 59: 71–73, 1938; 60: 68–70,
  1939; 61: 79–81, 1940; 62: 73–75, 1941.
  Covers the years: 1937–1940.
Browning, J   A
  Ontario. Canadian Mining Journal 82 (no. 2): 109–112, 1961.
  Mineral industries.
Browning, J   C
  Mining in Ontario – 1944. Canadian Mining Journal 66: 95–99, 1945.
— Mining in Ontario in 1941; large base metal expansion features year's
  production. Canadian Mining Journal 63: 80–83, 1942.
— Mining in Ontario, 1942; mica discovery at Eau Claire an important event.
  Canadian Mining Journal 64: 81–83, 1943.
— Ontario annual review. Canadian Mining Journal 70(no. 2): 99–106, 1949;
  71(no. 2): 98–105, 1950; 72(no. 2): 81–87, 1951; 73(no. 2): 90–98, 1952;
  74(no. 2): 94–100, 1953: 75(no. 2): 92–98, 1954; 76(no. 2): 84–88, 1955;
  77(no. 2): 94–97, 1956.
  Covers the years: 1948–1955.

— Ontario annual review; development of uranium mines raises value of mineral production to new record despite price decline in base metals. Canadian Mining Journal 79(no. 2): 115–119, 1958.

— Ontario annual review; increased production follows return of army personnel. Canadian Mining Journal 67: 101–106, 1946.

— Ontario annual review; increased uranium production raises 1958 total above 1957. Canadian Mining Journal 80(no. 2): 114–117, 1959.

— Ontario mining in 1943; gratifying showing in face of discouraging conditions. Canadian Mining Journal 65: 84–87, 1944.

— Ontario mining review. Canadian Mining Review 69(no. 2): 102–108, 1948.

— Ontario mining review – 1946; discriminatory taxation and dollar parity disturbing factors. Canadian Mining Journal 68: 97–103, 1947.

[Bruce, E   L   ]

Future of the Ontario iron deposits. Queen's Quarterly 32: 170–181, 1924.

— Precious metal mining in northern Ontario. Journal of the Canadian Bankers' Association 32: 346–356, 1925.

— The Swastika gold area. Canadian Mining Journal 34: 26–29, 1913.

Brumell, Nadine B

El Dorado to Omega Blue; notes on men and mining in eastern Ontario. Historic Kingston 14: 40–50, 1966.

Buckle, F   and Gordon R   Cameron.

Safety in Canada's deepest mine. Canadian Mining Journal 84(no. 9): 57–60, 1963.

Wright–Hargreaves Mine, Ontario.

Bucksar, Richard G

Elliot Lake. Habitat 8(1): 20–25, 1965.

— Timmins, the Porcupine and gold. Habitat 12(2): 7–12, 1969.

Building the nickel refinery at Port Colborne, Ontario. Canadian Mining Journal 38: 173–174, 1917.

Burke, J   II   G

The Haliburton country – land of promise. Canadian Geographical Journal 62: 106–111, 1961.

Burrows, A   G

Eldorado copper mine. Canadian Mining Journal 28(no. 5): 76, 1907.

— Geological features of the Porcupine area. Canadian Mining Journal 37: 218–222, 1916.

— The Porcupine gold area. Canadian Mining Journal 32: 526–531, 1911; 37: 93–96, 1916.

— South Lorrain silver area. Canadian Mining Journal 30: 434–437, 1909.

Burrows, A   G   and P   E   Hopkins.

Boston Creek gold area. Canadian Mining Journal 37: 399–402, 1916.

— Mines of Kirkland Lake area. Canadian Mining Journal 46: 971–974, 1002–1003, 1925.

Caillaud, Frédéric Romanet du

Les mines de nickel de la region de Sudbury. Société Historique du Nouvel-Ontario. Documents Historiques 38: 6–41, 1960.

Cain, W   C
Forest management in Ontario. Forestry Chronicle 15: 16–28, 1939.
Campbell, L   Clayton.
Ontario petroleum and its products. Canadian Magazine of Politics,
Science, Art and Literature 5: 323–325, 1895.
Canada's iron ore resources. Industrial Canada 19(no. 11): 144–148, 1919.
Reprinted from *Canadian Official Record.*
Canadian coal for Ontario. Industrial Canada 3: 435, 1903.
The Canadian Copper Company. Canadian Mining Review 19: 128–129, 1900.
The Canadian Copper Company's plant at Copper Cliff, Ontario. Canadian
Mining Review 23: 4–7, 1904.
Canadian Gold Fields Limited; the works of the Deloro Gold Mine. Canadian
Mining Review 19: 160–161, 1900.
Carlson, H   D
Base metal exploration... in the Kenora area. Canadian Mining Journal
77(no. 4): 87–89, 1956.
Carter, W   E   H
Gold mining in western Ontario, a lesson from mining history. Canadian
Mining Journal 32: 312–315, 1911.
— The mines of Ontario. Canadian Mining Review 23: 193–200, 222–227,
1904; 24: 34–37, 57–59, 1905.
— The Porcupine gold area. Canadian Mining Journal 31: 361–366, 1910.
Casey Cobalt Mining Company's fifth annual report. Canadian Mining Journal
34: 105–108, 1913.
Changes in Ontario mining tax. Canadian Mining Journal 38: 188, 1917.
Charleton, A   G
Mining in northern Ontario. Canadian Mining Journal 34: 729–742, 1913.
Clark, J   M
The Mines Act of Ontario. Canada Law Journal 42: 89–96, 1906.
— The Ontario mining law. Canadian Mining Review 19: 48–50, 1900.
Cleland, Ralph H
Accident experience in the mining industry of Ontario, 1938. Canadian
Mining Journal 60: 533–536, 1939.
— Accident experience in the mining industry; increased labour turnover
affects frequency rate. Canadian Mining Journal 63: 518–523, 1942.
— Accident experience in the mining industry of Ontario; to learn from the
experience of others may be helpful. Canadian Mining Journal 62: 454–458,
1941.
Clevenger, G   H
The mill and metallurgical practice of the Nipissing Mining Co., Ltd.,
Cobalt, Ontario. Canadian Mining Journal 35: 555–558, 558–590, 1914.
Cobalt; the greatest mining camp of the Temiskaming district. Mer Douce 1(3):
4–6, 1921.
Cobalt camp. Canadian Mining Review 27: 127–128, 1906.
Cobalt companies. Canadian Mining Review 28: 23–25, 1907.
The Cobalt district. Canadian Mining Review 28: 19–20, 1907.

Cobalt Lake. Canadian Mining Journal 28(no. 10): 240–242, 1907.

Cobalt metal revives the Cobalt camp. Canadian Mining Journal 75(no. 6): 70–72, 1954.

Cobalt – present and future. Canadian Mining Journal 29(no. 10): 200–203, 1908.

Cobalt shipments. Canadian Mining Review 27: 139, 1906.

Cochrane, Thomas S
   Mines Branch Elliot Lake Laboratory. Canadian Mining Journal 89(no. 8): 43–44, 1968.

Cockeram, Alan.
   Brief account of the history [of] central Patricia gold mines. Canadian Mining Journal 70(no. 11): 70–71, 1949.

Cockshutt, Henry.
   Ontario's natural resources in review; the rich heritage of the people of the province and the responsibilities attaching to their possession. Industrial Canada 25(no. 8): 41–43, 70, 1924.

Cole, Arthur A
   Canadian Mining and Finance Co.'s power plant at Timmins, Ontario. Canadian Mining Journal 36: 443, 1915.

— Mineral resources of northern Ontario. Canadian Mining Journal 44: 181–183, 1923.

— Mineral resources of Temiskaming. Mer Douce 1(3): 7–10, 1921.

— The mining industry in relation to the Temiskaming and Northern Railway. Canadian Mining Journal 35: 294, 1914.

— Mining royalties at Cobalt. Canadian Mining Journal 36: 373–374, 1915.

— Ore testing and sampling services. Canadian Mining Journal 71(no. 10): 172–175, 1950.

— The relation of transportation to mining in Cobalt. Canadian Mining Journal 33: 795–796, 1912.

— Report on Cobalt district for year . Canadian Mining Journal 29(no. 9): 168–171, 1908; 30: 323–329, 1909; 31: 45–47, 1910.
   Title varies: Cobalt in 1908; Cobalt during, 1909.

— Review of mining in Cobalt during 1910. Canadian Mining Journal 32: 36–40, 1911.

— Abstract of report. Canadian Mining Journal 31: 199–207, 1910.

— Smelting the Cobalt silver ores. Canadian Mining Journal 34: 763–764, 1913: 35: 20–21, 1914.

Coleman, A   P
   Chief minerals of the Sudbury district. Canadian Mining Journal 37: 388–389, 1916.

— The gold fields of western Ontario. Canadian Mining Review 15: 233–235, 1896.

— The Massey copper mine area. Canadian Mining Journal 35: 378–379, 1914.

— The Moose Mountain iron range. Canadian Mining Journal 34: 573, 1913.

— The nickel deposits of Sudbury district. Canadian Mining Journal 34: 552, 1913.

Collins, E   A
Canada's nickel industry. Canadian Geographical Journal 13: 256–275, 1936.

Collins, W   H
Gowganda mining division, district of Nipissing, Ontario. Canadian Mining Journal 30: 369–371, 392–394, 1909.

— Gowganda silver deposits. Canadian Mining Journal 35: 168–169, 1914.

Colvocoresses, G   M
Gowganda during 1911. Canadian Mining Journal 33: 256–260, 1912.

Concerning western Ontario gold fields. Canadian Mining Review 18: 219–220, 1899.

Coniagas Mines, annual report. Canadian Mining Journal 36: 16–18, 1915.

The Consolidated Lake Superior Company. Canadian Mining Review 21: 109–110, 1902.

The Consolidated Ophir Mines, Ltd.; Lake of the Woods. Canadian Mining Journal 33: 122–124, 1912.

Cook, S   J
Half a century in Canada's mineral industry, 1879–1929. Canadian Mining Journal 50 (Fiftieth Anniversary Number): 40–49, 1929.

Copper-nickel mining in Ontario. Canadian Mining Review 21: 258–260, 1902.

Corkill, E   T
Mica in Ontario. Canadian Mining Journal 28(no. 9): 196–200, 1907.

Corless, C   U
Manitoba and Ontario; a striking parallel. "Address to the Winnipeg Board of Trade." Canadian Mining Journal 46: 202–205, 1925.
Mineral industries,

— The mineral wealth of Ontario. Canadian Mining Journal 45: 332–333, 1924.

The corundum industry of Ontario. Canadian Mining Review 23: 191–193, 1904.

The corundum lands of Ontario. Canadian Mining Review 17: 192–193, 1898.

Corundum mining in Ontario. Canadian Mining Review 24: 159, 1905.

Coste, D   A
History of natural gas in Ontario. Welland County Historical Society. Papers and Records 2: 94–104, 1926.

Coste, Eugene.
Natural gas in Ontario. Canadian Mining Review 19: 70–76, 1900.

— The new Tilbury and Romney oil fields of Kent county, Ontario. Canadian Mining Journal 28(no. 11): 265–268, 1907.

Cowan, Hugh.
The development of a great industry. Mer Douce 1(5): 6–7, 1921.
Mining in Ontario.

Cowan, James A
White metal milestone. Canadian Geographical Journal 18: 34–51, 1939.

Craick, W
    From prison camp to industrial town. Industrial Canada 31(10): 53–55,
    1931.
    Kapuskasing.
Craig, Roland D
    The forest resources of Canada. Economic Geography 2: 394–413, 1926.
Crawford, M   Gail.
    The redoubtable carriage. York Pioneer 53–63, 1975.
Crosbie, H   W   and M   Ardenne.
    Progress and problems of forestry in the Trent district. Forestry Chronicle
    16: 138–148, 1940.
Crozier, A   R
    Fuels of Ontario. Canadian Mining Journal 71(no. 10): 166–168, 1950.
Crume, R   L
    Prospecting and development in Algoma district. Canadian Mining Journal
    48: 70–71, 1927.
— Prospecting in northwestern Ontario. Canadian Mining Journal 47: 1142,
    1926.
Cumming, Jas. D
    Gowganda notes. Canadian Mining Journal 30: 229, 1909.
Cunningham, L   J
    A description of recent silver deposits, Cobalt, Ontario. Canadian Mining
    Journal 85(no. 5): 49–53, 1964.
Cunningham, Noel.
    Metallurgical practice in the Porcupine district. Canadian Mining Journal
    36: 103–105, 1915.
Cuthbertson, G   A
    The Bruce Mine; a brief history of Canada's pioneer copper mine. Canadian
    Mining Journal 60: 424–426, 1939.
— First large scale silver mining operations commenced in Canada – Silver
    Islet, off Thunder Cape, Lake Superior, 1869. Canadian Mining Journal 61:
    604–605, 1940.
— Hard rock gold mining methods begin production in Ontario, 1870.
    Canadian Mining Journal 61: 677, 1940.
— Mechanical drilling in the Goderich – Maitland River area, Ontario,
    commenced 1868 (first salt wells developed in Canada). Canadian Mining
    Journal 61: 532–533, 1940.
Davies, John C
    Geology and mineral exploration in the Kenora – Fort Frances area.
    Canadian Mining Journal 87(no. 4): 81–85, 1966.
Davis, H   P
    The Vipond Mine of the Porcupine Gold Mines Co. Canadian Mining
    Journal 32: 697–699, 1911.
Davis, John.
    The iron ore industry. Canadian Geographical Journal 49: 204–217, 1954.

Dawson, John A
    Graphite gold ore from Kirkland Lake district, Ontario. Canadian Mining
    Journal 35: 578, 1914.
Dawson, John A   M
    The pioneering of nepheline syenite in eastern Ontario. Canadian Mining
    Journal 82(no. 1): 31–34, 1961.
DeKalb, Courtenay.
    Mining in eastern Ontario. Canadian Mining Review 20: 181–185,
    205–206, 230–232, 1901.
The Deloro Mining and Reduction Company. Canadian Mining Journal 28(no.
    19): 517–522, 1907.
Denis, Keith.
    Oliver Daunais – the "Silver King". Thunder Bay Historical Museum
    Society. Papers and Records 2: 12–21, 1974.
de Schmid, Hugh S
    On the mica deposits of Ontario and Quebec. Canadian Mining Journal 32:
    763–765, 1911.
Development of Canada's oil fields. Industrial Canada 49(no. 9): 77–80, 1949.
Dillon, J   C
    Forest protection in Ontario. Canadian Geographical Journal 46: 42–59,
    1953.
Discovering a mine; the diary of John MacFarlane, joint discoverer with H.H.
    Howell, on September tenth, in the year 1928, of the Pickle Crow mine in
    northwestern Ontario. Canadian Mining Journal 56: 562–566, 1935.
The discovery of copper-nickel ores in Sudbury district. Canadian Mining
    Journal 37: 386, 1916.
Dividends from northern Ontario gold and silver mines. Canadian Mining
    Journal 38: 289, 1917.
    Extracted from *The Northern Miner*.
Dobie, Draper.
    Bruce Mines; early history of one of Ontario's oldest mines. Canadian
    Mining Journal 45: 1195, 1924.
Douglas, Gilean.
    A lode on his mind. Canadian Mining Journal 73(no. 5): 76–77, 1952.
    Bob MacGregor – prospector in the Porcupine area.
Douglas, Gilean and Bob MacGregor.
    Diamond rush in Canada. Canadian Mining Journal 73(no. 1): 63–64,
    1952.
Durzi, K   and F   Kutas.
    Oil and natural gas in Ontario. Ontario Economic Review 2: no. 9, 1964.
Early days at Cobalt. Canadian Mining Journal 38: 359–360, 1917.
An eastern Ontario gold mine. Canadian Mining Journal 33: 700–703, 1912.
Emery, V   H
    McIntyre–Porcupine Mines. Ltd. Canadian Mining Journal 32: 555–557,
    1911.

Evans, J   W
    The gold bearing sands of the Vermillion River. Canadian Mining Review
    18: 72–74, 1899.
Explorations in northern Ontario. Industrial Canada 1: 313, 1901.
    Mineral exploration.
Fairlie, M   F
    Mining and concentration of corundum in Ontario. Canadian Mining
    Review 21: 88–90, 1902.
Fake mining meeting; standard mining exchange hold a convention of alleged
    Ontario mining men and railroads a number of resolutions affecting mining
    – a lively session. Canadian Mining Review 22: 38–39, 1903.
The Falconbridge story. Canadian Mining Journal 80(no. 6): 105–230, 1959.
Fellows, Patrick.
    Mining in northeastern Ontario. Monetary Times 128(5): 72, 74–75, 1960.
— Survey of mining activity in northeastern Ontario. Monetary Times
    129(10): 76–78, 1961.
The financial results of gold mining in northern Ontario. Canadian Mining
    Journal 41: 699–700, 1920.
Ferguson, Stewart A
    Prospecting activities in Bateman township Red lake area, Ontario.
    Canadian Mining Journal 81(no. 4): 76–77, 1960.
— Recent exploration for gold in the Red Lake area. Canadian Mining
    Journal 84(no. 4): 70–72, 1963.
Fish, Richard.
    Sturgeon Lake mines: new Ontario producer. Canadian Mining Journal
    96(no. 1): 40–43, 1975.
The Foley Mine, Shoal Lake, Ontario. Canadian Mining Review 16: 41–42,
    1897.
Forbes, D   L   H
    Treatment of gold ore at Dome mine, South Porcupine, Ontario. Canadian
    Mining Journal 35: 77–85, 1914.
Foster, Ralph E
    Hydro-electric power and Ontario gold mining. Canadian Mining Journal
    67: 1946.
    5 parts.
    Contents: Part 1, The development of gold mining in Ontario, 67: 155–168;
    Part 2, Hydro-electric power requirements at gold mining properties, 67:
    253–258; Part 3, Hydro-electric power supply to the gold mining areas, 67:
    634–639, 720–725, 788–795; Part 4, Relationship between power supplier
    and mine customer, 67: 867–874; Part 5, Conclusion, 67: 957–959.
Foster, W   T
    Forest protection in Ontario. Canadian Geographical Journal 60: 38–57,
    1960.
Fournier, F   L
    Exploring offshore in Ontario. Canadian Mining Journal 80(no. 4): 96–99,
    1959.

Futterer, Edward.
   Living conditions at Red Lake. Canadian Mining Journal 55: 467–468, 1934.
Gardner, Gérard.
   La région de la baie James. L'Actualité Èconomique 22: 220–260, 1946.
Gauthier, Henri.
   Historique de la région minière de Sudbury. Société Historique du Nouvel-Ontario. Documents Historiques 3: 26–55, 1943.
Geological survey notes from Cobalt mining camp. Canadian Mining Review 27: 40–41, 1906.
Giblin, P   E
   Recent exploration and mining developments in the Batchawana area of Ontario. Canadian Mining Journal 87(no. 4): 77–80, 1966.
Gibson, C   S
   Fire prevention at Ontario mines. Canadian Mining Journal 70(no. 8): 75–80, 1949.
Gibson, Homer L
   Gold and silver mining in northern Ontario – (retrospective and prospective). Canadian Mining Journal 38: 113–114, 1917.
Gibson, Thomas W
   Mineral discoveries in Ontario. Canadian Mining Journal 47: 61, 1926. From article in *Mail and Empire* annual review number.
— Mineral mine production of Ontario, 1914. Canadian Mining Journal 36: 186–189, 1915.
— The minerals of Canada. Industrial Canada 5: 703–704, 1905.
— Mining in Ontario, 1911. Canadian Mining Journal 33: 56–58, 1912; 34: 746–759, 1913; 56: 52–57, 1935.
— The mining industry of Ontario. Canadian Mining Journal 44: 619–621, 1923.
— Ontario in 1910. Canadian Mining Journal 32: 11–13, 1911.
— Ontario nickel mines. Canadian Mining Journal 37: 124, 1916.
— Ontario's estimated output, 1907. Canadian Mining Journal 29: 654, 1908.
— The year in Ontario. Canadian Mining Journal 31: 47–50, 1910; 34: 45–46, 1913; 44: 8–9, 1923.
Gilbert, M   C
   Lake Shore gold mine. Canadian Geographical Journal 17: 44–57, 1938.
Globe, A   P
   Concentrating methods at the McKinley – Darragh mine, Cobalt, Ontario. Canadian Mining Journal 32: 438–440, 1911.
Godson, T   E
   The Hollinger fire inquiry; Report of the Commission. Canadian Mining Journal 49: 878–880, 1928.
— The Hollinger fire; part 1 of the Report of the Commissioner appointed by the Ontario government. Canadian Mining Journal 49: 464–468, 1928.
— Ontario mining laws. Canadian Mining Journal 45: 573–574, 1924.

— A short summary of the mining act of Ontario. Canadian Mining Journal
44: 626, 1923.
Gold and silver mining in northern Ontario. Canadian Mining Journal 35:
298–300, 1914; 42: 10–13, 1921.
Gold in western Ontario. Canadian Mining Review 15: 187–188, 1896.
Gold mines of Kirkland Lake district. Canadian Mining Journal 37: 591–592,
1916.
Gold mines of northern Ontario. Canadian Mining Journal 37: 204–217, 1916.
Gold mining at Kirkland Lake. Canadian Mining Journal 47: 525–534, 1926.
Gold mining in Ontario. Canadian Mining Journal 33: 748, 1912.
Gold mining in Ontario. Canadian Mining Review 14: 164, 219, 1895; 15:
29–30, 1896.
Gold mining in Ontario; operations in the Seine and Lake of the Woods district.
Canadian Mining Review 14: 169–170, 1895.
Gold mining in Ontario; the Lake Harold mine. Canadian Mining Review 15:
37–38, 1896.
Golden jubilee of a great silver camp. Canadian Mining Journal 74(no. 8):
47–52, 1953.
Cobalt, Ontario.
Goodwin, W   L
The Helen iron district. Canadian Mining Journal 32: 600–604, 1911.
— The new silver district. Queen's Quarterly 13: 154–159, 1905/1906.
Goodwin, W   M
Notes on prospecting in Ontario. Canadian Mining Journal 31: 177–178,
1910.
Gorman, W   J
Steep Rock iron mine. Canadian Geographical Journal 25: 246–262, 1942.
Gould, E   C
Northeastern Ontario: its organization and outlook. Monetary Times
128(5): 64, 66, 70, 1960.
Graham, S   N
The McIntyre Mine and Mill, Porcupine. Canadian Mining Journal 33:
233–235, 1912.
Gratifying progress in Ontario. Canadian Mining Review 20: 256, 1901.
Metalliferous mines.
Gray, Alexander.
Canada's nickel industry. Canadian Mining Journal 34: 613–617, 647–650,
678–680, 1913.
— Hollinger nearing 1,000,000 tons; what Hollinger 1921 operations look like
and what is expected in 1922. Canadian Mining Journal 42: 978–980, 1921.
— How London views Cobalt. Canadian Mining Journal 28(no. 13): 335–336,
1907.
Greer, W   L   C
The Fort William water supply 1905–1909. Thunder Bay Historical
Museum Society. Papers and Records 2: 1–3, 1974.

Griffin, Selwyn P
    Fishing in Ontario. Canadian Forum 10: 324–328, 1930.
Gwillim, J   C
    Copper ores of the Sudbury – Soo district. Canadian Mining Journal 29:
    680–681, 1908.
Haight, H   V
    Steam-driven air compressors in Cobalt. Canadian Mining Journal 31:
    209–210, 1910.
Haileybury Mining Institute. Canadian Mining Journal 65: 859–860, 1944.
Hair, C   H
    Infection of injuries to accidents in the mining industry of Ontario.
    Canadian Mining Journal 61: 376–378, 1940.
Hall, Albert E
    A Sudbury ore chute. Canadian Mining Journal 37: 117–118, 1916.
Hall, Oliver.
    Mining at Noranda. Canadian Institute of Mining and Metallurgy.
    Transactions 40: 141–164, 1937.
Hancock, H   Sydney, Jr.
    Mining engineering in connection with Fort William's water supply.
    Canadian Mining Journal 31: 330–334, 1910.
Harding, W   D
    Prospecting classes; Ontario Department of Mines. Canadian Mining
    Journal 71(no. 10): 179–182, 1950.
Hardman, John E.
    The gold fields of Ontario. Canadian Mining Review 17: 156–163, 184–190,
    1898.
— A new mineral area in Ontario. Canadian Mining Review 24: 95–98,
    157–158, 1905.
Hassan, A   A
    Preliminary notes on geology of the Porcupine district of Canada. Canadian
    Mining Journal 31: 561–562, 1910.
Hatch, Hamlin Brooks.
    The porcupine gold district. Canadian Mining Journal 31: 306–308, 1910.
— Summer route to the Porcupine. Canadian Mining Journal 31: 327–329,
    1910.
Haultain, H   E   T
    Corundum at Craigmont. Canadian Mining Journal 28(no. 12): 291–296,
    1907.
— The Larder Lake district. Canadian Mining Journal 29(no. 16): 395–396,
    1908.
Hawley, John R   and Kim H   Shikaze.
    The problem of acid mine drainage in Ontario. Canadian Mining Journal
    92(no. 6): 82–84, 1971.
Hay, A   M
    The new Porcupine gold fields. Canadian Mining Journal 31: 53–56, 1910.
The Helen and Victoria mines. Industrial Canada 51(no. 9): 62–63, 65, 1951.

Hellens, A   D
    Recent developments in the Cobalt area. Canadian Mining Journal 73(no.
    6): 73–78, 1952.
Hendry, W
    Non-fatal hoisting accidents in Ontario mines 1965–69. Canadian Mining
    Journal 91(no. 9): 68–73, 1970.
Herapath, Theodora.
    Buried treasure. Canadian Mining Journal 87(no. 11): 63–64, 1966.
    Historical account of efforts to locate oil in southern Ontario.
Herridge, A   J
    The development of forestry policy. Ontario Economic Review 2: no. 4,
    1964.
Hille, F
    A few remarks on some of the gold deposits of Ontario. Canadian Mining
    Journal 33: 332–333, 1912.
— Recent progress in the mineral industry in the Thunder Bay and Rainy
    River districts. Canadian Mining Journal 30: 114–116, 1909.
— The western Ontario gold fields and their genesis. Canadian Mining Review
    16: 153–158, 1897.
Hilyard, H   A
    The nickel regions of Canada. Canadian Magazine of Politics, Science, Art
    and Literature 1: 305–313, 1893.
Hipel, N   O   (comp.).
    The history and status of forestry in Ontario. Canadian Geographical
    Journal 25: 110–145, 1942.
Hodgson, R   T
    An exploration of the corundum lands of Ontario. Queen's Quarterly 6:
    293–297, 1898/1899.
Hogg, Nelson.
    Rush Lake gold mines; preliminary report on Keith township property.
    Canadian Mining Journal 67: 1109–1112, 1946.
Hollinger Gold Mines Limited annual report. Canadian Mining Journal 34:
    241–250, 1913; 35: 121–126, 1914; 36: 113–122, 1935.
Hollinger merger announced. Canadian Mining Journal 37: 236–237, 1916.
The Hollinger Mill. Canadian Mining Journal 33: 230–231, 1912.
Hollinger Reserve mines of Porcupine. Canadian Mining Journal 32: 804–806,
    1911.
Hopper, C   H
    The engineer and the diamond drill in northern Ontario. Canadian Institute
    of Mining and Metallurgy. Transactions 46: 480–505, 1943.
Hopkins, Percy E
    The Kowkash gold area. Canadian Mining Journal 36: 583–584, 1915; 37:
    181–184, 1916.
— Larder Lake gold area. Canadian Mining Journal 40: 68–71, 1919.
— A recent discovery in northern Ontario. Canadian Mining Journal 39:
    56–57, 1918.

Hore, Reginald E
    Amalgamation and cyanidation of Cobalt silver ores. Canadian Mining
    Journal 34: 568–572, 1913.
— Characters on the Cobalt silver ores. Canadian Mining Journal 33: 850–853,
    1912.
— Concentration of Cobalt silver ores. Canadian Mining Journal 34: 402–406,
    1913.
— The Errington lead-zinc copper mine. Canadian Mining Journal 50: 26–27,
    1929.
— Gold mining in northern Ontario. Canadian Mining Journal 42: 552–564,
    1921.
— Gold mining in Ontario; a plea for recognition of a partnership of interest.
    Canadian Mining Journal 42: 274–275, 1921.
— Kirkland Lake gold deposits. Canadian Mining Journal 34: 424–431, 1913.
— Magmatic origin of Sudbury nickel-copper deposits. Canadian Mining
    Journal 34: 437–441, 1913.
— Nipissing picking and jigging plant, Cobalt, Ontario. Canadian Mining
    Journal 34: 363–365, 1913.
— Opening a new northern empire. Canadian Mining Journal 48: 943–945,
    1927.
    Red Lake, Ontario.
— Ores and rocks of the Cobalt region. Canadian Mining Journal 29(no. 13):
    300–301, 1908.
— Porcupine gold deposits. Canadian Mining Journal 31: 649–656, 1910.
— Porcupine goldfield in winter. Canadian Mining Journal 32: 82–86, 1911.
— The Porcupine trail. Canadian Mining Journal 31: 617–622, 1910.
— Tough–Oakes gold mine, Kirkland Lake, Ontario. Canadian Mining
    Journal 35: 259–263, 1914.
How to develop new Ontario; a graphic description of the climate and resources
    of the great undeveloped territory lying between Quebec and Manitoba.
    Industrial Canada 3: 485–486, 1903.
Howard, Frances L
    The lumbermen of the Ottawa valley. Women's Canadian Historical Society
    of Ottawa. Transactions 3: 22–26, 1910.
Howe, C   D
    Forest management in Ontario. Engineering Journal 20: 45–50, 1937.
Hubbell, A   H
    Sudbury stepping up production. Engineering and Mining Journal 137:
    453–459, 1936.
Hughes, Benjamin.
    Gold mining at Porcupine and Kirkland Lake, Ontario. Canadian Mining
    Journal 35: 635–636, 1914.
— Northern Ontario – the land of promise. Canadian Mining Journal 33:
    150–151, 1912.

Hughes, James M
    Ontario's 1970 Mining Amendment Act. Canadian Mining Journal 92(no.
    9): 36–40, 1971.
Hunter, W   D   G
    The development of the Canadian uranium industry: an experiment in
    public enterprise. Canadian Journal of Economics and Political Science 28:
    329–352, 1962.
Huntoon, Louis W
    Character of ore deposit and probable milling methods at Porcupine.
    Canadian Mining Journal 32: 811–814, 1911.
Hurst, M   E
    Iron in Ontario. Canadian Mining Journal 71(no. 10): 144–151, 1950.
Huston, C   C
    Gold in Ontario. Canadian Mining Journal 71(no. 10): 116–128, 1950.
Ignatieff, N.
— Story of McIntyre. Canadian Geographical Journal 14: 506–517, 1937.
Interesting case to mine owners – Adams V. Culligan – Howe V. Culligan –
    Judgement given by Chief Justice Falconbridge at Toronto, January, 1902.
    Canadian Mining Review 21: 39, 1902.
International Geological Congress; Sudbury – Cobalt – Porcupine excursion.
    Canadian Mining Journal 34: 504–509, 535–541, 1913.
The International Nickel Co. of Canada Ltd. Canadian Mining Journal 42:
    909–911, 1921.
International Nickel Company's good record. Canadian Mining Journal 47:
    611–612, 1926.
International Nickel's new laboratory. Industrial Canada 38(no. 9): 66–67,
    1938.
Iron ores produced by Moose Mountain, Ltd., Ontario. Canadian Mining
    Journal 36: 682, 1915.
Jacobs, E
    The Canadian Mining Institute Porcupine trip. Canadian Mining Journal
    33: 219–222, 1912.
James, Tennyson D
    Exploring in the Abitibi region. Ontario Agricultural College Review 16(4):
    16–22, 1904.
James, V   A
    The Preston East Dome Mine. Canadian Mining Journal 62: 503–506,
    1941.
Jessup, Britt.
    Northeastern Ontario – rich past – booming present – glorious future.
    Monetary Times 128(5): 60–62, 1960.
Jewett, G   A
    Exploration in northwestern Ontario. Canadian Mining Journal 95(no. 4):
    20–23, 1974.

Johnston, James.
Cyaniding silver ores at Nipissing Mine, Cobalt. Canadian Mining Journal 35: 99–101, 1914.
Jones, A   R   R
Thomas W. Gibson; a brief biography of the man who is the guide, philosopher, and friend of mining in Ontario. Canadian Mining Journal 50: 766–767, 1929.
Jordon, F   A
Moose Mountain iron mine. Canadian Mining Journal 33: 807–810, 1912.
Kelly, Kenneth.
The changing attitude of farmers to forest in nineteenth century Ontario. Ontario Geography 8: 64–77, 1974.
Kelsey, Arthur E
With the Mining Congress. Canadian Mining Journal 48: 820–822, 1927.
Kennedy, Howard.
Ontario Royal Commission on Forestry. Industrial Canada 48(no. 5): 70–72, 1947.
Kerr, D   G
Air compression by water power: the installation at the Belmont gold mine. Canadian Mining Review 22: 50–55, 1903.
— Corundum in Ontario. Canadian Mining Review 27: 152–157, 1906.
Kerr, H   L
Larder Lake. Canadian Mining Journal 29(no. 19): 489–490, 1908.
Kerr Lake Mining Company annual report. Canadian Mining Journal 24: 639–642, 1913; 35: 713–716, 1914; 36: 696–699, 1915.
Kirkgaard, J   P
The Harris system of pumping by compressed air, as applied to the Deloro Mine. Canadian Mining Review 21: 93–95, 1902.
Knight, Cyril W
Prospecting in Ontario – historical sketch. Canadian Mining Journal 71(no. 10): 76–87, 1950.
— Roasting of the argentiferous cobalt-nickel arsenides of Temiskaming, Ontario, Canada. Canadian Mining Journal 28(no. 4): 54, 1907.
Knight, G   and T   S   Cochrane.
Mines Branch Dust Laboratory. Canadian Mining Journal 88(no. 10): 79–82, 1967.
Kon, William E
Boom town into company town: the story of Sudbury. New Frontier 1(7): 6–9, 1936.
Lamble, B   C
The sampling and assaying of molybdenum ores; as practiced by the Orillia Molybdenum Company, Ltd., Orillia, Canada. Canadian Mining Journal 37: 185–186, 1916.
Lang, A   H
Discovery and benefits of the Marmora iron deposit. Canadian Mining Journal 91(no. 8): 47–49, 1970.

A Larder Lake wild cat. Canadian Mining Journal 28(no. 16): 420, 1907.
Large increase in Ontario's metal production. Canadian Mining Journal 37:
    555–556, 1916.
Leach, Norman L
    The Moose Mountain iron range, with special reference to the properties of
    Moose Mountain, Limited. Canadian Mining Journal 29(no. 6): 76–77,
    1908.
Leduc, Paul.
    Mining industry in Ontario. Royal Canadian Institute. Proceedings s.3A, 2:
    7–25, 1937.
Lees, Richard.
    Forestry problems in Ontario. Queen's Quarterly 11: 109–113, 1903/1904.
Lee–Whiting, Brenda B
    The Alligator – unique Canadian boat. Canadian Geographical Journal 76:
    30–33, 1968.
— The Craigmont corundum boom, 1900–13. Canadian Geographical Journal
    90(no. 4): 22–29, 1975.
Leslie, A   P
    DDT in Ontario's forests, Canadian Geographical Journal 31: 186–199,
    1945.
— Forest research in Ontario. Canadian Geographical Journal 44: 70–91,
    1952.
— Some historical aspects of forestry in Ontario. Forestry Chronicle 26:
    243–250, 1950.
Limestones of Ontario. Canadian Mining Review 24: 102–105, 109, 1905.
List of Canadian operating mining companies. Canadian Mining Journal
    29(no. 17): 437–444, 1908.
Loney, E   D
    The discovery of the McIntyre and Hollinger mines; the story of the famous
    prospectors of northern Ontario. Canadian Mining Journal 53: 21–26, 1932.
— The early history of Errington Mine. Canadian Mining Journal 48:
    582–583, 1927.
— The nickel industry – some further history. Canadian Mining Journal 50:
    50–52, 1929.
— A promising future for Sudbury district. Canadian Mining Journal 48:
    497–498, 1927.
— Prospecting for copper in Ontario. Canadian Mining Journal 48: 221–223,
    1927.
— A review of the Porcupine district. Canadian Mining Journal 49: 344–346,
    1928.
— Some account of the early history of the nickel industry, Canadian Mining
    Journal 49: 1004–1006, 1928.
Loring, Frank C
    The widening of the Cobalt silver belt. Canadian Mining Journal 30:
    237–238, 1909.

Losee, W   H
    A brief history of Canadian mining. Canadian Mining Journal 60: 643–671,
    1939.
Lower, A   R   M
    The assault on the Laurentian barrier, 1850–1870. Canadian Historical
    Review 10: 294–307, 1929.
— Lumberjack's River. Queen's Quarterly 60: 24–40, 1953.
— Report of the Ontario Royal Commission on Forestry. Canadian Journal of
    Economics and Political Science 14: 507–510, 1948.
The Lucky Cross mines – Swastika. Canadian Mining Journal 33: 20–22, 1912.
Luthi, Anna.
    The forest ranger. Sylva 11 (2): 4–12, 1955.
Lyall, K   D   and R   O   Tervo.
    Rock breakage research at the Mines Branch Elliot Lake Laboratory .
    Canadian Mining Journal 89(no. 11): 69–71, 1968.
McAskill, J   I
    Mining law – its development and application in Ontario. Canadian Mining
    Journal 57: 309–315, 1936.
McClelland, W   R
    Nickel – an expanding Canadian industry. Canadian Mining Journal 74
    (no. 12): 60–63, 1953.
McCrea, Charles.
    Fifty years of mining in Ontario. Canadian Mining Journal 50 (Fiftieth
    Anniversary Number): 74–79, 158–162, 1929.
— Gold mining industry in Ontario. Canadian Mining Journal 55: 55–57,
    1934.
— Mineral wealth of Ontario. Canadian Mining Journal 47: 73–74, 1926.
— Mining in Ontario. Canadian Mining Journal 46: 738, 1925.
    From *Financial Times*.
— The mining industry of Ontario. Industrial Canada 32(no. 2) : 41–44, 54,
    1931.
— Mining investments in Ontario. Canadian Mining Journal 47: 308–309,
    1926.
— Willet Green Miller. Canadian Mining Journal 47: 1107–1110, 1926.
McCrodan, P   B
    Underground fire at McIntyre Porcupine Mines Limited. Canadian Mining
    Journal 86(no. 9): 66–75, 1965.
McCulloch, R
    Uranium and nuclear energy in Ontario. Ontario Economic Review 1: no.
    5, 1963.
McDermott, Walter.
    The Silver Islet vein, Lake Superior. Canadian Mining Journal 30: 135–138,
    1909.
Macdonald, C   E
    Canada's nickel – its history and uses. Industrial Canada 35(no. 11): 31–34,
    1935.

McDonald, J   A
Dominion and Ontario regulations for the disposal of mining claims,
compared. Canadian Mining Journal 36: 74–75, 1915.
— The recent gold discovery at Kowkash, northern Ontario. Canadian Mining
Journal 36: 628, 1915.
— The staking out of working permits in Ontario. Canadian Mining Journal
36: 7, 1915.
MacDonald, John A
A plan for reforestation relief works projects in southern Ontario. Forestry
Chronicle 11(2): 133–153, 1935.
MacDougall, G   A
Algonquin Park. Forestry Chronicle 12: 85–91, 1936.
MacGregor, Alpine R
Early Porcupine history. Canadian Mining Journal 49: 721–723, 1928.
— Hermit of the wilds. Canadian Mining Journal 74(no. 1): 64–66,.1953.
Adolph Liebault, district of Patricia, Ontario.
— A pioneer prospector; an intimate sketch. Canadian Mining Journal 58:
18–22, 1937.
J. Russell Cryderman, northwestern Ontario.
MacGregor, Bob.
Trail breakers of Canada's golden pre-cambria; men who "cracked open the
North" but who failed to make the "Big Stake". Canadian Mining Journal
67: 13–19, 1946.
McGregor, W   Grant.
Bemocked of destiny. Bruce County Historical Society. Yearbook 9–10,
1971.
Aeneas McCharles, Huron township, developed the North Star Nickel Mine
southwest of Sudbury. Later became the International Nickel Company.
McGuire, B   J   and H   E   Freeman.
Gold mining in northern Ontario. Canadian Geographical Journal 44:
252–265, 1952.
— Wealth from the Canadian Shield. Canadian Geographical Journal 38:
198–227, 1949.
McInnes, W
The gold fields of Ontario. Canadian Mining Review 16: 172–173, 1897.
McIntyre–Porcupine Mines, Ltd. annual report. Canadian Mining Journal 36:
475–478, 1915.
McKay, Robert.
Discovery and production; some contrasts between the law of discovery and
production in England and in Ontario. Canada Law Journal 39: 762–779,
1903.
Mackellar, Peter.
The gold bearing veins of Bag Bay near Lake of the Woods. Canadian
Mining Review 18: 144–147, 1899.
— The Otter Head tin swindle. Thunder Bay Historical Society. Papers 4:
11–13, 1912/1913.

— The Little Pic copper mine. Thunder Bay Historical Society. Papers 14: 6–10, 1923.

— The Little Pic silver mine. Thunder Bay Historical Society. Papers 14: 4–5, 1923.

The McKinley–Darragh–Savage mines of Cobalt, Limited; abstract of general manager P.A. Robbins report for the year 1909. Canadian Mining Journal 31: 292–298, 337–343, 1910.

McLaren, D   C

The Eau Claire mica fields; a search for a lost mine. Canadian Mining Journal 66: 297–299, 1945.

— Madsen Red Lake gold mines. Canadian Mining Journal 68: 791–808, 1947.

— Milling cobalt ore at Silanco; benefication of a complex cobalt ore. Canadian Mining Journal 66: 141–145, 1945.

— The Onakawana lignite development; coal shortage hastens commercial development. Canadian Mining Journal 67: 1013–1022, 1946.

— Pickle Crow gold mines; community life maintained as permanent feature of camp. Canadian Mining Journal 65: 755–765, 1944.

— The Young–Davidson Mine; simplicity and regularity outstanding feature of mining system. Canadian Mining Journal 67: 5–12, 1946.

MacLean, John.

The town that rocked the oil cradle. Imperial Oil Review 39(3): 6–10, 1955.

MacLeod, G   W

The Goudreau gold area. Canadian Mining Journal 44: 295–297, 1923.

MacLeod, John.

The 1955 accident record. Canadian Mining Journal 77(no. 9): 99–100, 1956.

McMartin, John. Canadian Mining Journal 39: 175, 1918.

McMillan, J   G

Early development of Ontario mining; interesting side-lights on the rugged prospectors of Sudbury. Canadian Mining Journal 64: 561–564, 1943.

— Early mining days in the Kirkland–Larder Lake district. Canadian Mining Journal 65: 296–299, 1944.

McNaught, W   K

Ontario's true national policy in regard to white and black coal. Industrial Canada 11: 131–135, 1910.

McNulty, Clara Wilson.

The Provincial Institute of Mining, Haileybury, Ontario. Canadian Mining Journal 72(no. 1): 59–61, 1951.

McPhail, G   G

Operation stench gas what's that smell?; thirty years of mine rescue training in Ontario. Canadian Mining Journal 82(no. 9): 84–89, 1961.

McPherson, William Batten.

Notes on mining laws in Canada. Canadian Mining Journal 49: 740–744, 1928.

McRae, J   A

A comparison of gold and silver production in Ontario; gold output likely to exceed value of silver output by 1920. Canadian Mining Journal 40: 956, 1919.
— General description of status of the mining industry of Kirkland Lake. Canadian Mining Journal 42: 260–261, 1921.
— The historical achievements of Cobalt and Porcupine. Canadian Mining Journal 42: 725, 1921.
— A historical review of the silver and gold production of northern Ontario. Canadian Mining Journal 41: 6–7, 1920.
— The history and romance of oldest mine in Canada. Canadian Mining Journal 42: 665–667, 1921.
Wright Mine, Lake Temiskaming.
— The Kirkland Lake Proprietary, 1919, Ltd. Canadian Mining Journal 41: 929–930, 1920.
— The Lightning River Gold Mines, Ltd. Canadian Mining Journal 41: 842–843, 1920.
— McIntyre–Porcupine Mines, Ltd.; an up-to-date analysis of a great gold mine. Canadian Mining Journal 51: 973, 976, 1930.
— The McIntyre Porcupines Ltd.; making strong bid for position of second greatest gold mine in Canada. Canadian Mining Journal 41: 862–863, 1920.
— Metal mining in northern Ontario. Canadian Mining Journal 47: 1189–1190, 1926.
— Mines are not all profitable; ninety percent of earnings in successful northern Ontario mines are paid out in wages and materials. Canadian Mining Journal 40: 419–420, 1919.
— The Nipissing Mining Company. Canadian Mining Journal 41: 483, 1920.
— Northern Ontario gold mines in 1918 produced about $9,168,000, despite handicaps. Canadian Mining Journal 39: 416–417, 1918.
— Ontario mines in 1929. Canadian Mining Journal 51: 4–7, 1930.
— Ontario's mines in 1930; steady expansion in the three great camps of the Province. Canadian Mining Journal 52: 16–19, 1931.
— Pandora financed for mine development; present conditions compared with early history of Ontario mines. Canadian Mining Journal 52: 93–94, 1931.
— The Porcupine power controversy. Canadian Mining Journal 42: 906, 1921.
— Precious metal mining in northern Ontario; gold production will shortly exceed silver output. Canadian Mining Journal 40: 484–485, 1919.
— Present position of the gold mining industry of northern Ontario . Canadian Mining Journal 41: 526, 1920.
— Progress in northern Ontario. Canadian Mining Journal 47: 322–323, 1926.
— Prospecting for coal in northern Ontario. Canadian Mining Journal 47: 512, 1926.
— A review of the Kirkland Lake goldfield; the richest half mile in the world. Canadian Mining Journal 50: 476–478, 1929.
— A review of mining in Ontario during 1928. Canadian Mining Journal 49: 1074–1077, 1928.

— A review of the gold and silver production of northern Ontario during the first half of 1920. Canadian Mining Journal 41: 565–566, 1920.

— A review of the productive status of the gold mines of northern Ontario. Canadian Mining Journal 40: 854, 1919.

— The rise of the Hollinger mines. Canadian Mining Journal 42: 49–50, 1921.

— Silver mining in Ontario. Canadian Mining Journal 48: 11, 1927.

— The Sudbury and Sault Ste. Marie areas. Canadian Mining Journal 48: 515, 1927.

— The treasure vault of Ontario. Canadian Mining Journal 41: 419–420, 1920.

— The wealth of the hinterland of Ontario. Canadian Mining Journal 40: 147–148, 1919.

The magnetite mines of the Mineral Range Iron Mining Company, Limited, at Bessemer, Hastings county, Ontario. Canadian Mining Journal 28(no. 17): 451–453, 1907.

Malcolm, Wyatt.
The mining and metallurgical industries; section 1 – mining industry. Industrial Canada 19 (no. 9): 156–160, 1919.

Mallory, Enid Swerdfeger.
Ottawa lumber era. Canadian Geographical Journal 68: 60–73, 1964.

Malone, Colleen.
Sault Ste. Marie area attractive to investors. Monetary Times 129(10): 62, 67, 1961.

Mamen, C
From taconite to pellets at the Adams Mine. Canadian Mining Journal 86(no. 5): 65–71, 1965.

— Goderich Mine goes into production. Canadian Mining Journal 80(no. 12): 59–63, 1959.

— An iron tonic for Red Lake; Stelco's Griffith Mine. Canadian Mining Journal 89(no. 11): 48–52, 1968.

— Ontario annual review; new record $640,915,058; copper makes biggest gain; nickel and iron also strong. Canadian Mining Journal 78(no. 2): 103–107, 1957.

Marsh, W   H   C
For investors opportunity knocks many times and places in northeastern regions of Ontario. Monetary Times 129(10): 40–42, 44, 1961.

Memorandum presented on forestry; views of the Association are laid before the Ontario Royal Commission on Forestry. Industrial Canada 47(no. 9): 148–149, 1947.

Metal production in Ontario. Canadian Mining Journal 36: 745, 1915.

Mickle, G   R
House cleaning applied to mineral lands in Ontario. Canadian Mining Journal 31: 67, 1910.

— The Kent gas field. Canadian Mining Journal 31: 623–626, 1910.

— Probable effect of the acreage tax on mining lands in Ontario. Canadian Mining Journal 30: 195–197, 1909.

Mikado Gold Mining Company. Canadian Mining Review 20: 168, 1901.

Miller, Willet G
  Clay and the clay industry in Ontario. Canadian Mining Review 28: 48–49,
    1907.
— Cobalt and adjacent areas. Canadian Mining Journal 34: 87–90, 1913.
— The Cobalt area. Canadian Mining Journal 34: 546–548, 574–576, 1913.
— Cobalt-nickel arsenides and silver in Ontario. Canadian Mining Review 22:
    244–249, 1903.
— Eastern Ontario: a region of varied mining industries. Canadian Mining
    Review 21: 116–122, 1902.
— The iron ore fields of Ontario. Canadian Mining Review 20: 151–158, 1901.
— Mines and mining at Cobalt. Canadian Mining Journal 28(no. 3): 7–11,
    1907.
— Topaz, tins and granites in Ontario. Canadian Mining Journal 32: 582–583,
    1911.
— Undeveloped mineral resources of Ontario. Canadian Mining Review 23:
    110–114, 1904.
Miller, Willet G   and Cyril W   Knight.
  Revision of pre-Cambrian classification in Ontario. Canadian Mining
    Journal 36: 265–266, 1915.
Mills, S   Dillon.
  Some recent rock movements in the Laurentian and Huronian areas.
    Canadian Mining Review 23: 174–177, 1904.
Milner, James B
  The Ontario Water Resources Commission Act, 1956. University of Toronto
    Law Journal 12: 100–102, 1957.
The Mine Centre mining district, Ontario. Canadian Mining Journal 33:
    584–585, 1912.
Mineral production of Ontario. Canadian Mining Journal 32: 185–186, 1911;
    33: 191, 1912; 34:178–179, 589, 1913; 35: 196–198, 1914; 36: 330, 598,
    1915; 37: 110, 1916; 38: 100–101, 1917; 39: 112–114, 1918; 41: 211,
    1039–1040, 1920; 45: 581–583, 1924.
Mineral rights in Ontario. Canadian Mining Journal 75(no. 5): 71, 1954.
Minerals of Hastings county, Ontario. Canadian Mining Journal 51: 845–846,
    1930.
Mining accidents in Ontario in 1914. Canadian Mining Journal 36: 277–278,
    1915.
Mining in Ontario. Canadian Mining Journal 35: 39, 1914; 36: 39, 1915; 37:
    37–38, 1916.
Mining in Ontario. Canadian Mining Review 14: 216, 1895; 15: 115, 1896; 16:
    2–4, 1897; 17: 181–182, 1898; 18: 128–130, 1899.
Mining in Ontario; county of Frontenac and Lake of the Woods. Canadian
    Mining Review 18: 275–276, 301, 1899.
Mining in the Parry Sound district. Canadian Mining Review 19: 266, 1900.
Mining Institute; eastern Ontario and the eastern townships organize district
    branches. Canadian Mining Review 21: 164–166, 1902.

Mining progress in Ontario. Canadian Mining Review 20: 21–22, 103, 170, 1901; 21: 241–242, 1902.

Mining prosperity in Ontario. Canadian Mining Review 21: 48–49, 1902.

Moddle, D   A

Assaying in Ontario. Canadian Mining Journal 71(no. 10): 176–178, 1950.

Modern operation and welfare. Canadian Mining Journal 72(no. 4): 66–67, 1951.

Kerr–Addison Mine.

Moore, E   S

The Sturgeon Lake gold field. Canadian Mining Journal 32: 701–707, 1911.

Moore, Lloyd J

Developments in the Red Lake gold area. Canadian Mining Journal 47: 770–772, 1926.

Moore, Phil H

A suggestion about the treatment of Porcupine ores. Canadian Mining Journal 32: 560–562, 1911.

More nickel insanity. Canadian Mining Review 20: 28–29, 1901.

Morrison, R   G   K

Report on rockburst situation in Ontario mines. Canadian Mining and Metallurgical Bulletin 35: 225–272, 1942.

The Moss gold mine; story of the first substantial gold discovery in Ontario sixty years ago which is now on the point of production. Canadian Mining Journal 52: 446–448, 1931.

Motter, W   D   B   , Jr.

The Canada Iron Mines, Limited. Canadian Mining Journal 34: 395–399, 1913.

The Murray Mine. Canadian Mining Journal 38: 177, 1917.

The Natural Gas Conservation Act of Ontario. Canadian Mining Journal 42: 273, 1921.

The New Golden Twins, Limited. Canadian Mining Review 17: 146–148, 1898.

New Golden Twins (Ontario) swindle; collapse of the action for libel against the "Critic" arising out of the "Review's" expose. Canadian Mining Review 18: 10–11, 1899.

New mine rescue stations in northwestern Ontario. Canadian Mining Journal 65: 552, 1944.

The new Ontario Mining Act. Canadian Mining Review 19: 61–62, 1900.

The new trail to Gowganda. Canadian Mining Journal 30: 139–141, 1909.

Newman, Frank S

Development of reforestation in Ontario. Royal Canadian Institute. Proceedings s.3A, 7: 37–38, 1942–1943.

Newton–White, E

Trouble in the woods. Canadian Forum 14: 383–384, 1934.

Nichol, William.

Recent discoveries of cobalt-nickel ores in new Ontario. Queen's Quarterly 11: 313–317, 1903/1904.

The nickel agitation. Canadian Mining Review 19: 65–67, 1900.

Nickel legislation; a review of the grounds upon which the Dominion
    government was asked to disallow the Ontario Mines Act. Canadian Mining
    Review 20: 104–107, 1901.
Nickel legislation; strong delegation of Canadian mining men present to
    Dominion cabinet a strong plea for disallowance of Ontario act. Canadian
    Mining Review 20: 88–89, 1901.
Nipissing Mining Company, Limited, annual report. Canadian Mining Journal
    35: 295–297, 1914; 36: 280–283, 1915.
Northern Ontario mines in 1916. Canadian Mining Journal 38: 40–41, 1917.
    From Gibson's *Fortnightly Review*.
Notes concerning northern Ontario. Canadian Mining Review 23: 171–172,
    1904.
Notes from La Seine, Ontario. Canadian Mining Review 15: 45, 1896.
Nova Scotia coal for Ontario. Industrial Canada 3: 312–313, 1903.
O'Connor, Charles H
    Mineral deposits north of Sault Ste. Marie, Ontario. Canadian Mining
    Journal 36: 297–300, 1915.
O'Connor, J   J
    Government assistance required for Ontario iron-ore mining. Canadian
    Mining Journal 41: 404–406, 1920.
— Mining activities in western Ontario. Canadian Mining Journal 47: 266,
    1926.
— The Rainy Lake gold area, Ontario. Canadian Mining Journal 41: 85–86,
    1920.
— Silver mine to re-open near Port Arthur. Canadian Mining Journal 41:
    1043, 1920.
Official conference on Ontario iron ore. Canadian Mining Journal 43: 446–448,
    1922.
Oil fields of Ontario. Industrial Canada 7: 356, 1906.
Oko, M   U
    Monitoring waste water quality at Falconbridge's Sudbury operation.
    Canadian Mining Journal 92(no. 6): 72–76, 1971.
On the discoveries of cobalt-silver ores in Ontario. Canadian Mining Review
    24: 69–70, 72–75, 1905.
On the trail to Red Lake. Canadian Mining Journal 47: 411–412, 1926.
One view of Porcupine. Canadian Mining Journal 32: 284–285, 1911.
Ontario. Canadian Mining Journal 86(no. 4): 85–87, 1965.
    Mineral industry review.
Ontario and the iron trade. Canadian Mining Review 22: 123–124, 1903.
Ontario feldspar. Canadian Mining Journal 28(no. 7): 153, 1907.
Ontario forestry report. [editorial] Canadian Forum 27: 147–148, 1947.
Ontario geological surveys. Canadian Mining Journal 74(no. 12): 55, 1953.
Ontario gold mining committee interim report – March 1955. Canadian Mining
    Journal 76(no. 5): 66–67, 1955.
Ontario government gold concessions. Canadian Mining Review 16: 270–271,
    1897.

Ontario iron ore bounty to be doubled. Canadian Mining Journal 45: 1173, 1924.

The Ontario mineral industry in 1899. Canadian Mining Review 18: 303–305, 1899.

Ontario mineral output first quarter of 1910. Canadian Mining Journal 31: 399, 1910.

Ontario mineral production. Canadian Mining Journal 79(no. 12): 61, 1958.

Ontario mineral production in first quarter of 1914. Canadian Mining Journal 35: 458–459, 1914.

The Ontario Mines Act. Canadian Mining Review 19: 101–102; 109–111, 1900.

The Ontario Mines Act: its unconstitutionality. Canadian Mining Review 19: 102–104, 1900.

The Ontario mines report for 1896. Canadian Mining Review 16: 337–338, 1896.

The Ontario mining deal. Canadian Mining Review 16: 102–103, 1896.

Ontario mining in 1954. Canadian Mining Journal 76(no. 4): 71, 1955.

Ontario Mining Institute; holds a successful meeting at Rat Portage – numerous resolutions affecting the mineral industry adopted. Canadian Mining Review 15: 199–200, 1896.

Ontario mining intelligence. Canadian Mining Review 24: 180, 1905.

Ontario mining legislation. Canadian Mining Journal 28(no. 3): 11–13, 1907.

Ontario Mining Tax Act. Canadian Mining Journal 41: 959, 1920.

Ontario Nickel Commission. Canadian Mining Journal 36: 468–470, 1915.

Ontario Nickel Commission's Report. Canadian Mining Journal 38: 145, 1917.

Ontario production of metals during first nine months of 1913. Canadian Mining Journal 34: 759–760, 1913.

Ontario's fuel supply. Canadian Mining Journal 47: 487, 1926.

Ontario's gold mining industry expanding. Canadian Mining Journal 38: 478–479, 1917.

Ontario's growing mineral industry. Canadian Mining Review 22: 187, 1903.

Ontario's iron ore industry. Canadian Chemistry and Metallurgy 21: 90–91, 1937.

Ontario's lumber cut. Industrial Canada 12: 602, 1911.

Ontario's metal production. Canadian Mining Journal 37: 290, 467, 1916.

Ontario's mineral production. Canadian Mining Journal 32: 598–599, 1911.

Ontario's minerals. Canadian Mining Review 22: 188–189, 1903.

Opening of the Dome Mine, Porcupine. Canadian Mining Journal 33: 263–264, 1912.

The operations and plants of International Nickel Company of Canada Limited. Canadian Mining Journal 58: 581–748, 1937; 67: 307–554, 1946.

The Ophir decision. Canadian Mining Review 19: 3, 1900.

The Ophir litigation. Canadian Mining Review 18: 305–306, 1899.

Ore shipment sampling in Cobalt. Canadian Mining Journal 32: 617–622, 1911.

Our iron industries in Ontario. Canadian Mining Review 20: 276–277, 1901.

Our mineral exhibit at the Pan-American Exposition. Canadian Mining
    Review 20: 196–200, 1901.
The outlook for mining in northern Ontario. Canadian Mining Journal 40: 171,
    1919.
Parkinson, N   F
    Ontario Mining Association. Canadian Mining Journal 71(no. 10): 88–92,
    1950.
Pearce, Richard.
    The story of Temiskaming's first mining company. Northern Miner annual
    number 22(no. 27): 65, 72, 1936.
Pease, O   Clifford.
    Ontario's new policy for forest protection; the use of a fleet of seaplanes for
    patrolling the forests of northern Ontario adopted – great saving of timber.
    Industrial Canada 25(no. 1): 64c, 1924.
— Patricia – the land of fabled wealth; an account of the conditions governing
    this part of Ontario and the efforts being made to deal with them. Industrial
    Canada 26(no. 7): 42–44, 1925.
Pemberton, R   H   and H   O   Seigel.
    Airborne radioactivity tests – Elliot Lake area, Ontario. Canadian Mining
    Journal 87(no. 10): 81–87, 1966.
Phelps, Edward.
    The Canada Oil Association – an early business combination. Western
    Ontario Historical Notes 19: 31–39, 1963.
The Porcupine mining district. Canadian Mining Journal 32: 340–341, 1911.
Porcupine Vipond Mines, Limited, annual report. Canadian Mining Journal
    36: 349–350, 1915.
The pre-Cambrian geology of southeastern Ontario. Canadian Mining Journal
    35: 541–542, 1914.
Present conditions at Cobalt and Porcupine. Canadian Mining Journal 36:
    231–232, 1915.
Price, S
    Extracts from the report of S. Price, limitation of the hours of labour of
    underground workmen in the mines of Ontario. Canadian Mining Journal
    34: 278–283, 1913.
The projected custom sampling plant – to be erected this year in Cobalt,
    Ontario. Canadian Mining Journal 30: 580–584, 1909.
Proposed reduction plant of the Dome Mines Syndicate, Porcupine, Ontario.
    Canadian Mining Journal 32: 126–127, 1911.
Provincial mineral exhibits at the Canadian National Exhibition . Canadian
    Mining Journal 29(no. 18): 462–467, 1908.
The public policies of International Nickel. Inco Triangle 3(no. 2): 10–11, 1939.
    Reprinted from December 1938 issue of Engineering and Mining Journal.
Public spirit at Central Patricia. Canadian Mining Journal 66: 313, 1945.
Pugh, Donald E
    Ontario's great clay belt hoax. Canadian Geographical Journal 90: 19–24,
    1975.

Pye, E   G
    Current activities and trends in exploration in Ontario. Canadian Mining
    Journal 91(no. 4): 112–117, 1970; 91(no. 5): 56–57, 1970.
—   100 years of mining in Ontario. Canadian Mining Journal 88(no. 4): 85–89,
    1967.
Pyrite mining in Ontario. Canadian Mining Journal 37: 422, 1916.
[R   C   R   ]
    Prominent men in the Canadian mining industry. (1) John E. Hammell.
    Canadian Mining Journal 49: 825–827, 1928.
Ramsay, J   D
    The Maple Mountain mining district of Ontario. Canadian Mining Journal
    30: 526–527, 1909.
Randall, Charles A
    Metallurgy at Tough–Oakes Gold Mines, Limited. Canadian Mining
    Journal 37: 225–229, 1916.
Raymond, R   W
    The Ontario Mines Act. Canadian Mining Review 16: 283–284, 1897.
Rea, T   H
    The Rea Mine, Porcupine. Canadian Mining Journal 33: 16–18, 1912.
Recent developments in the Cobalt district. Canadian Mining Journal 37:
    302–304, 1916.
Recent developments in the Sudbury district. Canadian Mining Journal 37:
    391–392, 1916.
The Red Lake gold area; the assured success of the Howey, coupled with
    promising prospects discovered recently suggest a field of considerable
    importance. Canadian Mining Journal 52: 589–592, 1931.
Red Lake gold fields. Canadian Mining Journal 47: 601–604, 1926.
Regional review. Canadian Mining Journal 92(no. 2): 61–70, 1971; 93(no. 2):
    58–65, 1972; 94(no. 2): 49–52, 1973; 95(no. 2): 44–50, 1974.
Reid, J   A
    Silver in Ontario. Canadian Mining Journal 71(no. 10): 129–133, 1950.
Renewal of mining activity in the Thunder Bay district. Canadian Mining
    Review 27: 128, 1906.
Rennie, James.
    Claims assessment in the province of Ontario. Canadian Mining Journal 31:
    210–211, 1910.
Report of Ontario Nickel Commission. Canadian Mining Journal 38: 168–173,
    1917.
Report of the Ontario Bureau of Mines. Canadian Mining Journal 28(no. 4):
    57, 1907; 29: 618–620, 649–650, 1908; 30: 83, 718–724, 1909.
    Covers the years: 1906–1909.
Restaking of mining claims in Ontario; the Knox case. Canadian Mining
    Journal 40: 384–386, 1919.
Review by provinces. Canadian Mining Journal 90(no. 2): 68–71, 1969; 91(no.
    2): 69–74, 1970.

Review of operations at the Dome Mine, South Porcupine. Canadian Mining
   Journal 34: 37–38, 1913.
Rice, H   R
   Renabie mines; Missinabie's pioneer gold producer. Canadian Mining
   Journal 70(no. 1): 61–67, 1949.
Richards, George C
   A review of silicosis and dust testing in Ontario. Canadian Mining Journal
   60: 121–126, 1939.
Rickard, T   A
   The gold and silver of Ontario. Canadian Mining Journal 65: 688–696,
   1944.
— The nickel of Sudbury. Canadian Mining Journal 63: 785–792, 1942.
— The Silver Islet. Canadian Mining Journal 63: 565–569, 1942.
Roach, A   G
   Retreatment of corundum tailings at Craigmont. Canadian Mining Journal
   68: 563–568, 1947.
Roberts, Hugh M
   Iron mines of Steep Rock Lake, Ontario. Inland Seas 6: 139–143, 1950.
Roberts, Leslie.
   Cities in the bush. 1. Central Patcum Pickle Crow. Canadian Mining
   Journal 58: 540–545, 1937.
— 2. Red Lake revisited. Canadian Mining Journal 58: 795–799, 1937.
Robertson, James A
   Recent geological investigations in the Elliot Lake – Blind River uranium
   area, Ontario. Canadian Mining Journal 88(no. 4): 120–126, 1967.
Rogers, G   R
   The Porcupine fire. Canadian Mining Journal 32: 489–492, 1911.
Rogers, W   R
   Ontario's growing mining industry; abstract of a paper presented at the
   recent Quebec meeting of the Engineering Institute of Canada. Canadian
   Mining Journal 48: 180–181, 1927.
— Production of metals in Ontario. Canadian Mining Journal 55: 58–60, 1934.
Rogers, W   R   and A   C   Young.
   Metal production of Ontario; first nine months 1928. Canadian Mining
   Journal 49: 1010–1013, 1928.
Ross, J   C
   The development of northern Ontario by the mining industry. Canadian
   Mining Journal 34: 727, 1913.
Rowe, R   C
   Brief historical sketch of the Howey Mine. Canadian Mining Journal 55:
   434–437, 1934.
— Cobalt – 1927. Canadian Mining Journal 48: 871, 1927.
— The discovery of Silver Islet; being extracts from the diary of Thomas
   MacFarlane who discovered the Silver Islet Silver Mine in 1868; together
   with a foreword and some notes. Canadian Mining Journal 57: 222–227;
   266–271, 1936.

— The district of Patricia. Canadian Mining Journal 55: 470–474, 1934.
— The Kenty gold prospect; a brief review of Ontario's most promising gold
    prospect. Canadian Mining Journal 54: 49–51, 1933.
— A review of silver mining in Ontario. Canadian Mining Journal 48:
    916–918, 1927.
Safety at Central Patricia. Canadian Mining Journal 70(no. 8): 95, 1949.
The St. Anthony gold mine. Canadian Mining Journal 32: 387–392, 1911.
Sampling of high grade Cobalt silver ores. Canadian Mining Journal 32:
    660–663, 1911.
Sancton, George E
    Methods of concentration at Cobalt, Ontario. Canadian Mining Journal
    29(no. 18): 458–461, 1908.
Saville, Thomas.
    The Red Lake trail. Canadian Mining Journal 47: 484, 1926.
Sclanders, Ian.
    The amazing Jake Englehart. Imperial Oil Review 39(4): 2–7, 1955.
Sergiades, A   O
    Ontario – its mining potential today and tomorrow. Canadian Mining
    Journal 89(no. 5): 74–77, 1968.
Sherk, Florence N
    Peter McKellar. Thunder Bay Historical Society. Papers 18 and 19: 9–10,
    1926/1927, 1927/1928.
Shikaze, K
    Mine tailings dam construction in Ontario. Canadian Mining Journal
    91(no. 6): 49–51, 1970.
Sider, F   E
    Profit and conflict: early lumbering on Lake of the Woods. Sylva 14(5):
    4–12, 1958.
Silicosis in Ontario; Mr. Gillis' charge and Ontario Mining Association's reply.
    Canadian Mining Journal 62: 316–317, 1941.
Silicosis research in Ontario. Canadian Mining Journal 60: 478–481, 1939.
Silver deposits of the Cobalt district. Canadian Mining Journal 37: 291–297,
    1916.
Silver mining in Ontario; an important consolidation of some of the mines of
    Lake Superior. Canadian Mining Review 21: 202–204, 218–219, 1902.
Silvester, G   E
    History of Canadian nickel industry. Industrial Canada 21(no. 7): 132–136,
    1920.
Sinclair, D   G
    The new Temiskaming testing laboratories; new type sampling plant of
    outstanding interest. Canadian Mining Journal 66: 531–540, 1945.
Sinclair, the progress of mining in Ontario in the past ten years. Canadian
    Mining and Metallurgical Bulletin 29: 503–508, 1936.
Smith, Alexander H
    The Porcupine fire. Canadian Mining Journal 32: 487–489, 1911.

Smith, D   E
> Pronto uranium mines from inception to start of shaft sinking operations –
> early history. Canadian Mining Journal 76(no. 10): 67–69, 1955.
Smith, D   E   and D   H   James.
> Mineral exploration of Algoma Central Railway lands. Canadian Mining
> Journal 82(no. 4): 97–98, 1961.
Smith, George H
> Natural gas discovered when petroleum was sought. Welland County
> Historical Society. Papers and Records 2: 105–111, 1926.
Smith, J   R
> Progress of the Red Lake safety group. Canadian Mining Journal 74(no. 9):
> 90–91, 1953.
Smith, J   Burley.
> Description of the Sultana quartz lode and the sinking of the Burley shaft in
> Bald Indian Bay, Lake of the Woods. Canadian Mining Review 18: 64–71,
> 1899.
Spearman, Charles.
> The Kowkash district, Ontario. Canadian Mining Journal 36: 585–588,
> 1915.
— Microscopic characters of the ore deposits and rocks of the Kirkland Lake
> district, Ontario. Canadian Mining Journal 35: 329–332, 1914.
— Ore deposits of the Kirkland Lake district. Canadian Mining Journal 34:
> 599–601, 1913.
— Rocks and ore deposits at Sesekinaka, Ontario. Canadian Mining Journal
> 36: 69–73, 1915.
Spencer, W   H
> The Porcupine gold fields. Canadian Mining Journal 31: 137–138, 1910.
The Staff, International Nickel Company of Canada Ltd. Ontario nickel
> industry. Canadian Mining Journal 71(no. 10): 134–143, 1950.
Steele, Chas   F,
> Origin and history of the development of natural gas. Welland County
> Historical Society. Papers and Records 2: 116–123, 1926.
Stewart, Keith J
> Canada: a regional review of mining activity. Canadian Mining Journal
> 96(no. 2): 44–45, 51–55, 1975.
Stewart, R   B
> West Shining Tree gold area. Canadian Mining Journal 34: 696–698, 1913.
Sudbury, Cobalt and Porcupine. Canadian Mining Journal 34: 431–436, 1913.
Sudbury's nickel industry. Canadian Mining Journal 37: 488–489, 1916.
The "Sultana Mine, Ltd." Canadian Mining Review 18: 1–2, 1899.
The Sultana Ophir. Canadian Mining Review 22: 37, 1903.
The Sultana Ophir legislation. Canadian Mining Review 20: 162, 1901.
Sunday staking is legal in Ontario. Canadian Mining Journal 40: 405, 1919.
Surface prospecting at Cobalt. Canadian Mining Journal 34: 393–394, 1913.
Sutherland, T   F
> Mines inspection in Ontario. Canadian Mining Journal 44: 627–628, 1923.

— Ontario's mines. Canadian Mining Journal 45: 551–553, 1924.
— Sudbury – Ontario's first mining camp. Canadian Mining Journal 44: 629–630, 1923.
Swastika and Kirkland Lake gold area. Canadian Mining Journal 34: 765–766, 1913.
Taylor, Rex.
    After twenty-five years; a few intimate glimpses of the pioneer days of Porcupine. Canadian Mining Journal 57: 320–324, 1936.
Thompson, Phillips.
    Ontario's mining progress in the last decade. Canadian Mining Journal 29: 650–652, 1908.
Thomson, G   W
    Diamond drill results at Pearl Lake Porcupine, Ontario. Canadian Mining Journal 33: 238–241, 1912.
Thomson, James E
    Non-ferrous base metal deposits in Ontario. Canadian Mining Journal 71(no. 10): 152–154, 1950.
Timmins, Noah A
    A reminiscent history. Canadian Mining Journal 56: 352–362, 1935.
    Hollinger gold mines.
Timmins, Noah A   the man and his times. Canadian Mining Journal 57: 65–66, 1936.
Toombs, R   B   and T   H   Janes.
    The Canadian mineral industry in 1965 and its position in provincial economies, 1950–64. Canadian Mining Journal 87(no. 2): 81–99, 1966.
— One hundred years of progress. Canadian Mining Journal 88(no. 2): 99–124, 1967.
The treatment of Porcupine gold ores. Canadian Mining Journal 37: 223–224, 1916.
Tremblay, Maurice.
    North of the Great Lakes lies treasure. Canadian Geographical Journal 22: 286–307, 1941.
Tremblay, Rodolphe.
    Timmins Métropole de l'or. Société Historique du Nouvel-Ontario. Documents Historiques 22: 4–48, 1951.
Tretheway, W   G   Canadian Mining Journal 47: 295, 1926.
Tretheway annual report. Canadian Mining Journal 34: 137–139, 1913.
Tyrrell, Joseph B
    Memorial to Willet Green Miller. Canadian Mining Journal 47: 973–976, 1926.
— The occurrence of gold in Ontario. Canadian Mining Journal 35: 230–235, 1914.
— Silver veins in South Lorrain, Ontario. Canadian Mining Journal 34: 329–330, 1913.
— Vein formation at Cobalt, Ontario. Canadian Mining Journal 28(no. 12): 301–303, 1907; 33: 171–172, 1912.

Tyrrell, Joseph B   managing director of Kirkland Lake Gold Mining
    Company. Canadian Mining Journal 47: 514–515, 1926.
Valuable discovery of corundum. Canadian Mining Review 15: 231, 1896.
Vandergrift, J   W
    The Lucky Cross mines, Swastika. Canadian Mining Journal 32: 597–598,
    1911.
VanHise, C   R
    The geology of the Cobalt district. Canadian Mining Journal 28(no. 4):
    44–45, 1907.
Varela, Raymond.
    Let's forget Elliot Lake. Canadian Commentator 4(5): 7–9, 1960.
Visits to Ontario metal mines. Canadian Mining Journal 48: 823–826, 1927.
[W   M   G   ]
    Falconbridge nickel mine; description of the mine and the 250 ton smelter in
    the Sudbury district, Ontario. Canadian Mining Journal 51: 988–991, 1930.
Walker, T   L
    Ores of Worthington Mine, Sudbury district, Ontario. Canadian Mining
    Journal 36: 667–668, 1915.
Walli, O   E
    The Provincial Institute of Mining, Haileybury, Ontario. Canadian Mining
    Journal 80(no. 7): 67–69, 1959.
Wansbrough, V   C
    Importance of Ontario in Canadian Mining. Canadian Mining Journal
    71(no. 10): 93–95, 1950.
Warren, (E.D.) & Co. Cobalt and Porcupine shares during 1911. Canadian
    Mining Journal 33: 59, 1912.
Watson, R   B
    Summary of work done at Nipissing and LaRose for 1910. Canadian Mining
    Journal 32: 42–43, 1911.
Webb, J   E
    The call of the north; exploring and mining possibilities in northern
    Ontario. Canadian Mining Journal 46: 397–399, 1925.
Wells, J   Walter.
    Mining in eastern Ontario. Canadian Mining Review 19: 140–143, 1900.
Where Moose Mountain ore will be handled. Canadian Mining Journal 28(no.
    20): 562, 1907.
Whitman, Alfred R
    Structural features of the Porcupine ore deposits. Canadian Mining Journal
    36: 589–596, 1915.
Wilkie, George.
    Canada and its nickel. Canadian Magazine of Politics, Science, Art and
    Literature 47: 259–265, 1916.
— Ground rent for provincial forest land in Ontario. Canadian Journal of
    Economics and Political Science 22: 63–72, 1956.

Williams, H   H   Carnegie.
 The Bruce mines, Ontario, 1846–1906. Canadian Mining Journal 28(no. 4):
 47–51, 1907.
Williams, M   Y
 Oil prospecting in southwestern Ontario. Canadian Mining Journal 39:
 48–49, 1918.
Williams, W   R
 Big tugs and big rafts; a story of Georgian Bay lumbering. Inland Seas 3:
 11–16, 1947.
Willmott, A   B
 Canadian nickel industry. Industrial Canada 6: 635–637, 1906.
— The exploration of the Ontario iron ranges. Canadian Mining Review 23:
 154–156, 1904.
— Gowganda & Elk Lake Railway. Canadian Mining Journal 32: 474–479,
 1911.
— Iron mining in northern Ontario. Canadian Mining Journal 28(no. 3):
 22–24, 1907.
— The iron ores of Ontario. Canadian Mining Journal 29(no. 6): 77–84, 1908.
— The undeveloped iron resources of Canada. Canadian Mining Journal 32:
 519–524, 1911.
Wilmott, A   W
 Notes on the Michipicoton gold field. Canadian Mining Review 17: 73–74,
 1897.
Wilson, Alfred W   G
 The Mond Nickel Company's smelting plants at Victoria mines and
 Coniston, Ontario. Canadian Mining Journal 35: 667–671, 1914.
— The occurrence of pyrites in Canada. Canadian Mining Journal 34:
 219–223, 236–239, 308–311, 1913.
Winchell, Horace V
 An epidemic of mismanagement. Canadian Mining Review 16: 303–304,
 1896.
With Miller at Cobalt in 1904. Canadian Mining Journal 46: 501–502, 1925.
Work at the Seneca Mine, Peterson Lake, Cobalt. Canadian Mining Journal
 34: 251–252, 1913.
[Wright, Douglas]
 Red Lake. Canadian Mining Journal 47: 692–693, 1926.
Wright, Sydney B
 The treatment of auriferous mispickel ores at Deloro, Ontario. Canadian
 Mining Review 20: 53–56, 1901.
The year in Ontario: Canadian Mining Review 22: 1–2, 1903.
Young, A   C
 Chronological history of mining in Ontario. Canadian Mining Journal 51:
 669, 1930.
— Diamond drilling in Ontario: an increasingly important factor in the
 industry. Canadian Mining Journal 51: 788–789, 1930.

— Industrial minerals in Ontario. Canadian Chemistry and Process Industries 23: 449–451, 1939.
— Mining in Ontario. Canadian Mining Journal 57: 61–64, 1936; 58: 66–71, 1937.
Covers the years: 1935, 1936.

Young, Cyril T
Mining possibilities along Canadian Northern Railway, West Shining Tree to Nipigon. Canadian Mining Journal 37: 515–516, 1916.

Young, H   G
Concentration at Hudson Bay Mines, Ltd., Cobalt, Ontario. Canadian Mining Journal 32: 722–725, 1911.

Young, M   E   and E   E   Mumford.
Safety practices at Inco. Canadian Mining Journal 84(no. 9): 73–77, 1963.

Young, Paul E
Pronto uranium mines; the Pronto property – its story. Canadian Mining Journal 76(no. 10): 66, 1955.

Zahary, G
Ground control research program at the Mines Branch, Elliot Lake Laboratory. Canadian Mining Journal 90(no. 1): 55–56, 1969.

Zavitz, E   J
Development of forestry in Ontario. Forestry Chronicle 15: 36–43, 1939.
— Forest fire protection in Ontario. Mer Douce 2(2): 12–13, 1922.
— Forestry in southern Ontario. Ontario Agricultural College Review 22: 124–128, 1909.
— Reforestation in Ontario. Canadian Geographical Journal 34: 156–180, 1947.

Theses

Baba, Nobuyoshi.
A numerical investigation of Lake Ontario: dynamics and thermodynamics. Princeton, New Jersey [1974]
264 p.
Ph.D. thesis, Princeton University (microfilm 75-20,610).   DA

Ball, Norman Roger, 1944–
Petroleum technology in Ontario during the 1860. [Toronto] c1972.
334 leaves. illus., facsims., map.
M.A. thesis, University of Toronto.
Chiefly pre-Confederation.   OTU

Barbour, Wilson.
Entrepreneurial risk and reward; a study in raising risk capital for Canadian mining. [Toronto] 1962.
iv, 96 leaves.
M.B.A. thesis, University of Toronto.   OTU

Barnett, Donald Frederick, 1940–
    Output variability in the Canadian base-metal mining industry, 1949 to
    1963. Kingston, Ontario: 1966.
    vi, 224 leaves. figs., charts, tables (part fold.).
    M.A. thesis, Queen's University.   OKQ
Beach, Noel.
    Nickel capital: a study of the relationship between a town and an industry.
    Sudbury, Ontario: 1974.
    117 leaves. charts, maps.
    B.A. thesis, Laurentian University.   OSUL
Bedell, Frank G
    The Sudbury mining district. Lawrence, Kansas: 1906.
    39 leaves.
    B.S. thesis, University of Kansas.   U. Kansas
Buik, William Albert.
    Noranda Mines Limited; a study in business and economic history.
    [Toronto] 1958 [c1973]
    210, xxi leaves. illus., maps.
    M.A. thesis, University of Toronto (microfilm 16095).   OTU
Burwash, Edward Moore Jackson, 1873–
    An examination of the Huronian rocks along the boundary line between
    Nipissing and Algoma, with reference to minerals of economic value.
    [Toronto] 1897.
    25 leaves.
    M.A. thesis, University of Toronto.   OTU
Carswell, Gordon Ernest, 1924–
    The water supply problem in southwestern Ontario. [London, Ontario]
    1951.
    xii, 158 leaves. graphs, tables, maps.
    M.Sc. thesis, The University of Western Ontario.   OLU
Coad, Paul Randell.
    The Potter Mine. Toronto: c1976.
    xvii, 239 leaves. illus., col. plates, figs. (part col. part fold.), maps (part col.
    part fold.).
    M.Sc. thesis, University of Toronto.   OTU
Collin, Arthur Edwin, 1929–
    A study of the rivers of southwestern Ontario. [London, Ontario] 1957.
    vii, 64 leaves. diagrs., maps.
    M.Sc. thesis, The University of Western Ontario.   OLU
Dagher, J   H
    Effect of the National Oil Policy on the Ontario petroleum refining industry.
    Montreal, Quebec: 1968.
    vii, 823, 18 [226] leaves. illus.
    Thesis, (degree not indicated) McGill University (microfilm 2643).   Can

Downey, Terrance James, 1944–
  The political economy of uranium: Elliot Lake 1948–1970. London,
  Ontario: 1972.
  vii, 186 leaves. tables, maps (part fold.).
  M.A. thesis, The University of Western Ontario (microfilm 12532).   OLU
Eagan, William Edward, 1943–
  Joseph Burr Tyrrell, 1858–1957. London, Ontario: 1971.
  xv, 339 leaves. maps.
  Ph.D. thesis, The University of Western Ontario.   OLU
Ferguson, Stewart Alexander, 1913–
  Ore deposits of the Kamiskotia area, Ontario. [Toronto] 1945.
  103 leaves. illus., maps (6 fold in back pocket).
  Ph.D. thesis, University of Toronto.   OTU
Foster, Ralph Edwin.
  Hydro-electric power and Ontario gold mines. [Toronto] 1939.
  180 leaves. tables, charts (fold.), maps (fold.).
  M.A. thesis, University of Toronto.   OTU
Goltz, Eileen.
  Papertown (Espanola). Sudbury, Ontario: 1974.
  70 leaves. maps, tables.
  B.A. thesis, Laurentian University.   OSUL
Good, Stewart Wesley, 1948–
  Hardwood stand structure as it relates to site index determination and
  woodlot management. [Toronto] c1976.
  v, 56 leaves. tables, figs.
  M.Sc.F. thesis, University of Toronto.   OTU
Harvey, Robert Mackay.
  A study of the Falconbridge Nickel Mines and the marketing of nickel.
  Kingston, Ontario: 1935.
  vi, 140 leaves. tables, charts (part fold.), forms (part fold.), maps (fold in
  back pocket).
  B.Com. thesis, Queen's University.   OKQ
Hilborn, William Harvey. 1921–
  Forests and forestry of the Norfolk sand plain. London, Ontario: 1970.
  ix, 120 leaves. tables, maps (part fold.).
  M.A. thesis, The University of Western Ontario.   OLU
Hodgins, Larry E
  Economic geography of the Lake Timagami district. [Toronto] 1958.
  vi, 107 leaves. diagrs., maps.
  B.A. thesis, University of Toronto.   OTU
Ivey, T   J
  Iron ores of Ontario. [Toronto] 1896.
  21 leaves.
  M.A. thesis, University of Toronto.   OTU

Janssen, Rodney David, 1947–
    Inco and the Canadian nickel industry: the need for new directions by
    government. London, Ontario: 1975.
    vii, 130 leaves.
    M.A. thesis, The University of Western Ontario (microfilm 14575).   OLU
Kuo, Hsiao-Yu.
    Rare earth elements in the Sudbury nickel irruptive. Hamilton, Ontario:
    1975 [c1976]
    xvii, 242 leaves. illus., maps.
    Ph.D. thesis, McMaster University (microfilm 26163).   Can
Kureth, Elwood John Clark, 1929–
    The geographic, historic and political factors influencing the development of
    Canada's chemical valley. Ann Arbor, Michigan: 1971.
    vi, 179 leaves. illus., maps.
    Ph.D. thesis, The University of Michigan (microfilm 72-29,124).   DA
Kwong, Yan-Tat John.
    Distribution of gold in an archean greenstone belt as exemplified by the
    Kakagi Lake area, northwestern Ontario. Hamilton, Ontario: 1975 [c1976]
    ix, 82 leaves. illus., maps.
    M.Sc. thesis, McMaster University (microfilm 26166).   Can
Lake, Lera L
    Gold mining in northern Ontario. [Toronto] 1948.
    92 leaves. illus., maps (part col. part fold.).
    B.A. thesis, University of Toronto.   OTU
McCoy, Leslie Stuart, 1938–
    A socio-economic study of the use of forest land for timber production and
    recreation. [Toronto] c1972.
    viii, 188 leaves. tables, figs., maps (part fold.).
    M.Sc.F. thesis, University of Toronto.   OTU
MacLeod, William George.
    Kirkland Lake, a geographical study of a northern Ontario frontier mining
    community. [Toronto] 1954.
    i–[vii] 97 leaves. illus., figs. (part fold.), maps (part col.).
    B.A. thesis, University of Toronto.   OTU
McNutt, James Frederick Kirby.
    Multiple use of the boreal forest in northern Ontario by wood based
    industries. [Toronto] 1967.
    xi, 109 leaves. tables, figs., maps (part col.).
    M.B.A. thesis, University of Toronto.   OTU
McQuarrie, David Ian, 1947–
    Stand structure of the boreal forest in northeastern Ontario. [Toronto]
    c1975.
    xvi, 270 leaves. illus., plates (part col.), maps (part col.).
    M.Sc.F. thesis, University of Toronto (awarded 1976).   OTU

Riva, Harry John.
   Effectiveness of the Securities Act, 1966 (Ontario) with respect to securities
   issued by junior mining-exploration companies. [Toronto: 1969]
   26 [4] leaves.
   M.B.A. thesis, University of Toronto.   OTU
Sloan, Stephen F
   A conceptual approach to regional natural resources management based
   upon comparative analysis. Syracuse, New York: 1969.
   346 p.
   Ph.D. thesis, State University College of Forestry at Syracuse University
   (microfilm 70-0572).   DA
Sommerville, Robert Stewart.
   The mining industry in relation to development in northern Ontario during
   the period 1911–1918. [Toronto: 1933]
   65 leaves. (handwritten).
   Undergraduate commence thesis, University of Toronto.   OTU
Steadman, James.
   The North American mining frontier: a comparison of two mining camps,
   Cobalt, Ontario and Leadville, Colorado. Sudbury, Ontario: 1969.
   66 leaves. charts, maps. photos.
   B.A. thesis, Laurentian University.   OSUL
Taylor, Sandra Gail, 1942–
   Forest productivity in the Simcoe uplands region. A study of the effects of soil
   moisture availibility and fertility status on the growth of plantation red pine.
   Kingston, Ontario: 1970, c1971.
   xi, 272 leaves. tables, figs., maps (part fold.).
   M.Sc. thesis, Queen's University (accepted 1971).   OKQ
Thomson, James Edgar.
   The Atikokan iron deposits, Rainy River district. [Toronto] 1929.
   51 leaves. photos., maps (1 col. fold. in pocket).
   M.A. thesis, University of Toronto.   OTU
Yamaguchi, Takashi.
   The single-enterprise town of Wawa and Algoma Ore Properties Limited; a
   geographical study of a northern Ontario frontier mining community.
   [Toronto] 1960.
   xv, 103 leaves. illus., maps (part col.).
   M.A. thesis, University of Toronto.   OTU

HEAVY AND CONSUMER GOODS INDUSTRIES

Bibliography
Mid-Canada Development Foundation.
   Mid-Canada bibliography. [Toronto? 1970?]
   1 v. (various pagings).   OTU

Ontario Paper Company Limited.
   Utilization of waste sulphite liquor; a bibliography of the literature from
   1917 to early 1943. Compiled by B.R. Mead, R.F. patterson and J.M.
   Pepper, under the direction of Harold Hibbert. [Thorold, Ontario; 1947]
   107 p.   OTU

Monographs and Pamphlets
Abitibi Power & Paper Company.
   An illustrated story of the development of the newsprint paper mill of the
   Abitibi Power & Paper Company Iroquois Falls, Ontario. [Montreal:
   Ronalds Co.] 1924.
   26 leaves. chiefly illus.   OTAR
Aikenhead Hardware Limited.
   Building Toronto [1830–1930]. A story of growth of a great city and the
   development of a great enterprise. [Toronto? 1930?]
   [19] p. illus., ports.   OTAR
Aikman, Cecil Howard.
   The automobile industry of Canada. Toronto: Published by Macmillan
   Company of Canada for the Department of Economics and Political
   Science, McGill University [1926]
   48 p. (McGill University economic studies, no. 8).   OTU
Aylmer Express.
   Industrial and farming number of the *Aylmer Express* for the town of Aylmer
   and the township of Malahide, 1913. Authorized by Aylmer and Malahide
   Councils. Aylmer, Ontario: D.H. Price, 1913.
   72 p. illus., map, ports.   OTAR
Battelle Memorial Institute.
   Report of economic development opportunities for Greater Windsor –
   Canada's 10th largest community. Windsor, Ontario: The Greater Windsor
   Industrial Commission [1958]
   32 p. diagrs., graphs, map, tables.   OTU
— Summary report on economic development opportunities for the Sudbury
   area, Ontario. Columbus, Ohio: The Institute, 1959.
   1 v. (various pagings).   OTMCL
The Beacon, Stratford, Ontario.
   The Beacon's magazine of industry, reviewing historically the development
   of a progressive community descriptive of and illustrating Perth county
   (Stratford, St. Mary's, Mitchell, Listowel, Tavistock, Milverton). Compiled
   by C.M. Nichols. Stratford, Ontario: The Stratford Beacon [1911]
   60, 44 [4] illus., ports.   OLU
Benson, George F   1864–1953.
   Historical record of the Edwardsburg and Canada Starch Company.
   [Cardinal, Ontario: 1958]
   xvii, 280 p. illus., facsims., ports.   OTAR

The big tough expensive job: Imperial Oil and the Canadian economy; edited
by James Laxer and Anne Martin. [Toronto] Press Porcépic [c1976]
xi, 256 p. illus., ports., tables.   OTU
Binder Twine Festival, Kleinburg, Ontario, 1969.
Kleinburg Binder Twine Festival, September 6th, 1969. n.p. [1969?]
30 p. illus., port.   OTU
Bishop, Wilfred L
Men and pork chops: a history of the Ontario Pork Producers Marketing
Board. With a foreword by George Stuart Atkins. London, Ontario: Phelps
Publishing Company, 1977 [c1976]
viii, 184 p. illus., ports.   OLU
Bixby, (M.G.) & Co., publishers.
Industries of Canada: historical and commercial sketches: London,
Woodstock, Ingersoll, Guelph, Berlin, Waterloo, St. Thomas, Windsor and
environs. Its prominent places and people; representative merchants and
manufacturers, its improvements, progress and enterprise. Toronto: M.G.
Bixby & Co., 1887.
164 p. illus.   OLU
— Industries of Canada: historical and commercial sketches; London, Guelph,
Berlin, Brantford, Paris, Waterloo, Chatham and environs. Its prominent
places and people; representative merchants and manufacturers; its
improvements, progress and enterprise. Toronto: M.G. Bixby & Co., 1886.
156 p. illus.   OLU
— Industries of Canada: historical and commercial sketches: Toronto, and
environs. Toronto: M.G. Bixby & Co., 1886.
224 p. illus., ports.   OTURS
Booth, John Franklin, 1895–
The effect of volume on the cost of manufacturing cheese in Ontario and
Quebec factories, 1931. n.p. [1933]
1 v. (various pagings). tables.   OIIQ
Bourrie, Joseph N
Collingwood industrially. Collingwood, Ontario: Board of Trade, 1944.
1 v. (unpaged). illus., ports.   OKQ
Brantford, Ontario.
City of Brantford, province of Ontario, Canada: its advantages as a
manufacturing and business centre. Brantford, Ontario [City Council] 1880.
16 p. illus.   OLU
Brantford Development Commission.
Survey of manufacturing concerns, 1976. Brantford, Ontario [1976]
52 leaves.   OBRT
Brantford Industrial Commission.
Industrial development activities in the city of Brantford 1970. Brantford,
Ontario [1971]
8 leaves.
Chairman: C.T. Beaman.   OBRT

Brewster, Winfield, 1879–1962.
  Hespeler yarns; odds and ends about the textile trade at Hespeler, and some
  of the people concerned therewith. [Hespeler, Ontario] 1953.
  46 [25] p. facsims.   OTU
British Whig, Kingston, Ontario.
  Special industrial souvenir number. Published by authority of the Kingston
  Board of Trade. Kingston, Ontario: The British Whig, 1909.
  65 p. illus., ports.   OKQ
Brown, John James, 1916–
  The inventors: great ideas in Canadian enterprise. [Toronto: McClelland
  and Stewart Limited, 1967]
  128 p. illus., (part col.), ports.   OTU
Brown, (J.S.) & Sons, publisher.
  Industrial and picturesque Paris, Canada. [Paris, Ontario: 1901]
  1 v. (unpaged). chiefly illus.   OTAR
Bryan, George J
  Toronto: a progressive centre of trade and commerce; its industrial
  advantages, educational facilities and pleasure attractions. Toronto: W.S.
  Johnston & Co'y., 1906.
  40 p. illus., map.   OTAR
Campbell, Marjorie Freeman, 1896–1975.
  Niagara; hinge of the golden arc. [Foreword by Louis Blake Duff] Toronto:
  The Ryerson Press [c1958]
  xviii, 356 p. illus., port., map.   OTU
Canada. Bureau of Statistics.
  Manufacturing industries of the province of Ontario, 1942. Ottawa: General
  Manufactures Branch, Bureau of Statistics, 1944.
  38 p. tables.   OONL
Canada. National Capital Commission. Information and Historical Division.
  The Rideau Falls, New Edinburgh 1831–1962: an early industrial area.
  Ottawa: The Commission [1962]
  5, 10 leaves. maps.   OTAR
Canadian Industrial Record.
  Special number descriptive of and illustrating Brantford, Berlin, Waterloo,
  Galt, Stratford, Woodstock and vicinity. n.p. [1910?]
  39 p. illus., ports.   OLU
Canadian Locomotive Co. Ltd.
  Centenary 1850–1950. Kingston, Ontario: The Company [c1950]
  24 p. illus., ports.   OKP
Canadian Pacific Railway Company. Department of Industrial Development.
  The province of Ontario [industrial study] Toronto: Canadian Pacific
  Railway Company, 1959.
  91 leaves. map, tables.   OTU
Carol, Hans.
  The geographic identification of regional growth centres and development

regions in southern Ontario: a report to the Regional Development Branch, Department of Economics and Development, province of Ontario. Toronto: 1966.

49 p. tables.   OONL

Carruthers, George, 1869–1947.

Paper-making. Part I, First hundred years of paper-making by machine; Part II, First century of paper-making in Canada. Toronto: The Garden City Press Co-operative, 1947.

xxiv, 712 p. illus., ports., plan, maps (fold.).   OTU

Chown, W   F

Wholesale marketing of fresh fruits and vegetables in the city of Toronto. Ottawa: Department of Agriculture, 1940.

%L58 p. illus., graphs, tables. (Canada. Department of Agriculture. Economic Division. Marketing Service. Publication 673. Technical bulletin 23).   OONL

Cockshutt, William Ashton, 1892–

Brief history of Cockshutt Farm Equipment Limited as told by W. Ashton Cockshutt to the Historical Society of Brantford. n.p.: 1960.

11 leaves.   OBRT

— Supplement added April 1967.

1 leaf [i.e. leave 12]   OBRT

Conference on Productivity through new Technology, Ryerson Polytechnical Institute, 1965.

Papers prepared for the Conference held at Ryerson Polytechnical Institute, Toronto, May 27–28, 1965. Conference edition. Sponsored by Economic Council of Canada and Ontario Economic Council. Toronto: 1965.

6 parts. illus., diagrs.

Contents: 1, The tools of modern management by Gerald G. Fisch; 2, Practical application of data processing in medium sized and smaller manufacturing companies, by H.S. Gellman, R.C. Carroll; 3, A practical approach to automatic production by J.W. Abrams, R.W.P. Anderson, D.J. Clough; 4, Advances in metal working by J. Van de Vigte; 5, Improving material movement through the manufacturing cycle by James A. Brown in association with B.D. Beamish; 6, The economic justification of new equipment by C.C. Edge.

These papers were also published as Conference Papers by the Queen's Printer in Ottawa.   OTU

Consumers' Gas Company of Toronto.

First century of Consumer's Gas, 1848–1948, including the one hundred annual report. [Toronto] The Company, 1948.

1 v. (unpaged). illus., map, ports.   OTAR

— Sixty years. Toronto: Consumers' Gas Company, 1934.
    23 leaves. facsims., ports.   OTAR
A corner in old Toronto at Front and York Sts. now in the year nineteen
    hundred and twenty-eight occupied by the firm of W.R. Johnston &
    Company, Limited, for sixty years manufacturing clothiers. Toronto:
    Published by Rous & Mann for W.R. Johnston [1928]
    [16] p. illus., port.   OTURS
County of Halton, Ontario, Canada: in the heart of Canada's greatest industrial
    area. n.p. [1948]
    64 p. illus.   OTAR
Cumberland Land Company, Limited.
    Brantwood ... Oakville, Ontario [c1913]
    1 v. (unpaged). illus.   OTAR
Davis, Bruce Pettit.
    The Davis family and the leather industry, 1834–1934, by Bruce Pettit Davis
    and Carroll Langstaff Davis. Toronto: The Ryerson Press, 1934.
    145 p. illus., ports.   OTAR
Denison, Merrill, 1893–1975.
    Harvest triumphant: the story of Massey–Harris. A footnote to Canadian
    history. Toronto: McClelland & Stewart, 1948.
    xii, 351 p. illus. (part col.).   OTU
— New York: Dodd, Mead & Company, 1949.
    xii, 351 p. illus. (part col.).   OTU
Dulmage, Harry B
    Industrial growth patterns and strategy in small Ontario municipalities.
    Belleville, Ontario: Harry Dulmage Associates Limited, 1970.
    vi, 57 p. graphs, map, tables.
    From M.B.A. thesis, Queen's University 1969.
    Thesis not located.   OTU
Duncan, James Stuart, 1893–
    Not a one-way street: the autobiography of James S. Duncan. Toronto:
    Clarke, Irwin & Company Limited, 1971.
    262 p. illus., ports.   OTU
    Mr. Duncan was Vice-President of Massey–Ferguson and Chairman of
    Ontario Hydro.   OTU
East York, Ontario. Planning Board.
    The Leaside industrial area study 1973 [report by Richard Woods, based on
    his studies, and reports and studies of East York and Metro Planning Board].
    [Toronto] The Board, 1973.
    1 v. (various pagings). maps (part col.).   OTU
Eastern Ontario Development Association.
    Industry grows in eastern Ontario, the heart of Canada's multi-billion dollar
    market. [Ottawa, 1955]
    [20] p. illus., maps.   OTU

Electrical Development Company (Ontario), appellant.
Memorandum concerning recent provincial legislation and executive action
in Canada with special reference to the Niagara question in the Ontario
Legislature. n.p. [1917]
22 leaves.   OTU
Ellah, Robert T
Lower Rideau Lake commercial fishery 1966–1967. Kemptville, Ontario
[1968?]
14 leaves, map, tables.   OTAR
Essex County, Ontario. Planning and Industrial Promotion Committee .
A prospectus of Essex county, Ontario, Canada. [Windsor, Ontario] The
Committee [1972]
1 v. (unpaged). maps (part fold.), tables.   OWA OKQ
Expositor Press Brantford, Ontario.
Industrial edition: Guelph, Berlin, Waterloo, Galt, Preston and Hespeler.
Brantford, Ontario: Expositor Press, 1903.
24 p. illus., ports.   OTAR
Field, Neil Collard, 1930–
Geographical aspects of industrial growth in the Metropolitan Toronto
region, by N.C. Field and D.P. Kerr. [Toronto] 1968.
vi, 97 p. ([Ontario] Department of Treasury and Economics, Regional
Development Branch. Research paper, no. 1).   OTUSA
Ford, Marjory A
Annual landings of fish on the Canadian side of the Great Lakes from 1867
to 1939 as officially recorded. Ottawa: E. Cloutier, printer to the King's
Most Excellent Majesty, 1943.
91 p. tables.   OTY
Fox, William.
The mill, produced and designed by William Fox; photography by Bill
Brooks; written by Janice Tyrwhitt; illustrations by Helen Fox. [Toronto]
McClelland and Stewart [c1976]
224 p. illus. (part col.).   OTAR
The Freeholder, Cornwall, Ontario.
Cornwall: the factory town, 1901: 20th century souvenir of the Freeholder.
Cornwall, Ontario: Freeholder, 1901.
[100] p. illus.   OKQ
General Steel Wares Limited.
100 years of progress, 1847–1947. [London, Ontario: 1947]
[20] p. illus., ports.   OTAR
George, Roy Edwin, 1923–
A leader and a laggard; manufacturing industry in Nova Scotia, Quebec
and Ontario. [Toronto] University of Toronto Press [c1970]
xiv, 220 p. (Atlantic provinces studies, 2).   OTU

Gillen, Mollie (Woolnaugh).
The Masseys founding family. Toronto: The Ryerson Press [c1965]
174 p. illus., ports. OTU
Guelph, Ontario – the royal city: a city of great enterprises – wholesale and
manufacturing agricultural resources unsurpassed. [Guelph? Ontario:
1907?]
18 p. illus. OOA
Guthrie, John Alexander, 1907–
The newsprint paper industry; an economic analysis. Cambridge,
Massachusetts: Harvard University Press, 1941.
xxiii, 274 p. illus. (Harvard economic studies, v. 68). OTU
Hamilton, Ontario. Commissioner of Industries and Publicity.
Hamilton, Canada, the city of opportunity, Hamilton [Reid Press] n.d.
48 p. illus. (part fold.). OTU
Hamilton, the Birmingham of Canada. Hamilton, Ontario: Times Printing Co.,
1892.
[106] p. illus. OTU
Hare, H   R
The dairy farm business in Ontario: an economic survey of farms producing
milk for fluid consumption conducted in co-operation with The Economics
and Animal Husbandry Departments, Ontario Agricultural College,
Guelph. Ottawa [Department of Agriculture] 1940.
65 p. tables. OONL
Haviland, William E
Trade liberalization and the Canadian pulp and paper industry, by W.E.
Haviland, N.S. Takacsy, E.M. Cape. [Toronto] Published for the Private
Planning Association of Canada by University of Toronto Press [c1968]
vi, 107 p. graphs, tables. OTU
Hay township. A study of industry, past and present. Zurich, Ontario: 1972.
48 p. illus., tables.
"A report of a summer project carried out by seven area students, financed
by an Opportunities for Youth grant." OLU
Hazen and Whipple, New York.
Toronto water works filtration plant [plans. New York? 1909]
[1] p. 36 fold. plans. OTURS
Henderson, Dorothy (McLaughlin), 1900–
Robert McLaughlin: carriage builder. Sketches by Douglas C. Henderson.
[Oshawa, Ontario: Alger Press, 1968]
53 p. illus. OTU
— [Toronto: Griffin Press Limited, c1972]
70 p. illus. OTU

Herr, James A
  Breweries and soda works of St. Thomas, 1833–1933: an illustrated history
  for bottle collectors. St. Thomas, Ontario: The Author, 1974.
  44 p. illus. (Ontario series, v. 1).   OOC
Hodge, Gerald.
  Patterns and parameters of industrial location in the Toronto urban field.
  [Toronto] Centre for Urban and Community Studies, University of Toronto,
  1970.
  17, 7, 2 leaves. 7 col. maps. ([Environment study] Research paper, no. 28).
                                                                          OTU
— Theory and reality of industrial location in the Toronto region. A report to
  the Regional Development Branch, Ontario Department of Treasury and
  Economics. Toronto: 1970.
  iv, 30 leaves. maps, tables.   OONL
Huff, Harry Bruce.
  An economic appraisal of the market for Ontario flue-cured tobacco, by
  H.B. Huff, B.B. Perkins and S.M. Smith. [Guelph, Ontario: School of
  Agricultural, Economic and Extension Education, Ontario Agricultural
  College, University of Guelph, 1972]
  ix, 81 p. graphs, tables.   OTU
Innis, Harold Adam, 1894–1952 (ed.).
  The dairy industry in Canada, by J.A. Ruddick and others. Edited by H.A.
  Innis. Toronto: The Ryerson Press, 1937.
  xxxii, 299 p. illus., tables.   OTU
Jackson, John Nicolas, 1925–
  The industrial structure of the Niagara peninsula, by John N. Jackson and
  Carole White. St. Catharines, Ontario: Department of Geography, Brock
  University, 1971.
  ix, 321 p. illus., maps (part fold.).   OSTCB
Jaffray, James P
  The highly industralized and strikingly beautiful Grand River valley
  described from Port Dover and Dunnville to Elora and Fergus. [Galt,
  Ontario] The Author, 1932.
  136 p. illus.   OTU
— Kitchener, the industrial city; the birthplace of the great Niagara power
  movement; a city that leads all others in Canada in the manufacture of tires,
  rubber footwear, shirts and collars, felt boots and shoes, furniture, leather,
  pork products and buttons; phonographs and radio truck equipment.
  [Kitchener, Ontario: The Author, 1929?]
  96 p. illus.   OTU
— Picturesque and industrial city of Galt, Ontario, Canada. [Galt: Jaffray,
  1924]
  90 p. illus.   OTU
Jaffray Bros., publishers.
  Picturesque and industrial Galt. Galt, Ontario: Jaffray Bros., 1902.
  152 p. illus., ports.   OLU

Jones, Gwen.
  Black gold built Bothwell. Story by Gwen Jones, research by Audrey Kelly.
  [Bothwell, Ontario] The Bothwell Times, 1967.
    1 v. (unpaged). illus., facsims., ports., map.   OTU
Kemptville, Ontario. Industrial Committee.
  A brief outline of advantages offered to new industry at Kemptville, Ontario.
  Kemptville, Ontario [1944]
    20 p. illus., map.   OTAR
Kerr, Donald Peter, 1920–
  Manufacturing in downtown Toronto, by Donald Kerr and Jacob Spelt.
  [Ottawa; E. Cloutier, Queen's Printer, 1958]
    20 p. maps, tables.
    "Reprinted from *Geographical bulletin*, no. 10, 1957."   OTU
— Manufacturing in suburban Toronto., [by] Donald Kerr and Jacob Spelt.
  Presented at the eighth annual meeting of the Canadian Association of
  Geographers, Edmonton, 1958. n.p. [1958]
    [11] 19 p. illus., maps.   OTU
Kilbourn, William Morley, 1926–
  The elements combined; a history of The Steel Company of Canada. Wood
  engravings by Rosemary Kilbourn. Toronto: Clarke, Irwin & Company
  Limited [c1960]
    xxii, 335 p. illus., col. diagrs., col. tables.   OTU
Kingston, Ontario. Board of Trade.
  Kingston: the industrial centre of eastern Ontario [containing a
  comprehensive review of the natural advantages and resources of Kingston
  together with historical reviews of those representative concerns and
  biographical sketches of prominent men who have materially assisted in
  placing this community in a high position in the industrial, commercial and
  social world] Kingston, Ontario: The British Whig, 1909.
    65 p. illus., ports., map.   OK
Kingston, Ontario. Industrial Commission.
  Kingston, Ontario presents your industrial site. [Kingston, Ontario] 1967.
    15 p. map, plans.   OKQ
Kingston, Ontario. Junior Chamber of Commerce.
  Industrial survey. Kingston, Ontario. [Foster and North, 1950]
    20 p. illus., map.   OKQ
Lamorie, Andrew [pseud.]
  How they sold our Canada to the U.S.A. New rev. enl. ed. Toronto: NC
  Press Limited, 1976.
    133 p.   OONL
Lauriston, Victor, 1881–1973.
  Blue flame of service: a history of Union Gas Company and the natural gas
  industry in southwestern Ontario, by Victor Lauriston, edited by Ted Karry.
  Chatham, Ontario: Union Gas Company of Canada, Limited, 1961.
    viii, 126 p. illus., map, ports.   OLU

— A century of milling, 1848–1948: the story of The T.H. Taylor Company
   Limited, Chatham, Ontario. [Chatham, Ontario: 1949]
   35 p. illus., ports.   OOA
Law Society of Upper Canada.
   Developments in company law. Toronto: R. DeBoo, 1968.
   396 p. (*Its* special lectures, 1968).
   Corporation law in Ontario.   OLU
Leaside, Ontario. Town Council. Publicity and Industrial Committee.
   The story of Leaside. [Leaside, Ontario] The Council [1931]
   32 p. illus., map, ports.   OTAR
Leonard, (E.) & Sons.
   100 years, 1834–1934 [with an introduction by Fred Landon. London,
   Ontario: 1934].
   25 p. illus., facsims., ports.   OLU
Leonard, Frank E   1848–1923.
   The Honorable Elijah Leonard. A memoir [London, Ontario: Advertiser
   Printing Company, 1894?]
   51 p. illus., port.   OTAR
London, Ontario.
   City of London industrial survey. [London, Ontario: 1953]
   59 leaves. illus., plates.   OONL
London, Ontario. Chamber of Commerce.
   London, Canada: the centre of Canada's greatest economic area. [London,
   Ontario: The Author, 192–?]
   48 p. chiefly illus.   OLU
London, Ontario. City Council.
   London, Ontario, Canada the forest city, resources and advantages. London,
   Ontario: The London Advertiser Job, 1909.
   64 p. illus.   OLU
London, Ontario. Industrial Commission.
   Industrial survey, London, Ontario, Canada. [London, Ontario] n.d.
   32 p.
   Industrial commissioner: W.H.A. Sparling.   OLU
London, Ontario: its advantages and attractions as a place of residence,
   business, investment & manufacturing. [London, Ontario: H.C. Allison
   Printing & Novelty Co.] 1892.
   32 p. illus.   OL
Lumber trade of the Ottawa valley with a description of some of the principal
   manufacturing establishments 2d ed. Ottawa: Times Steam Printing and
   Publishing Company, 1871.
   61 p. tables.
   No first edition located.   OKQ
McLaughlin, Robert James, 1860–
   Daily journal for 1884. Toronto [1964?]
   1 v. (unpaged). ports.   OTAR

Macmillan, David S   (ed.).
  Canadian business history: selected studies, 1497–1971. Toronto:
  McClelland and Stewart Limited [c1972]
  346 p. tables.   OTU
McPherson, Robin M
  A history of the chemical industry in Lambton county, by R.M. McPherson
  and R.W. Ford. Sarnia, Ontario: Dow Chemical of Canada Ltd. [1964]
  16 p. illus., ports.   OTU
Map & Advertising Company, Limited.
  Guidal commercial directory atlas of Wellington county (province of
  Ontario)... Compiled and drawn from government surveys and best
  available data... Toronto: Map & Advertising Company Limited, 1917.
  14 leaves. col. maps.   OLU
Marshall, James S
  William M. Mercer Limited: the first quarter century, 1945 to 1970.
  [Toronto: Wm. M. Mercer, Ltd., 1976]
  ix, 234 p. port.   OTAR
Martin, Larry.
  Commodity future markets: hedging opportunities for Ontario grain, corn
  and soybean producers. [Guelph, Ontario] School of Agricultural Economics
  and Extension Education, University of Guelph, 1973.
  v, 90 p. graphs, tables.   OTU
Massey–Harris Company Limited.
  Commemorating the one-hundredth anniversary of the founding of
  Massey–Harris Company. An historical review of invention and progress
  and development and their contribution to agriculture from 1847 to the
  present day. n.p.: 1947.
  60 p. illus. (part col.), ports.   OKQ
— Massey–Harris: an historical sketch 1847–1920. Toronto: Massey–Harris
  Company, Ltd., 1920.
  44 p. illus., facsims., ports.   OTAR
Merritt, William Hamilton, 1855–1918.
  Notes on the possibilities of iron and steel production in Ontario . Toronto:
  The Copp, Clark Company, Limited, 1892.
  16 p. tables.   OKQ
Metropolitan Toronto. Industrial Commission.
  Toronto: the exciting city. [Toronto: 1967]
  1 v. (unpaged). chiefly illus. (part col.).   OTAR
Metropolitan Toronto. Works Commissioner.
  Report on refuse and industrial waste disposal. [Toronto] 1956.
  50 leaves. tables.   OTUL
Mid-Canada Development Conference, Lakehead University, 1969.
  Essays on mid-Canada. Essais sur le Canada-médian. Presented at the first
  session, Mid-Canada Development Conference, August, 1969. [Toronto:
  Maclean–Hunter, c1970]
  484 p. graphs, illus., ports., tables.   OTU

— Mid-Canada conference task force reports/Conference du Canada-médian rapports des comités. A companion volume to *"Mid-Canada report/*Un compagnon à rapport sur le Canada-médian". [Toronto: Mid-Canada Development Foundation, Inc. c1971]
    1 v. (various pagings). map.   OTU
— Mid-Canada report. Rapport sur le Canada-médian. [Toronto] Mid-Canada Development Foundation [1971]
    xi, 114 p. illus., port.   OTU
Morgan, E   P
    Hamilton and its industries: being a historical and descriptive sketch of the city of Hamilton and its public and private institutions, manufacturing and industrial interest, public citizens, etc. Hamilton, Ontario: E.P. Morgan and F.L. Harvey, 1884.
    67 p. illus.   OOA
— 2d ed. Hamilton, Ontario: Spectator Printing Co., 1884.
    52 p. illus.   OKA
Morrison, Edith Lennox.
    William Tyrrell of Weston, by Edith Lennox Morrison and J.E. Middleton. Toronto: Macmillan Company of Canada Limited, 1937.
    xv, 152 p. front., illus., ports.   OTU
Muller, Robert Andrew, 1943 –
    A simulation of adjustment to the costs of pollution control in the pulp and paper industry. Hamilton, Ontario: Department of Economics, McMaster University, 1975.
    32 leaves. illus., tables. (Department of Economics, McMaster University. Working paper no. 75–05).   OTU
Murray, J   Alex.
    A cross-sectional analysis of Canadian public attitudes toward U.S. equity investment in Canada, by J. Alex Murray and Lawrence Le Duc. [Toronto]: Ontario Economic Council] 1975.
    vi, 83 leaves. illus. (Ontario Economic Council. Working paper no. 2/75).
                                     OTER
Naylor, Robin Thomas, 1945–
    The history of Canadian business, 1867–1914. Toronto: James Lorimer & Company, 1975.
    2 v.
    Contents: v. 1, The banks and financial capital; v. 2, Industrial development.   OTU
Nelson, Frederick.
    Toronto in 1928 A.D. Toronto: National Business Methods & Publishing Company [1908, sic]
    48 p.   OTU
Neufeld, Edward Peter, 1927–
    A global corporation: a history of the international development of Massey–Ferguson Limited. [Toronto] University of Toronto Press, 1969.
    ix, 427 p. illus. (part col.), charts, tables.   OTU

Ontario.
   Submission of the government of Ontario to the Royal Commission on the
   Automotive Industry, presented by Leslie M. Frost, prime minister of
   Ontario, October, 1960. [Toronto: 1960]
   42 leaves. diagrs. (part fold.), tables (part fold.).   OTU
Ontario. Commission to inquire into the requirements of Great Lakes Lumber
   & Shipping Limited, respecting saw-log supplies.
   Proceedings, December 8, 1943–January 19, 1944.
   4 v. [i.e. 622 typewritten pages]
   Commissioner: Donald P. Guthrie.
   No report was located.   OTAR
Ontario. Commission under the designation Fame inquiry in respect of the
   affairs of Farmers' Allied Meat Enterprises Co-operatives Limited.
   Report. [Toronto: 1965]
   114 p.
   Commissioner: Campbell Grant.   OTAR
Ontario. Flue-cured Tobacco Industry Inquiry Committee.
   Report. [Toronto] 1964.
   1 v. (various pagings).
   Chairman: Ford A. Stinson.   OTU
Ontario. Legislative Assembly. Select Committee on Company Law.
   Interim report. [Toronto] 1967.
   xi, 155 p.
   Chairman: Allan F. Lawrence.
— Proceedings July 14, 1965–August 3, 1967.
   6 v. [i.e. 3170, 39 typewritten pages]   OTAR OTUL
— Report on co-operatives. [Toronto: Queen's Printer, 1971]
   v, 113 p.
   Chairman: Gordon R. Carton.   OTAR OTUL
   Proceedings, January 21, 1970–February 17, 1971.
   5 v. [i.e. 1582–5439 typewritten pages]
   Paging follows from *Proceedings on Credit Unions*.   OTAR
— Report on credit unions. [Toronto] 1969.
   vi, 111 p.
   Chairman: Gordon R. Carton.   OTAR OTUL
   Proceedings, October 8, 1968–September 29, 1969.
   4 v. [i.e. 1581 typewritten pages]   OTAR
— Report on mergers, amalgamations and certain related matters. [Toronto:
   Queen's Printer, 1973]
   iii, 73 p.
   Chairman: William Hodgson.   OTAR OTUL

Background papers to Ontario Legislative Assembly Select Committee on Company Law
Beck, Stanley M
    An analysis of Foss v. Harbottle, prepared for the Select Committee on
    Company Law. [Kingston, Ontario] 1966.
    79 leaves.   OTAR
  — Corporate amalgamations and shareholders' rights, prepared for the Select
    Committee on Company Law. [Kingston, Ontario] 1966.
    58 leaves.   OTAR
Iacobucci, Frank.
    Business combinations: proposals for legislation, prepared for the Select
    Committee on Company Law. Toronto: 1970.
    84 leaves.   OTAR
McNairn, Colin H
    Termination of corporate existence. A paper prepared for the Select
    Committee on Company Law. Toronto: 1970.
    93 leaves.   OTAR
Palmer, E   E
    An analysis of the law relating to corporate management in Ontario. A
    report prepared for the Select Committee on Company Law. [Toronto?]
    1966.
    220 leaves.   OTAR
Smyth, J   E
    A critical appraisal of the role of the auditor. A research paper prepared by
    J.E. Smyth with the assistance of M.A. Prabhu and P.L. Howell for the
    Select Committee on Company Law. [Toronto] 1967.
    vi, 133 leaves.   OTAR

Ontario. Legislative Assembly. Select Committee on Economic and Cultural
    Nationalism.
    Preliminary report. [Toronto] 1972.
    iv, 15 leaves.
    Chairman: Russell D. Rowe.   OTAR
  — Interim report: advertising and the advertising industry. [Toronto] J.C.
    Thatcher, Queen's Printer, 1974.
    28 p.   OTAR
  — Interim report: capital markets, foreign ownership and economic
    development. [Toronto] 1974.
    v, 103 p.   OTAR
  — Interim report: colleges and universities in Ontario. [Toronto] 1973.
    139 p. tables.   OTAR OTER
  — Interim report: foreign ownership of Ontario real estate. [Toronto] J.C.
    Thatcher, Queen's Printer, 1973.
    60 p.   OTAR
  — Interim report: natural resources, foreign ownership and economic
    development. [Toronto: J.C. Thatcher, Queen's Printer] 1974.
    vi, 103 p.   OTAR

— Report. Toronto: J.C. Thatcher, Queen's Printer, 1975.
2 v.
Contents: Final report on cultural nationalism; Final report on economic
nationalism.   OTAR
— Briefs.
113 v.   OTAR
— Proceedings, January 12, 1972–January 16, 1973.
23 v. [i.e. 2,695 typewritten pages]   OTAR

*Background papers to Ontario Legislative Assembly Select Committee on Economic and
Cultural Nationalism*
Kates, Peat, Marwick & Co.
Attitude of community leaders and the general public in four Ontario
communities, prepared as part of a study on foreign ownership: corporate
behaviour and public attitudes, for the Select Committee on Economic and
Cultural Nationalism, by Kates, Peat, Marwick & Co. in association with
Canadian Facts Co. Ltd. [Toronto: J.C. Thatcher, Queen's Printer] 1973.
112, 10 p. graphs, tables.   OTU OTAR
— Community leaders and general public attitudes in four Ontario
communities, prepared as part of a study on foreign ownership, corporate
behaviour and public attitudes for the Select Committee on Economic and
Cultural Nationalism, by Kates, Peat, Marwick & Co. in association with
Canadian Facts Co. Ltd. [Toronto] 1973.
105 leaves. graphs, tables.   OTAR
— Employee attitudes, prepared as part of a study on foreign ownership:
corporate behaviour and public attitudes for the Select Committee on
Economic and Cultural Nationalism, by Kates, Peat, Marwick & Co. in
association with Canadian Facts Co. Ltd. [Toronto: J.C. Thatcher, Queen's
Printer] 1974.
163 p. graphs.   OTAR
— Foreign ownership: architecture and engineering consulting, prepared as
part of a study on foreign ownership corporate behaviour and public
attitudes for the Select Committee on Economic and Cultural Nationalism.
[Toronto: J.C. Thatcher, Queen's Printer] 1973.
134 p. chart, graphs, tables.   OTAR
— Foreign ownership: corporate behaviour and public attitudes, overview
report, prepared for the Select Committee on Economic and Cultural
Nationalism. [Toronto: J.C. Thatcher, Queen's Printer] 1974.
236 p. graphs, tables.   OTAR
— Foreign ownership and forest-based industries, prepared as part of a study on
foreign ownership: corporate behaviour and public attitudes for the Select
Committee on Economic and Cultural Nationalism. [Toronto: J.C.
Thatcher, Queen's Printer] 1973.
124 p. graphs, map, tables.   OTU OTAR

— Foreign ownership and the advertising industry, prepared as part of a study on foreign ownership: corporate behaviour and public attitudes for the Select Committee on Economic and Cultural Nationalism. [Toronto: J.C. Thatcher, Queen's Printer] 1973.
  216 p. tables.   OTAR
— Foreign ownership and the auto parts industry, prepared as part of a study on foreign ownership: corporate behaviour and public attitudes for the Select Committee on Economic and Cultural Nationalism. [Toronto: J.C. Thatcher, Queen's Printer] 1973.
  114 p. graphs, tables.   OTAR
— Foreign ownership and the electronics industry, prepared as part of a study on foreign ownership: corporate behaviour and public attitudes, for the Select Committee on Economic and Cultural Nationalism. [Toronto: J.C. Thatcher] 1973.
  99 p. tables.   OTU OTAR
— Foreign ownership and the mining industry, prepared as part of a study on foreign ownership: corporate behaviour and public attitudes for the Select Committee on Economic and Cultural Nationalism. [Toronto: J.C. Thatcher] 1973.
  119 p. tables.   OTAR
Neilson, William A   W
  The Australian regulation of foreign direct investment: recent experience relevant to Canadian policies. A report prepared for the Ontario Select Committee on Economic and Cultural Nationalism. [Toronto] J.C. Thatcher, Queen's Printer, 1973.
  98 p.   OTAR

Ontario. Legislative Assembly. Special Committee charged with the revision of the Companies Act (Ontario) and related acts
  Report. Toronto: Baptist Johnston, printer to the Queen's Most Excellent Majesty, 1953.
  17 p.
  Chairman: A.K. Roberts.   OTAR
— Proceedings, May 5, 1952–December 10, 1953 [sic]
  26 v. [i.e. 3,337 typewritten pages]
  v. 24, pp. 3129–3168 missing.   OTAR
Ontario. Royal Commission appointed to inquire into the egg industry in Ontario.
  Report. [Thunder Bay, Ontario: 1972]
  x, 105 leaves. tables.
  Commissioner: James Ross.   OTAR
— Proceedings, December 15, 1971–February 9, 1972.
  13 v. transcript.   OTAR

Submission to the Ontario Royal Commission appointed to inquire into the egg industry in Ontario
National Farmers Union.
Submission to the Ontario inquiry into egg marketing. Presented at Toronto January 7, 1972. n.p.: 1972.
14 leaves.   OTU

Ontario. Royal Commission on certain Sectors of the Building Industry.
Report. [Toronto] Queen's Printer for Ontario [1974]
2 v. illus., facsims., ports.
Commissioner: Harry Waisberg.   OTAR OTUCR
Ontario. Royal Commission on Industrial Safety.
Report. [Toronto: 1961]
87 p. tables.
Chairman: P.J. McAndrew.   OTAR OTU
— Report of hearings, June 2–December 2, 1960.
10 v. [i.e. 2682 typewritten pages]   OTAR
Ontario. Royal Commission on Petroleum Products Pricing.
First report [Toronto] 1975.
1 v. (various pagings). graphs, tables.
Commissioner: Claude M. Isbister.   OTAR
— Supplement to First report. [Toronto] 1976.
1 v. (various pagings). tables.   OTAR
— Report. [Toronto] 1976.
iv, 192 p. graphs, tables.   OTAR
— Proceedings, August 15, 1975–April 22, 1976.
38 v. [i.e. 5001 typewritten pages]   OTAR
Ontario. Securities Commission.
Canadian provincial securities administrators; national policies, Alberta, British Columbia, Manitoba, New Brunswick, Ontario, Prince Edward Island, Quebec, Saskatchewan. [Toronto] 1971.
41 leaves.   OTUL
— Initial summary of insider trading reports. Toronto [1967]
167 p.   OONL
— Report of Commissioner D.S. Beatty on matters related to the financing of mining exploration and development companies. Toronto [1968]
41 p.   OONL

Background reports to the Ontario Securities Commission
Canadian Manufacturers' Association. Ontario Division.
A brief on Bill 154, the Securities Act, 1972, to the Ontario Securities Commission from the Canadian Manufacturers' Association, Ontario Division. [Toronto] The Association, 1972.
8 leaves.   OTU

Investment Dealers Association of Canada.
    Brief to the Ontario Securities Commission: cornerstone prospectus and
    offering circular. Prepared by a special committee. [Toronto] 1971.
    13 leaves.
    Chairman: J.R. Crysdale, of Mills, Spence & Co., Limited.   OTU
Toronto Stock Exchange.
    Submission to the Ontario Securities Commission on Bill 154 – the Securities
    Act, 1972. [Toronto] n.p.: 1973.
    51, 16 p.   OTU

Ontario. Securities Commission. Committee on the problems of disclosure raised
    for investors by business combinations and private placements.
    Report. [Toronto: Ontario Securities Commission] 1970.
    v, 200 p. tables.
    Chairman: H.S. Bray.   OTUCR
Ontario. Securities Commission. Securities Industry. Ownership Committee.
    Report. Toronto: Ontario Securities Commission, 1972.
    xiii, 192 p. illus., forms, tables.
    Chairman: E.A. Royce.   OTUCR
Ontario Economic Council.
    Report of a meeting concerning education as it relates to Ontario forest-
    based industry, September 2nd, 1965. [Toronto? 1965]
    15 leaves. 8 diagrs.,   OTU
— Skill acceleration: eighteen growth companies explain how they develop
    extra employee skill-power. [edited by B.T. Richardson] Toronto: 1967.
    84 p. illus.
    Chairman: William H. Cranston.   OTER
Ontario Flue-cured Tobacco Growers' Marketing Board.
    Submission to the Federal Conference on Smoking and Health, the
    Department of National Health and Welfare by the Ontario Flue-cured
    Tobacco Growers' Marketing Board and Burley Tobacco Marketing
    Association of Ontario. Presented in Ottawa on November 25th, 1963. n.p.
    [1963]
    28 p. illus.   OTU
Ontario Paper Company, Limited.
    No newsprint for sale: or, why proration should not be extended to the
    Ontario Paper Company – a noncommercial newsprint manufacturer.
    [Thorold, Ontario: 1941]
    31 p. illus.   OTU
Ottawa. Industrial and Publicity Commission,
    Ottawa, the capital of Canada. Ottawa: Industrial and Publicity
    Commission [19—].
    32 p. illus.   OTU

Ottawa industrial edition, Ottawa, Ontario, Canada the capital city.
  Representative merchants and manufacturers who have contributed to make
  the capital city famous. n.p.: 1909.
  24 p. illus., ports.   OOA
Our Dominion: mercantile and manufacturing interests, historical and
  commercial sketches of Ottawa and environs. Toronto: The Historical
  Publishing Company of Canada, 1887.
  259 p. illus., ports.   OOA
Pearson, Norman, 1928–
  Parry Sound: feasibility of a planned industrial estate. [Guelph, Ontario]
  Centre for Resources Development, University of Guelph, 1971.
  89 leaves. tables. (University of Guelph. The Centre for Resources
  Development. Publication no. 49).   OLU
Peat, Marwick and partners.
  Potential distribution of service industries. Prepared by Peat, Marwick and
  partners and [I.B.I.] group. [Toronto] Municipality of Metropolitan Toronto
  Planning Department, 1975.
  1 v. (various pagings). maps, tables. (Background studies in the metropolitan
  plan preparation programme)   OTUSA
Perry, Robert Louis, 1927–
  Galt, U.S.A. The American presence in a Canadian city. Toronto:
  Maclean–Hunter Limited [1971]
  137 p. illus., ports., tables.
  A *Financial Post* book.   OTU
Peterborough, Ontario. City Council. Manufacturers' Committee
  Peterborough, Ontario, where industry prospers and people enjoy life.
  Peterborough, Ontario: City Council, Manufacturers' Committee [1936]
  [25] p. illus., map.   OTU
Petrie, Auldham Roy, 1921–
  Samuel McLaughlin. [Don Mills, Ontario] Fitzhenry & Whiteside Limited
  [c1975]
  61 p. illus., ports.   OONL
Petrolia, Canada, 1862–1908: its advantages as a commercial and residential
  centre. [London, Ontario: London Advertiser, 1908]
  64 p. chiefly illus., ports., map.   OLU
Philips Planning and Engineering Limited.
  Burlington waste reclamation pilot study: final report, 1972. Prepared for
  the Waste Management Branch of the Ontario Ministry of the Environment
  and the town of Burlington, Ontario. [Burlington, Ontario: 1972]
  60 p. illus.   OONL
Phillips, William Gregory, 1921–
  The agricultural implement industry in Canada: a study of competition.
  [Toronto] University of Toronto Press, 1956.
  xi, 208 p. illus., diagrs., tables (Canadian studies in economics, no. 7). OTU

Piper, (W.S.) Limited.
Sixty years in business, 1884–1944. Fort William, Ontario [1944?]
[12] p. illus., ports.   OTU
Port Industry Task Force.
Report. [Toronto] The Task Force [c1975]
vii, 97 p. illus., maps, tables.
Toronto harbour and industries.   OTU
Priamo, Carol.
Mills of Canada. Toronto: McGraw–Hill Ryerson [c1976]
192 p. illus. (part col.).   OOA
Prothero, Frank.
The good years: a history of the commercial fishing industry on Lake Erie.
Belleville, Ontario: Mika Publishing, 1973.
160 p. illus., graphs, map, ports.   OTU
— Men 'n boats: the fisheries of the Great Lakes. [Port Stanley, Ontario: The
Great Lakes Fisherman, 1975?]
174 p. illus., ports.   OLU
Queen's University. Institute of Local Government.
Single-enterprise communities in Canada. A report to Central Mortgage
and Housing Corporation. [Ottawa: Central Mortgage and Housing
Corporation] 1953.
v, 312 p. illus.   OKQ
Ray, David Michael, 1935–
Market potential and economic shadow; a quantitative analysis of industrial
location in southern Ontario. Chicago [Department of Geography,
University of Chicago, 1965]
xvii, 164 p. illus., maps. (Chicago. University. Department of Geography.
Research paper no. 101).
Sarnia, Ontario. Industrial Development Committee.
Sarnia and district: facts and figures. [Sarnia, Ontario: 1971?]
30 p. tables.   OONL
Scarborough, Ontario. Council.
Scarborough; industrial pulse of Toronto. [Scarborough, Ontario: Township
of Scarborough Printing Department, 1959?]
[33] p. illus., maps.   OTU
Shackleton, Philip.
Potteries in nineteenth century Ontario. Ottawa: National Historic Sites
Service, 1964.
1 v. (unpaged). (National Historic Parks and Sites Branch.MRS no. 2).   OTAR
Shaw, Robert B
History of the Comstock patent medicine business and Dr. Morse's Indian
root pills. Washington, D.C.: Smithsonian Institution Press, 1972.
48 p. illus., facsims. (Smithsonian studies in history and technology, no. 22).
                                                                       OTAR

Simcoe – Georgian Area Task Force.
Simcoe – Georgian area development strategy study. Second interim report: alternative development strategies. [Midhurst, Ontario] 1975.
1 v. (various pagings). fold maps, tables. OMI
— Simcoe – Georgian area development strategy study: the development strategy. [Toronto] Simcoe – Georgian Area Task Force, c1976.
viii, S1–S17, 120 p. plates, maps (part col., part fold.). OTMCL
Spelt, Jacob, 1919–
Toronto. With a chapter on the economic structure of Toronto by Donald P. Kerr. [Toronto] Collier–Macmillan Canada, Ltd. [c1973]
183 p. illus., maps. (Canadian cities series). OTU
Strathroy, Ontario. Industrial Commission.
The town of Strathroy industrial survey. Strathroy, Ontario [1957?]
23 p. illus., map. OTU
A study of profitability for 16 Canadian food companies: prepared for the Ministry of Consumer and Commercial Relations, province of Ontario. [Toronto: Ministry of Consumer and Commercial Relations, province of Ontario] 1974.
2 v. OTU
Sullivan, Alan, 1868–1947.
The rapids. Toronto: Copp Clark Co., Limited, 1920.
336 p. OTU
— Introduction by Michael Bliss [Toronto] University of Toronto Press [c1972]
xx, 263 p. illus. (Social history of Canada series).
Francis H. Clergue's industrial empire at Sault Ste. Marie, 1884–1903. OTU
Tait, Lyal, 1911–
Tobacco in Canada. [Tillsonburg, Ontario: Flue-cured Tobacco Growers' Marketing Board, 1968]
xii, 560 p. illus. (part col.).
"Sponsored by the Ontario Flue-cured Tobacco Growers' Marketing Board to commemorate the one hundredth anniversary of Canada's confederation 1867–1967 and the tenth anniversary of Canada's tobacco auction system 1957–1967." OTU
Terdik, John.
The changing patterns of the distribution and composition of manufacturing industries in the city of Brantford from 1844 to 1925. [Brantford, Ontario] 1972.
52 leaves. maps. OBRT
Times Printing Company, Hamilton, Ontario.
Hamilton, the Birmingham of Canada. Hamilton, Ontario: The Times Printing Company, 1893.
127 p. illus. OKQ
Tomkins, Doreen Margaret, 1930–
Southern Ontario: workshop of the nation by Doreen Margaret Tomkins, George S. Tomkins and Neville V. Scarfe. Toronto: W.J. Gage Limited, c1970.
51 p. illus., maps. (Regional studies of Canada). OKQ

Toronto. City Planning Board.
   Central area plan review: central industrial district proposals. [Toronto]
   1976.
   iii, 164 p. illus., maps (part fold.).   OONL
— Industrial prospects in the city of Toronto [by] City of Toronto Planning
   Board [and] Metropolitan Toronto Industrial Commission. [Toronto] 1965.
   iv, 74 p. illus., maps, tables.   OTUSA
— Industry and warehousing in the city of Toronto. Prepared for the City of
   Toronto Planning Board by Donald Kerr and Jacob Spelt. [Toronto] 1961.
   70 [4] leaves. map, tables.   OTU
— Report on industry. [Toronto] 1971.
   2 v. illus., forms, maps (part fold.).
   Contents: 1, Survey of the western area; 2, Survey of the central area.   OTU
— Report on industry survey of the northern and eastern areas. [Toronto] 1973.
   64 p. illus., diagrs., map, plans, tables.   OTUSA
Toronto. City Planning Board. Industry Work Group.
   Industrial relocation & its impact on employees: summary report. [Toronto]
   The Group, c1975.
   9 p. diagrs.   OTUSA
— A place for industry: a discussion paper on the future of industry in the city
   of Toronto/City of Toronto Planning Board, Industry Work Group.
   [Toronto] The Group, 1974.
   ii, 59 p. illus., tables.   OTU
Toronto. King – Parliament Site Office.
   A policy for industrial firms in King – Parliament: draft proposals, City of
   Toronto Planning Board, King – Parliament Site Office. [Toronto] 1975.
   64 p. 15 leaves of plates, illus., maps. (Report 6).   OONL
Toronto. Township Planning Board.
   Industrial development study. n.p.: 1958.
   52 leaves.   OTUSA
Toronto Industrial Commission.
   Canada's national market; a brief analysis of official data prepared for the
   information of manufacturers. Toronto: Toronto Industrial Commission,
   c1938.
   20 p. figs., col. maps.   OTU
— Five years of industrial progress in the Toronto area. [Toronto: The
   Commission 1934?]
   [16] p. illus., map.   OTAR
— Toronto and the Toronto area. Toronto: The Commission [1932?]
   48 p. illus.   OTAR
Tucker, Edward J   (comp.).
   75th birthday, 1848–1923: the Consumers' Gas Company of Toronto.
   [Toronto] Consumers' Gas [1923]
   132 p. illus., ports., diagrs.   OOA

Walker, David F   (ed.).
 Industrial development in southern Ontario. Selected essays, edited by
 David F. Walker & James H. Bater. Waterloo, Ontario: Published by the
 Department of Geography, Faculty of Environmental Studies, University of
 Waterloo with the assistance of the Industrial Developers' Association of
 Canada [c1974]
 xv, 306 p. graphs, illus., map, plans, tables. (Department of Geography,
 Publication series no. 3, University of Waterloo).   OTU
Walton, Howard R
 Hiram Walker (1816–1896) and Walkerville from 1858. New York: The
 Newcomen Society of North America, 1958.
 24 p. illus. port.   OKQ
Wanamaker, Castello Loral Roy, 1896–
 A history of the first mills of 7th town, now Ameliasburgh township, Prince
 Edward county, Ontario. n.p. [1970?]
 11 leaves.
 Chiefly pre-Confederation.   OTAR
Waterford, Ontario. Chamber of Commerce.
 Industrial survey of Waterford, Ontario, Canada. [Waterford, Ontario:
 Industrial Commission] 1949.
 16 p. illus., plan, map.   OLU
Webster, Donald Blake, 1933–
 The Brantford pottery, 1849–1907; history and assessment of the stoneware
 pottery at Brantford, Ontario, including results of excavations and analysis
 of products. [Toronto] Royal Ontario Museum [1968]
 80 p. illus., maps (Royal Ontario Museum. Art and Archaeology.
 Occasional paper 13).   OTU
— Early Canadian pottery. Toronto: McClelland and Stewart [c1971]
 256 p. illus. (part col.).
 Several chapters on Ontario.   OTU
— The William Eby pottery, Conestogo, Ontario, 1855–1907. [Toronto: Royal
 Ontario Museum, 1971]
 54 p. illus., maps, plans.   OTU
Weller, James.
 Rouge industrial district study. Prepared by James Weller for Metropolitan
 Toronto Planning Board and Borough of Scarborough Planning Board.
 [Toronto] 1973.
 xi, 214 p. diagrs., illus., maps.   OTUSA
Wells, Norman E
 Medals and tokens of Industrial Exhibition Association of Toronto.
 Peterborough, Ontario: Pronto–Print, 1975.
 70 p. illus., facsims.   OTU
Wiegman, Carl.
 Trees to news, a chronicle of the Ontario Paper Company's origin and
 development. [Toronto] McClelland & Stewart, 1953.
 xii, 364 p. illus., map, port., tables.   OTU

Wilson, Alan.
  John Northway: a blue serge Canadian. Toronto: Burns & MacEachern
  [1965]
  xv, 235 p. illus., map, port.   OTU
Winter, James Ralph, 1930–
  Sudbury – an economic survey, by J.R. Winter. Research assistant: J.L.
  Thibault. [Sudbury, Ontario] Sudbury and District Industrial Commission
  and Laurentian University Press, 1967.
  72 p. tables.   OTU
Yeager, William.
  The cabinet makers of Norfolk county [1st ed.] Simcoe, Ontario: Norfolk
  Historical Society, 1975.
  iii, 154 p. illus.   OTU
Yeates, Maurice H   1938–
  Impact of industrial incentives: southern Georgian Bay region, Ontario, by
  Maurice H. Yeates and Peter E. Lloyd. Ottawa: Policy and Planning
  Branch, Department of Energy, Mines and Resources [1963]
  xi, 85 p. tables. (Geographical paper no. 44).   OTUSA
— Main Street: Windsor to Quebec city. Toronto: The Macmillan Company
  of Canada Limited in association with the Ministry of State for Urban
  Affairs and Information Canada, 1975.
  xiv, 431 p. illus., diagrs., col. maps, tables.   OTUSA

Periodical Articles
The Algoma Steel Company, Limited. Industrial Canada 2: 325–327, 1902.
Algoma Steel's developments. Industrial Canada 39(no. 9): 58–60, 1939.
Allan, Duncan.
  Concentration and competition in Ontario's fluid milk industry. Ontario
  Economic Review, 3(no. 7): 3–15, 1965.
Anthes, L   L
  Highlights in history of Toronto Branch. Industrial Canada 50(no. 10):
  53–56, 1950.
  Canadian Manufacturers' Association.
Art as an important factor in industry; Toronto manufacturers appeal to
  Ontario members, C.M.A., for Ontario College of Art. Industrial Canada
  27(no. 4): 90–91, 1926.
Atikokan iron works. Industrial Canada 8: 95–96, 1907.
The attack on the automotive industry; far-reaching effect of the reduction in
  duties announced in the Budget resolutions. Industrial Canada 27(no. 1):
  39–43, 1926.
The automobile industry in Canada. Industrial Canada 7: 781–784, 1907.
Automobiles of Canadian make. Industrial Canada 9: 582–583, 1909.
The Automotive Building, Canadian National Exhibition, Toronto. Royal
  Architectural Institute of Canada. Journal 6: 401–407, 1929.
  Plates: pp. 397–399.

"Automotive industry's growth in fifty years". Industrial Canada, 50(no. 9): 112–125, 1950.

Backus, (Mrs.) John C
The Backhouse Mill. Western Ontario Historical Notes 14(no. 1): 21–23, 1957.

Bacso, Jean.
The Davisville Pottery. York Pioneer 32–38, 1975.
— Potters of the Don valley. York Pioneer 71(1): 20–28, 1976.

Baker, M   B
Our visible supply of brick. Canadian Mining Journal 30: 100–102, 1909.

Baking industry maintains high standards; establishment of Trent Institute at Guelph, Ontario is evidence of Canadian bakers' desire to continue their reputation for fine quality in their products. Industrial Canada 27(no. 9): 131, 1927.

Bartley, T   H
Industrial expansion in Metropolitan Toronto. Industrial Canada 54(no. 5): 57–59, 1953.

Bell, Frederick.
Group hospital plans benefit Canadian industry. Industrial Canada 44(no. 7): 92–94, 1943.
Ontario plan.

Bergey, J   C
The Ontario egg trade. Ontario Agricultural College Review 26: 288–289, 1914.

Biddell, J   L
Mechanics' Lien legislation; the albatross of the construction industry. Royal Architectural Institute of Canada. Journal 42(no. 3): 28–38; (no. 4): 56–60, 1965.

Big tannery rebuilt. Industrial Canada 20(no. 3): 276, 1919.
Hastings, Ontario.

Biscuits and confectionery. Industrial Canada 5: 746–747, 1905.

Bitzer, Irmgard.
Moritz Lindner – Berlin toymaker. Waterloo Historical Society. Annual Volume 59: 75–76, 1971.

Black, I   W
A new industry in Canada; the Ontario Potteries plant Oshawa, Ontario. Canadian Mining Journal 45: 814–817, 1924.

Bland, Warren R
The changing location of metal-fabricating and clothing industries in southern Ontario: 1881–1932. Ontario Geography 9: 34–57, 1975.
— The location of manufacturing in southern Ontario in 1881. Ontario Geography 8: 8–39, 1974.

Blenkinsop, L   J
Dofasco's development. Industrial Canada 51(no. 9): 56–58, 1951.

Bodnar, Laszlo.
    Potato marketing in Ontario. Ontario Economic Review 6(no. 3): 4–12,
    1968.
Booth, J   F
    Apple prices and premiums paid for preferred varieties. Economic Annalist
    1(no. 4): 1–2, 1931.
    Norfolk Fruit Growers' Association, Simcoe, Ontario, 1908–1929.
— The purchase of apples by consumers in Montreal and Toronto. Economic
    Annalist 1(no. 11): 1–4; (no. 12): 1–3, 1931.
Boucher, G   P   and D   J   Packman
    The dairy farm business in eastern Ontario 1947–1948. Economic Annalist
    19: 63–67, 1949.
Bowman, Henry B
    Preston's furniture industry and Percy R. Hilborn. Waterloo Historical
    Society. Annual Volume 60: 78–87, 1972.
The Brantford banquet; The Canadian Manufacturers' Association royally
    entertained the manufacturers of Brantford – a unique "Made in Canada"
    banquet. Industrial Canada 3: 360–365, 1903.
Brewing and distilling. Industrial Canada 5: 750–751, 1905.
Britton, John N   H
    The influence of corporate organization and ownership linkages of industrial
    plants: a Canadian enquiry. Economic Geography 52: 311–324, 1976.
    Primarily southern Ontario.
Brock, R   W
    Hamilton as an industrial centre occupies commanding position in Ontario.
    Industrial Canada 30(no. 11): 52–58, 1930.
— Industrial growth of the Niagara peninsula based largely on power
    development. Industrial Canada 30(no. 11): 68–73, 120, 1930.
— The Larder Lake district. Canadian Mining Journal 29: 621–624, 656–659,
    1908.
Brown, J   N   M
    The Ontario wine industry. Canadian Business 17(9): 72–75, 120, 122, 160,
    1944.
Business in Kinburn – 1906. Huron Historical Notes 9: 9–11, 1973.
"Buy Canadian" at the "Ex" Industrial Canada 63(no. 5): 43–44, 1962.
C.G.E. Peterborough works has "million-dollar" corner. Industrial Canada
    52(no. 4): 48–50, 1951.
    Canadian General Electric Co.
Cameron, W   G   R
    Preliminary indexes of production in Ontario. Ontario Economic Review 2:
    no. 6, 1964.
Cameron, W   Walter.
    Regulation and distribution of securities in Ontario. University of Toronto
    Law Journal 10: 199–212, 1954.
The Canada Foundry Company. Industrial Canada 2: 334, 1902.

Canada Iron Furnace; new plant at Midland, Ontario. Canadian Mining
Review 19: 161, 1900.
Canada Iron Furnace Company. Industrial Canada 2: 329–330, 1902.
Canada's automobile industry grows. Industrial Canada 20(no. 9): 183–184,
248–250, 1920.
Canada's pioneer locomotive builders. Industrial Canada 50(no. 9): 71–72,
1950.
Canadian Locomotive Co., Kingston.
The Canadian furniture industry. Industrial Canada 3: 370–372, 1903.
The Canadian Locomotive Company, Limited; history of the works at
Kingston. Queen's Quarterly 10: 455–465, 1902/1903.
The Canadian Manufacturers' Association; a retrospect. Industrial Canada 2:
80–82, 1901.
Carter, W   E   H
Peat fuel; something about the processes employed in producing out of
Canada's waste bogs a commercial substitute for coal. Industrial Canada 5:
436–438, 1905.
Carthy, Helen E
Port Arthur, Ontario; its industrial development. Thunder Bay Historical
Society. Papers 16 and 17: 39–51, 1924/1925, 1925/1926.
Casey, Thomas W
Napanee's first mills and their builder. Ontario Historical Society. Papers &
Records 6: 50–54, 1905.
Cawkell, William,
The furniture manufacturing industry. Industrial Canada 19(no. 9):
172–173, 1919.
Celebrating notable achievements of Canada's wartime industry. Industrial
Canada 44(no. 7): 84–86, 1943.
Fleet Aircraft, Ltd., Fort Erie.
Chambers, Edward J   and Gordon W   Bertram.
Urbanization and manufacturing in central Canada, 1870–1890. Canadian
Political Science Association. Conference on Statistics 225–258, 1964.
Charlesworth, J   L
Canada's automobile industry comes of age; a review of the position of one of
our largest industries after 21 years of life. Industrial Canada 26(no. 6): 59,
75, 1925.
— Hamilton, scene of C.M.A.'s 1925 convention; a brief account of the city's
growth – the part industry has played in its progress – its many and varied
attractions. Industrial Canada 26(no. 1): 36–39, 1925.
Clark, S   D
The Canadian Manufacturers' Association; a political pressure group.
Canadian Journal of Economics and Political Science 4: 505–523, 1938.
— The Canadian Manufacturers' Association and the tariff. Canadian Journal
of Economics and Political Science 5: 19–39, 1939.

Complete fine new office building; Barber–Ellis, Limited, now occupy
    commodious fire-proof structure in Toronto. Industrial Canada 23(no. 4):
    54, 1923.
Cooper, Reed T
    The growth and development of the furniture industry in Ontario. Ontario
    Economic Review 2: no. 12, 1965.
— Progress under the Automotive Free Trade Agreement: some comments.
    Ontario Economic Review 4(no. 5–6): 3–6, 1966.
Couling, Gordon.
    Stone masonry in Waterloo county. Waterloo Historical Society. Annual
    Volume 63: 32–43, 1975.
Coumans, Camilla.
    102-year-old Bruce county industry closes its doors. Bruce County Historical
    Society. Yearbook 45–46, 1973.
Craick, W   Arnot
    Contrasts of half a century point to the benefits of protection; reminiscenses
    of a Brantford manufacturer. Industrial Canada 21(no. 8): 82–83, 1920.
    C.H. Waterous.
— Peterborough as an industrial centre. Industrial Canada 18: 1121–1128,
    1917.
Cramp Steel Company, Limited. Industrial Canada 2: 331–333, 1902.
Dack, W   L
    Canada's steel industry expands in a big way. Canadian Geographical
    Journal 91(no. 4): 32–41, 1975.
Dales, John Harkness.
    Fuel, power and industrial development in central Canada. American
    Economic Review 43: 181–202, 1953.
[Davies, E   ]
    The glass industry in Wallaceburg. Western Ontario Historical Notes 3: 90,
    1945.
Davis, M   B and R   L   Wheeler.
    The apple industry of Canada – development – marketing. Canadian
    Geographical Journal 17: 104–121, 1938.
Davis, R   H
    Stainless steel program at Atlas Steels. Industrial Canada 51(no. 9): 53–55,
    58, 1951.
Dean, H   B
    The Ontario Industrial Education Council. Industrial Canada 51(no. 8): 37,
    1950.
Death of a great industrial leader; Lloyd Harris, a former vice-president of the
    C.M.A. dies suddenly at Brantford. Industrial Canada 26(no. 6): 63, 84,
    1925.
Death of prominent C.M.A. member; James Peter Murray, founder of Toronto
    Carpet Manufacturing Co., dies in his 77th year. Industrial Canada 30(no.
    2): 75, 1929.
A devoted member of the Association who left his mark on its work; an
    appreciation. Industrial Canada 21(no. 7): 61–62, 1920.
    Ernest George Henderson, manager of Canadian Salt Co., Windsor.

Dick, W   J
   By-product coke ovens of the Algoma Steel Company, Sault Ste. Marie,
   Ontario. Canadian Mining Journal 35: 487, 1914.
Diesel locomotive plant opened (General Motors, London, Ontario). Industrial
   Canada 51(no. 5): 71–74, 1950.
Dolgoy, Sidney.
   The development of Ontario's textile industry. Ontario Economic Review
   4(no. 3): 3–10, 1966.
Dominion of Canada industrial exhibition. Industrial Canada 3: 454–456, 1903;
   4: 173–175, 1903.
Drugs and chemicals. Industrial Canada 5: 767–768, 1905.
Dunham, B   Mabel
   Mills and millers of western Ontario. Western Ontario History Nuggets 9:
   1–9, 1946.
Edmonds, William Lewis.
   Making life pleasanter for the workers in a frontier industry. Industrial
   Canada 21(no. 10): 70–72, 1921.
   Espanola, Ontario.
— A notable experiment in welfare work. Industrial Canada 19 (no. 2): 62–64,
   1918.
   Massey – Harris Co., Toronto.
Elford, Jean.
   Sarnia, Canada's "chemical valley". Canadian Geographical Journal 55:
   170–185, 1957.
Elford, Jean and Edward Phelps.
   Oil, then to now. Canadian Geographical Journal. 77: 164–171, 1968.
   Sarnia & Petrolia, Ontario.
Elliott, T   R
   The motor car industry makes victory its business. Canadian Geographical
   Journal 25: 298–313, 1942.
The embarrassment of success. Industrial Canada 64(no. 5): 61–63, 1963.
   Greb Shoes – Kitchener.
Engines and boilers. Industrial Canada 5: 719–720, 1905.
Ferguson, G   Howard.
   Decentralization of industry and metropolitan control. Town Planning 2(4):
   5–12, 1923.
— Progress of Ontario Research Foundation; an outline of some of the
   achievements of the Foundation – work in the interests of the metal and
   woollen industries – agricultural problems. Industrial Canada 30(no. 10):
   77–79, 81, 88, 1930.
Findlay, M
   Notes on the Ontario and Alberta industrial standards legislation. Canadian
   Journal of Economics and Political Science 2: 419–420, 1936.
The first hundred years. Industrial Canada 72(no. 3): 99–124, 1971.
   Canadian Manufacturers' Association history.
The first 75 years. Imperial Oil Review 39(4): 9–20, 1955.
Fleming, Donald M
   Toronto and its future. Industrial Canada 50(no. 10): 56–59, 1950.

Fox, W   Sherwood.
    The mill at Ghost Lake; a story of pioneering in "The Bruce". Queen's
    Quarterly 50: 14–24, 1943.
— The mill at Stokes Bay. Queen's Quarterly 51: 398–407, 1944.
Frost, Leslie M
    Ontario and her future. Industrial Canada 58(no. 3): 103–108, 1957.
Fulton, David
    Canadian industrial designers; Ernest Orr. Industrial Canada 63(no. 5):
    35–36, 1962.
Furniss, I   F
    Basic parameters of the primary dairy industry in Ontario and Quebec.
    Canadian Farm Economics 5(no. 4): 11–24, 1970; 6(no. 2): 24–47, 1971.
Furniture. Industrial Canada 5: 736–737, 1905.
Gardiner, Frederick G
    Metropolitan Toronto. Industrial Canada 54(no. 3): 89–93, 1953.
Gas Co. celebrate 100 years. Industrial Canada 48(no. 12): 100, 1948.
    Consumer's Gas Co. of Toronto.
Georgetown's imaginative bid for more industry. Industrial Canada 60(no. 7):
    52–54, 1959.
Get Trenton plant. Industrial Canada 20(no. 5): 112, 1919.
Gilbertson, F   S
    Progress at Terrace Bay mill. Industrial Canada 48(no. 7): 89–91, 112, 1947.
Gilmour, Frederick W
    Penetanguishene and the men behind the industries. Mer Douce 2(3): 6–12,
    29–30, 1923.
[Grant, G   M   ]
    The Jason of Algoma; an account of the wonderful industrial development
    in new Ontario. Canadian Magazine of Politics, Science, Art and Literature
    15: 483–494, 1900.
A great Canadian industry. Methodist Magazine 47: 505–515, 1898.
    Massey–Harris Co.
Greater production effort of Toronto plant. Industrial Canada 19(no. 8): 61,
    1918.
    Garden production at Dunlop Co.
Greening W   E
    The lumber industry in the Ottawa valley and the American market in the
    nineteenth century. Ontario History 62: 134–136, 1970.
Greenman, E   F
    An early industry on a raised beach near Killarney, Ontario. American
    Antiquity 8: 260–265, 1943.
Griffin, Fred V
    Impressions of Ontario's northland. Industrial Canada 45(no. 7): 85–86,
    1944.
Griffin, Watson.
    Canadian iron and steel. Canadian Mining Journal 31: 231–234, 1910.

— Construction of 110 koppers by-product regenerative coke ovens for the
   Algoma Steel Company at Sault Ste. Marie, Ontario, Canada. Canadian
   Mining Journal 32: 333–340, 1911.
Growth in manufacturing in Toronto. Industrial Canada 2: 282, 1902.
The growth of a town. Industrial Canada 9: 31–32, 1908.
   Welland, Ontario.
Gunn, Donald W
   Provincial taxation of paid-up capital of foreign corporations. Canadian Bar
   Review 19: 31–36, 1941.
Gunn, James T
   The building guild movement. Canadian Forum 1: 138–139, 1921.
Haanel, Eugene.
   Smelting iron ore by electricity. Industrial Canada 6: 565–569, 1906.
Hall, John T
   Hamilton as an industrial centre. Industrial Canada 6: 725–731, 1906.
The Hamilton Centennial Exhibition. Industrial Canada 14: 184–188, 1913.
Hamilton industry which will soon be operating. Industrial Canada 24(no. 9):
   170, 1924.
   By-product coke ovens.
The Hamilton Steel & Iron Co., Limited. Industrial Canada 2: 331, 1902.
Hannah, J   A
   Industry, health and medical economics; explanation of the co-operative
   plan devised by Associated Medical Services Incorporated in Ontario.
   Industrial Canada 38(no. 8): 36–37, 1937.
Harry, George.
   Ontario has a plan for development. Industrial Canada 57(no. 5): 60–61,
   1956.
Harwood, Elizabeth.
   Webb's mills at Springdale. York Pioneer and Historical Society. Annual
   Report 76–95, 1969.
Hasselbring, A   and George W   McLeod.
   An iron ore industry for Ontario; a practical proposal from two mining
   engineers. Canadian Mining Journal 44: 52–54, 1923.
Haviland, William E
   Major developments in the marketing of leaf tobacco in Ontario. Economic
   Annalist 21: 6–10, 1951.
Hay, Keith A   J
   Trends in the location of industry in Ontario 1945–1959. Canadian Journal
   of Economics and Political Science 31: 368–381, 1965.
Hedley, Zilla.
   Kingarf saw mill. Bruce County Historical Society. Yearbook 12, 1970.
Hewitt, D   F
   Industrial minerals in Ontario. Canadian Mining Journal 71(no. 10):
   155–165, 1950.
— The limestone industries of Ontario. Canadian Mining Journal 79(no. 4):
   91–92, 1958.

Hewitt, D   F   and A   N   Deland.
   Urban expansion and the mineral industries in the Toronto – Hamilton
   area. Canadian Mining Journal 84(no. 4): 102–104, 1963.
Hilborn, Miriam.
   The E.T. Coleman hardware store in New Dundee. Waterloo Historical
   Society. Annual Volume 50: 79, 1962.
— The New Dundee flour mills. Waterloo Historical Society. Annual Volume
   50: 78–79, 1962.
— The Poth Furniture Factory in New Dundee. Waterloo Historical Society.
   Annual Volume 50: 80, 1962.
Honey, Peter.
   The growth and development of primary iron and steel in Ontario. Ontario
   Economic Review 2: no. 8, 1964.
— The growth and development of the motor vehicle industry in Ontario.
   Ontario Economic Review 3: no. 2, 1965.
Hoskins, R   G
   Hiram Walker and the origins and development of Walkerville, Ontario.
   Ontario History 64: 122–131, 1972.
House, Arthur W
   Electronics in industry – the new industrial revolution. Industrial Canada
   53(no. 4): 38–41, 1952.
— Seventy-six years of Canada's annual "world's fair". Industrial Canada
   55(no. 3): 60–63, 1954.
— Trial by ordeal. Industrial Canada 54(no. 4): 36–38, 44, 1953.
   Canadian Standards Association.
Hutchison, Helen.
   John Thomson, pioneer in paper-making, father of the pulpwood industry in
   Canada. Historic Kingston 10: 15–21, 1962.
Inch, Murray.
   Sketch of the life of George Sleeman – an early settler in Guelph. Western
   Ontario Historical Notes 18: 20–21, 1962.
Inco and its employees. Industrial Canada 37(no. 7): 44–45, 1936.
Industrial air raid precautions; Ontario firms given widespread exemption from
   lighting restrictions. Industrial Canada 42(no. 12): 113–114, 1942.
Industrial conditions in Toronto. Industrial Canada 11: 27–29, 1910.
Industrial re-training in Ontario. Canadian Mining Journal 40: 459–460, 1919.
The industrial towns of Waterloo county. Mer Douce 3(2): 47–52, 1924.
Iron and steel. Industrial Canada 5: 713–716, 1905.
Irwin, Alan Maurice.
   Are we developing a Canadian Lyons? Industrial Canada 24(no. 10): 70–71,
   1924.
Jackes, Lyman B
   What workmen think of moving pictures in the factory. Industrial Canada
   21(no. 5): 89, 1920.
   Goodyear Co., New Toronto.
Jet engine plant opens at Malton. Industrial Canada 53(no. 6): 78–80, 1952.

Jewellery and silverware. Industrial Canada 5: 760–761, 1905.

The John Inglis Company; equipment and products of this long-established firm. Canadian Mining Journal 44: 183–185, 1923.

[John Watson catalogue]. Waterloo Historical Society. Annual Volume 59: 48–50, 1971.

John Watson Ayr Foundry – 1868.

John Watson of Ayr, 1820–1903. Waterloo Historical Society. Annual Report 17: 143–148, 1929.

Johnson, Harry G
The Bladen plan for increased protection of the Canadian automotive industry. Canadian Journal of Economics and Political Science 29: 212–238, 1963.

Johnston, James.
The mill and metallurgical practice of the Nipissing Mining Company, Limited. Canadian Mining Journal 35: 205–210, 238–241, 1914.

Jones, A   R   R
Ontario Wind Engine and Pump Co., Ltd. Canadian Mining Journal 42: 894–896, 1921.

Jones, Clarence
The grain trade of Montreal. Economic Geography 1: 53–72, 1925.
Includes Ontario ports.

Jones, J   C   H
Mergers and competition: the Brewing Case. Canadian Journal of Economics and Political Science 33: 551–568, 1967.

Jones, Lawrence F
The automobile industry in Canada's economy. Canadian Geographical Journal 37: 86–98, 1948.

Kealey, Gregory.
Artisans respond to industrialism: shoemakers, shoe factories and the Knights of St. Crispin in Toronto. Canadian Historical Association. Historical Papers, 137–157, 1973.

Keir, Robert J
Sudbury desperately in need of secondary industry. Monetary Times 130(11): 80–81, 1962.

Kennedy, Walter.
Steel manufacture at Collingwood. Industrial Canada 1: 157–159, 1901.

Kerr, Donald.
The geography of the Canadian iron and steel industry. Economic Geography 35: 151–163, 1959.

Kerr, Donald and Jacob Spelt.
Manufacturing in suburban Toronto. Canadian Geographer 3: 11–19, 1958.
— Some aspects of industrial location in southern Ontario. Canadian Geographer 4: 12–25, 1960.

Kewley, E   T
Contribution of Dominion Power and Transmission Company to industrial growth. Industrial Canada 30(no. 11): 66–67, 1930.

Khan, C   Rafiq A
The structure and concentration of Ontario manufacturing and its relative
position in Canada. Ontario Economic Review 1: no. 6, 1963.
Kilbourn, William.
— Hamilton, a city shaped by industry. Royal Architectural Institute of
Canada. Journal 40(no. 4): 51–55, 1963.
Killikelly, Desmond.
The steel industry of Canada. Canadian Geographical Journal 16: 212–245,
1938.
Kingston Diesel Day. Industrial Canada 52(no. 5): 57–58, 1951.
[Kreiner, H   C   ]
John Bramm – Kitchener's first brickmaker. Waterloo Historical Society.
Annual Volume 59: 36–37, 1971.
Laidlaw Lumber Company Limited, Weston, Ontario. Royal Architectural
Institute of Canada. Journal 33: 253–263, 1956.
Lambert, E   F
Canada's new nickel refining industry. Industrial Canada 19(no. 7): 54–56,
1918.
Lang, W   R
The chemical industries of the Dominion, 1905. Industrial Canada 5:
486–491, 551–555, 611–616, 630, 1905.
Lee–Whiting, Brenda.
Daniel Sarazin still makes birchbark canoes. Canadian Geographical
Journal 72: 124–129, 1966.
— Saga of a nineteenth century sawmill. Canadian Geographical Journal 74:
46–51, 1967.
Leung, Felicity Hale.
Roller milling at the St. Jacob's flour mill from 1888–1889. Waterloo
Historical Society. Annual Volume 63: 13–28, 1975.
Lewis, Robert S
The Lake Superior iron ore industry. Mining Magazine 44(6): 342–348,
1931.
Livingston, Harry P
James Livingston. Waterloo Historical Society. Annual Report 9: 189–191,
1921.
Locate in Cobourg; the Langslow, Fowler Company, of Rochester, are to
establish Canadian subsidiary. Industrial Canada 21(no. 1): 88, 1920.
Locomotive shops opened at Stratford; new plant for locomotive repair and
construction. Industrial Canada 9: 665, 1909.
Longenecker, Charles.
Algoma Steel Corporation, Ltd.: its products have greatly promoted the
industrial growth of the Dominion of Canada. Blast Furnace and Steel Plant
30: 112–135, 1942.
Macdonald, H
Taxing business in province of Ontario. Industrial Canada 23(no. 4): 50,
1922.

— The Toronto branch reviews its work. Industrial Canada 19(no. 2): 56–58,
1918; 20(no. 2): 51–53, 1919; 21(no. 2): 75–78, 1920.
Title varies: v. 21, Toronto branch reviews its year.
Canadian Manufacturers' Association.

MacDonald, Neil B
A comment: the Bladen plan for increased protection for the automotive
industry. Canadian Journal of Economics and Political Science 29: 505–515,
1963.

McDougall, Harry.
Canada makes a comeback in hydrofoil development. Industrial Canada
67(no. 8): 39–42, 1966.

Macfarlane, J   C   [et al.]
Report of the Legislation Committee; careful review of federal and
provincial legislation of past year affecting manufacturers. Industrial
Canada 23(no. 3): 149–155, 1922.

MacGillivray, Kenneth.
Canada on wheels. Canadian Geographical Journal 48: 70–83, 1954.
Automotive industry.

McGuire, B   J
Aluminum – the story of fifty years of growth by the Canadian industry.
Canadian Geographical Journal 43: 144–163, 1951.

— Steel forges ahead. Canadian Geographical Journal 45: 174–191, 1952.

McIntosh, J   M
Kitchener and Waterloo branch is organized. Industrial Canada 21(no. 2):
58, 1920.
Canadian Manufacturers' Association.

McIntosh, J   M
The produced in Canada effort in Ontario. Industrial Canada 29(no. 9):
149, 1929.

McKellar, Peter.
The original Kaministiquia Club. Thunder Bay Historical Society. Papers
6: 7–9, 1915.

— Shipping trade of Fort William; extracts from the *Fort William Daily Times –
Journal* of Nov. 20, 1915 re the grain, flour and shipping industries of
Thunder Bay district up to date. Thunder Bay Historical Society. Papers 7:
17–21, 1916.

Mackenzie, G   C
The mining and metallurgical industries, section II – metallurgical industry.
Industrial Canada 19(no. 9): 160–162, 1919.

McLeod, Donald J
A brief history of petroleum refining in western Ontario. Quarterly Review
of Commerce 4: 10–14, 1936.

MacNab, John E
Toronto's industrial growth to 1891. Ontario History 47: 59–80, 1955.

McNaught, W   K
   Report of Industrial Exhibition Committee. Industrial Canada 2: 110–112,
   1901.
McNeill, A
   The apple industry of Ontario. Ontario Agricultural College Review 17:
   456–460, 1905.
Machinery. Industrial Canada 5: 717–718, 1905.
Malone, Hal.
   Chrysler Canada gives ex-prisoners a chance. Industrial Canada 73(no. 7):
   28–30, 1973.
The manufacture of automobiles and trucks. Industrial Canada 33(no. 9):
   82–83, 1933.
Manufacturing expansion – the road to full employment; Ontario Industrial
   Development Conference calls for manufacturing speed-up. Industrial
   Canada 61(no. 8): 56–58, 1960.
Marsh, H   H
   Industrial growth in Hamilton. Industrial Canada 13: 858–859, 1913.
Marsh, W   H   C
   New activity in northeastern Ontario – business highlights of 1962.
   Monetary Times 130(11): 36–38, 40, 42, 1962.
Marshall, Alex.
   A unique exhibition held at Kitchener. Industrial Canada 20(no. 4): 57,
   1919.
Midland no. 1; Canada's Iron Furnace: Co's new furnace at Midland blown in
   with befitting ceremony. Canadian Mining Review 19: 272–277, 1900.
Midland's semicentennial, an historic review of fifty years of development of its
   resources, industries and commerce. Mer Douce 2(1): 5–12; 2(2): 22–23,
   1922.
Milling. Industrial Canada 5: 740–741, 1905.
More power for Ontario industry; new DeCew Falls plant opened. Industrial
   Canada 44(no. 7): 90–91, 1943.
Morine, A   B
   Ontario company law. Canada Law Journal 45: 145–155, 338–346, 1909.
Mulvey, Thomas.
   Company law in Ontario. Canada Law Journal 43: 81–85, 1907.
— Ontario company law. Canada Law Journal 45: 220–231, 1909.
Munro, Ross.
   The Snider flour mills, Waterloo. Waterloo Historical Society. Annual
   Report 15: 383–384, 1927.
   Reprinted from Saturday Night Sept. 10, 1927.
Musgrave, J   E   T
   Canadian tobacco. Canadian Geographical Journal 8: 177–289, 1934.
   Industry in southern Ontario.
New Aguasabon plant in operation. Industrial Canada 49(no. 7): 116, 1948.
   Terrace Bay, Ontario.
New beet-sugar factories. Industrial Canada 2: 334, 1902.

New blast furnace in Port Arthur. Industrial Canada 7: 656, 1907.

New industry for Hamilton. Industrial Canada 20(no. 2): 106, 1919.

The new northland; a description of part of northern Ontario and two of its industrial pioneers. Canadian Mining Journal 44: 240–242, 1923.

New Plant of the Steel Company of Canada at Hamilton, Ontario. Canadian Mining Journal 34: 488–489, 1913.

New spinning and worsted mill for Toronto. Industrial Canada 19(no. 9): 220, 1919.

New Toronto industry; the Arco Company, of Cleveland, Ohio, are establishing a Canadian plant. Industrial Canada 21(no. 1): 88, 1920.

New Wingham industry. Industrial Canada 20(no. 3): 262, 1919.

Newlands, David L
    The Ahrens Pottery. Canadian Antiques Collector 11(no. 5): 33–37, 1976.
    Near Paris Ontario.

— The Egmondville Pottery: Huron county, Ontario, 1852–1910. Canadian Antiques Collector 10: 22–25, 1975.

— The Edmondville Pottery revisited: Huron county, Ontario, 1852-1910. Canadian Antiques Collector 11(no. 3): 19–23, 1976.

Newman, W   M
    Wiarton's busy mills were centre of industry in Bruce peninsula. Western Ontario Historical Notes 4: 84–91, 1946.
    Reprinted from *Canada Lumberman* 1931.

Niagara District Industrial Association Congress. Industrial Canada 21(no. 4): 80, 92, 1920.

Oberholtzer, R   S
    One hundred and fifty years of change along the Preston – Kitchener roadway. Waterloo Historical Society. Annual Volume 51: 80–81, 1963.

Ontario: accent on production. Industrial Canada 53(no. 9): 64–72, 1953.

Ontario division's efforts to secure power. Industrial Canada 21(no. 8): 88–89, 1920.

Ontario shoe manufacturers. Industrial Canada 20(no. 10): 61, 1920.

Orchard, L   B
    The Atikoken Iron Company. Canadian Mining Journal 29(no. 5): 36–39, 1908.

Panabaker, D   N
    Glimpses of the industrial activities of Waterloo county about fifty years ago. Waterloo Historical Society. Annual Report 21: 32–44, 1933.

— Pioneer woolen mills in Preston, Hespeler and vicinity; Waterloo county, Ontario and their connection with later textile industries. Waterloo Historical Society. Annual Report 21: 45–52, 1933.

— The town of Hespeler; a sketch of the early years of its development, including some general references to the settlers associated with its early industries. Waterloo Historical Society. Annual Report 10: 213–224, 1922.

— Waterloo Historical Society. Annual Volume 60: 36–49, 1972.

Panabaker, J   D
    David Norman Panabaker. Waterloo Historical Society. Annual Report 27:
    86–89, 1939.
Paraskevopoulos, Christos C
    Regional growth patterns in Canadian manufacturing industry: an
    application of the shift and share analysis. Canadian Journal of Economics
    7: 121–125, 1974.
Paterson, Donald M
    The impact of large scale industrial developments, with special reference to
    the new Ford plant near Oakville, Ontario. Royal Architectural Institute of
    Canada. Journal 30: 166–168, 1953.
Pease, O   C
    In Ontario's industrial northland; a survey of conditions at the present time
    in the territory between Fort William and North Bay. Industrial Canada
    23(no. 4): 55–56, 1922.
— Northern Ontario's industrial potentialities; rapid development of the
    mineral and other resources of the region points to a future of manufacturing
    activity. Industrial Canada 25(no. 5): 47–49, 1924.
— Produced-in-Canada campaign organized in Ontario. Industrial Canada
    26(no. 9): 130–131, 1926.
Peat making at government plant. Industrial Canada 11: 33–35, 1910.
The piano and organ industry; a valuable department of Canadian industrial
    life – extensive growth in recent years – description of the process of
    manufacture. Industrial Canada 4: 362–367, 1904.
The pioneers of Canadian industry. Industrial Canada 32(no. 3): 269–314;
    32(no. 4): 46–49, 1931.
    Short sketches of industries in existence since 1871.
Pitkin, Frank C
    Dexter D'Everardo. Welland County Historical Society. Papers and Records
    3: 86–103, 1927.
Plans of the Industrial Exhibition Association. Industrial Canada 1: 106–107,
    1900.
The plant and equipment of the Cobalt Hydraulic Company. Canadian Mining
    Journal 30: 611–617, 1909.
Polymer Corporation. Royal Architectural Institute of Canada. Journal 24:
    421–429, 1947.
Porter, Dana.
    Industrial Ontario. Industrial Canada 48(no. 9): 83–85, 1948.
Portland cement. Industrial Canada 5: 769–771, 1905.
Price, W   J
    An Ontario live stock industry. Ontario Agricultural College Review 11(2):
    7–10, 1899.
A producer gas plant; the McClary Mfg. Co. of London have a gas power plant
    in satisfactory operation. Industrial Canada 8: 710, 1908.

[Pryce, Nona Beck]
The Becks of Doon. Waterloo Historical Society. Annual Volume 54: 59–61, 1966.
Rannie, William F
Old, big, colourful: the distilling industry. Canadian Geographical Journal 93(no. 3): 20–27, 1976.
Ray, D   Michael.
The location of United States manufacturing subsidiaries in Canada. Economic Geography 47: 389–400, 1971.
Reaburn, Ronald and Tauline Reaburn.
Line kilns – remnants of pioneer technology. Canadian Geographical Journal 86: 14–17, 1973.
Review of industrial conditions in Canada. Industrial Canada 24(no. 9): 109–153, 1924.
Reynolds, Marion R
History of Walkey's Feed Mill, Harriston, Ontario, 1856–1944. Western Ontario Historical Notes 22: 53–56, 1966.
Richmond, D   R
Whither the tourist industry. Ontario Economic Review 1: no. 4, 1903.
Robb, G   A
The tourist industry in Ontario. Royal Architectural Institute of Canada. Journal 23: 183–188, 1946.
Rolph, Frank.
A review of Toronto's industrial position. Industrial Canada 10: 35–37, 1909.
Russell, Loris S
"Carbide" Willson. Canada: an historical magazine 3(no. 1): 20–33, 1975.
Thomas Leopold Willson.
Sanders, C   F
Brantford Ontario, is an important industrial centre. Industrial Canada 36(no. 1): 45–46, 1935.
Saunders, J   H
Furniture manufacturers hold an exhibition. Industrial Canada 21(no. 10): 68–69, 1921.
— Large boiler-making industries amalgamate; Babcock–Wilcox & Goldie–McCulloch, Limited, combine interests of Canadian, British and United States firms. Industrial Canada 24(no. 8): 58–59, 1923.
— Textile manufacturers hold successful exhibition in Toronto during February. Industrial Canada 22(no. 11): 49–50, 1922.
Saywell, J   T
The early history of Canadian oil companies: a chapter in Canadian business history. Ontario History 53: 67–72, 1961.
Scott, B   S
Oil refining in London. Western Ontario Historical Notes. 6: 38–45, 1948.

Scott, Helene.
    Stokes Bay area mills. Bruce County Historical Society. Yearbook 22, 24, 48,
    1973.
Scott, W   J
    Industrial fire losses in Ontario. Industrial Canada 47(no. 3): 271–272, 1946.
The Seaforth salt works. Huron Historical Notes 9: 40–41, 1973.
    From Huron *Expositor*, 1881,
Shipley, W   C
    Dairy factories in eastern Ontario and southern Quebec. Economic Annalist
    19: 17–20, 1949.
Shorter hours in Ontario shoe factories. Industrial Canada 20(no. 1): 74–75,
    1919.
Slater, David W
    Decentralization of urban peoples and manufacturing activity in Canada.
    Canadian Journal of Economics of Political Science 27: 72–84, 1961.
Smaill, William.
    Iron making in Ontario; opening of the new furnaces of the Hamilton Iron
    and Steel Co., Ltd., at Hamilton, Ontario. Canadian Mining Review 15:
    38–39, 1896.
Smith, Arthur Q
    Industrial gas in Canada. Industrial Canada 49(no. 5): 88–90, 1948.
Smith, H   B
    A review of some aspects of our potato industry. Ontario Agricultural
    College Review 20: 22–26, 1907.
Snider, C   M
    New machinery for historic mill. Waterloo Historical Society. Annual
    Report 39: 22–25, 1951.
    St. Jacobs flour mill.
Snider, Muriel.
    Ajax is growing according to plan. Industrial Canada 53(no. 5): 49–51, 54,
    1952.
— In Scarborough even the boom is booming. Industrial Canada 53(no. 4):
    35–37, 41, 1952.
Some of Canada's industrial laboratories, illustrated and described. Industrial
    Canada 46(no. 9): 104–158; 46(no. 12): 65–68, 1946.
Sparrow, L   J
    Apprentice training at C.G.E. Co.'s Peterborough works. Industrial Canada
    47(no. 4): 63–66, 1946.
Steed, Guy P   F
    Centrality and locational change: printing, publishing, and clothing in
    Montreal and Toronto. Economic Geography 52: 193–205 1976.
Stelco's first fifty years. Industrial Canada 60(no. 11): 62, 1960.
Stelco's Hugh Hilton; man at the top. Industrial Canada 60 (no. 11): 63–64,
    1960.

Stelter, Gilbert A
    Community development in Toronto's commercial empire: the industrial
    towns of the nickel belt, 1883–1931. Laurentian University Review 6(no. 3):
    3–53, 1974.
Stewart, J   L
    Canada's motor car industry. Canadian Geographical Journal 14: 198–225,
    1937.
Stirrett, J   T
    Factories in northeast Ontario. Industrial Canada 12: 918–920, 1912.
— Factory building in eastern Ontario. Industrial Canada 13: 1576–1580,
    1913.
— Factory building in western Ontario. Industrial Canada 13: 1454–1460,
    1913.
Stock, F   W
    The flax industry in Ontario. Ontario Agricultural College Review 31:
    413–415, 1919.
The story of Ontario's industrial progress: the great achievement of John
    McClary. Mer Douce 2(2): 8–11, 1922.
Strongly against reciprocity; by an overwhelming majority the Toronto Board of
    Trade passes a resolution protesting against the reciprocity agreement.
    Industrial Canada 11: 835–836, 1911.
Sweeney, H   M
Qualities of cold drawn steel. Industrial Canada 51(no. 9): 51–52, 1951.
    Union Drawn Steel Co., Ltd., Hamilton.
Synopsis of proceedings before the Tariff Commission in Quebec and Ontario.
    Industrial Canada 21(no. 9): 138–143, 254; 21(no. 10): 54–60, 91, 1921.
Tabisz, E   F
    Progress in laboratory testing in Toronto. Industrial Canada 53(no. 3):
    131–134, 1952.
Talbot, Allen G
    Ontario origin of the Canadian explosive industry. Ontario History 56:
    45–57, 1964.
Taylor, R   Bruce.
    Corporation taxes in Ontario and Quebec. Industrial Canada 49(no. 3):
    273–274, 1948.
Telfer, A   F
    Work of the CSA approvals laboratories. Industrial Canada 54(no. 3):
    173–176, 1953.
    Canadian Standards Association.
Ten storeys up in ten days. Industrial Canada 11: 142–143, 1910.
Tobacco and cigars. Industrial Canada 5: 752–753, 1905.
Toronto branch gives many scholarships. Industrial Canada 21(no. 8): 87, 1920.
Toronto Industrial Exhibition. Industrial Canada 1: 210–211, 1901.
Toronto Industrial Exhibition; discussion of its organization by the
    manufacturers. Industrial Canada 1: 104–106, 1900.

Toronto Public Library.
  Canadian firms 100 or more years old. Industrial Canada 49(no. 4): 67;
  49(no. 6): 141; 49(no. 7): 90, 1948.
Toronto's big machine in the making. Industrial Canada 9: 749, 1909.
  For pumping station.
Toronto's new electric steel plant. Canadian Mining Journal 39: 174, 1918.
Toronto's water filtration plant. Industrial Canada 12: 57–58, 1911.
The tour of the manufacturing cities of western Ontario. Industrial Canada
  21(no. 12): 81–82, 1921.
Turn of the tide reported from Canada's principal industrial centres; a series of
  encouraging reports. Industrial Canada 21(no. 11): 52–59, 1921.
Van Every, Margaret.
  Francis Hector Clergue and the rise of Sault Ste. Marie as an industrial
  centre. Ontario History 56: 191–202, 1964.
Veitch, Sherry.
  James Livingston of Baden. Waterloo Historical Society. Annual Volume
  55: 59–60, 1967.
Walker, David F
  The energy sources of manufacturing industry in southern Ontario,
  1871–1921. Ontario Geography 6: 56–66, 1971.
Walker, Dean.
  IBM's 4,000,000 hours of safety. Industrial Canada 60(no. 8): 39–43, 1959.
Walsh, Thomas E
  What London did for made-in-Canada. Industrial Canada 21(no. l): 81–82,
  1920.
Warner, Clarence M
  John Thomson: inventor of a process for making wood pulp. Lennox and
  Addington Historical Society. Papers and Addresses 2: 21–25, 1910.
Waterman, H   E
  Hamilton branch closed successful year. Industrial Canada 21(no. 2): 79–80,
  1920.
Watson, J   K
  Chemical industries of western Ontario. Western Ontario Historical Notes 5:
  37–42, 1947.
Watson, J   W
  The changing industrial pattern of the Niagara peninsula. Ontario
  Historical Society. Papers & Records 37: 49–58, 1945.
Weiler, E   J
  Aged in wood. Bruce County Historical Society. Yearbook 26, 1968.
  Manufacture of the Iron threshing machine in Mildmay, Ontario.
Welfare plans of a Hamilton industry. Industrial Canada 36(no. 5): 38–39,
  1935.
  Canadian Westinghouse, Ltd.
Welsh, Arthur.
  Developing and expanding supply sources in Ontario. Industrial Canada
  49(no. 9): 122–123, 1949.

Westinghouse opens television plant in Brantford, Ontario. Industrial Canada
    55(no. 4): 54–56, 1954.
Westman, A   E   R
    Natural gas in the war industries of Ontario. Canadian Chemistry and
    Process Industries 25: 111–112, 1941.
— Research for industry in Ontario. Industrial Canada 47(no. 3): 176–183,
    1946.
Williams, W   R
    John Island's stolen sawmill. Inland seas 8: 139–140, 1952.
— The Midland blast furnace. Inland Seas 19: 308–310, 1963.
Williamson, O   T   G
    Commercial fishing: a new prospect for James Bay. The Quarterly no.
    61(June): 5, 12–13, 1961.
Wilton, David A
    An econometric model of the Canadian automotive manufacturing industry
    and the 1965 automotive agreement. Canadian Journal of Economics 5:
    157–181, 1972.
Woltz, G   L
    The status of the Ontario bacon industry. Ontario Agricultural College
    Review 25: 458–461, 1913.
Wong, Cheuk C
    The spatial structure of manufacturing industries in Ontario. Ontario
    Geography 4: 45–55, 1969.
Wonnacott, Paul.
    Canadian automotive protection: content provisions, the Bladen plan, and
    recent tariff changes. Canadian Journal of Economics and Political Science
    31: 98–116, 1965.
Wonnacott, Paul and R   J   Wonnacott.
    The automotive agreement of 1965. Canadian Journal of Economics and
    Political Science 33: 269–284, 1967.
Wood, W   H
    The western Ontario peninsula. Industrial Canada 30(no. 12): 51–73, 100,
    1930.
Wooding, F   H
    Draculas of the Great Lakes. Canadian Geographical Journal 55: 2–13,
    1957.
Woollens. Industrial Canada 5: 754–755, 1905.
Zimmerman, Idessa.
    Birth of the button in Canada. Waterloo Historical Society. Annual Volume
    46: 17–25, 1958.

Theses

Acheson, Thomas William, 1936–
    The social origins of Canadian industrialism: A study in the structure of
    entrepreneurship. [Toronto] c1971.
    ix, 484 leaves. tables. fold. map.
    Ph.D. thesis, University of Toronto (microfilm 25450).   OTU

Arathoon, David Nigel.
   The impact of industrial development on Saltfleet township 1964–1971.
   [Waterloo, Ontario] 1973.
   xii, 429 leaves. tables.
   M.A. thesis, University of Waterloo.   OWTU
Athey, Vincent Miles.
   Locational change in the cheese industry of eastern Ontario. Ottawa: 1976.
   vi, 51 leaves. graphs, maps.
   B.A. research essay, Carleton University.   OOCC
Bain, David.
   Urban industrial structure and net migration in southern Ontario. [Toronto]
   1973.
   v, 68 leaves. tables, maps.
   B.A. thesis, University of Toronto.   OTU
Ballabon, Maurice Bernard.
   Areal differentiation of the manufacturing belt in central Canada.
   [Montreal, Quebec] 1955.
   ix, 379 leaves.
   Ph.D. thesis, McGill University.   QMM
Bauer, Gary Brian.
   Industrial location in small Ontario municipalities: a case study of Elmira,
   Ontario. Waterloo, Ontario: 1976.
   vii, 125 leaves. charts, maps.
   B.A. thesis, Wilfrid Laurier University.   OWTL
Blackbourn, Anthony, 1938–
   Locational patterns of American-owned industry in southern Ontario.
   [Toronto] 1968.
   xiii, 189 leaves. diagrs., maps,
   Ph.D. thesis, University of Toronto (microfilm 3892).   OTU
Blair, Alexander Marshall, 1932–
   Geographic aspects of the cement industry in southwestern Ontario. London,
   Ontario: 1961.
   xiii, 168 leaves. photos., tables, maps (part fold.).
   M.A. thesis, The University of Western Ontario.   OLU
Bondy, Donald Victor.
   The post war industrial development of the city of Chatham. [London,
   Ontario] 1949.
   v, 37 p. map, tables.
   B.A. thesis, The University of Western Ontario.   OLU
Borsook, Benjamin.
   The output capacity of the Canadian iron and steel industry, with an
   introductory survey of the iron and coal resources of Canada. Toronto: 1934.
   61 leaves. tables, charts (part fold.), diagrs.
   M.A. thesis, University of Toronto.   OTU

Brown, Morgan.
   Tobacco industry in south western Ontario. Kingston, Ontario: 1930.
   iv, 71 leaves. figs. (part col.), maps.
   B.Com. thesis, Queen's University.   OKQ
Brown, W   J
   Industrial council Massey–Harris Co., Limited and additional personnel
   features of the same firm. [Kingston, Ontario] 1927.
   26 leaves.
   B. Com. thesis, Queen's University.   OKQ
Byrnes, Thomas Clohecy.
   The automotive industry in Ontario. [Toronto] 1951.
   iv, 129 leaves. illus., maps.
   M.A. thesis, University of Toronto.   OTU
Camenzuli, Francis Xavier.
   Effects of peripheral commercial developments on the central business
   district: a case study of the town of Aurora. London, Ontario: 1976.
   ix, 93 leaves. illus., graphs, map, tables.
   B.A. thesis, The University of Western Ontario.   OLU
Cartwright, Donald Gordon, 1933–   [sic]
   Cheese production in southwestern Ontario. London, Ontario: 1965.
   xiii, 152 leaves. illus., tables, maps.
   M.A. thesis, The University of Western Ontario.   OLU
Child, Arthur James Edward.
   The predecessor companies of Canada Packers Limited: a study of
   entrepreneurial achievement and entrepreneurial failure. [Toronto] 1960.
   260 leaves. tables.
   M.A. thesis, University of Toronto.   OTU
Christie, Robert C   1937–
   The development of the furniture industry in the southwestern Ontario
   furniture manufacturing region. London, Ontario: 1964.
   xxiii, 136 leaves. illus., tables, maps.
   M.A. thesis, The University of Western Ontario.   OLU
Clement, Wallace.
   The corporate elite: economic power in Canada. Ottawa: 1973.
   [ix] 439 leaves.
   M.A. thesis, Carleton University.   OOCC
— The Canadian corporate elite: an analysis of economic power, with a
   foreword by John Porter. Toronto: McClelland & Stewart Limited [c1975]
   xxvii, 479 p. tables. (Carleton Library, no. 89).   OTU
Cockayne, Shelagh Elizabeth, 1948–
   The spatial impact of the equalization of industrial opportunity programmes
   in the eastern Ontario economic region. London, Ontario: 1971.
   x, 143 leaves. graphs, tables, maps.
   M.A. thesis, The University of Western Ontario (microfilm 8547).   OLU

Collins, Lyndhurst, 1941–
 Industrial migration and relocation: a study of European branch plants,
 with special reference to Metropolitan Toronto. [Toronto] 1966.
 xii, 142 leaves. tables, diagrs., maps.
 M.A. thesis, University of Toronto.   OTU
— Markov chains and industrial migration; forecasting aspects of industrial
 activity in Ontario. [Toronto] c1970.
 x, 280 leaves. diagrs., maps, tables.
 Ph.D. thesis, University of Toronto.   OTU
Craddock, William John, 1938–
 An analysis of the markets for Ontario winter wheat. [Toronto] 1963.
 viii, 146 leaves. tables, figs.
 M.S.A. thesis, University of Toronto.   OTU
Curzon, Peter Brenchley.
 A study of cream procurement, butter manufacture and marketing by
 selected creameries in Ontario. [Toronto] 1956.
 73 leaves. tables, figs.
 M.S.A. thesis, University of Toronto.   OTU
Davidson, Jean.
 A study of the factors influencing the restructuring of the Ontario dairy
 industry 1960–1972. [Toronto] 1973.
 43 [6] leaves. figs., maps (part col.).
 B.A. research paper, University of Toronto.   OTU
Delaney, E   C
 Stores and materials control with reference to the Canadian Locomotive Co.,
 Ltd., Kingston, Ontario. [Kingston, Ontario: 1928]
 64 leaves. (handwritten), forms.
 B.Com. thesis, Queen's University.   OKQ
De Schiffart, Johan P
 Strathroy and its central place functions. [Toronto] 1970.
 ii, 35 leaves. illus., maps.
 B.A. research paper, University of Toronto.   OTU
Dickson, Ross D
 An examination of manufacturing in the Windsor – London region of
 Ontario. [Waterloo, Ontario] 1975.
 v, 85 leaves. maps, tables.
 B.A. thesis, Wilfrid Laurier University.   OWTL
Dill, Hubert Clark.
 A financial analysis of some recent consolidations in the pulp and paper
 industry. [Toronto] 1931.
 134 leaves.
 M.A. thesis, University of Toronto.   OTU
Domokos, Richard J
 Locational patterns of the Canadian pig iron industry, 1896–1926.
 Edmonton, Alberta: 1972.
 vi, 90 leaves. graphs, map, tables.
 M.A. thesis, University of Alberta (microfilm 13351).
 Ontario and Nova Scotia.   AEU

Drysdale, Douglas Paul.
   A study of the forest industry in Simcoe county and the factors relating to its
   present and future importance in that economy. [Toronto] 1957.
   229 leaves. tables (part fold.), (col. fold.) map in back pocket.
   M.Sc.F. thesis, University of Toronto.   OTU
Duggal, Ajudhia Nath.
   Earning capacity of the inputs used in the local feed-mills in south western
   Ontario. [Toronto] 1960.
   86 leaves. tables, figs., map.
   M.S.A. thesis, University of Toronto (accepted 1961).   OTU
Elz, Klaus Dieter.
   Some economic aspects of production control in the flue-cured tobacco
   industry of Ontario. [Toronto] 1960.
   [vii] 156 leaves. tables, figs., map.
   M.S.A. thesis, University of Toronto.   OTU
Faye, G   David.
   Past development and future prospects of manufacturing industry in
   Oakville, Ontario. [Toronto] 1968.
   i, 110 leaves. illus., maps (part col.).
   B.A. thesis, University of Toronto.   OTU
Fleming, Marion.
   A geographical study of the industries on Toronto's waterfront; appendix.
   [Toronto] 1948.
   1 v. (unpaged). 31 fold. maps.
   B.A. thesis, University of Toronto.   OTU
Foster, Gail Penelope Susan, 1947–
   Industrial growth in Barrie and Orillia. [Toronto] 1968.
   43 leaves.
   B.A. research project, University of Toronto.   OTU
Foster, Robert John .
   Entry in the Ontario cement industry. Toronto: c1973.
   v, 95 leaves. tables.
   M.A. thesis, Queen's University (microfilm 15004).   OKQ
Fraser, James Millan.
   The smallmouth bass fishery of South Bay. [Toronto] 1953.
   vi, 74 leaves. illus., map.
   M.A. thesis, University of Toronto.   OTU
Fukuda, Kenneth.
   The role of manufacturing in the economic development of eastern Ontario.
   [Toronto] 1971.
   iii, 80 leaves. tables, figs., fold. map.
   B.A. thesis, University of Toronto.   OTU
Gerland, Martin Edward.
   Industrial location in Galt; a study of the factors of industrial location in
   Galt from the founding of the town to 1958. [Toronto] 1959.
   x, 64 leaves. illus., maps.
   B.A. thesis, University of Toronto.   OTU

Gilmour, James Muckle, 1939–
    The economic geography of the pulp and paper industry in Ontario.
    [Toronto] 1964 [c1976]
    vi [7] 166 leaves. tables, maps.
    M.A. thesis, University of Toronto (microfilm 27485).   OTU
— Structural and spatial change in manufacturing industry: south Ontario,
    1850–1890. [Toronto] c1970.
    xiv, 448 leaves. diagrs., maps.
    Ph.D. thesis, University of Toronto (microfilm 9137).   OTU
— Spatial evolution of manufacturing: southern Ontario 1851–1891 . [Toronto]
    Published for the University of Toronto, Department of Geography by the
    University of Toronto Press [c1972]
    xvi, 214 p. illus., maps. (University of Toronto. Dept. of Geography.
    Research publication, 10).
    Based on author's thesis, University of Toronto.   OTV
Girard, Ghislain I
    The tender tree fruit industry in Canada with particular reference to
    Ontario: an analysis of shipping and demand. Ottawa: 1964.
    150 leaves. charts, tables.
    M.A. thesis, University of Ottawa.   OOU
Girvin, James E
    A study of personnel administration as practised at Silverwood Dairies
    Limited. [London, Ontario] 1946.
    vi, 149 leaves. charts, tables.
    M.A. thesis, The University of Western Ontario.   OLU
Green, Terence S
    A locational study of the furniture industry in southern Ontario. [Toronto]
    1967.
    ii [iii] 40 [2] leaves. maps, tables.
    B.A. research paper, University of Toronto.   OTU
Halpern, Anne Louise, 1951–
    Household woodenware of 19th century Ontario: references in the settler
    literature and a listing of the manufacturing companies. [Toronto] c1975.
    iii, 231 leaves. illus., photos., facsims.
    M.Muscol. thesis, University of Toronto.   OTU
Harvey, Edgar L
    The pulp and paper industry of Ontario. [Toronto] 1949.
    56 leaves. illus., maps (part col.).
    B.A. thesis, University of Toronto.   OTU
Haslett, Earl Allan, 1926–
    Factors in the growth and decline of the cheese industry in Ontario
    1864–1924. [Toronto] c1969.
    vi, 185 leaves. figs., tables, map.
    Ph.D. thesis, University of Toronto (microfilm 6313).   OTU

— Some economic aspects of the late potato industry in Ontario. [Toronto] 1953.
[vii] 143 leaves. tables.
M.S.A. thesis, University of Toronto. OTU
Hay, Keith Alexander James.
Trends in the location of industry. [Toronto] 1962.
101 leaves. maps (part fold., part col.), diagrs., tables.
M.S.A. thesis, University of Toronto. OTU
Heidenreich, Conrad Edmund, 1936–
The junction of West Toronto; an industrial area. [Toronto] 1961.
62 [24] leaves. illus., col. diagrs., col. maps (part fold.).
B.A. thesis, University of Toronto. OTU
Heit, Michael Joseph James.
A procedure for evaluating the feasibility of tourist accommodation development as applied to southern Ontario. College Station, Texas: 1975.
165 p.
Ph.D. thesis, Texas A & M University (microfilm 76-12,672). DA
Hewitt, John Anthony.
Development of Deep River as a new industrial frontier community. Ottawa: 1974.
vii, 49 leaves. illus., graphs, maps, tables.
B.A. research essay, Carleton University. OOCC
Hewson, Donald James.
The influence of transportation costs on the pattern of product distribution in the petroleum industry: study area, southern Ontario . [Toronto] 1967.
59 [1] leaves. illus., col. maps.
B.A. thesis, University of Toronto. OTU
Hodgson, Michael John.
Locational factors in the brewing industry in the province of Ontario. Ottawa: 1968.
ix, 79 leaves. graphs, maps (part fold).
B.A. research essay, Carleton University. OOCC
Houston, Stephen Robert.
Analysis of intracity industrial location, London, Ontario. London, Ontario: 1973.
vii, 86 leaves. illus., graphs, maps, tables.
B.A. thesis, The University of Western Ontario. OLU
Hrabovsky, John P
Some aspects of vertical integration in the Ontario hog industry. [Toronto] 1960.
122 leaves. tables, figs., map.
M.S.A. thesis, University of Toronto. OTU
Huhn, Frank Jones, 1945–
Lake sediment records of industrialization in the Sudbury area of Ontario. [Toronto] c1974.
84 leaves. tables, figs., plates, maps.
M.Sc. thesis, University of Toronto. OTU

Hyde, Martin James.
    Indian commercial fisheries in the Patricia district of Ontario: an economic
    analysis. Montreal, Quebec: 1963.
    viii, 360 leaves.
    Ph.D. Thesis, McGill University.   QMM
Ireland, Carole Anne.
    The early tanning industry in Ontario. [Toronto] 1967.
    29 [11] leaves. illus., maps.
    B.A. thesis, University of Toronto.   OTU
Jeffrey, John Stephen.
    The replacement of Galt by Kitchener as the major centre of the golden
    triangle. Waterloo, Ontario: 1968.
    iii, 46 leaves. diagrs., maps.
    B.A. thesis, Waterloo University College.   OWTL
Keizer, Elliott R
    Rural industralization: a case study of the wooden household furniture
    industry in the Georgian Bay region. [Guelph, Ontario] 1971.
    xv, 194 leaves. diagrs., maps, tables.
    M.Sc. thesis, The University of Guelph.   OGU
Kenyon, Nancy Louise.
    The marketing of hogs in Ontario. [Toronto] 1958.
    iii, 107 leaves. tables, figs., map.
    M.A. thesis, University of Toronto.   OTU
Kneutzwiser, Reid Douglas.
    A methodology for estimating tourist spending in Ontario counties.
    Waterloo, Ontario: 1973.
    v, 52 leaves. illus., maps.
    M.A. thesis, University of Waterloo (microfilm 22314).   Can
Kolle, William Joseph.
    A financial analysis of the Lake of the Woods Milling Company, Limited.
    Kingston, Ontario: 1930.
    iv, 30 [3] leaves.
    B.Com. thesis, Queen's University.   OKQ
Kotseff, Lawrence E
    Location and linkage: a study of the inter industry relationships within the
    Ontario economy. Toronto: 1975.
    vii, 122 leaves. diagrs., tables.
    M.A. research paper, York University.   OTY
Lander, John Brandon.
    Factors of industrial location as an explanation of regional growth
    differentials in Ontario, 1961 to 1971. Waterloo, Ontario: 1976.
    v, 158 leaves. map, tables.
    B.A. thesis, Wilfrid Laurier University.   OWTL
Lang, Sophie Janine.
    Georgetown, Acton and Milton: a study in industrial geography. [Toronto]
    1956.
    49 leaves. illus., maps (part col. part fold.).
    B.A. thesis, University of Toronto.   OTU

Lee, Judith Mary.
Inventive activity and its relation to industrial development in southern
Ontario, 1881–1911. [Waterloo, Ontario] 1972.
xi, 209 leaves. graphs, maps, tables.
M.A. thesis, University of Waterloo.   OWTU
Lee, Seward David.
The cement industry of Ontario. [Toronto] 1962.
[iv] 45 leaves. illus., map, diagrs.
B.A. thesis, University of Toronto.   OTU
Liddle, David Brian.
The intrametropolitan location of manufacturing and the industrial land
market: a case study of the Toronto region. [Toronto] 1968.
viii, 130 leaves. tables, figs, maps (part col.).
M.A. thesis, University of Toronto.   OTU
Loch, Francis J   P
The Kitchener rubber industries: a geographic analysis. Waterloo, Ontario:
1966.
ix, 104 leaves. maps, tables.
B.A. thesis, Waterloo University College.   OWTL
Lorch, Brian James.
An inter-regional analysis of the growth rate of manufacturing employment
in the province of Ontario 1960–1972. Waterloo, Ontario: 1975.
vi, 167 leaves. tables.
M.A. thesis, Wilfrid Laurier University.   OWTL
Lundman, Susan Brenda.
An economic analysis of the nursing home industry in Ontario. Montreal,
Quebec: 1975 [c1976]
ii, 96 leaves.
M.A. Thesis, McGill University (microfilm 27201).   Can
McArthur, Neil Max, 1921–
A geographical study of present and potential industrial development in
towns of the London area. [London, Ontario] 1950.
x, 162 leaves. illus., plates, graphs, maps.
M.A. thesis, The University of Western Ontario.   OLU
McCrimmon, J   S   G
An economic study of Algoma Steel Corporation, Limited. [Toronto] 1960.
ii, 79 leaves.
M.B.A. thesis, University of Toronto (accepted 1961).   OTU
McCutcheon, Richard Paul Wesley, 1938–
Market potential as a factor in change in manufacturing in Ontario,
1951–1961. London, Ontario: 1971.
xvii, 381, xviii–xix leaves. tables, maps (part fold.).
M.A. thesis, The University of Western Ontario (microfilm 9002).   OLU
McDaniel, Robert, 1926–
A military geography of the Great Lakes area with emphasis on industrial
dispersion and defence. [London, Ontario] 1954.
xi, 189 leaves. chart, maps.
M.A. thesis, The University of Western Ontario.   OLU

McKie, Donald Craig, 1944–
    An Ontario industrial elite: the senior executive in manufacturing industry.
    [Toronto] c1974.
    318, xxvi, 90 [10] leaves. tables.
    Ph.D. thesis, University of Toronto (microfilm 27500).   OTU
Main, Oscar Warren, 1916–
    The Canadian nickel industry, 1885–1939; a study in market control and
    public policy. [Toronto] 1952.
    348 leaves.
    Ph.D. thesis, University of Toronto (accepted 1953).   OTU
Marshall, Brian Gordon.
    Industrial attitudes toward water use and selected water management
    problems: a study of the Grand River watershed. [Waterloo, Ontario] 1972.
    xi, 144 leaves. diagrs., tables, maps.
    M.A. thesis, University of Waterloo.   OWTU
Martine, Gloria Ann.
    The role of the Welland Canal in industrial location. [Toronto] 1961.
    61 leaves. illus. (part col.), col. maps.
    B.A. thesis, University of Toronto (microfilm 16116).   OTU
Mock, Dennis Ronald, 1944–
    Agglomeration and industrial linkages: case studies of Metropolitan
    Toronto. Toronto, c1976.
    xiii, 264 leaves. tables, figs., maps.
    Ph.D. thesis, University of Toronto.   OTU
— External economies in intrametropolitan industrial location: review and
    measurement. [Toronto] 1968.
    ii, 70 leaves.
    M.A. research paper, University of Toronto.   OTU
Morgan, Lewis Wayne.
    Geographic association and inter-industry linkages in southern Ontario.
    Toronto: 1972.
    76 leaves. illus., maps.
    B.A. research paper, University of Toronto.   OTU
Morris, William Alfred.
    Pembroke, a study of the town and its industries. [Hamilton, Ontario] 1956.
    v, 117 leaves. illus., plates, maps, graphs.
    B.A. thesis, McMaster University.   OHM
Munn, John Eric, 1945–
    Tourism in the district of Cochrane. [Toronto] 1968.
    40 leaves. facsim., maps (part col.).
    B.A. thesis, University of Toronto.   OTU
Murphy, Lynda Susan.
    Selected factors in location of the petrochemical industry. [Toronto] 1966.
    63 [9] leaves. illus., maps.
    B.A. thesis, University of Toronto.   OTU

Neal, Stanley Frederick.
A study of the Metropolitan Toronto fluid milk shed. [Toronto] 1962.
42, ix leaves. photos., maps (part fold., part col.).
B.A. thesis, University of Toronto.   OTU
Neill, Robert Foliet.
Industrial galaxy; an exploratory survey of industrial galaxies in Canadian economic development. [Toronto] 1960.
128 leaves.
M.A. thesis, University of Toronto.   OTU
Neimanis, Viesturs Peteris.
Geographic analysis of the growth problems of Cornwall's manufacturing industries, 1950–1971. Ottawa: 1972.
vi, 65 leaves. diagrs., fold. table.
B.A. research essay, Carleton University.   OOCC
O'Connor, Kevin.
Industrial structure and urban growth of Canadian cities, 1951–1961.
Hamilton, Ontario: 1974 [c1975]
ix, 184 leaves. illus., maps.
Ph.D. thesis, McMaster University (microfilm 22646).   Can
Petegorsky, David.
The financial history of the Abitibi Power and Paper Company Limited.
Kingston, Ontario: 1931.
iii, 70 leaves. tables (part fold.).
B. Com. thesis, Queen's University.   OKQ
Phelps, Edward Charles Howard, 1939–
John Henry Fairbank of Petrolia (1831–1914): a Canadian entrepreneur.
London, Ontario: 1965.
vi, 322 leaves. illus., facsims.
M.A. thesis, The University of Western Ontario.   OLU
Porteous, S   Douglas.
Brock Street/Spadina Avenue from 1850 to 1900: a study of development.
Toronto: 1975.
iii, 63 leaves. illus.
B.A. thesis, University of Toronto.   OTU
Power, Graham Clifford, 1935–
An analysis of the geographical factors determining the northern limits of the pulp and paper industry in northern Ontario. Montreal, Quebec: 1959.
iii, 87 leaves.
M.A. thesis, McGill University.   QMM
Priamo, Carol Anne, 1947–
A study of the early grist mills of southern Ontario: 1783–1867 . [Toronto] c1975.
v, 103 [1] leaves. illus., figs.
M. Museol. thesis, University of Toronto.   OTU
Prior, Leonard L
Sault Ste. Marie and Algoma Steel Corporation, Ltd. [Toronto] 1956.
107 leaves. illus., diagrs., maps.
M.A. thesis, University of Toronto.   OTU

Quinton, David Maurice.
    Postwar developments in Ontario's cement industry. Kingston, Ontario:
    1971, c1972.
    iv, 88 leaves. tables, map.
    M.A. thesis, Queen's University (awarded 1972).   OKQ
Raizada, Harish Chandra, 1937–
    An input-output model of Ontario forest products economy. [Toronto] 1973.
    vi, 96 leaves. tables (part fold.).
    M.Sc.F. thesis, University of Toronto.   OTU
Roberts, Richard Delwyn.
    The changing patterns in distribution and composition of manufacturing
    activity in Hamilton between 1861 and 1921. [Hamilton, Ontario] 1964.
    vi, 174 leaves. illus., graphs, maps (part fold.), tables.
    M.A. thesis, McMaster University.   OHM
Robinson, Janet.
    A history of Ashbridge's Bay: from marshland to industrial district.
    [Toronto] 1975.
    v, 100 leaves. illus.
    B.A. research paper, University of Toronto.   OTU
Rose, Courtice George, 1944–
    An analysis of inputs to manufacturing industries in the Lake Erie region.
    London, Ontario, 1970.
    ix, 117 leaves. graphs, tables, maps.
    M.A. thesis, The University of Western Ontario (microfilm 7236).   OLU
Rose, Daniel James
    An opinion survey regarding the potential development of the northern
    Ontario beef industry. [Guelph, Ontario] 1967.
    viii, 79, 7, 2 leaves. tables.
    M.Sc. thesis, University of Guelph.   OGU
Roseman, Frank, 1934–
    The Canadian brewing industry: the effect of mergers and provincial
    regulations on economic conduct and performance. Evanston, Illinois: 1968.
    vi, 292 leaves. illus.
    Ph.D. thesis, Northwestern University (microfilm 69-1920).   DA
Rotman, Joseph Louis.
    The fuel oil 2 home heating market in Metropolitan Toronto. [Toronto]
    1960.
    127 leaves. tables.
    M.Com. thesis, University of Toronto.   OTU
Roytenberg, Max Menachem.
    The marketing of Ontario cheddar cheese: the cheese industry in Ontario
    and the operations of the Ontario Cheese Producers' Marketing Board
    1951–1957. [Toronto] 1957.
    ix, 117 leaves. tables, figs.
    M.S.A. thesis, University of Toronto.   OTU

Saleh, Mohammed Ebrahin, 1941–
    Spatial patterns of the hotel industry of London, Ontario. London, Ontario:
    1972.
    xv, 196 leaves. graphs, tables, maps.
    M.A. thesis, The University of Western Ontario.   OLU
Scott, Benjamin Samuel.
    The economic and industrial history of the city of London, Canada from the
    building of the first railway 1855 to the present 1930. [London, Ontario:
    1930]
    [8] 340 [2] leaves. facsims., tables.
    M.A. thesis, The University of Western Ontario.   OLU
Seifried, Neil Robert Michael, 1936–
    A study of changes in manufacturing in midwestern Ontario, 1951–1964. St.
    Louis, Missouri: 1969.
    Ph.D. thesis, University of Washington (microfilm 69-20,271).   DA
Semple, Robert Keith.
    A manufacturing geography of the paper industry in Metropolitan Toronto.
    [Toronto: 1965]
    v, 68 leaves. illus., maps (part col., part fold.).   OTU
Shervill, Robert Paul.
    Attitudes toward Dofasco industrial development in Bayham and Malahide
    townships. London, Ontario: 1973.
    ix, 50 leaves. illus., graphs, tables.
    B.A. thesis, The University of Western Ontario.   OLU
Sigsworth, Grant W
    An economic study of manufacturing industries in Oshawa, Ontario.
    Waterloo, Ontario: 1965.
    vii, 74 leaves. graphs, maps.
    B.A. thesis, Waterloo University College.   OWTL
Silva, Wanniaratchige Percy Terrence, 1930–
    Some aspects of the development of the fruit and vegetable canning industry
    in southern Ontario. [Toronto] 1962.
    vii, 82 leaves. tables, photos, maps (part fold.).
    M.A. thesis, University of Toronto.   OTU
Slater, John Morton.
    Supply management in relation to the marketing of milk in Ontario.
    [Toronto] 1963.
    viii, 161 leaves. tables, figs.
    M.S.A. thesis, University of Toronto.   OTU
Smart, John David.
    The Patrons of Industry in Ontario. Ottawa: 1969.
    167 leaves. fold. map.
    M.A. thesis, Carleton University (microfilm 3923).   OOCC

Smith, Sheila M
   An economic appraisal of the Ontario flue-cured tobacco industry, with
   particular emphasis on exports to the United Kingdom. [Guelph, Ontario]
   1970.
   ix, 154 leaves. diagrs., tables.
   M.Sc. thesis, The University of Guelph.   OGU
Smyth, J   H
   A study of problems affecting timber production from private lands in
   southern Ontario. [Toronto] 1970.
   xiii, 219 leaves. tables (part fold.), figs., maps (part fold., part col.).
   M.Sc.F. thesis, University of Toronto.   OTU
Spence, Madeline Karen Ann.
   Woodstock as an industrial centre: a study in industrial development.
   [Toronto] 1966.
   viii, 52 leaves. diagr., maps.
   B.A. thesis, University of Toronto.   OTU
Spricenieks, Alfred.
   Historical geography of industrial development of Kitchener, Waterloo,
   Bridgeport 1801–1956. Waterloo, Ontario: 1961.
   ix, 87 leaves. maps (part fold.), tables.
   B.A. thesis, Waterloo University College.   OWTL
Stapells, Herbert Gordon.
   The recent consolidation movement in Canadian industry. [Toronto] 1922.
   264 leaves + appendix.
   M.A. thesis, University of Toronto.   OTU
Stewart, James Innes.
   Problems in industrial location in Ontario. [Toronto] 1960.
   81 leaves.
   M.A. thesis, University of Toronto.   OTU
Storoy, Robert H
   Industrialization in Canada: the emergence of the Hamilton working class
   1850–1870. Halifax: 1975.
   vi, 242 [9] leaves.
   M.A. thesis, Dalhousie University (microfilm 28959).   Can
Surtees, William.
   The dairy industry of Oxford county, Ontario. [Hamilton, Ontario] 1963.
   xiii, 162 leaves. illus., maps (part fold.), diagrs., tables.
   M.A. thesis, McMaster University.   OHM
Taylor, Susan M
   Vaughan Acres: a suburban industrial development. [Toronto] 1970.
   vi, 51 leaves. illus., maps (part col.).
   B.A. research paper, University of Toronto.   OTU
Thomas, John Phillips, 1945–
   The spatial influence of industries in small urban centres on the regional
   labour force. London, Ontario: 1970.
   xi, 122 leaves. diagrs., maps, tables.
   M.A. thesis, The University of Western Ontario (microfilm 7242).   OLU

Thomas, Paul Frank.
Rexdale: a case study in suburban industry. [Waterloo, Ontario] 1968.
xvi, 248 leaves. illus., maps.
M.A. thesis, University of Waterloo (microfilm 7880). OWTU

Tosine, Tonu Peep.
Cheese factories in the Quinte – St. Lawrence area of Ontario, 1865–1905.
Toronto: 1974.
xiii, 135 leaves. graphs, facsim., maps.
M.A. thesis, York University (microfilm 21568). OTY

Turner, Helen Suzanne.
Hanover: a study of manufacturing in a small town. [Toronto] 1966.
iv, 51 [4] leaves. illus., fold. chart, maps (part fold., part col.).
B.A. thesis, University of Toronto. OTU

Vance, Robert Cameron, 1914–
The tobacco economy and its effect on the lives of the people in those
portions of the new belt lying in the counties of Norfolk, Elgin, Oxford,
Middlesex and Brant. [London, Ontario] 1952.
xii, 124, xii [11] leaves. illus., tables, maps.
M.A. thesis, The University of Western Ontario. OLU

Walker, David Frank, 1940–
The role of coal as a location factor in the development of manufacturing
industry in southern Ontario, 1871–1921. [Toronto] 1967 [c1975]
vii, 137 leaves. illus., figs., maps (part col.).
M.A. thesis, University of Toronto (microfilm 22792). OTU

Walker, John Henry.
The building material industries of the Niagara Escarpment; a study of
changing locational patterns. Toronto: 1965.
vii, 150 leaves. illus., plates, tables, maps.
M.A. thesis, University of Toronto. OTU

Wallbridge, John Francis.
A study of the Lake Superior Corporation. Kingston, Ontario: 1929.
i, 43 leaves. tables, graphs.
B.Com. thesis, Queen's University. OKQ

Wallis, James E.
An evaluation of the manufacturing potential for building stone and
industrial silico products from limestones and sandstones of the Kingston
area. Kingston, Ontario: 1967.
[i–xv] 141 leaves. illus., tables, figs., map.
M.Sc. thesis, Queen's University. OKQ

Ward, Harold Bernard.
Hamilton, Ontario, as a manufacturing centre. Chicago: 1935.
366 p. illus., maps.
Ph.D. thesis, University of Chicago. DA
— Chicago: Private edition distributed by the University of Chicago libraries,
1937.
v, 335–366 p. illus., maps. OTU

Ward, Horace Frederick, 1916–
   The geographic study of an industrial core, London, St. Thomas and Port
   Stanley. London, Ontario: 1950.
   xvi, 224 leaves. graphs, photos, tables, maps (part fold.).
   M.Sc. thesis, The University of Western Ontario.   OLU
Watson, Harold John .
   The evolving structure of the residential construction industry: London,
   Ontario, 1920–1975. London, Ontario: 1976.
   ix, 109 leaves. graphs, tables.
   B.A. thesis, The University of Western Ontario.   OLU
Wells, William Douglas, 1945–
   The Hamilton region, 1800–1882; the interrelationships between
   transportation and industrial development. [Waterloo, Ontario] 1973.
   142 leaves. maps.
   M.A. thesis, University of Waterloo.   OWTU
Whebell, Charles Frederick John, 1930–
   The industrial development of Haldimand county. [London, Ontario] 1955.
   xi, 84 leaves. photos, tables, maps (part fold., part col.).
   M.Sc. thesis, The University of Western Ontario.   OLU
Wild, David.
   A geographic analysis of the egg industry in Ontario. [Toronto] 1969.
   81 leaves. illus., maps (part col., part fold.).
   M.A. research paper, University of Toronto.   OTU
— The poultry meat industry in Ontario. [Toronto] 1968.
   iii, 81 leaves. tables, graphs, col. maps (part fold.).
   B.A. thesis, University of Toronto.   OTU
Wilkes, George Clarkson.
   Taxation of the forest industries in Ontario. [Toronto] 1952.
   203 leaves.
   M.Sc.F. thesis, University of Toronto.   OTU
Williams, Glen Sutherland.
   The Ontario Department of Trade and Development; a case study of
   capitalist public policy in relation to industrial growth. Toronto: 1971.
   ix, 82 [1] leaves.
   M.A. thesis, York University.   OTY
Williamson, Rutherford Wainwright.
   The Ontario flue-cured tobacco industry. Kingston, Ontario: 1935.
   iii, 79 leaves. tables, maps.
   B. Com. thesis, Queen's University.   OKQ
Wood, John Wyatt.
   Some aspects of the marketing and pricing of broilers in Ontario. [Toronto]
   1961.
   vii, 94 leaves. tables, figs.
   M.S.A. thesis, University of Toronto.   OTU
Youngman, Gordon F
   The industrial development of Leaside. [Toronto] 1949.
   73 leaves. illus., maps (part col. fold.).
   B.A. thesis, University of Toronto.   OTU

Yule, Lesley.
Richmond Hill: a case study in industrial geography. [Toronto] 1962.
34, xi [i–xi] leaves. photos., maps (part fold.).
B.A. thesis, University of Toronto. OTU

Zemek, Joe-Anne E
An analysis of the manufacturing trend in Ontario, 1956–1971. Waterloo,
Ontario: 1976.
v, 150 leaves. maps, tables.
B.A. thesis, Wilfrid Laurier University. OWTL

Zin, Michael. •
An evaluation of the accounting provisions in the Companies Act, Canada
and the Corporations Act, Ontario. Lansing, Michigan: 1962.
183 p.
Ph.D. thesis, Michigan State University (microfilm 62-04476). DA

TRANSPORTATION, COMMUNICATIONS, POWER

Bibliography
Canada. Bureau of Statistics.
Bibliographical list of references to Canadian railways, 1829–1938. Ottawa:
1938.
v, 99 p. OTU

Chew, (Mrs.) Anne Rose (Cushman), 1901–
... References on the Great Lakes – St. Lawrence waterway project by Anne
C. Chew and Arthur C. Churchill, under the direction of Everett D.
Edwards... Washington, D.C. [1940]
v, 189 p. (U.S. Department of Agriculture. Library. Bibliographical
contributions no. 30, ed. 2). OWAL

Metropolitan Toronto and Region Transportation Studies.
Selection of readings on metropolitan transportation administration.
[Toronto] 1967.
[43 [ ] leaves. OTMCL

— Study reports and publications; a bibliography of reports and publications
prepared by or on behalf of the Metropolitan Toronto and Region
Transportation Study. [Toronto] 1968.
28 leaves. OTU

Ontario. Community Planning Branch.
[A bibliography of reports and publications for the Metropolitan Toronto
and Region Transportation Study. Toronto: 1968].
28 p. OTUSA

Towle, Edward L 1929– (ed.).
Bibliography on the economic history and geography of the Great Lakes –
St. Lawrence drainage basin. Preliminary draft. Rochester, New York:
Canadian Studies Program, 1964.
41 leaves. OLU

Monographs and Pamphlets

Abouchar, Alan Joseph.
   The analysis of property values and subway investment and financing
   policies. Toronto: Institute for the Quantitative Analysis of Social and
   Economic Policy, University of Toronto, 1973.
   42 leaves. map.
   "Based on the experience of Metro Toronto."   OLU
Acres, Henry Girdlestone, 1880–1945.
   Water powers of Canada: the province of Ontario. Ottawa: Department of
   the Interior [c 1915]
   41 p. illus., map.   OTAR
Acres, (H.G.) & Company Limited.
   Niagara Falls traffic survey, 1961–1981; summary report. [Niagara Falls,
   Ontario: 1963?]
   [12] p. col. maps, diagrs.   OONL
— Traffic study. Niagara Falls, Ontario: The Corporation of the City of
   Niagara Falls, 1963.
   2 v. diagrs., fold. maps (part col.).
   Contents: v. 1, Text, tables, figures; v. 2, Plates, appendixes.   OTUSA
Acres, (H.G.) Limited.
   Guelph transit study: report to the Guelph Transportation Commission,
   Guelph, Ontario, Canada. [Niagara Falls, Ontario] 1971.
   xi, 227 p. illus., graphs, fold. maps.   OKQ
Adams, Edward Dean, 1846–1931.
   Niagara power: history of the Niagara Falls Power Company, 1886–1918;
   evolution of its central power station and alternating current system.
   Niagara Falls, New York: Privately printed for the Niagara Falls Power
   Company, 1927.
   2 v. illus., maps (part fold. part col.), plans, facsims., diagrs., ports.   OTMCL
Agassiz, Garnault.
   Lake Superior to the sea: an inland water voyage on the Great Lakes and
   far-famed St. Lawrence and Saguenay rivers, Montreal: Canada Steamship
   Lines, Limited, n.d.
   96 p. illus.   OTU
Aitken, Hugh George Jeffrey, 1922–
   The Welland Canal Company: a study in Canadian enterprise. Cambridge,
   Massachusett: Harvard University Press, 1954.
   ix, 178 p. charts, map, tables.
   Pre-Confederation.   OTAR
Allen, Robert Thomas, 1911–
   The Great Lakes. [Toronto: Natural Science of Canada Limited, c1970].
   160 p. illus. (part col.).   OONL
Ambridge, Douglas White, 1898–
   Frank Harris Anson (1859–1923): pioneer in the north. New York:
   Newcomen Society in North America, 1952.
   24 p. illus.   OOA

Andreae, Christopher A
    A historical railway atlas of southwestern Ontario. London, Ontario: The
    Author, c1972.
    25 p. maps.   OTU
Ashworth, Edward Montague, 1880–1954.
    Toronto Hydro recollections. [Toronto] University of Toronto Press [c1955]
    x, 224 p. illus., port., tables.   OTAR
Background reading materials, workshop on the use of sanctions in controlling
    behaviour on the roads, December 13 and 14, 1972, Centre of Criminology,
    University of Toronto. [Toronto] The Centre [c1972]
    5, ii, 121, 18 p.   OTUCR
Bailey, J   C
    A synopsis of the Hudson's Bay railways and the capabilities and possibilities
    of the country traversed by the same. [Toronto: Hart & Riddell, 1898]
    7 p.   OTAR
Barnard, (Peter) Associates.
    Waterloo area regional transit study. Phase 1, report. Prepared by Peter
    Barnard Associates in association with Read Voorhees and Associates Ltd.
    [Toronto: Peter Barnard Associates, 1971]
    xi, 53 leaves. graphs, maps.   OTDT
Barry, James P
    Georgian Bay, the sixth great lake. Toronto: Clarke, Irwin Company
    Limited, 1968.
    190 p. illus., facsims., maps.   OTU
Beasley, Norman.
    Freighters of fortune: the story of the Great Lakes. [1st ed.] New York:
    Harper and Bros., 1930.
    ix, 311 p. plates.
    Chiefly United States.   OTV
Beauchemin–Beaton–Lapointe Inc.
    Rapid transit appraisal study for the Regional Municipality of Ottawa –
    Carleton, by Beauchemin–Beaton–Lapointe Inc., M.M. Dillon Ltd.,
    DeLeuw Cather, Canada Ltd., 1976. Ottawa: 1976.
    1 v. (various pagings). maps, tables.   OTDT
Beaumont, Ralph, 1951–
    The great horseshoe wreck, by Ralph Beaumont and James Filby.
    [Cheltenham, Ontario: Boston Mills Press, c1974]
    [40] p. illus., facsims., maps. (Credit valley series, no. 4).   OTU
Beck, (Sir) Adam, 1857–1925.
    An address on the work of the [Hydro-Electric] Commission and its relation
    to the county of Huron. [Goderich, Ontario] The Signal Press [1911]
    13 p.   OOA
— The conservation of the water powers of Ontario. Address delivered before
    the Commission for the Conservation of National Resources at Ottawa,
    January 19, 1910. n.p.: 1910.
    22 p. tables.   OTAR

— Errors and misrepresentation made by the Hydro-Electric Inquiry
  Commission (known as the Gregory Commission) respecting the publicly
  owned and operated hydro-electric power undertaking of municipalities in
  the province of Ontario. Toronto: 1925.
  53 p.   OTU
— The Hydro-Electric Power Commission of Ontario. Address by Sir Adam
  Beck at the Public Ownership Conference, September 10th to 13th, 1923 at
  Toronto. [Toronto?: 1923?]
  15 p.   OTU
— The Hydro-Electric Power Commission of Ontario: its origin,
  administration and achievements. Toronto: 1924.
  19 p. illus., map.   OKQ
— Re "Murray report" on electric utilities: refutation of unjust statements
  contained in a report published by the National Electric Light Association
  entitled "Government owned and controlled compared with privately owned
  and regulated electric utilities in Canada and the United States" respecting
  the Hydro-Electric Power Commission of Ontario. Toronto: 1922.
  xii, 53 p. tables (1 fold.).   OTU
— Re "Sutherland Commission" majority report: statement respecting findings
  and other statements contained in majority report of the Commission
  (known as the "Sutherland Commission") appointed to inquire into the
  subject of hydro-electric railways. Toronto: 1922.
  43 p. fold. maps.   OTU
— Statement *re* enormous losses occasioned by the diversion of water from the
  Great Lakes to the Mississippi River by the Sanitary District of Chicago.
  Toronto: 1923.
  7 p.   OTAR
— A statement by Sir Adam Beck protesting against the exportation of electric
  power, with special reference to the proposed lease of the "Carillon" power
  site. Toronto: 1925.
  11 p.   OTU
— Unjust and harmful proposals published by authority of an organization
  known as the Canadian Deep Waterway and Power Association...
  examined and exposed. Toronto: 1925.
  12 p.   OKQ
— Water power statement... before the Committee on Water Power of the
  House of Representatives, sixty-five Congress, second session. Washington,
  D.C. 1918.
  71 p. tables.   OTU
Bell Telephone Company of Canada.
  Communications for northwestern Ontario. n.p.: 1964.
  [12] p. illus., map.   OONL
Biggar, Emerson Bristol, 1853–1921.
  Hydro-electric development in Ontario: a history of water power
  administration under the Hydro-Electric Power Commission of Ontario.
  Toronto: The Biggar Press Ltd [c1920]
  202 p. front., illus., diagr., fold. map, port.   OTAR

Blaine, William Edward, 1930–
Ride through the garden of Canada: a short history of the Hamilton,
Grimsby and Beamsville Electric Railway Company, 1894–1931. Grimsby,
Ontario: c1967.
26 [45] p. illus., facsims., ports.   OTU
Blanchard, Raoul, 1877–1965.
L'ouést du Canada français. Montreal: Beauchemin, 1953–54.
2 v. illus., maps (part fold.).
Contents: v. 1, Montreal et sa region; v. 2, Les pays de l'Ottawa, L'Abitibi –
Témiscamingue.   OTU
Bolton, Reginald Pelham, 1856–1942.
An expensive experiment: the Hydro-Electric Power Commission of
Ontario. New York: Baker & Taylor, 1913.
281 p. illus., ports.   OTU
Bonis, Robert Raynes, 1906–
Hydro-electric power in Scarborough. Scarborough, Ontario: Scarborough
Public Utilities Commission, 1966.
32 p. illus., graphs, maps, ports.   OONL
Bonsor, N   C   1944–
Transportation rates and economic development in northern Ontario.
Toronto: Published for the Ontario Economic Council by University of
Toronto Press, 1977.
91 p. graphs, tables. (Ontario Economic Council. Research studies, 7). OONL
Bookbinder, James H
Multiple queues of aircraft under time-dependent conditions: policy options
for Toronto International Airport, by James H. Bookbinder and Harvinder
Luthra. [Toronto] Joint Program in Transportation, 1974.
ii, 27 leaves. graphs. (Joint Program in Transportation. Research report, no.
22).   OTU
Boorse, J   W
Rapid transit in Canada. Philadelphia: Almo Press [c1968]
vii, 104 p. illus., plans.   OONL
Bowen, Dana Thomas, 1896–
Lore of the lakes, told in story and picture. Daytona Beach, Florida: D.T.
Bowen, 1940.
xv, 314 p. plates (part col.), diagr., front.   OKQ
— Shipwrecks of the lakes, told in story and picture. Daytona Beach, Florida:
Dana Thomas Bowen, 1952.
xv, 368 p. illus.   OMI
Bracebridge, Ontario. Council.
Bracebridge and its water powers. Bracebridge, Ontario: Bracebridge
Council and Board of Trade, 1903.
28 p. illus.   OTAR
Brazer, Marjorie Cahn, 1927–
Well-favoured passage; exploring the waters, land and history of Lake
Huron's north channel. Toronto: Peter Martin Associates [c1975]
xii, 160 p. illus., maps.   OTU

Brimacombe, Philip, 1949–
    The story of Bronte Harbour. Oakville, Ontario: Oakville Historical
    Society; Cheltenham, Ontario: Boston Mills Press [c1976]
    38 p. illus., (Halton county series, 2).   OONL
— The story of Oakville Harbour: a history. Cheltenham, Ontario: Boston
    Mills Press and the Oakville Historical Society, 1975.
    [43] p. illus., maps. (Halton county series, no. 1).   OTU
Bromley, John F
    Fifty years of progressive transit 1921–1971: a history of the Toronto Transit
    Commission by John F. Bromley and Jack May. New York: Electric
    Railroader's Association, c1973.
    176 p. illus., facsims., maps, charts.   OTU
Brown, George Williams, 1894–1963.
    The deepening of the St. Lawrence. Toronto: The Author, 1928.
    [20] p.
    "Reprinted by permission from *The Round Table*".   OTU
Bruce Mines and Algoma Railway.
    The greater Ontario to be developed by the Bruce Mines and Algoma
    Railway which is the western Ontario route to Hudson Bay. n.p. [1901?]
    31 p. tables, col. fold. map.   OTAR
Bruce Mines and Algoma Railway. n.p. [1902?]
    15 p. illus., map (part fold.).   OTAR
Buchanan, Edward Victor, 1887–
    A history of electrical energy in London. Prepared for the Ontario Hydro
    Centennial Hall of Memory project. [London, Ontario: Public Utilities
    Commission, 1966]
    91 p. illus., ports.   OLU
— London's water supply: a history. [London, Ontario] London Public
    Utilities Commission [1968]
    112 p. illus., ports.   OTU
Building rights over subway sites. [Toronto] Municipality of Metropolitan
    Toronto [1966?]
    2 v. plans.   OTUSA
Bullock, F   J
    Ships and the seaway. Toronto: J.M. Dent & Sons (Canada) Limited
    [c1959]
    115 p. illus.   OKQ
Burton, Ian.
    Accessibility in northern Ontario: an application of graph theory to a
    regional highway network. [Toronto] Department of Geography, University
    of Toronto, 1962.
    25 leaves. figs., tables.   OTU
Bushell, George.
    An optimizing model of traffic assignment for the freeway system of southern
    Ontario. [Toronto] Centre for Urban and Community Studies, University of
    Toronto, 1970.
    75, 2 leaves. graphs, maps, tables. (Research paper, no. 40).   OTU

Calvin, Delano Dexter, 1881–1948.
  A saga of the St. Lawrence timber and shipping through three generations.
  Toronto: The Ryerson Press [c1945]
  x, 176 p. illus., diagrs.   OLU
Campbellford, Canada, the great cheap power town. Campbellford, Ontario:
  Despatch Electric Presses, 1912.
  12 p. illus.   OKQ
Canada. Airport Inquiry Commission.
  Report. Ottawa: Information Canada, 1974.
  viii, 723 p. maps.
  Toronto airport.   OTU
Canada. Department of Public Works.
  Georgian Bay ship canal: report upon survey with plans and estimates of
  cost 1908. Ottawa: C.H. Parmelee, printer to the King's Most Excellent
  Majesty, 1909.
  xxii, 601 p. fold. maps, tables.   OMI
— Maps.
  3 v.   OMI
— Memorandum, with accompanying plans and documents relative to the past
  and present state of the harbour of Toronto, province of Ontario. Prepared
  by direction of the Hon. H.B. Langevin, C.B., minister of public works.
  Ottawa: Department of Public Works, 1881.
  xiii, 137 p. chart, plan, table.   OOA
— Report of the Chief Engineer of Public Works on the enlargement of the
  Welland Canal. Ottawa: 1872.
  59 p. (Canada. Sessional papers no. 6. Appendix no. 7, 1873).   OONL
Canada. Department of Railways and Canal.
  August sixth, nineteen thirty-two, the opening of the Welland Ship Canal. A
  Canadian conception, a Canadian achievement. [Ottawa: F.A. Acland,
  printer to the King's Most Excellent Majesty, 1932]
  43 p. illus., maps, plans.
  Cover title: The Welland Ship Canal: new links in the world's greatest
  inland waterway.   OTL OONL
— Reference and guide book of the Trent Canal including Kawartha lakes,
  Lake Simcoe, Lake Couchiching. Peterborough, Ontario: the Peterborough
  Examiner, Limited, 1911.
  50 p. iillus. fold. maps.   OKQ
— Report... on the necessity of deepening the Welland Canal, and on
  transportation, commerce and canal tolls, affecting the St. Lawrence water-
  route to the sea-board, by Robert C. Douglas, assistant engineer,
  Department of Railways and Canals. Ottawa: MacLean, Roger & Co.,
  1884.
  v, 115 p. tables.   OONL
— Welland Ship Canal, 1934. Ottawa: J.O. Patenaude, printer to the King's
  Most Excellent Majesty, 1935.
  31 p. map, table.   OTL OONL

— Welland Ship Canal (under construction), also brief historic reference to past and present Welland. Ottawa: Thomas Mulvey, printer to the King's Most Excellent Majesty, 1920.
     23 p. illus., maps, tables.   OOA
Canada. Geological Survey.
     National transcontinental railway; resources of the country between Quebec and Winnipeg along the line of the Grand Trunk Pacific Railway. Compiled ... by H.M. Ami. Ottawa: S.E. Dawson, printer to the King's Most Excellent Majesty, 1903.
     179 p. 1 col. map. (Canada. Parliament. Sessional paper no. 143, 1903).
                                                                                    OTU
Canada. Parliament.
     Reports of the "late House of Assembly," "House of Commons," and the "Legislative Assembly" of Ontario, in relation to the Huron and Ontario Ship Canal. 4th ed. Printed by order of the Council of the Corporation of the City of Toronto, in accordance with resolution passed Monday the 20th February, 1871. Toronto: Printed by Hunter, Rose & Company, 1871.
     30 [1] p.   OTURS
Canada. Transport Commission.
     Toronto commuter rail study. [Ottawa] Canadian Transport Commission, 1972.
     xii, 174 p. maps, tables..
     Cover: Final report.   OONL
Canada. Transport Commission. Research Branch.
     Intercity passenger transport study: a study of passenger transport in the urbanized corridor between Windsor, Ontario and Quebec city, P.Q. with a comparison of alternate strategies in the Montreal – Ottawa – Toronto portion of this corridor. [Ottawa: Information Canada, 1970]
     103 p. graphs, maps, tables.   OTUSA
Canada. Transport Service Appraisal Division.
     Midwestern Ontario: Bruce public transport study, 2d. ed. Ottawa: Canadian Transport Commission, Systems Analysis and Research Data Base Branch, 1973–1974.
     3 parts. illus. (part col.). (*Its* Report, 75–77).
     Contents: Part 1, Review of public transport system; Part 2, Comparative analysis of some preliminary alternative systems; part 3, Transportation habits and attitudes.   OTU
Canada – Ontario Rideau – Trent – Severn Study Committee.
     Optimum recreational development in the Lake Simcoe – Couchiching area: a supplementary reports of CORTS. Toronto: 1973.
     27 p. illus., maps.   OTAR
Canadian Archaeological Divers Society.
     The wreck of the S.S. Alexandria. n.p.: 1967.
     [8] p. illus.
     A ship wrecked off Scarborough Bluffs.   OTAR

Canadian Facts Company.
Metro-Toronto transportation study, northern region, February/March
1969. Conducted for the York Centre Commuter Committee, Toronto,
Ontario. Toronto [1969]
ii, 18, 5, 5 p. map.
Cover title: Go – north. OTU
Canadian Federation of Boards of Trade and Municipalities.
Canada's canal problem and its solution: a reply to the Toronto Board of
Trade. [Ottawa: 1912?].
64 p. fold. map.
Trent waterways. OTU
Canadian Federation of Mayors and Municipalities. Urban Transportation
Committee.
Submission to the Federal – Provincial Tax Structure Committee: financial
requirements to meet urban transportation needs in Canadian metropolitan
regions. Montreal [1969?]
96 p. diagrs., tables. OONL
Canadian Nuclear Association.
The role of nuclear power in Ontario: submission to the Royal Commission
on Electric Power Planning. [Toronto] The Association, c1976.
1 v. (various pagings). diagrs. OTU
Canadian Urban Transportation Conference, 1st, Toronto, 1969.
Proceedings. Edited by John Steel. Ottawa: Canadian Federation of Mayors
and Municipalities [1969]
vi, 377 p. ports.
Cover title: Opportunity or chaos. OTU
— Regional study papers. Prepared by the regional study groups for the first
Canadian Urban Transportation Conference, 9–12 February, 1969,
Toronto. Compiled and edited by John Steel. Ottawa: Canadian Federation
of Mayors and Municipalities [1969?]
iii, 120 p. ports. OTU
— Study papers. Prepared for the regional study groups and the first Canadian
Urban Transportation Conference, 9–12 February, 1969, Toronto.
Compiled and edited by John Steel. Ottawa: Canadian Federation of
Mayors and Municipalities [1969?]
vi, 331 [7] p. illus., map, ports. OTU
Carter, DeWitt, 1849–1933.
The Welland Canal: a history. Port Colbourne, Ontario: Privately printed
for Helen Carter, 1960.
117 p. port., tables. OTU
Chevrier, Lionel, 1903–
The St. Lawrence Seaway. Toronto: Macmillan Company of Canada
Limited, 1959.
x, 174 p. illus., maps. OTU

Clauson, Fred M
    The story of the Rideau Falls hydro-electric plant. Rideau Falls, Ontario:
    The Author [c1969]
      1 v. (various pagings). illus.   OTAR
The Commercial Press.
    Welland Ship Canal inauguration. St. Catharines, Ontario: The
    Commercial Press [1930]
      126 p. illus., ports., map.   OTAR
Cooke, John Robert.
    "Hydro" service considered in some of its important economic aspects; an
    address given before the Liberal–Conservative Summer School at
    Newmarket, September, 4th to 9th, 1933. n.p.: 1933.
      18 p.   OTU
Coombs, Albert Ernest, 1871–1957.
    History of the Niagara Peninsula and the new Welland Canal. Toronto:
    Historical Publishing Association, 1930.
      428 p. illus., ports.   OTU
Cooper, Douglas H   1915–
    Controlled access highways – Ontario's new intercity expressway; remarks to
    the Community Planning Association of Canada, Toronto, April 13, 1962.
    [Toronto: 1962]
      11 leaves.   OONL
Cornick, H   F
    The Saint Lawrence Seaway. With J.G.G. Kerry's winter navigation on the
    St. Lawrence. Reprinted from Nov. and Dec. 1950 issues of *The Dock and*
    Harbour Authority.
      16 p. illus., maps.   OKQ
Correspondence and documents relating to the Great Lakes – St. Lawrence
    basin development 1938–1941. Ottawa: Edmond Cloutier, printer to the
    King's Most Excellent Majesty, 1941.
      vi, 73 p. map.   OOA
Costain, Thomas Bertram, 1885–1965.
    The chord of steel; the story of the invention of the telephone. [1st ed.]
    Garden City, New York: Doubleday & Company Inc., 1960.
      238 p. illus., ports.   OTU
Cowan, Percy John.
    The Welland Ship Canal between Lake Ontario and Lake Erie, 1913–1932.
    Reprint of articles appearing in *Engineering* during the years 1929, 1930 and
    1931, by Major P.J. Cowan ... in collaboration with officials of the
    Department of Railways and Canals. London: Offices of Engineering, 1935.
    [iv] 254 p. illus., maps., fold. plates, diagrs.
    At head of title: Department of Railways and Canals, Canada.   OOA
Crain, John Ernest, 1921–
    The Noronic is burning! Don Mills, Ontario: General Publishing Co.
    Limited [1976]
      117 p. illus., facsims.   OOA

Credit Valley Railway Company.
The Esplanade difficulty. Reply to the statements of the Grand Trunk and Northern Railway companies in the matter of the disputed entrance to Toronto Harbour. Legal argument in favour of the Credit Valley's contention, appeal to Parliament. Toronto: Globe Printing Company, 1880.
27 p. OOA

Cruickshank, Ernest Alexander, 1854–1939.
The centenary of the Welland Canal. [Welland, Ontario: Tribune–Telegraph Press, 1924.
35 p. port. OKQ

Cumberland, Frederick Barlow, 1846–1913.
A century of sail and steam on the Niagara River. Toronto: Musson Book Company Limited [c1913]
xvi, 198 p. plates, ports. OTU

Cumberland, Frederic William, 1820–1881.
Railways to Grey: being a letter to the warden, reeves, and deputy reeves, of the South Riding of the county of Grey. Toronto: Globe Printing Company, 1867.
33 p. fold. map. OKQ

Currie, Archibald William, 1908–
Canadian transportation economics. [Toronto] University of Toronto Press [c1967]
viii, 719 p. OTU
— The Grand Trunk Railway of Canada. Toronto: University of Toronto Press, 1957.
viii, 556 p. illus., map. OTU

Currier, J E W (comp.).
Railway legislation of the Dominion of Canada from 1867 to 1905 inclusive. 2d ed. Ottawa [Department of Railways and Canals] 1905.
232 p.
No copy of first edition located. OLU

Cuthbertson, George A
Freshwater: a history and a narrative of the Great Lakes. Toronto: The Macmillan Company of Canada Limited, 1931.
315 p. illus. (part col.).
Chiefly pre-Confederation. OTU OMI

Damas and Smith Limited.
Regional municipality of Niagara traffic operations study, regional roads – Welland. Toronto: Damas and Smith Limited, 1974.
34, xii leaves. graphs., fold. map, tables. OTDT
— Town of Renfrew traffic planning report 1967–1990. Toronto [1971]
93 p. diagrs., maps (part col.), tables. OLU

DeLeuw Cather Canada Ltd.
Traffic operations study of the regional road system in Niagara Falls, the Regional Municipality of Niagara. [Toronto: DeLeuw Cather Canada Ltd., 1975]
149 p. diagrs., maps, tables. OTDT

DeLeuw Cather & Company of Canada Limited.
London urban transportation study: final report by DeLeuw Cather in
association with Earl Berger Limited [et al. London, Ontario: DeLeuw
Cather & Company Ltd.] 1973–1974.
3 v. illus., maps (part col.).
Contents: v. 1, Traffic operations; v. 2, Transit operations; v. 3, Systems
planning and railways.   OLU
— A new procedure for urban transportation planning: report on the first cycle
of a research project for the Department of Highways, Ontario. [Toronto?]
DeLeuw Cather & Company of Canada Limited, 1969.
76, 63 leaves. graphs., tables.   OTDT
— North-east corridor GO – urban study: preliminary evaluation cycle, by
DeLeuw–Dillon in association with Earl Berger Limited [et al.]. Toronto:
Metropolitan Toronto Planning Board, 1973.
2 v. illus., diagrs.
Contents: v. 1, Identification of routes and factors; v. 2, Study design. OTUSA
Denison, Merrill, 1893–1975.
The people's power; the history of Ontario Hydro. [Toronto] McClelland &
Stewart Limited [c1960]
viii, 295 p. illus., ports., fold. maps, facsims.   OTU
Dewees, Donald Norman, 1941–
Congestion costs in urban motoring: some Toronto estimates. Toronto:
Centre for Urban and Community Studies, University of Toronto, 1976.
38 p. (Centre for Urban and Community Studies, University of Toronto.
Research paper, no. 71).   OLU
— Some effects of conversion from streetcar to subway transit lines in Toronto.
Toronto: Centre for Urban and Community Studies, University of Toronto,
1976.
37 p.   OTU
Diamond & Myers.
Pickering impact study: a study prepared for the City of Toronto Planning
Board of the impact of the proposed New Toronto International Airport and
the North Pickering community, by Diamond & Myers, Jack B. Ellis &
Associates, Institute of Environmental Research Inc. Toronto: Diamond &
Myers, 1974.
2 v. graphs.
Contents: v. 1, Summary report; v. 2, Study report.   OTU
Dillon, (M.M.) Limited.
Sudbury area transportation study: a plan for progress. [Sudbury, Ontario]
1965.
[16] p. illus., col. maps.   OTUSA
— Traffic study for the Corporation of the City of Woodstock, Ontario.
London, Ontario: M.M. Dillon and Company Limited, 1962.
102 leaves. graphs, maps.   OWO

Dorman, Robert (comp.).
    A statutory history of the steam and electric railways of Canada, 1836–1937,
    with other data relevant to operation of the Department of Transport.
    Ottawa: J.O. Patenaude, printer to the King's Most Excellent Majesty,
    1938.
        765 p.   OLUL
Due, John Fitzgerald, 1915–
    The intercity electric railway industry in Canada. [Toronto] University of
    Toronto Press [c1966]
        x, 118 p. illus., maps, tables. (Canadian studies in economics, 18).
    One chapter plus devoted to Ontario.   OTU
Duff, Louis Blake, 1878–1959 (ed.).
    Welland Ship Canal. Edited by Louis Blake Duff [et al.]. St. Catharines,
    Ontario: The Commercial Press [1930]
        126 p. illus.   OTU
Eastern Ontario Development Council.
    Review of the Rideau – Trent – Severn. Report. [Ottawa] 1972.
        32, 3 leaves.   OONL
Eldon, Donald.
    The past, present and future of the London Street Railway Company.
    [London, Ontario: 1948]
        54 p. map, tables.   OL
Evening Journal, St. Thomas, Ontario.
    St. Thomas, Ontario: the railway city. Souvenir edition [St. Thomas,
    Ontario] 1891.
        38 p. illus.   OSTT
Extracts from and copies of the official documents and the correspondence
    between the Toronto Railway Company and the City in reference to the
    paving of the track allowances of the railway, and the explanatory comments
    on the merits of the case. [Toronto] 1893.
        26 p.   OTAR
Fairfax, Gerald, 1945–
    Communications and conveyance in the province of Upper Canada,
    1600–1870 with special emphasis on the effects of transport network growth
    on settlement and development in Frontenac county. n.p: 1970.
        iii, 37 leaves. maps.   OKQ
Farrell, Marvin William, 1920–
    The Guelph Junction Railway, 1884–1950. [Guelph, Ontario: Guelph
    Junction Railway Co., 1951]
        25 leaves. tables.   OOA
Filby, James Frederick, 1925–
    Credit Valley Railway: the third grant: a history. Cheltenham, Ontario:
    Boston Mills Press, c1974.
        107 p. illus., maps, port. (Credit valley series, no. 1).   OTU

Filey, Michael, 1941–
    Trillium and Toronto Island. Toronto: Peter Martin Associates Limited
    [1976]
    96 p. illus., facsims., ports.   OONL
Firestone, Otto Jack, 1913–
    Broadcast advertising in Canada, past and future growth. Ottawa:
    University of Ottawa Press, 1966.
    xvi, 358 p. diagrs., tables. (Ottawa. University. Social science studies, no. 3).
                                                                            OTU
Folkes, Patrick Regan, 1941–
    Shipwrecks of the Saugeen, 1828–1938: a history of marine disasters of Bruce
    county: Clark Point – Tobermory – Owen Sound. [Willowdale, Ontario:
    1970]
    85 leaves. illus., maps.   OTU
— Shipwrecks of Tobermory, 1828–1935. [Willowdale, Ontario: c1969]
    [2] 38 [1] leaves. illus., maps.   OTURS
Found, William Charles, 1940–
    A conceptual approach to rural land use – transportation modelling in the
    Toronto region, by Wm. C. Found and C.D. Morley. [Toronto: University
    of Toronto – York University Joint Program in Transportation] 1972.
    iv, 266 p. illus., tables. (Joint Program in Transportation. Research report,
    no. 8).   OTU
Foundation of Canada Engineering Corporation Limited.
    Functional report on proposed Don Valley Parkway to the Municipality of
    Metropolitan Toronto, October 1955, by Fenco – Harris, a joint venture of
    Foundation of Canada Engineering Corporation limited and Frederic R.
    Harris of Canada, Ltd. [Toronto: 1955]
    25 leaves. illus., maps (part fold., part col.), diagrs., plans.   OTU
Fowle, Otto, 1852–1920.
    Sault Ste. Marie and its great waterway. New York: G.P. Putnam's & Sons,
    1925.
    xxi, 458 p. plates, map.
    Chiefly pre-Confederation.   OTU
French, Maida Parlow.
    Apples don't just grow. Toronto: McClelland & Stewart Limited [c1954]
    viii, 226 p.
    Iroquois and the St. Lawrence Seaway.   OKQ
Frost, Leslie Miscampbell, 1895–1973.
    Forgotten pathways of the Trent. [Don Mills, Ontario] Burns &
    MacEachern Limited [1973]
    111 p. illus., facsims., maps.
    Chiefly pre-Confederation.   OTU
Fuller, Samuel Street, 1838–   (comp.).
    Book of clippings re the Stratford and Huron Railway, compiled by Mr.
    Fuller, president of the railway, 1880.
    100 p.   OLU

Gaby, Frederick Arthur, 1878–
    Canadian electrical development; electrical service for rural districts as
    provided by the Hydro-Electric Power Commission of Ontario. [Toronto?
    1928?]
    16 p. illus.
    "Reprinted from *World Power* September and October 1927.   OTU
— The power situation in Ontario: a statement made at the request of the
    Executive of the Ontario Municipal Electric Association, Toronto, April 6,
    1935. Toronto: Power Securities Protective Association [1935?]
    16 p.   OTU
— Some interesting aspects of the Hydro system including an historical review
    of its policies and achievements and a consideration of the lessons to be
    learned therefrom; address to Ontario Municipal Association and
    Association of Municipal Electrical Utilities at Ottawa, June 26, 1931. n.p.
    [1931]
    44 p. illus., map.   OTU
— Trends of electrical demands in relation to power supplies: The Hydro-
    Electric Power Commission of Ontario. Toronto: 1933.
    31 p. diagrs. (part fold.), table.   OTU
Gardiner, Frederick Goldwin, 1895–
    Traffic, transit and transportation. [Toronto] The Ontario Good Roads
    Association, 1956.
    14 p.   OTU
Gartner, Nathan.
    Platoon profiles and link delay functions for optimal coordination of traffic
    signals on arterial streets. University of Toronto – York University Joint
    Program in Transportation. Toronto: 1972.
    52 p. graphs, maps. (Research report no. 9).   OTU
George, Ewart B   1903–
    The steam age in western Ontario: a railroad anthology. 2d. ed. London,
    Ontario: F.J. Ram, 1976.
    ix, 125 p. illus., fold. map.
    No first edition located.   OTU
Geraghty, E
    Telephone history, London, Ontario 1880–1972. Montreal: Telephone
    Historical Collection, 1972.
    67 leaves.   OONL
Gibson, Jesse.
    Thomas Bone: the sailor's friend; the story of his work on the Welland
    Canal. Toronto: The Upper Canada Tract Society [1908]
    158 p. front. (port.), plates.   OTAR
Glazebrook, George Parkin de Twenebrokes, 1899–
    A history of transportation in Canada. Foreword by H.A. Innis. Toronto:
    The Ryerson Press, 1938.
    xxv, 475 p. fold. maps.   OTU
— 2d. ed. [Toronto] McClelland and Stewart [1964]
    2 v.
    Contents: v. 1, Continental strategy to 1867; v. 2, National economy
    1867–1936.   OTUSA

Gonem, Amiram.
  The Spadina Expressway in Toronto: decision and opposition.
  [Philadelphia, Pennsylvania: University of Pennsylvania, Wharton School of
  Finance and Commerce] 1970.
  ii, 22 p. (Research on conflict in locational decisions. Discussion paper, 5).
                                                                          OTU
Go– north commuter study. Prepared for York Centre Commuter Committee
  May 11, 1969. n.p.: 1969.
  1 v. (various pagings). tables.   OTU
Graham, Bernard Mearl, 1908–
  North Bay Hydro, 1885–1973. Don Mills, Ontario [T.H. Best Printing
  Company Limited, c1973]
  v, 157 p. illus., facsims., ports.   OTU
Graham, Percy Wentworth.
  Sir Adam Beck. London, Ontario: The Carl Smith Publishing Company,
  c1925.
  [64] p. port.   OLU
Grand River Parkway Conference, Brantford, Ontario, 1962.
  Grand River Conference report. n.p. [Niagara Regional Development
  Association, 1962]
  30 p.   OTU
Grand Trunk Railway Company of Canada.
  Annotated time table of the tour through Canada of their Royal Highnesses
  the Duke and Duchess of Cornwall and York, embracing that portion of the
  Grand Trunk Railway System traversed by their Royal Highnesses...
  through the provinces of Ontario and Quebec, October, 1901. [Montreal:
  Grand Trunk Railway, 1901]
  1 v. illus.   OTU
— Across Niagara's gorge. n.p. [19—]
  24 p. illus., map.
  Map dated 1906.   OTURS
Grant, Peter S   (ed.).
  Telephone operation and development in Canada, 1921–1971: papers on
  institutional and regulatory aspects. Toronto: Faculty of Law, University of
  Toronto, 1974.
  xiv, 401 p. diagrs., tables.   OONL
Griffin, Kevin Christopher, 1947–
  Ships of the Great Lakes and Saint Lawrence. 1st ed. rev. Stratford, Ontario:
  Griffin Publications, 1968.
  60 p.
  1st ed. March 1968, rev. June 1968.   OONL
Grindlay, Thomas.
  The independent telephone industry in Ontario: a history. Toronto: Ontario
  Telephone Services Commission, 1975.
  316 p. illus., facsims., ports.   OTAR

Guelph, Ontario. Transportation Study Committee.
   City of Guelph transportation plan to 100,000 persons and beyond [a joint
   municipal–consultant undertaking, Marshall Macklin Monaghan Limited
   providing the study director and other advisory staff. Guelph, Ontario: The
   Committee, 1974]
   107 p. illus. (part col.), maps.
   Chairman: William P. Taylor.   OTU
Guillet, Edwin Clarence, 1898–1975.
   Pioneer travel in Upper Canada. [Toronto] University of Toronto Press
   [1966, c1933]
   241 p. illus., ports., facsims.
   Chiefly pre-Confederation.   OKQ
—— Pioneer travel. Toronto: Ontario Publishing Co. Ltd., 1939.
   vii, 175 p. illus. (Early life in Upper Canada series, book 4).   OTAR
—— The story of Canadian roads. [Toronto] University of Toronto Press [c1966]
   246 p. illus.   OTAR
Gzowski, (Sir) Casimir Stanislaus, 1813–1898.
   Description of the International Bridge constructed over the Niagara River,
   near Fort Erie, Canada and Buffalo, United States of America. Toronto:
   Copp, Clark & Co., 1873.
   65 p. plates (part fold.).   OTURS
Hamilton Harbour Commissioners.
   Port of Hamilton. Hamilton, Ontario: The Author, 1951.
   [48] p. illus. (part col.), maps (part fold.), ports.   OTU
Harrington, Lyn, 1911–
   Covered bridges of central and eastern Canada, by Lyn and Richard
   Harrington. Toronto: McGraw–Hill Ryerson, Limited [c1976]
   88 p. illus. (part col.), maps.
   Ontario: pp. 74–80.   OONL
Harris, R   C
   Report to the Civic Transportation Committee on radical railway entrances
   and rapid transit for the city of Toronto, by R.C. Harris, F.A. Gaby and E.L.
   Cousins. [Toronto] 1915.
   2 v. maps (part col.), diagrs., plans (part fold).
   Contents: v. 1, Text; v. 2, Plans.   OTU
Hatcher, Harlan Henthorne, 1898–
   The Great Lakes. Toronto: Oxford University Press, 1944.
   xi, 384 p. front., illus., maps, plates.   OTSTM
—— Lake Erie. Indianapolis: Bobbs–Merrill [c1945]
   416 p. plates, ports., maps. (The American lakes series).   OLU
—— A pictorial history of the Great Lakes, by Harlan Hatcher and Erich A.
   Walter. New York: Crown Publishers [c1963]
   344 p. illus. (part col.), ports., maps.   OTU
Havighurst, Walter, 1901–
   The long ships passing: the story of the Great Lakes. Illustrated by John
   O'Hara Cosgrave II. New York: Macmillan Company, 1942.
   viii, 291 p. front., illus. map.   OTU

Heisler, John P
    The canals of Canada. Ottawa: Department of Indian and Northern Affairs,
    1973.
    183 p. illus. (Canadian historic sites: occasional papers in archaeology and
    history no. 8).   OTU
Heyl, Erik.
    Early American steamers. Buffalo, New York: The Author, 1953.
    4 v. illus.   OMI
Hills, Theo L
    The St. Lawrence Seaway. London: Methuen & Co. Ltd. [1959]
    157 p. illus., map.   OTU
A history of the Welland Ship Canal. n.p.: 1925.
    12 leaves.   OTURS
Hitchock, John R
    The impact of expressways on adjacent apartments; a case study of
    Metropolitan Toronto [by] John R. Hitchock and Alan Waterhouse.
    [Toronto] University of Toronto – York University Joint Program in
    Transportation, 1973.
    iii, 129 p. illus. (Joint Program in Transportation. Research report, no. 10).
                                                                            OTU
Hodge, Gerald.
    Regional impact of a new international airport for Toronto; a report for
    Ontario Department of Treasury and Economics, Regional Development
    Branch, and Canada Department of Transport Air Services [by] Gerald
    Hodge, with the assistance of Robert Morrow. Toronto: 1970.
    vi, 90 leaves. illus., fold. maps.   OTUSA
Hodgson, Michael John.
    A dynamic programming model of highway network development.
    [Toronto] Centre for Urban and Community Studies, University of Toronto,
    1971.
    29, 2 leaves. graphs, tables. ([Environment Study] Research paper no. 43).
                                                                            OTU
— A highway link addition model for southwestern Ontario. [Toronto]
    Department of Geography, University of Toronto, 1969.
    47, 3 [1] leaves. figures, maps. (Environment study. Research report no. 19).
                                                                            OTU
Hogg, Thomas H
    Hydro. Ontario's successful experiment in public ownership. [Princeton,
    New Jersey: University Press] 1941.
    31 p.   OKQ
Holgate, Henry.
    Report on the St. Lawrence waterway project, by H. Holgate and J.A.
    Jamieson. Montreal: Board of Trade [1929]
    46 p. map, tables.   OTU

Horsley, David B
  Manual of motor vehicle law, with special reference to the Ontario Highway
  traffic act. Toronto: Carswell Co., 1963.
  xxviii, 466 p. illus.   OONL
— Supplement. 2d. 1965. [Toronto] Carswell Co., 1965.
  iv, 77 p.   OONL
— 2d ed. Toronto: Carswell co., 1974.
  lxv, 568 p.   OONL
Hulbert, Arthur Butler, 1873–1933.
  The Niagara River. New York: Putnam, 1908.
  xiii, 319 p. illus., maps, parts.   OTU
Humphries, W
  Great fury: an introduction to marine history. [London, Ontario: Concept
  Printing, 1959?]
  1 v. (unpaged). illus., facsims.   OLU
Hynes, Cecil Vernon, 1920–
  Michigan and Ontario trade and transport reciprocity. East Lansing,
  Michigan: Institute for International Business Management Studies,
  Division of Research, Graduate School of Business Administration,
  Michigan State University, 1966.
  x, 133 p. illus., maps.   OTU
Inverhuron Harbour Committee, Bruce County, Ontario.
  The question of a harbour of refuge on the Canada coast of Lake Huron,
  discussed at some length by the Inverhuron Harbour Committee, county of
  Bruce, 1869. Toronto: Hunter, Rose & Co., 1869.
  31 p. 2 fold maps.
  Chairman: Alex. McBean.
  Cover title leaves "Canada" out of the title.   OTURS
Ireland, Tom.
  The Great Lakes – St. Lawrence deep waterway to the sea. New York: G.P.
  Putnam's Sons 1934.
  xiv, 223 p. illus., map.   OTU
Jackson, John Nicolas, 1925–
  Welland and the Welland Canal: the Welland Canal by-pass. Belleville,
  Ontario: Mika Publishing Co., 1975.
  214 p. illus., maps, plans.   OTU
Jacobs & Davies, Inc.
  Report of Messrs. Jacobs & Davies on street railway transportation in the
  city of Toronto. [Toronto?] 1910.
  43 p. tables.   OTU
Jazairi, N   T
  Indexes of average railway freight rates: 1954–1968. [Toronto] University of
  Toronto – York University, Joint Program in Transportation, 1971.
  32 leaves. tables. (Joint Program in Transportation. Research report, no. 1).
                                                                           OTU

Jeffery, R   T
    History of Ottawa River Power Development and Eastern Power Purchase
    agreements. [Toronto] 1951.
    24 v. maps.   OTH
Joint Program in Transportation.
    Two-year review of the University of Toronto – York University Joint
    Program in Transportation. Prepared by the Executive Committee of the
    Joint Program. [Toronto] 1972.
    iv, 41 p.
    Cover title: A review of program: 1970–72.   OTU
Joint Technical Transportation Planning Committee.
    Spadina rapid transit system alignment study; evaluation of the relative
    performance of five selected alignments. Report. [Toronto] 1971.
    4, 22, 8, 7 leaves. col. illus., col. maps.
    Co-chairmen: William Bidell, Wojciech Wronski.   OTU
Jury, William Wilfrid, 1890–
    The Nine-Mile Portage from Kemp Enfeldt Bay to the Nottawasaga River. I
    Historical significance of the Portage. II Report on search for Nine-Mile
    Portage, by Wilfrid Jury and Elsie McLeod Jury. London, Ontario: The
    University of Western Ontario, 1956.
    35 p. maps, table. (Museum of Indian Archaeology, The University of
    Western Ontario. Museum bulletin no. 11).   OKQ
Kakabeka Falls Land and Electric Company Limited.
    Kakabeka Falls. [Port Arthur] n.d.
    1 v. (unpaged). illus., map.   OTAR
Kates, Peat, Marwick & Co.
    Thunder Bay transit study: final report. [Toronto] 1971.
    1 v. (various pagings). illus., fold. maps   OONL
Keefer, George Alexander, 1836–1912.
    Report on the preliminary examination of the Ontario and Quebec railway
    from Ottawa to Toronto. Ottawa: Bell & Woodburn [1872]
    21 p. fold. map.   OKQ
Keefer, Robert, 1871–
    Memoirs of the Keefer family. Norwood, Ontario: Norwood Register Press,
    1935.
    26 p. illus., ports.   OTU
Keefer, Samuel, 1811–1890.
    Report on opening out navigation from Rice Lake to Bay of Quinte, by
    Samuel Keefer and James Lyons. Peterborough, Ontario: J.R. Stratton
    "Examiner" Steam Presses, 1882.
    8 p.   OKQ
Keefer, Thomas Coltrin, 1821–1915.
    Canadian water ways from the Great Lakes to the Altantic. Boston: Damrell
    and Upham, 1893.
    18 p. fold. plan.
    "The World's Columbian Water Commerce Congress, Chicago, 1893." OKQ

Keyser, Walter.
The introduction of Bell's telephone in London, Ontario: an early history of the telephone and of the developments which led to the establishment of telephone service in London, Ontario. Canada: 1875–1880. [London, Ontario: 1951]
29, 6 leaves. OONL
Kipping, J   R
Rapid transit for Toronto: an economical solution, by J.R. Kipping and E. Perkons. n.p. [c1970]
25 p. illus., maps. OTAR
Kitchener Light Commissioners.
The origin of the Ontario hydro-electric power movement. [Kitchener, Ontario: The Quality Printers, Limited, 1919]
14 p. illus., chart, facsims., ports. OOA
Knowles, John D
Sudbury – Copper Cliff Suburban Electric Railway Company. [Toronto] Upper Canada Railway Society [1952]
8 leaves. illus., maps. (Upper Canada Railway Society. Bulletin 34). OSU
Kovack, Carol.
The who, when and why of subway usage: a report on the Toronto subway with a focus on social and recreational trips for the Department of Housing and Urban Development. [Washington] Department of Housing and Urban Development, c1971.
1 v. (various pagings). illus., maps. OTU
Laidlaw, George, 1828–1889.
Cheap railways. Letter to the people of Bruce and Grey, showing the advantages, practiceability and cost of a cheap railway from Toronto, through these counties with an appendix addressed to the people of Ontario and Victoria. Toronto: Globe Printing Company, 1867.
34 p. OTAR
Landon, Fred, 1880–1969.
Lake Huron. Indianapolis: Bobbs–Merrill [1944]
398 p. plates, ports., maps. (The American lake series). OTU
— Reprinted. New York: Russell & Russell, 1972.
379 p. plates, illus., maps, ports. OONL
Leaning, John.
A proposal for the roadway environment in the existing community [report prepared for the National Capital Commission. Ottawa: 1970]
22 leaves. illus., maps, plans. OTUSA
LeBourdais, Donat Marc, 1887–1964.
Canada and the atomic revolution. [Toronto] McClelland & Stewart Limited [c1959]
xix, 199 p. illus., maps, ports. OTU
Legge, Charles, 1829–1881.
Preliminary report on various routes for connecting Long Point and the

town of Picton (Prince Edward district) with the Grand Trunk Railway of
Canada. Montreal: John Lovell, 1872.
19 p.   OKQ
Legget, Robert Ferguson, 1904–
  Canals of Canada. Vancouver, British Columbia: Douglas, David &
  Charles, 1976.
  x, 261 p. illus., maps. (Canals of the world).   OTAR
— Ottawa waterway: gateway to a continent. Toronto: University of Toronto
  Press [c1975]
  xi, 291 p. illus., maps. diagrs.   OTU
— Railroads of Canada. Vancouver, British Columbia: Douglas, David and
  Charles [1973]
  255 p. illus., maps (Railroad histories of the world).   OOA
— Rideau waterway. Toronto: University of Toronto Press, 1955.
  xiv, 249 p. illus., maps.   OTU
  Reprinted. Toronto: University of Toronto Press [1962]
  xiv, 249 p. illus., plates, maps (Canadian University paperbacks, 3). OONL
  Rev. ed. Toronto: University of Toronto Press, 1972.
  ix; 249 p. illus., maps.   OTU
Levy, Daniel.
  Innovation in transit in medium size Canadian cities. Toronto: University of
  Toronto – York University Transportation Centre, 1976.
  62 p. illus.
  Six Ontario cities used.   OLU
Linden, Allen Martin, 1934–
  The report of the Osgoode Hall study on compensation for victims of
  automobile accidents. Toronto: The Author [c1965].
  1 v. (various pagings). tables.   OTU
A link in the chain: ship canal between Lake St. Clair and Lake Erie. [Ottawa:
  1897]
  70 p. maps (part fold.).   OTAR
London Street Railway Co.
  Souvenir. London, Ontario [C.E. Tolmie and C.R. Sanagan] 1905.
  64 p. illus.   OLU
Lord, Ian James, 1938–
  Modelling the impact of proposed transportation networks on the Toronto-
  centred region [by] Ian James Lord [and] John Robert Miron. [Toronto]
  University of Toronto – York University Joint Program in Transportation,
  1971.
  30 leaves. maps, tables. (Joint Program in Transportation. Research report,
  no. 2).   OTU
— Centre for Urban and Community Studies, Department of Urban and
  Regional Planning, University of Toronto, 1971.
  30 [2] leaves. maps, tables. (Urban Environment Study. Research paper no.
  45).   OTU

Low, Richard A
    Traffic study of the city of Kingston. Kingston, Ontario: Town Planning
    Commission of the City of Kingston, 1942.
    33 p. illus., map, plan (fold.), tables.   OKQ
Lowry, E   A
    The facts about public ownership, Ontario's costly mistake. [Toronto:
    Ontario Power Digest] c1934.
    15 p.   OTH
Lussier, Roger.
    Les medias francophones d'information en Ontario, par Roger Lussier et
    Jean Laurin. n.p. [1973?]
    47, 10 feuille.   QQLA
Lyon, de Brouwer & Co. Ltd.
    Attitudes and motivation study of automobile commuters who travel to work
    from suburban areas in and around Metropolitan Toronto. Prepared for
    DeLeuw Cather & Company of Canada Ltd. Montreal: 1964.
    69, 10 leaves. maps, tables.   OTUL
MacBeth, Roderick George, 1858–1934.
    Empire of the north, northern Ontario. Toronto: Temiskaming and
    Northern Ontario Railway, 1912.
    16 p. illus. (Temiskaming and Northern Ontario Railway. Pamphlet no. 10).
                                                                           OKQ
McCann, David T
    Preliminary transportation-oriented development norms and strategy for the
    national capital region. [Ottawa ?] Planning and Urban Design Division,
    National Capital Commission, 1970.
    [28] leaves. illus., maps.   OTUSA
McDougall, John Lorne, 1900–
    The St. Lawrence waterway: a study of economic aspects. Kingston:
    Canadian Electrical Association [1941?]
    28 p. illus.   OTU
MacElwee, Roy Samuel, 1883–
    Economic aspects of the Great Lakes – St. Lawrence ship channel, by R.S.
    MacElwee and A.H. Ritter. New York: Ronald Press Company, 1921.
    291 p. illus., charts, maps (part fold.).   OTU
McIlwraith, Thomas F
    The Toronto, Grey and Bruce Railway 1863–1884. Toronto: Upper Canada
    Railway Society, 1963.
    27 p. illus., facsims., maps. (Upper Canada Railway Society, Bulletin 56).
    2nd printing in 1971.   OMI OTAR
McKean, Fleetwood Kingsley, 1910–
    Railroad reaches town: a history of railroading in Parry Sound and
    Georgian Bay. First train, Toronto to Parry Sound arrived in 1906,
    Canadian Northern Railway. [Parry Sound, Ontario] Parry Sound
    Historical Society [1962]
    6 leaves.   OOA

MacKenzie, Catharine Dunlop.
    Alexander Graham Bell, the man who contracted space. Boston and New
    York: Houghton Miffin Company, 1928.
    xiii, 382 p. front., plates, ports., facsims.   OKQ
MacKinnon, Ross Douglas.
    The highway system of southern Ontario and Quebec: some simple network
    generation models, by Ross D. MacKinnon and M. John Hodgson.
    [Toronto] Department of Geography, Centre for Urban and Community
    Studies, University of Toronto, 1969.
    44, 2 leaves. fig., maps. (Environment study. Research report no. 18).   OTU
— A note on the changing spatial pattern of traffic flow on a major
    transportation facility: Highway 401, Ontario. [Toronto] Centre for Urban
    and Community Studies, University of Toronto, 1970.
    21, 2 leaves. graphs, tables. (Environment study. Research paper no. 39).
                                                                              OTU
McKitrick, A   M
    Steam trains through Orangeville: a history. Cheltenham, Ontario: The
    Boston Mills Press, 1976.
    [48] p. illus., maps. (Credit valley series 12).   OTAR
MacLean, John.
    Railways to the north-west; a letter to the people of the counties of
    Wellington, Grey and Bruce. Hamilton, Ontario: "Spectator" Steam Press,
    1867.
    27 p.   OKQ
McLeod, Murray G
    A comprehensive survey of passengers flying from Toronto International
    Airport, May–June 1968. [Toronto: Institute for Aerospace Studies,
    University of Toronto] 1969.
    v, 24 [53] p. graphs, map, tables.   OONL
McPhedran, Marie, 1900–
    Cargoes on the Great Lakes. Illustrations by Dorothy Ivens. Toronto:
    Macmillan Company of Canada, 1956 [c1952]
    226 p. illus. map.   OTRM
Malkus, Alida Sims.
    Blue-water boundary: epic highway of the Great Lakes and the Saint
    Lawrence. New York: Hastings House [c1960]
    308 p. illus.   OTU
Mansfield, John Brandt.
    History of the Great Lakes. Illustrated. Chicago: J.H. Beers & Co., 1899.
    2 v. illus., ports., maps, tables.
    Contents: v. 1, History; v. 2, Biographical.   OTU
— Reprinted. Cleveland Ohio: Freshwater Press Inc., 1972.
    2 v. illus., ports., maps, tables.   OKQ OTAR
Margison, (A.D.) and Associates Limited.
    London area traffic plan 1959–1980. Toronto: 1960.
    105 p. maps (part col.), tables.   OLU

Marshall, Macklin Monaghan Limited.
    City of Orillia transit operations study. [Don Mills, Ontario: 1971]
    73 leaves. graphs, maps, tables.
    Project director: Mario Bruno.   OONL
Martin, Hugh (ed.).
    Central Ontario railway. Toronto: Model Railroad Club of Toronto,
    Incorporated [1969?]
    22 p. illus.   OKQ
Martin, Patrick.
    An analysis of person travel demand: a behavioral approach. [Ottawa]
    Department of Civil Engineering, Faculty of Engineering, Carleton
    University, 1973.
    ix, 127 leaves. graphs.   OTU
Martin, Thomas E
    Proposal for non aviation uses study for the Toronto Island Airport.
    [Toronto: Martin, 1975]
    [2] 19 leaves.   OTUSA
Massey, Hector John, 1931–
    People or planes, by Hector Massey and Charles Godfrey. Toronto: Copp
    Clark Limited [1973]
    109 p. maps.   OTU
Mavor, James, 1854–1925.
    Niagara in politics; a critical account of Ontario Hydro-Electric
    Commission. New York: E.P. Dutton & Company [1925]
    vi, 255 p.   OTU
—— Public ownership and the Hydro-Electric Commission of Ontario ; being a
    reprint of a series of articles which appeared in the *Financial Post* of Canada,
    Toronto, between July 15 and December 23, 1916 written by James Mavor
    ... together with leading and other articles on the same subject published at
    various dates also in the *Financial Post*. Toronto: Maclean Publishing Co.,
    1917.
    72 p.   OTU
Menefee, Ferdinand Northrup, 1886–
    The St. Lawrence Seaway. Ann Arbor, Michigan: Edwards Brothers Inc.,
    1940.
    xiv, 325 p. illus., maps, diagrs., tables.   OTU
Metcalfe, Willis, 1913–
    Canada & steam on Quinte waters. 2d [ed. rev.] Picton, Ontario: Prince
    Edward Historical Society, 1968.
    288 [13] p. illus., maps (part fold.), ports.   OOA
—— Marine memories. Picton, Ontario: The Picton Gazette [c1975]
    123 p. illus., facsims., ports. (Gazette Canadiana series).   OTU OTAR
Metropolitan Railway Company, Toronto.
    Bond Lake and the highlands of York, Thornhill, Richmond Hill, Aurora,
    Newmarket and intermediate points, via the Metropolitan Railway Co., and

Bond Lake to Schomberg via the Schomberg and Aurora Railway Co.;
guide and time table. [Toronto: Bryan Publishing Co., 1904]
24 p. illus.   OTURS
Metropolitan Toronto. Department of Roads.
    Contract for Lakeshore Expressway roadwork; Humber River to Spencer
    Avenue Station 36 + 00 to Station 164 + 50. Contract no. 25–56, B.W.
    Bemrose, deputy road commissioner, L.B. Allen, commissioner of works and
    roads. Toronto [Lakeshore Expressway Consultants] 1956.
    1 v. (various pagings).   OTU
Metropolitan Toronto. Department of Roads and Traffic.
    Functional design report south from Eglinton Avenue: William R. Allen
    Expressway and rapid transit line. [Toronto] 1970.
    16, A–Y, 3 leaves. illus., graphs, maps (part fold.).   OTUMA
— William R. Allen Expressway and rapid transit line; a summary of answers
    to technical questions raised at the Transportation Committee hearings.
    [Toronto] 1970.
    1 v. (various pagings).
    Covering letter signed: S. Cass, commissioner of roads and traffic, W.
    Wronski, commissioner of planning.   OTUMA
Metropolitan Toronto. Metropolitan Commissioners of Planning, Parks, Roads
    and Traffic.
    Toward a Metropolitan Toronto bicycle route system. [Toronto] 1973.
    1 v. (various pagings). fold. maps.   OTUSA
Metropolitan Toronto. Planning Board.
    Metropolitan Toronto transportation research program report number one.
    [Toronto] 1962.
    1 v. (various pagings). graphs, fold. maps, tables.   OTUL
— A planning review and appraisal of the William R. Allen Expressway and
    rapid transit line. Prepared by the staff of the Metropolitan Toronto
    Planning Board. [Toronto] 1970.
    119, 23, 5 p. illus., maps (part fold.).   OTUSA
— Report on east-west subway. Toronto: Metropolitan Toronto Planning
    Board, 1957.
    1 v. (various pagings). 1 plan, tables.
    Final summing up by the technical staff of the Planning Board.   OTU
— Report on the Metropolitan Toronto transportation plan. [Toronto] 1964.
    82, xv p. diagrs., plans (part col., part fold.).   OTU
— Report on the need for a long range waterfront plan from Clarkson to
    Carruthers Creek. Adopted by Metropolitan Toronto Planning Board,
    October 18, 1961. Joint report submitted to the Metropolitan Parks and
    Recreation Committee, November 2, 1961 by the Commissioner of
    Planning, the Parks Commissioner, and the Works Commissioner [Toronto:
    1961]
    49 leaves. fold. col. plan.   OTU
— Report on traffic, employment and assessment trends in downtown Toronto.
    Toronto: 1963.
    17 leaves. diagrs., tables.   OTUL

Metropolitan Toronto. Planning Board. Research Division.
Preliminary impressions to 1971. Prepared by the Research and
Transportation Divisions of the Metropolitan Toronto Planning Board,
1974. [Toronto: 1972]
xiii, 117 p. diagrs. (part fold. col.), maps, tables.   OTU
Metropolitan Toronto. Planning Board. Transportation and Services Division.
Lakeshore Expressway extension Leslie Street to Highway no. 2A. Toronto
[1957]
9 leaves. 9 fold. maps.   OTUMA
— Report on the study and analysis of the truck survey, prepared for the
municipality of Metropolitan Toronto by the M.T.P.B. Transportation
Division. Toronto: 1956.
1 v. (various pagings).   OTUL
Metropolitan Toronto and Region Transportation Study.
GO – transit Commuter Rail Project. [Conducted by the Metropolitan
Toronto and Region Transportation Study and GO – transit with the co-
operation of Canadian National Railways, Toronto, Ontario. Toronto]
1967–68.
9 v. in 10 parts. illus., fold. maps.
v. 1 and 8 not published.
Contents: Special report no. 2, The commuter train survey of May 17, 1967;
Special report no. 3, GO – transit commuter train survey of July 5th, 1967;
Special report no. 4(A), GO – transit commuter train survey of November 1,
1967 (part A) (afternoon peak trains); Special report no. 4(B), Survey of off
peak travellers on GO – transit, November 1, 1967; Special report no. 5, A
report on market and service analysis, phase 1: Establishment of research
specifications; Special report no. 6, Vehicle and person counts on other
modes before GO – transit operation; Special report no. 7, Benchmark
household survey; Special report no. 9, Second household survey.   OTU
— Growth and travel, past and present; a study of the basic components of
growth in the Toronto-centred region, and their relationship to travel
characteristics and demand. [Toronto: 1966]
vii, 94 p. illus., diagrs. (part col.), col. maps. (*Its* report no. 1).   OTU
— A new look for commuters in Canada. By R.D. Cowley, chairman,
Technical Advisory Committee. [Toronto, 1967]
40 leaves. illus., 2 fold. maps.   OTUSA
— Prospectus submitted to members of the Executive Committee in conformity
with order-in-council no. 4092/62. [Toronto] 1963 reprinted 1966.
23 leaves. map.   OTUL
— Transcript of public hearings held during the period November 18 to
December 9, 1965. [Toronto] 1965.
1 v. (various pagings). maps, tables.   OTUL
— Transportation for the regional city; statement of principles and
recommendations. A report by the Technical Advisory and Coordinating
Committee presenting the essential findings and recommendations that the

Committee feels are significant to the subject of regional transportation policy. [Toronto] 1967.
[24] p. map. (*Its* report no. 3).   OTU

Background papers to Metropolitan Toronto and Region Transportation Study
DeLeuw Cather & Company Limited
    Report on Commuter Rail Project for the lakeshore corridor: Burlington – Toronto – Dunbarton. Prepared for the Executive and Technical Committees, Metropolitan Toronto and Region Transportation Study. [Toronto] 1965.
    106 leaves: graphs, maps (part fold.), tables.
    "Study of regional economic prospects for Metropolitan Toronto and Region Transportation Study".   OTU
— Report on study of existing railway lines facilities required for establishment of commuter or rapid transit services. Toronto: 1963.
    39 p. illus., 6 plates, 2 col. maps.
    "Prepared for the Executive and Technical Committees, Metropolitan Toronto and Region Transportation Study."   OTU
Finnis, Frederic H
    Metropolitan Toronto and region transportation study; administrative and financial structure of transportation in the study area. [Toronto] Metropolitan Toronto and Region Transportation Study, 1966.
    76 leaves. charts, maps, tables.   OTUSA
Kates, Peat, Marwick & Co.
    Comparison of 1964 observed and simulated trip interchanges on a spider network. Prepared for the Metropolitan Toronto and Region Transportation Study. Toronto: 1967.
    13 leaves. fold. diagrs., fold. maps, fold. tables.   OTUL
— A forecast of the 1980 travel demand in Metropolitan Toronto and surrounding region for the 7–9 a.m. period; a report on the 1980 demand project. Prepared for the Metropolitan Toronto and Region Transportation Study. [Toronto?] 1967.
    95 p. illus., graphs.   OTUSA
— 1964 trip demand on commuter rail facilities for the 7–9 a.m. peak period. Prepared for the Metropolitan Toronto and Region Transportation Study. [Toronto] 1967.
    1 v. (various pagings). diagrs., col. maps (part fold.), plans, tables.   OTUL
— Technical report on the calibration of a regional traffic prediction model for the a.m. peak period. Prepared for the Metropolitan Toronto and Region Transportation Study and the Metropolitan Toronto Planning Board. [Toronto] 1967.
    65 p. illus., col. charts, col. maps.   OTU
— Vehicle and transit speed maps for the M.T.A.R.T.S. region. Prepared for the Metropolitan Toronto and Region Transportation Study. Toronto: 1967.
    7, 26, A2, B2, leaves. tables.   OTUL

Kates, Peat, Marwick & Co. Transportation Division.
  Contract 1x: Comparison of 1964 observed and simulated trip interchanges
  on a spider network. Prepared for the Metropolitan Toronto and Region
  Transportation Study. [Toronto] 1967.
  13 leaves. fold. maps, fold. tables.   OTU
Ontario. GO – transit.
  GO – transit. Government of Ontario transit; a new approach to urban
  transportation. [Report prepared by W.T. Howard, Government of Ontario
  Transit, E.A. Ingraham, Department of Highways and R.B. McEwen
  Metropolitan Toronto and Region Transportation Study. Toronto: Cape &
  Company Limited, 1968]
  36 p. illus., maps.   OTU
Robinson, R   A
  Assessing the impact of the Lakeshore commuter rail service to real estate
  values and land use. Prepared by R.A. Robinson for the Metropolitan
  Toronto and Region Transportation Study. [Toronto] 1966.
  22, 4 leaves.   OTU
Traffic Research Corporation Limited.
  An analysis report on the 1964 home interview survey, conducted jointly by
  Metropolitan Toronto and Region Transportation Study and Metropolitan
  Toronto Planning Board. Prepared for the Metropolitan Toronto and
  Region Transportation Study. [Toronto] 1965.
  1 v. (various pagings). illus., maps, charts, tables.   OTU
— The three-way modal split analysis, prepared for the Metropolitan and
  Region Transportation Study. [Toronto] 1965.
  iv, 61 leaves. graphs, maps, tables.   OTUL

Metropolitan Toronto Transportation Plan Review.
  [Reports by the] Municipality of Metropolitan Toronto, Toronto Transit
  Commission and the Ministry of Transportation and Communications,
  Ontario. Toronto: 1971–1975.
  59 v. charts, maps (part fold.).
  Contents: v. 1, Prospectus; v. 2, Appraisal; v. 3, Public participation
  program; v. 4, The objectives of transportation finance; v. 5, Land use
  change – transportation implications; v. 6, Pedestrian connection between
  TTC main station and Danforth Station; v. 7, Existing transportation; v. 8,
  Evaluation of transportation alternatives; v. 9, Existing transportation; v. 10,
  Applications of new transit technology: north east sector of Metropolitan
  Toronto; v. 11, Existing transportation: school busing; v. 12, Transportation
  finance; v. 13, Evaluation of transportation alternatives; v. 14, Urban
  resources book; v. 15, A catalogue of transportation concepts proposed for
  Metropolitan Toronto; v. 16, Review of transportation needs, priorities and
  programs; v. 17, Transportation organizational alternatives; v. 18, Strengths
  and weaknessess: public transport; v. 19, Strengths and weaknesses: road

system; v. 20, Strengths and weaknesses: parking; v. 21, Strengths and
weaknesses: goods movements; v. 22, Strengths and weaknesses: pedestrians
and bicycles; v. 23, Strengths and weaknesses: taxi cabs; v. 24, Land use and
transportation; v.25, Strengths and weaknesses: the environment and the
transportation system; v. 26, Strengths and weaknesses: summary; v. 27,
Transportation finance: 1962 to 1981; v. 28, number not used; v. 29,
Population and employment forecasts for 1981; v. 30, Phase one review; v.
31, number not used; v. 32, Short term alternatives: dial-a-bus plan; v. 33,
Transportation for the disabled; v. 34–v. 35, numbers not used; v. 35a, Car
pooling: summary; v. 35b, Car pooling: analysis; v. 36, Staggered working
hours; v. 37–v. 39, numbers not used; v. 40, Preliminary review of the
Scarborough expressway; v. 41, Metropolitan parking organization; v. 42,
The Scarborough expressway: a summary of the current status; v. 43, A
review of the proposed additions to Toronto's subway system; v. 44, Review
of the Highway 400 extension; v. 45, Review of the Richview expressway; v.
46, number not used; v. 47, The Scarborough expressway: a planning
review; v. 47a, The Scarborough expressway: a planning review, appendix;
v. 48, A review of the crosstown expressway; v. 49–v. 60, numbers not used;
v. 61, Public participation program: summary report; v. 62, Development
and land use and transportation alternatives; v. 63, Performanace and
impact of the alternatives: year 2000; v. 63.3, Transportation system
elements; v. 63.4, Travel demand procedures; v. 63.5, Truck movements; v.
63.6, 1981 Travel demand; v. 63.7, Development effects; v. 63.8, Central
area; v. 63.9, Environmental effects; v. 63.11, Income distribution effects; v.
63.12 Social effects; v. 63.15, Eglinton transit development corridor; v. 63.16,
Eglinton – Kennedy urban centre; v. 64, Choices for the future: summary
report.   OTMCL
— Transportation information for the various Metropolitan areas. Toronto:
   1973.
   2 v. in 15 parts. maps.
   Contents: v. 1, part 1, The central city area; v. 1, part 2, West Toronto; v. 1,
   part 3, Bathurst – St. Clair area; v. 1, part 4, The North Toronto area; v. 1,
   part 5, Yonge – St. Clair area; v. 1, part 6, East Toronto area; v. 1, part 7,
   Scarborough area; v. 1, part 8, An evaluation of light rail traffic in the
   Scarborough corridor; v. 2, part 1, Borough of York; v. 2, part 2, Central
   and west central Etobicoke area; v. 2, part 3, Community of Rexdale and
   Thistletown; v. 2, part 4, West York, Downsview and York University area;
   v. 2, part 5, Lawrence/Keele/Hwy. 400 area; v. 2, part 6,
   Lawrence/Bathurst/Dufferin area; v. 2, part 7, Area north of Hwy. 401 and
   south of Steeles Ave. between Dufferin and Yonge streets; v. 2, part 8,
   Leaside area Borough of East York.   OTU
Michaud, William.
   Pioneer railways of central Ontario from the past to the present: Rideau
   area of the Canadian National Railways. n.p. [1964]
   20 p. illus., maps (part fold.).   OTAR

Midland, Ontario. Chamber of Commerce.
    Power and water in Midland, Ontario. [Midland, Ontario] Published jointly
    by Midland Chamber of Commerce and Midland Public Utilities
    Commission [1961?]
    8 p. illus., map, tables.   OONL
Mika, Nick, 1912–
    Railways of Canada: a pictorical history, by Nick and Helma Mika.
    Toronto: McGraw–Hill Ryerson Limited [1972]
    176 p. illus., facsims., ports.   OTU
Mills, John M   1931–
    Cataract traction; the railways of Hamilton. Toronto: [Joint publication:
    Upper Canada Railway Society, Ontario Electric Railway Historical
    Association] 1971.
    116 p. illus., maps. (Canadian traction series, v. 2).   OTU
— History of the Niagara, St. Catharines and Toronto railway. [Toronto]
    Upper Canada Railway Society; Scarborough, Ontario: Ontario Electric
    Railway Historical Association [1967]
    118 p. facsims., illus., maps (part col.). (Canadian traction series, v.1).   OTU
Mississauga urban development and transportation study [by the Mississauga
    council... et al.] Mississauga, Ontario: City of Mississauga, 1975.
    5 v. illus., maps.
    "Final reports".
    Contents: v. 1, Mississauga evaluation and recommendations; v. 2,
    Mississauga transportation, v. 3, Mississauga centres; v. 4, Mississauga
    finance; v. 5, Mississauga development controls.   OTU
Montreal Engineering Company, Limited.
    Energy demand forecast, Ontario and Quebec, 1962–1975, by Montreal
    Engineering Company, Limited and Purvin & Gertz Inc. [Calgary, Alberta:
    Home Oil Co., 1962]
    37 p. col. diagrs., tables.   OONL
Montreal, Ottawa & Georgian Bay Canal Company.
    Memorandum on the growth of the traffic on the Great Lakes and the
    proposed Ottawa ship navigation. Ottawa: The Author, 1901.
    35 p. illus., maps (fold. col.).   OTU
Moore, James.
    History of the Ontario West Shore Railway, by James Moore and Sandra
    Robinson. n.p.: 1974.
    iii, 97 p.
    Funded by Opportunities for Youth 1974 Project no. 37 4K 2911.   OTAR
Morden, James Cochenour.
    Falls view bridges and Niagara ice bridges by James C. Morden. Collapse of
    Falls view bridge and ice jam of 1938 by W. Bruce Leslie. 4th ed. Niagara
    Falls, Ontario: Published and printed by F.H. Leslie, Limited, 1938.
    24 p. illus.
    1st edition, February 17, 1938.
    2nd edition, February 22, 1938.
    3rd edition, February 25, 1938.
    4th edition, March 4, 1938.
    Only the 4th edition was examined.   OTU

Morningstar, C   K
  From dobbin to diesel: the story of public transportation in London,
  Canada. [London, Ontario: London Transportation Commission, 1973]
  53 p. illus., maps.
  Editor: William E. Corfield.   OLU
Moulton, Harold Glenn, 1883–1965.
  The St. Lawrence navigation power project, by Harold G. Moulton, Charles
  S. Morgan and Adah L. Lee. Washington D.C.: The Brookings Institute,
  1929.
  xvi, 675 p. tables, fold. map.   OONL
Mucklestone, Raymond Frank.
  A brief report on the Rideau Canal system. n.p. [1965]
  11 leaves.   OONL
Municipal and Regional Water Management Symposium, University of
  Western Ontario, 1966.
  The water cycle: source of use of, disposal of, re-use of water. [Conference,
  London, Ontario] October 5, 1966. London, Ontario: Regional Economic
  Council, Lake Erie Economic Region, 1966.
  1 v. (various pagings).   OTU
Murray, William Spencer, 1873–1942.
  Government owned and controlled compared with privately owned and
  regulated utilities in Canada and the United States. William S. Murray,
  Murray & Flood. New York: New York city, National Electric Light
  Association, 1922.
  1, 233, iv p. maps (part fold.), diagrs.
  Deals chiefly with Hydro-Electric Power Commission of Ontario.   OTU
— Report on hydro-electic railways: Toronto – Hamilton – Niagara Falls,
  Toronto and Eastern and Hamilton – Galt – Guelph – Elmira. [Toronto]
  Hydro-Electric Power Commission of Ontario [1920]
  15 p.   OTAR
Muskoka Navigation Company.
  Muskoka lakes, highlands of Ontario: guide book. Montreal: Desbarats
  [1902?]
  48 p. illus.   OKQ
New Democratic Party (Ontario).
  Public car insurance for Ontario: policies of the New Democratic Party.
  [Toronto: 1971]
  11 [1] p.   OTURS
Niagara Navigation Company Limited.
  Niagara river line and Toronto [including] Buffalo, Niagara Falls, Lewiston,
  Queenston, Niagara-on-the-Lake and Toronto. [2d ed.] Toronto [Niagara
  Navigation Company 1903]
  32 p. illus., map.   OTAR
— The Niagara – Toronto route. [Toronto: Niagara Navigation Company,
  1905]
  48 p. illus., map.   OTAR

— Niagara – Toronto route, via the lower Niagara River and Lake Ontario.
[Toronto: Niagara Navigation Company, 1906]
44 p. illus., map.   OTAR
Nipissing & James Bay Railway.
Description of the country traversed by this railway between Lake Nipissing
& James Bay giving the resources of the same, as well as the districts
adjacent thereto, together with other useful information relating to Hudson's
Bay and Strait. Toronto: Copp, Clark & Co., 1884.
54 p. fold. map, tables.   OKQ
Nock, Oswald Stevens.
Algoma Central Railway. London: Adam and Charles Black [c1975]
190 p. illus. (part col.), maps, facsims.   OTAR
Northeastern Ontario Development Association.
A report on the possible effects of a seaport at Moosonee on the economy of
northeastern Ontario. Prepared for the Ontario government at the request of
Hon. William M. Nickle, minister, planning and development. North Bay,
Ontario [1960]
41 leaves. maps, tables.
H.F. Wiemer, consultant.   OTU
Nowlan, David Michael, 1936–
The anatomy of an expressway evaluation. [Don Mills, Ontario]
Collier–Macmillan Canada, c1972.
[12] p. illus.
The Spadina Expressway.   OTUSA
— The bad trip; the untold story of the Spadina Expressway, by David and
Nadine Nowlan. Toronto: House of Anansi, 1970.
105 p. illus., map.   OTU
Nunn, Paul N
The development of the Ontario power company ... Niagara Falls, Ontario:
Ontario Power co., [c1905]
35 p. illus., diagrs., plans.   OTU
Nute, Grace Lee, 1895–
Lake Superior. [1st ed.] Indianapolis: Bobbs–Merrill Company [1944]
376 p. plates, ports., map, facsim. (The American lakes series).   OTU
Ontario.
Submission of the government of Ontario to the Royal Commission on
Transportation, March 14, 1960. Presented by Leslie M. Frost, prime
minister of Ontario. [Toronto: 1960]
37 leaves. diagrs. tables.   OTU
Ontario. Advisory Committee on Energy.
Energy in Ontario: the outlook and policy implications. Toronto:
1972–1973.
2 v. diagrs., tables.
Chairman: John J. Deutsch.
Contents: v. 1, Summary of findings and recommendations for the
development of energy policy in future; v. 2, Energy in Ontario.   OTU

— Submissions.
    36 v.   OTAR
— Minutes of meetings, October 21, 1971–January 30, 1973.
    1 v. (various pagings).   OTAR

Background papers to Ontario Advisory Committee on Energy.
Angus, (H.H.) & Associates Ltd.
    Ontario air quality – 1991. Report to Air Management Branch, Department
    of the Environment. [Toronto] 1972.
    19 leaves. 53 maps.
    "Consultant's report to Advisory Committee on Energy".   OTAR
Bergougnou, Maurice A
    Environmental effects of lignite gasification and fluidized bed boiler power
    generation. [London, Ontario: 1972]
    10 leaves. diagr.
    "Consultant's report to Advisory Committee on Energy".   OTAR
Corpus Publishers Services Limited.
    Feedstock requirements for the Ontario petrochemical industry. A study
    carried out for the Ontario Advisory Committee on Energy. Toronto: 1972.
    210 leaves. tables.   OTAR
Corpus Research Services.
    Nuclear energy and the Ontario commitment. [Toronto] 1971.
    97 leaves. tables.
    "A Corpus background study for the Advisory Committee on Energy."
                                                         OTAR
Foster Economic Consultants Ltd.
    Prospective prices for energy consumed in Ontario 1972–1985. Prepared for
    the Advisory Committee on Energy, government of Ontario. Calgary,
    Alberta: 1972.
    1 v. (various pagings).   OTAR
Hanson, Eric J
    Some aspects of the administration of provincial energy policy in Ontario.
    [Prepared for] Advisory Committee on Energy. [Toronto] 1972.
    21 leaves.   OTAR
Hill, Philip G
    Effect of new technology on energy demand in automotive transportation.
    [Prepared for] Advisory Committee on Energy. [Kingston, Ontario] 1972.
    [11] leaves.   OTAR
— Effect of new technology in automotive transportation on energy demand in
    Ontario. A study prepared for the Ontario Advisory Committee on Energy.
    Consultants: G.F. Marsters, E.J. Wright. Kingston, Ontario: 1972.
    122 leaves. graphs, plans, tables.   OTAR
— Industrial energy demand in Ontario. A study prepared for the Ontario
    Advisory Committee on Energy. [Kingston, Ontario] 1972.
    38 leaves. graphs, tables.   OTAR

Laughlin, R   G   W
An examination of the technical and economic feasibility of producing
pipeline quality gas from the James Bay lignite deposits for the Ontario
Advisory Committee on Energy by R.G.W. Laughlin, C.K. Brown. Sheridan
Park, Ontario: Ontario Research Foundation, 1972.
2 v. graphs, tables.   OTAR

Ontario. Hydro-Electric Power Commission.
Submission by George Gathercole to the Ontario Advisory Committee on
Energy. [Toronto] 1972.
28 leaves.   OTAR

Oosthuizen, P   H
Effects of technology on residential and commerical energy demand in
Ontario. A study for the Ontario Advisory Committee on Energy, prepared
by P.H. Oosthuizen, C.K. Rush, P.G. Hill. Consultant: H.G. Conn.
Kingston, Ontario: 1972.
91 leaves. graphs, tables.   OTAR

Purvin & Gertz Inc.
A study of technological changes influencing future energy supplies for
Ontario. Prepared for the Ontario Advisory Committee on Energy.
[Toronto?] 1972.
55 leaves.   OTAR

Robertson, (David S.) & Associates, Limited.
Uranium supply and demand for Advisory Committee on Energy. Toronto:
1972.
iii, 53 leaves. graphs, tables.   OTAR

Sievwright, (E.C.) Associates Limited.
The Ontario energy outlook to 1985 prepared for Advisory Committee on
Energy Ontario. Toronto: 1972.
141 leaves. tables.   OTAR

Studnicki–Gizbert, K   W
Regulatory and developmental policies. A discussion paper prepared at the
request of the Advisory Committee on Energy. [Toronto: 1972]
32 p.   OTAR

Urwick, Currie & Partners Ltd.
Forecast of capital expenditures on energy transmission facilities for Ontario.
[Prepared for the Advisory Committee on Energy, Toronto: 1972]
1 v. (various pagings).   OTAR

Yovanovich, M   M
Heat loads upon the environment within the province of Ontario 1970–2000.
[Prepared for] the Advisory Committee on Energy. Waterloo, Ontario: 1972.
5 leaves.   OTAR

Ontario. Commission appointed to inquire into hydro-electric railways.
Report containing majority and minority reports and appendices. Printed by

order of the Legislative Assembly of Ontario. Toronto: Clarkson W. James,
printer to the King's Most Excellent Majesty, 1921.
234 p. maps. tables.
Chairman: R.F. Sutherland.   OTAR
— Minutes of the meetings of the Radial Railway Commission (Secretary's
Minute Book) July 28, 1920–June 22, 1922.
60, 2 handwritten pages.   OTAR
Ontario. Commission of inquiry concerning the causes of destruction of dams
near the town of Napanee.
Report. [Napanee, Ontario: 1911]
4 typewritten pages.
Commissioner: William Rankin.   OTAR
— Proceedings, July 19th, 1910–October 26, 1910.
2 v.   OTAR
Ontario. Commission of inquiry into charges by E.C. Settell with regard to the
administration of the affairs of the Hydro-Electric Power Commission of
Ontario.
Report. n.p.: 1924.
94 typewritten pages.
Commissioner: Colin G. Snider.   OTAR
— Proceedings, October 23–November 12, 1924.
949 typewritten pages.   OTAR
Ontario. Commission of inquiry into Ontario provincial air service.
Report. [Toronto] 1934.
15 typewritten pages.
Commissioner: D.W. Lang.   OTAR
— Proceedings, August 3–September 21, 1934.
xi, 1384 typewritten pages.   OTAR
Ontario. Commission of inquiry re waterworks regulations and Electrical
Development Company.
Report. [Toronto] 1918.
8 typewritten pages.
Commissioners: Sir William Meredith, Hon. Mr. Justice Sutherland, Hon.
Mr. Justice Kelly.   OTAR
— Proceedings, October 11, 1917–February 2, 1918.
212 typewritten pages.   OTAR
Ontario. Commission on Railway Taxation.
Report. Printed by order of the Legislative Assembly. Toronto: L.K.
Cameron, printer to the King's Most Excellent Majesty, 1905.
219 p.
Chairman: H.J. Pettypiece.   OTAR
Ontario. Department of Energy and Resources Management. Conservation
Authorities Branch.
History of the Rideau waterway. Toronto: 1970.
83 p. illus., fold. maps (part col.).   OTAR

Ontario. Department of Highways.
 A co-operative study of the county roads of Ontario concerning future road
 needs, projected financial resources and desirable administrative
 arrangementsxxcarried out by the counties of the Province and the
 Department of Highways. [Toronto] Department of Highways, 1966.
 38 p. illus., tables.   OTL

Road needs studies
Brant County Roads Needs Study. Technical Co-ordinating Committee.
 Road needs study, county of Brant 1969–1979. [Brantford, Ontario: Brant
 County Roads Committee, 1975?]
 52 p. illus., maps, tables.   OBRT
— 1976 update. Brantford, Ontario: County of Brant Engineering Department,
 1976.
 19 p. maps, tables.   OBRT
Bruce County. County Council.
 Road needs study 1969–1979 the county of Bruce. [Walkerton, Ontario:
 County Council, 1970]
 45 p. graphs, maps, tables.   OTDT
Bruce, (Douglas B.) & Associates.
 County of Waterloo road needs study 1965. Port Credit, Ontario: 1965.
 70 p. graphs, maps (part fold.), tables.   OLU
Damas and Smith Limited.
 County of Waterloo road needs study, 1969. [Toronto?] Damas and Smith
 Limited, 1969.
 1 v. (various pagings). graphs, maps, tables.   OTDT
DeLeuw Cather & Company of Canada Ltd.
 County of Kent roads needs study, 1969. London, Ontario: DeLeuw Cather
 Company of Canada, 1971.
 45 p. charts, maps, tables.   OTDT
DeLeuw Cather & Company of Canada Limited.
 County of Lambton roads needs study. [London, Ontario: DeLeuw Cather
 & Company of Canada Limited, 1965]
 43 p. charts (part fold.), graphs, maps, tables (part fold.).   OLU
— 1969. [London, Ontario: DeLeuw Cather & Company Ltd., 1970]
 1 v. (various pagings). graphs, maps, tables.   OTDT
Dillon, (M.M.) Limited.
 County of Middlesex roads needs study. London, Ontario: M.M. Dillon
 Limited, 1965.
 22 leaves. graphs, fold. maps (part col.), tables.   OLU
— Technical appendix. London, Ontario: M.M. Dillon Limited, 1965.
 139 leaves. graphs, tables.   OLU
— The road system regional roads needs study for the Regional Municipality of
 Ottawa – Carleton, by a Consortium of M.M. Dillon Ltd. and DeLeuw
 Cather and Company of Canada Ltd. [Ottawa: The Corsortium, 1968]
 1 v. (unpaged). fold. col. maps   OTDT

Duncan Hopper & Associates Limited.
    The Corporation of the County of Wellington road needs study, 1964.
    [Guelph, Ontario] 1964.
    vii, 111 p. graphs, maps, tables.   OLU
— 1969. [Weston, Ontario] Duncan Hopper & Associates Ltd., 1970.
    vii, 97 p. graphs, fold. maps, tables.   OTDT
— County of Dufferin road needs study, 1969. [Weston, Ontario: Duncan
    Hopper & Associates Limited, 1970]
    vi, 70 p. graphs, maps. tables.   OTDT
— [County of Halton] road needs study, 1969. [Weston, Ontario] Duncan
    Hopper & Associates Limited, 1970.
    vi, 91 p. graphs, maps, tables.   OTDT
Graham, Berman and Associates Ltd.
    United Counties of Prescott and Russell roads needs study 1969–1979.
    Ottawa: Graham, Berman and Associates Ltd. [1971?]
    40 p. charts, graphs, fold. maps, tables.   OTDT
Haldimand County. Road Needs Study Coordinating Committee.
    Road needs study 1969. [Cayuga, Ontario: The Committee, 1971]
    63 p. graphs, fold. map, tables.   OTDT
Huron County. Road Committee.
    Road needs study, county of Huron 1969–1979. [Goderich, Ontario: Huron
    County Council, 1970]
    49 p. illus., maps, graphs, tables.   8TDT
Kostuck, (R.M.) Associates Ltd.
    United Counties of Leeds and Grenville road needs study, 1970–1979.
    [Brockville, Ontario] R.M. Kostuck Associates Ltd. [1969?]
    75 p. charts, fold. maps, tables.   OTDT
— United Counties of Stormont, Dundas and Glengarry roads needs study,
    1970–1979. [Brockville, Ontario] R.M. Kostuck Associates Ltd. [1969?]
    59 p. graphs, fold. maps, tables   OTDT
Lanark County. Co-ordinating Committee.
    Road needs study county of Lanark, 1969–1979. [Perth, Ontario] The
    Committee, 1970.
    55 p. illus., charts, maps (part fold.), tables.   OTDT
— Road needs study county of Lanark 1964–1974. [Perth, Ontario] The
    Committee, 1965.
    23 p. charts, fold. maps, tables.   OTDT
Lennox and Addington County, Ontario.
    Road needs study, December 1965. [Napanee, Ontario: 1965?]
    51 leaves. maps (part fold. part col.), tables.   OKQ
McCormick, Rankin & Associates Limited.
    County of Bruce [road] needs study update, 1971: statistical summary. n.p.:
    1971.
    16 leaves. graphs, tables.   OTDT
— County of Huron [road] needs study update, 1971: statistical summary. n.p.:
    McCormick, Rankin & Associates Limited, 1971.
    17 leaves. graphs, tables.   OTDT

— County of Simcoe [road] needs study update 1971: statistical summary. n.p.:
McCormick, Rankin & Associates Limited, 1971.
    27 leaves. graphs, tables.   OTDT
Middlesex County. Road Department.
    County of Middlesex road needs study 1970–1979. [London, Ontario: 1971]
    80 p. illus., chart, maps, tables.   OTDT
Oxford County. Roads Committee. Co-ordinating Committee.
    Oxford county report on road needs study, by Co-ordinating Committee,
    Vance, Needles, Bergendoff & Smith Ltd.; and Ure and Smith. Woodstock,
    Ontario: 1965.
    1 v. (various pagings). graphs, tables.   OLU
Oxford County. Technical Co-ordinating Committee.
    County of Oxford 1976–1985 road needs study. [Woodstock, Ontario: 1975?]
    1 v. (various pagings). graphs, maps (part fold.), tables.   OTDT
Peel County. Co-ordinating Committee.
    Road needs study county of Peel 1969–1979. [Brampton, Ontario] Co-
    ordinating Committee [1970?]
    1 v. (various pagings). illus., graphs, fold. maps, tables.   OTDT
Perth County. Co-ordinating Committee.
    Road needs study county of Perth 1969–1979. [Stratford, Ontario] The
    Committee [1970?]
    59 p. illus., charts, fold. maps, tables.   OTDT
Prince Edward County. Co-ordinating Committee.
    Road needs study 1969–1979 county of Prince Edward. Picton, Ontario:
    The Committee [1969?]
    45 p. charts, maps, tables.   OTDT
Procter & Redfern Limited.
    Regional Niagara roads needs study report 1970–1980, by Proctor &
    Redfern Limited and William L. Sears & Associates Limited. [Toronto:
    Proctor & Redfern Limited, 1971]
    2 v. graphs, fold. maps, tables.   OTDT
Regional Municipality of Ottawa – Carleton. Roads Department.
    1970 roads needs study. [Ottawa: The Regional Municipality of Ottawa –
    Carleton, 1971]
    34 p. illus., maps, tables.   OTDT
Regional Municipality of Waterloo. Technical Co-ordinating Committee.
    Road needs study and maintenance management system 1975–1984.
    [Kitchener, Ontario 1975?]
    78 leaves. illus., fold., maps, tables.   OTDT
Renfrew County. Roads and Bridges Committee.
    County of Renfrew road needs study 1969–1979. Pembroke, Ontario: The
    Committee [1969?]
    90 p. fold. maps, charts, tables.   OTDT
Sears, (William L.) and Associates Limited.
    Road needs study for the Indian reserves of the Six Nations of the Grand

River and the Mississaugas of the New Credit. Hamilton, Ontario: William
L. Sears and Associates Limited, 1966.
    vi, 125 leaves. graphs, maps, tables.   OTDT
Simcoe County.
    Road needs study Simcoe county, 1964–1974. [Barrie, Ontario] n.d.
    45 p. graphs, fold. maps, tables.   OTDT
—— 1969–1979. [Barrie, Ontario] n.d.
    59 p. illus., graphs, maps (part fold.).   OTDT
Six Nations Council.
    Road needs study 1974–1983. Six Nations of the Grand River and
    Mississaugas of the New Credit Indian reserves. [Ohsweken, Ontario] Six
    Nations Council, 1973.
    50 leaves. illus., graphs., tables, maps.   OTDT
Spriet, (A.M.) and Associates Limited.
    Road needs study, county of Elgin. [London, Ontario: A.M. Spriet &
    Associates Ltd., 1965]
    80 p. illus., graphs, maps, tables.   OLU
—— London, Ontario: A.M. Spriet & Associates Ltd. [1970]
    93 p. illus., maps, tables.   OTDT
—— Road needs study county of Oxford [1975–1979]. London, Ontario: A.M.
    Spriet & Associates Ltd., 1970.
    129 p. illus., maps, tables.   OTDT
Tomlinson, (J.M.) & Associates Ltd.
    County of Frontenac road needs study 1965. n.p.: J.M. Tomlinson &
    Associates Ltd., 1965.
    1 v. (various pagings). graphs, maps, tables.   OTDT
—— Road needs study, county of Brant. n.p.: 1965.
    44, A20 leaves. graphs, maps (part fold.), tables.   OLU
Toronto and York Roads Commission.
    County [road] needs study and report 1965 to 1975. [Don Mills, Ontario:
    1965]
    15 leaves. 44 p. of tables, graphs.   OTDT
—— York county [road] needs study and report 1969 to 1979. Interim report.
    [Don Mills, Ontario: 1970]
    26 leaves. graphs, tables, fold. maps.   OTDT
Totten Sims Hubicki Associates Limited.
    County of Frontenac roads needs study 1970–1979. [Kingston, Ontario:
    Totten Sims Hubicki Associates Limited, 1971]
    iv, 23, 18 leaves. graphs, fold. maps, tables.   OTDT
—— County of Grey roads needs study: report on updating 1969–1970 . [Owen
    Sound, Ontario] 1971.
    27 leaves. fold. map, tables.   OTDT
—— County of Grey roads needs study 1970–1979. [Owen Sound, Ontario:
    Totten Sims Hubicki Associates Limited, 1971]
    81 p. fold. maps, tables.   OTDT

— County of Hastings road needs study 1970–1979. [Cobourg, Ontario: Totten Sims Hubicki Associates Limited, 1971]
v, 100 leaves. graphs, fold. maps, tables.   OTDT
— County of Lennox and Addington roads needs study 1970–1979. Kingston, Ontario: Totten Sims Hubicki Associates Limited, 1971.
69 p. charts, fold. maps, tables.   OTDT
— County of Ontario road needs study report 1965–1975. Cobourg, Ontario: Totten Sims and Associates Limited, 1965.
vii, 149, 56 p. charts, fold. col. maps, tables.   OLU
— County of Ontario roads needs study 1970–1979. [Whitby, Ontario: Totten Sims Hubicki Associates Limited, 1971]
87 p. graphs, maps (part fold.), tables.   OTDT
— County of Peterborough road needs study, 1970–1979. Cobourg, Ontario: Totten Sims Hubicki Associates Limited, 1971.
67 p. charts, fold. maps, tables.   OTDT
— County of Victoria roads needs study 1970–1979. [Whitby, Ontario: Totten Sims Hubicki Associates Limited [1971]
86 p. graphs, fold. maps, tables.   OTDT
— United Counties of Northumberland and Durham road needs study 1970–1979. [Cobourg, Ontario: Totten Sims Hubicki Associates Limited, 1971]
iv, 80 leaves, graphs, fold. maps, tables.   OTDT
— The Regional Municipality of Durham, 1976–1985 road system study. [Whitby, Ontario: Totten Sims Hubicki Associates Limited, 1976]
79 p. illus., maps, tables.   OTDT
Wentworth County. Co-ordinating Committee.
Road needs study county of Wentworth 1969–1970. Hamilton, Ontario: The Committee, 1971.
59 p. charts, maps, tables.   OTDT
Wentworth County. Road Needs Study Co-ordinating Committee.
County of Wentworth road needs study. [Hamilton, Ontario: 1965]
28 p. graphs, maps (part fold.), tables.   OLU

Ontario. Government Committee on Restructuring of Public Utilities.
Report. [Toronto] 1974.
131 leaves.
Chairman: W.M. Hogg.   OTU
Ontario. Hydro-Electric Inquiry Commission.
Final report with appendices. [Toronto: 1924]
239 typewritten pages. charts, maps.
Chairman: Walter D. Gregory.   OTAR
— Interim reports, 1922–1924.
21 v. in 24 parts. typewritten.   OTAR
Ontario. Hydro-Electric Power Commission.
Bulk power rates for 1975. [Toronto: The Commission] 1974.
5 v. diagrs., tables.
"Submission to the Ontario Energy Board."   OTU

— Financial policies and objectives. [Toronto: The Commission] 1974.
  3 v. diagrs., tables.
  "Submission to the Ontario Energy Board."   OTU
— The gifts of nature: a story of electricity at work in the province of Ontario.
  [Toronto] Ontario Hydro, 1961.
  44 p. illus. map.   OTAR
— Gifts of nature: electricity, the life-blood of modern society... [Toronto]
  Ontario Hydro, 1974.
  64 p. illus., map.   OTAR
— Hydro and the environment. [Toronto: 1973]
  32 p. illus.   OONL
— The Hydro-Electric Power Commission of Ontario: its origins,
  administration and achievement. Toronto: 1928.
  39 p. plates, illus., tables.   OTAR
— Hydro-electric power in the Niagara district, province of Ontario, Canada.
  n.p. [1921?]
  35 p. illus., fold. col. map.   OTAR
— Hydro golden jubilee. Toronto: The Commission, 1956.
  40 p. illus., ports.
  A special issue of the Ontario Hydro News.   OKQ
— ... The Nipigon hydro-electric power development constructed and operated
  for the municipalities of the Thunder Bay district by the Hydro-Electric
  Power Commission of Ontario. Toronto: 1922.
  38 p. tables, front, plates, maps.   OOA
— The organization of the Hydro-Electric Power Commission of Ontario.
  Toronto: The Commission [1948]
  [16] p. ports., fold. map, tables, chart.   OTU
— Paid-for propaganda? Who instigates attacks on Hydro? Important facts
  brought to public attention by the Hydro-Electric Power Commission of
  Ontario. Toronto: 1934.
  27 p.   OTAR
— Power development on the Niagara River. [Toronto] n.d.
  34 p. illus., maps, plans.   OTAR
— Statement and engineering report submitted to the International Joint
  Commission respecting the proposal to develop the St. Lawrence River,
  1921. Toronto: 1925.
  ix, 119 p. fold. col. plates (incl. maps, plans).   OONL
— System expansion program. [Toronto: The Commission] 1973.
  4 v. illus.
  "Submission to the Ontario Energy Board."   OTU
Ontario. Legislative Assembly. Select Committee appointed to enquire into
matters concerning certain divisions of the Department of Highways.
  Report. Toronto [1955]
  200, 17, 21, viii leaves.
  Chairman: A. Kelso Roberts.   OTAR
— Minority report. [Toronto: 1955?]
  22 leaves.   OTAR

— Proceedings, April 14, 1954–January 27, 1955.
28 v. [i.e. 2,583 typewritten pages] OTAR
— Index of witnesses, April 14–September 8, 1954.
11 leaves. OTAR
Ontario. Legislative Assembly. Select Committee appointed to inquire into various contracts between the Hydro-Electric Power Commission of Ontario and certain Quebec power companies.
Reports of majority and minority groups. [Toronto] 1939.
54 p.
Chairman: G.D. Conant. OTAR
— Proceedings, May 2–June 17, 1938.
11 v. [i.e. 1516 typewritten pages] OTAR
— Re: Ontario – Quebec Ottawa River power agreement: correspondence between Hon. G.D. Conant, premier of Ontario and Dr. T.H. Hogg, chairman, Hydro-Electric Power Commission of Ontario including report of Dr. Hogg. n.p.: 1943.
20 p. OTAR
Ontario. Legislative Assembly. Select Committee inquiring into Hydro's proposed Bulk Power Rates.
Interim report. [Toronto] 1975.
1 v. (various pagings).
Chairman: Donald C. MacDonald. OTAR
— Final report: a new public policy direction for Ontario Hydro. [Toronto] 1976.
1 v. (various pagings). diagrs., graphs, tables. OTAR
— Proceedings, November 3, 1975–June 9, 1976.
72 v. (various pagings). OTAR
Ontario. Legislative Assembly. Select Committee on Automobile Insurance.
Interim report. [Toronto] 1961.
27 leaves. tables.
Chairman: James N. Allan. OTAR OTUL
— Second interim report. [Toronto] 1961.
10 p. OTAR OTUL
— Final report. [Toronto] 1963.
11 p. OTAR OTUL
Ontario. Legislative Assembly. Select Committee on central registration of documents of title and pledge respecting chattels and certificates of title of ownership of motor vehicles.
Report. [Toronto: 1955]
22 p.
Chairman: Robert Macaulay. OTAR
— Report. [Toronto] 1956.
11 p. OTAR
— Minutes, May 10, 1954–January 24, 1955.
1 v. (various pagings). OTAR
— Minutes, September 29, 1955–January 20, 1956.
1 v. (various pagings). OTAR

— Proceedings, November 2–December 6, 1955.
  4 v. [i.e. 410 typewritten pages]   OTAR
— Briefs.
  14 v.   OTAR
Ontario. Legislative Assembly. Select Committee on Highway Safety.
  Report. [Toronto] 1955.
  36 p.
  Chairman: W.M. Nickle.   OTAR OTUL
— Proceedings, April 27–August 27, 1954.
  16 v. [i.e. 2391 typewritten pages]   OTAR
— Index of witnesses, April 27–June 30, 1954.
  12 leaves.   OTAR
— Index of witnesses, April 27–August 27, 1954.
  19 leaves.   OTAR
— Briefs.
  26 v.   OTAR
Ontario. Legislative Assembly. Select Committee on Huron and Ontario Ship
  Canal.
  Report. Toronto: Hunter, Rose & Co., 1871.
  11 p.
  Chairman: Wm. Lount.   OTAR
— Reports of several committees of the Legislative Assembly of the late
  Province of Canada, the House of Commons and the Legislative Assembly of
  Ontario on the Huron and Ontario Ship Canal. 2d ed. Printed by
  subscription of members of the Legislative Assembly of Ontario. Toronto:
  Hunter, Rose & Company, 1871.
  30 p.   OTAR
Ontario. Legislative Assembly. Select Committee on lake levels of the Great
  Lakes.
  Report. Toronto: Baptist Johnston, printer to the Queen's Most Excellent
  Majesty, 1953.
  [15] 149 leaves. illus., col. maps (part fold.), 34 plates (part fold.), tables.
  Chairman: P.F. Villeneuve.   OTAR OTU
— Proceedings, April 30–July 25, 1952.
  13 v. [i.e. 1835 typewritten pages]   OTAR
Ontario. Legislative Assembly. Select Committee on Motorized Snow Vehicles
  and All-terrain Vehicles.
  Interim report. [Toronto] 1973.
  39 leaves.
  Chairman: Alex Carruthers.   OTAR
— Final report. [Toronto] 1974.
  26 leaves.   OTAR
— Minutes, July 12, 1972–March 4, 1974.
  38 folders.   OTAR
— Briefs.
  134 v.   OTAR

Ontario. Legislative Assembly. Select Committee on Public Utilities .
Municipal trading and municipal ownership or operation of public utilities,
to which is added, the return ordered by the Legislative Assembly on June
12, 1903, of the reproductive undertakings operated by municipalities in
Ontario. Printed by order of the Legislative Assembly of Ontario. Toronto:
L.K. Cameron, printer to the King's Most Excellent Majesty, 1903.
246 p. tables.
Chairman: J.M. Gibson.   OTAR

Ontario. Legislative Assembly. Select Committee on Railway Accidents.
Report. 1880.
3 handwritten pages.
Chairman: James Young.   OTAR
— Minutes, January 23–March 2, 1880.
19 typewritten pages.   OTAR

Ontario. Legislative Assembly. Select Committee on the Huron and Ontario
Ship Canal.
Report. 1879. Printed by order of the Legislative Assembly. Toronto: C.
Blackett Robinson, 1879.
23 p. illus., map.
Chairman: J.H. Widdifield.   OTL

Ontario. Legislative Assembly. Select Committee on the Hydro-Electric Power
Commission of Ontario New Head Office Building.
Report. [Toronto] 1973.
ii, 12 p.
Chairman: John P. MacBeth.   OTAR OTUL
— Proceedings, May 9–September 17, 1973.
21 v. [i.e. 2672 typewritten pages]   OTAR

Ontario. Legislative Assembly. Select Committee on Toll Roads.
Report. [Toronto: 1956]
43 p. tables (part fold.).
Chairman: J.P. Robarts.   OTAR
— Report on toll roads and highway financing. [Toronto: 1957]
54 p. graphs, maps (part fold.), tables (part fold.).   OTAR
— Proceedings, April 19, 1955–December 20, 1956.
40 v. [i.e. 3,741 typewritten pages]   OTAR
— Indices, v. 1–7.
19 leaves.   OTAR
— Revised index, v. 1–10.
32 leaves.   OTAR
— Indices. v. 1–39.
310 leaves.   OTAR

Ontario. Legislative Assembly. Select Committee on Wooden Railways.
Report. Toronto: Hunter, Rose & Co., 1869.
10 p.
Chairman: John Carnegie.   OTAR

Ontario. Legislative Assembly. Special Committee to consider, revise and
    consolidate the laws respecting motor vehicles.
    Report. 1923.
    5 typewritten pages.
    Chairman: A.M. Rankin.   OTAR
— Proceedings, September 6–November 28, 1922.
    6 v. [i.e. 732 typewritten pages]   OTAR
Ontario. Public Roads and Highways Commission.
    Report. Printed by order of the Legislative Assembly of Ontario. Toronto:
    L.K. Cameron, printer to the King's Most Excellent Majesty, 1914.
    277 p. illus., graphs, fold. col. maps, tables.
    Commissioners: C.A. Magrath, W.A. McLean, A.M. Rankin.   OTAR
— Summary of evidence at public meetings of the Commission, October 28,
    1913–January 22, 1914.
    Various typewritten pages.   OTAR
Ontario. Royal Commission appointed to inquire into certain matters
    concerning The Hydro-Electric Power Commission of Ontario.
    Report. Toronto: Herbert H. Ball, printer to the King's Most Excellent
    Majesty, 1932.
    11 p.
    Commissioners: William Renwick Riddell, George H. Sedgewick.   OTAR
Ontario. Royal Commission appointed to investigate charges relating to the
    purchase of land in the city of Sarnia by the Hydro-Electic Power Commission
    of Ontario from Dimensional Investments Limited.
    Report. [Toronto: 1960]
    133 typewritten pages.
    Commissioner: G.A. McGillivray.   OTAR
— Appendices to report.
    1 v. (various pagings). charts, maps.   OTAR
    Proceedings, April 19 September 19, 1960.
    23 v. in 6 parts [i.e. 3951 typewritten pages]   OTAR
Ontario. Royal Commission on Automobile Insurance Premium Rates.
    Report. Printed by order of the Legislative Assembly of Ontario. Toronto:
    Herbert H. Ball, printer to the King's Most Excellent Majesty, 1930.
    116 p. tables.
    Commissioner: Frank E. Hodgins.   OTAR
— 2d ed. Printed by order of the Legislative Assembly of Ontario. Toronto:
    Herbert H. Ball, printer to the King's Most Excellent Majesty, 1930.
    116 p. tables.   OTAR
— Interim report on compulsory insurance and safety responsiblity laws.
    Toronto: 1930.
    99, 98 typewritten pages   OTAR
— Compulsory insurance and safety responsibility laws; interim report. 3d ed.
    Printed by order of the Legislative Assembly. Toronto: Herbert H. Ball,
    printer to the King's Most Excellent Majesty, 1930.
    85, 19 [2] p.   OTAR

Ontario. Royal Commission on Transportation.
  Report, 1938. Toronto: T.E. Bowman, printer to the King's Most Excellent
  Majesty, 1939.
  xii, 293 p. graphs, tables (part fold.).
  Chairman: E.R.E. Chevrier.   OTAR
— Proceedings, November 29, 1937–June 29, 1938.
  12 v. [i.e. 9947 typewritten pages]   OTAR
— Briefs.
  88 v.   OTAR
— Memorandum accompanying printed report entitled Report on annual
  highway costs, province of Ontario, made to the Railway Association of
  Canada, by C.B. Breed, Clifford Older and Wm. S. Downs, February 21,
  1938; memorandum by C.B. Breed, April 20, 1938. n.p. [1938?]
  62 leaves. illus., fold. map.   OTV
Ontario. Royal Commission on Violence in the Communications Industry.
  Interim report. [Toronto] 1976.
  1 v. (various pagings).
  Chairman: Judy LaMarsh.   OTAR
— Rapport interimaire. [Toronto] 1976.
  1 v. (various pagings).   OTAR
— Report. [Toronto: The Royal Commission on Violence in the
  Communications Industry 1977?]
  7 v. illus., tables.
  Contents: v. 1, Approaches, conclusions and recommendations; v. 2,
  Violence and the media: a bibliography; v. 3, Violence in television, films
  and news; v. 4, Violence in print and music; v. 5, Learning from the media;
  v. 6, Vulnerability to media effects; v. 7, The media industries: from here to
  where.   OTAR
— Proceedings, October 24, 1975–May 27, 1976.
  71 tapes.   OTAR
Ontario. Royal Commission to inquire into the purchase of the bonds of the
  Ontario Power Service Corporation by the Hydro-Electic Power
  Commission of Ontario and the government of Ontario.
  Report. [Toronto: 1934]
  43 typewritten leaves.
  Commissioners: Frances Robert Latchford, Robert Smith.   OTAR
— Proceedings, July 13–August 23, 1934.
  17 v. [i.e. 2472 typewritten pages]
  OTAR has v. 2, 16, 17.   OTAR
Ontario. Solandt Commission.
  Interim report. [Results of hearings on the Nanticoke to Pickering power
  line. Toronto] 1972.
  1 v. (various pagings). map.
  Chairman: Omond M. Solandt.   OTUL
— "Closing the generation gap." A public inquiry into the transmission of
  power between Nanticoke and Pickering. [Toronto: 1974]
  1 v. (various pagings). tables.   OTAR

— "Transmission." A public inquiry into the transmission of power between
Lennox and Oshawa. [Toronto: 1975]
xi, 213 p. diagrs., maps (part fold.), tables.   OTAR
— Proceedings July 31, 1972–January 20, 1975.
201 tapes.   OTAR

Background reports to Ontario Solandt Commission
B.H.I. Limited.
An environmental study to select hydro transmission corridors for the
Solandt Commission. [Toronto: 1973]
1 v. (various pagings). illus. (part fold.), maps (part fold.).   OTAR
— An abstract. [Toronto? Drewmark Graphics Limited, 1973]
32 p. fold. illus., fold. maps.   OTAR
Commonwealth Associates Inc.
Ontario Hydro 500kv transmission line right of way Lennox – Oshawa
environmental report. [Jackson, Michigan: 1974]
285 p. diagrs., maps, tables.
Report submitted to Ontario Hydro in conjunction with the Solandt
Commission.   OTAR
Sparling, Tom W
An evaluation of alternate routes, for the Solandt Commission's public
inquiry into the transmission of power between Lennox and Oshawa.
Toronto: 1974.
i, 11 leaves. map.   OTMCL

Ontario. Task Force Hydro.
Report. [Toronto: 1972–1973]
5 v. charts, diagrs., tables.
Chairman: John B. Cronyn.
Contents: v. 1, Hydro in Ontario: a future role and place; v. 2, Hydro in
Ontario: an approach to organization; v. 3, Nuclear power in Ontario; v. 4,
Hydro in Ontario: financial policy and rates; v. 5, Hydro in Ontario: a
policy for make or buy.
The Task Force was established by the Committee on Government
Productivity of Ontario.   OTAR
— Synopsis of the submissions from the public. [Prepared by] C. Nutch.
[Toronto] 1972.
37 leaves. fold. chart.   OTAR
Ontario. Temiskaming and Northern Ontario Railway inquiry.
Report. Toronto: T.E. Bowman, printer to the King's Most Excellent
Majesty, 1935.
25 p.
Commissioner: Armand Racine.   ·   OTAR

— Proceedings, August 14th–September 12th, 1934.
    3 v. [i.e. 758 typewritten pages]   OTAR
Ontario Council of University Librarians.
    Inter-university transit system anniversary report 1967–1968. [Toronto?]
    Committee of Presidents of Universities of Ontario [1968]
    20 p. illus., map.   OTER
Ontario Educational Television Committee.
    Brief presented to the Board of Broadcast Governors on Educational
    Television. n.p. [1960]
    1 v. (various pagings).
    Chairman: J.B. McDonnell.   OTER
Ontario Municipal Electric Association,
    Electric power in Ontario: hydro, a municipal co-operative. [Toronto] The
    Association [1970]
    54 p. illus., map, ports.   OONL
Ontario Northland Transportation Commission.
    The end of an era, last run of the steam locomotive on Ontario Northland
    Railway, June 24th & 25th, 1957. [North Bay, Ontario: The Daily Nugget,
    1957]
    11 p. illus.   OKQ
Ontario Power Commission.
    Official report. Toronto: Monetary Times Printing Company of Canada
    Limited [1906]
    [76] p. illus., maps, ports., tables.
    Chairman: E.W.B. Snider.   OTU
The open gate: Toronto Union Station. Edited by Richard Bébout. Original
    photos by John Taylor. Commentary on historical photos by Mike Filey.
    [Toronto] Peter Martin Associates [1972]
    xvi, 125 p. illus., plans.   OTU
The Ottawa River Canal; its advantages as a route from lake to tidewater. n.p.
    [1895?]
    [7] p.
    Reprinted from *The New York Times*, July 16, 1895.   OKQ
Parker, (C.C.) & Parsons, Brinckerhoff, Ltd.
    Hamilton area transportation plan; prepared for the Corporation of the City
    of Hamilton, Ontario. Hamilton, Ontario [1963?]
    iv, 162 p. illus., maps (part col.).   OTU
Parkway Consultants.
    Niagara Escarpment scenic drive feasibility study. [Prepared for the Tri-
    county Committee counties of Lincoln, Welland, Wentworth by Parkway
    Consultants. Don Mills, Ontario: 1968]
    144 p. illus., maps (part fold.).   OTU
Passfield, Robert W
    Historic bridges on the Rideau waterways system: a preliminary report.
    [Ottawa] Parks Canada, Department of Indian and Northern Affairs, 1976.
    viii, 129 p. illus. (National Historic Parks and Sites Branch. Manuscript
    report no. 212).   OTAR

Petrie, Auldham Roy, 1921–
    Alexander Graham Bell. Don Mills, Ontario: Fitzhenry & Whiteside
    [c1975]
    61 p. illus., ports.   OTER
Plantown Consultants Limited.
    Interim report on: services, utilities, and communications for: The North
    Pickering Project. [Toronto: Ministry of Housing, Ontario] 1974.
    1 v. (various pagings). fold. map.   OTUSA
Plewman, William Rothwell, 1880–
    Adam Beck and the Ontario Hydro. Toronto: The Ryerson Press [c1947]
    xxi, 494 p. illus., diagrs., ports.   OTU
Poot, Peter.
    Scarborough local transportation study; a study of local responsibilities with
    respect to transportation and of facilities provided and planned by other
    jurisdictions. Prepared for the Mayor and members of the Council of the
    Borough of Scarborough and the Chairman and members of the Planning
    Board of the Borough of Scarborough, by Peter Poot, under the direction of
    R.K. Brown, D.F. Easton and W.J. Bolton. [Scarborough, Ontario: 1968]
    131 p. illus., fold. maps.   OTUSA
Port Arthur, Ontario. Board of Trade.
    The Welland Canal or Georgian Bay Canal which? [Port Arthur, Ontario:
    Board of Trade [1913]
    16 p. illus.   OTAR
Pound, Arthur, 1884–1966.
    Lake Ontario. [1st ed. Indianapolis: Bobbs – Merrill Co., c1945]
    384 p. illus., maps, ports. (The American lakes series).   OTU
Preston, Richard Arthur.
    The history of the port of Kingston. [Toronto: 1955]
    [28] p.   OONL
Pritchard, Jean, 1940–
    The Welland Canal, yesterday, today, tomorrow. Written and compiled by
    Jean and Allan Pritchard. Edited by Francis J. Petrie. Niagara Falls,
    Ontario: Jean R. Dingman, c1970.
    28 p. illus. maps.   OTU
Proctor, Redfern, Bousfield & Bacon.
    Land use and population aspects, Kenora traffic planning study. Toronto:
    1968.
    26 leaves. diagrs., form, 2 fold. maps.   OTU
— London area transportation study; report on recommended land use,
    prepared for the Corporation of the City of London. [Toronto] 1964.
    iv, 22 leaves. maps.   OTUSA
Pursley, Louis H   1907–
    Street railways of Toronto, 1861–1921. Los Angeles, California: Interurbans
    Electric Railway Publications [1958]
    155 p. illus., maps.
    Fifteenth anniversary issue of *Interurbans* Special 25.   OTAR

— The Toronto trolley car story, 1921–1961. [Los Angeles, California:
Interurbans, 1961]
164 p. illus., maps.
Interurbans, Special 29.   OTAR
Quaife, Milo Milton, 1880–1959.
Lake Michigan. Indianapolis: The Bobbs–Merrill Company [c1944]
384 p. plates, ports. (The American lakes series).
Chiefly United States of America.   OTAR
Ratigan, William.
Great lakes shipwrecks & survivals. Pictures by Reynold H. Weidenaar. [2d
ed.] Grand Rapids, Michigan: Wm. B. Eerdmans Publishing Company
[1969]
333 p. illus.   OTU
Read, Voorhees & Associates Limited.
Grimsby traffic study. n.p.: 1971.
1 v. (various pagings). graphs, plans, maps.   OTU
Regional Municipality of Hamilton – Wentworth. Planning and Development
Department.
Transportation: a sub study of the regional official plan. [Hamilton,
Ontario: 1975–1976]
4 v.   OHM
Regional Municipality of Ottawa – Carleton. Department of Traffic
Engineering Services.
Churchill – Richmond Road area traffic study for the city of Ottawa:
existing conditions. [Ottawa] 1973.
24 p. maps.   OONL
— Queensway Terrance North area traffic study for the city of Ottawa: existing
conditions. [Ottawa] 1973.
23 p. maps.   OONL
— Whitehaven area traffic study for the city of Ottawa: existing conditions and
survey results. [Ottawa] 1973.
50 p. diagrs., maps, tables.   OONL
Rice, Ronald G
An interactive transportation gaming model for Metropolitan Toronto:
progress report, by R.G. Rice, W.C. Found, S.F. Gribble. Toronto:
University of Toronto – York University Joint Program in Transportation
1974.
v, 79 leaves. charts, illus. (Joint Program in Transportation. Research report
no. 17).   OTU
Richardson, Ronald E
Shaping Canada's environment: building for people. Freeway and
downtown – new frameworks for modern needs, by Ronald E. Richardson,
George H. McNevin and Walter G. Rooke. Toronto: The Ryerson Press;
Maclean–Hunter Limited [c1970]
120 p. illus., maps.   OTU

Richelieu and Ontario Navigation Co.
>   From Niagara to the sea: the finest inland water trip in the world. Official
>   guide 1899. Issued by the Passenger Department of the Richelieu and
>   Ontario Navigation Company. Montreal: Desbarats & Co. [c1898]
>   176 p. illus.   OKQ

Rideau waterway guide, by boat and car through the Rideau lakes and the
>   Rideau Canal. Complete with maps and tour information. Ottawa: Robert
>   Haig Publishing Company, n.d.
>   72 p. illus., maps.   OTU

Roebuck, Arthur Wentworth, 1878–1971.
>   The wreck of the Hydro. Toronto: Ontario Liberal Association, 1933.
>   15 p.   OTAR

Runnalls, John Lawrence, 1901–
>   The Irish on the Welland Canal. St. Catharines, Ontario: St. Catharines
>   Public Library, 1973, 1974 printing.
>   67 p. [4] leaves of plates. illus., maps.   OTU

St. Catharines, Ontario, and the Welland Ship Canal: the open door to
>   Canadian and British Empire Markets. [St. Catharines, Ontario:
>   Commercial Press, 1933]
>   7, 32 p. illus., map.   OTAR

St. Lawrence Power Project.
>   Four years of construction progress, August, 1954–August, 1958 . Project
>   dedicated, September 5, 1958. Power Authority of the state of New York and
>   the Hydro-Electric Power Commission of Ontario. n.p.: 1958.
>   [37] p. illus., map, ports.   OKQ

Saint Lawrence Seaway Authority.
>   The Saint Lawrence Seaway under construction. [Ottawa: Queen's Printer,
>   1957]
>   [30] p. illus., map (fold. col.).   OKQ

Salen, Richard Karl, 1953–
>   Guidebook and history of Tobermory Manitoulin Ferry Service, by Rick
>   and Jack Salen. Tobermory, Ontario: Mariner Chart Shop [c1975]
>   43 p. illus., maps.   OTU

— The Tobermory shipwrecks: a history and description [by Rick and Jack
>   Salen] New 2d ed. Tobermory, Ontario: Mariner Chart Shop [c1976]
>   83 p. illus., col. maps.   OONL

Sault Ste. Marie and Hudson's Bay Railway Co.
>   The great northern sea of Canada, how to utilize it most easily,
>   economically, expeditiously, extensively, and profitably; special report of the
>   original (charter) directors... with a supplementary statement by the
>   Toronto directorate. Toronto: 1897.
>   14 p. 2 col. maps.   OTURS

Scott, Harley E
>   Tales of the Muskoka steamboats: a history of Muskoka. Bracebridge,
>   Ontario: Herald–Gazette Press, 1969.
>   47 p. illus., maps.   OTSTM

Seagrams Limited.
    The St. Lawrence Seaway: the realization of a mighty dream. [Montreal:
    1954]
    40 p. illus. (part fold.).   OKQ
Senecal, Janet Nita.
    Home on the St. Lawrence River. [Gananoque, Ontario: 1000 Islands
    Publishers Ltd., 1973]
    186 p. illus.   OKQ
Sheffe, Norman, 1924–
    Casimir Gzowski. Don Mills, Ontario: Fitzhenry & Whiteside Limited
    [1975]
    60 p. illus., facsims., maps, ports.   OONL
Sinclair, Gordon Allan, 1900–
    Will Gordon Sinclair please sit down. [Toronto] McClelland and Stewart
    Limited [c1975]
    222 p.   OTU
Slater, D   W
    Kingston transportation study: projections of the population and
    employment in the study areas as a whole and in traffic zone. Prepared by
    D.W. Slater and S. Fyfe. Kingston, Ontario: Queen's University [1962]
    40 leaves. tables.   OKQ
Smith, Gavin John Anthony, 1947–
    Transportation and urban design: a systems approach to Toronto's future
    transportation network. Toronto: Department of Geography and Centre for
    Urban and Community Studies, University of Toronto, 1970.
    36 leaves. diagrs., maps. (Environment study. Research paper, no. 23).   OTU
Special International Niagara Board.
    Final report: the preservation of Niagara Falls. Ottawa: F.A. Acland,
    printer to the King's Most Excellent Majesty, 1930.
    xiv, 394 p. illus., graphs, tables.   OONL
Spencer, Joseph William Winthrop, 1851–1921.
    The duration of Niagara Falls and the history of the Great Lakes, 2d ed.
    New York: The Humboldt Publishing Co. [c1895]
    126 p. illus., front., maps, tables.   OTU
— The falls of Niagara: their evolution and varying relations to the Great
    Lakes; characteristics of the power, and the effects of its diversion. Ottawa:
    S.E. Dawson, printer to the King's Most Excellent Majesty, 1907.
    xxxi, 490, 4 p. illus., maps (part fold.).   OTU
Stein, C   E
    The wreck of the Erie Belle [the story of the old boiler of Boiler Beach]
    Wheatley, Ontario: Ship 'N Shore Publishing Company [c1970]
    iv, 28 p. illus.   OTU
Stephens, George Washington, 1866–1942.
    The St. Lawrence waterway project: the story of the St. Lawrence River as
    an international highway for waterborne commerce. Montreal: Carrier and
    Co. [c1930]
    460 p. illus., maps.   OTU

Stevens, George Roy, 1892–1975.
Canadian National Railways. Toronto: Clarke, Irwin & Company Limited, 1960–1962.
2 v. illus., maps, ports., tables.
Contents: v. 1, Sixty years of trial and errors (1836–1896). With a foreword by Donald Gordon and an introduction by S.W. Fairweather; v. 2, Towards the inevitable 1896–1922. With a foreword by O.M. Solandt.   OTU
— History of the Canadian National Railways. New York: Macmillan [1973]
xii, 538 p. illus.   OTU
Stevens, John R
Lighthouses of the Great Lakes, Ontario. Ottawa: National and Historic Parks Branch, 1965.
iii, 174 p. illus., maps. (National Historic Parks and Sites Branch. MRS no. 94).   OTAR
Stewart, James.
"On to the Bay". [Extension of Temiskaming and Northern Ontario Railway from Cochrane to Tide Water, Moose Factory, James Bay] n.p. [1918?]
16 p. illus., maps.   OTU
Stewart, McLeod, 1847–1926.
Ottawa an ocean port, and the emporium of the grain and coal trade of the Northwest; 2d ed. a paper read before the Ottawa Board of Trade on Monday the 6th of November, 1893. Ottawa: Printed by Thoburn & Co., 1895.
vi, 23 p. illus.   OTURS
Stories of the inside passage and the 30,000 islands of Georgian Bay from Midland to Penetanquishene to Parry Sound and Pointe-au-Baril: Trade route of Ancient Huronia. Midland, Canada: Midland Press Limited, n.d.
23 p. illus., map.   OMI
Streetcars for Toronto Committee.
A brief for the implementation of light rapid transit as the intermediate capacity mode in Metropolitan Toronto. [Toronto] 1973.
21 [7] 5 p.   OTU
Taber, Arthur Walter Hall, 1902–
Electricity and Fort William: history of the development of electricity in the city of Fort William, 1898–1967. [Fort William, Ontario: Times Journal Commercial Printers, 1967]
79 p. illus., ports.   OTAR
Talman, James John, 1904–
The development of the railway network of southwestern Ontario to 1876. [Toronto: 1953]
8 p.
From the Canadian Historical Association, 1953.   OKQ
Tatley, Richard.
Steamboating in Muskoka; a condensed history of the steamboats in

Muskoka from 1866 to the present time. Bracebridge, Ontario: Muskoka Litho [c1972]
101 p. illus. OMI OTAR
Tennant, Robert Dawson, 1942–
Ontario's government railway: genesis and development. [Halifax: Tennant Publishing House, 1972, c1973]
xv, 109 p. illus., graphs, maps. OTU
Thomson, Lesslie Rielle, 1886–1958.
The St. Lawrence problem, some Canadian economic aspects. [Montreal? 1929?]
112 p. illus., maps, diagrs., tables. OOA
Thomson, Thomas Kennard, 1864–1952.
The development of power in the Niagara River as a national necessity to conserve over 10,000,000 tons of coal yearly. n.p.: 1917.
[2] 44 leaves. illus., maps (part col.), plan. OTU
Three quarters of a century: the Muir Brothers and their work for Great Lakes shipping, 1850–1925. n.p. [1925?]
10 leaves.
Port Dalhousie. OTAR
Toronto. Board of Trade.
Canada's canal problem and its solution. [Toronto: Board of Trade, 19—]
11 p.
Trent waterways. OTU
— Canada's transportation problem from a national standpoint: the short line railway over the portage from Toronto to Georgian Bay. Toronto: Board of Trade, 1900.
38 p. map. OTU
Toronto. City Planning Board.
Evaluation of W.R. Allen Expressway. [Toronto] 1970.
51, 7, 4, 3, 4 leaves. illus. (part fold.), fold. maps, tables. OTUSA
Toronto. Electric Commissioners.
Report of an investigation ordered by the Toronto Electric Commissioners into the conclusions of the city auditors as to the financial position of the Toronto hydro-electric distributing system. [Toronto: 1913]
38 p. tables.
Chairman: P.W. Ellis. OTU
Toronto. University. Department of University Extension.
A verbatim report of the lectures given in the course on traffic... at the University of Toronto, October 17th, 1944–February 27th, 1945. [Toronto: 1945]
314 leaves. tables.
Sponsored by the Canadian Industrial Traffic League. OTU
Toronto and Georgian Bay Ship Railway.
Facts for the people. n.p.: 1888.
12 p. fold. map. (Industrial Exhibition, 1888). OOA

Toronto and Hamilton Highway Commission.
> Report covering the work of the Toronto and Hamilton Highway
> Commission from the time of its appointment to December 31, 1921.
> [Toronto: 1922]
> 56 p. illus., fold. plan, tables.
> Chairman: George H. Gooderham.   OTAR

Toronto Daily Star.
> A Canadian view of the St. Lawrence project, being a series of seven articles
> published in the *Toronto Daily Star* in the month of December, 1927. Toronto:
> The Star, 1927.
> 29 p. map.   OTU
> — The St. Lawrence project: comment on the criticism of the Jackman
> pamphlet made by Dr. Thomas H. Hogg, chairman of the Ontario Hydro-
> Electric Commission, in an address before the Empire Club of Toronto,
> April 11, 1940. With rejoinder by Prof. Jackman, as published in the *Toronto
> Daily Star*, April 16, 1940. Fort Erie, Ontario: Review Company, 1940.
> 8 p.   OTU

Toronto, Grey and Bruce Railway.
> Great railway meeting at Orangeville convened by Joseph Pattullo, mayor
> of Orangeville held on Friday, 7th September, 1877 to consider the
> advisability to widening the gauge of the Toronto, Grey and Bruce Railway.
> Speech of the President of the Railway Company. Toronto: Globe Printing
> Company, 1877.
> 17 p. tables.   OKQ
> — Railway for Grey, facts for the rate-payers concerning the Toronto, Grey
> and Bruce Railway. n.p. [1871?]
> 14 p.   OKQ

Toronto Harbour Commissioners.
> Facts concerning Toronto harbour. Toronto [1929?]
> [24] p. illus., map.   OTURS
> — [Toronto: Hunter–Rose Co. Ltd., 1933?]
> 61 p. illus., fold. plan, tables.
> "Plan" missing from copy examined.   OTU
> — The port and harbour of Toronto 1834–1934, centennial year. [Toronto:
> Press of the Hunter–Rose Co. Ltd., 1934?]
> 63 p. illus., ports.   OTU
> — Toronto waterfront development, 1912–1920. Toronto [Brigdens Limited,
> 1920 ?]
> 32 p. illus. (part col.), 3 fold. plans.
> Chairman: Lionel H. Clarke.   OTURS

Toronto Transit Commission.
> General plans for Bloor and University rapid transit subways. [Toronto]
> 1956.
> [5] leaves. 144 leaves of plans.   OTU
> — Bloor – University – Danforth subway: Bloor – Queen "U" subway. Final
> discussion with Metro planning staff. [Toronto: 1958]
> 11 leaves.   OTU

— Metro centre; a review of the transportation elements. Prepared by the staffs
  of Toronto Transit Commission, Department of Highways, Ontario [and]
  Metropolitan Toronto Planning Board. [Toronto] 1971.
  vii, 42, A1–A6 p. illus., plans.   OTU
— Transit in Toronto, 1849–1967, the story of the development of public
  transportation in Toronto, from horse cars to a modern high speed subway
  system. Toronto: The Commission, 1967.
  65 p. illus., maps (part col.).   OONL
  [2d ed. Toronto: 1969]
  72 p. illus., maps (part col.).   OTAR
  [3d ed. rev. Toronto: 1971]
  68 p. illus., maps (part col.).   OTAR
Toronto Transportation Commission.
  Outline of the history and operations of the Toronto Transportation
  Commission and its subsidiary Gray Coach Lines, Ltd. presented to the
  Royal Commission on Transportation at Toronto, January 19, 1932.
  [Toronto] 1932.
  38 p. graphs, tables.   OTAR
— Rapid transit for Toronto [a statement of policy] Toronto: Toronto
  Transportation Commission, 1945.
  32 p. illus., maps (part col.), plans.   OONL
— Ten years of progressive public service 1921–1931. [Toronto: Toronto
  Transportation Commission and Gray Coach Lines, 1931]
  1 v. (unpaged). illus., map.   OTAR
— Wheels of progress: a story of the development of Toronto and its public
  transportation services. [Toronto: Toronto Transportation Commission,
  1940?]
  116 p. illus., tables, diagrs., map.   OONL
  [2d ed. Toronto: 1942]
  116 p. illus., diagrs., tables.   OTU
  [3d ed. Toronto: 1944?]
  117 p. illus., maps, diagrs., tables.   OTU
  [4th ed. Toronto: 1946?]
  114 p. illus., maps, diagrs., tables.   OOA
  [5th ed. Toronto: 1953]
  128 p. illus., diagrs., maps, tables.   OTU
Traffic Research Corporation Limited.
  The control of traffic signals in Metropolitan Toronto with an electronic
  computer: a report on the pilot study of the automatic control of traffic
  signals conducted for the traffic engineering departments of the city of
  Toronto and the municipality of Metropolitan Toronto. [Toronto] 1961.
  191 leaves. illus., charts, graphs, tables.   OTU
The Trent valley route: the waterway of Canada. n.p.: 1898.
  [30] p. fold. plan.   OOA

Union Forwarding and Railway Company's Steamers.
>   Tourists' and travellers' guide to the Upper Ottawa, by the Union
>   Forwarding and Railway Company's Steamers and Brockville & Ottawa
>   Railway. Ottawa: Bell & Woodburn, 1869.
>   8 p.   OTAR
Urban bus transit: a planning guide, John Shortreed, editor. Waterloo, Ontario:
>   Transport Group, Department of Civil Engineering, University of Waterloo,
>   1974, 1975 printing.
>   xi, 356 p. illus., maps. (Publication series – Transport Group, Department of
>   Civil Engineering, University of Waterloo [12]).   OTU
Voskuil, Walter Henry, 1892–
>   The economics of water power development. Chicago: A.N. Shaw Company,
>   1928.
>   xii, 225 p. illus., maps, tables, diagrs.   OTU
Wade, John H   T
>   Mount Hope airport noise survey: present levels and predicted increases
>   with expansion. Prepared by J.H.T. Wade and H. Gidamy. Hamilton,
>   Ontario: Centre for Applied Research and Engineering Design,
>   Incorporated, 1973.
>   52 leaves. diagrs. (part fold), illus., maps.   OTU
Waterloo – South Wellington area study.
>   Transportation technical supplement. Completed under the direction of the
>   Transportation Technical Advisory Committee. Final report part two. n.p.:
>   1973.
>   117 p. graphs, maps, tables.   OONL
The Welland Ship Canal. n.p.: 1926.
>   33 [7] leaves. tables.   OTU
Wells, Kenneth McNeill, 1905–
>   Cruising the Georgian Bay. Decorative map by Lloyd Scott. [1st ed.]
>   Toronto: Kingswood House, 1958.
>   140 p. illus., maps (part aerial).   OTU
— Revised and enl. Toronto: Kingswood House, 1961.
>   xv, 183 p. illus., maps (part aerial).   OTU
— Cruising the North Channel. Endpaper maps by Lloyd Scott. [1st ed.]
>   Toronto: Kingswood House, 1960.
>   xv, 232 p. illus., maps.   OTU
— Cruising the Rideau waterway. Toronto: McClelland and Stewart [1965]
>   90 p. maps.   OTU
— Cruising the Trent – Severn waterway. [1st ed.] Toronto: Kingswood House,
>   1959.
>   120 p. illus., maps.   OONL
>   A revised and enlarged edition. Toronto: McClelland and Stewart Limited
>   [c1959]
>   100 p. map.   OONL
— Trailer boating where the North begins. Endpaper map designed by Lloyd
>   Scott. [1st ed.] Toronto: Kingswood House, 1961.
>   104 p. illus., maps.   OTU

West, Bruce.
    The firebirds [an account of the first 50 years of the Ontario Provincial Air
    Service] by Bruce West; illustrated by James Lumbers. [Toronto] Ministry
    of Natural Resources, 1974.
    xiv, 258 p. illus.   OTU

Williamson, Ethel.
    A light on the seaway. [St. Catharines, Ontario: Cyril E. Williamson, 1972]
    123 p. illus., ports., map.   OKQ

Williamson, Owen Templeton Garrett, 1883–
    Ontario Northland Railway: yesterday and tomorrow. [North Bay, Ontario]
    Ontario Northland Transportation Commission [1959]
    [16] p. illus., ports., map.   OTU

Willmot, Elizabeth A   1918–
    Meet me at the station. [Toronto] Gage Publishing [1976]
    114 p. illus., facsim.
    Ontario railway stations.   OTU

Willoughby, William R
    The St. Lawrence waterway; a study in politics and diplomacy. Madison:
    University of Wisconsin Press, c1961.
    381 p. illus.   OTU

Wills, Harold A   1907–
    The public utilities of Cochrane, Ontario, 1910–70. Retrospect in the
    Diamond Jubilee year. [Cochrane, Ontario: Public Utilities Commission,
    1970]
    28 p. illus.   OLU

Wilson, Dale, 1936–
    Tracks of the black bear: the story of the Algoma Central railroad.
    [Toronto] Green Tree Publishing Co. [c1974]
    [72] p. illus., map.   OTU

Wilson, Idele Louise.
    The St. Lawrence Seaway; it's Canada's river for Canada's future. Start
    digging now! Toronto: United Electrical, Radio & Machine Workers of
    America, 1954.
    20 p. illus.   OOA

Wright, Conrad Payling.
    The St. Lawrence deep waterway: a Canadian appraisal. Toronto:
    Macmillan Company of Canada Limited, 1935.
    xx, 450 p. maps, tables.   OTUL

Young, Anna Grace Peterson, 1898–
    Great Lakes' saga: the influence of one family on the development of
    Canada shipping on the Great Lakes, 1816–1931. Pencil sketches by Evan
    Macdonald. Charts by Ivan S. Brookes. Owen Sound, Ontario: Richardson,
    Bond & Wright [1965]
    xiii, 157 p. illus., maps, ports., facsims.   OTU

— Off watch: today and yesterday on the Great Lakes. Foreword by Fred
    Landon. Toronto: The Ryerson Press [c1957]
    xviii, 166 p. illus., map.   OTU

Periodical Articles

Accidents on Ontario railways. Railway and Marine World 9: 457, 1906.

Adams, Roy N
  Sir Adam Beck. Hydro-Electric Power Commission of Ontario. Bulletin 24:
  237–240, 1937.

The Aguasabon power project. Industrial Canada 48(no. 7): 92–95, 1947.

Aikin, J   Alexander.
  The St. Lawrence waterway project. Queen's Quarterly 30: 53–65, 1922; 39:
  111–129, 1932.

Ainslie, Jason.
  The great storm of 1913. Huron Historical Notes 10: 22–23, 1974.
  On Lake Huron.

All-year car ferries; boats which ply between Canadian and U.S. lake ports
  winter and summer. Industrial Canada 8: 709, 1908.

Angel, Arthur D
  The Great Lakes – St. Lawrence project. Land Economics 26: 222–231,
  1950.

Apropos the St. Lawrence waterway: will we... or won't we? Canadian Business
  13(2): 18–21, 1940.

Armour; Stuart.
  The St. Lawrence Seaway – how is it faring? Industrial Canada 60(no. 4):
  45–52, 1959.

Armstrong, Alan H
  Loss of a link with Toronto's past. Royal Architectural Institute of Canada
  Journal 30: 187, 1953.
  Passenger train shed – Great Western Railroad.

Armstrong, Frederick H
  John Armour of Dunnville: from canal supervisor to village patriarch.
  Inland Seas 29: 83–90, 1973.

Arthur, Paul.
  CBC – TV/Toronto. Canadian Art 15: 40–49, 1958.

Ashley, C   A
  The T.T.C. Canadian Forum 32: 73–74, 1952.
— T.T.C. finances. Canadian Forum 30: 73–74, 1950.

Baechler, Glenn H
  Waterloo county's romance with the automobile. Waterloo Historical
  Society. Annual Volume 59: 8–19, 1971.

Ballert, Albert G
  Commerce of the Sault canals. Economic Geography 33: 135–148, 1957.
— The major ports of the Great Lakes – their tonnages and principle traffic in
  1948. Inland Seas 8: 113–117, 1952.
— The ports and commerce of Georgian Bay. Inland Seas 11: 26–34, 119–125,
  1955.
— The Soo versus the Suez. Canadian Geographical Journal 53: 160–167,
  1956.

Bannister, J   A
   Port Dover Harbour. Ontario History 41: 57–88, 1949.
— Some north shore ports. Inland Seas 16: 299–308, 1960; 17: 31–38, 1961.
   North shore of Lake Erie.
— The white sails of Dover; part II. Inland Seas 5: 18–24, 1949.
Barker, Gerry.
   The loss of the steamer Atlantic. Inland Seas 20: 211–214, 1964.
Barry, James P
   The Wolseley expedition crosses the Great Lakes. Inland Seas 24: 91–107.
   1968.
Baxter, Kevin.
   "Ready about!" Inland Seas 29: 186–189, 1973.
   Owned and Operated by Toronto Brigantine, Inc.
Bayley, W   S
   The geographic effects of the proposed Great Lakes – St. Lawrence
   waterway. Economic Geography 1: 236–246, 1925.
Bechtol, Arthur.
   New Ferguson highway opening up northern Ontario. Canadian Mining
   Journal 50: 342–343, 1929.
Bernhardt, Clara.
   CKPC's early years in Preston. Waterloo Historical Society. Annual Volume
   57: 64–69, 1969.
Best, Kathleen E
   The economic aspects of the St. Lawrence waterway plan. Essays on
   Canadian Economic Problems 2: 7–17, 1928/1929.
Biss, Irene M
   The contracts of the Hydro-Electric Power Commission of Ontario.
   Economic Journal 46: 549–554, 1936.
— Recent power legislation in Ontario. Canadian Journal of Economics and
   Political Science 2: 212–215, 1936.
Bladen, M   L
   Construction of railways in Canada to the year 1885. Contributions to
   Canadian Economics 5: 43–60, 1932.
— Construction of railways in Canada Part II from 1885 to 1931. Contributions
   to Canadian Economics 7: 61–107, 1934.
Blaine, William E
   Ride through the garden of Canada. Wentworth Bygones 10: 48–52, 1973.
   Hamilton, Grimsby and Beamville Electric Railway Co.
Blust F   A
   The water levels of Lake Ontario. Inland Seas 18: 136–139, 1962.
Bond, C   C   J
   Tracks into Ottawa: the construction of railways into Canada's capital.
   Ontario History 57: 123–134, 1965.
Bonbright, J   C
   Power aspects of the St. Lawrence waterway. Canadian Journal of
   Economics and Political Science 8: 176–185, 1942.

Bradshaw, W   R
  The Georgian Bay archipelago. Canadian Magazine of Politics, Science, Art
  and Literature 15: 16–23, 1900.
Brady, A
  The Ontario Hydro-Electric Power Commission. Canadian Journal of
  Economics and Political Science 2: 331–353, 1936.
Breithaupt W   H
  The railways of Ontario. Ontario Historical Society. Papers & Records 25:
  12–25, 1929.
— Waterloo county railway history. Waterloo Historical Society. Annual
  Report 5: 14–23, 1917.
Bridle, A
  How the Grand Trunk handles freight. Industrial Canada 11: 136–138,
  1911.
Brock, R   W
  The Welland Ship Canal and its place in the progress of the Niagara
  peninsula. Industrial Canada 30(no. 11): 62–65, 1930.
Brown, A   Grant.
  Automobiles in Canada. Canadian Magazine of Politics, Science, Art and
  Literature 21: 327–334, 1903.
Brown, George W
  The St. Lawrence waterway in the nineteenth century. Queen's Quarterly
  35: 628–642, 1928.
— Some aspects of the St. Lawrence deepening project. Journal of the
  Canadian Bankers' Association 36: 177–185, 1929.
Brown, Harry W
  The coming of the telephone to Kitchener. Waterloo Historical Society.
  Annual Report 28: 98–101, 1940.
Brown, R   R
  Great Western Railway of Canada, growth chart. Western Ontario
  Historical Notes 6: 8–9, 1948.
[Brown, S   B   ]
  The Great Lakes – St. Lawrence Seaway and power project. Industrial
  Canada 52(no. 9): 60–62, 1952.
Brown, W   Russell.
  Ships at Port Authur and Fort William. Inland Seas 1(no. 4): 45–51, 1945.
Buchanan, E   V
  Reminiscences. Western Ontario Historical Notes 14(no. 5): 26–38, 1958.
  Ontario Hydro.
Building a causeway of rock across an arm of Rainy Lake. Industrial Canada
  14: 298–300, 1913.
Building railway in settled country; interesting features in work of construction.
  Industrial Canada 12: 261–263, 1911.
  Canadian northern Ontario railroad.

Burpee, Lawrence J
    Great Lakes, an international heritage. Canadian Geographical Journal 19:
        156–183, 1939.
Bush, Edward F
    Thomas Coltrin Keefer. Ontario History 66: 211–222, 1974.
Cahan, C   H
    The St. Lawrence waterways. Dalhousie Review 8: 490–499, 1928/1929.
Calvin, D   D
    A lake-built ocean vessel. Queen's Quarterly 40: 58–64, 1933.
— Rafting down the St. Lawrence. Canadian Geographical Journal 67:
        158–165, 1963.
        Reprinted from October 1931 issue.
Camm, R   W
    The Great Western empire. Western Ontario Historical Notes 6: 10–18,
        1948.
Campbell, Marjorie Freeman.
    Seventy years with Hamilton's street railway. Wentworth Bygones 2: 16–22,
        1960.
    Reprinted from Centennial number of the *Hamilton Spectator* July, 1946.
The Canadian Niagara Power Co. Industrial Canada 2: 16, 1901.
A Canadian northern railway lake port. Railway and Marine World 11: 9, 11,
        1908.
        Owen Sound.
Carnochan, Janet.
    Bridges over the Niagara River. Niagara Historical Society. Records of
        Niagara 36: 31–37, 1924.
Carriage and wagons. Industrial Canada 5: 727–729,1905.
Carter, DeWitt.
    Port Colborne harbour, etc. Railway and Marine World 10: 701, 1907.
Carty, Arthur C
    Sir Adam Beck. Waterloo Historical Society. Annual Report 13: 159–166,
        1925.
The case of the vanishing towns. Industrial Canada 60 (no. 4): 55–57, 1959.
        St. Lawrence Seaway.
Changes in street paving practice in Toronto. Engineering and Contract Record
        48: 584–586, 1934.
Chapman, A   H
    The new Toronto Hydro-Electric Building. Royal Architectural Institute of
        Canada. Journal 10: 152–156, 1933.
Chapter on Chatham. Hydro News 32(6): 7–9, 13, 1945.
Chevrier, Lionel.
    Opening our waterways. Canadian Spokesman 1(4): 28–35, 1941.
— The St. Lawrence Seaway and power project. Geographical Journal 119:
        400–419, 1953.

Clark, R   J
Electric railway development in Ontario. Railway and Marine World 10: 515, 517, 1907.
Clement, S   B
Construction of T. & N.O. Railway extension to James Bay. Canadian Engineer 66(20): 1–6, 1934.
Cody, William M
Who were the five Johns? Wentworth Bygones 5: 14–17, 1964.
Dickenson, Gibson, Moodie, Patterson, Sutherland, Cataract Power Co., Hamilton.
Cole, Arthur A
Ontario's route to the sea. Canadian Geographical Journal 5: 130–153, 1932.
Collins, Bill.
The sportman's special. Canadian Geographical Journal 47: 14–20, 1953.
Railway in Haliburton.
Common, Lela F
The Ontario Northland Railway to Moosonee. Canadian Geographical Journal 78: 62–67, 1969.
Conferences on hydro-electric power shortage. Industrial Canada 19(no. 7): 53, 1918.
Connor, James MacArthur.
The danger to the 'Hydro'. Canadian Forum 7: 140–141, 1927.
Conquering patriotism reigns; Toronto's great tribute to Sir Thomas Shaughnessy. Railway and Marine World 11: 457, 459, 461, 1908.
The construction of the C.P.R. lake and rail in 1878 at the French River. Thunder Bay Historical Society. Papers 18 and 19: 47–49, 1926/1927 and 1927/1928.
Cooke, Henry R
Transportation for Metropolitan Toronto. Community Planning Review 21(no. 1): 23–30, 1971.
Couture, Joseph-Marie.
De L'Aviron . . . A . . . L'Avion. Société Historique du Nouvel-Ontario. Documents Historiques 39–40: 7–133, 1961.
Cowan, John M
The Great Western Railway. Wentworth Bygones 5: 2–13, 1964.
Craick, W   Arnot.
The linking of Montreal and Toronto; fifty years of railroad communication. Canadian Magazine of Politics, Sciences, Art and Literature 28: 40–44, 1907.
Craig, Thelma.
The B.&W. becomes a memory. Canadian National Magazine 38(9): 8–9, 19–20, 1952.
Railroad between Brockville and Westport, Ontario.

Cronyn, V   P
    Grade separation and arterial highway planning in London, Ontario. Town
    Planning 7: 144–146, 1928.
Currie, A   W
    Freight rates and regionalism. Canadian Journal of Economics and Political
    Science 14: 427–440, 1948.
— Rate control on Canadian public utilities. Canadian Journal of Economics
    and Political Science 12: 148–158, 1946.
— The St. Lawrence waterway. Queen's Quarterly 58: 558–572, 1951.
Curry, Frederick C
    The Rideau Canal system. Inland Seas 21: 210–216, 1965.
— The St. Lawrence canals. Inland Seas 10: 214–215, 1954.
— St. Lawrence steamboat days. Inland Seas 7: 264–271, 1951.
Dainton, Douglas G
    Transportation facilities in northeastern Ontario. Monetary Times 128(5):
    87, 89, 1960.
Davies, Frank.
    Design and Toronto's subway. Canadian Art 11: 145–147, 1954.
Day, J   W   H   and B   J   Thomson.
    Medico-legal identification of disaster victims. Canadian Bar Review 28:
    661–671, 1950.
    "Noronic" disaster, Toronto Harbour, September 17, 1949.
Dempsey, John B
    Canada Steamship Lines, Limited: World's largest inland water
    transportation company. Inland Seas 15: 4–14, 1959.
Denis, Keith (comp.).
    Shipwrecks on Lake Superior's north shore since 1816. Thunder Bay
    Historical Museum Society. Papers and Records 3: 22–26, 1975.
Details of Toronto's proposed subway system. Canadian Transportation 48:
    205–213, 1945.
Detweiler envisioned St. Lawrence Seaway in 1912. Waterloo Historical Society.
    Annual Volume 47: 18–20, 1959.
Developments at the Canadian "Soo". Industrial Canada 2: 40, 1901.
Dill, Charles W
    Wings over Ontario. Canadian Geographical Journal 52: 42–63, 1956.
Dixon, Ronald.
    International bridge opening, big day for Sault Ste. Marie. Monetary Times
    130(11): 66, 68, 1962.
Dobbin, F   H
    An hydraulic lift lock. Canadian Magazine of Politics, Science, Art and
    Literature 23: 425–428, 1904.
Dodds, Ronald.
    Long Branch: Canada's first flying school. Canadian Geographical Journal
    88(no. 4): 22–29, 1974.

Doherty, L   A   W
>The Great Lakes as a transportation artery. Industrial Canada 33(no. 9):
>88–93, 1933.

Donohoe, E   F   Jr.
>From covered wagon to steam railway: Kitchener's saga of transportation
>links Conestoga wheel ruts and steel rails in industrial development.
>Canadian National Magazine 32(4): 6, 16–17, 1946.

Dosey, Herbert W
>Algoma argosy. Inland Seas 10: 9–13, 1954.

Dowling, Edward J
>Car ferries on the Detroit River. Western Ontario Historical Notes 10:
>97–102, 1952.

Draper, D   C
>Traffic law enforcement. Industrial Canada 47(no. 3): 265–267, 1946.

Due, John F
>Railways into Huron, Grey and Bruce. Western Ontario History Nuggets
>23: 1–11, 1955.
>One map, unpaginated included at the end of the article.

— Sir Adam Beck and the Hydro radial proposals. Upper Canada Railway
>Society. Bulletin 50: n.d.

Duffell, S
>Roads to resources; western Ontario project. Canadian Mining Journal
>82(no. 4): 77–79, 1961.

Duncan, James S
>Highway to the inland seas. Canadian Geographical Journal 58: 152–160,
>1959.

Dunlap, David A   Canadian Mining Journal 45: 1101, 1924.

Dunning, Phil.
>Montgomery Inn. Canadian Collector 10(no. 4): 23–27, 1975.

Eadie, James A
>Edward Wilkes Rathbun and the Napanee Tamworth and Quebec
>Railway. Ontario History 63: 112–130, 1971.

Earl, W   M
>A review of Ontario's new highway safety legislation. Industrial Canada
>49(no. 3): 247–248, 1948.

Electric power from Niagara. Industrial Canada 6: 590, 1906.

Electric railways; a Toronto railway judgment. Railway and Marine World 12:
>49, 51, 1909.

Electric railways; Niagara, St. Catharines and Toronto railway. Railway and
>Marine World 9: 213–215, 1906.

Electric railways; the Hamilton Street Railway case. Railway and Marine
>World 10: 267, 269, 1907.

Electrical apparatus. Industrial Canada 5: 721–722, 1905.

Elford, Jean.
>The St. Clair River: center span of the Seaway. Canadian Geographical
>Journal 86: 18–23, 1973.

— Tunnels along the St. Lawrence Seaway. Canadian Geographical Journal
   91(no. 4): 25–31, 1975.
— What lake tankers mean to central Canada. Canadian Geographical
   Journal 88(no. 5): 24–31, 1974.
Ellis, P   W
   Electric power development at Niagara. Industrial Canada 4: 358–359,
   1903.
Elson, John M
   Ontario Hydro 60-cycle changeover reaches 250,000 mark. Industrial
   Canada 52(no. 8): 126, 1952.
Facilities and traffic of the port of Hamilton. Canadian Railway and Marine
   World 38: 477–478, 1935.
Facilities and traffic of the port of Toronto. Canadian Railway and Marine
   World 38: 427–432, 1935.
Fenwick, A   R
   Wings over the bush. Canadian Geographical Journal 29: 156–185, 1944.
Fessenden, R   A
   Special articles [in relation to Ontario Power Commission]. Industrial
   Canada 6: 648–652, 1906.
Fiftieth anniversary of Hydro. Waterloo Historical Society. Annual Report 41:
   9, 1953.
The 50th anniversary of the Hydro-Electric Power Commission of Ontario –
   1906–1956. Waterloo Historical Society. Annual Report 44: 11–12, 1956.
A fight for access to the waterfront. Industrial Canada 8: 351, 1907.
   Toronto waterfront.
Filey, Mike.
   Trillium – 1910: side-paddle ferry re-joins Toronto Islands fleet. York
   Pioneer 71(2): 17–21, 1976.
The first sod of the Canadian Pacific turned. Thunder Bay Historical Society.
   Papers 7: 13–16, 1916.
   Reprinted from: *Toronto Globe*, June 10, 1875.
Fleming, Roy F
   Disaster on the Thames River, near London, Ontario. Inland Seas 15:
   299–305, 1959.
— Shipwrecks of Lake Ontario. Inland Seas 32: 216–220, 1976.
— The White Cloud Island tragedy of 1869. Inland Seas 6: 126–127, 1950.
   Wiarton, Colpoy's Bay.
Foley, K   W
   St. Lawrence Seaway – impact on Ontario. Ontario Economic Review 7(no.
   4): 3–12, 1969.
Foresaw Niagara Falls development. Industrial Canada 21(no. 9): 210, 1921.
Fox, William Sherwood.
   Wreck of the steamer Simcoe. Inland Seas 8(no. 4): 29–32, 1952.
Freeman, R   E
   The St. Lawrence – Great Lakes deep waterway. Nineteenth Century 97:
   815–822, 1925.

Gaby, F   A
    The safety employment of electrical apparatus; rules and regulations
    adopted by the Hydro-Electric Power Commission of Ontario to protect life
    and property from the hazards arising from the use of electricity. Industrial
    Canada 27(no. 5): 44–47, 51, 1926.
— Some interesting aspects of the Hydro system. Hydro-Electric Power
    Commission of Ontario. Bulletin 18: 273–290, 331–341, 356–367, 1931.
Galt, Preston and Hespeler Street Railway. Railway and Marine World 10:
    271, 1907.
The Georgian Bay ship waterway. Industrial Canada 7: 790–792, 1907.
Gigantic power development underway at Niagara Falls. Industrial Canada
    52(no. 10): 132, 1952.
Gilbertson, F   S
    Increased power for Ontario. Industrial Canada 48(no. 4): 66–71, 1947.
Gilpin, W   E
    A telegraph in Hanover in the twenties. Bruce County Historical Society.
    Yearbook 35–39, 1975.
Goforth, William Wallace.
    The economic consequences of the St. Lawrence project; a Canadian view.
    Queen's Quarterly, 35: 148–155, 1927.
Gould, Filomena.
    A sixth great lake. Inland Seas 23: 121–128, 1967.
Graham, John.
    Reflections on a planning failure: Ontario Hydro's proposed Nanticoke to
    Pickering transmission corridor. Plan Canada 13: 61–72, 1973.
Grant, Alexander J
    Welland Ship Canal. Welland Historical Society. Papers and Records 3:
    58–70, 1927.
Gray, Edward C
    Siting Hydro transmissions lines: the Solandt Commission and the
    Nanticoke – Pickering decision. Plan Canada 15: 164–175, 1975.
The Guelph and Goderich Railway. Railway and Marine World 10: 805, 807,
    1907.
[Gutelius, F   P   et al.]
    Toronto Union Station, tracks, etc. Railway and Marine World 11: 163,
    1908.
Hales, David.
    A railway through the Kawarthas: the Ontario and Quebec Railway.
    Canadian Rail no. 287: 372–383, 1975.
Hall, David J
    The development of roads in Elgin county, Ontario 1850–1880. Western
    Ontario Historical Notes 26: 36–48, 1972.
Hall, G   Edward.
    Sir Adam Beck. Western Ontario Historical Notes 16: 19–27, 1960.
Hallman, D   E
    Lakehead Harbour. Lakehead University Review 6: 73–84, 1973.

Hammond, M   O
> A river of Ontario. Canadian Magazine of Politics, Science, Art and
> Literature 54: 515–521, 1920.
> Grand River.

Harrington, Lyn.
> The Dawson route. Canadian Geographical Journal 43: 136–143, 1951.
> — Historic Rideau Canal. Canadian Geographical Journal 35: 278–291, 1947.

Harrington, Lyn and Richard Harrington.
> The Welland Canal. Canadian Geographical Journal 34: 202–215, 1947.

Hearn, Richard L
> Ontario Hydro – a pattern for progress. Canadian Geographical Journal 50:
> 216–227, 1955.

Heating apparatus. Industrial Canada 5: 723–724, 1905.

Hebden, Joan (ed.).
> The old P.D. Thunder Bay Historical Museum Society. Papers and Records
> 4: 1–2, 1976.
> Port Arthur, Duluth & Western Railroad.

Heenan, Warren.
> Rapid transit and property values. Community Planning Review 17(1): 4–9,
> 1967.

Hewitt, W   H
> Transportation from the steel to Red Lake. Canadian Mining Journal 55:
> 468–469, 1934.

Heyl, Erik.
> Railroad ferry boats on the Niagara River. Inland Seas 17: 97–104,
> 225–226, 1961.
> — The steamboat Kingston; was she built into the steamboat Bavarian. Inland
> Seas 16: 309–312, 1960.

Hilborn, Ivan M
> Independent telephone systems. Waterloo Historical Society. Annual
> Volume 46: 39–41, 1958.

Hirthe, Walter M
> Where is the Two Friends? Inland Seas 31: 186–191, 1975.
> Ship built at Port Burwell.

Hoan, Daniel W
> The St. Lawrence Seaway – navigation aspects. Canadian Geographical
> Journal 36: 52–69, 1948.

Hogg, Thomas H
> The eastern Ontario system. Hydro-Electric Power Commission of Ontario.
> Bulletin 25: 342–351, 1938.
> — The Georgian Bay system. Hydro-Electric Power Commission of Ontario.
> Bulletin 25: 297–303, 1938.
> — The Hydro-Electric Power Commission of Ontario: a study in public service.
> Hydro-Electric Power Commission of Ontario. Bulletin 29: 1–15, 1942.
> — Ontario Hydro's Thunder Bay development. Electrical News and
> Engineering 51 (17): 16–17, 36, 1942.

— Power development in northern Ontario. Engineering Journal 20: 124–130, 1937.
— Hydro today and the frequency problem. Industrial Canada 47(no. 1): 78–81, 1946.
— Hydro power for industry. Industrial Canada 41(no. 2): 37–39, 1940.
Holton, F   J   [et al.]
   History of the Windsor and Detroit ferries. Essex Historical Society. Papers and Addresses 3: 5–23, 1921.
Hopkins, E   C
   Toronto Harbour; significant history – magnificent plans. York Pioneer and Historical Society. Annual Report 23–32, 1970.
House, Arthur W
   A million horsepower in the making. Industrial Canada 53(no. 12): 49–52, 1953.
   Niagara Falls.
Howard, W   A
   The Ontario Car Ferry Company 1905–1950. Inland Seas 6: 111–113, 1950.
Hudson, T   C
   The southern Ontario district (across the system). Canadian National Railways Magazine 20(July): 8–9, 1934.
Hulchanski, John David.
   Citizen participation planning: a look at the Metropolitan Toronto Transportation Plan Review. Plan Canada 14: 23–29, 1974.
Hutchison, Helen.
   From Fifth Lake to the falls: one hundred years of water power, problems and perils on the Napanee River. Lennox and Addington Historical Society. Papers and Records 15: 28–57, 1976.
L'Hydro-Electric Commission de l'Ontario. L'Actualité Economique 7: 376–379, 1931.
The Hydro-Electric Power Commission of Ontario. Mer Douce 3(2): 53–57, 1924.
Hydro-electric progress in construction and investigation; an official review. Industrial Canada 22(no. 3): 192–194, 1921.
Hydro electric shortage in Ontario. Industrial Canada 20(no. 10): 51–52, 1920.
"Hydro" service in eastern Ontario. Industrial Canada 31(no. 2): 71–75, 1930.
International rate case; an important ruling in transportation case. Industrial Canada 8: 19–21, 1907.
   Freight rates in Ontario.
An interview with Captain Dick of the S.S. Rescue. Thunder Bay Historical Society. Papers 14: 13–14, 1923.
   Copied originally from the Kingston Whig, into the Thunder Bay Sentinal of June 28, 1886.
Irwin, William Gilbert.
   The development of the Sault Ste. Marie Canal. Canada Educational Monthly 24: 295–298, 1902.

Jackman, W   T
   Canada's weal not fostered by the St. Lawrence waterway plan. Railway
   Age 92: 599–602, 1932.
— The St. Lawrence waterway project. Canadian Political Science Association.
   Papers and Proceedings 4: 213–244, 1932.
Jackson, G   G
   Highways and by-ways: the Welland Ship Canal. Commonwealth and
   Empire Review 56(4): 245–247, 1932.
James, T   C
   Expansion of Hydro service in northern Ontario mining districts. Canadian
   Mining Journal 60: 811–816, 1939.
— Power supply in northern Ontario mining districts. Hydro-Electric Power
   Commission of Ontario. Bulletin 23: 326–345, 1936.
Johnson, Robert C
   Logs for Saginaw; the development of raft-towing on Lake Huron. Inland
   Seas 5: 37–41, 83–90, 1949.
Joining two countries by a tunnel; trains will run between Windsor and Detroit
   through twin tubes under the river. Industrial Canada 8: 478–479, 1908.
Jones, A   B
   The new Welland Ship Canal. Military Engineer 23: 527–531, 1931.
Jones, Clayton M
   A Canadian highway of power. Canadian Magazine of Politics, Science, Art
   and Literature 37: 101–108, 1911.
   Ontario Hydro.
Jones, Roger M
   The Yankcanuck. Inland Seas 2(no. 4): 270–272, 1946.
Jurisdiction over electric railways. Railway and Marine World 11: 127, 129,
   1908.
Kaplan, Harold.
   The Toronto Transit Commission: a case study of the structural – functional
   approach to administrative organizations. Canadian Journal of Economics
   and Political Science 33: 171–189, 1967.
Kehoe, J   J
   The Sault Ste. Marie Ship Canal. Canadian Magazine of Politics, Science,
   Art and Literature 1: 589–594, 1893.
Keith, A   G
   Rapid transit in Toronto. Royal Architectural Institute of Canada. Journal
   24: 390–401, 1947.
Kenn, John M
   The Saint Clair River railroad tunnel. Inland Seas 31: 175–185, 1975.
Kenora Railway Y.M.C.A. Railway and Marine World 12: 327, 1909.
Kensit, H   E   M
   Romance of water power. Canadian Geographical Journal 6: 35–48, 1933.
Kerry, J   G   G
   Proposed T. & N.O. Railway extension to James Bay. Canadian Mining
   Journal 35: 349–352, 1914.

Keyser, Walter.
  Excerpts from *The Introduction of Bell's Telephone in London, Ontario, 1875–1880*.
  Western Ontario Historical Notes 9: 95–100, 1951.
Kilbourn, Elizabeth.
  Toronto's new airport. Canadian Forum 43: 257–258, 1964.
King, Francis.
  The problem of the upper St. Lawrence. Queen's Quarterly 36: 2–19, 1929.
— The upper St. Lawrence. Queen's Quarterly 27: 379–395, 1920.
King, John.
  Canadian Pacific Railway construction in 1875 at Fort William. Thunder
  Bay Historical Society. Papers 18 and 19: 44–46, 1926/1927 and 1927/1928.
Kitchener converts to natural gas. Waterloo Historical Society. Annual Volume
  46: 53–57, 1958.
Knight, Cyril W
  The destruction of a valuable water-power on the Frederick House River,
  near Porcupine. Canadian Mining Journal 32: 91–93, 1911.
Konarek, J
  Algoma Central and Hudson Bay Railway: the beginnings. Ontario History
  62: 73–81, 1970.
Kuschel, George F
  Canada Southern Bridge Company. Western Ontario Historical Notes 10:
  92–97, 1952.
Landon, Fred.
  The end of coastal steamer service on Georgian Bay. Inland Seas 11: 68–70,
  1955.
— Engines salvaged from lake depths powered the Manitoba. Inland Seas 26:
  313–315, 1970.
— From cattle boat to passenger steamer. Inland Seas 17: 187–189, 1971.
— John Davis Barnett, 1849–1926. Ontario Library Review and Book-
  Selection Guide 10: 75–77, 1926.
— John Davis Barnett, L.L.D. Waterloo Historical Society. Annual Report 19:
  290–294, 1931.
— The Keefer Lakehead terminal. Inland Seas 18: 267–272, 1962.
— The loss of the Bannockburn. Inland Seas 13: 303–305, 1957.
  On Lake Superior, November 1902.
— The Midland City. Inland Seas 8: 212–213, 1952.
— November shipping disasters. Inland Seas 11: 221–222, 1955.
— The old Huronic. Inland Seas 6: 199–201, 1950.
— Shipbuilding at Midland, Ontario. Inland Seas 6: 131, 1950.
— Sixty years of the C.P.R. Great Lakes fleet. Inland Seas 1(1): 3–7, 1945.
— Some Great Lake tragedies. Western Ontario Historical Notes 5: 31–36,
  1947.
— Their greatness touched the land. Inland Seas 25: 3–11, 1969.
Langton, J   G
  The place of Toronto Harbour in the industrial development of the City.
  Industrial Canada 31(no. 1): 83–83, 1930.

— Toronto Harbour improvements in 1928. Industrial Canada 29(no. 9): 134–135, 1929.

Lee, T   R
Water use in the Great Lakes basin. Canadian Geographical Journal 82: 200–206, 1971.

Lee–Whiting, Brenda.
Energy crisis of 1905 ruined Osceola. Canadian Geographical Journal 93(no. 2): 32–37, 1976.

Legget, Robert F
The St. Lawrence Seaway. Canadian Forum 19: 381–383, 1940.

Leitch, Adelaide.
Nottawasaga – river of the Ontario heartland. Canadian Geographical Journal 79: 122–129, 1969.

Lewis, Alex C
Improving Toronto Harbour. Industrial Canada 13: 728–730, 1912.
— Progress of Toronto Harbour works. Industrial Canada 16: 44–46, 1915.

Low, C   M
Lake Joseph Transportation Company. Canadian Mining Journal 70(no. 8): 121–122, 1949.

Lower, Arthur R   M
The Mariposa Belle. Queen's Quarterly 58: 220–226, 1951.
Inland lake steamer, 1880's–1910.

Lowitt, Richard.
Ontario Hydro: a 1925 tempest in an American teapot. Canadian Historical Review 49: 267–274, 1968.

Lumby, J   R
The port of western Canada. Canadian Magazine of Politics, Science, Art and Literature 28: 33–39, 1907.
Fort William.

Lyon–Fellowes, Evelyn.
Bridge building on the Pagwachnan. Ontario History 54: 191–198, 1962.

McCannel, James.
Shipping on Lake Superior. Thunder Bay Historical Society. Papers 18 and 19: 11–20, 1926/1927, 1927/1928.
— Shipping out of Collingwood. Ontario Historical Society. Papers & Records 28: 16–24, 1932.
— The steamer "Rescue", a pioneer in Great Lakes shipping. Thunder Bay Historical Society. Papers 14: 11–13, 1923.
Collingwood to Fort William run.

Macaulay, Gordon.
Ferries out of Owen Sound. Inland Seas 21: 1965.
2 parts.
Part 1, By ear, by nose, and by God 21: 92–109, 1965; Part 2, Stalwart ladies 21: 194–209, 1965.
— The largest Canadian freighter. Inland Seas 10: 139, 1954.
Colonial Steamship Lines, Port Colborne, Ontario.

— The Soo Locks – second century. Inland Seas 11: 85–88, 1955.

McClure, Donelda.
Hydro Charlie. Bruce County Historical Society. Yearbook 25–27, 1975.
C.J. Halliday of Chesley, Ontario.

McDiarmid, O   J
Some aspects of the Canadian automoblie industry. Canadian Journal of
Economics and Political Science 6: 258–274, 1940.

McDonald, William A
The Caribou retires. Inland Seas 3: 118–119, 1947.
Owen Sound, Georgian Bay.

McDougall, J   L
The St. Lawrence Seaway – the realization of the dream. Industrial Canada
57(no. 3): 186–191, 1956.

McDowell, Franklin Davey.
One hundred years of the Great Western Railway. Wentworth Bygones 9:
2–8, 1971.

McFall, A   David.
Major John Barnett. York Pioneer and Historical Society. Annual Report
72–73, 1972.

MacGibbon, D   A
Economic aspects of the proposed St. Lawrence shipway. Queen's Quarterly
36: 449–467, 1929.

McGuire, B   J
Via the Port of Toronto. Canadian Geographical Journal 57: 118–131, 1958.

McIntyre, Wallace.
Niagara Falls power redevelopment. Economic Geography 28: 261–273,
1952.

MacIver, R   M
The power problem in Ontario. Canadian Forum 2: 486–488, 1922.

McKean, Fleetwood K
Oscar Wing – A captain of the lakes. Inland Seas 22: 137–141, 1966.
— The wreck of the S.S. Waubuno. Inland Seas 21: 302–305, 1965.
Parry Sound, November 22, 1879.

McKee, Samuel.
Canada's bid for the traffic of the middle west: a quarter century of the
history of the St. Lawrence waterway 1849–1874. Canadian Historical
Association. Historical Papers 26–35, 1940.

McKellar, Peter.
How Nepigon Bay lost the C.P.R. shipping port on the Great Lakes. Thunder
Bay Historical Society. Papers 3: 25–27, 1911/1912.
— The Thunder Bay Harbour; this paper treats [of] some of the critical crises
through which the Twin City harbours have passed. Thunder Bay Historical
Society. Papers 5: 19–21, 1914.

McKinnon, Florence.
The Bruce municipal telephone. Bruce County Historical Society. Yearbook
17–19, 1974.

McLean, S   J
Ontario Railway and Municipal Board. Railway and Marine World 9:
505–507, 1906.
McMillan, Ruth F
The Welland canals. Inland Seas 23: 316–319, 1967.
MacPhail, Andrew.
Sir Sandford Fleming. Queen's Quarterly 36: 185–204, 1929.
Magrath, C   A
Ontario Hydro Commission's activities. Canadian Engineer 59: 521–527,
1930.
— Power Commission uses Canadian products, policy of the Hydro-Electric
Power Commission of Ontario. Industrial Canada 29(no. 2): 150–151, 1929.
Mallory, Enid Swerdfeger.
The Trent – Severn waterway in Ontario. Canadian Geographical Journal
66: 140–153, 1963.
Marcolin, Lorenzo.
Canadian Pacific Railway Company steamship lines – last of an era. Inland
Seas 22: 3–16, 1966.
Marine department; Ontario and the Great Lakes. Railway and Marine World
9: 45–47, 103, 167–169, 227–229, 293–295, 359–361, 427–429, 487–489, 559,
619, 685, 687, 761, 1906; 10: 55, 57, 129, 131, 201, 203, 283, 359, 361, 363,
443, 445, 529, 531, 615, 617, 691, 693, 775, 777, 779, 855, 857, 941, 942,
1907; 11: 59, 133–135, 215, 217, 291, 293, 363, 365, 441, 519, 521, 591–593,
675, 677, 749–751, 823, 825, 899, 901, 1908; 12: 61, 63, 143, 220–221,
293–295, 373, 375, 457, 459, 531, 533–534, 621, 623, 701, 703, 783, 785,
859–861, 941, 943, 1909.
Marple, David.
The utility of quantitative sources in the study of transportation and the
growth of Ontario and Quebec urban hierarchy, 1861–1901: an example.
Urban History Review [2](2): 2–7, 1973.
Marshall, J   A   P
Post-war planning for Ontario county and township roads. Engineering and
Contract Record 57: 14–16, 34–35, 1944.
Matheson, Madeline L
The Welland Canal. Women's Canadian Historical Society of Ottawa.
Transactions 2: 64–74, 1909.
Mayer, Harold M
Great Lakes – overseas an expanding trade route. Economic Geography 30:
117–143, 1954.
Meakin, Alexander C
Changes at historic North Channel. Inland Seas 19: 241–242, 1963.
Owen Sound Transportation Company.
Men of the month; the progress of Ontario's government railway. Industrial
Canada 9: 514, 1909.
Merrilees, Andrew.
The railways of Hamilton. Wentworth Bygones 11: 34–48, 1975.

Milestone for Ontario Hydro. Industrial Canada 51(no. 4): 40–41, 1950.
  DesJoachims, Ottawa River.
Millar, Gerald and W   H   VanAllen.
  The Lakehead; an up-to-date harbour. Canadian Geographical Journal 64:
  174–179, 1962.
Mills, James Cooke.
  The gateway to the inland seas; the Sault Ste. Marie Canal and its
  importance to the water-borne commerce of Canada. Canadian Magazine of
  Politics, Science, Art and Literature 38: 27–35, 1912.
— The Welland Canal; its relation to the water-borne commerce in Canada.
  Canadian Magazine of Politics, Science, Art and Literature 34: 403–414,
  1910.
Mitchell, H
  Study of the automobile industry in Canada; interesting three year cycles in
  production and their explanation – estimate of consumption and an
  examination of the efficiency of labour in the industry. Industrial Canada
  29(no. 5): 44–46, 1928.
Mitchell, James.
  Deep waterways movements. Their origin and progress in Ontario. Ontario
  Historical Society. Papers & Records 19: 134–138, 1922.
Modern bridge construction. Industrial Canada 8: 888, 1908.
  French River, Ontario.
Montgomery, Paul.
  Ontario's newest north: the real reasons for the extension of the T. & N.O.
  Railway to the shores of James Bay. Saturday Night 46(36): 17, 22, 1931.
Moore, Lloyd.
  This year's progress on the Welland Ship Canal. Industrial Canada
  23(no. 8): 52–54, 1922.
Morgan, Robert J
  The Georgian Bay Canal. Canadian Geographical Journal 78: 90–97, 1969.
Morrison, Lauchlen P
  Recollections of the Great Lakes, 1874–1944. Inland Seas 4: 219–227, 1948;
  5: 48–51, 1949; 7: 118–127, 1951.
Morrison, Neil F
  Lauchlen Maclean Morrison, captain of the Great Lakes. Inland Seas 4:
  22–28, 1946.
— The life and times of Captain James Donaldson Morrison. Western Ontario
  Historical Notes 9: 3–15, 1951.
  Inland Seas 16: 180–189, 1960.
— Welland Canal anniversary. Inland Seas 10: 287–288, 1954.
Moulton, Harold G   [et al.]
  The St. Lawrence navigation and power project: a reply. Journal of Political
  Economy 38: 345–353, 1930.
Murphy, Rowley W
  C.H.J. Snider. Inland Seas 28: 152, 1972.
— Ghosts of the Great Lakes. Inland Seas 17: 88–96, 195–201, 1961.

— Gibralter Point light. Inland Seas 3: 150–154, 248–253, 1947.
Toronto.
— A history of the Royal Canadian Yacht Club, 1852–1952. Inland Seas 8:
75–82, 193–202, 1952.
— Memories of the third Welland Canal. Inland Seas 19: 260–265, 1963; 20:
21–29, 120–128, 295–302, 1964.
— Resurrection at Penetanguishene. Inland Seas 10: 3–8, 1954.
— Water against land. Inland Seas 4: 75–82, 1948.
— The Welland canals. Inland Seas 15: 172–179, 1959.
Nelles, H   V
Public ownership of electrical utilities in Manitoba and Ontario, 1906–30.
Canadian Historical Review 57: 461–484, 1976.
New Ontario road projects. Canadian Mining Journal 74(no. 11): 82, 1953.
The new T.T.C. subway. Royal Architectural Institute of Canada. Journal 31:
137–162, 1954.
New Union Station for Toronto. Railway and Marine World 10: 93, 95, 1907.
Niagara Navigation Co.'s new steamer. Railway and Marine World 9: 223,
1906.
Steamer "Cayuga."
Niagara, St. Catharines and Toronto railway. Railway and Marine World 11:
513–515, 1908.
The Noronic. Inland Seas 5: 55, 1949.
Burning of the Noronic in Toronto Harbour September, 1949.
The Northern Light Railway Company. Canadian Mining Journal 42:
446–447, 1921.
Northern Navigation Co. of Ontario. Railway and Marine World 9: 105–109,
1906; 10: 105, 107, 1907.
Noxon, William C
Hydro-electric development in Ontario, Canada. United Empire n.s. 16:
285–296, 1925.
Nuclear power station. Canadian Mining Journal 83(no. 7): 61, 1962.
The O.N.R.: quiet consistent service. Canadian Transportation 61(7): 25–28,
1958.
The Ogoki saga. Inland Seas 4: 15–21, 1948.
Ontario Hydro's project to divert waters of the Ogoki River in northern
Ontario.
Ontario. Department of Highways.
Compare 1962 with 1952 maps: road system is transformed. Monetary
Times 30(11): 86–92, 1962.
Ontario electric railway merger. Railway and Marine World 12: 611, 1909.
Ontario general railway legislation. Railway and Marine World 9: 331, 1906.
The Ontario government railway. Canadian Mining Journal 45: 584–585, 1924.
Ontario Hydro and Ontario history. Ontario History 45: 86–87, 1953.
Ontario Hydro changeover. [editorial] Canadian Forum 28: 243–244, 1949.
Ontario Hydro's Otter Rapids project booms round-the-clock. Roads and
Engineering Construction 98(4): 100–103, 1960.

Ontario jurisdiction over railways, etc. Railway and Marine World 10: 175, 1907.

Ontario Northland Railway. Canadian Mining Journal 67: 249, 1946.

Ontario railway subsidies. Railway and Marine World 10: 397, 1907.

Ontario Railway and Municipal Board. Railway and Marine World 9: 403, 1906.

Ontario Railway and Municipal Board rules. Railway and Marine World 9: 507, 509, 1906.

Ontario's last covered bridge. Waterloo Historical Society. Annual Volume 47: 27–28, 1959.
    West Montrose.

Ontario's place in [the] power industry. Industrial Canada 32(no. 9): 90–95, 1932.

Orford, McLeod.
    The last trip of the J.F. Card. Inland Seas 22: 192–195, 1966.

The Owen Sound Transportation Co., Ltd. Inland Seas 24: 250, 1968.

Pammett, Howard.
    The steamboat era on the Trent – Otonabee waterway, 1830–1950. Ontario History 56: 66A–103, 1964.

Parry Sound marine depot, etc. Railway and Marine World 12: 935, 937, 1909.

[Parsons, W   Barclay, et al.]
    Toronto Union Station, tracks, etc. Railway and Marine World 10: 679, 681, 719, 721, 723, 1907.

Paterson, W   H
    Rapid transit in Toronto. Royal Architectural Institute of Canada. Journal 24: 389, 393, 1947.

Patton, Harold S
    Canada's advance to Hudson Bay. Economic Geography 5: 215–235, 1929.

Patton, M   J
    The water-power resources of Canada. Economic Geography 2: 168–196, 1926.

Pequegnat, Marcel.
    Grand River Commission. Waterloo Historical Society. Annual Report 30: 211–224, 1942.

Phelan, Thomas N
    The rules of the road in the operation of motor vehicles. Canadian Bar Review 2: 307–322, 1924.
    The Highway Traffic Act, Ontario.

Pierce, John G
    Transit bearing north. Sylva 10(1): 8–17, 1954.

A plan for improving Toronto Harbour. Industrial Canada 9: 374–375, 1908.

Porte Dauphine: Great Lakes investigator. Canadian Geographical Journal 65: 170–173, 1962.

The ports of Fort William and Port Arthur. Canadian Railway and Marine World 38: 523–526, 1935.

Power at Cobalt. Canadian Mining Journal 30: 429–430, 1909.

Power development at Niagara. Hydro-Electric Power Commission of Ontario.
Bulletin 25: 391–400, 1938.
Power development in Cobalt; Mines, Power Ltd. Cobalt. Canadian Mining
Journal 30: 461, 1909.
Power development at Niagara; a short account of the hydraulic and electrical
development work now under way at Niagara Falls, Ontario. Industrial
Canada 5: 369–372, 1905.
Power shortage in Ontario. Industrial Canada 49(no. 6): 89–90, 1948.
Power situation in Ontario is discussed. Industrial Canada 21(no. 6): 88–89,
1920.
Preston, R   A
The history of the Port of Kingston. Historic Kingston 3: 3–25, 1954.
Ontario History 46: 201–211, 1954; 47: 23–38, 1955.
A public utility reports. [editorial] Canadian Forum 31: 99–100, 1951.
Toronto Transit Commission.
Quaife, M   M
A salute to the Soo Canal. Inland Seas 11: 80–84, 1955.
The R. Bruce Angus. Inland Seas 10: 213, 1954.
Railway legislation in Ontario. Railway and Marine World 9: 209, 1906.
Raney, W   E
The pedestrian and the street car. Canada Law Journal 50: 121–139, 1914.
Raper, Charles L
The St. Lawrence waterway. Current History 51(7): 28–29, 57, 1940.
Rapid transit system for queen city. Industrial Canada 50(no. 8): 54–57, 1949.
Ray, D   Michael.
Cultural differences in consumer travel behaviour in eastern Ontario.
Canadian Geographer 11: 143–156, 1967.
Reaburn, Pauline.
Power from the old mill streams. Canadian Geographical Journal 90(no. 3):
22–27, 1975.
Recent Ontario legislation. Railway and Marine World 9: 315, 1906; 11: 327,
1908; 12: 353, 1909.
Remick, Teddy.
The finding of the vanished Waubuno. Inland Seas 16: 289–290, 1960.
Report of Ross and Holgate, consulting engineers to the Ontario Power
Commission, as to users' requirements and cost of power. Industrial Canada
6: 653–671, 1906.
Report of the Ontario Power Commission. Industrial Canada 6: 638–647, 1906.
Reves, Haviland F
The Detroit, Belle Isle and Windsor Ferry Company 1891–1907. Inland Seas
20: 148–149, 1964.
Reynolds, C   E
Ontario's Northland Railway. Toronto Board of Trade. Journal 41(12):
27–32, 1951.

Rice, Doreen.
    Algoma central steamships. Inland Seas 23: 225–230, 1967; 26: 263–265,
    1970.
— Boats and ships of the circle route. Inland Seas 18: 62–65, 1962.
    Sault Ste. Marie, Ontario.
— Sault Ste. Marie ferries. Inland Seas 20: 115–119, 1964.
Rice, H   R
    Ontario Hydro project at Niagara Falls. Canadian Mining Journal
    74(no. 5): 63–68; 74(no. 6): 77–83, 1953.
Richards, Terence.
    Proposals for a Chatham ship canal, 1857–1893. Inland Seas 24: 202–209,
    1968.
Robbins, J   E
    Provincial power commissions in Canada. Industrial Canada 31(4): 50–52,
    104, 106, 1930.
    Ontario: pp. 51–52.
Roberts, V   M
    Toronto Harbour. Canadian Geographical Journal 15: 88–105, 1937.
Roebuck, A   W
    Exhaustive summary of Hydro affairs. Hydro-Electric Power Commission of
    Ontario. Bulletin 23: 69–108, 1936.
— Toronto's place in the Hydro system. Hydro-Electric Power Commission of
    Ontario. Bulletin 23: 321–325, 1936.
Rogers, W   R
    Water powers in the Porcupine area. Canadian Mining Journal 34: 21–23,
    1913.
Russell, A   L
    A brief history of Port Arthur Harbour. Thunder Bay Historical Society.
    Papers 6: 21–26, 1915.
Rutherford, James H
    Early navigation on the Georgian Bay. Ontario Historical Society. Papers &
    Records 18: 14–20, 1920.
Saca, David P
    Seaway at the cross roads. Canadian Forum 39: 99, 1959.
— Seaway prospects. Canadian Forum 38: 99–100, 1958.
Sainsbury, George V
    Re-routing the historic Welland Canal. Canadian Geographical Journal
    88(no. 3): 36–43, 1974.
Sandwell, Bernard K
    The St. Lawrence waterway. Canadian Geographical Journal 1: 619–634,
    1930.
Schmidt, John T   and Andrew W   Taylor.
    The electric railways of Waterloo county. Waterloo Historical Society.
    Annual Report 44: 22–36, 1956.

Scott, C W
  Power development at Niagara Falls, a great factor in progress of old
  Ontario. Industrial Canada 30(no. 11): 59–61, 67; 30(no. 12): 74–76, 93,
  1930.
Seeley, Sylvia.
  Remedial works programme at Niagara Falls, 1957. Canadian Geographical
  Journal 56: 38–42, 1958.
Sharlin, Harold I
  The first Niagara Falls power project. Business History Review 35: 59–74,
  1961.
Shipbuilding at Collingwood. Industrial Canada 2: 42, 1901.
Shipbuilding in Port Arthur. Industrial Canada 14: 911–912, 1914.
Shipping record of the Port of Goderich for 1882. Inland Seas 1(no. 3): 54–55,
  1945.
Ships and shipbuilding on upper lakes. Industrial Canada 9: 362–364, 1908.
  Mainly Collingwood, Ontario.
Shortt, George.
  The Ottawa River. Canadian Geographical Journal 2: 115–134, 1931.
Simpson, J
  The Trent and Murray canals. Women's Canadian Historical Society of
  Ottawa. Transactions 2: 56–63, 1909.
Sinclair, Robert A
  The 1913 storm once again. Inland Seas 27: 194–198, 207–211, 1971.
Skelton, O D
  The Canadian Northern. Queen's Quarterly 22: 102–111, 1914/1915.
— A seaport for Ontario. Queen's Quarterly 16: 375, 1908/1909.
Smith, Cecil B
  The relation of forests to water powers. Industrial Canada 6: 424–425, 1906.
— Ontario's water powers. Queen's Quarterly 13: 127–133, 1905/1906.
Smith, D E [et al.]
  The Algoma Central Railway company's mineral evaluation program.
  Canadian Mining Journal 85(no. 6): 56–60, 1964.
Smith, George.
  The Blue Water Highway Association. Western Ontario Historical Notes 25:
  20–28, 1969.
Smith, R H
  Great Lakes water levels; a look at the problem of control. Canadian
  Geographical Journal 72: 112–123, 1966.
Smith, R M
  King's highway of Ontario. Canadian Geographical Journal 16: 158–193,
  1938.
— Queen Elizabeth Way. Canadian Geographical Journal 40: 163–179, 1940.
Snider, Winifred.
  E.W.B. Snider, 1842–1921: an appreciation. Waterloo Historical Society.
  Annual Report 44: 8–11, 1956.
  Hydro-Electric Commission of Ontario.

Southworth, Thomas.
    The Lake Nippissing and James Bay Railway. Industrial Canada 2: 3–4,
    1901.
Springer, H   Isabel.
    A history of the Hamilton Street Railway Company. Wentworth Bygones 2:
    22–23, 1960.
Sprock, Albert F
    The Norisle of Owen Sound and Tobermory. Inland Seas 22: 318–320, 1966.
Stafford, Sarah.
    Railway builders of Canada. Thunder Bay Historical Society. Papers 8:
    21–23, 1917.
Stamp, Robert M
    J.D. Edgar and the Pacific Junction Railway: the problems of a nineteenth
    century Ontario railway promoter. Ontario History 55: 119–130, 1963.
Stead, Robert J   C
    Taming the St. Lawrence. Canadian Geographical Journal 51: 176–189,
    1955.
Stirling, Grande.
    The St. Lawrence Seaway – power development. Saturday Night 56(40): 6,
    1941.
Strike, W   Ross.
    Proposals on hydro frequency standardization in Ontario. Industrial
    Canada 47(no. 10): 51–53, 1947.
Swinyard, Thomas to [Edward William] Harris on the merger of the Grand
    Trunk and the Great Western. Western Ontario Historical Notes 10: 44–47,
    1952.
    Merger in 1882.
Sydor, Leon P
    The St. Lawrence Seaway: National shares in seaway wheat benefits.
    Canadian Journal of Economics 4: 543–555, 1971.
T. & N.O. extensions and a customs smelter. Canadian Mining Journal 48:
    303–304, 1927.
    Timiskaming and Northern Ontario Railroad.
Talman, James J
    The development of the railway network of southwestern Ontario to 1876.
    Canadian Historical Association. Historical Papers 53–60, 1953.
Temiskaming and Northern Ontario Railway; operated by a commission –
    owned by the province of Ontario. Canadian Mining Journal 50(Fiftieth
    Anniversary Number): 151–153, 1929.
Tennant, R   D   Jr.
    The Ottawa Electric Railway. Canadian Rail 216: 319–329, 1969.
That controversial Seaway! Industrial Canada 60(no. 4): 43–44, 52, 1959.
Thom, Robert W
    The lone sailor. Inland Seas 10: 140–141, 1954.
— The sinking of the Ottawa. Inland Seas 9: 296–297, 1953.
— The wreck of the Mary Ward. Inland Seas 4: 234–237, 1948.
    Craigleith, Ontario.

Thom, Robert William, 1875–1955. Inland Seas 11: 150, 1955.

Thomas, Redmond.
The beginnings of navigation and the tourist industry in Muskoka. Ontario History 42: 101–105, 1950.

Thompson, Ralph.
The St. Lawrence waterway treaty. Current History 36: 693–696, 1932.

Thomson, Lesslie R
The report of the Chevrier Commission. Canadian Journal of Economics and Political Science 5: 220–225, 1939.

— The St. Lawrence navigation and power project. Journal of Political Economy 38: 86–107, 1930.

— The St. Lawrence navigation and power project: a rejoinder. Journal of Political Economy 38: 479–482, 1930.

— The St. Lawrence waterway and the Canadian railways. Queen's Quarterly 36: 729–738, 1929.

Thomson, T   Kennard.
A comprehensive project for developing power in the Niagara River. Industrial Canada 21(no. 9): 144–146, 1921.

Tinkiss–Good, Mabel.
In the path of progress: St. Lawrence valley sites threatened by the Seaway. Ontario History 45: 165–175, 1953.

Tipton, Thomas L   M
At the mouth of the Grand. Canadian Magazine of Politics, Science, Art and Literature 1: 347–355, 1893.

Todd, John.
The Grand Trunk Pacific's Lake Superior Branch. Canadian Rail no. 296: 258–272, 1976.

Toronto and York Radial Railway. Railway and Marine World 10: 431, 1907.

Toronto International Airport. Royal Architectural Institute of Canada. Journal 41(no. 2): 58–72, 1964.

Toronto subway progress. Canadian Mining Journal 83(no. 7): 53–56, 1962.

Toronto Railway Co.'s employes [sic.] Railway and Marine World 10: 607, 1907.

Toronto Transit Commission opens Canada's first subway. Industrial Canada 54(no. 12): 78, 1954.

The Toronto viaduct question. Railway and Marine World 11: 495, 1908.

Toronto's high-pressure water system. Industrial Canada 9: 511, 1909.

Toronto's port and harbour, 1834–1934. Canadian Railway and Marine World 37: 450–453, 1934.

Toronto's proposed east-west subway route. Canadian Transportation 48: 389–394, 1945.

Toronto's proposed north-south subway route. Canadian Transportation 48: 325–331, 1945.

Transportation for Red Lake area. Canadian Mining Journal 47: 448–449, 1926.

Tunnel trains operated by electricity. Industrial Canada 9: 439, 1908.
St. Clair tunnel.

Tyrrell, Joseph B
    Arrivals and departures of ships; Moose Factory, Hudson Bay, province of
    Ontario. Ontario Historical Society. Papers & Records 14: 163–168, 1916.
Unscheduled launching. Inland Seas 25: 248, 1969.
Van Allen, W   H
    Canal systems of Canada. Canadian Geographical Journal 61: 152–169,
    1960.
Van Steen, Marcus.
    The Trans-Canada Highway makes road-building history north of Lake
    Superior. Canadian Geographical Journal 65: 174–181, 1962.
Walker, David F
    Transportation of coal into southern Ontario, 1871–1921. Ontario History
    63: 15–30, 1971.
Walker, Dean.
    When 60 seconds can cost $15,000.00. Industrial Canada 62(10): 15–23,
    1962.
    TV Commercial production mainly in Toronto.
Walker, Frank N
    The Great Western Railway of Canada. Western Ontario Historical Notes
    10: 110–127, 1952.
Walton, Ivan H
    Developments on the Great Lakes, 1815–1943. Michigan History 27:
    72–155, 1943.
Warner, Fayette S
    The St. Lawrence waterway project. American Academy of Political and
    Social Science. Annals 135: 60–67, 1928.
The waterway pact – a new era for Canada? Canadian Comment 1(8): 6–9,
    1932.
Webster, A   R
    Electric power for Ontario mines. Canadian Mining Journal 48: 184–188,
    1927.
When father was a lad... 65 years ago. Bruce County Historical Society.
    Yearbook 13–14, 1972.
    From *Wiarton Echo*.
Williams, David.
    Shipping on the upper lakes. Huron Institute. Papers and Records 1: 43–59,
    1909.
Williams, W   R
    Assiniboia and Keewatin celebrate golden anniversary. Inland Seas 13:
    148–149, 1957.
— Butcher's Boy and Butcher's Maid. Inland Seas 9: 224–225, 1953.
— The foundering of Manasoo and Hibou. Inland Seas 15: 283–287, 1959.
— The gale-shattered Waubuno. Inland Seas 11: 52–55, 1955.
— The Georgian Bay survey of 1885–1888. Inland Seas 13: 10–16, 1957.
— Georgian Bay's first lighthouse centennial. Inland Seas 12: 134–135, 1956.
— The Jane Miller mystery. Inland Seas 21: 300–301, 1965.

— Killarney Harbour. Inland Seas 17: 52–55, 1961.
— Kincardine and her nuclear power. Inland Seas 17: 284–288, 1961.
— The Leafield was unlucky. Inland Seas 3: 143–144, 1947.
— Lonely Island's lofty light. Inland Seas 6: 275, 1950.
— Lumber carriers of the lakes. Inland Seas 11: 203–207, 1955.
— The New England Transportation Company. Inland Seas 14: 50–54, 1958.
   Hamilton, Ontario.
— The Northwest Transportation Company. Inland Seas 18: 112–118, 1962.
— Whalesback Rock. Inland Seas 23: 33–34, 1967.
Willmot, Elizabeth A
   Petersburg railway station. Waterloo Historical Society. Annual Volume 61:
   4–8, 1973.
Willoughby, William R
   Power along the St. Lawrence. Current History 34: 283–290, 1958.
Wilson, Bertram H
   Transportation to Pickle Lake mining area. Canadian Mining Journal
   70(no. 8): 122–124, 1949.
Winter car ferries; Canadian transportation requires their operation in spite of
   ice and snow. Industrial Canada 12: 927, 1912.
   Windsor – Detroit car ferries.
Wolff, Julius F
   The shipwrecks of Lake Superior, 1900–1909. Inland Seas 27: 28–38,
   113–118, 127–130, 174–187, 297–306, 1971; 28: 51–63, 1972.
Wood, Harold A
   The St. Lawrence Seaway and urban geography, Cornwall – Cardinal,
   Ontario. Geographical Review 45: 509–530, 1955.
Woodhouse, T   Roy.
   Hamilton – the first telephone exchange in the British Empire. Wentworth
   Bygones 3: 24–29, 1962.
World's greatest lift lock; formal opening of hydraulic lift lock at Peterboro,
   some interesting facts regarding its construction and operation. Industrial
   Canada 5: 19, 1904.
The wreck of the "Asia"; the greatest of the tragedies of sea-faring life on the
   Bay. Mer Douce 1(5): 9–12, 1921.
The wreck of the Victoria. London and Middlesex Historical Society.
   Transactions 7: 63–65, 1915.
On May 24, 1881 – sinking of excursion steamer near London.
Wyer, Ramon.
   Fact and fallacy on the St. Lawrence. Harvard Business Review 13:
   344–352, 1935.
Yarham, E   R
   The St. Lawrence waterway. United Empire n.s. 28: 431–435, 1932.
Yates, George W
   The Welland Canal. Canadian Geographical Journal 2: 22–37, 1931.
Young, Anna G
   Captains in procession. Inland Seas 13: 299–302, 1957.

— "Great beyond their knowing". Inland Seas 21: 267–276, 1965; 22: 29–34, 1966.
Gildersleeve family of Kingston.
— A Great Lakes saga. Historic Kingston 14: 78–87, 1966.
— The Mackays of Owen Sound. Inland Seas 14: 302–305, 1958.
— The rough diamond. Inland Seas 18: 107–111, 1962.
Captain Peter Campbell.
— Sarnia from the Port-side. Inland Seas 12: 104–109, 1956.
Zeleznik, Robert A
Welland Canal weekend. Inland Seas 15: 319, 1959.

Theses

Ahmed, Sadrudin Abdulmalek, 1936–
The relationship of personality characteristics and television programme preference and viewing behaviour: a study of London, Ontario, housewives. London, Ontario: 1973.
xii, 165 leaves.
Ph.D. thesis, The University of Western Ontario (accepted 1974) (microfilm 20473).   OLU
Andrew, Wayne C
An examination of Williamsburg township in relation to the St. Lawrence Seaway. [Toronto] 1966.
iv, 53 leaves. photos, col. maps (part fold.).
B.A. thesis, University of Toronto.   OTU
Armstrong, Donald John.
A plan for the expansion of the port of Toronto: project. [Toronto] 1964.
iv, 42 [13] leaves. maps (part fold.).
M.Sc. student project, University of Toronto.   OTU
Azuma, Cathrine.
The Spadina Subway: projected land uses. [Toronto] 1976.
ii, 54 [5] leaves. maps (part col.).
B.A. research project, University of Toronto.   OTU
Bateman, Allan J
Home and workplace separation: an analysis of the journey to work in Toronto. London, Ontario: 1974.
vi, 80 leaves. diagrs., maps, tables.
M.A. research paper, The University of Western Ontario.   OLU
Blowes, William James, 1925–
Commodity movement by truck from south-western Ontario points to southern Ontario destinations. [London, Ontario] 1952.
v, 174 leaves. tables (part fold.), diagrs., fold. map.
M.Sc. thesis, The University of Western Ontario.   OLU
Boak, Christopher.
Projected household formation and long-range demands for housing in Ontario as related to electric utility planning. [Toronto] 1966.
ix, 102 leaves. tables, figs.
M.B.A. thesis, University of Toronto.   OTU

Brownell, George Walter, 1923–
    A study of the role played by Great Lakes package freighters between the
    industries of southwestern Ontario and the consumer market of western
    Ontario. [London, Ontario] 1951.
    xii, 135 leaves. tables, fold. maps.
    M.A. thesis, The University of Western Ontario.   OLU
Burn, Douglas.
    The role of mass media in local orientation. [Toronto] 1976.
    [ii] 55 leaves. tables, maps.
    B.A. research project, University of Toronto.   OTU
Burwash, E   M
    Canadian transportation on the Great Lakes. [Toronto] 1951.
    96 leaves. illus., maps (part col.).
    B.A. thesis, University of Toronto.   OTU
Bushell, George.
    An optimizing model of traffic assignment for the freeway system of southern
    Ontario. [Toronto: 1970]
    75 leaves. illus., maps.
    M.A. research paper, University of Toronto.   OTU
Cadwell, James Roy.
    The incidence and causes of automobile accidents in Ontario. [Toronto]
    1932.
    24 leaves. tables, graphs, form.
    M.A. thesis, University of Toronto.   OTU
Cain, Peter Francis.
    The Grand River Railway: a study of a Canadian intercity electric railroad.
    [Waterloo, Ontario] 1972.
    v, 66 leaves. graphs.
    B.A. thesis, Waterloo University College.   OWTL
Camm, Robert Wendell.
    History of the Great Western Railway (of Canada). [London, Ontario] 1947.
    viii, 454 p. illus., fold. maps.
    M.A. thesis, The University of Western Ontario.   OLU
Carr, Robert, 1945–
    A study of some factors relating to pedestrian collisions. Kingston, Ontario:
    1970, c1971.
    x, 168 leaves. tables, figs., facsim.
    M.Sc. thesis, Queen's University.   OKQ
Charboneau, Mark.
    D.B. Detweiler and E.W.B. Snider and the cooperative municipal electric
    power movement of Ontario. [Waterloo, Ontario] 1972.
    ii, 85 leaves.
    B.A. thesis, Waterloo University College.   OWTL
Charlton, Christina.
    An attempt to isolate development factors for prediction purposes: the
    Spadina Subway, a specific case. Toronto: 1976.
    vii, 103 [3] leaves. maps (part col.).
    B.A. research project, University of Toronto.   OTU

Che, Janet Mui Ho.
  Consumer behaviour and the journey to shop: an exploratory approach.
  Waterloo, Ontario: 1971 [c1974]
  iii, 80 leaves. illus.
  M.A. thesis, University of Waterloo (microfilm 18118).   Can
Cosens, C   W   DeWitt.
  The economic value of the water powers of Ontario. London, Ontario: 1916.
  46 leaves.
  [B.A. paper, The University of Western Ontario?]   OLU
Crawford, Richard Paul.
  Journey to work patterns in Sarnia, 1906–1970. London, Ontario: 1973.
  ix, 50 leaves. graphs, tables.
  B.A. thesis, The University of Western Ontario.   OLU
Dahms, Fredric Arthur, 1935–
  Commuting in Waterloo county. London, Ontario: 1962.
  xii, 115 leaves. photos., graphs, tables, maps (part fold.).
  M.A. thesis, The University of Western Ontario.   OLU
Dewar, Kenneth Cameron, 1944–
  State ownership in Canada: the origins of Ontario Hydro. [Toronto] c1975.
  386 leaves.
  Ph.D. thesis, University of Toronto.   OTU
Doucet, Michael J
  Daily patterns of urban transit use: a case study of the Leaside bus route.
  [Toronto] 1970.
  vii, 60 leaves. illus., maps.
  B.A. research paper, University of Toronto.   OTU
Douglas, David James A
  Towards an analysis of the functional efficiency of the rural service center.
  An essay in functional efficiency analysis of the rural service center in the
  context of regional economic development. [Toronto] 1968
  vi, 248 leaves. diagrs., forms, maps.
  M.A. thesis, University of Toronto (accepted 1969).   OTU
Duff, Douglas R
  Consumer hehavioural travel patterns in eastern Ontario with respect to
  certain goods and services. [Toronto] 1971.
  77 leaves. tables, maps.
  B.A. thesis, University of Toronto.   OTU
Ferris, Terry Thomas McCallum.
  History of the London and Port Stanley railway, 1852–1946. [London,
  Ontario] 1946.
  viii, 324 leaves. illus., port, tables, map.
  M.A. thesis, The University of Western Ontario.   OLU
Fine, Richard Michael, 1951–
  A sign-post aided, dead reckoning automatic vehicle monitoring system for
  Metropolitan Toronto. [Toronto] 1975.
  v, 103 leaves. tables, figs., map.
  M.A.Sc. thesis, University of Toronto (awarded 1976).   OTU

George, Victor Alan, 1924–
    The Rideau corridor: the effect of a canal system on a frontier region,
    1832–1895. Kingston, Ontario: c1972.
    vii, 233 [1] leaves. figs. (part fold.), maps (part fold.).
    M.A. thesis, Queen's University (accepted 1973) (microfilm 12,997).   OKQ
Goldberg, Toby, 1938–
    An examination, critique and evaluation of the man communications
    theories of Marshall McLuhan. Madison, Wisconsin: 1971.
    iii, 576 leaves.
    Ph.D. thesis, University of Wisconsin (microfilm 71-20,664).   DA
Goldi, Joan Catherine Hassard.
    A study of the Port of Toronto. [Toronto] 1966.
    48 leaves. tables (part fold.), diagrs.
    B.A. thesis, University of Toronto.   OTU
Grant, John Andrew, 1946–
    An analysis of expressway location. Kingston, Ontario: c1971.
    v, 85 leaves. table, figs., map.
    M.A. thesis, Queen's University.   OKQ
Grenfell, D   Paul.
    Road transport in Ontario, of the type which involves the haulage of small
    and package freight and the trans-shipment of it through transport terminals
    seen from the point of view of the terminals in their nature and operation.
    Toronto: 1958.
    xiv, 95, xv–xvi leaves. illus., maps.
    B.A. thesis, University of Toronto.   OTU
Gwodz, F   J
    Solar heating of buildings. [Toronto] 1954.
    65 leaves. plans, figs., tables.
    M.A.Sc. thesis, University of Toronto.   OTU
Haigh, John Bryan, 1940–
    The use of travel patterns in delimitation of regional boundaries. Kingston,
    Ontario: c1971.
    xiii, 217 [1] leaves. tables (part fold.), figs., maps.
    M.Sc. thesis, Queen's University.   OKQ
Hall, Carl Ansel St. Clair, 1932–
    Electrical utilities in Ontario under private ownership, 1890–1914.
    [Toronto] c1968.
    270 leaves. tables, map.
    Ph.D. thesis, University of Toronto (microfilm 15394).   OTU
Haritos, Zissis, 1940–
    Rational road pricing policies in Canada. [Toronto] c1972.
    xii, 385 leaves. tables, figs.
    Ph.D. thesis, University of Toronto (microfilm 14852).   OTU
Harmelink, M   D
    A study of trip generation figures for a small city as affected by sampling
    rate. Kingston, Ontario: 1963.
    vii, 85, A-1–A-53 leaves. tables, figs., fold. map.
    M.Sc. thesis, Queen's University. (restricted)   OKQ

Harper, George Coy, 1937–
A study of trip attraction characteristics within two Ontario cities. Kingston,
Ontario: 1964.
1 v. (various pagings). tables, figs., maps (1 fold.).
M.Sc. thesis, Queen's University.   OKQ
Harrison, Chester Morgan.
The Temiskaming and Northern Ontario Railway. Kingston, Ontario:
1934.
vi, 69 leaves. tables (part fold.).
B.Com. thesis, Queen's University.   OKQ
Hodgson, Michael John, 1942–
A highway link addition model for southwestern Ontario. [Toronto] 1969.
47 [1]–3 leaves. illus.
M.A. research paper, University of Toronto.   OTU
— Highway network development and optimal accessibility change in the
Toronto-centred region. [Toronto] c1973.
vii, 228 leaves. tables, figs.
Ph.D. thesis, University of Toronto (microfilm 17272).   OTU
Howard, William Ralph.
The problem of the St. Lawrence waterway. [Toronto] 1934.
188 leaves. illus., graph, fold. col. maps.
M.A. thesis, University of Toronto.   OTU
Howell, Peter A
Characteristics of Oakville travel habits. [Toronto] 1975.
1 v. (various pagings). tables.
B.A. research project, University of Toronto.   OTU
Hubbell, MacPherson.
Kingston public utilities. Kingston, Ontario: 1936.
v, 93 leaves. tables, charts.
B.Com. thesis, Queen's University.   OKQ
Hughes, John C
Recent changes in Toronto's St. Clair – Yonge area and the relation of the
Yonge Street Subway. [Toronto] 1970.
vi, 73 leaves. illus., maps (part col.).
B.A. thesis, University of Toronto.   OTU
Hunsberger, Brian A
The railroad and functional urban transition in Stratford, Ontario .
Waterloo, Ontario,1972.
iv, 63 leaves. illus., map.
B.A. thesis, Waterloo Lutheran University.   OWTL
Kajioka, John T
Transportational geography Ottawa. [Toronto] 1955.
xiv, 75 [16] leaves. illus., 14 fold. part col. maps in pocket.
B.A. thesis, University of Toronto.   OTU
Keogh, Brian Michael, 1942–
The role of travel in the recreational day-trip. London, Ontario: 1969.
xi, 148 leaves. graphs, tables, maps.
M.A. thesis, The University of Western Ontario (microfilm 5041).   OLU

Kovaleski, Irena, 1946–
  The impact of the development of the Trans-Canada Highway on selected
  northern Ontario towns. [Toronto] 1969.
  41, xii leaves. maps.
  B.A. research paper, University of Toronto.   OTU
Kruse, William Carl.
  The Ontario Northland railway: a resource development agency. [Waterloo,
  Ontario] 1966.
  vii, 62 leaves. maps.
  B.A. thesis, Waterloo Lutheran University.   OWTL
Lau, Richard.
  Air passenger flow of Toronto. [Toronto] 1971.
  v, 75 leaves. illus., maps.
  B.A. thesis, University of Toronto.   OTU
— Distribution of accessibility in Metropolitan Toronto (1964–1969). [Toronto]
  1973.
  ii, iv, 87 leaves. illus., maps.
  M.A. research paper, University of Toronto.   OTU
Leslie, Donald.
  An investigation into the intensity and extent of carbon monoxide
  concentrations about highway sites. [Toronto] 1970.
  iii, 25 leaves. tables.
  B.A. research paper, University of Toronto.   OTU
Lindsay, Jill.
  Peterborough on the waterways: a study of the changing uses of the local and
  regional watercourses. [Toronto] 1970.
  vii, 87 leaves. col. illus., maps.
  B.A. research paper, University of Toronto.   OTU
Linseman, K   G
  A study of driver behaviour at stop sign intersections. Kingston, Ontario:
  1963.
  xi, 101 leaves. illus., figs. (1 fold.).
  M.Sc. thesis, Queen's University. (restricted)   OKQ
Little, Arthur Graham.
  The Temiskaming and Northern Ontario Railway. [Toronto] 1933.
  54 leaves.
  Undergraduate Commerce thesis, University of Toronto.   OTU
Lockie, Robert Dale, 1948–
  The GO train – a cost-benefit analysis. Kingston, Ontario: c1972.
  ii, 83 leaves. tables, charts, map.
  M.A. thesis, Queen's University (microfilm 11710).   OKQ
Lustig, Gwen C
  Owen Sound: a port on Georgian Bay. [Toronto] 1947.
  50 leaves. illus., maps (part fold. col.).
  B.A. thesis, University of Toronto.   OTU

McArthur, Neil Max, 1921–
    River to seaway. Ann Arbor, Michigan: 1955.
    vi, 172 leaves. illus., maps.
    Ph.D. thesis, The University of Michigan (microfilm 00-12613).   DA
McGuire, Paul.
    An analysis of the development of Ontario's rail network: 1853–1880.
    [Toronto] 1975.
    v, 73 leaves. illus.
    "Submitted to the Geography Department, University of Toronto. April,
    1975."   OTU
McNicol, Sharon Lee.
    Truck transportation and industrial location. [Toronto] 1968.
    iv, 57 leaves. tables, diagrs., map.
    B.A. thesis, University of Toronto.   OTU
Mah, William.
    A study of standards in bus transit planning. [Toronto] c1976.
    vii, 117 leaves. illus., maps.
    M.A.Sc. thesis, University of Toronto.   OTU
Malkoff, Jack J
    Public ownership in action: an analysis of the Ontario Hydro-Electric Power
    Commission after a quarter of a century of operation. New York: 1938.
    70 leaves.
    M.A. thesis, Columbia University.   Columbia
Markovich, Robert, 1940–
    The evolution of public transport networks in Windsor (Ontario) and
    London (Ontario), 1872–1968. Windsor, Ontario: 1971.
    viii, 91 leaves. graphs, maps, tables.
    M.A. thesis, University of Windsor.   OWA
Martin, David James.
    Richelieu and Ontario Navigation Company; the merger of 1911.
    [Waterloo, Ontario] 1968.
    ii, 28 leaves.
    B.A. thesis, Waterloo University College.   OWTL
Martin, Lloyd Frederick.
    The economic supply of electricity and the problem of environmental
    control. [Toronto] 1971.
    v, 66 leaves. tables, figs.
    B.A. thesis, University of Toronto.   OTU
Mathews, Dryden.
    The Detroit Edison Company and Toronto Hydro-Electric System,
    1915–1935. Kingston, Ontario: 1937.
    v, 63 leaves. tables, graphs.
    B.Com. thesis, Queen's University.   OKQ
Mellen, Frances Nordlinger, 1941–
    The development of the Toronto waterfront during the railway expansion
    era, 1850–1912. [Toronto] c1974.
    xi, 386 leaves. illus., figs., maps.
    Ph.D. thesis, University of Toronto (microfilm 31286).   OTU

Michna, Felix Walter, 1946–
Evaluating landscapes for travelling and viewing potential: an examination
of the Ontario Land Inventory's methodology. [Toronto: 1975]
viii, 162 leaves. tables, figs. (part fold), col. photos, fold. maps.
M.Sc.F. thesis, University of Toronto.   OTU
Mink, Frank Joseph.
Project appraisal in Ontario's public utility sector. [Toronto] 1968.
iii, 51 leaves. forms.
M.B.A. thesis, University of Toronto.   OTU
Moras, Harold.
A study of the development of the public transportation system in the city of
Toronto from 1861–1921. [Toronto] 1970.
v, 70 leaves. tables, charts, maps.
B.A. thesis, University of Toronto.   OTU
Morgan, Robert James, 1938–
The Georgian Bay Canal. Kingston, Ontario: 1964.
iv, 143 leaves. maps (part fold.).
M.A. thesis, Queen's University.   OKQ
Morrall, John Frankland, 1942–
Work trip distribution and modal split in the Metropolitan Toronto region.
Waterloo, Ontario: 1971.
viii, 156 leaves. illus., maps.
Ph.D. thesis, University of Waterloo (microfilm 7971).   OWTU
Morrissey, Frederic Patric.
A study of the Hydro-Electric Power Commission of Ontario. New York:
1951.
295 p.
Ph.D. thesis, Columbia University (microfilm 00-02841).   DA
Newton, Antony Herbert, 1946–
An analysis of the location of Class A common carrier truck terminals in the
Metropolitan Toronto planning area from 1940–1971. London, Ontario:
1973.
x, 87 leaves. graphs, tables, maps.
M.A. thesis, The University of Western Ontario (microfilm 16436).   OLU
O'Mara, James.
The Toronto Harbour Commissioners: their role in the development of the
city's waterfront. [Toronto: 1974]
vii, 98 leaves. maps (part col.).
B.A. research paper, University of Toronto.   OTU
Onn, Gerald Alfred, 1932–
The history of the London Street Railway Company (1873–1951). London,
Ontario: 1958.
xii, 375 leaves. illus., photos, maps.
M.A. thesis, The University of Western Ontario.   OLU

Opheim, Lee Alfred, 1930–
  Twentieth century shipwrecks in Lake Superior. Norman, Oklahoma: 1971
  [c1972]
  ix, 353 leaves. illus., maps.
  Ph.D. thesis, University of Oklahoma (accepted 1972) (microfilm
  72-23,989).   DA
Overgaard, Herman Olaf Johan.
  Water problems in southwestern Ontario. New York: 1960.
  308 p.
  Ph.D. thesis, Columbia University (microfilm 60-03126).   DA
Overton, David James Bryan, 1943–
  An examination of models of port development: Lake Erie north shore,
  1784–1870. London, Ontario: 1970.
  xii, 157 leaves. graphs, tables, maps.
  M.A. thesis, The University of Western Ontario (microfilm 7231).   OLU
Owen, Leonard Anderson, 1941–
  Sir Adam Beck and the hydro-electric radial railways. London, Ontario:
  1967.
  vi, 224 leaves. maps.
  M.A. thesis, The University of Western Ontario.   OLU
Owens, Gilbert Brian, 1950–
  Evaluating a highway locational model: the London 402 controversy.
  London, Ontario: 1975.
  x, 113 leaves. illus., maps.
  M.A. thesis, The University of Western Ontario (microfilm 24629).   OLU
Patten, Harold Eugene.
  The undeveloped water power resources of New York State: an examination
  of the Ontario Hydro-Electric Power System as a model plan for their
  development. New York: 1930.
  55 leaves.
  M.A. thesis, Columbia University.   Columbia
Patterson, Ross Henry, 1947–
  Prohibition and disqualification from driving in Ontario. Kingston, Ontario:
  c1972.
  x, 236 leaves. illus.
  LL.M. thesis, Queen's University (microfilm 13027).   OKQ
Perera, Maximus Herbert, 1934–
  A study of the transit systems of small cities in Ontario. [Toronto] 1975.
  x, 171 leaves. tables (1 fold.).
  M.A.Sc. thesis, University of Toronto.   OTU
Pisarzowski, Gerald Paul, 1948–
  Public reaction to the Spadina Expressway. [Toronto] 1971.
  48 leaves. fold. map.
  B.A. thesis, University of Toronto.   OTU

Plewes, James Campbell, 1944–
    The urban rush-hour: an analysis of the Yonge Street Subway system.
    Kingston, Ontario: 1970 [c1971]
    ix, 162 leaves. tables, figs.
    M.A. thesis, Queen's University.   OKQ
Polano, Gary.
    Parking study of Windsor's downtown business district. Part A, consumer
    survey report: an investigation of the habits and attitudes of a sample of
    Windsor consumers towards the downtown shopping area. [Windsor,
    Ontario] 1969.
    100 leaves. map, tables.
    M.B.A. thesis, University of Windsor.   OWA
Porter, William Charles.
    Some problems in regional organization of a large public utility. [Toronto]
    1964.
    v, 79 leaves. illus., facsim., map.
    M.B.A. thesis, Unversity of Toronto.   OTU
Potts, James Malcolm, 1950–
    Concept and location algorithm for a multi-purpose communications
    corridor. London, Ontario: 1975.
    ix, 170 leaves. fold. maps, tables.
    M.A. thesis, The University of Western Ontario.
    Eric Economic Region.   OLU
Pulley, Christine.
    Some aspects of an urban arterial retail ribbon. [Toronto: 1968]
    31 leaves. illus.
    B.A. research paper, University of Toronto.   OTU
Ramsden, Margaret Charlotte.
    The history of the shipping companies on the Great Lakes. [Toronto] 1929.
    199 leaves.
    M.A. thesis, University of Toronto.   OTU
Reynolds, Timothy Malcolm.
    Interpreting the demand surface of a single transport mode: taxicab
    movements in Kingston. Kingston, Ontario: 1975.
    xi, 228 leaves. illus., maps.
    M.A. thesis, Queen's University (microfilm 26306).   OKQ
Riddell, John Barry.
    Toward an understanding of the friction of distance; an analysis of long
    distance telephone traffic in southwestern Ontario. [Toronto] 1965.
    viii, 125 leaves. diagrs., maps (part col.).
    M.A. thesis, University of Toronto (accepted 1966).   OTU
Romero, Louis J
    Automobile warranties in North America with special reference to the
    Ontario situation. Toronto: 1972.
    ix, 126, A1–75, B1–6 leaves.
    LL.M. thesis, York University (microfilm 12601).   OTY

Scott, William Stratton.
   The effect of road de-icing salts on sodium and chloride in two Metropolitan
   Toronto stream systems. Toronto: 1976.
   xvi, 211 leaves. charts, graphs, maps.
   M.A. thesis, York University (microfilm 30944).   OTY
Shortreed, J   H
   Automobile driver characteristics in speed transition zones of small
   municipalities. Kingston, Ontario: 1962.
   v, 137 leaves. illus., figs, map.
   M.Sc. thesis, Queen's University.   OKQ
Sitwell, Oswald Francis George.
   The Great Lake ports of Ontario: a survey of the trade of the Great Lake
   ports of Ontario in the years 1952–1957. [Toronto] 1959.
   89 leaves, fold. map, tables (part fold.).
   M.A. thesis, University of Toronto.   OTU
Smith, Gavin John Anthony, 1947–
   Transportation and urban design: a systems approach to Toronto's future
   transportation network. [Toronto] 1969.
   36, 2 leaves. maps (part fold.).
   M.A. research paper, University of Toronto.   OTU
Smith, William Randy.
   Rail network development and changes in Ontario's urban system,
   1850–1890. Toronto: 1975.
   vi, 106 leaves. charts, maps, tables.
   M.A. research paper, York University.   OTY
Snaith, William.
   Thesis on the construction plant, equipment, and structures of the Niagara
   power development scheme of the Hydro-Electric Power Commission of
   Ontario. Toronto: 1920.
   2 v. diagrs. (part fold., part col.), maps (part fold., part col.), plans (part
   fold.), fold. table.
   C.E. thesis, University of Toronto.   OTU
Stewart, Gregory John, 1946–
   The routing of public transit facilities within an urban area: a linear
   programming approach. Kingston, Ontario: 1970, c1971.
   xii, 202 leaves. tables (one fold), figs.
   M.A. thesis, Queen's University (accepted 1971) (microfilm 7576).   OKQ
Tarver, Glenn Donald, 1942–
   Toronto International Airport: a study of time and space. [Toronto] 1965.
   iii, 56 [4] leaves. col. illus.
   B.A. thesis, University of Toronto.   OTU
Taylor, Robert Stanley, 1917–
   The historical development of the four Welland canals, 1824–1933.
   [London, Ontario] 1950.
   ix, 228 leaves. facsims., illus., maps.
   M.A. thesis, The University of Western Ontario.   OLU

Thompson, Allan Russell.
  The relationship of transportation costs and industrial location in the
  Niagara peninsula. Toronto: 1972.
  xiii, 226 leaves. illus., maps.
  M.A. thesis, York University (microfilm 12609).   OTY
Underwood, Thomas Joseph, 1927–
  A spatial analysis of children's preferences for city streets as travel routes.
  London, Ontario: 1974.
  xiii, 226 leaves. diagrs., illus., maps, tables.
  Ph.D. thesis, The University of Western Ontario (accepted 1975) (microfilm
  24689).   OLU
Vardon, J   L
  Some factors affecting merging traffic on the outer ramp of highway
  interchanges. Kingston, Ontario: 1959.
  viii, 144 leaves. illus., tables, figs.
  M.Sc. thesis, Queen's University.   OKQ
Waite, William David, 1944–
  Road transportation in Ontario: problems in planning. London, Ontario:
  1966.
  xi, 124 leaves. charts (part fold.), tables, maps.
  M.A. thesis, The University of Western Ontario.   OLU
Ward, David Hadley.
  The development of ports on the Great Lakes. Toronto: 1930.
  124 leaves. illus., plans, photos, maps (part col., part fold.).
  Commerce undergraduate thesis, University of Toronto.   OTU
Warling, John Douglas.
  The electric power industry in Ontario: an analysis of the operations of an
  integrated power system. [Toronto] 1965.
  vii, 75 leaves. illus., maps.
  B.A. thesis, University of Toronto.   OTU
Waters, Nigel Michael, 1950–
  The growth of the southern Ontario railway system: a network analysis.
  London, Ontario: 1973.
  xi, 148 leaves. graphs, tables, maps.
  M.A. thesis, The University of Western Ontario (microfilm 16463). OLU
Watson, J   S
  Solar energy heating. [Toronto] 1951.
  43 leaves. figs., tables.
  M.A.Sc. thesis, University of Toronto.   OTU
Wells, William Douglas, 1945–
  How railways came to Ontario: the historical geography of railway
  development to 1880. Waterloo, Ontario: 1968.
  viii, 76 leaves. fold. maps.
  B.A. thesis, Waterloo University College.   OWTL
West, G   H
  The collection of solar energy. [Toronto] 1952.
  94 leaves. fold. plans, tables, figs.
  M.A.Sc. thesis, University of Toronto.   OTU

Westland, Stuart Ian.
  The land transport geography of Hamilton, Ontario. [Hamilton, Ontario]
  1950.
  x, 193 leaves. maps (part fold.), tables.
  M.A. thesis, McMaster University.   OHM
Wheeler, James Francis, 1946–
  Examination of the journey-to-work trip as a basis for the definition of
  regional boundaries for transportation planning. Kingston, Ontario: 1969.
  x, 133 leaves. tables, figs., maps (part fold.).
  M.Sc. thesis, Queen's University.   OKQ
Whitton, Stephen Lewis.
  An economic analysis of the policy of the Highway Department of Ontario.
  Kingston, Ontario: 1936.
  iii, 87 leaves. tables, charts, maps.
  B.Com. thesis, Queen's University.   OKQ
Wilson, Neil Alexander, 1948–
  Evolution of network configurations and optimal link additions in the
  northern Ontario highway network. Kingston, Ontario: 1975.
  xi, 176 leaves. illus., maps.
  M.A. thesis, Queen's University (microfilm 26326).   OKQ
Wilson, Norman D
  The street system: its function and structure. [Toronto] 1923.
  91 leaves. charts, figs. (part fold.), plates, maps (part fold.).
  C.E. thesis, University of Toronto.   OTU
Wilton, JoAnn.
  Activity systems and conflicting urban core influences: a study of the impact
  of Toronto on the trip orientations and the perceptions of the residents of the
  suburban city of Mississauga. Toronto: 1976.
  vii, 133 leaves. graphs, maps, tables.
  M.A. thesis, York University (microfilm 30959).   OTY
Wishart, Robert B
  The expenditures upon, and changes in, the connecting waterways of the
  Great Lakes. [Toronto] 1931.
  127 leaves. illus., figs., fold. col. map in pocket.
  Undergraduate Commerce thesis, University of Toronto.   OTU
Wong, Ping-Hou.
  The electric rate of the Hydro-Electric Power Commission of Ontario. New
  York: 1941.
  25 leaves.
  M.A. thesis, Columbia University.   Columbia
Woods, John Kenneth, 1931–
  The harbours of the north shore of Lake Erie from Port Dover to
  Leamington. London, Ontario: 1955.
  xiv, 145 leaves. graphs, photos, tables, maps (part col.).
  M.A. thesis, The University of Western Ontario.   OLU

Yao, Joseph Yung-tsin.
  Electricity consumption in Ontario's commercial market – developments
  and potentials. [Toronto] 1967.
  vii, 98 leaves. tables, figs.
  M.B.A. thesis, University of Toronto. (restricted)   OTU
Zaryski, William James.
  The location of marinas as outlets for petroleum products: the case of
  Western Muskoka. [Toronto] 1968.
  43 leaves. figs., tables, map (fold. in pocket).
  B.A. thesis, University of Toronto.   OTU

TRADE

Monographs and Pamphlets
Antelle, Yvonne.
  Do you fear poverty? Honest Ed welcomes you. Winnipeg, Manitoba:
  Greywood Publishing Limited [c1967]
  120 p. illus.   OTU
Bassett, John M
  Timothy Eaton. Don Mills, Ontario: Fitzhenry and Whiteside, Limited
  [c1975]
  59 p. illus., facsims., ports.   OONL
Batten, Jack.
  Honest Ed's story: the crazy rags to riches story of Ed Mirvish. Toronto:
  Doubleday Canada Ltd., 1972.
  237 p. illus.   OTU
Berlin, Ontario. Board of Trade.
  Busy Berlin will just suit you. [Berlin, Ontario: The Board of Trade, 1910]
  16 p. illus.   OTU
Bowman, Fred.
  Trade tokens of Ontario. Published under the auspices of The Canadian
  Numismatic Research Society. n.p.: 1966.
  109 p.   OLU
Brewster, Winfield, 1879–1962.
  The street of business: Queen Street, Hespeler, Ontario. [Hespeler, Ontario:
  T & T. Press] c1954.
  94 p. illus.   OTU
Burton, Charles Luther, 1876–1961.
  A sense of urgency: memoirs of a Canadian merchant. [Robert Simpson
  Company] Toronto: Clarke, Irwin & Company Limited, 1952.
  vi, 363 p. illus., port.   OTU
Canadian exhibitor.
  Colonial Indian Exhibition London, 1886. Toronto: Trades Publishing
  Company, 1886.
  1 v. (unpaged). illus.
  Chiefly county of Wentworth, Ontario.   OKQ

Collard, (Henrietta) Elizabeth, 1917–
    Nineteenth-century pottery and porcelain in Canada. Montreal: McGill
    University Press, 1967.
    xx, 441 p. illus., ports.   OTAR
Eaton, Flora McCrae, 1901–
    Memory's wall: autobiography. With a foreword by Arthur Meighen.
    Toronto: Clarke, Irwin & Company Limited, 1956.
    xii, 214 p. ports.   OTU
Eaton's.
    The story of a store: the history of Eaton's from 1869. Toronto: The T.
    Eaton Co., Limited, 1947.
    52 p. illus., ports.   OKQ
Engelhardt, George W
    Toronto, Canada: the book of its Board of Trade for general circulation
    through the business community 1897-98. [Toronto: R.G. McLean, 1897?]
    181 p. illus., ports., map.   OKQ
Fudger, Harris Henry, 1852–1930.
    Memoir and writings Harris Henry Fudger, 1852–1930. Compiled by his
    daughter. Toronto: Privately printed, 1931.
    119 p. illus., ports.
    Simpson (Robert) Co. Ltd., Toronto.   OKQ
Fyfe, Stewart, 1928–
    The economic basis of Kingston's development. n.p. [1968]
    15 leaves. tables.   OKQ
Galbraith, Thomas, Jr.
    General financial and trade review of the city of Toronto for 1880. Toronto:
    Globe Printing Company, 1881.
    104 p. tables.   OTURS
Geldart, Winston J   1914–1967.
    For want of a nail: the story of Cochrane–Dunlop Hardware Ltd. n.p. [1966]
    viii, 104 p. illus., port.   OTU
George, A   Robert.
    The House of Birks: a history of Henry Birks & Sons. [Montreal] 1946.
    51 p. illus., ports.   OTAR
Glenerin Hall, Erindale, Ontario. A convalescent home for employees of
    Simpson's and Simpson–Sears. Erindale, Ontario: 1956.
    12 p. illus.   OTSTM
Golden jubilee, 1869–1919. A book to commemorate the fifieth anniversary of
    the T. Eaton Co. Limited. Toronto: The T. Eaton Co. Limited [c1919]
    289 p. illus., facsims., ports.   OTU
Hopkins, John Castell, 1864–1923.
    The Toronto Board of Trade: "a souvenir". A history of the growth of the
    Queen City and its Board of Trade, with biographical sketches of the
    principal members thereof. Montreal & Toronto: Sabiston Lithographic &
    Publishing, 1893.
    273 p. illus., ports.   OTAR

Johnston, Hugh, 1840–1922.
  A merchant prince: life of Hon. Senator John Macdonald. Toronto: 1893.
  321 p. port.   OTU
Larkin, Jackie.
  Toronto Trades Assembly, 1871–1971 [notes on history compiled by J.
  Larkin. Toronto] Labour Council of Metropolitan Toronto [1971?]
  40 p. illus.   OTU
McAree, John Verner, 1876–1958.
  Cabbagetown store. Toronto: The Ryerson Press [c1953]
  [113] p. illus.   OTU
Macpherson, Mary Etta.
  Shopkeepers to a nation: the Eatons. Toronto: McClelland and Stewart
  Limited [c1963]
  122 p. illus.   OTU
Metrolpolitan Toronto. Planning Board. Research Division.
  Shopping centres and strip retail distribution, Metropolitan Toronto
  planning area, 1966. [Toronto] 1967.
  32 leaves. maps.   OTUSA
— 1969 [report. Toronto] 1970.
  42 p. maps, tables.   OTUMA
Nasmith, George Gallie.
  Timothy Eaton. Toronto: McClelland & Stewart [c1923]
  xi, 312 p. illus., ports.   OTU
Ontario.
  Submission of the government of Ontario to the Royal Commission on Price
  Spreads of Food Products, Sept. 15, 1958. Presented by the Honourable
  Leslie M. Frost. [Toronto: 1958]
  1 v. (various pagings). diagrs., tables (part fold.).   OTU
Pasternak, Jack.
  The Kitchener market fight. Toronto: Samuel Stevens, Hakkert Company,
  1975.
  236 p. illus., diagrs.
  An account of the controversy over the razing of the old Kitchener market
  and city hall to make way for urban renewal.   OTUSA
Peters, W   R
  The market for farm products in urban centres in northern Ontario, by
  W.R. Peters and E.P. Reid. Ottawa: Department of Agriculture, Marketing
  Service, Economic Division, 1945.
  130 p. tables.   OONL

Ramlalsinch, Roderick D
 A study of the decline of trade at the port of Toronto. Downsview, Ontario:
 York University, 1975.
 76 p. (Department of Geography, York University. Discussion paper, no.
 12).   OTU
Reliance Engravers Limited.
 Number 104 Bond Street: a brief historical sketch of Toronto – especially as
 pertaining to number 104 Bond Street and vicinity. Toronto: Reliance
 Engravers Limited [1972?]
 9 p. illus., map.   OTAR
Simmons, James William, 1936–
 Toronto's changing retail complex; a study in growth and blight. Chicago
 [Department of Geography] University of Chicago, 1966.
 ix, 126 p. illus. (part fold.), maps. (Research paper no. 104).   OTU
Simpson, (Robert) Co.
 The story of Simpson's: 68 years of progress. [Toronto] Wood, Gundy &
 Company Limited [1940]
 11 p. illus., tables.   OTAR
— Thumbnail sketches. Toronto: 1927.
 15 p. illus.   OKQ
Sioux Lookout, Ontario. Junior Chamber of Commerce.
 Sioux Lookout: a progressive northwestern Ontario community. [Sioux
 Lookout: 1953]
 [19] p.   OONL
Smith, (Walter A.) and Company.
 A study of the development of retail facilities in the Ottawa – Hull region:
 prepared for the Regional Municipality of Ottawa – Carleton. Richmond
 Hill, Ontario: W.A. Smith, 1972.
 2, 94 leaves. maps, tables.   OONL
Stanford, Geoffrey H   1906–
 To serve the community: the story of Toronto's Board of Trade. Toronto:
 Published for the Board of Trade of Metropolitan Toronto by University of
 Toronto Press, 1974.
 270 p. illus., port.   OTAR
Stephenson, William.
 The store that Timothy built. [Eaton 1869–1969] Toronto: McClelland and
 Stewart Limited [c1969]
 255 p. illus. (part col.), facsims., ports.   OTU
Toronto. Board of Trade. Book Publishers' Branch.
 Report on the Canadian book trade, 1944. [Toronto: 1944?]
 vii, 50 p.   OKQ
Toronto. City Planning Board.
 Toronto's retail strips: a discussion paper on the viability and future of strip
 retailing in the city. [Toronto] 1976.
 75 p. 17 leaves of plates. illus., maps.   OONL

Toronto business sketches, being descriptive notices of the principal business
  establishments in this city. Toronto: The Daily Telegraph Printing House,
  1867.
  116 p.   OLU
Toronto Industrial Commission.
  The Canadian market: an analysis showing that one-third of the country's
  buying power is concentrated within 100 miles of Toronto. Toronto: The
  Commission [1934?]
  24 p. illus., chart, maps.   OTU
Williams, James Richard Mackenzie, 1923–
  Resources, tariffs, and trade: Ontario's stake. Toronto: Published for the
  Ontario Economic Council by University of Toronto Press [c1976]
  viii, 117 p. (Ontario Economic Council research studies, no. 6).   OTU OKQL

Periodical Articles
Acland, James.
  Toronto's civic square and the Eaton Centre. Journal of Canadian Studies
  1(no. 1): 52–53, 1966.
Aitkin, Douglas.
  Basis of sales of retail business in London, Ontario. Quarterly Review of
  Commerce 11: 147–156, 1944.
Anderson, R   W   and C   T   Craddock.
  Ontario grain corn marketing. Canadian Farm Economics 9(no. 2): 1–8,
  1974.
Armbrust, Duncan.
  Merchandising on the frontier. Canadian Magazine of Politics, Science, Art
  and Literature 40: 377–385, 1913.
Assaly, Louis C   W
  Chain and independent grocery store prices in London, Ontario. Quarterly
  Review of Commerce 7: 287–298, 1940.
Bennett, Thomas A
  Direct marketing of fresh fruit and vegetables – a look at farmer's markets in
  Canada. Canadian Farm Economics 9(no. 5): 1–8, 1974.
Blackburn, Stephen.
  The late Arthur Harvey, F.R.S.C. and R.A.S.C. Royal Society of Canada.
  Transactions s. 2, 11(sect. 2): 31–36, 1905.
Boucher, G   P
  More facts concerning milk consumption in Canada. Economic Annalist 6:
  56–59, 1936.
— Some facts about cheese consumption in certain localities of Canada.
  Economic Annalist 7: 55–57, 1937.
— Some facts concerning milk consumption in Canada. Economic Annalist 6:
  35–37, 1936.

Brouillette, Benoît.
Les courants commerciaux de l'Ontario avec l'extérieur. Royal Society of
Canada. Transactions s. 4, 7: 133–156, 1969.
Campbell, B   A
Additional facts with respect to the Ottawa public market. Economic
Annalist 8: 44–45, 1938.
— The retailing of fruits and vegetables by four chain stores in Toronto.
Economic Annalist 7: 59–62, 1937.
Campbell, B   A   and F   H   Gorsline.
Turnover of fruits and vegetables in Ottawa by independent retail stores.
Economic Annalist 8: 31–32, 1938.
Chown, W   F
The Toronto wholesale fruit and vegetable trade. Economic Annalist 7: 4–8,
1937.
— The wholesale fruit trade – a comparison of trading results in 1929 and 1936.
Economic Annalist 8: 75–77, 1938.
Toronto and Montreal.
The city of London, Ontario. Monetary Times 117(8): 24–26, 28, 107, 1949.
The city of Oshawa. Monetary Times 116(7): 22–26, 105, 1948.
The city of Ottawa. Monetary Times 115(4): 30–34, 100, 1947.
The city of Peterborough. Monetary Times 115(8): 28–32, 110, 1947.
The city of St. Catharines. Monetary Times 118(1): 28–32, 34, 1950.
The city of Toronto. Monetary Times 116(5): 26–28, 30, 91, 92, 1948.
The city of Windsor. Monetary Times 114(10): 32–37, 144, 1946.
Cressman, Ella M
Kitchener market. Waterloo Historical Society. Annual Volume 61: 64–66,
1973.
Dampier, J   Laurence.
Early history of Smallman & Ingram, Limited. Quarterly Review of
Commerce 3: 131–139, 1936.
Dawson, Kenneth C   A
Underwater search for lost fur trade goods in northern Ontario. Thunder
Bay Historical Museum Society. Papers and Records 3: 27–32, 1975.
Enterprising Elmira, Waterloo Historical Society. Annual Report 33: 35–38,
1945.
Faulds, T   B
Factors influencing prices of Ontario fruit. Ontario Agricultural College
Review 22: 196–200, 1910.
Fitzpatrick, J   M
Consumer acceptance of Ontario fresh market peaches. Economic Annalist
25: 58–59, 1955.

Fortin, L and W R Peters.
    The milk market in the Ontario gold belt. Economic Annalist 12: 40–45, 1942.
Hopper, W C
    Charge account records of purchases of cheese by 92 families in the cities of Oshawa and Montreal. Economic Annalist 6: 89–90, 1936.
— The national aspect of the Toronto market for fresh fruits & vegetables. Economic Annalist 7: 26–29, 1937.
— Producers returns from sales of fruits and vegetables on consignment to Toronto commission merchants. Economic Annalist 7: 78, 1937.
— Sales of fruits and vegetables by growers in five districts adjacent to Toronto. Economic Annalist 7: 92–94, 1937.
Hugo–Brunt, Michael.
    Yorkdale shopping centre: a study. Royal Architectural Institute of Canada. Journal 41(no. 6): 38–47, 1964.
Investigation into alleged combine; inquiry made into distribution of fruits and vegetables produced in Ontario. Industrial Canada 27(no. 5): 82, 1926.
Johnston, Charlotte I
    Consumer acceptance of grade A lean bacon in Montreal, Edmonton and Toronto. Economic Annalist 28: 39–47, 1958.
— Consumption of cheese in certain rural areas of Quebec and Ontario, 1954. Economic Annalist 26: 11–18, 1955.
— Preliminary comparison of consumption of various agricultural products in Canada. Economic Annalist 7: 24–25, 1937.
Lang, Elizabeth.
    The Herman Kavelman store, New Dundee, Ontario. Waterloo Historical Society. Annual Volume 50: 81–84, 1962.
McCalla, Douglas.
    The decline of Hamilton as a wholesale center. Ontario History 65: 247–254, 1973.
McClure, Donelda.
    Old Chesley business. Bruce County Historical Society. Yearbook 16–18, 1976.
    James Milne.
McFall, Jean.
    John Paul of Weston. York Pioneer and Historical Society. Annual Report 29–31, 1958.
Mckenzie, N M W J
    Hudson Bay reminiscences. Thunder Bay Historical Society. Papers 11: 19–24, 1920.
Marketing of produce by 93 vegetable and flower growers in Ottawa district. Economic Annalist 8: 14–15, 1938.
Michell, H
    The co-operative store in Canada. Queen's Quarterly 23: 317–338, 1915/1916.
Milk and the consumer. Canadian Forum 27: 201–202, 1947.
    Royal Commission on Milk in Ontario.

Milky way milestone. [editorial] Canadian Forum 27: 172–173, 1947.
    Royal Commission on Milk in Ontario.
Mitchell, E   W   L
    The financing and marketing of the Niagara fruit crop. Journal of the
    Canadian Bankers' Association 32: 446–449, 1925.
Moodie, R   R
    Development of the home market in Ontario. Industrial Canada 25(no. 9):
    141–143, 1925.
Myers, Frank A
    History of the Hudson's Bay Company post at Little Current, Ontario.
    Inland Seas 15: 88–96, 222–232, 276–282, 1959; 16: 47–59, 1960.
Neill, N   P
    The value of the whitefish industry. Industrial Canada 13: 64–65, 1912.
Ontario commission urges improvements in marketing. Economic Annalist
    1(no. 2): 4, 1931.
    Fruit and vegetable production.
Ontario opens new trade and travel centre. Industrial Canada 73(no. 5): 25,
    1972.
Orford, McLeod.
    The Orford Store. Bruce County Historical Society. Yearbook 21–23, 1967.
Patterson, Norman.
    Evolution of a department store. Canadian Magazine of Politics, Science,
    Art and Literature 27: 425–438, 1906.
    Simpson's.
Pearson, G   G
    Grain corn and orderly marketing. Canadian Farm Economics 4(no. 2):
    1–7, 1969.
Poole, Nancy.
    "A man of trust and probity": Sidney Warner. Lennox and Addington
    Historical Society. Papers and Records 14: 64–75, 1972.
Rachlis, M
    Marketing Ontario grain corn. Economic Annalist 19: 134–136, 1949.
Rayner, L   C
    The distribution of perishable foods in Metropolitan Toronto. Canadian
    Farm Economics 1(no. 4): 19–23, 1966.
Reid, Ewart P
    Some observations on the organization and operation of 25 Ontario markets.
    Economic Annalist 8: 58–64, 72–74, 1938.
Reid, Ewart P   and W   R   Peters.
    The marketing of dairy products in the Ontario and Quebec gold belts.
    Economic Annalist 13: 31–32, 42–44, 1943.
Retson, G   C
    Four year summary of labour earnings, costs and prices in fluid milk market
    zones of Ontario. Economic Annalist 12: 20–23, 1942.
Ritchie, T
    Early brick masonry along the St. Lawrence in Ontario.
    Royal Architectural Institute of Canada. Journal 37: 115–122, 1960.

— Joseph van Norman, ironmaster of Upper Canada. Canadian Geographical
    Journal 77: 46–51, 1968.
Roper, E   M
    The industrial development of Ottawa and Hull. Women's Canadian
    Historical Society of Ottawa. Transactions 3: 13–21, 1910.
Roytenberg, M   M
    The development and organization of the Ontario Cheese Producers'
    Marketing Board. Economic Annalist 30: 56–60, 1960.
Seiling, Kenneth and Warren D   Stauch.
    The Brubacher grocery store in Elmira. Waterloo Historical Society. Annual
    Volume 61: 20–23, 1973.
Survey of the marketing of fruits and vegetables in the city of Toronto and
    surrounding district. Economic Annalist 6: 48, 1936.
Teeswater creamery. Bruce County Historical Society. Yearbook 29, 1968.
The Teeswater Creamery Limited. Bruce County Historical Society. Yearbook
    18–21, 1973.
Thom, Ronald J
    Toronto's civic square and the Eaton Centre. Journal of Canadian Studies
    1(no. 1): 49–51, 1966.
Thompson, Walter A
    Consumer purchasing outside the city of London. Quarterly Review of
    Commerce 2(no. 2): 15–23, 1935.
Toner, G   C
    The Great Lakes fisheries; unheeded depletion. Canadian Forum 19:
    178–180, 1939.
Wallace, W   Stewart.
    The post on Bear Island. Queen's Quarterly 46: 185–189, 1939.
Wallis, Hugh M
    James Wallis, founder of Fenelon Falls and pioneer in the early development
    of Peterborough. Ontario History 53: 257–271, 1961.
Waterloo Market closes. Waterloo Historical Society. Annual Volume 53:
    70–73, 1966.
Willis, R   B
    Retail mortality, London, Ontario, Part I: independent grocery stores.
    Quarterly Review of Commerce 10: 162–168, 1944.
Wilson, Alan.
    John Northway's career: an approach to Canadian history. Ontario History
    56: 37–44, 1964.
Woollam, G   E   and K   E   Cann.
    The effects of beef quality on prices in the Toronto area – 1954. Economic
    Annalist 25: 66–68, 1955.
Wray, John B
    One hundred and twenty-six years of arrangement by Blachford and Wray.
    Wentworth Bygones 8: 60–65, 1969.

Zeller homesteads at Breslau. Waterloo Historical Society. Annual Volume 59: 61–63, 1971.

Theses
Anderson, Jack M
  The Brampton central business district: a study in temporal change. [Toronto] 1975.
  36 leaves. tables, figs.
  B.A. research paper, University of Toronto.   OTU
Barber, John Barron.
  Changes in retail trading areas in Ontario. Kingston, Ontario: 1935.
  iv, 80 leaves. tables, charts, fold. map.
  B.Com. thesis, Queen's University.   OKQ
Black, Gordon David.
  The central business district of Niagara Falls. [Toronto] 1963.
  vi, 52 leaves. illus. (part fold.), maps (part col., part fold.).
  B.A. thesis, University of Toronto.   OTU
Bradley, Peter James, 1942–
  Commercial tourist establishments in the Madawaska valley area of southern Ontario. London, Ontario: 1966.
  xii, 198 leaves. fig., plates, tables, maps.
  M.A. thesis, The University of Western Ontario.   OLU
Chan, Chew Ee Kwa, 1948–
  A study on the location of importers in Canada. Windsor, Ontario: 1974.
  viii, 123 leaves. diagrs., maps, tables.
  M.A. thesis, University of Windsor (microfilm 23864).   OWA
Corking, Carolyn Jennifer.
  The historical development of the morphology and function in the central business district, Ottawa, Ontario. [Toronto] 1968.
  v, 62 leaves. maps (part col., part fold.), fold. plans.
  B.A. thesis, University of Toronto.   OTU
Cosgrove, Denis E
  Dry and fancy goods wholesaling in nineteenth century Toronto. [Toronto: 1971]
  v, 94 leaves.
  M.A. research paper, University of Toronto.   OTU
Cowell, Gregory Thomas.
  Functional change in Hamilton's central business district: 1853–1921. [Hamilton, Ontario] 1974.
  ix, 136 leaves. illus., maps, graphs, tables.
  M.A. thesis, McMaster University.   OHM
Crysler, Robert.
  Commercial activity patterns of Collingwood, Ontario. [Toronto] 1974.
  vi, 73 leaves. illus., maps.
  B.A. thesis, University of Toronto.   OTU

Cutler, Phil G
    General trends in retail trade location in the city of Welland. Waterloo,
    Ontario: 1966.
    ii, 47 p. illus., maps, diagrs.
    B.A. thesis, Waterloo Lutheran University.   OWTL
Darling, Howard Jackson.
    Cold storage in the marketing of Ontario fruits and vegetables. [Toronto:
    1938]
    215 leaves.
    M.A. thesis, University of Toronto.   OTU
Darrell, Jennifer.
    The effects of the two universities in Waterloo, Waterloo Lutheran
    University and the University of Waterloo, on retail trade in the city of
    Waterloo. Waterloo, Ontario: 1966.
    viii, 92 leaves. fold. maps, tables.
    B.A. thesis, Waterloo Lutheran University.   OWTL
Dike, Marion Louise, 1943–
    The changing economic structure of Kirkland Lake. London, Ontario: 1969.
    xii, 89 leaves. graphs, tables, maps.
    M.A. thesis, The University of Western Ontario (microfilm 3765).   OLU
Ellinger, Kurt Robert.
    The Toronto milk market 1938 to 1955; an analysis of supply,
    transportation, and distribution. [Toronto] 1957.
    vii, 82 leaves. tables, maps (part col.).
    M.S.A. thesis, University of Toronto.   OTU
Elliott, Bryan Robert.
    Examination of travel time, trade and settlement patterns in eastern
    Ontario, 1941–1971. Ottawa: 1975.
    1 v. (various pagings). maps, tables.
    B.A. research essay, Carleton University.   OOCC
Evans, William Watson.
    Economic account of the city of Owen Sound. London, Ontario: 1910.
    48 leaves.
    B.A. thesis, The Western University of London, Ontario.   OLU
Foty, Marta, 1942–
    Kensington Market, a geographical analysis. [Toronto] 1964.
    xi, 82 leaves. illus., maps (1 fold.).
    B.A. research paper, University of Toronto.   OTU
Foucault, Ernest Allan, 1951–
    A planning policy for single-enterprise communities in northeastern
    Ontario. London, Ontario: 1976.
    ix, 117 leaves. maps, tables.
    M.A. thesis, The University of Western Ontario (microfilm 28223). OLU
Friar, John.
    Hamilton's central business district. [Hamilton, Ontario] 1963.
    ix, 174 leaves. illus., fold. maps.
    M.A. thesis, McMaster University.   OHM

Gordon, Mary E
    Urban renewals impact on selected small retailers. Waterloo, Ontario: 1972.
    vii, 92 leaves. graphs, maps, tables.
    B.A. thesis, Waterloo University College.   OWTL
Halsey, David John.
    The development of the Market Square plaza, Kitchener, and its associated
    impact upon the 'downtown' commercial structure. [Waterloo, Ontario]
    1976.
    xiii, 126 leaves. illus., graphs, maps, plans.
    M.A. thesis, University of Waterloo.   OWTU
Havran, Martin J
    The growth of Windsor, Ontario, 1854–1900. Detroit, Michigan: 1953.
    1 v. (various pagings).
    M.A. thesis, Wayne University.   OTAR
Heidenreich, Conrad Edmund, 1936–
    A study of functions and form in business districts of some small urban
    centres in southern Ontario. [Toronto] 1964.
    vi, 123, vii–xxix leaves. 31 illus. (part col.), diagrs. (part fold., part col.),
    maps (part col.).
    M.A. thesis, University of Toronto (accepted 1965).   OTU
Hoffman, Edith Patience McGregor.
    Scrap metal wholesaling in Metropolitan Toronto: a study in urban
    geography [Toronto] 1965.
    vi, 52 leaves. photos, maps (part col., part fold.).
    B.A. thesis, University of Toronto.   OTU
Hynes, Cecil Vernon.
    An analysis of Michigan and Ontario trade and transport reciprocity.
    Lansing, Michigan: 1965.
    310 p.
    Ph.D. thesis, Michigan State University (microfilm 65-08387).   DA
Ilori, Christopher Oladosu.
    Analysis of retail store merchandising reaction of, and consumer preferences
    for, butter and margarine. [Toronto] 1958.
    vi, 69 leaves. tables, fig., maps.
    M.S.A. thesis, University of Toronto (accepted 1959).   OTU
Jogaratnan, Thambapillai.
    The marketing of soybeans in Ontario, 1945–1954. [Toronto] 1956.
    iii, 110 leaves. tables.
    M.S.A. thesis, University of Toronto.   OTU
Keyes, Robert J
    Postwar changes in ribbon retailing. [Toronto] 1970.
    v, 68 [2] leaves. illus., maps (part col. part fold.).
    B.A. research paper, University of Toronto.   OTU
Koblyk, George Ronald.
    The Ottawa Street business district and the greater Hamilton shopping
    centre: a study in commercial location. [Hamilton, Ontario] 1960.
    [viii] 120 leaves. illus., maps (part fold., part col.).
    B.A. thesis, McMaster University.   OHM

Long, Johannes Christopher.
   Local improvements in the Kingsway business district: a case study of
   commercial adjustment and renewal in an unplanned retail centre. Toronto:
   1975.
   viii, 122 leaves. illus., maps.
   B.A. research paper, University of Toronto.   OTU
Malachowski, Jacqueline H
   Functional change in the central area. [Toronto] 1972.
   v, 39 leaves. illus., maps.
   B.A. thesis, University of Toronto.   OTU
Marshall, John Urquhart.
   The Avenue Road – Eglinton commercial district: a study in urban
   geography. [Toronto] 1961.
   47 leaves. illus., col. diagr., maps (part col., part fold.).
   B.A. thesis, University of Toronto.   OTU
Morrison, Charles A
   Attitudes to growth and development in boomtown Toronto. [Toronto]
   1974.
   88 leaves. illus. (part col.).
   B.A. thesis, University of Toronto.   OTU
Norris, Darrell Alan.
   Business location and consumer behaviour 1882–1910: eastern Grey county,
   Ontario. [Hamilton, Ontario] 1976.
   xv, 231 leaves. illus., maps, graphs.
   Ph.D. thesis, McMaster University (microfilm 29699).   OHM
Plamondon, Maurice.
   Economic implications of the price ceiling policy on whole milk marketing
   in Ontario. [Toronto] 1943.
   60 leaves.
   M.S.A. thesis, University of Toronto.   OTU
Pope, Edward Franklin.
   The development of certain cost curves and the analysis of associated factors
   for milk production on farms selling milk in three Ontario markets.
   [Toronto] 1957.
   ix, 114 leaves. tables, figs.
   M.S.A. thesis, University of Toronto.   OTU
Punter, Lesley B
   Shopping centre development in small cities and towns in Ontario. Toronto:
   1975.
   89 leaves. graphs, maps, tables.
   M.A. research paper, York University.   OTY
Richmond, Gerald M
   Retailing on the Danforth. [Toronto] 1970.
   vi, 44 leaves. tables, maps (part col., part fold. in pocket).
   B.A. research paper, University of Toronto.   OTU

Riddell, John Barry.
    Waterloo county; retail trade in the study of central places. [Toronto] 1963.
    vii, 53 leaves. illus., col. diagrs., maps (part col.).
    B.A. thesis, University of Toronto.   OTU
Riddett, Robert Harry, 1944–
    Urban renewal as a catalyst of change in retail business: the case of civic
    square, Hamilton, Ontario. London, Ontario: 1969.
    ix, 139 leaves. graphs, tables, maps.
    M.A. thesis, The University of Western Ontario (microfilm 5053).   OLU
Rogers, Donald C   1948–
    The cognitive structure of urban shopping centres. Kingston, Ontario:
    c1973.
    viii, 142 leaves. tables, maps.
    M.A. thesis, Queen's University.   OKQ
Shimwell, Frank Harvey Joseph.
    The physical composition and dynamic of centre city with special reference
    to Ottawa. Montreal, Quebec: 1970.
    viii, 30, R1–44, 31–113 leaves. illus., maps.
    M.Arch. thesis, McGill University (microfilm 6048).   Can
Short, Frederick Walter.
    Fruit marketing with special reference to the Niagara peninsula of Ontario.
    Saint Paul, Minnesota: 1947.
    241 leaves. illus., tables.
    Ph.D. thesis, University of Minnesota.   U. Minnesota
Shouldice, William Neil.
    London's changing retail pattern. London, Ontario: 1973.
    xi, 73 leaves. illus., maps, plates, tables.
    B.A. thesis, The University of Western Ontario.   OLU
Skey, Boris Peter.
    Co-operative marketing of agricultural products in Ontario. Toronto: 1933.
    272 leaves. tables.
    Ph.D. thesis, University of Toronto.   OTU
Smart, Russell Charles.
    The history of Yorkdale shopping centre, a marketing viewpoint. [Toronto]
    1966.
    vii, 86 leaves. tables (part fold.), figs., plans.
    M.B.A. thesis, University of Toronto.   OTU
Sneddon, Richard, 1935–
    The central business district of Peterborough, Ontario: retail function and
    structure. Chicago, Illinois: 1962.
    v, 64 leaves. tables, maps.
    M.A. thesis, University of Chicago.   OTU
Spatafora, Vito.
    An historical economic analysis of the distribution of winery-owned stores in
    Ontario: 1927–1971. Waterloo, Ontario: 1973.
    iii, 117 leaves. maps, tables.
    B.A. thesis, Waterloo University College.   OWTL

Steele, June Karenina, 1943–
　　Consumer behavior; shopping activity patterns in Kingston. Kingston,
　　Ontario: 1972, c1973.
　　x, 153 leaves. tables, figs., maps.
　　M.A. thesis, Queen's University (accepted 1973) (microfilm 13708).　　OKQ
Stone, David Paul, 1947–
　　The changing retail systems of Gerrard Street – aspects of three systems.
　　[Toronto] 1968.
　　62 leaves. illus., maps (part col.).
　　B.A. research paper, University of Toronto.　　OTU
Stubbs, Alan Geoffrey S
　　A comparative retail study of Tillsonburg and Ingersoll, Ontario. London,
　　Ontario: 1976.
　　viii, 70 leaves. graphs, maps, tables.
　　B.A. thesis, The University of Western Ontario.　　OLU
Syld, Hasan Ali.
　　The growth of cooperative marketing and merchandising associations in
　　Ontario. [Toronto: 1956]
　　ii, 75 leaves. tables.
　　M.A. thesis, University of Toronto.　　OTU
Weber, Robert E
　　Parking study of Windsor's downtown shopping district, part B, an appraisal
　　of the activities and attitudes of Windsor's downtown retail merchants with
　　regard to parking conditions in the central business district. [Windsor,
　　Ontario] 1969.
　　77 leaves. tables.
　　M.B.A. thesis, University of Windsor.　　OWA
Wiggan, Michael John.
　　A spacial equilibrium model of swine marketed under the Ontario hog
　　producers marketing scheme. [Toronto] 1963.
　　viii, 123 leaves. illus., maps (1 fold. in pocket), diagrs., tables.
　　M.S.A. thesis, University of Toronto.　　OTU
Williams, Gregory P　1947–
　　An analysis of locational factors of wholesaling functions in Windsor,
　　Ontario with emphasis upon grocery wholesalers. Windsor, Ontario: 1974.
　　viii, 139 leaves. illus., graphs (part col.), maps, tables.
　　M.A. thesis, University of Windsor (microfilm 23966).　　OWA
Winter, John Orville.
　　The centre of a city; an examination into the fringe of Toronto's central
　　business district. [Toronto] 1966.
　　x, 131 leaves. tables, photos, maps.
　　M.A. thesis, University of Toronto.　　OTU
Yeung, Yue Man, 1938–
　　The commercial structure of London, Ontario. London, Ontario: 1966.
　　xi, 119 leaves. charts, graphs, tables, maps.
　　M.A. thesis, The University of Western Ontario.　　OLU

Zieber, George Henry.
  Toronto's central business district. [Toronto] 1961.
  xiv, 67 leaves. illus. (part col.), maps (part col., part fold.).
  M.A. thesis, University of Toronto.   OTU

BANKING AND FINANCE

Monographs and Pamphlets
Allen, Robert Thomas, 1911–
  "What do you do here?" "I'm Chairman of the Board"; an informal look at
  London Life entering its second century. [London, Ontario: London Life
  Insurance Company, 1974]
  52 p. illus.   OOA OL
Bank of Montreal.
  Toronto's first bank, 1818: still growing with the city. [Toronto: Bank of
  Montreal, 1937]
  [10] p. illus.   OTAR
Bank of Toronto.
  75 years of service. Toronto: The Bank [1931]
  31 p. illus., ports., facsims.   OTU
Beaverbrook, William Maxwell Aitken, Baron, 1879–1964.
  Courage: the story of Sir James Dunn. Fredericton, New Brunswick:
  Brunswick Press [c1961]
  280 p. ports. (part col.), facsims.   OTU
Campbell, James A
  The story of the London Life Insurance Company, London, Canada.
  London, Ontario: London Life Insurance Company Printing Department,
  1965–1966.
  2 v. illus., facsims., ports.
  Contents: v. 1, 1874–1918; v. 2, 1919–1963.   OLU
Canada Permanent Trust Company.
  A Toronto landmark. One of Toronto's busiest corners: then and now,
  1834–1934. Toronto: The Author, 1934.
  [10] p. illus.   OTAR
Carruthers, Douglas H
  Report on insurance study to Superintendent of Insurance, Ministry of
  Consumer and Commercial Relations, Ontario. [Toronto] Carruthers,
  1973–1975.
  4 v.   OTMCL
Catalogue of fire insurance plans of the Dominion of Canada 1885–1973.
  Catalogue des plans d'assurance du Canada 1885–1973. London, Ontario:
  Phelps Publishing Company, n.d.
  28 p. map.
  Ontario: pp. 1–8.   OKQ

Clarkson, (Gordon) & Co.
  Report on investigation into the affairs of Prudential Finance Corporation
  limited and its subsidiary and affiliated companies. Toronto: 1967.
    1 v. (various pagings). fold. tables.   OTU
Confederation Life Insurance Company, 1871–1971. Toronto: Confederation
  Life Insurance Company, 1971.
    64 p. illus., ports.   OTU
Consumer credit and the lower income family; a legal study and report of a
  survey of 235 families in Hamilton, 1967. Ottawa: Canadian Welfare
  Council, 1970.
    175 p. forms, tables.   OTU
Dominion Bank.
  Fifty years of banking service, 1871–1921. [Toronto] Dominion Bank [c1922]
  227 p. plates, ports.
  "Written by Dr. O.D. Skelton in co-operation with a small committee of the
  Bank's officials".   OTU
Field, Frederick William, 1884–
  Capital investments in Canada: some facts and figures respecting one of the
  most attractive investment fields in the world. 1st ed. Montreal: Monetary
  Times of Canada [1911]
    244 p.
  No copy of second edition located.   OTU
— 3d ed. Montreal: Monetary Times of Canada [1914]
    286 p. tables.   OTU
A fraternity of fellowship; presenting the London Life Men's Club in its first 50
  years. [London, Ontario: London Life Insurance Co., 1974]
    1 v. (unpaged). illus.   OL
Glazebrook, George Parkin de Twenebrokes, 1899–
  Sir Edmund Walker. With a foreword by Sir Robert Falconer. [London]
  Oxford University Press, 1933.
    xv, 160 p. ports.   OTU
Goad, Charles Edward   –1910.
  Insurance plan of Kingston, Ontario. Montreal: The Author, 1892.
    25 p. of maps.   OKQ
— Insurance plan of the city of Toronto, Ontario. Rev. ed. Montreal: 1889.
    2 v. maps.   OTY
— Insurance plan of the city of Toronto [1903–1913]. Toronto: The Author,
  1914–1917.
    8 v.   OTY
— Reference book to accompany insurance plans for Stratford, Goderich, Galt,
  Brampton, Chatham, Windsor, Strathroy, Ingersoll, Woodstock, Simcoe,
  Paris, Dundas. Montreal: Chas. E. Goad, 1882.
    15 books in 1 v.
    Books 1, 7, 10 are missing.   OTAR

Griffin, Frederick, 1889–1946.
  Major-General Sir Henry Mill Pellatt: a gentleman of Toronto, 1859–1939.
  With a foreword by Sir William Mulock. Toronto: Ontario Publishing Co.
  Limited [1939?]
  30 p. illus., ports.   OTU
Hanson, Eric John, 1912–
  Fiscal needs of the Canadian provinces. Toronto: Canadian Tax
  Foundation, 1961.
  vii, 107, 230 p. tables.   OTU
Howard, B   C
  Prudential Finance Corporation limited [et al.] interim report of
  investigation by B.C. Howard. [Toronto: 1967]
  14 [7] leaves. forms.   OTU
Kenyon, Ron, 1931–
  To the credit of the people. Toronto: Ontario Credit Union League, Limited
  [1976]
  303 p. illus., ports.
  History of Ontario credit unions.   OTU
Lambton Loan and Investment Company, Sarnia, Ontario.
  One hundred years of service: the record of the Lambton Loan and
  Investment Company, Sarnia, Ontario. [Sarnia, Ontario: The Company,
  1944]
  39 p. illus., port.   OTU
Landon, Fred, 1880–1969.
  John George Richter, 1854–1932: a brief record of his life and activities, with
  particular reference to his connection with the London Life Insurance
  Company over a period of fifty years. [London, Ontario: 193–]
  24 p. port.   OTU
Lash, G   Herbert.
  Century of fulfilment 1864–1964: a commentary on the times and events in
  the history of the Huron & Erie Mortgage Corporation [London, Ontario:
  Canada Trust – Huron & Erie, 1964?]
  12 p. illus.   OTAR
MacBeth, Roderick George, 1858–1934.
  Sir Augustus Nanton: a biography. Toronto: Macmillan Co. of Canada
  Limited, 1931.
  vi, 130 p. illus., port.   OTU
McKague, William Allison.
  Ontario. Toronto: Monetary Times of Canada, 1924.
  14 p. (The finances of the Canadian provinces series).   OTU
Neufeld, Edward Peter, 1927–
  The financial system of Canada: its growth and development. Toronto:
  Macmillan Company of Canada Limited [c1972]
  645 p. diagrs., tables.   OTU
— Money and banking in Canada: historical documents and commentary.
  [Toronto] McClelland and Stewart [c1964]
  369 p. (Carleton library no. 17).   OTU

Ontario.
　　Submission of the government of Ontario to the Royal Commission on
　　Banking and Finance. Ottawa: Royal Commission on Banking and Finance,
　　1962.
　　ix, 51 p. OONL
Ontario. Committee on Rural Credits.
　　Report. Printed by order of the Legislative Assembly of Ontario. Toronto:
　　Clarkson W. James, printer to the King's Most Excellent Majesty, 1921.
　　45 p.
　　Chairman: W.T. Jackson. OTU
Ontario. Insurance Commission.
　　Report with appendices. Printed by order of the Legislative Assembly of
　　Ontario. Toronto: A.T. Wilgress, printer to the King's Most Excellent
　　Majesty, 1919.
　　107 p.
　　Commissioner: Hon. Mr. Justice Masten. OTAR
Ontario. Interdepartmental Task Force on Foreign Investment.
　　Report. [Toronto: Published by the Economic Planning Branch,
　　Department of Treasury and Economics for the Task Force on Foreign
　　Investment] 1971.
　　iii, 52 leaves. tables.
　　Chairman: C.P. Honey. OTUL
Ontario. Interministerial Committee on Commodity Futures Trading.
　　Report. Toronto: Ministry of Consumer and Commercial Relations, 1975.
　　ix, 127 p.
　　Chairman: Harry S. Bray. OTU
Ontario. Legislative Assembly. Select Committee on Consumer Credit.
　　Final report [Toronto: 1965]
　　ix, 285 p. facsims., tables.
　　Chairman: Henry J. Price. OTUL
— Proceedings, June 24, 1963–November 25, 1964.
　　29 v.
　　v. 1–2, 29 missing. OTAR
— Proceedings, March 25–May 4, 1965.
　　3 v. OTAR
Ontario. Medical Services Insurance Committee.
　　Report. [Toronto] 1964.
　　71 p. facsim.
　　Chairman: J. Gerald Hagey. OTU
— Proceedings. Toronto: Verbatim Reporting Service Official Reporters
　　1963–1964.
　　11 v. OTU
Ontario. Royal Commission on Atlantic Acceptance.
　　Report. [Toronto] 1969.
　　4 v.
　　Commissioner: Samuel H.S. Hughes. OTAR OTU

— Proceedings, October 12, 1965–September 12, 1968.
   127 v. [i.e. 16,764 typewritten pages].   OTAR
Ontario. Royal Commission to investigate trading in the shares of Windfall Oils
   and Mines Limited.
   Report. [Toronto] 1965.
   xviii, 177 p. diagrs. (fold. col.).
   Commissioner: Arthur Kelly.   OTAR OTU
— Proceedings, February 25–June 25, 1965.
   5194 typewritten pages.   OTAR
Perkins, Brian Banbury, 1934–
   Co-operatives in Ontario: their development and current position. Guelph,
   Ontario: Department of Agricultural Economics, Ontario Agricultural
   College, 1960.
   vii, 137 p.   OTMCL
Ross, Victor Harold, 1878–1934.
   History of the Canadian Bank of Commerce, with an account of other banks
   which now form part of its organization. Toronto: Oxford University Press,
   1920–1934.
   3 v. illus., ports.
   v. 1–2 written by Victor Ross; v. 3 written by A. St. L. Trigge.   OTU
Rowat, William Andrew, 1884?–
   Backward glances: memoirs of a minister's son; an autobiography of a
   banker. Illustrations by Wm. Purcell. Original unabridged ed. n.p. [1971?]
   151 p. illus.   OTU
Schull, John Joseph, 1910–
   100 years of banking in Canada; a history of the Toronto – Dominion Bank.
   Illustrated by Merle Smith. [Toronto] Copp Clark Publishing Co. Limited
   [c1958]
   ix, 222 p. illus., tables.   OTU
Stevens, George Roy, 1892–1975.
   The Canada Permanent story, 1855–1955. [Toronto: Canada Permanent
   Mortgage Corp.] 1955.
   60 p. illus., ports.   OTU
Stewart, J   Cunningham.
   The Post Office Savings Bank System of Canada: provinces of Ontario and
   Quebec. Its history and progress. A paper read before the Economic Section,
   British Association at its meeting in Montreal, August, 1884. Montreal:
   Gazette Printing Company, 1884.
   20 p. tables (part fold.).   OOA
The story of the Canada Permanent Mortgage Corporation, 1855–1925.
   Toronto: Head Office, 1925.
   127 p. illus., ports., tables.   OTU
Toronto Stock Exchange.
   Brief to the Royal Commission on Banking and Finance. [Toronto?] 1962.
   xii, 111 p.   OTU
— Appendices. [Toronto?] 1962.
   [42] p. fold. map, diagrs., tables.   OTU

Wellington Fire Insurance Company.
  An historical review 1840–1925. [Guelph, Ontario: The Company, 1925]
  1 v. (unpaged). illus., facsims., ports. OTAR

Periodical Articles
Agar, T   J
  The twelve commandments in insuring an automobile. Canadian Bar
  Review 6: 94–103, 1928.
Appleton, John.
  Changes in provincial legislation affecting banks in 1924. Journal of the
  Canadian Bankers' Association 32: 165–176, 1925.
Beavers, B   W   F
  The history of the Usborne and Hibbert Insurance Company [sic] : part 2.
  Western Ontario Historical Notes 10: 10–13, 1952.
— History of the Usborne and Hibbert Mutual Fire Insurance Company [sic];
  part 1. Western Ontario Historical Notes 9: 149–156, 1951.
Clarke, William N   and J   Graham Esler.
  Bank of London in Canada. Western Ontario Historical Notes 26: 1–12,
  1972.
Colby, C   W
  Sir Edmund Walker. Canadian Banker 56(2): 92–101, 1949.
— Sir Edmund Walker. Dalhousie Review 4: 152–161, 1924.
Evans, Gladstone.
  Head office building for Imperial Bank of Canada. Royal Architectural
  Institute of Canada. Journal 13: 2–11, 1936.
Fletcher, Stephen M
  Canada Life – a first for Hamilton. Wentworth Bygones 10: 37–38, 1973.
Foster, R   Leighton.
  The influence of legislation on the development of life insurance in Canada.
  Canadian Bar Review 31: 786–797, 1953.
— The operation of the Ontario rating law; address given before the eighth
  annual conference of provincial Superintendents of Insurance. Industrial
  Canada 26(no. 7): 39–41, 86, 88, 1925.
Gilbert, Edward Jackson, 1890–1959. Canadian Journal of Economics and
  Political Science 25: 509, 1959.
Gosselin, A
  Rural credit in Canada – part II. Economic Annalist 1(no. 11): 5–8, 1931.
Interim report on automobile insurance. Industrial Canada 30(no. 11): 97, 106,
  108, 1930.
Jamieson, Spruce.
  One hundred and fifty years ago – since. Canadian Banker 52: 102–137,
  1945.
McCrea, Charles.
  British capital for Ontario. Canadian Mining Journal 45: 999, 1924.

Macnab, Alan.
  The Toronto – Dominion Bank. Canadian Paper Money Journal 12: 84–88,
  95, 1976.
Marshall, J
  Bank inspection. Queen's Quarterly 16: 201–202, 1908/1909.
Master minds of Canada: no. 1 – Sir John Aird. Canadian Magazine of Politics,
  Science, Art and Literature 63: 92–94, 1924.
  President of the Bank of Commerce.
Masters, D   C
  Canadian bankers of the last century: 1. Wilham McMaster. Canadian
  Banker 49: 389–396, 1942.
— Toronto vs. Montreal; struggle for financial hegemony, 1860–1875.
  Canadian Historical Review 22: 133–146, 1941.
Mathers, A   S
  The Bank of Nova Scotia building. Royal Architectural Institute of Canada.
  Journal 28: 317–337, 1951.
  In Toronto.
Michell, H
  Profit sharing and producers' co-operation in Canada. Queen's Quarterly
  25: 299–324, 1917/1918.
  Chiefly Ontario.
Minty, Leonard Le M
  Ontario Government Savings Bank and farm loan scheme. Economica 2:
  246–255, 1922.
Morris, R   Schofield.
  Bank of Montreal building, Toronto. Royal Architectural Institute of
  Canada. Journal 26: 365–379, 1949.
— The Manufacturers' Life Insurance Company building. Royal Architectural
  Institute of Canada. Journal 30: 316–326, 1953.
  In Toronto.
New building will house a city population. Industrial Canada 51(no. 5): 49,
  1950.
  Bank of Nova Scotia Building in Toronto.
Parkin, (John B.) Associates.
  The Sun Life building (Toronto). Royal Architectural Institute of Canada.
  Journal 38: 41–52, 1961.
Phelen, R   G
  Automobile insurance – Ontario – section 205(1) of the Insurance Act –
  requirements of proof. Canadian Bar Review 25: 1153–1155, 1947.
Richards, A   E
  Acts of incorporation of co-operative associations in Canada. Economic
  Annalist 5: 3–8, 1935.
Shaw, Lillian M
  The Stinson family of Hamilton. Wentworth Bygones 7: 42–44, 1967.
Smith, Gerald F
  The trial of Billy Ponton: Dominion Bank robbery. Napanee: August 27th,
  1897. Lennox and Addington Historical Society. Papers and Records 14:
  11–21, 1972.

Stirrett, J   R
  The ethics of stock-market speculation in Toronto. Canadian Forum 26:
    208, 1946.
The Toronto Stock Exchange. Royal Architectural Institute of Canada. Journal
    14: 58–66, 1937.
Turner, A   H
  Credit unions in Canada. Economic Annalist 10: 84–88, 1940; 11: 4–8,
    1941.
Wallace, W   Stewart.
  Clarence Bogert. Canadian Banker 45: 20–24, 1937.
Waterloo Mutual – century old. Waterloo Historical Society. Annual Volume
    51: 75–79, 1963.
Wilkes, F   Hilton.
  The Canada Permanent building, Toronto. Royal Architectural Institute of
    Canada. Journal 7: 181–191, 1930.

Theses

Bartlett, Christopher David Sloan.
  A study of some factors affecting growth in Ontario co-operatives. [Toronto]
    1963.
  vii, 122 leaves.
  M.S.A. thesis, University of Toronto.   OTU
Braid, Andrew Falcnor, 1916–
  The role of directors of local co-operatives in Ontario, Canada, in continuity
    and change. Ithaca, New York: 1961.
  xiv, 266 leaves. map, diagrs., tables.
  Ph.D. thesis, Cornell University (microfilm 61-05179).   DA
Dunning, Gregory Roy, 1950–
  Insider trading in corporate securities in Canada. A comparative study of
    insider trading legislation in Ontario, Canada and the Commonwealth.
    [Toronto: 1975?]
  viii, 146 [6] leaves.
  LLM. thesis, University of Toronto (awarded 1976).   OTU
Frost, Alfred John.
  An analysis of Ontario mutual fire insurance companies operating on the
    premium note plan. Kingston, Ontario: 1930.
  42 leaves.
  B.Com. thesis, Queen's University.   OKQ
Lawson, William Morse.
  Market efficiency and the interaction among the three classes of participants
    trading on the Toronto Stock Exchange. Toronto: 1974.
  x, 195 leaves. tables.
  Ph.D. thesis, York University (microfilm 21553).   OTY

McCutcheon, Wilfred Whyte.
  Economic organization and development of the United Farmers Co-
  operative Company, Limited. [Toronto] 1948 [c1976]
  [4] 168, 5 [1] leaves.
  M.S.A. thesis, University of Toronto (microfilm 25491).   OTU
Macdonald, John Atwood Ross.
  A financial history of Ontario, 1939–1947. Worcester, Massachusetts: 1950.
  138 leaves.
  M.A. thesis, Clark University.   Clark U.
McKie, Donald Craig, 1944–
  The use of credit and its effect on life style in a student group. Toronto: 1969.
  67, xxi leaves. tables.
  M.A. thesis, York University (microfilm 3436).   OTY
McKinney, Edward Harvey.
  The organization of the investment field in Ontario. [Toronto] 1922.
  151 leaves.
  M.A. thesis, University of Toronto.   OTU
Manga, Pranlal, 1944 –
  A benefit incidence analysis of the public medical and hospital insurance
  programs in Ontario. Toronto: c1976.
  xxi, 332 leaves. tables, figs.
  Ph.D. thesis, University of Toronto.   OTU
Noble, Keith Robert.
  The disclosure of corporate financial information in Ontario. [Toronto]
  1966.
  55 leaves.
  M.B.A. thesis, University of Toronto.   OTU
Russell, David.
  … A financial history of Hamilton. [Hamilton, Ontario] 1936.
  108 leaves. tables.
  B.A. thesis, McMaster University.   OHM
Saidi, Harum, 1948–
  Victims of automobile accidents and insurance compensation – the struggle
  continues. [Toronto] 1975.
  iv, 189 leaves.
  LL.M. thesis, University of Toronto.   OTU
Simpson, Edward Barclay.
  Some aspects of the issuing of public offerings of non-mining corporate
  securities, registered in Ontario, 1959–1961. [Toronto] 1962.
  ii, 50 leaves. tables.
  M.B.A. thesis, University of Toronto.   OTU
Walker, E   David.
  Cooperative mergers: a study of united cooperatives of Ontario's merger
  strategy. [Guelph, Ontario] 1971.
  vi, 116 leaves. tables.
  M.Sc. thesis, The University of Guelph.   OGU

Whytock, Donald Brown.
   An analysis of the investments of Ontario trust corporations. Kingston,
   Ontario: 1931.
   iv, 86 leaves. figs., tables (part fold.).
   B.Com. thesis, Queen's University.   OKQ

INDUSTRIAL RELATIONS

Bibliography
Blount, Gail (comp.).
   Collective bargaining in Canadian education: an annotated bibliography.
   [Toronto] Ontario Institute for Studies in Education [c1975]
   x, 38 p. (Ontario Institute for Studies in Education. Bibliography series no.
   1).   OTER
Isbester, Alexander Fraser, 1932–
   Industrial and labour relations in Canada: a selected bibliography by A.F.
   Isbester, D. Coates and C.B. Williams. Kingston, Ontario: Industrial
   Relations Centre, Queen's University, 1965.
   120 p. (Industrial Relations Centre. Queen's University. Bibliography series
   no. 2).   OTU

Monographs and Pamphlets
Abella, Irving Martin, 1940–
   Nationalism, communism and Canadian labour: the CIO; the Communist
   Party, and the Canadian Congress of Labour, 1935–1956. [Toronto]
   University of Toronto Press [c1973]
   vii, 256 p.   OTAR
Abella, Irving Martin, 1940–   (ed.).
   On strike: six key struggles in Canada 1919–1949. Toronto: James Lewis &
   Samuel, 1974.
   xv, 196 p. (Major strikes in Canadian history, 1).
   Includes the Stratford chicken pluckers strike, 1933; the Ford Windsor
   strike, 1945; the Oshawa strike, 1937.   OTU
The Artistic Woodwork strike, 1973: a lesson for the Canadian Labour
   movement. Toronto: Right to Strike Committee [1974?]
   28 p. illus. (Right to Strike Committee, pamphlet no. 1).   OTU
Bromke, Adam, 1928–
   The Labour Relations Board in Ontario; a study of the administrative
   tribunal. Montreal: Industrial Relations Centre, McGill University [1961]
   ii, 104 p. table.   OTU
Caloren, Fred, 1934–
   Layoffs, shutdowns and closures in Ontario manufacturing, mining and
   trade establishments January 1971–June 1972. Ottawa: University of
   Ottawa, 1974.
   ix, 298, A78 p. maps, tables.   OTU

Cameron, James Carruthers, 1894–
   The status of trade unions in Canada, by J.C. Cameron and F.J.L. Young.
   Kingston, Ontario: Department of Industrial Relations, Queen's University,
   1960.
   169 p.   OTU
Canada. Department of Labour.
   Wages and hours of labour in Canada, 1920–30. Ottawa: F.A. Acland,
   printer to the King's Most Excellent Majesty, 1931.
   104 p. tables. (Wages and hours of labour. Report no. 14).   OONL
Canadian Labor Party. Ontario Section.
   Programme and standing orders as amended July 1, 1921. Toronto: Allied
   Printing, 1921.
   11 p.   OKQ
Crispo, John Herbert Gillespie, 1933–
   Nurses and their employers: the need for a fresh approach. A report
   prepared for the Board of Directors of the Registered Nurses' Association of
   Ontario. [Toronto] 1963.
   16 p.   OTU
Crysdale, R   C   Stewart, 1914–
   Social effects of a factory relocation: a case study of social and political
   consequences of job displacement. [Toronto: Religious-Labour Council of
   Canada and United Steelworkers of America, 1965]
   25 p. tables.   OTU
Cunningham, Rosella, 1915–
   An analysis of the supervisory process in Middlesex – London District Health
   Unit in 1973. [Toronto: 1973?]
   iv, 167 leaves.   OTU
Deutsch, Antal, 1936–
   Provincial legislation governing municipal labour relations: a comparative
   study of provincial labour legislation governing municipal employer –
   employee relations. [Montreal] Canadian Federation of Mayors and
   Municipalities [1960]
   viii, 61 leaves.   OTU
Eleen, John W   1923–
   Shutdowns: the impact of plant shutdown, extensive employment
   terminations and layoffs on the workers and the community. Prepared by
   John W. Eleen and Ashley G. Bernardine. [Toronto?] Ontario Federation of
   Labour, Research Department, 1971.
   v, 135 p. illus., form.   OTU
Farmer – Labour – Teachers' Conference, 8th, Port Elgin, Ontario, 1967.
   Report of the eighth Farmer – Labour – Teachers' Conference, UAW
   Education Centre, Port Elgin, June 17–18, 1967. n.p.]] 1967]
   35 p.
   Cover title: Community colleges: the new colleges of arts and technology in
   Ontario: Farmer – Labour – Teachers' Conference, 1967.

Sponsored jointly by Canadian Labour Congress and Ontario Federation of
Labour.
Editor: M. Lazarus.   OTV
Farmer – Labour – Teacher Conference, 11th, Port Elgin, Ontario, 1970.
Report of the 11th Farmer – Labour – Teacher Conference, UAW Education
Centre, Port Elgin, June 20–21, 1970. n.p. [ ] 1970]
47 p.
Cover title: Solution to pollution; matter of life and death, Farmer – Labour
– Teacher Conference, 1970.
Sponsored by the Ontario Federation of Labour in cooperation with the
Canadian Labour Congress.
Editor: M. Lazarus   OTV
Ferris, John.
Algoma's industrial and trade union development. [Sault Ste. Marie,
Ontario] The Author, 1951.
122 p. illus.   OTU OTAR
Finkelman, Jacob, 1907–
The Ontario Labour Relations Board and natural justice. Kingston,
Ontario: Industrial Relations Centre, Queen's University, 1965.
iv, 60 p. (Queen's University. Industrial Relations Centre. Reprint series, no.
7).   OTUCR
Ford Motor Company of Canada, Limited.
To complete the record of the strike at Ford of Canada. the twelve-day
wildcat strike ended Friday, Dec. 14, 1951 after a secret ballot by members
of the unions. Windsor, Ontario: The Company, 1951.
14 p.   OW
— The truth about the work stoppage at the Ford – Windsor plants, April
22–24, 1943. Windsor, Ontario: The Company, 1943.
14 p. illus.   OTAR
Ford Motor Company of Canada, Limited. Public Relations Division.
Canadian newspaper editors view the Ford strike. Toronto: The Company,
1954.
88 p.   OONL
Forsey, Eugene Alfred, 1904–
The Canadian labour movement, 1812–1902. Ottawa: Canadian Historical
Association, 1974.
23 p. (Canadian Historical Association booklets no. 27).   OTU
French, Doris Cavell Martin, 1918–
Faith, sweat and politics: the early trade union years in Canada. [Toronto]
McClelland and Stewart [c1962]
154 p.   OTU
Goldenberg, Hyman Carl, 1907–
In the matter of the arbitration between Hydro-Electric Power Commission
of Ontario and the Ontario Hydro Employees' Union, Local 1000, N.U.P.S.E.
– C.L.C.: award of H. Carl Goldenberg, arbitrator, July 26, 1962. [Toronto?
1962?]
25 leaves.   OTU

Submissions to H.C. Goldenberg
Ontario. Hydro-Electric Power Commission.
  Submission to H. Carl Goldenberg, arbitrator, appointed by the Lieutenant
  Governor in Council, pursuant to bill 163, an act respecting a certain
  dispute between the Hydro-Electric Power Commission of Ontario and the
  Ontario Hydro Employees Union, Local 1000, N.U.P.S.E. – C.L.C. Compiled
  by Labour Relations Division. [Toronto?] 1962.
  2 v. illus.   OTU
— Rebuttal. [Toronto?] 1962.
  41 leaves. diagrs.   OTU
Ontario Hydro Employees Union. Local 1000.
  A brief presented by the Ontario Hydro Employees Union, Local 1000,
  N.U.P.S.E. – C.L.C. to the Ontario Hydro Electric Power Commission. n.p.
  [1962?]
  2 v. in 1, diagrs.   OTU

Greening, W   E
  Paper makers in Canada: a history of the Paper Makers Union in Canada.
  n.p.: International Brotherhood of Paper Makers, 1952.
  96 p. map.   OTHOP
Hann, Russell G   (comp.).
  Primary sources in Canadian working class history, 1860–1930, by Russell
  Hann, Gregory Kealey, Linda Kealey & Peter Warrain. Kitchener,
  Ontario: Dumont Press, 1973.
  169 p.   OTU
Hayes, James K
  Perspectives on management rights: the curious logic of the argument for
  reducing industrial discord by removing the mid-term strike bar from labour
  relations legislation. Don Mills, Ontario: Ontario Federation of Labour
  1974.
  1, 87 p. table.   OLU
Horne, Gilbert Richard.
  A survey of labour market conditions, Windsor, Ontario, 1964: a case study
  by G.R. Horne, W.J. Gillen and R.A. Helling. Prepared for the Economic
  Council of Canada. [Ottawa: Roger Duhamel, Queen's Printer, 1965]
  i, 34 p. (Economic Council of Canada. Special study no. 2).   OTU
Industrial democracy and Canadian labour. [Toronto] Ontario Woodsworth
  Memorial Foundation and Praxis Research Institute for Social Change
  [c1970]
  71 p.   OTU
Industrial unionism in Kitchener, 1937–47: researched and written by students
  in the Department of History, Wilfrid Laurier University: edited by Terry
  Copp. Elora, Ontario: Cumnock Press, c1976.
  viii, 99 [30] p. [8] leaves of plates. illus., ports.   OTU
Isbester, Alexander Fraser, 1932–
  Teachers and collective bargaining in Ontario: a means to what end, by

Fraser Isbester and Sandra Castle. [Hamilton, Ontario] Faculty of Business, McMaster University, 1971.
47 p. table. (McMaster University. Faculty of Business. Working paper series no. 1). OTC

Kelly, Laurence Alexander, 1936–
Settlement methods in Ontario collective bargaining; 1970–1973.
[Kingston, Ontario] Queen's University, Industrial Relations Centre [c1974]
12 p. tables. (Industrial Relations Centre, Queen's University. Research and current issues series, no. 22). OTU

Kennedy, Douglas Ross, 1921–1954.
The Knights of Labour in Canada. London, Ontario: The University of Western Ontario, 1956.
127 p. front. (port.), tables. OTAR

Law Society of Upper Canada. Department of Continuing Education.
Strikes, lockouts, picketing, and injunctions. Toronto: The Society, 1974.
139 p. OLU

Laxer, Robert Mendel, 1915–
Canada's unions. Toronto: James Lorimer Company, 1976.
xvi, 341 p. OTU

Lazarus, Morden, 1907–
Years of hard labour: an account of the Canadian workingman, his organizations and tribulations over a period of more than a hundred years. [Don Mills, Ontario: Published by Co-operative Press Associates for the Ontario Federation of Labour, c1974]
116 p. charts, illus., ports., tables. OTU

Lipton, Charles, 1916–
The trade union movement of Canada, 1827–1959. Montreal: Canadian Social Publications Limited, 1966.
xiii, 366 p. OTU
— 2d ed. Montreal: Canadian Social Publications, 1968.
xiii, 366 p. OTU
— 3d ed. Toronto: NC Press, 1973.
xiii, 384 p. illus. OTU

Little, Walter.
Collective bargaining in the Ontario government service. A report of the special adviser. [Toronto] 1969.
viii, 104 p.
Special Adviser: Walter Little. OTAR

Logan, Harold Amos, 1889–
The history of trade-union organization in Canada. Chicago: University of Chicago Press [c1928]
xiii, 427 p. OTU
— Trade unions in Canada: their development and functioning. Toronto: Macmillan Company of Canada Limited, 1948.
xvi, 639 p. illus., charts (fold.), tables. OTU

Miller, Richard Ulric (ed.).
  Canadian labour in transition, edited by Richard Ulric Miller and Fraser
  Isbester. Scarborough, Ontario: Prentice–Hall of Canada Ltd. [1971]
  xviii, 266 p.   OLU
Morris, Leslie Tom, 1904–1964.
  The big Ford strike. [Toronto: Ontario Committee Labor – Progressive
  Party, 1945?]
  7 p.   OKQ
Ontario. Commission of inquiry into wages and living conditions of the men
  employed by the Hydro-Electric Power Commission at the Queenston –
  Chippawa Development.
  [Preliminary report] n.d.
  5 typewritten pages.
  Chairman: Edgar Watson.   OTAR
— Report. [Toronto: 1920]
  4 typewritten pages.   OTAR
— Proceedings, May 20, 26–28, 1920.
  208 typewritten pages.   OTAR
Ontario. Commission on laws relating to the liability of employers to make
  compensation to their employees for injuries received in the course of their
  employment.
  Interim report with the evidence taken and the brief of the Canadian
  Manufacturers' Association. Printed by order of the Legislative Assembly of
  Ontario. Toronto: L.K. Cameron, printer to the King's Most Excellent
  Majesty, 1912.
  478 p.
  Commissioner: William Meredith.   OTAR
— Second interim report with draft of an act to provide for compensation to
  workmen for injuries sustained and industrial diseases contracted in the
  course of their employment. Printed by order of the Legislative Assembly of
  Ontario. Toronto: L.K. Cameron, printer to the King's Most Excellent
  Majesty, 1913.
  40 p.   OTAR
— Final report and second interim report. Printed by order of the Legislative
  Assembly of Ontario. Toronto: L.K. Cameron, printer to the King's Most
  Excellent Majesty, 1913.
  58 p.   OTAR
— Final report with appendices. Printed by order of the Legislative Assembly.
  Toronto: L.K. Cameron, printer to the King's Most Excellent Majesty,
  1913.
  xx, 733 p.   OTAR
Ontario. Committee of inquiry into negotiation procedures concerning
  elementary and secondary schools of Ontario.
  Report: professional consultation and the determination of compensation for
  Ontario teachers. [Toronto] 1972.
  iv, 106 p. tables.
  Chairman: R.W. Reville.   OTER OTUL

Background papers to Ontario Committee of inquiry into negotiation procedures concerning
   elementary and secondary schools of Ontario.
Isbester, Alexander Fraser, 1932–
   Brief to the Special Committee of inquiry into negotiation procedures.
   [Hamilton? 1971].
   [10] leaves.
   Elementary and secondary schools.   OTER
Ontario Association of Education Administrative Officials.
   Professional consultation and the determination of compensation for Ontario
   teachers: the report of the Committee of inquiry, June 1972, "The Reville
   report"; an assessment and reaction. [Toronto: 1973]
   13 leaves.   OTER
Ontario Federation of Labour.
   [Brief submitted to the] Committee of inquiry into negotiation procedures
   concerning the primary [sic] and secondary schools of Ontario. [Toronto?
   1971?]
   6 leaves.   OTER
Ontario School Trustees' Council.
   A submission to the Minister of Education in response to the report of the
   Committee of enquiry into negotiation procedures concerning elementary
   and secondary schools of Ontario, June, 1972. [Toronto] 1972.
   18 p.   OTER
Ontario Secondary School Teachers' Federation.
   A brief to the Committee of inquiry into negotiation procedures concerning
   primary [sic] and secondary schools of Ontario. [Toronto: 1971?]
   1 v. (various pagings).   OTER
— The O.S.S.T.F. position on the Reville Committee report: an overview.
   [Toronto: 1972]
   4, 24 leaves. chart.   OTER
— The O.S.S.T.F. response: professional consultation and the determination of
   compensation for Ontario teachers, the report of the Committee of inquiry.
   [Toronto: 1973]
   15 p. chart.
   President: Daryl Hodgins.   OTER
Ontario Separate School Trustees' Association.
   Brief presented to the Committee of inquiry into negotiation procedures.
   [Toronto: 1971]
   15, 7, 3 leaves.   OTER
Ontario Teachers' Federation.
   A submission to the Minister of Education in response to the report of the
   Committee of inquiry into negotiation procedures, June, 1972. Toronto
   [c1972]
   22 p. chart.   OTER
— A submission to the Minister's Committee on negotiation procedures.
   Toronto: [c1971]
   64 p. illus.   OTER

Ontario. Committee on Child Labour.
> Report. Printed by order of the Legislative Assembly of Ontario. Toronto:
> L.K. Cameron, printer to the King's Most Excellent Majesty, 1907.
> 13 p.
> Chairman: Nelson Monteith.   OTAR

Ontario. Legislative Assembly. Select Committee on Industrial Rehabilitation.
> Report. Printed by order of the Legislative Assembly of Ontario. Toronto:
> Clarkson W. James, printer to the King's Most Excellent Majesty, 1921.
> 17 p.
> Chairman: J. McNamara.   OTAR

Ontario. Legislative Assembly. Select Committee on Labour Relations.
> Interim report. [Toronto: 1958]
> 5 [5] leaves.
> Chairman: James A. Maloney.   OTAR

— Report. [Toronto: 1958]
> 64 p.   OTAR

— Minutes, April 17, 1957–July 10, 1958.
> 1 v. (various pagings).   OTAR

— Minutes, January 15, 1959.
> 2 leaves.   OTAR

— Summary of recommendations contained in Briefs submitted by employee
> organizations, employer organizations and other groups and individuals
> concerning the Labour Relations Act or its administration, 1957-58.
> [Toronto: 1958]
> 62 leaves.   OTAR

— Proceedings, June 24, 1957–May 15, 1958.
> 51 v. [i.e. 4280 typewritten pages]   OTAR

— Briefs.
> 97 v.   OTAR

— [Miscellaneous publications. Toronto: 1958?]
> 1 v. (various pagings).   OTUL

— Jurisdictional disputes in the construction industry. [Toronto] Ontario
> Department of Labour, 1958.
> 32, 4 leaves.   OTUL

— Time lapse in disputes disposed of by the conciliation system under the
> Ontario Labour Relations Act: [report. Toronto] Ontario Department of
> Labour, 1958.
> 1 v. (various pagings).   OTU

Ontario. Legislative Assembly. Select Committee regarding collective
> bargaining between employers and employees.
> Proceedings, February 25–March 18, 1943.
> 13 v. [i.e. 1765 typewritten pages.]
> Chairman: J.H. Clark.   OTAR

Ontario. Royal Commission of Inquiry on Labour Disputes.
> Report, August 1968. [Toronto: Queen's Printer, 1968]
> xxv, 263 p. tables.
> Commissioner: Ivan C. Rand.   OTAR OTU

— Proceedings, January 11–June 2, 1967.
  5432 typewritten pages.   OTAR
— Briefs.
  75 v.   OTAR
— Summaries of the proceedings and briefs.
  2 v.   OTAR
— Press clippings.
  3 v.   OTAR

Papers re Ontario Royal Commission of Inquiry on Labour Disputes
Fisher, Douglas Mason, 1919–
  What do you know about the Rand report? Is it "a textbook for the
  promotion of conflict and turmoil in Ontario's industrial relations"? By
  Douglas Fisher and Harry Crowe. [Toronto: Ontario Federation of Labour,
  1969]
  [12] p. ports.
  "Six articles reprinted from *Toronto Telegram* between September 12th and
  20th, 1968."   OTL
Ontario Federation of Labour.
  Submission of the Ontario Federation of Labour to Hon. Dalton Bales in
  regards to the report of the Royal Commission Inquiry into Labour Disputes
  in the province of Ontario. [Don Mills, Ontario: Ontario Federation of
  Labour] 1969.
  17 p.   OTY

Ontario. Royal Commission on Labour – Management Relations in the
  Construction Industry.
  Report. [Toronto] 1962.
  xi, 79 p.
  Commissioner: H. Carl Goldenberg.   OTU
— Draft memorandum.
  4 v. typewritten.   OTAR
— Public hearings, October 18, 1961–November 7, 1961.
  6 v. in 2. facsims., tables.   OTURS
— Summary of recommendations made to the Royal Commission at the public
  hearings. Prepared by T.N. Eberlee. 1961.
  11 leaves.

Background papers to Ontario Royal Commission on Labour – Management Relations in the
  Construction Industry
Hall, John.
  Labour – management relations in the construction industry: chronicle of
  events 1957–1961. Royal Commission on Labour – Management Relations
  in the Construction Industry. [Toronto] 1961.
  11 leaves.   OTAR

Memorandum on minimum wages in the construction industry. Prepared for
    the Royal Commission on Labour – Management Relations in the
    Construction Industry in Ontario. [Toronto] 1961.
    140 leaves.   OTAR
Memorandum on the Industrial Standards Act of Ontario 1935–1961 .
    Prepared for the Royal Commission on Labour – Management in the
    Construction Industry. [Toronto] 1961.
    2 v.
    Contents: Part 1, The history of the Act and the development of its
    administration; Part 2, Schedules in effect in construction by industry and
    zone, as at the end of each fiscal year, 1935-36 to 1960-61.   OTAR

Ontario. Royal Commission on compulsory arbitration in disputes affecting
hospitals and their employees.
    Report. [Toronto] 1964.
    62 p.
    Chairman: C.E. Bennett.   OTUL
Ontario. Royal Commission re: Individual Dump Truck Owners Association
    and International Brotherhood of Teamsters, Chauffeurs, Warehousemen
    and Helpers.
    Report. [Toronto: 1958]
    105 typewritten pages.
    Commissioner: W.D. Roach.   OTAR
— Proceedings, March 24–July 2, 1958.
    9 v. [i.e. 1947 typewritten pages]   OTAR
Ontario Federation of Labour.
    Summary of policies, 1957–1970. Don Mills, Ontario: The Federation, 1970.
    37 p.   OONL
Ontario Federation of Labour. Committee on Labour Relations Legislation.
    Report. Toronto: Thistle Printing Co. [1957]
    1 v. (various pagings).   OTAR
Portis, Bernard.
    The effect of advance notice in a plant shutdown: a study of the closing of
    the Kelvinator plant in London, Ontario, by B. Portis and Michel G. Suys.
    [London, Ontario: School of Business Administration, The University of
    Western Ontario, 1970]
    43 p.   OTU
Queen's University.
    Recent Canadian collective bargaining agreements. Kingston, Ontario:
    Industrial Relations Section [School of Commerce & Administration]
    Queen's University, 1943.
    vi, 133 p. (Queen's University. Industrial Relations Section. Bulletin no. 7).
                                                                     OKQ

Reed, G   W
    White-collar bargaining units under the Ontario Labour Relations Act.
    Kingston, Ontario: Industrial Relations Centre, Queen's University, 1969.
    xi, 56 [5] p. (Research series, no. 8).   OTU
Registered Nurses' Association of Ontario.
    Brief presented by Registered Nurses Association of Ontario in support of
    special legislation entitled the Nurses' Collective Bargaining Act, 1965.
    [Toronto, 1965?]
    [6] p.   OTU
— Collective bargaining progress report 1945–1968. Toronto [1969]
    125 p. diagrs.   OTU
Robin, Martin, 1936–
    Radical politics and Canadian labour, 1880–1930. Kingston, Ontario:
    Industrial Relations Centre, Queen's University, 1968.
    xi, 321 p.   OTU
Sayles, Fern Almer, 1896–1959.
    Welland workers make history. [Welland, Ontario: c1963]
    221 p. illus., port.   OTU
Schulz, Patricia V
    East York Workers' Association: a response to the Great Depression .
    Toronto: New Hogtown Press [c1975]
    74 p. illus.   OONL OTU
Scott, Francis Reginald, 1899–
    Labour conditions in the men's clothing industry. A report by F.R. Scott and
    H.M. Cassidy. Toronto: Published for the Institute of Pacific Relations by
    Thomas Nelson & Sons, Limited [c1935]
    x, 106 p. tables.
    Ontario and Quebec.   OTMCL
Scott, Jack.
    Sweat and struggle: working class struggles in Canada, 1789–1899.
    [Vancouver, British Columbia] New Star Books [c1974]
    209 p. illus., ports.   OTU
Shapiro, Jack R   (ed.).
    Golden jubilee. Division 113, Toronto Street Railway, Motor Coach and
    Maintenance Employees' Union; affiliated with International Amalgamated
    Association of Street Electric Railway and Motor Coach Employees of
    America (A.F. of L.). 50 years of organization, 1899–1949. [Toronto: Golden
    Jubilee Committee of Division 113, Toronto Street Railway and Motor
    Coach Employees' Union, 1949]
    116 p. illus., ports.   OTU
Spencer, Byron G
    Determinants of the labour force participation of married women: a micro-
    study of Toronto households. Hamilton, Ontario: Department of Economics,
    McMaster University, 1972.
    29 leaves. tables. (Department of Economics, McMaster University.
    Working paper, no. 72–08).   OTU

Spicer, Elizabeth, 1916–
>   Our odyssey – thirty years: a history of the London Library Employees'
>   Union, Local 217 (Canadian Union of Public Employees) November
>   1945–1975. London, Ontario: London Public Libraries, Galleries, Museums,
>   1976.
>   53 p.   OL

Stone, Ken.
>   Steel strike, Hamilton 1946. Toronto: Canadian Party of Labour [1946]
>   24 p. illus.   OLU

Sudbury Mine, Mill & Smelter Workers Union, Local 598.
>   A short history of struggle for the Union at Inco–Falconbridge. [Sudbury,
>   Ontario: The Union] 1965.
>   [131] p. illus.   OSU

Teachers' collective bargaining in Ontario: an introduction. [Toronto]
>   Department of Adult Education, Ontario Institute for Studies in Education,
>   1976.
>   39 p. (Interaction of law and education, no. [3]).   OTER

Thunder Bay Labour History Interview Project.
>   Thunder Bay labour history. Thunder Bay, Ontario: Resource Centre,
>   Confederation College, 1973.
>   21 leaves.   OTU

Toronto. University. Board of Governors.
>   Memorandum of agreement [between] the Governors of the University of
>   Toronto and the Canadian Union of Public Employees and its local 1230.
>   March 1, 1970. [Toronto: Printed by Thistle Printing Limited, 1970]
>   [2] 36 p.   OTU

Toronto and District Labour Council.
>   The truth, the whole truth and nothing but the truth. [Toronto] Toronto
>   District Trades and Labour Council [1935?]
>   14 p.   OTU

Toronto Hydro-Electric System.
>   Labour, 1915. Statement of the Toronto Electric Commissioner, Nov. 2nd,
>   1915; majority report of the Arbitrators; minority report of the Arbitrators.
>   n.p.: 1915.
>   30 p.   OOA OTAR

Toronto Transit Commission.
>   Summing up and award of arbitration proceedings February 1929 by and
>   between Toronto Transportation Commission and Toronto Railway
>   Employees Union. Compiled by W.D. Robbins. Toronto: 1929.
>   152 p. ports.   OTAR

Whittingham, Frank J
>   Minimum wages in Ontario: analysis and measurement problems. Kingston,
>   Ontario: Industrial Relations Centre, Queen's University, 1970.
>   xi, 55 p. tables. (Industrial Relations Centre, Queen's University. Research
>   series, no. 11).   OTU

Willes, John Allen.
    The craft bargaining unit: Ontario and U.S. labour board experience.
    Kingston, Ontario: Industrial Relations Centre, Queen's University, 1970.
    xiii, 43 p. fold. map. (Queen's University. Industrial Relations Centre.
    Research series, no. 19).   OTAR
Wills, Harold A   1907–
    Strike: a right or a crime? Cobalt, Ontario: Highway Book Shop [c1974]
    38 p.   OTU
Wood, William Donald, 1920–
    The current industrial relations scene in Canada (1974). Kingston, Ontario:
    Industrial Relations Centre, Queen's University [1974]
    1 v. (various pagings). illus., graphs, tables.   OKQ
Woods, Harry D   1907–
    Labour policy and labour economics in Canada, by H.D. Woods and Sylvia
    Ostry. Toronto: Macmillan Company of Canada Limited, 1962.
    xvii, 534 p.   OTAR
Zwelling, Marc, 1946–
    The report of the Strike-breaking Committee of the Ontario Federation of
    Labour and the Labour Council of Metropolitan Toronto. Written by Marc
    Zwelling for the Ontario Federation of Labour and the Labour Council of
    Metropolitan Toronto. Don Mills, Ontario: Ontario Federation of Labour
    and Labour Council of Metropolitan Toronto [1972]
    322 [24] p. illus.   OTU
— The strikebreakers: the report of the Strikebreaking Committee of the
    Ontario Federation of Labour and the Labour Council of Metropolitan
    Toronto. Written by Marc Zwelling for the Ontario Federation of Labour
    and the Labour Council of Metropolitan Toronto. Toronto: 1972.
    161 p.   OTU

Periodical Articles

Armstrong, Charles W
    Pickets round the Tely. Canadian Forum 21: 233–235, 1941.
Arthurs, H   W
    Labour law – secondary picketing – per se liability – public policy. Canadian
    Bar Review 41: 573–586, 1963.
Biss, Irene M
    The dressmakers' strike. Canadian Forum 11: 367–369, 1931.
Brewery arbitrators' award. Industrial Canada 5: 326–327, 1904.
Brewin, F   A
    The Ontario collective bargaining act. Canadian Forum 22: 344–345, 1943.
Brown, Arnold E
    A "newspaper" fights a miners' strike. Canadian Forum 21: 301–304, 1942.
Browning, J   C
    Labour situation at Sudbury. Canadian Mining Journal 63: 720, 1942.

Cameron, James C
    Compulsory arbitration of industrial disputes. Industrial Canada 53(no. 3):
    198–202, 1952.
Campbell, G   G
    Staff coordination and employee relations. Canadian Mining Journal 62:
    507–510, 1941.
    Preston East Dome mine.
The Canadian Locomotive Co.'s strike. Railway and Marine World 9: 17, 1906.
Capes, Judith.
    Unions in the public libraries of Ontario. IPLO Quarterly 17: 125–154, 1976.
The carpenters' strike. Industrial Canada 7: 118, 1906.
Chester, Leonard A
    Unions come to public libraries. Ontario Library Review 50: 7–9, 1966.
The Chatham plan; Chamber of Commerce adopts resolution on the subject of
    industrial relations. Industrial Canada 22(no. 1): 118–120, 1921.
Clark, S   D
    The Canadian Manufacturers' Association; a study in collective bargaining
    and political pressure. University of Toronto Studies. History and Economics
    7: xiii, 1–107, 1939.
Cohen, J   L
    Injunctions against picketing. Canadian Forum 16(September): 10–12,
    1936.
Collective bargaining, Ontario. Industrial Canada 44(no. 8): 93–94, 1943.
Collective bargaining bill; Legislature adopts bill based on Select Committee's
    report. Industrial Canada 44(no. 1): 112, 1943.
Crawford, Arthur W
    Labour and industry in Ontario. Canadian Unionist 7: 221–223, 1934.
Creighton, D   G
    George Brown, Sir John Macdonald, and the "workingman"; an episode in
    the history of the Canadian labour movement. Canadian Historical Review
    24: 362–376, 1943.
Crispo, John H   G
    Labour – management relations in the construction industry: the findings of
    the Goldenberg Commission. Canadian Journal of Economics and Political
    Science 29: 348–363, 1963.
Crysler, A   C
    Actions by or against trade unions in Ontario. Canadian Bar Review 39:
    30–42, 1961.
Cunningham, W   B
    Labour relations boards and the courts. Canadian Journal of Economics and
    Political Science 30: 499–511, 1964.
Dewdney, Patricia.
    United we stand; London's library strike. Ontario Library Review 54:
    159–161, 1970.

Dymond, W   R
    Union – management co-operation at the Toronto factory of Lever Brothers
    Limited. Canadian Journal of Economics and Political Science 13: 26–67,
    1947.
Fleming, Arthur.
    Collective bargaining legislation. Royal Architectural Institute of Canada.
    Journal 20: 61, 1943.
Forsey, Eugene.
    The Toronto Trades Assembly, 1871–1878. Canadian Labour 10(6): 17–19;
    10(7–8): 21–22; 10(10): 23–24, 1965; 11(3): 20–22; 11(4): 37–40; 11(7–8):
    24–26; 11(9): 14–16; 11(10): 17–18; 11(11): 27–28; 11(12): 25–26, 1966.
Fraser, Frank.
    Labor cracks the rubber front. Canadian Forum 19: 7–8, 1939.
    Kitchener strike.
Gerring, Howard.
    Jimmy Simpson. Canadian Forum 18: 229, 1938.
Goldblatt, Murray.
    The prize in Sudbury. Canadian Forum 41: 146–147, 1961.
Grube, G   M   A
    Defeat at Kirkland Lake. Canadian Forum 21: 358–359, 1942.
— Legislating for labor. Canadian Forum 23: 30–31, 1943.
— The strike at Kirkland Lake. Canadian Forum 21: 299–301, 1942.
— Two strikes in steel. Canadian Forum 21: 77–80, 1941.
    National Steel Car, Hamilton.
Hamilton Electric Railway employees' agreement. Railway and Marine World
    10: 115, 117, 1907.
Hamilton's union label case. Industrial Canada 6: 516, 1906.
Hart, C   W   M
    Industrial relations research and social theory. Canadian Journal of
    Economics and Political Science 15: 53–73, 1949.
    Trade unionism in Windsor.
Hessel, R   H
    The Labour movement in London: some personal recollections. Western
    Ontario Historical Notes 21: 49–50, 1965.
Labor and wages – Kirkland Lake and Cobalt. Canadian Mining Journal 40:
    456, 1919.
The labor dispute at Cobalt. Canadian Mining Journal 37: 482–487, 1916.
Labor questions on Ontario lines. Railway and Marine World 9: 549, 551, 1906.
Labour situation at Kirkland Lake; mine operators tell their story. Canadian
    Mining Journal 62: 774–780, 1941.
Landon, Fred.
    Knights of Labour, predecessor of the c.i.o. Quarterly Review of Commerce
    4: 133–139, 1937.

Laskin, Bora.
    Collective bargaining in Ontario: a new legislative approach. Canadian Bar
    Review 21: 684–706, 1943.
— Recent labour legislation in Canada. Canadian Bar Review 22: 776–792,
    1944.
Lazarus, Felix.
    The Oshawa strike. Canadian Forum 17: 88–89, 1937.
Leach, James D
    The Workers' Unity League and the Stratford furniture workers: the
    anatomy of a strike. Ontario History 60: 39–48, 1968.
The liability of trade unions. Industrial Canada 5: 556, 1905.
List, Wilfred.
    U.A.W.: Windsor business barometer. Saturday Night 67(11): 21, 26, 1951.
MacEwan, Ross.
    The steel strike is settled – temporarily! Canadian Forum 22: 342, 1943.
Mackintosh, Margaret.
    Government intervention in labour disputes in Canada. Queen's Quarterly
    31: 298–328, 1924.
    Ontario: pp. 300–303.
— Government intervention in labour disputes in Canada. Queen's University.
    Bulletin of the Departments of History and Political Science 47: 1–30, 1924.
    Ontario: pp. 3–6,
— Legislation concerning collective labour agreements: (part II) Canada.
    Canadian Bar Review 14: 220–246, 1936.
    Part I concerns countries other than Canada.
MacLeod, Clare R
    Anatomy of a teachers' strike. Education Canada 13(no. 4): 47–50, 1973.
    Windsor strike.
Metallic boycotters must pay heavy damages. Industrial Canada 6: 278, 1905.
    Labour dispute in Toronto.
Midanik, S
    Problems of legislation relating to collective bargaining. Canadian Journal
    of Economics and Political Science 9: 348–356, 1943.
Morrison, Jean.
    Labour in Fort William and Port Arthur, 1903–1913. Thunder Bay
    Historical Museum Society. Papers and Records 1: 23–30, 1973.
Muir, J   Douglas.
    Decentralized bargaining: its problems and direction in the public education
    systems of Ontario and the western provinces. Relations Industrielles 26:
    124–145, 1971.
Munro, Duff.
    Labor legislation 1939. Canadian Forum 19: 74–75, 1939.
Nicholls, G   V   V
    Mediation, conciliation and arbitration of labour disputes in Canada.
    Industrial Canada 39(no. 5): 43–47, 1938.

O'Donoghue, John G
Daniel John O'Donoghue, father of the Canadian labor movement.
Canadian Catholic Historical Association. Report 87–96, 1942–43.
Ontario Collective Bargaining Act. Industrial Canada 14(no. 6): 127–128, 1943.
Painters guilty of conspiracy; St. Catharines unionists convicted of conspiring to
deprive a fellow-workman of employment. Industrial Canada 5: 387, 1905.
Pearce, C   A
Trade unions in Canada; Canadian Bar Review 10: 349–360, 414–422,
524–532, 1932.
3 parts.
Part 1, The legal status; Part 2, The right to strike in Canada; Part 3, The
right to picket in Canada.
Phillips, W   G
Industrial problems confronting Toronto. Industrial Canada 12: 49–52,
1911.
Phillips, William G
Government conciliation in labour disputes: some recent experience in
Ontario. Canadian Journal of Economics and Political Science 22: 523–534,
1956.
— Lessons from the Ford strike. Canadian Forum 34: 245–247, 1955.
Porter, Dana.
The civil status and disabilities of trade unions in Ontario. Canadian Bar
Review 21: 215–232, 1943.
Scott, Jean Thomson.
The conditions of female labour in Ontario. University of Toronto. Studies
in Political Science. s. 1, no. 3: 83–113, 1892.
Session of Provincial legislature; discussion of resolution to refer collective
bargaining to a committee. Industrial Canada 43(no. 11): 106–107, 1943.
Shorter hours and increased wages asked by Cobalt Miners' Union. Canadian
Mining Journal 40: 421–422, 1919.
The status of unions established. Industrial Canada 7: 929–931, 1907.
Submission on collective bargaining; Division's brief to Select Committee of
Legislature presented by chairman. Industrial Canada 43(no. 12): 106–109,
1943.
Ontario Division of Canadian Manufacturers' Association.
The Sultana Mine dispute. Canadian Mining Review 15: 217, 1896.
The T.T.C. strike. Canadian Forum 31: 242, 1952.
Thompson, A   C
Collective labour agreements. Canadian Bar Review 24: 167–177, 1946.
Trade unions and restraint of trade. Canadian Bar Review 6: 210–211, 1928.
Judgement of the Ontario Supreme Court.
Traill, W   A
Making things pleasant for the workers. Industrial Canada 19(no. 6): 62–63,
1918.
A triumph for arbitration. Industrial Canada 7: 113, 1906.
Dispute between Toronto Street Railway Co. and its employees.

Theses

Abella, Irving Martin, 1940–
  The struggle for industrial unionism in Canada: the CIO, the Communist
  party and the Canadian Congress of Labour, 1936–1956. [Toronto] c1969.
  vii, 419 leaves.
  Ph.D. thesis, University of Toronto (microfilm 21375).   OTU
Adams, Robert McDonald.
  The development of the United Steelworkers of America in Canada:
  1936–1951. Kingston, Ontario: 1952.
  233 [5] leaves.
  M.A. thesis, Queen's University.   OKQ
Albright, Wilfred Paul.
  The impact of the unions on wages of supermarket cashiers in southern
  Ontario. Buffalo, New York: 1970.
  202 p.
  Ph.D. thesis, State University of New York at Buffalo (microfilm 71-07139).
                                                                            DA
Biely, Robert Bernard.
  A study of the general contractors' section of the Toronto Construction
  Association. [Toronto] 1967.
  ii, 48 leaves.
  M.B.A. thesis, University of Toronto.   OTU
Blais, Gilles.
  Collective bargaining for teachers in Canada: a comparative study. Los
  Angeles, California: 1972.
  227 p.
  Ph.D. thesis, University of California, Los Angeles (microfilm 73-1688).
  "Collective bargaining systems in Quebec, Ontario and British Columbia
  are studied".   DA
Blank, Henry Christopher, 1950–
  Industrial relations in Sarnia, Ontario, with specific reference to the Holmes
  Foundry Strike in March, 1937. London, Ontario: 1975.
  viii, 211 leaves.
  M.A. thesis, The University of Western Ontario (microfilm 24493).   OLU
Bradfield, Frederick Michael, 1942–
  The sources of wage and labour efficiency differences between Ontario and
  Quebec. Providence, Rhode Island: 1971.
  vi, 120 leaves.
  Ph.D. thesis, Brown University (microfilm 72-8087).   DA
Cahan, Jacqueline Flint.
  A survey of the political activities of the Ontario labour movement,
  1850–1935. [Toronto] 1945 [c1974]
  ii, 96 [6] leaves.
  M.A. thesis, University of Toronto (microfilm 17755).   OTU

Cako, Stephen Charles.
  Labour's struggle for union security: the Ford of Canada strike Windsor
  1945. [Guelph, Ontario] 1971.
  vi, 153 leaves.
  M.A. thesis, The University of Guelph.   OGU
Caldwell, Douglas Neil, 1949–
  The United Electrical, Radio and Machine Workers, District Five Canada,
  1937 to 1956. London, Ontario: 1976.
  xii, 193 leaves. tables.
  M.A. thesis, The University of Western Ontario (microfilm 28179).   OLU
Collins, Thomas Ernest, 1951–
  The retail, wholesale and department store union: the political behaviour of
  a trade union in Ontario. London, Ontario: 1974.
  ix, 143 leaves. diagrs., map.
  M.A. thesis, The University of Western Ontario (accepted 1975) (microfilm
  24516).   OLU
Crispo, John Herbert Gillespie, 1933–
  Collective bargaining in the public service: a study of union – management
  relations in Ontario Hydro and TVA. Cambridge, Massachusetts: 1960.
  2 v. [xiii, 500, 1 leaves.] tables, charts.
  Ph.D. thesis, Massachusetts Institute of Technology.   OTH
Dakin, J   E
  Arbitration in the Canadian automobile industry. Kingston, Ontario: 1951.
  v, 209 leaves.
  M.Com. thesis, Queen's University.   OKQ
Danylak, Olga Mary.
  Fair employment practices in Ontario: attitudes of employers toward
  minority groups with particular reference to large and small manufacturers.
  [Toronto] 1964.
  iv, 100 leaves.
  M.S.W. thesis, University of Toronto.   OTU
Davis, William Lester, 1905–
  A history of the early labor movement in London, Ontario. [London,
  Ontario] 1930.
  ix, 140 leaves.
  B.A. thesis, The University of Western Ontario.   OLU
Drexler, John.
  Regional wage rate differentials in Canada. Windsor, Ontario: 1968.
  vi, 38 leaves. charts, tables.
  Geography thesis, University of Windsor.   OWA
Eastman, Sheila Baldwin MacQueen, 1926–
  Multiple–employer collective bargaining: three case studies. [Toronto] 1952.
  v, 278 leaves.
  Ph.D. thesis, University of Toronto.   OTU
Edgar, William Wilkie.
  Railway labour legislation in Great Britain and Canada. [Toronto] 1905.
  41 leaves.
  M.A. thesis, University of Toronto.
  Ontario: pp. 32–35.   OTU

Elliott, Thomas L
　　Decentralization at Chrysler Canada Ltd. "A study of the organizational
　　changes in the manufacturing division of Chrysler Can. Ltd. from the period
　　of 1959 through 1969". [Windsor, Ontario] 1970.
　　iii, 40 leaves. charts, tables.
　　M.B.A. thesis, University of Windsor.   OWA
Ephron, Harman Saul.
　　A study of the internal workings of the International Typographical Union
　　during the forty-four hour strike. [Toronto] 1924.
　　iv, 175 leaves.
　　M.A. thesis, University of Toronto (accepted 1925).   OTU
Fraser, Donald.
　　Collective bargaining for professional engineers in Ontario. Toronto: 1973.
　　[6] 118 leaves.
　　LL.M. thesis, York University (microfilm 17111).   OTY
Freeman, George Edwin.
　　Wage bargaining in the newspaper industry. [Toronto] 1946.
　　82 leaves.
　　M.A. thesis, University of Toronto.   OTU
Fullan, Michael, 1940–
　　Workers' receptivity to industrial change in different technological settings.
　　[Toronto] c1969.
　　viii, 345 leaves. tables.
　　Ph.D. thesis, University of Toronto.   OTU
Goldberg, Theodore Irving, 1923–
　　Trade union interest in medical care and voluntary health insurance: a
　　study of two collectively bargained programmes [Toronto] 1962.
　　2 v. [xiii, 504 leaves] tables.
　　Ph.D. thesis, University of Toronto.   OTU
Green, Reuben, 1924–
　　The wage structure in Windsor, Ontario 1955–65. Windsor, Ontario: 1966.
　　ix, 110 leaves. charts, tables.
　　M.A. thesis, University of Windsor.   OWA
Haney, Reginald A
　　Police labour relations in Ontario under the Police Act, 1946–1973.
　　Toronto: 1974.
　　vi, 346 leaves. tables.
　　LL.M. thesis, York University (microfilm 21545).   OTY
Hjorleifson, Geoffrey Ronald.
　　The reaction of the Canadian non-ferrous mining industry to collective
　　bargaining at the International Nickel Company of Canada, Sudbury,
　　Ontario. Winnipeg, Manitoba: 1971.
　　xii, 313 leaves. illus., maps.
　　M.A. thesis, University of Manitoba (microfilm 7442).   Can

Kelly, R   M
 The impact of the hospital disputes investigation act on collective bargaining
 in hospitals in Ontario. [Toronto] 1969.
 iii, 42 leaves.
 M.B.A. thesis, University of Toronto.   OTU
Kipp, Margaret Anne.
 Labourism and socialism in the labour politics of Windsor, Ontario. Ottawa:
 1972.
 70 leaves.
 B.A. research essay, Carleton University.   OOCC
Lang, John B
 Lion in a den of Daniels: a history of the International Union of Mine, Mill
 and Smelter Workers in Sudbury, Ontario, 1942–1962. [Guelph, Ontario]
 1970.
 iv, 335 leaves.
 M.A. thesis, The University of Guelph.   OGU OTAR
McKenna, Bessie Josephine.
 The industrial relations of women in Toronto. Toronto: 1915.
 M.A. thesis, University of Toronto.
 No copy located.
Marshall, John Roy.
 Labour legislation in Ontario. [Toronto] 1903.
 47 leaves.
 M.A. thesis, University of Toronto.   OTU
Martin, William Stewart Arnold, 1924–
 A study of legislation designed to foster industrial peace in the common law
 jurisdictions of Canada. [Toronto] 1954 [c1976]
 xxiv, 520 leaves.
 Ph.D. thesis, University of Toronto (microfilm 25493).   OTU
O'Connor, Thomas Francis, 1940–
 Plant shutdown and worker attitudes; the case of Kelvinator. London,
 Ontario: 1970 [c1971]
 ix, 98 leaves. illus.
 M.A. thesis, The University of Western Ontario (microfilm 7228).   OLU
Olley, Robert Edward.
 Construction wage notes in Ontario: 1864 to 1903. Kingston, Ontario: 1961.
 vi, 121 leaves. tables (part fold.).
 M.A. thesis, Queen's University.   OKQ
Patton, J   A
 Employee assessment scale: development and research: Canadian Industries
 Limited, Nylon division, Kingston, Ontario. [Kingston, Ontario] 1951.
 1 v. (various pagings).
 M.A. thesis, Queen's University.   OKQ
Porter, Allan Ames.
 Conciliation in the province of Ontario as a means of settling industrial
 disputes. [Toronto: 1956]
 M.A. thesis, University of Toronto.   OTU

Purdon, Andrew.
  The functions of the industrial relations department of the International
  Harvester Company of Canada, Limited. Kingston, Ontario: 1929.
  ii, 29 leaves.
  B.Com. thesis, Queen's University.   OKQ
Renaud, Robert.
  The dimensions of alienation: a survey of organized industrial workers.
  Windsor, Ontario: 1972.
  v, 93 leaves.
  M.A. thesis, University of Windsor (microfilm 14777).   Can
Rutherford, William Herbert, 1876–
  The industrial worker in Ontario [Toronto] 1914.
  123 p.
  D.Paed. thesis, University of Toronto.   OTU
St-Arnaud, Pierre, 1948–
  Une étude sur le choix des representants à la négociation collective dans
  l'industrie de la construction en Ontario et au Québec. Kingston, Ontario:
  c1973.
  x, 266 [1] leaves.
  LL.M. thesis, Queen's University.   OKQ
Saunders, George S
  The movement of union and non-union wage rates in the Ontario iron and
  steel products industries, 1946–1954. Madison, Wisconsin: 1959.
  424 p.
  Ph.D. thesis, University of Wisconsin (microfilm 59-05822).   DA
Schonning, Egil, 1907–
  Union, management relations in the pulp and paper industry of Ontario and
  Quebec, 1914–1950. [Toronto] 1955.
  3 [5] 277 leaves. tables, charts.
  Ph.D. thesis, University of Toronto.   OTU
Sharpe, Kenneth Francis.
  Collective bargaining in a quasi-monopoly: a case study of Air Terminal
  Transport Limited. [Toronto] 1969.
  43 [2] leaves.
  M.B.A. thesis, University of Toronto.   OTU
Sippel, Donald G
  A survey of the financial effects of the 1967 Ford strike. [Windsor, Ontario]
  1968.
  iv, 33 leaves. tables.
  M.B.A. thesis, University of Windsor.   OWA
Stapleton, John James, 1941–
  A case study of the 1970 salary negotiations between the Metropolitan
  Separate School Board and the teachers of districts 29 and 32. [Toronto]
  c1971.
  vi, 223 leaves. figs.
  M.A. thesis, University of Toronto.   OTU

Starr, Gerald Frank, 1942–
    Union–nonunion wage differentials: a cross-sectional analysis. [Toronto]
    c1973.
    viii, 188 leaves.
    Ph.D. thesis, University of Toronto (microfilm 17288).   OTU
Stortz, Thomas Gerald John.
    Ontario labour and the First World War. Waterloo, Ontario: 1976.
    viii, 326 leaves.
    M.A. thesis, University of Waterloo.   OWTU
Stunden, Nancy.
    Stratford strikes of 1933. Ottawa: 1975.
    x, 108 leaves.
    M.A. research essay, Carleton University.   OOCC
Veres, Louis Joseph, 1932–
    History of the United Automobile workers in Windsor 1936–1955. London,
    Ontario: 1956.
    vii, 179 leaves. graphs, tables
    M.A. thesis, The University of Western Ontario.   OLU
Voigt, Barbara Carole.
    A comparison of Alberta, British Columbia, and Ontario industrial relations
    systems in the health care industry. Edmonton, Alberta: 1976.
    xiv, 221 leaves. charts, tables.
    M.B.A. thesis, University of Alberta.   AEU
Waisglass, Harry Jacob.
    A case study in union – management cooperation. [Toronto] 1948.
    174 leaves.
    M.A. thesis, University of Toronto.   OTU
Warrian, Peter, 1945–
    The challenge of the one big union movement in Canada, 1919–1921.
    Waterloo, Ontario: 1971 [c1975]
    iii, 137 [i.e. 139 [ ] leaves.
    M.A. thesis, University of Waterloo (microfilm 22316).   Can
Wick, E   Marshall.
    An analysis of briefs submitted to the Bennett Commission on compulsory
    arbitration in disputes affecting hospitals and their employees in Ontario.
    [Toronto] 1964.
    vii, 38 leaves.
    M.B.A. thesis, University of Toronto.   OTU
Williamson, David Robert, 1942–
    Wage change determinants in the construction industry, Ontario,
    1960–1970. London, Ontario: 1973.
    xvi, 338 leaves. illus., maps, tables.
    Ph.D. thesis, The University of Western Ontario (microfilm 16464).   OLU
Wolfenden, Warren Reginald, 1947–
    An examination of the factors influencing the bargaining process in Ontario

water resources commission municipal regulatory proceedings. London,
Ontario: 1972.

x, 107 leaves.

M.A. thesis, The University of Western Ontario (accepted 1973) (microfilm
14062).   OLU

Wong, Chee H

Study of the relationship between the workers' favorability toward union
and toward management. [Guelph, Ontario] 1968.

44 leaves.

M.A. thesis, The University of Guelph.   OGU

Wood, William Donald.

Unionization of office workers in Ontario. Kingston, Ontario: 1952.

ix, 134 leaves. tables (part fold.).

M.A. thesis, Queen's University.   OKQ

Young, Frederick John Lenahe.

The limits of collective bargaining in the Canadian automobile industry.
Kingston, Ontario: 1952.

vi, 166 leaves.

M.A. thesis, Queen's University.   OKQ

Zerker, Sally Friedberg, 1928–

A history of the Toronto Typographical Union, 1832–1925. [Toronto: 1972]

iii, 450 leaves. tables.

Ph.D. thesis, University of Toronto (microfilm 13091).   OTU

6

Social History

GENERAL

Bibliography
Ontario. Office on Aging.
> Bibliography on aging and religion and aging. Prepared for the Conference on Aging and its Implications for Theological colleges and training schools.[Toronto] 1968.
> 26 leaves. OTE

[Scott, Joyce]
> A checklist of lodge and fraternal society material in the regional history collection. Western Ontario Historical Notes 25: 7–16, 1969.

Monographs and Pamphlets
Acton, Janice (ed.).
> Women at work, Ontario 1850–1930. [Edited by Janice Acton, Penny Goldsmith and Bonnie Shepard. Toronto: Canadian Women's Educational Press, 1974]
> vi, 405 p. OTER

Adams, Ian.
> The real poverty report, by Ian Adams [et al.] Edmonton: M.G. Hurtig Limited [c1971]
> xii, 255 p. illus. OTU

Addiction Research Foundation of Ontario.
> The first twenty years. [Toronto? 1970?]
> [34] p. illus., map. OTUCR

Alcoholism and Drug Addiction Research Foundation of Ontario.
> The chronic drunkeness offender, chapter XVII: first offenders, a comparison. Toronto: The Foundation [1966?]
> 122 [2] leaves. OTU

Allemang, Margaret.
  Report of a project to implement, assess and refine a decentralized system to
  facilitate patient-centred care. Reported by Margaret N. Allemang.
  [Toronto] School of Nursing, University of Toronto, 1971.
  100 p. tables.   OTU
— Request for the development of a nursing research unit at Sunnybrook
  Hospital; Toronto. [Toronto] University of Toronto, 1967.
  27 leaves. diagr.   OTU
Allen, Richard.
  The social passion: religion and social reform in Canada, 1914–28.
  [Toronto] University of Toronto Press [c1971]
  xxv, 385 p. illus., ports.   OTU
Arndt, Ruth (Spence).
  Prohibition in Canada: a memorial to Francis Stephens Spence. Toronto:
  Ontario Branch of Dominion Alliance [c1919]
  xvi, 624 p. tables.   OTU
Association for Civil Liberties.
  A brief... to the Premier of Ontario. Toronto: Morris Printing Co., 1949.
  14 p.   OTU
Aston, William H
  History of the 21st regiment, Essex fusiliers of Windsor, Ontario, Canadian
  militia; with a brief history of the Essex frontier, the war of 1812, Canadian
  rebellion of 1837, Fenian raids, war in South Africa, etc., including an
  account of the different actions in which the militia of Essex have been
  engaged. Windsor, Ontario: Record Printing Company Ltd., 1902.
  7–124 p. front., illus., ports.   OLU
[Bartlett, Jack Fortune]
  1st Battalion, The Highland Light Infantry of Canada, 1940–1945. Galt,
  Ontario: Highland Light Infantry of Canada Association, 1951.
  126 p. illus., fold. maps.
  This was a Galt based unit.   OTU
Bassett, John M
  Laura Secord, by John M. Bassett and A. Roy Petrie. Don Mills, Ontario:
  Fitzhenry & Whiteside, Limited [c1974]
  59 p. illus., facsims., ports.
  Chiefly pre-Confederation.   OONL
Benson, Margaret.
  Admissions to the provincial correctional centre for women in Ontario.
  Toronto: Elizabeth Fry Society [1971]
  x, 111 leaves. graphs, tables. (Elizabeth Fry Society, Toronto. Working
  paper, no. 5).   OTUCR
— Adult female offenders: an examination of the nature of their offences and
  criminal process and service patterns [a summary of the findings of seven
  independent but related research studies. Ottawa] Solicitor General of
  Canada [1974?]
  35, 46 leaves.   OTUCR

— The Elizabeth Fry Society, Toronto: clients, contact patterns and agency
   services. Toronto: Elizabeth Fry Society [1973]
   vii, 115 p. graphs, tables. (Elizabeth Fry Society, Toronto. Working paper,
   no. 6).   OTUCR
— Fines imposed on women in the provincial courts, Toronto. Toronto:
   Elizabeth Fry Society [1973]
   v, 44 leaves. (Elizabeth Fry Society, Toronto. Working paper, no. 7).   OTUCR
— From arrest to trial for female offenders appearing in the former Magistrates'
   Courts in Toronto from September 1961 to February 1962. Toronto:
   Elizabeth Fry Society [c1969?]
   v, 47 leaves. (Elizabeth Fry Society, Toronto. Working Paper, no. 2).   OTUCR
— Statistics of criminal and other offences as related to adult women convicted
   in Canada with special reference to Ontario and York county. Toronto:
   Elizabeth Fry Society [1968]
   vi, 58 leaves. graphs. (Elizabeth Fry Society, Toronto. Working paper, no.
   1).   OTUCR
— Women on probation in Metropolitan Toronto. Toronto: Elizabeth Fry
   Society [1969?]
   viii, 82 leaves. graphs. (Elizabeth Fry Society, Toronto. Working paper, no.
   3).   OTUCR
Binnie, Susan.
   Parole and Ontario reform institution inmates. Toronto: Centre of
   Criminology, University of Toronto, 1974.
   xvi, 163 p. graphs. (Research report of the Centre of Criminology, University
   of Toronto).   OTU
Birchall, Reginald.
   The story of his life, trial and imprisonment as told by himself. Toronto: The
   National Publishing Company [1890]
   xxv, 70 p. illus., facsims.   OLU
Black, Ernest Garside, 1893–
   A stuff gown and a silk one. Scarborough, Ontario: Talisman Publishing
   [c1974]
   151 p.
   Ontario social life & customs.   OTU
Blishen, Bernard Russell, 1919–   (ed.).
   Canadian society: sociological perspective, edited by Bernard R. Blishen [et
   al.] Toronto: The Macmillan Company of Canada Limited, 1961.
   xiii, 622 p. diagrs., tables.   OTU
— Rev. ed. Toronto: Macmillan of Canada, 1964.
   xiii, 541 p. diagrs., tables.   OTU
— 3d ed. Toronto: Macmillan of Canada, 1968.
   xiii, 877 p. tables.   OTU
— Abridged ed. Toronto: Macmillan of Canada, 1971.
   xiii, 575 p. graphs, tables.   OTU
Boss, William.
   The Stormont, Dundas and Glengarry Highlanders, 1783–1951. Ottawa:
   Runge Press, 1952.
   x, 449 p. illus. (1 col.), ports., map.   OTU

Bourne, Paula Theresa (O'Neill), 1941–
    Women in Canadian society. [Toronto] Ontario Institute for Studies in
    Education [c1976]
    x, 158 p. (Canadian critical issues series).   OONL
Bradwin, Edmund William, 1877–1954.
    The bunkhouse man: a study of work and pay in the camps of Canada,
    1903–1914. New York: Columbia University Press, 1928.
    306 p. illus., tables.   OTU
— With an introduction by Jean Burnet. [Toronto] University of Toronto Press
    [c1972]
    xv, 249 p. illus., maps. (The social history of Canada).   OTU
Brantford Courier.
    Military section: response of Brantford and Brant county to the call.
    Brantford, Ontario: The Courier, 1916.
    pp. 25–32. illus., ports.
    December 16, 1916 issue.   OBRT
The Brantford Expositor.
    Christmas number, 1916: the third war Christmas. Brantford, Ontario: The
    Expositor, 1916.
    32 p. illus., ports.
    December 1916 issue.   OBRT
Brett, Katharine Beatrice, 1910–
    Women's costumes in early Ontario. [Toronto] Royal Ontario Museum,
    University of Toronto [c1965]
    [1] 16 [1] p. illus. (Royal Ontario Museum series. What? why? when? how?
    where? who? no. 1).   OTU
— Women's costume in Ontario (1867–1907), [Toronto] Royal Ontario
    Museum, University of Toronto [c1966]
    [1] 16 [1] p. illus. (Royal Ontario Museum series. What? why? when? how?
    where? who? no. 14).   OTU
Brough, James.
    "We were five"; the Dionne Quintuplets' story from birth through girlhood
    to womanhood, by James Brough with Annette, Cecile, Marie and Yvonne
    Dionne. New York: Simon and Schuster, 1965.
    256 p. ports.   OTAR
Bruce, Herbert Alexander, 1868–1963.
    Our heritage and other addresses. Toronto: Macmillan Company of Canada
    Limited, 1934.
    xvi, 392 p. ports.   OTAR
Buckingham, John B
    A short history of Court Pride of Ontario, no. 5640, Hamilton, Ontario,
    Canada, Ancient Order of Foresters: with introduction by J. Watson Stead,
    editor of the *Ancient Forester*. Hamilton, Ontario: McPherson & Drope, 1896.
    41 p. port.   OKQ

Bull, William Perkins, 1870–1948.
From Brock to Currie; the military development and exploits of Canadians in general and of the men of Peel in particular, 1791 to 1930. Toronto: Perkins Bull Foundation [1935]
xxiv, 772 p. illus., plates, port., maps, plans, facsims.   OTU
— From medicine man to medical man: a record of a century and a half of progress in health and sanitation as exemplified by developments in Peel. Toronto: The Perkins Bull Foundation, George J. McLeod, Ltd. [c1934]
xviii, 457 p. illus. (part col.), ports.   OTU
— From the Boyne to Brampton; or John the Orangeman at home and abroad. Toronto: Perkins Bull Foundation [c1936]
365 p. illus., plates, port., facsims., maps.   OTU
Bureau of Municipal Research, Toronto.
Interim report on the Juvenile Court of Toronto; the detention home. Toronto: Bureau of Municipal Research [1920]
14 p. diagrs., table.   OTU
Burton, Charles Luther, 1876–1961.
Address at the opening of the new Granite Club, Toronto, September 16, 1926. n.p. [1926]
11 leaves.   OTAR
Burton, Eli Franklin, 1879–1948 (ed.).
Canadian naval radar officers, the story of university graduates for whom preliminary training was given in the Department of Physics, University of Toronto. Toronto: University of Toronto Press, 1946.
63 p. illus., ports.   OTU
Caillaud, F   Romanet du.
Le nouvelle-Ontario (Canada). Paris: Société de Geographie Commerciale, 1906.
18 p.
"Extrait du *Bulletin de la Société de Géographie Commerciale de Paris.*"   OKQ
Campbell, Marjorie Freeman, 1896–1975.
Torso. Toronto: Macmillan of Canada, c1974.
x, 198 p. plates, illus.,   OTU
Campbell, Mary Imogene Clark, 1901–
100 years: Orphans Home and Widows Friend Society, 1857–1957. [Kingston, Ontario: 1957?]
51 p. illus.   OTU
— A short history of the Women's Aid of the Kingston General Hospital, 1905–1968. [Kingston, Ontario: 1968]
66 p.   OTU

Canada. Army. Argyll and Sutherland Highlanders of Canada (Princess
    Louise's).
    The Argyle and Sutherland Highlanders of Canada (Princess Louise's)
    1928–1953. Compiled by officers of the Regiment; ed. by H.M. Jackson.
    [Hamilton, Ontario] 1953.
    407 p. illus., ports., maps, plans, tables.   OTU
Canada. Army. Essex Scottish Regiment. 1st Battalion.
    I Battalion, the Essex Scottish Regiment (allied with the Essex Regiment)
    1939–1945; a brief narrative. [Aldershot, England: Wellington press, 1946]
    95 p. illus., ports.   OTU
Canada. Army. Fusiliers.
    The log; containing an account of the 7th Fusiliers' trip from London,
    Ontario to Clark's Crossing, N.W.T. Also, the official reports of the officers in
    charge of boats. London, Ontario: Free Press Printing Company, 1888.
    47 p.   OTURS
Canada. Army. The Lorne Scots (Peel, Dufferin and Halton Regiment).
    A brief historical sketch of The Lorne Scots (Peel, Dufferin and Halton
    Regiment). Brampton, Ontario: Regimental Headquarters, Brampton
    Armoury, 1943.
    24 p. 1 col. illus., facsims.   OTU
— The Lorne Scots (Peel, Dufferin and Halton regiment. Allied with: xx the
    Lancashire fusiliers). [Brampton, Ontario: Charters Publishing Co. 1962]
    47 p. illus. (part col.).   OTU
Canada. Army. 7th Toronto Regiment of Royal Canadian Artillery.
    7th Toronto Regiment, Royal Regiment of Canadian Artillery, 1866–1966.
    Compiled by A.D. Camp and L.F. Atkins. [Toronto? 1966?]
    33 p. illus., ports.   OTU
Canada. Army. Stormont, Dundas and Glengarry Highlanders.
    A brief history, 1784–1945. Presented to members of the first battalion upon
    their return from overseas. Cornwall, Ontario [1945]
    40 p. illus.   OKQ
Canada. Commission of inquiry into certain disturbances at Kingston
    Penitentiary during April, 1971.
    Report submitted to Paul A. Faguy, commissioner Canadian Penitentiary
    Services, Solicitor General's Department. Ottawa: Information Canada
    [1973]
    63 p.
    Chairman: J.W. Swackhamer.   OTUCR
Canada. Commissioners appointed to enquire into the affairs of the Kingston
    Penitentiary.
    Report. Ottawa: S.E.Dawson, Queen's Printer, 1897.
    44 p.
    Commissioners: E.A. Meredith, James Noxon, O.K. Fraser.   OKQ
Canada. Committee on Youth.
    It's your turn ... a report to the Secretary of State. [Ottawa: Information
    Canada, 1971]
    xvi, 216 p. illus.
    Chairman: David Hunter.   OLU

Canada. Correctional Investigator.
    Report of inquiry: Millhaven incident, 3rd November, 1975. [Ottawa] The
    Investigator, 1976.
    97 [8] p. plan.
    Commissioner: Inger Hansen; Commission counsel: Brian A. Crane.   OTUCR
Canada. Royal Commission on Health Services.
    [Report. Ottawa: Roger Duhamel, Queen's Printer] 1964–1965.
    2 v. diagrs., tables.
    Chairman: Emmett M. Hall.   OTU

Background papers to Canada Royal Commission on Health Services
Hamilton, John Drennan, 1911–
    Brief to the Royal Commission on Health Services presented on behalf of the
    teaching hospitals of the University of Toronto, by John Hamilton and R.M.
    Janes. [Toronto?] 1962.
    25, 84 leaves.   OTUFP
Ontario.
    Submission of the province of Ontario to the Royal Commission on Health
    Services. [Toronto] 1962.
    1 v. (various pagings).   OTUH
Ontario College of Pharmacy, Toronto.
    Submission to the Royal Commission on Health Services. [Toronto: 1961?]
    30 leaves.   OTUFP
Ontario Medical Association.
    Brief submitted to the Royal Commission on Health Services. [Toronto]
    1962.
    1 v. (various pagings). tables.   OTU
Ontario Retail Pharmacists Association.
    The submission to the Royal Commission on Health Services. [Toronto:
    1961?]
    43 leaves.   OTUFP
Registered Nurses Association of Ontario.
    Brief to the Royal Commission on Health Services, Toronto: 1962.
    iv, 36 leaves. charts, tables.   OTU

Canadian Association of Social Workers. Central Ontario Branch.
    The war on poverty in Hamilton; papers presented at two panel discussions
    sponsored by the Central Ontario Branch of the Canadian Association of
    Social Workers, April 25, 1966–June 6, 1966. Hamilton, Ontario: 1966.
    1 v. (various pagings).   OTU
Carter, John Smyth, 1877–   (ed.).
    A story of twenty-five years 1917–1942, Kiwanis Club of Toronto (a silver
    anniversary review). Toronto: The Kiwanis Club of Toronto, Inc., 1942.
    125 p. illus., facsims., ports.   OTMCL

Chambers, Ernest John, 1862–1925.
"The Duke of Cornwall's Own Rifles"; a regimental history of the Forty-
third Regiment, active militia of Canada. Ottawa: E.L. Ruddy, 1903.
82 p. illus., port.   OTURS
— The Queen's Own Rifles of Canada; a history of a splendid regiment's
origin, development and services, including a story of patriotic duties well
performed in three campaigns. Toronto: E.L. Ruddy, 1901.
156, lix p. illus., port.   OTURS
Chandler, Charles M
The militia in Durham county, 1812–1936: an outline of history of the
Durham Regiment. [Bowmanville, Ontario: Canadian Statesman &
Bowmanville News, 1936]
19, 7 leaves. ports.   OTMCL
Chappell, Frank (comp.).
Oshawa Rotary in retrospect [1920–1952. Oshawa, Ontario: General
Printers, Limited, 1952]
102 p. ports.   OTAR
Clark, Samuel Delbert, 1910–
The social development of Canada; an introductory study with select
documents. Toronto: University of Toronto Press, 1942.
x, 484 p.
Ontario: pp. 204–307.   OTU
Collard, Constance Eileen McCarthy, 1912–
The cut of women's 19th century dress. Burlington, Ontario: Costume
Society of Ontario, 1972.
2 parts. illus.   OLU
— Clothing in English Canada, circa 1867–1907. [Burlington, Ontario: The
Author, c1975]
71 p. illus., facsims.
Sequel to *Early clothing in southern Ontario* which is pre-Confederation.   OOA
— From toddlers to teens; an outline of children's clothing circa 1780 to 1930.
[Burlington, Ontario: The Author, c1973]
58 p. illus.   OLU
— Patterns of fashions of the 1870's. Burlington, Ontario: Joseph Brant
Museum [c1971]
22 p. illus.   OTSTM
Collinson, J   H
The recruiting league of Hamilton, by J.H. Collinson and Mrs. Bertie Smith.
[Hamilton, Ontario: 1919?]
44 p. ports.   OH
Committee for Survey of Hospital Needs in Metropolitan Toronto.
Active treatment hospitals in Metropolitan Toronto. [Toronto] 1963.
iv, 207 p. fold. maps, tables. (*Its* Study part 5).
Director of Study: Harvey Agnew.
Chairman: C.C.Calvin.   OTU
— Ambulance services. [Toronto] 1965.
15 p. (*Its* Study, part 18).   OTU

— The capital financing of Metropolitan Toronto hospitals. [Toronto] 1964.
27 p. (*Its* Study part 19).   OTU
— Care of the chronically ill in Metropolitan Toronto. [Toronto] 1965.
iii, 85 p. (*Its* Study part 7).   OTU
— The continuing program. [Toronto?] 1965.
41 p. (*Its* Study, part 20).   OTU
— Credits & purpose of study and terms of reference, summary of
recommendations, definitions and terminology and the community served.
[Toronto] 1965.
4 v. in 1. (*Its* Study, parts 1–4).   OTU
— Education and the provision of personnel [Toronto] 1963.
vi, 179 p. tables. (*Its* Study, part 16).   OTU
— Home care. [Toronto] 1964.
23 p. (*Its* Study, part 14).   OTU
— Hospital accommodation and facilities for children in Metropolitan
Toronto. [Toronto] 1962.
75 p. fold. map, tables. (*Its* Study, part 6).   OTU
— Isolation care. [Toronto] 1964.
13 p. (*Its* Study, part 9).   OTU
— Medical and dental professions and hospitals. [Toronto] 1964.
ii, 69 p. (*Its* Study, part 15).   OTU
— Mental care in Metropolitan Toronto. [Toronto] 1965.
ii, 65 p. (*Its* Study, part 11).   OTU
— The provision of community social services in Metropolitan Toronto.
[Toronto] 1965.
25 p. (*Its* Study, part 12).   OTU
— Rehabilitation & convalescent care. [Toronto] 1964.
ii, ii, 67 p. fold. map. (*Its* Study, part 8).   OTU
— Tuberculosis care. [Toronto] 1963.
21 p. (*Its* Study, part 10).   OTU
Conroy, Mary, 1935–
300 years of Canada's quilts. Toronto: Griffin House, 1976.
ix, 133 p. illus.   OONL
Consultation for Action on Unreached Youth, Lake Couchiching, Ontario,
1964.
The report and recommendations. [Toronto: 1964]
58 p.
"Sponsored by Social Planning Council of Metropolitan Toronto."   OONL
The Corrective Collective.
Never done: three centuries of women's work in Canada. [Toronto]
Canadian Women's Education Press [c1974]
150 p. illus.   OLU
Corrigall, David James.
The history of the Twentieth Canadian Battalion (Central Ontario
Regiment), Canadian Expeditionary Force, in the Great War, 1914–1918.
Toronto: Stone and Cox Limited, 1935.
xvii, 323, 268 p. illus., maps (part fold.), port.   OTU

Costume Society of Ontario. Workshop, 1st Burlington, Ontario, 1971.
Fashions of the seventies, 1870–1879: style, cut and construction. Papers of
the first workshop of the Society held in Burlington, Ontario, April 30th,
May 1st and 2nd, 1971. Burlington, Ontario: Costume Society of Ontario,
1972.
1 v. (unpaged). illus.   OTU
Courtis, Malcolm C   1934–
Attitudes to crime and the police in Toronto; a report on some survey
findings, by M.C. Courtis, assisted by I. Dussuyer. [Toronto] Centre of
Criminology, University of Toronto, 1970.
189 leaves. illus., forms, tables.   OTUCR
Crooks, E   M   (Ellis).
Hillcrest Convalescent Home, the early story of Hillcrest Convalescent
Hospital. [Toronto: 1953]
71 p. tables.   OTU
Currie, Emma Augusta (Harvey), 1829–1913.
The story of Laura Secord and Canadian reminiscences. St. Catharines,
Ontario: 1913.
254 p. illus., facsims., ports.   OTU
Defries, Robert Davies, 1889–   (ed.).
The federal and provincial health services in Canada; a volume
commemorating the fiftieth year of the Canadian Public Health Association
and the Canadian Journal of Public Health, 1910–1959. [1st ed. Toronto]
Canadian Public Health Association, 1959.
147 p. diagrs., maps.
Ontario: pp. 79–92.   OTU
Denberg, Dave.
Perspectives on the impaired driver and a recommended program. Toronto:
Addiction Research Foundation, 1973.
iii, 82, iv, 9 leaves.   OTUCR
Denison, George Taylor, 1839–1925.
Recollections of a police magistrate. With an introduction by Dr. A.H.U.
Colquhoun. Toronto: The Musson Book Company Limited [c1920]
xiv, 263 p. front.
Police Court of Toronto.   OTU OLU
Dobson, Henry.
The early furniture of Ontario & the Atlantic provinces: a record of pieces
assembled for the Country Heritage Loan Exhibition from private
collections across Canada. [Toronto] M.F. Feheley [c1974]
1 v. (unpaged). chiefly illus.   OTV
Dominion Alliance for the Total Suppression of the Liquor Traffic. Ontario
Branch.
Ontario six years dry, 1916, September 17th, 1922. Toronto: The Alliance
[1922]
31 p. graphs, tables.   OTURS

Doucet, Michael John.
    Nineteenth century residential mobility: some preliminary comments.
    [Toronto] Department of Geography, York University, 1972.
    64 p. charts, maps, tables. (Discussion paper no. 4).
    Area covered is Yorkville in 1872.   OTU
Downsview Weston Action Community. Youth Committee.
    We're exploding: a proposal for a 5 year youth crime prevention program in
    District 10 submitted to the Solicitor General of Canada. Toronto: The
    Committee, 1975.
    2 v. maps.
    Contents: [v. 1] We live here; [v. 2] Background.   OTU
Dunlop, Sheila O
    An examination of the Metropolitan Toronto Police Community Service
    Officer Program: from two viewpoints: the police and the community by
    Sheila O. Dunlop and Denise M.A. Greenway. [Toronto] 1972.
    x, 165 leaves. tables.   OTUCR
Easton, George.
    Travels in America. With special reference to the province of Ontario as a
    home for working men. Glasgow: John S. Marr, 1871.
    183 p.   OTU
Edwards, Nina L
    The story of the first Canadian Club told on the occasion of its diamond
    jubilee 1893–1953. [Hamilton, Ontario: Canadian Club of Hamilton, 1953]
    32 p. illus., ports.   OTU
Equal Rights Association for the province of Ontario.
    Ordinances and by-laws. Toronto: Hunter, Rose & Co., 1889.
    14 p.   OTU
Fish, Lawrence A   1923–
    The history of the Ontario Rifle Association, 1868–1973. Oakville, Ontario:
    c1974.
    1 v. (unpaged). illus.   OTAR
Forbes, Elizabeth (comp.).
    With enthusiasm and faith: history of the Canadian Federation of Business
    and Professional Women's Clubs – La Fédération Canadienne des Clubs de
    Femmes de Carrières Liberales et Commerciales, 1930–1972. [Ottawa]
    Canadian Federation of Business and Professional Women's Clubs, 1974.
    174 p. ports.   OTER
Forcese, Dennis P
    The Canadian class structure. Toronto: McGraw–Hill, Ryerson Limited
    [c1975]
    x, 148 p. graphs, map, tables.   OTU
Foster, Margaret Helen, 1896–
    The first fifty years; a history of the University Women's Club of Toronto,
    1903–1953. [Toronto: University Women's Club of Toronto, 1953]
    v, 50 p. illus.   OTU

Fotheringham, John Brooks.
  The retarded child and his family: the effects of home and institution, by
  John B. Fotheringham, Mora Skelton and Bernard A. Hoddinott. [Toronto:
  Ontario Institute for Studies in Education, c1971]
  ix, 115 p. (Ontario Institute for Studies in Education. Monograph series, 11).
                                                                                           OTU
Fraser, Alexander, 1860–1936.
  The 48th Highlanders of Toronto, Canadian Militia, the origin and history
  of this regiment, and a short account of the Highland regiments from time to
  time stationed in Canada. Toronto: E.L. Ruddy, 1900.
  128 p. illus., port.   OTURS
Frost, Leslie Miscampbell, 1895–1973
  Fighting men, with a foreword by Thomas H.B. Symons. Toronto: Clarke,
  Irwin & Company Limited, 1967.
  xxv, 262 p. illus., facsims., ports.   OTU
Gilling, W   (ed.).
  Ontario Provincial Police 60th anniversary, 1909–1969. [Toronto: 1969?]
  1 v. (unpaged). illus., facsims., ports.   OLU
Glazebrook, George Parkin de Twenebrokes, 1899–
  Life in Ontario; a social history. Drawings by Adrian Dingle. [Toronto]
  University of Toronto Press [c1968]
  [x] 316 p. illus., map.   OTU
— [Reprinted 1971]
  [x] 316 p. illus., map. (Canadian university paperbacks, no. 100).   OTU
Grant, Don W
  "Carry on": the history of the Toronto Scottish Regiment (M.G.) 1939–1945.
  Illustrated with photographs from the Canadian Army Photo Section,
  C.M.H.Q. cartoons and maps by the author. n.p. [c1949]
  xiii, 175 p. illus., ports., maps.   OOA
Grosman, Brian Allen, 1935–
  Police command: decisions & discretion. Toronto: Macmillan of Canada,
  c1975.
  154 p.   OTU
Groves, Hubert (comp.).
  Toronto does her "Bit". Compiled by Hubert Groves assisted by Walter G.
  Fessey, Margaret Lillis Hart. Toronto: Municipal Intelligence Bureau
  [1918]
  72 p. port.
  "Record of what city of Toronto has done in the Great War".   OTU
Guinsburg, Thomas N   (ed.).
  Perspectives on the social sciences in Canada. Edited by T.N. Guinsburg and
  G.L. Reuber. Toronto: University of Toronto Press, 1974.
  viii, 196 p. tables.   OTER
Ham, George H
  Reminiscences of a raconteur between the '40s and the '20s. Toronto: The
  Musson Book Company Limited [c1921]
  xvi, 330 p. illus., fold. map, ports.   OKQ

Hamilton, John.
  A Christian home for men; the Working Men's Home, 59 Frederick St.,
  Toronto. [Toronto: 1901?]
  [4] p.   OTURS
Harshaw, Josephine Perfect.
  When women work together: a history of the Young Women's Christian
  Association in Canada. [Toronto: Young Women's Christian Association of
  Canada, c1966]
  209 p. illus., ports.   OTAR
Hedley, James Alexander, 1844–1916.
  Notes of a hunting trip with the Dwight Wiman Club in the Muskoka
  district, Canada. [Toronto?] 1884.
  77 p.   OTU
Herrington, Walter Stevens, 1860–1947.
  The history of the Grand Lodge of Canada in the province of Ontario,
  1855–1930. Hamilton, Ontario: Robert Duncan Co., [c1930]
  354 p. ports., tables.   OTU
— The war work of the county of Lennox and Addington; published under the
  auspices of the Lennox and Addington Historical Society, by Walter S.
  Herrington and A.J. Wilson. Napanee, Ontario: Beaver Press, 1922.
  278 p. plates, front., ports.   OTU
Hill, Douglas Arthur, 1935–
  The Scots to Canada. London: Gentry Books [c1972]
  vii, 136 p. illus., maps.   OTU
Hopkins, John Castell, 1864–1923.
  Historical sketch of the Canadian Club movement: with appointments and
  elections to the presidency of Canadian public bodies in 1907. [Toronto]
  Canadian Annual Review, 1907.
  23 p. ports.
  Contains information re founding in Ontario 1871?–1907.   OTU
— The origin and history of Empire Day. n.p. [1910]
  23 p.   OTAR
Hunter, Alfred Taylour.
  History of the 12th regiment York Rangers with some account of the
  different raisings of militia in the county of York. Toronto: Murray Printing
  Company, Limited [1912?]
  90 p. illus., ports., maps.   OTU
Iroquois Post and Matilda Advocate.
  Lieutenant Colonel Lorne Winfield Mulloy: Memorial supplement.
  [Iroquois, Ontario: 1932]
  4 p. ports.   OKQ
Jackson, Harold McGill, 1898–
  The Queen's Rangers in Upper Canada 1792 and after. [Montreal:
  Industrial Shops for the Deaf, 1946?]
  117 p.
  Chiefly pre-Confederation.   OTU

— The Royal Regiment of Artillery, Ottawa, 1855–1952; a history. [Ottawa]
1952.
418 p. port., maps, tables.   OTU
Jackson, J   E   Winston.
Migration to northern mining communities; structural and social-
psychological dimensions, by J.E. Winston Jackson [and] Nicholas W.
Poushinsky. Winnipeg: Centre for Settlement Studies, University of
Manitoba, 1971.
xvi, 158 p. illus. (Manitoba. University. Center for Settlement Studies. Series
2: research reports no. 8).   OTU
James, Lois, 1928–
Influence in the prison environment. Toronto: Centre of Criminology,
University of Toronto, 1974.
xvii, 152 p. (Research report of the Centre of Criminology, University of
Toronto).   OTU
— Prisoners' perceptions of parole: a survey of the national parole system
conducted in the penitentiaries of Ontario, Canada. [Toronto] Centre of
Criminology, University of Toronto [c1971]
xix, 281 p. graphs, tables.   OTU
John Howard Society of Ontario.
Thirty years on! 1929–1959. [Toronto: John Howard Society] 1959.
[4] p. illus., ports.   OKQ
Johnston, W   Sandfield (comp.).
Odd Fellowship in Ontario up to 1923. Published under authority of the
Grand Lodge of Ontario I.O.O.F. Toronto: Macoomb Press, 1923.
332 p. ports.   OTAR
Johnston, Walter Stafford, 1911–
The fighting Perths; the story of the first century in the life of a Canadian
county regiment. Illustrated by Jack M. Dent. [Stratford, Ontario: Perth
Regiment Veterans Association, c1964]
133 p. illus., fold. map.   OONL
— History of Perth county to 1967, by W. Stafford Johnston and Hugh J.M.
Johnston. Maps by James Anderson. Stratford, Ontario: County of Perth,
1967.
xv, 481 p. illus., facsim., ports., maps (part col.).   OTU
Jones, James Edmund, 1866–1939.
Pioneer crimes and punishments in Toronto and the Home district; an
account of the many activities of the magistrates both in criminal and civil
matters, drawn largely from records hitherto for the most part unpublished.
Foreword by W.L. Smith. Toronto: G.A. Morang, 1924.
xvi, 195 p. illus.
Chiefly pre-Confederation.   OTU
Joy, Richard J
Languages in conflict: the Canadian experience. With a preface by Frank G.
Vallee. Toronto: McClelland and Stewart Limited, 1967.
xiii, 149 p.   OTU

Kealey, Gregory Sean, 1948–
    Hogtown: working class Toronto at the turn of the century. [Toronto] New
    Hogtown Press, c1974.
    30 p. illus., tables.
    First edition 1972 has title: *Working class Toronto at the turn of the century.*   OONL
— Working class Toronto at the turn of the century. [Toronto: New Hogtown
    Press, 1972]
    23 p. illus.   OTU
Kelner, Merrijoy Sharon, 1927–
    The health of Yorkville; draft of final report by Merrijoy Kelner [et al.
    Toronto] Behaviourial Science, University of Toronto, 1970.
    xi, 194 leaves. diagr.   OTU
Kerr, Vivien R
    A flame of compassion: a history of the Provincial Council of Women of
    Ontario. Foreword by John Robarts. [Toronto: The Author, 1967]
    x, 134 p.   OTU
Kileeg, John.
    Village service unit for alienated youth: the "Trailer" in Yorkville; a report
    to the Social Planning Council of Metropolitan Toronto. [Toronto] 1968.
    17 leaves.   OTU
King, John S
    The early history of the Sons of England Benevolent Society, including the
    origin, principles and progress; as well as a biographical sketch of the
    founders with an account of the organization of the Grand Lodge. Toronto:
    Bros. Thos. Moore & Co., 1891.
    51 p.   OTAR
— Health needs in Kingston and district. [Kingston, Ontario] The Council,
    1967.
    v, 90 p. tables.   OKP
Kirby, William, 1817–1906.
    Letter of Mr. William Kirby referring to the military grounds, Niagara-on-
    the-Lake, Ontario. Niagara, Ontario: 1905.
    2 p.   OKQ
Kiwanis Club, London, Ontario.
    Via Kiwanis: a history of the Kiwanis Club of London 1916–1964. [London,
    Ontario: Kiwanis Club of London Inc., 1965]
    96 p. illus., facsims.   OLU
Kohn, Paul Max.
    Drug use, drug-use attitudes, and the authoritarianism-rebellion dimension.
    Toronto: York University, 1970.
    17 p. tables. (York University. Institute for Behaviourial Research).   OTU
Lamb, Marjorie, 1949–
    The Boyd gang, by Marjorie Lamb, Barry Pearson. Toronto: Peter Martin
    Associates Limited [c1976]
    x, 256 p. illus., ports.   OOA

Langman, Robert Clare, 1924–
    Poverty pockets: a study of the limestone plains of southern Ontario.
    Toronto: McClelland and Stewart Limited [c1975]
    95 p. illus., maps.   OONL
Langstaff, James Miles, 1883–1917.
    A memorial. [Toronto: Miln–Bingham Co., Ltd. 1918?]
    75 p. ports.   OTU
Lavell, W   Stewart.
    Pioneering with youth: history of the Young Men's Christian Association of
    Kingston, Canada, 1855–1935. Kingston, Ontario: Hanson & Edgar
    Limited, 1936.
    147 p. illus., diagr., ports.   OTAR
League for Social Reconstruction. Research Committee.
    Social planning for Canada. Toronto: Thomas Nelson & Sons Limited
    [c1935]
    xv, 528 p. tables.   OTU
— With an introduction by F.R. Scott [et al.] Toronto: University of Toronto
    Press [c1975]
    xxiv, xv, 528 p. tables. (The social history of Canada).   OTU
Leriche, William Harding, 1916–
    A study of an in-hospital prepaid medical care plan in Ontario, with
    relevant background data on Physicians' Services Incorporated, by W.
    Harding Leriche, W.B. Stiver and W.S. Major. Toronto: Physicians'
    Services Incorporated, 1962.
    xii, 270 p. tables. (Physicians' Services Incorporated. Special report no. 1).
                                                                                                      OONL
Linden, Allen Martin, 1934–
    The report of the Osgoode Hall study on compensation for victims of crime.
    Toronto: The Author, 1968.
    117 leaves. tables.
    Metropolitan Toronto used for the study.   OTU
Little, Charles Herbert, 1907
    The Rideau Club: a short history: the first 100 years, 1865–1965. [Ottawa:
    Rideau Club, 1965]
    68 p. illus., facsims.   OKQ
Lorimer, James, 1942–
    The Ex: a pictorial history of the Canadian National Exhibition. [Toronto]
    James Lewis & Samuel [c1973]
    viii, 136 p. illus., facsims.   OTUSA
Macdonald, Adrian, 1889–   (ed.).
    Gone are the days: a new horizons project by the senior scribes. Toronto:
    Gall Publications [c1975]
    206 p. illus.
    Covers the period 1895–1914 which "saw a complete transformation of the
    way of life of the people of Ontario".   OTU

MacDonald, James C
    Provisional memorandum on the Juvenile Court of the Juvenile and Family
    Court of Metropolitan Toronto. Prepared for the instruction of duty counsel
    in Metropolitan Juvenile Court for the York area, the Ontario legal aid
    plan. [Toronto] 1967.
    44 p.   OTUCR
Macdonell, Archibald Cameron, 1864–1941.
    Early history of the Stormont, Dundas & Glengarry Highlanders.
    [Kingston? Ontario] British Whig Job Dept., 1921.
    12 p.   OTAR
Macfarlane, Dianne.
    Background papers for the Crime Prevention Workshop convened by the
    Centre of Criminology, University of Toronto May 21st and 22nd, 1975.
    [Toronto: Centre of Criminology, University of Toronto, c1975]
    ii, 55 p.   OTUCR
McKay, Kenneth W
    The court houses of a century [1800–1900]: a brief historical sketch of the
    court houses of the London district, the county of Middlesex and county of
    Elgin. With an introduction by James H. Coyne. St. Thomas, Ontario: The
    Elgin County Council, 1901.
    [28] p. illus., plan, ports.   OOA
McKee, S   G   E
    Jubilee history of the Ontario Women's Christian Temperance Union,
    1877–1927. Whitby, Ontario: C.A. Goodfellow & Son [1927?]
    167 p. illus., ports.   OTU
Mackie, John.
    To the Orangemen of Kingston. Kingston, Ontario: [1889]
    14 p.   OKQ
MacLachlan, K   Gordon.
    And the poor shall always be among you. Petrolia, Ontario: 1973.
    59 p. illus.
    Social programs in Ontario pp. 21–33.   OLU
Madawaska Club, Go Home Bay, 1898–1923. n.p. [1923?]
    56 p. illus., maps.   OKQ
— 1898–1948. [Midland, Ontario: Midland Press, 1948?]
    68 p.   OLU
— 1898–1973. [Toronto: Imperial Press, c1974]
    112 p. illus., diagrs.   OKQ
Mann, William Edward, 1918–   (comp.).
    Canada: a sociological profile. [Toronto] Copp Clark Publishing Company
    [c1968]
    xii, 522 p. illus., tables.   OTU
— Deviant behaviour in Canada. Toronto: Social Science Publishers [c1968]
    328 p. tables.   OTU
— Social and cultural change in Canada. Vancouver: Copp Clark Publishing
    Company [c1970]
    2 v. maps, tables.   OTU

— Social deviance in Canada. Toronto: Copp Clark Publishing Company
[1871]
412 p. diagrs., tables.
"New, revised and enlarged edition of: *Deviant behaviour in Canada*".   OTU
— Society behind bars: a sociological scrutiny of the Guelph Reformatory.
Toronto: Social Science Publishers [c1967]
xi, 164 p. tables.   OTU
Marsh, Leonard Charles, 1905–
Report on social security for Canada. Prepared for the Advisory Committee
on Reconstruction. Ottawa: Edmond Cloutier, printer to the King's Most
Excellent Majesty, 1943.
145 p. tables.   OTU
— With a new introduction by the author and a preface by Michael Bliss.
Toronto: University of Toronto Press [c1975]
xxxi, 330 p. (The social history of Canada).   OTU
Martin, O   T   G
"Oxford's big black wall". The story of the Oxford Rifles in three centuries.
n.p.: 1936.
Newspaper clippings.   OLU
Maxwell, G   Dean.
The first one hundred years: a history of Wilson Lodge A.F. & A.M., no. 86
Grand Lodge of Canada in the province of Ontario. Toronto: 1957.
vii, 63 p. illus., facsims., ports.   OTAR
Metropolitan Toronto. Board of Commissioners of Police.
Report on an inquiry into allegations made against certain members of the
Metropolitan Toronto police. [Toronto] 1970.
99 leaves.
Chairman: Judge C.O. Bick.   OTUCR
Millar, W   C
From Thunder Bay through Ypres with the fighting 52nd. n.p.: 1918.
101 p. illus., port.   OTU
Miller, Hanson Orlo, 1911–
The London Club. [London, Ontario: 1954]
39 p. illus.   OLU
Morgan, John Stewart, 1911–
The abolition of poverty: two proposals, by John S. Morgan and Melville H.
Watkins [Papers presented at the Conference on "Poverty and Planning"
sponsored by the Woodsworth Foundation, held in Toronto, January 21–22,
1966. Toronto: Ontario Woodsworth Memorial Foundation, 1966]
16 p.   OTU
Morley, T   P   (ed.).
The opening of the Neurosurgical Unit, Toronto General Hospital,
November 8, 1958. Toronto: 1960.
68 p. fold. col. illus., plans.   OTU

Moss, Susanne, 1935–
    Too many tears. Preface by Pierre Berton. [Toronto] McClelland & Stewart
    [c1974]
    128 p.
    A story of a handicapped in Toronto.   OTU
Mowat, Farley, 1921–
    The regiment. [1st ed.] Toronto: McClelland and Stewart Limited [1955]
    xix, 312 p. illus., maps.   OTU
  — [2d ed. Toronto] McClelland & Stewart Limited [c1973]
    xvii, 317 p. illus., maps.
    History of the Hastings and Prince Edward Regiment.   OTU
Murray, William Waldie, 1891–1956 (comp.).
    The history of the 2nd Canadian Battalion (East. Ontario Regiment),
    Canadian Expeditionary Force in the Great War, 1914–1918. [Ottawa: The
    Historical Committee, 2nd Battalion, C.E.F.] 1947.
    xix, 408 p. illus., ports., maps.   OTU
National Club, Toronto.
    The national century: a history of the National Club, 1874–1974. Toronto:
    1974.
    xi, 93 p. illus., ports.   OTAR
Norton, Lewis Adelbert, 1819–
    Life and adventures of Col. L.A. Norton. Oakland, California: Pacific Press
    Publishing House, 1887.
    viii, 492 p. front., port.
    London, Ontario, 1874: pp. 368–379.   OL
Official programme and souvenir of the Royal tour showing the progress of their
    Royal Highnesses the Duke and Duchess of Cornwall and York through
    Quebec and Ontario, 1901. Toronto: Hunter, Rose Company, Limited
    1901.
    1 v. illus., ports.   OTU
Ontario. Commission of enquiry into matters relating to the Middlesex county
    gaol located at London, Ontario.
    Report. Simcoe, Ontario: 1928.
    21 typewritten leaves.
    Commissioner: Arthur T. Boles.   OTAR
  — Proceedings, January 5–February 7, 1928.
    515 typewritten pages.   OTAR
Ontario. Commission of inquiry as to the arrest and detention of Robert Wright
    and Michael Griffin.
    Report. [Toronto: 1954]
    35 typewritten leaves.
    Commissioner: W.B. Roach.   OTAR
  — Proceedings, November 4–24, 1954.
    2 v. [i.e. 1652 typewritten pages]   OTAR

Ontario. Commission of inquiry into charges against David Hastings, police
    magistrate of Dunnville.
    Report. [Toronto: 1921]
    19 typewritten leaves.
    Commissioner: John A. Patterson.   OTAR
Ontario. Commission of inquiry into charges of violations of the Ontario
    Temperance Act in Brockville.
    Report. [Brockville, 1921]
    5 typewritten pages.
    Commissioner: J.H. Dowsley.   OTAR
Ontario. Commission of inquiry into the affairs of the Guelph Reformatory.
    Report [Toronto: 1937]
    36 typewritten pages.
    Commissioner: James E. Madden.   OTAR
— Proceedings, January 26–February 24, 1937.
    15 v. [i.e. 2567 typewritten pages]   OTAR
Ontario. Commission of inquiry into the Industrial Farm, Langstaff and the
    Women's Farm, Concord.
    Report. [Toronto: 1926]
    7 typewritten pages.
    Commissioners: A.L. McPherson, Col. W.W. Denisom.   OTAR
— Proceedings, January 22–March 22, 1926.
    342 typewritten pages.   OTAR
Ontario. Commission of inquiry re Magistrate Frederick J. Bannon and
    Magistrate George W. Gardhouse.
    [Report. Toronto] 1968.
    xi, 69 p.
    Commissioner: Campbell Grant.   OTAR OTU
— Proceedings, July 15–22, 1968.
    1165 typewritten pages.   OTAR
Ontario. Commission of inquiry re Ontario Provincial Police.
    Inquiry re alleged improper relations between personnel of the Ontario
    Provincial Police and persons of known criminal activity. [Toronto: William
    Kinmond, Queen's Printer, 1970]
    x, 118 p.
    Commissioner: Campbell Grant.   OTAR OTU
— Proceedings, September 14–October 13, 1970.
    18 v. [i.e. 3335 typewritten pages]   OTAR
Ontario. Commission of inquiry re Provincial Judge Lucien Coe Kurata.
    [Report] [Toronto: 1969]
    xiv, 140 p.
    Commissioner: Donald A. Keith.   OTAR OTU
— Proceedings, March 18–April 2, 1969.
    695 typewritten pages.   OTAR
— Proceedings of the Judicial Council for Provincial Judge December 23 and
    26, 1968.
    200 typewritten pages.   OTAR

Ontario. Commission of inquiry respecting the appointment and resignation of
Daniel McCaughrin, police magistrate.
Report. [Toronto: 1934]
8 typewritten leaves.
Commissioner: Robert Grant Fisher. OTAR
Ontario. Commission on the methods employed in caring for and treating the
insane.
Report. Printed by order of the Legislative Assembly of Ontario. Toronto:
L.K. Cameron, printer to the King's Most Excellent Majesty, 1908.
12 p.
Chairman: W.A. Willoughby. OTAR
Ontario. Commission to enquire into and report upon the workings of the Deaf
and Dumb Institute at Belleville.
Report and recommendations. [Toronto: 1907]
25 typewritten pages.
Commissioner: A.J. Russell Snow. OTAR
— Proceedings, 1907.
2 v. [i.e. 196 typewritten pages] OTAR
Ontario. Commission to enquire into and report upon the workings of the
Institute for the Blind at Brantford.
Report and recommendations [Toronto: 1907]
50 typewritten pages.
Commissioner: A.J. Russell Snow. OTAR
— Proceedings, November 29th, 1906–January 4, 1907.
2 v. [i.e. 894 typewritten pages] OTAR
Ontario. Commission to enquire into prison and reformatory system of Ontario.
Report. Printed by order of the Legislative Assembly. Toronto: Warwick &
Sons, 1891.
799 p.
Chairman: John Woodburn Langmuir. OTL
Ontario. Commission to inquire into the administration, management, conduct
and welfare of the Industrial Farm at Burwash, Ontario.
Report. [Toronto: 1918]
42 typewritten leaves.
Commissioner: Emerson Coatsworth. OTAR
— Evidence, November 19–27, 1917.
481 typewritten pages. OTAR
Ontario. Commission to inquire into the seizure of a railway car of whiskey at
Chatham.
Report. [Chatham, Ontario: 1921]
16 typewritten pages.
Commissioner: Judge Talbot MacBeth OTAR
— Evidence, June 29–30, 1920.
204 typewritten pages. OTAR

Ontario. Commission to investigate charges made by George A. Laing against
the police magistrate and license inspector of Welland.
Report. St. Catharines, Ontario: 1921]
11 typewritten pages.
Commissioner: John Samuel Campbell.   OTAR
— Evidence, October 31, 1921–November 10, 1921.
107 typewritten pages.   OTAR
Ontario. Committee of enquiry into the health care system in the Ministry of
Correctional Services.
Report to the Minister. Toronto: 1972.
xi, 435 p. tables.
Committee of one: E.H. Botterell.   OTU
Ontario. Committee of inquiry into hospital privileges in Ontario.
Report to A.B.R. Lawrence, minister of health. [Toronto] 1972.
viii, 36 p.
Chairman: S.G.M. Grange.   OTU
Ontario. Committee on Interim Research Project on Unreached Youths.
Alienation, deviance and social control: a study of adolescents in
Metropolitan Toronto, by John A. Byles. Toronto: 1969.
xviii, 254 p. diagrs., tables.
Chairman: Trevor F. Moore.   OTU
— Final report. Toronto: Department of Education, 1969.
9 p.   OTU
Ontario. Committee on the Healing Arts.
Report, 1970. [Toronto: Queen's Printer, 1970]
4 v. tables.
Chairman: Ian R. Dowie.   OTU
— Proceedings, February 13, 1967–December 10, 1968.
64 v. typescript.   OTU
— Briefs.
108 v.   OTU
— Highlights of the report. n.p. [1970]
26 leaves.   OTU

Background papers on the Ontario Committee on the Healing Arts
Bichan, Joan (comp.).
Summary of recommendations contained in: (1) Task Force reports on the
cost of health services in Canada (2) Report of the Committee on the
Healing Arts (3) Report on the activities of the Ontario Council of Health.
[Toronto?] 1970.
2 v.   OTU
Chemical Engineering Research Consultants, Ltd., Toronto.
Private clinical laboratories in Ontario: a study for the Committee on the
Healing Arts. [Toronto: Queen's Printer] 1970.
xiii, 76 p. tables.   OTU

Fraser, R   D
    Selected economic aspects of the health care sector in Ontario: a study for
    the Committee on the Healing Arts, 1970. [Toronto: Queen's Printer, 1970]
    xxxii, 479 p. diagrs., tables.   OTU
Grove, J   W
    Organized medicine in Ontario: a study for the Committee on the Healing
    Arts. [Toronto: 1969?]
    xi, 327 p.   OTU
Hall, Oswald, 1908–
    The paramedical occupations in Ontario: a study for the Committee on the
    Healing Arts. [Toronto: Queen's Printer] 1970.
    xiii, 140 p. tables.   OTU
Hanly, Charles Mervyn Taylor, 1930–
    Mental health in Ontario: a study for the Committee on the Healing Arts.
    [Toronto: Queen's Printer] 1970.
    xv, 436 p. tables.   OTU
House, R   K
    Dentistry in Ontario: a study for the Committee on the Healing Arts, 1970.
    [Toronto: Queen's Printer, 1970]
    xi, 274 p. tables.   OTU
Landauer, Michael.
    Social work in Ontario: a study for the Committee on the Healing Arts,
    1970. [Toronto: Queen's Printer, 1970]
    1 v. (various pagings). tables.   OTU
Lee, John Alan.
    Sectarian healers and hypnotherapy: a study for the Committee on the
    Healing Arts. [Toronto: Queen's Printer] 1970.
    x, 173 p.   OTU
Macnab, Elizabeth.
    A legal history of the health professions in Ontario: a study for the
    Committee on the Healing Arts, 1970. [Toronto: Queen's Printer, 1970]
    xii, 152 p.   OTU
Murray, V   V
    Nursing in Ontario: a study for the Committee on the Healing Arts, 1970.
    [Toronto: Queen's Printer, 1970]
    xiv, 284 p.   OTU
Toronto. University. Faculty of Pharmacy.
    A submission to the Minister of Health on certain recommendations of the
    Committee on the Healing Arts. [Toronto] 1970.
    27 leaves.   OTUFP

Ontario. Health Planning Task Force.
    Report. [Toronto] 1974.
    xiv, 77 p. illus., charts, map.
    Chairman: Dr. J.F. Mustard.   OTU

Ontario. Health Survey Committee.
    Report. [Toronto 1950–51]
    3 v. in 1 [iii, 450 p.] maps, tables.
    Chairman: George G. Davis.   OTU
Ontario. Hospital Inquiry Commission.
    Report. [Toronto: c1974]
    61 p.
    Chairman: D.L. Johnston.   OTU
Ontario. Inter-ministerial Committee on Drinking and Driving.
    Drinking – driving in the province of Ontario: a report to the Provincial
    Secretary for Justice. [Toronto] 1974.
    xv, 107 p. diagrs., tables.
    Chairman: Howard Morton.   OTUCR
Ontario. Legislative Assembly. Committee on a memorial of the recent war for
    the province of Ontario.
    Report. Printed by order of the Legislative Assembly of Ontario. Toronto:
    Clarkson W. James, printer to the King's Most Excellent Majesty, 1921.
    6 p.
    Chairman: H.S. Cooper.   OTAR
— Proceedings, November 30, 1920–October 25, 1922.
    1 v. (various pagings).   OTAR
— Minutes, January 5–12, 1923.
    2 v. (unpaged).   OTAR
— Report. 1923.
    5 typewritten pages.   OTAR
Ontario. Legislative Assembly. Select Committee appointed to enquire into the
    working of the Tavern and Shop License Act of 1868.
    Minutes, February 19–March 28, 1873.
    11 handwritten pages.
    Chairman: S. Farewell.   OTAR
Ontario. Legislative Assembly. Select Committee on the Cost of Drugs.
    Report. [Toronto: 1963]
    93 p. tables.
    Chairman: H.L. Rowntree.   OTAR OTUFP
— Minutes, June 14, 1960–April 13, 1962.
    1 v. (unpaged).   OTAR
— Briefs.
    39 v.   OTAR
— Proceedings, June 14, 1960–November 16, 1961.
    31 v. [i.e. 3134 typewritten pages]   OTAR
— Index to proceedings:
    31 v. (one volume for each volume of proceedings).   OTAR
Ontario. Legislative Assembly. Select Committee on the Liquor Traffic.
    Report. [Printed by order of the Legislative Assembly. Toronto: 1874]
    74 p. tables.
    Chairman: A. Farewell.   OTAR

Ontario. Legislative Assembly. Select Committee: *re* public health.
   Report. 1878.
   4 handwritten pages.
   Chairman: [A?] Crooks.   OTAR
— Minute book, January 22–March 1, 1878.
   15 handwritten pages.   OTAR
— Proceedings, January 29, 1878.
   66 handwritten pages.   OTAR
Ontario. Legislative Assembly. Special Committee appointed in respect to the
   administration of and amendments to the Ontario Temperance Act.
   Report. 1921.
   4 typewritten pages.
   Chairman: H.C. Dixon.   OTAR
— Minority report.
   1 typewritten page.   OTAR
— Proceedings, October 19–December 10, 1920.
   3 v. [i.e. 242 typewritten pages]   OTAR
— Minutes, February 2, l921
   6 typewritten leaves.   OTAR
Ontario. Legislative Assembly. Special Committee on Prison Labor .
   Report. Printed by order of the Legislative Assembly of Ontario. Toronto:
   L.K. Cameron, printer to the King's Most Excellent Majesty, 1908.
   44 p.
   Chairman: J.P. Downey.   OTAR
Ontario. Police Commission. Advisory Committee on General Police Training.
   Steering Sub-Committee on Police Training in Ontario.
   Report. [Toronto] The Sub-Committee, c1976.
   99 p.   OTUCR
Ontario. Police Commission on Organized Crime.
   Report to the Attorney General for Ontario on organized crime, January
   31st, 1964. n.p.: 1964.
   223 leaves. facsims.
   Chairman: Bruce J.S. Macdonald.   OTU
Ontario. Public Inquiry into Laurentian Hospital, Sudbury.
   [Report] Sudbury, Ontario: 1976.
   v, 235 p.
   Commissioner: Carl Weisberg.   OTUL
Ontario. Rehabilitation Committee.
   Digest of (second series) rehabilitation conferences of delegates of Ontario
   community committees and employer interests – permanent and temporary
   along with necessary government personnel. Sponsored by the governments
   of the Dominion of Canada and the province of Ontario. Toronto: Ontario
   Rehabilitation Committee [1947]
   279 p.
   Chairman: A. Bruce Matthews.   OTU

— The Veterans' stepping stones for future security. [Toronto] Ontario
   Rehabilitation Committee, n.d.
   40 p. illus.   OTAR
Ontario. Royal Commission appointed to enquire into certain charges against
   the Warden of the Central Prison and into the management of the said
   prison.
   Report of evidence. Printed by order of the Legislative Assembly. Toronto:
   Warwick & Sons, 1886.
   181 p.
   Chairman: James Shaw Sinclair.   OTL
— Report of commissioners. Toronto: Warwick & Sons, 1886.
   63 p.   OTL
— Summary of Commissioners findings.
   18 typed leaves.   OTAR
— Newspaper clippings 1885.
   93 p.   OTAR
Ontario. Royal Commission appointed to enquire into conditions at the Don
   Jail, Toronto.
   Report. [Toronto: 1952].
   65 typewritten pages.
   Commissioner: Ian M. Macdonell.   OTAR
— Proceedings, October 20–November 18, 1952.
   19 v. [i.e. 3242 typewritten pages].   OTAR
Ontario. Royal Commission appointed to examine into and report upon the
   safety of premises in the province of Ontario hired for use by the public as
   places of public assembly.
   Report. [Toronto] 1944.
   51 typewritten pages.
   Commissioner: Ian M. Macdonald.   OTAR
— Proceedings, July 5–November 1, 1944.
   4 v. [i.e. 1519 typewritten pages]   OTAR
Ontario. Royal Commission appointed to inquire into the internal management
   of the Ontario Hospital, Mimico.
   Report. [Toronto: 1935]
   28 typewritten leaves.
   Commissioner: William Belmont Common.   OTAR
— Proceedings, August 6–9, 1935.
   833 typewritten pages.   OTAR
Ontario. Royal Commission appointed to inquire into the value of the Central
   Prison labour.
   Report of evidence taken before the Royal Commission. Toronto: Hunter,
   Rose & Co. 1877.
   310 p.
   Chairman: W. Pearce Howland.   OTL
Ontario. Royal Commission on Crime.
   Report. [Toronto: 1963]
   383 leaves.
   Commissioner: Wilfrid D. Roach.   OTAR

— Proceedings, March 20–October 23, 1962.
   68 v. [i.e. 13626 typewritten pages]   OTAR
— Investigative briefs.
   21 v.   OTAR
Ontario. Royal Commission on Police Matters.
   Report. [Toronto: 1919]
   58 typewritten pages.
   Chairman: Sir William R. Meredith.   OTAR
— Proceedings, February 6, 1919–April 14, 1919.
   3 v. [i.e. 2110 typewritten pages]   OTAR
Ontario. Royal Commission on Public Welfare.
   Report to the Lieutenant-Governor in Council. Toronto: Herbert H. Ball,
   printer to the King's Most Excellent Majesty, 1930.
   ii, 108 p.
   Chairman: P.D.Ross.   OTAR
Ontario. Royal Commission on the conduct of police forces at Fort Erie on the
   11th of May, 1974.
   [Report. Toronto: 1975]
   91 leaves.
   Commissioner: John A. Pringle.   OTAR
— Proceedings, July 22–August 14, 1974.
   11 v. [i.e. 2,084 typewritten pages]   OTAR
Ontario. Royal Commission on the operation of the Mental Health Act.
   Report. [Toronto: 1930]
   84 typewritten pages.
   Chairman: Clifford R. Magone.   OTAR
Ontario. Royal Commission on the use of radium and x-rays in the treatment of
   the sick.
   Report. Printed by order of the Legislative Assembly of Ontario. Toronto:
   Herbert H. Ball, printer to the King's Most Excellent Majesty, 1932.
   171 p. tables.
   Chairman: Henry John Cody.   OTAR
Ontario. Royal Commission re: East Windsor Health Association.
   Report. n.p. [1952]
   183 typewritten pages.
   Commissioner: Gordon L. Fraser.   OTAR
— Proceedings, April 3–August 22, 1952.
   18 v. [i.e. 7926 typewritten pages]   OTAR
Ontario. Royal Commission re: statement in the Toronto *Globe and Mail* that
   many Toronto reliefees had died of malnutrition due to the inadequacy of
   the past relief schedules.
   Report. [Toronto: 1942]
   3 typewritten pages.
   Commissioner: Smirle Lawson.   OTAR

Ontario. Royal Commission to inquire into alleged abuses occurring in the
    vicinity of Niagara Falls.
    Report. [Brantford, Ontario: 1873]
    6 handwritten pages.
    Commissioner: E.B. Wood.   OTAR
— Evidence, July 11, 1873–August 7, 1873.
    22 handwritten pages.   OTAR
Ontario. Royal Commission to inquire into and report upon the events and
    circumstances connected with the arrest of Albert Dorland and William
    Toohey.
    Report. [Toronto: 1933]
    43 typewritten pages.
    Commissioner: Mr. Justice Courtney Kingstone.   OTAR
— Proceedings, April 10, 1933–July 17, 1933.
    9 v. [i.e. 4190 typewritten pages]   OTAR
Ontario. Royal Commission to inquire into any charge or complaint made
    against any police officer or public official in a report made by provincial
    constable J.E. Keays.
    Report. [Toronto: 1949]
    35 typewritten leaves.
    Commissioner: J. Keiller MacKay.   OTAR
Ontario. Royal Commission to inquire into the finances, administration and
    personnel of the Windsor Metropolitan General Hospital.
    Proceedings, April 25–June 30, 1949.
    1267 typewritten pages.
    Commissioner: Eric W. Cross.   OTAR
— Appendices to the Proceedings.
    5 parts in various typewritten pages.
    No report for this Commission was located.   OTAR
Ontario. Royal Commission to investigate allegations relating to coroners'
    inquests.
    Report. [Toronto: 1968]
    xiii, 132 p.
    Commissioner: William D. Parker.   OTAR
Ontario. Royal Commission to investigate the Victoria Industrial School,
    Mimico.
    Report. [Toronto: 1921]
    7 typewritten pages.
    Chairman: Dr. John Waugh.   OTAR
— Report of the Special Committee of Enquiry. Toronto: 1921.
    4 typewritten pages.   OTAR
Ontario. Task Froce on Employment Opportunities for the Welfare Recipients.
    Report. Toronto: Department of Social and Family Services, 1972.
    xvi, 208 p. charts.
    Chairman: Barry B. Swadron.   OTUL

Ontario. Task Force on Health Research Requirements.
Report. [Toronto: Ministry of Health] 1976.
xix, 165 leaves.   OTU

Background papers to Ontario Task Force on Health Research Requirements
Toronto. University. Faculty of Medicine.
Brief on health research to the Ontario Government Task Force on Health
Research Requirements. [Toronto] The Faculty, 1974.
3 v.
Chairman: H.E. Petch.   OTU

Ontario. Task Force on Policing in Ontario.
The police are the public & the public are the police [report to the Solicitor-
General. Toronto: 1974]
183 p. illus., diagrs.
Chairman: Edward B. Hale.   OTUCR
Ontario Conference on Aging, 1st, University of Toronto, 1957.
Aging is everyone's concern: the proceedings of the first Ontario Conference
on Aging, held at University of Toronto, May 31st–June 31th [sic] 1957.
[Toronto] General Committee of the First Ontario Conference on Aging and
University Extension, University of Toronto [1957]
vii, 208 p.   OTU
Ontario County Rehabilitation Conference, Oshawa, 1963.
[Proceedings of the Ontario County Rehabilitation Conference held in the
city of Oshawa on February 27th, 28th and March 1st, 1963] Oshawa,
Ontario: Ontario Department of Health, Ontario County Rehabilitation
Council, 1963.
252 leaves.   OTU
Ontario Economic Council.
Health: issues and alternatives 1976. [Toronto] The Council [1976]
vii, 54 p. tables.   OONL
— Ontario: a society in transition. [Toronto: 1972]
91 p.   OTER
Ontario Federation of Labour. Research Department.
Poverty in the midst of plenty. [Toronto: Ontario Federation of Labour,
1964]
58 p.   OKQ OTU
Ontario Psychogeriatric Association.
Care of the difficult patient. Proceedings of [the second annual meeting of
the Ontario Psychogeriatric Association, Stratford, Ontario, September
1975] focussed upon our treatment of the elderly at risk. Edited by J.A.
Dykes. Kingston, Ontario [1975]
119 p.   OTU

Ontario Welfare Council.
  Study of nursing home facilities in Ontario, 1964–1965. Toronto [1965]
  1 v. (various pagings). illus. (part fold.), tables.   OTU
Ontario Welfare Council. Action Committeee on Youth.
  Report on inquiry regarding accommodation needs of youth in the province
  of Ontario. Toronto [1970]
  1 v. (various pagings).   OTU
Oronhyatekha, 1841–1907.
  History of the Independent Order of Foresters. Toronto: Hunter, Rose &
  Co., 1894.
  vii, 862 p. ports.   OTAR
Ossenberg, Richard J   1934 –   (comp.).
  Canadian society: pluralism, change and conflict. Scarborough, Ontario:
  Prentice–Hall of Canada Ltd. [c1971]
  x, 214 p.   OTU
Osterhoff, A   H
  Restrictions on the property right in Ontario: a study produced for the
  Ontario Real Estate Association, by A.H. Osterhoff, W.B. Rayner, P.E.
  Vivian. [London, Ontario: 1973]
  vi, 65 p.   OTU
Ottawa. Protestant Children's Village.
  One hundred years, 1868–1964. Ottawa [1964]
  86 p. illus.   OTU
Ottawa. Welfare Council.
  Survey of Ottawa's child and family services. Ottawa: The Council, 1953.
  66 leaves.   OONL
Packard, Dorothy A   (comp.).
  The Women's Auxiliary to the Norfolk General Hospital: 50 years of
  dedicated voluntary service. [Simcoe, Ontario: Norfolk Historical Society,
  1974?]
  1 v. (unpaged).   OTAR
Panabaker, Katherine.
  The story of the Girl Guides in Ontario. [Toronto] Girl Guides of
  Canada/Guides du Canada Ontario Council [c1966]
  118 p. illus., ports.   OTAR
Peace souvenir: activities of Waterloo county in the Great War 1914–1918.
  Kitchener, Ontario: Daily Telegraph, 1919.
  70, xxxvi p. illus.   OTU
Penal Reform for Women Joint Committee. History Committee.
  A brief summary of the work of the penal reform for women 1953–1960.
  Compiled by Elsie Gregory MacGill. n.p.: 1966.
  6 p.   OTU
Perry, Charles Ebenezer, 1835–1917.
  Lectures on Orangeism and other subjects. Toronto: William Briggs, 1892.
  ix, 131 p. port.
  Ontario: pp. 107–109.   OKQ

Petticoats '67. Y.W.C.A. of Canada centennial publication. [Toronto: 1967]
    36 p. ports.   OTAR
Pierce, Lorne Albert, 1890–1961 (ed.).
    Everett Boyd Jackson Fallis. [Toronto: Methodist Book and Publishing
    House, 1924?]
    1 v. (unpaged). illus., facsims., ports.   OKQ
Porter, John, 1921–1979.
    The vertical mosaic: an analysis of social class and power in Canada.
    Toronto: University of Toronto Press [1965]
    xxi, 626 p.   OTUCR
Queen's Own Rifles of Canada.
    Illustrated historical album of the 2nd Battalion of the Queen's Own Rifles
    of Canada, 1856–1894. Toronto: Toronto News Co., 1894.
    80 p. ports.   OTURS
— Souvenir history of the Queen's Own Rifles, Toronto. [Toronto: Imperial
    Publishing Co., 1898?]
    [82] p. illus., ports.   OTURS
Reid, Linda.
    The self concept of the adult female offender. Toronto: Elizabeth Fry
    Society, [1971]
    iii, 86 leaves. (Elizabeth Fry Society, Toronto. Working paper, no. 4).
                                                                    OTUCR
Roberts, V   M   (comp.).
    The trail of the Canadian National Exhibition; an illustrated historical
    souvenir. Compiled and edited by V.M. Roberts, Toronto: Noble Scott
    Limited, 1925.
    63 p. illus., facsim., maps (1 fold.), ports., plans.   OTU
Roberts, Wayne, 1944–
    Honest womanhood: feminism, femininity and class consciousness among
    Toronto working women, 1893–1914. Toronto: New Hogtown Press [c1976]
    60 p. illus.   OONL
Rogers, Robert Louis, 1919–
    History of the Lincoln and Welland Regiment. [St. Catharines, Ontario.
    Lincoln and Welland Regiment] 1954.
    465 p. illus., maps, tables.   OTU
Ross, Murray George, 1911–
    The Y.M.C.A. in Canada: the chronicle of a century. Toronto: The Ryerson
    Press [1951]
    xvii, 517 p. illus., facsims.   OTU
Ross, Richard M
    The history of the 1st Battalion Cameron Highlanders of Ottawa (MG). With
    a foreword by Colonel Cameron M. Edwards. [Ottawa: Runge Press, 1946?]
    96 p. illus., maps, port.   OTU
Rotary Club, Brockville, Ontario.
    History Rotary Club of Brockville, Ontario. [Brockville, Ontario] 1955.
    33 p. illus.   OKQ

St. Andrew's Society of Toronto.
    One hundred years of history, 1836–1936. Toronto: Murray Printing
    Company Limited, 1936.
    xx, 154 p. front (port.).   OTER
Salvation Army.
    Fair Canada's dark side! being a description of the Canadian rescue work
    and of the children's shelter. Toronto: Salvation Army, 1892.
    30 p. illus.   OTMCL
Samuel, Sigmund, 1867–1961.
    In return: the autobiography of Sigmund Samuel. [Toronto] University of
    Toronto Press [c1963]
    viii, 166 p. illus., ports.   OTAR
Saunders, Ivan James, 1944–
    A history of Martello towers in the defence of British North America,
    1796–1871. Ottawa: Department of Indian and Northern Affairs, 1976.
    169 p. illus., plans, maps. (Canadian Historic Sites. Occasional papers in
    Archaeology and History no. 15).   OTAR
Saunders, Leslie Howard, 1899–
    The story of Orangeism, its origin and history for a century and a quarter in
    Canada particularly Ontario West. Toronto: Grand Orange Lodge of
    Ontario West, 1941.
    38 p. illus., ports.   OTAR
—— 3d ed. printing revised. [Toronto: Britannica Printers 1960]
    48 p. illus., ports.
    Contains also: Directory of all lodges which originated in or existed in
    Ontario West since 1830. [48] p.   OTAR
—— The story of Orangeism: the highlights in its origin and a century and a
    quarter of service to the Christian church, Canada, and the empire; with a
    record of the Orange Lodges operating in Ontario West since 1830.
    Compiled for the Grand Orange Lodge of Ontario West by Leslie H.
    Saunders. Toronto: The Author, 1941.
    1–20, 47, 21–39 p. ports.   OTU
Senior, Hereward.
    Orangeism: the Canadian phase. Toronto: McGraw–Hill Ryerson Limited
    [c1972]
    xi, 107 p. illus. (The Frontenac library, 4).   OTAR
Sherbourne House Club, 1917–1947. [Toronto: 1916–47]
    32 v. illus., fold. map, ports.
    Cover title: Scrapbooks covering all aspects of life at Sherbourne House
    Club, Toronto, established by H.H. Fudger, President of the Robert
    Simpson Company, as a residence for girls employed by the Company.
                                                                        OTURS
Shillington, C   Howard.
    The road to Medicare in Canada: the story of the development of medical
    care insurance in Canada with special emphases on the role of the physician
    sponsored non-profit prepayment plans [Toronto: Del Graphics Publishing
    Department, c1972]
    208 p.   OTU

The Sigmund Samuel story. [Toronto: Brigdens, 1959]
    [24] p. illus. (part col.), ports. (1 col.), facsims.   OTU
Simmons, James William, 1936–
    Patterns of interaction within Ontario and Quebec. [Toronto] Centre for
    Urban and Community Studies, University of Toronto, 1970.
    532 p. maps. (Centre for Urban and Community Studies. Research paper
    no. 41).   OTU
Smith, Goldwin, 1823–1910.
    The St. George's Society and Mr. Goldwin Smith. [Toronto? Privately
    printed, 1893?]
    13 p.   OTER
— Social problems: an address delivered to the Conference of Combined City
    Charities of Toronto, May 20th, 1889. Toronto: C. Blackett Robinson, 1889.
    20 p.   OKQ
Social Planning Council of Greater Niagara. Action Committee on Chemical
    Abuse. Youth Resources Committee.
    Kolauge evaluation. Niagara Falls, Ontario [1970?]
    1 v. (various pagings).   OTU
Social Planning Council of Hamilton and District.
    Papers presented at Clergy – Social Workers' Conference: theme – Aging in
    the modern world. Hamilton, Ontario: 1964.
    25 leaves.   OTU
Social Planning Council of Kingston and District. Needs and Resources
    Committee.
    Health, welfare and recreation needs in Kingston and District. [Kingston,
    Ontario] The Council, 1967.
    v, 90 p. tables.   OK
Social Planning Council of Metropolitan Toronto.
    The aging: trends, problems, prospects. Toronto: 1973.
    1 v. (various pagings). maps.   OTU
— Comparative study of two citizen participation models (design). Toronto:
    1971.
    34 leaves.   OTU
Social Planning Council of Metropolitan Toronto. Committee on Juvenile
    Delinquency.
    Report of the Committee on Juvenile Delinquency to the Minister of
    Justice's Committee on Juvenile Delinquency. [Toronto] 1962.
    1 v. (various pagings).   OTU
Social Planning Council of Metropolitan Toronto. Committee on Needs of the
    Retarded.
    A report on the needs of the retarded in Metropolitan Toronto. Toronto
    [1961]
    1 v. (various pagings). diagrs., tables.
    Chairman: Aileen Klaehn.   OTU
Social Planning Council of Metropolitan Toronto. Committee on Survey of
    Services for Older People in Metropolitan Toronto.
    Report. [Toronto] 1961.
    2, 83 leaves. fold. map, tables (part fold.).   OTU

Social Planning Council of Metropolitan Toronto. Department of Research and
Development.
Social opportunity project; a report of a survey relating to urban migrants
and receiving areas in Metropolitan Toronto. [Toronto] 1968.
95, 6 p. map.   OTU
Social Planning Council of Metropolitan Toronto. East York Area. Committee
on Aging.
A study of the needs of senior citizens in receipt of service from East York
Agencies. [Toronto?] 1961.
iii, 15, 4 leaves. forms, tables.   OTU
Social Planning Council of Metropolitan Toronto. Neighbourhood Service
Unit.
Report; a project of co-ordinated services [1965–1967. Toronto: 1968]
56 p. plan.   OTU
Social Planning Council of Metropolitan Toronto. North Toronto District
Association. Committee on Aging.
Report on the needs of the aging in North Toronto. [Toronto] 1961.
8 p.   OTU
Social Planning Council of Metropolitan Toronto. Study Committee on Homes
for the Aged.
Report. Toronto: 1963.
2 v.
Chairman: J.S. Kennedy.   OTU
Socialization and values in Canadian Society. Toronto: McClelland & Stewart,
1975.
2 v. tables. (The Carleton Library).
Contents: v. 1, Political socialization, ed. by Elia Zureik [et al.] v. 2,
Socialization, social stratification and ethnicity, ed. by Robert M. Pike and
Elia Zureik.   OTU
Stanley, George Francis Gilman, 1907–
In the face of danger; the history of the Lake Superior Regiment. With an
introduction by R.A. Keene, and maps by C.C.J. Bond. Port Arthur,
Ontario: Lake Superior Scottish Regiment [1960]
357 p. illus., ports., maps, tables.   OTU
— A short history of Kingston as a military and naval centre, by George F.G.
Stanley and Richard A. Preston [Kingston: Royal Military College, 1950]
37 p. illus., ports.   OTU
Stephenson, Marylee (ed.).
Women in Canada. Toronto: New Press, 1973.
xvii, 331 p.   OTU
Stevens, George Roy, 1892–1975.
The incompleat Canadian [an approach to social history] Decor by J.W.
McLaren. n.p. [c1965]
214 p. illus., ports.   OTU
Stormont, Dundas and Glengarry Highlanders: a brief chronological history.
Ottawa: 1943.
4 leaves.   OTAR

Swettenham, John Alexander (ed.).
    Valiant men: Canada's Victoria & George Cross winners. Toronto:
    Hakkert, 1973.
    xiii, 234 p. illus., ports.   OTU
Thomas, Hartley Munro, 1896–
    UWO contingent COTC; the history of the Canadian Officers Training Corps
    at the University of Western Ontario. London, Ontario: The University of
    Western Ontario, 1956.
    422 p. illus., ports.   OTU
Thompson, J   F
    A century of masonry in Norfolk county. Waterford, Ontario: Star Print,
    1904.
    1 v. (unpaged). ports.
                                                                               OTAR
Thorburn, John, 1830–1911?
    History of the first century of the St. Andrew's Society of Ottawa, by John
    Thorburn and A.E. Cameron, 1846–1946. [Ottawa: The Society, 1946]
    219 p. ports.
    "Thorburn had written the history up to 1908 and Cameron carried it on to
    1946".   OOA
— The St. Andrew's Society of Ottawa, 1846–1897: sketch of the first half
    century. Ottawa: Haldane & Co., 1898.
    44 p.   OTAR
Thorburn, Maria J   I
    The orphan's home of the city of Ottawa. Sketch of the first forty years
    1864–1904. Toronto: William Briggs, 1904.
    vi, 80 p. illus., ports.   OONL
Toronto. Department of Public Health.
    Report on Pilot Home Care Program, city of Toronto, 1958–1964. With
    appropriate reference to a successor, a Home Care Program for
    Metropolitan Toronto. [Toronto: 1964?]
    42 [20] p. tables.   OTU
Toronto. General Hospital. Trustees.
    Answer of the Trustees of the Toronto General Hospital to the report of the
    Inspector of Prisons, etc., lately presented to the Legislative Assembly.
    Toronto: Printed at the Leader Office, 1871.
    27 p.   OTURS
Toronto. Mayor's Task Force re: the disabled and elderly.
    Report. "This city is for all its citizens." [Toronto: 1973]
    102 p. illus.
    Chairman: Gerald Clarke; co-chairman: Anne Johnston.   OTU
Toronto. South of Carlton Working Committee. Skid Row Subcommittee .
    Skid Row Subcommittee report. Toronto: City of Toronto Planning Board,
    1974.
    22 p.
    Chairman: Ron Jenkins.   OTU

Toronto. University. Department of University Extension.
   Proceedings of conference on earning opportunities for older people,
   February 26th and 27th, 1954, with bibliography of gerontological
   publications. Toronto: 1954.
   72, 8 leaves.
   "This conference was arranged in co-operation with the Old Age Division of
   the Welfare Council of Toronto and District.   OTU
Toronto. University. Student Health Organization.
   The Alexandra Park health care study [by Paul Finnegan et al. Toronto]
   1971.
   iv, 84 p. illus., tables.
   Chairman, SHOUT: Paul Finnegan.   OTU
— Attitudes toward and use of health services in area of downtown Toronto.
   [Toronto: 1970?]
   81 leaves.   OTU
Tresidder, Marion.
   A study of the needs of cancer patients in Waterloo county; a joint project of
   the Ontario Cancer Treatment and Research Foundation and the Ontario
   Division Canadian Cancer Society. A report of the welfare survey conducted
   in Waterloo county, August 1, 1956 to July 31, 1957. Toronto: 1957.
   25 [11] leaves. tables.   OTU
Turner, Robert Edward.
   The Forensic Clinic of the Toronto Psychiatric Hospital. n.p.: 1965.
   15, ii leaves.   OTU
Visiting Homemakers Association.
   Homemaker service for older people: a pilot project undertaken by the
   Visiting Homemakers Association at the request of the Social Planning
   Council of Metropolitan Toronto. [Toronto] 1961.
   60, x p. tables.   OTU
Ware, Francis B
   The story of the seventh regiment, fusiliers of London, Canada 1899 to 1914
   with an epilogue "A few days with the fusiliers at war". London, Ontario
   [Hunter Printing Company] 1945.
   xiii, 190 p. illus., ports.   OLU
Watson, W   S
   Semper paratus: an unofficial history of the Brockville Rifles. Brockville,
   Ontario: Recorder Printing Company of Brockville Limited c1966.
   138 p. illus., ports.   OOA
Weatherbe, K   (comp.).
   From the Rideau to the Rhine and back: the 6th Field Company and
   Battalion Canadian Engineers in the Great War. Toronto: The Hunter-
   Rose Co., Limited 1928.
   519 p. illus., maps, ports.   OLU
Withrow, Oswald Charles Joseph, 1878–1946.
   The romance of the Canadian National Exhibition. [1st ed.] Toronto:
   Reginald Saunders [1936]
   xiv [157] p. front. illus., port.   OTU

Wodson, Harry Milner, 1874–1952.
    The whirlpool, scenes from Toronto police court. Illustrated by Malcolm
    Lennox. Toronto: 1917.
    208 p. illus., port.   OTU
Working Women's Association.
    Working in hospitals. Vancouver, British Columbia [1974?]
    23 p. illus.   OPAL
Workshop Education for Aging, Toronto, 1962.
    Proceedings. Toronto: Ontario Society on Aging [1962]
    78 p.   OTU
Workshop on Aging, Toronto, 1961.
    Community councils and committees on aging. Toronto: Ontario Society on
    Aging [1961?]
    1 v. (various pagings).   OTU
Youmans, Letitia Creighton, 1827–1896.
    Campaign echoes: the autobiography of Mrs. Letitia Youmans, the pioneer
    of the White Ribbon movement in Canada. Written by request of the
    Provincial Women's Christian Temperance Union of Ontario. Introduction
    by Miss Frances E. Willard. Endorsed by Lady Henry Somerset. 2d ed.
    Toronto: William Briggs [1893]
    xvi [17]–311 [1] p. front., illus.
    No first edition located.   OTV
Zavitz, Edgar M
    A history of the Society of Friends of Lobo township. [London, Ontario: A.
    Talbot & Co.] 1917.
    8 p. port.   OOA

Periodical Articles

Aikenbrack, Wesley M
    Three vignettes of violence in the county: 1. The murder of Maggie Howard.
    Lennox and Addington Historical Society. Papers and Records 15: 115–121,
    1976.
Ascher, Elizabeth C
    Number One Company, Niagara. Niagara Historical Society. Papers and
    Records 26: 60–73, 1926?
Bailey, Don.
    Both sides of the poverty wall. Canadian Forum 50: 206–207, 1970.
— Down and out in Toronto. Canadian Forum 50: 64–66, 1970.
Barratt, T   R
    An analysis of mortality patterns in Ontario. Ontario Economic Review
    10(no. 4): 2–21, 1972.

Barrie, E   G
    History of the militia in Waterloo county. Waterloo Historical Society.
    Annual Report 19: 266–271, 1931.
Bates, Gordon.
    A survey of the incidence of venereal diseases in Toronto in 1943. Canadian
    Journal of Public Health 35: 234–240, 1944.
Batten, Jack H
    Two notes on public morality. Canadian Forum 40: 73–74, 1960.
Bayly, E
    Canadian criminal law and procedure as administered in the province of
    Ontario. Canadian Bar Review 4: 552–560, 1926.
Bower, Joseph H   W
    Serving sick children. Royal Architectural Institute of Canada. Journal 28:
    155–158, 191, 1951.
Boylen, J   C
    York county's regiment; an historical sketch. York Pioneer and Historical
    Society. Annual Report 23–43, 1949.
Braid, Andrew.
    Windsor St. Andrew's Society. Essex Historical Society. Papers and
    Addresses 3: 24–32, 1921.
Brink, G   C
    Recent advances in tuberculosis control in Ontario. Canadian Journal of
    Public Health 32: 502–508, 1941.
Bruce, L   M
    Waterloo county great war memorials. Waterloo Historical Society. Annual
    Report 11: 22–37, 1923.
The Canadian National Exhibition. Industrial Canada 7: 109, 1906.
Card, S
    The Ontario reformatory for boys. Methodist Magazine 39: 308–311, 1894.
Carter, John.
    Temperance and local option in Bruce and Grey counties: a summary of
    events and reactions up to 1916. Bruce County Historical Society. Yearbook
    21–25, 1976.
The combined Y.M.C.A. and Y.W.C.A. buildings at Windsor, Ontario . Royal
    Architectural Institute of Canada. Journal 3: 223–226, 1926.
Coumans, Camilla C
    St. Agatha Orphanage. Waterloo Historical Society. Annual Volume 54:
    31–32, 1966.
Coutts, E   N
    History of Freeport Sanitorium. Waterloo Historical Society. Annual Report
    31: 11–28, 1943.
Croft, William F
    Sidelights on the Hamilton police force. Wentworth Bygones 7: 64–66, 1967.
Daly, Conway.
    Intrigue, Ontario style. Canadian Forum 45: 41–43, 1965.

Davison, J F
   Marriage and divorce. Canadian Bar Review 5: 654–663, 1927.
Decarie, M G
   Paved with good intentions: the prohibitionists' road to racism in Ontario.
   Ontario History 66: 15–22, 1974.
Denis–Nathan, H
   The Highland Fusiliers of Canada. Waterloo Historical Society. Annual
   Volume 60: 60–62, 1972.
Denison, R L
   Colonel Richard Lippincott Denison, the first of Dovercourt; first president
   of the York Pioneers. York Pioneer and Historical Society. Annual Report
   18–32, 1969.
Denton, Frank T and Peter J George.
   The influence of socio-economic variables on family size in Wentworth
   county, Ontario, 1971: a statistical analysis of historical micro-data.
   Canadian Review of Sociology and Anthropology 10: 334–345, 1973.
Dicken's Snow Shoe Club visits Presqu'Isle. Western Ontario Historical Notes 3:
   9–11, 1945.
   Article appeared originally in *Owen Sound Times* in early 1870's. Interesting
   description of a social event & provides information on shipping in Georgian
   Bay & development of Presqu' Isle.
Dobbs, Kildare.
   Shocking charge. Canadian Forum 40: 100–101, 1960.
Doering, John Frederick.
   More folk customs from western Ontario. Journal of American Folk-Lore 58:
   150–155, 1945.
— Pennsylvania German folk medicine in Waterloo county, Ontario. Journal
   of American Folk-Lore 49: 194–198, 1936.
Doering, John Frederick and Eileen Elita Doering.
   Some western Ontario folk beliefs and practices. Journal of American Folk-
   Lore 51: 60–68, 1938.
Dosey, Herbert W
   The spirits of '26. Inland seas 9: 119–124, 1953.
   Great Lakes shipments of liquor.
Durward, D N
   The Highland Light Infantry of Canada. Waterloo Historical Society.
   Annual Report 33: 8–16, 1945.
   Waterloo county.
Eadie, James A
   Three vignettes of violence in the county: 3. The navvy riots on the N.T.Q.
   Railway. Lennox and Addington Historical Society. Papers and Records 15:
   127–129, 1976.
Edmison, J
   The history of Kingston Penitentiary. Historic Kingston 3: 26–35, 1954.
Elte, Hans.
   The Group Health Centre at Sault Ste. Marie, Ontario. Royal Architectural
   Institute of Canada. Journal 41(no. 9): 45–53, 1964.

Enns, Gerhard.
    Waterloo North and conscription 1917. Waterloo Historical Society. Annual
    Volume 51: 60–69, 1963.
Evans, Robert G   and Hugh D   Walker.
    Information theory and the analysis of hospital cost structure. Canadian
    Journal of Economics 5: 398–418, 1972.
    British Columbia and Ontario compared..
Fire department's old steam pumper now on display in Pioneer Museum.
    Western Ontario Historical Notes 10: 8–10, 1952.
    From: *Goderich Signal–Star*, Feb. 28, 1952.
Forsey, Eugene.
    Distribution of income in Ontario. Canadian Forum 21: 374–376, 1942.
The Fort York Armoury, Toronto. Royal Architectural Institute of Canada.
    Journal 12: 162–165, 1935.
Gray, Pearl M
    The Women's Industrial Farm. Ontario Agricultural College Review 28:
    438–440, 1916.
    Concord, Ontario.
Green, David.
    Waterloo county's militia. Waterloo Historical Society. Annual Volume 54:
    62–68, 1966.
Greenland, Cyril.
    Mary Edwards Merrill 1858–1880: "the psychic". Ontario History 68:
    81–92, 1976.
    From Picton, Ontario.
Harding, Frank N
    Colonel Pollard and Dr. Watt of Meaford. Western Ontario Historical Notes
    3: 63–64, 1945.
Hill, Daniel G
    The role of a human rights commission: the Ontario experience. University
    of Toronto Law Journal 19: 390–401, 1969.
Hitchins, F   H
    Service aviation in western Ontario. Western Ontario Historical Notes 13: i,
    ii, 1–64, 1955.
Hulet, Marion and Katherine Hebblethwaite.
    Blair Athol. Waterloo Historical Society. Annual Volume 54: 33–35, 1966.
    Orphanage for boys in Galt.
In memoriam. Lt. Col. Harry E. Pense, D.S.O., M.C. Historic Kingston 10: 1,
    1962.
An institution of historical significance the new secular training school for girls.
    Waterloo Historical Society. Annual Report 21: 59–60, 1933.
    Reformatory, Galt, Ontario.
Jarvis, Julia.
    The founding of the Girl Guide movement in Canada, 1910. Ontario
    History 62: 213–219, 1970.

Jones, James Edmund.
Legal aid for the poor. Canadian Bar Review 9: 271–276, 1931.
Jordan, W   G
The temperance question in Ontario. Queen's Quarterly 34: 474–477, 1927.
Keffer, Marion Christena.
Major Addison Alexander Mackenzie, M.C., M.P.P. York Pioneer, 2–14, 1975.
Kirkwood, Hilda.
New ideas in reformatory training. Canadian Forum 33: 225–226, 1954.
Brampton, Ontario Reformatory.
Kurokawa, Minako.
Psycho-social roles of children in a changing society. Canadian Review of Sociology and Anthropology 6: 15–35, 1969.
Waterloo county.
Laycock, Joseph E
Juvenile courts in Canada. Canadian Bar Review 21: 1–22, 1943.
Leys, James Farquharson.
Major Robert Tait Mckenzie: the life of a remarkable man. Canadian Army Journal 9(1): 96–106, 1955.
Light, Frank G
The Galt Club Limited. Waterloo Historical Society. Annual Volume 52: 87–88, 1964.
McAree, John Verner.
Ontario's outworn police system. Canadian Magazine of Politics, Science, Art and Literature 33: 11–16, 1909.
MacDonell, Mary E
What the women of Chatham did during Great War. Kent Historical Society. Papers and Addresses 6: 38–48, 1924.
McIntyre, Hugh.
Some aspects of health administration in northern Ontario. Canadian Journal of Public Health 27: 592–596, 1936.
Mckinnon, N   E
Mortality reductions in Ontario, 1900–1942. Canadian Journal of Public Health 35: 481–484, 1944.
MacLean, Mary R
Colonel Elizabeth Smellie [1884–1968] Thunder Bay Historical Museum Society. Papers and Records 3: 16–18, 1975.
McLeod, W   J
Canada's greatest prison. Canadian Magazine of Politics, Science, Art and Literature 6: 3–16, 1896.
Kingston Penitentiary.
Mathers, A   S   and E   W   Haldenby.
Modernization of the Toronto General Hospital. Royal Architectural Institute of Canada. Journal 38: 57–70, 1961.
The Medical Arts Building, Toronto. Royal Architectural Institute of Canada. Journal 7: 59–65, 1930.
Plates: p. 55, 57.

Millgate, Michael.
    Faulkner in Toronto: a further note. University of Toronto Quarterly 37:
    197–202, 1968.
— William Faulkner, cadet. University of Toronto Quarterly 35: 117–132,
    1966.
Morrison, J   Earl.
    Three vignettes of violence in the county: 2. The Tamworth tragedy, 1914.
    Lennox and Addington Historical Society. Papers and Records 15: 122–126,
    1976.
Murray, E   H
    Ontario's summer estates. Canadian Geographical Journal 30: 80–99, 1945.
New system of prison labor. Industrial Canada 8: 642–643, 1908.
A notable Diamond Jubilee celebration; Canadian National Exhibition
    completes sixty years of service to the Dominion. Industrial Canada 39(no.
    4): 29–33, 1938.
Oliver, Edward B
    Department of Health. Thunder Bay Historical Society. Papers 5: 29–33,
    1914.
— The influenza epidemic of 1918–19. Thunder Bay Historical Society. Papers
    10: 9–10, 1919.
The Ontario safety associations. Industrial Canada 16: 1176–1177, 1916.
Osborne, A   C
    Old Penetanguishene: sketches of its pioneer naval and military days.
    Pioneer Papers 5: 3–82, 1912; 6: 87–164, 1917.
Past and present: the Y.M.C.A. at the O.A.C. 1888–1915. Ontario Agricultural
    College Review 27: 154–157, 1915.
Patterson, Norman.
    The exhibition habit. Canadian Magazine of Politics, Science, Art and
    Literature 27: 291–298, 1906.
    Toronto Exhibition.
Penlington, N
    Ontario's contribution to the South African War. Ontario History 42:
    171–181, 1950.
Prat, Hyperbole.
    Canada's cluttered show window. Canadian Forum 30: 145–146, 151, 1950.
    Canadian National Exhibition.
The prison system of Ontario. Methodist Magazine 39: 99–102, 1894.
Raney, W   E
    Intoxicating liquors. Canada Law Journal 34: 722–723, 1898.
    Law in Ontario.
Rawlins, J   W
    Examination of well water at Copper Cliff. Canadian Mining Journal 29:
    687–688, 1908.
Report on the administration of justice in Ontario. Canadian Bar Review 19:
    128–131, 1940.

Robertson, D   E
    Medico-legal evidence. Canadian Bar Review 16: 185–192, 1938.
Sellers, A   Hardisty.
    Highlights on hospitalization in Ontario. Canadian Journal of Public
    Health 31: 595–606, 1940.
Smellie, Thomas S   T
    The origin and history of the Fort William Relief Society. Thunder Bay
    Historical Society. Papers 3: 17–19, 1911/1912.
Smyth, D   McCormack.
    A plan for improving quality of daily human life. Ontario Education Review
    3 (no. 4): 3, 1968.
Somerville, W   L
    Fort Henry, Kingston, Ontario. Royal Architectural Institute of Canada.
    Journal 16: 136–137, 1939.
Spurr, John W
    The Kingston Garrison, 1815–1870. Historic Kingston 20: 14–34, 1972.
Stanley, George F   G
    Kingston and the North West Rebellion 1885. Historic Kingston 9: 31–45,
    1960.
Swainson, Donald.
    Schuyler Shibley and the underside of Victorian Ontario. Ontario History
    65: 51–60, 1973.
[Swanson, W   W   ]
    Canadian reformatory methods. Queen's Quarterly 18: 83–85, 1910/1911.
Thom, Robert W
    Kionontio. Western Ontario Historical Notes 5: 86–90, 1947.
    Summer residence of B.B. Osler near Collingwood.
Torrance, Gordon V
    The history of law enforcement in Hamilton from 1833 to 1967. Wentworth
    Bygones 7: 67–78, 1967.
Vivian, Percy.
    Panel discussion on hospital building. Royal Architectural Institute. Journal
    25: 289–292, 1948.
Wright, Florence.
    The Niagara Camp [1915]. Niagara Historical Society. Papers and Records
    28: 54–60, 1915?
Zavitz, Edgar M
    Society of Friends of Lobo township. London and Middlesex Historical
    Society. Transactions 8: 47–52, 1916.

Theses

Aharan, Charles Hart, 1924–
    The interdependence of personal and cultural variables in alcoholism.
    London, Ontario: 1966.
    viii, 141 leaves. tables.
    Ph.D. thesis, The University of Western Ontario.   OLU

Allen, Hugh A   J
    An investigation of water hardness, calcium and magnesium in relation to
    mortality in Ontario. Waterloo, Ontario: 1972.
    112 [i.e. 113] A1–86, Bb1–10 leaves. illus.
    Ph.D. thesis, University of Waterloo (microfilm 12898).   Can
Amos, Jack Loyal.
    Vocational rehabilitation; a comparison of programs for the physically
    handicapped. [Toronto] 1942.
    138 leaves.
    M.A. thesis, University of Toronto.   OTU
Anderson, Frank W
    Ontario's extra mural permit system [Toronto] 1957.
    v, 120 leaves.
    M.S.W. research report, University of Toronto.   OTU
Appleby, Edith E
    Rehabilitation services for the female offender in the province of Ontario.
    [Toronto] 1948.
    vi, 96 leaves.
    M.S.W. thesis, University of Toronto.   OTU
Arkilander, Alan.
    North Bay and the Bomarcs, 1957–1964. Sudbury, Ontario: 1973.
    48 leaves. table.
    B.A. thesis, Laurentian University.   OSUL
Avrith, Gale, 1950–
    The Sir Alfred: the social organization of a bar. [Toronto: 1976?]
    ii, 128 leaves. illus.
    M.A. thesis, University of Toronto.   OTU
Baehre, Rainer Karl.
    From pauper lunatics to Bucke: studies in the management of lunacy in 19th
    century Ontario. Waterloo, Ontario: 1976.
    v, 277 leaves.
    M.A. thesis, University of Waterloo.   OWTU
Barclay, Emma Koenig.
    Temperance movements in Canada in the nineteenth century. Toronto:
    1941.
    M.A. thesis, University of Toronto.
    No copy located.
Beaudry, Mary Rose, 1947–
    A study of adoption breakdowns in Ontario, by Mary Rose Beaudry and
    Claude Bertrand. Windsor, Ontario: 1974.
    viii, 115 leaves. tables.
    M.S.W. thesis, University of Windsor (microfilm 23858).   OWA
Blackburn, Walter W
    One hundred graduates of B.T.S. A study of the effects of treatment of
    delinquent boys in the Ontario Training School for Boys, Bowmanville, by
    Walter W. Blackburn and William T. McGrath. [Toronto] 1948.
    ix, 165 leaves.
    M.S.W. thesis, University of Toronto.   OTU

Bliss, John William Michael, 1941–
A living profit: studies in the social history of Canadian business, 1883–1911. [Toronto] c1972.
vi, 464 leaves.
Ph.D. thesis, University of Toronto (microfilm 12926).   OTU

Brett, Fred W
A history of the Big Brother Movement of Toronto, Incorporated, 1912–1939. An historical analysis of the developments in the history of the Big Brother Movement of Toronto, Incorporated, from 1912 to 1939, inclusive. [Toronto] 1953.
v, 241 leaves. illus., charts.
M.S.W. research project, University of Toronto.   OTU

Briault, Margaret A
History of the Toronto Mental Health Clinic 1946–1954, with particular reference to a change in function. [Toronto] 1954.
iii, 137 leaves.
M.S.W. research report, University of Toronto.   OTU

Brown, M   Jennifer.
Influences affecting the treatment of women prisoners in Toronto, 1880 to 1890. [Waterloo, Ontario] 1975.
vi, 146 leaves. tables.
M.A. thesis, Wilfrid Laurier University.   OWTL

Bryers, John Alexander.
A study of drop-in-centres in Metropolitan Toronto with special reference to the teenage respondents' pattern of participation in community sponsored youth services and their perception of drop-in-centre programs and staff. [Toronto] 1967.
ii [i] 113 leaves. tables.
M.S.W. thesis, University of Toronto.   OTU

Bull, Michael A   1950–
An exploratory study of fatherled families in the Windsor – Essex area, by Michael A. Bull, Theresa Ann Eve. Windsor, Ontario: 1976.
xii, 271 leaves. tables.
M.S.W. thesis, University of Windsor (microfilm 29119).   OWA

Carlesimo, Peter, 1947–
The Refugee Home Society: its origin, operation and results, 1851–1876. Windsor, Ontario: 1973.
190 leaves. map.
M.A. thesis, University of Windsor (microfilm 19866).
Essex county.   OWA

Carruthers, Russell Garfield.
Social and economic aspects of family life, in a selected area in Ontario. [Toronto] 1925.
vi [vii–xi] 212 leaves. illus., tables.
M.A. thesis, University of Toronto.   OTU

Christie, Howard Angus, 1949–
    The function of the tavern in Toronto 1834 to 1875, with special reference to
    sport. Windsor, Ontario: 1973.
    vii, 89 leaves. maps.
    M.P.E. thesis, University of Windsor (microfilm 19872).   OWA
Decarie, Malcolm Graeme, 1933–
    The prohibition movement in Ontario: 1894–1916. Kingston, Ontario:
    c1972.
    v, 370 leaves.
    Ph.D. thesis, Queen's University (microfilm 12706).   OKQ
Denys, Jozef Gerard, 1940–
    An exploratory and descriptive study of the behaviour and attitudes of
    Ontario teenagers to alcohol & drugs. [Windsor, Ontario] 1968.
    1 v. (various pagings). facsims., tables.
    M.A. thesis, University of Windsor (degree granted 1969).   OWA
Dingman, Frank S
    The story of the Wellington county family court. [Toronto] 1948.
    198 leaves. fig., maps.
    M.S.W. thesis, University of Toronto.   OTU
Falconer, Mardi Jane.
    The family life of the aged in Metropolitan Toronto. [Toronto] 1964 [c1975]
    vii, 80 leaves. tables, map.
    M.S.W. thesis, University of Toronto (microfilm 21645).   OTU
Farquharson, William Andrew Fletcher, 1940–
    Peers as helpers: personal change in members of self-help groups in
    Metropolitan Toronto. [Toronto] c1975.
    ix, 224 leaves. tables.
    Ed.D. thesis, University of Toronto (microfilm 27841).   OTU
Gandy, John Manuel, 1918–
    The exercise of discretion by the police in the handling of juveniles. Toronto:
    1967.
    x, 400 leaves. table, chart.
    D.S.W. thesis, University of Toronto.   OTU
Goldberg, Grace Safeer.
    Parents without partners; an exploratory study of men and women who are
    single parents, and who are separated, divorced or widowed, and who are
    members of Parents Associated in Metropolitan Toronto with emphasis on
    the organization itself, its history and development, and the use its members
    make of it. [Toronto] 1964.
    viii, 199 leaves. tables.
    M.S.W. thesis, University of Toronto.   OTU
Goldblatt, Sylvia.
    Social integration or isolation among residents of public housing projects.
    [Toronto] 1965.
    170 leaves.
    M.S.W. thesis, University of Toronto.   OTU

Greene, Barbara H
    The volunteer in community service. [Toronto] 1948.
    iv, 78, 3 leaves.
    M.S.W. thesis, University of Toronto.   OTU
Grehwe, Regina Augusta.
    Warrendale's place in the community. [Toronto] 1963.
    vii, 60 leaves. tables, 1 fold. leaf of col. graphs.
    M.S.W. thesis, University of Toronto.   OTU
Griffin, Douglas Keith, 1941–
    An analysis of staff perspectives in five Ontario correctional centres.
    [Toronto] c1976.
    iii, 450 leaves.
    Ph.D. thesis, University of Toronto.   OTU
— A comparison of staff and inmate attitudes in an Ontario correctional centre.
    [Toronto] c1972.
    iii, 148 leaves.
    M.A. thesis, University of Toronto.   OTU
Gross, Dora Pishker.
    A study of the Ontario Training School for Girls. [Toronto] 1955.
    iv, 169 leaves. tables.
    M.S.W. research report, University of Toronto.   OTU
Hallowell, Gerald Allan.
    Prohibition in Ontario, 1919–1923. Ottawa: 1966.
    155 leaves.
    M.A. thesis, Carleton University (microfilm 1067).   OOCC
— Ottawa: Love Printing Service, 1972.
    xi, 180 p. (Ontario Historical Society. Research publication, no. 2). OTU
Heilbron, Herman Julius.
    Parents without partners; an exploratory study of men and women who are
    single parents due to divorce, separation, and widowhood, and who are
    members of Parents Associated in Metropolitan Toronto, with special
    emphasis on divorce. [Toronto] 1963.
    vi [vii] 248 leaves.
    M.S.W. thesis, University of Toronto.   OTU
Heins, Terence John.
    Determinants of outcome in residential homes for special care. Hamilton,
    Ontario: 1974 [c1975]
    xi, 117 leaves. illus.
    M.Sc. thesis, McMaster University (microfilm 22609).   Can
Holy, M   M
    Growth and sewage treatment in Ontario 1901–1971. [Toronto] 1972.
    72 leaves. tables, charts, maps.
    B.A. thesis, University of Toronto.   OTU
Keddie, Vincent Gordon.
    A study of manual workers' attitudes toward social class in four Ontario
    communities. Hamilton, Ontario: 1974 [c1975]
    xv, 399 leaves.
    Ph.D. thesis, McMaster University (microfilm 22626).   Can

Kingston, George Byron.
  Unemployment and relief in Ontario 1929–1937. Kingston, Ontario: 1937.
  74 leaves. graphs, tables (part fold.).
  B.Com. thesis, Queen's University.   OKQ
Kirby, J   Michael.
  Some aspects of the military history of London, Ontario 1850–1900.
  [Guelph, Ontario] 1972.
  vi, 149 leaves. tables.
  M.A. thesis, The University of Guelph.   OGU
Kumove, Leon.
  Voluntary group sponsorship of handicapped refugees. [Toronto] 1965.
  iv, 118 leaves. tables.
  M.S.W. thesis, University of Toronto.   OTU
Lappin, Bernard William, 1916–
  Stages in the development of community organization work as a social work
  method. Toronto: 1965.
  iv, 395 leaves.
  D.S.W. thesis, University of Toronto.   OTU
Lee, Jean Elizabeth.
  Drop-in centres of Metropolitan Toronto; a descriptive study of the families
  of the teens in attendance. [Toronto] 1967.
  x, 112 leaves. tables.
  M.S.W. thesis, University of Toronto.   OTU
McClellan, Ross Adams.
  The developmwnt of the Credit Counselling Service of Metropolitan
  Toronto. [Toronto] 1967.
  iii, 138 leaves. charts.
  M.S.W. thesis, University of Toronto.   OTU
McCollum, Edith Mary.
  A study of male juvenile delinquency in the city of Toronto. [Toronto] 1932.
  63 leaves. tables, fold. maps.
  M.A. thesis, University of Toronto.   OTU
McDermott, Joseph.
  Rebellious youth in conflict with the law: a study in juvenile delinquency.
  [Toronto] 1932.
  115 leaves.
  M.A. thesis, University of Toronto.   OTU
McDougall, Allan Kerr.
  Control of the police in Ontario. Ottawa: 1967.
  ii, 218 leaves.
  M.A. thesis, Carleton University.   OOCC
Main, William.
  A study of Lambert Lodge Home for the Aged. [Toronto] 1951.
  v, 109 leaves. tables.
  M.S.W. thesis, University of Toronto.   OTU

Miers, David Robert.
    Responses to victimisation: a study of compensation to victims of criminal
    violence in Ontario and Great Britain. Toronto: 1976.
    271 leaves.
    D.Jur.thesis, York University (microfilm 30927).   OTY
Nagel, Harry N
    Employment problems of male offenders on parole. A study of twenty-seven
    men released from penitentiary on Ticket-of-leave and supervised by the
    John Howard Society of Ontario in Toronto. [Toronto] 1957.
    x, 208 leaves. tables.
    M.S.W. research report, University of Toronto.   OTU
Nease, Barbara Jane S
    An ecological approach to the measurement of juvenile delinquency in
    Hamilton. [Toronto] 1965 [c1974]
    3, ix, 199 leaves. tables, map.
    M.S.W. thesis, University of Toronto (microfilm 20591).   OTU
Neidhardt, Wilfried Steffen, 1941–
    The Fenian Brotherhood and southwestern Ontario. London, Ontario: 1967.
    viii, 146 leaves.
    M.A. thesis, The University of Western Ontario.   OLU
Newman, Albert F   1930–
    Alcoholism in Frontenac county: a survey of the characteristics of an
    alcoholic population in its native habitat. Kingston, Ontario: 1965.
    1 v. (various pagings). tables.
    Ph.D. thesis, Queen's University.   OKQ
Olliffe, June Muriel.
    The family life of the aged in Metropolitan Toronto; a descriptive study of
    seventy members of the Second Mile Club of Metropolitan Toronto with
    special reference to income and housing [Toronto] 1965.
    vi, 154, 22 leaves. tables, map.
    M.S.W. thesis, University of Toronto.   OTU
Pickard, Toni, 1942–
    Preliminary proposal program design for the psycotherapy unit of the
    Regional Medical Centre, Millhaven, Ontario. Kingston, Ontario: 1970,
    c1971.
    289 [24] 5, 6 [1] leaves. plan.
    LL.M. thesis, Queen's University (microfilm 7564) (restricted)   OKQ
Piva, Michael J
    The condition of the working class in Toronto, 1900–1921. Montreal,
    Quebec: 1975 [c1976]
    ix, 360 leaves. illus., map.
    Ph.D. thesis, Concordia University (microfilm 25349).   Can
Ratz, Jane Elizabeth.
    An analysis of seven hundred weekly food records of low income families and
    the practical application of the information thus obtained. [Toronto] 1951.
    40 leaves. illus.
    M.A. thesis, University of Toronto.   OTU

Reed, Paul Branwell, 1944–
    Life style as an element of social logic: patterns of activity, social
    characteristics, and residential choice. [Toronto] c1976.
    1 v. (various pagings).
    Ph.D. thesis, University of Toronto.   OTU
Rickard, Philip, 1918–
    A model for the delivery of health care in Ontario with special emphasis on
    the central role of the hospital and its inter-relationship with the public
    health and practitioner services. Kingston, Ontario: c1972.
    vi, 78 leaves. figs., maps.
    M.P.A. thesis, Queen's University (microfilm 11715).   OKQ
Roberts, Judy.
    The attitudes of unrepresented inmates on remand in the Toronto jail to
    lawyers and the Ontario Legal Aid Plan. [Toronto] c1972.
    93 [16] leaves.
    M.A. thesis, University of Toronto.   OTU
Robinson, Ruth B
    Truant – Delinquents: a study based on the records of the Toronto Juvenile
    Court Clinic for the years 1946–47. [Toronto] 1948.
    v, 56 leaves. charts, form.
    M.S.W. thesis, University of Toronto.   OTU
Ross, Mary Alexandra.
    A statistical study of the mortality from diphtheria in Ontario for the years
    1880 to 1925. [Toronto: 1928]
    29 leaves.
    M.A. thesis, University of Toronto.   OTU
— A survey of mortality of diphtheria, scarlet fever, whooping cough, measles,
    tuberculosis, typhoid fever, influenza and other respiratory diseases, and
    diabetes for fifty years in Ontario, and an analysis of the results of the use of
    toxoid in the prevention of diphtheria in Toronto school children. [Toronto:
    1934]
    1 v. (various pagings). tables, graphs.
    Ph.D. thesis, University of Toronto.   OTU
Ross, Murray George, 1911–
    The Toronto Y.M.C.A. in a changing community, 1864–1940. [Toronto] 1947.
    176 leaves.
    M.A. thesis, University of Toronto.   OTU
Ross, Thomas McCallum.
    Pre-payment of prescriptions and the "Green Shield" plan. [Toronto] 1961.
    81 leaves. map.
    M.B.A. thesis, University of Toronto.   OTU
Sargant, Glenn Edward.
    An analysis of social well being in Ontario with some implications for
    behaviour. [Toronto] 1976.
    101 leaves. tables, charts, map.
    B.A. thesis, University of Toronto.   OTU

Sharma, Ram Karan, 1935–
    Benefit-cost analysis and public health: a case study of the tuberculosis
    control program in Ontario 1948–1966. London, Ontario: 1973.
    xiii, 221 leaves. tables.
    Ph.D. thesis, The University of Western Ontario (microfilm 14973).   OLU
Sloman, Joan Grace.
    A study of recent trends in infant mortality rates in Ontario. [Toronto] 1965.
    vi, 149 leaves. diagrs.
    M.A. thesis, University of Toronto.   OTU
Smith, Edward Stuart Orford.
    Lung cancer mortality in Ontario with special reference to the influence of
    urbanization. [Toronto] 1968.
    xi, 133 leaves. tables (part fold.), figs.
    M.Sc. thesis, University of Toronto.   OTU
Stern, William I
    Young adult drinking habits: the drinking habits of thirty members of Club
    Cosmo, a group in the University Settlement, Toronto. [Toronto] 1952.
    vii, 105 leaves. illus., maps.
    M.S.W. thesis, University of Toronto.   OTU
Stirrett, Marjorie M
    Changes in food habits in Ontario in relation to public health. [Toronto]
    1956.
    93 leaves. illus., charts.
    M.A. thesis, University of Toronto.   OTU
Stoetzer, Louis Arthur.
    The violation of probation in Ontario: a descriptive study of 241 female
    probation violators who were supervised during the period 1956–1961 by
    probation officers attached to the Adult Probation Office, Toronto, Ontario.
    [Toronto] 1963.
    x, 222 leaves. tables.
    M.S.W. thesis, University of Toronto.   OTU
Vos, Walter John L
    Fair accommodation practices in Ontario. A study of the Ontario Human
    Rights Commission, with particular reference to complainants who referred
    cases to the Commission regarding alleged discrimination in public
    accommodations and to their attitudes toward the Commission and its
    programmes. [Toronto] 1964.
    ix, 110 leaves + appendices. tables.
    M.S.W. thesis, University of Toronto.   OTU
Warren, Sharon Ann, 1947–
    The regionalization of health services in southern Ontario. London,
    Ontario: 1971.
    viii, 120 leaves.
    M.A. thesis, The University of Western Ontario (microfilm 8569).   OLU
Warriner, Walter L
    Medical services for old age pensioners in Ontario. [Toronto] 1950.
    v, 88 leaves. table, form, map.
    M.S.W. thesis, University of Toronto.   OTU

Way, Ronald Lawrence.
    Defences of the Niagara frontier (1764–1870). [Kingston, Ontario] 1938.
    79, xxiii leaves. illus., plans (part fold.), maps.
    M.A. thesis, Queen's University.   OKQ
West, William Gordon, 1945–
    Serious thieves: lower class adolescent males in a short-term deviant
    occupation. Evanston, Illinois: 1974.
    x, 348 leaves.
    Ph.D. thesis, Northwestern University.   OTUCR
Wilson, Nora R
    A study of the Victor Home for Unmarried Mothers. [Toronto] 1961.
    iv, 218 leaves.
    M.S.W. research report, University of Toronto.   OTU
Wong, Lam Wo, 1939–
    An exploratory study of the evaluative practices of the member agencies of
    the United Community Services of Greater Windsor. Windsor, Ontario:
    1974.
    ix, 212 [i.e.211] leaves. illus.
    M.S.W. thesis, University of Windsor (microfilm 23969).   Can

RURAL SOCIETY

Monographs and Pamphlets
Abell, Helen Caroline, 1917–
    Rural families and their homes; based on a longitudinal study of Ontario
    rural families. [Waterloo, Ontario] School of Urban and Regional Planning,
    University of Waterloo, 1971.
    vi, 66, 1–6, 2–9 p. illus.   OTU
Adam, Graeme Mercer, 1839–1912.
    Muskoka illustrated; with descriptive narrative of this picturesque region.
    Toronto: William Bryce [1888]
    20 p. plates, maps.   OTURS
Bartlett, L
    "Uncle Joe Little." Life and memoirs of Joseph Russell Little. Toronto:
    William Briggs, 1903.
    xv, 251 p.
    Life in Lambton county in the 19th century.   OLU
Blake, Verschoyle Benson, 1899–1971.
    Rural Ontario. By Verschoyle Benson Blake and Ralph Greenhill.
    [Toronto] University of Toronto Press [1969]
    viii, 173 p. illus.   OTU
Boyle, Harry Joseph, 1915–
    Homebrew and patches. With a foreword by Harry Halliwell. Toronto:
    Clarke, Irwin & Company Limited, 1963.
    x, 173 p.   OTU

— Don Mills, Ontario: Paperjacks [1972]
    x, 173 p.
    Ontario in the 30's.   OTU
— Memoirs of a Catholic boyhood. [1st ed.] Toronto: Doubleday, Canada,
    1973.
    192 p.
    Rural Ontario during the depression.   OTU
— Mostly in clover. With a foreword by Burton T. Richardson. Toronto:
    Clarke, Irwin & Company Limited, 1961.
    x, 227 p. illus.
    Boyhood in rural Ontario.   OTU
— With a pinch of sin. [Huron county] New York: Doubleday Company, 1966.
    230 p.   OTU
Brown, William McEvery.
    The Queen's bush: a tale of the early days of Bruce county. Owen Sound,
    Ontario: Richardson, Bond & Wright, 1967.
    vi, 295 p. illus., fold. map.
    A reprint of the 1932 edition, published by John Bale, Sons & Danielsson,
    London. No Copy located.   OTU
Byrnes, J   D
    Greater Ontario, or new Ontario. [Toronto: Forward Movement
    Committee, Presbyterian Church of Canada, 1918?]
    11 p. illus.
    Northern Ontario.   OTAR
Cameron, Daniel George, 1856–
    Twigs from the oak and other trees. Regina: Commercial Printers, 1933.
    283 p. plates, ports.
    Life in the Ottawa valley.
    Chiefly pre-Confederation.   OKQ
Campbell, Hugh A   1888–
    Life and adventure of a pioneer. Newmarket, Ontario: Northland Printers
    Ltd., 1970.
    257 p. illus.
    Chiefly of life in northern Ontario.   OTU
Carmichael, Hugh G
    Who's where on the Muskoka Lakes. Bracebridge, Ontario: Muskoka
    Publishing, 1976.
    268, 18 p. maps.   OONL
Clay, John .
    My recollections of Ontario. Chicago: Printed for private circulation, 1918.
    60 p. front., illus. (part fold., part col.), ports.
    "Originally written for the *Farmer's Magazine*, Toronto, Ontario."   OTU
Countryside in Ontario Conference, London, Ontario, 1974.
    Proceedings. Edited by M.J. Troughton, J.G. Nelson and S. Brown. London,
    Ontario: The University of Western Ontario, 1974.
    vi, 260 p.   OTU

Dickson, James.
    Camping in the Muskoka region. Toronto: C. Blackett Robinson, 1886.
    164 p. front.   OTU
— Camping in the Muskoka region: a story of Algonquin Park. Toronto: The
    Ryerson Press for Ontario Department of Lands and Forests [1960, c1959]
    164 p. illus., fold. map.
    Reprinted from 1886 edition.   OTU
Dixon, Andrew.
    What most people don't see at Grand Bend. Illustrated by K.R. Philip
    Miller. London, Ontario: A. Talbot Ltd., c1963.
    26 p. illus.   OTMCL
Douglas, Jack, 1908–
    Shut up and eat your snowshoes. New York: G.P. Putnam's Sons [c1970]
    251 p.
    Life in northern Ontario.   OTU
The first Women's Institute in the world was founded in Stoney Creek, Feb. 19,
    1897. [Stoney Creek: 1966]
    11 p.   OTAR
Fraser, Joshua, fl. 1858–1883.
    Shanty, forest and river life in the backwoods of Canada, by the author of
    "Three months among the moose". Montreal: John Lovell & Son, 1883.
    361 p. illus.
    Perth, Ontario.   OKQ
Galbraith, John Kenneth, 1908–
    Made to last. London: Hamish Hamilton [1964]
    144 p.
    Life in Elgin county.
    Canadian edition (Toronto: Macmillan) published under title *The Scotch*.
                                                                       OTU
— The Scotch. With illustrations by Samuel H. Bryant. Toronto: The
    Macmillan Company of Canada Ltd. [c1964]
    ix, 145 p. illus.   OTU OKQ
Green, Gavin Hamilton, 1862–
    The old log house and bygone days in our villages. Goderich, Ontario:
    Signal–Star Press, 1948.
    201 p. illus., ports.   OTU
Guillet, Edwin Clarence, 1898–1975.
    Early life in Upper Canada. With 318 illustrations, including 16 in colour,
    selected and arranged by the author. Toronto: Ontario Publishing Co.,
    Limited, 1933.
    xliii, 782 p. illus., maps.
    Chiefly pre-Confederation.   OTU
— [Toronto] University of Toronto Press, 1963.
    xliii, 782 p. illus., maps.
    A reprint of the 1933 edition.   OTU

— Pioneer days in Upper Canada. [Toronto] University of Toronto Press [1963
  c1933]
  216 p. illus.
  Chiefly pre-Confederation.   OTU
— Pioneer inns and taverns. Toronto: Ontario Publishing Co., Limited,
  1954–1958.
  4 v. illus. (part col.), facsims., port.
  v. 1 was published by the author.
  Contents: v. 1, Ontario, with detailed reference to Metropolitan Toronto
  and Yonge Street to Penetanguishene. v. 2, The province of Quebec, the
  Ottawa valley, and American inns, with special reference to the New York –
  Buffalo route via the Hudson River and the Erie Canal; v. 3, Quebec to
  Detroit, with a detailed coverage of the province of Ontario; v. 4,
  Continuing the detailed coverage of Ontario with a concluding estimate of
  the position of the innkeeper in community life.   OTU
— Pioneer life in the county of York. Toronto: Hess–Trade Typesetting
  Company, 1946.
  xi, 166 p. illus., ports.   OTU
— Pioneer settlements in Upper Canada. [Toronto] University of Toronto Press
  [1969, c1933]
  118 p. illus., map.
  Chiefly pre-Confederation.   OTU
— Pioneer social life. Toronto: Ontario Publishing Co., 1938.
  124 p. col. front., illus. (Early life in Upper Canada series, book 3).
  Chiefly pre-Confederation.   OTAR
Haight, Canniff, 1825–1900.
  Country life in Canada fifty years ago: personal recollections and
  reminiscences of a sexagenarian. Toronto: Hunter, Rose & Co., 1885.
  xi, 303 p. illus., ports.   OLU
— Country life in Canada. With a new introduction by Arthur R.M. Lower.
  Belleville, Ontario: Mika Silk Screening Limited, 1971.
  ii, xi, 303, 5 p. illus. (Canadiana reprint series, no. 2).
  Original was published in 1885.   OTU
Hale, J   R
  Twenty-five years of Women's Institute activities in East Simcoe. [Orillia,
  Ontario: Orillia Packet & Times, 1935]
  29 p.   OTAR
Hathaway, Ann, 1849–
  Muskoka memories: sketches from real life. Toronto: William Briggs, 1904.
  viii, 227 p. illus., ports.   OTU
Hett, Francis Paget.
  Georgina: a type study of early settlement and church building in Upper
  Canada. Toronto: The Macmillan Company of Canada Limited, 1939.
  xvi, 128 p. illus.
  Chiefly pre-Confederation.   OLU

Hinds, A   Leone.
    The pioneer inns and taverns of Guelph. Illustrated by Hugh Douglass.
    [Cheltenham, Ontario: The Boston Mills Press, c1977?]
    1 v. (unpaged). illus. (Waterloo – Wellington county series, 2)   OTAR
Howard, David James, 1884–
    The true life story of David James Howard. [2d ed. Thornhill, Ontario:
    York Printing House Ltd., 1972]
    [144] p. illus., ports., map.
    First edition, 1971. No copy located.   OTU
Kelley, Thomas Patrick, 1909–
    The black Donnellys. Toronto: Harlequin Books [1954]
    160 p.   OTU
— Vengeance of the black Donnellys: Canada's most feared family strikes back
    from the grave. Winnipeg: Greywood Publishing [c1962]
    190 p.   OTU
King, Harriett Barbara.
    Letters from Muskoka, by an emigrant lady. London: Richard Bentley and
    Son, 1878.
    xii, 289 p.
    The 1870's.   OKQ
Landon, Fred, 1880–1969.
    Up the proof line. The story of a rural community. Compiled for Douglas B.
    Weldon by Fred Landon and Orlo Miller. With a foreword by Arthur R.
    Ford. London, Ontario: Hunter Printing Company Limited, 1955.
    85 p.   OTU
Langman, Robert Clare, 1924–
    Patterns of settlement in southern Ontario: three studies. [Toronto]
    McClelland and Stewart Limited [c1971]
    ix, 141 p. illus., graphs, plans, maps, tables.   OTU
Leverette, Clarke Edward, 1936–
    Our fourth concession: a 19th century history of lots nine to twelve of the
    fourth concession, London township. Illustrations by Hillary M. Hallpike.
    London, Ontario: The Northridge – Stoneybrook Community Association,
    1969.
    iii, 36 p. illus., maps.   OTAR
MacDougall, John, 1842–1917.
    Rural life in Canada: its trends and tasks. With an introduction by James
    W. Robertson. Toronto: The Westminister Company, Limited, 1913.
    248 p. illus.   OTAR
McKenzie, Ruth.
    Laura Secord: the legend and the lady. Toronto: McClelland & Stewart
    [c1971]
    142 p. illus., ports.   OTU
MacTavish, Newton McFaul, 1875–1941.
    Newton MacTavish's Canada: selected essays of Newton MacTavish, edited

and with an introduction by Ellen Stafford. With illustrations by Richard
Taylor. Toronto: Baxter Pub. Co. [c1963]
176 p. illus.
Stories of rural Ontario.   OTU
Miller, Hanson Orlo, 1911–
Death to the Donnellys. Toronto: Macmillan of Canada [c1975]
228 p.   OTU
— The Donnellys must die. Toronto: Macmillan of Canada, 1962.
244 p. ports., facsims.   OTU
Minhinnick, Jeanne, 1903–
At home in Upper Canada. Illustration design and drawings by John
Richmond. Toronto: Clarke, Irwin & Company Limited, [c1970]
228 p. illus., facsims.
Chiefly 1783–1867.   OKQ
Moodie, Susannah (Strickland), 1803–1885.
Roughing it in the bush; or, Forest life in Canada. With an introductory
chapter in which Canada of the present is contrasted with Canada of forty
years ago. Toronto: Hunter, Rose, 1871.
538 p. illus.
The original work tells of life in Ontario circa 1832. An additional chapter
contrasts 1832 with 1871.   OTU
Morenus, Richard.
Crazy white man. Illustrated by William Lackey. London: Hammond,
Hammond & Co. [c1954]
256 p. map.
Life in northern Ontario.   OTU
Morphy, E   M
A York pioneer looking back, 1834–1884 at youthful days, emigration and
the drinking customs of fifty years ago also at the cranks met with in the
Emerald Isle and Canada: with amusing incidents and anecdotes of the
early settler in the latter place... and a brief sketch of the York Pioneers'
Society. [Toronto: Budget Press, 1890]
32 p.
Chiefly pre-Confederation.   OTURS
Munro, William F
The backwoods life. Toronto: Hunter, Rose & Co., 1869.
79 p.
Corning Mills, Ontario.   OLU
— The backwoods' life: an interesting story of pioneer days in Melancthon
township. Shelburne, Ontario: The Free Press, 1910.
59, viii p. ports.
Reprint of the 1869 edition.   OTAR
Nasby, David, 1945–
Permanence and change; a rural Ontario document. [Toronto: House of
Anansi Press Limited, c1973]
66 p. chiefly illus.   OTU

Ontario. Commission in the matter of application for patent of lots 94 and 95 in
  3rd concession S.W. of Toronto and Sydenham Road township of Glenelg.
  Report. [Toronto: 1925]
  10 typewritten pages.
  Commissioner: F.E. Titus.   OTAR
— Proceedings, March 28, 1925.
  30 typewritten pages.   OTAR
Ontario. Commission in the matter of application for patent of north one-half of
  lot number seven, ninth concession, township of Glenelg, county of Grey,
  province of Ontario.
  Report. [Toronto: 1931]
  6 typewritten pages.
  Commissioner: Fernando Elwood Titus.   OTAR
— Evidence, June 1, 1931.
  16 typewritten pages.   OTAR
Ontario. Commission of enquiry Kapuskasing colony.
  Report. Printed by order of the Legislative Assembly of Ontario. Toronto:
  A.T. Wilgress, printer to the King's Most Excellent Majesty, 1920.
  15 p.
  Chairman: W.F. Nickle.   OTAR
Pinkerton, Kathrene.
  Wilderness wife. New York: Carrick and Evans, Inc. [c1939]
  327 p.
  A story of northern Ontario.   OTU
Powell, M   Viola.
  Forty years agrowing: a history of Ontario Women's Institutes. Port Perry,
  Ontario: Port Perry Star, 1941.
  95 p. illus., ports.   OTAR
Russell, Loris Shano, 1904–
  A heritage of light: lamps and lighting in the early Canadian home.
  [Toronto] University of Toronto Press [c1968]
  344 p. illus.   OTU
— Lighting the pioneer Ontario home. [Toronto] Royal Ontario Museum,
  University of Toronto, 1966.
  [1] 16 [1] p. illus. (Royal Ontario Museum series. What? why? when? how?
  where? who? no. 12).   OTU
St. John, Judith.
  Where the saints have trod. London: Oxford University Press, 1974.
  xi, 107 p.
  Reminiscences of early life in rural Ontario, fifty years ago.   OONL
Scott, James, 1916–
  Huron county in pioneer times... illustrations by C.W. Jefferys and Donald
  Vincent. Seaforth, Ontario: Huron County Historical Committee, 1954.
  87 p. illus.
  Chiefly pre-Confederation.   OTU
— The settlement of Huron county. Toronto: The Ryerson Press [c1966]
  xvi, 328 p. illus., ports.   OTU

Shaw, Bertha Mary Constance, 1880–
    Born to grow old. Timmins, Ontario: Northern Stationery and Printing
    Company, 1960.
        163 p.
        Reminiscences of a teacher in northern Ontario.   OTU
— Broken threads: memories of a northern Ontario school-teacher. [1st ed.]
    New York: Exposition Press [c1955]
        153 p.   OTU
— Laughter and tears; memories from between the limestone hills and the blue
    Georgian Bay, Ontario. [1st ed.] New York: Exposition Press [c1957]
        183 p.   OTU
Stewart, Frances (Browne), 1794–1872.
    Our forest home being extracts from the correspondence of the late Frances
    Stewart. Compiled and edited by her daughter, Eleanor Susannah Dunlop.
    [2d ed] Montreal: Gazette Printing and Publishing Co., 1902.
        300, xci p. plates.
        Peterborough, Ontario, chiefly pre-Confederation.
        A first edition was published in Toronto, 1889. No copy was located.   OTURS
Swain, John Gwynn.
    Letters to his mother, written on his entrance into life, aged seventeen, giving
    a description of his voyage to Canada and adventures at Lake Superior.
    Edinburgh [Turnbull & Spears] 1869.
        111 p. illus.   OTU
Temiskaming and Northern Ontario Railway Commission.
    Opportunities for settlers in the northland: Temiskaming, new Ontario,
    1911. Toronto: 1911.
        20 p. illus. (*Its* pamphlet no. 8).
        Chairman: J.L. Englehart.   OTU
— A plain tale of plain people: pioneer life in new Ontario. The great clay belt.
    Toronto: Temiskaming and Northern Ontario Railway Commission [1913?]
        42 p. illus. (*Its* pamphlet no. 12).   OTU
Thompson, Ronald T   F   (ed.).
    Life from old letters, 1795–1886, glimpses into the past Canada, Britain and
    the United States; a review of 500 letters and documents. [Victoria, British
    Columbia, c1969]
        68 leaves.   OTU
        A companion volume to *Reminiscences of a Canadian pioneer* by Samuel
        Thompson.   OTU
Tivy, Louis, 1902–1972 (ed.).
    Your loving Anna. Letters from the Ontario frontier. [Toronto] University of
    Toronto Press [c1972]
        120 p. illus., map.
        Anna Leveridge settled with her husband in Hastings county in 1883. An
        account of life in Ontario at that time.   OTU

Trumble, David, 1867–
    When I was a boy, edited by Glen Ellis. Don Mills, Ontario: J.M. Dent &
    Sons (Canada) Limited [c1976]
    107 p. illus., ports.   OONL
Victorian Cobourg: a nineteenth century profile, J. Petryshyn, editor-in-chief;
    associate editors, D.M. Calnan, T.W. Crossen, L.Dzubak. Belleville,
    Ontario: Mika Publishing Company, 1976.
    238 p. illus., ports., tables.
    Chiefly pre-Confederation.   OTU
Walker, Annie E
    Fifty years of achievement: in commemoration of the 50th anniversary of the
    founding of the Women's Institutes of Ontario, by Annie Walker, Edith M.
    Collins and M. McIntyre Hood. [Toronto] Federated Women's Institutes of
    Ontario, 1948.
    163 p. illus., ports.   OTU
Ward, Duren James Henderson, 1851–
    Dorchester early settlers: living round-about the center of the township of
    North Dorchester, Middlesex county, Upper Canada from 1850 to 1870.
    Denver, Colorado: Up the Divide Publishing Co., 1927.
    96 p. illus., map, ports.   OKQ
Ward, Edward H   K   1903–
    Early homesteaders of Parry Sound: as told by descendants of the Haines
    family, researched and compiled by E.H.R. Ward and Moira M. Ward.
    Barrie, Omtario: Industrial Printing, 1974.
    201 p. illus., facsims., geneal., tables, maps, ports.   OTAR
Waterston, Elizabeth, 1922–   (ed.).
    On middle ground: landscape and life in Wellington county 1841–1891,
    edited by Elizabeth Waterston and Douglas Hoffman. [Guelph, Ontario:
    The University of Guelph, 1974]
    79 p. illus., maps, tables.   OTU
Wilson, Andrew.
    A history of old Bytown and vicinity, now the city of Ottawa. Ottawa: Daily
    News, 1876.
    89 p.   OTURS
Wilson, (Mrs.) George.
    The history of North Middlesex District Women's Institute: 1903 golden
    anniversary 1953 [by Mrs. George Wilson and Mrs. Harman Morton]. n.p.
    [1953]
    32 p.   OLU
Wilson, Robert.
    A retrospect: a short review of the steps taken in sanitation to transform the
    town of muddy York into the queen city of the west. Toronto: The Carswell
    Co. Ltd., 1934.
    37 p.   OTAR

Wood, Agnus Campbell.
    Old days on the farm... Toronto: McClelland, Goodchild & Stewart
    [c1918]
    x, 255 p. illus.
    Pioneer life in Ontario.   OTMCL
Wood, J   David (ed.).
    Perspectives on landscape and settlement in nineteenth century Ontario.
    Toronto: McClelland and Stewart in association with the Institute of
    Canadian Studies, Carleton University, c1975.
    xxviii, 213 p. illus., maps, tables.   OTU

Periodical Articles

Abbott, J   Kerr.
    Will rural democracy dwindle. Ontario Agricultural College Review 26:
    222–225, 1914.
Abell, Helen C
    Attitudes of some rural leaders in Simcoe county, Ontario. Economic
    Annalist 27: 40–42, 1957.
Abell, Helen C   and D   Dyck.
    Children of rural families of Ontario and Prince Edward Island. Economic
    Annalist 32: 65–69, 1962.
Ball, Rosemary R
    "A perfect farmer's wife": women in the 19th century rural Ontario.
    Canada: an historical magazine 3(no. 2): 2–21, 1975.
    Recollections of Rev. Leonard Bartlett. Western Ontario Historical Notes 17:
    69–88, 1961.
    Notes to the manuscript compiled by Edward Phelps.
Brown, Harry W
    The second Betzner reunion. Waterloo Historical Society. Annual Report 8:
    133–139, 1920.
Burton, Patricia.
    Memoirs of David McCloy 1832–1917. Waterloo Historical Society. Annual
    Volume 59: 82–88, 1971.
Carnochan, Janet.
    Women's Institutes and specially that of Niagara-on-the-Lake. Niagara
    Historical Society. Transactions 37: 32–51, 1925.
Cudmore, S   A
    Rural depopulation in southern Ontario. Royal Canadian Institute,
    Transactions s. 4, 9: 261–267, 1912.
Curtis, Mary Lou (ed.).
    The Garbutt letters. Thunder Bay Historical Museum Society. Papers and
    Records 4: 12–23, 1976.
    Charles Oliver Garbutt.

Dean, W   G
    Human geography of the Lower Albany River basin. Geographical Bulletin
    10: 56–75, 1957.
Dunnett, Carol.
    Mrs. Ophelia Rife; a warm and tender tribute. Waterloo Historical Society.
    Annual Report 44: 43–54, 1956.
Ferris, Diana.
    Availability and use of mass information media in rural Ontario. Economic
    Annalist 32: 137–142, 1962.
Gagan, David.
    Geographical and social mobility in nineteenth-century Ontario: a
    microstudy. Canadian Review of Sociology and Anthropology 13: 152–164,
    1976.
Garland, M   A
    Rural work in western Ontario. Canadian Welfare 20(6): 28–31, 1944.
Grant, Melvin.
    James Grant. Western Ontario Historical Notes 4: 5–11, 1946.
    New Ontario area.
Hart, F   C
    History, purpose, and development of community halls in rural
    communities. Ontario Historical Society. Papers & Records 30: 106–110,
    1934.
Hepburn, Olive E
    Nina Moore Jamieson; writer, philosopher, teacher and friend of the
    Ontario rural scene. Bruce County Historical Society. Yearbook 39–41,
    1972.
Historic landmark about to vanish; much of the old history of Fort William
    centers around the McKellar homestead, which was built fifty years ago, and
    was the home of Fort William's first mayor, and the social center of the
    settlement for many years. Thunder Bay Historical Society. Papers 8: 9–10,
    1917.
    From: *Daily Times–Journal*, Jan. 26, 1917.
Home, Ruth M
    The diary of Aaron Wismer (1844–1931), Jordan, Ontario. Ontario History
    51: 39–42, 1959.
Jones, D   H
    The rural scenery of Ontario. Ontario Agricultural College Review 21:
    148–153, 1908.
Joynt, Carey B
    Social changes in Huron county – 1880–1945. Huron Historical Notes 12:
    11–13, 1976.
    Western Ontario Historical Notes 7: 23–26, 1949.
Laidler, George.
    The story of the Land family. Wentworth Bygones 1: 14–26, 1958.

Lee–Whiting, Brenda.
    The Opeongo Road – an early colonization scheme. Canadian Geographical
    Journal. 74: 76–83, 1967.
Macdonald, Ronald.
    Social life in rural districts.Ontario Agricultural College Review 22:
    399–404, 1910.
Mackay, L   A
    The Ontario small-town labourer and farm-hand. Canadian Forum 12: 174,
    1932.
Maynard, (Mrs.) G   Gordon.
    Historical research by Women's Institutes of Ontario. Western Ontario
    Historical Notes 2: 54–56, 1944.
Michie, G   H   and W   C   Found.
    Rural estates in the Toronto region. Ontario Geography 10: 15–26, 1976.
Nisbet, Charlotte Vidal.
    The Talfourd family. Western Ontario History Nuggets 6: 1–8, 1945.
The observations of a fire ranger. Ontario Agricultural College Review 23:
    412–421, 1911.
Ontario Women's Institutes. Economic Annalist 1(no. 12): 9, 1931.
Page, Stewart L
    The philosophy of rural community life. Ontario Library Review 35: 35–40,
    1951.
    Simcoe county.
Pennington, Doris Tucker.
    Life and times of Frank Carter, 1853–1941. Bruce County Historical Society.
    Yearbook 7–13, 1975.
Putnam, G   A
    Farmers' Institutes in Ontario. Ontario Agricultural College Review 20:
    193–197, 1908.
Ransford, Henry.
    Dates and events connected with my family (1667 : 1881). Western Ontario
    History Nuggets 28: 1–81, 1959.
Reid, Timothy E
    Rural poverty crisis: Ontario. Canadian Forum 48: 279–280, 1969.
Walker, Gerald.
    Social interaction in the Holland Marsh. Ontario Geography 8: 52–63,
    1974.
Ward, J   T
    General amenities at Central Patricia and Pickle Crow. Canadian Mining
    Journal 70(no. 8): 119–120, 1949.
Wetherell, Alice.
    The diary of Augusta Silverthorn. Ontario History, 45: 75–81, 1953.
Worrall, Robert J
    The resettlement of Bruce county. Bruce County Historical Society.
    Yearbook 31–35, 1975.

Theses
Alderdice, Kenneth Roy.
   The geography of Albion township. Hamilton, Ontario: 1963.
   132 leaves. illus., graphs, maps (part fold.).
   B.A. thesis, McMaster University.   OHM
Balutanski, Olga.
   Regional geography of Etobicoke township. [Toronto] 1949.
   74 [1] leaves. illus., maps.
   B.A. thesis, University of Toronto.   OTU
Bateman, Robert McLellan.
   Central Haliburton: a geographic study. [Toronto] 1954.
   viii, 146 leaves. illus. (part col.), diagrs. (part col.), col. maps (part fold.).
   B.A. thesis, University of Toronto.   OTU
Beacock, Mary Elinor, 1929–
   A geographic study of Elizabethtown and Brockville. [Toronto] 1952.
   vii, 104 leaves. illus., maps (part col.).
   B.A. thesis, University of Toronto.   OTU
Berton, Marianne M.
   The development of small nucleated settlements in Carleton county .
   [Toronto] 1960.
   xi, 204 leaves. illus., maps (part fold., part col.).
   B.A. thesis, University of Toronto.   OTU
Bland, Peter B
   The survival of the hamlet in Muskoka. [Toronto] 1971.
   v, 68 leaves. tables, maps (part fold.).
   B.A. research paper, University of Toronto.   OTU
Bousfield, John Reginald, 1929–
   The town of Cobourg and Hamilton township: a regional study. [Toronto]
   1951.
   133 [1] leaves. illus. (part col.), maps (part col.).
   B.A. thesis, University of Toronto.   OTU
Brown, Charles G
   A geographical study of Malahide township. [Toronto] 1951.
   ix, 112 [2] leaves. illus., maps.
   B.A. thesis, University of Toronto.   OTU
Brown, W   Stuart.
   Caledon township: a geographical survey. [Toronto] 1951.
   117 leaves. illus., maps.
   B.A. thesis, University of Toronto.   OTU
Calder, George.
   A geographical survey of the district of Parry Sound. [Toronto] 1949.
   1 v. (various pagings). illus., maps.
   B.A. thesis, University of Toronto.   OTU
Copeland, R   A
   The town of Barrie and its island: a geographic study. [Toronto] 1951.
   vi, 122 leaves. illus. (part col.), diagrs., maps.
   B.A. thesis, University of Toronto.   OTU

Cox, Kenneth Wayne.
    A functional classification of small towns in Waterloo county. Waterloo, Ontario: 1969.
    vi, 66 leaves. graphs, maps.
    B.A. thesis, Waterloo University College.   OWTL
Cramm, Earl Wesley Reid.
    An analysis of the urban process in Pickering township. [Toronto] 1962.
    xiii, 126 leaves. illus., diagrs., maps.
    M.A. thesis, University of Toronto.   OTU
Cunningham, Griffiths Laurence.
    The geography of Louth township. [Toronto] 1955.
    [9] 94 leaves. illus., maps (part col.).
    B.A. thesis, University of Toronto.   OTU
—— The Manitoulin district: a geographic survey. [Toronto] 1957.
    xii, 133 leaves. illus., maps (5 fold.).
    M.A. thesis, University of Toronto.   OTU
Davis, Robert A
    Evolution of the settlement pattern of Scarborough township: a rural-urban fringe study. [Toronto] 1948.
    87 leaves. illus., maps (part col., part fold.).
    B.A. thesis, University of Toronto.   OTU
Dean, William George, 1921–
    Toronto township: a geographical reconnaissance. [Toronto] 1949.
    iii, 108 [1] leaves. illus., maps (part col., part fold.).
    B.A. thesis, University of Toronto.   OTU
Edwards, Karen Louise.
    A geographical study of Mono township. [Hamilton, Ontario] 1964.
    74 leaves. illus., graphs, maps, tables.
    B.A. thesis, McMaster University.   OHM
Ellis, Brent Barkley.
    A geographical study of Walpole township. [Hamilton, Ontario] 1961.
    100 leaves. illus., maps, graphs.
    B.A. thesis, McMaster University.   OHM
Evenden, Leonard Jessie.
    A geographical study of Keppel township. Hamilton, Ontario: 1960.
    117 leaves. illus., maps.
    B.A. thesis, McMaster University.   OHM
Firstbrook, Elizabeth Holland, 1934–
    Port Credit: a port of the past or of the future? a geographical study of the development of a village on Lake Ontario, between the ever increasing cities of Toronto and Hamilton. [Toronto] 1957.
    77 [1] leaves. illus., maps (part fold., part col.).
    B.A. thesis, University of Toronto.   OTU
Fors, Eric Hugo.
    The Porcupine district: a regional study. [Toronto] 1956.
    ii, 86 leaves. illus. (part col.), maps (part col., part fold.), fold. plan.
    B.A. thesis, University of Toronto.   OTU

Fraser, John Keith Campbell.
    A geographic study of the northern coasts of lakes Huron and Superior.
    [Toronto] 1953.
    2 v. [396 leaves] illus., maps (part fold., part col.).
    M.A. thesis, University of Toronto (accepted 1955).   OTU
Frid, Bradley Robert.
    South Grimsby township, a geographical study. [Hamilton, Ontario] 1959.
    96 leaves. illus., maps, tables.
    B.A. thesis, McMaster University.   OHM
Game, Kathleen.
    A study of Walkerton and its rimland. [Toronto] 1949.
    1 v. (various pagings). illus., maps (2 fold. in pocket).
    B.A. thesis, University of Toronto.   OTU
Gawinski, T   G
    The township of North York: a study of Toronto's rural-urban fringe.
    [Toronto] 1951.
    79 [2] leaves. illus., maps.
    B.A. thesis, University of Toronto.   OTU
Geen, Robert Cecil.
    A regional study of Bromley township, Renfrew county, Ontario. [Hamilton,
    Ontario] 1956.
    50 leaves. illus., diagrs., maps.
    B.A. thesis, McMaster University.   OHM
George, Isabelle E
    Hullett township in Huron county: a study of a township in southwestern
    Ontario on a regional basis. [Toronto] 1950.
    98 leaves. illus., maps (part col.).
    B.A. thesis, University of Toronto.   OTU
George, Victor Alan, 1924–
    Wallaceburg, Ontario: a geographical study of a town and its rimland.
    [Toronto] 1952.
    iv, 125 leaves. illus., maps (part col., part fold.).
    B.A. thesis, University of Toronto.   OTU
Hall, Kenneth Murray.
    Flos township: a study in settlement and land utilization. [Hamilton,
    Ontario] 1954.
    v, 88 leaves. plates, maps (part fold.), graphs.
    B.A. thesis, McMaster University.   OHM
Helm, Michael.
    Civil disorders in Biddulph township, 1850–1880; a case study of the
    Donnelly murders. Montreal, Quebec: 1970.
    iv, 101 leaves.
    M.A. thesis, Sir George Williams University (microfilm 6334).   Can
Hill, Peter Leslie.
    A geographical study of Moulton and Sherbrooke townships. Hamilton,
    Ontario: 1959.
    vii, 116 leaves. illus., maps (part fold.).
    B.A. thesis, McMaster University.   OHM

Hitchman, Elaine.
 Second homes and their conversion to principal residences: a case study in
 the district municipality of Muskoka. Toronto: 1976.
 xiii, 175 leaves. tables, fold. map.
 M.A. thesis, York University (microfilm 30906).   OTY
Innis, Donald Quayle.
 The rural-urban fringe of Toronto. [Toronto] 1947.
 103 leaves. illus., maps8
 B.A. thesis, University of Toronto.   OTU
Irwin, Sheila A
 A geographic study of the township of Gloucester. [Toronto] 1952.
 vii, 115 leaves. illus. (part col.), maps (part col.).
 B.A. thesis, University of Toronto.   OTU
Jamieson, Ronald Keith.
 A residential subdivision in Shumiah, Ontario. Winnipeg: 1957.
 48 leaves.
 M.Sc. thesis, University of Manitoba.   MWU
Jarrett, Rob.
 Settlement and development of the Yonge Street area, York Mills to Steeles
 Avenue, 1774 to 1922. [Toronto] 1974.
 iii, 55 leaves. illus., maps.
 B.A. research paper, University of Toronto.   OTU
Kidd, George Albert.
 A sociological survey of an Ontario rural community. [Toronto: 1936]
 108 [1, iv] leaves.
 M.A. thesis, University of Toronto (microfilm 27892).   OTU
Kirk, Donald William.
 The Listowel region of southwestern Ontario. [Toronto] 1945.
 iii, 175 leaves. illus., maps (part fold.).
 M.A. thesis, University of Toronto.   OTU
LaRocque, Alex. J
 Winchester and Mountain townships: a geography of Mountain and
 Winchester township, Dundas county. [Toronto] 1948.
 110 leaves. illus., maps (part col.).
 B.A. thesis, University of Toronto.   OTU
Lee, Chun-fen, 1912–
 The middle Grand River valley of Ontario; a study in regional geography
 [Toronto] 1943.
 [24] 471 [1] leaves. illus., diagrs., maps (part fold.).
 Ph.D. thesis, University of Toronto.   OTU
Legg, C   L
 Rural progress in old Ontario. Hamilton, Ontario: 1915.
 80 leaves.
 M.A. thesis, McMaster University.   OHM
Leigh, Keith William.
 Some aspects of the historical geography of Orillia. [Toronto] 1970.
 v, 73 leaves. tables, maps.
 B.A. research paper, University of Toronto.   OTU

Lemp, William Eric.
    A geographical study of Hullett township. Hamilton, Ontario: 1961.
    vi, 138 leaves. illus., maps (part fold., part col.), charts, tables.
    B.A. thesis, McMaster University.   OHM
Lewis, Malcolm Reginald.
    A geographical study of Bertie township. [Hamilton, Ontario] 1964.
    vi, 143 leaves. illus., maps (part fold.), charts, tables.
    B.A. thesis, McMaster University.   OHM
Lockhead, C   H
    Reach and Scugog townships: a geographical survey. [Toronto] 1950.
    122 [1] leaves. illus., maps (part fold., part col.).
    B.A. thesis, University of Toronto.   OTU
Longley, Robert Prescott.
    Rural credits in Ontario. [Toronto] 1932.
    81 [10] leaves.
    M.S.A. thesis, University of Toronto.   OTU
Lustig, Joan Lenore.
    Port Elgin and Southampton: a study of two lakeside towns. [Toronto] 1957.
    31 [1] leaves. illus., col. diagrs., maps (part fold., part col.).
    B.A. thesis, University of Toronto.   OTU
Lustig, Marie E
    Elderslie and Brant: a geographic study of two townships in Bruce county,
    Ontario. [Toronto: 1944]
    55 leaves. illus., maps (part col., part fold.).
    B.A. thesis, University of Toronto.   OTU
McCullough, Sheila.
    Bowmanville, Ontario: a geographical study of a southern Ontario town.
    [Toronto] 1954.
    iv, 73 [1] leaves. illus., maps (part col.).
    B.A. thesis, University of Toronto.   OTU
McCutcheon, Murray K
    Mulmur and Melancthon; a geographical survey of the two northern
    townships of Dufferin county. [Toronto] 1950.
    v, 167 leaves. illus., maps. (1 fold. in pocket, col.).
    B.A. thesis, University of Toronto.   OTU
McCutheon, Henry Richard.
    A geographic study of East Gwillimbury township. Hamilton, Ontario:
    1964.
    117 leaves. illus., maps (part fold.), graphs.
    B.A. thesis, McMaster University.   OHM
MacKenzie, Albert Edward Douglas, 1936–
    Lord Selkirk's Baldoon experiment. London, Ontario: 1968.
    vi, 184 leaves. facsims., illus., maps.
    M.A. thesis, The University of Western Ontario.   OLU

MacKenzie, Marilyn Beatty.
   A geographical study of North Dumfries township. [Hamilton, Ontario]
   1958.
   111 leaves. illus., maps (part fold.).
   B.A. thesis, McMaster University.   OHM
McLean, William Alexander.
   A geographical study of the township of Whitby and the town of Whitby.
   Hamilton, Ontario: 1959.
   104 leaves. illus., maps (part col.).
   B.A. thesis, McMaster University.   OHM
MacLeod, Peter Kenneth.
   Gualainn Ri Gualainn: a study of concentrations of Scottish settlement in
   nineteenth century Ontario. Ottawa: 1972.
   xiii, 258 leaves. graphs, maps, facsims., tables.
   M.A. thesis, Carleton University.   OOCC
Mandziuk, Diane.
   Delhi: growth problems of a small town. [Toronto] 1967.
   viii, 58 leaves. illus., maps (1 col. fold.).
   B.A. thesis, University of Toronto.   OTU
Mason, Reginald Wray.
   Dereham township, a study in settlement and land utilization. [Hamilton,
   Ontario] 1953.
   viii, 78 leaves. illus., maps, diagrs.
   B.A. thesis, McMaster University.   OHM
Moore, Kate.
   Regional geography of Bruce peninsula. [Toronto] 1948.
   68 [1] leaves. illus., maps (part fold. col.).
   B.A. thesis, University of Toronto.   OTU
Moore, Sandra Maureen, 1947–
   Yorkville 1808–1883. [Toronto] 1968.
   iii, 48 leaves. maps (part fold., part col.).
   B.A. research paper, University of Toronto.   OTU
Morrison, Neil Farquharson, 1896–
   Essex county, province of Ontario; a geographical study. [Ann Arbor,
   Michigan: 1944]
   v, 245 leaves. illus., diagrs., maps.
   Ph.D. thesis, The University of Michigan.   DA
Munro, J   H
   The township of Kincardine: a geographical survey. [Toronto] 1951.
   81 [1] leaves. illus., maps.
   B.A. thesis, University of Toronto.   OTU
Murdoch, Louise Helen.
   A study of the hopes, aspirations and attitudes of the traditional rural
   disadvantaged families which may be used by the helping professions to
   motivate these families to upgrade themselves. [Toronto] 1968.
   ii, 140 leaves. tables (part fold.).
   M.S.W. thesis, University of Toronto.   OTU

Nesbit, Douglas C
    Geographic studies in the town of Napanee. [Toronto] 1949.
    103 [1] leaves. illus., maps (part col.).
    B.A. thesis, University of Toronto.   OTU
Neyland, David Lawrence Michael.
    A geographical study of Townsend township. [Hamilton, Ontario] 1960.
    v, 131 leaves. illus., maps, graphs.
    B.A. thesis, McMaster University.   OHM
Nitkin, David Alexander.
    Pelee Island: the future or a future? [Toronto] 1968.
    viii, 152 [1] leaves. illus., maps.
    B.A. thesis, University of Toronto.   OTU
O'Neill, John William.
    Whitby, Ontario: a study of the urban geography of a town. [Toronto] 1954.
    77 leaves. illus., maps (part col.).
    B.A. thesis, University of Toronto.   OTU
Owen, Marjory R
    Nottawasaga township: a regional study. [Toronto] 1950.
    v, 119 [1] leaves. illus., maps.
    B.A. thesis, University of Toronto.   OTU
Parson, Helen Edna.
    Nepean township since 1951: a geographical analysis of the processes of
    change. Ottawa: 1967.
    vii, 41 leaves. graphs, maps, tables.
    B.A. research essay, Carleton University.   OOCC
Patterson, H   S
    A geographical survey of Albion township. [Toronto] 1950.
    151 leaves. illus., maps (1 fold. col. in pocket).
    B.A. thesis, University of Toronto.   OTU
Pisko, Milan.
    A geographic analysis of the township of Mersea: an exercise in applied
    geography with a view to evolving a zoning by-law. [Windsor, Ontario]
    1972.
    xii, 153 leaves. illus., graphs, maps, tables.
    M.A. thesis, University of Windsor.   OWA
Porter, Earl F
    The geography of Nelson and Trafalgar townships in Halton county,
    Ontario: a regional study. [Toronto] 1950.
    vii, 135 leaves. illus., maps.
    B.A. thesis, University of Toronto.   OTU
Reid, John Christopher.
    A geographical study of Gainsborough township. [Hamilton, Ontario] 1959.
    iv, 105 leaves. illus., maps (part fold., part col.).
    B.A. thesis, McMaster University.   OHM

Reid, John G
    Clarke township, Durham county, Ontario; a geographical survey.
    [Toronto] 1953.
    65 [2] leaves. illus., col. maps.
    B.A. thesis, University of Toronto.   OTU
Reid, Norman Edward.
    A geographical study of Blenheim township. [Hamilton, Ontario] 1958.
    86 leaves. illus., maps, (part col., part fold.), diagrs.
    B.A. thesis, McMaster University.   OHM
Ridge, F   Gerald.
    Barton township: a study in rural-urban relationships. [Hamilton, Ontario]
    1950.
    vii, 110 p. plates, maps (part fold.).
    B.A. thesis, McMaster University.   OHM
Robson, W   T
    The Severn valley: a geographical study on the Shield. [Toronto] 1949.
    60 [1] leaves. illus., maps (part fold., part col.).
    B.A. thesis, University of Toronto.   OTU
Roulston, Pauline J
    The urbanization of nineteenth-century Orangeville, Ontario: some
    historical and geographical aspects. [Toronto] 1974.
    94 leaves. tables, maps.
    M.A. research paper, University of Toronto.   OTU
Roy, Joan M
    A geographic study of Nepean township. [Toronto] 1952.
    viii, 144 leaves. illus., maps (part col.).
    B.A. thesis, University of Toronto.   OTU
Seymour, Lee, 1949–
    Social interaction of senior citizens in St. Mary's, Ontario. London, Ontario:
    1973.
    xii, 170 leaves. tables, maps.
    M.A. thesis, The University of Western Ontario (microfilm 16450).   OLU
Shindman, B
    A geographic reconnaissance of Lambton county. [Toronto] 1948.
    115 leaves. illus., maps (part fold., part col.).
    B.A. thesis, University of Toronto.   OTU
Sim, Victor W
    Binbrook township: a study in settlement and land utilization. [Hamilton,
    Ontario] 1952.
    v, 106 leaves. plates, maps (part fold.).
    B.A. thesis, McMaster University.   OHM
Sled, George William.
    A geographical study of Culross township. Hamilton, Ontario: 1963.
    96 leaves. illus., maps (part fold.).
    B.A. thesis, McMaster University.   OHM

Sloan, Hugh.
　　Aspects of temporality and townscape with a perspective on Ontario towns.
　　[Toronto] 1976.
　　ii, 103 leaves. illus.
　　M.A. research paper, University of Toronto.   OTU
Smith, James Dennis.
　　The Blezard valley. Hamilton, Ontario: 1956.
　　iii, 62 leaves. illus., maps (part fold.).
　　B.A. thesis, McMaster University.   OHM
Snelgrove, Howard Baron.
　　Hope township: a regional study. [Toronto] 1952.
　　v, 72 leaves. illus., diagrs. (part col.), maps (part col.), col. plans.
　　B.A. thesis, University of Toronto.   OTU
Spearin, Charles Edward.
　　A geographic study of Brighton township. Hamilton, Ontario: 1960.
　　vi, 95 leaves. illus., maps (part fold.).
　　B.A. thesis, McMaster University.   OHM
Stager, John K
　　Ancaster township: a study in settlement and land utilization. [Hamilton,
　　Ontario] 1951.
　　1 v. (unpaged). plates, maps (part fold., part col.), diagrs.
　　B.A. thesis, McMaster University.   OHM
Stone, Wilfrid Gerard, 1911–
　　A geographical survey of Pelee Island. [London, Ontario] 1949.
　　xv, 162 leaves. illus., graphs, photos, maps (part fold.).
　　M.Sc. thesis, The University of Western Ontario.   OLU
Stymeist, David Harold, 1946–
　　The permanent resident – outsider distinction in Sioux Lookout, Ontario: an
　　analysis of a local social system. [Toronto] c1975.
　　vii, 232 leaves. tables, figs., map.
　　Ph.D. thesis, University of Toronto (awarded 1976)   OTU
Thomson, Helen Dianne.
　　A geographical study of Amabel township. Hamilton, Ontario: 1957.
　　120 leaves. illus., maps (part fold., part col.).
　　B.A. thesis, McMaster University.   OHM
Timms, Sidney.
　　A geographical study of Saugeen township. [Hamilton, Ontario] 1963.
　　132 leaves. illus., maps (part fold.), graphs.
　　B.A. thesis, McMaster University.   OHM
Toiviainen, Martin.
　　A geographical study of Nassagawega and Esquesing townships. [Toronto]
　　1951.
　　[7] 128 [2] leaves. illus., maps.
　　B.A. thesis, University of Toronto.   OTU
Truemner, Roger B
　　Hay township: a geographical study of Hay township, Huron county,
　　Ontario. [Toronto] 1950.
　　116 leaves. illus., maps (1 col. fold. in pocket).
　　B.A. thesis, University of Toronto.   OTU

Usher, Anthony J
    Northeastern Ontario in 1900. [Toronto] c1973.
    [5] 104 leaves. illus. (col.), maps (part col.).
    M.A. research paper, University of Toronto.   OTU
Washington, John Calvert.
    A geographical study of Bosanquet township. [Hamilton, Ontario] 1961.
    vi, 112 leaves. illus., maps (part fold.), graphs.
    B.A. thesis, McMaster University.   OHM
Waters, John William, 1924–
    A geographical study of the villages in the London area. [London, Ontario]
    1950.
    xv, 175 leaves. charts, plates, maps (part col.).
    M.Sc. thesis, The University of Western Ontario.   OLU
Watts, Frederick B
    Pelee Island, Ontario: a regional study. [Toronto] 1951.
    69 [1] 2 leaves. illus., maps (part col.).
    B.A. thesis, University of Toronto.   OTU
Weatherhead, Barbara.
    A regional study of the townships of Augusta and Edwardsburg, and the
    town of Prescott. [Toronto] 1952.
    85 leaves. illus., col. maps.
    B.A. thesis, University of Toronto.   OTU
Wonders, William C
    "The Penetanguishene peninsula": a geographic study of the townships of
    Tiny & Tay, Simcoe county, Ontario. [Toronto] 1946.
    128 leaves. illus., maps (part fold. & col.).
    B.A. thesis, University of Toronto.   OTU
Woodruff, James Frederick, 1920–
    Present and future settlement in the Hearst – Nipigon region. Ann Arbor,
    Michigan: 1952.
    vi, 148 leaves. illus., maps (part fold.), diagrs.
    Ph.D. thesis, The University of Michigan (microfilm 00-03822).   DA
Young, R   G
    A geographic reconnaissance of Durham county. [Toronto] 1949.
    119 [1] leaves. illus., maps (part col.).
    B.A. thesis, University of Toronto.   OTU
Zeigler, Wolfgang Frederick.
    A geographical study of Blandford township. [Hamilton, Ontario] 1964.
    108 leaves. illus., maps.
    B.A. thesis, McMaster University.   OHM

URBAN SOCIETY

Bibliography
Stelter, Gilbert Arthur, 1933–
    Canadian urban history: a selected bibliography. Sudbury, Ontario:

Laurentian University Press, 1972.
ii, 61 p. (Laurentian University social science research publication, no. 2).
Ontario: pp. 42–52.   OTU
— Community development in northeastern Ontario: a selected bibliography,
compiled by Gilbert A. Stelter and John Rowan. (Sudbury, Ontario:
Laurentian University Press, 1972)
56 leaves.   OTU
— Current research in Canadian urban history. Urban History Review [4](3):
27–36, 1975.
List of Canadian masters and doctoral theses.

Monographs and Pamphlets
Adam, Graeme Mercer, 1839–1912.
Illustrated Toronto, the queen city of the west. Montreal: J. McConniff,
1891.
61 p. illus.   OTRM
Toronto of today, with a glance at the past. Bryce's souvenir guide to
Toronto. [Toronto: Wm. Bryce] 1887.
15 p. illus., map.   OKQ
— Toronto, old and new: a memorial volume, historical, descriptive and
pictorial, designed to mark the hundredth anniversary of the passing of the
Constitutional Act of 1791, which set apart the province of Upper Canada
and gave birth to York (now Toronto) to which is added a narrative of the
rise and progress of the professions, and the growth and development of the
city's industries and commerce, with some sketches of the men who have
made or are making the provincial capital. With an introduction by the
Rev. Henry Scadding. Toronto: The Mail Printing Company, 1891.
212 p. illus., ports.   OKQ
— Facsimile edition. [Toronto: Coles Publishing Company, c1972]
212 p. illus. (Coles Canadiana Collection).   OTER
Barrett, Frank Alexander, 1935–
Residential search behavior: a study of intra-urban relocation in Toronto.
Toronto: Atkinson College, York University, 1973.
vii, 257 p. (Geographical monographs, no. 1).   OTMCL
Birch, Cecil Mackintosh.
An analysis of occupational unemployment in Greater Windsor, January
1962–June 1964. Prepared for the Greater Windsor Industrial Commission
by Cecil M. Birch & J. Blake Gertz. [Windsor, Ontario] 1964.
v, 118 leaves. graphs, tables.   OTU OWA
Blumenfeld, Hans.
Report on households and families in Metropolitan Toronto, 1951–1956.
[Toronto] Metropolitan Toronto Planning Board, 1958.
5, 13 leaves. tables.   OTU
Bureau of Municipal Research, Toronto.
Citizen participation in Metro Toronto: climate for cooperation? Toronto:
1975.
68 p.   OTU

Butler, Juan.
Cabbagetown diary: a documentary. [Toronto] Peter Martin Associates,
Limited [c1970]
206 p. OTU
Casa Loma; Canada's famous castle. [Toronto: Kiwanis Club of West Toronto]
n.d.
32 p. illus., ports. OTU
Chisamore, Dale.
Brockville: a social history, 1890–1930 by Dale Chisamore [et al.] Brockville,
Ontario: The Waterway Press, 1975.
iv, 126 p. tables. OTU OOA
Clark, Christopher St. George.
Of Toronto the good: a social study, the queen city of Canada as it is.
Montreal: The Toronto Publishing Company, 1898.
210 p. OONL
— [Toronto: Coles Publishing Co., c1970]
210 p. (Coles Canadiana Collection). OONL
Clark, Samuel Delbert, 1910– (ed.).
Urbanism and the changing Canadian society. [Toronto] University of
Toronto Press [c1961]
vii, 150 p. tables. OTU
Collier, Donald F
Ascent from skid row: the Bon Accord community 1867–1973, by Donald F.
Collier and S.A. Somfay. Toronto: Addiction Research Foundation of
Ontario, 1974.
108 p. illus. OTMCL
Conference on Urban Growth, University of Guelph, 1973.
The implications of the urbanization of Toronto on the rest of Ontario;
conference summary. [Guelph, Ontario: University of Guelph? c1973?]
64 p. OTU
Corelli, Rae, 1927–
The Toronto that used to be. [Toronto; Toronto Star, c1964]
61 p. illus., map.
"Contents of this volume appeared originally as an exclusive series of articles
in the news columns of the *Toronto Daily Star*". OTU
Davidson, Emily Delatre, 1874–1954.
Stories my mother told me, and memories of my own. [Toronto: 1967]
[1] 20 leaves.
Toronto social life & customs. OTURS
Eastview, Ontario. Council.
La nouvelle cité; Eastview, the new city. [Eastview, Ontario: The Council]
1963.
68 p. illus., ports., fold. map. OTU
Firth, Sophia.
The urbanization of Sophia Firth. [Toronto] Peter Martin Associates
Limited [c1974]
271 p.
One story of Toronto's poor. OTU

Garvin, Amelia Beers (Warnock), 1878–1956.
>   Toronto: romance of a great city. Decorative maps drawn by Lloyd Scott.
>   Toronto: Cassell & Company Ltd. [c1956]
>   262 p. illus., maps, ports.   OKQ

Goheen, Peter George.
>   Victorian Toronto, 1850–1900; pattern and process of growth. Chicago,
>   Illinois: University of Chicago, Department of Geography, 1970.
>   xiii, 278 p. illus., charts. (Chicago. University. Department of Geography.
>   Research paper, no. 127).   OTU

Harris, (Mrs.) Amelia, 1798–1882.
>   Extracts from the diary of Mrs. Amelia Harris, of London, Ontario, between
>   1857 and 1877. Edited by Fred Landon, and published in the London Free
>   Press between July 14 and November 17, 1928.
>   68 p.   OTURS

How to have a good time in and about Toronto; a complete alphabetically
>   arranged guide to all places of interest, amusements, resorts, etc., in and
>   about Toronto, giving brief descriptions, locations, how to get there and
>   prices, together with time tables of railroads and excursion steamers and
>   much miscellaneous matter; summer edition. Toronto: Supplement Co.,
>   1885.
>   63 p. map.   OTURS

Jackes, Lyman B   1889–1958.
>   Tales of North Toronto. Toronto: North Toronto Business Men's
>   Association, 1948–[52]
>   2 v. illus., maps, ports.   OQK

Jackson, John Nicholas, 1925–
>   The Canadian city: space, form, quality. Toronto: McGraw–Hill, Ryerson
>   Limited [c1973]
>   xi, 237 p. illus., plans.
>   Deals chiefly with southern Ontario (and especially St. Catharines, the
>   Niagara peninsula and Toronto).   OTU

Kumove, Leon.
>   The social structure of Metropolitan Toronto, prepared by Leon Kumove.
>   [Toronto] Municipality of Metropolitan Toronto Planning Department,
>   1975.
>   iii, 319 p. maps. (Background studies in the metropolitan plan preparation
>   programme; v [no. 10]).   OTU

Lamont, Graham.
>   Toronto and York county: a sample study. [Don Mills, Ontario] J.M. Dent
>   & Sons (Canada) Limited [c1970]
>   vii, 120 p. illus. (part col.), maps (part col.), diagrs.   OTAR

London, Ontario. Chamber of Commerce.
>   Seventy-five years of service in community building. London, Canada,
>   1857–1934. [London, Ontario: 1935]
>   1 v. (various pagings). illus. (part col.), plates, ports., maps.   OLU

Lorimer, James, 1942–
    Working people; life in a downtown city neighbourhood [by] James Lorimer
    [and] Myfanwy Phillips. Toronto: James Lewis & Samuel Ltd., 1971.
    xi, 273 p. illus., ports.
    Downtown Toronto.   OTU
Lucas, Rex A   1924–
    Minetown, milltown, railtown; life in Canadian communities of single
    industry. [Toronto] University of Toronto Press [c1971]
    xii, 433 p. map.   OTU
Macbeth, Madge Hamilton (Lyons), 1898–
    Over my shoulder. Foreword by B.K. Sandwell. Toronto: The Ryerson Press
    [c1953]
    170 p. illus.
    Ottawa social life and customs.   OTU
Maher, Charlotte.
    Survey of goals, programmes and clientele of eight multifunctional
    community agencies which have requested grants from the metropolitan
    corporation. [Toronto] 1972.
    88 leaves. maps, tables.   OTU
Mann, William Edward, 1918–   (ed.).
    The underside of Toronto. Toronto: McClelland and Stewart Limited
    [c1970]
    346 p. tables.   OTU
Murdie, Robert A   1939–
    Factorial ecology of Metropolitan Toronto, 1951–1961: an essay on the
    social geography of the city. Chicago: Department of Geography, University
    of Chicago, 1969.
    xi, 212 p. maps, tables. (Chicago. University. Department of Geography.
    Research paper, no. 116).   OTU
Niagara Falls, Ontario. Planning Department.
    Buckley Avenue senior citizens' project. Niagara Falls, Ontario: 1974.
    50 leaves. chart, maps (part fold.), tables.   OONL
ODA Operation Drug Alert Week.
    Proceedings: September 14th to 18th, 1970, Niagara Falls, Ontario.
    [Niagara Falls, Ontario: 1970]
    v, 69 p.   OTU
Pineo, Peter Camden, 1934–
    Basic characteristics of a neighbourhood; preliminary report, North End
    study. Rev. [Ottawa?] 1966.
    30 leaves.
    Hamilton.   OTU
Project 70 looks back at 69. [Toronto] Project '70 [1970]
    1 v. (various pagings).
    Chairman: R. Gerstein; consulting secretary: John Fisher.
    "Under the auspices of the Social Planning Council of Metropolitan
    Toronto".
    Yorkville.   OTUCR

Project 70 looks back. [Toronto] Social Planning Council of Metropolitan
   Toronto [1971]
   1 v. (unpaged).   OTU
Project 71 looks back. [Toronto: Social Planning Council of Metropolitan
   Toronto, 1971?]
   42 leaves.   OTU
Proulx, David.
   Pardon my lunch bucket: a look at the new Hamilton with a bit of old
   thrown in. Text: David Proulx, design: Joe Urban. [Hamilton, Ontario]
   Corporation of the City of Hamilton [1971?]
   1 v. (unpaged). chiefly illus.   OKQ
Rogers, Kenneth H
   Street gangs in Toronto: a study of the forgotten boy. Foreword by R.S.
   Robertson. Toronto: The Ryerson Press [c1945]
   x, 114 p. illus., fold. map.
   pp. 113–114 which contain a poem are missing from the copy examined.
                                                                         OTU
Rosenfeld, Max.
   A blot on the face of the city: the story of Inglewood, Toronto's notorious
   slum empire, by Max Rosenfeld and Earle Beattie. [Toronto: c1956]
   28 p. illus., ports., facsims.
   "Reprint of article published in *The Telegram*, October 11–24, 1955.   OONL
Sawle, George Robert Tregerthen, 1877–
   Hometown: historical sketches of persons & spicy incidents from the late
   years of the 19th century & the early decades of the 20th. Welland, Ontario:
   The Author, 1959.
   92 p.   OTAR
Seeley, John R   1913–
   Crestwood heights, by J.R. Seeley, R.A. Sim and E.W. Loosley, in
   collaboration with Norman W. Bell and D.F. Fleming. [Toronto] University
   of Toronto Press [c1956]
   vi, 505 p. illus.   OTU
Silbert, Morris.
   A study of pensioners living in segregated high-rise apartment buildings in
   the city of Hamilton. Hamilton, Ontario: School of Social Work, McMaster
   University, 1971.
   18 leaves. tables.   OTER
Smallwood, Frank, 1927–
   Metro Toronto: a decade later. Toronto: Bureau of Municipal Research
   [1963]
   v, 41 p. tables.   OTULS
Smart, Reginald George, 1936–
   The Yorkville subculture; a study of the life styles and interactions of hippies
   and non-hippies. Prepared from the field notes of Gopala Alampur by
   Reginald G. Smart and David Jackson. [Toronto] Addiction Research
   Foundation, 1969.
   87 [1] 5, ix p. illus. (Addiction Research Foundation. Project J-183). OTUCR

Thernstrom, Stephen (ed.).
    Nineteenth-century cities: essays in the new urban history. Edited by
    Stephen Thernstrom and Richard Sennent. New Haven and London: Yale
    University Press, 1969.
    xiii, 430 p. tables.
    Hamilton: pp. 209–244.   OTU
Toronto Island Residents Association.
    Save Island homes. [Toronto: The Coach House Press] 1974.
    1 v. (unpaged). illus.   OLU
The Toronto News.
    The night hawks of a great city, as seen by the reporters of "The Toronto
    News". Toronto: Edmund & Sheppard, 1885.
    65 p. illus.
    The Toronto Daily News Library. Toronto by gaslight, no. 1.   OTURS
United Community Services of Greater London. Committee on Drug
    Dependencies.
    Report & recommendations of the Committee on Drug Dependence.
    London, Ontario: 1970.
    1 v. (various pagings). graphs, tables.   OTU
United Community Fund of Greater Toronto.
    Re-examination project; report. Toronto: 1971.
    iii, 55, xxi p. illus.   OTU
Walker, Frank Norman, 1892–
    Sketches of old Toronto. [Don Mills, Ontario] Longmans Canada [1965]
    xii, 350 p. illus., maps, ports.   OTU
Wolforth, John R
    Urban prospects, by John Wolforth and Roger Leigh [Toronto] McClelland
    and Stewart Limited [c1971]
    x, 171 p. graphs, illus., maps, tables.   OTU
Woodsworth, James Shaver, 1874–1942.
    My neighbour: a study of city conditions; a plea for social service. Toronto:
    Missionary Society of the Methodist Church [1911]
    341 p. illus. ports.   OTU
— 2d ed. Toronto: Missionary Society of the Methodist Church [1913]
    341 p. illus., ports.   OTU
— With an introduction by Richard Allen. [Toronto] University of Toronto
    Press [c1972]
    xix, 216 p. illus., maps, ports. (Social history of Canada).   OTU

Periodical Articles
Adamson, Anthony.
    Form and the 20th century Canadian city. Queen's Quarterly 69: 49–68,
    1962.
    Mostly Ontario cities.

Alcorn, Richard S   and José E   Igartua.
    Du rang à la ville: le processus d'urbanisation au Québec et en Ontario.
    Revue d'histoire de l'Amérique française 29: 417–420, 1975.
Barnett, A   N
    Potential homogeneous social bonds in metropolitan Sudbury. Laurentian
    University Review (3): 71–100, 1971.
Batten, Jack H
    Underworld Toronto. Canadian Forum 41: 149–151, 1961.
Bell, Margaret.
    Toronto's melting pot. Canadian Magazine of Politics, Science, Art and
    Literature 41: 234–242, 1913.
Clarke, Lionel H
    Putting on a new front on Toronto. Canadian Magazine of Politics, Science,
    Art and Literature 42: 205–215, 1914.
Colbourne, Maurice.
    Mittens and mud. Canadian Forum 14: 300–301, 1934.
    Toronto morality squad.
De Brisay, Richard.
    The opportunity of the city. Canadian Forum 5: 364–366, 1925.
    Toronto, economic & social problems.
Denton, Frank T   and Peter J   George.
    An exploratory statistical analysis of some socioeconomic characteristics of
    families in Hamilton, Ontario, 1871. Histoire sociale/ Social History 5(1):
    16–44, 1970.
Fox, Joan.
    The facts of life, Toronto style. Canadian Forum 45: 79–80, 1965.
Garner, Hubert.
    Christmas Eve in Cabbagetown. Canadian Forum 17: 354–355, 1938.
— Toronto's Cabbagetown. Canadian Forum 16: 13–15, 1936.
Hambly, W   B
    Cabbage Town. York Pioneer and Historical Society. Annual Report 33–44,
    1969.
Horn, Michiel.
    Keeping Canada "Canadian": anti-communism and Canadianism in
    Toronto 1928–29. Canada: an historical magazine 3(no. 1): 34–47, 1975.
Jackson, David.
    Warrendale. Canadian Forum 47: 77–78, 1967.
Jaffray, William.
    A day at the Waterloo Poor House and what I learned there. Waterloo
    Historical Society. Annual Volume 57: 72–78, 1969.
    Lecture delivered on June 20, 1870 at the Town Hall, Berlin.
Jones, Murray V
    Metropolitan man, some economic and social aspects. Plan Canada 4:
    11–23, 1963.
    Metropolitan Toronto.

Kasahara, Yoshiko.
    A profile of Canadian metropolitan centres. Queen's Quarterly 70: 303–313
    1963.
Kelner, Merrijoy.
    Ethnic penetration into Toronto's elite structure. Canadian Review of
    Sociology and Anthropology 7: 128–137, 1970.
Lamontagne, Leopold.
    Petticoats and coifs in old Kingston. Historic Kingston 9: 21–30, 1960.
Lee, Chun-fen.
    Twin cities of Waterloo and Kitchener. Economic Geography 22: 142–147,
    1946.
Lemon, J   T
    Study of the urban past: approaches by geographers. Canadian Historical
    Association. Historical papers, 179–190, 1973.
Lotto, Victor.
    The Clochard in Toronto. Canadian Forum 41: 29, 1961.
MacDermaid, Anne.
    Kingston in the eighteen-nineties; a study of urban-rural interaction and
    change. Historic Kingston 20: 35–45, 1972.
Mutambirwa, C   C
    An analytical model of a small urban community: the case of the city of
    Woodstock. Ontario Geography 6: 29–46, 1971.
Providing for Toronto's unemployed. Industrial Canada 9: 106, 1908.
Stelter, Gilbert A
    The origins of a company town: Sudbury in the nineteenth century.
    Laurentian University Review (3): 3–37, 1971.
Steward, Hartley.
    Farewell to Chinatown. Toronto Life 3(4): 42–46, 78–79, 1969.
Taylor, Griffith.
    The seven ages of towns. Economic Geography 21: 157–160, 1945.
    Toronto.
— Topographic control in the Toronto region. Canadian Journal of Economics
    and Political Science 2: 493–511, 1936.
— Towns and townships in southern Ontario. Economic Geography 21: 88–96,
    1945.
Urwick, E   J
    Toronto and its slums. Commerce Journal. Annual Review 34–35, 1935.
Watson, J   W
    Hamilton and its environs. Canadian Geographical Journal 30: 240–252,
    1945.
Whitaker, Russell.
    Sault Ste. Marie, Michigan and Ontario: a comparative study in urban
    geography. Bulletin of the Geographical Society of Philadelphia 32: 88–107,
    1934.

Theses

Barlow, James F
    Windsor, a suburb or satellite of Detroit? – a geographic approach to this
    problem. [Windsor, Ontario: 1967]
    v, 46 leaves. graphs, tables.
    Geography thesis, University of Windsor.   OWA
Barrett, Frank Alexander, 1935–
    The search behaviour of recent house movers: a study of intra-urban
    relocation in Toronto. [Lansing, Michigan] 1973.
    xi, 238 [21] leaves. illus., maps.
    Ph.D. thesis, Michigan State University (microfilm 73-29,664).   DA
Baxter, Wayne C   1946–
    Labour mobility between Windsor and Detroit. Windsor, Ontario: 1971.
    vii, 112 leaves. charts, tables.
    M.A. thesis, University of Windsor.   OWA
Beaman, Jay Gilmore, 1939 –
    A framework for modelling geographic mobility with test applications to the
    analysis of mobility data for thirteen Canadian cities. Ithaca, New York:
    1973.
    xv, 235 leaves. illus.
    Ph.D. thesis Cornell University (microfilm 73-14726).   DA
Bierenacki, Conrad M
    Urban migration rates: their concept, measurement and ecological
    correlates. [Toronto] 1976.
    viii, 97 leaves. tables, figs., maps.
    M.A. research paper, University of Toronto.   OTU
Bollons, Frank.
    A social and living space patterning study of the city of Ottawa. Ottawa:
    1969.
    66 leaves. maps, tables.
    B.A. research essay, Carleton University.   OOCC
Bonk, Stella Stephanie.
    The historical geography of the city of Ottawa. [Hamilton, Ontario] 1953.
    77 leaves. illus., maps.
    B.A. thesis, McMaster University.   OHM
Bremer, Hans H
    The Toronto Distress Centre; the social organization of telephone
    befriending. Toronto: 1971.
    viii, 160 leaves.
    M.A. thesis, York University (microfilm 8956).   OTY

Bunting, Trudi Elizabeth, 1944 –
Behaviour systems in the city: a conceptual and analytical approach to the investigation of household activites. [Toronto] 1975.
viii, 270 leaves. diagrs. (part fold.), tables.
Ph.D. thesis, University of Toronto.
City: Kitchener – Waterloo.. OTU

Burns, Robert Joseph, 1944 –
The first elite of Toronto: an examination of the genesis, consolidation and duration of power in an emerging colonial society. London, Ontario: 1974.
vii, 359 leaves.
Ph.D. thesis, The University of Western Ontario. OLU

Carter–Edwards, Dennis Russell.
Toronto in the 1890's: a decade of challenge and response. Vancouver, British Columbia: 1973.
vii, 180 leaves.
M.A. thesis, University of British Columbia (microfilm 22045). Can

Cave, L   S
Some human aspects of the new town concept – a case study of Bramalea. [Toronto] 1970.
iv, 72 [1] leaves. illus. (part col.), fold. maps
B.A. thesis, University of Toronto. OTU

Clark, Kenneth Lloyd.
Social relations and urban change in a late nineteenth century southwestern Ontario railway city: St. Thomas, 1868 to 1890. Toronto: 1976.
xiii, 171 leaves. graphs, maps, tables.
M.A. thesis, York University. OTY

Clements, Audrey Lorraine.
Social need in an urban renewal area; a comparison of social need in Alexandra Park as seen by two groups of respondents: the materialist and social observers. [Toronto] 1964.
v, 107 leaves.
M.S.W. thesis, University of Toronto. OTU

Cruikshank, Tom.
An assessment of the new town of Meadowvale. [Toronto] 1976.
i, 59 leaves. col. illus., maps (part fold.).
B.A. research project, University of Toronto. OTU

Crysdale, Robert Cecil Stewart, 1914–
Occupational and social mobility in Riverdale, a blue collar community. [Toronto] c1968.
ix, 417 leaves. tables, fold. map.
Ph.D. thesis, University of Toronto (microfilm 15390). OTU

Czyz, Michael Frederick.
West Hamilton, a study in urban geography. Hamilton, Ontario: 1959.
vii, 95 leaves. illus., maps.
B.A. thesis, McMaster University. OHM

Dynes, Stephen W
    The spatial and social implications of whitepainting. [Toronto] 1974.
    77 [25]. illus., maps.
    B.A. thesis, University of Toronto.   OTU
Egri, Esther J
    Whitepainting in the city of Toronto: a behavioral approach to spatial
    processes. [Toronto] 1976.
    iv, 70 leaves. maps.
    B.A. thesis, University of Toronto.   OTU
Freedman, Harry Ajzen.
    Intra-urban mobility in Toronto: a study in micro-migration analysis. State
    College, Pennsylvania: 1967.
    viii, 101 leaves. figs., maps.
    M.Sc. thesis, Pennsylvania State University, Graduate School, Department
    of Geography.   OTU
Goheen, Peter George.
    Geographic aspects of the urban development of Grey county. [Hamilton,
    Ontario] 1962.
    135 leaves. illus., maps (part fold.).
    B.A. thesis, McMaster University.   OHM
Graff, Harvey Jay, 1949–
    Literacy and social structure in the nineteenth-century city. Toronto: 1975.
    x, 578 leaves. tables, figs.
    Ph.D. thesis, University of Toronto.   OTU
Grant, Janet Elaine.
    Spatial distribution and concomitant social changes in Chinatown, Toronto:
    1900–1973. Toronto: 1974.
    75 leaves. illus., maps.
    B.A. thesis, University of Toronto.   OTU
Graham, Joan Elizabeth.
    Weston's position in the metropolitan area. [Toronto] 1955.
    78 [1] leaves. illus., maps (1 fold., part col.).
    B.A. thesis, University of Toronto.   OTU
Giuliani, Gary Erzi Anthony.
    Legal predicaments of Toronto west enders and their interaction with the
    West End Legal Aid Clinic. Hamilton, Ontario: 1975 [c1976]
    ix, 134 leaves. illus.
    M.A. thesis, McMaster University (microfilm 26134).   Can
Guyatt, Doris Elsie, 1929–
    Adolescent pregnancy: a study of pregnant teenagers in a suburban
    community in Ontario. [Toronto] c1976.
    304 leaves. figs., tables.
    D.S.W. thesis, University of Toronto.   OTU
Hahn, David Robert.
    The geography of urban fire hazards. [Toronto] 1968.
    iv, 38 [18] leaves. diagrs., tables.
    B.A. thesis, University of Toronto.   OTU

Hall, John Gordon.
  The historical development of Front Street, 1850–1900: a street geography.
  [Toronto] 1968.
  35 leaves. diagrs., maps.
  B.A. thesis, University of Toronto.   OTU
Hooper, Nadine Aurep.
  Toronto, a study in urban geography. [Toronto] 1941 (c1974)
  vi, 98 leaves. maps (fold.),
  M.A. thesis, University of Toronto (microfiche 19714).   OTU
Horne, Kathryn Anne.
  English as a second language in Metropolitan Toronto. (Toronto) c1969.
  1 v. (various pagings).
  M.A. thesis, University of Toronto.   OTU
Houston, Susan Elisabeth, 1937–
  The impetus to reform: urban crime, poverty and ignorance in Ontario
  1850–1875. [Toronto] c1974.
  v, 466 leaves.
  Ph.D. thesis, University of Toronto (microfilm 27954).   OTU
Jackson, John Talbot, 1946–
  The house as a visual indicator of social status change: the example of
  London, Ontario, 1861 to 1915. London, Ontario: 1973.
  x, 165 leaves. graphs, photos., sketches, tables, maps.
  M.A. thesis, The University of Western Ontario (microfilm 16421).   OLU
Jackson, William Arthur Douglas, 1923–
  A geographical study of early settlement in southern Ontario. (Toronto)
  1948.
  xi, 200 leaves. illus., maps (part fold.), plans (part fold.).
  M.A. thesis, University of Toronto (accepted 1949).   OTU
— The lands along the upper St. Lawrence; Canadian–American development
  during the nineteenth century. [College Park, Maryland] 1953.
  xviii, 260 leaves. illus., maps (part fold.), tables.
  Ph.D. thesis, University of Maryland.   U. Maryland
Jacob, Andrew L
  Interaction in urban systems: a Canadian illustration. [Toronto] c1971.
  v, 93 leaves. illus., maps.
  M.A. research paper, University of Toronto.   OTU
Jacobs, Abraham Hersch.
  Perception of urban places in the Niagara peninsula. Ottawa: 1971.
  vi, 183 leaves. diagrs., maps.
  M.A. thesis, Carleton University.   OOCC
Keith, Margaret Pearl.
  Testing the theory of increasing societal scale: the ecology of Toronto,
  1951–1961. Winnipeg, Manitoba: 1973.
  x, 130 leaves. illus., maps.
  M.A. thesis, University of Manitoba (microfilm 15505).   Can

Kelner, Merrijoy Sharon, 1927–
 The elite structure of Toronto: ethnic composition and patterns of
 recruitment. [Toronto] c1969.
 251 leaves. map.
 Ph.D. thesis, University of Toronto (microfilm 4501).   OTU
Kitamura, Yae, 1930–
 Bloor Street. (Toronto) 1957.
 iii, 60 leaves. illus., col. maps (1 fold., in pocket).
 B.A. thesis, University of Toronto.   OTU
Krueger, Ralph Ray, 1927–
 Urban blight with specific reference to London, Ontario. [London, Ontario]
 1955.
 x, 156 leaves. illus., plates, maps (part fold.).
 M.A. thesis, The University of Western Ontario.   OLU
Lewis, Victor George.
 Earlscourt, Toronto, a descriptive, historical and interpretative study in
 urban class development. Toronto: 1920.
 iii, 108 leaves. illus., charts, map.
 M.A. thesis, University of Toronto.   OTU
Lutes, Jack R
 Social and economic differences between public assistance families and self
 supporting families in Regent Park (South). [Toronto] 1954.
 viii, 90 leaves. tables.
 M.S.W. research report, University of Toronto.   OTU
Lutman, John Howard, 1948–
 The Hoyt concept and London, Ontario: a case study of the Dundas Street –
 Queens Avenue high income sector. London, Ontario: 1976.
 viii, 248 p. illus., maps, tables.
 M.A. thesis. The University of Western Ontario. (restricted)   OLU
Luxton, Margaret Joan, 1946–
 A study of urban communes and co-ops in Toronto. [Toronto] c1973.
 147 leaves. figs.
 Phil.M. thesis, University of Toronto.   OTU
McCallum, John Hall.
 Burlington: an urban study. [Hamilton, Ontario] 1957.
 vii, 138 leaves. illus., maps.
 B.A. thesis, McMaster University.   OHM
McLeod, Barbara.
 Woodstock: the centre of Oxford county. [Toronto: 1948]
 79 [2] leaves. illus., maps (part fold.).
 B.A. thesis, University of Toronto.   OTU
MacLeod, Douglas.
 Orillia, a geographic study of a southern Ontario town. [Toronto] 1953.
 xi, 78 leaves. illus., col. maps.
 B.A. thesis, University of Toronto.   OTU

Martin, Jean Pierre.
    Sudbury: étude economique et humaine de la ville et de son bassin. Paris:
    1971.
    37 feuilles.
    Thesis, doctorat de troisième cycle, University of Paris.   U.Paris
Meeker, Josephine Patricia.
    The social geography of the city of Hamilton. [Hamilton, Ontario] 1953.
    vii, 136 leaves. illus., diagrs., maps.
    B.A. thesis, McMaster University.   OHM
Melanson, Harold.
    Urban and economic development in northern Ontario. Kingston, Ontario:
    1962.
    iv, 56 leaves.
    B.A. thesis, Queen's University.   OKQ
Miyauchi, Judy Shigeko.
    An exploratory study of the institutional arrangements for the aged in
    Metropolitan Toronto with special emphasis on their liaison with the
    community and its services. [Toronto] 1965.
    131 leaves. tables.
    M.S.W. thesis, University of Toronto.   OTU
Plewes, Melvyn Edward.
    An analysis of urbanization in Albion township. Waterloo, Ontario: 1967.
    117 leaves. diagrs., maps, tables.
    B.A. thesis, Waterloo University College.   OWTL
Rees, Ronald.
    Brampton, Ontario: an urban study. [Toronto] 1960.
    119 leaves. illus., facsim., maps.
    M.A. thesis, University of Toronto.   OTU
Rempel, Martin C
    The intra-urban migrational process: a case study: the city of Waterloo.
    Waterloo, Ontario: 1975.
    vi, 108 leaves. graphs, maps, tables.
    B.A. thesis, Wilfrid Laurier University.   OWTL
Roberts, Ellis Noel Rees, 1947–
    Environment, community and lifestyle: components of residential
    preferences for cities. [Toronto] c1976.
    xv, 260 leaves.
    Ph.D. thesis, University of Toronto.   OTU
Russwurm, Lorne Henry, 1929–
    Expanding urbanization in the London to Hamilton area of western
    Ontario: 1941–1961. Urbana, Illinois: 1964.
    ix, 245 leaves. diagrs., maps (part fold.).
    Ph.D. thesis, University of Illinois (microfilm 65-03664).   DA
— The rural-urban fringe with comparative reference to London, Kitchener –
    Waterloo and Sarnia. [London, Ontario] 1961.
    xii, 207 leaves. illus., maps (part fold.) tables.
    M.A. thesis, The University of Western Ontario.   OLU

Shulman, Norman, 1942–
   Urban social networks: an investigation of personal networks in an urban
   setting. [Toronto] 1972.
   x, 199 leaves. tables.
   Ph.D. thesis, University of Toronto (microfilm 13074).   OTU
Smith, Roger J
   Characteristics of the urban heat island at Georgetown, Ontario. [Toronto:
   1971]
   47 leaves. illus.
   B.A. thesis, University of Toronto.   OTU
Smythe, James M
   A regional survey of Toronto Island. [Toronto] 1949.
   140 [1] leaves. illus. (1 in pocket), maps (part col.).
   B.A. thesis, University of Toronto.   OTU
Stephens, Maureen Walsh.
   Social need in an urban renewal area; an exploratory study of the needs of
   newcomers in Alexandra Park. [Toronto] 1964.
   iii, 107 leaves. maps.
   M.S.W. thesis, University of Toronto.   OTU
Thomson, Claire Walker.
   North Bay and region. [Hamilton, Ontario] 1953.
   v, 93 leaves. illus., maps.
   B.A. thesis, McMaster University.   OHM
Tumpane, Mary Denise Catherine.
   Yorkville; an exploratory study of the Toronto Telegram's coverage of
   Yorkville. [Toronto] 1968.
   v, 92 leaves. tables., graphs.
   M.S.W. thesis, University of Toronto.   OTU
Tweed, Edwin.
   The evolution of St. Catharines, Ontario. [Hamilton, Ontario] 1960.
   xii, 283 leaves. illus., maps (part fold.).
   M.A. thesis, McMaster University.   OHM
Van der Laan, Herman.
   Social participation and spatial differentiation: a pilot study of social
   participation among residents of differently designed high-rise apartment
   buildings. London, Ontario: 1974.
   vi, 79 leaves. illus., tables.
   M.A. research paper, The University of Western Ontario.   OLU
Wallace, John Kenyon.
   A spatial analysis of crime distribution in Metropolitan Toronto. Toronto:
   1975.
   viii, 130 leaves. maps, tables.
   M.A. research paper, York University.   OTY

Wargon, Harold, 1932–
    Yonge Street; a study in urban geography. [Toronto] 1956.
    vi, 63 leaves. illus., maps.
    B.A. thesis, University of Toronto.   OTU
Wasteneys, Hortense Catherine Fardell, 1925–
    The adequacy of the social services made available to displaced families in
    Toronto. [Toronto] 1950.
    iii, 143 leaves.
    M.S.W. thesis, University of Toronto.   OTU
Weis, Sorele.
    Social need in an urban renewal area; the neighbourhood as an element in
    developing a social plan for Alexandra Park. [Toronto] 1964.
    iii, 143 leaves. tables, maps.
    M.S.W. thesis, University of Toronto.   OTU
Weller, James Paul.
    The evolution of Toronto: a geographic study. Columbus, Ohio: 1963.
    86 leaves.
    M.A. thesis, Ohio State University.   Ohio State
Wretham, Blake Allan.
    Functional analysis of settlements and metropolitan dominance: Toronto
    and York County, 1921–1966. Waterloo, Ontario: 1970.
    xi, 119 leaves. diagrs. (part fold.), tables.
    M.A. thesis, University of Waterloo.   OWTU
Yates, Gary Wilfred.
    Ethnic origin and occupation of Sandy Hill, 1925–1950–1971. Ottawa:
    1974.
    viii, 81 leaves. maps (part fold.), tables.
    B.A. research essay, Carleton University.   OOCC

NATIVE PEOPLES

Bibliography

Abler, Thomas Struthers, 1941–   (comp.).
    A Canadian-Indian bibliography, 1960–1970 by Thomas S. Abler, Douglas
    Sanders & Sally Weaver. Toronto: University of Toronto Press [c1974]
    xii, 732 p. maps.
    Includes Case laws digest prepared by Douglas E. Sanders.   OMI OTU
The Canadian Indian; Grey-Bruce counties. Bruce County Historical Society.
    Yearbook 27, 1970.
Leigh, Dawson M   (comp.).
    Huronia in print. Midland, Ontario: Huronia Historic Sites and Tourist
    Association [195–?]
    [12] p.
    Contents: Bound books on Huronia; pamphlets on Huronia; books and
    pamphlets by or about Stephen Leacock.   OTU

Whiteside, Don, 1931–
  Aboriginal people: a selected bibliography concerning Canada's first people.
  Ottawa: National Indian Brotherhood [1973]
  345 p.   OTU

Monographs and Pamphlets

The attitudes of Toronto students towards the Canadian Indians [by Sandy
    McKay and others] Toronto: The Indian–Eskimo Association of Toronto,
    1971.
  28 p.   OTER
Beattie, Jessie Louise, 1896–
  The split in the sky. Toronto: The Ryerson Press [c1960]
  xii, 214 p. illus.
  Stories from the Grand River Reservation.   OTAR
Beveridge, Louise B   (comp.).
  Projects and people: Ontario Indian research and related projects; an
  inventory prepared for the Ontario Economic Council. [Toronto: Ontario
  Economic Council, 1969]
  1 v. (unpaged). map.   OTER
Bishop, Charles Aldrich, 1935–
  The northern Ojibwa and the fur trade: an historical and ecological study.
  Toronto: Holt Rinehart Winston of Canada, Limited [c1974]
  xx, 379 p. illus. (Cultures and communities: a series of monographs on native
  peoples).   OTU
Boyle, David, 1842–1911.
  Rock paintings at Lake Massanog and Temagami district, Ontario 1896 and
  1906. Toronto: Canadiana House, 1971.
  11 p. illus.
  Reprint of 1896 and 1906 edition which were not located.   OONG
Burnford, Sheila (Every).
  Without reserve. Illustrated by Susan Ross. Toronto: McClelland and
  Stewart Limited [c1969]
  242 p. illus., map.
  The Ojibwa & Cree in northwestern Ontario.   OBRWI OTU
Canada. Department of Citizenship and Immigration. Indian Affairs Branch.
  Census of Indians in Canada, 1949. Ottawa: Edmond Cloutier, Queen's
  Printer, 1952.
  38 p. tables.   OONL
— Indians of Ontario. Ottawa: Indian Affairs Branch, 1962.
  42 p.   OONL
Canada. Department of Indian Affairs and Northern Development.
  Indians of Ontario (an historical review). Ottawa: Indian Affairs Branch,
  1966.
  40 p. illus.   OLU

Canada. Geographic Board.

    Handbook of Indians of Canada. Ottawa: C.H. Parmelee, printer to the King's Most Excellent Majesty, 1913.

    x, 632 p. fold. col. map. (Canada. Geographic Board. Tenth report. Appendix).   OBRWI

Canada. Treaties.

    Copy of the treaty made October 31, 1923 between His Majesty the King and the Chippewa Indians of Christian Island, Georgina Island and Rama. Ottawa: F.A. Acland, printer to the King's Most Excellent Majesty, 1932.

    8 p.   OMI

Canadian Civil Liberties Education Trust.

    Indian life and Canadian law: a report on the Ontario north. Toronto: 1973.

    41 p. illus.   OTU

The Canadian Indian in Ontario's school texts: a study of social studies textbooks grades 1 through 8. Report prepared for the University Women's Club of Port Credit, 1968. Toronto: c1968.

    41 leaves.

    Prepared by Rosamand M. Vanderburgh.   OTER

Chance, Norman Allee, 1927– (ed.).

    Conflict in culture: problems of developmental change among the Cree; working papers of the Cree Developmental Change Project. Ottawa: Canadian Research Centre for Anthropology, St. Paul University, 1968.

    104 p. illus., map. tables.   OTER

Coatsworth, Emerson S

    The Indians of Quetico, from field notes and research by Robert C. Dailey. [Toronto] Published for the Quetico Foundation by University of Toronto Press, 1957.

    x, 58 p. illus. (Quetico Foundation series no. 1).   OTU

Cooper, John Montgomery, 1881–1949.

    The northern Algonquian supreme being. Washington: Catholic University of America, 1934.

    78 p.   OTU

Craig, John.

    No word for good-bye. Illustrated by Harri Aalto. [Toronto] Peter Martin Associates Limited [c1969]

    194 p.

    Indian life in northwestern Ontario.   OBRWI

Cumming, Peter A 1938– (ed.).

    Native rights in Canada, edited by Peter A. Cumming and Neil H. Mickenberg. 2d ed. Toronto: The Indian–Eskimo Association of Canada in association with General Publishing Co., Limited [c1972]

    xxiv, 352 p. maps.

    Ontario: pp. 107–117.

    No copy of first edition located.   OBRWI

Dewdney, Selwyn Hanington, 1909–
    Indian rock paintings on the Great Lakes, by Selwyn Dewdney and
    Kenneth E. Kidd. [Toronto] Published for the Quetico Foundation by
    University of Toronto Press [c1962]
    viii, 127 p. illus. (part col.), map.   OTU
—— 2d ed. [Toronto] Published for the Quetico Foundation by University of
    Toronto Press [c1967]
    x, 191 p. illus. (part col.), map.   OBRWI OTU
—— The sacred scrolls of southern Ojibwa. Toronto: Published for the Glenbow –
    Alberta Institute Calgary, Alberta by University of Toronto Press [c1975]
    viii, 199 p. illus., map.   OBRWI
—— Thcy shared to survive: the native peoples of Canada. Toronto: Macmillan
    of Canada [c1975]
    210 p. illus.   OTU
Dickason, Olive Patricia.
    Indian arts in Canada. Ottawa: Department of Indian Affairs & Northern
    Development [1972]
    138 p. illus. (part. col).   OTU
Dunning, Robert William, 1918–
    Social and economic change among the northern Ojibwa. [Toronto]
    University of Toronto Press [c1959]
    xiv, 217 p. illus., maps, diagrs., tables.   OBRWI OTU
Emerson, John Norman, 1917–
    Understanding Iroquois pottery in Ontario; a rethinking. Mississauga,
    Ontario: Ontario Archaeological Society [1968]
    iv, 132 p. illus. (Ontario Archaeological Society. Special publication).   OTU
Farrand, (Mrs.) B   C
    Indians at Sarnia. Bright's Grove, Ontario: G.L. Smith, 1975.
    3 leaves.
    Reprint of 1899 edition.   OONL
Fenton, William Nelson, 1908–
    Symposium on local diversity in Iroquois culture. Washington, D.C.:
    Smithsonian Institution, Bureau of American Ethnology, 1951.
    v, 187 p. illus., music.
    Ontario: pp. 169–187.   OLU
Ficek, Richard.
    Information needs of native peoples in the city of Toronto. Toronto:
    Practicum in Community Service, Faculty of Library Science, University of
    Toronto, 1974.
    60 p. illus.   OTULS
Fisher, Olive M
    Totem, tipi and tumplini. Stories of Canadian Indians, by Olive M. Fisher
    and Clara L. Tyner with illustrations by Annora Brown. London: J.M. Dent
    [c1955]
    xi, 264 p.   OBRWI

Flint Institute of Art.
    The art of the Great Lakes Indians. An exhibition organized March 25–July
    1, 1973. n.p. [1973]
    xxxviii, 114 p. illus., maps.   OBRWI
Graham, Elizabeth Jane, 1941–
    Medicine man to missionary: missionaries as agents of change among the
    Indians of southern Ontario, 1784–1867. Toronto: Peter Martin Associates
    [c1975]
    xi, 125 p. maps. (Canadian experience series).   OTER
Greene, Alma, 1896–
    Forbidden voice: reflections of a Mohawk Indian. Illustrations and cover
    design by Gordon McLean. [London] Hamlyn, n.d.
    157 p. illus.
    Grand River area.   OBRWI
— Tales of the Mohawks. Illustrations by R.G. Miller [Toronto] J.M. Dent &
    Sons (Canada) Limited [c1975]
    186 p. illus.   OBRWI
Haycock, Ronald Graham.
    The image of the Indian; the Canadian Indian as a subject and a concept in
    a sampling of the popular national magazines read in Canada, 1900–1970.
    [Waterloo, Ontario: Waterloo Lutheran University, 1971]
    vi, 98 p. (Waterloo Lutheran University monograph series, 1).   OTU
Hayes, John F   1904–
    Wilderness mission: the story of Sainte-Marie-among-the-Hurons . Toronto:
    The Ryerson Press [c1969]
    118 p. illus.   OMI
Heidenreich, Conrad Edmund, 1936–
    The Huron: a brief ethnography. [Toronto: Department of Geography,
    York University, 1972]
    ii, 104 p. illus. (Discussion paper, no. 6).   OLU
Houston, James A   1921–
    Ojibwa summer. Text by James Houston. Photos by B.A. King. [Don Mills,
    Ontario] Longman Canada, 1972.
    1 v. (unpaged). chiefly illus.
    Indians around Georgian Bay and Lake Simcoe summer of 1971.   OTU
Jacobson, Eleanor Mary Roach, 1928–
    Bended elbow. Kenora, Ontario: Central Publications [1975–76]
    2 v. illus.
    Indians in Kenora, Ontario.   OTU
Jenness, Diamond, 1886–1965.
    The Indians of Canada. Ottawa: F.A. Acland, printer to the King's Most
    Excellent Majesty, 1932.
    x, 446 p. illus. (part col.). (National Museum of Canada. Bulletin 65). OONL
— The Ojibwa Indians of Parry Sound, their social and religious life. Ottawa:
    J.O. Patenaude, King's Printer, 1935.
    vi, 115 p. (Canada. Department of Mines. National Museum of Canada.
    Bulletin no. 78. Anthropological series, no. 17).   OKQ

Joblin, Elgie Ellingham Miller, 1909–
    The education of the Indians of western Ontario. Toronto: Department of
    Education Research, Ontario College of Education [University of Toronto]
    1947.
    138 p. diagrs., map, tables. (Department of Educational Research. Bulletin
    no. 13).   OTER
Johnston, Basil.
    Ojibway heritage. [Toronto] McClelland and Stewart Limited [1976]
    170 p. illus., map.   OBRWI
Jury, Elsie McLead (Murray).
    The Hurons by Elsia [sic.] McLeod Jury and Wilfrid Jury. Midland,
    Ontario: 1960.
    36 p. illus., map.   OTU
Jury, William Wilfrid, 1890–
    Huronia: yesterday, today and tomorrow. [Midland, Ontario: Huronia
    Historic Sites and Tourist Association, 1953?]
    29 p.   OTU
Kenora, Ontario. Concerned Citizens Committee.
    While people sleep: sudden deaths in Kenora area. A study of sudden deaths
    amongst the Indian people of the Kenora area, with primary emphases on
    apparent alcohol involvement. Kenora, Ontario: Grand Council Treaty no.
    3. [c1973?]
    x, 32 p. tables.   OTU
Kurath, Gertrude Prokosch.
    Dance and song rituals of Six Nations Reserve Ontario. Ottawa [Roger
    Duhamel, Queen's Printer]1968.
    xiv, 205 p. (National Museum of Canada. Bulletin no. 220. Folklore series
    no. 4).   OBRWI
Landes, Ruth, 1908–
    Ojibwa sociology. New York: Columbia University Press, 1937.
    144 p. charts.   OTMCL
— New York: AMS Press [1969]
    144 p. illus. (Columbia. Contributions to anthropology, v. 29).   OTSTM
— The Ojibwa woman. New York: Columbia University Press, 1938.
    viii, 247 p.   OTU
— New York: AMS Press [1969]
    viii, 247 p.   OTU
McDiarmid, Garnet Leo, 1924–
    The challenge of a differential curriculum: Ontario's Indian children.
    [Toronto] Ontario Institute for Studies in Education [196?]
    13 [11] leaves. tables.   OTER
McEwen, Ernest R
    Community development services for Canadian Indian and Metis
    communities. Toronto: Indian–Eskimo Association of Canada, 1968.
    52 p.   OONL

MacLean, John, 1851–1928.
  Canadian savage folk: the native tribes of Canada. Toronto: William Briggs,
  1896.
  viii, 641 p. illus., ports. OMI
Major, Frederick William, 1874–   (comp.).
  Manitoulin, the isle of the Ottawas. Being a handbook of historical and
  other information on the Grand Manitoulin Island. Gore Bay, Ontario:
  Recorder Press [1934]
  iv, 84 p. port.
  "Reprinted from the *Gore Bay Recorder*. OTU
  Gore Bay, Ontario: Recorder Press, c1934, 1974.
  84 p. OTAR
Manuel, George.
  The fourth world: an Indian reality by George Manuel and Michael
  Posluns. Foreword by Vine Deloria, Jr. [Don Mills, Ontario]
  Collier–Macmillan Canada, Ltd. [c1974]
  xvi, 278 p. illus. OBRWI
Marois, Roger J   M
  L'Archeologie des provinces de Quebec et d'Ontario. Ottawa: National
  Museums of Canada, 1975.
  vii, 117 p. (National Museum of Man Mercury series). OTAR
Mead, Margaret, 1901–   (ed.).
  Cooperation and competition among primitive peoples. [1st ed.] New York:
  McGraw–Hill Book Company Inc., 1937.
  xii, 531 p. illus.
  Chapter 3, The Ojibwa of Canada by Ruth Landes – southwest Ontario.
  OTU
Montour, Enos T   1899–
  The feathered U.E.L.'s: an account of the life and times of certain Canadian
  native people. Toronto: The Division of Communication, The United
  Church of Canada [1973]
  148 p. illus., ports. OBRWI
Monture, Ethel Brant.
  Canadian portraits: Brant, Crowfoot, Oronbyatekha, famous Indians.
  Toronto: Clarke, Irwin & Company Limited, 1960.
  vii, 160 p. illus., ports. OBRWI
Morin, Léopold, 1912–
  Moosonee Indians' integration. Moosonee, Ontario [A.B.C. Studio] 1971.
  56 p. illus. OTU
Morris, William James.
  Report to the Department of Citizenship and Immigration concerning the
  integration of Indians in the district of Red Lake, Ontario. Toronto:
  Department of Anthropology, University of Toronto, 1958.
  159 p. OORD

Mortimore, George Ernest, 1921–
    The Indian in industry: roads to independence. [Ottawa: Department of
    Indian Affairs and Northern Development, Indian Affairs Branch, 1965]
    27 p. illus.
    Also issued in French under title: Les indiens et l'industrie; les chemins de
    l'independence.   OTY
Nagler, Mark, 1939–
    Indians in the city: a study of the urbanization of Indians in Toronto.
    Ottawa: Canadian Research Centre for Anthropology, Saint Paul
    University, 1970.
    xiv, 107 p.   OTV
    2d ed. Ottawa: Canadian Research Centre for Anthropology, St. Paul
    University [c1970] 1973.
    xiv, 107 p.   OTRM
New Democratic Party (Ontario).
    Indians, do we care? [Toronto: 1966]
    [2] 9 p.   OTURS
Noon, John A
    Law and government of the Grand River Iroquois. New York: Johnson
    Reprint Corporation [1964, c1949]
    186 p. (Viking Fund publications in Anthropology no. 12).   OTU
Ojibway Warrior's Society in occupied Anicinabe Park, Kenora, Ontario,
    August, 1974. Toronto: Better Read Graphies, 1975.
    ii, 32 p. illus.   OTU
Ontario. Legislative Assembly. Select Committee appointed to enquire into civil
    liberties and rights with respect to the Indian population of Ontario, and
    matters relevant thereto.
    Report. [Toronto: 1954]
    23 p. tables.
    Chairman: W.A. Goodfellow.   OTAR
— Proceedings, April 27, 1953–January 18, 1954.
    15 v. [i.e. 417 typewritten pages]   OTAR
Ontario. Task Force on the Education needs of Native Peoples.
    Summary report. Toronto: 1976.
    44 p.   OONL
Pelletier, Wilfred.
    No foreign land: a biography of a North American Indian by Wilfred
    Pelletier and Ted Poole. New York: Pantheon Books [c1975]
    xi, 212 p.
    Manitoulin Island.   OBRWI
Plain, Aylmer Nicholas.
    A history of the Sarnia Indian Reserve based on the personal
    reminisiences of the author. Bright's Grove, Ontario: George Smith, 1975.
    19 p.   OONL

Powell, Edna.
Indian artifacts of Lambton county, by Edna Powell and Dorothy Stanton.
[Sarnia, Ontario: Lambton County Historical Society, 1972?]
[44] p. illus. OTU
Ray, Arthur Joseph.
Indians in the fur trade: their role as hunters, trappers and middlemen in
the lands of southwest of Hudson Bay, 1660–1870. [Toronto] University of
Toronto Press [c1974]
xii, 249 p. diagrs., maps. OTU
Redsky, James.
Great leader of the Ojibway: Mis-quona-queb. Edited by James R. Stevens.
Toronto: McClelland and Stewart Limited [c1972]
127 p. illus., map. OBRWI
Reid, C B
The Boys site and the early Ontario Iroquois tradition. Ottawa: National
Museums of Canada, 1975.
vi, 129 p. illus., maps. (National Museum of Man Mercury series). OTAR
Renaud, André.
Indian education today. [Ottawa: Indian and Eskimo Welfare Oblate
Commission, 1958?]
49 p. OTU
Robertson, J Heather.
Reservations are for Indians. Toronto: James Lewis and Samuel, 1970.
303 p. OTU
Scott, Duncan Campbell, 1862–1947.
Administration of Indian affairs in Canada. [Montreal] Canadian Institute
of International Affairs, 1931.
27 p. tables. OTURS
Sieber, Sylvestre Anthony Michael, 1908–
The Saulteaus Indians. Rev. ed. Techy, Illinois: The Mission House, 1950.
159 leaves. OTU
Six Nations Indians yesterday and today, 1867–1942. [Brantford, Ontario:
1942]
61 p.
"Written to celebrate the Diamond Anniversary of the Six Nations
Agricultural Society. OTAR
Smith, Leslie Kean, 1898–1968.
Historical references to Sarnia Indian Reserve, by Leslie K. Smith and
George L. Smith. Bright's Grove, Ontario: George Smith, 1976.
[10] leaves. OTAR
Speck, F G
Family hunting territories and social life of various Algonkian bands of the
Ottawa valley. Ottawa: Government Printing Bureau, 1915.
30 p. charts. (Canada. Department of Mines. Geological Survey. Memoir
70). OBRWI

— Myths and folk-lore of the Temiskaming Algonquin and Timagami Ojibwa.
Ottawa: Government Printing Bureau, 1915.
iii, 87 p. illus., map. (Canada. Department of Mines. Geological Survey.
Memoir 71).   OBRWI
Stymeist, David H
Ethnics and Indians: social relations in a northwestern Ontario town.
Toronto: Peter Martin Associates Limited [c1975]
viii, 98 p.   OTU
Symons, Harry L
Ojibway melody. Toronto: The Author, 1946.
viii, 294 p.   OKQ
Tait, Lyal, 1911
The Petuns Tobacco Indians of Canada. Port Burwell: Eric publishers,
1971.
133 p. illus., facsims., maps.
History of Indians living in Ontario prior to Confederation.   OTU
Van Steen, Marcus.
Pauline Johnson: her life and work. Toronto: Hodder and Stoughton
[c1965]
279 p.   OBRWI
Vastokas, Joan M   1938–
Sacred art of the Algonkians: a study of the Peterborough petroglyphs, by
Joan M. Vastokas and Romas K. Vastokas. Peterborough, Ontario:
Mansard Press [c1973]
xiv, 164 p. illus.   OTAR
Weaver, Sally Mae, 1940–
Medicine and politics among the Grand River Iroquois: a study of the non-
conservatives. [Ottawa: National Museum of Man, 1972]
xiii, 182 p. illus. (Publications in ethnology series, no. 4).
Covers the period 1600–1966.   OBRWI OTU
Woodland Indian Cultural Educational Centre.
Indian Hall of Fame. Brantford, Ontario [1976?]
1 v. (unpaged). ports.   OBRWI

Periodical Articles
Baker, Jocelyn.
Ojibway of the Lake of the Woods. Canadian Geographical Journal 12:
47–54, 1936.
Baldwin, William W
Social problems of the Ojibwa Indians in the Collins area in northwestern
Ontario. Anthropolica 5: 51–123, 1957.
Brant–Sero, J   Ojijatekha.
The Six-Nations Indians in the province of Ontario, Canada. Wentworth
Historical Society. Transactions 2: 62–73, 1899.

Buller, Grace.
Native peoples and library service in Ontario. Ontario Library Review 59: 4–9, 1975.

Burnham, J   Hampden.
The coming of the Missisagas. Ontario Historical Society. Papers & Records 6: 7–11, 1905.

Cadot, J   C
Bruce county and work among the Indians. Ontario Historical Society. Papers & Records 17: 21–24, 1920.

Carruthers, Janet.
Land of the Ojibway. The Beaver (Outfit) 282 (4): 42–45, 1952.
Lake-of-the-Woods.

Chamberlain, Alexander Francis.
Tribal divisions of the Indians of Ontario. Ontario Historical Society. Papers & Records 12: 199–202, 1914.

Chance, Norman A   and John Trudeau.
Social organization, acculturation and integration among the Eskimo and Cree: a comparative study. Anthropologica n.s. 5: 47–56, 1963.
Winisk.

Chitwood, Prince and Sandra Woolfrey.
Archaeological excavation of New Aberdeen. Waterloo Historical Society. Annual Volume 63: 29–31, 1975.

Coburn, Kathleen.
The case of Mr. Ojibway. Canadian Forum 22: 215–217, 1942.

Currell, Harvey.
Deluxe camping with the Indians. Bruce County Historical Society. Yearbook 36–37, 1970.

Dilling, H   J
Educational achievement and social acceptance of Indian pupils integrated in non-Indian schools of southern Ontario. Ontario Journal of Educational Research 8: 47–57, 1965–66.

Dunning, R   W
Rules of residence and ecology among the northern Ojibwa. American Anthropologist n.s. 61: 806–816, 1959.
— Some implications of economic change in northern Ojibwa social structure. Canadian Journal of Economics and Political Science 24: 562–566, 1958.
— Some problems of reserve Indian communities: a case study. Anthropologica n.s. 6: 3–38, 1964.

Flannery, Regina.
The position of woman among the eastern Cree. Primitive Man 8: 81–86, 1935.

Gardiner, Herbert F
Centenary of the death of Brant. Ontario Historical Society. Papers & Records 9: 33–54, 1910.

Garrard, Charles.
Note concerning the Honsberger collection, Niagara peninsula, Ontario. Anthropological Journal of Canada 7(no. 2): 15, 1969.
Godsell, Philip H
The Ojibwa Indian. Canadian Geographical Journal 4: 51–66, 1932.
Jamieson, Elmer and Peter Sandiford.
The mental capacity of southern Ontario Indians. Journal of Educational Psychology 19: 313–328; 536–551, 1928.
Johnson, Frederick.
The Algonquin at Golden Lake, Ontario. Indian Notes 5: 173–178, 1928.
— Notes on the Ojibwa and Potawatomi of the Parry Island Reservation, Ontario. Indian Notes 6: 193–216, 1929.
Jury, Wilfrid.
Have you some Indian relics? Ontario Library Review and Canadian Periodical Index 28: 388–392, 1944.
Keppler, Joseph.
Cayuga adoption custom. Indian Notes 3: 73–75, 1926.
Knechtel, Fritz.
The Nodwell Indian village. Bruce County Historical Society. Yearbook 28–31, 1970.
— The Nodwell Indian village park. Bruce County Historical Society. Yearbook 23–25, 1971.
Kurath, Gertrude Prokosch.
Iroquois mid winter medicine rites. International Folk Music Council. Journal 3: 96–100, 1951.
LaViolette, Gontran.
Notes on the aborigines of the province of Ontario. Anthropologica 4: 79–106, 1957.
Lee, Thomas E
Footprints in Essex. Anthropological Journal of Canada 5(no. 1): 12–24, 1967.
Liebon, Elliot and John Trudeau.
A preliminary study of acculturation among the Cree Indians of Winisk, Ontario. Arctic 15: 190–204, 1962.
Mallory, Gordon and Enid Mallory.
The Peterborough petroglyphs. Canadian Geographical Journal 62: 130–135, 1961.
Montgomery, Malcolm.
The Six Nations Indians and the MacDonald franchise. Ontario History 57: 13–25, 1965.
Moses, Elliott.
Seventy-five years of progress of the Six Nations of the Grand River. Waterloo Historical Society. Annual Volume 56: 19–26, 1968.
Panabaker, D N
Indian trails – bridle paths – gravel roads, concrete highways in Waterloo county. Waterloo Historical Society. Annual Report 23: 160–164, 1935.
Radin, Paul.
Ethnological notes on the Ojibwa of southeastern Ontario. American Anthropologist n.s. 30: 659–668, 1928.

Randle, Martha Champion.
Educational problems of Canadian Indians. Food for Thought 13(6): 10–14, 1953.
Ridley, Frank.
The Ontario Iroquoian controversy. Ontario History 55: 49–59, 1963.
Ringland, Mabel Crews.
Indian handicrafts of Algoma. Canadian Geographical Journal 6: 185–201, 1933.
Rogers, Edward S
Changing settlement patterns of the Cree – Ojibwa of northern Ontario. Southwestern Journal of Anthropology 19: 64–88, 1963.
Saindon, J   E
Mental disorders among the James Bay Cree. Primitive Man 6: 1–12, 1933.
Sanford, John T
Seguiandah reviewed. Anthropological Journal of Canada 9(no. 1): 2–15, 1971.
Scott, Lloyd and Douglas Leechman.
The Swampy Cree. The Beaver (Outfit) 283 (3): 26–27, 1952.
Shaw, R   W
The Indian in our literature. Ontario Library Review 17: 52–56, 1933.
Skinner, Alanson.
Bear customs of the Cree and other Algonkian Indians of northern Ontario. Ontario Historical Society. Papers & Records 12: 203–209, 1914.
Smith, Donald B
Grey Owl. Ontario History 63: 160–176, 1971.
Speck, F   G
Algonkian influence upon Iroquois social organization. American Anthropologist n.s. 25: 219–227, 1923.
Tisdall, Frederick F   and Elizabeth Chant Robertson.
Voyage of the medicine men. The Beaver (Outfit) 279(3): 42–46, 1948.
James Bay Indians, nutrition and health.
Turner, G   H   and D   J   Penfold.
The scholastic aptitude of the Indian children of the Caradoc Reserve. Canadian Journal of Psychology 6: 31–44, 1952.
Van Steen, Marcus.
Brantford's Royal Chapel. Canadian Geographical Journal 57: 136–141, 1958.
Mohawk Chapel.
Vivian, R   P   [et al.]
The nutrition and health of the James Bay Indian. Canadian Medical Association. Journal 59: 505–518, 1948.

Theses

Baldwin, W   W
> Social problems of the Ojibwa Indians in the Collins area of northwestern
> Ontario. [Toronto] 1956.
> 72 leaves.
> M.A. thesis, University of Toronto.   OTU

Brant, Marlene J
> Parental neglect in Indian families: a descriptive study of twenty case
> records of Indian families whose children became permanent wards of the
> Children's Aid Society of Metropolitan Toronto. Toronto: 1959.
> 105 [12] leaves.
> M.S.W. thesis, University of Toronto (microfilm 27473).   OTU

Cargill, Isabel Agnes, 1933–
> An investigation of cognitive development among infants on a Canadian
> Indian reservation. [Toronto] 1970.
> 191 leaves. tables, figs.
> M.A. thesis, University of Toronto.   OTU

Chawla, Saroj.
> Indian children in Toronto: a study in socialization. Toronto: 1971.
> ii, 106 leaves. illus., chart.
> M.A. thesis, York University (microfilm 9343).   OTY

Christie, Thomas Laird, 1938–
> Reserve colonialism and sociocultural change. [Toronto] c1976.
> v, 295 leaves.
> Ph.D. thesis, University of Toronto.   OTU

Cooper, Virginia J
> Political history of the Grand River Iroquois 1784–1880. Ottawa: 1975.
> iv, 108 leaves. illus.
> M.A. thesis, Carleton University.   OOCC

Dilling, Harold John.
> Educational achievement and social acceptance of Indian pupils integrated
> in non-Indian schools of southern Ontario. [Toronto] 1965 [c1974]
> xviii, 440 leaves. tables, fig., map.
> Ed.D. thesis, University of Toronto (microfilm 17261).   OTU

— Integration of the Indian Canadian in and through schools, with emphasis
> on the St. Clair Reserve in Sarnia. [Toronto] 1961.
> viii, 171 leaves. illus., photos, tables.
> M.Ed. thesis, University of Toronto (accepted 1962).   OTU

Emerson, John Norman, 1917–
> The archaeology of the Ontario Iroquois. Chicago, Illinois: 1954.
> viii, 279 [i.e. 278] leaves. illus., maps.
> Ph.D. thesis, University of Chicago (microfilm).   OOA

England, Raymond Edward.
> The planning and development process in Indian reserve communities.
> Waterloo, Ontario: 1969 [c1971]
> xiv, 272 leaves. illus., maps.
> Ph.D. thesis, University of Waterloo (microfilm 7865).   OWTU

Fransen, Jack Jacob.
    Employment experiences and economic position of a selected group of
    Indians in Metropolitan Toronto. [Toronto] 1964 [c1976]
    v, 105 leaves.
    M.S.W. thesis, University of Toronto (microfilm 25475).   OTU
Freedman, Catherine Jan.
    Anduhyaun: a Toronto residence for Canadian Indian girls migrating to the
    city for retraining. Toronto: 1974.
    105 leaves.
    M.A. thesis, York University (microfiche 30902).   OTY
Gleason, Aileen May.
    A study of the relationships that exist between the deceleration in academic
    achievement of Indian children integrated in the separate schools of Fort
    Frances, Ontario, and their social acceptance and personality structure.
    Winnipeg: 1970.
    x, 126 leaves. illus., maps.
    M.Ed. thesis, University of Manitoba (microfilm 7440).   Can
Goldenson, Karen, 1945–
    Cognitive development of Indian elementary school children on a southern
    Ontario reserve. [Toronto] 1970.
    81 leaves. tables, figs.
    M.A. thesis, University of Toronto.   OTU
Hamori–Torok, Charles, 1932–
    The acculturation of the Mohawks of the Bay of Quinte. [Toronto] 1966.
    iii, 183 leaves. tables, maps.
    Ph.D. thesis, University of Toronto (microfilm 1059).   OTU
Hoffmann, Hans.
    Assessment of cultural homogeneity among the James Bay Cree. New
    Haven, Connecticut: 1957.
    iv, 301 leaves. map.
    Ph.D. thesis, Yale University.   Yale
Jamieson, Elmer.
    The mental capacity of southern Ontario Indians. [Toronto: 1928]
    x, 216 leaves. tables, diagrs.
    D.Paed. thesis, University of Toronto.   OTU
Joblin, Elgie Ellingham Miller, 1909–
    The education of the Indians of western Ontario. [Toronto] 1946 [c1976]
    vii, 157 leaves. graphs, tables, maps.
    M.A. thesis, University of Toronto (microfilm 17781).   OTU
Keating, William James Joseph, 1945–
    The relationship of home environmental variables to level of acculturation
    and cognitive patterns of Ojibwa pre-school children. [Toronto] c1976.
    iv, 61 leaves. tables.
    M.A. thesis, University of Toronto.   OTU

Latus, Gerald Robert.
    Academic achievement, personality and boarding home habits of Ojibwa
    high school students. Thunder Bay, Ontario: 1974 [c1975]
    vi, 104 leaves.
    M.A. thesis, Lakehead University (microfilm 23680).   Can
Pugh, Donald Edward.
    Cultural optimality: a study of the rise and decline of the Cree culture of
    north eastern Ontario. Ottawa: 1972.
    i, 300 leaves. maps.
    M.A. thesis, Carleton University.   OOCC
Rogers, Jean Hayes, 1928–
    Participant identification and role allocation in Ojibwa. [Toronto] c1973.
    x, 314 leaves. charts, diagrs.
    Ph.D. thesis, University of Toronto (microfilm 22357).   OTU
St. John, Joan.
    Northwestern Ontario Indian childrens' [sic] scores on the WISC in relation
    to the normative population. Thunder Bay, Ontario: 1973 [c1976]
    iv, 58 leaves. illus., map.
    M.A. thesis, Lakehead University (microfilm 24468).   Can.
Schmalz, Peter Stanley.
    The history of the Saugeen Indians. [Waterloo, Ontario] 1972.
    v, 403 leaves. illus.
    M.A. thesis, University of Waterloo.   OWTU
Shimony, Annemarie Anrod.
    Conservatism at Six Nations Reserve. New Haven, Connecticut: 1958.
    vii, 580 leaves.
    Ph.D. thesis, Yale University.   Yale
— Conservatism among the Iroquois at the Six Nations Reserve. [Ohsweken,
    Ontario] New Haven, Conn.: Department of Anthropology, Yale
    University, 1961.
    302 p. (Yale University publications in Anthropology, no. 65).   OTU
Smith, June Elizabeth.
    Anomie: a definition of the concept and an application to the Canadian
    Indian reservation. [Hamilton, Ontario] 1963.
    v, 131 leaves. tables.
    M.A. thesis, McMaster University.
    Indians of Manitoulin Island.   OHM
Szathmary, Emöke Jolan Erzsébet, 1944–
    Genetic studies on two Ontario Ojibwa Indian communities. [Toronto]
    c1974.
    xii, 281 leaves. tables, figs., maps.
    Ph.D. thesis, University of Toronto (microfilm 27518).   OTU
Trudeau, Jean.
    Cultural change among the Swampy Cree Indians of Winisk, Ontario.
    Washington, D.C.: 1966.
    182 p.
    Ph.D. thesis, Catholic University of America (microfilm 67-01842).   DA

Tucker, Morton Irving, 1920–
    Windigo psychosis, a study of a relationship between belief and behaviour
    among the Indians of northeastern Canada. [Toronto] 1956.
    v, 400 leaves. maps (fold.).
    Ph.D. thesis, University of Toronto.   OTY
Vlassoff, Carol.
    Native Indians in Canada: the problem of identity. London, Ontario: 1974.
    v, 177 leaves. maps, tables.
    M.A. research paper, The University of Western Ontario.   OLU
Wagman, Barbara Ann, 1947–
    Preschool and childhood cognitive development of Indians at Curve Lake
    Reserve. [Toronto] 1970.
    85 leaves. tables, figs.
    M.A. thesis, University of Toronto.   OTU
Weaver, Sally Mae, 1940–
    Health, culture and dilemma: a study of the non–conservative Iroquois, Six
    Nations Reserve, Ontario. [Toronto] c1967.
    xi, 435 leaves. tables, diagrs., maps.
    Ph.D. thesis, University of Toronto (microfilm 1864).   OTU
Wright, James Valliere, 1932–
    The Ontario Iroquois tradition. Madison, Wisconsin: 1964.
    x, 342 leaves. diagrs., tables.
    Ph.D. thesis, University of Wisconsin (microfilm 64-07111).   OTU
— Ottawa [Roger Duhamel, Queen's Printer] 1966.
    xii, 195 p. illus., diagr., tables. (National Museum of Canada. Bulletin no.
    210. Anthropological series no. 75).   OBRWI

MINORITIES

Bibliography
Anderson, Grace Merle, 1923–
    A selected bibliography on Portuguese immigration. [Toronto: 1969]
    iv, 5 p.   OTU
Blizzard, Flora Helena.
    West Indians in Canada: a selective annotated bibliography. Guelph,
    Ontario: 1970.
    41 leaves. (The Library, University of Guelph. Bibliography series, no. 1).
    OTU
Dworancyek, Marian Joseph, 1944–
    Minority groups in Metropolitan Toronto: a bibliography. [Toronto]
    Ontario Ministry of Labour, Research Branch Library, 1973.
    57 p.   OTU
— Supplement to the 1973 bibliography. Toronto: Research Library, Ontario
    Ministry of Labour, 1975.
    48 p.   OONL

Gregorovich, Andrew Svyatoslav, 1935–
    Canadian ethnic groups bibliography; a selected bibiliography of ethno-
    cultural groups in Canada and the province of Ontario. Toronto: Ontario
    Department of the Provincial Secretary and Citizenship, 1972.
    xvi, 208 p.   OTU
Malycky, Alexander.
    [Bibliography and checklist of ten Canadian enthic groups] Canadian
    Ethnic Studies 1(no. 1): 1–163, 1969 (+ vi); 2(no. 1): xii, 1–249, 1970; 5(no.
    1–2): x, 1–408, 1973.
Ontario Human Rights Commission. Special Projects, Education and Research
    Division.
    Minority group research in Ontario; selected bibliography of graduate
    research carried out at the University of Toronto in the areas of human
    rights and minority groups in Ontario. Prepared by the Special Projects
    Education and Research Division of the Ontario Human Rights
    Commission [Toronto: 1969?]
    8 leaves.   OTU
Suski, Edwin.
    Finnish-Canadian bibliography: Ontario. Canadian suomalaisten arkisto:
    Luettelo. Sudbury, Ontario: 1973.
    46 p.   OTAR

Monographs and Pamphlets
Adachi, Ken Ichi, 1913–
    The enemy that never was: a history of the Japanese Canadians. [Toronto]
    McClelland and Stewart [c1976]
    vi, 456 p. illus., ports.   OONL
Anderson, Grace Merle, 1923–
    Channels of employment: the Portuguese in Toronto. [Waterloo, Ontario]
    1971.
    26 leaves.   OTU
— A future to inherit: Portuguese communities in Canada, by Grace M.
    Anderson and David Higgs. [Toronto] McClelland and Stewart in
    association with the Multiculturalism Program, Department of the Secretary
    of State of Canada [c1976]
    202 p. illus. (Generations: a history of Canada's peoples).   OTU OONL
— Illegal immigration: a sociologically unexplored field. Waterloo, Ontario:
    Department of Sociology and Anthropology, Waterloo Lutheran University
    [1971]
    42 leaves. diagrs.   OTU
— Networks of contact: the Portuguese and Toronto. [Waterloo, Ontario:
    Wilfrid Laurier University c1974]
    xv, 195 p. diagrs., tables.   OTER

Ashworth, Mary.
Immigrant children and Canadian schools. [Toronto] McClelland and
Stewart Limited [c1975]
xii, 228 p. tables.   OTU
Balikci, Asen.
Remargues sur la structure de groupe ethnique bulgare et Macédonien de
Toronto. Ottawa: Musée national du Canada, 1956.
iii, 225 feuilles. illus.   OOSS
Baronas, Kazys (ed.).
Lietuwiai Hamilton 1948–1954. [Toronto: Foto-Lith, 1954]
201 p. illus., ports.
Chiefly illustrations of the Lithuanian Canadian Federation of Hamilton.
                                                                                     OTU
Beattie, Jessie Louise, 1896–
Black Moses: the real Uncle Tom. Toronto: The Ryerson Press [c1957]
xiii, 215 p. illus., port.   OOA
Bossin, Hye.
A tattler's tales of Toronto. Toronto: Handy Library, n.d.
64 p.   OTU
Bovay, Emile H
Le Canada et les suisses, 1604–1974. Fribourg, Suisse: Editions
Universitaires [c1976]
xii, 334 p. illus. (part col.), facsims., ports., maps.   OTAR
Brantford and District Citizenship Council.
History of ours; French, German, Hungarian, Italian, Polish, Ukrainian.
[Brantford, Ontario: 1967]
66 p. [19] leaves of plates. illus. (part col.).   OONL
Burkholder, Lewis J   1875–   (comp.).
A brief history of the Mennonites in Ontario, giving a description of
conditions in early Ontario – the coming of the Mennonites into Canada –
settlements – congregations – conferences – other activities – and nearly four
hundred ordinations; written and compiled under the direction of the
Mennonite Conference of Ontario. [Toronto: Livingstone Press] 1935.
358 p. illus., ports., maps, facsims.   OTU
Canada. Department of Manpower and Immigration.
Three years in Canada: first report of a longitudinal survey on the economic
and social adaptation of immigrants. [Ottawa: Information Canada, 1974]
152 p. tables, charts.   OOU
Canadian Jewish Congress. Central Region.
Highlights of Toronto's Jewish history. Toronto: The Congress [1957]
11, 14 leaves.   OTU
Canadian Jewish Congress. Central Region. Archives Committee.
A sense of Spadina. Toronto: The Author [1974]
12 p. illus., map.   OONL
Canadian Jewish Congress, Central Region. Research Committee.
The Jewish community of Chatham, Ontario: a self-survey. Toronto: 1952.
[17] leaves. map, chart, tables.   OTU

— The Jewish community of Cornwall, Ontario: a self-survey. Toronto: 1955.
[18] leaves. map, chart, tables.   OTU
— The Jewish communities of Galt, Preston and Hespeler, Ontario: a self-
survey. Toronto:1954.
[15] leaves. map, chart, tables.   OTU
— The Jewish community of London, Ontario: a self-survey. Toronto: 1959.
38 leaves. charts, tables, map.   OTU
— The Jewish community of Niagara Falls: a self-survey. Toronto: 1953.
[15] leaves. map, chart, tables.   OTU
— The Jewish community of Peterborough, Ontario: a self-survey. Toronto:
1956.
[15] leaves, chart, tables.   OTU
— The Jewish community of Port Colborne, Ontario: a self-survey. Toronto:
1952.
[14] leaves. map, tables.   OTU
— The Jewish community of St. Catharines, Ontario: a self-survey. Toronto:
1951.
[15] sheets. map, tables.   OTU
— The Jewish community of Sault Ste. Marie, Ontario: a self-survey. Toronto:
1954.
[14] leaves. fold. map., charts, tables.   OTU
— The Jewish community of Sudbury, Ontario: a self-survey. Toronto: 1953.
[20] leaves. map, chart, tables.   OTU
— The Jewish community of Welland, Ontario: a self-survey. Toronto: 1951.
[22] leaves. map, charts, tables.   OTU
— The smaller Jewish communities of Ontario; their history and population
characteristics; based on self-surveys of ten Ontario Jewish communities.
Toronto: 1956.
25 leaves. tables.   OTU
Conference on Future Immigration Policy, Toronto, 1974.
Proceedings of the Conference on Future Immigration Policy: what do we
want? ... sponsored by the Inter-Agency Council for Services to Immigrants
and Migrants in cooperation with the Department of Adult Education,
Ontario Institute for Studies in Education. Toronto: 1974.
143, 7 leaves. charts, tables.   OTU
Danziger, Kurt.
The socialization of immigrant children. [Toronto: Ethnic Research
Program, Institute for Behaviorial Research, York University, 1971?]
171 leaves. tables.
A study of Italians, chiefly Toronto.   OTU
Davies, Blodwen, 1897–1966.
A string of amber: the heritage of the Mennonites. Vancouver: Mitchell
Press Limited [c1973]
228 p. illus.   OTU

Degh, Linda.
    People in the tobacco belt: four lives. Ottawa: National Museums of
    Canada, 1975.
    xx, 277 p. illus. (National Museum of Man Mercury series).
    Hungarian immigrants at Delhi, Ontario.   OLU
Elliott, Jean Leonard.
    Minority Canadians. Scarborough, Ontario: Prentice–Hall of Canada Ltd.
    [c1971]
    2 v.
    Contents: v. 1, Native peoples; v. 2, Immigrant groups.   OTU
Epp, Frank Henry, 1929–
    Mennonites in Canada, 1786–1920: the history of a separate people
    illustrated by Douglas Ratchford. Toronto: Macmillan of Canada, c1974.
    xii, 480 p. illus.   OTU
Ferguson, Edith Anne, 1903–
    Immigrants in Canada. [Toronto] Guidance Centre, Faculty of Education.
    University of Toronto [c1974]
    48 p. (Social problems in Canada, 3).   OTC
— Newcomers and new learning; a project of the International Institute of
    Metropolitan Toronto 1964–1966. [Toronto: International Institute of
    Metropolitan Toronto, 1966]
    114 p. fold. map, tables.   OTER
— Newcomers in transition: an experimental study project conducted by the
    International Institute of Metropolitan Toronto to study the relation
    between rural immigrants and Toronto community services, March 1,
    1962–March 1, 1964. [Toronto: International Institute of Metropolitan
    Toronto, 1964]
    128 p. maps, plan.   OTU
Fretz, J   Winfield.
    The Mennonites in Ontario. Waterloo, Ontario: The Mennonite Historical
    Society of Ontario, 1967.
    43 p. illus.   OTAR
Gellner, John, 1907–
    The Czechs and Slovaks in Canada, by John Gellner and John Smerek.
    [Toronto] University of Toronto Press [c1968]
    x, 172 p. illus., ports.   OTER
German Canadian Yearbook, 1973–1975. Toronto: Historical Society of
    Meckleburg Upper Canada Inc., 1973–1975.
    2 v. for the years: 1973, 1975. illus.
    Contains several articles on Ontario.   OTU
Germania Club of Hamilton, Ontario.
    Germania 100 jahre. [Radaktion Eugene Rapp. Hamilton, Ontario: The
    Club, 1964]
    216 p. illus., ports.
    Text in German and English.   OTU

Gingerich, Orland.
    The Amish of Canada. Waterloo, Ontario: Conrad Press [1972]
    244 p. illus., map, ports.
    Several sections on Ontario.   OTU
Gregorovich, Andrew Svyatoslav, 1935–
    Chronology of Ukrainian Canadian history. Toronto: Ukrainian Canadian
    Committee, 1974.
    64 p.   OTU
Grygier, Tateusz, 1915–
    The integration of immigrants in Toronto. Final report by T. Grygier and J.
    Spencer to the Social Planning Council of Metro [sic] Toronto. Toronto:
    School of Social Work, University of Toronto, 1963.
    25, 15 leaves.   OONL
Hamilton, Jon R
    Portuguese in transition. [Toronto: Research Department, Board of
    Education for the city of Toronto, 1970]
    109 p. tables.   OONL
Harney, Robert F   1939–
    Immigrants: a portrait of the urban experience, 1890–1930, by Robert F.
    Harney and Harold Troper. Toronto: VanNostrand Reinhold Ltd. [c1975]
    x, 212 p. illus., ports, map, facsims.   OTU
Head, Wilson A.
    The Black presence in the Canadian mosaic: a study of perception and the
    practice of discrimination against Blacks in Metropolitan Toronto.
    Submitted to the Ontario Human Rights Commission. [Toronto] 1975.
    ii, 235, 18 p. facsims.   OTAR
Helling, Rudolf Anton, 1929–
    The position of Negroes, Chinese and Italians in the social structure of
    Windsor, Ontario; a report submitted to the Ontario Human Rights
    Commission. Windsor, Ontario: 1965.
    iii, 124 p. maps.   OTU
Hostetler, John Andrew, 1918–
    Amish society. Baltimore: Johns Hopkins Press, 1963.
    xviii, 347 p. illus., diagrs., maps.
    Includes Amish communities in Ontario.   OONL
Indians in Ontario, Conference Victoria University, 1974.
    Report, April 1975. Toronto: Victoria University, 1975.
    x, 23 leaves.
    East Indians in Ontario.   OTU
Inter-Agency Council for Service to Immigrants and Migrants.
    Those people; a report on the accessibility of health, education and social
    services to the immigrant population to Metropolitan Toronto. Prepared by
    the Inter-Agency Council for Services to Immigrants and Migrants, assisted
    by the Local Initiatives Programme Project 311-1081. Editor: Kay Brown.
    Toronto [1973]
    xiv, 132, A1–A10, 65 p. tables.   OTU

Jamieson, Annie Straith.
    William King, friend and champion of slaves. Toronto: Missions of
    Evangelism [c1925]
    209 p. illus., ports.   OKQ
Jurkszus, Jadwiga.
    Toronto Tronto Trana, by Jadwiga Jurkszus and Adam Tomaszewscy.
    Toronto: The Authors, 1967.
    188 p. illus., port.
    Poles in Toronto.   OTU
Kayfetz, Ben G
    Toronto Jewry; an historical sketch. [Toronto] Centennial Research
    Committee [of the] Canadian Jewish Congress, Central Region [and the]
    United Jewish Welfare Fund of Toronto, 1957.
    7, 4 leaves.
    Contents: Toronto Jewry; an historical sketch, by B. G. Kayfetz; Our first
    100 years, by Julius Hayman.   OTU
King, William Lyon Mackenzie, 1874–1950.
    Toronto Jewry 60 years ago. Toronto: Canadian Jewish Congress Central
    Region, 1958.
    4 p.
    "An excerpt from the Toronto *Mail & Empire* of September 25th, 1897."
    Reprinted under present title in 1958.   OTU
Kirschbaum, Joseph M
    Slovaks in Canada. [Toronto] Canadian Ethnic Press Association of Ontario
    [c1967]
    xvi, 468 p. illus., ports.
    Several sections on Ontario.   OTU
Kosa, John (ed.).
    Immigrants in Canada, by Imre Bernolak [et al.] Montreal: 1955.
    63 p. tables.   OTU
— Land of choice: Hungarians in Canada. [Toronto] University of Toronto
    Press, 1957.
    104 p. illus., charts, tables.   OTU
Krychowski, T   W   (ed.).
    Polish Canadians: profile and image. Six studies in English, summaries in
    French. Toronto: Canadian Polish Congress, Polish Canadian Research
    Institute, 1969.
    111 p. diagrs., tables.   OTU
Kurlents, Alfred.
    Eestlased Kanadas, by Alfred Kurlents, Richard Antik and Jean Olvet.
    Toronto: KEAK, 1975.
    xvii, 670 p. illus., graphs.
    Estonians in Canada.   OOA
Lappin, Adah.
    The story of the Jewish community of Toronto, 1856–1957. Toronto: Bureau
    of Jewish Education, 1957.
    36 p.   OTCJCA

Lieberson, Stanley, 1933–
> Language and ethnic relations in Canada. New York: John Wiley & Sons
> [1970]
> xii, 264 p. graphs, map, tables.   OTU

Lithuanians in Canada by Pr. Gaida [et al.] Ottawa: Lights Printing and
> Publishing Co. Ltd., 1967.
> xx, 370 p. illus., maps, ports. (Canada Ethnica v).
> Chiefly Ontario.   OTU

Makowski, William Boleslaus, 1924–
> History and integration of Poles in Canada. Published by the Canadian
> Polish Congress Niagara Peninsula, Canada. [Lindsay, Ontario: John
> Deyell Limited] 1967
> 274 p. illus., ports. tables.   OTU

Mennonite Historical Society of Ontario.
> Sesquincentennial of the Amish Mennonites in Ontario. Edited by Dorothy
> Sauder. Sponsored by the Mennonite Historical Society of Ontario and the
> Western Ontario Mennonite Conference. n.p. [1972]
> 50 p. illus., facsims., maps, ports.   OTAR

Migus, Paul (ed.).
> Sounds Canadian: languages and cultures in multi-ethnic society. [Toronto]
> Peter Martin Associates [c1975]
> 261 p. (Canadian Ethnic Studies Association series, v. 4).   OTU

Nagata, Judith A
> English language classes for immigrant women with pre-school children. By
> Judith A. Nagata, Joan Rayfield [and] Mary Ferraris. [Toronto] 1970.
> 116 leaves. (York University, Toronto. Ethnic Research Programme.
> Research report, 2).
> "A report presented to the Citizenship Branch Office of the Provincial
> Secretary and Citizenship, Ontario, 1970."   OTU

Ontario Economic Council.
> Immigrant integration: a report. Our obligations – political, social and
> economic – to the 1,700,000 people who have come to Ontario in the past
> quarter century. [Toronto] 1970.
> xi, 55 p.
> Chairman: Wm. H. Cranston.   OTER

Ontario Welfare Council.
> From immigrant to Canadian. Toronto: The Author, 1958.
> [19] p.   OKQ

Order of the Sons of Italy of Ontario.
> [Submission to the] Special Joint Committee of the Senate and House of
> Commons on Immigration, March 16, 1967. Ottawa: 1967.
> pp. 728–730. (Canada. Special Joint Committee of the Senate and House of
> Commons on Immigration. Minutes of Proceedings and Evidence no. 14,
> 1967).   OONL

Palmer, Howard, 1946–   (ed.).
 Immigration and the rise of multiculturalism. Vancouver: Copp Clark
 [c1975]
 viii, 216 p. (Issues in Canadian history).   OTER
Perry, Charlotte Bronte.
 The history of the coloured Canadian in Windsor, Ontario 1867–1967.
 [Windsor, Ontario: Printed by Sumner Printing and Publishing Company
 Ltd., c1967]
 211 p. illus., ports., maps. (The Long Road, v. 1).   OTU
Project Bay Street [compiled by Carol Bell et al.] Sponsored by Finlandia Club
 and Department of Secretary of State. [Thunder Bay, Ontario] 1974.
 [150] leaves. map.
 Finns in Thunder Bay.   OONL
Purbhoo, Mary.
 Transition from Italian, by Mary Purbhoo and Stan Shapson. [Toronto:
 Research Department, Board of Education] 1975.
 ii, 99 p. diagrs.,tables. (Research service report 133).   OTER
Radecki, Henry.
 A member of a distinquished family: the Polish group in Canada, by Henry
 Radecki and Benedykt Heydenkorn. Toronto: McClelland and Stewart in
 association with the Multiculturalism Program, Department of the Secretary
 of State of Canada, 1976.
 240 p. illus. (Generations: a history of Canada's people).   OOA
Reid, William Stanford, 1913–   (ed.).
 The Scottish tradition in Canada. Toronto: McClelland and Stewart, in
 association with the Multiculturalism Program, Department of the Secretary
 of State of Canada, 1976.
 xi, 324 p. (Generations: a history of Canada's peoples).   OONL
Richmond, Anthony H   1925–
 Ethnic residential segregation in Metropolitan Toronto. [Toronto] York
 University. Institute for Behavioural Research, Ethnic Research
 Programme, in association with the Survey Research Centre, 1972.
 vi, 90 leaves. illus. (York University, Toronto. Ethnic Research report, E5).
                                                                              OTU
— Immigrants and ethnic groups in Metropolitan Toronto. [Toronto] Institute
 for Behavioural Research, York University, 1967.
 iii leaves. 101 [11] p. (York University, Toronto. Institute for Behavioural
 Research. Ethnic Research Programme. Research report, E1).   OTU
Rose, Albert, 1917–   (ed.).
 A people and its faith: essays on Jews and reform Judaism in a changing
 Canada. [Toronto] University of Toronto Press, 1959.
 xiv, 204 p.   OTU
— Social needs of the aged in Toronto. [Toronto: United Jewish Welfare Fund
 1957?]
 12 p.
 "Needs of the aged in the Jewish community of Toronto."   OTU

Rosenberg, Louis, 1893–
    Canada's Jewish community: a brief survey of its history, growth and
    characteristics. Montreal: Bureau of Social and Ecomonic Research,
    Canadian Jewish Congress [195?]
    16 leaves. map, tables. (Canadian Jewish population studies. Canadian
    Jewish community series no. 1).   OTU
— Canada's Jews: a social and economic study of the Jews in Canada. With a
    foreword by Doctor Arthur Ruppin. Montreal: Bureau of Social and
    Economic Research, Canadian Jewish Congress, 1939.
    xxiv, 418 p. diagrs., tables.   OTU
— Chronology of Canadian Jewish history. [Montreal: National Bicentenary
    Committee of the Canadian Jewish Congress, 1959]
    24 p.
    Chronology covers: 1697–1934.   OTU
— Language and mother tongue of Jews in Canada. Montreal: Bureau of
    Social and Economic Research, Canadian Jewish Congress, 1957.
    38, 20 p. tables. (Canadian Jewish population studies. Population
    characteristics series, no. 1).
    Reprinted from Our Library 1914–1957 Jewish Public Library, Montreal,
    1957.   OTU
— Some aspects of the historical development of the Canadian Jewish
    community. Montreal: Bureau of Social and Economic Research, Canadian
    Jewish Congress, 1960.
    pp. 121–142. (Canadian Jewish population studies. Population
    characteristics series, no. 4).
    Reprinted from Publication of the American Jewish Historical Society v. 50,
    no. 2, December, 1960.   OTU
— Two centuries of Jewish life in Canada: 1760–1960. Montreal: Bureau of
    Social and Economic Research, Canadian Jewish Congress [1961?]
    pp. 28–49. (Canadian Jewish population studies. Population characteristics
    series, no. 3).
    Reprinted from The American Jewish Year Book v. 62, 1961.   OTU
Rosenberg, Stewart E   1922–
    The Jewish community in Canada. Toronto: McClelland and Stewart
    Limited, 1970–1971.
    2 v. illus., ports.
    Contents: v. 1, A history; v. 2, In the midst of freedom.   OTU
Sack, Benjamin Gudman, 1890–1967.
    History of the Jews in Canada from the earliest beginnings to the present
    day, Montreal: Canadian Jewish Congress, 1945.
    vi, 285 p.
    The work was projected as two volumes. Only one volume was located.   OOA
— History of the Jews in Canada. Translated by Ralph Novek. Montreal:
    Harvest House [1965, c1964]
    xviii, 299 p.   OOA

Sauder, Dorothy.
    Trail's end, the Oxbow. [Bloomington, Ontario: Bloomington Mennonite
    Church, 1972]
    18 leaves. illus., ports.
    Mennonites in Ontario.   OONL
Schreiber, Jan Edward, 1941–
    In the course of discovery: West Indian immigrants in Toronto schools.
    Toronto: Board of Education for the city of Toronto [1970]
    70 p. map.   OTER
Social Planning Council of Metropolitan Toronto.
    The adoption of Negro children; a community-wide approach. [Toronto]
    1966.
    73 leaves. ports.   OTU
— A study of needs and resources of immigrants in Metropolitan Toronto.
    Toronto: 1970.
    82, 5, 2, 11, 6, leaves. tables.   OTU
Social Planning Council of Metropolitan Toronto. Immigration Section.
    Community planning for immigration. Reports and papers presented at the
    Immigration Conference and annual meeting. Toronto: The Council, 1961.
    57 leaves.   OONL
Social Planning Council of Metropolitan Toronto. Urban Alliance on Race
    Relations.
    Law enforcement and race relations. Toronto: The Council, 1976.
    1 v. (various pagings).   OTUCR
Stoll, Joseph.
    Recent Amish immigration to Ontario. n.p. 1966.
    [28] leaves. map.   OWTU
Toronto. Board of Education. Research Department.
    Immigrants and their education. [Toronto: 1965]
    17 leaves.   OTER
Toronto. City Planning Board.
    A report on the ethnic origins of the population of Toronto, 1960. [Toronto]
    1961.
    10 leaves. 22 maps.   OTU
Toronto Anti-Draft Programme.
    Manual for draft–age immigrants to Canada. Edited by Mark Satin. [2d
    ed.] Toronto: House of Anansi, 1968.
    87 p.   OTU
Tulloch, Headley, 1934–
    Black Canadians: a long line of fighters. Toronto: NC Press Limited, 1975.
    186 p. illus.   OTU
Turek, Victor, 1910–   (ed.).
    The Polish past in Canada. Contributions to the history of the Poles in
    Canada and the Polish-Canadian relations. Introduction by Watson
    Kirkconnell ... Toronto: Polish Alliance Press Limited, 1960.
    138 p. illus., ports., map. (Polish Research Institute in Canada. Studies 3).
                                                                          OTAR

Ukrainian Literary Society of T. Shevehenko, Kenora, Ontario.
   Ukrainians in Kenora: a jubilee book of Ukrainian Literary Society of T.
   Shevehenko, 1915–1965. Edited by Ol'ha Woycenko. Kenora, Ontario:
   1965.
   296 p. illus., ports.
   Title page and text in Ukrainian. Added t.p. in English.   OONL
Ukrainian National Federation of Canada. Toronto Branch.
   Propamiatna knyzhka. Toronto: 1950.
   1 v. (unpaged).   OTU
Ulemaailmsed Eesti Päevad, Toronto, 1972.
   Ulemaailmsed Eesti Päevad, 1972. The Estonian World Festival, 1972.
   [Toronto] Ulemaalimsete Eesti Päevade 1972 Peakomitee, 1973.
   1 v. (unpaged). illus. (part col.).
   English and Estonian.   OTU
United Jewish Welfare Fund of Toronto. Social Planning Committee.
   Report on health and welfare needs and services of the Toronto Jewish
   community. Toronto: 1969.
   xii, 185 p.   OTMCL
Vlassis, George Demetrios.
   The Greeks in Canada. Ottawa: 1942.
   147 p.   OTU
Winks, Robin W
   The Blacks in Canada: a history. Montreal: McGill–Queen's University
   Press, [c1971]
   xvii, 546 p. maps.   OTU
Wilmer, Leslie D
   Fairview Mennonite home. Elmira, Ontario: Bauman Printing for
   Mennonite Conference of Ontario, 1963.
   30 p. illus., ports.   OTAR
Wolfgang, Aaron, 1933–   (ed.).
   Education of immigrant students: issues and answers. [Toronto] Ontario
   Institute for Studies in Education [c1975]
   viii, 224 p. (Ontario Institute for Studies in Education. Symposium series 5).
                                                                        OTER
Woodyard, Monty.
   Components of the in-migration stream in central Canada. [Toronto] Centre
   for Urban and Community Studies, University of Toronto, 1972.
   44 p. tables. (Environment study. Research paper no. 57).   OTU
Zettlemoyer, Nancy Elizabeth.
   An assessment of immigrant needs and their fulfillment in Metropolitan
   Windsor, by Nancy E. Zettlemoyer, Paul Lassaline and Rudolf A. Helling.
   Windsor, Ontario: Windsor Citizenship Committe [sic] 1961.
   56 leaves. tables, maps.   OTU

Ziegler, Suzanne Gross, 1940–
  Characteristics of Italian householders in Metropolitan Toronto, by Suzanne
  Ziegler in association with Anthony H. Richmond. [Toronto] The Survey
  Research Centre, York University, 1972.
  125 leaves. tables. (York University. Institute for Behavioural Research.
  Ethnic Research Programme). OTU

Periodical Articles
Ascher, Elizabeth C
  Polish relief work at Niagara. Niagara Historical Society. Papers and
  Records 35: 27–43, 1923.
Bernhardt, Clara.
  Pennsylvania German folklore to the fore. Ontario History 45: 45–46, 1953.
Boudreau, Joseph A
  Interning Canada's "enemy aliens", 1914–1919. Canada: an historical
  magazine 2(no. 1): 15–27, 1974.
  Camp at Kapuskasing discussed.
Cowan, Jennie F
  Principal immigration groups of Waterloo county. Waterloo Historical
  Society. Annual Report 42: 26–27, 1954.
Demko, Donald.
  Cognition of southern Ontario cities in a potential migration context.
  Economic Geography 50: 20–34, 1974.
Dunham, B   Mabel.
  Mid-European backgrounds of Waterloo county. Ontario Historical Society.
  Papers & Records 37: 59–70, 1945.
German Peace Festival, 1871. Waterloo Historical Society. Annual Volume 54:
  78–80, 1966.
Harney, Robert F
  Chiaroscuro: Italians in Toronto, 1885–1915. Italian Americana 1: 142–167,
  1975.
Harrington, Lyn.
  Ontario's Klondike gardens: new settlers find new homes in a new land –
  after as earlier reclaimed it from a marsh near Grand Bend. Farmer's
  Magazine, Toronto 46 (6): 9, 36, 44, 1949.
Havel, J   E
  Some effects of the introduction of a policy of bilingualism in the polyglot
  community of Sudbury. Canadian Review of Sociology and Anthropology 9:
  57–71, 1972.
Heick, Welf H
  The Lutherans of Waterloo county during World War I. Waterloo
  Historical Society. Annual Volume 50: 23–32, 1962.
Hicks, Wesseley.
  Toronto's Czechs: how they've settled in. Toronto Life 3(3): 42–45, 75, 1969.

Hilborn, Ella.
    The history of the Negro population of Collingwood. Huron Institute. Papers
    and Records 1: 40–42, 1909.
Himel, Irving.
    Dresden. Canadian Forum 35: 148–149, 1955.
    Racial discrimination in Dresden, Ontario.
Integration through education. Industrial Canada 64(10): 42–45, 1964.
    Italian immigrants.
Jansen, Clifford J
    Leadership in the Toronto Italian ethnic group. International Migration
    Review n.s. 4: 25–43, 1969.
Kalbfleisch, Herbert K
    German or Canadian? Waterloo Historical Society. Annual Report 40:
    18–29, 1952.
    German settlers in Waterloo county.
— A short sketch of the German element in the townships of Stephen, Hay and
    Stanley of Huron county. Huron Historical Notes 8: 6–13, 1972.
Kero, Reino.
    Emigration from Finland to Canada before the first World War. Lakehead
    University Review 9: 7–16, 1976.
Kouhi, Christine.
    Labour and Finnish immigration to Thunder Bay, 1876–1974. Lakehead
    University Review 9: 17–40, 1976.
Kurman, Louis A
    The Hamilton Jewish community. Wentworth Bygones 8: 8–12, 1969.
Lee–Whiting, Brenda B
    First Polish settlement in Canada. Canadian Geographical Journal 75:
    108–112, 1967.
    Wilno district of Ontario.
Lenhard, J   A
    German Catholics in Ontario. Canadian Catholic Historical Association.
    Report 41–45, 1936–1937.
McKegney, Patricia.
    The German schools of Waterloo county, 1851–1913. Waterloo Historical
    Society. Annual Volume 58: 54–67, 1970.
Marston, Wilfred G
    Social class segregation within ethnic groups in Toronto. Canadian Review
    of Sociology and Anthropology 6: 65–79, 1969.
Milnes, Humphrey.
    German folklore in Ontario. Journal of American Folk-Lore 67: 35–43,
    1954.
Mollica, Anthony.
    Italian in Ontario. Canadian Modern Language Review 22(3): 19–23, 1966.
Morrison, Jean.
    Ethnicity and class consciousness: British, Finnish and South European

workers at the Canadian Lakehead before World War I. Lakehead University Review 9: 41–54, 1976.

Nagata, Judith A
Adaption and integration of Greek working class immigrants in the city of Toronto, Canada: a situational approach. International Migration Review n.s. 4: 44–70, 1969.

Ossenberg, Richard J
The social integration and adjustment of post-war immigrants in Montreal and Toronto. Canadian Review of Sociology and Anthropology 1: 202–214, 1964.

Phelan, Josephine.
A programme for the Italian community. Ontario Library Review 47: 168–170, 1963.
Toronto Public Libraries.

Ramcharan, Subhas.
The economic adaptation of West Indians in Toronto, Canada. Canadian Review of Sociology and Anthropology 13: 295–304, 1976.

Richmond, Anthony H
Toronto's ethnic ghettoes. Canadian Forum 52(May): 58–60, 1972.

Saarinen, Oiva W
The pattern and impact of Finnish settlement in Canada. Terra 79, 4: 113–120, 1967.

Sas, Anthony.
Dutch concentrations in rural southwestern Ontario during the post-war decade. Association of American Geographers. Annals 48: 185–194, 1958.

Shantz, Elven.
Mennonite groups in Waterloo county and adjacent area. Waterloo Historical Society. Annual Volume 55: 18–29, 1967.

Sherk, A   B
The Pennsylvania Germans of Waterloo county, Ontario. Ontario Historical Society. Papers & Records 7: 98–109, 1906.

Shoemaker, Alfred L
Pennsylvania Dutch Canada. Dutchman 7(4): 8–14, 1956.

Smucker, Barbara C
They found a home in Canada. Waterloo Historical Society. Annual Volume 62: 16–25, 1974.
Russian Mennonite migration to Canada and Waterloo county.

Toews, David.
The Mennonites of Canada. Mennonite Quarterly Review 11: 83–91, 1937.

Troper, Harold.
Images of the *foreigner* in Toronto, 1900–1930: a report. Urban History Review [4](2): 1–7, 1975.

Weirmair, K
The economic adjustment of Hungarian refugees in Toronto. Migration News 21: 7–12, 1972.

Theses

Abrams, Percy.
> A study of the Jewish immigrants in Hamilton and their relationship with
> the Jewish Community Centre. [Toronto] 1955.
> vii, 157 leaves. tables, fig.
> M.S.W. research report, University of Toronto.   OTU

Allen, Martha Isobel Gerard, 1917–
> A survey of the Finnish cultural economic, and political development in the
> Sudbury district of Ontario. [London, Ontario] 1954.
> vii, 121 leaves. fold. map.
> M.A. thesis, The University of Western Ontario.   OLU

Anderson, Grace Merle, 1923–
> The channel facilitators model of migration: a model tested using
> Portuguese blue-collar immigrants in Metropolitan Toronto. [Toronto]
> c1971.
> xiii, 363 leaves. tables, figs.
> Ph.D. thesis, University of Toronto (microfilm 31153).   OTU

Armogan, George Alan P   1939–
> An inquiry into the lives of Black West Indian children in Toronto schools.
> [Toronto] c1976.
> 221 leaves.
> M.A. thesis, University of Toronto.   OTU

Baker, Sylvia Kathleen.
> Integration of Jewish immigrants from Morocco into the Toronto
> community; a comment on the relationship between integration and
> disciplinary problems with their children experienced by parents from
> Morocco. [Toronto] 1965.
> vii, 96 leaves. tables.
> M.S.W. thesis, University of Toronto.   OTU

Baranyi, Nicholas.
> The relationship between the level of formal education and integration of
> immigrants. [Toronto] 1963, c1974.
> iv, 120 leaves. maps.
> M.S.W. thesis, University of Toronto (microfilm 17752).   OTU

Barrett, Frank Alexander, 1935–
> Post war European immigrants in Metropolitan Toronto: a social
> geography. [St. Paul, Minnesota] 1963.
> xv, 114 leaves. illus., maps.
> M.A. thesis, University of Minnesota.   OTY

Baumgartel, Bernd W
> A study of some aspects of juvenile delinquency among children of
> immigrants. [Toronto] 1955 [c1976]
> v, 71 leaves. tables, form.
> M.S.W. thesis, University of Toronto (microfilm 26037).   OTU

Becker, Billie Roxanne Gail.
  Fair employment practices in Ontario; attitudes of employers toward the
  employment of Jewish persons. [Toronto] 1964.
  xvi, 169 leaves. tables.
  M.S.W. thesis, University of Toronto.   OTU
Beserve, Christopher Abilogun, 1941–
  Relationship between home environment and cognitive and personality
  characteristics of working-class West Indian pupils in Toronto: consequences
  for their education [Toronto] c1976.
  xiii, 276 leaves. map.
  Ph.D. thesis, University of Toronto (microfilm 30333).   OTU
Binns, Margaret Alice, 1946–
  Cultural pluralism in Canada: an exploratory study of the Italians and the
  Ukrainians in London, Ontario. London, Ontario: 1971.
  xi, 106 leaves. charts, tables.
  M.A. thesis, The University of Western Ontario (microfilm 10756).   OLU
Bolotta, Angelo.
  An analysis of the savings and investment habits of Metropolitan Toronto's
  Italian community. [Toronto] 1973.
  iv, 61 leaves. tables, maps.
  B.A. research paper, University of Toronto.   OTU
Budd, William.
  The scholarship intake procedure of the Toronto Jewish camp council in
  1950. [Toronto] 1950.
  v, 96 leaves. illus.
  M.S.W. thesis, University of Toronto.   OTU
Burnham, Carol.
  Changes in services to recent immigrants by selected agencies in
  Metropolitan Toronto during the period 1960–66, with emphasis on agency
  interaction with the social planning council. [Toronto] 1967.
  iii [iv–v] 124 leaves. tables.
  M.S.W. thesis, University of Toronto.   OTU
Cangona, Lino, 1929–
  Employment factors affecting the integration of immigrant families: a
  comparative study of the adjustment of British, German, Hungarian and
  Italian immigrant husbands in the economic life of Canada. [Toronto] 1963.
  v, 192 leaves.
  M.S.W. thesis, University of Toronto (accepted 1964).   OTU
Chandler, David Ballantine, 1937–
  The residential location of occupational and ethnic groups in Hamilton.
  [Hamilton, Ontario] 1965.
  viii, 162 leaves. graphs, maps, tables.
  M.A. thesis, McMaster University.   OHM
Chlebowski, Tadeuez Stephen.
  Polish reception area analysis in Toronto. Waterloo, Ontario: 1973.
  v, 76 leaves. maps, tables.
  B.A. thesis, Waterloo University College.   OWTL

Cobbledick, Eleanor.
    The integration of immigrants and the cohesiveness of their extended
    families. [Toronto] 1963.
    v, 131 leaves. tables, charts.
    M.S.W. thesis, University of Toronto.   OTU
Colalillo, Guiliana Giovanna, 1950–
    Culture conflict in the adolescent Italian girl. [Toronto] c1974.
    ii, 103 leaves tables.
    M.A. thesis, University of Toronto (awarded 1975).   OTU
Cole, Joyce Lilian.
    West Indian teachers and nurses in Ontario, Canada: a study of migration
    patterns. [Hamilton, Ontario] 1967.
    iv, 114 leaves. tables.
    M.A. thesis, McMaster University.   OHM
Davies, Yvonne S
    The participation of women in the activities of the United Jewish Welfare
    Fund of Toronto. [Toronto] 1949.
    iv, 59 leaves. charts (fold.).
    M.S.W. thesis, University of Toronto.   OTU
Davison, Anne M
    An analysis of the significant factors in the patterns of Toronto Chinese
    family life as a result of the recent changes in immigration laws which
    permitted the wives of Canadian citizens to enter Canada. [Toronto] 1952,
    c1975.
    [7] 79 leaves. illus.
    M.S.W. thesis, University of Toronto (microfilm 21633).   OTU
Economopoulou, Louesa, 1950–
    Assimilation and sources of culture tension of second generation Greek pre-
    adolescents in Toronto. [Toronto] c1976.
    1 v. (various pagings). tables.
    M.A. thesis, University of Toronto   OTU
Einbinder, Esther.
    An exploratory study of attitudes toward Jews in the city of Toronto.
    [Toronto] 1934.
    59 leaves.
    M.A. thesis, University of Toronto.   OTU
Elliott, Una.
    Comparative roles of the people of Italian and Netherlandish origin in the
    creation of a homogenous population in the city of London. London,
    Ontario: 1964.
    xvi, 112 [20] leaves. graphs, tables, maps.
    M.A. thesis, The University of Western Ontario.   OLU
Feldbrill, Zelda.
    The adjustment of European youth in the Toronto Jewish Community.
    [Toronto] 1952.
    vii, 87 leaves. tables, fig.
    M.S.W. research report, University of Toronto.   OTU

Fenton, Charles Stephen.
    Assimilation processes among immigrants: a study of German and Italian
    immigrants to Hamilton. [Hamilton, Ontario] 1968.
    1 v. (various pagings). graphs.
    M.A. thesis, McMaster University.   OHM
Ferraris, Mary.
    Factors influencing the integration of a group of Italian women immigrants
    in Toronto. Toronto: 1969.
    xi, 209 leaves. tables.
    M.A. thesis, York University (microfilm 4794).   OTY
Foster, Matthew James.
    Ethnic settlement in the Barton Street region of Hamilton, 1921–1961.
    [Hamilton, Ontario] 1965.
    xiii, 236 p. illus., fold. maps.
    M.A. thesis, McMaster University.   OHM
Fu, Carly Yee Bing.
    A study of social adjustment of the Chinese family in Toronto. [Guelph,
    Ontario] 1966.
    vi, 78, 10 leaves. tables,
    M.Sc. thesis, The University of Guelph.   OGU
Galbraith, Christine Isobel Macintosh.
    Interethnic comparisons of factors relating to the integration of immigrants.
    [Toronto] 1963, c1974.
    113 leaves. tables, graphs.
    M.S.W. thesis, University of Toronto (microfilm 1770).   OTU
Gerendas–Giannone, Otto.
    Integration of Jewish immigrants from Morocco into the Toronto
    community; a comparative study of the employment experiences of French-
    Moroccan and Tangerian immigrants of Jewish faith to Metropolitan
    Toronto. [Toronto] 1965.
    viii, 107 leaves.
    M.S.W. thesis, University of Toronto.   OTU
Glickman, Yaacoo, 1936–
    Organizational indicators and social correlates of collective Jewish identity.
    [Toronto] c1976.
    2 v. [xvii, 683 leaves]
    Ph.D. thesis, University of Toronto.   OTU
Goldberg, Samuel Lawrence.
    Economic and social aspects of the location of Jews in Ottawa, 1891–1931.
    Ottawa: 1976.
    vii, 75 leaves. maps (part fold.), tables.
    B.A. research essay, Carleton University.   OOCC
Grant, Charity L
    Occupational adjustment of immigrants. [Toronto] 1955.
    74 [3] leaves. tables.
    M.S.W. research paper, University of Toronto.   OTU

Graumans, Joe, 1943–
   The role of ethnic-religious organizations in the assimilation process of
   Dutch Christian Reformed and Catholic immigrants in south western
   Ontario. Windsor, Ontario: 1973.
   vii, 99 leaves. tables.
   M.A. thesis, University of Windsor (microfilm 19894).   OWA
Greenberg, Zeev.
   Israeli immigrants in Toronto. Toronto: 1971.
   xii, 125 leaves. tables.
   M.A. thesis, York University (microfilm 7771).   OTY
Hahn, Eva Brass.
   Admissions to the New Jewish Home for the Aged, Toronto. [Toronto] 1958.
   viii, 111 leaves.
   M.S.W. research report, University of Toronto.   OTU
Heintz, Gladys.
   German immigration into Upper Canada and Ontario from 1783 to the
   present day. Kingston, Ontario: 1938.
   147, xv leaves. illus., chart, maps (part col. part fold.).
   M.A. thesis, Queen's University.   OKQ
Helling, Rudolf Anton, 1929–
   A comparison of the acculturation of immigrants in Toronto, Ontario and
   Detroit, Michigan. Detroit, Michigan: 1962.
   282 p.
   Ph.D. thesis, Wayne State University (microfilm 68-06642).   DA
Herniman, Charles Albert, 1943–
   Ethnic type and rural land ownership Mersea township, Ontario. London,
   Ontario: 1969.
   ix, 83 leaves. tables, maps (part fold.).
   M.A. thesis, The University of Western Ontario (accepted 1970) (microfilm
   5769).   OLU
Hill, Daniel Grafton, 1923–
   Negroes in Toronto; a sociological study of a minority group. [Toronto] 1960
   [c1974]
   vi, 410 [8] leaves. tables, maps (part fold.).
   Ph.D. thesis, University of Toronto (microfilm 17270).   OTU
Kim, Bo-Kyung, 1937–
   Attitudes, parental identification, and locus of control of Korean, New
   Korean-Canadian and Canadian adolescents. [Toronto] c1976.
   x, 174 leaves.
   Ph.D. thesis, University of Toronto.   OTU
Kirshenblatt–Gimblett, Barbara, 1942–
   Traditional storytelling in the Toronto Jewish community: a study in
   performance and creativity in an immigrant culture. Bloomington, Indiana:
   1972.
   ix, 508 leaves. illus.
   Ph.D. thesis, Indiana University (microfilm 73-2724).   DA

Knott, John Werner.
Spoken Yiddish; a study of the Lithuanian and the Polish dialect of Yiddish
in Toronto. [Toronto] 1963.
47 leaves.
M.A. thesis, University of Toronto.   OTU
Ko, Eva Maria Bik-Chi Li.
Survey of the leisure time activities of the Chinese in downtown Toronto.
[Toronto] 1964.
iv, 97 leaves.
M.S.W. thesis, University of Toronto.   OTU
Kohn, Ruby Gaibath.
The Jewish vocational service of Toronto. A study of how the functions
originally proposed for one Toronto agency were adapted to meet the
changing needs of the local Jewish community during the period of 1947 to
1949. [Toronto] 1950.
115 leaves. tables.
M.S.W. thesis, University of Toronto.   OTU
Labarge, Claire Munroe.
Jewish youth in the community: Jewish identity and its relationship to
choice of friends and use of services. [Toronto] 1968.
vi, 91 leaves. tables, figs., map.
M.S.W. thesis, University of Toronto.   OTU
Lai, Vivien.
The assimilation of Chinese immigrants in Toronto. Toronto: 1970.
1 v. (various pagings). illus.
M.A. thesis, York University (microfilm 6667).   OTY
Lam, Yiu Tong.
Ethnic community and identification: a survey of the male Chinese
immigrants in Toronto. Waterloo, Ontario: 1976.
xi, 179 leaves. tables.
M.A. thesis, University of Waterloo.   OWTU
Lamb, John Douglas.
A neighbourhood business street as an expression of Italian urban culture.
[Toronto] 1965.
iv, 52 leaves. illus., maps (part col. 1 fold.).
B.A. thesis, University of Toronto.   OTU
Lappin, B   W
Joint fund-raising in Toronto: the role of the Jewish community. [Toronto]
1947.
v, 90 leaves.
M.S.W. thesis, University of Toronto.   OTU
Lazarou, Linda Hoermann.
Integration of Jewish immigrants from Morocco into the Toronto
community: social and community relationships. [Toronto] 1966.
v, 89 leaves. tables.
M.S.W. thesis, University of Toronto.   OTU

Lemay, Roger.
  Une enquête préliminaire des préférences ethniques à Ottawa. Ottawa:
  1952.
  105 leaves. tables.
  M.A. thesis, Université d'Ottawa.   OOU
McKenzie, Thomas Rose.
  The past and present status of the teaching of English to non-English
  speaking immigrants to Canada, with special reference to Ontario.
  [Toronto] 1954.
  v, 179 leaves. tables, figs., map.
  Ed.D. thesis, University of Toronto.   OTU
McMahen, Janice A
  Berlin becomes Kitchener, a breach in the German tradition of an Ontario
  city. [Waterloo, Ontario] 1973.
  ii, 75 leaves.
  B.A. thesis, Waterloo Lutheran University.   OWTL
Makabe, Tomoko, 1944–
  Ethnic group identity: Canadian-born Japanese in Metropolitan Toronto.
  [Toronto] c1976.
  ix, 283 leaves. tables, maps.
  Ph.D. thesis, University of Toronto.   OTU
Matsumoto, Norman S
  The influence of ethnicity on residential mobility: the case of the Japanese in
  Metropolitan Toronto 1945–1975. [Toronto] 1976.
  v, 79 leaves. tables, maps.
  B.A. thesis, University of Toronto.   OTU
Morton, William Jerome Eugene.
  Fair accommodation practices in Ontario; a study of the Negro
  complainants's and leaders' knowledge of and attitudes toward the Ontario
  human rights code and Commission. [Toronto] 1966 [c1974]
  ix, 140, 11 leaves. tables.
  M.S.W. thesis, University of Toronto (microfilm 19726).   OTU
Munro, Peter Fraser.
  An experimental investigation of the mentality of the Jew in Ryerson public
  school. Toronto: University of Toronto Press, 1926.
  55 p. tables, diagrs.
  D.Paed. thesis, University of Toronto.   OTU
Murdie, Robert.
  A geographic study of the Mennonite settlement in Waterloo county.
  Waterloo, Ontario: 1961.
  x, 91 leaves. illus., maps, tables.
  B.A. thesis, Waterloo University College.   OWTL
Nizamuddin, Khondakar, 1937–
  Some behavioural characteristics of migrants from India and Pakistan in
  Windsor, Ontario, Canada: a case study. Windsor, Ontario: 1976.
  vi, 99 leaves, graphs, maps, tables.
  M.A. thesis, University of Windsor.   OWA

Norman, Anne Catherine.
  Fair employment practices in Ontario: attitudes of employers toward the
  employment of Negroes. [Toronto] 1961.
  iii, 145 leaves.
  M.S.W. thesis, University of Toronto (microfilm 31297).   OTU
Olyan, Sidney D
  Democracy in action: a study of the Co-operative Committee on Japanese
  Canadians. [Toronto] 1951.
  ii, 116 leaves.
  M.S.W. thesis, University of Toronto.   OTU
Osten, Ellen Sue.
  Sub-group response toward legislation against hate propaganda in the
  Jewish community of Toronto. [Toronto: 1967]
  117 [3] leaves.
  M.S.W. thesis, University of Toronto.   OTU
Petroff, Lillian, 1951–
  The Macedonian community in Toronto to 1930. [Toronto] c1976.
  142 leaves. maps.
  M.A. thesis, University of Toronto.   OTU
Pirie, Margaret Cameron.
  Patterns of mobility and assimilation: a study of the Toronto Jewish
  community. New Haven, Connecticut: 1957.
  xxxv, 400 leaves. maps.
  Ph.D. thesis, Yale University.   Yale
Ramcharan, Subhas.
  The adaptation of West Indians in Canada. Toronto: 1974.
  xviii, 319 leaves. tables.
  Ph.D. thesis, York University (microfilm 20024).   OTY
Rappak, Peter G
  Patterns of ethnic occupational assimilation and mobility: a case study of
  Polish immigrants in Toronto. Hamilton, Ontario: 1976 [c1977]
  ix, 215 leaves. tables.
  M.A. thesis, McMaster University (microfiche 29716).   OHM
Rashleigh, Edward Thornton.
  South Rosedale; clan stability and clan change in a central residential
  district. Toronto [1960]
  52 leaves.
  M.A. thesis, University of Toronto.   OTU
Richter, Manfred Martin, 1929–
  The phonemic system of the Pennsylvania German dialect in Waterloo
  county, Ontario. [Toronto] c1969.
  iv, 173 leaves.
  Ph.D. thesis, University of Toronto (microfilm 21404).   OTU
Schaefer, Thomas L
  Russian Mennonite immigration and settlement in Waterloo county
  1924–1925. Waterloo, Ontario: 1974.
  56 leaves. map.
  B.A. thesis, Wiifrid Laurier University.   OWTL

Sgro, Salvatore.
    Minority groups in the tertiary activity system: the Italian presence in
    Metropolitan Toronto. [Toronto] 1972.
    88 leaves. diagrs., maps, tables.
    B.A. thesis, Erindale College, University of Toronto.   OTU
Shiff, Murray.
    The youth program of the Canadian Jewish Congress in Ontario. [Toronto]
    1952.
    118 leaves.
    M.S.W. research report, University of Toronto.   OTU
Sibbald, Patricia A
    Study of a multi-ethnic transient area of Toronto. [Toronto] 1962.
    vi, 140 leaves. tables, maps.
    M.S.W. research report, University of Toronto.   OTU
Sidlofsky, Samuel, 1926–
    Post-war immigrants in the changing metropolis, with special reference to
    Toronto's Italian population. [Toronto] c1969.
    iv, 312 leaves. maps (part fold.), fold. table.
    Ph.D. thesis, University of Toronto (microfilm 7935).   OTU
Simpson, Donald George, 1934–
    Negroes in Ontario from early times to 1870. London, Ontario: 1971.
    2 v. [1, iii, 993 leaves]
    Ph.D. thesis, The University of Western Ontario (microfilm 8008).   OLU
Smith, Claudette Pamela.
    West Indian migration to Kitchener – Waterloo, Ontario. [Waterloo,
    Ontario] 1975.
    vii, 158 leaves. tables.
    M.A. thesis, University of Waterloo.   OWTU
Smith, Mary Ann, 1943–
    The attitudes of new Canadian high school students and their achievement
    in English. ['Toronto] c1974.
    iv, 148 leaves.
    M.A. thesis, University of Toronto.   OTU
Southgate, H   Jane.
    An examination of the position of the Mennonites in Ontario under the
    jurisdiction of the Military Service Act, 1917. [Waterloo, Ontario] 1976.
    116 leaves.
    M.A. thesis, Wilfrid Laurier University.   OWTL
Spack, Margaret.
    Integration of Jewish immigrants from Morocco into the Toronto
    community: the use of and attitudes towards the social services. [Toronto]
    1965.
    v, 90 leaves. tables.
    M.S.W. thesis, University of Toronto.   OTU
Speisman, Stephen Alan.
    The Jews of Toronto: a history to 1937. Toronto: 1975.
    2 v.
    Ph.D. thesis, University of Toronto. (restricted)   OTU

[Starodub, Linda]
    An examination of the attitudes affecting the morphology of Italian
    neighbourhoods in Toronto. [Toronto] 1973.
    67 [2] leaves. maps.
    B.A. research paper, University of Toronto.   OTU
Stiles, Elizabeth Alice.
    Fair accommodation practices in Ontario; a study of the education
    programme of the Ontario Human Rights Commission, with specific
    reference to nineteen community organizations concerned with ethnic
    groups. [Toronto] 1964.
    vi, 76 leaves. tables.
    M.S.W. thesis, University of Toronto.   OTU
Tanser, Harry Ambrose, 1897–
    The settlement of Negroes in Kent county, Ontario, and a study of the
    mental capacity of their descendants. [Toronto: 1939]
    xviii, 301 leaves. tables, diagrs., maps, plates.
    D.Paed. thesis, University of Toronto.   OTU
— [Chatham, Ontario: Shepherd Publishing Co., c1939]
    187 p. diagrs., tables.   OTU
— Westport, Connecticut: Negro University Press [c1970]
    187 p. diagrs., maps, ports.   OTU
Taylor, Edward.
    Conflict, group affiliation and social adjustment: the case of the West
    Indians in Toronto. [Guelph, Ontario] 1969.
    vii, 229 leaves. diagrs., maps, tables.
    M.A. thesis, The University of Guelph.   OGU
Thompson, Alford Wingrove, 1939–
    Assimilation of West Indians in London and Hamilton, Ontario. London,
    Ontario: 1970.
    xiii, 130 leaves. tables.
    M.A. thesis, The University of Western Ontario (microfilm 7241).   OLU
Tull, Anne Liis.
    The residential distribution and mobility of the Estonian population in
    Metropolitan Toronto: consequences for the preservation of ethnicity.
    Toronto: 1975.
    vi, 68 leaves. illus., maps.
    B.A. research paper, University of Toronto.   OTU
Turner, Joanne Catherine.
    A study of the relationship between the integration of immigrant parents
    and their acceptance of and involvement in the Canadian school. [Toronto]
    1963.
    v, 123 leaves. tables.
    M.S.W. thesis, University of Toronto.   OTU
Turrittin, Jane Sawyer.
    Networks to jobs: case studies of West Indian women from Montserrat.
    [Toronto] c1975.
    [i–iv] 176 leaves.
    Phil M. research paper, University of Toronto.   OTU

Venditti, Mario P
    The Italian ethnic community of Metrpolitan Toronto: a case in
    intra–urban network. Toronto: 1975.
    vii, 107 leaves. illus., maps (part col.).
    M.A. research paper, York University.   OTY
Vincent, Patrick.
    The assimilation process: with special reference to Italian children in the
    Hamilton school system. Hamilton, Ontario: 1968.
    218 leaves.
    M.A. thesis, McMaster University.   OHM
Vuorinen, Saara Sofia.
    Ethnic identification of Caribbean immigrants in the Kitchener – Waterloo
    area. Waterloo, Ontario: 1973 [c1974]
    178 leaves.
    Ph.D. thesis, University of Waterloo (accepted 1974) (microfilm 19358).   Can
Wangenheim, Elizabeth Dean.
    The social organization of the Japanese community in Toronto: a product of
    crisis. [Toronto] 1956.
    163 leaves.
    M.A. thesis, University of Toronto.   OTU
Woollatt, Margarete.
    The German Canadians of Berlin (Kitchener), Ontario, in the first World
    War. [Waterloo, Ontario] 1968.
    iii, 43 leaves. tables.
    B.A. thesis, Waterloo Lutheran University.   OWTL
Yiu, Esther Kam-Yu.
    Youth in need: a study of the need for after-school programs geared to the
    acculturation of Chinese immigrant youth from downtown Toronto.
    [Toronto] 1968.
    vi, 156 leaves. tables.
    M.S.W. thesis, University of Toronto.   OTU
Zador, Thomas Henry.
    Integration of Jewish immigrants from Morocco into the Toronto
    community: an exploratory study of Sephradic Jewish immigrants who came
    to Canada after Morocco gained independence in 1956; with special
    reference to their psychological-emotional as well as socio-economic
    satisfactions and dissatisfactions in Canada. [Toronto] 1965.
    vi, 162 leaves. tables.
    M.S.W. thesis, University of Toronto.   OTU
Ziegler, Suzanne Gross, 1940–
    The adaptation of Italian immigrants to Toronto: an analysis. Boulder,
    Colorado: 1971.
    viii, 162 leaves. illus.
    Ph.D. thesis, University of Colorado (microfilm 72-3723).   DA

FRANCO-ONTARIANS

Bibliography
Canada. Department of the Secretary of State. Research and Planning Branch. Bilingualism Development Programme.
Selected bibliography on Francophone minorities in Canada. [Ottawa] 1972.
2 v.
Also published in French.   OONL
Fortin, Benjamin.
Bibliographie analytique de l'Ontario français, par Benjamin Fortin, Jean–Pierre Gaboury. [Ottawa] Cahiers de Centre de recherche en civilization canadienne-française, editions de l'Université d'Ottawa, 1975.
xii, 236 p.   OOU
Lortie, Monique.
Les relations biculturelles au Canada: memoire bibliographique.
Contribution à l'étude des Sciences de l'homme no. 1: 11–55, 1952.

Monographs and Pamphlets.
Allaire, Yvan.
Situation socio-économique et satisfaction des chefs de ménage franco-ontariens, by Yvan Allaire and Jean-Marie Toulouse. Ottawa: [Public par L'Association Canadienne-Française de l'Ontario] 1973.
vii, 182, A150 p. charts, tables. (Recherche sur la situation economique des franco-ontariens v. 1).   OTU
L'Association canadienne des èducateurs de langue française.
Esquisses de Canada français. Montreal: Editions Fide's [c1967].
450 p. illus., fold. map, ports.   OTU
—— Répertoire des institutions d'enseignement française v. 1–7, 1956/57–1962/63. Quebec: Editions L'ACELF [1956]–1962.
7 v. for the years: 1956-1957, 1957-1958, 1958-1959, 1959-1960, 1960-1961, 1961-1962, 1962-1963.   OONL
L'Association canadienne des éducateurs de langue française. 14, congrès, 1961.
Avenir du Canada et culture française. Québec: editions L'ACELF, 1961.
176 p. (Travaux du xive congrés).   OTU
L'Association canadienne des éducateurs de langue française. 19, Congres, 1966.
Culture française, sauvegards de l'identité canadienne . Quebec: editions L'ACELF, 1967.
196 p. (Actes du xixe congrés).   OTU
Association canadienne-française d'education d'Ontario.
Bi-lingualism in Ontario: common sense and prejudice. Ottawa: 1912.
27 p. (Association canadienne-française d'education d'Ontario, publication no. 5).   OTU OKQ
—— 1910–1960. Rapport général des fêtes du cinquantenaire et du quinzième

congrès général de l'Association candaienne-française d'educations
d'Ontario, les 20, 21 et 22 avril 1960. [Ottawa: Le Droit, 1960]
180 p. illus., ports.   OOA
— Programme d'enseignement bilingue d'Ontario. Deuxieme convention
biennale des canadiens français de la province d'Ontario. Ottawa: 1912.
7 p.   OTER
Association des écoles secondaires privées franco-ontariennes.
   Les écoles secondaires privées franco-ontariennes: situation actuelle;
   perspective d'avenir. Memoire de la Commission d'étude de l'AESPFO. 2e ed.
   [Ottawa?] 1966.
   vii, 151 feuilles. cartes, tabl.   OOU
Barrette, Victor, 1888–
   Moi, franco-ontarien: mes droits, mes devoirs. Sudbury, Ontario. Société
   historique de Nouvel-Ontario, 1947.
   32 p. (Collection franco-ontarienne no. 2).   OTU OOU
Belcourt, Napoléon Antoine, 1860–1932.
   French in Ontario. Ottawa: Imprimeau du "Droit," 1915.
   9 p.
   Reproduced from the *University Magazine*, December, 1912.   OKQ
Boileau, Gilles.
   Les canadiens français dans l'est de l'Ontario [la terre et les hommes] Etude
   préparée par Gilles Boileau, réalisée en collaboration avec l'Union des
   cultivateurs franco-ontariens. n.p.: 1964.
   74 leaves. map, tables, graphs. (La sociéte canadienne d'establissement
   rural).   OOU OTU
— Saint Albert: étude de geographie humaine. En collaboration avec l'Union
   des cultivateurs franco-ontariens. Ottawa: La sociétê canadienne
   d'etablissement rural, 1958.
   45 p.   OOU
Boucher, Jacqueline, 1946–
   Rapport de comité cultural provincial de l'Association canadienne-française
   de l'Ontario, 1969–1970.
   Ottawa: The Association, 1970.
   33 p.   OOU
Bref historique des canadiens-français d'Ontario. Ottawa: Le Droit, 1934.
   16 p.   OTU
Canada. Information Canada.
   Les canadiens français d'un ocean à l'autre. [Ottawa: 1971]
   19 p. illus.   OONL
Canada. Royal Commission on Bilingualism and Biculturalism.
   Report. Ottawa: Queen's Printer, 1967–1969 [i.e. 1970]
   4 v. in 5. maps (part fold.).
   Co-chairmen: A. Davidson Dunton and André Laurendeau replaced in
   1968 by John–Louis Gagnon.   OTU
— Bilingualism and biculturalism: an abridged version of the Royal

Commission report by Hugh R. Innis. Toronto: McClelland and Stewart, in co-operation with The Secretary of State Department, and Information Canada [c1973]
186 p.   OTU

Background papers to Canada Royal Commission on Bilingualism and Biculturalism
L'Association canadienne-française d'education d'Ontario.
Memoire à la Commission royale d'enquête sur le bilinguisme et le biculturalisme. [Ottawa: Imprimerie Gatineau Ltée] 1964.
55 p.   OOL
Baird, Norman B
Finances of bilingual elementary schools in Ontario. [Ottawa?] 1965.
1 v. (various pagings). diagrs. (part col.), tables. (Canada. Royal Commission on Bilingualism and Biculturalism. Research report. Division 6, no. 6).   OOA
Bryan, Nancy.
Ethnic participation and language use in the public service of Ontario. Report presented to the Royal Commission on Bilingualism and Biculturalism [Ottawa] 1967.
2 v. charts (part fold.), tables.   OONL
Carlton, R
Kapuskasing and district community study. [Ottawa: 1965?]
275 p. charts, facsims., maps, tables. (Canada. Royal Commission on Bilingualism and Biculturalism. Research report. Division 5–A, no. 10). OOA
Cook, George Ramsay, 1931–
Provincial autonomy, minority rights and the compact theory, 1867–1921. [Ottawa: Information Canada, 1969, reprinted 1970]
81 p. (Canada. Royal Commission on Bilingualism and Biculturalism. Studies, 4).   OTMCL
Henripin, Jacques.
Etude des aspects demographiques des problemes ethniques et linguistiques au Canada. Rapport de recherche préparé pour la Commission royale de'enquête sur le bilinguisme et le biculturalisme. [Ottawa] 1966.
1 v. (unpaged). tables.   OONL
Hurley, James Ross.
The teaching of and teaching in a language other than English in the provinces of Ontario, Manitoba, Saskatchewan, Alberta and British Columbia: PRECIS. Prepared by J.R. Hurley and W.T.R. Wilson for H.B. Neatby. [Ottawa?] 1965.
1 v. (various pagings). tables. (Canada. Royal Commission on Bilingualism and Biculturalism. Research report. Division 6, no. 19).   OOA
Meisel, John.
Ethnic relations in Canadian voluntary associations, by John Meisel and Vincent Lemieux. [Ottawa: Information Canada, 1972]
xiv, 354 p. (Canada. Royal Commission on Bilingualism and Biculturalism. Documents [monographic series] 13).   OTU

Orlikow, Lionel.
    Report on second-language teaching in the western provinces and in
    Ontario. [Ottawa? 1966?]
    1 v. (various pagings). tables (part fold.). (Canada. Royal Commission on
    Bilingualism and Biculturalism. Research report. Division 6, no. 22).   OOA
Painchaud, Louis.
    Descriptions du bilinguisme et du biculturelisme de l'Université
    Laurentienne et du Collège militaire royal de Saint-Jean. Préparé pour la
    Commission royale d'enquête sur le bilinguisme et le biculturalisme. [Final
    report] Sherbrooke, Quebec: 1966.
    207 leaves. tables.   OONL
Sheppard, Claude Armand, 1935–
    The law of languages in Canada. [Ottawa: Information Canada, 1971]
    xix, 414 p. (Canada. Royal Commission on Bilingualism and Biculturalism.
    Studies, 10).   OTU
Smiley, Donald Victor.
    Constitutional adaptation and Canadian federalism since 1945. [Ottawa:
    Information Canada, 1971]
    viii, 155 p. (Canada. Royal Commission on Bilingualism and Biculturalism.
    Documents, 4).   OTU
Trudel, Marcel.
    Canadian history textbooks: a comparative study, by Marcel Trudel and
    Geneviève Jain. [A study prepared for the Royal Commission on
    Bilingualism and Biculturalism. Ottawa: Queen's Printer, 1970]
    xx, 149 p.   OTU

Carrière, Laurier.
    Le vocabulaire français des écoliers franco-ontariens. [Montreal] Institut
    Pédagogique Saint-Georges, Université de Montreal, 1952.
    110 p.   OTER
Chaperon–Lor, D
    Une minorité s'explique: les attitudes de la population francophone du nord-
    est ontarien envers l'education de langue francaise. [Toronto: Ontario
    Institute for Studies in Education, 1974]
    iix, 94 p. (Ontario Institute for Studies in Education. Occasional papers 14).
                                                                            OOU OTER
Charlebois, R   P   Charles.
    Les canadiens-français d'Ontario et la presse. Rapport a la premiere
    convention biennale des canadiens-français d'Ontario. Ottawa:
    L'Association canadienne-française d'education d'Ontario, 1912.
    42 p.   OTU

Charron, Alphonse-T
La langue française et les petits canadiens français de l'Ontario. Etude lue
en séance de la société du parler française au Canada, à l'Université Laval
(Quebec) le 4 février 1914. Quebec: Imp. l'Action Sociale Ltée., 1914.
29 p. (L'Association canadienne-française d'education de l'Ontario.
Publications). OOU OOA

Choquette, Robert, 1938–
Language and religion: a history of English-French conflict in Ontario.
Ottawa: University of Ottawa Press, 1975.
xii, 264 p. (Cahiers d'histoire de l'Université d'Ottawa, no. 5). OTU

Colloque sur la situation de la recherche sur la vie française en Ontario,
Ottawa, 1974.
Actes du colloque sur la situation de la recherche sur la vie française en
Ontario: tenu a l'Université d'Ottawa les 28 et 29 Novembre 1974. Organizé
par le Centre de recherche en civilization canadienne-française de
l'Université d'Ottawa. [Ottawa: Centre de recherche en civilization
canadian-française de l'Université d'Ottawa et l'Association canadienne-
française pour l'advancement des sciences, 1975]
277 p. map, graphs, tables. OTAR

Comeau, Paul-André.
Les facettes d'un système scolaire, by Paul-André Comeau [et al. Rapport
préliminaire soumis au Comité de recherche de l'Association des commission
des écoles bilingues de l'Ontario] Ottawa: Faculté des sciences societes,
l'Université d'Ottawa, 1971.
180 leaves. tables. OOU OONL

— Les franco-ontariens et le College Algonquin, par Paul A. Comeau [et al.
Ottawa] Université d'Ottawa, 1969.
1 v. (various pagings). OTER

Congrès d'education des canadiens-français d'Ontario, Ottawa, 1910.
Rapport officiel des séances tenues à Ottawa du 18 au 20 janvier 1910:
questions d'education et d'interet général. Ottawa: L'Association
canadienne-française d'education, 1910.
363 p. ports. OTER

— Système scolaire de la province d'Ontario. Etude publiée par la Commission
constituante du Congres d'éducation des canadiens-français d'Ontario, qui
s'ouvrirs à Ottawa, le mardi 18 janvier, 1910. Hawkesbury, Ontario:
Imprimere du Moniteur, 1909.
28 p. OTER

Congrès de la langue française au Canada, 3d, Quebec, 1952.
Mémoires. Quebec: Les Editions Ferland, 1953.
390 p.
Several papers on franco-ontariens. OTU

Constantineau, Albert, 1866–1944.
La langue française dans l'Ontario: mémoire lu à la séance publique de la
Société du parler français au Canada, 22 févier, 1911. Quebec: L'Action
sociale Ltée, 1911.
15 p. OOU

Cyr, Roger, 1929–
    The Canada français d'outre-frontières: l'Ontario. St. Hyacinthe, Quebec:
    Editions Alerte [1960?]
    12 p.   OOU
Desroches, Jocelyn.
    Les diplômés des programmes de formation professionnelle de deux ans des
    écoles secondaires de langue francaise de l'Ontario et le marché du travail
    par Jocelyn Desroches et Jean-Paul Breton. [Toronto] Ontario Institute for
    Studies in Education, 1973.
    viii, 109, 9 leaves.   OTER
Dionne, Narcisse Eutrope, 1848–1917.
    Fête nationale des canadiens-français célébrée à Windsor, Ontario, le 23 juin
    1883. Quebec: Imprimerie Léger Brousseau, 1883.
    152 p.   OOU
Lefranc, J   P
    Catéchisme des caisses populaires, sociétés coopératives d'épargne et de
    crédit, destiné à vulgariser l'idée de l'association coopérative. Explication de
    cette oeuvre économique sa nature, ses propriétés, son fonctionmement et ses
    bienfaits. Quebec: La Propaganda des, bons livres, 1910.
    vii, 82 p.
    Cover title is 1911.   OONL
Les Franco-ontariens. [Travaus de recherche présentés] Sciences politiques 424
    Collège universitaire Glendon août. 1970. n.p.: 1970.
    3 v.
    Class reports presented to Professor M.K. Spicer.   OOU
Gaudrault Pie-Marie, 1889–1953.
    Le milieu facteur de culture francaise. [Ottawa] Association canadienne-
    française d'education d'Ontario, 1934.
    21 p.   OOA
Gauthier, Annette La Casse, 1916–
    Genese de nos paroisses regionales: nord-ouest Quebecois et est Ontarien
    Rouyn Quebec: Société Saint-Jean-Baptiste de l'ouest quebecois, 1972.
    1 v. (unpaged). illus.   OTU
Gold, Gerald Lewis.
    Communities and culture in French Canada, by Gerald L. Gold and Marc-
    Adelard Tremblay. Toronto: Holt, Rinehart and Winston of Canada,
    Limited [c1973]
    xiii, 364 p. diagrs., maps, port., tables.   OTU
Gosselin, Paul-Emile.
    Le conseil de la vie française [1937–1967] Quebec: Les Editions Ferland,
    1967.
    168 p. ports.
    Ontario: pp. 114–154.   OTU
— L'empire français d'Amerique. Quebec: Les Editions Ferland, 1963.
    144 p. illus., maps, ports., tables.
    Ontario: pp. 66–82.   OTU

Granger, Pierre.
　　Aux canadiens-français de l'Ontario: raisons d'esperer. Saint Hyacinthe,
　　Quebec: Le Rosaire, 1915.
　　22 p.   OKQ
Grant, George Monro, 1835–1902 (ed.).
　　French Canadian life and character, with historical and descriptive sketches
　　of the scenery and life in Quebec, Montreal, Ottawa and surrounding
　　country: illustrated by wood engraving from original drawings by F.B.
　　Schell, L.R. O'Brien, W.T. Smedley, T. Moran, G. Gibson [et al.] Chicago:
　　Belford, 1899.
　　249 p. illus.   OTU
Groulx, Lionel Adolphe, 1878–1967.
　　Le français au Canada. Paris: Libraries Delagrove, 1932.
　　234 p.
　　Contents: Part 1, Quebec; Part 2, Acadie, Manitoba and Ontario.   OTU
— Nos luthes constitutionnelles. Montréal: Le Devoir, 1915–1916.
　　5 parts.
　　Contents: 1, La constitution de l'Angleterre – Le Canada politique en 1791;
　　2, La question des subsides; 3, La responsabilité ministrérielle; 4, La liberté
　　scolaire; 5, Les droits du français.
　　Chiefly pre-Confederation.   OTMCL
Hurtubise, Raoul.
　　Les Canadiens français et le nouvel-Ontario. Montreal: L'Oeuvre des tracts,
　　1939.
　　16 p.   OKQ
Jackson, John David, 1932–
　　Community and conflict [a study of French-English relations in Ontario].
　　Toronto: Holt, Rinehart & Winston of Canada [c1975]
　　viii, 181 p. illus., tables, maps.   OTU
Landry, Philippe.
　　Memoire sur la question scolaire de l'Ontario. [Quebec: 1915]
　　38 p.   OTER
— La question scolaire de l'Ontario: le desaveu. Quebec: Imp. Dussault &
　　Proulx, 1916.
　　34 p.   OTER
Langlois, Georges.
　　Histoire de la population canadienne-française. Montreal: Albert Lévesque,
　　1934.
　　309 p. tables. (Documents historique).   OTU
Laplante, M   Marc, 1934–
　　Le developement de la culture française à Sudbury, Ontario. n.p.: 1968.
　　87 feuilles. tabl.   OOU
Lemieux, Germain, 1914–
　　Les vieux m'ont conté: contes franco-ontariens, recueillis et annotés.
　　Montreal: Les Editions Bellarmin, 1973–1974.
　　8 v. (Centre franco-ontarien de folklore, Université d'Sudbury).   OTU

Longpré,Alfred.
    L'Eveil de la race, un épisode de la résistance franco-ontarienne (Pembroke,
    1923–27). Preface de Victor Barrette. n.p.: Les Editions de Droit [1930]
    63 p. plates, ports.   OTU
Maheu, Robert.
    Les francophones du Canada 1941–1991. Montreal: Parti pris, 1970.
    119 p. tabl.   OONL
Marion, Marie Albert.
    Le probleme scolaire étudie dans ses principes. Ed. revue et di minuée.
    Ottawa: Ottawa Printing Co., 1920.
    325 p.   OTU
Moore, William Henry, 1872–1960.
    The clash: a study in nationalities. Toronto: J.M. Dent & Sons, Limited,
    1918.
    xxiii, 333 p. tables.
    Chiefly Quebec and Ontario.   OTU
Morley, Percival Fellman, 1884–1936.
    Bridging the chasm: a study of the Ontario – Quebec question. Toronto:
    J.M. Dent and Sons, 1919.
    [xi] 182 p.   OTV
Mougeon, Raymond.
    L'acquisition et la maitrise de l'anglais parle par les jeunes bilingues de
    Welland, par Raymond Mougeon et Pierre Hébrard. Toronto: Ontario
    Institute for Studies in Education, 1975.
    v, 150 p. tables.   OTER
Nevers, Edmond de, 1862–1906.
    L'avenir du peuple canadien-français, Montreal: Fides [1964]
    332 p. port.   OTU
O'Hagan, Thomas, 1855–1939.
    The French language in Ontario. An address delivered March 6th, 1914,
    under the auspices of St. John the Baptist Society, at the Monument
    National, Montreal. Windsor, Ontario: The Record Printing Co. Limited,
    1914.
    8 p.   OOA
Ontario. Comité franco-ontarien d'enquête culturelle.
    Rapport. Ottawa: 1969.
    253 p. diagrs., cartes, tabl.
    Chairman: Roger Saint-Denis.   OTU
— Survey of the cultural life of franco-ontariens, abridged version. Ottawa:
    1969.
    74 p.   OTU
    La vie culturelle des franco-ontariens. Rapport. Ottawa: 1969.
    259 p. diagrs., carte, tabl.   OOU
Ottawa. Universite. Centre de recherche en civilization canadienne-française.
    Francophonie: L'Ontario et l'ouest canadien. Bibliographie sommaire.
    Ottawa: 1976.
    8 leaves.   OOU

— Inventaire des documents de l'Association canadienne-française d'Ontario, by Bibliotheque Morisset et Centre de recherche en civilization canadienne-française, Universite d'Ottawa. Ottawa: 1976.
iv, 204 p. (Documents de travail du CRCCF, no. 4).   OOU
— Repertoire des chercheurs sur la vie française en Ontario. 2d ed. Ottawa: Centre de recherche en civilization canadienne-française, Université d'Ottawa, 1976.
1 v. (unpaged).   OOU
Plante, Albert, 1908–
Vingt-cinq ans de vie française: Le collège de Sudbury. Montreal: Imprimerie du Messenger, 1938.
150 p.   OTREC
Prince, Vincent.
Statut particulier et minorité francophones en dehors du Québec. Dans *Le Québec dans le Canada de demain*. Montréal: Editions du jour [1967] v.2: 159–167.
Monographic publication of a Supplement of Le Devoir, June 30, 1967.
    OOSS.
Robert, E   André.
French-Canadian youth outside the province of Quebec, a report submitted to the Committee on Youth. Edited by Frank Vallee. n.p.: 1970.
143 leaves. (Canada. Committee on Youth. Report [no. 12]).   OTER
Roy, Ferdinand, 1873–
L'Appel aux armes et la réponse canadienne-française: étude sur le conflit des races. 3e ed. Quebec: Garneau, 1917.
44 p.   OTURS
Rumilly, Robert, 1897–
Le probleme national des Canadiens français. Montreal: Fides [c1961]
146 p.   OTU
Saint-Pierre, Telesphore, 1869–
Historire des canadiens du Michigan et du comté d'Essex, Ontario. Montreal: Gazette, 1895.
348 p.   OTU
Sanouillet, Michel-Eugène, 1924–
Separatism and the franco-ontariens. Adapted from the French of Maurice Tremblay. Reprinted from Les Nouvelles françaises. [Toronto] Librairie Française [c1962]
28 p.
Text in English and French.   OTU
— Le separatisme quebécoes et nous. Toronto: Editions de Nouvelles Françaises [1962]
28 p.   OTU
Savard, Pierre.
Arts with a difference: a report on French-speaking Ontario. Presented to the Ontario Arts Council by Pierre Savard, Rhéal Beauchamp, Paul Thompson. [Ottawa] 1977.
xiii, 206 p. maps, tables.   OOU

Simard, Georges, 1878–1956.
    Études canadiennes, éducation, politique, choses d'église. Montréal, Quebec:
    Editions Beauchemin [etc., etc.] 1938.
    2 leaves, 218 p. 3 leaves. (Les publications seriées de l'Université d'Ottawa,
    iv).   OTSTM
Skelton, Oscar Douglas, 1878–1941.
    The language issue in Canada. Kingston, Ontario: Jackson Press, 1917.
    40 p. (Queen's University. Department of History and Political and
    Economic science. Bulletin, no. 23).
    Ontario: pp. 11–15, 28–29.   OTV
Stanfield, David.
    How to live French in Toronto. [Toronto] Ontario Educational
    Communications Authority, c1975.
    32 p. illus., maps.   OTER
Tesiorowski, Jan, 1914–
    Canadiens français, puissance du nombré; étude statistque sur le
    bi-linguisme. Montréal: Librairie Beauchemins [1966]
    50 p. tables.   OTU
Tremblay, Jules, 1879–1927.
    La français en Ontario. Montreal: Arthur Nault, 1913.
    34 p.
    Descours prononcé au ralliement des franco-canadiens du nouvel Ontario, à
    Sturgeon Falls, le mardi 24 juin 1913.   OKQ
Tremblay, Laurent, 1905–
    Entre deux livraisons, 1913–1963. Ottawa: Editions Le Droit, 1963.
    216 p. illus.   OTU
Trofimenkoff, Susan Mann, 1941–
    Action francaise; French Canadian nationalism in the twenties. Toronto:
    University of Toronto Press [c1975]
    x, 157 p.   OTU
Wade, Mason, 1913–
    La dualité canadienne: essais sur les relations entre Canadiens français et
    Canadiens anglais. Ouverage réalisé par Mason Wade en collaboration avec
    un Comité du Conseil de recherche en sciences sociales du Canada soux la
    direction de Jean C. Falardeau. Toronto: Presses Universitaires Laval,
    University of Toronto Press [c1960]
    xxv, 427 p. diagrs., tables.   OTU
— Regionalism in the Canadian community, 1867–1967. Canadian Historical
    Association centennial seminars. [Toronto] University of Toronto Press
    [c1969]
    x, 300 p.
    Contents: Chapter 1, Regionalism and confederation by Paul W. Fox;
    Chapter 6, The viability of French groupings outside Quebec, by Frank G.
    Vallee and Norman Shulman.   OTU

Periodical Articles

Alie, Laurent.
L'Ultramontanisme au xixe siecle: une ideologie qui se manifeste encore dans le milieu francophone nord-Ontarien. Laurentian University Review 5(no. 4): 105–120, 1973.

Archambault, Jean.
Mqr. Stéphane Côté, P.D., V.G., (1876–1952). Société Historique de Nouvel-Ontario. Documents Historiques 30: 6–48, 1955.

Arès, Richard.
Comportement linguistique des minorités françaises au Canada. Relations 24: 108–110, 1964.

— Francophones et anglophones au Canada: le recensement de 1971... et l'évolution des 40 derniéres années. Relations 32: 170–172, 1972.

— La grande pitié de nos minorités française. Relations 23: 65–68, 1963.

— Positions au française au Canada: bilan général. Relations 14: 260–263, 1954.

— Positions du français en Ontario et au Québec. Relations 14: 220–224, 1954.

— Le recensement de 1961–IV. Chez les minorités: langues officielles et langues maternelles. L'Action Nationale 52: 1012–1036, 1963.

— Un siècle de vie française en dehors du Québec. Revue d'Histoire de l'Amérique française 21: 533–570, 1967.

Association canadienne-française d'éducation d'Ontario.
Situation et satisfaction économiques des franco-ontariens. Vie française 27: 240–242, 1972–73.

Beauregard, Ludger.
Le Canada française par la carte. Revue de géographie de Montréal 22: 35–44, 1968.

Belcourt, Guillaume.
Situation actuelle des canadiens-français de l'Ontario-nord. Relations 19: 205–207, 1959.

Belcourt, N   A
The French Canadians outside of Quebec. American Academy of Political and Social Science. Annals 107: 13–24, 1923.

Bouchette, Errol.
L'Ontario français économique. Revue franco-américaine 9: 389–409, 1912.

Buisson, Augustin.
Paroisses françaises principales de la peninsule de Niagara. La Société Canadienne d'Histoire de l'Eglise Catholique. Rapport 11–19, 1962.

Cadieux, Lorenzo.
Frédéric Romanet du Caillaud "Comte" de Sudbury (1847–1919). Société Historique du Nouvel-Ontario. Documents Historiques 55–57: 17–141, 1971.

Canada: IV. The French language in Ontario. The Round Table 4: 149–154, 1913.

Cantin, Narcisse M. Huron Historical Notes 8: 33–35, 1972.
Resident of French settlement (later St. Joseph), Ontario.

Charbonneau, Louis.
    Cinquante ans de vie franco-ontarienne. Relations 20: 96–97, 1960.
— L'Ontario français. Culture 8: 78 –83, 1947.
Chartier, Chanoine Emile.
    La race canadienne-française: étude ethnologique et statistique. Revue
    Trimestrielle Canadian 7 (June): 113–136, 1921.
Chauvin, F   X
    Les canadiens-français d'Essex et de Kent. Relations 6: 365–369, 1946.
Choquette, Robert.
    Linguistic and ethnic factors in the French-Irish Catholic relations in
    Ontario. Canadian Catholic Historical Association. Study Sessions, 35–43,
    1972.
Comeau, Paul-André.
    Acculturation ou assimilation: technique d'analyse et tentative de mesure
    chez les franco-ontariens. Canadian Journal of Political Science 2: 158–172,
    1969.
Conseil de la Vie Française.
    Enquête économique du Conseil de la Vie Française [... sur les possibilités
    d'echanges économiques entre les groupes françaises au Canada]. Vie
    française 18: 205–238, 1963–64.
Courteau, Guy.
    Le docteur J.-Raoul Hurtubise M.D., M.P. (1882–1955). 40 ans de vie
    française à Sudbury. Société Historique du Nouvel-Ontario. Documents
    Historiques 58–60: 13–134, 1971.
— Le docteur Joseph-Raoul Hurtubise, M.D., Senateur. La Société
    Canadienne d'Histoire de l'Eglise Catholique. Rapport 53–70, 1960.
Courteau, Guy and Lorenzo Cadieux.
    Letters, allocutions de Son Excellence Monseignieur Alexsandre Carter.
    Société Historique du Nouvel-Ontario. Documents Historiques 42–43: 7–94,
    1962.
Delaby; Jean.
    La race française au Canada d'après le recensement de 1931. France-
    Amerique 155–158, 1934.
Dorais, Fernand (ed.).
    Numero spécial sur le fait français du nord de l'Ontario . Laurentian
    University Review 3(no. 4): 4–106, 1971.
Dugré, Alexandre.
    Notre histoire en cinq actes. Société Historique du Nouvel-Ontario.
    Documents Historiques 21: 3–35, 1951.
Enquête sur l'Ontario français. Vie française 22: 76–81, 1967–68.
Les États généraux du Canada français: Assises nationales. L'Action Nationale
    58: 3–646, 1969.
Folklore franco-ontarien, chansons. Société Historique du Nouvel-Ontario.
    Documents Historiques 17: 3–48, 1949.

Fortier, René.
Co-operative associations among French-speaking groups in Ontario.
Economic Annalist 18: 56–60, 1948.
Frémont, Donatien.
Les établissements français à l'ouest du Lac Supérieur; esquisse de
géographie humaine. Mémoires de la Société royale du Canada, s.3.
48(sect.1): 7–12, 1954.
Gauthier, Alphonse.
Héros dans l'ombre, mais héros quand même: Joseph Jennesseaux, s.j., Jean
Véroneau, s.j., Georges Lehoux, s.j. Société Historique du Nouvel-Ontario.
Documents Historiques 32: 4–44, 1956.
Jackson, John D.
A study of French-English relations in an Ontario community; towards a
conflict model for the analysis of ethnic relations. Canadian Review of
Sociology and Anthropology 3: 117–131, 1966.
Joubert, Leonidas.
Des groupements français au Canada. Etudes Economiques. Publications de
l'Ecole des Hautes Etudes Commerciales de Montréal 5: 75-118, 1935.
Ontario: pp. 95–104.
Les jumelles Dionne. Société Historique du Nouvel-Ontario. Documents
Historiques 19: 37–48, 1950.
Labelle, Jules.
La jeunesse et la vie franco-ontarienne. La vie franco-ontarienne 1(no. 6): 2,
1966.
Lacasse, Gustave.
Soixante-et-quinze ans de vie Catholique et francaise en Ontario. Canadian
Catholic Historical Association. Report 19–28, 1940–1941.
Lamontagne, Léopold.
Kingston's French heritage. Historic Kingston 2: 27–39, 1953.
Lemieux, Germain.
Chansonnier franco-ontarien. Société Historique du Nouvel-Ontario.
Documents Historiques 64: 1–135, 1974; 66: 1–138, 1975.
— Chanteurs franco-ontariens et leurs chansons. Société Historique de Nouvel-
Ontario. Documents Historiques 44–45: 7–112, 1963–1964.
— Contes populaires franco-ontariens. Société Historique du Nouvel-Ontario.
Documents Historiques 25: 3–39, 1953; 35: 7–59, 1958.
— Folklore franco-ontarien chansons. La Société Historique du Nouvel-
Ontario. Documents Historique 17: [1]–48, 1949; 20: [1]–47, 1950.
— Index analytique des 35 documents de la Société Historique du Nouvel-
Ontario. La Société Historique du Nouvel-Ontario. Documents Historiques
36: 2–47, 1959.
— Les jongleurs de billochet conteurs et contes franco-ontariens. Société
Historique du Nouvel-Ontario. Documents Historiques 61–63: 17–131,
1972.

Maistre, Gilbert.
    Canadiens-français vivant hors du Quebec et moyens d'information en
    langue française. Vie française 25: 57–83, 1970–71.
Maizen, Arnold.
    Le développement des service de langue français par la bibliothèque
    régionale Algonquin. Ontario Library Review 58: 76–79, 1974.
Majerus, Yvette.
    Le journal du Père Dominique du Ranquet, S.J. Société Historique du
    Nouvel-Ontario. Documents Historiques 49–50: 7–56, 1967.
Marion, Séraphin.
    Le pacte fédératif et les Catholiques de l'Ontario. Les Cahiers des Dix 30:
    69–101, 1965.
— Le pacte fédératif et les minorités française au Canada. Les Cahiers des Dix
    29: 89–113, 1964.
— Vie française 20: 200 –228, 1965 –66.
Maxwell, Thomas R
    La population d'origine française de l'agglomération métropolitaine de
    Toronto. Recherches sociographiques 12: 319–344, 1971.
Perrault, Marcel G
    Enquête royale sur l'education. Culture 7: 342–352, 1946.
Prince, Vincent.
    Progrès du bilinguisme en 1968 au Canada. Vie française 23: 159–167,
    1968–69.
Racette, Oscar.
    M. Jean-Baptiste Dubuc. Société Historique du Nouvel-Ontario. Documents
    Historiques 1: 26–28, 1942.
Regimbal, Albert.
    Le française en Ontario-sud. Relations 5: 258–260, 1945.
Ryan, C
    French minorities in Canada. Canadian Forum 43 (March): 1964.
Skelton, O   D
    The language issue in Canada. Queen's Quarterly 24: 438–468, 1916–1917.
    Ontario: pp. 446–452.
Soeurs grises de la Croix, fédération des femmes canadiennes-françaises
    Orphelinat d'Youville. Société Historique du Nouvel-Ontario. Documents
    Historique 9: 3–41, 1945.
Spicer, Keith.
    La tradition et l'avenir français de l'Ontario. Vie Française 22: 61–66, 1967.
Tremblay, Jean-Jacques.
    L'Ontario français. Vie française 11: 234–237, 1957.
— Problèmes franco-ontariens. Relations 13: 332–334, 1953.
Welch, David.
    Les communications francophones du sud de l'Ontario. Quebec-Amerique
    Avril: 1–14, 1969.

Wilkins, D   F   H
    The French in eastern Ontario. Canada Educational Monthly 9: 213–219,
    1887.
Yon, Armand.
    L'Ottawa vue par les français: depuis le xvii e siècle jusqu' à nos jours.
    Revue de l'Université d'Ottawa 8: 381–408, 1938.

Theses
Beattie, Christopher Fraser.
    Minority men in a majority setting: middle-level francophones at mid-career
    in the anglophone public service of Canada. Berkeley, California: 1970.
    425 leaves.
    Ph.D. thesis, University of California at Berkeley (microfilm 71-20771).   DA
— Minority men in a majority setting: middle level francophones in the
    Canadian public service. Toronto: McClelland and Stewart, c1975.
    xi, 224 p. illus. (The Carleton Library, no. 92).
    Based on his doctoral thesis.   OTU
Benoit, Frère.
    Au siècle d'enseignement français en Ontario. Montreal: 1945.
    193 p.
    M.A. thesis, Université de Montreal.   OOU
Cartwright, Donald Gordon, [sic] 1934–
    French Canadian colonization in eastern Ontario to 1910: a study of process
    and pattern. London, Ontario: 1973.
    xiv, 333 leaves. maps (part fold.).
    Ph.D. thesis, The University of Western Ontario (microfilm 16400).   OTU
Cuthbert Brandt, Gail.
    J'y suis, j'y reste: the French Canadians of Sudbury, 1883–1913. Toronto:
    1976.
    xiv, 287 [i.e. 289] leaves. illus., maps.
    Ph.D. thesis, York University (microfilm 30887).   Can
Hopkinson, Marvin Walter, 1944–
    The London region and the French-Canadian question 1864–1890. London,
    Ontario: 1969.
    vi, 316 leaves. maps (part. col.).
    M.A. thesis, The University of Western Ontario (microfilm 5037).   OLU
Jackson, John David, 1932–
    Toward a theory of social conflict: a study of French-English relations in an
    Ontario community. Lansing, Michigan: 1967 [c1968]
    [4] ii–xiii, 493 leaves. maps.
    Ph.D. thesis, Michigan State University (microfilm 68-7906).   DA
Jocas, Yves de.
    Analyse écologique de la ville d'Ottawa. Quebec: 1955.
    135 leaves. illus., cartes, graph.
    M.Sc. thesis, Université Laval.   QQLA

Lapalme, Victor, 1943–
   Les franco-ontariens et la politique provinciale. Ottawa: 1968.
   v, 131 feuilles. illus., carte, graphs.
   M.A. thesis, Université d'Ottawa.   OOU
McDonald, Robert Burns.
   French Canadian settlement in eastern Ontario; the case of Russell
   township. Ottawa: 1967.
   vi, 53 leaves, maps, tables.
   B.A. research essay, Carleton University.   OOCC
Martineau, Gloriana J
   La survivance française dans les comtes de Prescott et Russell. [Montreal,
   Quebec] 1947.
   viii, 144 leaves.
   M.A. thesis, McGill University.   QMM
Maxwell, Thomas Robert, 1911–
   The French population of Metropolitan Toronto: a study of ethnic
   participation and ethnic identity. [Toronto] c1971.
   ix, 263, 19 leaves.
   Ph.D. thesis, University of Toronto (microfilm 11607).   OTU
— The invisible French: the French in Metropolitan Toronto. [Waterloo,
   Ontario: Wilfrid Laurier University Press, c1977]
   xv, 174 p. graphs, map, tables.
   Originally presented as the author's thesis (Ph.D.), University of Toronto,
   1971.   OONL
Mercer, Warwick McMillan, 1944–
   The Windsor French: study of an urban community. Windsor, Ontario:
   1974.
   viii, 157 leaves. illus., diagrs., maps, tables.
   M.A. thesis, University of Windsor.   OWA
Morin, Fernand.
   L'exercice du droit de vote et la protection des actionnaires minoritaires dans
   les compagnies ontariennes et québecoises. Toronto [1960]
   97 leaves.
   Ll.M. thesis, University of Toronto.   OTUL
Ossenberg, Richard J   1934–
   Idealogy in a plural society: Canadian dualism and the issue of immigration.
   Buffalo: 1966.
   iv, 166 leaves.
   Ph.D. thesis, State University of New York at Buffalo (microfilm).   OTER
Szmidt, Yvette, 1944–
   L'interogation totale dans le parler franco-canadien de Lafontaine, Ontario
   ses formes et ses modalités intonatives. [Toronto] c1976.
   iv, 274 leaves. tables, figs., map.
   Ph.D. thesis, University of Toronto.   OTU

Wilkins, James Robert.
   The analysis of residence patterns as an indication of the degree of
   assimilation of ethnic groups, case study: the French Canadians of Sarnia.
   Waterloo, Ontario: 1967.
   vi, 53 leaves. maps (part fold.), tables.
   B.A. thesis, Waterloo University College.   OWTL
Wrenn, Phyllis Margaret, 1941–
   Declarative melodic structures in Canadian French as spoken at Lafontaine,
   Ontario. [Toronto] c1974.
   326 leaves. tables, figs.
   Ph.D. thesis, University of Toronto (microfiche).   OTU

EDUCATION: GENERAL

Bibliography
Alexander, William E   (comp.).
   Educational planning at the provincial level: a partially annotated
   bibliography of the OISE Department of Educational Planning's writings and
   research activities relevant to planning at the provincial level, compiled by
   William E. Alexander and Judy LeGros. Toronto: Ontario Institute for
   Studies in Education, 1971.
   v, 10 leaves.   OTER
Auster, Ethel.
   Meeting Ontario's need for education information: an evaluation of the
   SDC/ERIC on-line bibliographic search service. Prepared for the Office of the
   Coordinator of Field Development, Department of Educational
   Administration and the Library, Ontario Institute for Studies in Education
   by Ethel Auster and Stephen B. Lawton. [Toronto] Ontario Institute for
   Studies in Education, 1973.
   92 leaves. diagrs.   OTER
Cockburn, Ilze (comp.).
   Open education: an annotated bibliography. [Toronto] Office of the
   Coordinator of Field Development [Ontario Institute for Studies in
   Education] 1973.
   [14] p.   OTER
— [Toronto] Library. Reference and Information Services, Ontario Institute
   for Studies in Education, 1973.
   viii, 34 p.   OTER
Corman, Linda (comp.).
   Community education in Canada: an annotated bibliography. [Toronto]
   Ontario Institute for Studies in Education [c1975]
   xi, 55 p.. (Ontario Institute for Studies in Education. Bibliography no. 2).
                                                                                OTER

Draper, James A   (comp.).
  Canadian theses in adult education: a look at the '70's. Compiled by James
  A. Draper and Jeffrey Field. [Toronto: Department of Adult Education,
  Ontario Institute for Studies in Education, 1974?]
  [15] leaves.   OTER
— University of Toronto theses research relating to adult education: an
  interdisciplinary analysis, 1900–1970, by James A. Draper, assisted by Ross
  Kidd and Dale Shuttleworth. [Toronto] Department of Adult Education,
  Ontario Institute for Studies in Education [1974]
  76 p.   OTER
Gillespie, Jack.
  A guide to educational records in the possession of county boards of
  education, eastern Ontario. [Toronto] Department of History and
  Philosophy, Ontario Institute for Studies in Education [c1972]
  ii, 331 p. map. (Ontario Institute for Studies in Education. Department of
  History and Philosophy Educational records series, no. 10).   OTER
Hill, T   L   (comp.).
  Adult education: bibliography. Thunder Bay, Ontario: Northwestern
  Centre, Ontario Institute for Studies in Education [1972]
  56 p.   OTER
Hoy, Eileen M   (comp.).
  Select bibliography of recent material on teaching machines and
  programmed learning. [Toronto: Ontario Educational Research Council,
  1963]
  18 leaves.   OTU
The interaction of law and education; working notes towards a selected
  bibliography. [Toronto] Department of Adult Education, Ontario Institute
  for Studies in Education, 1974.
  30 leaves. (Interaction of law and education, no. [1]).   OTER
McRobbie, K   A
  A survey and listing of educational research studies completed or in progress
  in Ontario during the period July 1st, 1958 to June 30th, 1959. Ontario
  Journal of Educational Research 3: 39–83, 1960–61.
Metropolitan Toronto. School Board. Study of Educational Facilities.
  SEF annotated bibliography of research on open plan schools. [Toronto]
  1974.
  90 p.   OTC
Ontario Institute for Studies in Education. Library. Reference and Information
  Services.
  Non-grading: an annotated bibliography. [Toronto: 1970]
  viii, 32 p. (*Its* Current bibliography, no. 1 rev.).   OTER
— Open plan: an annotated bibliography. [Toronto] 1970.
  viii, 22 p. (*Its* Current bibliography, no. 2).   OTER
Ontario Teachers' Federation. Curriculum Committee.
  Catalogue of school board publications. Toronto: Ontario Teachers'
  Federation [1976]
  40 p.   OTER
  Chairman: Paul Kennedy.   OTER

Reynolds, David Roy, 1912–
 A guide to educational materials in municipal records, records of committees
 and commissions and other miscellaneous papers in the Ontario Archives.
 [Toronto] Department of History and Philosophy, Ontario Institute for
 Studies in Education [c1976]
 123 p. (Educational records series 8).   OTER
— A guide to items relating to education in newspapers in the Ontario
 Archives. [Toronto] Department of History and Philosophy, Ontario
 Institute for Studies in Education [1971]
 90 p. (Archive series 3).   OTER
— A guide to items relating to education in papers of the Prime Minister's
 Department (Record group 3) in the Ontario Archives. [Toronto]
 Department of History and Philosophy, Ontario Institute for Studies in
 Education [c1974]
 v, 121 p. (Educational records series 6).   OTER
— A guide to pamphlets in the Ontario Archives relating to educational
 history, 1803–1967. Toronto: Department of History and Philosophy,
 Ontario Institute for Studies in Education, 1971.
 iv, 104 p. (Archive series 1).   OTER
— A guide to periodicals and books relating to education in the Ontario
 Archives. [Toronto] Department of History and Philosophy, Ontario
 Institute for Studies in Education [c1976]
 iii, 149 p. (Educational records series 7).   OTER
— A guide to published government documents relating to education in
 Ontario [c1792–1948. Toronto] Department of History and Philosophy,
 Ontario Institute for Studies in Education [1972]
 i, 47 p. (Archive series 2).   OTER
— A guide to sources in educational history from the Private Manuscripts
 Section of the Archives of Ontario. [Toronto] Department of History and
 Philosophy, Ontario Institute for Studies in Education [c1973]
 ii, 197 p. (Educational records series no. 5).   OTER
Rideout, Brock.
 City school district reorganization: an annotated bibliography:
 centralization and decentralization in the government of metropolitan areas
 with special emphasis on the organization, administration and financing of
 large-city school systems by E. Brock Rideout and Sandra Najat. [Toronto]
 Ontario Institute for Studies in Education [1967]
 v, 93 p. (Ontario Institute for Studies in Education. Educational research
 series, no. 1).   OTU
Savage, H   W
 Second survey and listing of educational research completed or in progress in
 Ontario: July 1st, 1959 to June 30th, 1960. Ontario Journal of Educational
 Research 4: 1–30, 1961–62.
Smith, Albert H   (comp.).
 A bibliography of Canadian education. Toronto: Department of
 Educational Research, University of Toronto [c1938]
 302 p. (Department of Educational Research. Bulletin no. 10).
 Ontario: pp. 172–231.   OTER

Toronto. University. Ontario College of Education. Department of Educational
Research.
Theses in education, Ontario College of Education, University of Toronto,
since 1898 (including theses in pedagogy from Queen's University,
1911–1925). Toronto: Department of Educational Research, Ontario
College of Education, University of Toronto, 1949.
ii, 31 leaves. (Educational research series, no. 20).   OTER
Tracz, George Stephen, 1938–
Research into academic staff manpower and salary issues: a selective
bibliography. Toronto: Department of Educational Planning, Ontario
Institute for Studies in Education, 1974.
ii, 35 leaves.   OTER
Zimmerman, A   J
Ontario Educational Research Council Fourth survey and listing of
educational research completed or in progress in Ontario July 1st, 1963, to
June 30th, 1965. Ontario Journal of Educational Research 8: 287–323,
1965/66.
— A survey of educational research in Metropolitan Toronto: studies
conducted by Metropolitan Area Boards, completed or in progress in the
period September 1, 1961 to June 30, 1963. [Toronto: Metropolitan Toronto
Educational Research Council, 1963]
iii, 39 leaves. table.   OTU
— Third survey and listing of educational research completed or in progress in
Ontario: July 1st, 1960 to June 30th, 1963. Ontario Journal of Educational
Research 7: 61–98, 1964–65.

Monographs and Pamphlets
Accidents will happen: an inquiry into the legal liability of teachers and school
boards. [Toronto] Department of Adult Education, Ontario Institute for
Studies in Education, 1976.
49 p. (Interaction of law and education, no 1)   OTER
Alexander, Robert.
Some recollections of the early history of the Ontario Educational
Association. Toronto: Morang & Co., Limited, 1904.
31 p. ports., illus.   OTU
Althouse, John George, 1889–1956.
Addresses: a selection covering the years 1936–1956. Toronto: W.J. Gage,
1958.
243 p.   OTU
— The structure and aims of Canadian education. Toronto: W.J. Gage [1950]
77 p. (The Quance lectures in Canadian education, 1).   OTU
Anderson, James Thomas Milton, 1878–1946.
The education of the new Canadian: a treatise on Canada's greatest
educational problem. London: J.M. Dent & Sons Ltd., 1918.
271 p. front., plates, ports.   OOA

Anglican Church of Canada. Provinces. Ontario.

Memorandum presented by the Anglican bishops of Ontario to the Prime Minister of Ontario and members of the provincial Legislature. [Toronto: 1962]

7 leaves.

On education (religious). OONL

Anglin, R W

The roll of honour of the Ontario teachers who served in the Great War 1914–1918. Issued by authority of the Minister of Education. [Toronto: The Ryerson Press, 1922]

72 p. OTER

Ault, Orvill E

The training of special teachers or the relation of certain problems to the training of teachers in the United States, Ontario, France, Scotland and Germany. Ottawa: 1936.

196 p. OTER

Baird, Norman B

Educational finance and administration for Ontario. Toronto: Department of Educational Research, Ontario College of Education, University of Toronto, 1952.

v, 33 p. (Department of Educational Research. Bulletin no. 14). OTER

Bancroft, George Winston.

A survey of criticisms, comments and suggestions concerning adult education in London, Ontario, 1966. [London, Ontario] London Council for Adult Education [1966]

57 leaves. OONL

Bannister, John Arthur.

Early educational history of Norfolk county. Toronto: University Press, 1926.

194 p. illus., maps, plans.

Chiefly pre-Confederation. OTU

Bell, John Charles.

Responsibilities of provincial departments of education for school library service. [Vancouver] British Columbia School Librarians' Association, 1973.

6 p. (British Columbia School Librarians Association. Occasional paper, no. 6). OONL

Benzon, Ralph.

Educational finance in Ontario: a report prepared for the Ontario Teachers' Federation, Educational Finance Committee. [Toronto: Ontario Teachers' Federation] 1971.

19 leaves. tables. OTC

Brown, Arthur Edwin.

The Toronto early identification and development program, by A.E. Brown, G.D. Landrus and E.R. Long. Toronto: Board of Education, 1974.

217 p. graphs, tables. OTER

Burgoyne, Lola Martin (comp.).
    A history of the home and school movement in Ontario. [Toronto] Charters
    Publishing Co. Ltd. [1935]
    vii, 205 p. illus., ports.   OTC
Byrne, Niall (ed.).
    Must schools fail? The growing debate in Canadian education. Edited by
    Niall Byrne and Jack Quarter. [Toronto] McClelland and Stewart Limited
    [c1972]
    xi, 301 p. chart.   OTU
Cameron, Maxwell A   1907–1951.
    The administration of education in Ontario. Rev. ed. Toronto: Ontario
    College of Education, 1941.
    48 leaves. tables. (Department of Educational Research, Ontario College of
    Education, University of Toronto. Educational series, no. 1).   OTC
— The administration of education in Ontario, by Maxwell A. Cameron and
    A.C. Lewis. Rev. ed. [Toronto] Department of Educational Research,
    Ontario College of Education, University of Toronto, 1945.
    48 leaves.   OTC
— 4th rev. [ed. Toronto] Department of Educational Research, Ontario
    College of Education, University of Toronto, 1939 [i.e. 1950]
    45 leaves.   OTC
— The financing of education in Ontario. Toronto: Department of Educational
    Research, University of Toronto [c1936]
    175 p. illus. (Department of Educational Research, University of Toronto.
    Bulletin no. 7).   OTER
Campbell, Ken, 1934–
    "Tempest in a teapot": the exposure of a "sex and security scandal" at the
    heart of our society. [Cambridge, Ontario: Coronation Publications, c1975]
    303 p. illus.
    Community and school in Ontario.   OONL
Campbell, Sylvia F
    Continuing education for women in Metropolitan Toronto. A study
    prepared for Atkinson College. Toronto: York University, 1965.
    28, xviii leaves.   OONL
Canada.
    Review of educational policies in Canada: Ontario report. Submission of the
    Minister of Education and the Minister of Colleges and Universities for the
    province of Ontario. [Ottawa?] 1975.
    180 p. charts, map, tables.   OTER
Canada. Bureau of Statistics.
    Educational attainment in Canada: some regional and social aspects, by
    Michel D. Lagacé. [Ottawa: Roger Duhamel, Queen's Printer] 1968.
    53 p. tables. (Canada. Bureau of Statistics. Special labour force studies, 7).
                                                                           OKQL

The Chairman of the board: an examination of his role. Edited by Edward S.
  Hickcox, assisted by William H. Stapleton [Toronto] Ontario Institute for
  Studies in Education [c1970]
  vi, 49 p. (Ontario Institute for Studies in Education. Monograph series, no.
  8).
  Chairman of a board of education.   OTU
Cheal, John E
  Investment in Canadian youth: an analysis of differences among Canadian
  provincial school systems. Toronto: Macmillan Company of Canada [c1963]
  xiii, 167 p. diagrs., tables.   OTU
Cohen, Allan.
  Adult education in Metropolitan Toronto: a situation report, by Allan
  Cohen [et al. Toronto: Research Department, Board of Education for the
  city of Toronto] 1967.
  89 leaves. diagrs., tables.   OONL
Commission on Emotional and Learning Disorders in Children. Ontario
  Committee.
  Report. A supplementary publication to *One million children.* Toronto: 1970.
  xi, 121, xii–xxii leaves.   OTER
Conference on Canadian Studies, 1st Toronto, 1969.
  Focus on Canadian studies; report of the Conference on Canadian Studies,
  sponsored by the Ontario Institute for Studies in Education, February
  20–22, 1969. Edited by Edward H. Humphreys. [Toronto: 1970]
  ix, 125 p. (Ontario Institute for Studies in Education. Monograph series, no.
  6).   OTU
Cook, Gail Carol Annabel, 1940–
  Effect of metropolitan government on resource allocation: the case of
  education in Toronto. Toronto: Institute for Quantitative Analysis of Social
  and Economic Policy, University of Toronto, 1972.
  13 leaves. tables.   OTER
Council of Ministers of Education of Canada.
  Review of educational policies in Canada [by the Council of Ministers of
  Education in co-operation with the federal government. Toronto? Council of
  Ministers of Education? 1975]
  6 v. diagrs., graphs, maps.
  Contents: [v. 1] Introduction [v. 2] Western region [v. 3] Ontario [v. 4]
  Quebec [v. 5] Atlantic region [v. 6] Government of Canada.   OONL
Crawford, Kenneth Grant, 1904–
  Provincial grants to Canadian schools, 1941 to 1961. Toronto: Canadian
  Tax Foundation [1962]
  vii, 259 p. tables. (Canadian tax papers no. 26).
  Ontario: pp. 76–147.   OLU
Crawford, Patricia J   1940–
  The effects of high-rise living on school behaviour, by Patricia Crawford and
  Albert E. Virgin. North York, Ontario: Department of Educational
  Research Services, 1971.
  i, 76 leaves. tables.   OTER

— School achievement: a preliminary look at the effects of the home, by
Patricia Crawford and Gary Eason. [Toronto: Research Department, Board
of Education] 1970.
50 leaves. tables. (Research service report).   OTER
Cudmore, Sedley Anthony, 1879–1945.
Historical statistical survey of education in Canada [by S.A. Cudmore and
M.C. Maclean] Ottawa: Thomas Mulvey, printer to the King's Most
Excellent Majesty, 1921.
120 p. graphs, tables. (Canada. Bureau of Statistics, Education Statistics
Branch).   OLU
D'Oyley, Vincent Roy.
Testing: the first two years of the Carnegie study 1959 to 1961, analysis of
scores by course, sex and size of municipality. [Toronto] Department of
Educational Research, Ontario College of Education, University of Toronto,
1964.
ix, 53 p. diagrs., tables. (Carnegie study of identification and utilization of
talent in high school and college. Bulletin no. 6).   OTER
Education and society: six studies [Toronto] Innis College, University of
Toronto, 1970.
iv, 168 p. diagr., tables.   OTER
Educational problems and how they have been met: an intelligent and
statesmanlike conception. [Toronto: W.S. Johnston & Co'y. Limited, 1919?]
27 p. tables.   OTU
Ellis, Maxyne Evelyn Dormer, 1925–
The M.T.E.R.C.: an account of its activities and accomplishments. [Toronto:
Metropolitan Toronto Educational Research Council] 1967.
23 [6] leaves. (Research publication no. 7).   OTER
— Seven thousand men (who are members of the OPSMTF) Toronto: [Ontario
Public School Men Teachers' Association, 1971]
ii, 67 leaves. tables.   OTER
— A study of age-grade statistics in Metropolitan Toronto, by M.E. Dormer
Ellis and A.J. Zimmerman. [Toronto: Metropolitan Toronto Educational
Research Council 1968]
i, 19 [67] leaves. tables. (Research publication no. 9).   OTER
Elwood, Bryan C
Project SAMPS: Student Accommodation Management and Planning
System; development and application in Waterloo county. A summary
report to the Waterloo County Board of Education, prepared by the
Department of Educational Planning, The Ontario Institute for Studies in
Education. Project directors: Bryan C. Elwood and Ted G. Vangel.
[Toronto] The Ontario Institute for Studies in Education, 1972.
1 v. (various pagings). charts, tables.   OTER
— Student transportation: comparing alternative methods of providing the
service. [Toronto] Ontario Institute for Studies in Education [c1970]
vii, 24 p. illus., maps. (Ontario Institute for Studies in Education.

Department of Educational Planning. County School Board Project.
Reports, no. 2). OTU
Environics Research Group.
Quality of education in Ontario; a survey of the parents perspectives.
Principal investigators: Michael J. Adams, Frederic L. Buckland [and]
Lynda J. Tribbling. [Toronto: Conducted for the] Department of Education,
1972.
178 leaves. OTER
Farewell, John Edwin Chandler, 1840–1923.
A paper on technical education. Whitby, Ontario: [1899?]
8 p.
"Read before the Ontario Educational Association at the Easter meeting,
1899." OTAR
Fraser, Charles G
The teachers' trip to northern Ontario: the story of a happy week. n.p.:
1920.
16 p. illus. OTU
French, Doris Cavell Martin, 1918–
High button bootstraps: Federation of Women Teachers Associations of
Ontario: 1918–1968. Toronto: The Ryerson Press [c1968]
205 p. illus. OTU
Frye, Northrop, 1912–   (ed.).
Design for learning: reports submitted to the Joint Committee of the
Toronto Board of Education and the University of Toronto. Edited, with an
introduction by Northrop Frye. [Toronto] University of Toronto Press
[c1962]
x, 148 p. OTU
Ganley, Rosemary (ed.).
Technology and change: the crisis in Canadian education, edited by R.
Ganley and R. Wood. [Toronto] McClelland and Stewart [c1975]
63 p. illus. (Foundations of Contemporary Canada series no. 4). OTER
Giles, Thomas Edward, 1931–
Educational administration in Canada. Calgary, Alberta: Detselig
Enterprise [c1974]
240 p. diagrs. OTER
Green, Gavin Hamilton, 1862–
The old log school and Huron old boys in pioneer days. Goderich, Ontario:
Signal Star Press, 1939.
217 p. illus., ports. OTU
Guillet, Edwin Clarence, 1898–1975.
In the cause of education; centennial history of the Ontario Educational
Association 1861–1960. Toronto: University of Toronto Press, 1960.
xxiv, 472 p. illus., ports., facsims. OTU
Halpern, Gerald.
The Ottawa drug survey – univariate results, by G. Halpern and G. Mori.
Ottawa: Research Office, Ottawa Board of Education, 1970.
87 p. tables. OTU

Handa, Madan Lai, 1931–
    Manipulating educational expenditure: dilemmas for the '70's. [Toronto]
    The Ontario Institute for Studies in Education [c1972]
    25 p. (Ontario Institute for Studies in Education. Monograph series, no. 13).
                                                                         OTER
— Towards a rational educational policy: an econometric analysis of Ontario
    (Canada) 1950–1965 with tests 1966–68 and projections 1969–75. Toronto:
    Ontario Institute for Studies in Education [c1972]
    xiii, 272 p. graphs, tables. (Ontario Institute for Studies in Education.
    Occasional papers, 10).   OTER
Harris, Robin Sutton, 1919–
    Quiet evolution; a study of the educational system of Ontario. [Toronto]
    University of Toronto Press [c1967]
    xiv, 168 p. charts, maps.   OTU
Harvey, Edward B
    An evaluation of student guidance information service: final report, by E.B.
    Harvey, V.L. Masemann and Arminée Kazanjian. [Toronto] Department of
    Sociology in Education, Ontario Institute for Studies in Education [1974?]
    xiii, 228 leaves. tables.   OTER
— Occupational graduates and the labour force, by Edward B. Harvey and
    Vandra L. Masemann. [Toronto] Department of Sociology, Ontario
    Institute for Studies in Education, 1973.
    2 v. [viii, 568 leaves] tables.   OTER
— [Toronto: Ontario Institute for Studies in Education, c1975]
    vii, 204 p. tables.   OTER
Hennessy, Peter H
    Teacher militancy: a comparative study of Ontario, Quebec and New York
    teachers, 1975. Ottawa: Canadian Teachers' Federation, 1975.
    80 p. tables.   OONL
Herbert, John David (ed.).
    Psychology in teacher preparation. Edited by John Herbert and David P.
    Ausubel. [Toronto] Ontario Institute for Studies in Education [c1969]
    vii, 128 p. tables. (Ontario Institute for Studies in Education. Monograph
    series, no. 5).   OTU
Heyman, Richard D
    Studies in educational change, by Richard D. Heyman, Robert F. Lawson
    and Robert M. Stamp. Toronto: Holt, Rinehart and Winston of Canada
    [1972]
    ix, 259 p. illus.   OOU
Historique de l'Association des enseignants franco-ontariens. [Ottawa: Le Droit,
    1964?]
    80 p. illus. table.   OOU
Hodgetts, A   B
    What culture? what heritage? a study of civil education in Canada. Toronto:
    Ontario Institute for Studies in Education [c1968]
    122 p. (Ontario Institute for Studies in Education. Curriculum series, 5).
                                                                         OTU

Hodgins, John George, 1821–1912.
   Documentary history of education in Upper Canada from the passing of the
   Constitutional Act of 1791, to the close of Rev. Dr. Ryerson's administration
   of the Education Department in 1876. Edited under the direction of the
   Honourable the Minister of Education with explanatory notes by J. George
   Hodgins. Toronto: Warwick Bros. & Rutter, 1894–1910.
   28 v.
   Contents: v. 1(1790–1830), 1894; v. 2(1831–1836), 1894; v. 3(1836–1846),
   1895; v. 4(1841–1843), 1897; v. 5(1843–1846), 1897; v. 6(1846), 1899; v.
   7(1847–1848), 1900; v. 8(1848–1849), 1901; v. 9(1850–1851), 1902; v.
   10(1851–1852), 1903; v. 11(1853–1855), 1904; v. 12(1855–1856), 1905; v.
   13(1856–1858), 1906; v. 14(1858–1860), 1906; v. 15–16(1860), 1906; v.
   17(1861–1863), 1907; v. 18(1863–1865), 1907; v. 19(1865–1867), 1907; v.
   20(1867–1869), 1907; v. 21(1868–1869), 1907; v. 22(1869–1871), 1908; v.
   23(1871–1872), 1908; v. 24(1872), 1908; v. 25(1871–1874), 1908; v.
   26(1874–1875), 1908; v. 27(1875–1876), 1908; v. 28(1876), 1910.   OTU
— The establishment of schools and colleges in Ontario, 1792–1910. Toronto:
   L.K. Cameron, printer to the King's Most Excellent Majesty, 1910.
   3 v. illus., ports.   OTER
— Historical and other papers and documents illustrative of the educational
   system of Ontario: 1792–1876. Printed by order of the Legislative Assembly.
   Toronto: L.K. Cameron, printer to the King's Most Excellent Majesty,
   1911–1912.
   6 v.
   Contents: v. 1, 1792–1853; v. 2, 1856–1872; v. 3 1853–1868; v. 4 1858–1876;
   v. 5 1842–1861; v. 6, 1862–1871.   OTER
Holland, John W   1929–
   Educational futures for the city of Brantford and Brant county, by John W.
   Holland, Saeed Quazi, Joya Sen. Prepared for Brantford Regional Board of
   Trade, July 1970. [Brantford: 1970]
   130 leaves. maps, tables.   OTER
Hope, John Andrew, 1890–1954.
   Where knowledge is free. Toronto: University of Toronto Press, 1954.
   [4] 11 p.
   "An address delivered at the reunion dinner of the University College
   Alumni Association, University of Toronto, May 28, 1954."   OTU
Hopkins, Robert A
   The long march; history of the Ontario Public School Men Teachers'
   Federation. Toronto: Baxter Publishing [c1969]
   392 p. port., tables.   OTU
Husby, Philip James.
   Educational effort in five resource frontier communities. Winnipeg: Centre
   for Settlement Studies, University of Manitoba, 1971.
   x, 57 p. (Manitoba. University. Centre for Settlement Studies. Series 2:
   Research reports, no. 7).
   Red Lake, Ontario is the frontier community studied in Ontario.   OTU

Jackson, Dorothy Newsom Ridgway, 1906–
    A brief history of three schools: the School of Expression, the Margaret
    Eaton School of Literature and Expression, the Margaret Eaton School,
    1901–1941. [Toronto: 1953]
    35 p. illus., ports.   OTU
James, George M
    Standing before kings. Belleville, Ontario: The James Texts [c1924]
    258 p.
    Education.   OTAR
Johnson, Francis Henry, 1908–
    A brief history of Canadian Education. Toronto: McGraw–Hill Company of
    Canada, Limited [c1968]
    viii, 216 p.   OTER
Jones, (Murray V.) and Associates.
    School enrolment forecast, 1966–1976; a report prepared for the Board of
    Education, township of Etobicoke. Toronto: 1966.
    51 leaves. illus., maps, graphs, tables.   OONL
Kapos, Andrew.
    Toronto speaks: a survey of the educational adjustment and leisure time
    activities of adult residents in the west and central areas of the city of
    Toronto. [Toronto: University of Toronto Press, 1960]
    36 p. illus., diagrs., tables.   OTU
Kaposy, John.
    Open education: the St. Daniel's experience, by John Kaposy, H.G. Hedges
    with contributions by Lydia Dedo [et al. St. Catharines, Ontario] Niagara
    Centre, Ontario Institute for Studies in Education and Wentworth county
    Roman Catholic Separate School Board, 1974.
    viii, 142 p. illus.   OTER
Katz, Michael Barry, 1939–
    The Canadian Social History Project: interim report no. 4. Toronto:
    Department of History and Philosophy of Education, Ontario Institute for
    Studies in Education, 1972.
    iv, 351 p. maps, tables.
    Chiefly pre-Confederation.   OTC
— Education and social change: themes from Ontario's past, edited by Michael
    B. Katz and Paul H. Mattingly. New York: New York University Press,
    1975.
    xxxi, 324 p. illus., tables.   OLU
Keith, Janet.
    The Collegiate Institute Board of Ottawa: a short history, 1843–1969.
    [Ottawa: Kent Reproduction, 1969?]
    1, 115 p. illus., ports.   OTU
Kelly, M   Frances.
    Report on Canadian education in Ontario province. [Toronto? 197–?]
    1 v. in 2 parts.

Contents: Part 1, An analysis of educational opportunity: 1966–1967; Part
2, The colleges of applied arts and technology: problems of role, staff, and
relationship.   OTER

Khan, Sar Bilund, 1936–
A factor analytic study of the Ontario tests for admission to college and
university. [Toronto: Department of Measurement and Evaluation, Ontario
Institute for Studies in Education, 1969?]
1 v. (various pagings).   OTER

Kidd, James Robbins, 1915–
18 to 80, continuing education in Metropolitan Toronto: a report of an
enquiry concerning the education of adults in Metropolitan Toronto.
Toronto: Board of Education [c1960]
153 p. diagrs., tables.   OTU

Klinck, George, 1862–1944.
The development and progress of education in Elmira and vicinity. Elmira:
The Author, 1938.
[12] 57 [5] p. illus., port.   OTU

Knoepfli, Heather E
Project: learning for change; a study of learning needs and interests of
Ontario adults, by Heather E. Knoepfli and David J. Saul. [Toronto]
Ontario Educational Communications Authority, 1973.
iii, 136 leaves. forms.   OTER

Kovaloff, Alexander A
An updated survey of career opportunities for four year high school and
community college graduates. [Toronto] Ontario Educational Research
Council, 1970.
60 p.   OTER

La Légalité, C   de.
The juridical and pedagogical position of English–French schools in
Ontario. Ottawa: Imprimerie du Droit, 1915.
40 p.   OTU

Lambert, Richard Stanton, 1894–
School broadcasting in Canada. [Toronto] University of Toronto Press
[c1963]
xii, 223 p. illus.   OTER

Langford, Howard David.
Educational service, its functions and possibilities. New York: Teachers
College, Columbia University, 1931.
vi, 212 p.
Education in Ontario.   OTU

Levine, Jack Bernard, 1941–
Institutional survival through integrated systems; projection analysis.
Toronto: 1970.
37 leaves.   OTU

Lewis, A   C
  Handbook on the administration of education in Ontario. Rev. ed.
  [Toronto] Department of Educational Research, Ontario College of
  Education, University of Toronto, 1954.
  iii, 58 leaves. diagrs., tables. (Educational Research series, no. 1).   OTER
London Home and School Council.
  History 1905–1939. London, Ontario [1939]
  28 p.   OL
Long, John A
  Educational survey prepared for the Leaside Board of Education. Toronto:
  Department of Educational Research, Ontario College of Education
  [University of Toronto] 1945.
  29 leaves.   OTER
Longtin, Nicolas.
  Les garanties du français et le réglement XVII: dialogue entre Nicholas
  Longtin, Maître d'école, et Louis Bérubé, ouvier. Montreal: Imprimerie du
  Devoir, 1927.
  64 p.   OOU
Loubser, Jan J   1932–
  The York county Board of Education: a study in innovation, by Jan J.
  Loubser, Herbert Spiers and Carolyn Moody. [Toronto] Ontario Institute
  for Studies in Education [c1972]
  v, 54 p. illus., map. (Ontario Institute for Studies in Education. Profiles in
  practical education, no. 5).   OTER
McCrimmon, Abraham Lincoln, 1865–1935.
  The educational policy of the Baptists of Ontario and Quebec. Foreword by
  D.E. Thomson. Toronto: McMaster University, 1920.
  35 p.   OTU
McDiarmid, Garnet Leo, 1924–   (ed.).
  From quantitative to qualitative change in Ontario education: a festschrift
  for R.W.B. Jackson. Toronto: Ontario Institute for Studies in Education,
  1975.
  xv, 190 p. (Ontario Institute for Studies in Education. Symposium series, 6).
  History of education in Ontario.   OTER
— Teaching prejudice: a content analysis of social studies textbooks authorized
  for use in Ontario, by Garnet McDiarmid and David Pratt. [Toronto] The
  Ontario Institute for Studies in Education [c1971]
  x, 131 p. (Ontario Institute for Studies in Education. Curriculum series, no.
  12).   OTER
MacDonald, Mary (comp.).
  Researches and studies, completed and ongoing, in connection with
  bilingualism, second-language teaching, and French or English as second
  languages: The Ontario Curriculum Institute and the Ontario Institute for
  Studies in Education, 1960–1970. [Toronto: 1970]
  10 leaves.   OTER

Mackenzie, J   G   D
   Educational suggestions: compiled from reports of J.G.D. Mackenzie,
   inspector of high schools. Toronto: Rowsell & Hutchison, 1882.
   60 p.   OTER
McMurrich, William Barclay, 1872–1908.
   The school law of Ontario, edited by W.B. McMurrich and H.N. Roberts.
   Toronto: Goodwin Law Book and Publishing Company (Limited), 1894.
   xxvi, 625 p.   OTU
McNeil, Neil, Archbp., 1851–1934.
   The school question of Ontario, by the Archbishop of Toronto. Toronto:
   Extension Print, 1931.
   31 p.   OTU
McReynolds, William Peter.
   A model for the Ontario educational system. A report on the project titled
   "Technology, education and employment – a study of interactions: part 1 – a
   macro-model of the Ontario educational system". [Toronto] Department of
   Educational Planning, Ontario Institute for Studies in Education [1969]
   xiii, 177 p. graphs, tables. (Ontario Institute for Studies in Education.
   Department of Educational Planning. Educational Planning occasional
   papers no. 8).   OTER
Metropolitan Toronto. School Board.
   Quality teaching study: a composite report of three major studies conducted
   by the Teachers' Salary Committee, the Teacher Workload Committee and
   the Quality Teaching Committee. [Toronto] 1969.
   1 v. (various pagings). illus.   OONL
Metropolitan Toronto. School Board. Advisory Council.
   A study of school finance in the metropolitan area [a report by Brock
   Rideout and George Gray. Toronto: 1957]
   iii, 74 leaves. tables.
   Chairman Advisory Council: C.C. Goldring.   OTU
Metropolitan Toronto. School Board. Research Department.
   A survey of outdoor education in Metropolitan Toronto: attitudes, activities
   and facilities. [Toronto] 1970.
   1 v. (various pagings). diagrs., tables.   OTC
Metropolitan Toronto. School Board. Special Committee.
   The case for equalization of educational opportunity in Metro Toronto.
   [Toronto] The Board, 1962.
   79 p. charts, tables.   OTER
Metropolitan Toronto Separate School Board.
   New Canadian educational program: report. [Toronto: 1966]
   23 [20] leaves. map.
   Education of foreign students in Toronto.   OONL
Minorities, schools, and politics. Essays by D.G. Creighton [et al.] Introduction
   by Craig Brown. [Toronto] University of Toronto Press [c1969]
   xi, 111 p.

Contents: John A. Macdonald Confederation and the Canadian west,
D.G.Creighton; Manitoba schools and Canadian nationality, 1890–1923,
W.L. Morton; Church, schools, and politics in Manitoba, 1903–1912,
Ramsay Cook; The campaign for a French Catholic school inspector in the
North-West Territories, 1898–1903, Momoly B. Lupul; The Ontario
bilingual schools issue: sources of conflict, Marilyn Barber; Clerics,
politicians, and the bilingual schools issue in Ontario, 1910–1917, Margaret
Prang.   OTU

Moffat, Harding Pyle, 1905–
Educational finance in Canada. Toronto: W.J. Gage Limited [1958]
95 p. (Quance Lectures in Canada Education, series 9).   OTU

Monroe, David.
The organization and administration of education in Canada. Ottawa:
Department of the Secretary of State, 1974.
xii, 219 p. charts, tables.
Ontario: pp. 43–64.   OONL

Mowat, Susanne (Clarke), 1942–
Cost analysis of New Canadian instruction. [Toronto: Research
Department, Board of Education for the City of Toronto] 1968.
ii, 30 leaves. tables.   OONL

— Main Street school and regional reception centres: a comparison of
"graduates". [Toronto: Research Department, Board of Education] 1969.
52 leaves. diagrs., tables. (Research service report).   OTER

Myers, Douglas.
Educating teachers: critiques and proposals, edited by Douglas Myers and
Fran Reid. [Toronto] Ontario Institute for Studies in Education [c1974]
156 p. (Ontario Institute for Studies in Education. Symposium series 4).
                                                                                      OTER

Neatby, Hilda Marian, 1904–1975.
So little for the mind. Toronto: Clarke, Irwin & Company Limited, 1953.
ix, 384 p.   OTU

Newnham, William Thomson, 1923–
The professional teacher in Ontario, the heritage responsibilities, and
practices, by W.T. Newham and A.S. Noase, Toronto: The Ryerson Press
[c1965]
233 p. illus.   OTER

— Rev. ed. Toronto: The Ryerson Press [c1967]
290 p.   OTU

— 3d ed. Toronto: The Ryerson Press [c1970]
309 p. illus., charts, facsims., maps.   OTU

North Bay, Ontario. Teachers' College.
An historical sketch of N.B.N.S.-N.B.T.C., 1909–1959. [North Bay, Ontario:
1959]
11 p. illus.   OTU

North York, Ontario.
North York info: through fifty years of development. Willowdale, Ontario:
1972.
32 p. illus.   OLU

North York, Ontario. Board of Education.
   5-year guidelines study 1970. [North York, Ontario: 1970?]
   ix, 246 p. illus. (part col.), map.   OTER
— A report on the community – the school. [North York] 1972.
   81 p. tables.   OTER
OISE-CPAC Waterfront Workshop, 1st, Toronto, 1969.
   The waterfront is for living and learning. [Toronto: Ontario Institute for
   Studies in Education, 1969]
   iv, 47 leaves.   OTU
Oksanen, Ernest H
   Student performance in introductory courses in economics and other social
   sciences, by Ernest H. Oksanen and Byron G. Spencer. Hamilton, Ontario:
   Department of Economics, McMaster University, 1975.
   15 leaves. (Department of Economics, McMaster University. Working
   paper, no. 75–03).   OTU
Ontario. Commission to enquire on a charge made against the Central
   Committee from the Honourable the Minister of Education.
   Central Committee inquiry: Report. Printed by order of the Legislative
   Assembly. Toronto: Hunter, Rose & Co., 1878.
   254 p.
   Chairman: Christopher Salmon Patterson.   OTL
Ontario. Commission to inquire into the Building Department of the Board of
   Education of the city of Toronto.
   Report. [Toronto: 1919]
   91 typewritten pages.
   Commissioner: Haughton I.S. Lennox.   OTAR
Ontario. Committee on Drug Information and Education.
   Report... to the Hon. A.B.R. Lawrence, minister of health. [Toronto: 1971]
   35 leaves.
   Chairman: James W.F. Bain.   OTER
Ontario. Committee on the Teaching of French.
   Report. [Toronto] Ontario Ministry of Education [1974?]
   59 p.
   Chairman: Robert Gillin.   OTER
Ontario. Educational Resources Allocation System Task Force.
   An initial statement. Rev. ed. [Toronto] 1973.
   iv, 12 p. illus.
   Director: D.S. Lawless.   OTER
— E.R.A.S. in practice: the development and implementation of a systematic
   decision-making process. [Toronto] 1974.
   27 p. charts. (*Its* Working paper no. 6).   OTER
— Evaluation in school systems: a component of an educational resources
   allocation system. [Toronto?] 1973.
   8 p. illus. (*Its* Working paper no. 3).   OTER
— Goals and objectives for school systems: a component of an educational
   resources allocation system. [Toronto?] 1973.
   15 p. (*Its* Working paper no. 1).   OTER

— The initial stage in implementing an E.R.A.S. [Toronto] 1974.
   15 p. charts. (*Its* Working paper no. 5).   OTER
— Program accounting and budgeting: a component of an educational
   resources allocation system. [Toronto?] 1973.
   6 p. illus. (*Its* Working paper no. 4).   OTER
— Program and staff development in the context of the educational resources
   allocation system. [Toronto] 1975.
   8 p. charts. (*Its* Working paper no. 8).   OTER
— Program structure: a component of an educational resources allocation
   system. [Toronto?] 1973.
   15 p. charts. (*Its* Working paper no. 2).   OTER
— Programming: the second stage of an educational resources allocation
   system. [Toronto] 1975.
   15 p. charts. (*Its* Working paper no. 7).   OTER
Ontario. General Advisory Committee on Industrial Training.
   Report. [Toronto] Department of Labour, 1968.
   17 p.
   Chairman: C. Ross Ford.   OTER
Ontario. Interministerial Textbook Committee.
   Report to Deputy Minister of Education, Deputy Minister of Labour.
   [Toronto?] 1972.
   14 leaves.
   Chairman: Daniel G. Hill.   OTER
Ontario. Legislative Assembly. Select Committee on Manpower Training.
   Report. [Toronto] 1963.
   126 p. chart.
   Chairman: J.R. Simonett.   OTUL OTAR
— Briefs.
   46 v.   OTAR
Ontario. Legislative Assembly. Select Committee on the Utilization of
   Educational Facilities.
   Interim report number one. [Toronto] 1973.
   1 v. (various pagings).
   Chairman: Charles E. McElveen.   OTAR OTER
— Interim report number two. [Toronto] 1973.
   1 v. (various pagings). diagrs.   OTAR OTER
— Interim report number three. [Toronto] 1974.
   1 v. (various pagings).   OTAR OTER
— Final report ["What happens next is up to you". Toronto] 1975.
   1 v. (various pagings).   OTAR OTER
— Briefs.
   416 v.   OTAR
— Minutes, January 25, 1972–December 10, 1974.
   3 v. (various pagings).   OTAR
— Committee meeting, transcript of tape, December 18, 1972–December 10,
   1974.
   41 v. (various pagings).   OTAR

— Detailed accounts of visits and meetings, January 26–November 9, 1972.
   6 v. (various pagings). OTAR
Ontario. Ministry of Education. Task Force on Organization.
   Structure for education administration: report. [Toronto: 1973]
   94 p. illus., maps, charts, graphs. OTER
Ontario. Provincial Conference on Aims and Objectives of the Education of the
   Deaf Individual in Ontario. Toronto: 1973.
   Proceedings, Queen's Park, October 16th–17th. [Toronto] Ontario Ministry
   of Education, 1973.
   109 p. OTU
Ontario. Royal Commission on the question of prices of school books, royalties,
   etc.
   Report. Toronto: Warwick Bros. & Rutter, 1898.
   19 p.
   Chairman: Edward Morgan. OTL
— Report. Toronto: Warwick Bros. & Rutter, 1898.
   16 p.
   Cover for this edition states imprint: L.K. Cameron, printer to the King's
   Most Excellent Majesty, 1898. OTAR
Ontario. Royal Commission to inquire into the administration, management
   and welfare of the Ontario School for the Blind.
   Report and recommendations. Printed by order of the Legislative Assembly
   of Ontario. Toronto: A.T. Wilgress, printer to the King's Most Excellent
   Majesty, 1917.
   35 p.
   Commissioner: Norman Blain Gash. OTAR
Ontario. Study Team on the Sharing or Transfering of Education Facilities.
   Report to the Minister of Education ... February, 1973. [Toronto: 1973]
   20 p.
   Co-chairmen: R.J. Marrese and J.R. Christie. OTER
Ontario. Task Force on School Health Services.
   Report. [Toronto] Ontario Ministry of Health, 1972.
   v, 37 leaves.
   Chairman: Jean F. Webb. OTER
Ontario. Text Book Commission.
   Report [and appendices]. Printed by order of the Legislative Assembly of
   Ontario. Toronto: L.K. Cameron, printer to the King's Most Excellent
   Majesty, 1907.
   389 p.
   Commissioners: Thomas Wilson Crothers and John Alexander Cooper. OTC
— Report. 1907.
   16 p. OTAR
Ontario Association for Continuing Education.
   Planning and purpose in adult education in Ontario: the report of the
   founding conference of the Ontario Association for Continuing Education.
   Toronto: 1966.
   25, 9 leaves. OTULS

Ontario Association for Curriculum Development.
    Standards in education in Ontario schools. Report of the eighth annual
    conference, Ontario Association for Curriculum Development. Vancouver,
    British Columbia: Copp Clark Publishing Co., Limited [c1958]
    vi, 186 p.   OTER
Ontario Association for Emotionally Disturbed Children.
    A brief to the Honourable W.G.Davis, minister of education, province of
    Ontario, concerning the improvement of educational facilities for
    emotionally disturbed children. Presented March 1964. Toronto: 1964.
    16 leaves.
    Chairman: Don Hurley.   OTU
Ontario Association for the Mentally Retarded.
    Education for living: a curriculum for the life experience training. [Toronto:
    197–?]
    iii, 79 leaves.   OTER
Ontario Association of Education Administrative Officials.
    A proposal to establish the Ontario Council for Leadership in Educational
    Administration, submitted to the W.K. Kellogg Foundation [Toronto] 1972.
    iii, 53 [20] leaves. tables.   OTER
Ontario Conference on Continuing Education, Windsor, Ontario, 1964.
    [Proceedings. Toronto] Ontario Association for Curriculum Development
    [1964?]
    48 p.
    Chairman: Eldon P. Ray.   OTER OTULS
Ontario Conference on Education, Windsor, Ontario, 1962.
    The quest for excellence in education. November 23, 24 and 25, 1961.
    [Toronto: Ontario Association for Curriculum Development, 1961]
    156 p.   OTER
— Working papers. n.p. [1961?]
    2 v.   OTER
Ontario Curriculum Institute,
    New design for learning, highlights of the reports of the Institute, 1963–1966.
    Edited and with introductions by Brian Burnham. [Toronto] Published for
    the Ontario Institute for Studies in Education by University of Toronto Press
    [c1967]
    xi, 326 p. illus., diagrs., tables. (Ontario Institute for Studies in Education.
    Curriculum series no. 1).   OTER
Ontario Curriculum Institute. Study Committee on Instructional Aids and
    Techniques.
    Technology in learning: an interim report. [Toronto] 1965.
    105 p. illus. (part col.), col. map, ports.   OONL
Ontario Economic Council.
    Assessing educational requirements for skillpower; a look at how five
    manufacturers and three service businesses in Ontario view the educational
    requirements of their 28,500 employees between 1965 and 1970. [Toronto]
    Ontario Economic Council, 1966.
    24 p. charts.   OTER

— Education: issues and alternatives, 1976. [Toronto: 1976]
vii, 41 p.
Chairman: G.L. Reuber.   OTER
Ontario Educational Association.
Centennial year book, 1860–1960. [Toronto: 1960]
208 p. illus., ports.
"Accounts of proceedings of the Convention of the Ontario Educational
Association on the occasion of its Centennial held in Toronto, April 18th to
22nd, 1960.   OTC
— Jubilee banquet, Convocation Hall, University of Toronto, April 18, 1911.
[Toronto: 1912]
97 p. ports.   OTER
Ontario Educational Research Council.
Proceedings of the workshop on classroom research. [Toronto: 1965]
29 leaves.   OONL
Ontario Federation of Home and School Associations.
Through the years with the Ontario Federation of Home and School
Associations: a review of accomplishments, interests, hopes, 1919–1963.
[Toronto: The Association 1963]
37, vi p.   OONL
— 1919–1969. [Toronto: The Association, 1969?]
47, vii p.   OTER
Ontario Institute for Studies in Education.
English: four essays: the aims and problems of English in school, community
colleges and universities of Ontario. [Toronto: The Institute, c1968]
47 p. (Ontario Institute for Studies in Education. Curriculum series, 3).   OTU
— School boards cooperating in some OISE research and development projects
and studies. [Toronto] 1969.
1 v. (unpaged).   OTER
Ontario Institute for Studies in Education. Department of Adult Education.
Report of informal discussion of continuing education for women, May 9,
1968. [Toronto] 1968.
1 v. (various pagings). illus.
Chairman: Marion Royce.   OTER
Ontario Institute for Studies in Education. Department of Educational
Administration.
Developing school systems: planning, organization, and personnel; a manual
for trustees, administrators, and teachers by T.B. Greenfield [et al.] Toronto:
c1969.
xi, 177 p. illus., diagrs.   OTER
Ontario Institute for Studies in Education. Department of Educational
Planning.
The growth of York South region, by Upinder Dugal [et al. Toronto]
Ontario Institute for Studies in Education, 1968.
101 leaves. maps, graphs, tables.   OTER

Ontario Institute for Studies in Education. Mid-northern Centre.
  Sudbury Board of Education Open Schools Project. Sudbury, Ontario: 1972.
  14, 2 leaves. tables.   OTER
Ontario Institute for Studies in Education. Office of the Coordinator of
  Research and Development Studies.
  Ontario Institute for Studies in Education activities related to minority
  groups in the educational system. [Toronto] 1973.
  26 p.   OTER
Ontario Institute for Studies in Education. Trent Valley Centre.
  The continuing evaluation of POISE, a report of results. [Peterborough,
  Ontario] Trent Valley Centre, Ontario Institute for Studies in Education
  [1972]
  1 v. (various pagings). tables.   OTER
— The Trent Valley Centre projection, 1971–1972: report, by H. Russell, K.
  Leithwood and P. Baxter. Peterborough, Ontario [1972?]
  83 leaves.   OTER
Ontario Public and Separate School Inspectors.
  The training of teachers-in-service. Toronto: Clarke, Irwin & Company
  Limited, 1936.
  vii, 294 p. charts.   OTER
Ontario School Trustees Council.
  Brief, presented to Leslie M. Frost, prime minister, province of Ontario and
  members of Cabinet, December, 1956. [Toronto? 1956]
  15 leaves.
  Chairman: D.F. Hassard.   OTER
— Resolutions presented for the consideration of the Honourable William G.
  Davis, minister of education, October 26th, 1966. [Toronto: 1966]
  30 leaves.   OONL
— Submission to the Minister of Education on redraft of Bill 275. Toronto:
  1974.
  37, 24 leaves.   OTER
Ontario School Trustees' Council. Curriculum Committee.
  Educational articulation in Ontario: a survey. [Toronto: Ontario School
  Trustees' Council] 1964.
  32 p.
  Chairman: Elise Grossberg.   OTER
Ontario Secondary School Teachers' Federation. Comité d'étude sur l'homme
  dans la société.
  Rapport. [Toronto] Comité de langue française de l'O.S.S.T.F. 1972.
  [38] p. illus.   OTER
Ontario Secondary School Teachers' Federation. Educational Finance
  Committee.
  The finance and administration of education in English-speaking countries,
  together with a suggested programme of reform for Ontario. [Toronto?
  1935?]
  36 p. tables.   OTER

Ontario Secondary School Teachers' Federation. Ontario Secondary Education
    Commission. Non-Graded Schools Committee.
    Education for the '70's: the non-graded school; a report. [Toronto: 1969]
    31 p. ports.
    Chairman: R.J. Hunter.   OTER
— Education for the '70's: papers 1–6; report. [Toronto: 1971]
    1 v. (various pagings). illus.
    Chairman: J. Kar.   OTER
Ontario Secondary School Teachers' Federation. Salary Committee.
    The school and the community, prepared to set forth the advantages of
    salary schedules for teachers, together with suggestions for financing same.
    Toronto [1939]
    32 p.   OTC
Ontario Separate School Trustees' Association.
    Brief presented to the Prime Minister and the Minister of Education of the
    province of Ontario, by the Ontario Separate School Trustees Association
    and l'Association des commissions des écoles bilingues d'Ontario, October,
    1966. Toronto [1966]
    20, 20 p. tables.
    Text in English and French.   OONL
— Equal opportunity for continuous education in separate schools of Ontario.
    A brief presented to Hon. John P. Robarts, Hon. Wm. G. Davis and the
    members of the Legislative Assembly. Toronto: 1969.
    47 p. illus.   OTAR
— A statement on the reorganization of school zones as applied to the separate
    schools of Ontario. [Toronto? 1968]
    13 [3] 6 leaves.   OTER
Ontario Teachers' Federation.
    Beyond the classroom: a report on professional activities by the teachers of
    Ontario. [Toronto: 1959]
    [15] p. illus.   OTAR
— Innovative schools in the province of Ontario 1976. Toronto: 1976.
    [35] leaves.   OTER
— OTF at 20: recollections of the first two decades of the Ontario Teachers'
    Federation. Toronto [1964?]
    51 p. illus., ports.   OTER
— Ontario teachers: the Ontario Teachers' Federation report to cabinet.
    [Toronto] Ontario Teachers' Federation, 1976.
    24 p. illus.   OONL
Ontario Teachers' Federation. Advisory Committee for York County.
    Report. [Toronto] 1968.
    1 v. (various pagings). diagrs., tables.   OTER
Ontario Teachers' Federation Commission.
    Pattern for professionalism. Report of the OTF Commission to the Board of

Governors of the Ontario Teachers' Federation. [Toronto: Ontario
Teachers' Federation] 1968.
63 p.
Chairman: Brother Omer Deslauriers.   OTOTF
Ontario Teachers' Federation. Committee on Integration of Total School
    Program K-13.
    Integration of total school program K-13: a report. [Toronto] Ontario
    Teachers' Federation, 1973.
    v, 142 p.
    Chairman: C. Mayer.   OTER
Ontario Teachers' Federation. Optimum Size Committee.
    A comparative survey of school districts in Ontario. [Toronto] 1967.
    1 v. (various pagings). tables.
    Research advisor: Edward H. Humphreys.   OTER
— The consolidation of Ontario school districts: a survey. [Toronto] 1965.
    71 p. tables.
    Chairman of Committee: Marion Evans.   OTER
Ontario Teachers' Federation. Students' Rights and Responsibilities
    Committee.
    The right to responsibility. [Toronto?] 1970.
    79 leaves.   OLU
Ontario Teachers' Federation. Symposium on Teacher Education, Toronto,
    1971.
    Concepts in teacher education. Toronto: Ontario Teachers' Federation
    [1971]
    204 p.   OTER
Ontario Teachers' Federation. Working Conditions Committee.
    An interim survey report from the OTF Committee on Working Conditions.
    Toronto: Ontario Teachers' Federation, 1972.
    xiv, 96 p. tables.
    Chairman: René Bisnaire.   OTER
— A survey report from the OTF Committee on Working Conditions comparing
    1970–71 and 1973–74. [Toronto] Ontario Teachers' Federation, 1974.
    72, 7 p. tables.   OTER
Ottawa School Division. Interim School Organization Committee.
    Report to the Ottawa Board of Education. [Ottawa] 1969.
    1 v. (various pagings). charts, tables.
    Chairman: Eileen Scotton.   OTER
The Ottawa school question; printed privately for R. Mackell, J.F. Lanigan,
    H.F. Sims, A.J. Brennan, M.J. O'Neill and James Finn, Ottawa separate
    school trustees, Ottawa, June, 1914. Ottawa: 1914.
    47 p.   OTU
The Ottawa separate school case. Ottawa: Printed privately, 1915.
    15 p.   OTU

Owen, Joslyn.
New education in Canada. [Aspects of changing policy in three provinces.
Ottawa? c1969]
77 leaves.
Ontario: pp. 4–16.   OTER
Palmer, Judith A 1941–
Home environment and achievement. [Toronto] Research Department
[Board of Education] 1967.
29 leaves. tables.   OTER
Past principals of Ontario normal schools. [Toronto?] 1905.
1 v. (unpaged). ports.   OTER
Patterson, Robert Steven.
Profiles of Canadian educators. Edited by Robert S. Patterson, John W.
Chalmers and John W. Friesen. [Toronto] D.C. Heath Canada Ltd. [c1974]
409 p. illus.   OTU
Peel County, Ontario. Board of Education.
The administrative organization of the Peel Board of Education. n.p.: 1974.
41 leaves. chart, graphs.   OTER
Phillips, A   J
Relative difficulties of the fundamental facts in arithmetic based on a study
of errors made by Ontario children, by A.J. Phillips and H.M. Fowler.
[Toronto] Department of Educational Research, Ontario College of
Education, University of Toronto, 1946.
ii, 33 leaves. (Educational Research series, no. 13).   OTER
Phillips, Charles Edward, 1897–
The development of education in Canada. Illustrated by Fay Edwards and
Priscilla Hutchings. Toronto: W.J. Gage and Company Limited, 1957.
xiii, 626 p. illus., ports.   OTU
Plumptre, Adelaide M
The non-academic child. A reprint of two papers by Adelaide M. Plumptre
and E.P. Lewis. Ottawa: The Canadian Council on Child and Family
Welfare, 1931.
15 p. (C.C.C.F.W. Public's no. 50).   OOCW
Proctor, Redfern, Bousfield & Bacon.
City of London school study, prepared for the Board of Education for the
city of London, 1964. Toronto: 1964.
76 leaves. diagrs., maps.   OTUSA
Putman, John Harold, 1866–1940.
Fifty years at school: an educationalist looks at life. Toronto: Clarke, Irwin
& Company Limited, 1938.
xv, 253 p.   OTU
Reich, Carol Musselman, 1943–
Ontario Secondary School Teachers' Federation Task Force on Women
report: the effect of sexism on the career development of teachers by Carol
Reich and Helen La Fountaine. [Toronto] Ontario Secondary School
Teachers' Federation, 1976.
101, xxii p. graphs, map, tables.   OONL

Richardson, William Leeds.
     The administration of schools in the cities of the Dominion of Canada.
     Toronto: J.M. Dent & Sons, Limited [1921]
     xviii, 315 p. diagrs., tables.   OTER
Rideout, E   Brock.
     Survey of 1960 elementary school grants, by E. Brock Rideout and R.W.B.
     Jackson. Toronto: Department of Educational Research, University of
     Toronto, 1961.
     1 v. (unpaged). tables.   OTER
Robinson, Stephen B
     Do not erase: the story of OSSTF [by S.G.B. Robinson. Toronto: Ontario
     Secondary School Teachers' Federation, c1971]
     viii, 324 p. ports.   OTER
Rosenthal, Ron.
     A study of the social, vocational and educational capability of the adult
     hemophiliac in Ontario, by Ron Rosenthal, Mira Friedlander and Richard
     Nelson. Toronto: The Author, 1973.
     11 p. 49 leaves.   OTU
Ross, J   Douglas, 1930–
     Education in Oshawa from settlement to city. Oshawa, Ontario: County
     Board of Education, 1970.
     [ix] 220 p. illus.   OTAR
Roth, John .
     West Indians in Toronto: the students and the schools, written by John
     Roth; edited by Z. Akonde [et al. Toronto] MERS Learner Characteristics
     Committee, Board of Education for the Borough of York [197–]
     i, 68 p. map.   OONL
Russell, H   Howard, 1928–
     The Peterborough project: a case study of educational change and
     innovation, by H.H. Russell, K.A. Leithwood and R.P. Baxter. [Toronto]
     Ontario Institute for Studies in Education [c1973]
     v, 142 p. diagrs., tables. (Research in Education series no. 2).   OTER
Ryan, Doris W
     The education of adolescents in remote areas of Ontario. [Toronto: Ontario
     Institute for Studies in Education, c1976]
     xiv, 386 p. tables.   OTER
Ryerson, Adolphus Egerton, 1803–1882.
     Report on institutions for the deaf and dumb in Europe and in the United
     States of America, with appendices and suggestions for their establishment in
     the province of Ontario. Toronto: *Daily Telegraph* Printing House, 1868.
     58 p.
—   Rev. Dr. Ryerson's defence against the attacks of the Hon. George Brown,
     managing director of the *Globe* newspaper and his assistants relative to the
     Ontario system of public instruction and its administration. Toronto: Copp,
     Clark Co., 1872.
     viii, 95 p.   OTURS

St. John, Clinton.
  Ontario study of vocational-technical training: a preliminary report.
  Toronto: Ontario Institute for Studies in Education, 1967.
  iii, 29, 7, 6, 3, 3 leaves.   OTER
Scott, J   Glenn (ed.).
  The planning process: a system perspective for school boards [edited by] J.
  Glenn Scott and David J. Ducharme. [Toronto] Department of Educational
  Administration in cooperation with the Office of Field Development,
  Ontario Institute for Studies in Education [c1972]
  vi, 81 p. diagrs., tables.
  Educational planning for Ontario.   OTER
Seath, John, 1844–1919.
  Some needed educational reform. President's address [at the] annual
  convention of the Ontario Educational Association. [Toronto] 1903.
  16 p.   OTU
Selby–Smith, Christopher, 1942–
  Concerning the growth of provincial expenditures on education in Ontario,
  1938–1966, by Christopher Selby–Smith and Michael Skolnik. [Toronto]
  Ontario Institute for Studies in Education [c1969]
  36 p. tables. (Ontario Institute for Studies in Education. Occasional papers,
  3).   OTU
Shuttleworth, Dale E
  The community school and social reconstruction: a demonstration project.
  [Toronto: Ontario Educational Research Council, 1967?]
  31, 6 leaves.
  Toronto.   OTER
Simard, (J.F.) Company Limited.
  General information concerning the school system of Ontario and
  particularly the allotment of legislative grants. Ottawa: 1958–1959.
  xxxi, 24, 4 p. tables.   OTAR
Sissons, Charles Bruce, 1879–1965.
  Bilingual schools in Canada. London: J.M. Dent & Sons, Ltd., 1917.
  242 p.
  Ontario: pp. 13–113.   OTU
— Church & state in Canadian education: an historical study. Toronto: The
  Ryerson Press [c1959]
  x, 414 p. ports.
  Ontario: pp. 3–125.   OTU
Skene, Dora L
  The "culturally deprived" in school and society: selected approaches.
  [Toronto: Board of Education, Research Department] 1966.
  91 leaves. illus.
  "A cooperative project of the Kenora School Board and the Board of
  Education for the city of Toronto".   OTER

Skolnik, Michael L
  Some economic aspects of the relationship between education and
  employment of technicians and technologists in Ontario, by M.L. Skolnik
  and Gillian Bryce. [Toronto] Ontario Institute for Studies in Education,
  1971.
  vi, 66 leaves. diagrs., tables.   OTER
Smart, Reginald George, 1936–
  The extent of drug use in metropolitan schools: a study of changes from 1968
  to 1970, by Reginald G. Smart, Dianne Fejer, Jim White. Toronto:
  Addiction Research Foundation, 1970.
  49, A82 leaves. graphs, table.   OTU
Squair, John, 1850–1928.
  An open letter to the people of Ontario on the teaching of French . Toronto:
  University of Toronto Press, 1918.
  [8] p.   OTU
— John Seath and the school system of Ontario. [Toronto] Printed for the
  author by the University of Toronto Press, 1920.
  124 p. port.   OTER
Stabler, Martin.
  Explorations in a night culture, or, After dinner walks in night school. A
  report for the Ontario Association for Continuing Education, by Martin
  Stabler with the cooperation of the Ministry of Community & Social
  Services, Youth and Recreation Branch. [Toronto: Ontario Association for
  Continuing Education, c1972]
  viii, 67 p. illus.   OTER
Stanley, J   R
  Our St. Mary's schools: an historical sketch. [St. Mary's, Ontario] The St.
  Mary's Journal. [1909?]
  37 p.   OTER
Staples, R   O
  The rural teacher: selection, training and in service guidance. Toronto: The
  Ryerson Press [c1947]
  81 p.   OTER
Stephen, A   G   A   (ed.).
  Private schools in Canada: a handbook of boys' schools which are members
  of the Canadian Headmasters' Association. [Toronto] Published for the
  Canadian Headmasters' Association by Clarke, Irwin & Company Limited,
  1938.
  viii, 133 p.   OTER
Stokes, Shirley, 1920–
  The shortest shadow: a descriptive study of the members of the Federation of
  Women Teachers' Associations of Ontario. [Toronto: Federation of Women
  Teachers' Associations of Ontario, 1969?]
  2, 3, 120, 2, 11 leaves.   OTER

Structure, decision-making and communication in the Waterloo county school
    system: an evaluation report, by T. Barr Greenfield [et al.] Toronto: Ontario
    Institute for Studies in Education, 1974.
    iv, 94 leaves.   OTER
The structure and process of decision-making in a school system: an evaluation
    report on organizational change in Grey county, by T. Barr Greenfield [et
    al. Toronto] Department of Educational Administration, Ontario Institute
    for Studies in Education, 1972.
    iv, 46 leaves.   OTER
Stuhr, Christian A   1942–
    Patterns of parental mobility in an inner-city Toronto school. [Toronto:
    Research Department, Board of Education] 1967.
    51 leaves. tables.   OTER
Thompson, Ivor William.
    A method for developing unit costs in educational programs, by I. Wm.
    Thompson and P.A. Lapp. [Toronto? Committee of Presidents of
    Universities of Ontario] 1970.
    v, 65 p. tables. (CPUO report, no. 70–3).   OTU
Thorson, Sondra.
    Communities in transition: toward school district re-organization. [Toronto]
    Ontario Institute for Studies in Education, 1971.
    75 leaves. tables.
    York county.   OTER
The thrift campaign in the schools of Ontario, with a brief sketch of what
    Ontario has done in the war. n.p.: n.d.
    viii, 59 p. ports.   OTAR
Tisdall, Clark and Lesly Ltd.
    1966 attitudes study: (trustees – board and department officials) [toward
    the] Federation of Women Teachers' Associations of Ontario. [Toronto:
    1967?]
    22 leaves.   OONL
Toronto. Board of Education.
    Brief on French instruction. [Toronto] 1973.
    61 p.   OTER
— Centennial story. The Board of Education for the city of Toronto,
    1850–1950. Prepared by the staff of the Board, under the direction of E.A.
    Hardy. Honora M. Cochrane, editor. Toronto: Thomas Nelson & Sons
    (Canada) Limited [1950]
    xi, 306 p. front., illus., plates (part col.), ports.   OTER OKQ
— Learnxs: learning exchange system. Toronto: 1973.
    12 leaves. diagrs.   OTER
Toronto. Board of Education. Office of the Director of Education.
    Preliminary report on the results of the French survey. [Toronto: 1973?]
    49 leaves. tables.   OTER
Toronto. Board of Education. Research Department.
    Adult education in Metropolitan Toronto; a situation report. [Toronto: The
    Author] 1967.
    89 leaves. diagrs., tables.   OTER

— An experimental study of television as a medium of French instruction. [Toronto] 1962.
    63 leaves. tables.   OTER
Toronto. Board of Education. Work Group on Vocational Schools.
    Vocational schools in Toronto: an interim report. [Toronto] 1973.
    73 leaves.
    Chairman: G. Cressy.   OTER
Toronto Normal School.
    Jubilee celebration (October 31st, November 1st and 2nd, 1897) 1847–1897.
    Biographical sketches and names of successful students 1847 to 1875.
    Toronto: Warwick Bro's & Rutter, 1898.
    vii, 203 p. illus.   OTU
Toronto Normal School. Centennial Committee.
    Toronto Normal School, 1847–1947. [Toronto: School of Graphic Arts, 1947]
    76 p. illus., ports.   OTER
Tough, Allen MacNeill.
    Learning without a teacher; a study of tasks and assistance during adult self-teaching projects. [Toronto] Ontario Institute for Studies in Education [1967]
    92 p. (Ontario Institute for Studies in Education. Educational research series, no. 3).   OTU
Tracz, George Stephen, 1938–
    A computerized system for school bus routing, by G.S. Tracz and M.J. Norman. [Toronto] Ontario Institute for Studies in Education [c1970]
    vi, 29 p. illus., maps. (Department of Educational Planning. Reports of the County School Board Project, no. 1).   OTU
— The dynamics of teacher costs: a dollar flow analysis, by G.S. Tracz and W.A. Burtnyk. Toronto: Department of Educational Planning, Ontario Institute for Studies in Education, 1974.
    iii, 22 p. tables.   OTER
— Teacher cost models, by G.S. Tracz and W.A. Burtnyk. Toronto: Department of Educational Planning, Ontario Institute for Studies in Education, 1972.
    vii, 90 leaves. diagrs., tables.   OTER
Traub, Ross E
    Openness in schools: an evaluation study by Ross Traub, Joel Weiss and Charles Fisher, with Donald Musella and Sar Khan. [Toronto: Ontario Institute for Studies in Education, c1976]
    69 p. tables. (Research in education series, 5).
    Wentworth county, Ontario.   OTER
Wahlstrom, Merlin W
    Assessment of student achievement, a survey of the assessment of student achievement in Ontario by Merlin W. Wahlstrom and Raymond R. Danley. [Toronto: Ontario Institute for Studies in Education, 1976.
    x, 121 p. tables.   OTER

— A survey of assessment of student achievement in Ontario: final report, by
Merlin Wahlstrom and Dawn Whitmore. [Toronto] Educational Evaluation
Center, Ontario Institute for Studies in Education, 1974.
150, 16, 10, 2 leaves.   OTER

Waniewicz, Ignacy.
Demand for part-time learning in Ontario. Toronto: Published for the
Ontario Educational Authority by the Ontario Institute for Studies in
Education, 1976.
216 p. tables.   OTER

Watson, Cicely, 1921–
Financing education, the next ten years. [Toronto] Department of
Education Planning, The Ontario Institute for Studies in Education [1970]
12 leaves. tables. (Ontario Institute for Studies in Education. Department of
Educational Planning. Educational Planning Occasional papers no. 12).
                                                                                          OTER

— School planning manual, by Cicely Watson, Saeed Quazi. Toronto: Ontario
Institute for Studies in Education, 1973.
iii, 225 p. illus.   OTU

— Specifying future educational needs in a changing political climate.
[Toronto] Department of Educational Planning, Ontario Institute for
Studies in Education [1971]
[37] leaves. tables. (Ontario Institute for Studies in Education. Department
of Educational Planning. Educational Planning Occasional Papers no.
8/71).   OTER

Watson, Cicely, 1921–   (ed.).
Educational planning: papers of the invitational conference, March 20–22,
1967. Sponsored by the Policy and Development Council, Ontario
Department of Education in conjunction with the Department of
Educational Planning, Ontario Institute for Studies in Education. [Toronto:
1967]
76 p. illus.   OTER

Weir, George Moir, 1885–1949.
The separate school question in Canada. Toronto: The Ryerson Press
[c1934]
ix, 298 p. illus.
Ontario: pp. 118–173.   OTU

Welch, Robert, 1928–
Address by the Hon. Robert Welch, minister of education, to the chief
education officer, and senior program officials of Ontario school boards as
part of the Seminar on Program Development, 1972, Ontario Room,
Macdonald Block, January 17, 1972. [Toronto] 1972.
27 leaves.   OTER

— How the Ontario school system can serve the multicultural nature of this
province. An address by the Minister of Education, Provincial Secretary for
Social Development to Ukrainian Alumni Association, St. Vladimir
Institute, January 26, 1972. Toronto: 1972.
30 leaves.   OONL

Wickins, Cecil James, 1898–
  Research departments established by boards of education in Ontario; a
  study prepared for the Ontario Educational Research Council. [Toronto:
  Ontario Educational Research Council, 1966?]
  v, 60 leaves.   OTER
Wilson, Arthur Lawrence.
  Assessment act, Public schools act and Separate schools act, condensed and
  classified. Toronto: Shepard Bros. [1898]
  127 p.   OTAR$8
Wilson, John Donald, 1936–   (ed.).
  Canadian education: a history, edited by J. Donald Wilson, Robert M.
  Stamp and Louis Philippé Audet. Scarborough, Ontario: Prentice–Hall
  [1970]
  xiv, 528 p. illus., ports.
  Several chapters on Ontario.   OTU
Wilson, R   A   P
  Financing public education in Ontario, 1975. [Toronto] OSSTF, 1975.
  107 p. graphs, tables.   OTER
Winchester, John.
  Report of investigation Board of Education contracts. Toronto: 1913.
  198 p.
  Toronto Board of Education contacts.   OTU
Wittenberg, Alexander Israel, 1926–
  General education as a challenge for creative scholarship. Toronto: York
  University [c1964]
  viii, 45 p.   OTU
Women Teachers' Association of Toronto.
  The story of the Women Teachers' Association of Toronto. Toronto:
  Thomas Nelson & Sons Limited [1930–1963]
  2 v.
  Contents: v. 1, 1892–1930 by the Association; v. 2, 1931–1963 by Eva K.
  Walker.
  v. 2 was published by Copp Clark Publishing Co. Limited.   OTER
Wright, Edgar Norman, 1932–
  Learning English as a second language: a summary of Research Department
  studies [Toronto: Research Department, Board of Education for the city of
  Toronto] 1970.
  14 leaves.   OONL
— Parents occupations, student's mother tongue and immigrant status : further
  analysis of the every student survey data, by E.N. Wright and D.B. McLeod.
  [Toronto: Research Department, Board of Education for the city of
  Toronto] 1971.
  23 leaves. maps, tables.   OONL
— Programme placement related to selected countries of birth and selected
  languages (further every student survey analysis). [Toronto: Research
  Department, Board of Education for the city of Toronto] 1971.
  31 leaves. tables.   OONL

— Student's background and its relationship to class and programme in school, the every student survey. [Toronto: Research Department, Board of Education] 1970.
61 leaves. tables. (Research service [no. 91]).   OTER

— Students of non-Canadian origin: age on arrival, academic achievement and ability, by E.N. Wright, C.A. Ramsey [Toronto: Research Department, Board of Education] 1970.
40 leaves. diagrs., tables.

Wright, J   R
Development alternatives: Ontario Teachers' Federation Eagle Lake property, by J.R. Wright and W.B. Cormack. [Guelph, Ontario] Centre for Resources Development, University of Guelph, 1970?]
iv, 109 leaves. [18] leaves of maps.   OLU

York County, Ontario. Board of Education. Committee on an Alternative to the Present Educational Trends.
An alternative. Report. [Toronto] Division of Planning and Development, York County Board of Education, 1970.
21 leaves.   OTER

Young, Vivienne.
Patterns of dropping out, by Vivienne Young and Carol Reich. [Toronto: Research Department, Board of Education] 1974.
55 p. tables. (Research service report 129).   OTER

Zsigmond, Z   E
Enrolment in educational institutions by province, 1951-2 to 1980-81 by Z.E. Zsigmond and C.J. Wenaas. Ottawa: Queen's Printer, 1970.
viii, 303 p. charts, tables. (Economic Council of Canada. Staff study no. 25).
                                                                                    OKQ

Periodical Articles

The administrators of educational affairs in Ontario. Canada Educational Monthly 25: 437, 1903.
Richard Harcourt, minister of education; John Miller, deputy minister of education.

Alexander, R
Some recollections of the early history of the Ontario Educational Association. Canada Educational Monthly 26: 197–201, 1904.

Anderson, Joan.
Teacher militancy: an appraisal. Ontario Education 6(no. 1): 2–10, 1974.
Ontario teachers.

Appleby, Barry and Peter P. Ferlejowski.
Opportunity through on-the-job training. Ontario Economic Review 4(no. 1–2): 5–8, 1966.

Bancroft, George W
Socio-economic mobility and educational achievement in southern Ontario. Ontario Journal of Educational Research 5: 27–31, 1962–63.

Barrett, Harry O
    The Ontario Educational Research Council. Ontario Journal of
    Educational Research 1(no. 2): 143–144, 1958–59.
Better education. Canadian Forum 29: 195–196, 1949.
Boyce, Gerald E
    The Bayside property and school, 1784–1874. Ontario History 64: 181–200,
    1972.
Bryant, J   E
    The administration of our educational affairs. Canada Educational Monthly
    5: 322–325, 1883.
Burns, William.
    The Ontario College of Preceptors. Canada Educational Monthly 8:
    350–351, 1886.
Canada: II. The bilingual school question. The Round Table 18: 163–170, 1927.
Canada: III. The bilingual school question in Ontario. The Round Table 5:
    661–669, 1915.
Canada: III. French in the schools. The Round Table 3: 144–151, 1912.
Canada: IV. French in the schools. The Round Table 2: 354–357, 1912.
Charbonneau, Louis.
    La situation des écoles bilingues de l'Ontario en 1950. Culture 11: 90–95,
    1950.
Children's recreational reading in Ontario; a survey and a report. Ontario
    Library Review 39: 76–77, 1955.
Cowley, R   H
    The Macdonald school gardens. Queen's Quarterly 12: 390–419, 1904/1905.
[Davis, William G   ]
    From the Minister [of Education]. Ontario Education Review 11,
    November, 1967.
Donovan, Cornelius: printer, teacher, educator. Wentworth Historical Society.
    Papers and Records 11: 43–45, 1924.
Douglass, Hugh.
    The story of Rockwood Academy. Wentworth Bygones 8: 47–59, 1969.
Driscoll, Helen.
    The changing status of teachers of retarded children in Ontario. Ontario
    Education Review 4(no. 5): 1, 1970.
Dunlop, W   J
    Workers' Educational Association of Ontario. Social Welfare 7: 229–230,
    1925.
Easton, J   A   G
    The school building problem. Royal Architectural Institute of Canada.
    Journal 25: 185–191, 1948.
Education Centre, Toronto. Royal Architectural Institute of Canada. Journal
    39: 43–50, 1962.
Faith, hope and electricity. [editorial] Canadian Forum 28: 52, 1948.
    Education in Ontario.

Faught, (Rev.) D   T
    Report on the work of the Ontario Teachers' Federation Mathematics
    Commission. Ontario Journal of Educational Research 3: 120–128, 1960–61.
Fitzpatrick, A
    Education on the frontier. Queen's Quarterly 21: 62–68, 1913/1914.
Gavin, F   P
    Vocational training for adults in Ontario. Ontario Library Review and
    Book-Selection Guide 9: 30–32, 1924.
Girls' colleges. Canadian Magazine of Politics, Science, Art and Literature 24:
    377–379, 1905.
    In Toronto.
Glenn, Willis.
    From the President. Ontario Education Review 2, October, 1967; 2,
    January, 1968.
    Comments on the development and changes in education in Ontario.
Godbout, Arthur.
    The history of franco-ontarian schools. Orbit 2(2): 5, 1971.
Grant, W   L
    The education of the brilliant child. Queen's Quarterly 35: 370–383, 1928.
— What is wrong with education in Ontario? Canadian Forum 3: 104–105,
    1923.
Haileybury Mining School. Canadian Mining Journal 40: 455, 1919.
Hanly, Charles.
    The Toronto teach-in. Canadian Forum 45: 130–131, 1965.
Hardy, E   A
    The Ontario Educational Association: a history and a criticism. Canada
    Educational Monthly 25: 101–108, 1903.
— Literature under the new regulations. Canada Educational Monthly 25:
    388–390, 1903.
Haultain, Arnold.
    The new Ontario "readers". Canadian Magazine of Politics, Science, Art
    and Literature 33: 539–542, 1909.
Heaton, Ernest.
    Ontario's weakness. Canadian Magazine of Politics, Science, Art and
    Literature 8: 265–268, 1897.
    Education system.
Hodgins, Nora, honoured by OEA with Greer Award. Ontario Education Review
    7(no. 1) [4] 1974.
Hunt, C   H   and F   Forster.
    Educational facilities. Canadian Mining Journal 70(no. 8): 118–119, 1949.
    At Central Patricia, Pickle Crow.
Jones, Frank E
    The social origins of high school teachers in a Canadian city. Canadian
    Journal of Economics and Political Science 29: 529–535, 1963.
    Hamilton.

Joyner, Beryl L
    Economic education. Ontario Economic Review 4(no. 8–9): 4–9, 1966.
Junior Achievement grows in Ontario. Ontario Education Review 8, January,
    1968.
Katz, Michael Barry.
    Education and social change in English-speaking Canada. History of
    Education Quarterly 12: 251–459, 1972.
Keirstead, W   C
    Taxation for school purposes: the support and administration of education in
    the provinces of Canada. Canadian Chartered Accountant 30: 129–137,
    1937.
Lalonde, André.
    Le Règlement XVII et ses répercussions sur le nouvel-Ontario. Société
    Historique du Nouvel-Ontario. Documents Historiques 46–47: 7–71, 1965.
Lavell, W   Stewart.
    New theories at work in Canadian schools. Queen's Quarterly 46: 312–319,
    1939.
Lawr, D   A
    Agricultural education in nineteenth-century Ontario: an idea in search of
    an institution. History of Education Quarterly 12: 334–357, 1972.
Lowes, Barry.
    The real issues between trustees and teachers. Ontario Education Review 5,
    11, October 1967.
    Metro Toronto School Board.
McCaffrary, C   J
    The real issues between trustees and teachers; the Toronto problem – this
    year and next. Ontario Education Review 5, November 1967.
McCulley, Joseph.
    Private schools of Ontario. Canadian School Journal 13: 63–67, 1935.
McGready, S   B
    On the training of teachers for rural schools. Ontario Agricultural College
    Review 20: 363–367, 1908.
McKellar, Carlotta S   and Jessie M   Oliver.
    School history of the Canadian Head of the Lakes. Thunder Bay Historical
    Society. Papers 8: 13–17, 1917.
McKenzie, Douglas W
    Reminiscences of a rural school teacher at Purpleville – 1912–13. York
    Pioneer, 26–31, 1975.
McRobbie, K   A
    An interim report on experiments in several Ontario schools with the New
    Castle textfilm method of teaching reading in the primary grades. Ontario
    Journal of Educational Research 3: 191–197, 1960–61.
— The Toronto New Castle textfilm reading experiment. Ontario Journal of
    Educational Research 3: 133–168, 1960/61.

Madge, Helen L
  Educational achievement levels in Ontario. Ontario Economic Review 3(no. 6): 3–9, 1965.
Marshall, J
  The public schools, high schools and universities. Queen's Quarterly 14: 81–82, 1906/1907.
Mehmet, Ozay.
  Evaluation of institutional and on-the-job manpower training in Ontario. Canadian Journal of Economics 4: 362–373, 1971.
Moore, Edna L
  School health service in Ontario. The School (Secondary Edition) 29: 10–12, 1940.
Morgan, J   R   H
  The Ontario Curriculum Institute. Ontario Journal of Educational Research 7: 133–137, 1964–65.
Morrison, George W
  Adult education in Simcoe county. Canadian Forum 28: 135–136, 1948.
Mr. Drew on education. [editorial] Canadian Forum 23: 171, 1943.
[Nelson, A   E   ]
  Schools then and now; a century of schools in Perth. Western Ontario Historical Notes 11: 8–13, 1953.
Ontario Provincial Library Council.
  Brief to the Select Committee on the Utilization of Educational Facilities. Ontario Library Review 57: 15–17, 1973.
Pammett, Jon H
  The development of political orientations in Canadian school children. Canadian Journal of Political Science 4: 132–141, 1971.
Park, H   G
  The organization of the teachers of Ontario. Canada Educational Monthly 26: 228–231, 1904.
Pitman, Walter.
  The big blue schoolhouse: the Davis era in Ontario education. Canadian Forum 52 (October-November): 62–65, 1972.
Pomeroy, Elsie.
  School books for the lone frontier; miles from anywhere children are being taught, by an amazing development of the correspondence school idea. Canadian Magazine of Politics, Science, Art and Literature 78 (December): 12, 32–33, 1932.
Prentice, Alison.
  Education and the metaphor of the family: the Upper Canada example. History of Education Quarterly 12: 281–303, 1972.
  Chiefly pre-Confederation.
The Principal of Upper Canada College. Canada Educational Monthly 17: 247–249, 1895.
The proposed provincial board for teachers' certificates. Queen's Quarterly 11: 330–334, 1903/1904.

Quinlan, Frank.
    Students are not permitted. Orbit 5(5): 22–23, 1974.
    Historical collection of textbooks at Ontario Institute for Studies in
    Education.
Regulation XVII. Queen's Quarterly 35: 216, 1927.
Robbie, Roderick G
    Study of educational facilities. Ontario Education 1(5): 23–25; 1(6): 18–19,
    33–35, 1969.
Ross, George W
    How teachers are trained in the province of Ontario, Canada. Canada
    Educational Monthly 15: 295–300, 1893.
Rutledge, John R
    George Rutledge, 1794–1873; first schoolmaster of Loughborough township.
    Historic Kingston 15: 3–14, 1967.
Sandiford, Peter.
    The county board. Canadian Forum 3: 200–201, 1923.
— Local units for education. Canadian Forum 9: 308–309, 1929.
— Salaries of teachers in Ontario. The School 3: 176–182; 251–254, 1914.
Sexton, Anne M
    Obituary; John Arthur Bannister, 1875–1965. Western Ontario Historical
    Notes 21(no. 2): i–ii, 1965.
Sissons, C   B
    Little men and big issues. Canadian Forum 2: 522–524, 1922.
    Educational problems in Toronto.
Smith Report takes school tax pressure off property owners. Ontario Education
    Review 3, October, 1967.
Stamp, Robert M
    Empire day in the schools of Ontario: the training of young imperialists.
    Journal of Canadian Studies 8(no. 3): 32–42, 1973.
— Urbanization and education in Ontario and Quebec, 1867–1914. McGill
    Journal of Education 3: 127–135, 1968.
Stevens, V   S
    Vocational guidance in Ontario. Ontario Library Review 19: 63–64, 1935.
[Stewart, E   E   ]
    Position paper; a working paper from the Department of Education –
    proposed changes in teacher certification in Ontario. Ontario Education
    Review 5(no. 2): 1971.
Stewart, G   F
    The deaf children of Ontario. Canada Educational Monthly 24: 272–275,
    1902.
Strang, H   I
    Ontario Teachers' Association. Canada Educational Monthly 9: 249–255,
    1887.

Survey of educational research in Canada 1953 to 1955-56. Ontario Journal of Educational Research 1(no. 1): 3–141, 1958–59.
　　Ontario: pp. 59–99.
Sutherland, Neil.
　　"To create a strong and healthy race": school children in the public health movement, 1880–1914. History of Education Quarterly 12: 304–333, 1972.
　　Primarily Ontario.
Sykes, W　J
　　Adult education in Ottawa. Ontario Library Review and Book-Selection Guide 9: 35–36, 1924.
Teachers oppose county base for proposed new boards. Ontario Education Review 1, 4, 6, December, 1967.
Telford, Murray M
　　Oliphant's first seat of learning. Bruce County Historical Society. Yearbook 41–44, 1975.
[W　M　C　]
　　Educational reforms in Canada. Queen's Quarterly 34: 477–480, 1927.
Wilkins, Harold T
　　Schools on wheels in the wilds. United Empire n.s. 24: 510–513, 1933.
　　Northern Ontario.
Will, J　S
　　Education in Ontario – Prolegomena. Canadian Forum 16: 11–12, 1936.
Wilson, David J
　　Community co-operation in education. Industrial Canada 51(no. 4): 46–48, 1950.
　　Galt, Ontario.
Winks, Robin W
　　Negro school segregation in Ontario and Nova Scotia. Canadian Historical Review 50: 164–191, 1969.

Theses
Abray, William Ewart.
　　A critical evaluation of the Ontario Department of Education concert plan and its general effect on music education in the province of Ontario.
　　Rochester, New York: 1953.
　　vii, 131 leaves. illus., maps.
　　M.A. thesis, Eastman School of Music, University of Rochester.　U Rochester
Allen, Howard C
　　The organization and administration of the educational system of the provinces of Quebec and Ontario. Syracuse, New York: 1938.
　　vii, 117 leaves. tables.
　　Ph.D. thesis, Syracuse University.　DA
Andress, Donald Douglas, 1942–
　　The impact of apartment building and townhouse development on school planning London, Ontario. London, Ontario: 1967.
　　xv, 166 leaves. fig. (part col.), tables, graphs, maps (part fold.).
　　M.A. thesis, The University of Western Ontario (microfilm 1562).　OLU

Ansara, Joseph, 1934–
   A comparison in practice teaching patterns between Faculty of Education,
   University of Toronto and Toronto Teachers' College students in the junior
   high school. [Toronto] c1973.
   116, xxx leaves. tables.
   M.A. thesis, University of Toronto.   OTU
Armstrong, David Patrick, 1941–
   Corbett's house: the origins of the Canadian Association for Adult Education
   and its development during the directorship of E.A. Corbett, 1936–1951.
   [Toronto] 1968.
   i, 197 leaves.
   M.A. thesis, University of Toronto.   OTU
Arnold, Donald John.
   Attitudes of public school and municipal recreation authorities in
   southwestern Ontario toward policies for the joint acquisition, development,
   and utilization of school facilities for school and recreational use.
   Bloomington, Indiana: 1970.
   163 p.
   Re.D. thesis, Indiana University (microfilm 71-06947).   DA
Ault, Orvill Everitt, 1899–
   The relation of certain problems to the training of teachers in the United
   States, Ontario, France, Scotland and Germany. Edinburgh: 1935.
   332 leaves.
   Ph.D. thesis, University of Edinburgh.   U. Edinburgh
Baird, Norman Barnes.
   Educational finance and administration for Ontario. [Toronto] 1946.
   xii, 297 leaves. tables, figs., maps.
   D.Paed. thesis, University of Toronto.   OTU
Bancroft, George Winston, 1922–
   Occupational status, mobility and educational achievement of 522 males in
   southern Ontario. [Toronto] 1960.
   viii, 205 leaves. tables.
   Ph.D. thesis, University of Toronto.   OTU
Bates, Duane Adair, 1940–
   The status of music education in 1969–70 in the cities of southern Ontario
   having a population in excess of 100,000. Urbana, Illinois [1972]
   vii, 180 leaves. illus.
   Ed.D. thesis, University of Illinois at Urbana – Champaign (microfilm
   73-17,109).   DA
Beaudin, Sandra Jane.
   An examination of selected aspects of the language, arts, curricula, in four
   Canadian provinces; New Brunswick, Ontario, Alberta and British
   Columbia. Montreal, Quebec: 1970 [c1971]
   iv, 237 leaves.
   M.A. thesis, McGill University (microfilm 9202).   Can

Bhatia, Kamala Ghosh, 1917–
An explication of the perceptions of Marshall McLuban as indicated in his major works with a view to discovering his underlying philosophy and its educational and sociological implications. Buffalo, New York: 1970.
vi, 149 leaves.
Ph.D. thesis, State University of New York at Buffalo (microfilm 71-7147).
DA

Boyce, Eleanor.
Canadian readers since 1846: a study of their merits and weaknesses as instruments of education. Winnipeg: 1949.
vi, 251 leaves. tables.
Ph.D. thesis, University of Manitoba.
OTER

Branscombe, Frederic Ray.
The pre-service professional training of teachers in the province of Ontario, Canada, as it relates to instruction in the selection, production and utilization of audio-visual instructional materials. New York: 1969.
2 v. [xi, 504 leaves] tables.
Ph.D. thesis, New York University (microfilm 70-5954).
OTER

Brewin, Margaret Judith.
The establishment of an industrial education system in Ontario. [Toronto] c1967.
56 leaves.
M.A. thesis, University of Toronto.
OTU

Brooke, Wilfrid Michael, 1938–
The adult basic education teacher in Ontario: his background, problems, and need for continuing professional education. [Toronto] 1968.
iv, 113 leaves. tables.
M.A. thesis, University of Toronto (accepted 1969).
OTU

— An investigation of certain factors contributing to dropping out in an Ontario adult basic education program. [Toronto] c1973.
vii, 242 leaves.
Ph.D. thesis, University of Toronto (microfilm 16620).
OTU

Brown, Wilfred John, 1936–
Interprovincial educational differences in Canada: alternative measures of their underlying causes and their allocations. [Toronto] c1969.
ix, 155 leaves. tables, figs.
M.A. thesis, University of Toronto (microfilm 27474).
OTU

Bryans, Wendy Elizabeth, 1950–
Virtuous women at half the price: the feminization of the teaching force and early women teacher organizations in Ontario. [Toronto] 1974.
125 leaves.
M.A. thesis, University of Toronto (microfilm 31173).
OTU

Buiston, Geoffrey Victor Frank, 1944–
Temporary systems in a school district organisation: experience in the Hastings county Board of Education. [Toronto] c1976.
80 leaves.
M.A. thesis, University of Toronto.
OTU

Cameron, David Murray, 1940–
    The politics of education in Ontario, with special reference to the financial
    structure. [Toronto] c1969.
    xiii, 565 leaves. diagrs.
    Ph.D. thesis, University of Toronto (microfilm 5221).   OTU
Cameron, Maxwell A   1907–1951.
    The financing of education in Ontario. [Toronto] 1935.
    ix, 396 leaves. tables (part fold.), figs., fold. maps.
    Ph.D. thesis, University of Toronto.   OTU
Campbell, Judith, 1942–
    A study of the teacher education participation of Ontario teachers of English
    as a second language to adults. [Toronto] c1973.
    v, 156 leaves. tables.
    M.A. thesis, University of Toronto.   OTU
Cann, Marjorie Mitchell.
    An historical study of the office of coordinator of teacher education in the
    Canadian provinces of New Brunswick, Ontario, Saskatchewan, Alberta and
    British Columbia. Ann Arbor, Michigan: 1957.
    iv, 143 leaves.
    Ph.D. thesis, The University of Michigan (microfilm 58-00890).   OTER
Carlton, Richard Austin Michael, 1934–
    Differential educational achievement in a bilinqual community. [Toronto]
    c1967.
    vi, 341 leaves. diagrs., maps.
    Ph.D. thesis, University of Toronto (microfilm 12930).   OTU
Carter, Bruce Northleigh.
    James L. Hughes and the gospel of education: a study of the work and
    thought of a nineteenth century Canadian educator. [Toronto] 1966 [c1974]
    xv, 513 leaves.
    Ed.D. thesis, University of Toronto (accepted 1967) (microfilm 17757).   OTU
Cook, Brian Wayne.
    An assessment of the priorities for continuing education in Perth county,
    Ontario. Guelph, Ontario: 1973.
    v, 81 leaves. illus., maps.
    M.Sc. thesis, University of Guelph (microfilm 17976).   OGU
Cook, Gail Carol Annabel, 1940–
    Effect of federation on education expenditures in Metropolitan Toronto.
    Ann Arbor, Michigan [1968]
    vii, 91 leaves. illus., map.
    Ph.D. thesis, The University of Michigan (microfilm 69-12,078).   DA

Croal, Albert George.
  The history of the teaching of science in Ontario, 1800–1900. [Toronto]
  1940.
  234 leaves.
  D.Paed. thesis, University of Toronto.   OTU
Dalziel, Graham Garriock, 1947–
  Training teachers for the north: the early development of teacher training in
  North Bay, Ontario, 1905–1920. [Toronto: 1976]
  ii, 104 leaves.
  M.A. thesis, University of Toronto.   OTU
Davey, R   Barrie.
  The value of school records in interpreting the present standing of pupils.
  [Toronto] 1934.
  31 leaves.
  M.A. thesis, University of Toronto.   OTU
Dennison, Donald Gordon.
  The development of vocational education in Canada: a study of
  intergovernmental relations and their constitutional implications. Ottawa:
  1970.
  125, vii leaves.
  M.A. thesis, Carleton University.   OOCC
Ditchburn, Peter Bernard.
  A survey of selected characteristics of Australian teachers in Ontario, 1969.
  Calgary, Alberta: 1970.
  xiv, 158 leaves. illus.
  M.Ed. thesis, University of Calgary (microfilm 7656).   Can
Dunlop, Florence S
  Subsequent careers of non-academic boys, Ottawa. New York: 1935.
  95 p. tables.
  Ph.D. thesis, Teachers College, Columbia University.
  Ottawa special classes.   DA
— Ottawa [National Printers Limited, 1935]
  93 p. tables.   OTER
Fagbamiye, Olukayode Emmanuel Michael, 1940–
  Conflict and school district reorganization in thirty-eight southern Ontario
  counties. [Toronto] c1971.
  x, 229 leaves. tables.   OTU
  Ph.D. thesis, University of Toronto (microfilm 11570).   OTU
Flaherty, Mary Josephine, 1934–
  An enquiry into the need for continuing education for registered nurses in
  the province of Ontario. [Toronto] 1965.
  viii, 176 leaves. tables.
  M.A. thesis, University of Toronto (accepted 1966).   OTU
Fraser, Brian John, 1947–
  Education for neighbourhood and nation: the educational work of St.
  Christopher House, Toronto, 1912–1918. [Toronto] c1975.
  133 leaves.
  M.A. thesis, University of Toronto (accepted 1976).   OTU

Gaitskell, Charles Dudley.
  Art education in the province of Ontario. [Toronto] 1947.
  v, 185 leaves.
  D.Paed. thesis, University of Toronto.   OTU
Gopie, Hilton Walter, 1936–
  The relationship of personality and environmental variables to vocational
  choice. [Toronto] c1970.
  ix, 178 leaves. diagrs., tables.
  Ed.D. thesis, University of Toronto.   OTU
Goulson, Carlyn Floyd.
  An historical survey of royal commissions and other major governmental
  inquiries in Canadian education. [Toronto] 1966.
  v, 509, xxxviii leaves.
  Ed.D. thesis, University of Toronto (microfilm 27487).   OTU
Graham, Carol Ann.
  Yorkville: an exploratory study of the attitudes of Yorkville youth towards
  the educational system. [Toronto] 1968.
  vii, 124 leaves. tables.
  M.S.W. thesis, University of Toronto (microfilm 17775).   OTU
Greene, Ralph Irving, 1936–
  Various ways in which new Canadians might learn English outside the
  classroom without formal assistance. [Toronto] c1972.
  xiii, 517 leaves. tables.
  Ed.D. thesis, University of Toronto.   OTU
Haché, Jean Baptiste, 1940–
  Language and religious factors in Canadian ethnic politics of education:
  case study in power mobilization. [Toronto] 1976.
  xiv, 377 leaves.
  Ph.D. thesis, University of Toronto.   OTU
Hardy, John Howard, 1891–1945.
  Teachers' organizations in Ontario; an historical account of their part in
  Ontario educational development, and their influence on the teacher and
  teaching, 1840–1938. [Toronto] 1938.
  269 leaves.
  D.Paed. thesis, University of Toronto (accepted 1939).   OTU
Husby, Philip James.
  The relationship between education and earnings among the Canadian
  provinces. Edmonton, Alberta: 1968.
  xvi, 185 leaves.
  Ph.D. thesis, University of Alberta (microfilm).   OTER
Jain, Geneviève Laloux.
  Les manuels d'histoire du Canada et le nationalisme en Ontario et au
  Québec, 1867–1914. Montreal, Quebec: 1970.
  3, 497 [i.e. 501] feuillets.
  Ph.D. thèse, Université McGill (accepted 1970)(microfilm 7068).   Can

— Les manuels d'histoire du Canada au Québec et en Ontario, de 1867 à 1914. Quebec: Presses de l'Université Laval, 1974.
250 p. (Histoire et sociologie de la culture, 6). OTU
Johnson, Francis Henry.
Changing conceptions of discipline and pupil-teacher relations in Canadian schools. [Toronto] 1952.
xii, 429 leaves.
D.Paed. thesis, University of Toronto. OTU
Jones, Alan H
The role of pressure groups in the educational system of the province of Ontario. [Ann Arbor, Michigan] 1961.
v, 140 leaves.
M.A. thesis, The University of Michigan (microfilm). OTER
Jones, Frank Arthur.
The preparation of teachers in Ontario and the United States. Ottawa: 1916.
105 p.
D.Paed. thesis, Queen's University. OKQ
— The preparation of teachers in the province of Ontario, Canada. [Chicago] 1916.
v, 146 leaves.
M.A. thesis, University of Chicago (microfilm). OTER
Jones, Michael Allen Westover, 1942–
Neighbourhood learning centres, a study in community co-operation. [Toronto] c1976.
118 leaves. tables.
M.A. thesis, University of Toronto. OTU
Keys, George Eric Maxwell.
Certain aspects of guidance in western Australia, New South Wales and Ontario. [Toronto] 1959.
vi, 424 leaves. fold. tables.
Ed.D. thesis, University of Toronto. OTU
Klassen, Peter George.
A history of Mennonite education in Canada, 1786–1960. [Toronto] 1970 [c1975]
xii, 444 leaves. illus., tables, maps.
Ed.D. thesis, University of Toronto (microfilm 22337). OTU
Knoepfli, Heather Elizabeth Blaine, 1942–
The origin of women's autonomous learning groups. [Toronto] c1971.
xii, 284 leaves. tables, fig.
Ph.D. thesis, University of Toronto. OTU
Lajoie, Joseph Jean Guy, 1942–
A study of the Ryerson–Charbonnel controversy and its background. Ottawa: 1971.
vii, 75 leaves.
M.A. thesis, University of Ottawa. OOU

Lamy, Paul Gerard.
   A study of the social and political orientations of a sample of Quebec
   French-speaking and Ontario English-speaking school children. [Hamilton,
   Ontario] 1969.
   107 leaves. tables.
   M.A. thesis, McMaster University.   OHM
Lansdell, Clyde Edison, 1935–
   Moral education in Ontario – past, present, and future (an example of how
   social change is effected). [Toronto] 1976.
   M.A. thesis, University of Toronto.   OTU
Larson, Kenneth Louis.
   Metropolitan school government: its development and operation in Toronto.
   Berkeley, California: 1964.
   328 p.
   Ph.D. thesis, University of California, Berkeley (microfilm 64-13040).   DA
Lécuyer, André, 1924–
   Analysing, reporting, and validating a design to evaluate developmental
   agencies in the field of education. [Toronto] c1976.
   ix, 252 leaves.
   Ed.D. thesis, University of Toronto.   OTU
Lindsey, Barbara.
   Henri Bourassa, French Canada and the Ontario school question.
   [Waterloo, Ontario] 1968.
   43 leaves.
   B.A. thesis, Waterloo University College.   OWTL
Lorenz, Lyle Charles.
   A documentary approach to the teaching of a local history social studies
   unit. Calgary, Alberta: 1971.
   x, 226 leaves. illus.
   M.Ed. thesis, University of Calgary (microfilm 10193).   Can
McCaw, William Ralph, 1927–
   Non-institutional training of retarded children in Ontario. Evanston,
   Illinois: 1956.
   171 p.
   Ph.D. thesis, Northwestern University (microfilm 00-19020).   DA
— Toronto: Published in collaboration with the Ontario Association for
   Retarded Children by The Ryerson Press [1956]
   v, 91 p. forms, tables.   OTU
McNeil, Rosemary M   1936–
   The special education teacher in Ontario: analysis of factors influencing
   recruitment and retention. Windsor, Ontario: 1972.
   vi, 112 leaves. tables.
   M.A. thesis, University of Windsor (microfilm 14756).   OWA
McQueen, James.
   The development of the technical and vocational schools of Ontario. [New
   York: 1934]
   65 [2] leaves.
   M.A. thesis, Columbia University.   OTER

Mehmet, Ozay, 1938–
  Optimum choice between institutional and on-the-job adult manpower
  training activities in the province of Ontario. [Toronto] c1968.
  256 leaves. tables.
  Ph.D. thesis, University of Toronto (microfiche 19724).   OTU
Merchant, Francis Walter.
  The Ontario examination systems. London, Ontario: The London Printing
  & Lithographing Company (Limited), 1903.
  42 p.
  D.Paed. thesis, University of Toronto.   OTU
Miller, Albert Herman, 1926–
  The theory and practice of education in Ontario in the 1860's. [Vancouver,
  British Columbia] 1968.
  vii, 455 leaves. illus., facsims.
  Ed.D. thesis, University of British Columbia (microfilm) (microfilm 2384).
                                                                         OTER
Molnar, Patricia Ann.
  Some factors influencing educational and occupational aspirations of youth
  in northeastern Ontario. [Guelph, Ontario] 1974.
  xiii, 141 leaves. map, tables.
  M.Sc. thesis, The University of Guelph (microfilm 20137).   OGU
Morrow, L[eslie] Donald, 1949–
  Selected topics in the history of physical education in Ontario: from Dr.
  Egerton Ryerson to the Strathcona Trust 1844–1939. Edmonton, Alberta:
  1975.
  xvi, 408 p. illus., facsims., tables.
  Ph.D. thesis, University of Alberta (microfilm 26853).   AEU
O'Driscoll, Denis Christopher, 1929–
  Ontario attitudes towards American and British education, 1792–1950: a
  comparative study of international images. [Ann Arbor, Michigan] 1974.
  viii, 236 leaves. diagrs., tables.
  Ph.D. thesis, The University of Michigan.   OTER
Peterson, Robert James, 1939–
  Apprenticeship in Ontario, 1911–1965. [Toronto] c1971.
  158 leaves.
  M.A. thesis, University of Toronto.   OTU
Reid, Una Vivienne, 1935–
  A survey of resources for continuing education in nursing in northeastern
  Ontario. Vancouver, British Columbia: 1975 [c1976]
  ix, 214 leaves. map.
  M.S.N. thesis, University of British Columbia (microfilm 25977).   Can
Ruth, Sister.
  Henry Carr C.S.B., 1880–1963, Canadian educator, by Sister M. Ruth
  (Irene Anna Poelzer). Saskatoon: c1968.
  iv, 105 leaves.
  M.Ed. thesis, University of Saskatchewan.   SSU

Selby, John.
Local autonomy and central control in Ontario education: a study of inter-organizational relationships. Hamilton, Ontario: 1973 [c1974]
xii, 280 leaves.
Ph.D. thesis, McMaster University (microfilm 19455).   Can

Sheldon, Mary Elizabeth.
Administration and finance of education in Canada with special reference to Ontario. Hamilton, Ontario: 1939.
viii, 121 leaves.
M.A. thesis, McMaster University.   OHM

Shorey, Leonard Ludwig, 1925–
Teacher participation in continuing education activities. [Toronto] c1969.
xvii, 258 leaves. diagrs., fold. tables.
Ph.D. thesis, University of Toronto (microfilm 7934).   OTU

Stapleton, John James, 1941–
The politics of educational innovations: a case study of the credit system in Ontario. [Toronto] c1975.
xv, 299 leaves. tables, figs.
Ph.D. thesis, University of Toronto.   OTU

Stewart, William J.
Bishop Alexander MacDonell and education in Upper Canada. [Ottawa: 1942]
1 v. (unpaged).
M.A. thesis, University of Ottawa (microfilm).   OTER

Teepirach, Sakol.
A study of industrialized techniques of construction in school building in Ontario with reference to their use in Thailand. [Toronto] 1968.
1 v. (various pagings). illus., tables, plans (part fold.), charts, diagrs., maps.
M.Arch. thesis, University of Toronto.   OTU

Thomas, J   M
A study of teachers' retirement schemes in Canada including a review of the social philosophy and general principles underlying a sound retirement scheme. [Toronto] 1942.
v, 277 leaves.
D.Paed. thesis, University of Toronto.   OTU

Topley, Derrick Norman, 1926–
The professional policies of the Ontario Secondary School Teachers' Federation, 1919–1966. [Toronto] c1969.
v, 316 leaves.
Ed.D. thesis, University of Toronto.   OTU

Tsuji, Gerry K
The geography of education: a case study. Toronto: 1974.
v, 97 leaves. illus., tables, maps.
B.A. thesis, University of Toronto.   OTU

Vinet, Robert Gary.
　　An analysis of the educational effort of a single enterprise community: Red
　　Lake, Ontario. [Winnipeg, Manitoba] 1970.
　　x, 124 leaves. illus.
　　M.Ed. thesis, University of Manitoba (microfilm) (microfilm 5567). OTER
Wagner, Edith Mary.
　　Education as revealed in family papers, Ontario, 1800–1900. [Toronto]
　　1954.
　　viii, 90 leaves.
　　M.A. thesis, University of Toronto. OTU
Weinzweig, Paul Alan, 1943–
　　Socialization and subculture in elite education; a study of a Canadian boys'
　　private school. [Toronto] c1970.
　　2 v. [i.e. v, 342, 30 leaves] tables.
　　Ph.D. thesis, University of Toronto (microfilm 28015).
　　Upper Canada College. OTU
Wilkinson, Bruce William.
　　Some economic aspects of education in Canada. [Cambridge,
　　Massachusetts] 1964.
　　xii, 299 leaves. illus.
　　Ph.D. thesis, Massachusetts Institute of Technology (accepted 1965). OTER

EARLY CHILDHOOD EDUCATION

Monographs and Pamphlets

Blatz, William Emet, 1895–1964.
　　Nursery education, theory and practice, by William E. Blatz, Dorothy
　　Millechamp and Margaret Fletcher. New York: William Morrow and
　　Company, 1936.
　　xv, 365 p. illus., forms, tables.
　　Includes a discussion of the programme followed at St. George's School for
　　Child Study, University of Toronto. OTU
— Parents and the pre-school child, by William E. Blatz and Helen McM.
　　Bott. London: J.M. Dent & Sons, 1928.
　　xi, 306 p. forms, tables.
　　"The inquiry here presented has been conducted in the St. George's School
　　for Child Study at the University of Toronto". OTU
Burnham, Brian.
　　Evaluating an alternative to "junior kindergartens"; research on four-year-
　　olds who enrolled in regular kindergarten classes in York county, 1969–72.
　　[Aurora, Ontario: York County Board of Education] 1973.
　　5 leaves. OTER
Canadian Council on Child and Family Welfare.
　　The day nursery in the programme of child care. Ottawa: The Council
　　House, 1933.
　　30 p. (Publication no. 65).
　　Toronto. OH

Gaitskell, Charles D
    Art education in the kindergarten, by Charles D. Gaitskell and Margaret R.
    Gaitskell. Toronto: The Ryerson Press [c1952]
    viii, 40 p. illus.   OTER
O'Bryan, Kenneth G
    The junior kindergarten study, by K.G. O'Bryan (principal investigator)
    O.M. Kuplowska and H.M. O'Bryan. [Toronto: Ontario Institute for
    Studies in Education, c1975]
    v, 133 p.   OTER
Palmer, Judith A   1941–
    The effects of junior kindergarten on achievement: the first five years.
    [Toronto: Research Department, Board of Education for the city of
    Toronto] 1966.
    43 leaves.   OONL
— Appendix. 1966.
    59 leaves. tables.   OONL
— "Pre-school" education, pros and cons: a survey of "pre-school" education
    with emphasis on research, past, present and future. [Toronto: Research
    Department, Board of Education for the city of Toronto] 1966.
    23 leaves.   OONL
Reich, Carol Musselman, 1943–
    Follow-up of the Montessori programme. [Toronto: Research Department,
    Board of Education] 1974.
    9 leaves. (Research service report 128).   OTER
— Preschool education for inner-city children: preliminary results of an
    experimental Montessori programme. [Toronto: Research Department,
    Board of Education] 1971.
    22 p. tables. (Research service report 102).   OTER
Rogers, Rex S   1943–
    The school achievement of kindergarten pupils for whom English is a second
    language: a longitudinal study using data from the study of achievement, by
    R.S. Rogers and E.N. Wright. [Toronto: Board of Education, Research
    Department] 1969.
    26 leaves. diagrs., tables.   OTER
Scarborough, Ontario. Social Planning Council.
    Scarborough Day Care Committee brief. Toronto: Social Planning Council
    of Metropolitan Toronto, 1959.
    10 leaves.   OTU
Social Planning and Research Council of Hamilton and District. Committee on
    Day Care for Children.
    Day care needs of children in Hamilton and district. Hamilton, Ontario:
    Social Planning and Research Council of Hamilton and District, 1971.
    1 v. (various pagings).
    Chairman: J.G. Lambertus.   OTER

Social Planning and Research Council of Hamilton and District. Task Force on
Day Care.
　Day care '73: interim report to the Board of Directors. Hamilton, Ontario:
　Social Planning and Research Council of Hamilton and District, 1973.
　24 leaves.　　　　　　　　　　　　　　　　　　　　　　　　OONL
Social Planning Council of Metropolitan Toronto.
　Report on family day care of children. A report of a Co-ordinating
　Committee based on a study of experimental programs undertaken by
　Protestant Children's Homes, St. Christopher House, Victoria Day Nursery.
　Toronto [1966]
　1 v. (various pagings). illus.　　　　　　　　　　　　　　　OTU
Social Planning Council of Metropolitan Toronto. Committee on Day Care of
Children.
　Day care for children in Metropolitan Toronto; a report. [Toronto] 1968.
　a–c, 71, xxii p. map, tables.　　　　　　　　　　　　　　　OTU
— Summary statement. Toronto [1968]
　11 leaves.　　　　　　　　　　　　　　　　　　　　　　　OTU
Social Planning Council of Metropolitan Toronto. North York and Weston
Area Social Planning Committee. Governing Committee.
　Meeting day care needs in North York township; day care report to the
　Reeve and members of Council of the township of North York. [Toronto:
　Social Planning Council of Metropolitan Toronto] 1966.
　1 v. (various pagings). map.　　　　　　　　　　　　　　　OTU
South River, Ontario. East Parry Sound Board of Education.
　Kindergarten and early childhood education: research and inquiry. [South
　River, Ontario] 1972.
　1 v. (various pagings). illus.　　　　　　　　　　　　　　　OTER
Toronto. Board of Education. Research Department.
　Study of achievement, Toronto, stage 1; a profile of junior kindergarten
　pupils. [Toronto: 1961]
　[16] leaves. tables.　　　　　　　　　　　　　　　　　　　OONL
— Study of achievement: junior kindergarten: who is served and who goes.
　[Toronto] 1965.
　31 leaves. diagrs., tables.　　　　　　　　　　　　　　　　OONL

Periodical Articles
Rubin, Kenneth H
　Day care and early childhood education in Ontario: a Canadian
　perspective. Child Care Quarterly 4(3): 150–155, 1975.

Theses
Church, Edward John Maxwell, 1915–
　An evaluation of preschool education in Canada. [Toronto] 1950.
　v, 186 leaves.
　Ph.D. thesis, University of Toronto.　　　　　　　　　　　OTU

Corbett, Barbara Elizabeth.
 The public school kindergarten in Ontario 1883 to 1967: a study of the
 Froebelian origins, history, and educational theory and practice of the
 kindergarten in Ontario. [Toronto] c1968.
 vii, 277 leaves.
 Ed.D. thesis, University of Toronto (awarded 1969).   OTU
Fancy, Gail P
 Working mothers and private day nurseries. [Toronto] 1965.
 ix, 133 leaves. tables.
 M.S.W. thesis, University of Toronto.   OTU
Lewis, Herbert Samuel.
 Pre-school education in Metropolitan Toronto and market opportunities for
 educational publishers. [Toronto] 1967.
 iii, 76 [1] [1]–9 leaves.
 M.B.A. thesis, University of Toronto.   OTU
MacGregor, Mary Elizabeth.
 Day care as a service in the community; an exploratory study of the use
 made of the private day care nursery school by working mothers. [Toronto]
 1965.
 v, 154 leaves. tables.
 M.S.W. thesis, University of Toronto.   OTU
MacKenzie, John Angus.
 The working mother and private nurseries: an exploratory study of married
 working mothers in intact families who placed their children in two private
 day nurseries in Metropolitan Toronto, with special emphasis on the role of
 the father in a family with a working mother. [Toronto] 1965.
 v, 84 leaves. tables.
 M.S.W. thesis, University of Toronto.   OTU
Nosal, Ann Marie.
 Working mothers and private day nurseries; an exploratory study of
 working women who place their children in two private day nurseries in
 Metropolitan Toronto, with emphasis on "middle class culture". [Toronto]
 1965.
 v, 105 leaves. tables.
 M.S.W. thesis, University of Toronto.   OTU
Summers, Georgina M.
 A study of the Sacred Heart Orphanage. [Toronto] 1951.
 viii, 96 leaves.
 M.S.W. thesis, University of Toronto.   OTU

PRIMARY AND SECONDARY EDUCATION

Bibliography
Cockburn, Ilze (comp.).
  Elementary teacher education certification: an annotated bibliography,
  1963–1973. Toronto: Library, Reference and Information Services, Ontario
  Institute for Studies in Education, 1974.
  x, 44 p.   OTER
Guillet, Edwin Clarence, 1898–1975.
  Bio-bibliography of Dr. Edwin C. Guillet. Kingston, Ontario: Douglas
  Library, Queen's University, 1970.
  x, 23 p. port. (Douglas Library. Occasional papers, no. 3).
  Edited by Margaret Clogg.   OTU
Taylor, Ruth (comp.).
  The nongraded school: an annotated bibliography. [Toronto] The Library,
  Reference and Information Services, Ontario Institute for Studies in
  Education, 1973.
  x, 40 p. (Current bibliography no. 5).   OTER

Monographs and Pamphlets
Addiction Research Foundation.
  A preliminary report on the attitudes and behaviour of Toronto students in
  relation to drugs. Toronto: 1969.
  1 v. (various pagings). graphs, tables.   OTU
Alcoholism and Drug Addiction Research Foundation of Ontario.
  The extent of drug use in Metropolitan Toronto schools: a study of changes
  from 1968 to 1970. Toronto: The Foundation, 1970.
  1 v. (various pagings). tables.   OTMCL
Amoss, Harold Edwin, 1880–
  Elementary science in the secondary schools of Ontario. Toronto: University
  of Toronto Press, n.d.
  125 p.   OTER
— Training handicapped children, by H.E. Amoss and L. Helen DeLaporte.
  Toronto: The Ryerson Press [c1933]
  328 p. illus.
  Ontario public and separate schools.   OTER
Arnoldi, Frank.
  Upper Canada College, 1829–1904. An epoch in Canadian history: an
  appreciation. Toronto: The Upper Canada College Old Boy's Association
  [1904]
  1 v. (unpaged). illus., ports.   OTAR
Attendance at school in Ontario, the right and the duty. [Toronto] Ontario
  Institute for Studies in Education, 1976.
  ii, 36, 12 leaves. (Interaction of law and education, no. [2]). OTER

Bamijoke, Folorunso.
> The role of the secondary school vice principal: survey of the secondary
> school vice principals of the Etobicoke Board of Education, by Folorunso
> Bamijoke, Donald Musella and Steven Lawton. [Toronto] Department of
> Educational Administration, Ontario Institute for Studies in Education,
> 1973.
> v, 85 leaves.   OTER

Bargen, Peter Frank.
> The legal status of the Canadian public school pupil. Toronto: Macmillan
> Company of Canada Limited [c1961]
> xiv, 172 p.
> Separate schools for Negroes in Ontario: pp. 33–36.   OTU

Barker, Catherine (comp.).
> Innovations in Ontario schools, 1968-69: a compendium. [Toronto] Liaison
> Section, Office of Development, Ontario Institute for Studies in Education,
> 1969.
> 52 leaves.   OTER

Beattie, Kim, 1900–1963.
> Ridley: the story of a school. With collaboration in research by A.H.
> Griffith. St. Catharines, Ontario: Ridley College [1963]
> 2 v. illus., ports., tables.   OTU

Belcourt, Napoléon Antoine, 1860–1932.
> Bilingualism: address delivered before the Quebec Canadian Club at
> Quebec, Tuesday, March 28th 1916. Quebec: Telegraph Print., 1916.
> 16 p.
> Bi-lingualism in Ontario schools.   OTU

Bell, Walter Nehemiah.
> The development of the Ontario high school [1790–1882. Toronto]
> University of Toronto Press [c1918]
> 161 [3] p. tables.   OTU

Bennett, John Martin.
> Separate Catholic schools in northern Ontario: Pembroke to Manitoba
> boundary. n.p. [1959]
> 1 v. (unpaged).   OTAR

Bordeleau, Gabriel.
> Sondage sur les inventions educatives et professionnelles des éléves franco-
> ontariens des écoles secondaires de l'Ontario en 12e et 13e années
> (1974–1975) par Gabriel Bordeleau, Louis M. Desjardins. [Toronto?] Le
> Conseil consultatif des affairs franco-ontariennes, 1976.
> iv, 111 p.   OTY

Brault, Lucian, 1904–
> Bref exposé de l'enseignement bilingue au xxe siècle dans l'Ontario et les
> autres provinces. [Kingston, Ontario: Privately printed] 1966.
> 36 p.   OTU

Brehaut, Willard, 1928–
  Ontario elementary school teachers' evaluation of their teacher preparation
  programme final report. A research project conducted by Willard Brehaut,
  principal investigator and Mohindra Gill, co-investigator, with the
  assistance of Gurpyari Kobly and Alexander Gray. [Toronto] Ontario
  Institute for Studies in Education, 1975.
  1 v. (various pagings). tables.   OTER
— A preliminary look at the Carnegie students in grade 12 in Ontario schools;
  analysis of the replies from the student and staff questionnaires. [Toronto]
  Department of Educational Research, Ontario College of Education,
  University of Toronto, 1964.
  vi, 15 p. tables. (Carnegie Study of Identification and Utilization of Talent
  in High School and College. Bulletin no. 8).   OTER
— Survey of achievement in English and Arithmetic in grades 9 and 10 of
  Ontario secondary schools. Toronto: Department of Educational Research.
  Ontario College of Education [University of Toronto] 1959.
  vi, 18 p. tables. (Educational research series, no. 30).
  At head of title: The Ontario Secondary School Headmasters' Association
  Study. Report no. 1.   OTER
— Survey of achievement in grades 9 and 10 of Ontario secondary schools.
  Toronto: Department of Educational Research, Ontario College of
  Education [University of Toronto] 1961.
  viii, 31 p. map. tables. (Educational research series, no. 33).
  At head of title. The Ontario Secondary School Headmasters' Association
  Study. Report no. 2.   OTER
— A survey of factors related to variations in the cost of transportation of
  elementary and secondary school pupils in Ontario, 1953-54. [Toronto]
  Department of Educational Research, Ontario College of Education,
  University of Toronto, 1955.
  vi, 81 p. tables. (Information series, no. 1).   OTER
Brown, Corbin A
  Elementary school supervision in Ontario. Toronto: The Ryerson Press
  [c1949]
  76 p. (The Ryerson Educational Monographs).   OTER
Brown, Wilfred John, 1936–
  The impact of federal financial support on elementary and secondary
  education in Canada. Ottawa: Canadian Teachers' Federation, 1974.
  284 p. graphs, tables.   OONL
Bruce Township School Area Board.
  History of schools of Bruce township. [Bruce township, Ontario: 1965]
  49 p. illus., ports.   OTU
Bryant, John Ebenezer, 1849–
  Agriculture in public schools. An address delivered before the members of
  the Ontario Teachers' Association at their thirteeth annual convention held
  at Niagara-on-the-Lake, August, 1890. Toronto: Warwick & Sons, 1891.
  28 p.   OOA

Bureau of Municipal Research. Toronto.
    Biographies of individual schools under the Toronto Board of Education.
    Toronto: Bureau of Municipal Research, 1920–21.
    2 v.
    Contents: v. 1, York Street School; v. 2, Park School.   OTU
— Interim reports of the Toronto school survey. Toronto: Bureau of Municipal
    Research, 1920–21.
    5 parts. in 2 v. plan, diagrs.   OTU
— Measurement of educational waste in the Toronto public schools: an
    historical and statistical statement... with suggestions for improvements in
    administrative methods. Toronto: The Bureau, 1920.
    33 p. tables.   OONL
Burnham, Brian.
    A day in the life: case studies of pupils in open plan schools. [Toronto]
    Research Office, Division of Planning and Development, York County
    Board of Education, 1970.
    62 leaves.   OTER
— The elementary school in Ontario, 1966–1969: practices and trends in
    program development, organization and resources. [Toronto] Office of
    Development, Ontario Institute for Studies in Education [1969]
    73 p. tables.   OTER
— The secondary school in Ontario, 1966–1969: practices and trends in
    program development, organization and resources. [Toronto] Office of
    Development, Ontario Institute for Studies in Education [1969]
    72 p. tables.   OTER
Burnham, Brian (comp.).
    New designs for learning: highlights of the reports of the Ontario
    Curriculum Institute, 1963–1966. Edited and with an introduction by Brian
    Burnham. [Toronto] Published for the Ontario Institute for Studies in
    Education by University of Toronto Press [c1967]
    xi, 326 p. Illus., group port. (Ontario Institute for Studies in Education.
    Curriculum series, no. 1).   OTU
Burwash, Nathanael, 1839–1918.
    Egeron Ryerson. Toronto: Morang & Co., Limited, 1903.
    303 p. port. (Makers of Canada, v. 13).   OTU
— Reprinted 1906 (Parkman edition).   OTU
— Reprinted 1910.
    Bound with: Leacock, Stephen; Baldwin, Lafontaine, Hincks.   OTU
Cameletti, John R
    A history of the separate schools in the city of Sault Ste. Marie. Sault Ste.
    Marie, Ontario: Sault Ste. Marie Separate School Board, 1967.
    32 p.   OTAR
Cameron, David Murray, 1940–
    Schools for Ontario; policy making, administration and finance in the
    1960's. [Toronto] University of Toronto Press [c1972]
    xvi, 331 p. illus., map, tables.   OTU

Canada. Bureau of Statistics.
Height and weight survey of Toronto elementary school children, 1939.
Ottawa: 1942.
36 p.   OOS
Canadian Council on Child Welfare.
Special training for school-age children in need of special care. Ottawa: The
Council House, 1925.
15 p. (Publication no. 16).
Ontario.   OONL
Canadian Facts Company Ltd.
A survey of further educational and career opportunities for graduates of the
four-year arts and science high school program , part II (Ontario outside
Metropolitan Toronto). Conducted for Ontario Educational Research
Council. [Toronto: 1968?]
1 v. (various pagings). tables.   OTER
Canadian Teachers' Federation. Research Division.
Teacher influence on curriculum: a study of the part played by teachers in
curriculum revision and implementation in Ontario, 1948–1958. Ottawa:
The Federation, 1959.
56 p. (Research study no. 4).   OTER
— Supplement. 1959.
xi, 127 leaves. tables.   OTER
Carter, Francis Gerard.
Judicial decisions on denominational schools. 1st ed. Toronto: Ontario
Separate School Trustees Association, 1962.
xvi, 373 p.   OTU
Charlton, John, 1829–1910.
Equal rights... open letter to Rev. Principal Caven, May 9, 1890. Ottawa:
1890.
4 p.
Separate school question in Ontario and Quebec.   OKQ
Clinton County Grammer School, Clinton, Ontario.
The grammar school system of Ontario: a correspondence between the
Board of Trustees of the Clinton County Grammar School and the Rev. E.
Ryerson. [Clinton, Ontario] Reprinted from the Clinton *New Era*, 1868.
19 p.   OOA
Comité de Theologiens de haute autorité sur les Ecoles Bilinques.
La crise scolaire dans l'Ontario. Travail sur les écoles bilinques. n.p.: 1914.
14 p.   OOA
Committee on the Implementation of Change in the Classroom.
Planning and implementing change in Ontario schools: a report. [Toronto]
Office of Development, Ontario Institute for Studies in Education [1967]
39 p. diagrs.   OTER
Conway, Clifford B
The hearing abilities of children in Toronto public schools. Toronto:

Department of Educational Research, Ontario College of Education
[University of Toronto c1937]
132 p. diagrs., tables. (Department of Educational Research. Bulletin no. 9).
OTER

Costisella, Joseph.
Le scandale des écoles séparées en Ontario. Montreal: Editions de l'homme
[c1962]
124 p.   OTU

Craven, William.
Equal rights: recent modifications of the separate school law are in substance
what our platform demands; all attempts to make party capital out of the
separate school question are either ignorant or dishonest. Toronto: 1890.
6 p.   OOA

Crawford, Patricia J   1940–
An evaluation of the French program in North York at the grade 6 level, by
Patricia Crawford and Lynne Brenner. [North York, Ontario: Board of
Education] 1972.
47 leaves. illus.   OTER

Cummings, Harley Richards, 1909–
The city of Ottawa public schools: a brief history by H.R. Cummings and
W.T. MacSkimming. With a foreword by Eileen Scotton. [Ottawa] Ottawa
Board of Education, 1971.
102 p. illus., ports.   OTER

— Dr. J.H. Putman, 1866–1940, by H.R. Cummings. Life with father by Irene
Putman. Ottawa: 1969.
17 p. port.
Cover title: John Harold Putman, Ottawa educationalist.
Contents: Dr. J.H. Putman 1866–1940, by H.R. Cummings; Life with
father, by Irene Putman.   OTER

Damania, Laura.
Egerton Ryerson. [Don Mills, Ontario: Fitzhenry & Whiteside, c1975]
59 p. illus., facsims., map, ports. (The Canadians).   OONL

Darrah, James Robert, 1927–
Roman Catholic separate school support. [St. Thomas, Ontario] Municipal
World Limited, c1963.
50 p. diagrs.   OONL

Davis, William Grenville, 1929–
The merit and value of a single, universally accessible, publicly-supported
secondary school system. [Toronto] 1971.
[7] p.
Also published in French.   OTER

— Le mérite et la valeur générale d'un système unique d'écoles secondaires
soutenu par l'Etat et accessible à tous. [Toronto] 1971.
11 leaves.
Also published in English.   OTER

Dawson, Donald Allan, 1940–
  Economics of scale in the public secondary school education sector in
  Ontario, by D.A. Dawson. Hamilton, Ontario: 1970.
  52 leaves. illus., diagrs. (Department of Economics, McMaster University.
  Working paper no. 70-04). OTU
Denniss, Gary.
  A brief history of the schools in Muskoka. Bracebridge, Ontario:
  Herald–Gazette Press, 1972.
  222 p. illus., maps, ports. OTU
Denton, Frank Trevor, 1930–
  The influence of socio-economic variables on family size and school
  attendance in Wentworth county, Ontario, 1871; a statistical analysis of
  historical micro-data by Frank T. Denton and Peter J. George. Hamilton,
  Ontario: Department of Economics, McMaster University, 1971.
  19 [6] leaves. (Working paper, no. 71-08). OTU
Dickson, George, 1946–   (ed.).
  A history of Upper Canada College, 1829–1892. With contributions of old
  Upper Canada College boys, lists of head-boys, exhibitioners, university
  scholars and medalists, and a roll of the school. Compiled and edited by
  George Dickson and G. Mercer Adam... Toronto: Rowsell and Hutchison,
  1893.
  327 p. front., illus., plates, ports. OTAR OKQ
Easson, McGregor.
  The intermediate school in Ottawa. [Ottawa] The Author [1934]
  123 p. tables. OTER
Easton, Patrick W
  Secondary school survivors: a follow-up study of students included in the
  1955–57 survey. [Toronto] Department of Educational Research, Ontario
  College of Education [University of Toronto] 1963.
  vi, 11 p. tables. (Educational research series, no. 34).
  At head of title: The Ontario Secondary School Headmasters' Association
  Study Report no. 3. OTER
Ecumenical Study Commission on Religious Education.
  A brief concerning religion in the public schools of Ontario for the
  Honourable the Minister of Education in Ontario. Toronto: Ecumenical
  Institute of Canada [1970]
  8 p.
  Chairmen: Canon H.L. Puxley. OTU
Educational Consultants of Canada.
  Feasibility report concerning the intregration of Jewish schools. [Willowdale,
  Ontario: Board of Education for the Borough of North York, 1974.]
  75 p. tables. OTY
— An interim report concerning the feasibility of the Board of Education of
  North York assuming responsibility for the "General studies" program in the
  private schools of the Board of Jewish Education, Toronto, Ontario. [Don
  Mills, Ontario] 1974.
  75 p. tables. OTC

Edwards, Edwin Wesley.
    The history of Alma College St. Thomas, Ontario. Printed by the authority
    of the College Board. [St. Thomas, Ontario] 1927.
    47 p. illus., ports.   OLU
Edwards, John Wesley, 1865–1929.
    The wedge: an exhaustive study of public and separate school legislation in
    the province of Ontario. Toronto: Sentinal Publishing Co. Limited, 1923.
    129 p. tables.   OTU
Ellis, Maxyne Evelyn Dormer, 1925–
    Elementary school teachers-in-training, their qualifications and success at
    teachers' colleges, by M. Dormer Ellis, Mohindra Gill and H.W. Savage
    [Toronto] Ontario Institute for Studies in Education, 1967.
    ix, 65 p. map, tables. (Atkinson Study of Utilization of Student Resources.
    Report no. 13).   OONL
— A survey of opinions concerning promotion policies and practices in the
    secondary schools of Metropolitan Toronto, by M.E. Dormer Ellis and
    Mohindra P. Gill. [Toronto: Metropolitan Toronto Educational Research
    Council] 1964.
    vii, 145 leaves. tables. (Research publication no. 4).   OTER
Ellis, W   S
    A report on elementary technical education for Ontario. Kingston, Ontario:
    Daily News Office, 1900.
    40 p.   OKQ
Equal Rights Association.
    Address by the Provincial Council to the people of Ontario dealing mainly
    with the separate schools. Toronto: Equal Rights Association [1890]
    8 p.   OTAR
Federation of Women Teachers' Associations of Ontario. Educational Studies
    Committee.
    A survey of the problems of female rural elementary school teachers in
    Ontario, 1960–61. [Toronto] The Federation, 1961.
    172 p. fold. map, tables.
    Chairman: Edith Fulcher.   OTER
Federation of Women Teachers' Associations of Ontario. Research Committee.
    Study of teacher workload, conducted by FWTAO Research Committee with
    the assistance of Research Seminar participants. Toronto: 1970?]
    38 p.   OONL
Federation of Women Teachers' Associations of Ontario. Status Committee.
    The relative achievement of pupils in schools of varying sizes. Toronto: 1965.
    vi, 37 p. tables.   OONL
Fenwick, George Roy.
    The function of music in education: incorporating a history of school music
    in Ontario. Toronto: W.J. Gage and Company Limited [c1951]
    v, 89 p.   OTER

Fleming, William Gerald, 1924–1975.
  Atkinson study of utilization of student resources. Report. [Toronto]
  Department of Educational Research, Ontario College of Education,
  University of Toronto, 1957–1967.
  13 v. tables, 4 supplementary volumes.
  Contents: no. 1, Background and personality factors associated with
  educational and occupational plans and careers of Ontario grade 13
  students; no. 2, Ontario grade 13 students: who are they and what happens
  to them? no. 3, Aptitude and achievement scores related to immediate
  educational and occupational choices of Ontario grade 13 students; no. 4,
  Ontario grade 13 students: their aptitude, achievement, and immediate
  destination; no. 5, Personal and academic factors as predictors of first year
  success in Ontario universities; no. 6, A first-year follow-up of Atkinson
  students who enrolled in hospital schools of nursing, by Willard Brehaut; no.
  7, A follow-up study of Atkinson students in certain non-degree courses of
  further education beyond secondary school; no. 8, Barriers to university: a
  study of students prevented from or delayed in attending university, by J.A.
  Pipher; no. 9, The use of predictive factors for the improvement of university
  admission requirements; no. 10, From grade 13 to employment: a follow-up
  study of students who entered employment immediately after leaving school
  by E.R. Eastwood and W.G.Fleming; no. 11, Characteristics and
  achievement of students in Ontario universities; no. 12, A follow-up study of
  Atkinson students who became secondary school teachers by Walter A.
  Cruickshank and Trevor J. Wigney; no. 13, Elementary school teachers-in-
  training: their qualifications and success at teachers' colleges, by M. Dormer
  Ellis, Mohindra Gill, and H.W. Savage; Supplementary report no. 1, An
  evaluation of the cooperative English test of effectiveness of expression for use
  in Ontario, by H.W. Savage; Supplementary report no. 2, The Kuder
  preference record – vocational as a predictor of post-high school educational
  and occupational choices; Supplementary report no. 3, An evaluation of the
  Brown Holtzman survey of study habits and attitudes for use in Ontario, by
  H.W. Savage; Supplementary report no. 4, An evaluation of the Kuder
  preference record: personal for use in Ontario.   OTU
— Education: Ontario's preoccupation. [Toronto] University of Toronto Press
  [c1972]
  xvi, 330 p. charts.
  Companion volume to: *Ontario's educative society*, by W.G. Fleming.   OTU
— Estimates of teacher supply and demand in Ontario secondary schools for
  1957–72. [Toronto] Department of Educational Research, Ontario College
  of Education, University of Toronto [c1956]
  v, 20 leaves. tables. (Information series, no. 3).   OTER
— Estimate of teaching supply and demand in Ontario secondary schools for
  1959–68. [Toronto] Department of Education Research, Ontario College of
  Education, University of Toronto, 1959.
  ii, 10 leaves. tables. (Information series, no. 12).   OTER

— Factors affecting the predictive accuracy of Ontario grade XIII results. Toronto: Department of Educational Research. Ontario College of Education, University of Toronto, 1955.
viii, 46 p. (Department of Educational Research. Bulletin no. 16).   OTER
— Ontario's educative society. [Toronto] University of Toronto Press [c1971–1972]
7 v. illus., maps, diagrs., tables.
Contents: v. 1, The expansion of the educational system; v. 2, The administrative structure; v. 3, Schools, pupils and teachers; v. 4, Post-secondary and adult education; v. 5, Supporting institutions and services; v. 6, Significant developments in local school systems; v. 7, Educational contributions of associations.   OTU
— A study of factors relating to achievement among rural elementary schools in an Ontario county: 1955-56 rural school survey. [Toronto] Department of Educational Research, Ontario College of Education, University of Toronto, 1959.
iv, 19 leaves. (Information series no. 11).   OTER
— A study of high school plans among grade 8 pupils in Oxford county: 1955-56 rural school survey. [Toronto] Department of Educational Research, Ontario College of Education, University of Toronto, 1958.
24 leaves. tables. (Information series, no. 8).   OTER
— A study of social and recreational activities of grade 9 students with different elementary school backgrounds: 1955-56 rural school survey. Toronto: Department of Educational Research, Ontario College of Education, University of Toronto, 1960.
vi, 40 leaves. tables. (Information series, no. 13).   OTER
— Survey of scholastic results of the class entering arts, University of Toronto, in 1949. [Toronto] Department of Educational Research, Ontario College of Education, University of Toronto [1955]
viii, 44 p. tables. (Information series, no. 2).   OTER
Flowers, John F
Some characteristics of the Carnegie students in grades 10 and 11 in Ontario schools: analysis of the replies from the student and staff questionnaires. [Toronto] Department of Educational Research, Ontario College of Education, University of Toronto, 1964.
vii, 24 p. graphs, tables. (Carnegie Study of Identification and Utilization of Talent in High School and College. Bulletin no. 7).   OTER
Fluxgold, Howard.
Federal financial support for secondary education and its effect on Ontario, 1900–1972. Toronto: Ontario Teachers' Federation [c1972]
viii, 168 p.   OTER
Flynn, Louis J   1902–
At school in Kingston, 1850–1973: the story of Catholic education in Kingston and district. [Kingston, Ontario: Frontenac, Lennox and Addington county Roman Catholic Separate School Board, 1973.
223 p. illus., port., map.   OTU

Foght, Harold Waldstein, 1869–
  The school system of Ontario with special reference to rural schools.
  Washington, D.C.: Government Printing Office, 1915.
  58 p. plates, maps. (United States Office of Education. Bulletin no. 32).
  OTER

Gaitskell, Charles Dudley.
  Art education in the province of Ontario. Toronto: The Ryerson Press
  [c1948]
  viii, 55 p.   OTU

Gauthier, Robert, 1902–
  Une étude sur l'etat des écoles bilingues de l'Ontario, by Robert Gauthier [et
  al.] n.p.: 1944.
  [25] p. illus., tabl.   OOU

Gilbert, Vernon K
  Let each become: an account of the implementation of the Credit Diploma
  in the secondary school of Ontario. [Toronto] Guidance Centre, Faculty of
  Education, University of Toronto [c1972]
  88 p.   OTER

Gill, Mohindra Pal.
  Current policies and practices concerning programs for emotionally
  disturbed children in the Ontario school system, 1972-73: a final report by
  M.P. Gill and H. Silverman. [Toronto] Ontario Institute for Studies in
  Education [1972]
  x, 199 leaves. map.   OTER

— Facts and opinions about Toronto pupils in grades 7 and 8: an analysis of
  the student and staff questionaires for the Toronto Extension of the Carnegie
  study by Mohindra Gill [et al. Toronto] Department of Educational
  Research, Ontario College of Education, University of Toronto, 1963.
  vii, 61 p. tables. (Carnegie Study of Identification and Utilization of Talent
  in High School and College. Bulletin no. 3).   OTER

Godbout, Arthur.
  L'Origine des écoles françaises dans l'Ontario. [Ottawa] Les Editions de
  l'Université d'Ottawa, 1972.
  xvi, 183 p. facsims.   OTER OOU

Great Britain. Board of Education.
  Secondary education in Ontario, prepared by E.G. Savage. London: H.M.
  Stationery Office, 1928.
  101 p. tables. (Educational pamphlets no. 53).   OTER

Greenfield, T   Barr.
  Developing and assessing objectives for school system planning: a report for
  the Board of Education for the Borough of York. [Toronto] Department of
  Educational Administration, Ontario Institute for Studies in Education,
  1972.
  62 leaves. tables.   OTER

Grey County, Ontario. Board of Education.
  Plans for education in Grey county. n.p.: 1972.
  14 leaves. diagrs.   OTER

Grey County, Ontario. Board of Education. Aims and Objectives Council, 1971.
Aims and objectives of education for Grey county. n.p. [1971]
21 leaves.   OTER
Grey County, Ontario. Board of Education. Aims and Objectives Council, 1972.
Aims and objectives of education for Grey county and suggested goals for
schools. n.p. [1972?]
22 leaves.   OTER
Groulx, Lionel Adolphe, 1878–1967.
L'Enseignement français au Canada. Montreal: Librairie Granger Frères,
1931–33.
2 v.
Contents: v. 1, Dans le Québec; v. 2, Les écoles des minorités.
Ontario: v. 2, pp. 194–239.   OTU
Groves, Lorne R
Aspects of educational administration, school organization and curriculum
development in England and Ontario; with particular reference to the pre-
secondary level. [London: 1970]
xiii, 261 leaves. 2 fold. illus., facsims., forms, maps, plans.
A report submitted to the Institute of Education, University of London,
England, for the Associateship Award, June 1970.   OTER
Gruneau Research Associates.
Attitudes toward elementary school teachers in Ontario: a research study.
Toronto: 1968.
iii, 68, 12 p.   OONL
Hale, Lynda.
The little red school house, compiled and written by Lynda Hale, Joy Nicol
and Carol Patterson. n.p. [1973?]
105 p. illus.
Schools in Wellington county.   OTAR
Hamilton, Ontario. Senior Public Schools Principals.
A study of the principles and practices of the senior public school in
Hamilton, Ontario. Editorial Committee: G.R. Force [et al.] Toronto:
Published for the Board of Education for the city of Hamilton by W.J. Gage
Limited [c1965]
xiii, 138 p. illus., ports.   OTER
Hanchard, Alan J
A study of public education in Ontario and the development and
organization of the authority responsible for its government and direction.
n.p.: 1966.
42, 6 p. [6] leaves. charts.   OTU
Hastings County, Ontario. Board of Education.
Reorganization of administration. n.p. [1973]
21 leaves.   OTER
Hedges, Henry George.
Using volunteers in schools [final report. St. Catharines, Ontario] Niagara
Centre, Ontario Institute for Studies in Education [1972]
1 v. (various pagings). graphs, tables.   OTER

Henderson, Edward Fawcett, 1870–
    Ontario school question: objection and replies. Toronto: The Author [1931]
    15 p.   OTU
History of the schools of St. Vincent township and other chronicles, 1847–1967.
    [Vina Rose Ufland, editor. Meaford?, Ontario: 1970]
    ix, 258 p. illus., ports.   OTU
Hodgins, John George, 1821–1912.
    The legislation and history of separate schools in Upper Canada: from 1841
    until the close of the Reverend Doctor Ryerson's administration of the
    Education Department in 1876: including various private papers and
    documents on the subject. Toronto: William Briggs, 1897.
    xi, 225 p.   OTER
— Ryerson memorial volume: prepared on the occasion of the unveiling of the
    Ryerson statue in the grounds of the Education Department on the Queen's
    birthday, 1889. Toronto: Warwick & Sons, 1889.
    x, 131 p. front.   OTU
Hofferd, George W
    A study of the content and methodology of Ontario lower school biology.
    Toronto: The University of Toronto Press, 1932.
    149 p. charts, tables.   OTER
Hogeboom, Alice Ethel, 1909–
    Chalk dust: the history of education in Kingston township. [Kingston,
    Ontario: The Author, c1969]
    240 p. illus., facsims., ports.   OTU
Horsey, Edwin Ernest, 1870–1953.
    A century and a half of secondary school education in Kingston, 1792–1942
    [by Edwin Horsey, et al. Kingston, Ontario: 1970?]
    1 v. illus.   OKQ
Houseley, Michael.
    A preliminary report on the Bickford Park project. [Toronto: Research
    Department, Board of Education] 1967.
    27 leaves. tables.   OTER
Hughes, James Laughlin, 1846–1935.
    A principle of education vindicated; reports on the teaching of English in the
    English-French schools of Ottawa and certain rural localities in Ontario, by
    James L. Hughes, C.B. Sissons, M.H. Staples, Aurelian Belanger issued by
    the R.C.S.S. Board of the city of Ottawa, February, 1924. Ottawa: Roman
    Catholic Separate School Board, 1924.
    28 p.   OTU
— [Toronto: Ontario Unity League, 1924]
    38 p.   OTAR
— The teaching of English in the English-French schools of Ottawa. Report of
    inspection. [Toronto] Unity League of Ontario [1923]
    [8] p.   OTU

Humphreys, Edward Harold, 1932–
      Interaction and concept change of secondary school teachers in the province
      of Ontario. [Toronto] Ontario Institute for Studies in Education, 1970.
      25 p. graphs, tables. (Ontario Institute for Studies in Education. Department
      of Educational Planning. Educational planning occasional papers, no. 16).
                                                                                                          OTER
— Interaction and prestige of secondary school teachers in the province of
      Ontario. [Toronto] Ontario Institute for Studies in Education [1970]
      22 leaves. tables. (Ontario Institute for Studies in Education. Department of
      Educational Planning. Educational planning occasional paper no. 15).
                                                                                                          OTER
— Schools in change: a comparative survey of elementary school services,
      facilities and personnel, 1965–1969. Published in cooperation with the
      Ontario Teachers' Federation. [Toronto] The Ontario Institute for Studies
      in Education [c1970]
      vii, 60 p. illus. (Ontario Institute for Studies in Education. Occasional
      papers, no. 6).   OTER
— Urban-rural disparity in Ontario elementary education. [Toronto] Ontario
      Institute for Studies in Education, 1970.
      45 leaves. (Ontario Institute for Studies in Education. Department of
      Educational Planning. Educational planning occasional papers, no. 18/70).
                                                                                                          OTER
Hunter, John Howard, 1839–1911.
      The Upper Canada College question. [Dundas, Ontario? 1868?]
      broadside   OTU
— The U.C. College question. An examination, in what is believed to be
      intelligible language, of three not very intelligible points: 1. How U.C.
      College came to be established in defiance of the Legislature; 2. How U.C.
      College has contrived to absorb more than one-half of the endowment of the
      provincial university; 3. Why U.C. College has been so long permitted to
      remain a charge on the grammar school endowment. With full references to
      original documents. Compiled by order of the Ontario Grammar School
      Masters' Association. Dundas: Printed by J. Somerville "True Banner"
      Power Press, 1868.
      55 p.   OTU
— The Upper Canada College question, opinions of the press, with strictures on
      articles that have recently appeared in certain Toronto newspapers. n.p.
      [1868]
      24 p.   OONL
In the matter of Roman Catholic separate schools, Ontario. n.p.: 1938.
      11 p.   OKQ
Inter-Church Committee on Protestant–Roman Catholic Relations.
      The separate school in Ontario. [Toronto: 1946?]
      47 p. graphs, maps.   OTER

Irvine, Florence Gladys, 1921–
Aims and objectives of education: towards change in Ontario. Toronto:
Ontario Teachers' Federation, 1968.
37 leaves. diagrs. OTOTF
Jackson, Robert William Brierley, 1909–1979.
Achievement in the skill subjects in public schools in four areas of Ontario:
1955-56 rural school survey. [Toronto] Department of Educational
Research, Ontario College of Education, University of Toronto, 1957.
12 leaves. tables. (Information series, no. 7). OTER
— The Atkinson study of utilization of student resources in Ontario; report
submitted to the National Conference of Canadian Universities, June 5,
1958. [Toronto] Department of Educational Research, Ontario College of
Education, University of Toronto, 1958.
vii, 53 p. tables. OTU
King, Alan John Campbell, 1933–
Innovative secondary schools. Published for the Faculty of Education,
Queen's University by the Ontario Institute for Studies in Education.
[Toronto: c1972]
v, 58 p. OTER
— The school in transition. A profile of a secondary school undergoing
innovation, by Alan J.C. King and Reginald A. Ripton. [Toronto: Ontario
Institute for Studies in Education, 1970]
52p. diagrs., tables.
"A joint project of the Ontario Institute for Studies in Education and the
Collegiate Institute Board of Ottawa." OTU
Kirkconnell, Watson, 1895–
A Canadian headmaster: a brief biography of Thomas Allison Kirkconnell
1862–1934. With a foreword by W.J. Alexander. Toronto: Clarke, Irwin &
Company Limited, 1935.
xi, 156 p. port. OTU
Klinck, G   A
L'enseignement du français dans nos écoles de langue anglaise . Quebec: Les
Presses Universitaires Laval, 1960.
14 p.
"Extrait de la *Revue de l'Université Laval* v. 15 no. 1, September 1960." OKQ
Laing, John.
Religious instruction in our public schools, being a number of letters
published in the Toronto *Mail*. Toronto: Mail Printing Co., 1883.
46 p. OTURS
Lawr, Douglas A   (ed.).
Educating Canadians: a documentary history of public education, edited by
Douglas A. Lawr and Robert D. Gidney. Toronto: VanNostrand Reinhold
Ltd. [c1973]
284 p. illus. OTU

Laxer, Gordon.
　　A study of student social and achievement patterns as related to secondary
　　school organizational structures, by Gordon Laxer, Ross Traub and
　　Katherine Wayne. Toronto: Educational Evaluation Center, Ontario
　　Institute for Studies in Education, 1973.
　　xii, 267 leaves. tables.   OTER
Lind, Loren Jay.
　　The learning machine: a hard look at Toronto schools. Toronto: Anansi
　　[c1974]
　　iv, 228 p. graphs, tables.   OTER
Longstaff, Frank R
　　Attitudes and perceptions of grade nine secondary school students, by Frank
　　R. Longstaff and Alan J.C. King. [Toronto: Scarborough Board of
　　Education and Ontario Institute for Studies in Education, 1967]
　　90 leaves. graphs, tables.   OTER
Love, J　　H
　　Welland county Roman Catholic Separate School Board: comparative study
　　of the effectiveness at the junior kindergarten level of certificated and non-
　　certificated teachers: final report, by J.H. Love and A.A. Shynal. St.
　　Catharines, Ontario: Niagara Centre, Ontario Institute for Studies in
　　Education, 1973.
　　1 v. (various pagings). graphs, tables.   OTER
Loyal Orange Association of British America, Ontario. Public School Defence
　　Committee.
　　Segregation is wrong. Brief presented to the Premier and members of the
　　Legislature in opposition to the request of the Roman Catholic Bishops for
　　further financial support for, and extension of, the separate school system.
　　n.p.: 1963.
　　14 leaves. tables.   OTU
　　Ontario government "foundation tax plan" transfers Protestant (and other
　　non-separate school) $$$ [sic] to Roman Catholic schools; Premier John
　　Robarts yields to R.C. bishops' demands and betrays public school
　　supporters. [Toronto: 1963]
　　[8] p. illus.   OONL
McBain, W　　J
　　The pattern of change in education: a study of the determinants of school
　　design in Ontario, by W.J. McBain, Y.Y. Jung and R.A. McNeilly.
　　Toronto: School of Architecture, University of Toronto, 1966.
　　1 v. (various pagings). tables.   OTER
McCutcheon, J　　M
　　Public education in Ontario. Toronto [T.H. Best Printing Co. Limited]
　　1941.
　　vii, 283 p.   OTAR
MacDougall, James Brown, 1871–1950.
　　Building the north. Toronto: McClelland and Stewart [c1919]
　　268 p. illus., plates, ports., diagrs.
　　Northern Ontario education.   OTU

MacEachern, D   G
　　Twenty questions, a quick look at 90,000 people: the grade 9 students in 800
　　Ontario schools. An analysis of the replies to the "student questionnaire"
　　from the Carnegie Study of Identification and Utilization of Talent in High
　　School and College. [Toronto] Department of Educational Research,
　　Ontario College of Education, University Qf Toronto, 1960.
　　v, 20 p. graphs, tables. (Carnegie Study of Identification and Utilization of
　　Talent in High School and College. Bulletin no. 1).   OTER
McMillan, George.
　　The agricultural high school in Ontario. Toronto: University of Toronto
　　Press, 1924.
　　129 p. diagrs., maps, tables.   OTER
The Maple Grove story, by Edra Thompson [et al. St. Catharines, Ontario]
　　Niagara Centre, Ontario Institute for Studies in Education, 1972.
　　vi, 83 [54] p. illus.
　　Volunteers in education in rural schools.   OTER
Martell, George (ed.).
　　The politics of the Canadian public school. Toronto: James Lewis &
　　Samuel, 1974.
　　vii, 257 p. illus.
　　Political aspects of the school system and teacher government confrontations
　　in British Columbia, Ontario and Quebec.   OTU
Massey, Norman Bland, 1910–
　　Canadian studies in Canadian schools. Toronto: Council of Ministers of
　　Education, 1971.
　　58, 70 leaves.
　　Text in the English and French languages.
　　A report for the Curriculum Committee of the Council of Ministers of
　　Education on the study of Canada, Canadians and life in Canada.   OLU
Melvin, Arthur Gordon, 1894–
　　The professional training of teachers for the Canadian public schools as
　　typified by Ontario. Baltimore: Warwick & York, Inc. 1923.
　　212 p.   OTC
Merchant, Francis Walter, 1855–1937.
　　The Ontario examination systems. London, Ontario: London Printing &
　　Litho Co., 1903.
　　42 p. graph.   OTU
— Report on the condition of English-French schools in the province of
　　Ontario. Printed by order of the Legislative Assembly of Ontario. Toronto:
　　L.K. Cameron, printer to the King's Most Excellent Majesty, 1912.
　　81 p. tables.   OTAR OLU

*Studies on the Merchant report on the condition of English-French schools in the province of
Ontario*
L'Association canadienne-française d'education d'Ontario.
    The bilingual schools of Ontario: a review of the report of Dr. Merchant.
    Ottawa: The Ottawa Printing Company, Limited, 1912.
    55 p.   OOA
— Écoles bilingues d'Ontario: étude de rapport du Dr. Merchant. Ottawa:
    Compagnie d'Imprimerie d'Ottawa, 1912.
    59 p. tables.   OTU
The French Canadian Educational Association of Ontario.
    The bilingual schools of Ontario: a review of the report of Dr. Merchant (a
    translation from the French original). Ottawa: The Ottawa Printing
    Company, Limited, 1912.
    55 p. tables.   OKQ OTU

Metropolitan Separate School Board.
    Metropolitan Separate School Board. [Toronto: 1965?]
    [18] p. illus., map.   OTU
Metropolitan Toronto. School Board. Advisory Council.
    Report on the organization of the intermediate grades. [Toronto: 1955]
    56 p. illus. (part col.).
    Chairman: C.C. Goldring.   OTER
Metropolitan Toronto. School Board. Study of Educational Facilities .
    Academic evaluation: an interim report. [Toronto] 1971.
    162 p. (*Its* report, E5 (draft)).   OTER
— [Toronto] 1972.
    214 p. graphs, tables. (*Its* report, E5 (interim)).   OTER
— Academic evaluation: a report on SEF open plan schools. [Toronto] 1975.
    xv, 289 p. graphs, plans, tables. (*Its* report E6).   OTER
— Education specifications and user requirements for elementary (K-6) schools.
    Toronto: The Ryerson Press, for the Study of Educational Facilities of the
    Metropolitan Toronto School Board, 1968.
    xvi, 208 p. illus. (part col.), ports. (*Its* report E1).   OTUSA
— Educational specifications and user requirements for intermediate schools.
    [Toronto: The Ryerson Press for the Study of Educational Facilities of the
    Metropolitan Toronto School Board, c1969.
    xiv, 254 p. illus. (*Its* report, E2).   OTUSA
— Educational specifications and user requirements for secondary schools.
    [Toronto: The Ryerson Press, for the Study of Educational Facilities of the
    Metropolitan Toronto School Board, c1970]
    xiv, 308 p. illus., tables. (*Its* report, E3).   OTUSA
— The function of the school in the community. [Toronto: 1967?]
    vii, 55, 12 p. illus. (*Its* report, E4).   OTER
— High-rise and mixed-use study. Toronto: The Board, c1970.
    xiii, 118 p. illus., diagrs., tables. (*Its* report, T3).   OTUSA

— Hints for survival in open plan school. [Toronto: 1973]
    13 p.   OTER
— Introduction to the first SEF building system. [Toronto: c1968]
    1 v. (loose leaf). illus. (part col.), diagrs. (part fold.). (*Its* report, T1).   OTU
— The Metropolitan Toronto School Board SEF building system. [Toronto:
    c1970]
    1 v. (various pagings). illus.   OTER OTUSA
— Short-term accommodation and relocatable facilities. [Toronto: c1970]
    xiv, 128 p. illus., plans. (*Its* report T4).   OTU
— Specifications for the first SEF building system. [Toronto: c1968]
    1 v. (loose leaf). illus. (*Its* report T2).   OTU
Metropolitan Toronto. Special Committee on Technical Education.
    Special report on the extension of technical education in Metropolitan
    Toronto, prepared by Lewis Beattie [et al. Toronto] 1959.
    30 p. fold. map.
    Chairman: Lewis Beattie.   OTER
Middlemiss, James, 1823–1907.
    Christian instruction in the public schools of Ontario. Toronto: William
    Briggs, 1901.
    239 p.   OTU
Moreland, Paul Arthur.
    Essay on commercial education in Ontario. Toronto: The Ryerson Press,
    1932.
    133 leaves.
    Title page states: vol. III. No other volumes were located.   OTC
Morgan, Dorothy Johnston, 1901–
    Chalkdust in my blood. Cornwall, Ontario: Vesta, 1975.
    154 p.   OTU
Mowat, (Sir) Oliver, 1820–1903.
    The separate schools. The no-popery cry. Protestantism not in danger.
    Memorandum December 2, 1886. Toronto: C. Blackett Robinson, 1886.
    26 p.   OTAR
— A speech delivered by Hon. Oliver Mowat in the Legislative Assembly
    March 25, 1890. Proposed amendments to the Act relating to separate
    schools. Toronto: Hunter, Rose & Co., 1890.
    19 p. (Provincial politics 1890, no. 4).   OKQ
— A speech delivered by Hon. Oliver Mowat, premier of Ontario at
    Woodstock, December 3, 1880. The sectarian issues and the history and
    present position of the public schools in the French districts of Ontario.
    Toronto: Hunter, Rose & Co., 1890.
    31 p. (Provincial politics 1890, no. 1).   OKQ
Munro, George, 1934–
    Team teaching in Ontario secondary schools 1964-1965, by George Munro
    and Gerald Wiley. [Toronto: Ontario Educational Research Council, 1966?]
    viii, 34 leaves.
    At least one leaf is missing at the end of the report.   OONL

Musella, Donald F
  Open concept programs in open area schools: final report, no. 5508.
  Submitted June 30, 1973 by Donald F. Musella and others. [Toronto]
  Department of Educational Administration, Ontario Institute for Studies in
  Education [1973]
  139 leaves.   OTER
New Democratic Party (Ontario).
  The financial crises in the Catholic high schools: a basis for discussion.
  [Toronto: c1969]
  15 [1] p.   OTURS
North York, Ontario. Board of Education. Ad Hoc Committee. Respecting
    Student Matters.
  Perceptions of school and education: a comparative study of three surveys
  conducted at the secondary school level. [North York, Ontario] 1972.
  19 p.   OTER
— Survey of parents of secondary school students: perceptions of school and
  education, a report. [North York, Ontario] 1972.
  31 p. tables.   OTER
— Survey of secondary school students' perceptions of school and education: a
  report. [North York, Ontario] 1972.
  74, 6 leaves. graphs, tables.   OTER
— Survey of secondary school teachers' perceptions of school and education: a
  report. [North York, Ontario] 1972.
  74 p. graphs, tables.   OTER
North York, Ontario. Board of Education. Advisory Vocational Committee.
  A study to determine the need for technical education in North York
  township, prepared for the Committee... by L.S. Beattie, editor and
  consultant [et al.] Willowdale, Ontario: 1963.
  v, 70 p. illus., graphs, tables.   OTU
Notes in regard to high school facilities in general and to Catholic high school
  facilities in particular in the neighbour cities of Fort William and Port
  Arthur. n.p.: 1960.
  5 leaves.   OTAR
Oliver, Michael Joseph.
  Marylake farm school, King, Ontario: an outline of its work and objects.
  Toronto: St. Michael's College, 1939.
  6 p. map.   OTMCL
Ontario. Commission relating to the Ottawa separate schools.
  Report. Toronto: Warwick Bros. & Rutter, 1895.
  51 p. tables.
  Chairman: J.T. Foley.   OTC
Ontario. Committee appointed to enquire into the condition of the schools
    attended by French-speaking pupils.
  Report. Printed by order of the Legislative Assembly. Toronto: Printed by
  the printer to the King's Most Excellent Majesty, 1927.
  149 p. tables.
  Chairman: F.W. Merchant.   OTER OTU

Ontario. Committee of enquiry into the cost of education in the province of
Ontario.
Report. Printed by order of the Legislation Assembly. Toronto: T.E.
Bowman, printer to the King's Most Excellent Majesty, 1938.
78 p. tables.
Chairman: D. McArthur. OTER
Ontario. Committee on French Language Schools in Ontario.
Report. [Toronto: Ontario Department of Education] 1968.
87 p. illus., tables.
Chairman: Roland R. Bériault.
Text in French and English. OTU
Ontario. Committee on High School Education.
Interim report. Printed by order of the Legislative Assembly. Toronto:
Clarkson W. James, 1921.
12 p.
Chairman: F.W. Merchant. OTU
Ontario. Committee on Planning, Construction and Equipment of Schools in
Ontario.
Interim report on elementary schools. [Toronto? 1945]
15 p. plans.
Chairman: Eric R. Arthur. OTER
Ontario. Committee on Religious Education in the Public Schools of Ontario.
Report, 1969: religious information and moral development. [Toronto:
Ontario Department of Education, c1969]
xiv, 119 p.
Chairman: J. Keiller Mackay. OTU

*Background papers to Ontario Committee on Religious Education in the Public Schools of
Ontario*
Canadian Jewish Congress. Central Region.
Brief to the Committee on Religious Education in the Public Schools of
Ontario. [Toronto] 1967.
vii, 83, A75 leaves. OTER
Catholic Church in Ontario. Bishops.
Brief presented to the Prime Minister of Ontario and to the members of the
Legislative Assembly. Toronto: English Catholic Education Association of
Ontario [1962]
16 p.
Religious education.
Crittenden, Brian S   1930–
Form and content in moral education: an essay on aspects of the Mackay
report. [Toronto] Ontario Institute for Studies in Education [c1972]
102 p. (Ontario Institute for studies in Education. Monograph series, 12).
OTER

Ecumenical Study Commission on Religious Education.
    Religion in our schools: an ecumenical reaction to the Keiller Mackay
    report/Ecumenical Study Commission. Toronto: Ecumenical Study
    Commission [1972]
    28 p.
    Chairman: Canon H.L. Puxley.   OTU
Ottawa. Université Saint-Paul.
    Mémoire de la Commission d'études du recteur de l'Université Saint-Paul
    sur le rapport J. Keiller Mackay concernant l'éducation religieuse dans les
    écoles de la province d'Ontario. Ottawa: Université Saint-Paul, 1969.
    49 p.   OOU

Ontario. Committee on the Costs of Education.
    Interim report. [Toronto] 1972–1977.
    7 v. graphs, tables.
    Chairman: T.A. McEwan.
    Contents: no. 1, OTER Report on the education of elementary and secondary
    teachers in Ontario: facilities, organization, administration; no. 2, OTER
    School building programs; no. 3, OTER Pupil transportation; no. 4, OTER
    Goals, alternatives, priorities, implementation, evaluation, adjustment,
    revised goals; no. 5, OTDU Educational agencies and programs; no. 6, OTDU
    Compensation in elementary and secondary education; no. 7, OTER
    Financing education in elementary and secondary schools.
— Transcript of public hearings held in Toronto, May 1 to June 26, 1972.
    2 v.   OTU
— Briefs.
    45 v.   OTER
Ontario. Legislative Assembly. Select Committee on Common and Grammar
    Schools.
    Report. [1869]
    2 handwritten pages.
    Chairman: C. Cameron.   OTAR
— Minutes, November 17–December 4, 1868.   OTAR
— Proceedings, January 13–19, 1869. Toronto: Hunter, Rose & Co., 1869.
    2 v.   OTAR
Ontario. Legislative Assembly. Select Committee on Upper Canada College.
    Proceedings, December 13, 1869.
    63 handwritten pages.
    Chairman: Mr. Carnegie.   OTAR
Ontario. Ministerial Commission on French Language Secondary Education.
    Report. Toronto: William Kinmond, Queen's Printer and Publisher, 1972.
    79 p. map.
    Chairman: T.H.B. Symons.
    Text in French and English.   OTU

Ontario. Ministerial Commission on the Organization and Financing of the
Public and Secondary School Systems in Metropolitan Toronto.
Report. [Toronto] Ministry of Education [1974?]
xiii, 311 p. graphs, tables.
Chairman: Barry Lowes. OTU
Ontario. Provincial Committee on Aims and Objectives of Education in the
Schools of Ontario.
Living and learning: report. [Toronto: Newton Publishing Co., 1968]
221 p. illus. (part col.), facsims., ports.
Co-chairmen: E.M. Hall and L.A. Dennis. OTU
— Report summary. [Abridged ed. Toronto] 1968.
56 leaves. OTU
— Abridged edition. 1968.
87 p. OTER
— Vivre et s'instruire. Ed. Abrégée. [Toronto: Newton Publishing Company,
1968]
82 p. illus. (part col.). OTER
— Documents: a selection of special presentations and research reports.
[Toronto?] 1968.
1 v. (various pagings). OTER

*Background papers to Ontario Provincial Committee on Aims and Objectives of Education in
the Schools of Ontario*
Canadian Mental Health Association. Ontario Division.
A brief to the Provincial Committee on Aims and Objectives of Education in
the Schools of Ontario. [Toronto: 1965?]
43 [4] leaves. OTER
Conference on the Report of the Provincial Committee on Aims and Objectives
of Education in the Schools of Ontario. Toronto, 1969.
Re-thinking education: proceedings. [Toronto] Ontario Institute for Studies
in Education [1969]
64 p. diagrs. OTER
Crittenden, Brian S   1930–   (ed.).
Means and ends in education; comments on *Living and learning*, edited by
Brian Crittenden. [Toronto: Hunter, Rose & Company, c1969]
128 p. (Ontario Institute for Studies in Education. Occasional papers, 2).
OTU
Daly, James William, 1932–
Education or molasses? A critical look at the Hall–Dennis report. Ancaster,
Ontario: Cromlech Press [c1969]
79 p. OTU
Federation of Women Teachers' Associations of Ontario. Committee to Study
Living and Learning.
A description of teacher opinion on some of the issues discussed in the
Hall–Dennis report, *Living and learning.* [Toronto, 1969]
44 leaves. tables.
Convener: Melba Woolley. OTU

Kent, Charles Deane.
    Ryerson cake with Dewey icing; some reflections on *Living and learning*: the
    report of the Provincial Committee on Aims and Objectives of Education in
    the Schools of Ontario (the Hall–Dennis report). London, Ontario: London
    Public Library and Art Museum, 1969.
    23 p. (London Public Library and Art Museum. Occasional paper, no. 8).
                                                                          OTU
Ontario Catholic Education Council.
    Brief submitted to the Hall Committee on Aims and Objectives in
    Education. [Toronto: Mission Press] 1966.
    iv, 44 p.   OTC
Sim, Robert Alexander.
    The education of Indians in Ontario. A report to the Provincial Committee
    on Aims and Objectives of Education in the schools of Ontario. North
    Gower, Ontario: 1967.
    [2] 106 leaves. tables.   OTURS

Ontario. Provincial Task Force on H.S.1.
    Report: a summary. [Toronto: 1973?]
    19 p.   OTER

Papers re: Ontario Provincial Task Force on H.S.1.
Leithwood, Kenneth Arthur, 1942–
    The individualized system: courses and patterns of student choice, by
    Kenneth A. Leithwood, John S. Clipsham, Cheryl Davies. Toronto: The
    Ontario Institute for Studies in Education [c1974]
    vii, 63 p. (The Ontario Institute for Studies in Education H.S.1. studies).
                                                                          OONL
Ontario Teachers' Federation.
    A brief to the Task Force on H.S.1. of the Ministry of Education. Toronto
    [1973]
    6 leaves.   OTER

Ontario. Royal Commission on Education.
    Report. Toronto: Baptist Johnston, printer to the King's Most Excellent
    Majesty, 1950.
    xxiii, 933 p. diagrs.
    Chairman: John A. Hope.   OTER
— Another issue.
    5 v.
    Manuscript.   OTER
— Proceedings. Toronto: 1945–46.
    8 v.

Contents: Second session: April 26, 27, 1945; third session, September 21,
1945; seventh session, January 7–11, 1946; eighth session, February 18, 19,
21, 22, 1946; ninth session part A March 18, 19, 1946, part B March 20–22,
1946; tenth session April 29, 30, May 1–3, 1946.   OTER
— Ninth session, private meetings March 21–22, 1946.
   14 v.   OTP
— [Proceedings of] private sessions. Toronto [1948–1950]
   19 v. [i.e. 6587 leaves]   OTER
— Excerpt from the proceedings at private session, December 7, 1945.
   [Toronto: 1945]
   32 leaves.   OTER
— Report of private sessions, January 9 and 11, 1946 [Toronto: 1946]
   76 leaves.   OTER
— Proceedings of meetings of majority report signatories. October 26, 1950.
   Toronto [1950]
   97 leaves.
   Official reporter: H.O. Taylor.   OTER
— Briefs submitted to the Royal Commission on Education. [Toronto:
   1945–1947]
   213 v.   OTER
— Complete list of briefs. n.p.: 1947.
   18 leaves.   OTER
— Clippings 1945–1950.
   650 p. (scrapbook).
   Also available on microfilm.   OTER
— Memoranda to the Royal Commission on Education. [Toronto: n.p:
   1945–1947]
   42 v.   OTER
— Miscellaneous correspondence and reports re the Royal Commission on
   Education. [Toronto: n.p: 1945–1947]
   34 v.   OTER
— Report on an emergency training scheme for teachers for the public and
   separate schools of Ontario. [Toronto? 1949]
   15 leaves. tables.
   Partial report issued prior to the completed final report.   OTER

Background papers to Ontario Royal Commission on Education
Amoss, Harry E   1880–
   Memorandum on special education for the Honourable Justice John A.
   Hope, Royal Commission on Education. [Prepared by H.E. Amoss and C.E.
   Strothers. Toronto: 1947]
   16 leaves. tables.   OTER
Henderson, Edward Fawcett, 1870–
   Historical sketch of the separate schools of Ontario and the Catholic

separate school minority report. Presented in conjunction with the Report of
the Royal Commission on Education in Ontario, 1950. Toronto: The
English Catholic Education Association of Ontario, 1950.
115 p.   OTER OTMCL
Minkler, Frederick.
The aims and objectives of education in Ontario... Report prepared for The
Royal Commission on Education. [Toronto? 1947?]
2 v.
Contents: v. 1, Part I, Extracts of recommendations and suggestions in Briefs
and Memoranda submitted to the Royal Commission on Education; v. 2,
Part II, suggestions concerning a philosophy of Education; Part III,
Suggestions concerning some practical implications.   OKQ
Ontario. Royal Commission on Education. Committee on Educational
Personnel.
Proceedings. [Toronto: 1946–1948]
6 v. [i.e. 2009 leaves.]
Committee chairman: W.L. Whitelock.
Official reporter: H.O. Taylor.   OTER
Ontario. Royal Commission on Education. Committee on Provincial and Local
School Administration.
Report of proceedings, Nov. 11, 12 and 13, 1946. [Toronto: 1946]
396 leaves.
Committee chairman: M.A. Campbell.   OTER
Ontario. Royal Commission on Education. Committee on Provincial and Local
School Administration. Travelling Committee.
Report. [Toronto? 1947?]
vii, 106 leaves. charts, tables.   OTC
Ontario. Royal Commission on Education in Ontario. Committee on the
Educational System.
Report of proceedings, Dec. 9, 10, 11, 1946.
425 leaves.
Committee chairman: C.R. Sanderson.   OTER
Ontario. Royal Commission on Education in Ontario. Committee on the
School.
Proceedings of May 27 & 28, 1947. Toronto [1947]
340 leaves.
Committee chairman: Fred Molineux.
Official reporter: H.O. Taylor.   OTER
Separate schools: documents presented to the Royal Commission on Education
in Ontario. Toronto: English Catholic Education Association of Ontario,
1946.
90 p.
Contents: Brief no. 146 submitted by The Ontario Catholic Education
Council on behalf of the Catholic separate schools of Ontario; The Roman
Catholic separate schools of Ontario second supplementary statement to

Brief no. 146; Statement of the Catholic bishops of Ontario; Educational
problems in Ontario. OOU
Silcox, Claris Edwin, 1888–1961.
The Hope report on education, a brief critique of the Report of the Royal
Commission of Education in Ontario. Toronto: The Ryerson Press [c1952]
69 p. OTU

Ontario. Royal Commission on Ottawa Collegiate Conditions.
Report. [Toronto: 1927]
20 typewritten pages.
Commissioner: John Fosbery Orde. OTAR
— Proceedings, November 9–11, 1926.
238 typewritten pages. OTAR
Ontario. The Grade 13 Study Committee, 1964.
Report submitted to the Honourable William G. Davis, minister of
education June 26, 1964. [Toronto] 1964.
35 p.
Chairman: F.A. Hamilton. OTU
Ontario Commercial Teachers' Association. Shorthand Survey Committee.
Selection and training of shorthand students in Ontario secondary schools; a
study conducted by the Shorthand Survey Committee of the Ontario
Commercial Teachers' Association and the Department of Educational
Research, Ontario College of Education, University of Toronto. Toronto: Sir
Isaac Pitman & Sons (Canada) Ltd. [c1949]
vii, 68 p. tables. OTER
Ontario English Catholic Teachers' Association.
Right or privilege? 1800–1867. [Toronto] c1971.
37 lesson sheets and 60 p. teachers' guide. (A documentary history of
separate schools in Ontario, part 1). OTER
— Survival . . . ? 1867–1949. Authors: R.T. Dixon and N.L. Bethune. [Toronto]
c1974.
56 sheets and 76 p. teachers' guide. (A documentary history of separate
schools in Ontario, part 2). OTER
Ontario Institute for Studies in Education.
Planning and implementing change in Ontario schools. A report of the
Committee on the Implementation of change in the Classroom. Toronto:
Office of Development, The Ontario Institute for Studies in Education
[1967]
39 p. OTU
— POISE; Peterborough operation: individualizing student education. A joint
endeavour of the Peterborough public schools and the Ontario Institute for
Studies in Education. Toronto: 1969.
x, 106 p. diagrs. OTER

Ontario Ladies College.
  Vox collegi: centennial edition, 1874–1974. [Whitby, Ontario: Ontario
  Ladies College c1974]
  173 p. illus., ports.   OONL
Ontario Normal School Teachers' Association. Committee on the Training of
  Elementary School Teachers.
  Report on the normal schools of the province of Ontario. [Toronto: 1950]
  103 leaves.   OTER
Ontario Public School Men Teachers' Federation.
  A programme for teacher education in Ontario. [Toronto: The Federation,
  1950]
  31 p.   OTER
Ontario Secondary School Teachers' Federation.
  Financing public education in Ontario, 1970. [Toronto: 1970?]
  57 p. tables.   OONL
— Statistical analysis of secondary school boards; including distribution of
  experience and certification rating, average years of experience, average
  salary. [Toronto] 1966.
  [14] leaves. tables.   OTER
— The status of the secondary school teacher in Ontario, a symposium. [Edited
  by Harry Oke Barrett] Toronto [W.J. Gage Limited] 1961.
  138 p. diagrs., forms, tables.   OTU
Ontario Secondary School Teachers Federation. Committee on Conditions of
  Work for Quality Education.
  Report. [Toronto] The Federation, 1974.
  3 v.
  Contents: v. 1, Statistical summary of secondary and junior high schools;
  v. 2, Statistical summary of teaching situations in secondary and junior high
  schools; v. 3 [Summary]   OTER
Ontario Secondary School Teachers' Federation. Provincial Research
  Committee.
  At what cost? A study of the role of the secondary school in Ontario. Toronto
  [c1976]
  140 p. illus., graphs, tables.   OTER
Ontario's school system. History of education in the Province: facts clearly
  stated. The past and the present. n.p. [1877?]
  29 p.   OTAR
Oro Township, Ontario. School Board. Historical Committee.
  A history of Oro schools, 1836 to 1966. [Compiled by Howard Campbell,
  chairman; Mrs. Victor Ross and Mrs. Albert Pearsall. n.p.: 1967]
  60 p. illus., maps, port.   OTAR
Ottawa Curriculum Committee.
  The Ottawa experiment: a report on the first six years of the Ottawa plan of
  grade 12 socialized classes in English, social studies, health and guidance,
  1945–1950. [Ottawa: 1950]
  32 leaves.
  Chairman: Michael McHugh.   OTER

Palmer, James Buchanan, 1914–
What every parent should know about the new Robarts plan for secondary schools. [Toronto: Daily Star, 1962]
[20] p. illus. (part col.), graph.   OONL
Parvin, Viola Elizabeth, 1922–
Authorization of textbooks for the schools of Ontario, 1846–1950 . [Toronto] Published in association with the Canadian Textbook Publisher's Institute by University of Toronto Press [c1965]
161 p.   OTER
Pierce, Lorne Albert, 1890–1961.
Fifty years of public service: a life of James L. Hughes. Toronto: S.B. Gundy, Oxford University Press [c1924]
256 p. port.   OTER
Plante, Albert, 1908–
Les écoles séparées d'Ontario. Montreal: [Les Editions Bellarmin, 1952]
103 p. tables.   OTU
— 2d ed. Montreal [Bellarmin, 1952]
103 p. (Relations, 3).   OTU
Quinn, Martin J
The case for Ontario separate schools. Toronto: The Catholic Taxpayers' Association of Ontario [1937]
22 p.   OTAR
— Injustice envers les écoles séparées, l'acte de l'évaluation municipal est défectueux, comparaison entre Ontario et Quebec. [Toronto? L'Association d'education de l'Ontario, 1931]
20 p.   OOU
— Same pertinent facts with notes, comments and quotations for the use of those who desire to understand and discuss publicly or privately, the situation of the separate schools in Ontario. 2d ed. Toronto: Catholic Taxpayers Association of Ontario, 1932.
22 p.   OTU
Radcliffe, Samuel John.
Retardation in the schools of Ontario. Toronto: Radcliffe [1921?]
63 p. charts, tables.   OTU
Ramsey, Craig A   1937–
Grade nine programme placement; non-Canadian born students, their placement in grade nine programmes and its relationship to other factors by C.A. Ramsey and E.N. Wright. [Toronto: Board of Education, Research Department] 1969.
34 leaves. diagrs., tables.   OTER
— Language backgrounds and achievements in Toronto schools, by C.A. Ramsey and E.N. Wright. [Toronto: Research Department, Board of Education] 1970.
36 leaves. diagrs., tables.   OTER
— Students of non-Canadian origin: a descriptive report of students in Toronto

schools, by C.A. Ramsey and E.N. Wright. [Toronto: Research Department,
Board of Education] 1969.
ii, 74 leaves. tables.   OTER
— Students of non-Canadian origin: the relation of language and rural-urban
background to academic achievement and ability, by C.A. Ramsey and E.N.
Wright. [Toronto: Board of Education, Research Department] 1969.
48 leaves. tables.   OTER
Reich, Carol Musselman, 1943–
A follow-up study of special vocational and special high school students, by
Carol M. Reich and Suzanne Zeigler. [Toronto] Research Department,
Board of Education] 1972.
73 p. diagrs., tables. (Research service report 102).   OTER
Renney, A   J
Some aspects of rural and agricultural education in Canada. Toronto:
Department of Educational Research, Ontario College of Education,
University of Toronto, 1950.
ix, 181 p. tables. (Educational research series, no. 21).
Ontario: pp. 62–82.   OTER
Robarts, John Parmenter, 1917–
Le français dans les écoles de l'Ontario. Allocution adressée par l'honorable
John P. Robarts, premier ministre de l'Ontario à l'Association canadienne
des éducateurs de langue-française à Ottawa, 24 août 1967. [Toronto]
Ministère l'Education, 1968.
14 p.
Text in French and English.   OOU
— French in Ontario's schools. Address by the Honourable John P. Robarts,
prime minister of Ontario to l'Association canadienne des éducateurs de
langue-française, Ottawa, August 24, 1967. [Toronto: Department of
Education, 1968]
13 p.   OOU
Robinson, Floyd Grant, 1931–   (comp.).
Volunteer helpers in elementary schools: a survey of current practice in the
Niagara region of Ontario and an analysis of instructional roles, conducted
and compiled by Floyd Robinson [et al. Toronto] Ontario Institute for
Studies in Education [c1971]
v, 33 p. tables.   OTER
Rogers, Rex S   1943–
Who leaves and why?: pupil attrition in Toronto public schools; selected
statistics from the study of achievement. [Toronto: Research Department,
Board of Education, 1969]
29 leaves. diagrs., tables.   OTER
Ross, George William, 1841–1914.
The school system of Ontario (Canada): its history and distinctive features.
New York: D. Appleton and Company, 1896.
xiv, 203 p.   OTER

— The separate school question and the French language in the public schools; report of the speech delivered by Hon. George W. Ross, minister of education, on the occasion of the Annual Demonstration of the Toronto Reform Association, June 29th, 1889. Toronto: Hunter, Rose & Co., 1889.
16 p. OKQ

Ryerson, Adolphus Egerton, 1803–1882.
My dearest Sophie: letters from Egerton Ryerson to his daughter, edited by C.B. Sissons. Toronto: The Ryerson Press [c1955]
xxxvi, 350 p. illus., ports., map. OTU OLU

— The story of my life (being reminiscences of sixty years' public service in Canada). Prepared under the supervision of his literary trustees... Edited by J. George Hodgins. Toronto: William Briggs, 1883.
xvi, 612 [10] p. illus., facsims., port. OTU

St. John, Joseph Bascom, 1906–
Separate schools in Ontario. n.p. [1963]
40 p. port.
"Reprinted from *The Globe and Mail* Canada's national newpaper." OTU

Saunders, Robert E
Financing public education in Ontario, 1970. [Toronto] Ontario Secondary School Teachers' Federation [1971?]
57 p. tables. OTER

Shain, Martin V
Communication, education and drugs: report on the first year of intervention in a St. Catharines high school, by Martin Shain in cooperation with Bill Riddell. [St. Catharines, Ontario: 1972]
136, 96 leaves. tables. OTUCR

Shukyn, Murray, 1938–
You can't take a bathtub on the subway; a personal history of SEED: a new approach to secondary school education [by] Murray Shukyn [and] Beverley Shukyn. Toronto: Holt, Rinehart and Winston of Canada Limited [c1973]
xiv, 235 p. illus. OTER

Shutt, Greta Mary, 1891–
The high schools of Guelph: being the story of the Wellington District Grammar School, Guelph Grammar School, Guelph High School, and Guelph's collegiate institutes. [Guelph, Ontario] Board of Education for the city of Guelph [c1961]
xi, 138 p. illus., ports., facsims., tables. OTU

Sissons, Charles Bruce, 1879–1965.
Egerton Ryerson. Toronto: The Ryerson Press [c1930]
30 p. port. OTU

— Egerton Ryerson: his life and letters. With a foreword by E.W. Wallace. Toronto: Clarke, Irwin & Company Ltd., 1937–1947.
2 v.
Contents: v. 1, 1826–1841; v. 2, 1841–1882. OTU

Sisters of St. Joseph.
The changing face of Catholic education in London 1858–1963: a study
prepared for the Separate School Board, London, Ontario. [London,
Ontario: 1963]
145 p. illus. ports.   OLSSJ
Smith, Waldo Edward Lovel, 1901–
Albert College, 1857–1957. [Belleville, Ontario: Ontario Intelligencer
Limited, 1957]
56 p. illus., facsims.   OTER
Social Planning Council of Metropolitan Toronto. Committee on School
Dropouts.
A report on school dropouts. Toronto: 1961.
6, 23, iv leaves.
Chairman: John Haddad.   OONL
Sowby, Cedric Walter, 1902–
A family writ large. [Don Mills, Ontario] Longman Canada [c1971]
278 p. illus., ports.
Sowby was principal of Upper Canada College from 1949–1965.   OTU
Stothers, Carman Edmund.
"V.K." a record of some of V.K. Greer's achievement. Islington, Ontario:
Folios & Small Editions [1964]
159 p. illus., port. facsims.   OTU
Stothers, Robert.
A biographical memorial to Robert Henry Cowley 1859–1927. Toronto:
Thomas Nelson & Sons, Limited [c1935]
xix, 151 p. ports.   OTU
Survey of use of standardized tests in Ontario elementary schools , by Dennis
Roberts [et al. Toronto] Department of Measurement and Evaluation,
Ontario Institute for Studies in Education, c1969.
71 p. tables.   OTER
Thomas, Clara Eileen (McCandless), 1919–
Ryerson of Upper Canada. Toronto: The Ryerson Press [1969]
151 p. illus., port.   OTU
Thornlea: a case study of the innovative secondary school, by Michael Fullan,
Glenn Eastabrook, Dan Spinner and Jan J. Loubser. [Toronto] Ontario
Institute for Studies in Education [c1972]
vi, 46 p. illus. (Ontario Institute for Studies in Education. Profiles in
practical education no. 6).   OTER
Toronto. Board of Education.
Dropouts in the secondary schools of Toronto 1952-1953. Toronto: The
Board [1953?]
[iv, 55] leaves. graphs, tables.
Committee: W.D.A. Douglas, Graham M. Gore and Paul A. Moreland.
                                                                                 OTER

Toronto. Board of Education. Research Department.
A follow-up study of the effects of aural-oral French instruction in the elementary school on pupils' achievement in a secondary school programme. [Toronto] 1962.
33 leaves. tables. OTER
— Grade 12 standardized departmental tests: a comparison of norms of students in the city of Toronto secondary schools and Ontario secondary schools. [Toronto: 1962?]
67 leaves. diagrs., tables. OTER
— A preliminary study of teaching load in six subject areas in the Toronto secondary schools. [Toronto: 1963]
40 leaves. tables. OTER
— A study of the effects of an acceleration programme in Toronto secondary schools. [Toronto] 1962.
45 leaves. diagrs., tables. OTER
— A survey of pupils learning English as a second language in the city of Toronto public schools, by the Research Department in cooperation with the Public School Principals' Association. Toronto: 1962.
58 p. illus., tables. OTULS
Toronto. Board of Education. Survey Committee on Forest Hill Public School.
Report. [Toronto: 1933]
1 v. (unpaged). tables.
Director: Peter Sandiford. OTER
Toronto. Board of Trade. Special Committee *re* Technical Education.
Report of the council of the Board of Trade *re* technical education: also an address by Jas. D. Allen. Subject: Technical education from a business standpoint, Dec. 8th, 1899. Toronto: Hunter, Rose Co., Limited, 1899.
19 p. OTURS
Toronto Secondary Schools. Association of Heads of Guidance Departments. Research Committee.
A study of thirty-two gifted students of the Toronto secondary schools. Toronto: The Committee, 1955.
[iv, 83] leaves. tables. OTER
Trumpour, Kenneth Ryerson.
A comparison of the Ontario elementary school principal and the English head teacher with reference to curriculum development especially in the field of mathematics. [London: 1968]
ii, 157 p. illus.
Submitted April, 1968 to the Institute of Education University of London for the award of Associateship of the Institute of Education. OTER
The truth nothing but the truth. Will you help us. Montreal: "Le Devoir" Printing, 1915.
25 p.
Bi-lingual and separate schools in Ontario. OTAR
Upper Canada College: a short history and documents [1829–1929. Toronto: The College] 1967.
26 p. illus. OTAR

Upper Canada Endowment and Extension Fund.
  Upper Canada College 1829–1920. [Toronto: 1920]
  30 p. illus., ports.   OOA
Walker, Franklin Arthur, 1921–
  Catholic education and politics in Ontario: a documentary study. [Toronto]
  Thomas Nelson & Sons (Canada) Limited [c1964]
  xiii, 507 p.
  Covers period 1867–1939.   OTER
— Toronto: Federation of Catholic Education Associations of Ontario [1976]
  xiii, 514 p.   OTER
— Catholic education and politics in Upper Canada: a study of the
  documentation relative to the origin of Catholic elementary schools in the
  Ontario school system. Toronto: J.M. Dent & Sons (Canada) Limited
  [c1955]
  xii, 331 p.   OTU
Watson, Cicely, 1921–
  The dropout: report of a pilot study of dropouts from grades 11, 12 and 13 of
  the secondary schools of thirteen Ontario Boards of Education, 1972-73, by
  Cicely Watson and Sharon Burnham. [Toronto] Department of Educational
  Planning, Ontario Institute for Studies in Education, 1973.
  114 p. tables. (Ontario Institute for Studies in Education. Department of
  Educational Planning. Occasional paper no. 73/74-3).   OTER
— The elementary teacher: a study of the characteristics and supply/demand
  relations of Ontario teachers, by Cicely Watson, Saeed Quazi and Russ
  Jones. [Toronto: Ontario Institute for Studies in Education, c1972]
  iii, 180 p. diagrs., tables.   OTER
— Future needs for elementary and secondary school classrooms in the county
  of Waterloo, by Cicely Watson and Saeed Quazi. [Toronto] Department of
  Educational Planning, Ontario Institute for Studies in Education, 1970.
  ix 120 p. diagrs., maps, tables.   OTER
— Ontario elementary school enrollment projections to 1901/0a, part o, 1971
  projection, by Cicely Watson, Saeed Quazi and Aribert Kleist. [Toronto]
  The Ontario Institute for Studies in Education [c1970]
  83 p. tables. (Enrollment projections series, no. 6).   OTER
— Ontario grade 13: three studies, by C. Watson and Patricia M. Lyle.
  [Toronto] Ontario Institute for Studies in Education [c1965]
  xiv, 149 p. tables. (Bulletin no. 23).   OTER
— Ontario preschool and elementary school enrollment projections to 1981-82,
  by Cicely Watson and Saeed Quazi. [Toronto] The Ontario Institute for
  Studies in Education, 1968.
  67 p. diagrs., tables. (Ontario Institute for Studies in Education. Enrollment
  projections series, no. 3).   OTU
— Ontario secondary school enrollment projections to 1981/82: 1969
  projection, by Cicely Watson, Saeed Quazi and Aribert Kleist. [Toronto]
  Ontario Institute for Studies in Education [c1970]

129 p. diagrs., map, tables. (Ontario Institute for Studies in Education.
Enrollment projections series, no. 5).   OTU
— The secondary teacher: a study of the characteristics and supply/demand
relations of Ontario teachers, by Cicely Watson, Saeed Quazi and Joy
Poyntz. [Toronto] Ontario Institute for Studies in Education [c1972]
iii, 151 p.   OTER
Weinrib, Alice.
   Report on the survey of teaching materials for the learning of French as a
   second language in Ontario elementary and secondary schools, 1969–1970.
   Toronto: Modern Languages Centre, Ontario Institute for Studies in
   Education, 1971.
   1 v. (various pagings). illus.   OTER
Weisbrod, Kathleen M
   School and general health characteristics of grade 9 students in Ontario: an
   analysis of replies to the Carnegie staff questionnaire, by K.M. Weisbrod
   and Willard Brehaut. Toronto: Department of Educational Research,
   Ontario College of Education, University of Toronto, 1963.
   viii, 51 p. graphs, tables. (Carnegie Study of Identification and Utilization of
   Talent in High School and College. Bulletin no. 2).   OTER
Wilkins, Cecil James, 1898–
   A study of reading in the schools of Metropolitan Toronto. Part I.
   Evaluation of reading tests in use in June 1964. [Toronto: Metropolitan
   Toronto Educational Research Council, 1964]
   32 [157] leaves. (Metropolitan Toronto Educational Research Council.
   Research publication no. 5).   OONL
Wilkinson, Cecil E
   History of education in Ontario: a historical sketch of Woodville School, S.S.
   11, Sophiasburg township, Prince Edward county. Illustrations by Bill
   O'Brien. [Scarborough, Ontario] 1967.
   58 p. illus., facsims.   OTU
Willison, (Sir) John Stephen, 1856–1927.
   Sir George Parkin: a biography. London: Macmillan and Co., Limited,
   1929.
   278 p. ports.   OTU
   Completed after the author's death by W.L. Grant.   OTU
Windsor, Ontario. Board of Education.
   Windsor schools excel; progressive march of education in Windsor in twenty-
   five years, 1892–1917. [Windsor, Ontario: 1917]
   16 p. illus., port.   OTU
Wright, Vicki.
   The rape of children's minds: a survey of the most frequently used grades 1,
   2 & 3 readers in the Borough of North York. [North York, Ontario: 1976]
   13–43 p.   OTER
Yau, Cecilia (comp.).
   The use of voluntary aides in the elementary school program: a survey of

current practice in the Niagara region and an analysis of instructional roles. Edited by Jane Hill. [St. Catharines, Ontario] Niagara Centre, Ontario Institute for Studies in Education [1970]
73 [20] p.   OTER
York County, Ontario. Board of Education. Division of Planning and Development.
Differential effects of alternate secondary school environments: review studies, 1972–73. [Toronto?] 1973.
iv, 76 leaves. tables. (Report no. 3).   OTER
York County, Ontario. Board of Education. Research Office.
Report of a study of grade 8 programs housed in Sutton, Huron Heights and Markham secondary schools, 1970 71. [Toronto] The Board, 1971.
12, 4, 3 leaves. tables.   OTER
Young, Archibald Hope, 1863–1935.
Upper Canada College, Toronto, 1829–1929. [Toronto: 1928?]
[14] p.   OKQ
— Upper Canada College and the University of Toronto. [Toronto: 1929]
[16] p. ports.
"Reprinted from the *University of Toronto Monthly*."   OTAR
Young, Archibald Hope, 1863–1935 (ed.).
The war book of Upper Canada College, Toronto: Edited for the Old Boys' Association. Toronto: Printers Guild, Limited, 1923.
xxvii, 322 p. ports.   OTU

Periodical Articles

Adler, Marilynne [et al.]
A study of the effects of an acceleration programme in Toronto secondary schools. Ontario Journal of Educational Research 6: 1–22, 1963–64.
Althouse, J   G
Significant trends in education in Ontario. University of Toronto Quarterly 25: 232–241, 1956.
Angle, P   E
The teaching of agriculture in the high schools of Ontario. Ontario Agricultural College Review 23: 1–5, 1910.
Asbury, F   C
The grade 12 departmental testing programme. Ontario Journal of Educational Research 3: 117–119, 1960–61.
Baldwin, Lawrence.
The Ontario educational system and voluntary schools. Canada Educational Monthly 20: 361–366, 1898; 21: 41–44, 1899.
Bamman, Haley P
Patterns of school attendance in Toronto, 1844–1878: some spatial considerations. History of Education Quarterly 12: 381–410, 1972.

Barber, Marilyn.
The Ontario bilingual schools issue: sources of conflict. Canadian Historical
Review 47: 227–248, 1966.
Barrett, Harry O
Administrative problems related to the gifted child in the Toronto secondary
schools. Ontario Journal of Educational Research 4: 31–37, 1961–62.
Beeckmans, Merlyn.
Not enough regimentation, politics in Ontario secondary schools. Ontario
Education Review 1(no.3): 3, 1975.
Bergey, Lorna L   (comp.).
The effect of Bill 54 in Wilmot township. Waterloo Historical Society.
Annual Volume 54: 69–76, 1966.
Bill that established township as smallest administration unit for education;
consolidation of small schools.
The Bilingual schools of Ontario. School and Society 26: 451–452, 1927.
Bradley, Robert B
Vocational education in the secondary school. Education Canada 15(4):
53–58, 1975.
Cameron, D   M
Projection of the costs of elementary and secondary education in Ontario to
1975. Ontario Journal of Educational Research 10: 33–48, 1967–68.
Cameron, Maxwell A
The cost of elementary and secondary education in Ontario. The School
(Secondary Edition) 26: 7–10, 1937.
Canada: I. French in the schools. The Round Table 6: 734–739, 1916.
Cappon, James.
Is Ontario to abandon classical education? Queen's Quarterly 12: 190–206,
1904/1905.
Carnahan, A   T
Geology and earth science in Ontario high schools. Canadian Mining
Journal 88 (no. 6): 54–56, 1967.
Carson, Kenneth O
An evaluation of the objectives and achievement of special classes for gifted
children in the Kingston public schools. Ontario Journal of Educational
Research 6: 23–36, 1963–64.
Chartrand, Adélard.
L'école française en Ontario. Relations 2: 322–325, 1942.
Clarke, Katharine Wallbridge.
The story of The Bishop Strachan School. The Bishop Strachan School
Association Bulletin 37: 19–50, 1949.
Connor, A   W
James W. Connor, B.A., 1843–1929. Waterloo Historical Society. Annual
Report 17: 153–158, 1929.
Principal of Berlin High School 1871–1901.
Corporal punishment in the schools of the city of Toronto. Canada Educational
Monthly 27: 326–331, 1905.

Cowley, R   H
    The improvement of Ontario rural schools. Queen's Quarterly 13: 246–258,
    1905/1906.
Crawford, Arthur W
    Co-operation between schools and industry; the scope and aim of technical
    schools, together with an account of some of the schemes in use in Canada to
    co-ordinate the schools with industry. Industrial Canada 28(no. 5): 40–46,
    1927.
Crawford, Douglas H
    School mathematics in Ontario: expansion and moderate reform,
    1894–1959. National Council of Teachers of Mathematics. Yearbook 32:
    385–411, 1970.
Dadson, D   F
    Local history in our schools. Ontario History 45: 59–67, 1953.
[Davis, William G   ]
    Education Minister outlines changes. Ontario Education Review 4, May
    1967.
Dawson, Donald A
    Economies of scale in the Ontario public secondary schools. Canadian
    Journal of Economics 5: 306–309, 1972.
Denton, Frank T   and Peter J   George.
    Socio-economic influences on school attendance: a study of a Canadian
    county in 1871. History of Education Quarterly 14: 223–232, 1974.
    Wentworth county, Ontario.
Desjarlais, Lionel.
    L'école franco-ontarienne de demain. L'école Ontarienne 22(no. 4) 127–134,
    1966.
Desormeaux, Ernest G
    L'école Catholique en Ontario. Relations 2: 268–271, 1942.
Dewart, E   H
    Maintain the unity of our school system. Canada Educational Monthly 25:
    178–182, 1903.
    Ontario – Church vs. public schools.
Diamond, Florence.
    School system – Wilmot township. Waterloo Historical Society. Annual
    Volume 50: 88–92, 1962.
Donovan, Michael J
    The establishment of Roman Catholic separate schools in Port Arthur in the
    1880's. Thunder Bay Historical Museum Society. Papers and Records 3:
    9–15, 1975.
Dorland, A   G
    A hundred years of Quaker education in Canada; the centenary of Pickering
    College. Royal Society of Canada. Transactions s. 3, (sect. 2), 36: 51–91,
    1942.
— The re-opening of Pickering College; a scheme of education for Canadian
    citizenship. Canadian Forum 7: 384–385, 1927.

Douglass, Hugh.
A brief survey of the history of Ontario public school texts. Waterloo
Historical Society. Annual Volume 51: 12–16, 1963.
Dyde, S   W
The draft education bill; the public school. Canada Educational Monthly
25: 252–255, 1903.
— The rural teacher in Ontario. Canada Educational Monthly 26: 309–314,
1904.
Dyson, C   E   Cyril.
Typical schools of the province of Ontario. Royal Architectural Institute of
Canada. Journal 4: 255–262, 302–308, 1927.
Edwards, C   B
London, public schools, 1848–1871. London and Middlesex Historical
Society. Transactions 5: 14–29, 1912/1913.
Ellis, W   S
Regarding the proposed revision of the curriculum. Canada Educational
Monthly 25: 52–58, 1903.
Flowers, John F
Some opinions of Ontario grade 12 students on religion, education, and
government. Ontario Journal of Educational Research 3: 25–34, 1960–61.
— The viewpoints of Ontario grade 12 students towards themselves and
Americans. Ontario Journal of Educational Research 1(no. 2): 173–178,
1958–59.
The future of grade thirteen: a symposuim. The Toronto Education Quarterly 1
(no. 3): 2–9, 1962.
German, John F
Ontario Ladies College, Whitby. Canadian Magazine of Politics, Science,
Art and Literature 5: 72–78, 1895.
Goldring, C   C
After-school activities in Toronto schools. The School (Elementary Edition)
24: 373–381, 1936.
Grant, W   L
A pioneer school of today. Canadian Forum 3: 264–266, 1923.
Gray, Lillian Collier.
Rural education in Ontario. Canadian Forum 26: 155–156, 1946.
Griggs, Hugh.
Blueprint of education: a digest of some of the recommendations placed
before the [Ontario] Royal Commission on Education. Canadian School
Journal 23: 339–341, 350, 1945.
Hamilton, R   S
The history of secondary education in Galt. Part 1. The Howe régime.
Waterloo Historical Society. Annual Report 29: 158–161, 1941.
Hellmuth Ladies' College, London. Western Ontario Historical Notes 15 (no.
3): 7–10, 1959.
Hopper, A   G
Secondary education in Ontario. Culture 5: 149–155, 1944.

Hope deferred. Canadian Forum 30: 241, 246, 1951.
   Hope Royal Commission on Education.
Hornady, Aline Grandier.
   John Moffat and the Komoka Academy. Western Ontario Historical Notes
   25: 1–7, 1969.
House, Arthur W
   C.M.A. scholarships; a helping hand for technical school students .
   Industrial Canada 55(no. 7): 41 – 42, 53, 1954.
   Central Technical School, Toronto.
Hurtubise, J   Raoul.
   Les écoles bilingues de Sudbury. Société Historique du Nouvel-Ontario.
   Documents Historiques 28: 21–42, 1955.
Hutton, Harry K
   Name your next new school after Sir George. Ontario Education Review
   3(no. 1): 6, 1968.
Jamieson, M
   Schools and schoolmasters of Bytown and early Ottawa. Women's Canadian
   Historical Society of Ottawa. Transactions 3: 36–44, 1910.
Johnston, M   A
   A brief history of elementary education in the city of Waterloo. Waterloo
   Historical Society. Annual Volume 53: 56–66, 1966.
Johnston, Marion.
   The development of special-class programmes for gifted children in the
   elementary schools of Ontario from 1910 to 1962. Ontario Journal of
   Educational Research 7: 39–48, 1964–65.
Jordan, W   G
   Bi-lingual schools in Ontario. Queen's Quarterly 19: 300–303, 1911/1912.
Keith, Virginia.
   Legal status of the Ontario public school inspector. Revue de l'Université
   d'Ottawa 36: 668–677, 1966.
King, Jane.
   Dickie settlement schools. Waterloo Historical Society. Annual Report 38:
   25–28, 1950.
   North Dumfries township.
Knight, A   P
   Junior matriculation. Queen's Quarterly 11: 418–420, 1903/1904.
— Medical inspection of schools. Queen's Quarterly 15: 138–146, 1907/1908.
Knight, J   H
   The amendments to regulations for 1903. Canada Educational Monthly 24:
   314–315, 1902.
— Compulsory attendance and the Truancy Act. Canada Educational
   Monthly 22: 222–223, 1900.
Lamont, Melville L
   Our country school. Huron Historical Notes 7: 20–23, 1971.
   Grey township.

Leitch, Adelaide.
    The woodland schools of Georgian Bay. Canadian Geographical Journal 48:
    22–25, 1954.
Lind, Loren.
    The rise of bureaucracy in Ontario schools. This Magazine Is About Schools
    6 (2): 104–119, 1972.
Lyle, Patricia M   and M   Dormer Ellis.
    Some changes in age-grade distributions in Ontario during the quarter
    century, 1936–1961. Ontario Journal of Educational Research 5: 41–63,
    1962–63.
McCready S   P
    Rural education in Ontario. Canadian Forum 13: 376–378, 1933.
Macdonald, J   F
    Men in Ontario high schools. Queen's Quarterly 26: 229–235, 1918/1919.
— Salaries in Ontario high schools. Queen's Quarterly 17: 132–139,
    1909/1910.
McGuigan, J   C
    École secondaire bilinque à Toronto. L'Action Nationale 48: 117–123, 1958.
Mackay, Alexander.
    Central Technical School of Toronto. Industrial Canada 16: 482–483, 488,
    1915.
Mackinnon, A   R
    Experimental study of learning French in the public schools undertaken by
    the Toronto Board of Education. Ontario Journal of Educational Research
    4: 43–50, 1961–62.
Macpherson, W   E
    The Ontario grammar schools. Queen's Quarterly 24: 193–214, 1916/1917.
— The Ontario grammar schools, Kingston, Ontario. Queen's University.
    Bulletin of the Departments of History and Political Science 21: 1–22, 1916.
Manning, W   R
    The proposed changes in the public and high school courses of study, etc., for
    Ontario. Canada Educational Monthly 26: 125–128, 1904.
Massey, Vincent.
    Primary education in Ontario. The University Magazine 10: 495–503, 1911.
Millar, John.
    The educational system of Ontario – its excellences and its defects. Canada
    Educational Monthly 26: 270–278, 1904.
Millar, W   C
    Rural school sanitation. Canadian Public Health Journal 24: 572–576, 1933.
    Northern Ontario.
Mitchell, C   H
    Vocational education in Ontario. Industrial Canada 47(no. 1): 73–75, 77,
    1946.
    Text of brief submitted to Royal Commission on Education by Ontario
    Division of Canadian Manufacturers' Association.

Mitchell, G   W
    The new Ontario school regulations. Queen's Quarterly 12: 28–33,
    1904/1905.
— The new regulations for Ontario high schools. Queen's Quarterly 11:
    275–280, 1903/1904.
— The new regulations for Ontario high schools. Canada Educational Monthly
    26: 121–124, 1904.
    Reprinted from *Queen's Quarterly*.
Moir, John S
    The origins of the separate school question in Ontario. Canadian Journal of
    Theology 5: 105–118, 1959.
Myers, Douglas.
    The Hall–Dennis report. Canadian Forum 48: 136–138, 1968.
Neilson, W   Allan.
    Upper Canada College. Canadian Magazine of Politics, Science, Art and
    Literature 1: 451–459, 1893.
Nelson, Fiona.
    Community schools in Toronto: a sign of hope. Canadian Forum
    52(Oct.–Nov.): 52–57, 1972.
Newcombe, Ervin Ernest.
    The development of elementary school teacher education in Ontario since
    1900. Ontario Journal of Educational Research 8: 59–72, 1965/1966.
Newly organized technical institutes in Ontario. School Progress 17(3): 29,
    1949.
O'Hagan, T
    Catholic education in Ontario. Canada Educational Monthly 1: 149–152,
    1879.
Ontario Educational Association. Ontario Trustees' and Ratepayers'
    Association. Rural Section.
    Rural education. [Brief submitted to the Royal Commission on Education]
    Canadian School Journal 23: 245–248, 1945.
Parnall, M   B
    The senior public school and the neighbourhood schools of Guelph. Ontario
    Journal of Educational Research 2: 37–38, 1959/60.
Pearce, Thomas.
    School history, Waterloo county and Berlin. Waterloo Historical Society.
    Annual Report 2: 33–48, 1914.
Pearce, Thomas. Waterloo Historical Society. Annual Report 2: 49–50, 1914.
    Educator in Waterloo county.
Phair, John T   [et al.]
    An experiment in health teaching in the schools of Ontario. The School
    (Secondary Edition) 25: 6–12, 1936.
Pharand, Donat.
    Le statut juridique de l'école dite "bilingue en Ontario". Presence no. 1:
    4–16, 1965.

Pierce, Lorne.
    James Laughlin Hughes, LL.D.: patriot, preacher, pedagogue, poet.
    Canadian Magazine of Politics, Science, Art and Literature 58: 57–62, 1922.
Pitman, Walter.
    Hall–Dennis – its impact on education for tomorrow. Ontario Education
    Review 3(no. 2): 7, 11, 1968.
Plante, Albert.
    Les écoles bilingues d'Ontario. Société Historique du Nouvel-Ontario.
    Documents Historiques 28: 4–20, 1955.
— Les écoles séparées d'Ontario. Relations 11: 171–175, 259–262, 291–295,
    330–334, 1951; 12: 47–50, 62–65, 102–105, 146–149, 188–190, 1952.
Poster, James.
    The public schools of Ontario. Canadian Monthly & National Review 1:
    483–496, 1872.
Prang, Margaret Clerics.
    Politicians, and the bilingual schools issue in Ontario, 1910–1917. Canadian
    Historical Review 41: 281–307, 1960.
Reed, F   H
    The agriculture course in secondary schools: the work in Victoria county.
    Ontario Agricultural College Review 20: 372–375, 1908.
Religious education in Ontario. Canadian Forum 24: 197, 272, 1944/1945.
Report of the Senate of Victoria University on the draft of proposed changes in
    the public and high school courses of study and organization and in the
    departmental examination system. Canada Educational Monthly 26:
    169–171, 1904.
Revision of the public school curriculum in Ontario. School and Society 44:
    770–771, 1936.
Robinson, George H
    English literature in Canadian schools. Canada Educational Monthly 1:
    507–514, 1879.
Rogers, George F
    Intermediate schools. The School 22: 746–754, 1934.
    Proposed intermediate schools in Ontario.
Rogers, W
    Single-grade and multiple-grade classrooms in the public schools of Ontario.
    Ontario Journal of Educational Research 4: 97–104, 1961–62.
Royce, Marion V
    Arguments over the education of girls – their admission to grammar schools
    in this province. Ontario History 67: 1–13, 1975.
The rural school – 1883. Bruce County Historical Society. Yearbook 54–56,
    1970.
Sage, Walter N
    The teaching of history in the elementary schools of Canada. Canadian
    Historical Association. Historical Papers 55–63, 1930.

Sandwell, B   K
    Canadian unity and the separate school problem of Ontario. Saturday Night
    61(35): 16–17, 1946.
Savage, H   W
    Ontario Department of Education grade 12 testing programmes. Ontario
    Journal of Educational Research 1(no. 2): 145–147, 1958–59.
Scott, Colin A
    Drawing in the high schools and collegiate institutes of Ontario. Canada
    Educational Monthly 13: 281–284, 1891; 14: 4–7, 1892.
Scott, J   Glenn.
    The urban elementary public school principal in Ontario – his status
    according to the expressed views of principals and senior adminstrative
    officials. Ontario Journal of Educational Research 8: 73–82, 1965–66.
Seath, John.
    Inspector Seath on Toronto's schools. Canada Educational Monthly 25:
    33–35, 1903.
— Some needed educational reforms. Canada Educational Monthly 25:
    200–203, 245–251, 1903.
Sissons, C   B
    Canadian political ideas in the sixties and seventies: Egerton Ryerson.
    Canadian Historical Association. Historical Papers 94–103, 1942.
— The Crown Hill School; a study in rural education. Canadian Forum 3:
    135–137, 1923.
— French in the schools of Ontario – sixty years after. Queen's Quarterly 28:
    254–263, 1920/1921.
— A real rural teacher. Canadian Forum 3: 233–235, 1923.
Smith, A   R   G
    Beginning and progress of school fairs in Ontario. Waterloo Historical
    Society. Annual Report 18: 171–174, 1930.
Smith, Florence.
    Survey of reading interests in the secondary schools of Hamilton. Ontario
    Library Review 32: 124–129, 1948.
Smith, Karen.
    Secondary education in Ilderton 1921–1929. Western Ontario Historical
    Notes 23: 22–26, 1967.
Somerville, Henry.
    School taxes in Ontario. The Canadian Messenger of the Sacred Heart
    46(no. 6): 359–364, 1936.
Stamp, Robert M
    Schools on wheels: the railway car schools of northern Ontario. Canada: an
    historical magazine 1(no. 3): 34–42, 1973.
Standing, T   W
    County Board of public instruction for the county of Brant (Ontario). The
    School 22: 755–757, 847–849, 1934.
    Historical sketch 1853–1907.

Steele, Catherine.
    Frances Ridley Havergal and Havergal College. York Pioneer 36–45, 1974.
Strang, H   I
    The effect of high school regulations on teachers. Canada Educational
    Monthly 19: 201–209, 1897.
— The requirements for junior matriculation. Canada Educational Monthly
    25: 163–165, 1903.
Sutherland, J   C
    At Dr. Tassie's. Canadian Magazine of Politics, Science, Art and Literature
    62: 261–265, 1924.
    Private school in Galt.
The teachers of the Pine Bush School (1847–1874). Canadian-German Folklore
    2: 49–52, 1969.
Teachers of the red brick school renamed Clearview School in 1874. Canadian-
    German Folklore 2: 53–55, 1969.
Trowsdale, G   C
    Vocal music in the common schools of Upper Canada: 1846–76. Journal of
    Research in Music Education 18: 340–354, 1970.
Turner, Joanne.
    The private school: how change is affecting Alma College. Orbit 5(5):
    19–21, 1974.
25 SEF schools for Metro Toronto by 1970; modular, flexible schools dictated by
    course content. Ontario Education Review 5, May 1968.
Wallace, Malcolm W
    Secondary school reform. Canadian Forum 1: 230–231, 1921.
Wallace, W   G
    A Tassie boy. Ontario History 46: 169–178, 1954.
Weaver, Emily P
    Upper Canada College; its boys and old boys. Canadian Magazine of
    Politics, Science, Art and Literature 54: 407–416, 1920.
Wetherell, Alice.
    James Elgin Wetherell, B.A., 1851–1940. Western Ontario Historical Notes 9:
    16–33, 1951.
Will, J   S
    French in the schools of Ontario. Canadian Forum 1: 70–72, 1921.
Willson, Alice M
    French in Ontario schools since the nineties. The School (Secondary
    Edition) 25: 404–408, 1937.
Wilson, L   Roberta.
    Book talks in Wentworth county schools. Ontario Library Review 36: 8–9,
    1952.
Woltz, G   L
    Secondary agricultural education in Ontario, Canada. Ontario Agricultural
    College Review 26: 486–504, 1914.

You and the law; The Public Schools Amendment Act, 1967. Ontario
   Education Review 2, November 1967.
You and the law; The Separate Schools Amendment Act, 1967, The Municipal
   and School Tax Credit Assistance Act, 1967, The Teaching Profession
   Amendment Act, 1967, The Municipality of Metropolitan Toronto
   Amendment Act, 1967. Ontario Education Review 8, October 1967.
Zieman, Margaret K
   The religious tradition in Ontario's public schools. Queen's Quarterly 77:
   205–210, 1970.

Theses
Acal, Alice.
   A study of the mutual attitudes of English (speaking) Canadian children and
   French (speaking) Canadian children in two elementary schools, and the
   relation of the attitudes of these children to their sociometric status.
   [Toronto] 1949.
   I v. (various pagings). figs. (part fold.).
   M.A. thesis, University of Toronto.   OTU
Ahlawat, Usha Kiran, 1946–
   A comparative study of curricular, pedagogical and organizational aspects of
   innovations in primary education in England and the province of Ontario,
   Canada. [Toronto] c1972.
   iii, 119 leaves.
   M.A. thesis, University of Toronto.   OTU
Aim, Edward Mason, 1943–
   Resources for secondary education in Ontario: their distribution and
   relationship to educational outputs. [Toronto] c1972.
   I v. (various pagings). tables, figs.
   Ph.D. thesis, University of Toronto (microfilm 12922).   OTU
Ainsworth, Philip John, 1944–
   Functions of the associations of elementary principals in the county boards of
   eastern Ontario. Kingston, Ontario: c1974.
   xi, 139 leaves. tables.
   M.Ed. thesis, Queen's University (microfilm 22433).   OKQ
Althouse, John George, 1889–1956.
   The Ontario teacher: an historical account of progress, 1800–1910.
   [Toronto] 1929.
   viii [i.e. vi] 362 leaves.
   D.Paed. thesis, University of Toronto.   OTU
— Toronto: Ontario Teachers' Federation, 1967.
   184 p.   OTU
— n.p: 1929.
   14 p.
   Abstract of the thesis.   OTU
Amoss, Harold Edwin, 1880–
   Elementary science in the secondary schools of Ontario. Toronto [1916]
   125 p.
   D.Paed. thesis, University of Toronto.   OTU

Anderson, Barry Douglas, 1942–
  Bureaucratization and alienation: an empirical study in secondary schools.
  [Toronto] c1970.
  xvi [1] 299 [25] leaves. figs., tables (part fold.).
  Ph.D. thesis, University of Toronto (microfilm 8785).   OTU
Anderson, John Alexander.
  An Ontario secondary school student information system. [Toronto] 1968.
  2 v.
  M.A. thesis, University of Toronto.   OTU
Armstrong, Alexander MacKenzie, 1942–
  Ontario elementary education expenditure patterns, 1970–1973. [Toronto]
  c1973.
  iii, 108 leaves. tables, figs.
  M.A. thesis, University of Toronto.   OTU
Awender, Michael, 1943–
  The status of political science teaching in the high schools of Ontario.
  [Windsor, Ontario] 1973.
  ix, 124 leaves. tables.
  M.A. thesis, University of Windsor (microfilm 19849).   OWA
Barber, Marilyn Jean, 1942–
  The Ontario bilingual schools issue 1910–1916. Kingston, Ontario: 1964.
  v, 178 ieaves.
  M.A. thesis, Queen's University.   OKQ
Bassett, Eva.
  Social problems dealt with by the guidance programme in a secondary
  school. [Toronto] 1954.
  iv, 89 leaves.
  M.S.W. research report, University of Toronto.   OTU
Batt, Douglas Murray.
  Catholic politics and separate schools in the province of Ontario . Ottawa:
  1970.
  92 leaves.
  B.A. research essay, Carleton University.   OOCC
Bell, Walter Nehemiah.
  The development of the Ontario high school. [Toronto] University of
  Toronto Press [c1918]
  161 [3] p.
  D.Paed. thesis, University of Toronto.   OTU
Benson, Ralph, 1941–
  Determinants of expenditure for public secondary education in the province
  of Ontario. [Toronto] c1975.
  vi, 98 leaves. tables, diagrs.
  Ph.D. thesis, University of Toronto.   OTU
Bishop, Gordon Dale, 1945–
  Community decision: a gamed-simulation designed as an aid for teaching
  local government and politics. London, Ontario: 1974.
  viii, 334 leaves. diagrs., tables.
  M.A. thesis, The University of Western Ontario (microfilm 23261).   OLU

Bondy, Daniel Norman, 1947–
    Perceived leader behavior of the physical education department head
    associated with situational variables in secondary schools. Windsor, Ontario:
    1972.
    xi, 159 leaves. graphs, tables.
    M.P.E. thesis, University of Windsor (microfilm 14727).   OWA
Box, Colin Edward, 1941–
    Drug education in Ontario, Canada: secondary public schools. Bloomington,
    Indiana: 1970.
    xi, 226 leaves. illus., map.
    Ph.D. thesis, Indiana University (accepted 1971) (microfilm 73-12889).   DA
Boyko, Michael Bernard, 1948–
    The history and development of mathematics instruction in the elementary
    schools of Ontario, 1960–1973. [Toronto] c1974.
    ii, 129 leaves.
    M.A. thesis, University of Toronto.   OTU
Brehaut, Willard, 1928–
    A survey of factors related to variations in the cost of transportation of
    elementary and secondary school pupils in Ontario, 1953-54. [Toronto]
    1955.
    76 leaves. forms, map.
    M.A. thesis, University of Toronto.   OTU
Brown, Corbin Alexander.
    Elementary school supervision in Ontario: an evaluation of certain aspects of
    the supervisory programme. [Toronto] 1948.
    vi, 349 leaves.
    D.Paed. thesis, University of Toronto (microfilm 31172).   OTU
Brown, Wilfred John, 1936–
    Redistributive implications of federal – provincial fiscal arrangements for
    elementary and secondary education in Canada. [Toronto] c1974.
    xi, 284 leaves.
    Ph.D. thesis, University of Toronto (microfilm 26041).   OTU
Campbell, John Duncan.
    The arithmetic of the elementary schools in Ontario. [Toronto] 1943.
    297 leaves. illus., facsims.
    D.Paed. thesis, University of Toronto.   OTU
Carlton, Sylvia.
    Egerton Ryerson and education in Ontario, 1844–1877. Philadelphia: 1950.
    117 p.
    Ph.D. thesis, University of Pennsylvania.   DA
Carnahan, Archibald Thomas, 1923–
    Audio-visual aids in the teaching of geography. [London, Ontario] 1952.
    viii, 132 leaves. tables.
    M.A. thesis, The University of Western Ontario.
    Survey conducted in a sample of rural and urban elementary and secondary
    schools in Ontario.   OLU

Carson, Kenneth Oliver.
An evaluation of segregation in the programme for gifted children in the
Kingston public schools. [Toronto] 1963.
vii, 213 [59] leaves. illus., tables.
M.Ed. thesis, University of Toronto. OTU
Chambers, David Lee, 1940–
An analysis of the professional preparation and attitudes of male secondary
school coaches in selected sports in the province of Ontario. Columbus,
Ohio: 1972.
iv, 146 leaves. illus.
Ph.D. thesis, Ohio State University (microfilm 73-11,469). DA
Chambers, Lucille Hanna, 1938–
Teachers' perceptions on the existing and desired levels of thinking fostered
by verbal problems in approved grade 11 mathematics textbooks in Ontario.
[Toronto] c1976.
ix, 190 leaves. tables, figs.
M.A. thesis, University of Toronto. OTU
Clubine, Gordon Laverne.
A plan for the improvement and extension of art education in Ontario
secondary schools. New York: 1952.
v, 218 leaves. illus.
Ed.D. thesis, Columbia University. OTER
Clubine, Ivan Ward.
The use of records and forms in the internal administration of Ontario
secondary schools. [Toronto] 1940.
x, 206 leaves. diagrs.
M.A. thesis, University of Toronto. OTU
— Teacher load in the secondary schools of Ontario. New York: 1944.
ix, 188 leaves. graphs, tables.
Ph.D. thesis, New York University. OTER
Cluley, Kenneth G   1939–
A study of congruence and dissonance between student needs and
environmental press in Ontario secondary schools. [Toronto: 1973]
v, 120 leaves. 7 pages. tables(part fold.), figs.
M.A. thesis, University of Toronto. OTU
Coleman, Herbert Thomas John, 1872–
Public education in Upper Canada. New York: 1907.
120 p.
Ph.D. thesis, Columbia University.
Chiefly pre-Confederation. OTER
Connaughton, Edward Anthony.
A study of the provisions made for the Catholic elementary schools of the
province of Ontario. Washington, D.C.: 1940.
94 leaves.
M.A. thesis, Catholic University of America. OTER

Conway, Clifford Bruce.
 The hearing abilities of children in Toronto public schools. [Toronto] 1937.
 vi, 202 leaves. tables, figs.
 D.Paed. thesis, University of Toronto.   OTU
Cooke, Geoffrey James, 1935–
 Teachers' roles and structural differentiation. [Toronto] c1971.
 v, 356 leaves.
 Ph.D. thesis, University of Toronto.
 Open and closed classes.   OTU
Copp, Harold W
 The history of physical education and health in the elementary and
 secondary schools of Ontario, Canada. [Ann Arbor, Michigan: 1933]
 85 p. illus., tables.
 M.A. thesis, The University of Michigan.   OTC
Crawford, Douglas Gordon, 1931–
 Family interaction, achievement – values and motivation as related to school
 dropouts. [Toronto] c1969.
 ix, 162 p. tables. diagrs.
 Ph.D. thesis, University of Toronto (microfilm 5223).   OTU
Davey, Ian Elliott, 1945–
 Educational reform and the working class: school attendance in Hamilton,
 Ontario, 1851–1891. [Toronto: 1975]
 vii, 349 leaves. tables.
 Ph.D. thesis, University of Toronto (microfiche 31193).   OTU
Dawson, Donald Allan, 1940–
 Economics of scale in the secondary education sector in the province of
 Ontario. London, Ontario: 1969.
 xii, 165 leaves. tables.
 Ph.D. thesis, The University of Western Ontario (microfilm 5311).   OLU
Dean, Ruth.
 A report of a survey of the graduates of the dietitians course from 1928 to
 1933 Central Technical School, Toronto. New York: 1935.
 21 leaves.
 M.A. thesis, Teachers College, Columbia University.   Columbia
Denys, Jozef Gerard, 1940–
 A comparative study of the effects of Roman Catholic high schools and
 public high schools on the Roman Catholic commitment of Roman Catholic
 students in southern Ontario. [Waterloo, Ontario] 1972.
 xi, 242 leaves. illus.
 Ph.D. thesis, University of Waterloo (microfilm 10838).   OWTU
Dhillon, Pritam Singh, 1923–
 An historical study of aims of education in Ontario, 1800–1900. [Toronto]
 1961.
 iv, 123 leaves.
 M.Ed. thesis, University of Toronto.   OTU

Dixon, Robert Grieves.
 A comparison of two junior high schools, one in Ohio and one in Ontario.
 [Toronto] 1958.
 viii, 233 leaves. tables.
 M.Ed. thesis, University of Toronto. OTU
Dixon, Robert Thomas, 1935–
 The Ontario separate school system and section 93 of the BNA Act. [Toronto]
 c1976.
 iv, 427 leaves.
 Ed.D. thesis, University of Toronto. OTU
Doan, Arthur Wallace Ross.
 The evaluation of elementary school buildings and grounds. [Toronto] 1932.
 [iv] 236 [2] leaves. tables, plates, figs., fold. blueprints.
 D.Paed. thesis, University of Toronto. OTU
— The public school buildings of Toronto. [Toronto] 1921.
 1 v. (unpaged).
 M.A. thesis, University of Toronto. OTU
Duhamel, Ronald Joseph, 1938–
 Various forms of support and non-support of bilingual immersion programs
 in schools. [Toronto] c1973.
 1 v. (various pagings).
 Ph.D. thesis, University of Toronto (microfilm 20554). OTU
Dukhan, Hamlyn.
 The development of the junior high school and the senior school in
 Metropolitan Toronto. [Toronto] 1959.
 viii, 130 leaves. tables, figs.
 M.Ed. thesis, University of Toronto. OTU
Dunkley, George Albert Charles.
 The status of music education in Ontario high schools. Rochester, New
 York: 1965.
 M.A. thesis, Eastmen School of Music, University of Rochester. U. Rochester
Dupuis, L   J
 A history of elementary teacher training in Ontario. Ottawa: 1952.
 vii, 135 leaves.
 M.A. thesis, University of Ottawa (microfilm). OTER
Duran, Marcela Sofia, 1945–
 Values and education: a study of the Spanish-speaking Latin American
 children in the junior schools of Metropolitan Toronto. [Toronto] c1975.
 ii, 96 leaves.
 M.A. thesis, University of Toronto. OTU
Easson, McGregor.
 The intermediate school in Ottawa. [Toronto] 1934.
 123 p. tables.
 D.Paed. thesis, University of Toronto. OTU

Elliott, Charles M
    Proposals for the improvement of the instructional leadership provided by
    elementary school inspectors in northern Ontario. New York: 1954.
    70 leaves. tables.
    Ph.D. thesis, Columbia University.   OTC
Ellis, Maxyne Evelyn Dormer, 1925–
    A study of personal characteristics, family background and school factors
    associated with the patterns of progress through the grades of grade 13
    students in Metropolitan Toronto. [Toronto] c1968.
    xiii, 487 leaves. tables.
    Ed.D. thesis, University of Toronto.   OTU
Emerson, Sandra Lynn, 1947–
    Population education: a survey in Toronto schools, with implications for
    curriculum development. [Toronto: 1975]
    v, 263 leaves. tables.
    M.Sc. thesis, University of Toronto.   OTU
Emery, John Whitehall.
    The library, the school, and the child. Toronto: Macmillan, 1917.
    ix, 216 p. illus.
    D.Paed. thesis, University of Toronto.   OTU
Fair, James William, 1937–
    Teachers as learners: the learning projects of beginning elementary–school
    teachers. [Toronto] c1973.
    viii, 205 leaves. tables.
    Ph.D. thesis, University of Toronto (microfilm 21639).   OTU
Ferguson, Robert Carlisle, 1938–
    Teachers and teacher aides: a case study of innovation in an elementary
    school. [Toronto] c1976.
    ix, 219 leaves. figs.
    Ed.D. thesis, University of Toronto.   OTU
Fisher, Charles Wilfred, 1941–
    Educational environments in elementary schools differing in architecture
    and program openness. [Toronto] c1973.
    x, 165 leaves. tables.
    Ph.D. thesis, University of Toronto (microfilm 17263).
    Wentworth county separate schools.   OTU
Fitzpatrick, Michael Joseph, 1944–
    The role of Bishop Michael Francis Fallon and the conflict between French
    Catholics and Irish Catholics in the Ontario bilingual schools question,
    1910–1920. London, Ontario: 1969.
    v, 188 leaves. map.
    M.A. thesis, The University of Western Ontario(microfilm 5312).   OTU
Fleming, William Gerald, 1924–1975.
    Factors affecting the predictive accuracy of Ontario upper school results.
    [Toronto] 1954.
    x, 276 leaves. tables (part fold.).
    Ed.D. thesis, University of Toronto.   OTU

Flowers, John Franklin.
    The viewpoints of Ontario grade twelve students toward themselves and
    Americans. [Toronto] 1958.
    viii, 269 leaves. tables.
    Ed.D. thesis, University of Toronto.   OTU
Fox, James Harold.
    The centralized control of secondary education in the province of Ontario.
    Cambridge, Massachusetts: 1937.
    xxiii, 554 p. graphs, tables.
    Ed.D. thesis, Harvard University.   OTER
Fris, Joe, 1942–
    Professional role aspirations and achievements among Ontario secondary
    school teachers. [Toronto] c1972.
    xi, 132 leaves. tables, fig.
    M.A. thesis, University of Toronto (microfilm 22749).   OTU
— Professionalization and militancy among Ontario secondary school teachers.
    [Toronto] c1976.
    xiii, 277 leaves. tables, figs.
    Ph.D. thesis, University of Toronto.   OTU
Gagné, Jacques Réal.
    Personalizing the educational experience and the Hall–Dennis report. [Ann
    Arbor, Michigan] 1972.
    vii, 226 p.
    Ph.D. thesis, The University of Michigan.   OOU OTER
Gilbert, Sidney Norman.
    Educational and occupational aspirations of Ontario high school students: a
    multivariate analysis. Ottawa: 1973.
    262 leaves. diagrs., tables.
    Ph.D. thesis, Carleton University (microfilm 20093).   OOCC
Glendenning, Donald Ernest Malcolm.
    Impact of federal financial support on vocational education in Canada.
    Bloomington, Indiana: 1964.
    ix, 207 p. tables.
    Ph.D. thesis, Indiana University.   OTU
Goldstick, Isidore.
    Modern languages in the Ontario high school: a historical study. Toronto:
    University of Toronto Press, 1928.
    245 p. tables, charts, diagrs.
    D.Paed. thesis, University of Toronto.   OTU
Gray, Douglas Andrew.
    The role of the department head in Ottawa high schools. Calgary, Alberta:
    1972.
    xii, 210 leaves. illus.
    M.Ed. thesis, University of Alberta (microfilm 13391).   Can
Gray, William Barrisdale.
    The teaching of mathematics in Ontario, 1800–1941. [Toronto] 1948.
    503 leaves. tables, figs.
    D.Paed. thesis, University of Toronto.   OTU

Grime, Alexander Roger.
   Geography in the secondary schools of Ontario, 1800–1900. [Toronto] c1968.
   vi, 174 leaves. illus., tables, figs., facsims., map.
   M.Ed. thesis, University of Toronto.   OTU
Hackett, Gerald Thomas, 1925–
   The history of public education for mentally retarded children in the
   province of Ontario, 1867–1964. [Toronto] c1969.
   v, 435 leaves. tables.
   Ed.D. thesis, University of Toronto (microfilm 77-20,791).   OTU
Haggerty, Terry Robert Russell, 1945–
   An analysis of the physical education supplies and capital, budgetary
   decision making processes in an Ontario secondary school system. London,
   Ontario: 1973.
   xi, 173 leaves. tables.
   M.A. thesis, The University of Western Ontario (microfilm 16417).   OLU
Hardy, Edwin Austin, 1867–1952.
   The public library: its place in our educational system. Toronto: William
   Briggs, 1912.
   iii [1] 223 p. illus.
   D.Paed. thesis, University of Toronto.   OTU
Hardy, Timothy Ashley, 1941–
   Teacher–student dyadic relationships in the elementary school classroom: a
   participant observation study. [Toronto] c1974.
   vii, 563 leaves.
   Ph.D. thesis, University of Toronto.   OTU
Hedges, Henry George, 1924–
   Volunteer parental assistance in elementary schools. [Toronto] c1972.
   viii, 369 leaves. tables.
   Ed.D. thesis, University of Toronto.   OTU
Hempstead, Howard.
   Reporting pupil progress to parents: a survey of the methods and an analysis
   of the report cards used in the elementary schools of selected Ontario school
   systems. [Toronto] 1961.
   [v] 132 leaves. map.
   M.Ed. thesis, University of Toronto.   OTU
High, Norman Henry.
   A study of educational opportunity in the provincially-controlled schools of
   Haldimand county, Ontario. New York: 1950.
   xv, 250 leaves. maps, tables.
   Ph.D. thesis, Cornell University.   OTER
Hillier, Robert Melville, 1917–
   A comparative study of provincial and Seventh-Day Adventist secondary
   and higher education in Ontario and Alberta. Lincoln, Nebraska: 1971.
   256 leaves. illus.
   Ed.D. thesis, University of Nebraska (microfilm 71-19,492).   OTER

Hofferd, George W
    A study of the content and methodology of Ontario lower school biology.
    Toronto: The University of Toronto Press, 1932.
    149 p. tables, charts.
    D.Paed. thesis, University of Toronto.   OTU
Holmes, Alfred.
    Voluntary reading of Toronto public school pupils; a quantitative and
    qualitative study. [Toronto] 1932.
    155 leaves.
    D.Paed. thesis, University of Toronto.   OTU
Humphreys, Edward Harold, 1932–
    Interaction, prestige and occupational concepts of secondary school teachers
    in the province of Ontario. [Toronto] c1968.
    xiv, 240 leaves. tables, figs. (part fold.).
    Ed.D. thesis, University of Toronto.   OTU
Irvine, Florence Gladys, 1921–
    A study of some curricular problems of selected rural elementary schools in
    Ontario, with particular reference to the occupational mobility of students.
    [Toronto] c1972.
    xvi, 559 leaves. tables.
    Ph.D. thesis, University of Toronto (microfilm 14860).   OTU
Johnston, Marion Campbell.
    The development of special class programmes for gifted children in the
    elementary schools of Ontario from 1910 to 1962. [Toronto] 1964.
    iv, 283 leaves. tables.
    Ed.D. thesis, University of Toronto.   OTU
Johnston, Ruth L
    An examination of the work of the educational social worker in York
    township public schools. [Toronto] 1947.
    iii, 78 leaves.
    M.S.W. thesis, University of Toronto.   OLU
Kendall, Joan Irene, 1952–
    The Black legend in Ontario: an examination of derogatory sterotypes of
    Latin Americans in primary and secondary school textbooks. London,
    Ontario: 1976.
    v, 112 p.
    M.A. thesis, The University of Western Ontario (microfilm 28256).   OLU
Lapp, Donald Arthur.
    The schools of Kingston: their first hundred and fifty years. [Kingston,
    Ontario] 1937.
    xi, 232 leaves. illus., tables, maps (part fold.).
    M.A. thesis, Queen's University.   OKQ
Leger, Raymond Joseph Jules.
    Critical teaching behaviours of the Ontario French-language elementary
    school teachers perceived by pupils. State College, Pennsylvania: 1971.
    136 p.
    Ed.D. thesis, Pennsylvania State University (microfilm 72-13886).   DA

Leonard, Alvin Kiel.
    Over-ageness and under-ageness in the elementary schools of Ontario.
    Toronto: 1926.
    iii, 46 leaves.
    M.A. thesis, University of Toronto.   OTU
Letourneau, Reginald.
    Pourquoi l'enseignement du français dans les high schools d'Ontario, est-il
    en partie une faillite? [Ottawa] 1932.
    51 leaves.
    M.A. thesis, University of Ottawa (microfilm).   OTER
Li, Janet.
    A comparison of written work performance by Chinese bilingual and
    Canadian monolingual children in grades five and six. [Toronto] 1970.
    73 leaves. tables.
    M.A. thesis, University of Toronto.   OTU
Londerville, John J   D
    The schools of Peterborough: their first hundred years. Kingston, Ontario:
    1942.
    x, 223 leaves. illus., chart, maps (part col. part fold.).
    M.A. thesis, Queen's University.   OKQ
Losier, Mary Carmel,   −1972.
    The history of the teaching of English literature in the public schools and
    high schools of Ontario. [Toronto] 1930 [c1976]
    119 [1] leaves.
    M.A. thesis, University of Toronto (microfilm 25490).   OTU
MacDonald, Donald D   −1947.
    Sight-saving classes in the public schools. [Toronto: 1923?]
    86 [2] p. illus., forms.
    D.Paed. thesis, University of Toronto.   OTU
Macdonald, George.
    Uniformity in the academic subjects of the industrial course: an investigation
    of the extent and effect of uniformity in the application of academic subjects
    to the Industrial Course in the technical schools of Toronto, 1945–1950.
    [Toronto] 1952.
    vi, 185 leaves. tables, figs.
    D.Paed. thesis, University of Toronto.   OTU
McIntosh, William John.
    A study in shop guidance at Jarvis School for Boys, Toronto. [Toronto] 1946.
    ix, 139 leaves. illus., tables.
    D.Paed. thesis, University of Toronto.   OTU
McMillan, George.
    The agricultural high school in Ontario. Toronto: University of Toronto
    Press, 1924.
    129 p. tables, diagrs.
    D.Paed. thesis, University of Toronto.   OTU

McNamara, John Andrew, 1943–
   A study of alternate school calendars: implications for the Ontario school
   system. [Toronto] c1969.
   107 leaves.
   M.A. thesis, University of Toronto.   OTU
McReynolds, William Peter, 1935–
   A model for the Ontario educational system. [Toronto] c1969.
   3, xx, 177 [44] leaves. figs., tables.
   Ph.D. thesis, University of Toronto (microfilm 7915).   OTU
Mark, Clarence Ellsworth.
   The public schools of Ottawa: a survey. Ottawa: Pattison Print, 1918.
   108 p. diagrs., map, plate.
   D.Paed. thesis, University of Toronto (accepted 1919).   OTU
Martin, Harold George.
   Grammar in Ontario elementary schools. [Toronto: 1931]
   158 leaves. diagrs., tables.
   D.Paed. thesis, University of Toronto.   OTU
— Toronto: The Ryerson Press [c1932]
   vii, 128 p. tables.   OTER
Mary of St. Catherine, Sister.
   The genesis of Catholic education in Renfrew. Ottawa: 1958.
   102 leaves.
   M.A. thesis, University of Ottawa.   OOU
Matthews, Carl Joseph.
   Intermediate schools in the Ontario separate school system. Toronto: 1961.
   20 leaves.
   M.Ed. thesis, University of Toronto.
   No copy located.
Matthews, William David Edison.
   The history of the religious factor in Ontario elementary education.
   [Toronto] 1950.
   xiii, 387 leaves.
   D.Paed. thesis, University of Toronto.   OTU
Meagher, Robert W
   An analysis of the Jesuit code of education in Canadian Jesuit high schools.
   Winnipeg: 1954.
   v, 159 leaves.
   M.Ed. thesis, University of Manitoba.   MWU
Melvin, Arthur Gordon, 1894–
   The professional training of teachers for the Ontario public schools.
   Baltimore: 1923.
   213 p.
   Ph.D. thesis, Columbia University.   Columbia
Milburn, Geoffrey.
   The Ontario grammar schools, 1853–1871. Durham, England: 1960.
   M.A. thesis, University of Durham.
   No copy located.

Mobley, Jack Arthur.
　　Protestant support of religious instruction in Ontario public schools. Ann
　　Arbor, Michigan: 1962.
　　150 p.
　　Ph.D. thesis, The University of Michigan (microfilm 62-03253).　　OTER DA
Mutimer, Brian T　　P　　1933–
　　Attitudes towards physical activity of grade 12 boys in two London high
　　schools. London, Ontario: 1969.
　　x, 150 leaves. illus., tables.
　　M.A. thesis, The University of Western Ontario (microfilm 5330).　　OLU
Newcombe, Ervin Ernest.
　　The development of elementary school teacher education in Ontario since
　　1900. [Toronto] 1965.
　　vii [ii] 289 leaves. illus., tables, facsims.
　　Ed.D. thesis, University of Toronto.　　OTU
O'Neill, Gilbert Patrick, 1944–
　　Post-secondary aspirations of high school seniors from different contextual
　　settings. [Toronto] c1976.
　　ii, ix, 202 leaves. tables, figs., maps.
　　Ph.D. thesis, University of Toronto (microfiche 30352).　　OTU
Orr, E　　Arnold.
　　The intermediate school – and Ontario. [Hamilton, Ontario] 1935.
　　96 leaves.
　　M.A. thesis, McMaster University.　　OHM
Parnall, Maxwell Bennett.
　　A study of the senior public school and the neighbourhood schools of
　　Guelph. [Toronto] 1958.
　　vi, 145 leaves. illus.
　　M.Ed. thesis, University of Toronto.　　OTU
Partlow, Hugh Russell.
　　A comparison of St. Catharines public school standards in arithmatic and
　　reading 1933–38 and 1952–54. [Toronto] 1955.
　　viii, 307 [4] leaves. tables. fig.
　　D.Paed. thesis, University of Toronto.　　OTU
Parvin, Viola Elizabeth.
　　Authorization of textbooks for the elementary schools of Ontario, 1846–1950.
　　[Toronto] 1961.
　　viii, 285 leaves. illus., facsims.
　　Ed.D. thesis, University of Toronto　　OTU
Perron, Rhéal Rolland.
　　A study of the non-repeating grade IX bilingual pupils of Sudbury in the
　　private and public secondary schools. [Toronto] 1965.
　　vi, 175 leaves. diagrs., forms.
　　M.Ed. thesis, University of Toronto.　　OTU
Phillips, Charles Edward, 1897–
　　The teaching of English in Ontario, 1800–1900. [Toronto: 1935] c1976.
　　v, 198, vi–xviii leaves.
　　D.Paed. thesis, University of Toronto (microfilm 15499).　　OTU

Pratt, David, 1939–
An instrument for measuring evaluative assertions concerning minority
groups and its application in an analysis of history textbooks approved for
Ontario schools. [Toronto] c1969.
200 leaves. tables, fig.
Ph.D. thesis, University of Toronto (microfilm 7923).   OTU
Pullen, Harry.
A study of secondary school curriculum change in Canada, with special
emphasis on an Ontario experiment. [Toronto] 1955 [c1976].
vi, 234 leaves. tables, charts, maps.
Ed.D. thesis, University of Toronto (microfilm 25501).   OTU
Putman, John Harold, 1866–1940.
Egerton Ryerson and education in Upper Canada. Toronto: William Briggs,
1912.
270 p.
D.Paed. thesis, Queen's University.   OKQ
Quick, Edison Junior.
The development of geography and history curricula in the elementary
schools of Ontario, 1846–1966. [Toronto] c1967.
365 leaves. tables.
Ed.D. thesis, University of Toronto.   OTU
Quinn, George William.
Impact of European immigration upon the elementary schools of central
Toronto, 1815–1915. [Toronto] 1968.
vi, 120 leaves. tables, graphs, maps.
M.A. thesis, University of Toronto.   OTU
Radcliffe, Samuel John.
Retardation in the schools of Ontario. [Toronto: 1922?]
59 p. diagrs.
D.Paed. thesis, University of Toronto.   ·   OTU
Robinson, George Carlton.
A historical and critical account of public secondary education in the
province of Ontario, Canada, 1782–1916. [Cambridge, Massachusetts:
1918?]
189 leaves. illus.
Ph.D. thesis, Harvard University (microfilm).   OTER
Robinson, Roosevelt MacDonald, 1935–
Communications and power within the York region system of education
during a period of transition, 1969–74. [Toronto] c1975.
x [1] 335 leaves. tables, figs., maps.
Ed.D. thesis, University of Toronto.   OTU
Rule, James William, 1946–
Innovation and experimentation in Ontario's public and secondary school
system 1919–1940. London, Ontario: 1974.
viii, 126 leaves.
M.A. thesis, The University of Western Ontario (awarded 1975) (microfilm
24653).   OLU

Ryerson, Donald Egerton.
   Musical education in secondary schools in Ontario: a critical survey.
   [Toronto] 1947.
   21 leaves.
   Mus.Bac. thesis, University of Toronto (awarded 1950).   OTU
Savage, Hubert William.
   A study of the factors affecting Ontario secondary school mathematics
   specialist teachers' knowledge of educational research. [Toronto] 1957.
   90 leaves. tables.
   M.Ed. thesis, University of Toronto.   OTU
Schalburg, Annette.
   School leaving at fifteen; a study of work permits issued by the Toronto
   Board of Education. Toronto: 1948.
   ix, 116 leaves. charts.
   M.S.W. thesis, University of Toronto.   OTU
Scott, John Glenn.
   The urban elementary public school principal in Ontario – his status
   according to the expressed views of principals and senior administrative
   officials. [Toronto] 1965.
   xi, 363 leaves. tables.
   Ed.D. thesis, University of Toronto.   OTU
Sedgwick, Mildred Sybil.
   A study of unlawful non-attendance (truancy) in the city of Toronto.
   [Toronto] 1939.
   40 leaves. tables, graphs.
   M.A. thesis, University of Toronto.   OTU
Semple, Stuart Ward, 1935–
   John Seath's concept of vocational education in the school system of
   Ontario, 1884–1911. [Toronto] 1964.
   [vi] 330 leaves. tables.
   M.Ed. thesis, University of Toronto (microfilm 22778).   OTU
Sheridan, Harold Stanley.
   The development of public elementary teacher education in Ontario, New
   York, and Michigan. Washington, D.C.: 1971.
   183 p.
   Ed.D. thesis, George Washington University (microfilm 72-07602).   DA
Simpson, John Garbutt.
   An objective study of the subject matter of the various fourth readers which
   have been authorized in Upper Canada and Ontario, giving an historical
   sketch of the same and stating what ... an ideal reader should contain and
   what its purpose should be. Toronto: 1922.
   98 leaves.
   M.A. thesis, University of Toronto.   OTU

Singhawisai, Wilars, 1934–
An analysis of degrees of concensus or role expectations of the district high
school principal in Ontario as perceived by the principals themselves, the
board mambers and the teachers. [Toronto] 1964.
xi, 271 leaves. tables, diagrs.
Ed.D. thesis, University of Toronto.   OTU
Smith, Alan Arthur.
A study of instrumental music in Ontario secondary schools during
1954–1955. [Toronto] 1956.
xii, 257 leaves. tables (part fold.), col. fold. map.
Mus.M. thesis, University of Toronto.   OTU
Sorley, Gordon D
Ontario Secondary School Teachers' Federation and economic and
protective priorities 1919–1974: a descriptive essay. Ottawa: 1974.
92 leaves.
M.A. research essay, Carleton University.   OOCC
Speare, Allan Denley, 1925–
Student mobility and academic achievement. [Toronto] c1971.
vii, 167 leaves. tables, figs., fold. form.
Ed.D. thesis, University of Toronto.   OTU
Spence, Ruth Elizabeth.
Education as growth: its significance for the secondary schools of Ontario.
Toronto: 1925.
viii, 183 p.
Ph.D. thesis, Columbia University.   OTER
Stamm, Carol A
The introduction and maintenance of an innovative program in Ontario at
the elementary school level: a case study. Montreal: 1976.
ii, 186 leaves. illus.
M.A. thesis, McGill University (microfiche 29461).   Can
Stamp, Robert Miles, 1937–
The campaign for technical education in Ontario, 1876–1914. London,
Ontario: 1970.
xi, 323, xii–xiii leaves. tables.
Ph.D. thesis, The University of Western Ontario (microfilm 6181).   OLU
Staples, Richard Osborne.
The Ontario rural teacher – selective professional training and in-service
guidance. [Toronto: 1946]
217 leaves.
D.Paed. thesis, University of Toronto.   OTU
Stewart, Edward Emslie, 1930–
The 1955 status of recommendations in the Report of the Royal Commission
on Education in Ontario, 1950. [Ann Arbor] 1956.
257 leaves. table.
M.A. thesis, The University of Michigan.   OTC

Stoddart, William Brunton.
    A critical analysis of the provisions for the gifted child in the Forest Hill
    school system: a case study. [Toronto] 1965.
    [viii] 386 leaves. tables, figs.
    Ed.D. thesis, University of Toronto.   OTU
Stokes, Shirley Grace, 1919–
    The career patterns of women elementary school principals in Ontario.
    [Toronto] c1974.
    xxi, 297 [4] leaves. 12, 11A pages. tables.
    M.A. thesis, University of Toronto.   OTU
Stratton, Hilton Anthony.
    London elementary school district enrollments in relation to socio-economic
    indicators. London, Ontario: 1976.
    vii, 78 leaves. maps, tables.
    B.A. thesis, The University of Western Ontario.   OLU
Tait, Eleanor M
    The growth of music in the schools of Ontario with a short account of the
    music, past and present, in the other provinces of Canada. [Toronto] 1952.
    44, [2] leaves.
    Mus. Bac. thesis, University of Toronto.   OTU
Tait, George Edward, 1910–
    A history of art education in the elementary schools of Ontario. [Toronto]
    1957 [c1976]
    x, 304 leaves. illus. (8 col.).
    Ed.D. thesis, University of Toronto (microfilm 25508).   OTU
— [Toronto] 1957.
    26 p.
    Abstract of a thesis for the degree of Doctor of Education, University of
    Toronto 1957.   OKQ
Tannis, Wendy Bunt, 1949–
    An analysis of the effects of social class, mother's working status, mother's
    occupation and mother's education on the educational and occupational
    aspirations of female grade 10 students in an Ontario community. Windsor,
    Ontario: 1972.
    viii, 115 leaves. tables.
    M.A. thesis, University of Windsor (microfilm 14792).   OWA
Thompson, Melville McClelland, 1949–
    An analysis of financial practices in secondary school physical education
    departments in Ontario. London, Ontario: 1973.
    xii, 159 leaves. illus., tables.
    M.A. thesis, The University of Western Ontario (accepted 1974) (microfilm
    20542).   OLU
Tobias, Henry.
    How high school students view their neighbourhood environment. [Toronto]
    1976.
    ii, 73 leaves. tables, maps.
    B.A. thesis, University of Toronto.   OTU

Treddenick, John Macauley, 1938–
An econometric analysis of public education activity in Ontario, 1947–1965.
Kingston, Ontario: 1969.
ix, 201 leaves. diagrs. tables, figs.
Ph.D. thesis, Queen's University (microfilm 3527).   OKQ
Trowsdale, George Campbell.
A history of public school music in Ontario. [Toronto] 1962.
2 v. [xviii, 566 leaves] tables, plates.
Ed.D. thesis, University of Toronto (microfilm 21416).   OTU
Underwood, Thomas Joseph, 1927–
Imbalances in school play facilities – case study: elementary schools in
London, Ontario. London, Ontario: 1971.
xiv, 125 leaves. graphs, photos, tables, maps.
M.A. thesis, The University of Western Ontario.   OLU
Vernon, Foster.
Some aspects of the development of public education in the city of St.
Catharines. [Toronto] 1959.
iv, 240 leaves. illus., facsim., map.
M.Ed. thesis, University of Toronto.   OTU
Vincent, Colin.
Spatial variations of educational opportunity in the publicly supported high
schools of Ontario. [Waterloo, Ontario] 1969.
vii, 122 leaves. illus., maps.
M.A. thesis, University of Waterloo (microfilm 11611).   OWTU
Waide, Frederick Gordon.
A history of primary education in Ontario and Quebec. New York: 1912.
106 p.
Ped.D. thesis, New York University.   DA
Warner, Lincoln Lloyd, 1940–
Relationships between student participation in decision-making on
discipline and the perceptions of students and teachers on selected aspects of
school life: a case study of Ontario secondary schools. [Toronto] c1975.
xiii, 231 leaves. tables.
M.A. thesis, University of Toronto.   OTU
Webster, Gary William, 1947–
The application of location – allocation models to the design of a public
facility system: a case study of the Kingston public school system. Kingston,
Ontario: c1972.
v, 73 leaves. tables, figs., maps.
M.A. thesis, Queen's University (accepted 1973) (microfilm 14077).   OKQ
White, Edwin Theodore, 1869–1929.
Public school textbooks in Ontario. London: The Chas. Chapman Co., 1922.
114 p.
D.Paed. thesis, University of Toronto.   OTU

White, Lloyd.
> Some aspects of commercial law in Ontario secondary schools. [Toronto]
> 1942.
> 4 v. tables.
> D.Paed. thesis, University of Toronto.   OTU

Wilkins, Cecil James.
> An administrative plan for the improvement of reading in the Toronto
> secondary schools. New York: 1952.
> 181 leaves.
> Ed.D. thesis, Columbia University.   Columbia

Williamson, Lloyd Paul.
> The image of Indians, French Canadians, and Americans in authorized
> Ontario high school textbooks, 1890–1930. Ottawa: 1969.
> v, 129 leaves.
> M.A. thesis, Carleton University.   OOCC

POST-SECONDARY EDUCATION

Bibliography

Bates, Hilary.
> A bibliography of Fred Landon. Ontario History 62: 5–16, 1970.

Campbell, Gordon.
> The community college in Canada: an annotated bibliography. Calgary,
> Alberta: Department of Educational Administration, The University of
> Calgary, 1971.
> v, 82 p.
> Ontario: pp. 74–78.   OTU

Harris, Robin Sutton, 1919–   (comp.).
> An annotated list of the legislative acts concerning higher education in
> Ontario. Compiled by Robin S. Harris with the assistance of Constance
> Allen and Mary Lewis. [Toronto] Innis College, University of Toronto,
> 1966.
> vi, 79 p.   OTER

— An index to the material bearing on higher education contained in J.G.
> Hodgins *Documentary history of education in Upper Canada* (Ontario) compiled by
> Robin S. Harris with the assistance of Constance Allen. [Toronto] Innis
> College, University of Toronto, 1966.
> vi, 60 p.   OTU

— A list of reports to the Legislature of Ontario bearing on higher education in
> the province, compiled by Robin S. Harris with the assistance of Constance
> Allen and Mary Lewis. [Toronto] Innis College, University of Toronto,
> 1966.
> v, 17 p.   OTU

Meikle, M   Duncan.
   A bibliography of George M. Wrong. Papers of the Bibliographical Society
   of Canada 14: 90–114, 1975.
Wales, Katharine and Elsie McLeod Murray.
   A bibliography of the works of George M. Wrong. Canadian Historical
   Review 29: 238–239, 1948.
Ward, Jane.
   The published works of H.A. Innis. Canadian Journal of Economics and
   Political Science 19: 233–244, 1953.

Monographs and Pamphlets
Academic career planning: the ivory tower and the crystal ball, report of the
   Joint COU/OCUFA Committee on the Study of Academic Career
   Development in Ontario Universities by G.W. Bennett [et al.]Toronto:
   Council of Ontario Universities, 1976.
   42 p. graphs, tables.   OTER
Acres, Mima A
   The junior college here and now. Ottawa: 1937.
   64 p. illus., tables.
   Junior colleges in Ottawa.   BVAU
Alderson, Henrietta Jane.
   Twenty-five years a-growing: the history of the School of Nursing,
   McMaster University. [Hamilton, Ontario] McMaster University, 1976.
   xiv, 333 p. illus., charts, graphs, ports., tables.   OONL
Alexander, William E
   Patterns in higher education: a case study of an educational institute.
   Toronto: Ontario Institute for Studies in Education, Department of
   Educational Planning, 1971.
   44 leaves.   OTER
Allen, James,   –1918.
   Facts concerning federation; an address to the Alumni Association of
   Victoria University at their annual meeting, Alumni Hall, Cobourg,
   Ontario, May 14th, 1889. n.p.: Published by order of the Alumni
   Association [1889?]
   37 p.   OTU
Allen, Moyra.
   Learning to nurse; the first five years of the Ryerson nursing program [by]
   Moyra Allen [and] Mary Reidy. [Toronto] Registered Nurses Association of
   Ontario, 1971.
   270 p. diagrs., tables.   OTU
Althouse, John George, 1889–1956.
   A tribute to Peter Sandiford, M.A., Ph.D., 1882–1941. n.p. [1941?]
   [5] p. port.   OTU
Andrews, (John) architects.
   Scarborough College; interim report on master plan. Toronto: 1968.
   [3] 12 [4] leaves. 7 plans.   OTU

Ashley, Anne, 1889–
    William James Ashley: a life by his daughter with a chapter by J.H.
    Muirhead and a foreword by Stanley Baldwin. London: P.G. King & Son
    Ltd., 1932.
    176 p. ports.   OTU
L'Association des anciens L'Université d'Ottawa/The University of Ottawa
    1848–1948. Ottawa: L'Association [1948?]
    39 p. illus., ports.   OOU
Association of Universities and Colleges of Canada. Commission on the
    Financing of Higher Education in Canada.
    Financing higher education in Canada; being the report of a Commission to
    the Association of Universities and Colleges of Canada, successor to the
    National Conference of Canadian Universities and Colleges, and its
    executive agency, the Canadian Universities Foundation. [Toronto]
    University of Toronto Press, 1965.
    xiv, 98 [6] p.
    Chairman: Vincent W. Bladen.   OTU

Background paper to Association of Universities and Colleges of Canada. Commission on the
    Financing of Higher Education in Canada
Canadian Association of College and University Libraries.
    Forecast of the cost of academic library services in Canada 1965–1975: a
    brief to the Bladen Commission on the Cost of Higher Education. [Waterloo,
    Ontario: University of Waterloo Press] 1964.
    ii, 37 leaves. tables.   OTU

Assumption College, Windsor, Ontario.
    The Ambassador of nineteen hundred and forty. Windsor, Ontario: 1940.
    192 p. front., illus., ports., map.
    A special edition issued in honour of the 70th anniversary year of the
    reorganized college, 1870–1940.   OLU
— Golden jubilee, 1870–1920. Sandwich, Ontario [1920?]
    158 p. illus., ports.   OTAR
— The nineteen forty-five Ambassador. [Windsor, Ontario: 1945]
    216 p. illus., ports.
    "Published by the students in commemoration of the 75th anniversary of the
    College, 1870–1945".   OLU
Assumption University, Windsor, Ontario.
    The Basilian Fathers, Assumption 1870–1970. Centennial Proceedings.
    [Windsor, Ontario] 1970.
    19 p.   OTSTM
— The Basilian Fathers, Assumption, 1870–1970. Centennial Souvenir.
    [Windsor, Ontario] 1970.
    13 p.   OTSTM

Ayers, H   D
>   Engineering at Guelph: a history 1874–1973, by H.D. Ayers and R.W.
>   Irwin. Guelph, Ontario: School of Engineering, University of Guelph [1973]
>   7 p. illus., ports. (Technical publication, no. 18).   OTU

Aylsworth, M   B
>   Alumni souvenir, illustrating buildings and faculties of the University of
>   Toronto and affiliated colleges. Arts and divinity edition. Compiled and
>   published by M.B. Aylsworth. Toronto [c1892]
>   [3] p. [24] leaves. illus., ports.   OTU

Ball, Donald James, 1950–
>   A short history of Engineering Science at University of Toronto. [Toronto]
>   1970.
>   6 [4] leaves. 2 diagrs.   OTU

Ballantyne, P   M
>   A history of Lakehead University: Lakehead Technical Institute,
>   1947–1956, Lakehead College of Arts, Science & Technology, 1957–1965,
>   Lakehead University, 1966. Port Arthur, Ontario: Friends of the Lakehead
>   University Library, 1966.
>   1 v. (various pagings). illus., facsims.   OPAL

Barber, Frank Louis, 1877–1945.
>   In memorium. Toronto: Published for Victoria University by Clarke, Irwin
>   & Company, Limited, 1948.
>   19 p.
>   Memorial address given by President Walter T. Brown.   OTAR

Bartell, R   Constance (Dunkin).
>   The history of the School of Nursing at the Toronto Western Hospital.
>   [Toronto] 1965.
>   iii, 40 leaves. illus., graphs, tables.   OTU

Bellisle, Henry S
>   The Institute of Mediaeval Studies. Toronto: The Institute of Mediaeval
>   Studies, St. Michael's College, 1933.
>   19 p.
>   "An address delivered by Rev. H.S. Bellisle at the Canadian Federation of
>   Catholic Alumnae Reunion, 1933".   OTSTM

Bensalem. [Toronto: 1974]
>   104 p. illus.
>   Erindale College, University of Toronto.   OTU

Bergevin, Jean Louis.
>   University of Ottawa: vocations to priesthood and liberal professions,
>   1848–1928/L'Université d'Ottawa: vocations sacerdotale et professions
>   liberales, 1848–1928. Ottawa: Editions de l'Université d'Ottawa, 1929.
>   147 p. illus., plates.   OTU OOU

Bissell, Claude Thomas, 1916–
>   An address: "Changing patterns of higher education in Canada: the
>   province of Ontario". [Toronto: 1965]
>   21 leaves.   OTU

— Halfway up Parnassus: a personal account of the University of Toronto
    1932–1971. [Toronto] University of Toronto Press [c1971]
    197 p. illus.   OTU
— Remarks on the challenge of expansion at the University of Toronto.
    [Toronto, 1959]
    [13] leaves. fold. plan.   OTU
— A role for Carleton. [Ottawa] Carleton College, 1956.
    16 p. illus., port.   OTU
— The strength of the university; a selection from the addresses of Claude T.
    Bissell. [Toronto] University of Toronto Press [c1968]
    vii, 251 p.   OTU
Bissell, Claude Thomas, 1916–   (ed.).
    University College: a portrait, 1853–1953. [Toronto] University of Toronto
    Press, 1953.
    xi, 148 p. illus.   OTU
Blake, Samuel Hume, 1835–1914.
    Mr. Blake's acknowledgment of the Report of "The Board of Governors" or
    "The teaching of religious knowledge in University College ultra vires" and
    other matters. Toronto: L.S. Haynes Press [1901]
    13 p.   OTU
— Wycliffe College: an historical sketch. [Toronto: 1910]
    43 p. plan, plate, port.   OTU
Bowes, Joseph Hetherington.
    Recollections of residence, by J.H.B. n.p. [191–]
    [14] p.   OTU
Brantford and Brant County. Post-Secondary Education Committee.
    Post-secondary education for Brantford and Brant county. [Brantford,
    Ontario] 1973.
    vii, 13 leaves. tables.
    Chairman: J.C. White.   OBRT
Brebner, John Bartlett, 1895–1957.
    Harold Adams Innis as historian. [Ottawa: Canadian Historical Association,
    1953]
    11 p.   OKQ
Brehaut, Willard.
    Report of a survey of programmes and courses in education in Canadian
    degree granting institutions, by Willard Brehaut and Kathleen Francoeur.
    [Toronto: Canadian Education Association] 1956.
    2 v. (Kellogg project in educational leadership).   OTER
Brock University. Founders' Committee.
    Statement of the Chairman regarding the site selected as the home of Brock
    University. St. Catharines, Ontario: 1963.
    23 p.   OSTCB
Brown, Walter T
    In memoriam: Margaret Addison 1868–1940. Toronto: Published for
    Victoria University by Clarke, Irwin & Company Limited, 1941.
    26 p. port.   OTU

Burwash, Nathanael, 1839–1918.
>The history of Victoria College. Toronto: Victoria College Press [c1927]
>xviii, 571 p. illus., ports.
>Due to Dr. Burwash's death, the work was completed and edited by F.H.
>Wallace.   OTU
— Some further facts concerning federation. [Toronto? 1890?]
>13 p.
>Reprinted from *Methodist Magazine*, February, 1890.   OTU
CUA/COU Joint Subcommittee on Finance/Operating Grants.
>Financing university programs in education: report on the special study of
>requirements for the formula financing of education programs in Ontario
>universities. [Toronto?] Released 1970, revised for publication 1971.
>76 p. tables.   OTU
Callaghan, Morley, 1903–
>The Varsity story. Toronto: Macmillan Company of Canada, Limited,
>1948.
>172 p. illus.   OTU
Calvin, Delano Dexter, 1881–1948.
>Queen's University at Kingston: the first century of a Scottish–Canadian
>foundation 1841–1941. Kingston, Ontario: The Trustees of the University,
>1941.
>xi, 321 p. illus., facsims., ports.   OTU
Cameron, Maxwell A   1907–1951.
>The relation between matriculation marks and the achievements of students
>in the universities of Ontario, by Maxwell A. Cameron and others. [Toronto]
>Department of Educational Research, Ontario College of Education,
>University of Toronto, 1939.
>vi, 128 leaves. tables. (Educational research series, no. 2).   OTER
Campbell, Marjorie Freeman, 1896–1975.
>The Hamilton General Hospital School of Nursing, 1890–1955. Toronto:
>The Ryerson Press [1956]
>xi, 172 p. illus., ports.   OTU
Campbell, Robert, 1835–1921.
>Statement regarding the present position of Queen's University. [Montreal:
>1909]
>19 p.   OTU
The Campus as the campus centre: a manual [by] D. Engel [et al.] Department
>of Architecture. Toronto: Students' Administrative Council, University of
>Toronto, 1971.
>88 p. illus., maps (part col., part fold.), plans (part col.).   OTER
Can light mingle with darkness? Can Trinity affiliate with Toronto? n.p.
>[1902?]
>16 p.   OTU
Canadensis (pseud.).
>University consolidation: a plea for higher education in Ontario. Toronto:
>Hunter, Rose, 1877.
>37 p.

Reprinted from *Belford's Magazine* for December, 1876, with extensive
additions.   OTU
Canadian Teachers' Federation. Research Division.
Four-year Bachelor of Education programs for elementary teachers in
Ontario. [Ottawa] 1962.
59 p. (*Its* Research memo no. 9).   OONL
A career of eminent service in education and agriculture. A few facts gleaned
from the life and career of James Mills. Toronto: William Briggs, 1917.
32 p.
Dr. Mills was President of the Ontario Agricultural College, Guelph
1879–1904.   OTU
Carleton College.
A summary report on graduates of Carleton College, 1946–53. Ottawa: The
College, 1954.
61 leaves.   OOCC
Carleton University.
Goals and requirements to 1975. Ottawa: The University, 1969.
82 leaves. graphs, tables.   OOCC
— Supplement, October 1975.
34 leaves. graphs, tables.   OOCC
— Submission to the Committee on University Affairs. [Ottawa: The
University] 1973.
v, 157 leaves. diagrs., tables.   OTU
Carleton University. Senate. Commission on Undergraduate Teaching and
Learning in the Faculty of Arts.
Preliminary report. Ottawa: The University, 1969.
60, xiii leaves.
Chairman: Muni Frumhartz.   OOCC
— Working papers, 1969.
3 v.   OOCC
Carleton University. Students' Council. New University Government Study
Committee.
Report. Ottawa: The University, 1969.
74 p. illus.
Co-chairmen: D.M. Rayside and J.C. Stevenson.   OOCC
Carrière, Gaston.
Un grand éducateur: le R.P. René Lamoureux. Ottawa: Editions de
l'Université, 1958.
137 p.
Fondateur de l'école normale de l'Université d' Ottawa.   OTU
— L'Université d'Ottawa, 1848–1861. Ottawa: Editions de l'Université
d'Ottawa, 1960.
94 p.   OOU
Chant, Clarence Augustus, 1865–1956.
Astronomy in the University of Toronto: the David Dunlap Observatory.
Toronto: University of Toronto Press, 1954.
v, 66 p. illus., ports.   OTU

Charlton, John, 1829–1910.
  Speeches and addresses, political, literary and religious. Toronto: Morang &
  Co., Limited, 1905.
  xi, 499 p. front.
  Queen's University: Presbyterian theological colleges. pp. 291–304.   OLU
Charron, Kenneth C
  Education of the health professions in the context of the health care system:
  the Ontario experience. Paris: Organization for Economic Co-operation and
  Development c1975.
  70 p. illus.   OTU
Clark, Arthur Lewis, 1873–1956.
  The first fifty years: a history of the Science Faculty at Queen's, 1893–1943.
  [Kingston: Queen's University, 1944]
  132 p. illus., ports., facsims.   OTU
Clark, Edmund.
  Student aid and access to higher education in Ontario, by Edmund Clark,
  David Cook, George Fallis, Michael Kent. [Toronto? 1969]
  145 leaves + appendix.   OTU
Clark, John Murray, 1860–1929.
  The functions of a great university, inaugural address delivered on
  November 16th, 1894. Toronto: The Bryant Press, 1895.
  18 p.
  University of Toronto.   OTER
Collection of miscellaneous material on Rochdale College 1968–1975.
  One box of files containing pamphlets, clippings, etc. about and by Rochdale
  College.   OTURS
Committee of Finance Officers. Universities of Ontario.
  Preliminary budget forecasts for provincially-assisted universities of Ontario,
  1st–2nd, 1974–1975. Toronto: Council of Ontario Universities, 1973–1974.
  2 reports for the years: 1974, 1975.   OTU
— Total revenue and expenses for provincially-assisted universities in Ontario.
  1st–2nd, 1973–1974. Toronto: Council of Ontario Universities, 1973–1974.
  2 reports for the years; 1973, 1974.   OTU
Committee of Presidents of Provincially-assisted Universities and Colleges of
  Ontario.
  Post-secondary education in Ontario: report to the Advisory Committee on
  University Affairs. [Toronto: University of Toronto Press, 1963]
  44 p.
  Chairman: Claude T. Bissell.   OTER
— 47 leaves. map, tables.   OTER
— The structure of post-secondary education in Ontario. [Toronto: University
  of Toronto Press, 1963]
  30 p. tables (*Its* Supplementary report no. 1).   OTER
— The city college. [Toronto: University of Toronto Press] 1965.
  15 p. (*Its* Supplementary report no. 2).   OTER

— University television. [Toronto: University of Toronto Press, 1965]
iv, 28 p. (*Its* Supplementary report no. 3).   OTER
Committee of Presidents of Provincially-assisted Universities and Colleges of
Ontario. Research Committee.
The health sciences in Ontario universities, recent experience and prospects
for the next decade; a report. 1966. [Toronto: University of Toronto Press,
1967]
26 p. tables.   OTULS
— The supply of librarians; a report to the Presidents of the Provincially-
assisted Universities of Ontario from the Presidents' Research Committee,
5th February, 1964. [Toronto?] 1964.
4 leaves.   OTULS
Committee of Presidents of Universities of Ontario.
Report to the Committee on University Affairs on the value of the basic
income unit for 1968-69. [Toronto] 1967.
38 leaves. graphs, tables.   OTER
Committee of Presidents of Universities of Ontario. Research Committee.
From the sixties to the seventies; an appraisal of higher education in Ontario
by the President's Research Committee for the Committee of Presidents of
Universities of Ontario, June, 1966. [Toronto: University of Toronto Press,
1967]
x, 101 p. diagrs., tables.
Chairman, President's Research Committee: Ross B. Willis.
Chairman: J.A. Corry.   OTU
Committee of Presidents of Universities of Ontario. Research Division.
Analysis of section sizes, fall, 1969. [Toronto?] 1971.
8 [30] leaves. forms, graphs, tables.   OTER
— Methodology of section size analysis. [Toronto?] 1971.
10, 3 leaves.   OTER
— Proposal for a central data bank on students and resources of Ontario
universities. [Toronto] 1969.
71, 46 leaves. graphs.   OTER
— Survey of citizenship of graduate students enrolled in master's and doctoral
degree programmes at Ontario universities 1969-70 (with comparative
statistics for 1968-69). Revised. Prepared for the Ontario Council on
Graduate Studies by the Research Division of the Committee of Presidents of
Universities of Ontario. [Toronto] 1970.
1 v. (unpaged). tables.   OTER
Committee of Presidents of Universities of Ontario. Subcommittee on Operating
Grants.
Brief to the Committee on University Affairs. [Toronto] 1970.
47 p. graphs, tables.   OTER
— Brief to the Committee on University Affairs: estimates of operating grant
requirements for 1970-71. Rev. 1970. [Toronto] 1970.
54 leaves. graphs, tables.   OTER

— Report to the Committee on University Affairs. Submission on the value of the basic income unit, 1969–1970. [Toronto] 1968.
40 leaves. graphs, tables.   OTER
Committee of Presidents of Universities of Ontario. Subcommittee on Research and Planning.
Aims and objectives of emerging universities: study paper. [Toronto? 1969]
14 leaves.   OTER
— Student participation in university government; a study paper prepared for the Committee of Presidents by its Subcommittee on Research and Planning. Toronto: The Committee, 1968.
[5] 21 p.
Chairman of Subcommittee: Bernard Trotter.   OTU
Committee of Presidents of Universities of Ontario. Subcommittee on the financing of Emergent Universities.
A formula for operating grants to emergent universities and emergent components of established universities. [Toronto] 1967.
9, 28 leaves. graphs, tables.   OTER
Committee Protesting against the Toronto Degrees.
Letter to the Right Hon. Lord Knutsford, H.M. secretary of state for the colonies, on the reply of the University of Trinity College, Toronto, in answer to the Memorial presented to his Lordship on March 6th, 1890 with regard to the issue in England of degrees by that University, together with an explanatory statement. London: C Jaques, 1890.
27 p.
"Signed: John Stainer, by request, and on behalf of the Committee".   OTU
Conference on University Education Relating to Aging and Teaching of Professional Skills in the Field of Gerontology, Toronto, 1965.
Proceeding of the Conference ... Osler Hall, Academy of Medicine, Toronto, Canada, March 26, 1965. Toronto: Ontario Department of Public Welfare, 1965.
133 leaves.   OTUFP
Cook, Gail Carol Annabel, 1940–
Student financial assistance programs; a report to the Ontario Committee on Student Awards, by Gail C.A. Cook and David A.A. Stager. Toronto: Institute for the Quantitative Analysis of Social and Economic Policy, University of Toronto, 1969.
xii, 297 leaves. illus.   OTU
Corbett, Edward Annand, 1887–1964.
Henry Marshall Tory, beloved Canadian. With an introduction by Robert C. Wallace. Toronto: The Ryerson Press [1954]
xi, 241 p. plates, ports.   OTAR
— Sidney Earle Smith. [Toronto] University of Toronto Press [c1961]
72 p. port.   OTU
Council of Ontario Universities.
Annual review 1st–7th, 1966/67–1974/75. Toronto: 1967–1975.

7 v. for the years: 1966/67; 1967/68; 1968/69; 1969/70; 1970/71; 1971/72;
1972/73–1974/75.
Contents: v. 1, System emerging; v. 2, Collective autonomy; v. 3, Campus
and forum; v. 4, Variations on a theme; v. 5, Participatory planning; v. 6,
Stimulus and response; [v. 7] New structure and environment.
Name of the organization varies: v. 1–4, Committee of Presidents of
Universities of Ontario; v. 5–7, Council of Ontario Universities.
1966/67–1969/70, 1971/72.   OTU
1970/71, 1974/75.   OTER
— Brief to the Canadian and Ontario governments on the financing of higher
education in Canada. [Toronto] 1976.
24 p. table.   OONL
— Brief to the Ontario Council on University Affairs: inflation and the
formula. Toronto: 1974.
1 v. (various paging).   OTU
— Building blocks: background studies on the development of a capital formula
for Ontario. Toronto: 1972–1973.
5 v. illus., diagrs., tables.
Contents: v. 1, Report of the task force – space and utilization; v. 2, Report
of the task force – space for education; v. 3, Report of the task force – space
for health services; v. 4, Report of the task force – building costs; v. 5, Report
of the task force – building life costs.   OTDU
— Capital financing, funding by formula and cyclic renewal: brief to the
Ontario Council on University Affairs. Toronto: The Council, 1974.
12 leaves. (*Its* publication 74-20).   OTU
— Commodity, firmness and delight: a study of architectural education in
Ontario. Toronto: 1976.
1 v. (various pagings). diagrs., tables.   OTER
— A comparative analysis of university calendar systems: brief to the Ontario
Committee on University Affairs. [Toronto] 1971.
1 v. (various pagings). graphs, tables.   OTER
— Equity for Ontario's universities: brief to the Ontario Council on University
Affairs. [Toronto] 1975.
27 p. tables.   OTER
— Graduate enrolments in relation to requirements for academic staff in
Ontario universities: brief to the Ontario Committee on University Affairs.
[Toronto: 1971]
1 v. (various pagings).   OTER
— Graduate student incomes in Ontario 1972-73. Introduction by Colin F.W.
Isaacs. [Toronto] The Council, c1974.
9 [28] p. chiefly tables.   OTU
— Inflation and the formula: brief to the Ontario Council on University
Affairs. Toronto: 1974.
12 [5] 6 leaves.   OTU
— The Ontario operating grants formula: a statement of principles to the

Ontario Council on University Affairs, June, 1974. Toronto: The Council, 1974.
51 p. (*Its* Publication 74-9).   OTU
— Review of the Ontario operating grants formula: interim report. [Toronto?] 1972.
24 leaves.   OTER
— Stability: a continuing issue; brief to the Committee on University Affairs. Toronto [1973]
23 leaves. tables.   OTER
— Statement by the Council of Ontario Universities and responses by Committee of Ontario Deans of Engineering, Ontario Council on Graduate Studies and Association of Professional Engineers of the province of Ontario to *Ring of iron*: a study of engineering education in Ontario. [Toronto] 1971.
98 p. graphs, tables.   OTER
— Statement on the principles which should govern the setting of tuition fees. Toronto: Council of Ontario Universities [c1976]
10, 2 p.
"Submitted to Ontario Council on University Affairs".   OTU
Council of Ontario Universities. Committee on Capital Financing.
Capital support: objectives, policy, implementation brief April 30, 1976. Toronto: Council of Ontario Universities, 1976.
1 v. (various pagings). tables.   OONL
— Report: cyclic renewal and the special problem of equipment: brief to the Ontario Council on University Affairs. Toronto: Council of Ontario Universities, 1975.
8 leaves.   OTU
Council of Ontario Universities. Committee on Operating Grants.
Approach to the eighties: demand, quality resources. Toronto: Council of Ontario Universities, 1976.
ii, 60 p. graphs, tables.
At head of title: Brief to the Ontario Council on University Affairs.   OTU
Council of Ontario Universities. Committee on Research and Planning.
"The ten o'clock scholar?" What a professor does for his pay [prepared by] Bernard Trotter, David L. McQueen, Bertrand L. Hansen for Committee on Research and Planning Council of Ontario Universities. May 1972. n.p.: 1972.
14 leaves. (*Its* report 72-8).   OTER
Council of Ontario Universities. Office of Library Coordination.
Guide to Ontario university libraries. Toronto: 1972.
1 v. (various pagings). charts, diagrs., maps.   OTULS
Council of Ontario Universities. Special Committee to Assess University Policies and Plans.
Report. Toronto: Council of Ontario Universities, 1976.
31 p.   OONL

Council of Ontario Universities. Sub-committee on Student Aid.
    Accessibility and student aid. Report of the Sub-committee on Student Aid
    of the Council of Ontario Universities. Toronto: 1971.
    149 p. charts.   OTU
— Undergraduate student aid and accessibility in the universities of Ontario.
    1970.
    165 p. (Appendix A).   OTU
Craick, William Arnot, 1880–1969 (comp.).
    The annals of nineteen-two; compiled for the 50th anniversary reunion,
    Class of 1902, University College, University of Toronto, Toronto, June 5, 6
    and 7, 1952. [Toronto: The Author] 1952.
    44 leaves.   OTU
Craigie, Edward Horne, 1894–
    A history of the Department of Zoology of the University of Toronto up to
    1962. [Toronto: University of Toronto Press, 1966?]
    108 p. illus., ports.   OTU
Creating a college of general education; a national consultation, the Georgian
    Bay region as a case study, Geneva Park, Orillia, Ontario, May 9–13, 1971.
    [Orillia? Ontario, 1971?]
    123 leaves.
    Sponsored by the Simcoe College Foundation.   OTU
Creighton, Donald Grant, 1902–
    Harold Adams Innis: portrait of a scholar. Toronto: University of Toronto
    Press [1957]
    146 p. port.   OTU
Crothers, Katherine Connell.
    With tender loving care: a short story of the K.G.H. Nursing School.
    Kingston, Ontario: The Author, 1973.
    101 p. illus., ports.   OONL
Dadson, Douglas French, 1913–   (ed.).
    On higher education: five lectures. Toronto: Published for the Ontario
    College of Education by the University of Toronto Press [c1966]
    x, 149 p. tables.
    Ontario: pp. 3–85.   OTU
The Daily Mercury, Guelph, Ontario.
    OAC centennial 1874–1974. [Guelph, Ontario] 1974.
    52 p. illus., ports.
    July 5, 1974 issue.   OGU
Dalton, F   Keith.
    A biography of the Reverend William Arthur Johnson, 1816–1880, founder
    of Trinity College School, Weston – Port Hope. Toronto: 1965.
    13 leaves.
    Compiled June 1963; revised July, 1964; additions May, 1965.   OKQ
Dewar, David G
    Queen's profiles. [Kingston, Ontario] Queen's University Office of
    Endowment and Public Relations, 1951.
    124 p. ports.   OKQ

Dewart, Edward Hartley, 1828–1903.
University federation, considered in its relation to the educational interests of the Methodist Church. [Toronto: Printed at the Christian Guardian Office, 1886]
16 p. OTU

Diltz, Bert Case, 1894–
Stranger than fiction. Toronto: McClelland and Stewart Limited [c1969]
128 p.
Autobiography of an Ontario educator. OTU

Dupuis, Nathan Fellowes, 1836–1917.
A sketch of the history of the medical college at Kingston during the first twenty-five years of its existence. [Kingston, Ontario; 1916?]
24 p. OKQ

Dutchak, Phyllis E
College with a purpose: a history of Kemptville College of Agricultural Technology, 1916–1973. Belleville, Ontario: Mika Publishing Company, 1976.
170 p. illus., ports. OTAR

Epp, Frank Henry, 1929–
Education with a plus: the story of Rosthern Junior College. Waterloo, Ontario: Conrad Press [c1975]
xxiv, 460 p. illus., ports., tables. OONL

La Faculté de médecine de l' Université d'Ottawa, 1945–1970. The Faculty of Medicine of the University of Ottawa. [Ottawa? University of Ottawa? 1970?]
167 p. illus. (part col.), facsim., ports. (part col.). OTU

[Falconer, (Sir) Robert Alexander] 1867–1943.
The suggestion to close the University of Toronto during the next academic year. [Toronto? 1917]
[4] p. OTU

Felstiner, James Purvin, 1932–
Detached work; a report of the first stage of the University Settlement project. [Toronto: Printed at the University of Toronto Press for University Settlement Recreation Centre] 1965.
xii, 51 p. map. OTU

— Youth in need; a report of the second stage of the University Settlement Project [by] James P. Felstiner [et al. Toronto: University Settlement Recreation Centre] 1966.
xiv, 88 p. illus., graphs. OTU

Fitzpatrick, Alfred, 1862–1936.
The university in overalls: a plea for part-time study. Toronto [Hunter–Rose Co. Limited] 1920.
xvi, 150, xxxi p. illus., ports., tables. OTER

— Reprinted [Frontier College Press, c1923]
xvi, 184 p. illus.
Frontier college. OTER

Flavelle, (Sir) Joseph Wesley, bart., 1858–1939.
> The present administration of the University of Toronto: address delivered
> ... to the members of the Canadian Club, Toronto, May 2nd, 1922.
> [Toronto, 1922?]
> 15 p.   OTU

Flenley, Ralph, 1886–   (ed.).
> Essays in Canadian history presented to George M. Wrong. for his eightieth
> birthday. Toronto: Macmillan Company of Canada, 1939.
> x, 372 p. port.   OTU

Floch, Wolfgang, 1930–
> The Ontario data of the Canadian Universities Foundation survey of the
> movement of university teaching staff, by Wolfgang Floch and Cicely
> Watson. [Toronto] Department of Educational Research, Ontario College of
> Education, University of Toronto, 1965.
> vii, 118 leaves. forms. (Toronto. University. Ontario College of Education.
> Department of Educational Research. Information series no. 15).   OTU

Foley, Roy S
> William James Dunlop: a brief biography. [Toronto: c1966]
> [54] p. port.   OTU

Fox, William Sherwood, 1878–1967.
> Sherwood Fox of Western: reminiscences. Toronto: Burns and McEachern,
> 1964.
> xvii, 250 p. illus., ports.   OTU
— Silken lines and silver hooks: a life-long fisherman recounts his catch.
> Illustrated by Clare Bice. Toronto: Copp Clark, Limited, 1954.
> xii, 152 p. illus.   OTU

Fraser, William Henry, 1853–1916.
> Pass French and German in the University of Toronto. Toronto: Printed at
> the office of "The Week" [1892?]
> 15 p.
> "Paper read ... before the Modern Language Association of Ontario, April
> 20, 1892".   OTU

Frost, Russell Welland, 1899–
> Concerning McMaster: the University's past and present in facts and
> figures. Hamilton, Ontario: McMaster University, 1947.
> 1 v. (unpaged). illus., port.   OHM

Frye, Northrop, 1912–
> By liberal things. Address by H. Northrop Frye on the occasion of his
> installation as Principal of Victoria College, University of Toronto, October
> 21, 1959. [Toronto] Clarke, Irwin & Company Limited [c1959]
> 23 p.   OTU

Galbraith, John, 1846–1914.
    Technical education; address delivered by Professor Galbraith at the
    opening of the engineering laboratory of the School of Practical Science,
    Toronto, February 24th, 1892. Toronto: Warwick & Sons, 1892.
        13 p.   OTU
Garratt, George Alfred, 1898–
    Forestry education in Canada. [Ste. Anne de Bellevue, Quebec] Canadian
    Institute of Forestry [c1971]
        viii, 408 p.   OTU
Gattinger, Friston Eugene, 1921–
    A century of challenge; a history of the Ontario Veterinary College.
    [Toronto] Published for the Ontario Veterinary College by the University of
    Toronto Press [c1962]
        xii, 224 p. illus., ports., diagrs., facsims., tables.   OTU
Geikie, Walter Bayne, 1830–1917.
    An address on the work of Trinity Medical College. Toronto: 1907.
        7 p.
        "Reprinted from the *Canada Lancet* for May, 1907.   OTU
The General Hospital versus University of Toronto. [Toronto: 1908]
        [1] 26 p.
        Articles reprinted from the *Evening Telegram*, May 2, 1908 to May 23, 1908.
                                                                              OTU
Gibson, James Alexander, 1912–
    Brock University 1963–1965: a retrospective report. [St. Catharines,
    Ontario: Brock University, 1965?]
        31 p. illus.   OLU
Gordon, Wilhelmina, 1886–
    Daniel M. Gordon, his life. Foreword by W.E. McNeill. Toronto: The
    Ryerson Press [c1941]
        xvii, 313 p. front., plates, ports.   OKQ
Graduate work in education in the province of Ontario. A report prepared at
    the request of Advisory Committee on Academic Planning [Council of
    Ontario Universities] by Harold Baker [et al. Toronto?] 1973.
        77 p. tables.   OTER
Grant, George Monro, 1835–1902.
    Speech to the General Assembly on the relation of Queen's University to the
    Church. Toronto: Presbyterian Printing and Publishing Co. Ltd., 1892.
        16 p.   OKQ
— A statement concerning Queen's submitted to the founders, the graduates
    and alumni and the benefactors and friends of the University. Kingston:
    [Queen's University] 1887.
        8 p. table.   OOA
Grant, William Lawson, 1872–1902.
    George Monro Grant, by William Lawson Grant and Frederick Hamilton.
    Edinburgh: T.C. & E.C. Jack, 1905.
        531 p. port.
        Grant was Principal of Queen's 1877–1902.   OTU

— Principal Grant, by William Lawson Grant and Frederick Hamilton.
Toronto: Morang & Co., Limited, 1904.
531 p. port.   OTU OTAR
Gray, V   Evan.
The university question, 1945. [Toronto: The Author, 1944]
15 p.
"To delegates to a special Baptist convention" on McMaster University.
                                                                OTU
Griffin, Virginia R
Freedom and frustration in the professional school: an experimental project
in curriculum change, School of Social Work, University of Toronto: an
evaluation. [Toronto] Department of Adult Education, Ontario Institute for
Studies in Education [1969]
vii, 57 leaves. illus.   OTER
Griffith, Byron Alexander, 1908–
University of Toronto enrolments projected to 1968-69. [Toronto] 1956.
8, 10 leaves. diagrs., tables.   OTU
Guelph, Ontario. University. Board of Undergraduate Studies. Study
Committee.
Undergraduate training in resources development: report. [Guelph,
Ontario] Centre for Resources Development, 1970.
163 leaves. (Guelph, Ontario. University. Centre for Resources
Development. Publication, no. 23).   OTU
Guelph, Ontario. University. Office of Continuing Education.
The Ontario aggregate industry problems and potentials, conference
summary. Guelph, Ontario: The Author, 1974.
62 leaves.   OGU
Guelph, Ontario. University. President's Task Force on the Status of Women.
Report. [Guelph, Ontario] 1975.
58 p. graphs, tables.   OONL
Guelph, Ontario. University. Spring Admissions Research Committee.
The students of the 1966 spring admissions programme at the University of
Guelph: their first semester. [Toronto: The Ontario Institute for Studies in
Education and the University of Guelph, 1966]
34 leaves. diagrs., tables. (The Guelph spring admissions research project.
Study no. 2).   OTER
— The students of the 1966 spring admissions programme at the University of
Guelph: who are they? why did they come? [Toronto: Ontario Institute for
Studies in Education and the University of Guelph, 1966]
23 [58] leaves. illus., map. (The Guelph spring admissions research project.
Study no. 1).   OTER
The Guelph Evening Mercury.
Ontario Agricultural College semi-centennial 1874–1924. Guelph, Ontario:
1924.
38 p. illus., ports.
June 7, 1924 issue.   OGU

Gullen, Augusta Stowe, 1857–1943.
    A brief history of the Ontario Medical College for women. n.p.: 1906.
    11 p.   OTAR
Gundy, Henry Pearson, 1905–
    Queen's University at Kingston. [Kingston? Cape and Company Limited,
    1966?]
    87 p. illus., facsims., ports.   OTU
Handa, Madan Lai, 1931–
    Unemployment, expected returns, and the demand for university education
    in Ontario; some empirical results by M.L. Handa and M.L. Skolnik.
    [Toronto] Department of Educational Planning, Ontario Institute for
    Studies in Education, 1973.
    32 leaves. tables.   OTER
Hanly, Charles Mervyn Taylor, 1930–
    Who pays? University financing in Ontario, by Charles Hanly, with N.
    Shulman and D.N. Swaan. Toronto: James Lewis & Samuel, 1970.
    168 p. illus. (OCUFA studies in higher education 1).   OTER
Hansen, B   L
    Report on a study of faculty activities at the University of Toronto, by B.L.
    Hansen and S. Sandler. [Toronto: Office of Institutional Research,
    University of Toronto] 1967.
    21 leaves. graphs, tables.   OONL
Harris, Robin Sutton, 1919–   (ed.).
    Cold iron and Lady Godiva: engineering education at Toronto, 1920–1972,
    edited by Robin S. Harris & Ian Montagnes. [Toronto] University of
    Toronto Press [c1973]
    x, 169 p. illus.   OTU
— The establishment of a provincial university in Ontario. [Toronto? 1965]
    34 leaves. tables.   OTU
— A history of higher education in Canada, 1663–1960. Toronto: University of
    Toronto Press [c1976]
    xxiv, 715 p. (Studies in the history of higher education in Canada, no. 7).
          OTER
Harry M. Cassidy Memorial Research Fund, Toronto.
    Exploring social frontiers: report 1952–1957. [Toronto] University of
    Toronto, School of Social Work [1957]
    15 [2] p. port.   OTU
— "Over and out"; final report of the Harry M. Cassidy Memorial Research
    Fund, March 1969. [Toronto] University of Toronto School of Social Work
    [1969]
    [8] p.   OTU
[Hartle, Douglas George]
    Expenditures on higher education in Ontario. [Toronto? 196–]
    15 p. 16–32 leaves. diagrs.   OTU

Heick, Welf Henry, 1930–   (ed.).
　　His own man: essays in honour of Arthur Reginald Marsden Lower. Edited
　　by W.H. Heick and Roger Graham. Montreal: McGill–Queen's University
　　Press, 1974.
　　xi, 187 p. port.   OTU
House, William Arthur, 1948–
　　The University of Windsor: a special study, by William House, Robert
　　McCrae and Robert Reynolds. [Windsor, Ontario: 1969]
　　2 parts.   OTU
Houwing, J   F   1926–
　　Changes in the composition of the governing bodies of Canadian universities
　　and colleges, 1965–1970. Ottawa: Research Division, Association of
　　Universities and Colleges of Canada, 1972.
　　vii, 65 p. tables.   OONL
—— Composition of governing bodies of Canadian universities and
　　colleges/Composition des organismes administratifs des universités et
　　collèges du Canada, 1975, by J.F. Houwing and A.M. Kristjanson. Ottawa:
　　Association of Universities and Colleges of Canada/Association des
　　universités et collèges du Canada, 1975.
　　iv, 51 p.   OTU
Hugo–Brunt, Michael.
　　University of Toronto, Scarborough College; a report from the planning
　　consultants [Michael Hugo–Brunt, Michael Hough and John Andrews.
　　Toronto: Printed by Elvidge Print. Co., 1963]
　　41 leaves. illus., maps, plans.   OTU
Humble, Archibald Herbert, 1909–
　　The school on the hill: Trinity College School 1865–1965, by A.H. Humble
　　with the collaboration of J.D. Burns. Port Hope, Ontario: Trinity College
　　School [c1965]
　　380 p. illus., ports.   OTAR OTU
In memoriam: Alfred Gandier, 1861–1932 (Emmanuel College). Toronto:
　　Published for Victoria University by Clarke, Irwin & Company Limited,
　　1934.
　　20 p. port.   OTU
In memoriam: Andrew James Bell, 1856–1932 (Victoria College). Toronto:
　　Published for Victoria University by Clarke, Irwin & Company Limited,
　　1934.
　　29 p. port.   OTU
In memoriam: Edward Wilson Wallace, 1880–1941 ... Toronto: Published for
　　Victoria University by Clarke, Irwin & Company Limited, 1942.
　　[4] 26 p. port.   OTU
In memoriam: John Fletcher McLaughlin, 1863–1933 (Emmanuel College).
　　Toronto: Published for Victoria University by Clarke, Irwin & Company
　　Limited, 1934.
　　24 p. port.   OTU

Innis, Mary Quayle, 1899–1972   (ed.).
  Nursing education in a changing society. [Toronto] University of Toronto
  Press [c1970]
  x, 244 p.
  "Published on the occasion of the fiftieth anniversary of the University of
  Toronto School of Nursing.   OTU
Jamieson, George H
  The biggest house on the block: Neill Wycik College, 1966–1972. [Toronto:
  Neill-Wycik College, c1974]
  92 p. illus.   OLU
Jansen, Clifford J   (ed.).
  Housing, transport and social participation at York University. Edited by
  Clifford Jansen and Patricia Pryse–White. [Toronto: York University,
  Institute for Behavioural Research] 1972.
  2 v. illus.
  Contents: v. 1, The University setting; v. 2, A survey of undergraduates.
                                                                        OTU
Johnston, Charles Murray, 1926–
  McMaster University. Toronto: Published for McMaster University by
  University of Toronto Press [c1976–
  2 v. illus., ports.
  Contents: v. 1, The Toronto years; v. 2, Not yet published, October, 1976.
                                                                        OTU
Joint COU/OCUFA Committee on the Study of Academic Career Development in
  Ontario Universities.
  Academic career planning: the ivory tower and the crystal ball, a report by
  C.W. Bennett [et al.] Toronto: Council of Ontario Universities, 1976.
  42 p. graphs, tables.   OTER
Judy, Richard White, 1932–
  Systems analysis for efficient resource allocation in higher education: a
  report on the development and implementation of CAMPUS techniques [by]
  Richard W. Judy [and] Jack B. Levine. [Toronto: 1969?]
  iii, 21 leaves.   OTU
— A research progress report. [Toronto: Printing House in Canada] 1970.
  24 p. (Institute for the Quantitative Analysis of Social and Economic Policy,
  University of Toronto).   OTU
Kenrick, Charles.
  Picturesque Trinity. Toronto: G.N. Morang [1903]
  21 p. plates.
  At head of title: Glimpses of Toronto.   OTU
Khan, Sar Biland, 1936–
  Prediction of first-year achievement in Ontario universities, by S.B. Khan,
  Pat Ransom and Martin Herbert. Toronto: Department of Measurement
  and Evaluation, Ontario Institute for Studies in Education [c1970]
  18, 68 leaves. tables.   OTER

— Prediction of university achievement at the University of Guelph, by S.B.
  Khan and Sherry McBain. Toronto: Department of Measurement and
  Evaluation, Ontario Institute for Studies in Education, 1970.
  15, 20 leaves. tables.   OTER
King, John, 1843–1916.
  McCaul, Croft, Forneri: personalities of early university days. Toronto:
  Macmillan Company of Canada, Limited, 1914.
  256 p. ports.   OTU
Kirkconnell, Watson, 1895–1977.
  A slice of Canada: memoirs. [Toronto] Published for Acadia University by
  University of Toronto Press [c1967]
  x, 393 p. illus., ports.   OTU
Kupsch, Walter Oscar, 1919–   (ed.).
  The university and the Canadian north: inventory of classes, research and
  special projects. Ottawa: Association of Universities and Colleges of Canada,
  1973.
  xlviii, 300 p. map.
  Bi-lingual.   OTU
Lakehead University. Commission on University Governmental Organization.
  Report. [Thunder Bay, Ontario] 1972.
  x, 123 leaves. charts.
  Chairman: Douglas Rome Lindsay.   OTER
Lakehead University. School of Library Technology.
  The history of the School of Library Technology, Lakehead University, from
  its inception 1966–1971. Thunder Bay, Ontario: 1971.
  11 leaves.   OPAL
Land, Reginald Brian, 1927–
  Education for librarianship: a memorandum prepared for the Ontario
  University Presidents, Research Committee, Subcommittee on
  Librarianship. Toronto [1964]
  1 v. (various pagings).   OTU
— Library school curricula; memorandum to members of the subcommittee on
  Librarianship of the Ontario University Presidents' Research Committee.
  Toronto [1965]
  8 p.   OTU
Langton, Hugh Hornby, 1862–1953.
  James Loudon and the University of Toronto. Toronto: University of
  Toronto Press, 1927.
  32 p. port.   OTU
— Sir Daniel Wilson. [Toronto: 1901]
  19 p.
  "Reprint for v. 5 of the *Review of historical publications relating to Canada*".
  "Chronological list of the published writings of Sir Daniel Wilson": p. 14–19.
                                                                           OTU
— Sir Daniel Wilson: a memoir. Edinburgh: Thomas Nelson & Sons Limited,
  1929.
  250 p. illus., port.   OTU

— Sir John Cunningham McLennan: a memoir. With a chapter on his
scientific work, by E.F. Burton. Toronto: University of Toronto Press, 1939.
123 p. illus., ports.   OTU

Lapp, Philip A
Ring of iron: a study of engineering education in Ontario, December 1970.
A report to the Committee of Presidents of Universities of Ontario, [by
Philip A. Lapp, John W.H. Hodgins and Colin B. MacKay. Toronto]
Committee of Presidents of Universities of Ontario, 1970.
iv, 157 p. illus., map, graphs.   OTER

— Undergraduate engineering enrolment projections for Ontario, 1970–80.
[Toronto: Committee of the Presidents of Universities of Ontario] 1969.
vi, 72 p. graphs, tables. (CPUO report, no. 70–1).   OTU

Lash, Zebulon Aiton, 1846–1920.
The University of Toronto: past and present. An address before the
University Club, Toronto, November, 1913. [Toronto: 1913]
12 p.   OTU OTAR

Laurentian University.
Presentation to the Ontario Council on University Affairs, December 13,
1974. Sudbury, Ontario: 1974.
6 p. tables.   OTER

— May, 1975. Sudbury, Ontario: 1975.
7 p. tables.   OTER

Laurentian University. Academic Planning Committee.
Planning for tomorrow: preliminary report, original text, March, 1973.
[Sudbury, Ontario] 1973.
1 v. (various pagings). graphs, tables.
Chairman: Wesley Cragg.
English and French text.   OTER

Law Society of Upper Canada. Special Committee on Law School.
Report, 14th February, 1957. Adopted by Convocation, 15th February,
1957. [Toronto: Published for the Law Society of Upper Canada by Richard
De Boo Limited, 1957]
15 p.
Chairman: C.F.H. Carson.   OLU

Law Society of Upper Canada. Special Committee on Legal Education.
Report. [Toronto] 1972.
iii, 62 p.
Chairman: B.J. MacKinnon.   OLU

Lawrence, Margaret Isabel.
History: the School for Nurses, Toronto General Hospital; commemorating
the fiftieth anniversary of its establishment, 1881–1931. Toronto: General
Hospital [1931?]
63 p. illus., ports.   BVAU

Lee, John A
Test pattern: instructional television at Scarborough College, University of
Toronto. [Toronto] University of Toronto Press [1971]
xix, 124 p.   OTU

Le Roy, Donald James, 1913–
   Lash Miller and a history of chemistry at the University of Toronto . [Paper
   presented at the] University Chemical Club Meeting... Wednesday,
   February 6, 1963, 8:00 p.m., Music Room, Hart House. Toronto: Lash
   Miller Chemical Laboratories, University of Toronto [1963]
   14 p.   OTUC
Letters and speeches on the University question. Toronto: T. Hill & Son,
   Caxton Press, 1884.
   116 p.   OTU
Lewis, Lesley Vanessa.
   Women and the colleges of applied arts and technology: a report to the
   Ministry of Colleges and Universities. Toronto: Ministry of Colleges and
   Universities, 1975.
   176 p.   OTU
London, Ontario. The University of Western Ontario.
   The Golden Jubilee endowment fund campaign, 1928. [London, Ontario:
   1928]
   10 pamphlets in 1 v. illus.
   Contents: Semi-centennial endowment fund campaign, 1878–1928; a portal
   to opportunity; Medicine and surgery; Arts and natural sciences; Public
   health; The education of women; Summer school and extension courses;
   The libraries; Physical education and athletics; The cost of education.   OLU
— "Let justice be done". An evaluation of the report of the President's
   Committee of Inquiry into Social Behaviour. London, Ontario: University
   Students' Council of the University of Western Ontario, 1968.
   67 leaves.
   Chairman: Michael Ledgett.   OTER
— 75th anniversary of the University of Western Ontario. Addresses delivered
   by the Right Honourable Vincent Massey, Principal Douglas William
   Logan... President Sidney Earle Smith, London, Ontario: 1953.
   28 p.   OLU
London, Ontario. University of Western Ontario. President's Advisory
   Committee on the Status of Women at the University of Western Ontario.
   Report. [London, Ontario: 1975]
   111 [28] p. graphs.
   Chairperson: B. Campbell.   OONL
London, Ontario. University of Western Ontario. President's Committee of
   Inquiry into Social Behaviour.
   Let right be done. Report. London, Ontario: 1968.
   55 p. chart, tables.
   Chairman: A.W.R. Carrothers.   OTER
London, Ontario. University of Western Ontario Medical Journal. Staff.
   Changes in medical education and other special articles on the history,
   growth and progress of the University of Western Ontario Faculty of
   Medicine, 1881–1965. The new medical sciences building officially opened

22nd October, 1965. [London, Ontario: University of Western Ontario]
1965.
32 p. illus., map.   OLU
Lord, A   R
   Report of the evaluation of the Metropolitan School of Nursing, Windsor,
   Ontario. n.p.: Canadian Nurses' Association [1952]
   54 p. tables.   OONL
Loudon, James, 1841–1916.
   The memoirs of James Loudon, President of the University of Toronto,
   1892–1906. [Toronto: 1964]
   1 v. (various pagings).
   Typescript with manuscript notes, letters and newspaper and magazine
   cuttings. Copy 2, xerox copy of the original.   OTU
— Queen's University and the university question, by President Loudon and
   Chancellor Burwash. n.p. [1903?]
   [1] 13 p.   OTU
Loudon, William James, 1860–1951.
   Studies of student life. [Toronto: Macmillan, 1923–194?]
   8 v.
   Contents: v. 1, The Onion Club; v. 2, An examination in logic; v. 3, Silas
   Smith of Coboconk; v. 4, A civil servant; v. 5, The golden age; v. 6, The
   yellow tortoise and other tales; v. 7, A merry Christmas and other tales; v. 8,
   Pioneers: being a short history of the founding of the Madawaska Club, and
   of its early settlement on Georgian Bay during the years 1898–1903.   OTU
Lower, Arthur Reginald Marsden, 1889–
   My first seventy-five years. Toronto: Macmillan of Canada, 1967.
   384 p. illus., ports.   OTU
MacClement, W   T
   Queen's in summer. [Kingston, Ontario: Jackson Press, 1926?]
   [8] illus.   OKQ
McCorkell, Edmund Joseph, 1891–
   Captain the Reverend William Leo Murray, 1890–1937.... a memoir.
   [Toronto: St. Michael's College] 1939.
   47 p. illus.   OTSTM
— Henry Carr, revolutionary. Toronto: Griffin House, 1969.
   x, 165 p. plates (incl. ports.).
   St. Michael's (Superior and President).   OTU
— The Pontifical Institute of Mediaeval Studies. Toronto: 1956.
   21 p. illus., ports.   OTSTM
— Seventy-fifth anniversary St. Michael's College in the University of Toronto
   [1852–1927. Toronto: The College, 1927]
   57 p. illus. (fold.), ports.   OTMCL
McElheran, Irene Beatrice (Brock), 1870–1955.
   That's what I'm here for: Robert B. McElheran, his days and his ways.
   Toronto: The Ryerson Press, 1955.
   xvii, 126 p. port.
   Wycliffe College.   OTF

Macfarland, Mary E
    History, School of Nursing, Toronto General Hospital, 1932–1967.
    [Toronto: Published for the Alumnae Association School of Nursing T.G.H.
    by McGaw–Jordan Limited 1968]
    60 p. illus., ports. (part col.), facsims.,   OTU
McGovern, Kathleen.
    Outline of the history of Loretto College. [Toronto: 1976]
    5 leaves.
    "Paper read before students and guests on the occasion of the annual dinner
    in honour of Mary Ward, January 22, 1976".   OTSTM
McIntyre, Gail.
    Women and Ontario universities: a report to the Ministry of Colleges and
    Universities, by Gail McIntyre and Janice Doherty. [Toronto] Ministry of
    Colleges and Universities, 1975.
    iii, 145 p. tables.   OTU
Mackinnon, Clarence, 1868–1937.
    The life of Principal Oliver. Toronto: The Ryerson Press [c1936]
    viii, 162 p. port.   OOA
McLay, Walter Scott Williams, 1870–
    McMaster University, 1890–1940. Hamilton, Ontario: McMaster
    University, 1940.
    20 p.   OHM
McLean, Catherine D
    Nurses come lately; the first five years of the Quo Vadis School of Nursing
    by Catherine D. McLean and Rex A. Lucas. [Etobicoke, Ontario: 1970]
    v, 50 p. diagr.   OTU
McMaster University.
    A frank statement: its origins, development, present status and future needs.
    [Hamilton, Ontario: The University, 1944]
    21 p. illus.   OTU
— McMaster University, 1887–1964. [Hamilton, 1964]
    [20] p. illus.   OTU
— McMaster University 1890–1940: the historical address and commemorative
    ode, presented at McMaster University 1940. Hamilton, Ontario: 1940.
    20 p.   OTU
— McMaster University in the post-war world. Published by authority of the
    Board of Governors. [Hamilton, Ontario] 1945.
    [16] p.   OTU
— A submission to the Ontario Council on University Affairs, November, 1974.
    [Hamilton, Ontario] 1974.
    83 leaves. tables.   OTER
— June, 1975. [Hamilton, Ontario] 1975.
    63 p. tables.   OTER
McMaster University. Alumni Association.
    Memoir of Daniel Arthur McGregor, late principal of Toronto Baptist
    College. 2d ed. Toronto: Dudley & Burns, 1891.
    245 p. port.
    No copy of first edition located.   OTU

McMaster University. Group for Equal Rights.
  The status of women at McMaster University: a report and petition of the
  Group for Equal Rights at McMaster. [Hamilton, Ontario] 1971.
  20 [4] leaves. diagrs., tables.   OTER
McMaster University. Senate Committee appointed to Investigate Charges
  made by Rev. Elmore Harris against the teaching of Prof. I.G. Matthews.
  Report. [Toronto: Standard Publishing Co., 1909]
  23 p.   OTU
McMaster University. Senate. Committee on Undergraduate Education.
  Report to the Senate of McMaster University of the Ad Hoc Committee on
  Undergraduate Education. [Hamilton, Ontario: 1971]
  137 p. illus.
  Chairman: G.S. Vichert.   OTER
MacMechan, Archibald McKellar, 1862–1933.
  Reminiscences of Toronto University. I. The Convocation Hall; II. Professor
  George Paxton Young. n.p. [189–?]
  15 p.   OTU
McNab, George Gibbon, 1875–
  The development of higher education in Ontario. Toronto: The Ryerson
  Press [c1925]
  267 p.   OTU
Macnaughton, John, 1858–1943.
  Essays and addresses, selected by D.D. Calvin. [Kingston, Ontario] Queen's
  University, 1946.
  x, 319 p. port.
  Professor of Greek at various Canadian universities.   OTU
McNeill, William Everett, 1876–
  The story of Queen's: an address delivered on student and alumni day,
  Queen's University centenary celebration, October 16–18, 1941. Kingston,
  Ontario: Queen's University, 1941.
  16 p.   OTAR
— Wallace of Queen's. [Kingston, Ontario: Queen's University, 1951]
  [12] port.   OTU
Madill, Alonzo James, 1874–
  History of agricultural education in Ontario. Toronto: University of Toronto
  Press, 1930.
  264 p. tables.   OTU
— Rev. ed. Toronto: University of Toronto Press, 1937.
  316 p. tables.   OTU
Main, Alex N
  Teaching and learning: an evaluation of the Ontario universities
  programme for instructional development, by Alex Main, Alwyn Berland
  and Peter Morand. [Toronto] 1975.
  vi, 89 p.   OTER

Malkin, Ray B
    The role played by Department of Extension, University of Toronto, in
    adult education. [Toronto] 1952.
    [2] 37 leaves.   OTU
Market Facts of Canada Limited.
    A survey concerning the "short-fall" in student attendance at Ontario
    colleges and universities. Submitted to [the] Ontario government,
    Department of Colleges and Universities. Toronto: 1972.
    77 leaves. tables.   OTER
Masters, Donald Campbell Charles, 1908–
    Protestant church colleges in Canada: a history. [Toronto] University of
    Toronto Press [c1966]
    viii, 225 p.   OTU
Memorials of Chancellor W.H. Blake, Bishop John Strachan, Professor H.H.
    Croft and Professor G.P. Young. Presented to the University of Toronto in
    the University Library, January 13, 1894. Toronto: Rowsell and Hutchison,
    1894.
    20 p.   OTU
Milnes, Humphrey Newton, 1919–
    The archives of University College; a study of our past with pictures and a
    commentary. [Toronto: University College Literary and Athletic Society,
    1959]
    [8] p. illus., ports. (University College gargoyle, v. 5, no. 12).   OTU
Mitchell, Charles Hamilton, 1872–1941.
    Policies for engineering education; an address... to the Council of the
    Faculty of Applied Science and Engineering, University of Toronto.
    [Toronto?] 1927.
    [19] 5, 5 leaves.   OTU
Mitchelson, Edward E
    The story of Brock University to date. St. Catharines, Ontario: The
    University, 1964.
    20 leaves.
    Distributed to members of Brock University Founders' Committee and
    members of Niagara Peninsula Joint Committee on Higher Education at the
    Welland Club April 22, 1964.   OSTCB
Montagnes, Ian, 1932–
    Plans for renovating University College. [Toronto: 1970]
    11 [2] p.   OTU
— An uncommon fellowship; the story of Hart House. [Toronto] University of
    Toronto Press [c1969]
    viii, 203 p. illus., plans, ports.   OTU
Moore, Elwood S   1878–
    An address on the life and work of the late Professor Arthur P. Coleman...
    delivered... on the occasion of an exhibition of Dr. Coleman's watercolours
    as Victoria University, Toronto, Canada. [Toronto: Victoria University,
    1944]
    [1] 9 leaves.   OTU

Morisset, Auguste Marie, 1900–
    La bibliothèque de l'Université d'Ottawa: son role et ses initiatives.
    Montreal: Imprimerie Populaire, 1945.
    8 p.
    "Reproduction d'un article paru dans *Le Devoir* du Septembre 1945".   OTU
Morley, William Felix Edmund, 1920–   (ed.).
    Ernest Cockburn Kyte; a tribute. Kingston, Ontario: Douglas Library,
    Queen's University, 1970.
    ix, 51 p. port. (Douglas Library. Occasional papers, no. 2).   OTU
Mulock, (Sir) William, 1844–1944.
    The University Act (Toronto) R.S.O. cap. 279; a review of university
    legislation and some of its results. An address delivered at the annual
    banquet of the Ottawa branch of The Alumni Association at the Chateau
    Laurier, Friday, March 21, 1924. [Ottawa? 1924?]
    12 p.   OTU
Needham, Robert W
    Sixty years of service: The University of Western Ontario from small
    beginnings has become one of the great centres of higher education. London,
    Ontario: University of Western Ontario, 1938.
    6 p.
    "Reprinted from *The London Free Press* July 28th, 1938.   OTU
Norman, Colin.
    The Queen's English: standards of literacy among undergraduates in the
    Faculty of Arts and Science at Queen's University, 1975-76, by Colin
    Norman, assisted by Stella Wynne–Edwards. Kingston, Ontario:
    Department of English, Queen's University, 1976.
    xi, 106 p. tables.   OTER
Notes on the special study on operating support for the emerging universities in
    Ontario for fiscal year 1968/1969, prepared for the Ontario Committee on
    University Affairs. [Toronto] 1968.
    17 leaves.   OTER
Ontario. Commission of inquiry as to the Ontario Agricultural College and
    Experimental Farm.
    Report. Printed by order of the Legislative Assembly. Toronto: Warwick
    and Sons, 1893.
    156 p.
    Chairman: John Winchester.   OTL
— Evidence taken by the Commission. Published by the Ontario Department
    of Agriculture. Toronto: Warwick Bros. & Rutter, 1894.
    iv, 655 p.   OTL
Ontario. Commission on Medical Education.
    Report and supporting statements on medical education in Ontario, 1917.
    Printed by order of the Legislative Assembly of Ontario. Toronto: A.T.
    Wilgress, printer to the King's Most Excellent Majesty, 1918.
    177 p.
    Commissioner: The Honourable Mr. Justice Hodgins.   OTU

Ontario. Commission on Post-Secondary Education in Ontario.
  Draft report. [Toronto: W. Kinmond, Queen's Printer, 1972]
  112 p. diagrs., tables.
  Chairman: Douglas T. Wright, April 15, 1969–February 22, 1972; D.O.
  Davis, February 23, 1972–
— Draft supplementary report on post-secondary education for the Franco-
  Ontarian population/Projet de rapport complémentaire sur l'éducation
  postsecondaire de la population franco-ontarienne. [Toronto: W. Kinmond,
  Queen's Printer, 1972]
  8, 8 p.
  In English and French.   OTU
— The learning society: report. Toronto: Ministry of Government Services,
  1972.
  vii, 266 p. illus., diagrs., tables.   OTU
— La société s'epanouit: rapport. [Toronto: Ministère des services
  gouvernementaux, 1972.
  vii, 287 p. illus., diagrs., tables.   OTU
— Briefs... [Toronto: 1971]
  46 v. (various pagings).   OTER
— Post-secondary education in North Bay and Sault Ste. Marie. [Toronto: W.
  Kinmond, Queen's Printer, 1972]
  43 p.   OTU
— Post-secondary education in Northwestern Ontario: a draft report.
  [Toronto] 1970.
  2 v. [108 leaves] map, tables.   OTER
— Post-secondary education in Northwestern Ontario. [Toronto: Queen's
  Printer, 1972]
  40 p. tables.   OTU
— Post-secondary education in Ontario: a statement of issues. [Toronto: 1970?]
  19 p.   OTER

Background reports to the Ontario Commission on Post-Secondary Education in Ontario
Adelman, Howard, 1938–
  The holiversity: a perspective on the Wright report. Toronto: New Press,
  1973.
  152 p.   OTER
Andrew Roman & Associates.
  Legal education in Ontario, 1970. A study prepared for the Commission on
  Post-Secondary Education in Ontario. Toronto: W. Kinmond, Queen's
  Printer, 1972.
  234, 159 p. tables.   OTU
Applied Research Associates.
  Certification and post-secondary education. A study prepared for the
  Commission on Post-Secondary Education in Ontario. [Toronto: W.
  Kinmond, Queen's Printer, 1972]
  110 p.   OTU

— Professional education: a policy opinion. A study prepared for the Commission on Post-Secondary Education in Ontario. [Toronto: W. Kinmond, Queen's Printer, 1972]
160 p.   OTU

Cook, Gail Carol Annabel, 1940–
Financing post-secondary education: an examination of the Draft report of the Commission on Post-Secondary Education in Ontario. By Gail C.A. Cook and David A.A. Stager. Toronto: Institute for the Quantitative Analysis of Social and Economic Policy, University of Toronto, 1972.
14 leaves.   OTER

Council of Ontario Universities.
Response to the report of the Commission on Post-Secondary Education in Ontario. Toronto [1973]
28 leaves. table.   OTU

— Responses to the Draft report of the Commission on Post-Secondary Education in Ontario. Toronto: 1972.
45 p.   OTER

D'Costa, Ronald B
Post-secondary educational opportunities for the Ontario Francophone population. A study prepared for the Commission on Post-Secondary Education in Ontario. Toronto: W. Kinmond, Queen's Printer, 1972.
iii, 109, 115 p. diagrs., tables.   OTULS

Environics Research Group.
Post-secondary educational opportunity for the Ontario Indian population. A study prepared for the Commission on Post-Secondary Education in Ontario. [Toronto: W. Kinmond, Queen's Printer, 1972]
187, 37, 14 p. tables.   OTU

Harvey, Edward B
Education and employment of arts and science graduates; the last decade in Ontario. A study prepared for the Commission on Post-Secondary Education in Ontario. [Toronto: W. Kinmond, Queen's Printer, 1972]
iv, 314 p.   OTU

Hickling–Johnston Limited.
Guidance. A study prepared for the Commission on Post-Secondary Education in Ontario. Toronto: W. Kinmond, Queen's Printer, 1972.
1 v. (various pagings). (Research study no. 19).   OTU

Holland, J
Manpower, forecasting and educational policy. A study prepared for the Commission on Post-Secondary Education in Ontario [by J. Holland and others. Toronto: W. Kinmond, Queen's Printer, 1972]
xviii, 267, 20 p. charts, tables.   OTU

Kates, Peat, Marwick and Company.
Libraries and information storage and retrieval systems. A study prepared for the Commission on Post-Secondary Education in Ontario. [Toronto: W. Kinmond, Queen's Printer, 1972]
1 v. (various paging). diagrs.   OTU

Kirkaldy, J   S
Social reporting and educational planning: a feasibility study. A study
prepared for the Commission on Post-Secondary Education in Ontario by
J.S. Kirkaldy and D.M. Black. [Toronto: Ministry of Government Services,
1972]
iv, 213 p. diagrs., tables.   OTU
Lennards, Jos L
The changing nature of post-secondary education: attitudes, costs and
benefits; a report to the Commission on Post-Secondary Education in
Ontario, by J. Lennards and Edward Harvey. n.p.: 1970.
189 leaves.   OTER
McLean, Neil.
The utilization of electronic technology in post-secondary education in
Britain and West Germany. A study prepared for the Commission on Post-
Secondary Education in Ontario. Toronto: W. Kinmond, Queen's Printer,
1972.
iv, 193 p. diagrs., tables.   OTU
Ontario Institute for Studies in Education. Department of Adult Education.
A response to the Draft report of the Commission on Post-Secondary
Education in Ontario... Toronto: The Institute, 1972.
34 p.   OTER
Smith, Anthony Harry, 1945–
The production of scientific knowledge in Ontario universities; an overview
of problems. A report prepared for the Commission on Post-Secondary
Education in Ontario. [Toronto: W. Kinmond, Queen's Printer, 1972]
iii, 174 p. tables.   OTER OTU
Sterling Institute Canada Limited, Toronto.
Manpower retraining programs in Ontario. A study prepared for the
Commission on Post-Secondary Education in Ontario. [Toronto: W.
Kinmond, Queen's Printer, 1972]
195 p. diagr., tables.   OTU
Systems Research Group.
Cost and benefit study of post-secondary education in Ontario, school year
1968-69. A study prepared for the Commission on Post-Secondary Education
in Ontario [under the direction of R.W. Judy. Toronto: W. Kinmond,
Queen's Printer, 1972]
1 v. (various pagings). illus., forms.   OTU
— Financing post-secondary education. A study prepared for the Commission
on Post-Secondary Education in Ontario [by the Systems Research Group
under the direction of R.W. Judy. Toronto: W. Kinmond, Queen's Printer,
1972]
158 p. diagrs., tables.   OTU
— The Ontario colleges of applied arts and technology. A study prepared for
the Commission on Post-Secondary Education in Ontario. [Toronto: W.
Kinmond, Queen's Printer, 1972]
iv, 150 [1] p. forms, map.   OTU

— Some economics of post-secondary education: a critical review. A study
prepared for the Commission on Post-Secondary Education in Ontario
[under the direction of R.W. Judy. Toronto: W. Kinmond, Queen's Printer,
1972]
1, 89 [A1]–A24 p. illus.   OTU
Toronto. University. School of Nursing.
Comments on the Draft report of the Commission on Post-Secondary
Education in Ontario. [Toronto: 1971?]
5 leaves.   OTU
Toronto. University. Students' Administrative Council.
The learning society. Report of the Commission on Post-Secondary
Education in Ontario. An abridged version. Toronto: SAC Press, 1973.
36 p.   OTU
Towards 2000; the future of post-secondary education in Ontario. With a
foreword by Claude Bissell. [Toronto] McClelland and Stewart [c1971]
xiii, 176 p. diagrs., tables.
"From the Report prepared for the Committee of Presidents of Universities
of Ontario by its Subcommittee on Research and Planning presented as a
brief to the Commission on Post-Secondary Education in Ontario.   OTU
Woods, Gordon and Company, Toronto.
Organization of the academic year. A study prepared for the Commission on
Post-Secondary Education in Ontario. Toronto: W. Kinmond, Queen's
Printer, 1972.
214, 10, 6 p. illus.   OTU

Ontario. Commission on the discipline and other matters of the University of
Toronto.
Report. Printed by order of the Legislative Assembly. Toronto: Warwick
Bros. & Rutter, 1895.
34 p.
Chairman: Thomas Wardlaw Taylor.   OTL
— Evidence.
25–217 typewritten pages.   OTL
— Proceedings: April 8, 1895 to April 22, 1895.
1083 typewritten pages.   OTAR
Ontario. Commission to inquire into certain misconduct at the Agricultural
College, Guelph.
Report. [Toronto: 1884]
5 handwritten pages.
Commissioner: John Winchester.   OTAR
— [Evidence received from students. 1884]
22 handwritten pages.   OTAR

Ontario. Commission to study the development of graduate programmes in
    Ontario universities.
    Report to the Committee on University Affairs and the Committee of
    Presidents of Provincially-assisted Universities. Toronto: 1966.
    vi, 110 p. map.
    Chairman: J.W.T. Spinks.   OTU

*Brief to Ontario Commission to study the development of graduate programmes in Ontario
universities*
Ontario Association of College and University Libraries.
    A brief to the Commission appointed to study the development of graduate
    programmes in Ontario universities. [Toronto?] 1966.
    6 leaves.   OTULS

Ontario. Commissioners appointed to inquire into and report upon the matters
    referred to in a resolution of the Senate of the University of Toronto.
    Report. Printed by order of the Legislative Assembly of Ontario. Toronto:
    L.K. Cameron, printer to the King, 1905.
    14 p.
    Chairman: W.R. Meredith.   OTU
Ontario. Council on University Affairs.
    Minutes of meetings, 1969–1974.
    9 v.
    Contents: [v. 1] 7th October, 1969–16th December, 1969; [v. 2] 5th January,
    1970–23rd June, 1970; [v. 3] 5th October 1970–26th January, 1971; [v. 4]
    9th February, 1971–7th June, 1971; [v. 5] 27th September, 1971–24th
    January, 1972; [v. 6] 7th February, 1972–26th June, 1972; [v. 7] 25th July,
    1972–16 January, 1973; [v. 8] February 5, 1973–February 12, 1974; [v. 9]
    February 13th, 1974–   OTU
— Statistical information on Ontario universities. Fall 1971. n.p.: 1972.
    145 p.   OTER

Briefs to the Ontario Council on University Affairs
Lakehead University.
    Brief to the Committee on University Affairs, November 24, 1970. [Thunder
    Bay, Ontario] 1970.
    1 v. (various pagings). graphs, tables.   OTER
— December 7, 1971. [Thunder Bay, Ontario] 1971.
    10, A31, B53 leaves. tables.   OTER
— October 16, 1973. [Thunder Bay, Ontario] 1973.
    73 leaves. tables.   OTER
Toronto. University.
    Statement of the University of Toronto to the Committee on University
    Affairs. [Toronto] 1970.
    2 v.   OTU

— A statement to the Committee on University Affairs by the University of
   Toronto. [Toronto] 1973.
   51, 4, 6 leaves. diagrs.
   In pocket: Brief from the Students' Administrative Council.
   11 p.   OTER
Trent University.
   Brief to the Ontario Council on University Affairs. [Peterborough, Ontario]
   1974.
   1 v. (various pagings). tables.   OTER
— [Peterborough, Ontario] 1975.
   1 v. (various pagings). tables.   OTER

Ontario. Legislative Assembly. Select Committee to which was referred the
   inquiry into the condition and management of the Agricultural College,
   Guelph.
   Report. 1874.
   5 handwritten pages.
   Chairman: James Bethune.   OTAR
Ontario. Legislative Assembly. Special Committee appointed to inquire into the
   organization and administration of the University of Toronto.
   Report. Printed by order of the Legislative Assembly. Toronto: Clarkson W.
   James, printer to the King's Most Excellent Majesty, 1923.
   20 p.
   Chairman: E.C. Drury.   OTAR
— Minutes of the sessions of the Special Committee, November 16,
   1922–January 17, 1923.
   5 v. [i.e. 1138 typewritten pages]   OTAR
— Minutes [Proceedings] October 25, 1922–April 27, 1923.
   1 v. (various pagings).   OTAR

Background papers to Ontario Legislative Assembly Special Committee appointed to inquire
   into the organization and administration of the University of Toronto
Toronto. University. Board of Governors.
   Memorandum from the Board of Governors of the University of Toronto for
   the Select Committee [sic] of the Legislature. [Toronto: 1923]
   [11] p.   OTU
The University of Toronto: concerning the events leading up to the
   appointment of a select committee of the Legislature of the province of
   Ontario, in the session of 1922, to enquire into the affairs of the University of
   Toronto and the Toronto General Hospital, with a summary of the Report
   of the Committee to the House. [Toronto? 1923?]
   21 p.   OTU

Ontario. Royal Commission on the University of Toronto.
Report. Printed by order of the Legislative Assembly of Ontario. Toronto:
L.K. Cameron, printer to the King's Most Excellent Majesty, 1906.
lx, 268 p.
Chairman: J.W. Flavelle.   OTU
— Clippings regarding the University Commission of 1906.
[31] p.   OTUAR
— [Papers] 1905–1908.
6 boxes.
Contents: 1, Act of 1906, earlier acts, Senate amendment of 1907, Report of
the Commission, Preliminary drafts of the report; 2, General correspondence
and papers; 3, General correspondence and papers, minute book; 4,
Submissions, Commission's reports on Trinity, 5, Reports and
recommendations submitted to the Commission by committees and
individuals; 6, Miscellaneous printed material.   OTUAR

Background papers to Ontario Royal Commission on the University of Toronto
Toronto. University of Trinity College.
Memorandum from the Convocation of Trinity College to the Royal
Commission appointed to enquire into the management and government of
the University of Toronto. [Toronto: 1905?]
[4]p.   OTU

Ontario. Royal Commission on University Finances.
Report. Printed by order of the Legislative Assembly of Ontario. Toronto:
C.W. James, printer to the King's Most Excellent Majesty, 1921.
2 v. illus., charts, diagrs., maps.
Contents: v. 1, Report; v. 2, Appendices.
Chairman: H.J. Cody.   OTU
— Evidence.
Various typewritten pages.   OTAR

Background papers to Ontario Royal Commission on University Finances
Queen's University. Trustees.
Report of the Trustees of Queen's University to the Royal Commission on
University Finance. [Kingston, Ontario: Queen's University, 1920]
62 p. map, tables.   OTU
Toronto. University.
Statement and reports presented to the University Commission [Finance] by
the Board of Governors and Senate of the University of Toronto. [Toronto]
1920.
71 p. diagrs., tables.   OTU
— A summary of the University's position, its work, and its needs, being

extracts from the statement presented on December 6th, 1920, to the Royal
Commission Investigating University Finances in Ontario. [Toronto]
University of Toronto Press [1921]
32 p. illus. OTU
Ontario Agricultural College. Macdonald Institute.
A fiftieth anniversary sketch of the development of Macdonald Institute,
Ontario Agricultural College. [Guelph, Ontario: 1953]
31 p. illus., ports. OGU
Ontario Agricultural College and Experimental Farm.
Diamond jubilee of the College. Guelph, Ontario: The College, 1934.
[16] p. illus. OTU
— Diamond jubilee of the College, June 1934. [Guelph, Ontario: The College,
1934]
[20] p. chiefly illus. OLU
— 1874–1924, semi-centennial of the college June, 1924 [half-century of the
O.A.C.: some of the events and the personalities which make up the history.
Guelph, Ontario: The College, 1924]
28 p. illus., ports. OGU
— History, activities and accomplishments. [Guelph, Ontario] Office of the
President [1934?]
21 leaves. OTU
— Ontario Agricultural College, 1874–1949. Proceedings of the celebration of
the seventy-fifth anniversary. Guelph, Canada: 1949.
27 p. OGU OTU
— 75th anniversary, 1949. Guelph, Ontario: 1949.
1 v. (unpaged). illus. (part col.), ports. OGU
Ontario Association for Continuing Education. Community Colleges
Committee.
The community colleges and their communities; a report prepared by
Dorene E. Jacobs. December, 1970. Revised for publication, August 1971.
[Toronto] 1971.
56 p. OTULS
Ontario Council of Deans of Medicine.
Specialized manpower production and research development in Ontario
faculties of medicine, 1969–1975. [Toronto] 1970.
92 p. OTER
Ontario Council of University Faculty Associations.
University education in Ontario; a brief presented to the Prime Minister of
Ontario. Ottawa: Canadian Association of University Teachers, 1963.
55 leaves. tables. OTER
— Revised. Ottawa: Canadian Association of University Teachers, 1964.
57 leaves. tables. OONL
Ontario Council on Graduate Studies.
Graduate planning in Ontario universities: a brief to be presented to OCUA
in June 1976. Toronto: Council of Ontario Universities, 1976.
1 v. (various pagings). graphs, tables. OONL

— Survey of employment of Ontario Ph.D. graduates – 1964–69. [Toronto]
   1970.
   5 p. 25 tables.   OTER
— Survey of nationality of graduate students enrolled in master's and doctoral
   degree programs at Ontario universities in 1968-69. n.p.: 1969.
   [2] 20 leaves.   OTU
Ontario Council on Graduate Studies. Advisory Committee on Academic
   Planning.
   Perspectives and plans for graduate studies, by the Advisory Committee on
   Academic Planning, Ontario Council on Graduate Studies. Toronto:
   Council of Ontario Universities, 1973–1975.
   18 v. in 23 parts.
   Contents: v. 1, Library science 1972; v. 2, Education 1973; v. 3, Economics
   1973; v. 4, Geography 1973; v. 5, Chemistry 1973; v. 6, Solid earth science
   1973; v. 7, Sociology 1973; v. 8, Anthropology 1974; v. 9, Political Science
   1974; v. 10, Physical education, kinesiology and related areas 1974; v. 11,
   Engineering, A. Chemical engineering 1974, B. Electrical engineering 1974,
   C. Metalurgical and materials engineering 1974, D. Mechanical engineering
   1974, E. Industrial engineering and system design 1974, F. Civil Engineering
   1975; v. 12, Religious studies 1974; v. 13, Planning and environmental
   studies 1974; v. 14, Physics and astronomy 1974; v. 15, History 1974; v. 16,
   Biophysics 1974; v. 17, Administration, business and management science
   1974; v. 18, Mathematical sciences 1975.   OTU
Ontario Council on Graduate Studies. Committee on Appraisal of Graduate
   Degree Programmes.
   The first three years of appraisal of graduate programmes [report prepared
   by M.A. Preston] Toronto: Committee of Presidents of Universities of
   Ontario [1970]
   17 p.   OTU
Ontario Council on Graduate Studies. Committee on Student Financial
   Support.
   Report. [Toronto] 1970.
   vi, 59 p.   OTER
Ontario Economic Council.
   Human resource development in the province of Ontario: education,
   retraining, immigration. Toronto: The Council, 1966.
   16 p.
   Chairman: William H. Cranston.   OONL
Ontario Institute for Studies in Education. Office of the Coordinator of
   Research and Development Studies.
   Studies of society and social issues: activities related to social studies at the
   Ontario Institute for Studies in Education. [Toronto] 1974.
   vii, 41 p.   OTER
Ontario Institute for Studies in Education. Professional Education Project.
   The advancement of professional education in Canada: the report of the

professional education project (Kellogg Foundation – Ontario Institute for Studies in Education). Written by John A.B. McLeish on behalf of J. Roby Kidd [et al. Toronto] 1973.
 59 p. illus.   OTER
Ontario Universities' Application Centre.
 The first three years, 1971–74. Toronto: Council of Ontario Universities, 1974.
 i, 47 p. (Council of Ontario Universities, 74-16).   OTU
Ontario Veterinary College, Guelph, Ontario..
 Ontario Veterinary College, Guelph, Ontario, Canada. Veterinary science and its opportunities; a brief outline of the College, the course of instruction and of the opportunities available to graduates in Veterinary Science. Under the Department of Agriculture of Ontario and affiliated with the University of Toronto. [Toronto: Press of the Hunter–Rose Co. Ltd., 192–?]
 15 [1] p. illus.   OTU
Ontario Welfare Council. Section on Aging.
 Survey of education related to aging offered in professional schools in Ontario. Toronto: Ontario Welfare Council, 1964.
 34, vi p. tables.   OTOWC
The opening ceremonies of Massey College, Friday, October 4th, 1963. [Toronto? 1963?]
 9 leaves.   OTU
Ottawa. Université.
 Aux Canadiens-français des États-Unis. Aperçu du plan d'études et de la méthode d'enseignement suivis au Collège d'Ottawa. Ottawa: 1882.
 22 p.   OTURS
— Histoire du passé, l'orientation de l'avenir. Ottawa: The Université d'Ottawa, 1935.
 43 p.
 Language question.   OTU
— L'Université d'Ottawa, une maison d'enseignement catholique et bilingue. Ottawa: The Université, 1931.
 11 p. illus.   OTU
Ottawa. Université. Bureau des gouverneurs. Sous-comite sur les structures de l'Université.
 Rapport. Ottawa: Université d'Ottawa [1968]
 39, 39 p.
 Texte anglais et français.   OONL
Ottawa. Université. Commission de révision des structures d'enseignement et de recherche.
 Strategie pour le changement. Rapport. [Ottawa: 1974–75]
 2 v. charts, tables.
 President: Denis Carrier.
 Also published in English.   OTER
— L'Université d'Ottawa c'est quoi? [Ottawa] 1972–1973.
 10 v.   OOU

Ottawa. Université. Groupe de Travail sur le Bilinguisme.
    Rapport. Ottawa: Université d'Ottawa, 1971.
    163 leaves. tables.
    Président: Hugues Morrissette.
    Also published in English.   OTER
Ottawa. University.
    A searchlight showing the need of a university for the English speaking
    Catholics of Canada. [Ottawa: The University, 1905?]
    48 p.   OTU
— Souvenir of the laying of the corner-stone of the new arts building. [Ottawa:
    University of Ottawa, 1904]
    61 p. illus., ports.   OTU
— L'Université d'Ottawa. The University of Ottawa. [Ottawa: 1957]
    55 p. illus.
    "Prepared on the occasion of the Conference of Learned Societies,
    University of Ottawa, 1957".   OTU
— To the Catholics of the province of Ontario, a plea in favour of higher
    education. Ottawa: Ottawa Printing, 1899.
    25 p. illus.   OOU
Ottawa. University. Board of Governors. Sub-committee on the Structure of the
    University.
    Report. Ottawa: University of Ottawa [1969]
    39, 39 p.
    Text in English and French on opposite pages.   OONL
Ottawa. University. Commission on the Revision of Teaching and Research
    Structures.
    Strategy for change. Report. [Ottawa: 1974–75]
    2 v. charts, tables.
    Chairman: Denis Carrier.
    Also published in French.   OTER
Ottawa. University. Legal Aid Planning Committee.
    Report. [Ottawa] The Committee, c1971.
    ii, 73 leaves. map, tables.   OTUCR
Ottawa. University. Publicity Bureau.
    The University of Ottawa. Ottawa: Publicity Bureau of the University
    [1935?]
    1 v. (unpaged). chiefly illus., ports.   OTU
Ottawa. University. School of Nursing.
    The University of Ottawa School of Nursing, 1933–1973. [Richelieu,
    Quebec: Imprimerie Notre Dame] 1973.
    145 p. ports.
    Text in English and French.   OOU
Ottawa. University. Task Force on Bilingualism.
    Report. Ottawa: Ottawa University, 1971.
    164 leaves. tables.
    Chairman: Hugues Morrissette.
    Also published in French.   OOU

Overduin, Henrich.
   People and ideas: nursing at Western, 1920–1970. [London, Ontario]
   Faculty of Nursing, The University of Western Ontario [1973]
   150 p. illus.   OLUM
Owen, Derwyn Randolph Grier, 1914–
   Trinity College [a history of the building and expansion programme
   1957–1963] a report. n.p. [1964?]
   [12] p. illus. (part col.).   OONL
Page, James E
   Canadian studies in community colleges: a report. [Toronto] Canadian
   Studies Office, Ontario Institute for Studies in Education [1973?]
   vi, 175 p.   OTER
Painchaud, Louis, 1927–
   Le bilinguisme à l'université, description du bilinguisme et du biculturalisme
   de l'Université d'Ottawa, de l' Université Laurentienne et du Collège
   militaire royal de Saint-Jean. Montreal: Beauchemin [1968]
   248 p. tables.   OOU
Payton, L   C
   Post-doctoral education in the Ontario universities 1969-70: a report
   submitted to the Council of Ontario Universities. [Toronto? Council of
   Ontario Universities] 1972.
   v, 75 p. forms, tables.   OTER
— Post-doctoral education in the Ontario universities, 1973-74: a report
   submitted to the Council of Ontario Universities. [Toronto?: Council of
   Ontario Universities] 1975.
   v, 63 p. forms.   OTER
— The status of women in the Ontario universities, a report to the Council of
   Ontario Universities. [Toronto] Council of Ontario Universities, 1975.
   21 p.   OTU
Pearson, Norman, 1928–
   Leisure research activities and teaching at the University of Guelph. Report
   to the Ontario Research Council on leisure. [Guelph, Ontario] Centre for
   Resources Development, University of Guelph, 1972.
   8 leaves. (Publication no. 62).   OTU
— Planning, resources and environmental studies at Canadian universities:
   study for the Ad Hoc Senate Committee on the Centre for Resources
   Development. [Guelph, Ontario] Centre for Resources Development,
   University of Guelph, 1972.
   31 leaves. graphs. (Publication no. 59).   OTU
Peitchinis, Stephen Gabriel, 1925–
   Financing post-secondary education in Canada. [Toronto: Council of
   Ministers of Education of Canada, 1971]
   iii, 451 p. tables.
   "A report commissioned by The Council of Ministers of Education of
   Canada".   OONL

Pettipiere, H   W
> Ontario universities application centre: a study of the needs and design of a
> centre for applications for admission to the universities of Ontario prepared
> for the Committee of Presidents of Universities of Ontario and the Ontario
> Universities Council on Admissions. [Guelph, Ontario?] 1971.
> 49 p. illus., forms.   OTER

Pickersgill, John Whitney, 1905–
> Address at the official opening of the School of Public Administration,
> Carleton College, Ottawa, October 23, 1953. Ottawa: The College, 1953.
> 17 leaves.   OOCC

Porter, Arthur, 1910–
> Towards a community university: a study of learning at Western. Report to
> the Senate of The University of Western Ontario. London, Ontario
> [Department of Information Services and University Publications] The
> University of Western Ontario, 1971.
> x, 235 p. illus.   OTU

Porter, Marion R
> Does money matter? Prospects for higher education, by Marion R. Porter,
> John Porter and Bernard R. Blishen. Toronto: Institute for Behavioural
> Research, York University [c1973]
> xiv, 304 p.   OTU

Position paper on developing a concept for health sciences education; University
> of Toronto study of health sciences. [Toronto] 1968.
> 1 v. (various pagings). diagrs.   OTU

Preliminary report; a study of 42 women who have children and who are in
> graduate programmes at the University of Toronto, May 1966. A project
> organized by Natalie Zemon Davis, Josephine Grimshaw, Elizabeth
> Mandell, Alison Smith Prentice [and] Germaine Warkentin. [Toronto:
> 1970?]
> [1] iii, 25 leaves.   OTU

Preston, Richard Arthur.
> Canada's RMC: a history of the Royal Military College. [Toronto] Published
> for the Royal Military College Club of Canada by the University of Toronto
> Press [c1969]
> xv, 415 p. illus., ports.   OTU

Quarter, Jack Joel, 1941–
> The student movement of the sixties; a social-psychological analysis.
> [Toronto] Ontario Institute for Studies in Education [c1972]
> x, 138 p. (Ontario Institute for Studies in Education. Occasional papers, 7).
> Toronto and United States.   OONL

Queen's College, Kingston, Ontario.
> Regulations affecting students being a compilation of statutes and by-laws.
> Kingston, Ontario: Creighton, 1870.
> 14 p.   OKQ

— Report of the general committee on the endowment of Queen's College.
> Kingston, Ontario: 1869.
> 5 p.   OKQ

Queen's University.
  Overseas record; record of graduates, alumni, members of staff, and students
  of Queen's University on active military (overseas) service, 1914–1917 (to
  June 1st, 1917). [Kingston: 1917?]
  44 p.   OTU
— Queen's 1841–1911; the making of Queen's. Kingston, Ontario: Queen's
  University, 1911.
  40 p. illus., port.   OKQ
— Queen's eighty-fifth anniversary reunion, 1841–1926, at Kingston,
  November 6th to 13th, 1926. [Kingston, Ontario: 1926]
  28 p. illus., ports.   OKQ
— Queen's in pictures. Kingston, Ontario: Queen's University, 1951.
  1 v. (unpaged). chiefly illus.   OKQ
— Queen's University, a centenary volume, 1841–1941. Toronto: The Ryerson
  Press [1942]
  xi, 189 p. front., plates.   OKQ
— Queen's University: an illustrated sketch of its foundation, growth and
  present proportions, published by *Queen's Quarterly* as a souvenir of the
  installation of Principal Gordon and the jubilee of the medical faculty,
  October 14th, 15th, 16th, 1903. [Kingston, Ontario] Queen's Quarterly,
  1903.
  42 p. chiefly illus. ports.   OKQ
— Queen's University Art Foundation; being a brief and informal account of
  the stewardship of a few friends of Queen's University, Kingston, Ontario,
  during the five years, 1940–1944. n.p. [1944]
  23 p.   OTU
— Queen's University at Kingston. [Commemorative publication marking the
  one hundred and twenty-fifth anniversary of the first classes held March 7,
  1842. Kingston: 1967.
  1 v. (unpaged). illus.   OTSTM
— Report of the Chancellor with regard to the scheme for confederating
  universities and colleges. Toronto: Grip Printing and Publishing Co., 1885.
  34 p.   OTURS
— Statement regarding the relations of Queen's University to the church.
  Kingston, Ontario [1903]
  8 p.   OOA
— Statement respecting the present position of Queen's University. Kingston,
  Ontario: The University, 1908.
  12 p.   OKQ
— University government at Queen's. I, Report of the Joint Committee on
  University Government; II, Second report of the Committee on Structure of
  the Senate. Kingston, Ontario: Queen's University, 1969.
  28 p.   OONL
Queen's University. Alumnae Association.
  Queen's University Alumnae Association 1900–1961 and women's residences

at Queen's. [Edited by Mary MacPhail Chown] Kingston, Ontario: The
University, 1965.
73 leaves.   OKQ
Queen's University. Alumni Association Conference.
The university question. A symposium. Kingston, Ontario: Daily News
Office, 1901.
12 p.   OTU
Queen's University. General Alumni Association.
Queen's University at Kingston, 1841–1941. Centenary booklet by the
General Alumni Association and the Alumnae Association. [Kingston,
Ontario: 1941?]
[24] p. illus., ports.   OTU
Queen's University. Institute of Intergovernmental Relations.
The functional spending priorities of Canadian governments, with particular
reference to education. [Ottawa: The University of Ottawa Press, c1970]
586 p. tables. (Commission on the Relations between Universities and
Governments: Studies on the university, society and government, v. 2).   OTU
Queen's University. Principal's Committee on Teaching and Learning.
Report. [Kingston, Ontario] Queen's University, 1969.
83 p. illus.
Chairman: G.A. Harrower.   OTER
Queen's University. Principal's Committee on the Status of Women at Queen's
University.
Report. [Kingston, Ontario: The University, 1974]
32 p. tables.
Chairman: Lin Good.
Queen's Gazette Supplement v. 6, no. 9, February 28, 1974.   OKQL
Radford, Peter F
Undergraduate physical education students: a preliminary study, by Peter
F. Radford and Geoff R. Gowan. [Hamilton, Ontario] School of Physical
Education and Athletics, McMaster University, 1969.
vi, 129 leaves. graphs, tables.   OTER
Ramsey, Craig A   1937–
The "graduate" study, by Craig A. Ramsey and E.N. Wright. [Toronto:
Research Department, Board of Education for the city of Toronto] 1969.
41 leaves. graphs, tables.   OONL
Rapport du Comité de recherche sur l'avenir du Collège, par André Bordealeau
[et autres]. 2e ed. Hearst, Ontario: Le Collège Universitaire de Hearst, 1972.
ii, 44, iv p. illus.
"There is no first edition, only a first impression".   OHC
Reed, Thomas Arthur, 1871–1958.
The architecture of the building. n.p. [1936?]
[4] p. illus.
University College.   OTU
— A history of the University of Trinity College, Toronto, 1852–1952.
[Toronto] University of Toronto Press, 1952.
xii, 313 p. ports., plates.   OKQ

Repo, Marjaleena.
   Who needs the Ph.D?: a case study of 190 Ph.D. level job seekers at
   University of Toronto. [Toronto] Graduate Students' Union, University of
   Toronto [1970]
   [4] 83 p. tables.   OTU
Robinson, Floyd Grant, 1931–
   Staff research in Canadian degree-granting universities and colleges, by F.G.
   Robinson and E. Haltrecht. [Ottawa? Canadian Council for Research in
   Education, 1964]
   ii, 54 p.   OTU
Robinson, Percy James, 1873–1953.
   University of Toronto (The provincial university of Ontario), a brief outline
   of its history and its administration, with illustrations of twenty-five of the
   university buildings. [Toronto] University Press [1924]
   18 p. illus.   OTU
Rodgers, Andrew Denny.
   Bernard Edward Fernow: a story of North American Forestry. Princeton,
   New Jersey: Princeton University Press, 1951.
   623 p. ports.
   Fernow and the Faculty of Forestry at Toronto: pp. 427–519.   OTU
Ross, Alexander Murdock, 1916–
   The college on the hill: a history of the Ontario Agricultural College
   1874–1974. Vancouver: Copp Clark Publishing, published in co-operation
   with O.A.C. Alumni Association [c1974]
   ix, 180 p. illus., facsims., ports.   OTU
Ross, George William, 1841–1914.
   The universities of Canada: their history and organization with an outline of
   British and American university systems. Toronto: Warwick Bros. & Rutter,
   1896.
   viii, 440 p.
   Ontario: pp. 7–146.
   "Appendix to the *Report of the Minister of Education, 1896*".   OTAR
Ross, Murray George, 1911–
   The new university. [Toronto] University of Toronto Press [1961]
   ix, 110 p.   OTU
— Those five years, 1960–1965. The President's report. [Toronto] York
   University [1965]
   123 p. illus., tables.   OTU
— Those ten years, 1960–70: the President's report on the first decade of York
   University. [Toronto] York University [1970]
   59 p. illus.   OTU
— The university: the anatomy of academe. New York: McGraw–Hill Book
   Company [c1976]
   xii, 310 p.   OTU
Ross, Murray George, 1911–   (ed.).
   New universities in the modern world. Toronto: Macmillan, 1966.
   x, 190 p. illus.
   York University: pp. 69–86.   OTU

Rothstein, Samuel, 1921–
  The university–the library: papers presented by Samuel Rothstein, Richard
  Blackwell and Archibald MacLeish at York University, Toronto, on the
  occasion of the dedication of the Scott Library, 30 October, 1971. Oxford:
  Shakespeare Head Press, 1972.
  [5] 62 p. illus.   OTU
Rowles, Dorothy.
  Report of the "Ryerson Project": a study of the development of a diploma
  program in nursing at the Ryerson Institute of Technology, Toronto,
  Ontario. [Toronto] Registered Nurses' Association of Ontario, 1963.
  35, xiii p.   OTU
Royal Military College of Canada.
  The Royal Military College, 1876 to 1919. 2d ed. [Kingston, 1920?]
  20 leaves.
  No copy of the first edition located.   OTU
Royal Society of Canada.
  Canadian universities today: symposium presented to the Royal Society of
  Canada in 1960. Les universités canadiennes aujourd' hui: colloque présenté
  à la Société royale du Canada en 1960. Edited by George Stanley & Guy
  Sylvestre. [Toronto] Published for the society by University of Toronto Press,
  1961.
  x, 97 p. diagrs. (*Its* Studia varia series, 6).   OTU
— Scholarship in Canada, 1967: achievement and outlook. Symposium
  presented to Section II of the Royal Society of Canada in 1967. Edited by
  R.H. Hubbard with an introduction by Watson Kirkconnell. [Toronto]
  Published for the Society by University of Toronto Press, 1968.
  xii, 104 p. (*Its* Studia varia 12).   OTSTM
Ryerson School Old Boys' Association.
  Memorial of Samuel McAllister, principal of Ryerson School 1877–1906.
  Toronto: The Author, 1907.
  45 p. facsim., port.   OTU
St. Michael's College.
  Seventy-fifth anniversary. St. Michael's College in the University of
  Toronto. [Toronto: 1927]
  57 p. illus., ports.   OTSTM
St. Michael's College, Toronto, Canada: the Catholic College of the University
  of Toronto. [Toronto] University of Toronto Press, 1923.
  13 p.   OTSTM
Scollard, Robert Joseph, 1908–
  A bibliography of the writings of Charles Collins, C.S.B., compiled by Robert
  J. Scollard, C.S.B. with an introduction by J. Francis Mallon, C.S.B. Toronto:
  The Basilian Press, 1974.
  24 p. (Basilian Historical Bulletin no. 9).   OTSTM
— The diaries and other papers of Michael Joseph Ferguson, C.S.B., a
  bibliography compiled by Robert J. Scollard, C.S.B. with an introduction by
  J. Stanley Murphy, C.S.B. Toronto: The Basilian Press, 1970.
  36 p. port., facsims. (Basilian Historical Bulletin no. 5).   OTSTM

— The diaries and other papers of Michael Joseph Mungovan, C.S.B., a bibliography compiled by Robert J. Scollard, C.S.B. Toronto: The Basilian Press, 1971.
  23 [1] p. facsims. (Basilian Historical Bulletin no. 6).   OTSTM
— Footprints in the sands of Cloverhill: anniversaries and notable events... St. Michael's College, 1852–1977. Toronto: University of St. Michael's College Archives, 1977.
  55 p. illus.   OTAR
Scott, James, 1916–
  Of mud and dreams: University of Waterloo 1957–1967. Toronto: The Ryerson Press [1967]
  xiii, 194 p. illus.   OTU
Seager, Charles Allen, Bp., 1872–1948.
  The University of Trinity College, its ideals and needs. [Toronto: 1925?]
  [8] p.   OTU
Seath, John, 1844–1919.
  University matriculation in Ontario: a paper (rev.) read April 16, 1892 before the Classical Mathematical, Modern Languages and Science Associations of Ontario. [Toronto: 1892]
  8 p.   OTMCL
Second chances for mature women; report of a talk-in with the Quo Vadis School of Nursing, March 3, 1971. Sponsored by Department of Adult Education, Ontario Institute for Studies in Education. [Toronto 1971]
  [3] 29 leaves.   OTU
Seminar on Part-time Study and Resources for Learning, Cambrian College, Sudbury, 1973.
  Part-time study and resources for learning. [Toronto? 1973]
  27 leaves.   OTER
Sheffield, Edward Fletcher, 1912–   (ed.).
  Agencies for higher education in Ontario: A series of seven seminars sponsored by the Higher Education Group, University of Toronto, January–February, 1973. [Toronto] Ontario Institute for Studies in Education [c1974]
  vi, 82 p. charts. (Symposium series 3).   OTER
Sheraton, James Paterson, 1841–1906.
  The history and principles of Wycliffe College; an address to the alumni... October 7th, 1891. Toronto: J.E. Bryant Co., 1891.
  32 p.   OTU
Shook, Laurence Kennedy, 1909–
  Catholic post-secondary education in English-speaking Canada: a history. [Toronto] University of Toronto Press [c1971]
  x, 457 p.
  Ontario: pp. 129–256, 275–313.   OTU
Short, Elizabeth (Smith), 1859–
  Historical sketch of medical education of women in Kingston. [Ottawa: 1916]
  13 leaves.   OKQ

Should Victoria University join the proposed federation of colleges? ... [n.p.
[1885]
   16 p.   OTU
Simard, Georges, 1878–1956.
   Un centenaire: Le pere Tabaret, et son oeuvre d'education. [Ottawa]
   Université d'Ottawa, 1928.
   40 p.   OTU
— L'Université d'Ottawa: I, histoire du passe; II, l'orientation de l'avenir. n.p.
   [1910?]
   42 p.   OOU
Sisam, John William Bernard, 1906–
   Forestry education at Toronto. [Toronto] University of Toronto Press [1961]
   116 p. illus., ports., tables.   OTU
Sissons, Charles Bruce, 1879–1965.
   A history of Victoria University. Toronto: University of Toronto Press, 1952.
   vii, 346 p. illus., ports.   OTU
— Nil alienum: the memoirs. [Toronto] University of Toronto Press [c1964]
   xii, 260 p.   OTU
Sixty years on – 1910–1970; a brief history of the University of Toronto schools.
   [Toronto: 1970]
   64 p. illus., ports.   OTU
Skelhorne, Jean M
   The adult learner in the university; does anybody care? A study of need
   based on an investigation of the facilities and services provided by the
   University of Toronto for mature, full-time undergraduate women.
   [Toronto] Department of Adult Education, Ontario Institute for Studies in
   Education, 1975.
   viii, 53 p. tables.   OTER
Smart, Reginald George, 1936–
   Effects of lowering the legal drinking age on post-secondary students in
   Metropolitan Toronto, by Reginald G. Smart and W. James White.
   Toronto: Addiction Research Foundation, 1972.
   1 v. (various pagings). tables.   OTUCR
Smyth, Delmar McCormack, 1922–
   Government for higher learning in Ryerson Polytechnical Institute. A report
   prepared for the Board of Governors of Ryerson Polytechnical Institute.
   [Toronto] 1970.
   v, 229 p. graphs, map, tables.   OTU OTER
Social Planning Council of Metropolitan Toronto. Section on Aging.
   Report of Committee on Training and Retraining Opportunities for Older
   People. [Toronto: 1958]
   15 leaves. 6 p.   OTU
Squair, John, 1850–1928.
   I. Admission of women to the University of Toronto and University College.
   II. Rectification of a passage in "Alumni Association in the University of
   Toronto" (1922). [Toronto] University of Toronto Press, 1924.
   [1] 34 p.   OTU

— Alumni associations in the University of Toronto. [Toronto] University of Toronto Press, 1922.
  [1] 45 p.   OTU

— The autobiography of a teacher of French, with preliminary chapters from various sources, being a contribution to the history of the University of Toronto. Toronto: University of Toronto Press, 1928.
  ix, 292 p. plates.   OTU

— Forty years ago; chairman's address at 1883 class reunion, June 8, 1923. [Toronto] University of Toronto Press, 1924.
  [1] 9 p.   OTU

Stager, David Arnold Albert, 1937–
  Some economic aspects of alternative systems of post-secondary education. A paper presented at the seventh Canadian Conference on Educational Research, Victoria, British Columbia January 28, 1969. [Toronto] 1969.
  49 p. tables.
  Higher education in Ontario.   OONL

Stevenson, Orlando John, 1869–1950.
  Ontario Agricultural College, semi-centennial 1874–1924: historical review. n.p. [1924?]
  24 leaves.   OGU

The student and the system: proceedings of the conference sponsored by the Graduate Students Association, OISE, November, 1969. Edited by Bruce Rusk, Tim Hardy and Bill Tooley. [Toronto] Ontario Institute for Studies in Education [c1970]
  viii, 78 p. (Ontario Institute for Studies in Education. Occasional papers no. 5).   OTER

Sudbury, Ontario. Université.
  50 ans: le Collège du Sacré-Coeur, Sudbury, 1963. [Sudbury, Ontario] 1963.
  66 p. illus., port.   OSUL

Sudbury Star.
  Laurentian University. [Sudbury, Ontario: 1964]
  [56] p. illus., ports., map.
  Issued as a supplement to the *Sudbury Star*, October 8, 1964.   OTU

Sutherland, Alexander, 1833–1910.
  The proposed plan of college confederation. Toronto: The Author, 1885.
  24 p. (Educational tracts for the times, no. 2).   OTURS

Symonds, Herbert, 1860–1921.
  Trinity University and university federation. An essay addressed to the Council of Trinity University and the members of Convocation. Peterborough: Peterborough Examiner Printing Co., 1894.
  26 p.   OTU

Symons, Thomas Henry Bull, 1929–
     The planning and operation of some new residential colleges at the
     University of Toronto; a report prepared for the Committee on Policy and
     Planning of the University of Toronto. [Toronto] 1961.
     36 leaves.   OTU
— To know ourselves: the report of the Commission on Canadian Studies.
     Ottawa: Association of Universities and Colleges of Canada, 1975–
     4 v.
     Only v. 1–2 had been published by December 1976.   OTU
— The University in summer; a report prepared for the Presidential
     Committee on Policy and Planning on the University of Toronto. [Toronto]
     1960.
     55, 5 leaves.   OTU
Talman, James John, 1904–
     Huron college, 1863–1963. London, Ontario: Huron College, 1963.
     xiii, 102 p. illus., ports.   OTU
— "Western", 1878–1953, being the history of the origins and development of
     The University of Western Ontario, during its first seventy-five years, by
     James J. Talman and Ruth Davis Talman. London, Ontario: The
     University of Western Ontario, 1953.
     xv, 185 p. illus., facsims., ports.   OTER
Tamblyn, William Ferguson, 1874–1956.
     These sixty years; an unconventional chronicle of the lives, the faith, the
     labour and the comradeship that have gone into the building of "Western's"
     household of learning. London, Ontario: The University of Western
     Ontario, 1938.
     iv, 135 p. plates, ports.   OLU OKQ
Taylor, Lieberfield and Heldman, Inc., New York.
     Ontario universities physical resources study; report to the Joint Sub-
     committee on Capital Studies of the Committee of Presidents of the
     Universities of Ontario and the Committee on University Affairs. Summary
     report. New York: 1972.
     131 p. illus., graphs.   OTU
Taylor, Robert Bruce, 1869–1954.
     Queen's and Canada. [Kingston, Ontario: Jackson Press] n.d.
     18 p. ports.   OTU
Thompson, Joseph A
     Report to the Committee concerning the property in the vicinity of No. 47
     Queen's Park in the city of Toronto [1920. Toronto] Aylesworth, n.d.
     28 p.   OTU
Toronto. University.
     As a tree with the passage of time. [Toronto: 1970]
     104 p. illus. (part col.), ports. (part col.).   OTU
— The benefactors of the University of Toronto after the great fire of 14th
     February, 1890. Toronto: Williamson Book Co., 1892.
     58 p. illus.
     Contains some history as well as a list of benefactors.   OTU

— Fasti from 1850 to 1887. Compiled and edited by W.J. Loudon and W.F.
  Maclean. Toronto: Williamson, 1887.
  95 leaves.   OTU
— Hart House, University of Toronto; illustrated from photographs by Mr.
  G.D. Haight. [Toronto] Published by order of the Board of Governors of the
  University of Toronto, 1921.
  [48] p. incl. illus. (facsim.), plates, plans.   OTU
— The need for scholarships: a brief outline of the necessity in the interests of
  educational democracy, for a large number of scholarships in the provincial
  university if the youth of Ontario are to enjoy equality of opportunity.
  Toronto: University of Toronto Press, 1921.
  [8] p.   OTMCL
— A record of proceedings at the celebration of the centenary of the University
  of Toronto, 1927. Published by authority of the Board of Governors of the
  University. Toronto: University of Toronto Press, 1929.
  135 p.   OTU
— Record of statements made at University of Toronto meeting with
  Committee on University Affairs, November 28th, 1972. [Toronto? 1972?]
  1 v. (various pagings).
  Deals with the changes necessary in moving from a bi-cameral to a uni-
  cameral organizational structure.   OTU
— Report on the Faculty of Applied Science and Engineering, by Dugald C.
  Jackson. [Toronto] 1940.
  v, 41 leaves.   OTU
— The University of Toronto and its colleges, 1827–1906. [Toronto] University
  Library, 1906.
  330 p. illus., ports., tables, fold. plan.   OTU
— University of Toronto installation lectures, 1958: 3 lectures by Frye,
  Kluckhohn and Wiggleworth. [Toronto: University of Toronto Press, 1959]
  [67] p.   OTU
— The University of Toronto: its work and needs. [Toronto] University of
  Toronto Press, 1943.
  30 p.   OTAR
— University of Toronto; the provincial university of Ontario: a brief sketch of
  its history and its organization compiled by the Registrar. Toronto: 1932.
  24 p. illus.
— University of Toronto roll of service. 1st ed. August 1914–August, 1917.
  [Toronto] University of Toronto Press [1917]
  xii, 212 p.   OTU
— Supplement,’August 1917–October 1918. [Toronto] University of Toronto
  Press [1918]
  vi, 120 p.   OTU
— University of Toronto roll of service, 1914–1918. [Toronto] University of
  Toronto Press, 1921.
  xlviii, 603 p.   OTU

— University of Toronto, the provincial university of Ontario; 1827–1927: The first one hundred years. Toronto: 1927.
31 p. illus.   OTU
— Universitatis Torontonensis liber aureus, chirographa continens eorum gros senatus universitatis propter egnegias vertutes gradii legum doctoris et doctoris-juris-civilis honoris causa est degratus 1894–1923. [Toronto: 1923?]
[28] leaves.   OTU
Toronto. University. Banting Institute.
A record of proceedings at the opening, 1930. Toronto: University of Toronto Press, 1931.
56 p.   OTU OTAR
Toronto. University. Board of Governors. Committee appointed to confer with the Bursar as to the capital and income accounts and other matters connected with the administration of his office.
Report. Adopted November 8th, 1893. Toronto: Warwick Bros. & Rutter, 1893.
31 p.
Report signed by B.E. Walker.   OTU
Toronto. University. Board of Governors. Connaught Laboratories Committee.
Connaught Laboratories, University of Toronto. [Toronto: 1930?]
62 p. illus., plans.   OTU
Toronto. University. Board of Governors. Special Committee on Religious Education.
Report. Toronto: University Press [1909?]
14 p.
Chairman: D. Bruce Macdonald.   OTU
Toronto. University. Chancellor's Committee.
Report. [Toronto 1958]
3 parts in 2.
Chairman: Samuel Beatty.
Alumni 'matters'.   OTU
Toronto. University. Charles H. Best Institute.
Opening ceremonies. September 15, 1953. [Toronto? 1954]
56 p. illus., ports. (col.).   OTU
Toronto. University. College of Education.
Prospect; initial faculty report on the role of the College of Education, University of Toronto. [Toronto] 1967.
[3] 20 [1] p.   OTU
Toronto. University. Commission on University Government.
Toward community in university government; report. [Toronto] University of Toronto Press [c1970]
240 p. tables.
Co-chairmen: L.E. Lynch, A.G. Webster.   OTU
Toronto. University. Committee of Alumnae Associations.
Dean of women; report of committee. [Toronto: 1909?]
12 p.
Report signed: Elizabeth R. Hendry, Secretary of committee.   OTU

Toronto. University. Committee on the Siting of Buildings and the Physical
Growth of the University.
Report. [Toronto?: 1949]
35 leaves. map. OTU
Toronto. University. Committee to investigate the pass and general courses.
Report. n.p. [1948?]
46 leaves. tables.
Chairman: Edgar McInnis. OTU
Toronto. University. Decanal Committee on Slavic Studies.
Russian and Eastern European Studies at the University of Toronto; a
report. July 18, 1961. [Toronto: 1961]
[1] 17 leaves. OTU
Toronto. University. Department of Classics.
Honour classics in the University of Toronto, by a group of classical
graduates, with a foreword by Sir Robert Falconer. [Toronto] University of
Toronto Press, 1929.
83 p. port. OTU OTTC
Toronto. University. Faculty of Applied Science and Engineering.
Brief on the proposed establishment of an undergraduate course in
administrative engineering. Toronto: 1944.
[2] 9 [3] leaves. OTU
— Recent progress and the present situation in the Faculty. [Toronto: 1930?]
11 p. OTU
Toronto. University. Faculty of Applied Science and Engineering. Committee of
the Whole Council.
Report no. 457. [Toronto, 1929]
[11] leaves. diagr.
Chairman: C.H.C. Wright. OTU
Toronto. University. Faculty of Applied Science and Engineering. Engineering
Society.
Brief on student opinion of curricula in the Faculty of Applied Science and
Engineering. [Toronto: 1943?]
74 p. OTU
— A preliminary policy position on objectives for an educational environment
in engineering. [Toronto: 1969?]
[8] p. OTU
Toronto. University. Faculty of Arts and Science.
New programme, 1969. [Toronto: University of Toronto Press, 1969]
1 v. (various pagings). OTV
— Supplement. [Toronto: University of Toronto Press, 1968?]
30 p. OTV
Toronto. University. Faculty of Dentistry. User's Committee.
The proposed expansion of postgraduate and graduate facilities of the
Faculty of Dentistry, University of Toronto; report. [Toronto: 1969]
[4] 36 [2] leaves.
Chairman: Arthur Murray Hunt. OTU

Toronto. University. Faculty of Medicine.
 Report of the committee appointed to consider the requirements of the
 Faculty in view of a possible grant of money from the Rockefellar
 Foundation. [Toronto: 1920?]
 [73] leaves.
 Chairman: Professor A. Primrose.   OTU
— Report of the Faculty of Medicine with reference to proposed introduction of
 chiropractic legislation. Toronto: 1922.
 15 leaves.   OTU
Toronto. University. Faculty of Medicine. Independent Planning Committee.
 Report of the Independent Planning Committee constituted by the Faculty
 Council of the Faculty of Medicine, University of Toronto. [Toronto] 1969.
 iv, 168, A1–A37 leaves.   OTU
Toronto. University. Graduate Students' Union.
 The graduate student at the University of Toronto, 1968 [by] Veronica
 Boag, Michael Pybus [and] John Winter. Toronto [1969]
 iv, 34 p.   OTU
Toronto. University. Institute of Child Study.
 Twenty-five years of child study: the development of the programme and
 review of the research at the Institute of Child Study, 1926–1951. [Toronto]
 University of Toronto Press, 1951.
 xiii, 182 p.
 Chairman: Mary L. Northway.   OONL
Toronto. University. Instructional Media Centre.
 Instructional Media Centre. [Toronto] The Centre, 1971.
 [8] p. illus.   OTU
Toronto. University. Knox College. Centenary Committee.
 The centenary of the granting of the charter of Knox College, Toronto,
 1858–1958. Toronto [1959]
 22 p. illus., ports.   OTU
Toronto. University. Off-Campus College Committee.
 First estimate of space requirements for two off-campus colleges in the
 University of Toronto. [Toronto] 1963.
 [2] 20 [1] leaves.   OTU
— A provisional plan for two off-campus colleges in the University of Toronto.
 [Toronto] 1963.
 15 [7] 6 leaves.
 Chairman: D.C. Williams.   OTU
Toronto. University. Planning Division.
 St. George campus, University of Toronto. [Toronto] 1968.
 [9] 21 [8] leaves. 1 illus., 5 plans (1 fold.). (*Its* Master plan framework,
 supplement, no. 1).   OTU
Toronto. University. Plateau Committee.
 Report to the Senate. [Toronto] 1956.
 12 leaves. tables.
 Chairman: G. deB. Robinson.   OTU

Toronto. University. Presidential Advisory Committee on Disciplinary
    Procedures.
    [Report. Toronto: 1969]
    [3] iv [1] 88 p.
    Chairman: D. Ralph Campbell.   OTU
Toronto. University. Presidential Advisory Committee on the Status and Future
    of Scarborough College.
    Report. [Toronto] 1971.
    1 v. (various pagings). tables.
    Chairman: F. Kenneth Hare.   OTU OTER
Toronto. University. Presidential Advisory Committee on Undergraduate
    Instruction in the Faculty of Arts and Science.
    Undergraduate instruction in Arts and Science: report. [Toronto: University
    of Toronto Press, 1967]
    ix, 148 p.
    Chairman: C.B. Macpherson.   OTU
Toronto. University. Presidential Users' Committee on the Space Needs in the
    Faculty of Applied Science and Engineering.
    Report. [Toronto] 1967.
    [4] 21 [10] leaves. 2 diagrs.,
    Chairman: Carson F. Morrison.   OTU
Toronto. University. President's Advisory Committee on Student Aid.
    Towards a policy of student aid. [Toronto: 1958]
    11 leaves.
    Chairman: Murray G. Ross.   OTU
Toronto. University. President's Committee on Graduate Studies.
    Report. [Toronto: 1947]
    15 leaves.
    Chairman: H.A. Innis.   OTU
Toronto. University. President's Committee on the School of Graduate Studies.
    Graduate studies in the University of Toronto: report... 1964-1965.
    [Toronto: Printed at the University of Toronto Press, 1965]
    viii, 140 p.
    Chairman: Bora Laskin.   OTU
Toronto. University. President's Long Range Planning Committee on Alumni
    Affairs.
    Alumni in the university community; report. [Toronto] University of
    Toronto, 1971.
    68 p. diagrs.   OTU
    Chairman: H. Ian Macdonald.   OTU
Toronto. University. St. Michael's College.
    Seventy-fifth anniversary. [Toronto? 1927?]
    48 p. fold. illus., ports.   OTU
Toronto. University. Scarborough College.
    The socio-economic environment of Scarborough College: the sixties. A
    study based on census material. West Hill, Ontario: 1972.
    x, 164 p. graphs, maps, tables.
    Study Committee: A.F.W. Plumptre [et al.]   OTU

Toronto. University. School of Hygiene.
     Hygiene building: request for consideration of renovation of existing
     teaching and research facilities and provision of additional facilities;
     statement prepared by A.J. Rhodes, director. Approved by Committee on
     Planning, School of Hygiene, and submitted to the President's Advisory
     Committee on Accommodation and Facilities February 10, 1966. [Toronto:
     1966]
     [1] 11, 103 leaves (6 fold.).   OTU
Toronto. University. School of Social Work.
     Fiftieth anniversary, 1914–1964, School of Social Work, University of
     Toronto. [Toronto: 1964?]
     [1] 63 [2] p. illus., ports.   OTU
— Directory of graduates. [Toronto] 1964.
     [3] xii, 54 p.   OTU
— Training for social work in the Department of Social Science, University of
     Toronto, 1914–1940. Toronto: University of Toronto Press, 1940.
     56 p. (Social science series, no. 1).
     "Published by the Department of University Extension of the University of
     Toronto to commemorate the twenty-fifth anniversary of the founding of the
     Department of Social Science".
     Contents: Foreword, by E.J. Urwick; The Department of Social Science,
     1914–1940, by A.C. McGregor; Social action or inaction: The challenge, by
     M. Hathway; Social philosophy and social work, by E.J. Urwick.   OTU
Toronto. University. Senate.
     Plan of organization of the School of Graduate Studies. [Toronto: 1922]
     [3] p.
     Chairman: J. Playfair McMurrich.   OTU
Toronto. University. Senate. Committee on Admission Standards.
     Report. [Toronto, 1964]
     [1] 5 [5] leaves.
     Chairman: R.S. Harris.   OTU
Toronto. University. Senate. Special Committee on the affiliation of colleges,
     schools and other institutions to the University of Toronto.
     Report. [Toronto: 1895?]
     9 p.
     Chairman: Thomas Hodgins.   OTU
Toronto. University. Senate. Committee on Control of Certificate and Diploma
     Courses.
     Report on graduate certificate and diploma courses. [Toronto] 1966.
     ix, 70 leaves. fold. tables.   OTU
— Report on undergraduate certificate and diploma courses. [Toronto] 1964.
     [1] vii, 65 leaves.   OTU
Toronto. University. Senate. Committee on the Present and Prospective
     Revenues of the University and University College.
     Revenues and requirements; report of a committee appointed by the Senate

of the University of Toronto, and also by the Board of Trustees, April 13th,
1891. Toronto: Warwick & Sons, 1891.
 94 p. tables.   OTU
Toronto. University. Senate. Special Committee on the Claims of the University
 against the late Province of Canada.
 Second report: Claim in respect of loans to Upper Canada College. n.p.
 [1895?]
 8 p.   OTU
Toronto. University. Senate. Special Committee Respecting Affiliation with the
 Universities of Oxford, Cambridge and Dublin.
 Papers relating to the application of the Senate of the University of Toronto
 to the universities of Oxford and Cambridge for the grant of special
 affiliation privileges to the University of Toronto. Printed by order of the
 Legislative Assembly of Ontario. Toronto: Warwick Bro's & Rutter, 1896.
 24 p.   OTU
Toronto. University. Senate. Standing Committee on the Faculty of Medicine.
 Report on the subject of reorganization, 1892. Printed by order of the
 Legislative Assembly. Toronto: Warwick & Sons, 1892.
 16 p.   OTU
Toronto. University. Special Committee on the Humanities.
 Report. n.p.: 1954.
 35 leaves.
 Chairman: M. St. A. Woodside.   OTU
Toronto. University. Students' Administrative Council.
 The *Varsity* war supplement. Toronto: Students' Administrative Council,
 University of Toronto [1915]
 54, 16 p. illus., ports.
 July 1915 issue.   OOA
Toronto. University. Students Administrative Council. Services Commission.
 A report on the University of Toronto bookstores. [Toronto: 1967?]
 [3] 21 p. diagr.   OTU
Toronto. University. Task Force to Review Policy and Procedures on Academic
 Appointments.
 Report. [Toronto: 1973]
 85 [22] leaves. graphs, tables.
 Committee of 11 members, no one is listed as chairman.   OONL
Toronto. University. Users' Committee for the Humanities and Social Sciences
 Research Library.
 Report of the Users' Committee appointed to prepare a programme for the
 construction of a building complex to house the Humanities and Social
 Sciences Research Library and the School of Library Science. [Toronto]
 University of Toronto, 1965.
 [1] vi, 77 leaves.
 Chairman: D.C. Williams.   OTU

Toronto. University. University Advisory Committee on Ex-Service Students.
    The veteran at Varsity; an enquiry concerning the impact of the veteran
    student on policy and practices in the University of Toronto, 1945–1951.
    [Toronto] Distributed by University of Toronto Bookstore [1951?]
    49 leaves. tables.
    Chairman: W. Line.   OTU
Toronto. University. University College. Class of 1883.
    Velut arbor aevo: University of Toronto, 1883–1933. [Toronto: 1933?]
    [1] 17 p.   OTU
Toronto. University. University College. Class of 1894.
    Interesting facts regarding the career of members of the Arts Class of '94.
    [Toronto: 1929?]
    [36] p. ports.   OTU
Toronto. University. Wycliffe College.
    Between the jubilees, 1927–1937; supplement to the Wycliffe College Jubilee
    Volume. [Toronto: 1937?]
    18 p. ports.   OTU
— [Honour roll of graduates and undergraduates of Wycliffe College who
    served in Canada and overseas during the First World War. Toronto: 1919?]
    Broadside.   OTU
— The jubilee volume of Wycliffe College. Toronto: Wycliffe College, 1927.
    301 p. illus., ports.   OTU
— The jubilee volume of Wycliffe College. Toronto: Wycliffe College, 1927 [i.e.
    1937?]
    [8] 318 p. plates, ports.   OTU
— Why Wycliffe is needed today. [Toronto: 1924]
    20 p.   OTU
— Wycliffe College diamond jubilee, September eleven to September fifteen,
    1937. [Orillia: Pocket-Times Press, 1937?]
    32 p.   OTU
— Wycliffe College jubilee celebration, 1877–1927. Toronto: Wycliffe College
    Jubilee Bulletin, v. 2, no. 1, 1927.
    8 p. illus., ports.
    "Newspaper issued to celebrate the Jubilee".   OOA
— Wycliffe College, Toronto, Canada: a glimpse of its life and work. [Toronto:
    Sevant Press, 1913?]
    16 p. illus., ports.   OKQ
Toronto. University of Trinity College.
    [History] Toronto [1914]
    30 leaves. chiefly illus.   OTU
— Memorials presented to Lord Knutsford, H.M. secretary of state for the
    colonies, with appendices, & etc. London: W. Brown, 1890.
    1 v. (various pagings). fold. table.
    At head of title: Faculty of Music.   OTU
Toronto. University of Trinity College. Association.
    A national university. [Toronto? 1875?]
    [1] 16 p.
    University consolidation.   OTU

Trinity College School.
　　Record. Jubilee number, May, 1915.
　　vi, 117, vii–xii p. illus., facsims., ports.　　　　　　　　　　　　OTAR
Trinity review.
　　Trinity, 1852–1952. Toronto: Trinity College, 1952.
　　vi, 186 p. illus., facsims.
　　"A history of Trinity College, University of Toronto".
　　"Published as a special centennial issue of *Trinity Review*, Trinity College,
　　Toronto, 1952".　　　　　　　　　　　　　　　　　　　　　　　OTU
Trott, Harold Williams, 1900–
　　Campus shadows. [Hemlock, New York] Grosset and Williams, 1946.
　　371 p.　　　　　　　　　　　　　　　　　　　　　　　　　　OKQ
Trotter, Bernard, 1924–
　　Television and technology in university teaching: a report to the Committee
　　on University Affairs, and the Committee of Presidents of Universities of
　　Ontario. [Toronto: Committee on University Affairs and the Committee of
　　Presidents of Universities of Ontario] 1970.
　　vii, 84 p. tables.　　　　　　　　　　　　　　　　　　　　　　OTU
Tupper, Kenneth Franklin, 1905–
　　Engineering, yesterday, today, and tomorrow; inaugural address as Dean of
　　the Faculty of Applied Science and Engineering, Convocation Hall, October
　　28th, 1949. [Toronto: Printed by the University of Toronto Press, c1950]
　　15 p.　　　　　　　　　　　　　　　　　　　　　　　　　　OTU
The University of Toronto; post-war expansion programme. [Toronto:
　　University of Toronto Press, 1944?]
　　32 p.　　　　　　　　　　　　　　　　　　　　　　　　　　OTU
University Planners, Architects and Consulting Engineers.
　　Report on the master plan for the York University campus, prepared for the
　　Board of Governors of York University. [Toronto: c1963]
　　79 p. illus., diagrs., maps, plans.　　　　　　　　　　　　　　OTURS
Vanderkamp, Joan Ruth Bushell, 1931–
　　Provincial programmes of aid to University students 1957-58 to 1960-61.
　　Programmes provinciaux d'aide aux étudiants d'université, 1957-1958 à
　　1960–1961. Ottawa: Canadian Universities Foundation/Fondation des
　　Universités Canadiennes, 1961.
　　27 p. tables. (Financing higher education in Canada no. 3).　　　OTU
Vaughan, Michael Bryan.
　　Graduate student morale at the University of Toronto. A submission to the
　　Committee on University Affairs. [Toronto] Graduate Students' Union,
　　University of Toronto [1969]
　　7 [4] leaves. diagrs.　　　　　　　　　　　　　　　　　　　OTU
Victoria University, Toronto.
　　On the old Ontario strand: Victoria's hundred years. Addresses at the
　　centenary of Victoria University, and the Burwash memorial lectures of the
　　centennial year. Toronto: 1936.
　　176 p. illus., music.　　　　　　　　　　　　　　　　　　　OTU

— The spirit of '29: Victoria University, 1829–1929. Emmanuel College,
   Victoria College. Toronto: The United Church Publishing House, 1929.
   32 p. illus., facsim., ports.   OKQ
Vigeant, Pierre.
   L'anglicisation à l'université d'Ottawa. Montreal: L'Action Nationale, n.d.
   31 p.   OKQ
Vincent, Joseph Ulric, 1872–
   La question scolaire. Ottawa: L'Ottawa Printing Co., Limitée [1915?]
   vi, 123 p.   OOU
Walker, (Sir) Byron Edmond, 1848–1924.
   [Letter to N. Burwash. Toronto? 1898?]
   8 p.
   Dated: Toronto, April 29th, 1898.
   Letter re federation of colleges.   OTU
Wallace, Robert Charles, 1881–1955 (ed.).
   Some great men of Queen's: Grant, Watson, Dupuis, Cappon, Jordan,
   Shortt. Toronto: The Ryerson Press [c1941]
   133 p.   OTU
— Freeport, New York: Books for Libraries Press [1969]
   133 p.   OLU
Wallace, William Stewart, 1884–1970.
   A history of the University of Toronto, 1827–1927. Toronto: University of
   Toronto Press, 1927.
   308 p. illus., facsims., ports.   OTU
— Report on the experiment in nursing education of the Atkinson School of
   Nursing, the Toronto Western Hospital, 1950–1955. [Toronto] University of
   Toronto Press [1955?]
   iii, 24 p. diagr.   OTU
Walmsley, Lewis Calvin, 1897–
   Bishop of Honan: mission and museum in the life of William C. White.
   Toronto: University of Toronto Press, c1974.
   xi, 230 [35] p. illus., maps.
   White was founder of the School of Chinese Studies at the University of
   Toronto.   OTU
Wasteneys, Hardolph.
   A brief account of the history of the organization of the Faculty of Medicine
   of the University of Toronto. [Toronto: 1952?]
   7 leaves.   OTU
Waterloo, Ontario. University. Faculty of Engineering.
   Research in Engineering. Waterloo, Ontario: 1964.
   39 p.   OWTU
Waterloo, Ontario. University. President's Advisory Committee on Equal
   Rights for Women and Men.
   Report. Waterloo, Ontario: 1973.
   8 p.
   "Supplement to *University of Waterloo Gazette*, November 21, 1973.   OONL

Watson, Cicely, 1921–
Enrollment in Ontario colleges of applied arts and technology: projections to 1981-82 (1970 projection) by Cicely Watson, Saeed Quazi and Farid Seddiqui. [Toronto] Ontario Institute for Studies in Education [c1972] 91 p. maps, tables (part fold.). (Ontario Institute for Studies in Education. Enrollment projections series, no. 7). OTER
— Innovation in higher education, Canadian case study: new college systems in Canada. Toronto: Department of Educational Planning, Ontario Institute for Studies in Education, 1971.
vii, 453 p. tables. OTER
— Ontario school and university enrollment projections to 1981-82, by Cicely Watson and Saeed Quazi. [Toronto] Ontario Institute for Studies in Education [c1966]
x, 68 p. diagrs. (Ontario Institute for Studies in Education. Enrollment projection series, no. 1). OTU
— Ontario university and college enrollment projections to 1881/82: 1968 projection, by Cicely Watson and Saeed Quazi. [Toronto: Ontario Institute for Studies in Education, c1969]
57 p. diagrs., tables (Ontario Institute for Studies in Education. Enrollment projection series, no. 4). OTU

Wees, Wilfred Rusk, 1899–
OISE and the schools: the Ontario Institute for Studies in Education and its involvement in the educational community. [Toronto: Ontario Institute for Studies in Education, 1971]
31 p. OTER

Weir, George Moir, 1885–1949.
Survey of nursing education in Canada. Toronto: The University of Toronto Press, 1932.
591 p. fold. map, diagrs. OTU

Weir, Jenny M
Nursing education at Queen's University: its future? by Jenny M. Weir and Evelyn B. Moulton. [Kingston, Ontario: 1964]
31 leaves. illus. OTU

Weldon, Kenneth Laurence.
Inter-provincial comparisons of costs and quality of higher education in Canada. [Toronto?] Committee of Presidents of Universities of Ontario, 1970.
54 leaves. graphs, tables. OTER

Wells, James Edward, 1836–1898.
Life and labors of Robert Alexander Fyfe, founder and for many years principal of the Canadian Literary Institute, now Woodstock College. Toronto: Printed for the author by W.J. Gage & Company [1885?]
466 p. OTER

West, Edwin George.
Student loans: a reappraisal ... with special reference to Ontario's and

Canada's changing needs in educational finance, by E.G. West, assisted by
Michael McKee. [Toronto] Ontario Economic Council, 1975.
212 [26] 11 p. (Ontario Economic Council. Working paper, no. 4).   OTER
Whig–Standard, Kingston, Ontario.
The Kingston Whig–Standard presents Queen's University Century II,
Souvenir edition. [Kingston, Ontario] 1964.
48 p. illus., ports.
"Issued October 16, 1964".   OKQ
Wilson, (Sir) Daniel, 1816–1892.
Coeducation; a letter to the Hon. G.W. Ross, M.P.P., minister of education.
Toronto: Hunter, Rose & Co., 1884.
15 p.   OTU
— A letter to the Hon. G.W. Ross, LL.D., minister of education, with resolutions
and letters from the Board of Trustees, the faculty, heads of universities,
graduates, & etc., in approval of college residence. Toronto: Rowsell &
Hutchison, 1890.
28 p.   OTU
— Medical education in Ontario; a letter to the Hon. G.W. Ross, LL.D.,
minister of education. Toronto: Rowsell & Hutchison, 1892.
12 p.   OTU
Windsor, Ontario. University.
The installation of a president, John Francis Leddy, University of Windsor,
September 26, 1964. A record of events and statements. [Windsor, Ontario]
1964.
[20] p. port.   OTU
Wipper, Kirk A   W
Retrospect and prospect; a record of the School of Physical and Health
Education, University of Toronto, 1940–1965. Presented in the twenty-fifth
anniversary year. [Toronto: 1965?]
[5] 39 p. illus., ports.   OTU
Wood, Herbert George, 1879–
Terrot Reavely Glover: a biography. Cambridge: Cambridge University
Press, 1953.
xii, 233 p. port.   OTER
Woodside, Moffatt St. Andrew, 1906–1970.
The Faculty of Arts; address by Dean Woodside to the Senate of the
University of Toronto, February 8th, 1957. [Toronto: 1957]
4 p.   OTU
Woodstock College.
Woodstock College memorial book. [Toronto] Memorial Committee,
Woodstock College Alumni Association [1951]
167 p. illus., ports.
"Published twenty-fifth anniversary of the closing of the school".   OTAR
Wright, Douglas T   1927–
The first five years of the co-operative engineering programme at the
University of Waterloo. [Montreal] 1963.

1 v. (various pagings). (Transactions of the Engineering Institute of Canada. v. 6). OONL
— Report on the organizational structure of the Ontario College of Art. Toronto: 1968.
23 p.
Study made for the Ontario Department of Education.
Cover title: Report on the Ontario College of Art. OTCA OTMCL

York/U of T Higher Education Seminar, 1973/74.
Ontario and its universities. [Toronto? 1974?]
12 p. OTU

York University .
Official opening, York University, Falconer Hall, Queen's Park, Toronto, September twelfth, 1960. [Toronto: 1960]
15 p. ports. OTAR

York University. Presidential Committee on Rights and Responsibilities of Members of York University.
Freedom and responsibility in the university; report. [Toronto] Published for York University by University of Toronto Press [c1970]
64 p.
Chairman: Bora Laskin. OTU

Young, Archibald Hope, 1863–1935.
The sites of Trinity College and St. Hilda's, 1798–1926. [Toronto: 1926]
[9] p. OTU
— The war memorial volume of Trinity College, Toronto. Edited by A.H. Young and W.A. Kirkwood. [Toronto] Printers Guild, Limited, 1922.
xvii, 165 p. illus., ports. OTU

Young, Clarence Richard, 1879–
Beating to windward; the early years of engineering education in Canada. Toronto: 1957.
x, 299 [i.e. 306] 5 p. illus., ports. OTU
— Early engineering education at Toronto, 1851–1919. [Toronto] University of Toronto Press [1958]
vi, 150 p. illus., ports., table. OTU
— Emil Andrew Wallberg, constructor and adventurer. [Toronto] Faculty of Applied Science and Engineering, University of Toronto [1951]
28 p. port. OTU

Young, Elrid Gordon, 1897–
The development of biochemistry in Canada. Toronto: University of Toronto Press [c1976]
vi, 129 p. OLU

Zabarchuk, Ted M
Some aspects of planning for post-secondary vocational institutions: a case study, the Ryerson Polytechnical Institute. [Toronto: Department of Education Planning, Ontario Institute for Studies in Education, 1971]
viii, 289 leaves. graphs, tables. OTER

Zeidler, Eberhard H
   Healing the hospital: McMaster Health Science Centre: its conception and
   evolution. Toronto: The Zeidler Partnership [c1974]
   165 p. illus., diagrs., plans.   OTU

Periodical Articles
Abbott, Richard D
   Legal studies at Carleton University. Canadian Legal Studies 2: 71–74;
   1964.
Abel, Albert S   [et al.]
   [New courses at the University of Toronto (School of Law)]. University of
   Toronto Law Journal 12: 81–94, 1957.
Abols, Gus.
   The CUG Report: a student's view. CAUT Bulletin 18(3): 25–31, 1970.
Additions to Trinity College, Toronto. Royal Architectural Institute of Canada.
   Journal 18: 182–185, 1941.
Adelman, Howard.
   A tale of two universities; university residences and campus planning,
   Toronto. Architecture Canada 46(no. 7–8): 53, 1969.
Ajax Division: University of Toronto. School Progress 14(no. 4): 29–33, 1946.
Alexander, D
   My impressions of O.A.C. life at Guelph, 1917. Ontario Agricultural College
   Review 29: 350–353, 1917.
Allcut, E   A
   Mechanical Building, University of Toronto. Royal Architectural Institute
   of Canada. Journal 26: 189–190, 1949.
Angus, Margaret.
   The old stones of Queen's, 1842–1900. Historic Kingston 20: 5–13, 1972.
Architectural education expansion in Ontario: report of the O.A.A. Study
   Committee. Architecture Canada 43(10): 5–9, 1966.
Architectural training in the Canadian universities: Toronto. Royal
   Architectural Institute of Canada. Journal 29: 140–143, 1952.
Armstrong, Fred.
   Fred Landon, 1880–1969. Ontario History 62: 1–4, 1970.
Arthur, A   Z
   Clinical training programs in Ontario: a survey report. Ontario Psychologist
   1: 65–110, 1969.
Arthur Eric R
   The master plan and the building. Royal Architectural Institute of Canada.
   Journal 31: 38–47, 1954.
   Victoria University.
— University of Toronto master plan. Royal Architectural Institute of Canada.
   Journal 30: 286–289, 1953.
Arthurs, H   W
   The affiliation of Osgoode Hall Law School with York University.
   University of Toronto Law Journal 17: 194–204, 1967.

Barabé, Paul-Henri.
  Mgr. Adélaid Langevin, O.M.I. educateur. Revue de l'Université d'Ottawa
  11: 338–348, 461–471, 1941.
Barnstead, Winifred G
  A new degree course in library science. Ontario Library Review 20:
  146–147, 1936.
Bassam, Bertha.
  University of Toronto Library School and its predecessors. Canadian
  Library Association. Bulletin 14: 211–215, 1958.
Batke, T   L
  Engineering education at Waterloo. Chemistry in Canada 11(8): 43–44, 46,
  1959.
— Graduate professional studies in engineering. Professional Engineer and
  Engineering Digest 25(6): 35–38, 1964.
  University of Waterloo.
Beals, C   S
  John Stanley Pluskett. Journal of the Royal Astronomical Society of Canada
  35: 401–407, Plate XII, 1941.
Beatty, J   David.
  History of medical education in Toronto. University of Toronto Medical
  Journal 47: 152–157, 1970.
Belcourt, Guillaume.
  Les luttes scolaires d l'Ontario-nord. Relations 19: 175–177, 1959.
Bell, J   Jones.
  Queen's University and its founders. Canadian Magazine of Politics,
  Science, Art and Literature 7: 19–27, 1897.
Benson, Eugene.
— The house that Davis built (or university education in the sixties). CAUT
  Bulletin 19(3): 3–12, 1971.
Benson, Lillian Rea.
  An O.A.C. student in the 1880's. Ontario History 42: 67–80, 1950.
Bernard, Guy.
  Ideologies et pedagogies dans l'ensiegnement secondaire francophone de
  l'Ontario: problématique de recherche. Laurentian University Review 6
  (no. 2): 105–109, 1974.
Bissell, Claude T
  The Duff–Berdahl Report at Toronto. Canadian Forum 46: 204–205, 1966.
— Internal university government. Association of Universities and Colleges of
  Canada. Proceedings 67–73, 1966.
— A proposal for university government at the University of Toronto. CAUT
  Bulletin 15(2): 42–46, 1966.
— University of Toronto expansion program. Royal Architectural Institute of
  Canada. Journal 37: 6–23, 1960.
Black, J   Laurence.
  Eastern European historical studies in Canadian universities since 1945.
  New Review 5(no. 4): 46–58, 1965.

— Slavic Studies at Laurentian University. New Review 9: 301–305, 1969.
Bladen, Vincent.
    In memoriam Sidney Earle Smith, 1897–1959.
    Canadian Forum 39: 31–32, 1959.
Blatz, W   E
    The St. George's School for Child study. University of Toronto Monthly 26:
    419–422, 1926.
Boland, Francis.
    Father Soulerin, C.S.B., founder and administrator. Canadian Catholic
    Historical Association. Report 13–27, 1956.
    St. Michael's College, Toronto.
Bouvier, Émile.
    L'Université Laurentienne de Sudbury. Relations 20: 120–123, 1960.
Boyd, O   H
    The new mining curriculum at Toronto University. Canadian Mining
    Journal 43: 359–360, 1922.
Brady, Alexander.
    Harold Adams Innis, 1894–1952. Canadian Journal of Economics and
    Political Science 19: 87–96, 1953.
Brebner, J   Bartlet.
    Harold Adams Innis as historian. Canadian Historical Association.
    Historical Papers 14–24, 1953.
— Oxford, Toronto, Columbia. Columbia University Quarterly 23: 224–240,
    1931.
Breithaupt, W   H
    Rockwood Academy and its founder, William Wetherald. Waterloo
    Historical Society. Annual Report 30: 208–211, 1942.
Brett, G   S
    Graduate work in Toronto in non-scientific subjects. National Conference of
    Canadian Universities. Proceedings 13: 41–44, 1929.
Brewer, Alan W
    Meteorology at the University of Toronto: 1. the past. Atmosphere 3(1): 4–8,
    1965.
    At end of article, stated to be continued. Never published.
Brewin, F   A
    Legal education in Ontario, 1935. Canadian Bar Review 13: 359–365, 1935.
Bringmann, Wolfgang G   [et al.]
    Psychology at Windsor. Canadian Psychologist 10: 371–382, 1969.
Brock stresses interdisciplinary relationships. Chemistry in Canada 21(June):
    37–38, 1969.
Brock University student centre, St. Catharines, Ontario. Canadian Architect
    21(June): 48–49, 1976.
Brown, Walter T
    Associated colleges in the University of Toronto. Association of American
    Colleges. Bulletin 19: 181–182, 1933.

Bucknall, Brian D   [et al.]
   Pedants, practitioners and prophets: legal education at Osgoode Hall to
   1957. Osgoode Hall Law Journal 6: 137–229, 1968.
Bulani, W
   Chemical engineering at Western. Chemistry in Canada 18(1): 52–53, 1966.
Burton, Robert.
   Queen's University, Kingston. Canada Educational Monthly 21: 195–201,
   1899.
Burwash, Nathanael.
   A review of the founding and development of the University of Toronto as a
   provincial institution. Royal Society of Canada. Transactions s. 2, 11(sect.
   2): 37–98, 1905.
Buttrick, John.
   Who goes to university in Ontario? This Magazine is about Schools 6(2):
   81–100, 1972.
Calais, Stuart.
   Canadian celebrities; no. 70 – Professor George M. Wrong. Canadian
   Magazine of Politics, Science, Art and Literature 27: 208–210, 1906.
Callaghan, Morley.
   "It was news in Paris – not in Toronto. Saturday Night 66(35): 8, 17–18,
   1951.
   Institute of Mediaeval Studies, Toronto.
Calvin, D   D
   "John". Queen's Quarterly 40: 357–364, 1933.
   Reverend John Macnaughton, Professor at Queen's, McGill, Toronto.
— Letters from 'T.R.'. Queen's Quarterly 50: 394–401, 1943.
   T.R. Glover – Queen's.
— The stamp of Queen's. Queen's Quarterly 48: 209–215, 1941.
Cameron, E   R
   Legal education in Ontario. Canadian Bar Review 2: 503–506, 1924.
Cameron, Malcolm H   V
   Medical education in Toronto. Calgary Associate Clinic. Historical Bulletin
   17(no. 4): 71–74, 1953.
Campbell, P   G   C
   A university forty years ago. Queen's Quarterly 48: 249–257, 1941.
Cappon, James.
   In Memoriam; John Fletcher. Queen's Quarterly 25: 133–140, 1917/1918.
   University of Toronto, Queen's
— In memoriam; Nathan F. Dupuis. Queen's Quarterly 25: 125–133,
   1917/1918.
   Queen's.
— Is Queen's to get justice? Queen's Quarterly 14: 239–241, 1906/1907.
   Financial dispute with Ontario government.
— President Falconer's matriculation scheme. Queen's Quarterly 20: 336–344,
   1912/1913.
   University of Toronto.

— Queen's University and the School of Mining. Queen's Quarterly 16: 87-90, 1908/1909.
— The religious test in Queen's constitution. Queen's Quarterly 19: 436–441, 1911/1912.
— A school of forestry. Queen's Quarterly 10: 503–505, 1902/1903.
— The situation in Queen's. Queen's Quarterly 17: 193–211, 1909/1910.
Carlyle, Randolph.
    The Royal Military College. Canadian Magazine of Politics, Science, Art and Literature 35: 121–129, 1910.
Caron, Georges.
    The Faculty of Law of the University of Ottawa. University of Toronto Law Journal 12: 292–295, 1958.
Carr, A   H
    Adult education – Queen's University. Ontario Library Review and Book-Selection Guide 9: 33–34, 1924.
Carr, Henry.
    The Very Reverend J.R. Teefy, C.S.B., LL.D. Canadian Catholic Historical Association. Report 85–95, 1939–1940.
    Teefy involved with University of Toronto.
Carrick, Donald D   [et al.]
    Education for the Bar; report of the Special Committee of Students of Osgoode Hall. Canadian Bar Review 12: 144–160, 1934.
Carrière, Gaston.
    Le Collège de Bytown. Revue de l'Université d'Ottawa 26: 56–78, 224–245, 317–349, 1956.
— À la mémoire d'un grand éducateur: Le Père Phillipe Cornellier. Revue de l'Université d'Ottawa 37: 5–10, 1967.
— Trois quarts de siècle au service des sciences sacrées(1889–1964). Revue de l'Université d'Ottawa 34: 234–248, 1964.
Castel, J   G
    [New developments at Osgoode Hall Law School]; public international law and comparative law. University of Toronto Law Journal 14: 108–114, 1961.
Cerwin, V   B
    Psychology of individual and social human learning at the University of Windsor. Canadian Psychologist 8A: 193–201, 1967.
Chant, C   A
    The death of Mrs. Dunlap. Journal of the Royal Astronomical Society of Canada 40: 245–247, plates 7 and 8, 1946.
    Donor of David Dunlap Observatory.
— John S. Plaskett at the University of Toronto. Journal of the Royal Astronomical Society of Canada 35: 412–414, 1941.
— Progress on the David Dunlap Observatory. Journal of the Royal Astronomical Society 27: 281–284, plates VI and VII, 1933.
— Recollections of astronomy in Canada. Journal of the Royal Astronomical Society of Canada 35: 97–104, 1941.

— The 74-inch telescope of the David Dunlap Observatory. Journal of the
Royal Astronomical Society of Canada 27: 401–402, plates IX and X, 1933.

Chapman, Howard.
The campus development plan. Royal Architectural Institute of Canada.
Journal 37: 24–26, 1960.

Childs, Sidney.
Trinity College, University of Toronto. Royal Architectural Institute of
Canada. Journal 2: 195–203, 1925.

Clark, William.
Trinity University, Toronto. Canada Educational Monthly 21: 115–118,
1899.

Clarkson, F   Arnold.
The medical faculty of the University of Toronto. Calgary Associate Clinic.
Historical Bulletin 13(no. 2): 21–30, 1948.

Cochrane, Charles Norris, 1889–1945. Canadian Journal of Economics and
Political Science 12: 95–97, 1946.

Code, J   E
Geology at institutions of technology and trades. Canadian Mining Journal
88(no. 6): 54, 56–58, 1967.

Cody, H   J
A chapter in the organization of higher education in Canada, 1905–6. Royal
Society of Canada. Transactions s. 3, 40(sect. 2): 87–99, 1946.
Chiefly University of Toronto.

— The recent Commission on University Finance. Canadian Club of Toronto.
Addresses 18: 178–191, 1920.

— The University of Toronto as a public servant. Canadian Club of Toronto.
Addresses 25: 134–148, 1927.

Cohen, Maxwell.
The condition of legal education in Canada. Canadian Bar Review 28:
267–314, 1950.

Collins, Peter.
An appraisal [Massey College]. Royal Architectural Institute of Canada.
Journal 40(no. 10): 39–48, 1963.

Commercial education; a new course at the University of Toronto. Industrial
Canada 2: 59–60, 1901.

Committee of the Canadian Bar Association on Legal Education.
Legal education in Canada. Canadian Bar Review 1: 671–684, 1923.

Community Colleges under way geared for 'tremendous growth'. Ontario
Education Review 9, October 1967.

Connell, J   C
The position of the Medical Faculty in the reorganized university. Queen's
Quarterly 17: 329–332, 1909/1910.
Queen's.

Connell, W   T
The Medical Faculty – Queen's University. Calgary Associate Clinic.
Historical Bulletin 13(no. 3): 45–50, 1948.

Cook, George L
   Alfred Fitzpatrick and the foundation of Frontier College (1899–1922).
   Canada: an historical magazine 3(no. 4): 15–39, 1976.
Cooper, John A
   The University of Toronto. Canadian Magazine of Politics, Science, Art and
   Literature 24: 569–570, 1905.
Corbett, Beatrice.
   Susan Moulton Fraser McMaster. Inland Seas 31: 192–200, 1975.
Corbett, E   A
   Atkinson College. Continuous Learning 2: 22–25, 1963.
Corry, J   A
   The Queen's University Faculty of Law. University of Toronto Law Journal
   12: 290–292, 1958.
— University – provincial government relations. Association of Universities and
   Colleges of Canada. Proceedings, 119–124, 1965.
Cosens, G   G
   Forestry education in the University of Toronto. Forestry Chronicle 22:
   250–252, 1946.
Crane, James W
   The University of Western Ontario. Calgary Associate Clinic. Historical
   Bulletin 13(no. 1): 1–3, 1948.
Creamer, LeRoy.
   The Faculty of Medicine of the University of Ottawa: Canada's only bi-
   lingual medical school. Canadian Doctor 20(Nov.): 28–32, 1954.
Creighton, Donald G
   An episode in the history of the University of Toronto. University of Toronto
   Quarterly 17: 245–256, 1948.
Cronkite, F   C
   Legal education – which trend? Canadian Bar Review 13: 375–385, 1935.
Crummy, Eber.
   Normal colleges for Ontario. Queen's Quarterly 14: 37–39, 1906/1907.
Cumberland, Barlow.
   The story of a university building. Canadian Magazine of Politics, Science,
   Art and Literature 17: 235–243, 1901.
   University of Toronto.
[D   M   G   ]?
   Queen's and the Assembly's Commission. Queen's Quarterly 11: 187–190,
   1903/1904.
Dandeno, J   B
   Agricultural education in Ontario. Agricultural Gazette of Canada 11:
   46–55, 1924.
Davenport, Bruce.
   McMaster – the septuagenarian youngster. Executive 2(6): 26–32, 1960.
The David Dunlap Observatory, University of Toronto. Royal Architectural
   Institute of Canada. Journal 12: 124–128, 1935.

Davis, W   E
    A community college for the Ottawa region. Continuous Learning 4:
    228–232, 1965.
Dawson, John A
    Professor A.P. Coleman honoured. Canadian Mining Journal 48: 201–202,
    1927.
De Kalb, Courtenay.
    The Kingston School of Mining. Canadian Mining Review 20: 81–82, 1901.
Denison, Shirley.
    Legal education in Ontario. Canadian Bar Review 2: 85–92, 1924.
Dickson, George.
    The Ontario College of Preceptors. Canada Educational Monthly 8:
    249–256, 1886.
Dittrick, Howard.
    The old days in Toronto: further reminiscences concerning faculty members
    of the Medical School of the University of Toronto at the turn of the century.
    Calgary Associates Clinic. Historical Bulletin 7(4): 6–9, 1943.
Donohoe, E   F
    St. Jerome's College, historical sketch. Waterloo Historical Society. Annual
    Report 28: 101–110, 1940.
Dorrance, Roy L
    The Department of Chemistry, Queen's University, Kingston, Ontario.
    Royal Institute of Chemistry. Journal 81: 560–566, 1957.
Douglas, A   Vibert.
    Canadian scientists report; x – Astronomy at Queen's University. Journal of
    the Royal Astronomical Society of Canada 52: 82–86, 1958.
Douglas, James.
    Dr. James Douglas. Queen's Quarterly 23: 239–240, 1915/1916; 23:
    240–247, 1915/1916.
Downie, John.
    Chemical engineering developments at Queen's. Chemistry in Canada
    20(2): 30–31, 1968.
Drummond, A   T
    A course in music at Queen's. Queen's Quarterly 9: 61–62, 1901/1902.
Drummond, Andrew. Queen's Quarterly 30: 351–352, 1923.
Duncanson, Blanche.
    The Nightingale School of Nursing, Toronto. Canadian Nurse 55: 802–804,
    1960.
Dunlop, W   J
    Adult education – University of Toronto. Ontario Library Review and
    Book-Selection Guide 9: 32–33, 1924.
Dunn, Wesley J
    Canada's eighth dental school is born. Canadian Dental Association.
    Journal 31: 693–699, 1965.
    The University of Western Ontario.
Dyde, S   W
    The future of Queen's. Queen's Quarterly 11: 191–192, 1903/1904.

— Should there be a Faculty of Education in the University? Queen's
  Quarterly 12: 165–177, 1904.
Dyson, F   W
  The David Dunlap Observatory, Toronto. Nature 135: 1082, 1935.
L'École de Psychologie et d'Éducation de l'Université d'Ottawa. Revue de
  l'Université d'Ottawa 33: 480–485, 1963.
Edinborough, Arnold.
  How to create a home-town college. Saturday Night 79(December): 18–21,
  1964.
Eggleston, Wilfrid.
  The dream of 'Georgie' Grant. Queen's Quarterly 60: 565–574, 1953.
Ellis, Roy G
  Faculty of Dentistry, University of Toronto. Canadian Dental Association.
  Journal 31: 330–337, 1965.
Ellis, Roy G   and Thomas Cowling.
  University of Toronto (Faculty of Dentistry). Dental Record 70: 114–122,
  1950.
Engineering at McMaster. Chemistry in Canada 13(2): 40–42, 1961.
Experimental Union. Ontario Agricultural College Review 8(3): 2–6, 1896.
F   S   H   and H   S   H
  The official opening of the David Dunlap Observatory. Journal of the Royal
  Astronomical Society of Canada 29: 265–298, plates II–IX, 1935.
Fairbairn, L   S
  Legal aid clinics for Ontario law schools. Osgoode Hall Law Journal 3:
  316–330, 1965.
Fairfax, John.
  Canadian universities and the last war. Canadian Forum 17: 127–128, 1937.
Falconer, Robert A
  English influence on the higher education of Canada. Royal Society of
  Canada. Transactions s. 3, 22(sect. 2): 33–48, 1928.
— Glimpses of the university at work from 1907 until the First World War.
  University of Toronto Quarterly 11: 127–139; 389–402, 1942.
— Maurice Hutton, (1856–1940). Royal Society of Canada. Proceedings. s. 2,
  34: 111–114, 1940.
— Scottish influence in the higher education of Canada. Royal Society of
  Canada. Transactions s. 3, 21: 7–20, 1927.
— The tradition of liberal education in Canada. Canadian Historical Review
  8: 99–118, 1927.
— University federation in Toronto. Dalhousie Review 3: 279–285, 1923–1924.
— University federation in Toronto. Royal Society of Canada. Transactions s. 3
  34(sect. 2): 43–54, 1940.
Farrant, R   H   and G   Thibaudeau.
  L'enseignement de la psychologie: à l'Université Laurentienne. Canadian
  Psychologist 9: 1–5, 1968.

Faure, Alexandre.
Les dix ans universitaire du séminaire: 1937–1947. Revue de l'Université d'Ottawa 17: 239–248, 1947.
Ferguson, Edna M
Early days at Macdonald. Ontario Agricultural College Review 21: 54–56, 1908.
Ferguson, George V
Charles Avery Dunning. Queen's Quarterly 65: 570–577, 1958.
Chancellor of Queen's, 1948–1958.
Ferguson, Katherine.
George Dalrymple Ferguson; first professor of history at Queen's University. Historic Kingston 14: 51–66, 1966.
The first sixty years of Waterloo Lutheran University. Waterloo Historical Society. Annual Volume 59: 71–72, 1971.
Fitzpatrick, Alfred.
Canadian industry and the Frontier College; an exposition of the objects of a unique Canadian educational institution. Industrial Canada 26(no. 7): 50–51, 65, 1925.
Fleming, Sandford.
The expansion of Queen's University. Canada Educational Monthly 25: 173–177, 1903.
Fleming,(Sir) Sandford. Queen's Quarterly 23: 124–128, 1915/1916.
Fleming, W   G
The Ontario Institute for Studies in Education – a serious Canadian investment in the scientific study of education. Canadian Education and Research Digest 6: 18–25, 1966.
Forbes, Guillaume.
Sur l'Université d'Ottawa. Revue de l'Université d'Ottawa 3: 409–414, 1933.
Forbes, W   G
The emerging concept of community colleges in Ontario. Chemistry in Canada 19(8): 17–18, 1967.
Ford, Arthur R
Fred Landon, journalist, librarian, historian. Ontario Library Review and Canadian Periodical Index 27: 119–120, 1943.
Forster, Leonard.
Ernst Stadler and the University of Toronto. University of Toronto Quarterly 29: 11–20, 1959.
Fra Domenico.
L'Institut d'écoles medievales d'Ottawa. Revue Dominicaine 37: 166–172, 1931.
Fraser, W   H
The University of Toronto and its presidents. Canadian Magazine of Politics, Science, Art and Literature 6: 541–550, 1896.

Friedmann, W
    Teaching and research in comparative law: recent developments at the
    University of Toronto School of Law. University of Toronto Law Journal 10:
    245–247, 1954.
Fry, H   S
    Student co-operative movement. Ontario Agricultural College Review 26:
    14–17, 1913.
Galbraith, John.
    The function of the School of Applied Science in the education of the
    engineer. University of Toronto Monthly 18: 150–157, 1917-1918.
Galbraith, The late dean. Canadian Mining Journal 35: 551–553, 1914.
Gallie, William Edward.
    The University of Toronto Medical School: fifty years' growth. Medical
    Graduate 3(2): 6–13, 1950–1957.
Garvey, Edwin.
    A Canadian university: pluralism in the university. Commonweal 73:
    458–462, 1961.
Gattinger, F   E
    The Ontario Veterinary College at Confederation. Canadian Veterinarian
    Journal 3: 97–100, 1962.
— Veterinary instruction at Queen's and O.A.C. Canadian Veterinarian Journal
    3: 174–180, 1962.
Geikie, Walter B
    An historical sketch of Canadian medical education. The Canada Lancet
    34: 225–236, 281–287, 1901.
Gibson, Frederick W
    President Franklin Roosevelt's visit to Queen's University, 18 August, 1938.
    Historic Kingston 22: 9–36, 1974.
Gibson, William.
    Senator The Hon. Michael Sullivan, M.D. Canadian Catholic Historical
    Association. Report 85–93, 1938–39.
Glover, T   R
    Symposium on the university question. Queen's Quarterly 8: 257–268,
    1900/1901.
Godfrey, C   M
    Trinity Medical School. Applied Therapeutics 8: 1024–1028, 1964.
Goodwin, W   L
    A school of forestry for Ontario. Queen's Quarterly 10: 77–80, 1902/1903.
Gordon, Daniel M
    Our late Chancellor. Queen's Quarterly 23: 111–123, 1915/1916.
    Sir Sandford Fleming – Queen's.
Graham, R   P   and L   H   Cragg.
    Department of Chemistry at McMaster University. Canadian Chemical and
    Process Industries 31: 822–824, 1947.
[Grant, D   M   ]
    Queen's and the War. Queen's Quarterly 22: 384–388, 1914/1915.

Grant, G   M
    "How we raised the $150,000"; a narrative of the endowment campaign of 1878. Douglas Library Notes 13(no. 2): 8–12, 1962.
— Important changes in the constitution of Queen's. Queen's Quarterly 8: 97–104, 1900/1901.
    The following article gives various views on Grant's report.
    Views of representative graduates on the above. Queen's Quarterly 8: 105–109, 1900/1901.
— Two experiments in university extension by a Canadian university. Canada Educational Monthly 14: 123–128, 1892.
    Queen's University.
— The university question. Queen's Quarterly 8: 211–220, 1900/1901.
Grant, W   L
    In memoriam G.M. MacDonnell. Queen's Quarterly 31: 365–370, 1924.
— Reminiscences. Queen's Quarterly 25: 141–147, 1917/1918.
    Nathan Dupuis.
Grant, W   L   and W   L   Goodwin.
    The late Chancellor Douglas. Queen's Quarterly 26: 1–6, 1918/1919.
Gray, W   A
    Early years in our medical school. University of Western Ontario Medical Journal 22: 106–112, 1952.
Grayhurst, Denis.
    Funding squeeze at Waterloo University. Canadian Magazine 1(2): 32, 1966.
Grelton, Robert.
    The winds of change: 1 – a new literacy. Canadian Architect 14(2): 32–39, 1969.
    Curriculum at University of Toronto School of Architecture.
Guillet, Edwin C
    The Victoria College manuscript discoveries. The New Outlook n.s. 7: 277, 300, 313, 322, 339, 346, 358, 372, 379, 394, 408, 420, 445, 454, 466, 480, 492, 494, 516, 540, 552–553, 564, 574, 586, 599, 610, 616, 1931.
Gundy, H   Pearson.
    Growing pains: the early years of Queen's Medical Faculty. Historic Kingston 4: 14–25, 1955.
— That man Grant. Douglas Library Notes 13(no. 2): 2–8, 1964.
Gwillim, J   C
    The Kingston School of Mining. Canadian Mining Review 24: 98–101, 1905.
— Nicol Hall, School of Mining, Kingston. Canadian Mining Journal 33: 264–265, 1912.
Gwyn, Norman B
    Details connected with the evolution of medical education in Toronto. University of Toronto Medical Journal 8: 224–229, 1931.
Habashi, Fathi.
    University news. Canadian Mining Journal 95(no. 1): 51–56, 1974.
    Queen's University.

Haldenby, Eric W
   The School of Hygiene, University of Toronto. Royal Architectural Institute
   of Canada. Journal 4: 279–289, 1927.
Hales, J   P
   The College poultry plant. Ontario Agricultural College Review 27: 28–30,
   1914.
Hamilton, J   D
   The future of medical education at the University of Toronto. Medical
   Graduate 8(1): 2–9, 1961–1962.
Hardie, Betty.
   Bertha Bassam retires. Ontario Library Review 48: 61–62, 1964.
   Director, University of Toronto Library School.
Harris, Charles W
   William Thomas Atkins, Professor of Surgery, Toronto School of Medicine.
   Canadian Journal of Surgery 5: 131–137, 1962.
Harris, Robin S
   The universities of Ontario. Canadian Geographical Journal 70: 2–19, 1965.
Hart, John.
   Brock University. School Progress 33(7): 41–43, 1964.
Haultain, H   E   T
   The University of Toronto and the mineral industry. Canadian Mining
   Journal 33: 394–399, 510–513, 1912.
Haydon, Andrew.
   Adam Shortt. Queen's Quarterly 38: 609–623, 1931.
Heard, John F
   Ruth Josephine Northcott. Journal of the Royal Astronomical Society of
   Canada 63: 225–226, 1969.
Heard, John F   and Helen Sawyer Hogg.
   Astronomy at the David Dunlap Observatory: 1935–1967. Journal of the
   Royal Astronomical Society of Canada 61: 257–276, 1967.
Hébert, Joseph.
   L'Université d'Ottawa: ses réalisations et ses espérances. Revue de
   l'Université d'Ottawa 7: 389–411, 1937.
Hellmuth, I
   Huron College and the Western University. Journal of the Synod of the
   Church of England of the Diocese of Huron. 26: 22–48, 1883.
Henderson, J   L   H
   The founding of Trinity College, Toronto. Ontario History 44: 7–14, 1952.
Historical sketch of University College. University College Bulletin 9–18, 1938.
Holmes, J   M
   The modern look: Carleton University. Chemistry in Canada 12(5): 39–41,
   1960.
Home, Paul.
   Legal education in Ontario. Canadian Bar Review 1: 685–693, 1923.

Hough, H
Victoria University – its history and educational work. Canadian Magazine of Politics, Science, Art and Literature 7: 205–215, 1897.
Housing and town planning course. Canadian Forum 23: 230, 1944.
University of Toronto.
How, H R
Ferment and transition at University of Toronto. Canadian Business 43(3): 60–62, 64, 66, 1970.
Howarth, Thomas.
Campus planning, York University. Royal Architectural Institute of Canada. Journal 38: 30–34, 1961.
Hugo–Brunt, Michael.
University of Toronto, Scarborough College. Royal Architectural Institute of Canada. Journal 41(no. 7): 61–65, 1964.
Hurley, James T
Thomas O'Hagan; pioneer poet and scholar. Canadian Catholic Historical Association. Report 79–87, 1950.
Hutt, H L
The Horticultural Department. Ontario Agricultural College Review 5(3): 18–19, 1893.
I B
The making of the president. Canadian Forum 50: 260–261, 1970.
University of Toronto.
In memoriam: Sir Robert Alexander Falconer, K.G.M.G. University of Toronto Quarterly 13: 135–174, 1944.
In memoriam: William John Alexander. University of Toronto Quarterly 14: 1–33, 1944.
Industrial education in Ontario. Industrial Canada 13: 1219–1223, 1913.
Innanen, K A and R W Nicholls.
Astronomy and astrophysics at York University. Journal of the Royal Astronomical Society of Canada 63: 87–89, 1969.
Innes, R
Student life at Macdonald College. Ontario Agricultural College Review 22: 328–331, 1910.
Innis, H A
William T. Jackman, 1871–1951. Canadian Journal of Economics and Political Science 18: 201–204, 1952.
Irving, J A
The achievement of George Sidney Brett (1879–1944). University of Toronto Quarterly 14: 329–365, 1945.
Isabelle, Laurent.
La psychologie à l'Université d'Ottawa. Canadian Psychologist 9: 6–12, 1968.
— Vingt-cinq ans en orientation à l'Université d'Ottawa. Council of Associations of University Student Personnel Services. Journal 2(1): 15–22, 1967.

Israel, Fred C
    The place of the Ontario"D" certificate in library education. Ontario
    Library Review 49: 181–182, 1965.
Ivanov, Peter Pavlovic.
    Le Centre Catholique de l'Université d'Ottawa: son idée et sa mission.
    Revue de l'Université d'Ottawa 21: 173–177, 1951.
Jackman, M   R
    The function and furnishing of the Union. Royal Architectural Institute of
    Canada. Journal 31: 48–54, 1954.
    Wymilwood – Union at Victoria University.
Jackson, Robert W   B
    The Ontario Institute for Studies in Education. Ontario Journal of
    Educational Research 8: 173–181, 1965–66.
James, C   C
    George Coulson Creelman, B.S.A.: President of the Ontario Agricultural
    College. Ontario Agricultural College Review 16(5): 14–16, 1904.
James, Lois.
    Will Scarborough College "flunk out"? Continuous Learning 7: 198–202,
    1968.
James, N   C
    The Western University. London and Middlesex Historical Society.
    Transactions 5: 41–47, 1914.
Jamieson, D   Park.
    A four-year law course in Ontario. Canadian Bar Review 31: 894–907, 1953.
Janes, J   R
    Geology of Canada: an outdoor approach to university education at the
    adult level. Continuous learning 9(May–June): 134–136, 1970.
Johnson, Arthur C
    York's plans crystallizing. School Progress 33(7): 36–38, 1964.
Jones, T   Lloyd.
    The Ontario Veterinary College is one hundred years old. Canadian
    Veterinarian Journal 3: 194–196, 1962.
Jordan, W   G
    Queen's and the Church. Queen's Quarterly 16: 258–260, 1908/1909.
— Queen's and the General Assembly. Queen's Quarterly 17: 86–97,
    1909/1910.
Juvet, C   S
    Training in public administration at Carleton University under Canada's
    external aid program. Canadian Public Administration 4: 396–405, 1961.
Kennedy, W   P   M
    Legal subjects in the universities of Canada. Society of Public Teachers of
    Law. Journal 10: 23–27, 1933.
Kent, Stanley R
    The Sample Room; School of Architecture, University of Toronto. Royal
    Architectural Institute of Canada. Journal 21: 76–77, 1944.

Kerr, W   B
    The pass student. Canadian Forum 8: 446–447, 1927.
Keyes, Mary Eleanor.
    John Howard Crocker LL.D., 1870–1959. Western Ontario History Nuggets
    32: 1–96, 1966.
Kilbourn, William.
    The McMaster University Act, 1957. Canadian Forum 37: 124, 1957.
Kingsford, William.
    Sir Daniel Wilson (Died, 6th August, 1892); in memoriam. Royal Society of
    Canada. Transactions s.1, 11(sect. 2): 55–65, 1893.
Kingston and its universities. Chemistry in Canada 16(2): 41–44, 1964.
Kingston School of Mining; new mining and metallurgy building and research
    laboratories. Canadian Mining Journal 33: 749, 1912.
Kirley, Kevin J
    A seminary rector in English Canada during and after the Second Vatican
    Council. Canadian Catholic Historical Association. Study Sessions 43:
    57–74, 1976.
    St. Basil's Seminary – Toronto St. Michael's.
[LaBrie, F   E]
    William Paul McClure Kennedy, 1879–1963. University of Toronto Law
    Journal 15: 255–258, 1964.
Laframboise, Jean-Charles.
    A l'aube d'un second siècle. Revue de l'Université d'Ottawa 19: 19–45,
    1949.
— L'Université d'Ottawa et l'Ontario français. Revue de l'Université d'Ottawa
    17: 395–404, 1947.
Land, R   Brian.
    University of Toronto School of Library Science. Canadian Library 22:
    223–225, 1966.
Landon, Fred.
    Adult education – The University of Western Ontario. Ontario Library
    Review and Book-Selection Guide 9: 34–35, 1924.
— J. Davis Barnett's gift to the Western University. Ontario Library Review
    and Book-Selection Guide 3: 16, 1918.
Langton, Hugh Hornby.
    Great technical schools: the University of Toronto, Toronto, Ontario,
    Canada. Technical World 2: 171–180, 1904.
Laskin, Bora.
    Cecil A. Wright – a tribute. Canadian Bar Review 45: 215–218, 1967.
Laurin, J. Rhéal.
    Mgr. Duhamel et l'Université Catholique d'Ottawa. Société Canadienne de
    l'histoire de l'Église Catholique. Rapport 19–29, 1956–1957.
— Canadian Catholic Historical Association. Report 19–29, 1957.
Lavell, Cecil F
    Queen's Faculty of Education. Queen's Quarterly 15: 134–137, 1907/1908.

Law, Harriet.
    Community colleges search for an identity. Canadian University 1(2):
    26–29, 1966.
Leal, H   Allan.
    Osgoode Hall Law School – today and tomorrow. University of Toronto Law
    Journal 12: 285–290, 1958.
Lemieux, Germain.
    Centre franco-ontarien de folklore à l'Université de Sudbury. Laurentian
    University Review 8(no. 2): 134–137, 1976.
Le Moine, Roger.
    Le Club des Dix à Ottawa. La Revue de l'Université Laval 20: 703–709,
    1966.
Library training school for 1917. Ontario Library Review and Book-Selection
    Guide 1: 90–92, 1917.
Lochhead, W
    The Macdonald College. Ontario Agricultural College Review 20: 8–12,
    1907.
— Nature study at the O.A.C. Ontario Agricultural College Review 15(5):
    13–15, 1903.
— Then and now: a decade of biology at the O.A.C. Ontario Agricultural
    College Review 14(6): 3–6, 1902.
Lorriman, F   R
    The Department of Chemistry, University of Toronto. Chemistry in Canada
    11(10): 38–39, 1959.
Loudon, James.
    An Ontario school of forestry. Canada Educational Monthly 25: 3–6, 1903.
Lower, Arthur R   M
    Adam Shortt, founder. Historic Kingston 17: 3–15, 1969.
— Queen's yesterday and today. Historic Kingston 20: 77–89, 1972.
— Queen's Quarterly 70: 69–75, 1963.
Ludwig, M   T
    Legal education; report of the Benchers of the Law Society of Upper
    Canada. Canadian Bar Review 13: 347–357, 1935.
Lusztig, Peter A   and Jack Haskett.
    A look at two Canadian business schools. Canadian Business 34(4): 96–100,
    102, 1961.
McCallion, William J   and Truman M   Norton.
    The Spitz Planetarium, McMaster University, Hamilton, Ontario. Journal
    of the Royal Astronomical Society of Canada 53: 149–153, 1959.
Macallum, Archibald Byron.
    The late Principal Grant and the university question. University of Toronto
    Monthly 5: 67–73, 1904.
— The new medical buildings of the University of Toronto. Science n.s. 17:
    813–817, 1903.
MacClement, W   T
    Queen's summer school. Queen's Quarterly 23: 177–180, 1915/1916.

McCorkell, Edmund J
Bertram Coghill Alan Windle, F.R.S., F.S.A., K.S.G., MD; LL.D., Ph.D., SC.D.
Canadian Catholic Historical Association. Report 53–58, 1958.
— Federation: the legacy of Father Carr. Basilian Teacher 8: 301–307, 1964.
McCreadie (Professor).
Training of teachers in agriculture. Ontario Agricultural College Review 21:
460–464, 1909.
Macdonald. Ontario Agricultural College Review 17: 182–186, 1904.
Macdonnell, G M and S W Dyde.
Queen's and her future. Queen's Quarterly 17: 218–236, 1909/1910.
McDougall, Robert L
The university quarterlies. Canadian Forum 38: 253–255, 1959.
Macgillivray, John.
German in schools and colleges. Queen's Quarterly 15: 211–215, 1907/1908.
Chiefly at Queen's.
McKay, G J
The mining and metallurgical laboratory; School of Mining, Kingston,
Ontario. Canadian Mining Journal 28(no. 14): 369–371, 1907.
MacKenzie, Norman.
The teaching of international law and international relations in Canadian
universities, 1931. Canadian Bar Review 10: 519–523, 1932.
Mackintosh, W A
Adam Shortt, 1859–1931. Canadian Journal of Economics and Political
Science 4: 164–176, 1938.
— William Clifford Clarke; a personal memoir. Queen's Quarterly 60: 1–16,
1953.
McLean, Helen.
Toronto University. Women's Canadian Historical Society of Ottawa.
Transactions 7: 12–15, 1917.
McMaster Divinity College, Hamilton, Ontario. Royal Architectural Institute
of Canada. Journal 38: 39–44, 1961.
McMaster plays the game; a novel teaching aid for commerce students.
Industrial Canada 60(10): 44–45, 1960.
McMaster University. School Progress 30(7): 28–33, 46, 1961.
MacMechan, Archibald.
The President of Toronto University. Canadian Magazine of Politics,
Science, Art and Literature 35: 248–250, 1910.
McNaught, Carlton.
Democracy and our universities. Canadian Forum 20: 333, 1941.
Macnaughton, John.
Principal Gordon. Queen's Quarterly 10: 249–252, 1902/1903.
McNeill, W E
James Cappon(1854–1939). Royal Society of Canada. Proceedings s.3, 34:
97–100, 1940.
MacPherson, L G
In memoriam – W.A. Mackintosh. Queen's Quarterly 78: 117–119, 1971.

MacRae, D   F
    Ernest Pascoe Goodwin: a Queen's man – class of '88. Historic Kingston 8:
    14–23, 1959.
McRae, D   G   W
    Architectural Draughting School: Training and Re-establishment Institute,
    Toronto. Royal Architectural Institute of Canada. Journal 22: 214–215,
    1945.
Madill, H   H
    Charles Henry Challenor Wright. Royal Architectural Institute of Canada.
    Journal 21: 94, 1944.
— School of Architecture, University of Toronto. Royal Architectural Institute
    of Canada. Journal 18: 26–28, 1941.
— University of Toronto School of Architecture. Royal Architectural Institute
    of Canada. Journal 22: 75–77, 1945; 26: 136–140, 1949.
— University of Toronto; undergrad activities at Varsity. Royal Architectural
    Institute of Canada. Journal 27: 128–132, 1950.
Mallory, James.
    "Teachers Unions". Queen's Quarterly 61: 53–62, 1954.
    CAUT – formation.
Mamen, C
    Annual review of mine technology – 1971; word from educational
    institutions. Canadian Mining Journal 93(no. 3): 63–68, 1972.
    Queen's University; Haileybury School of Mines.
Marsh, G   F
    The Ontario and Experimental Union. Ontario Agricultural College
    Review 6(5): 2–3, 1895.
Marshall, J
    The Faculty of Pedagogy. Queen's Quarterly 15: 81–83, 1907/1908.
    Queen's University.
— Reorganization of the Education Department. Queen's Quarterly 14: 76–81,
    1906–1907.
    University of Toronto.
Marshall, John.
    Major issues in library education: Toronto's approach to its new program.
    Saskatchewan Library 23(1): 3–18, 1969.
Martin, Chester.
    Professor George M. Wrong. Western Ontario Historical Notes 8: 52–54,
    1950.
    From St. Thomas *Times-Journal*.
Marvin, George.
    The heart of Toronto: unifying a great university. Outlook 143: 62–66, 1926.
    Hart House.
Mason, Thomas H
    The Experimental Union. Ontario Agricultural College Review 16(2): 9–12,
    1903.

Mate, Herbert V
Assumption University of Windsor. Ontario Library Review 43: 16–18, 1959.
Mathers, A   S
The William H. Wright Building. Royal Architectural Institute of Canada. Journal 15: 173–181, 190, 1938.
Matheson, John.
Professor Dupuis as a teacher of mathematics. Queen's Quarterly 25: 148–152, 1917/1918.
Meikleham, Marget H   C
Welcome to McMaster. Ontario Library Review 37: 7, 1953.
Merritt, William Hamilton.
Prospectors' classes and mineral collections in mining centres. Canadian Mining Review 15: 207–208, 1896.
Kingston School of Mining.
— The School of Mining and "Miners". Queen's Quarterly 1: 223–227, 1893/1894.
Miller, Frederick R
Archibald Byron Macallum, B.A., M.B., Ph.D., F.R.S. Western Ontario Historical Notes 8: 50–52, 1950.
Millman, P   M
Canada's third large observatory; the new David Dunlap Observatory of the University of Toronto. The Telescope 4(5): 58–65, 1934.
Milner, James B
Ontario legal education – some background facts. Canadian Bar Journal 5: 310–321, 1962.
Montagnes, James.
Ryerson – a training school for the most-wanted men of the 20th century. Canadian Business 32(9): 122–126, 1959.
Morgan, William. Queen's Quarterly 35: 336–337, 1928.
Morisset, Auguste-M
Twenty years of library education at the University of Ottawa. Canadian Library Association. Bulletin 14: 220–223, 1958.
Morrison, T   R
Reform as social tracking: the case of industrial education in Ontario. Journal of Educational Thought 8(2): 87–110, 1974.
Mowat (Professor J.B.).
Early reminiscences of Queen's University, Kingston. Canada Educational Monthly 17: 53–55, 1895.
Muldrew, W   H
The Macdonald Institute. Ontario Agricultural College Review 16(3): 63–65, 1903.
Mulock, William.
University federation of denominational colleges in Canada. Current History 27: 524–528, 1928.

Mungall, Constance.
    Co-operative education – how good is it? Canadian Business 40(10): 52–54,
    56, 58, 1967.
    University of Waterloo.
Munro, June E
    Library technician training in Ontario. Ontario Library Review 52: 3–5,
    1968.
Murray, Walter C
    State support and control of universities in Canada. Royal Society of
    Canada. Transactions s.3, 19(sect. 2): 19–32, 1925.
Myers, B   R   and J   S   Keeler.
    Engineering education in Canada and the co-operative electrical
    engineering program at the University of Waterloo. Institute of Radio
    Engineers. Transactions E4: 71–79, 1961.
Myers, Douglas.
    OISE and John Seeley. Canadian Forum 54(March): 3–4, 1975.
Neill, R   F
    Adam Shortt; a bibliographic comment. Journal of Canadian Studies 2(no.
    1): 53–61, 1967.
A new approach to campus recruiting. Industrial Canada 58(no. 7): 56–59,
    1957.
    University of Toronto Placement Service.
New laboratories of the Department of Mining Engineering, University of
    Toronto. Canadian Mining Journal 52: 375–376, 1931.
Newbigging, P   L
    Psychology at McMaster. Canadian Psychologist 1: 106–110, 1960.
Nicholls, R   W
    International Conference on Laboratory Astrophysics and opening of the
    Petrie Science Building, York University, Toronto, November 7–8, 1969.
    Journal of the Royal Astronomical Society of Canada 64: 66–68, 1970.
Nicholson, N   L
    The religious factor in the location of Ontario universities. Ontario
    Geography 7: 37–49, 1972.
Nikiforuk, Gordon.
    The Division of Dental Research, University of Toronto. Canadian Dental
    Association. Journal 28: 709–718, 1962.
The old and the new at Ottawa University. Chemistry in Canada 12(4): 36–38,
    1960.
Ontario Council of University Faculty Associations.
    University education in Ontario – a brief prepared for presentation to the
    Prime Minister of Ontario. CAUT Bulletin 12(3); 10–41, 1964.
The Ontario Institute for Studies in Education. Ontario Journal of Educational
    Research 8: 1–4, 1965–66.
The Ontario Law School. Canadian Magazine of Politics, Science, Art and
    Literature 1: 699–700, 1893.

Ontario's emerging CAATS – a survey and progress report. Canadian University 2(5): 60–64, 100, 1967.
[Osborne, Milton S]
    School of Architecture, University of Toronto. Royal Architectural Institute of Canada. Journal 35: 70–92, 1958.
Pakenham, W
    Technical education. Ontario Agricultural College Review 21: 1–5, 1908.
— Technical education in Ontario and the West. Canada Educational Monthly 25: 159–161, 218–222, 1903.
Panet, H   A   (Major-General).
    The Royal Military College. Canadian Geographical Journal 3: 441–454, 1931.
Panton, J   Hoyes.
    Natural History Department of the O.A.C. Ontario Agricultural College Review 5(3): 4–6, 1893.
Parker, Graham.
    Legal education in Ontario. Journal of Legal Education 27: 576–591, 1976.
Parkin, J   H
    The new aerodynamic laboratory of the University of Toronto. Engineering Journal 10: 390–399, 1927.
Pearce, Jon.
    Filling up the whole round: an interview with Tom Marshall. Queen's Quarterly 83: 413–423, 1976.
Pearson, Charles E
    Report of dental education in Ontario, Canada. Dominion Dental Journal 15: 304–309, 1903.
Pentland, Clare.
    Louis Aubrey Wood, 1883–1955. Canadian Journal of Economics and Political Science 22: 251–252, 1956.
Petrie, R   M
    Canadian scientists report; I. The growth of astronomy in Canada. Journal of the Royal Astronomical Society of Canada 50: 146–151, 1956.
Physics at the University of Ottawa. Physics in Canada 24(4): 13–17, 1968.
Plewes, A   C
    Chemical engineering training at Queen's. Chemistry in Canada 12(9): 88–90, 92, 1960.
Pomeroy, Elsie.
    Mary Electa Adams: a pioneer educator. Ontario History 41: 107–117, 1949.
Porter, George D
    Health work at the University. University of Toronto Monthly 31: 305, 1931.
Potter, Alex O
    Waterloo College. Waterloo Historical Society. Annual Report 37: 10–14, 1949.

Preston, Adrian.
    The founding of the Royal Military College; gleanings from the Royal
    Archives. Queen's Quarterly 74: 398–412, 1967.
Preston, R   A
    A business college student's letters, 1886–7. Historic Kingston 19: 81–86,
    1971.
Preston, Richard.
    R.M.C. and Kingston: the effect of imperial and military influences on a
    Canadian community. Ontario History 60: 105–123, 1968.
Priestley, F   E   L
    The future of the humanities in Ontario universities. Humanities Association
    Bulletin 19(1): 3–13, 1968.
Putnam, George A
    Dairy instruction in the province of Ontario. Ontario Agricultural College
    Review 21: 326–329, 1909.
Queen's and the Church. Queen's Quarterly 10: 122–123, 1902/1903.
Queen's Journal.
    Special memorial issue [for Principal Grant] 30(no.1): November 6, 1902.
Queen's University; an illustrated sketch of its foundation, growth and present
    proportions. Queen's Quarterly 10: 1902/1903; 11: 1903/1904.
Queen's University, Kingston, Ontario. Royal Architectural Institute of
    Canada. Journal 2: 213–221, 1925.
Quick, Don.
    Ontario: the CAATS: program and planning. Canadian University 3(4): 16,
    52, 1968.
[Radio Broadcast – CJBC(CBC)].
    A visit to Dunlap Observatory. Journal of the Royal Astronomical Society of
    Canada 38: 407–416, 1944.
Rand, I   C
    The new Faculty of Law in The University of Western Ontario. University
    of Toronto Law Journal 14: 107–108, 1960.
Reed, Alfred Z
    The organization of legal education in Ontario. Canadian Bar Review 13:
    371–374, 1935.
Reed, J   Hugo
    Reminiscences of the O.A.C. Ontario Agricultural College Review 31: 43–47,
    1918.
Research activity at Queen's University in 1970. Canadian Mining Journal
    92(no. 1): 64–65, 1971.
Reynolds, J   B
    James Mills, M.A., LL.D. Ontario Agricultural College Review 16(5): 9–13,
    1904.
— Our College. Ontario Agricultural College Review 13(3): 3–7, 1902.
— Prospects for agricultural education in Ontario. Ontario Agricultural
    College Review 8(2): 5–6, 1896.

Robertson, J   K
  An experiment in medical education. British Journal of Radiology. n.s. 27:
  593–603, 1954.
Robinson, Percy J
  Classical teaching in Ontario. University Magazine 13: 126–147, 1914.
Robson, John M
  The CUG Report, or, how to nail jelly to the wall. CAUT Bulletin 18(3):
  32–42, 1970.
Roedde, William A
  The provincial role in library education. Ontario Library Review 43:
  130–131, 1959.
Rogers, R   Vashon.
  Professor James Williamson, LL.D. Queen's Quarterly 3: 161–172,
  1895/1896.
Root, Donna L
  Dr. Fred Landon. Inland Seas 25: 250, 1969.
Ross, Peter N
  The establishment of the Ph.D. at Toronto: a case of American influence.
  History of Education Quarterly 12: 358–380, 1972.
Rotstein, Abraham.
  The makings of a president. Canadian Forum 48: 124–127, 1968.
Rounthwaite, Shelagh.
  Architectural education; University of Toronto. Royal Architectural
  Institute of Canada. Journal 24: 151–157, 1947.
The Royal Military College. Canadian Magazine of Politics, Science, Art and
  Literature 4: 261–268, 377–388, 428–442, 1895.
Ruth, Norbert J
  Assumption University and the University of Windsor. Basilian Teacher 8:
  154–168, 1964.
— A dean's look at a new university. Assumption University Alumni Times
  8(winter): 7–9, 1963.
— The University of Windsor: an example of ecumenical co-operation. Journal
  of Higher Education 38: 90–95, 1967.
The Ryerson Institute of Technology. School Progress 17(3): 30–33, 1949.
Ryerson Polytechnical Institute, Toronto. Architecture Canada 43(no. 10): 59,
  1966.
Sackett, F
  A task scarcely begun. Le Seminaire 9(March): 9, 13–19, 1944.
  Faculty of Canon Law, University of Ottawa.
Sandiford, Peter.
  The Department of Educational Research, University of Toronto. The
  School (Secondary Edition) 29: 433–438, 1941.
Saunders, Richard M
  Vers la bonne entente. Revue de l'Université Laval 3: 592–595, 1949.
School of Architecture, University of Toronto. Royal Architectural Institute of
  Canada. Journal 30: 59–83, 1953; 40(3): 56–68, 1963.

Separate Department of Astronomy created at the University of Western
    Ontario. Journal of the Royal Astronomical Society of Canada 60: 247–248,
    1966.
Shevenell, Raymond.
    L'Institut de Psychologie et le Centre d'Orientation. Revue de l'Université
    d'Ottawa 16: 234–242, 1946.
— The School of Psychology and Education at the University of Ottawa .
    Canadian Psychologist 3A: 7–10, 1962.
Shook, Lawrence K
    The coming of the Basilians to Assumption College; early expansion of St.
    Michael's College. Canadian Catholic Historical Association. Report 59–73,
    1951.
— Father Carr: educator, superior, friend. Basilian Teacher 8: 291–300, 1964.
— Marian pilgrimages of the Archdiocese of Toronto. Canadian Catholic
    Historical Association. Report. 53–65, 1954.
Short, R   C
    1 in 5 St. Lawrence students learn data processing. Ontario Education
    Review 4, January 1968.
Short course library training school. Ontario Library Review and Book-
    Selection Guide 1: 13–14, 1916.
Short course training school for librarianship. Ontario Library Review and
    Book-selection Guide 1: 35–36, 1916.
Shortt, Adam.
    Principal Grant. Queen's Quarterly 10: 1–4, 1902/1903.
— Random recollections of Queen's. Queen's Quarterly 27: 352–363,
    1919/1920; 28: 131–137, 1920/1921.
— Should we revise the constitution of Queen's? Queen's Quarterly 8: 112–114,
    1900/1901.
Shutt, Greta M
    Donald Bethune Shutt, B.S.A., C.S.I.(C), F.A.A.A.S. Bruce County Historical
    Society. Yearbook 40–41, 43, 1974.
Shuttleworth, A   E
    Chemical Department. Ontario Agricultural College Review 5(3): 7–8,
    1893.
Sidnell, Michael J
    Towards bureaupolitocracy. Journal of Canadian Studies 7(no. 2): 3–18,
    1972.
    Wright Report on Education.
Siegel, Ida L
    Toronto's Talmud Torah: then and now. Canadian Jewish Review 37(Sept.
    16): 16, 1955.
Silverthorn, Mary.
    Miss Bertha Bassam, director of the Library School, University of Toronto,
    1951–. Ontario Library Review 35: 259–260, 1951.

Simard, Georges.
La doctrine catholique et les universités: l'Université d'Ottawa 1889–1939.
Revue de l'Université d'Ottawa 9: 155–175, 1939.
— L'École supérieure de l'Université. Revue de l'Université d'Ottawa 1:
405–409, 1931.
— Le fondateur de L'Université d'Ottawa. Royal Society of Canada.
Transactions s.3, 37(sect.1): 117–121, 1943.
— Les Universités dan l'Église. Revue de l'Université d'Ottawa 5: 157–185,
1935.
Sir John A. Macdonald and Queen's. Queen's Alumni Review 41: 116–120,
1967.
pp. 118–119 are blank.
Sirluck, Ernest.
The future development of graduate programmes in Ontario. Queen's
Quarterly 75: 195–207, 1968.
Sisco, N   A
Canada's manpower training and education: a view from Ontario.
Canadian Education and Research Digest 7: 299–304, 1967.
— Two comments on Ontario's Community Colleges. Continuous Learning 5:
222–226, 1966.
Sissons, C   B
University federation at Toronto: a Canadian experiment. Canadian
Historical Review 31: 166–176, 1950.
Sissons, Constance Kerr.
Recollections of the Ontario School of Pedagogy, 1894–1895. Douglas
Library Notes 12(no. 2): 4–8, 1963.
Skinner, A   G
The Students' Co-operative Movement. Ontario Agricultural College
Review 29: 6–8, 1916.
Smiley, Barbara.
The Centre for Renaissance and Reformation Studies. Ontario Library
Review 60: 18–21, 1976.
Smith, Denis.
Trent University prepares for first classes. School Progress 33(7): 39–40, 51,
1964.
— University grants. Canadian Forum 43: 268–270, 1964.
Smith, J   Percy.
University – government relations: a case in point. CAUT Bulletin 16(4):
78–81, 1968.
Smith, Tony.
The pursuit of academerika; higher education in Ontario. Canadian Forum
50: 414–416, 1971.
Soberman, D   A
The Faculty of Law of Queen's University. University of Toronto Law
Journal 19: 420–423, 1969.

Some requirements for technical education in Toronto. Industrial Canada 12:
603–606, 1911.
Spetz, Theobald, C.R.D.D. Waterloo Historical Society. Annual Report 10:
261–264, 1922.
Spragge, George W
The Trinity Medical College. Ontario History 58: 63–98, 1966.
Sproatt, C   B
Emmanuel College and residences; Victoria University, Toronto. Royal
Architectural Institute of Canada. Journal 8: 181–188, 1932.
Squair, John.
French in the educational system of Ontario. University of Toronto Monthly
19: 291–296, 1919.
— Post-graduate courses in the University of Toronto. Canada Educational
Monthly 16: 242–244, 283–286, 1894.
Squirrell, W   J
The O.A. College – a brief history. Ontario Agricultural College Review 22:
103–107, 1909.
Stager, David.
The new look in educational research. Canadian Forum 46: 268–269, 1967.
Steiner, Simon D
Furniture design at Ryerson Institute. Royal Architectural Institute of
Canada. Journal 28: 212–213, 1951.
Stevens, Martin S
Co-operative education in engineering at University of Waterloo. Canadian
Mining Journal 83(no. 12): 54–57, 1962.
Stevenson, J   A
Hamilton Fyfe of Queen's. Queen's Quarterly 37: 586–592, 1930.
Stevenson, L
The Ontario Agricultural College. Ontario Library Review and Book-
Selection Guide 10: 36–37, 1925.
Stewart, E   E
Using formula financing; the province of Ontario's approach to campus
planning. Architecture Canada 46(no. 7–8): 41, 1969.
Stokes, H   W
McMaster's swimming pool reactor. Canadian Chemical Processing
43(April): 104–110, 1959.
Strachan, Daniel.
Rev. Daniel Miner Gordon, D.D., LL.D., C.M.G. Queen's Quarterly 25:
365–367, 1917/1918.
Straka, M   K
The colleges of applied arts and technology. Ontario Mathematics Gazette
7: 3–12, 1968.
Student residences, Brock University. Canadian Architect 15(November):
31–35, 1970.

Sudar, Dan D
  Ontario's first library technology course. Ontario Library Review 52: 6–11,
  1968.
Swan, C   M   J   F
  The roots of a university. Canadian Geographical Journal 57: 204–208,
  1958.
  Assumption University – University of Windsor.
Talbot, Joan.
  Miller Hall; commemorating a great geologist at Queen's University .
  Canadian Mining Journal 56: 473, 1935.
Talman, James J
  Rise of the University of Western Ontario. Western Ontario Historical Notes
  5: 26–31, 1947.
Tamblyn, W   F
  A university in the making. Canadian Magazine of Politics, Science, Art and
  Literature 56: 417–425, 1921.
  The University of Western Ontario.
Tansey, Charlotte.
  Other voices other classrooms; the Thomas More Institute and Rochdale
  College. Canadian Forum 48: 130–131, 1968.
Tarnopolsky, W   S
  The New Law School at the University of Windsor. University of Toronto
  Law Journal 19: 622–626, 1969.
Taylor, Griffith.
  Geography at the University of Toronto. Canadian Geographical Journal
  23: 152–154, 1941.
Taylor, K   W
  Economic scholarship in Canada. Canadian Journal of Economics and
  Political Science 26: 6–18, 1960.
Taylor, Richard K
  Wilfrid Laurier University. Waterloo Historical Society. Annual Volume 61:
  74–75, 1973.
Taylor, Robert Bruce.
  George Young Chown. Queen's Quarterly 28: 331–338, 1920/1921.
Taylor, Robert Bruce. Queen's Quarterly 25: 247–249, 1917/1918.
Technical education; memorandum submitted to Minister of Education for the
  province of Ontario – Commission to deal with the subject asked for.
  Industrial Canada 1: 154–155, 1901.
Technical education gets impetus in Hamilton; reorganization of Technical
  School described at annual meeting of Hamilton Branch – work of Branch
  reviewed. Industrial Canada 24(no. 2): 63, 1923.
Technical education in Canada; some general remarks on the situation in
  Ontario – present facilities and future needs – a prominent educationist on
  the subject – what technical education has done for Germany. Industrial
  Canada 5: 375–377, 1905.
Technical education in Toronto. Industrial Canada 10: 607–608, 1910.

Technicians for industry. Industrial Canada 58(no. 4): 47–49, 1957.

Thom, R   J
    Massey College. Royal Architectural Institute of Canada. Journal 40(no.
    10): 38, 1963.
— Massey College competition. Royal Architectural Institute of Canada.
    Journal 37: 488–492, 1960.
— Trent University, Peterborough, Ontario. Architecture Canada 43(no. 10):
    44–47, 1966.

Thomson, James S
    Sir Robert A. Falconer. Dalhousie Review 30: 361–368, 1950–1951.

Three-campus plan for York University. School Progress 31(7): 40–41, 64, 1962.

L'Université d'Ottawa. L'Action Nationale 32: 246–249, 1948.

Universities adopt new admission procedures. Ontario Education Review 1,
    November 1967.

The University Club – Toronto. Royal Architectural Institute of Canada.
    Journal 7: 128–137, 1930.

University College; President Wilson's address. Canada Educational Monthly
    7: 337–346, 1885.

University consolidation. Canada Educational Monthly 1: 1–7, 1879.

The University of Toronto and the war. Canadian Mining Journal 36: 147–148,
    1915.

The University of Toronto Commission. Canada Educational Monthly 27:
    292–295, 1905.

University of Toronto. Department of Architecture. Architecture Canada 46(no.
    4): 47–50, 1969.

University of Toronto [School of Architecture]. Royal Architectural Institute of
    Canada. Journal 28: 62–67, 1951.

University of Toronto School of Architecture proposes graduate design program.
    Royal Architectural Institute of Canada. Journal 40(no. 4): 81, 1963.

University of Waterloo, Waterloo, Ontario. Royal Architectural Institute of
    Canada. Journal 39: 45–54, 1962.

The University of Western Ontario. Royal Architectural Institute of Canada.
    Journal 2: 128–131, 1925.

Unwin, G   H
    The study of French at the O.A.C. Ontario Agricultural College Review 30:
    532–535, 1918.

Verney, Douglas V
    The government and politics of a developing university: a Canadian
    experience. The Review of Politics 31: 291–311, 1969.
    York University.

Waldon, Freda F
    W.G.B. Ontario Library Review 35: 203–205, 1951.
    Winifred G. Barnstead, director, Library School, University of Toronto.

Walker, C   E   1880–1942. Canadian Journal of Economics and Political
    Science 9: 75–76, 1943.

Walker, George C
The Faculty of Pharmacy, University of Toronto. American Journal of Pharmaceutical Education 28: 360–377, 1964.

Wallace, Malcolm W
Sir Robert Falconer as president of the University of Toronto. Canadian Journal of Religious Thought 9: 97–100, 1932.

Wallace, W   Stewart.
The life and work of George M. Wrong. Canadian Historical Review 29: 229–237, 1948.

Walters, Richard H
Psychology at the University of Waterloo. Ontario Psychological Association Quarterly 16(2): 5–9, 1963.

Waterloo School of Architecture. Architecture Canada 44(5): 57–59, 1967.

Waterloo's engineering students spend six months on the campus, six months on the job. Industrial Canada 60(7): 47–48, 1959.

Watson, John.
The degree of Ph.D. in philosophy. Queen's Quarterly 8: 73–75, 1900/1901.

— Thirty years in the history of Queen's University. Queen's Quarterly 10: 188–196, 1902/1903.

Watson, John, N   F   Dupuis and James Cappon.
Some considerations on Queen's position. Queen's Quarterly 17: 154–157, 1909/1910.

Wehlau, William.
New observatory of the University of Western Ontario. Journal of the Royal Astronomical Society of Canada 64: 1–4, 1970.

— New University of Western Ontario observatory opened. Journal of the Royal Astronomical Society of Canada 63: 318–319, 1969.

Weisdorf, Irving.
Game and government: university revisited. Canadian Forum 47: 272–276, 1968.
Rochdale College.

Wells, E   P
McMaster University. Canadian Magazine of Politics, Science, Art and Literature 3: 309–316, 1894.

White, S   J
University of Toronto exhibition architecture and you. Royal Architectural Institute of Canada. Journal 25: 152–157, 1948.

Whitney Hall, University of Toronto. Royal Architectural Institute of Canada. Journal 8: 115–120, 1932.

William Nichol. Canadian Mining Journal 45: 235, 1924.

Williams, D   C
The nature of the contemporary university. Association of Universities and Colleges of Canada. Proceedings, 104–111, 1968.

Wilson, G   E
Robert MacGregor Dawson, 1895–1958. Canadian Journal of Economics and Political Science 25: 210–213, 1959.

Wilson, R   A
    John Macnaughton: humanist. Queen's Quarterly 54: 84–89, 1947.
Wilson, R   F
    Legal education in Ontario. Canadian Bar Review 13: 366–370, 1935.
Winter, F   E
    Reform of university government at the University of Toronto. CAUT
    Bulletin 18(3): 16–24, 1970.
Woodhead, W   D
    John Macnaughton. Queen's Quarterly 50: 165–173, 1943.
The work of the Kingston School of Mining. Canadian Mining Journal 30:
    26–27, 1909.
Wright, A   H
    The medical schools of Toronto. Canadian Medical Association. Journal 18:
    616–620, 1928.
Wright, C   A
    The outlook for Ontario legal education. University of Toronto Law Journal
    12: 282–285, 1958.
Wright, C   H   C
    The University of Toronto. Royal Architectural Institute of Canada.
    Journal 2: 5–24, 1925.
Wright, Mary J
    Psychology at Western. Canadian Psychologist 4A: 15–18, 1963.
York University, Toronto. Royal Architectural Institute of Canada. Journal
    41(no. 7): 56–60, 1964.
Young, A   H
    Canadian celebrities; no. XV – the Reverend T.C.S. Macklem, M.A., LL.D.
    Canadian Magazine of Politics, Science, Art and Literature 15: 224–226,
    1900.
— Trinity University, Toronto. Canadian Magazine of Politics, Science, Art
    and Literature 7: 395–405, 1897.
Young, R   K
    The David Dunlap Observatory. Journal of the Royal Astronomical Society
    of Canada 29: 299–308, plates X–XVII, 1935.
— The David Dunlap Observatory. University of Toronto Quarterly 4:
    327–336, 1935.
— The 74-inch telescope of the David Dunlap Observatory. Journal of the
    Royal Astronomical Society of Canada 28: 97–119, 1934.
Younkie, Grace W
    School of Architectural Draughting opens in Toronto. Royal Architectural
    Institute of Canada. Journal 25: 428, 432, 1948.
Zavitz, C   A
    The Experimental Department of the Ontario Agricultural College. Ontario
    Agricultural College Review 5(3): 16–17, 1893.
— History and development of O.A.C. Ontario Agricultural College Review
    34(1): 1–8, 1921.

Theses

Appleyard, Reginald Thomas Peel.
The origins of Huron College in relation to the religious questions of the period. London, Ontario: 1937.
192 leaves.
M.A. thesis, The University of Western Ontario. OLU

Bachor, Patricia Angelica C 1949–
The interaction of learner characteristics and degree of learner control in CAI. [Toronto] c1976.
186 leaves. tables, figs.
Ph.D. thesis, University of Toronto. OTU

Barron, Marion, 1914–
Possible consequences for diploma nursing education in Ontario as a subsystem of colleges of applied arts and technology. Washington, D.C.: 1972.
viii, 103 leaves.
Ph.D. thesis, Catholic University of America (microfilm 72-21,563). DA

Bhatt, Perviz.
A study of the admissions' criteria of the School of Social Work, University of Toronto. [Toronto] 1957.
v, 90 leaves.
M.S.W. thesis, University of Toronto. OTU

Blais, Gérald.
Le Collège du Sacré Coeur, Sudbury, Ontario. Ottawa: 1968.
ix, 89 leaves.
M.A. thesis, Université d'Ottawa. OTER

Bowker, Alan Franklin, 1943–
Truly useful men: Maurice Hutton, George Wrong, James Mavor and the University of Toronto, 1880–1927. [Toronto] c1975.
ix, 457 leaves.
Ph.D. thesis, University of Toronto. OTU

Boyd, Marcia Ann, 1945–
Graduate dental education in Canada. Vancouver, British Columbia: 1974.
xi, 97 leaves. illus.
M.A. thesis, University of British Columbia (microfilm 19501). Can

Brehaut, Willard, 1928–
A quarter century of educational research in Canada: an analysis of dissertations (English) in education accepted by Canadian universities, 1930–1955. [Toronto] 1958.
xvii, 283 leaves.
Ed.D. thesis, University of Toronto. OTU

Cameron, Donald Alan, 1927–
An examination of social service programs in Ontario community colleges with special reference to field instruction. [Toronto] c1975.
vii, 302, A61 leaves. tables, charts.
D.S.W. thesis, University of Toronto (microfiche 31178). OTU

Casswell, Beverley Lois, 1939–
    Methodology for determining professional development needs of teachers for
    curriculum planning in diploma nursing education. [Toronto] c1974.
    vii, 133 leaves. tables, figs.
    M.A. thesis, University of Toronto.   OTU
Cheng, Chung-Sing, 1920–
    The main factors that led to the establishment of the University of Ottawa
    Teachers' College. Ottawa: 1960.
    xi, 245 leaves. tables.
    Ph.D. thesis, University of Ottawa.   OOU
Corbeil, Clement Pierre, 1947–
    Robert Falconer, philosopher of empire. [Toronto] c1969.
    52 leaves.
    M.A. thesis, University of Toronto (awarded 1970).   OTU
Crompton, Gordon Roland, 1948–
    A follow-up study of the graduates of the School of Social Work of the
    University of Windsor, by Gordon R. Crompton and Terrence Wm. Monk.
    Windsor, Ontario: 1974.
    iv, 131 leaves. tables.
    M.S.W. thesis, University of Windsor (microfilm 23873).   OWA
Daniel, Juri Vrezesnevski, 1923–
    Differentiated roles and faculty job satisfaction in departments of physical
    education and athletics in Ontario universities. Urbana, Illinois: 1971.
    v, 251 leaves. illus.
    Ph.D. thesis, University of Illinois at Urbana – Champaign (microfilm 72-
    12,129).   DA
Davis, Ruth Helen.
    The beginnings and developments of the University of Western Ontario
    1878–1924. [London, Ontario] 1925.
    150, xliii leaves. facsims.
    M.A. thesis, The University of Western Ontario.   OLU
Day, Georgia Marie Pippy.
    A history of secondary school teacher training at the Ontario College of
    Education. [Toronto: 1954]
    268 [1] leaves.
    M.A. thesis, University of Toronto.   OTU
Desroches, Jocelyn Jean-Yves, 1942–
    The concept and determinants of job satisfaction: an exploratory study in
    the colleges of applied arts and technology in Ontario. [Toronto] c1976.
    xvii, 379 leaves. tables, figs.
    Ph.D. thesis, University of Toronto.   OTU
Dhillon, Pritam Singh, 1923–
    The educational thought of J.G. Althouse. [Toronto] c1969.
    [iii] 265 leaves.
    Ed.D. thesis, University of Toronto.   OTU

Drache, Daniel Aaron, 1941–
    The ideology and reform and the Canadian university: a study in the
    structure of power in the Faculty of Arts and Science, the University of
    Toronto 1969. Kingston, Ontario: c1971.
    iv, 210 leaves.
    M.A. thesis, Queen's University (microfilm 9156). OKQ
Drake, David A
    Some factors affecting the withdrawal patterns of part time special students
    at Carleton University. Guelph, Ontario: 1973.
    viii, 93 leaves. illus.
    M.Sc. thesis, University of Guelph (microfilm 17981). OGU
Ford, Barbara Cecile, 1937–
    Factors involved in the reading ability of students in Ontario colleges of
    applied arts and technology. [Toronto] c1972.
    xi, 258 leaves. tables.
    Ph.D. thesis, University of Toronto (microfilm 14687). OTU
Godfrey, Charles Morris, 1917–
    The evolution of medical education in Ontario. [Toronto: 1974]
    vi, 235 leaves. illus., facsim.
    M.A. thesis, University of Toronto. OTU
Goss, Anthony John, 1937–
    The effectiveness of the colleges of applied arts and technology of Ontario.
    Buffalo, New York: 1972.
    1 v. (various pagings). illus.
    Ph.D. thesis, State University of New York at Buffalo (microfilm 73-5110).
                                                                          DA
Griffin, Amy Elizabeth.
    The improvement of the educational preparation of instructors in preservice
    programs in nursing in Ontario. New York: 1963.
    378 leaves.
    Ed.D. thesis, Columbia University (microfilm 64-08233). DA
Hamilton, Robert.
    The founding of McMaster University. [Hamilton, Ontario] 1938.
    1 v. (various pagings).
    B.D. thesis, McMaster University. OHM
Hitchman, Gladys Symons.
    The professional socialization of women and men in two Canadian graduate
    schools. Toronto: 1976.
    xix, 346 leaves. tables.
    Ph.D. thesis, York University (microfilm 26639).
    Toronto and York. OTY
Hodgins, Thomas Arnold, 1929–
    University education for elementary school teachers of Ontario, 1950–1970;
    a case study. Syracuse, New York: 1971.
    x, 431 leaves. illus., map.
    Ph.D. thesis, Syracuse University (microfilm 72-11845). DA

Hoichberg, Samuel W
    A study of relationships between a student's Ontario high school background
    and performance in the diploma course in agriculture at the Ontario
    Agricultural College, University of Guelph. [Guelph, Ontario] 1968.
    viii, 75 leaves. tables.
    M.Sc. thesis, The University of Guelph.   OGU
Hughes, Norah L
    A history of the development of ministerial education in Canada from its
    inception until 1925 in those churches which were tributary to the United
    Church of Canada in Ontario, Quebec and the Maritime provinces of
    Canada. Chicago: 1945.
    263 p.
    Ph.D. thesis: The University of Chicago.   DA
Hyman, Charles.
    An analysis of factors associated with variations in Canadian university
    operating expenditures in the decade 1960/61 to 1969/70. Edmonton,
    Alberta: 1972.
    xvii, 212 leaves.
    Ph.D. thesis, University of Alberta (microfilm 13419).   Can
— Federal aid to higher education with particular reference to universities in
    the period 1951–1967. Montreal: 1968.
    ix, 133 leaves.
    M.A. thesis, McGill University (microfilm).   QMM OTER
Karr, W   J
    The training of teachers in Ontario. Ottawa, Ontario: 1916.
    112 pages.
    D.Paed. thesis, Queen's University.   OKQ
Keddy, John Arthur.
    Selection of candidates for entrance to the Ontario College of Education.
    [Toronto] 1950.
    v, 183 leaves.
    D.Paed. thesis, University of Toronto.   OTU
Kefentse, Netto Akono, 1944–
    Universities and labour education in Ontario: a study into the politics of
    cooperation between unions and universities. [Toronto] c1975.
    ix, 194 leaves. tables, fig.
    M.A. thesis, University of Toronto (accepted 1976).   OTU
Kelly, Desmond Aylmer Gratten, 1920–
    A study of the student population at an Ontario college of applied arts and
    technology between 1967 and 1969 with an analysis of factors relating to
    academic success. [Toronto] c1970.
    vii, 205 leaves. tables, forms.
    Ed.D. thesis, University of Toronto.   OTU
Keyes, Mary Elizabeth, 1940–
    John Howard Crocker, LL.D. London, Ontario: 1964.
    viii, 163 leaves. illus., port.
    M.A. thesis, The University of Western Ontario.   OLU

Lafleur, Guy, 1942–
Griefs et movements sociaux; approche sociologique du malaise étudients à l'Université d'Ottawa. Ottawa: 1971, c1972.
xvii, 107 feuilles.
M.A. thesis, Université d'Ottawa. OOU

Laing, Martha Carol, 1946–
French in business education. [Toronto] c1975.
iii, 156 leaves. tables.
M.A. thesis, University of Toronto. OTU

Lawr, Douglas Archie, 1938–
Development of agricultural education in Ontario, 1870–1910. [Toronto] c1972.
263 leaves.
Ph.D. thesis, University of Toronto (microfilm 13789). OTU

Lewis, William H
Pharmaceutical education in Ontario 1867–1900. Toronto: 1953.
60 leaves.
B.Sc.Phm. thesis, University of Toronto. OTU

Long, John Clifford N
An historical study of the establishment of college systems in Ontario and Alberta in the 1960's. Calgary, Alberta: 1972.
x, 176 leaves. illus.
M.Ed. thesis, University of Calgary (microfilm 13898). Can

Louis, Cecil Alver, 1939–
The University of Toronto's student housing in Metropolitan Toronto. [Toronto] 1964.
v, 63 leaves. illus., 4 fold. maps.
B.A. thesis, University of Toronto. OTU

Lynch, Timothy, 1944–
The education and utilization of technologists in diagnostic radiology: a study of allied health education in Ontario. [Toronto] c1975.
1 v. (various pagings).
M.Sc. thesis, University of Toronto. OTU

Macfarlane, Gertrude Cécile.
Certain factors affecting mobility and the relationship between spatial and social mobility of university faculty, particularly scientists – Ontario, 1967–1968. Lansing, Michigan: 1969.
199 p.
Ph.D. thesis, Michigan State University (microfilm 70-16075). DA

McHoull, W Donald.
The founding and early history of Queen's University. [Kingston, Ontario] 1935.
xii, 228 leaves.
M.A. thesis, Queen's University. OKQ

Mackenzie, Ken L
    Harold A. Innis; a study of creative intellect. Vancouver, British Columbia:
    1971.
    v, 103 leaves.
    M.A. thesis, Simon Fraser University (microfilm 8768).   Can
McMackin, Paul Francis, 1945–
    A study in occupational mobility determinants of "Atkinson Engineering
    Graduates" from engineering to secondary school teaching in Ontario.
    [Toronto] c1975.
    iv, 66 leaves. tables.
    M.A. thesis, University of Toronto.   OTU
McNab, G   G
    The development of higher education in Ontario. [Kingston, Ontario: 1924]
    242 leaves.
    D.Paed. thesis, Queen's University.   OKQ
Maddocks, G   R
    A comparative analysis of approaches to planning development in post-
    secondary education. Edmonton, 1972.
    x, 210 leaves.
    Ph.D. thesis, University of Alberta.
    Ontario and Alberta studied.   AEU OTER
Madill, Alonzo J
    History of agricultural education in Ontario. Toronto: University of Toronto
    Press, 1930.
    264 p. tables.
    D.Paed. thesis, University of Toronto.   OTU
Marett, Clara M
    The Ontario Agricultural College (1874–1974): some developments in
    scientific agriculture. [Guelph, Ontario] 1975.
    v, 145 leaves.
    M.A. thesis, The University of Guelph (microfilm 22712).   OGU
Massot, Alain.
    Dimensions de l'assimilation des étudiants francophones à l'Université
    d'Ottawa. Ottawa: 1973.
    xxi, 232 feuilles. carte.
    M.A. thesis, Université d'Ottawa.   OOU
Meikle, William Duncan.
    The University of Toronto and the threatened dismissal of Professor Frank
    Underhill, 1940-41. [Ottawa] 1967.
    iii, 48 leaves.
    M.A. research essay, Carleton University.   OOCC
Melamed, Miriam.
    The history of the undergraduate department in the geography department
    inside the University of Toronto. [Toronto] 1976.
    35 leaves. illus.
    B.A. thesis, University of Toronto, Innis College.   OTU

Nicholson, Murdo Duncan.
    A study of Queen's commerce graduates 1921–1952. Kingston, Ontario
    [c1954]
    xi, 51 p. tables.
    B.Com. thesis, Queen's University.   OKQ
Nicholson, Norman L   1919–
    The evolution of graduate studies in the universities of Ontario, 1841–1971.
    [Toronto] c1975.
    ix, 377 leaves. tables (part fold.), figs.
    Ed.D. thesis, University of Toronto.   OTU
O'Bryan, Maureen Hazel, 1939–
    Physical education: a study of professional education in Ontario universities.
    [Toronto] c1973.
    324 leaves. tables, figs.
    Ph.D. thesis, University of Toronto (microfilm 21674).   OTU
O'Malley, Denis Anthony.
    The market for higher degree holders and the graduate education system in
    Canada. Edmonton, Alberta, 1975.
    xv, 219 leaves.
    Ph.D. thesis, University of Alberta.   AEU
Pal, Leslie Alexander, 1954–
    Scholarship and politics in the later writings of Harold Innis. Kingston,
    Ontario: 1976.
    183 leaves.
    M.A. thesis, Queen's University (microfilm 30196).   Can
Pelaia, Sebastian.
    University of Toronto's (St. George Campus) Faculty of Arts and Science,
    who attends and why. [Toronto] 1976.
    79 leaves. tables, figs.
    B.A. thesis, University of Toronto.   OTU
Perticaro, Barbara Fletcher.
    The relative statuses of academic men and women at York University .
    Toronto: 1975.
    xii, 95 [23] leaves. tables.
    M.A. thesis, York University (microfilm 23572).   OTY
Poulin, Gilles.
    L'Origine geographique des étudiants de l'Université d'Ottawa. Ottawa:
    1971.
    ix, 135 feuilles. cartes.
    M.A. thesis, Université d'Ottawa.   OOU
Prakash, Brahm, 1944–
    The demand for and financing of higher education in Canada. [Toronto]
    c1976.
    1 v. (various pagings).
    Ph.D. thesis, University of Toronto.   OTU

Quarter, Jack Joel, 1941–
    The student movement of the 1960's: a social–psychological analysis.
    [Toronto] c1970.
    [17] 221 leaves. illus.
    Ph.D. thesis, University of Toronto (microfilm 9562).   OTU
Robert, Bernard.
    Une étude de certaines caractéristiques des diplomes de l'école de
    Bibliothécairee de l'Université d'Ottawa pour les annes 1942–64. Ottawa:
    1967.
    xiii, 93 feuilles.
    M.Bibl. thesis, Université d'Ottawa.   OOU
Ross, Peter Noble, 1935–
    The origins and development of the Ph.D. degree at the University of
    Toronto, 1871–1932. [Toronto] c1972.
    xii, 381 leaves.
    Ed.D. thesis, University of Toronto.   OTU
Schram, James Galbraith.
    A method for assessing the cost-effectiveness of television and conventional
    instruction within the context of the university. Kingston, Ontario: 1971,
    c1972.
    v, 124 leaves. tables, figs.
    M.A. thesis, Queen's University.   OKQ
Shaw, Ernest Comfort.
    An analytical study of the correspondence courses conducted by the Ontario
    Agricultural College, Guelph, Ontario. [Toronto] 1964.
    1 v. (various pagings). diagrs.
    M.S.A. thesis, University of Toronto.   OTU
Smyth, Delmar McCormack, 1922–
    Some aspects of the development of Ontario colleges of applied arts and
    technology. [Toronto] c1970.
    391 leaves. tables, facsim.
    Phil.M. thesis, University of Toronto.   OTU
— Structures for university government to the beginning of the twentieth
    century with particular reference to American, British and Canadian
    institutions. [Toronto] c1972.
    651 leaves.
    Ph.D. thesis, University of Toronto (microfilm 17287).   OTU
Spencer, Leona Elizabeth, 1936–
    Mathematics in higher education: a history of the evolution of the
    mathematics curriculum at Queen's University and the University of
    Toronto 1840–1970. Kingston, Ontario: 1972 [c1973]
    ix, 200 leaves. tables, charts (part fold.).
    M.A. thesis, Queen's University. (accepted 1973) (microfilm 13042).   OKQ
Stager, David Arnold Albert, 1937–
    Monetary returns to post-secondary education in Ontario. Princeton, New
    Jersey: 1968, c1969.
    viii, 259 leaves. illus.
    Ph.D. thesis, Princeton University (microfilm 69-02783).   DA

Stewart, Edward Emslie, 1930–
   The role of the provincial government in the development of the universities
   of Ontario, 1791–1964. [Toronto] c1970.
   ii, 575 leaves.
   Ed.D. thesis, University of Toronto.   OTU
Swartz, Sydney Gary.
   Pharmaceutical education in Ontario 1900–1950. [Toronto] 1955.
   i, 57 leaves.
   B.Sc.Phm. thesis, University of Toronto.   OTU
Syposz, Dorothy Maisie, 1933–
   Trends for diploma programs in nursing in Ontario as reflected by the
   nursing literature and the opinions of selected nurse educators . [Toronto]
   c1971.
   viii, 203 leaves. tables.
   M.A. thesis, University of Toronto.   OTU
Teasdale, Elinor Constance.
   A study of graduates of the University of Toronto School of Social Work.
   [Toronto] 1950.
   viii, 133 leaves. tables, forms.
   M.S.W. thesis, University of Toronto.   OTU
Thompson, Nancy Ramsay, 1935–
   The controversy over the admission of women to University College,
   University of Toronto. [Toronto] c1974.
   144 leaves.
   M.A. thesis, University of Toronto.   OTU
Tough, Allen MacNeill.
   The development of adult education at the University of Toronto before
   1920. [Toronto] 1962.
   168 leaves.
   M.A. thesis, University of Toronto.   OTU
Valdés, Maria-Elena, 1934–
   A conceptual analysis of the domain of Spanish studies and its application in
   the curriculum of university education in Ontario. [Toronto] c1976.
   viii, 340 leaves. tables, figs.
   Ph.D. thesis, University of Toronto.   OTU
Vernon, Foster.
   The development of adult education in Ontario, 1790–1900. [Toronto]
   c1969.
   xi, 571 leaves. tables, figs.
   Ed.D. thesis, University of Toronto (microfilm 16136).   OTU
Ward, Muriel Alma, 1925–
   Some factors related to the mobility of teachers in diploma schools of nursing
   in the province of Ontario. [Toronto] c1970.
   iv, 48 leaves.
   M.Ed. thesis, University of Toronto.   OTU

Wasteneys; Hortense Catherine Fardel, 1925–
  A history of the University Settlement of Toronto, 1910–1958: an
  exploration of the social objectives of the University Settlement and of their
  implementation. [Toronto] c1975.
  iv, 345 leaves. illus., maps.
  D.S.W. thesis, University of Toronto (microfiche 31363).   OTU
Williams, Stephen Alfred, 1946–
  A study of the forestry education potential of a property in the Muskoka
  district, Ontario. [Toronto] c1972.
  1 v. (various pagings). tables, facsim., maps, col. photos.
  M.Sc.F. thesis, University of Toronto.   OTU
Woods, Mary Jean, 1944–
  An analysis of home economics programs in Ontario universities based on
  the development of four theoretical patterns. [Toronto] c1972.
  viii, 169 leaves. tables, figs.
  M.A. thesis, University of Toronto.   OTU
Zaharchuk, Ted Michael, 1942–
  Some aspects of planning for post-secondary vocational institutions: a case
  study, The Ryerson Polytechnical Institute. [Toronto] c1971.
  xi, 289 leaves. tables, figs.
  Ph.D. thesis, University of Toronto (microfilm 12242).   OTU

RELIGIOUS INSTITUTIONS

Bibliography
Hanrahan, James.
  A current bibliography of Canadian church history. Canadian Catholic
  Historical Association. Report 37: 101–126, 1970; 38: 71–97, 1971; 39:
  83–104, 1972; 40: 60–93, 1973.
Hanrahan, James and Brian F   Hogan.
  A current bibliography of Canadian church history. Canadian Catholic
  Historical Association. Report 42: 111–141, 1975.
Hogan, Brian F
  A current bibliography of Canadian church history. Canadian Catholic
  Historical Association. Report 43: 91–119, 1976.
Lucas, Glenn.
  Canadian Protestant church history to 1973. United Church of Canada.
  Committee on Archives. Bulletin 23: 5–50, 1974.
Sheehan, Michael M
  A current bibliography of Canadian church history. Canadian Catholic
  Historical Association. Report 31: 51–72, 1964; 32: 81–99, 1965; 33: 51–67,
  1966; 34: 77–93, 1967; 35: 117–135, 1968; 36: 79–101, 1969.

Monographs and Pamphlets

Alexis de Barbezieux, Father, 1854–1941.
  Histoire de la province ecclesiastique d'Ottawa et de la colonisation dans la
  vallee de l'Ottawa. Ottawa: Cie d'imprimerie d'Ottawa, 1897.
    2 v. illus., ports., fold. map.   OTU
Anderson, Allan James.
  The Anglican churches of Kingston. Kingston, Ontario [Diocese of Ontario
  Office] 1963.
    110 p. illus.   OTU
Anglican Church of Canada. Dioceses. Algoma.
  Algoma 100, 1873–1973: a documentary commemorating the centennial of
  the Diocese of Algoma. [Sault Ste. Marie, Ontario: The Diocese] c1973.
    163 p. illus.   OTU
— Centennial commemoration on hundred years of the Church of England in
  Sault Ste. Marie, Ontario 1832–1932. [Soo, Ontario: Cliffe Ptg. Co. Ltd.]
  1932.
    52 p. illus., port.   OTU
Anglican Church of Canada. Dioceses. Niagara.
  The history of the Diocese of Niagara to 1950 A.D. Published on the
  occasion of the 75th anniversary of the creation of the Diocese of Niagara in
  1875. Hamilton, Ontario: 1950.
    98 p. illus., facsims., map, ports.   OTAR
Anglican Church of Canada. Dioceses. Toronto.
  Jubilee of the Diocese of Toronto, 1830–1889. Record of proceedings
  connected with the celebration of the jubilee November 21st to the 28th,
  1889, inclusive. [Edited by] Henry Scadding and J. George Hodgins.
  Toronto: Rowsell & Hutchison, 1890.
    223 p.   OTU OTER
Anglican Church of Canada. Dioceses. Toronto. Woman's Auxiliary.
  These fifty years, 1886–1936. Woman's Auxiliary to the Missionary Society
  of the Church of England in Canada, and to Diocesan Missions. [Toronto]
  Toronto Diocesan Board [1936?]
    163 p. plates (encl. ports.).   OTU
Anglican churches, Elgin county. n.p. [1975?]
    [79] leaves. illus., ports.   OTAR
Anglican Women's Training College.
  The story of A.W.T.C. diamond jubilee [1893–1953. Toronto: Southam Press,
  1953?]
    47 p. illus., ports.   OTAR
The Archdiocese of Toronto and Archbishop Walsh. With introduction by His
  Grace the Archbishop. Jubilee volume 1842–1892. Toronto: George T.
  Dixon, 1892.
    15, xxx, 365 p. illus., ports.   OTU OTREC
Bailey, Thomas Melville, 1912–
  The Covenant in Canada: four hundred years of history of the Presbyterian
  Church in Canada. Hamilton, Ontario: The MacNab Circle, 1975.
    160 p. chiefly illus.   OTU

Balfour, Charles Wilfred.
Life and work and memoirs of George Thorneloe, Bishop of the Diocese of
Algoma (1897–1927), Metropolitan of Ontario and Archbishop of Ontario
(1915–1926). [Peterborough, Ontario: 1955]
112 p. illus., port. OTU
Baptist churches, Elgin county. n.p. [1975?]
[65] leaves. OTAR
Baptist Convention of Ontario and Quebec.
The Baptist year book historical number for Ontario, Quebec, Manitoba
and the North-West Territories and British Columbia, containing carefully
compiled information. [St. George, Ontario] 1900.
402 p. illus., ports. OLU
Bethune, Alexander Neil, 1800–1879.
Memoir of the Right Reverend John Strachan, first Bishop of Toronto.
Toronto: Henry Rowsell, 1870.
viii, 385 p. port. OKQ
B'nai B'rith. District no. 22. Grand Lodge.
History of the B'nai B'rith in eastern Canada. [Editor: Abel Selick, et al. 1st
ed. Toronto: c1964]
vii, 118 p. illus., map, ports. OTU
Boorman, Sylvia, 1923–
John Toronto: a biography of Bishop Strachan. Toronto: Clarke, Irwin &
Company Limited, 1969.
222 p. OKQ OTU
Brault, Lucien, 1904–
Sainte-Anne d'Ottawa: cent ans d'histoire, 1873-1973. [Ottawa: Imprimerie
Beauregard, 1973?]
80 p. illus., port. facsim. OTU
Brighty, Isabel McComb.
The Diamond Jubilee history of the Protestant Home of St. Catharines,
1874–1934: an historical sketch and record. St. Catharines, Ontario: 1934.
77 p. illus., ports. OTAR
Brown, Enid Essie (Hanes), 1887–
Stephenson township: its founders and early church life, 1868–1957, by Mrs.
Enid Brown (formerly Enid Hanes). [Utterson, Ontario] Women's
Association of Utterson United Church, 1958.
32 p. OTAR
Bull, William Perkins, 1870–1948.
From Macdonell to McGuigan: the history of the growth of the Roman
Catholic Church in Upper Canada. Toronto: Perkins Bull Foundation
[c1939]
501 p. illus., facsims., fold. maps, plan., plates, ports. OTSTM
— Spadunk: or, From paganism to Davenport United; a study of community
development, of the religious life around which it centered, and of the
pioneer personalities which gave shape to both. Toronto: Perkins Bull
Foundation, G.J. McLeod Ltd. [c1935]
467 p. illus., ports. (The Perkins Bull historical series). OTU

Burden, H   N
    Manitoulin; or, Five years of church work among Ojibway Indians and
    lumbermen, resident upon that Island or in its vicinity. London: Simpkin
    Marshall, Hamilton, Kent & Co., Ltd., 1895.
    164, v p. illus.   OKQ
Buskin, George.
    More than forty years in gospel harness: a tale of truth designed to profit the
    readers, young and old. [Berlin, Ontario] International Evangelical and
    Colportage Mission of Algoma and the Northwest, 1898.
    175 p. illus.
    Covers the years 1854–1899.
    The publication date is 1898, however concluding remarks are dated March
    1899.   OLU
Carrington, Philip, abp. 1892–
    The Anglican Church in Canada: a history. Toronto: Collins, 1963.
    320 p. illus., ports, maps.   OTAR
Catholic Church. Diocese of Toronto. Pastoral Research Committee.
    How Toronto Catholics see their church; a brief survey. [Toronto] 1972.
    1 v. (various pagings).   OTE
Champion, Thomas Edward, 1843–1910 (ed.).
    The Methodist Church of Toronto: a history of the Methodist denomination
    and its churches in York and Toronto, with biographical sketches of many of
    the clergy and laity. Toronto: G.M. Rose & Sons, 1899.
    388 p. plates.   OTU
Crowfoot, Alfred Henchman, 1881–1962.
    Benjamin Cronyn, first Bishop of Huron. [London, Ontario] Incorporated
    Synod of the Diocese of Huron, 1957.
    142 p. illus., map.   OKQ
— This dreamer: life of Isaac Hellmuth, second Bishop of Huron. Toronto:
    Copp Clark Publishing Co. Limited [c1963]
    ix, 86 p.   OTU
Crysdale, Robert Cecil Stewart, 1914–
    Religion in Canadian society, edited by Stewart Crysdale and Les
    Wheatcroft. [Toronto] Macmillan of Canada [c1976]
    xi, 498 p. tables.
    Ontario: pp. 113–126, 434–447.   OTU
Diamond Jubilee, St. Joseph's Convent, Toronto. In commemoration of the
    seventy-fifth anniversary of the coming of the Sisters of St. Joseph to
    Toronto, Canada. [Toronto: Brigdens Limited, 1926?]
    26 p. illus.   OTSTM
Edwards, Mary Elizabeth Currie.
    The Bronson home 1930–1965: a home for aged Protestant women. n.p.
    [1965]
    41 p. illus.   OTU

Falconer, R   H
>   The church in politics in Ontario. An address delivered before the annual
>   convention of the Canadian Secular Union, Sept. 9, 1894. Toronto: Printed
>   by C.M. Ellis & Co., 1894.
>   8 p.   OOA

Flint, David Moore, 1938–
>   John Strachan: pastor and politician. Toronto: Oxford University Press,
>   1971.
>   160 p. illus., ports. (Canadian lives).   OTU

Flynn, Louis J   1902–
>   Built on a rock: the story of the Roman Catholic Church in Kingston
>   1826–1976. Kingston, Ontario: Archdiocese of Kingston, 1976.
>   xviii, 409 p. illus., port.   OTU

Foisy, J   Albert, 1887–
>   Le Catholicisme en Ontario. Quelques statistiques. Preface par M. Phillippe
>   Landry. Ottawa: Imprimerie "Le Droit", 1918.
>   58 p. tables.   OKQ

Forsyth, Alex E
>   Reminiscences of the past and present of the early formation of the
>   Methodist Church in eastern Ontario. Cornwall, Ontario: The Standard
>   Printing House, 1907.
>   56 p. illus., ports.   OTAR

Fuller, Peter, 1826–1890.
>   Diary, 1826–1890. Edited by F. Stanley Knight. [Meaford, Ontario: Knight
>   Press, c1959]
>   34 p. port.
>   Chiefly Church of England history.   OTU

Geddes, Hilda.
>   Historical sketch of McDonald's Corners, Snow Road and Elphin. Snow
>   Road, Ontario: The Author, 1975.
>   iii, 62 p. illus., ports.
>   "The centenary of the Presbyterian Church in Canada, 1875–1975.   OONL

Gordon, Charles William, 1860–1937.
>   The life of James Robertson. Toronto: The Westminster Company Limited,
>   1909.
>   xi, 427 p. port.   OMI

Grant, Angus Murray.
>   From log school to United Church; from Brewster to Grand Bend. [London,
>   Ontario: c1965]
>   27 p. illus., ports.   OTU

Grant, John Webster, 1919–
>   The church in the Canadian era. The first century of confederation.
>   Toronto: McGraw–Hill, Ryerson, 1972.
>   xi, 241 p.   OTU

Green, Anson, 1801–1879.
  Life and times of the Rev. Anson Green, written by himself at the request of
  the Toronto Conference... With an introduction by S.S. Nelles. Toronto:
  Methodist Book Room, 1877.
  xix, 448 p. front.   OKQ
Green, Eda.
  Pioneer work in Algoma. Westminster: Society for the Propagation of the
  Gospel in Foreign Parts, 1915.
  viii, 93 p. front., plates.   OTAR
Hanrahan, James.
  The Basilian Fathers (1822–1972): a documentary study of one hundred and
  fifty years of the history of the Congregation of Priests of St. Basil. Toronto:
  The Basilian Press, 1973.
  vii, 263 p.   OONL
Harris, William Richard, 1847–1923.
  The Catholic Church in the Niagara Peninsula, 1626–1895. Toronto:
  William Briggs, 1895.
  352 p. illus., port., plates.   OTU
Henderson, John Lanceley Hodge, 1917–1973.
  John Strachan, 1778–1867. [Toronto] University of Toronto Press [c1969]
  vi, 112 p. (Canadian biographical studies, 1).   OTU
Hodgins, Bruce Willard, 1931–
  Paradis of Temagami: the story of Charles Paradis, 1848–1926, northern
  priest, colonizer and rebel. Cobalt, Ontario: Highway Book Shop, 1976.
  46 p. illus., facsims, map.   OOU
Hughes, James Laughlin, 1846–1935.
  Sketches of the Sharon Temple and of its founder David Willson. Toronto:
  The York Pioneer and Historical Society [1918?]
  16 p. illus., port.   OTURS
Hunt, Thomas J
  The story of Cormac and its Shrine of St. Ann. Toronto: Mission Press
  [1954]
  86 p. illus., ports.   OTU
Huron (Diocese).
  Constitution rules and canons of the Incorporated Synod of the Diocese of
  Huron, as well as those of the Provincial Synod, and Statutes of Parliament
  affecting ecclesiastical rights. London, Ontario: Herald Steam Printing
  Establishment, 1879.
  191 p.   OTURS
— A jubilee memorial: the story of the church and first fifty years of the Diocese
  of Huron 1857–1907. London, Ontario: The London Printing and
  Lithographing Company, Limited [1907]
  122 p. illus., ports.   OLU
Jefferson, Robert, bp. of Ottawa, 1881–
  Faith of our fathers; the story of the Diocese of Ottawa; about the building of

the diocese by Robert Jefferson, and about the people and their churches by
Leonard J. Johnson. Ottawa: Anglican Book Society [c1957]
230 p. illus., ports., facsims, map.
"Including the deaneries of Arnprior, Carleton, Lanark, Pembroke, Prescott,
Russell and Stormont."   OTU OOC
Johnston, John A
  Through the years with Ontario PYPS. [Toronto: Presbyterian Church in
  Canada, 1952?]
  26 p.   OTU
  A jubilee retrospect. Address delivered on the completion of fifty years of the
  ministry of Rev. John Wakefield, (1852–1902) with introductory sketch by
  Rev. E.B. Ryckman. Toronto: William Briggs, 1902.
  158 p.
  Methodism in Ontario in the 19th century.   OTU
Kalman, Harold David, 1943–
  Pioneer churches. Photos by John deVisser. [Toronto] McClelland &
  Stewart, 1976.
  192 p. illus. (part col.).   OOA
Kell, John Ambrose Campbell, 1897–
  Church life in Grey county: an historical supplement to "History of Grey
  county, 1972." [Owen Sound] Grey County Historical Society, 1972.
  26 p. map.   OONL
Kilbourn, William Morley, 1926–   (ed.).
  Religion in Canada: the spiritual development of a nation. [Toronto:
  McClelland & Stewart, 1974 c1968]
  128 p. illus. (part col.).   OTU
Lamb, Silas Horald, 1888–
  Profile. Hamilton, Ontario: The Author, 1973.
  ii, 139 p. illus., facsim., ports., tables.
  "The Baptist pastorate in Ontario."   OTAR
Lane, Grace H
  Brief halt at mile "50": a half century of church union. Toronto: United
  Church Publishing House, 1974.
  vii, 119 p. illus. (part col.).   OLU
Leckie, E   P
  The parish of Elmvale. n.p. [1963?]
  1 v. (various pagings).   OMI
Legros, Hector.
  Le diocese d'Ottawa, 1847–1948. [Ottawa: Le Droit Press, 1949]
  905 p. illus. (part fold.), ports (part fold.), fold. maps.   OTU
Lesage, Germain, 1915–
  L'évêque errant [Mgr. Ovide Charlebois] Ottawa: Les Editions de
  l'Université d'Ottawa, 1950.
  193 p. illus., ports, map.   OTU

Lewis, (Mrs.) J   T
    The life of John Travers Lewis. With a foreword by Sir Gilbert Parker.
    London: Skeffington & Son, Ltd. [19—]
    xix, 160 p. illus., ports.
    First Archbishop of Ontario.   OTAR
Liederbach, Clarence A
    Canada's Bishops: from 1120 to 1975: from Allen to Yelle. Preface by Most
    Reverend Philip Pocock. Cleveland, Ohio: Dillon/Liederbach Inc. [c1975]
    64 p.   OONL
London, Ontario (Diocese). French-Canadian priests.
    Cause des curés dénoncés, diffamés , ou suspendus ab officier par
    Monseigneur M.F. Fallon. n.p.: 1914.
    21 p.   OTURS
London, Ontario (Diocese). French Catholics.
    La situation religieuse des catholiques-français. n.p.: 1912–1914.
    2 v. (Memoire no. 1–2).   OTURS
Lucas, Glenn.
    Canadian Protestant church history to 1973. Toronto: Published by the
    Committee on Archives of the United Church of Canada in collaboration
    with Victoria University [c1974]
    56 p.   OTU
McCurdy, James Frederick, 1847–1935.
    Life and work of D.J. Macdonnell, minister of St. Andrew's Church,
    Toronto. With a selection of sermons and prayers, edited by J.F. McCurdy.
    Toronto: William Briggs, 1897.
    xii, 512 p. illus.   OTU
McKeown, Hugh Charles, 1841–1889.
    The life and labours of Most Reverend John Joseph Lynch, first archbishop
    of Toronto. Montreal: J.A. Sadlier, 1886.
    x, 343 p. port.   OTAR
McLean, Earl Reginald, 1886–
    Religion in Ontario schools based on the minutes of the Inter-Church
    Committee on religious education in schools 1922–1965. Toronto:
    Distributed by The Ryerson Press [1965]
    viii, 87 p.   OONL
McLeod, Duncan.
    Arch-bishop Lynch "premier of Ontario", unmasked. Peterborough,
    Ontario [Review Hydraulic Presses] 1884.
    20 p.   OTAR
McTavish, Duncan, 1889–1979.
    Looking back: memoirs. [London, Ontario: 1971]
    156 p. port.   OLU
— Scenes of my childhood. n.p.: n.d.
    56 p.
    Early 20th century Bruce county, Ontario.   OLU
— Tales that have been told. n.p.: n.d.
    234 p. port.   OLU

Mary St. Paul, Mother, 1858–
From Desenzano to "The Pines," a sketch of the history of the Ursulines of
Ontario, with a brief history of the Order, compiled from various sources, by
Mother M. St. Paul. With a foreword by A.P. Mahoney. Toronto:
Macmillan, 1941.
xvi, 387 p. plates, ports.   OTU
Methodist Church in Canada and Presbyterian Church in Canada.
County of Huron, Ontario: report on a rural survey of the agricultural,
educational, social and religious life; prepared for the Huron Survey
Committee by the Department of Temperance and Moral Reform of the
Methodist Church, the Board of Social Service and Evangelism, and the
Board of Sabbath Schools and Young Peoples Societies of the Presbyterian
Church, December–January, 1913–1914. [Toronto: William Briggs, 1914]
56 p. illus., plates, maps, tables.   OTU
Mitchell, David (ed.).
Life and labours of Rev. Anselm Schuster late city missionary in Belleville...
Belleville, Ontario: Daily Intelligencer Steam Printing House, 1886.
167 p.   OKQ
Moir, John Sargent, 1926–
Enduring witness: a history of the Presbyterian Church in Canada. Don
Mills, Ontario: United Publishers Representatives [1974?]
xiii, 311 p. illus.   OTU
Newton–White, Ernest, 1892–
Gillmor of Algoma: archdeacon and tramp. [Brampton, Ontario: Charters
Publishing Company Limited, c1967]
123 p. illus., port.   OTU
O'Dwyer, William Cornelius.
Highways of destiny: a history of the Diocese of Pembroke, Ottawa valley,
Canada. [Ottawa: Le Droit Printers, 1964]
xiii, 263 p. illus., fold. map, ports.   OTU
Oliver, Edmund Henry, 1882–1935.
The winning of the frontier. Toronto: United Church Publishing House
[c1930]
xii, 271 p. fold. table.   OTAR
O'Neil, J   H
Diary of a priest (containing a history of Catholicism of Tillsonburg,
Norwick, Langton, Port Burwell and Courtland, also a brief history of
tobacco with caricatures, pictures and anecdotes). [London, Ontario: 1970]
168 p. illus., map, ports.   OLU
Ontario. Royal Commission of inquiry respecting the arrest and detention of
Rabbi Norbert Leiner by the Metropolitan Toronto Police Force.
Report. [Toronto: 1962?]
99 p.
Commissioner: Dalton C. Wells.   OTURS
— Proceedings, February 8–June 5, 1962.
4 v. [i.e. 1292 typewritten pages]   OTAR

— Report. [Toronto: 1962]
    xxxiv, 101 typewritten pages.   OTAR
P.P.A. in Ontario: history and principles of the organization. n.p. [1894?]
    15 p.
    Protestant Protective Association.   OKQ
Page, A   F
    A history of the Basilian Order in Canada. Toronto: The Catholic Truth
    Society of Canada, 1924.
    55 p.   OTSTM
Penton, M   James.
    Jehovah's Witnesses in Canada: champions of freedom of speech and
    worship. Toronto: Macmillan of Canada [c1976]
    xi, 388 p.   OTU
Petersen, Olive MacKay.
    The land of Moosoneek. Schumacker, Ontario: Diocese of Moosonee, 1974.
    x, 252 p.   OONL
Pierce, Lorne Albert, 1890–1961 (ed.).
    The chronicle of a century, 1829–1929: the record of one hundred years of
    progress in the publishing concerns of the Methodist, Presbyterian and
    Congregational churches in Canada. Toronto: United Church Publishing
    House [1929]
    xvi, 271 p.   OTU
Platt, Pauline (Vipond) (ed.).
    The story of the Woman's Auxiliary in the Diocese of Ontario, edited by
    Mrs. Garfield A. Platt and Mrs. Herbert C. Secker. Kingston, Ontario
    [c1962]
    109 p. ports.   OONL
Poulin, Gonzalve, 1906–
    Paroisse du sacré-coeur [de Welland, 1919–1969] Welland, Ontario: Les
    Artisans [c1969]
    94 p. illus., ports.   OTU
Presbyterian churches, Elgin county. n.p. [1975?]
    [38] leaves. illus.   OTAR
Price, Neil Gladstone, 1916–
    Education – religion – politics in Ontario: a study of the religious influences
    in education and politics in Ontario. North Bay, Ontario: Northland
    Printers, c1966.
    46 p.   OONL
Proctor, Redfern, Bousfield & Bacon.
    Master plan for church extension in the Metropolitan Toronto Planning
    Area, prepared for the Incorporated Synod of the Diocese of Toronto,
    Anglican Church of Canada. [Toronto: Incorporated Synod of the Diocese
    of Toronto, Anglican Church of Canada, 1962]
    vii, 32, vii leaves. maps (part fold.), diagrs., tables.   OTUSA
Project Planning Associates Limited, Toronto.
    The Metro Toronto United Church study. [Toronto: 1968–69]
    5 v. in 3 parts. illus., maps (part fold.).

Contents: I, An inventory; II, Land use and population; III, Social factors; IV, Organization and government; V, Analysis: conditions, trends, and implications for the future of the United Church in Metropolitan Toronto.

OTU

Renison, Robert John, 1875–1957.
One day at a time: autobiography, edited by Margaret Blackstock. Toronto: Kingswood House, 1957.
x, 322 p. illus., ports.
Archbishop of Moosonee.   OTU

Rowley, Owsley Robert, 1868–1949 (comp.).
The house of bishops: portraits of the living archbishops and bishops of the Church of England in Canada, in order of their concentration, with short historical notes concerning them and their dioceses... Montreal: Morton, Phillips & Co., 1907.
1 v. (unpaged). ports.   OTAR

Ruggle, Richard, 1941–   (ed.).
Some men and some controversies: published on the occasion of the centennial of the Diocese of Niagara. Erin, Ontario: Press Porcépic, 1974.
155 [4] p. illus., ports.   OTU

Salvation Army.
The plan of campaign for 1893, or, The first decade of Salvation Army in Canada. [Toronto? 1893?]
48 p. illus., facsims., ports.   OTURS

Scollard, Robert Joseph, 1908–
Centennial of the Basilian Fathers at St. Mary's Church, Owen Sound, and its Mission Churches, 1863–1963; an address by the Rev. R.J. Scollard, C.S.B., to Granottier Council of the Knights of Columbus, Feb. 25th, 1963.
27 p.   OTSTM

Sketches of Toronto churches, Toronto: J. Ross Robertson, 1886.
145 p. illus., ports.
"Reprinted from the *Evening Telegram*, with the original illustrations."   OTAR

Skirving, Archibald H
The house on the hill: the story of the Society of Saint John the Evangelist in Canada. Bracebridge, Ontario: Society of Saint John the Evangelist, c1972.
147 p. illus., map, port.   OTU

Spetz, Theobald, 1850–1921.
The Catholic Church in Waterloo county, with a summary history of the Diocese of Hamilton, and a list of the clergy who laboured in its district from the beginning to the present. [Toronto?] The Catholic Register and Extension, 1916.
xiv, 262 p. illus., ports., map.   OTU

Stevenson, John C
One hundred years of Methodism in Lundy's Lane, Niagara Falls South. [Niagara Falls, Ontario: Quarterly Board, 1898?]
18 p.
Chiefly pre-Confederation.   OKQ

Strachan, John, 1778–1867.
John Strachan: documents and opinions. A selection edited and with an introduction by J.L.H. Henderson. Toronto: McClelland and Stewart Limited [c1969]
xi, 290 p. (The Carleton library, no. 44). OTU
Strakhovsky, Leonid Ivan, 1898–
Historical outline of the Russian Orthodox Church in North America and in particular of the Parish of the Cathedral of Christ the Saviour in the city of Toronto. n.p.: n.d.
15 leaves. OTU
Sutherland, Alexander, 1833–1910.
The Methodist Church and missions in Canada and Newfoundland; a brief account of the Methodist Church in Canada, what it is and what it has done. Toronto: Department of Missonary Literature of the Methodist Church, Canada [1906]
316 p. plates, ports. (Young People's Forward Movement for Missions. Text book, no. 4). OTE
Swan, William John Minto, 1900–
Props, bars and pulpits or Minto's minutes. Foreword by the Bishop of Toronto. Kingston, Ontario: Hanson & Edgar [1965]
143 p. ports. OTU
Teewhella, Ethel Wellson.
The Yonge Street Quakers. Aurora, Ontario: J.M. Walton, 1937.
15 p. OTAR
Trosky, Odarka Savella, 1932–
The Ukrainian Greek Orthodox Church in Canada. [Winnipeg: Bulman Bros. Limited 1968]
86 p. OTU
United Church of Canada, Elgin Presbytery. n.p. [1975?]
[101] leaves. illus., ports. OTAR
United Church Women, Kingston, Ontario.
The history of Kingston Presbytery churches. [Kingston, Ontario: The Author, c1968]
74 p. OK
Walker, William Wesley, 1858–1945.
By northern lakes; reminiscences of life in Ontario mission fields. Toronto: William Briggs, 1896.
viii, 168 p. front., illus., ports. OTU
Warder, Richard C
Northern exposure: tales of the north country. New York: Pageant Press, Inc. [c1957]
179 p.
The Diocese of Algoma. OTU
Watson, Budd, 1929–
Sainte-Marie reborn. Midland, Ontario: The Author [1970]
32 p. chiefly illus. OTAR

White, William Charles, bp. 1873–1960.
> Canon Cody of St. Paul's Church. Foreword by Frederick H. Wilkinson.
> Toronto: The Ryerson Press [c1953]
> ix, 220 p. illus., port.   OTU

Women's Institute (Canada). Picton Women's Institute.
> History of the churches of Prince Edward county: the Tweedsmuir book as
> compiled by the Picton Branch of Prince Edward county Women's
> Institutes. Rev. and edited by Patricia C. Taylor. [Picton, Ontario] Picton
> Gazette Pub. Co., 1971.
> 162 p. illus., ports.   OTU

Young, Archibald Hope, 1863–1935.
> Our church in Ontario. Toronto: The Church of England in Canada, 1933.
> 15 p. illus., port. (Our Church in Canada III).   OTU

— Partial chronology of the Church of England in Canada for the celebration
> of the 75th anniversary of the formation of the Synod of the Diocese of
> Toronto: the first with lay delegates to be established in the British Empire.
> Toronto: 1928.
> 24 p.   OTAR

Periodical Articles

Aboulin, J   J   M
> Notes on the parish of the Assumption, Sandwich. Essex Historical Society.
> Papers and Addresses 2: 76–90, 1915.

Anderson, Allan J
> The Anglican churches of Kingston. Historic Kingston 12: 27–33, 1964.

Archambault, Jean.
> Astorville. Société Historique du Nouvel-Ontario. Documents Historiques
> 23: 22–56, 1952.

Audet, Francis J
> Les frères Robillard. Bulletin des Recherches Historiques 47: 239–241, 1941.

Ballantyne, Francis.
> Historical sketches of the congregations in the London Presbytery of the
> Presbyterian Church in Canada. Western Ontario Historical Notes 20:
> 19–51, 1964; 21: 51–87, 1965.

Barabé, Paul-Henri.
> Mgr. Joseph-Thomas Duhamel: premier archevêque d'Ottawa. Revue de
> l'Université d'Ottawa 17: 181–207, 1947.

Battle, Thomas F
> The Right Reverend John Farrell, D.D., first bishop of Hamilton. Canadian
> Catholic Historical Association. Report 39–45, 1942–43.

Bauman, Salome.
> First Mennonite Church 1813–1963. Waterloo Historical Society. Annual
> Volume 51: 19–26, 28, 1963.

Bean, Gordon A
 The archives of the Archdiocese of Toronto. Canadian Catholic Historical
 Association. Study Sessions 97–100, 1970.
Beck, Jeanne M
 Henry Somerville and social reform: his contribution to Canadian Catholic
 social thought. Canadian Catholic Historical Association. Study Sessions
 91–108, 1975.
Bible scholar dies at 102. Bruce County Historical Society. Yearbook 28, 1974.
 Harris MacNeill.
Cadieux, Lorenzo.
 Fondateurs du Diocèse du Sault-Sainte Marie. Société Historique du
 Nouvel-Ontario. Documents Historiques 6: 3–45, 1944.
— Missionaires au Lac Nipigon. Société Historique du Nouvel-Ontario.
 Documents Historiques 33: 30–40, 1957.
Cappon, James.
 General Assembly at Winnipeg. Queen's Quarterly 16: 90–115, 1908/1909.
 Queen's University and its relation to Presbyterian Church.
Carrière, Gaston.
 Albert Perbal, o.m.i., missiologue (1884–1971). Revue de l'Université
 D'Ottawa 42: 162–166, 1972.
— Jean-Marie Nédélec, o.m.i., 1834–1896. Société Historique de Nouvel-
 Ontario. Documents Historiques 34: 6–42, 1957.
— Mattawa, centre religieux (1844–1900). La Société Canadienne d'Histoire
 de l'Eglise Catholique. Rapport 35–51, 1960.
Cassel, Winnifred M
 The parish of Wilmot. Waterloo Historical Society. Annual Volume 50:
 71–77; 1962.
Le centenaire de l'arrivée des Oblats au Canada. Revue de l'Université
 d'Ottawa 12: 236–241, 1942.
Chamberland, Joseph.
 Bonfield. Société Historique du Nouvel-Ontario. Documents Historiques 23:
 4–21, 1952.
Cleary, Francis.
 History of the parish of Assumption. Essex Historical Society. Papers and
 Records 2: 71–75, 1915.
Cressman, J Boyd.
 History of the first Mennonite Church of Kitchener, Ontario. Mennonite
 Quarterly Review 13: 159–186, 251–283, 1939.
Dehler, David.
 Church and state: the problem of inter-faith adoption in Ontario. Revue de
 l'Université D'Ottawa 36: 66–85, 317–346, 1966.
Deschamps, Lorenzo.
 Le développement de l'Englise Catholique à Sudbury. La Société
 Canadienne d'Histoire de l'Eglise Catholique. Rapport 23–33, 1960.

DeVilliers–Westfall, William E.
    The dominion of the Lord: an introduction to the cultural history of
    protestant Ontario in the Victorian period. Queen's Quarterly 83: 47–70,
    1976.
The diocese of Ottawa. Canadian Churchman 79: 38–39, 1952.
Dobie, Belle.
    Extracts from Rev. D.M. McKeracher's diary of 1873. Thunder Bay
    Historical Society Papers 11: 13–18, 1920.
Dunn, (Mrs.) J   P
    The Roman Catholic Church in Kent County. Kent Historical Society.
    Papers and Addresses 1: 22–29, 1914.
Eadie, James A
    The Pearson years. Lennox and Addington Historical Society Papers and
    Records 15: 58–90, 1976.
Electa, Sister Mary.
    The history of the community of the sisters of Providence of St. Vincent de
    Paul, Kingston. Historic Kingston 7: 28–42, 1958.
Evans, Kenneth C
    The intellectual background of Dr. John Travers Lewis, the first bishop of
    the Anglican Diocese of Ontario. Historic Kingston 10: 37–45, 1962.
Farrell, John K   A
    Michael Francis Fallon, Bishop of London, Ontario, Canada 1909–1913; the
    man and his controversies. Canadian Catholic Historical Association. Study
    Sessions 73–90, 1968.
Flynn, Louis J
    Bishop Edward John Horan. Historic Kingston 24: 43–54, 1976.
Geddes, J   G
    Notes of autobiography. Wentworth Historical Society. Journal and
    Transactions 1: 44–47, 1892.
    Rector of Hamilton 1835–1880.
Grant, A   M
    Early religious life and church organization in the Huron tract. Western
    Ontario Historical Notes 14(no. 4): 1–22; 14(no. 5): 1–25, 1958.
Greenfield, J   Katharine.
    The Reverend John Gamble Geddes and early days at Christ's Church,
    Hamilton. Wentworth Bygones 4: 9–21, 1963.
— The Reverend Thomas Geoghegan 1848–1906. Wentworth Bygones 11:
    9–19, 1975.
Hart, M   L
    Neil McNeil: Archbishop of Toronto. Canadian Magazine of Politics,
    Science, Art and Literature 41: 90–93, 1913.
Heick, Welf H
    Becoming an indigenous church: the Lutheran Church in Waterloo county,
    Ontario. Ontario History 56: 249–260, 1964.

Hepburn, Olive E
  Padre of the Bruce. Bruce County Historical Society. Yearbook 16, 1974.
  Canon R.W. James.
Hicks, A   A
  Growth of Methodism in Chatham and vicinity. Kent Historical Society.
  Papers and Addresses 4: 34–39, 1919.
Hovinen, Elizabeth.
  Quakers of Yonge Street. Canadian Geographical Journal 92(no. 1): 52–57,
  1976.
Howard, Canon.
  Notes on the history of the Church of England in Chatham, Ontario. Kent
  Historical Society. Papers and Addresses 3: 5–12, 1917.
Howard, Minnie.
  The Catholic Church in Collingwood. Huron Institute. Papers and Records
  1: 19–23, 1909.
Jenkins, Mariel.
  Life of Henry Scadding. York Pioneer and Historical Society. Annual
  Report 6–7, 1963.
Jordan, W   G
  Church union and after. Queen's Quarterly 34: 472–474, 1927.
— The higher criticism in Canada; II, The Canadian scene. Queen's Quarterly
  36: 31–47, 1929.
  Religious controversy – mainly Ontario.
Laderoute, F   X
  The church in the Ottawa valley. Canadian Catholic Historical Association.
  Report 55–68, 1944–45.
Larocque, Marcel.
  Corbeil. Société Historique du Nouvel-Ontario. Documents Historiques 23:
  57–64, 1952.
Lord, William D
  Early Methodism in Essex county, with special reference to the Woodslee
  charge. Western Ontario Historical Notes 20: 6–23, 1964.
McCannell, Ted.
  Unusual Indian church of the Bruce. Bruce County Historical Society.
  Yearbook 20–22, 1974.
MacDonald, Brother Prudent.
  The archives of the Christian Brothers in Toronto. Canadian Catholic
  Historical Association. Study Sessions 79–82, 1972.
MacDonald, Caroline – missionary. Huron Historical Notes 7: 18–20, 1971.
McFall, A   David (ed.).
  Pine Orchard Meeting House and burying ground. York Pioneer and
  Historical Society. Annual Report 31–51, 1967.
McFall, Jean.
  The last days of the Children of Peace. York Pioneer 22–33, 1973.
McKellar, P   D
  The Presbyterian Church in Chatham. Kent Historical Society. Papers and
  Addresses 2: 12–18, 1915.

McLelland, Joseph C
    The Macdonnell heresy trial. Canadian Journal of Theology 4: 273–284,
    1958.
    Daniel James Macdonnell – Toronto, 1870's.
Mage, Julius and Robert Murdie.
    The Mennonites of Waterloo county. Canadian Geographical Journal 80:
    10–19, 1970.
Maryan, Sister.
    The work of the congregation of the Good Shepherd in Toronto, 1875–1973.
    York Pioneer 38–48, 1974.
Margarita, M
    The Institute of the Blessed Virgin Mary. Canadian Catholic Historical
    Association Report. 69–81, 1944–45.
    Loretto Abbey, Toronto.
Melady, Thomas S
    A distinguish [sic] son of Huron county the Rev. Stephen Eckert, O.M.Cap.
    Canadian Catholic Historical Association. Report 95–100, 1940–41.
Millman, Thomas R
    The Church of England in western Ontario. Western Ontario Historical
    Notes 13: 1–27, 1955.
— The Conference on Christian Unity, Toronto, 1889. Canadian Journal of
    Theology 3: 165–174, 1957.
Mitchell, Eva.
    History of the Presbyterian Church in Collingwood. Huron Institute. Papers
    and Records 1: 24–32, 1909.
Morisseau, Henri.
    Le centenaire de l'arrivée des Oblats à Bytown (Ottawa) 1844–1944. Revue
    de l'Université d'Ottawa 14: 28–57, 174–202, 327–355, 459–497, 1944.
Morley, E   Lillian.
    The Milverton circuit of the Methodist Church. Western Ontario Historical
    Notes 9: 56–67, 1951.
Newlands, David L
    The Yonge Street Friends Meeting House 1810–1975. York Pioneer 41–49,
    1975.
Nock, David.
    Wilson, E.F.: early years as missionary in Huron and Algoma. Canadian
    Church History Society. Journal 15: 78–96, 1973.
d'Ostie, Reverend Soeur Sainte-Monique.
    Les Filles de Mère d'Youville dans la région de Sudbury. La Société
    Canadienne d'Histoire de l'Eglise Catholique. Rapport 83–91, 1960.
Parker, Harry E
    Early Presbyterianism in western Ontario. London and Middlesex Historical
    Society. Transactions 14: 9–79, 1930.
Pense, E   J   B
    The making of a bishop with the antecedents and history of a Canadian

Bishopric. Canadian Magazine of Politics, Science, Art and Literature 16:
228–234, 1901.
Kingston, Ontario.
Price, Brian J
The archives of the Archdiocese of Kingston. Canadian Catholic Historical
Association. Study Sessions 21–25, 1973.
Proulx, Adolphe.
Histoire du diocèse du Sault-Sainte-Marie. La Société Canadienne
d'Histoire de l'Eglise Catholic. Rapport 71–82, 1960.
Pym, Ernest J
Pioneer churches in Usborne. Huron Historical Notes 8: 22–25, 1972.
Ralston, David and Hugo McPherson.
The Ronald Chapel in Toronto Harbour. Canadian Art 23(2): 28–31, 1966.
Reed, T   A
A memoir of Canon Henry Scadding. D.D. (1813–1901). York Pioneer and
Historical Society. Annual Report 8–10, 1952.
The restoration of the study at Sharon. York Pioneer and Historical Society.
Annual Report 52–54, 1963.
Robin, J
The story of Fort William mission; with a brief sketch of some of its
missionaries. Thunder Bay Historical Society. Papers 4: 27–30, 1912/1913.
St. Kevin, Reverend Sister.
The early history of Notre Dame Convent in Kingston. Historic Kingston 9:
5–20, 1960.
St. Peter's Seminary, London, Ontario. Royal Architectural Institute of
Canada. Journal 7: 365–373, 1930.
Scollard, Robert J
Reverend William Richard Harris, 1846–1923. Canadian Catholic
Historical Association. Study Sessions 65–80, 1974.
— Roman Catholic history and archives in the province of Ontario. Families
13: 34–45, 1974.
Snyder, Marsha.
Thomas Vincent: Archdeacon of Moosonee. Ontario History 68: 119–135,
1976.
Stanley, George F   G
The Abbé of Abbey Dawn. Historic Kingston 18: 15–35, 1970.
Swayze, Beulah.
Dr. Carmichael of King. York Pioneer and Historical Society. Annual
Report 2–8, 1970.
Switzer, E   M
History of the Methodist Church in Collingwood. Huron Institute. Papers
and Records 1: 33–39, 1909.
Thivierge, Edgar.
A la naissance du diocèse d'Ottawa. Revue de l'Université d'Ottawa 7:
424–440, 1937; 8: 6– 30, 1938.

Thomas, Ernest.
Social reform and the Methodist Church. Canadian Forum 1: 264–266,
1921.
[W   G   L   ]
The Hamilton Assembly. Queen's Quarterly 27: 85–92, 1919/1920.
Wetherell, Alice.
William Nason of Weston, 1819–1890. York Pioneer and Historical Society.
Annual Report 62–69, 1964.

Theses

Ashley, Stephen M
The Salvation Army in Toronto 1882–1896. [Guelph, Ontario] 1969.
ix, 127 leaves.
M.A. thesis, The University of Guelph.   OGU
Baeszler, St. Alfred of Rome, Sister.
The congregation of Notre Dame in Ontario and the United States: the
History of Holy Angels' province. New York: 1944.
251 p.
Ph.D. thesis, Fordham University.   DA
Beck, Jeanne R   M
Henry Somerville and the development of Catholic social thought in
Canada: Somerville's role in the Archdiocese of Toronto, 1915-1943.
Hamilton, Ontario: 1977
xiii, 485 leaves.
Ph.D. thesis, McMaster University.
Boyle, George Alfred.
Higher criticism and the struggle for academic freedom in Canadian
Methodism. [Toronto] 1965.
iii, 458 leaves.
Th.D. thesis, Victoria University.   OTV
Brown, William Lorne.
The Sunday School movement in the Methodist Church in Canada,
1875–1925. [Toronto] 1959.
160 leaves.
Th.M. thesis, University of Toronto.   OTCC
Burnside, Albert.
The contribution of the Reverend Albert Carman to Albert College,
Belleville, and to the Methodist Episcopal Church in Canada 1857–1884.
[Toronto] 1962.
vii, 357 leaves.
Th.M. thesis, Emmanuel College, Victoria University.   OTE
Crysdale, Robert Cecil Stewart, 1914–
Industrialization and the churches in Canada. [Toronto] 1959.
viii, 270, xvi leaves.
M.Th. thesis, University of Toronto, Emmanuel College.   OTE

Dehler, David.
  Church and state: the problem of inter-faith adoption in Ontario. Ottawa:
  1965.
  vii, 90 leaves.
  M.A. thesis, University of Ottawa.   OOU
Doerksen, John George.
  History of education of the Mennonite bretheran of Canada. Winnipeg:
  1963.
  vii, 207 leaves.
  M.Ed. thesis, University of Manitoba.   OTER
Dorland, Arthur Garratt.
  A history of the Society of Friends (Quakers) in Canada. [Toronto: 1926]
  384 leaves. charts (part fold.), map.
  Ph.D. thesis, University of Toronto (accepted 1927).   OTU
Farrell, John Kevin Anthony, 1924–
  The history of the Roman Catholic Church in London, Ontario 1826–1931.
  [London, Ontario] 1949.
  203 leaves. tables.
  M.A. thesis, The University of Western Ontario.   OLU
Galvin, Martin John.
  Catholic–Protestant relations in Ontario, 1864–1875. [Toronto] 1962
  [c1974]
  251 leaves.
  M.A. thesis, University of Toronto (microfilm 17771).   OTU
Groenenberg, Adrians Laurens 1930–
  The social geography of the Netherlanders in south western Ontario with
  special reference to the role of the churches in the integration of the
  immigrants. London, Ontario: 1966.
  xi, 109, viii leaves. diagrs., graphs, tables, maps.
  M.A. thesis, The University of Western Ontario.   OLU
Hargraft, George Leslie.
  Adjustment problems of churches in downtown Toronto. [Toronto] 1949.
  41 leaves. fold. maps., fold. chart.
  M.A. thesis, University of Toronto.   OTU
Headon, Christopher Fergus.
  The influence of the Oxford Movement upon the Church of England in
  eastern and central Canada, 1840–1900. Montreal, Quebec: 1974.
  xv, 306 leaves.
  Ph.D. thesis, McGill University (microfilm 23089).   Can
Heick, Welf H
  The Lutherans of Waterloo county, Ontario: 1810–1959, a historical study.
  [Kingston, Ontario] 1959.
  vii, 219p.
  M.A. thesis, Queen's University.   OKQ
Hitchins, William English.
  The origins of the Diocese of Huron and its history to 1871. London,
  Ontario: 1934.
  144 [11] leaves. illus., map.
  M.A. thesis, The University of Western Ontario.   OLU

Hoover, John Douglas, 1937–
　　The Primitive Methodist Church in Canada 1829–1884. London, Ontario:
　　1970.
　　viii, 312 leaves. tables.
　　M.A. thesis, The University of Western Ontario (microfilm 6162).
　　Concentration is in Ontario.   OLU
Imai, Paul Ken.
　　The Japanese adjustment to Canadian life: the part played by the church in
　　that adjustment, with particular reference to the life of a Japanese Anglican
　　congregation in Toronto, since 1942. [Toronto] Trinity College, 1958.
　　120 leaves. fold. map.
　　M.Th. thesis, University of Trinity College.   OTTC
Kiesekamp, Burkhard, 1939–
　　Community and faith: The intellectual and ideological bases of the church
　　union movement in Victorian Canada. [Toronto] 1974.
　　iii, 331 leaves.
　　Ph.D. thesis, University of Toronto (accepted 1975).   OTU
Latowsky, Evelyn Kallen, 1929–
　　Three Toronto synagogues: a comparative study of religious systems in
　　transition. [Toronto] c1969.
　　vii, i, 343 leaves. graphs, figs., map.
　　Ph.D. thesis, University of Toronto (microfilm 21395).   OTU
Looy, Anthony Jacobus.
　　The Toronto Daily Globe and church-state relations, 1869–1878. Kingston,
　　Ontario: c1971.
　　59 [3] leaves.
　　M.A. thesis, Queen's University (microfilm 9854).   OKQ
McFaddin, Charles E
　　A study of the buildings of the Children of Peace, Sharon, Ontario.
　　[Toronto] 1953.
　　2 v.
　　M.A. thesis, University of Toronto.
　　Chiefly pre-Confederation.   OTU
Mercedes, Mother M
　　The history of the Ursulines of Ontario. London, Ontario: 1937.
　　[222] leaves. facsims., photos, ports.
　　M.A. thesis, The University of Western Ontario.   OLU
Mitchell, Bruce William.
　　Geography of irreligion in Ontario. Ottawa: 1974.
　　vi, 168 leaves. graphs, maps, tables.
　　B.A. research essay, Carleton University.   OOCC
Paul, Gerald Walton.
　　The Board of Evangelism and Social Service of the United Church of
　　Canada: an historical analysis of the enterprises of the board from 1925 to
　　1968. Vancouver, British Columbia: 1974 [c1975]
　　144 leaves.
　　Th.M. thesis, Vancouver School of Theology (microfilm 23670).   Can

Smith, D   Crawford.
>The history of the Presbyterian Church in Guelph, 1827–1927. Guelph,
>Ontario: 1955.
>224 leaves.
>Th.M. thesis, Knox College, University of Toronto.   OTK

Smith, Garry Douglas.
>The growth and distribution of Baptist churches in Ontario. Waterloo,
>Ontario: 1969.
>vii, 69 leaves. graphs, maps, tables.
>B.A. thesis, Waterloo University College.   OWTL

Smith, Lyman Eveleigh.
>Nineteenth century Canadian preaching in the Methodist, Presbyterian,
>and Congregational Churches. [Toronto] 1953.
>311 leaves.
>Th.D. thesis, University of Toronto, Emmanuel College.   OTE

Stewart, Robert Gordon.
>Radiant smiles in the dirty thirties: history and ideology of the Oxford
>Group Movement in Canada, 1932–1936. Vancouver, British Columbia:
>1974.
>143 leaves.
>M.Div. thesis, Vancouver School of Theology (accepted 1975) (microfilm
>23671).   Can

Thomas, Theodore Elia, 1927–
>The Protestant churches and the religious issue in Ontario's public schools: a
>study in church and state. New York: 1972.
>3, i, 350 leaves.
>Ph.D. thesis, Columbia University (microfilm 73-9049).   DA

Trosky, (Mrs.) Odarka Savella, 1932–
>A historical study of the development of the Ukrainain Greek Orthodox
>Church of Canada and its role in the field of education, 1918–1964.
>Winnipeg: 1965.
>iv, 191 leaves. illus.
>M.Ed. thesis, University of Manitoba (microfilm 48).   Can

Turner, Harry Ernest.
>The Evangelical movement in the Church of England in the Diocese of
>Toronto, 1839–1879. [Toronto] 1959.
>364 leaves.
>M.A. thesis, University of Toronto.   OTU

Westfall, William Edward de Villiers, 1945–
>The sacred and the secular: studies in the cultural history of Protestant
>Ontario in the Victorian period. [Toronto] c1976.
>385 leaves.
>Ph.D. thesis, University of Toronto.   OTU

Willis, Robert Charles, 1919–
>David Williams 1859–1904: the background of a bishop. [London, Ontario]
>1957.
>xiv, 174 leaves. photos.
>M.A. thesis, The University of Western Ontario.   OLU

THE PROFESSIONS

Monographs and Pamphlets

Academy of Medicine, Toronto.
> The map of the history of medicine of Canada. Commemorating the
> Diamond Jubilee of the Academy of Medicine, Toronto and the Centennial
> of Confederation of Canada. Painted by Charles F. Comfort. [Toronto]
> 1967.
> 32 p. map.   OTU

Allinson, Cyril Launcelot Cathrope.
> Notes on courts and court-buildings at Guelph, history of administration of
> justice in this area, Wellington county lawyers who attained special
> eminence, 1867–1967. Guelph, Ontario: 1967.
> 18 leaves.   OTU

Armstrong, Charles Harold Algeo, 1888–
> The honourable society of Osgoode Hall: with an appendix on the history
> and architecture of the fabric, by E.R. Arthur. Toronto: Clarke, Irwin &
> Company Limited 1952.
> 60 p. illus.   OTU

Association of Professional Engineers of the province of Ontario. Lambton
    Chapter.
> History of engineering in Lambton county, by Lambton Chapter APEO
> [under the general editorship of John J. Klauke. Toronto: Association of
> Professional Engineers of Ontario, 1972]
> 86 p. illus.   OTU

Becher, Henry Corry Rowley, 1817–1885.
> Diary, edited by E.J. Carty. London, Ontario: Advertiser, 1926.
> [27] p. illus., port.
> Covers the years 1836–1884.
> Articles published in the *London Advertiser* between November 6 and
> December 11, 1926.   OLU

Brien, James Wilbert, 1879–
> The medical men of Essex county. Windsor, Ontario: Windsor Daily Star,
> 1949.
> 63 p.   OLUM

Buchanan, Edward Victor, 1887–
> The professional engineers of London. Edited by R.K. Swartman. Line
> drawings by Silvia Clarke. [London, Ontario] London Branch, The
> Engineering Institute of Canada [c1972]
> 40 p. illus., ports.   OONL

Campbell, Marjorie Freeman, 1896–1975.
> Holbrook of the San. Toronto: The Ryerson Press [c1953]
> xi, 212 p. illus., port.   OTU

Canadian Medical Association.
  Richard Maurice Bucke: catalogue to the exhibition, Canadian Medical
  Association and Canadian Psychiatric Association annual meetings June
  10–14, 1963, Toronto. [Toronto: University of Toronto Press, 1963]
  [20] p. facsim., ports.   OLU
Canadian Medical Week, Hamilton, 1918.
  The Canadian Medical Week, Hamilton May 27–June 1, 1918. Published
  under the auspices of the Ontario Medical Association. Toronto: Macmillan
  Company of Canada Ltd., 1918.
  xv, 360 p.
  Ontario: pp. 183–199.   OTU
Canfield, Ethel.
  Pioneer doctors of Oxford county. n.p. [1944?]
  29 leaves.   OULM
Card, Raymond William George, 1893–
  The Ontario Association of Architects 1890–1950; a record of achievement
  from the year of incorporation, together with an account of earlier efforts of
  individuals and groups whose interest and professional integrity contributed
  much to the firm foundation on which the Association now stands. [Toronto]
  Printed for the O.A.A. at the University of Toronto Press, 1950.
  45 p. illus., ports.   OTRM
Carter, Francis Gerard.
  The Middlesex bench and bar. London, Ontario: Middlesex Law
  Association [1969]
  xv, 126 p. illus., ports.   OTU
Carter, John Smyth, 1877–
  Doctor M.W. Locke and the Williamsburg scene. Toronto: 1933.
  138 p. illus., ports. (Life portrayal series).   OTAR
Clute, Kenneth Fleury, 1918–
  The general practitioner: a study of medical education and practice in
  Ontario and Nova Scotia. [Toronto] University of Toronto Press [1963]
  xvi, 566 p. tables.   OTU
Corfield, William Elwyn, 1920–
  Towers of justice. 1st ed. London, Ontario: London & St. Thomas Real
  Estate Board, 1974.
  [36] p. illus., maps, ports, facsims., plans.   OONL
Court house: the Norfolk county court house [Simcoe, Ontario. Simcoe Ontario:
  Save our Court House Committee, Norfolk Historical Society, 1975]
  52 p. illus., facsims.   OTU
Courteau, Guy, 1897–
  Le docteur J.-Raoul Hurtubise, M.D., M.P., 1882–1955: 40 ans de vie française
  à Sudbury. Préface de Lorenzo Cadieux. Montréal: Les Éditions Bellarmin,
  1971.
  134 p. illus., ports.   OTER

Crate, Harold E   1902–
    Thorne, Gunn, Helliwell & Christenson: a history 1880–1970. Toronto:
    Thorne, Gunn, Helliwell & Christenson, 1970.
    112 p. illus., ports.
    Ontario: pp. 39–48.   OTU
Curtis, James Davis, 1868–
    Autobiography. St. Thomas, Ontario: 1972.
    43 leaves.   OSTT
— St. Thomas medical men of the past. n.p.: 1946.
    65 p. ports.   OLUM
— St. Thomas and Elgin medical men of the past. St. Thomas, Ontario: 1956.
    122 p. ports.   OLUM OTU
Dodge, David A
    Returns to investment in University training: the case of Canadian
    accountants, engineers and scientists. Kingston, Ontario: Industrial
    Relations Centre, Queen's University, 1972.
    xiv, 167 p. (Industrial Relations Centre, Queen's University. Research series,
    no. 17).   OTU
Durand, Charles, 1811–1905.
    Reminiscences. Toronto: Hunter, Rose Co., Ltd., 1897.
    xii, 534 p. front.
    A Toronto barrister reminiscences chiefly of life in Upper Canada.   OTU
Eisen, David, 1901–
    Toronto's Jewish doctors. [Toronto] Published through the co-operation of
    the Maimonides Medical Society of Ontario and the Toronto Centennial
    Committee of the Canadian Jewish Congress and the United Jewish Welfare
    Fund [1960]
    16 p. ports.   OONL
Evans, Anna Margaret, 1914–
    Century one: a history of the Ontario Veterinary Association, 1874–1974, by
    A. Margaret Evans, C.A.V. Barker. Guelph, Ontario: The Authors, 1976.
    xi, 516 p. illus., ports.   OONL
Faulkes, Tom.
    Statistical papers prepared for the Special study regarding the medical
    profession in Ontario, December, 1972 [a report by E.D. Pickering to the
    Ontario Medical Association. Toronto: 1973]
    [78] p. map, tables.   OTU
Ferguson, John.
    History of the Ontario Medical Association, 1880–1930. Toronto: Murray
    Printing Company, Limited, 1930.
    142 p.   OTU
Forster, Fred J   R   1874–
    The physicians of Perth. n.p.: 1953.
    20 leaves.   OLUM

Gimby, William Edwin, 1859–1950.
    History of the medical profession, Sault Ste. Marie, Ontario [Sault Star Job
    Department, 1922]
    67 leaves. ports.   OLUM
Greenland, Cyril.
    Charles Kirk Clarke: a pioneer of Canadian psychiatry. [Toronto] The
    Clarke Institute of Psychiatry, 1966.
    31 p. illus., port.   OTU
Groves, Abraham, 1847–1935.
    All in the day's work: leaves from a doctor's casebook. With a foreword by
    Ambrose Lorne Lockwood. Toronto: Macmillan Company of Canada
    Limited, 1934.
    xv, 181 p. illus., port.
    Medicine in Fergus, Ontario.   OTU
Gruneau Research Limited.
    Study of attitudes of registered nurses of Ontario. Toronto: 1964.
    45, 5 p. tables.   OTU
Hacker, Carlotta.
    The indomitable lady doctors. Toronto: Clarke, Irwin & Company Limited
    [c1974]
    259 p. ports.   OTU
Hamilton, James Cleland, 1836–1907.
    Osgoode Hall: reminiscences of the bench and bar. Toronto: Carswell
    Company Limited, 1904.
    xii, 196 p. plates, ports.   OTU
Harris, Seale.
    Banting's miracle: the story of the discoverer of insulin. With a foreword by
    Elliott P. Joslin. Toronto: J.M. Dent & Sons (Canada) Limited [c1946]
    xx, 245 p. illus., facsims, ports.   OTU
Houser, Lloyd J
    The Institute of Professional Librarians of Ontario: an analysis, 1954–1975.
    Toronto: IPLO., 1975.
    119 p.   OTULS
Howard, John George, 1803–1890.
    Incidents in the life of John G. Howard of Colborne Lodge, High Park, near
    Toronto; chiefly adapted from his journals. Toronto: Copp, Clark & Co.,
    1885.
    36, 15 p. illus., port.
    Chiefly pre-Confederation.   OTURS
Hughes, David J   1819–
    History of the Bar of the county of Middlesex, by Judge Hughes and T.H.
    Purdom. London, Ontario: Middlesex Historical Association [1912]
    51 p. ports.   OLU
Hunt, Frazier.
    The little doc: the story of Allan Roy Dafoe, the physician to the
    Quintuplets. New York: Simon and Schuster [c1939]
    xi, 300 p. port.   OTU

Johnston, William Victor.
    Before the age of miracles: memoirs of a country doctor. Foreword by E.K.
    Lyon. Toronto: Fitzhenry and Whiteside [1972]
    212 p. illus.
    History of Huron county.   OTU
Kaiser, Thomas Erlin, 1863–1940.
    A history of the medical profession of the county of Ontario. Edited by T.E.
    Kaiser under the auspices of the Ontario County Medical Association.
    [Oshawa, Ontario: Mundy-Goodfellow Printing Co. Limited] 1934.
    126 [2] p. ports.   OTU
Kenyon, Ron, 1931–
    The Ontario Dental Association; a profile, the first one hundred years.
    [Toronto: 1967]
    32 p. illus., facsims., ports.   OTU
Lauriston, Victor, 1881–1973.
    A centennial chronicle of Kent doctors. [Chatham, Ontario: Kent County
    Medical Society, 1967]
    248 p.   OTU
Law Society of Upper Canada.
    The Law Society of Upper Canada: a short account of the history of the Law
    Society of Upper Canada. Toronto: The Society, 1947.
    19 p. illus.
    150th anniversary.   OTU
— Law Society of Upper Canada, 1797–1972. [Toronto: 1973]
    v, 121 p.
    Special issues of *Law Society of Upper Canada Gazette* v. 6, 1972.   OTUL
— Osgoode Hall: a short account of the Hall, 1832–1932. [Toronto: Rous &
    Mann Limited] 1932.
    15 p. illus.   OTU
Legal aspects of architectural practice; a series of lectures presented by members
    of the Law Society of Upper Canada before the Ontario Association of
    Architects, 1963. [Toronto: Ontario Association of Architects, 1963]
    120 p.   OTU
— 2d ed. Toronto: Ontario Association of Architects, 1969.
    x, 137 p. forms.   OTUSA
Lewis, Ella N
    Early medical men of Elgin county. St. Thomas, Ontario: Sutherland Press,
    1931.
    60 p.   OTU
MacDermot, Hugh Ernest, 1888–
    History of the Canadian Medical Association, 1867–1921. Toronto: Murray
    Printing, 1935–58.
    2 v. plates, ports.   OTU
— One hundred years of medicine in Canada, 1867–1967. Toronto:
    McClelland and Stewart [c1967]
    224 p. illus., ports.   OTU

— Sir Thomas Roddick: his work in medicine and public life. Toronto: The
   Macmillan Company of Canada Limited, 1938.
   xiii, 160 p. front., plates, ports., facsims, map.   OTU
Manion, Robert James. 1881–1943.
   Life is an adventure. Toronto: The Ryerson Press [c1936]
   360 p. front.   OTV
Medicine on the march. [Toronto] University of Toronto [1948]
   [16] p.
   Issued to celebrate plan to build the Charles H. Best Institute.   OTU
People look at doctors, and other relevant matters; the Sunnybrook Health
   Attitude Survey [W. Harding Leriche et al. Toronto: Sunnybrook Hospital,
   c1971]
   xiv, 204 p. illus., graphs, tables.   OTU
Pickering, Edward A
   Special study regarding the medical profession in Ontario: a report to the
   Ontario Medical Association by Edward A. Pickering. [Toronto] 1973.
   125, 32, 36 p.
   Contents: Special study regarding the medical profession in Ontario; The
   economic position of Ontario physicians and the relation between the
   schedule of fees and actual income from fee practice, by A. Peter Ruderman;
   Citizen participation by Thelma McCormack.   OTU
Pratt, Viola Leone (Whitney), 1892–
   Canadian portraits; famous doctors: Osler; Banting; Penfield. Toronto:
   Clarke, Irwin and Company Limited, 1956.
   xi, 160 p. illus., ports.
   Banting: pp. 49–92.   OTAR
Registered Nurses' Association of Ontario.
   Interpretive information in respect to the history, organization and activities
   of the Registered Nurses' Association of Ontario. Toronto: 1963.
   54 p. chart.   OTU
Riddell, William Renwick, 1852–1945.
   The Bar and the courts of the province of Upper Canada, or Ontario.
   Toronto: Macmillan Company of Canada Limited, 1928.
   251 p. ports.
   Chiefly pre-Confederation.   OTU
— The legal profession in Upper Canada in the early periods. Toronto: Law
   Society of Upper Canada, 1916.
   vii, 194 p.
   Chiefly pre-Confederation.   OTAR
— The legal profession in Ontario and the Law Society of Upper Canada.
   Chicago: The Chicago Society of Advocates, 1915.
   pp. 35–65 *Book of the Chicago Society of Advocates*.   OTAR
Robinson, Marion O
   Give my heart: the Dr. Marion Hilliard story. Garden City, New York:
   Doubleday, 1964.
   x, 348 p. illus., ports.   OKQ

Rowland, John, 1907–
    The insulin man: the story of Sir Frederick Banting. New York: Roy
    Publishers, Inc. [c1965]
    140 p.   OKQ
Seaborn, Edwin, 1872–1951.
    The march of medicine in western Ontario. Toronto: The Ryerson Press
    [1944]
    xvi, 386 p. illus., ports.   OTU
Shulman, Morton, 1925–
    Coroner. Toronto: Fitzhenry & Whiteside [c1975]
    154 p. illus.   OTU
Skolnik, Michael L
    An analysis of projections of the demand for engineers in Canada and
    Ontario, and an inquiry into substitution between engineers and
    technologists by M.L. Skolnik and W.F. McMullen. [Toronto: Committee of
    Presidents of Universities of Ontario] 1970.
    xii, 64 p. graphs, tables. (CPUO report, no. 70-2).   OTU
Smiley, John R
    The untapped pool: a survey of Ontario nurses (1968) by John R. Smiley,
    Isabel Black, Andrew Kapos and Boyde G. Gill. n.p.: 1968.
    19 leaves.   OTU
Steering Committee on Negotiation Rights for Professional Staffs.
    Brief presented in support of special legislation entitled Professional
    Negotiations Act, 1966, to the Honourable John P. Robarts. [Toronto] 1966.
    14 p.
    Chairman: Edward G. Phillips; Counsel: Aubrey E. Golden.   OTU
Stevenson, Lloyd Grenfell, 1918–
    Sir Frederick Banting. Toronto: The Ryerson Press [c1964]
    xv, 446 p. facsims., ports.   OLUM
Waugh, William.
    Reminiscences of sixty years medical practice in the city of London. An
    address February 6, 1932. n.p.: 1932.
    9 leaves.   OLU
Wells, Kenneth E
    Highlights in the story of preventive medicine in Hamilton, Ontario,
    1778–1968. [Hamilton, Ontario: Hamilton – Wentworth District Health
    Unit, 1968?]
    15 p. illus.   OTU
Wilkie, George, 1867–
    The bench and bar of Ontario. Editors: George Wilkie, John A. Cooper and
    C.W. Benedict. Toronto: Brown–Searle Printing Co., 1905.
    7, 17–445 p. of ports.   OTU
Wodson, Harry Milner, 1874–1952.
    The justice shop. Toronto: Sovereign Press, 1931.
    119 p. port.   OTU

Periodical Articles

Anderson, H   B
  Evolution of medicine in Ontario. Canadian Practioner and Review 31: 673–682, 1906.
— An historical sketch of the medical profession of Toronto. Canadian Medical Association Journal 16: 446–452, 1926.

Ardagh, His Honour Judge.
  Some reminiscences (Apr. 22, 1892). Pioneer Papers 3: 25–39, 1910. Barrie, Ontario.

Arthur, Eric R
  W.A. Langton, 1854–1933. Royal Architectural Institute of Canada. Journal 10: 101–102, 1933.

Arthurs, H   W
  Authority, accountability and democracy in the government of the Ontario legal profession. Canadian Bar Review 49: 1–23, 1971.

Arthurs, H   W   [et al.]
  The Toronto legal profession: an exploratory survey. University of Toronto Law Journal 21: 498–528, 1971.

Association of Professional Engineers of Ontario, 1922–1972: Anniversary Issue. Engineering Digest 18(7), 1972.

Banks, Margaret A
  George Warburton Spragge, 1893–1976. Ontario History 68: 116–118, 1976.

Best, C   H
  Sir Frederick Banting. University of Toronto Quarterly 10: 249–254, 1941.

Bray, Reginald V
  The medical profession of the city of Chatham and county of Kent, a history. Kent Historical Society. Papers and Addresses 4: 5–12, 1919.

Brigstocke, R   W
  Doctor, poet and miner; reminiscences of Dr. William Henry Drummond. Canadian Mining Journal 54: 310–312, 1933.

Brown, John Nelson Elliott.
  A retrospect: the class of '92. Canada Lancet and Practitioner 81: 164–191, 1933.

Burden, H   J
  Alexander Frank Wickson. Royal Architectural Institute of Canada. Journal 14: 14, 1937.

Burton, W   F
  The development of law associations. Canada Law Journal n.s. 30: 2–6, 1894.
  Ontario Law Associations.

Cameron, (Sir) Matthew. Canada Law Journal n.s. 22: 243–244, 1886.

Card, Raymond.
  History of the Ontario Association of Architects, 1890–1950. Royal Architectural Institute of Canada. Journal 31: 432–439, 1954.

Cauley, John Stuart.
   1950 to 1954 [history of the Ontario Association of Architects]. Royal
   Architectural Institute of Canada. Journal 31: 440–441, 1954.
A chronicle of progress as revealed by the accomplishments of Toronto's city
   engineers from 1834 to 1934. Engineering and Contract Record 48: 570–577,
   1934.
Clarkson, F   Arnold.
   Dr. Bertram Spencer, M.B., M.R.C.S. Calgary Associates Clinic. Historical
   Bulletin 7(no. 3): 1–5, 1942.
   Toronto doctor.
— Dr. Thomas Chisholm, M.P. (1842–1931). Canadian Medical Association
   Journal 29: 82–86, 1933.
County law associations. Canada Law Journal n.s. 29: 3–5, 1893.
County of York Law Association. Canada Law Journal n.s. 34: 251, 1898.
Coyne, James H
   Richard Maurice Bucke. Royal Society of Canada. Transactions s. 2,
   12(sect. 2): 159–191, 1906.
Currelly, C   T
   Henry Sproatt, 1867–1934. Royal Architectural Institute of Canada.
   Journal 11: 151, 1934.
Curry, S   G
   History of the Architectural Guild of Toronto. Royal Architectural Institute
   of Canada. Journal 7: 317–318, 1930.
Duff, Lyman Poore.
   John Almon Ritchie, K.C. Canadian Bar Review 14: 412–417, 1936.
Engineers' Club of Toronto. Railway and Marine World 9: 73, 1906.
Falconbridge, Honourable Chief Justice (Sir) William Glenholme, knt. Canada
   Law Journal n.s. 56: 75–76, 1920.
Ferguson, Mr. Justice.
   Sir William Ralph Meredith, C.J.O. Canadian Bar Review 1: 555–556, 1923.
Field, F   M
   Ontario Bar Association. Canada Law Journal n.s. 51: 41–51, 1915.
Fisher, A   W
   Dr. Donald Blair Fraser; an Ontario physician. Calgary Associate Clinic.
   Historical Bulletin 13(no. 2): 35–38, 1948.
Galt, (Sir) Thomas. Canada Law Journal 30: 488–489, 1894.
Gibson, Thomas.
   Notes on the medical history of Kingston. Canadian Medical Association
   Journal 18: 331–334, 446–451, 1928.
Godfrey, C   M
   The deans of Toronto medicine. Academy of Medicine, Toronto. Bulletin
   39: 152–157, 1966.
Gregg, A   H
   Francis Spence Baker. Royal Architectural Institute of Canada. Journal 3:
   31, 1926.

Grey, Rodney.
 Can the Ontario benchers justify archaic plan for law school? Saturday
 Night 64(18): 6–7, 1949.
Hagarty, Chief Justice (Sir) John Hawkins. Canada Law Journal n.s. 33:
 337–340, 1897.
Hagarty, Chief Justice (Sir) John Hawkins, farewell. Canada Law Journal n.s.
 33: 476–477, 1897.
Hamilton Law Association. Canada Law Journal n.s. 22: 114–115, 1886.
Harrison, Robert Alexander; chief justice of Ontario. Canada Law Journal n.s.
 11: 309–312, 1875.
[Helmer, D'Arcy]
 OAA takes realistic look at future of profession in Ontario. Royal
 Architectural Institute of Canada. Journal 42(no. 4): 20–22, 1965.
G   F   H   [Henderson, G   F   ]
 The centenary of Osgoode Hall. Canadian Bar Review 10: 182–185, 1932.
— The late Mr. Justice Orde. Canadian Bar Review 10: 456–457, 1932.
— Wallace Nesbitt, K.C. Canadian Bar Review 8: 283–284, 1930.
Herrington, W   S
 Sir Glenholme Falconbridge, C.J.K.B. Canadian Bar Review 3: 225–235,
 1925.
[Hodgins, Frank E   ]
 The Ontario Bar Association. Canada Law Journal n.s. 46: 288–296, 1910.
Holmested, the late George Smith. Canadian Bar Review 6: 145, 1928.
Horne, James.
 R.M. Bucke, pioneer psychiatrist, practical mystic. Ontario History 69:
 197–208, 1967.
Houser, Lloyd.
 The Institute of Professional Librarians of Ontario: an analysis, 1954–1975.
 IPLO Quarterly 17: 3–119, 1975.
Howell, W   A. Haldimand County Historical Review 1: 6, 1936.
Hughes, Jean.
 Dr. Hugh Macmillan. Bruce County Historical Society. Yearbook 9–10,
 1972.
Institute of Professional Librarians; professional organizations, their problems,
 pitfalls and possibilities. Ontario Library Review 43: 279–282, 1959.
Irving Heward Cameron; the philosophical surgeon. Calgary Historical Clinic.
 Historical Bulletin 6(no. 1): 1–11, 1941.
Kinnear, Helen.
 The county judge in Ontario. Canadian Bar Review 32: 21–43, 127–160,
 1954.
Klotz, Otto Julius. Waterloo Historical Society. Annual Report 2: 50, 1914.
 Engineer, astronomer from Waterloo county.

Laidman, G   H   R
Dr. George Sherk. Haldimand County Historical Review 1(no. 2): 2, 1936.
Landon, Fred.
David Mills, the philosopher from Bothwell. Willison's Monthly 5(3): 8–9, 1929.
— Dr. James H. Coyne. Western Ontario Historical Notes 8: 55–58, 1950. From St. Thomas *Times–Journal*.
— Otto Julius Klotz. Waterloo Historical Society. Annual Report 40: 30–32, 1952.
Langton, Thomas. Canada Law Journal n.s. 51: 38–39, 1915.
Leather, Ted.
Casimir Gzowski. Waterloo Historical Society. Annual Volume 56: 27–32, 1968.
Leriche, Harding and W   B   Stiver.
The work of specialists and general practitioners in Ontario. Canadian Medical Association Journal 81: 37–42, 1959.
McGhie, A   G
The growth of medical practice and medical education in Canada. Wentworth Bygones 9: 48–55, 1971.
MacKenzie, Kenneth.
Ward Wright. Canadian Bar Review 18: 52–53, 1940.
MacMurchy, Angus.
George Smith Holmested; an appreciation. Canadian Bar Review 6: 451–454, 1928.
McNab, Gordon F
Thoughts on legal aid. Canadian Forum 47: 12–14, 1967.
Mathers, A   S
Thirty-five years of practice. Royal Architectural Institute of Canada. Journal 32: 462–464, 1955.
Meredith, Chief Justice. Canada Law Journal n.s. 30: 583–584, 1894. Supreme Court of Ontario.
Meredith, William Ralph.
An appreciation; Sir Walter Gibson Pringle Cassels. Canadian Bar Review 1: 297–298, 1923.
Mignault, Honourable Mr. Justice.
Sir Walter Cassels. Canadian Bar Review 1: 210–213, 1923.
Mills, David; minister of justice. Canada Law Journal n.s. 36: 393–396, 1900.
Moore, H   Napier.
Charles Barry Cleveland, 1880–1934. Royal Architectural Institute of Canada. Journal 11: 137–138, 1934.
Morley, T   P
The need for nursing reform in Ontario. Canadian Medical Association Journal 90: 684–686, 1964.
Morphet, Georgina.
William Burgess. Bruce County Historical Society. Yearbook 34–35, 1972.
Morton, Joseph Francis. Bruce County Historical Society. Yearbook 19, 1974.

Moss, (Sir) Charles. Canada Law Journal n.s. 33: 413–415, 1897.
Moss, the late Chief Justice Thomas. Canada Law Journal n.s. 17: 55–60, 1881.
Moss, Thomas, justice of the Court of Error and Appeal. Canada Law Journal
    n.s. 11: 312–313, 1875.
Mowat, the late Mr. Justice Herbert Macdonald. Canadian Bar Review 6:
    390–392, 1928.
Murphy, Charles.
    Harold Fisher. Canadian Bar Review 7: 15–17, 1929.
Nelligan, John P
    Lawyers in Canada: a half-century count. Canadian Bar Review 28:
    727–749, 1950.
[Nesbitt, Wallace]: the late chief justice of Ontario. Canadian Bar Review 1:
    557–558, 1923.
New registration regulations in Ontario. Royal Architectural Institute of
    Canada. Journal 40(no. 5): 18, 1963.
Nicholls, Albert G
    Insulin: a chapter in the romance of medicine. Queen's Quarterly 35:
    516–528, 1928.
O'Connor, Mr. Justice John. Canada Law Journal n.s. 22: 383–384, 1886.
Oryst, Sawchuk.
    OAA Diamond Jubilee. Royal Architectural Institute of Canada. Journal
    42(no. 4): 15–19, 1965.
Osler, Britton Bath. Canada Law Journal n.s. 35: 289–291, 1899.
Page, F   E
    Doctor Ward Woolner. Waterloo Historical Society. Annual Report 42:
    43–44, 1954.
Parker, Stuart C
    Samuel George Curry. Royal Architectural Institute of Canada. Journal 19:
    140, 1942.
Patterson, Mr. Justice Christopher Salmon. Canada Law Journal n.s. 29:
    600–602, 1893.
Pennington, Doris (contributed by Mrs. Dan McInnes).
    Profile of a country doctor. Bruce County Historical Society. Yearbook
    29–32, 1974.
Perdue, W   E
    The late Mr. Justice Cameron. Canadian Bar Review 1: 298–299, 1923.
Rand, I   C   [et al.]
    Rt. Hon. Sir Lyman Poore Duff, G.C.M.G.; 1865–1955. Canadian Bar Review
    33: 1113–1129, 1955.
Reed, T   A
    Toronto's early architects; many fine buildings still standing. Royal
    Architectural Institute of Canada. Journal 27: 46–64, 1950.
Resignation of Vice-Chancellor Mowat. Canada Law Journal n.s. 8: 264–265,
    1872.

Riddell, William Renwick.
      Osgoode Hall. Canadian Historical Association. Historical Papers and
      Addresses 32–34, 1922.
Roy, James A
      John A. MacDonald: barrister and solicitor. Canadian Bar Review 26:
      415–432, 1948.
Sage, Walter N
      Sandford Fleming, engineer. Queen's Quarterly 57: 353–361, 1950.
Scott, W   L
      John Skirving Ewart, K.C.; an appreciation. Canadian Bar Review 11:
      333–338, 1933.
Smith, W   Earl.
      The Law Society of Upper Canada: 1797–1947. Canadian Bar Review 26:
      437–443, 1948.
Somerville, W   L
      The Ontario Association of Architects and the public. Royal Architectural
      Institute of Canada. Journal 1: 101, 1924.
Spack, Vivian M
      The story of a pioneer doctor – Harmaunus Smith. Wentworth Bygones 5:
      40–43, 1964.
Spragge, John Godfrey. Canada Law Journal n.s. 20: 233–234, 1884.
Stanley, G   D
      Dr. Abraham Groves, 1847–1935: a great crusader of Canadian medicine.
      Calgary Associate Clinic. Historical Bulletin 13(no. 1): 4–10, 1948.
— Further notes on Irving Heward Cameron. Calgary Associate Clinic.
      Historical Bulletin 7(no. 2): 8–10, 1942.
— Dr. Hugh Lang of Granton; a family physician on the old Ontario Strand.
      Calgary Associate Clinic. Historical Bulletin 16(no. 4): 82–87, 1952.
— Dr. J.F. ("Windy") Ross; medical recollections of Toronto Varsity. Calgary
      Associate Clinic. Historical Bulletin 18(no. 4): 88–95, 1954.
Stevenson, G   H
      The life and work of Richard Maurice Bucke. American Journal of
      Psychiatry 93: 1127–1150, 1937.
Timothy, H   B
      Rediscovering R.M. Bucke. Western Ontario Historical Notes 21: 34–40,
      1965.
Wilson, (Sir) Adam. Canada Law Journal n.s. 23: 401–403, 1887; n.s. 28: 3–4,
      1892.
Wilson, Matthew.
      The Kent Bar. Kent Historical Society. Papers and Addresses 3: 13–23,
      1917.
Wollock, Jeffrey.
      Did Stinson Jarvis hypnotize "Kit of the Mail"? Ontario History 67:
      241–245, 1975.

Woods, Damon C
    Law enforcement and the judiciary in Ontario. American Bar Association
    Journal 18: 343–348, 1932.
Young, Lita.
    Dr. Thomas Bradley. Bruce County Historical Society. Yearbook 24–26,
    1972.

Theses
Aris, Dale Louise.
    The pressure politics of the Ontario Medical Association: a case study.
    [Guelph, Ontario] 1976.
    ii, 147 leaves.
    M.A. thesis, The University of Guelph (microfilm 28040).   OGU
Birkhans, Martin.
    The life and work of Francis L. Sullivan, architect, 1882–1929. [Toronto]
    1964 [c1976]
    xii, 187 leaves. 69 leaves of plates. ports., illus.
    M.Arch. thesis, University of Toronto.   OTU
Burridge, G   E
    Attitude and opinion survey of professional engineers in Ontario. [Toronto]
    1961.
    93 leaves.
    M.B.A. thesis, University of Toronto.   OTU
Fisher, Helen Elizabeth.
    Professional associations in Canada. [Toronto: 1925]
    209 leaves.
    Ph.D. thesis, University of Toronto.   OTU
— Professional associations in Ontario. [Toronto] 1924.
    1 v. (unpaged).
    M.A. thesis, University of Toronto.   OTU
Hammond, Bernard.
    Differential utilization patterns and public evaluation of physicians' services
    in a medically insured public: the case of Ontario. Toronto: 1975.
    xviii, 262 leaves. tables.
    Ph.D. thesis, York University (microfilm 25718).   OTY
Heys, Donald J
    The pharmacist; a new role and a new store. [Toronto] 1968.
    i, 47 leaves. tables, figs.
    M.B.A. thesis, University of Toronto.   OTU
Kergin, Dorothy Jean, 1928–
    An exploratory study of the professionalization of registered nurses in
    Ontario and the implications for the support of change in basic nursing
    educational programs. Ann Arbor, Michigan: 1968.
    x, 244 leaves. illus.
    Ph.D. thesis, The University of Michigan (microfilm 69-12,151).   DA

Klein, William John, 1941–
  Judicial recruitment in Manitoba, Ontario, and Quebec, 1905–1970 .
  [Toronto] c1975.
  xiv, 403 leaves, tables, fig.
  Ph.D. thesis, University of Toronto (microfiche 31260).   OTU
McDermott, Ray Earl, 1930–
  An analysis of public dental services in Toronto. [Toronto] c1973.
  ix, 115 leaves. tables, forms, maps (part fold.).
  M.Sc. thesis, University of Toronto.   OTU
Mackay, E   M
  A study of changes in the engineering profession in Ontario 1941–1959.
  [Toronto] 1961.
  iv, 39 leaves.
  M.B.A. thesis, University of Toronto.   OTU
Marsden, Lorna R   1942–
  Doctors who teach: an influence on health delivery in Ontario. Princeton,
  New Jersey [1972, c1973]
  245 leaves. illus.
  Ph.D. thesis, Princeton University (microfilm 72-29804).   DA
Orkin, Mark Merrill, 1917–
  Professional autonomy and the public interest: a study of the Law Society of
  Upper Canada. Toronto: 1971.
  xiv, 349 leaves.
  D.Jur. thesis, York University (accepted 1972) (microfilm 11610).   OTY
Warren, Sharon Ann, 1947–
  Physicians and health regionalization: patterns of response to government
  policy. London, Ontario: 1973.
  xiv, 196 leaves. illus.
  Ph.D. thesis, The University of Western Ontario (microfilm 17102).   OLUM

SOCIAL POLICY

Bibliography
Conservation Council of Ontario.
  A conservation bibliography. Toronto: The Council, 1972.
  12 p.   OONL

Monographs and Pamphlets
Agnew, George Harvey, 1895–1971.
  Canadian hospitals, 1920–1970: a dramatic half-century. [Toronto]
  University of Toronto Press [c1974]
  xvii, 276 p. illus., port.   OTU
Angus, Margaret Sharp, 1908–
  Kingston General Hospital: a social and institutional history. [Montreal:

Published for the Kingston General Hospital by McGill–Queen's University
Press, 1973]
205 p. illus., ports. OTU
Ausable River Conservation Authority.
Our valley. v. 1–3, July, 1952–1954. [Toronto] Ontario Department of
Planning and Development. Conservation Branch, 1952–1954.
3 v. for the years; 1952, 1953, 1954. OTMCL
— The pinery. n.p. [1953]
14 leaves. illus., maps. OTMCL
Braithwaite, John Victor Maxwell, 1911–
Sick kids: the story of the Hospital for Sick Children in Toronto. Toronto:
McClelland and Stewart, c1974.
204 p. [16] leaves of plates. OTU
Canadian Public Health Association.
The development of public health in Canada: a review of the history and
organization of public health in the provinces of Canada, with an outline of
the present organization of the National Health Section of the Department
of Pensions and National Health, Canada. [1st ed. Toronto: 1940]
x, 184 p. illus., diagrs., maps.
Ontario: pp. 67–85. OTU
Carman, R   S
Wilmot Creek drainage unit (northern part); a study in forest conservation
and land use. Toronto: Department of Lands and Forests. Forestry Branch,
1940.
55 leaves. illus., fold. maps. OKQ
Cassidy, Harry Morris, 1900–1951.
Public health and welfare reorganization in Canada: the postwar problem in
Canadian provinces. Toronto: The Ryerson Press [1945]
xi, 464 p. diagrs., tables.
Ontario: p. 335–363. OTU
— Unemployment and relief in Ontario, 1929–1932: a survey and report under
the auspices of the Unemployment and Research Committee of Ontario.
Toronto: J.M. Dent & Sons Limited [1932]
290, xiii p. tables. OTU
Catfish Creek Conservation Authority.
Our valley. v. 1, June, 1954. [Toronto] Ontario Department of Planning and
Development, Conservation Branch, 1954.
4 p. OTMCL
Child Welfare League of America.
Children's institutions in Metropolitan Toronto: a report prepared for the
Social Planning Council of Metropolitan Toronto. Approved by the Board
of the SPC. [Toronto] 1960.
154, xi, leaves. tables. OTUCR
The Children's Aid Society of the County of Norfolk.
Fiftieth anniversary 1956. [Simcoe? Ontario: 1956?]
1 v. (unpaged). facsim., ports. OLU

Clarke, Charles Kirk, 1857–1924.
   A history of the Toronto General Hospital, including an account of the
   medal of the Loyal and Patroitic Society of 1812. With twenty illustrations.
   Toronto: William Briggs, 1913.
   147 p. front., plates, ports.   OTU
Cochrane, Frank.
   The conservation of the natural resources of Ontario. An address delivered
   before the first annual meeting of the Commission of Conservation. Ottawa:
   1910.
   10 p.
   "Reprinted from the *First annual report of the Commission of Conservation*, 1910."
                                                                              OTAR
Conference on Conservation in Eastern Ontario, Queen's University, Kingston,
   Ontario, 1945.
   Conservation in eastern Ontario; papers and proceedings [1st ed.] Toronto:
   T.E. Bowman, printer to the King's Most Excellent Majesty, 1946.
   x, 132 p. illus., maps (part fold.).   OTU
Conference on Conservation in South Central Ontario, Ontario Training and
   Re-establishment Institute, Toronto, 1946.
   Conservation in south central Ontario; papers and proceedings. Toronto: B.
   Johnston, printer to the King's Most Excellent Majesty, 1948.
   x, 131 p. graphs, illus., maps.   OTU
Conference on River Valley Development in Southern Ontario, London,
   Ontario, 1944.
   River valley development in southern Ontario: papers and proceedings.
   Toronto: T.E. Bowman, printer to the King's Most Excellent Majesty, 1945.
   134 p. illus., maps (part fold.), diagrs., tables.   OTU
Conference on the conservation of the natural resources of the counties of
   Hastings, Lennox and Addington, Frontenac and Leeds, held at Queen's
   University, April 30, 1943. [Kingston, Ontario: 1943]
   40 p.   OTU
Conservation Council of Ontario.
   A report on land use. Toronto: The Council, 1960.
   39 p. maps (fold.).
   President: F.H. Kortright.   OTAR
— The urban landscape: a study of open space in urban metropolitan areas.
   [Prepared under the direction of Michael Hough et al.] Toronto: 1971.
   126 p. illus., maps.   OTU
Cosbie, Waring Gerald, 1894–
   The Toronto General Hospital 1819–1965: a chronicle. Toronto: Macmillan
   of Canada [c1975]
   vii, 373 p. illus., ports.   OTU
Coventry, A   F
   The need of river valley development in Ontario. Toronto: Department of
   Planning and Development. Conservation Branch [1937?]
   16 p. map.   OTAR

Credit Valley Conservation Authority.
    Black Creek plan. [Toronto] 1956.
    44 p. illus., map.   OTU OTMCL
Cronin, Fergus.
    End of an era: the story of Scarborough General Hospital. [Toronto: 1974]
    40 p. illus.   OTU
Denholm, Kenneth Andrew, 1894–1969.
    History of Parry Sound General Hospital. Edited by C.M.M. Higham.
    [Parry Sound, Ontario: Bookworm, c1973]
    xi, 44 p. illus.   OTU
Dillon, (M.M.) Limited.
    Grand River Conservation Authority, Cambridge, Ontario: report on
    Mohawk Lake study. Cambridge, Ontario [1973]
    15 leaves. illus., graphs, fold. maps.   OBRT
— Watershed report for Junction Creek Conservation Authority. Sudbury,
    Ontario: 1969.
    1 v. (various pagings). diagrs. (part fold.), fold. col. maps, tables.   OTU
Dolan, Thomas J
    Twenty years of conservation on the Upper Thames watershed, 1947–1967.
    London, Ontario: Upper Thames River Conservation Authority, 1969.
    iii, 110 p. illus., ports., fold. maps.   OTU
Don Valley Conservation Authority.
    Don Valley conservation trail. Toronto: 1954.
    56 p. illus., map.   OTMCL
— Our valley. v. 1–3, 1952–1954. [Toronto] Ontario Department of Planning
    and Development. Conservation Branch, 1952–1954.
    3 v. for the years: 1952, 1953, 1954.
    No issue for 1953 was located.   OTMCL
Donnison, David Vernon.
    Welfare services in a Canadian community: a study of Brockville, Ontario.
    [Toronto] University of Toronto Press [c1958]
    vii, 200 p. illus., tables.   OTU
Duncan, Dorothy Ellen, 1927–
    Pioneer Village: Black Creek Conservation area. Photos by Margaret
    Whitley. [Woodbridge, Ontario: Metropolitan Toronto and Region
    Conservation Authority, 1964]
    24 p. illus.   OTU
Dymond, Allan Malcolm, 1864–1912.
    The laws of Ontario relating to women and children. Toronto: Clarkson W.
    James, printer to the King's Most Excellent Majesty, 1923.
    196 p.   OTU
Etobicoke – Mimico Conservation Authority.
    Our valley. v. 1, June, 1954. [Toronto] Ontario Department of Planning and
    Development. Conservation Branch, 1954.
    5 p.   OTMCL

Flavelle, (Sir) Joseph Wesley, bart., 1858–1939.
   Statement made by J.W. Flavelle, chairman of the Board of Trustees,
   Toronto General Hospital, Thursday, June 19, 1913, on the occasion of the
   formal opening of the new hospital buildings on College St., Toronto.
   [Toronto: 1913]
   10 p. plan.   OTU
Friedland, Martin L
   Legal aid; working papers, prepared for the Joint Committee on Legal Aid.
   [Toronto] 1964.
   1 v. (various pagings). diagrs. (Programme in Criminal Studies, Osgoode
   Hall Law School).   OTUCR
Ganaraska River Conservation Authority.
   Our valley. v. 1, January–June, 1954. [Toronto] Ontario Department of
   Planning and Development. Conservation Branch, 1954.
   1 v.   OTMCL
Gibson, Rose Mary.
   St. Mary's of the Lake in Kingston, compiled and written for the silver
   anniversary of the hospital. [Kingston, Ontario: Maxwell Printers, 1971]
   48 p. illus., ports.   OKP
Gibson, Thomas, 1865–
   A short account of the early history of the Kingston General Hospital.
   [Kingston, Ontario: Hanson & Edgar, Ltd.] 1935.
   20 p.   OTU
Glasner, Avrum A
   Deliver us from evil, but lead us not into temptation, by Avrum A. Glasner
   and Jack A. Walker. [Toronto] 1964.
   72 leaves.
   Ontario laws relating to child welfare.   OTU
Gogo, Jean L   1901–
   A history of the Cornwall General Hospital. [Cornwall, Ontario: 1967]
   23 p. illus.   OTU
Grand Valley Conservation Authority.
   Grand Valley Conservation Authority, 1948–1958. [Galt, Ontario] 1959.
   1 v. (unpaged). illus., map, ports.   OTMCL
— Our valley. v. 1, January–June, 1954. [Toronto] Ontario Department of
   Planning and Development. Conservation Branch, 1954.
   1 v.   OTMCL
Guelph Conference on the Conservation of Natural Resources of Ontario, 1942.
   Conservation and post-war rehabilitation, a report prepared by the Guelph
   Conference... February, 1942. Toronto: 1942.
   15 p.   OTAR OTU
Hamilton – Wentworth Planning Area Board.
   A study of the Ancaster – Dundas valley system for conservation purposes,
   part II: appraisal and recommendations. Prepared for the Hamilton Region
   Conservation Authority. [Hamilton, Ontario: The Board, 1968]
   73 leaves. plates, fold. maps (part col.).   OH

Held, Frieda.
    A brief history of the Ontario Welfare Council, 1908–1959, by Frieda Held,
    Mary Jennison and Lillian Henderson. Toronto: Ontario Welfare Council,
    1959.
    v, 21 p.   OTU
The history of the Hospital for Sick Children, College Street, Toronto, Ont.,
    Canada, and the Lakeside Home for Little Children, summer branch of the
    hospital, Toronto Island. Rev. to 1918. Toronto [1918?]
    68 p. illus., ports.   OTU
Hodgins, John George, 1821–1912.
    Aims and objectives of the Toronto Humane Society. Toronto: William
    Briggs, 1888.
    xii, 231 p. illus.   OTAR
Humber Valley Conservation Authority.
    King Creek plan, 1952. [Toronto] 1954.
    48 p. illus., map.   OTMCL
— Our valley. v. 1–3, June, 1952–June 1954. [Toronto] Ontario Department of
    Planning and Development. Conservation Branch, 1952–1954.
    3 v. for the years: 1952, 1953, 1954. illus.   OTMCL
— The story of a flood. [2d. ed. Toronto: The Author, 1955]
    12 p. illus., map.   OTU
Hutton, William L
    A brief for sterilisation of the feeble-minded. Prepared at the request of the
    Association of Ontario Mayors at their annual conference, Orillia, June,
    1936.
    11 p. charts.   OTU
Jenkinson, Vivien M
    The nursing standards project to establish tools of measurement of the
    quantity and quality of nursing care at the Hospital for Sick Children,
    Toronto. Report for the Ministry of Health in the province of Ontario,
    prepared by Vivien M. Jenkinson, Edwin L. Weinstein. Toronto: 1975.
    77 [36] leaves. tables.   OTU
Junction Creek Conservation Authority.
    Mud Lake – nature study; conservation project by Junction Creek
    Conservation Authority and city of Sudbury Planning Board. [Sudbury,
    Ontario] 1963.
    30 leaves. fold. maps, plans.   OTUSA
Kennedy, Cecil Howard, 1910–
    The Kingston General Hospital: a summary of its growth, 1835–1954.
    [Kingston, Ontario: 1955]
    35 leaves.   OTU
Kortright, Francis H
    Ontario's future? Conservation or else. Toronto: Conservation Council of
    Ontario [1952]
    [20] p. illus.   OTU

Law Society of Upper Canada. Subcommittee on Community Services in
  Ontario.
  Supplementary report on aid to persons in remote areas of the province and
  in particular the Indian and Eskimo population of northern Ontario.
  [Toronto: 1974?]
  1 v. (various pagings). illus.
  Chairman: P.S. Fitzgerald.   OLU
Lobsinger, Irwin (comp.).
  Saugeen Valley Conservation Authority [twenty years of conservation on the
  Saugeen watershed, 1950–1970. Walkerton, Ontario?] Saugeen Valley
  Conservation Authority [1970?]
  x, 112 p. illus.   OTMCL
McInnis, Ronald W
  Welfare legislation and benefit plans in Canada. Toronto: Law Society of
  Upper Canada [c1974]
  xvi, 270 p.
  Ontario: pp. 35–50.   OLU
McKenna, Ward, 1914–
  Catfish Creek Conservation Authority March 14, 1950–July 11, 1975. n.p.
  [1975?]
  79 p. illus., facsims.   OLU
MacLaren, (James F.) Limited.
  Report on the Appleby Creek flood prevention channel south of New Street
  to Lake Ontario, for the Halton Region Conservation Authority. Windsor,
  Ontario: 1972.
  1 v. (various pagings). fold. plans.   OTU
Makuck, Stanley M
  A study of statutory powers to provide community services. Toronto: Centre
  for Urban and Community Studies, University of Toronto, c1976.
  93 [6] P.   OTU
Mann, William Edward, 1918–   (ed.).
  Poverty and social policy in Canada. Vancouver; Copp Clark Publishing
  Company [c1970]
  xiv, 434 p. tables.   OTU
Metropolitan Toronto. Council.
  Report upon a proposed realignment of the jurisdiction of the children's aid
  societies operating within the Metropolitan Toronto area. [Toronto: The
  Author, 1956]
  xxiv, 383 p. diagrs., tables (part fold.).
  Consultants: Elizabeth S.F. Govan, Mr. R.D. Moore, J.D. Woods and
  Gordon Limited.   OTU

Metropolitan Toronto and Region Conservation Authority.
  A compendium of information. [Toronto] 1965.
  [2] iii, 68 [1] leaves.   OTU
  [Toronto: 1972]
  iii, 102 leaves. fold. col. map.   OTU
  [Toronto] 1976.
  75 leaves.   OTMCL
— Conservation 1957–1967. Woodbridge, Ontario [1967?]
  57 p. illus., col. maps.   OTU
— The Metropolitan Toronto and region waterfront plan 1972–1976; schedule
  "C". [Toronto] 1972.
  B619–B679 p. maps.   OTUMA
— Ontario Regulation 253/64. [Made under the Conservation Authorities Act.
  Toronto: 1965?]
  227 p. chiefly maps.   OTU
— Plan for flood control and water conservation. Woodbridge, Ontario: 1959.
  xii, 167 p. illus., col. maps, diagrs., tables.   OTU
Moira River Conservation Authority.
  O'Hara Mill, an historical monument being preserved by Moira River
  Conservation Authority. n.p. [1955?]
  [15] p. illus., maps.   OTAR
— Our valley. v. 1–3, 1952–1954. [Toronto] Ontario Department of Planning
  and Development, Conservation Branch, 1952–1954.
  3 v. for the years: 1952; 1953; 1954.   OTMCL
Mulock, (Sir) William, 1844–1944.
  To the Senate of the University of Toronto. [Toronto? 1892?]
  15 p.
  History of Park Hospital.   OTU
Niagara Regional Development Association.
  Outline and proposal, recreation and conservation plan, Grand River, for
  zones 4 and 5. n.p. [1964?]
  11 leaves.   OTU
North Grey Conservation Authority.
  Report 1966. [Owen Sound, Ontario] North Grey and Sauble Valley
  Conservation Authorities [1966]
  28 p. illus., maps.   OTU
Ontario. Advisory Committee on Child Welfare.
  Report to the Minister of Public Welfare. [Toronto: 1964]
  vi, 75, vi, 43 leaves.
  Chairman: Charles J. Foster.   OTL
Ontario. Attorney General's Department. Committee on enforcement of the law
  relating to gambling.
  Report. [Toronto] 1961.
  2 v.
  Chairman: J.D. Morton.   OTU

Ontario. Bronte Creek Provincial Park Advisory Committee.
  Master plan. [Toronto: Ministry of Natural Resources, 1972]
  40 p. illus. (part fold.), plans.
  Chairman: Donald M. Blenkhorn.   OTU
— Policy recommendations report. [Toronto] Minister of Lands and Forests,
  1972.
  31 p. maps (part fold.).   OTU
Ontario. Commission in the matter of the Workmen's Compensation Act.
  Report. Printed by order of the Legislative Assembly of Ontario. Toronto:
  Herbert H. Ball, printer to the King's Most Excellent Majesty, 1932.
  17 p.
  Commissioner: W.E. Middleton.   OTAR
Ontario. Commission of inquiry in the matter of Valerie and Peggy wards in the
  care of the Children's Aid Society for the county of Waterloo, placed by it in
  the foster home of Mr. & Mrs. Arthur Timbrell.
  Report. n.p. [1968]
  147 p.
  Chairman: Harry Waisberg.
Ontario. Commission of inquiry into certain matters relating to and arising from
  the report of Professor Leonard Gertler dated June, 1968, entitled "Niagara
  Escarpment Study – Conservation and Recreation Report".
  Report. [Toronto: 1971]
  101 leaves.
  Commissioner: Colin E. Bennett.   OTL
— Proceedings, June 11–July 6, 1971.
  2 v. [i.e. 411 typewritten pages]
  Only v. 2 pp. 204–411 in OTAR.   OTAR
Ontario. Commission of investigation into the administration, management,
  conduct, discipline and welfare of the Ontario Hospital, Hamilton.
  Report. Hamilton, Ontario: 1920.
  20 typewritten pages.
  Commissioner: Colin G. Snider.   OTAR
— Proceedings, February 11–17, 1920.
  1 v. [i.e. 449 typewritten pages]   OTAR
Ontario. Commissioner appointed to report upon the Workmen's Compensation
  Act.
  Report. Toronto: Baptist Johnston, printer to the King's Most Excellent
  Majesty, 1950.
  125 p. tables.
  Commissioner: W.D. Roach.   OTU
Ontario. Department of Commerce and Development. Conservation Branch.
  Holland valley conservation report: land and forest. Toronto: 1961.
  18, 11, 18 leaves. illus., diagrs. (part col.), maps (part col.).   OTUSA
— North Grey region conservation report, 1961; summary. Toronto: 1961.
  127 p. illus. (part col.), fold. map.   OTUSA
— Otonabee region conservation report: forest. [Toronto] 1961.
  58 leaves. illus., diagrs., map, tables.   OTMCL
  Land. [Toronto] 1961.
  78 leaves. illus., diagrs., maps (part fold.).   OTMCL

— Spencer Creek conservation report, 1960. Toronto: 1960.
 1 v. (various pagings). illus., maps (part col.), diagrs., tables.   OTUSA
— Twelve Mile Creek conservation report, 1960. Toronto: 1960.
 1 v. (various pagings). illus., maps (part fold., part col.).
 The report covers forests, water, wildlife and recreation.   OTU
Ontario. Department of Energy and Resources Management. Conservation
Authorities Branch.
 Cataraqui region conservation report: history. Toronto [1968]
 76 p. illus., diagrs., maps.   OTU
 Land, forest, wildlife. Toronto: 1966.
 3, 48, 43 p. illus., diagrs. (part fold.), maps (part fold. col.).   OTU
 Recreation. Toronto: 1967.
 63 p. illus., col. fold. map.   OTU
 Water. Toronto: 1967.
 iv, 2, 41 p. illus.; diagrs., maps (part fold. col.), tables.   OTU
— Central Lake Ontario conservation report: water. Toronto: 1964.
 39 leaves. illus., diagrs. (part fold.), maps (part fold. col.), tables.   OTU
— Ganaraska region conservation report, 1966. Toronto [1966]
 1 v. (various pagings). illus. (part fold., part col.).
 "A supplement to the Ganaraska report, 1944."   OTU
— Hamilton region conservation report, 1968. Toronto [1968]
 43 p. illus., diagrs., maps (part fold., part col.).   OTU
— Holland valley conservation report: water. Toronto: 1966.
 71, iv leaves. illus., diagrs. (part fold.), maps (part fold. col.), tables.   OTU
— Kettle Creek conservation report, 1967. Toronto [1967]
 1 v. (various pagings). illus., diagrs., maps (part fold. col.).   OTAR
 Land, forest, wildlife. Toronto: 1966.
 3, 59, 8 p. illus., maps (part col., part fold.), tables.   OTAR
 Water. Toronto: 1967.
 34 p. illus., maps (fold. part col.).   OTU
— Lakehead region conservation report: land, forest. Toronto: 1966.
 iv, 70 p. illus. (part fold.), diagrs., maps (part col.).   OTU
 Recreation by [J.O. Farina] Toronto: 1964.
 16 p. illus., maps (part col. part fold.).   OTU
— Lower Thames valley conservation report, 1965. Toronto: 1965.
 1 v. (various pagings). illus., graphs, maps (part col.), tables.   OTAR
 Summary. Toronto [1967?]
 ix, 93 p. illus., maps (part col.).   OTU
 Water. Toronto: 1965.
 68 leaves. illus., diagrs. (part fold.), maps (part fold. col.).   OTU
— Lower Trent region conservation report. [Toronto] 1970.
 3 v. illus. (part fold. col.), maps (part fold. col.).
 Contents: 1, Report and plan; 2, Appendix; 3, History.   OTU
— Maitland valley conservation report, 1967. Toronto [1967]
 1 v. (various pagings). illus., diagrs., fold. maps (part col.), tables.   OTAR
 Land, forest, wildlife. Toronto: 1965.
 45, 51, 28 p. illus., diagrs. (part col.), maps (part fold., part col.).   OTU
 Water. Toronto: 1967.
 43, A1–5, B1–6 p. illus., diagrs., fold. maps, plans (part fold.), tables.   OTU

— Mississippi valley conservation report, 1970. [Toronto? 1970]
  3 v. illus., diagrs., maps (part fold. col.), tables.
  Contents: v. 1, Report and plan; v. 2, Appendix; v. 3, History.   OTU
— Napanee region conservation report: Salmon River section. Toronto [1967]
  67, 30, 40 leaves. illus., map (part fold.).   OTMCL
— Niagara peninsula conservation report; water. Toronto: 1964.
  2, ii, 73 leaves. illus., maps (part col., part fold.), diagrs. (part fold.), tables.
                                                                              OTU
— Nottawasaga valley conservation report, 1964. Toronto: 1964.
  1 v. (various pagings). illus. (part fold.), diagrs. (part fold.), col. maps (part
  fold.).   OTU
— Otonabee region conservation report, 1964. Toronto: 1964.
  1 v. (various reports). illus., graphs, maps (part fold., part col.), tables. OTAR
  Summary. Toronto: 1965.
  x, 152 p. illus. (part col.), diagrs., col. maps.   OTMCL
— Prince Edward region conservation report; land, forest, water, wildlife.
  Toronto: 1968.
  xv, 161 p. illus., diagrs. (part fold.), maps (part fold., part col.), tables.   OTU
  Recreation. Toronto: 1970.
  81 p. illus., maps (part fold.).   OTU
— Raisin River conservation report, 1966. Toronto: 1966.
  iii, 93 p. illus., diagrs. (part col. part fold.), maps (part fold., col.).   OTU
  Supplement. Toronto: 1969.
  v, 63 p. illus., diagrs. (part fold., part col.), fold. col. maps.   OTU
— Rideau valley conservation report: history, land use and forest, water
  biology, recreation. Toronto: 1968.
  330 p. illus., diagrs. (part fold.), maps (part fold., part col.), tables.   OTU
  Summary. [Toronto] 1970.
  177 p. illus., fold. col. map.   OTMCL
— Sault Ste. Marie region conservation report, 1969. Toronto: 1969.
  62 p. illus., diagrs., maps (part fold., part col.).   OTU
— Sydenham valley conservation report, 1965. Toronto: 1965.
  1 v. (various pagings). illus., diagrs., maps (part col., part fold.), plans. OTAR
  Summary. [Toronto] 1968.
  118 p. illus., diagrs., map.   OTMCL
  Water. Toronto: 1965.
  2, 77, iv leaves. illus. diagrs. (part col., part fold.), maps (part col., part fold.).
                                                                              OTU
Ontario. Department of the Environment.
  Niagara peninsula conservation report, 1972. [Toronto: 1972]
  2 v. illus., maps (part fold., col.).   OTU
Ontario. Department of Lands and Forests. Conservation Authorities Branch.
  Big Creek region conservation report: history [Toronto] 1963.
  277 leaves. illus., fold. maps, diagrs., tables.
  Chiefly pre-Confederation.   OTU
  Summary. [Toronto] 1963.
  x, 120 [1] p. front., illus., maps.   OTU

— Crowe valley conservation report, 1963. [Toronto: 1963]
    1 v. (various pagings). illus., fold. col. maps, diagrs., tables.   OTAR
    Water, wildlife. [Toronto] 1962.
    [xi] 2, 71, 5, iv leaves. illus., maps (part fold., part col.), diagrs. (part fold.),
    tables.   OTU
— Lower Thames valley conservation report, 1962: recreation. Toronto: 1962.
    18 leaves. illus., maps.   OTMCL
    Land, forest. [Toronto] 1963.
    33, 64 leaves. illus., col. map, diagrs., tables.   OTU
— Mattagami valley conservation report: water, forest. [Toronto] 1963.
    29 p. illus., maps (part fold.).   OTMCL
— Otonabee region conservation report; recreation. [Toronto] 1962.
    31 leaves. illus., maps (col. part fold.).   OTU
    Wildlife. [Toronto] 1962.
    34 leaves. illus., maps (part fold., part col.).   OTU
— Otter Creek conservation report, 1962; summary. [Toronto] 1962.
    x, 107 [2] p. illus., maps (part col.).   OTU
— Sauble valley conservation report, 1962. [Toronto: 1962]
    1 v. (various pagings). illus., graphs, maps (part fold. col.), tables.   OTAR
    Water, wildlife. [Toronto] 1963.
    67 leaves. illus., diagrs., maps (part fold. col.).   OTMCL
— Spencer Creek conservation report, 1962: history. Toronto: 1962.
    200 leaves. illus., maps (part fold., part col.), diagrs., tables.   OTU
— Sydenham valley conservation report, 1963; land, forest. [Toronto?] 1963.
    3, 25, 70 p. illus. (part fold.), maps (fold. col.), diagrs., tables.   OTU
    Recreation. Toronto: 1962.
    15 leaves. illus., map.   OTMCL
— Whiteman (Horner) Creek conservation report. [Toronto] 1962.
    2, 38, 3 leaves. illus., charts, maps (part fold., part col.).   OTAR
Ontario. Department of Planning and Development. Community Councils Co-
    ordinating Committee.
    Conservation tour of the Humber River watershed; sponsored by the
    Community Councils Co-ordinating Committee in co-operation with
    Department of Planning and Development, Conservation Branch, October
    23, 1946. [Toronto: 1946]
    [34] leaves. map.   OTU
Ontario. Department of Planning and Development. Conservation Branch.
    Ausable valley conservation report. [2d ed.] Toronto: 1949.
    1 v. (various pagings). illus. (part col.), maps (part col. fold.).   OTU
    Recommendations and summary. Toronto: B. Johnston, printer to the
    King's Most Excellent Majesty, 1951.
    73 p. illus., diagrs., maps.   OTUSA
— Big Creek region conservation report: forest. [Toronto] 1958.
    2, 47 leaves. illus., fold. maps, diagrs., tables.   OTU
    Land. [Toronto] 1958.
    2, 48 leaves. illus., col. maps (part fold.), tables.   OTAR
    Water. [Toronto] 1958.
    71, v, iv leaves. illus., fold. maps, tables.   OTAR
    Wildlife [Toronto] 1958.
    2, 29 leaves. fold. col. maps.   OTAR

— Big Creek valley conservation report, 1953. [Prepared by the staff of the
Conservation Branch of the Department of Planning and Development]
Toronto: 1953.
84 leaves. illus., maps, (part fold.), diagrs., tables.   OTU
— Catfish Creek conservation report, 1951, ground water; forestry. Toronto:
1951.
[12] 76, 62 leaves. illus., maps (part fold.), diagrs., tables.   OLU
— Central Lake Ontario conservation report: forest. [Toronto] 1960.
57 leaves. illus., diagrs., maps.   OTMCL
Land. [Toronto] 1960.
52 leaves. illus., diagrs., tables.   OTMCL
Recreation. [Toronto] 1960.
21 leaves. maps.   OTMCL
Wildlife. [Toronto] 1960.
32 leaves. illus., fold. col. map, plans.   OTMCL
— Credit valley conservation report, 1956. Toronto: 1956.
1 v. (various pagings). graphs, illus., maps (part fold., part col.), tables.
The report covers history, land, forestry, water, recreation and wildlife. OTU
1957: summary. Toronto: Baptist Johnston, printer to the Queen's Most
Excellent Majesty, 1957.
139 p. illus., fold. map.   OTUSA
— Conservation authorities in Ontario. Prepared for the members of the
Legislature. n.p.: 1955.
18 leaves. 32 plates. map.   OTAR
— Crowe valley conservation report: forest. [Toronto] 1960.
2, 55 leaves. illus., maps (part col.), diagrs., tables.   OTU
— Denfield Creek plan, 1956. Toronto: 1956.
52 leaves. col. fold. map, tables.   OTMCL
— Don valley conservation report. Toronto: 1950.
1 v. (various pagings). illus., maps, diagrs.
The report covers land use, forestry, water, wildlife and recreation.   OTU
Recommendations and summary. Toronto: Baptist Johnston, printer to the
King's Most Excellent Majesty, 1950.
95 p. illus., maps (part col. part fold.).   OTU
— Etobicoke valley report, 1947: recommendations and summary. Toronto:
Baptist Johnston, printer to the King's Most Excellent Majesty, 1947.
16 p. map.   OTMCL
— Ganaraska watershed: irrigation water supply survey, 1957. Toronto: 1957.
17, 3, v leaves. illus., tables.   OTAR
— Grand valley conservation report, 1954. Toronto: 1954.
1 v. (various pagings). illus., maps (part fold., part col.).   OTU
— Humber valley conservation report, 1948: recommendations and summary.
Toronto: Baptist Johnston, printer to the King's Most Excellent Majesty,
1948.
32 p. illus., maps.   OTMCL
— Junction Creek conservation report: land, forest. [Toronto] 1959.
13 leaves. illus.   OTU
Recreation. [Toronto] 1959.
16 leaves. illus., map, plans.   OTMCL

— Lower Saugeen valley conservation report: forest. [Toronto] 1959.
  48, 18 leaves. illus., fold. maps, tables.   OTU
— Luttrell's Creek conservation report. [Toronto] 1953.
  45 leaves. illus., fold. col. map.   OTMCL
— Middle Maitland valley conservation report, 1954. Toronto: 1954.
  v, 68, 73, iii leaves. illus., maps (part fold. col.), tables.
  "The report is in two sections: forestry and water".   OTU
— Moira valley conservation report, 1950. Toronto: 1950.
  1 v. (various pagings). illus., maps. (part fold., part col.), diagrs., tables. OTU
  Summary and recommendations. Toronto: Baptist Johnston, printer to the
  King's Most Excellent Majesty, 1950.
  53 p. illus., diagrs., maps   OTU
  [Recommendations and] summary. 2d ed. Toronto: Baptist Johnston,
  printer to the Queen's Most Excellent Majesty, 1955.
  123 p. illus., diagrs., maps (part fold.).   OTU
— Napanee valley conservation report, 1957. Toronto: 1957.
  1 v. (various pagings). illus., maps, diagrs., tables.   OTU
  1958, summary. Toronto: 1958.
  104 p. illus. (part col.), fold. col. maps, tables.   OONL
— Neebling valley conservation report, 1957. Toronto: 1957.
  1 v. (various pagings). illus., fold. col. maps, tables.   OTU
— Niagara peninsula conservation report: recreation. [Toronto] 1960.
  26 leaves. illus., maps (part fold. col.).   OTMCL
— Nith valley interim conservation report. Toronto: 1951.
  1 v. (various pagings). illus., diagrs.
  This report is in four sections: geography, forestry, water and wildlife. OTU
— North Grey region conservation report, 1959. Toronto: 1959.
  1 v. (various pagings). illus., fold. maps (part col.), tables.
  "The report covers history, land, forests, water, wildlife and recreation".
                                                                           OTU
— Ontario conservation authorities tour to the Muskingum, September 27th to
  October 1st. Toronto: 1948.
  63 leaves. illus., fold. col. map.
  A tour to explore conservation in Ohio state.   OTAR
— Otter valley conservation report, 1957. Toronto: 1957.
  1 v. (various pagings). illus., diagrs. (part col.), maps (part col., part fold.).
  "This report covers history, land, forestry, water and wildlife."
  Cover title: Otter Creek conservation report, 1957.   OTU
— Our valley: a report to the people of the nineteen authorities in Ontario. v.
  1–6, January 1955–Summer, 1960. [Toronto] Baptist Johnston, printer to
  the Queen's Most Excellent Majesty, 1955–1960.
  6 v. for the years: 1955, 1956, 1957, 1958, 1959, 1960. illus., maps.
  Sub-title varies.   OTMCL
— R.D.H.P. valley conservation report, 1956. Toronto: 1956.
  1 v. (various pagings). illus., maps (part fold., part col.).
  Cover title: Rouge Duffin Highland Petticoat conservation report.

"The reports covers history, land, forestry, water, recreation and wildlife.

OTU

— Report on stream conditions of Boyd Creek: a tributary of the Ganaraska
River. Toronto: 1953.
13 leaves. illus., fold. map, tables.   OTAR
— Sauble valley conservation report: forest. [Toronto] 1959.
2, 53, leaves. illus., col. map, diagrs., tables.   OTU
Land. [Toronto] 1960.
59 leaves. illus., diagrs.   OTU
— Saugeen valley conservation report, 1952. Toronto: 1952.
1 v. (various pagings). illus., graphs, maps (part fold., part col.), tables.

OTAR

— Sixteen Mile Creek conservation report, 1958. Toronto: 1958.
1 v. (various pagings). illus., col. maps (part fold.).
"The report covers land, forestry, water, recreation and wildlife.   OTU
— South Nation valley interim report. Toronto: 1948.
15, 102, 56, 19, 76 leaves. illus., diagrs., maps (part fold., part col.).   OTU
Recommendations and summary. Toronto: Baptist Johnston, printer to the
King's Most Excellent Majesty, 1950.
65 p. illus., graphs, maps (part fold.).   OTAR
— Speed valley conservation report, 1953. Toronto: 1953.
1 v. (various pagings). graphs, illus., maps (part fold., part col.), tables.
Report is in four sections, namely: land, forest, wildlife and water.   OTU
— The Thames valley report, 1946: introduction, summary and
recommendations. Toronto: T.E. Bowman, printer to the King's Most
Excellent Majesty, 1947.
15 p. map.   OTMCL
— Upper Holland valley conservation report, 1953. Toronto: 1953.
1 v. (various pagings). illus., diagrs., maps (part fold., part col.).
"The report is in five sections: history, land use, forestry, water and wildlife.

OTU

— Upper Saugeen valley conservation report, 1953; summary. Toronto: B.
Johnston, printer to the Queen's Most Excellent Majesty, 1953.
170 p. illus., diagrs., maps (part fold.).   OTU
— Upper Thames valley conservation report, 1952. Toronto: 1952.
1 v. (various pagings). illus. (part fold., part col.), diagrs., tables, fold. maps.
The report covers: land use, forestry, water, wildlife and recreation.   OTU
Ontario. Human Rights Commission.
Human rights in Ontario. [Toronto: 1965]
16 p. illus.
Chairman: Louis Fine.   OTU
— A brief pictorial history of Blacks in 19th century Ontario. [Toronto: 1971]
[30] p. chiefly ports., facsims.   OTAR
— A brief pictorial account of Japanese-Canadians in Ontario. Toronto: 1971.
[30] p. chiefly ports.   OTAR

— Case study and community action programs under the Ontario human
rights code and the Age Discrimination Act. [Toronto: Queen's Printer,
1968]
27 p. illus.   OTUL

Background report to the Ontario Human Rights Commission
Elkin, Frederick.
The employment of visible minority groups in mass media advertising; a
report submitted to the Ontario Human Rights Commission. Downsview,
Ontario: 1971.
iv, 79 leaves.   OTU

Ontario. Joint Committee on Legal Aid.
Report. [Toronto] 1965.
126 p.
Chairman: William B. Common.   OTUCR
Ontario. Legislative Assembly. Select Committee appointed to enquire into
certain matters concerning the administration of justice in the province of
Ontario.
Proceedings, April 24–October 4, 1951.
28 v. [i.e. 3,945 typewritten pages]
Chairman: Dana Porter.
No report was prepared due to the dissolution of the Committee upon the
dissolution of the Legislature October 6, 1951.   OTAR
Ontario. Legislative Assembly. Select Committee appointed to enquire into the
administration of justice.
Report. Toronto: T.E. Bowman, printer to the King's Most Excellent
Majesty, 1941.
79 p.
Chairman: G.D. Conant.   OTAR
— Proceedings, March 6–April 12, 1940.
941 typewritten pages.   OTAR

*Background report to Ontario Legislative Assembly Select Committee appointed to inquire into
the administration of justice*
Barlow, F   H
Interim and final reports on a survey of the administration of justice in the
province of Ontario, pursuant to the direction of the Honourable Gordon D.
Conant. [Toronto] 1939.
54 leaves.   OTAR

Ontario. Legislative Assembly. Select Committee appointed to inquire into the
affairs of the Toronto General Hospital.
Report. Toronto: Samuel Beatty, 1868.
20 p.
Chairman: A.W. Lauder.
The above is really the proceedings.   OTAR
— Report. [Toronto: 1868]
[7] handwritten pages.   OTAR
Ontario. Legislative Assembly. Select Committee appointed to study and report
upon problems of delinquent individuals and custodial questions, and the
place of reform institutions therein.
Report. Toronto: 1954.
455 leaves.
Chairman: W.J. Stewart.   OTAR
— Proceedings, April 20, 1953–February 5, 1954.
114 v. [i.e. 8185 typewritten pages]   OTAR
— Consolidated indices v. 1–106.
443 leaves.   OTAR
— Interim index.
9 v. in 10 parts.   OTAR
Ontario. Legislative Assembly. Select Committee on Aging and the Aged.
Interim report. [Toronto] 1965.
31 leaves. map, tables.
Chairman: Alex Carruthers.   OTAR
— Second interim report. Toronto: 1966.
46 leaves.   OTAR
— Final recommendations. Toronto [1967?]
vi, 43 p. tables.   OTAR
— Population growth in Ontario. [Toronto: 1964]
6 leaves. graph, tables. (Background paper no. 1).   OTAR
— Growth of the older population of Ontario, prepared by Lawrence
Crawford. [Toronto] 1964.
12 leaves. graphs, tables. (Background paper no. 2 part A).   OTAR
— Proceedings, December 14, 1964–January 12, 1967.
30 v. [i.e. 2738 typewritten pages]   OTAR
— Proceedings of the Committee July 14–August 25, 1964.
2 v. [i.e. 204 typewritten pages]   OTAR
Ontario. Legislative Assembly. Select Committee on Conservation.
Report. Toronto: Baptist Johnston, printer to the King's Most Excellent
Majesty, 1950.
xxi, 188 p. illus. (part col.), maps (part col., part fold.), tables.
Chairman: F.S. Thomas.   OTAR
Report. Toronto: Baptist Johnston, printer to the King's Nost Excellent
Majesty, 1950.
185 leaves. illus. (part col.), maps (part col., part fold.), tables.   OTAR
— Briefs.
111 v.   OTAR

Ontario. Legislative Assembly. Select Committee on Conservation Authority.
    Interim report. [Toronto] 1966.
    iii, 4 leaves.
    Chairman: D. Arthur Evans.   OTAR
— Report. [Toronto] 1967.
    135 p. tables, fold. col. maps.   OTAR
— Conservation authorities of the province of Ontario 1965 and 1966 ,
    prepared by H.G. Rowan. [Toronto] 1966.
    1 v. (various pagings).   OTAR
— Briefs, submissions.
    37 authorities.   OTAR
Ontario. Legislative Assembly. Select Committee on the Act to amend the
    Workmen's Compensation for Injuries Act 1886.
    Report. Printed by order of the Legislative Assembly. Toronto: Warwick &
    Sons, 1887.
    67 p.
    Chairman: C.F. Fraser.   OLU
— Proceedings, March 31–April 14, 1887.
    380 typewritten pages.   OTAR
Ontario. Legislative Assembly. Select Committee on the Cemeteries Act and
    related matters.
    Report. [Toronto: 1954]
    28 p.
    Chairman: J.N. Allan.   OTAR
— Report. [Toronto: 1954]
    34 leaves.   OTAR
— Proceedings, April 13, 1953–January 20, 1954.
    12 v. [i.e. 1301 typewritten pages]   OTAR
Ontario. Legislative Assembly. Select Committee on Youth.
    Preliminary report. [Toronto: 1964]
    40 leaves. graphs, tables.
    Chairman: C.J.S. Apps.   OTAR
— A progress report. [Toronto] 1965.
    24 leaves. graphs.   OTAR
— An interim report [Toronto] 1966.
    63 leaves.   OTAR OTUCR
— Report. [Toronto] 1967.
    x, 408 p. graphs, tables.   OTAR OTUL
— Terms of reference.
    7 v.   OTAR
— Minutes, June 4, 1964–December 29, 1964.
    309 leaves.   OTAR
— Briefs.
    530 v.   OTAR
— Summary of recommendations 1965.
    2 v. (v. 1, unpaged; v. 2, 105 leaves.)   OTAR

Ontario. Ministry of Natural Resources. Conservation Authorities Branch.
    Nottawasaga valley conservation report: water. Toronto: 1973.
    42 p. illus., diagrs., fold. col. maps, tables.   OTU
— South Lake Simcoe conservation report, 1973. [Toronto: 1973]
    115 p. illus., maps, tables.   OTU
Ontario. Ministry of the Environment. Conservation Authorities Branch.
    Long Point region conservation report; a supplement to Big Creek
    conservation report. Toronto: Department of the Environment, 1972.
    31 leaves. illus., diagrs. fold. col. maps.   OTU
Ontario. Royal Commission in the matter of Workmen's Compensation Act.
    Report. [Toronto?] 1967.
    xx, 217 p. fold. chart.
    Chairman: George A. McGillivray.   OTAR OTER
— Proceedings, August 16–November 29, 1966.
    21 v.   OTAR
— Briefs.
    68 v.   OTAR
Ontario. Royal Commission to inquire into the care and control of the mentally
    defective and feeble-minded and the prevalence of venereal disease.
    Report on the case and control of the mentally defective and feeble-minded
    in Ontario. Printed by order of the Legislative Assembly of Ontario.
    Toronto: A.T. Wilgress, printer to the King's Most Excellent Majesty, 1919.
    236 p.
    Commissioner: Frank Egerton Hodgins.   OTAR
— Report on venereal disease. Printed by order of the Legislative Assembly of
    Ontario. Toronto: A.T. Wilgress, printer to the King's Most Excellent
    Majesty, 1919.
    25 p.   OTAR
Ontario. Treasury Department. Regional Development Branch. Niagara
    Escarpment Study Group.
    Niagara Escarpment study: conservation and recreation report. Toronto:
    1968.
    ix, 96 p. illus., col. fold. maps, tables.   OTU
Ontario. Workmen's Compensation Board. Task Force.
    The administration of workmen's compensation in Ontario: report.
    [Toronto: 1973]
    xxvi, 117 p. charts, tables.
    Chairman: A.R. Aird.   OTER
Ontario Conservation and Reforestation Association.
    Summary of the Ganaraska report: a study in land use with
    recommendations for the rehabilitation of the area in the post-war period,
    with introduction, recommendations and table of projects and costs.
    [Toronto?] The Association, 1944.
    19 p. illus.   OONL

Ontario Federation of Labour.
  Brief to the government of Ontario concerning human rights. [Don Mills,
  Ontario: 1971?]
    12 leaves.   OONL
Ottawa General Hospital since 1867 to 1929. Souvenir book. Ottawa: 1929.
    64 p. illus., ports.   OOA
Putnam, Donald Fulton, 1903–
  The Don River system, by D.F. Putnam and L.G. Reeds. [Toronto]
  Conservation Branch, Ontario Department of Planning and Development,
  n.d.
    16 p. illus., graphs, map.   OTMCL
Red Cross (Canada). Ottawa and Ottawa Valley Branch. History Committee.
  To serve and to share: a short history of the Ottawa and Ottawa Valley
  Branch of the Canadian Red Cross Society: the story of sixty years of service,
  1914–1974. Ottawa: 1974.
    64 p. illus., ports.
    Chairman: Miriam Sheridan.   OONL
Red Cross (Canada). Toronto Branch.
  History Toronto Branch the Canadian Red Cross Society 1914–1948.
  [Toronto] The Toronto Red Cross [1949?]
    109 p. illus., ports.   OTAR
Regional Development of Community Services Conference, Hamilton, Ontario,
1963.
  Our growing community. [Hamilton, Ontario] 1963.
    ii, 28 leaves. illus., map.   OTU
Richardson, Arthur Herbert, 1890–1971.
  Conservation by the people: the history of the conservation movement in
  Ontario to 1970. Toronto: Published by the University of Toronto Press for
  the Conservation Authorities of Ontario [c1974]
    xi, 154 p. illus., fold. col. map.   OTU
— Draft of a proposed scheme for a Humber valley & Don valley greenbelt for
  submission to the Humber Valley Conservation Authority, the Don Valley
  Conservation Authority and the Toronto and York Planning Board.
  Toronto: 1953.
    23 leaves. fold. col. map, tables.   OTUSA
— A report on the Ganaraska watershed: a study in land use with plans for the
  rehabilitation of the area in the post-war period. With an introduction by
  R.C. Wallace. Toronto: Published jointly by the Dominion and Ontario
  governments by T.E. Bowman, printer to the King's Most Excellent
  Majesty, 1944.
    xxvi, 248 p. illus., diagrs., maps (part fold.), tables.   OTMCL
    2d ed. Toronto: Published jointly by the Dominion and Ontario
  governments by T.E. Bowman, printer to the King's Most Excellent Majesty
  [1946]
    xxvi, 253 p. illus., diagrs., maps (part fold.), tables.   OTMCL

Rolstin, Hilda Ruth, 1917–
   The Hospital for Sick Children, School of Nursing, Toronto, written by
   Hilda Rolstin for the Alumnae Association. [Toronto] 1972.
   94 p. illus., ports.
   Cover title: History of the School of Nursing, the Hospital for Sick Children.
                                                                                    OTU
Rouge, Duffin, Highland and Petticoat Creeks Conservation Authority.
   Our valley. v. 1, no. 1, June, 1954. [Toronto] Department of Planning and
   Development, Conservation Branch, 1954.
   1 v. illus.   OTMCL
Runnalls, John Lawrence, 1901–
   A century with the St. Catharines General Hospital, by John Lawrence
   Runnalls, assisted by Helen Beall Brown and Charles Douglas Complin. St.
   Catherines, Ontario: St. Catharines General Hospital, 1974.
   150 p. illus., ports.   OLU
Saugeen Valley Conservation Authority.
   Our valley. v. 1–3, April, 1952–June, 1954. [Walkerton, Ontario]
   1952–1954.
   3 v. for the years: 1952, 1953, 1954, tables.   OTMCL
Savage, Harvey.
   Legal aid pilot project: Islington Band – Whitedog Reserve. [Kenora?
   Ontario: 1974]
   1 v. (various pagings).
   "Ontario. The rules for determining financial eligibility for legal aid
   pursuant to the Legal act aid, Revised statutes of Ontario, 1970 and
   regulations. Revised August 1973" (5 leaves) inserted at end.   OTU
Simcoe County, Ontario. County Council. Special Committee on Post-war Soil
   Conservation and Land Utilization Programme.
   Report... which was unanimously adopted at the January session, 1944 by
   the Simcoe County Council. [Barrie, Ontario] Press of the Barrie Examiner
   [1944]
   8 p.
   Chairman: H. Eric Simpson.   OTMCL
Social Planning & Research Council of Hamilton and District.
   Manual of agency policies [rev. ed. Hamilton, Ontario] 1967.
   121 [6] p.   OTU
Social Planning Council of Hamilton and District.
   Analysis of a selected group of families whose children were admitted to the
   care of the children's aid societies in Hamilton between January 1st, 1957,
   and December 31st, 1959 by Kathleen Arnott. Hamilton, Ontario [1961]
   v, 32 p. tables.   OTU
Social Planning Council of Hamilton and District. Committee on Handicapped.
   A study of services and facilities for disabled people. [Hamilton] 1964.
   iv, 121 leaves. graphs, tables.   OTU

Social Planning Council of Metropolitan Toronto.
Community resources in Metropolitan Toronto with emphasis on youth oriented services. Toronto: 1971.
57 p. OTU
— Revised. Toronto: 1972.
85 p. OTU
— Families in high rise apartments. Toronto: 1973.
166 p.
Research staff: Alwyne Graham [et al.] Project director: Wilson A. Head.
OTU
— In search of a framework: a review of trends in the financing and delivery of community services. Prepared for the city of Toronto Neighbourhood Services Work Group. [Toronto: The Council] 1976.
2 v. charts, maps. OTU
— A preliminary study of the social implications of high density living conditions. Toronto: 1966.
35 leaves. OTU
— A report on maternity homes in Metropolitan Toronto. [Toronto] 1960.
xi, 73 leaves. OTU
— Report on the Conference on Drop-in-Centres for Young People, Toronto, June 7, 1966. Toronto: 1966.
11, 6 leaves. OOCW
— A study of the needs and resources for community supported welfare, health and recreation services in Metropolitan Toronto: workshop papers. Toronto: [1962?]
5 parts in 1. fold. maps.
Contents: Planning and co-ordination; The use of human resources; The "best pattern" of services for a metropolitan area; Financing; The respective responsibilities of government and voluntary agencies. OTU
— A study of the needs and resources for community supported welfare, health and recreation services in Metropolitan Toronto; a community self-study. [Toronto: c1963]
xii, 274 p. maps, tables. OTUSA
— Survey of personnel practices in voluntary social welfare organizations in Metropolitan Toronto. Toronto: 1964.
33 leaves. tables. OTU
— Trends affecting the development of social services in Metropolitan Toronto: report. 2d ed. [Toronto] 1970.
vi, 116 p. fold. map, graphs. OTU
Social Planning Council of Metropolitan Toronto. Committee on Homeless and Transient Men.
Report. [Toronto] 1960.
25 p.
Chairman: John L. Spencer. OTU

Social Planning Council of Metropolitan Toronto. Committee on Homemaker
Services for Older People.
Homemaker services for older people: report. Toronto: 1963.
27 [9] 3 p. tables.
Chairman: W.B. MacKinnon. OONL
Social Planning Council of Metropolitan Toronto. Committee to Consider and
Promote a Residence for Physically Incapacited Young Adults.
Residential care for physically incapacitated young adults, November 3,
1965. Toronto: Social Planning Council of Metropolitan Toronto [1965?]
41 leaves. tables. OTU
Social Planning Council of Metropolitan Toronto. Community Review &
Research Group.
Social policies for planning in Metropolitan Toronto. Project staff: George
Nicholson, Barbara Woolley. [Toronto: The Council] 1976.
17 p. OTU
Social Planning Council of Metropolitan Toronto. Department of Research and
Development.
Lakeshore district social study, 1968. [Toronto] 1969.
2, 28 leaves. tables. OTU
— Social development study of northwest Scarborough. [Toronto] 1970.
40 leaves. map, tables.
Project director: Wilson A. Head. OTU
Social Planning Council of Ottawa and District. Needs and Resources
Committee.
A survey of the needs and resources for community supported health, welfare
and recreation services in Metropolitan Ottawa. Rapport d'enquête sur les
besoins et les ressources dans les domaines de la santé, du bien-être et des
loisirs à Ottawa, Eastview, Gloucester, Nepean. Ottawa: Social Planning
Council of Ottawa and District, 1967.
viii, 152, vii, 59 p. map, tables. OTU
Splane, Richard Beverley, 1916–
Social welfare in Ontario 1791–1893: a study of public welfare
administration. [Toronto] University of Toronto Press [c1965]
xiv, 305 p. tables. OTU
[Stapleford, Frank N]
After twenty years: a short history of the Neighbourhood Workers'
Association, 1918–1938. [Toronto: The Association, 1938]
58 [2] p. ports., tables. OH OTE
Strong, Margaret Kirkpatrick.
Public welfare administration in Canada. Chicago: University of Chicago
Press [1930]
xiii, 246 p. OTU
Sudbury, Ontario. Planning Board.
Development plan for Minnow Lake conservation area. Junction Creek
Conservation Authority. Sudbury, Ontario: Sudbury Planning Board, 1969.
26 leaves. illus., fold. plan, map. OONL

Temins, Irving D   1921–
The law of divorce and domestic relations in Ontario. [New ed. Toronto]
Primrose Publishing Co. [1966]
110 p.
First edition *a guide to the Ontario law of marriage and divorce.*   OONL
Thomson, Thomas M
The Spenser story. [Spencer Creek, Ontario: Spencer Creek Conservation
Authority, 1965]
60 p. illus., map.   OTUSA
Toronto General Hospital. Social Service Association.
Social service in the Toronto General Hospital, 1911–1949; a history of the
Association and an account of the growth and development of the Social
Service Department. Toronto: 1950.
55 p. front.   OTU
Toronto. University. Faculty of Medicine.
Memorials presented to the Board of Trustee of the Toronto General
Hospital concerning reorganization of the staff of the hospital: including a
comparative statement of hospital statistics and hospital regulations,
collected from various parts of the world. [Toronto] University Press, 1906.
83 p.   OTU
Touzel, Bessie, 1904–
The province of Ontario: its welfare services. [Toronto] Community Welfare
Council of Ontario [1954]
xi, 94 p.
No second edition located.
— 3d ed. revised by Donald F. Bellamy, Lillian Henderson, editor. Toronto
[Ontario Welfare Council, 1960]
xvi, 102 p.   OTU
— 4th ed. revised by Lillian Burke. Toronto: Ontario Welfare Council [1962]
xviii, 110 p.   OTU
— 5th ed. revised by Margaret Cragg. Toronto: Ontario Welfare Council
[1965]
xvi, 116 p. tables.   OONL
— Its social services. 6th ed. revised by Margaret Cragg. Toronto: Ontario
Welfare Council [1968]
xiv, 128 p.   OTU
— 7th ed. revised by Helen Palmer. Toronto: Ontario Welfare Council [1971]
xiv, 127 p.   OTU
— Welfare services in Peel county, 1954, and recommendations for their
development; a report to the Peel County Welfare Committee of a study
made of the welfare services in the county of Peel during 1954, with
recommendations for their development in order to serve the people of the
county more effectively. Final ed. Toronto: Ontario Welfare Council [1954]
iv, 87 p. tables.   OTU
— Welfare services in York county, 1963, and recommendations for their

development. A report to the York County Welfare Committee of a study
made of the welfare services in the county of York during 1963, with
recommendations for their development in order more effectively to serve the
people of the county. [Toronto: Ontario Welfare Council, 1963]
35 [16] p. tables.   OTU
Tremblay, Jules, 1879–1927.
    L'Hospital public d'Ottawa. Ottawa: Syndicate des Oeuvres sociales, 1921.
    23 p.   OKQ
Upper Holland Valley Conservation Authority.
    Our valley. v. 1, November, 1954. [Toronto] Ontario Department of
    Planning and Development. Conservation Branch, 1954.
    4 p. maps.
    Only one issue published.   OTMCL
Upper Thames River Conservation Authority.
    Avon valley plan, 1952. [London, Ontario: 1952]
    51 p. illus., diagrs., maps (part. col.) issued separately.   OTU
— Our valley. v. 1–3, 1952–1954. [Toronto] Ontario Department of Planning
    and Development. Conservation Branch, 1952–1954.
— 3 v. for the years: 1952; 1953; 1954.   OTMCL
— Twenty five years of conservation on the Upper Thames watershed
    1947–1973. [Stratford, Ontario] The Authority [1973]
    iii, 122 p. illus., fold. map, ports.   OLU
Wahn, Edwin Valentine.
    The integration of hospital facilities and services in the north western area of
    Metropolitan Toronto. Some recommended future developments based on
    the findings of a study conducted under the direction of the District no. 2 Ad
    Hoc Hospital Planning Committee. [Toronto: Metropolitan Toronto
    Hospital Planning Council, 1970]
    01–04 leaves. 21, lviii p. maps.   OTUH
Waterloo, Ontario. University. Ecology and Resource Management Research
    Group.
    Hilborn conservation area study; resource inventory, development and
    management of the site, Preston, Ontario. [Waterloo] Division of
    Environmental Studies, University of Waterloo, 1971.
    iii, 119 leaves. illus., graphs, maps.   OTU
Watson, Cicely, 1921–
    Qualified manpower in Ontario, 1961–1986, by Cicely Watson and Joseph
    Butorac, Department of Education Planning, The Ontario Institute for
    Studies in Education. [Toronto: Ontario Institute for Studies in Education,
    c1968]
    xx, 356 p. diagrs., tables.   OTU
— A summary: qualified manpower in Ontario 1961–1986, by Cicely Watson
    and Joseph Butorac, Department of Educational Planning, The Ontario
    Institute for Studies in Education. [Toronto: Ontario Institute for Studies in
    Education, c1968]
    30 p. tables.   OTU

Watson, Ervin Herbert Alfred.
    History, Ontario Red Cross, 1914–1946. Toronto: Ontario Division
    Headquarters [1946]
    ix, 91 p. front., illus., ports.   OTU
Welfare Council of Greater Toronto.
    A guide to family spending in Toronto, Canada, 1949. [Toronto, Welfare
    Council of Greater Toronto, 1949]
    57 p. tables.   OTU
Welfare Council of Toronto and District.
    Cost of living: study of cost of standard of living in Toronto which should
    maintain health and self-respect. Toronto: The Council, 1939.
    43 p. illus., tables.   OTU
— Rev. ed. 1944.
    32 p. tables.   OTU
— A plan for the reduction of juvenile delinquency in Toronto. [Toronto] 1943.
    28 p.   OTU
Wolfenden, Hugh Herbert.
    The real meaning of social insurance: its present status and tendencies.
    Toronto: Macmillan Company of Canada Limited, 1932.
    xiv, 227 p.   OTU
Zemans, Frederick H
    Community legal services in perspective. [Toronto] Osgoode Hall Law
    School of York University, 1974.
    vii, 237 leaves.   OTU
Ziegel, Jacob S   (ed.).
    Law and social change, by H.W. Arthurs and others. Edited by Jacob S.
    Ziegel. Toronto: Osgoode Hall Law School, York University [c1973]
    128 p. (Osgoode Hall Law School. Annual lecture series, 1971–1972).   OTU

Periodical Articles
Allward, Hugh L
    The planning of Sunnybrook Hospital. Royal Architectural Institute of
    Canada. Journal 26: 313–322, 1949.
Baxter, Ian F   G
    Family law reform in Ontario. University of Toronto Law Journal 25:
    236–280, 1975.
— The law of domestic relations, 1948–1958. Canadian Bar Review 36:
    299–332, 1958.
Bell, Frederick.
    Step towards the economic goal. Canadian Forum 23: 111–112, 1943.
    Ontario plan for hospital care.
Berry, A   E
    Milk control regulations in Ontario, 1936. Canadian Journal of Public
    Health 27: 504–510, 1936.

Bradbrook, Adrian J
    The role of judicial discretion in child custody adjudication in Ontario.
    University of Toronto Law Journal 21: 402–408, 1971.
Brown, W   Gordon and Charles Walker.
    Mental hospitals legislation in Ontario. University of Toronto Law Journal
    15: 208–213, 1963.
Burgess, T   J   W
    A historical sketch of our Canadian institutions for the insane. Royal Society
    of Canada. Transactions s. 2, 4(sect. 4): 3–122, 1898.
Case history on the Chest [editorial]. Canadian Forum 30: 100, 1950.
    Toronto's welfare problems.
Connor, E   S
    Medical services; Pickle Lake area. Canadian Mining Journal 70(no. 8):
    117–118, 1949.
Conservation programme begun in Simcoe county. Farmer's Advocate 79: 176,
    199, 1944.
Coventry, Alan F
    An Ontario experiment in the conservation of resources. Industrial Canada
    40 (3): 131–137, 1939.
Crayston, E   G
    A look at workmen's compensation. Canadian Mining Journal 85(no. 10):
    87–90, 1964.
Davison, J   F
    The problem of liquor legislation in Canada. Canadian Bar Review 4:
    468–482, 1926.
Dawson, Marshall.
    Ontario procedure in settlement of workmen's compensation claims.
    Monthly Labour Review 42: 1–9, 1936.
Defects in Ontario compensation act. Industrial Canada 15: 730–731, 1915.
Dunham, B   Mabel.
    Waterloo county house of industry and refuge. Waterloo Historical Society.
    Annual Report 35: 19–29, 1947.
Eberlee, T   M   and D   G   Hill.
    The Ontario Human Rights Code. University of Toronto Law Journal 15:
    448–455, 1964.
Forest conservation in Ontario. Industrial Canada 47(no. 11): 72, 126, 1947.
Fowler, Gordon.
    Entourage development and facilities. Royal Architectural Institute of
    Canada. Journal 26: 323–326, 1949.
    Sunnybrook Hospital.
Gibson, J   M
    The Children's Act. Methodist Magazine 39: 39–48, 1894.
Gilbertson, Forbes.
    The Don: an urban river struggling for survival. Canadian Geographical
    Journal 84: 62–69, 1972.

Gillis, Robert Peter.
The Ottawa lumber barons and the conservation movement 1880–1914.
Journal of Canadian Studies 9(no. 1): 14–30, 1974.
Govan, James.
The Hospital for Sick Children. Royal Architectural Institute of Canada.
Journal 28: 153–154, 1951.
Gray, K   G
The Mental Hospitals Act, 1935 (Ontario). University of Toronto Law
Journal 2: 103–113, 1937.
Green, Bernard.
Trumpets, justice and federalism: an analysis of the Ontario Training
Schools Act of 1965. University of Toronto Law Journal 16: 407–423, 1966.
Greenland, Cyril.
Services for the mentally retarded in Ontario, 1870–1930. Ontario History
54: 267–274, 1962.
Haffey, Helen.
Six cots and a prayer that becomes a famous children's hospital. York
Pioneer, 15–25, 1975.
Sick Children's Hospital.
Hall, Oswald.
The social consequences of uranium mining. University of Toronto
Quarterly 26: 226–243, 1957.
Hawes, Fred J
Apprenticeship and apprenticeship training. Royal Architectural Institute of
Canada. Journal 20: 162, 1943.
Hayley, Margaret A
Industrial noise deafness and compensation. Canadian Mining Journal
90(no. 9): 52–54, 1969.
Henderson, Nora Frances.
Child welfare in Ontario. Canadian Welfare 20(3): 28–29, 1944.
Hill, Daniel G
Human rights legislation in Ontario. International Conference on Social
Welfare. Report of the Canadian Committee 14: 95–99. 1968.
Hollis, K   E
Sunnybrook in operation. Royal Architectural Institute of Canada. Journal
26: 310–312, 1949.
Keirstead, W   C
Succession duties in Canadian provinces. Journal of Political Economy 30:
137–154, 1922.
Kenndey, W   P   M
Medico-legal developments in Ontario. University of Toronto Law Journal
5: 458–459, 1944.
LaBatt, C   B
Ontario Workmen's Compensation Act; provision abolishing actions at law.
Canada Law Journal 50: 201–204, 1914.

Laidlaw, John B
    What Toronto can do to relieve its depression. Canadian Club of Toronto.
    Addresses 33: 269–297, 1936.
Land and forest conservation and development in northeastern Ontario.
    Monetary Times 128(5): 82, 84–85, 1960.
Lavell, Alfred E
    The beginning of Ontario mental hospitals. Queen's Quarterly 49: 59–67,
    1942.
Lecours, Antonio.
    L'enseignement à l'hôpital sous l'assurance-hospitalisation en Ontario.
    Union Medicale du Canada 90: 515–518, 1961.
Legge, B   J
    Compensation and accident prevention. Industrial Canada 69(10): 18–19,
    1969.
Lemon, Charles.
    Historical comments on the origin and development of some of the laws of
    Ontario. Wentworth Historical Society. Journal and Transactions 4:
    98–108, 1905.
Love, John L
    The founding of St. Joseph's Hospital. Thunder Bay Historical Museum
    Society. Papers and Records 2: 4–11, 1974.
MacDonald, A   L
    Child trespassers. Canadian Bar Review 8: 8–25, 1930.
McIntosh, J   M
    A differential rating scheme for Ontario. Industrial Canada 37(no. 10):
    40–41, 1937.
    Workmen's Compensation Act.
— The Ontario Workmen's Compensation Act. Industrial Canada 35(no. 5):
    31–34, 1934.
McRuer, J   C   [et al.]
    Punishment of juveniles and young persons: being a report of a committee of
    the Canadian Bar Association appointed to review legislation on this subject.
    Canadian Bar Review 22: 585–597, 1944.
The Malton Convalescent Centre. Industrial Canada 50(no. 5): 140–142, 1949.
    Ontario Workmen's Compensation Board.
Manson, Freda.
    The Ontario Child Welfare Act of 1965. University of Toronto Law Journal
    17: 207–217, 1967.
Morrison, T   R
    "Their proper sphere" feminism, the family, and child-centered social
    reform in Ontario, 1875–1900. Ontario History 68: 45–79, 1976.
Murphy, E   P
    Sunnybrook Hospital, Toronto. Royal Architectural Institute of Canada.
    Journal 26: 309, 1949.

Nelligan, John P
Legal aid in Canada: existing facilities. Canadian Bar Review 29: 589–620,
1951.
— Legal aid in Canada: the need. Canadian Bar Review 31: 752–769, 1953.
Ontario. Department of Health.
The development of public health in Ontario. Canadian Public Health
Journal 26: 110–123, 1935.
Ontario adopts incentive plan for workmen's compensation assessment.
Industrial Canada 57(no. 10): 50–51, 1957.
The Ontario hospital insurance proposal. Canadian Forum 36: 266–267, 1957.
Ontario minimum wage rates. Canadian Textile Journal 55(no. 3): 23–24, 1938.
Ontario workmen's compensation. Industrial Canada 51(no. 10): 44–45, 1951.
Ontario Workmen's Compensation Act; already most generous Act in world –
no reason for increasing burden on industry. Industrial Canada 27(no. 10):
69, 1927.
Ontario Workmen's Compensation Act is international model. Industrial
Canada 54(no. 6): 58–60, 1953.
Parry, Judge.
Legal aid: a message from Ontario. Fortnightly Review n.s. 118: 626–633,
1925.
Philip, William.
The Grand River conservation scheme. Industrial Canada 43(no. 2): 50–51,
1942.
Pioneering family welfare in Toronto. Canadian Welfare Summary 15(3):
49–55, 1939.
Piva, Michael J
The workmen's compensation movement in Ontario. Ontario History 67:
39–56, 1975.
Pratten, J   S
Early history of the Rockwood Hospital. Historic Kingston 17: 50–68, 1969.
Recreational opportunities for workers. Industrial Canada 21(no. 1): 78–79,
1920.
Brantford, Ontario.
The Red Lake Memorial Hospital. Canadian Mining Journal 70(no. 8): 69,
1949.
Reed, T   A
The Toronto General. Calgary Associate Clinic. Historical Bulletin 9(no. 1):
13–18, 1944.
Report of the Committee on welfare. Industrial Canada 20(no. 2): 53–56, 1919.
Richardson, A   H
Conservation authorities in southern Ontario. Canadian Geographical
Journal 45: 86–103, 1952.
Sanders, Constance E
The Red Cross Society celebrates its 60th anniversary in Cambridge
September 9, 1914–September 9, 1974. Waterloo Historical Society. Annual
Volume 62: 51–63, 1974.

Sharpe, Frank T
    The outlook for the non-academic child. Social Welfare 12: 125–128, 1930.
    Big Brother Movement, Toronto.
Somerville, W   L
    Red Cross Lodge, Sunnybrook Hospital. Royal Architectural Institute of
    Canada. Journal 26: 352–355, 1949.
Stanford, E   N
    Ganaraska: a conservation blueprint. Canadian Business 17(7): 50–51, 130,
    132, 1944.
Supreme Court of Ontario decision on architect's liability. Royal Architectural
    Institute of Canada. Journal 17: 217, 1940.
Tompkins, George.
    A history of the Kitchener – Waterloo Hospital. Waterloo Historical Society.
    Annual Volume 52: 44–60, 1964.
Wallace, Elisabeth.
    The origin of the social welfare state in Canada, 1867–1900. Canadian
    Journal of Economics and Political Science 15: 383–393, 1950.
Wood, Alfred.
    The largest sick children's hospital in the world. Canadian Magazine of
    Politics, Science, Art and Literature 12: 314–318, 1899.
Workmen's compensation. Canadian Forum 1: 40–42, 1921.
Workmen's compensation; results are announced under the fourth year of
    operation of the Ontario act. Industrial Canada 20(no. 4): 116, 1919.
Workmen's compensation for injuries. Canada Law Journal 33: 135–136, 1897.

Theses
Bain, Ian William.
    The role of J.J. Kelso in the launching of the child welfare movement in
    Ontario. [Toronto] 1955 [c1976]
    185 leaves.
    M.S.W. thesis, University of Toronto (microfilm 25456).   OTU
Baker, Walter, 1929–
    The place of the private agency in the administration of government
    policies. A case study: The Ontario Children's Aid System, 1893–1965.
    Kingston, Ontario: 1966.
    iv, 344 [1] leaves.
    Ph.D. thesis, Queen's University.   OKQ
Bear, Murray Ross.
    The impact of social change on the organization of welfare services in
    Ontario from 1891–1921: the development, organization and administration
    of The Workmen's Compensation Act of 1914. [Toronto] 1966 [c1974]
    vi, 107 leaves.
    M.S.W. thesis, University of Toronto (microfilm 21377).   OTU
Bell, Marion M
    The history of the Catholic Welfare Bureau. [Toronto] 1949.
    iv, 122 leaves.
    M.S.W. thesis, University of Toronto.   OTU

Binsell, Raymond A
　A study of flood control and future development in downtown Brampton.
　[Toronto] 1971.
　vii, 45 leaves. illus., maps (part col.).
　B.A. research project, University of Toronto.　　　　　　　　OTU
Bissell, Muriel Dorothea.
　Group intervention in family relationships as exemplified by The Children's
　Aid Society of Guelph and Wellington county. [Toronto] 1938.
　156 leaves.
　M.A. thesis, University of Toronto.　　　　　　　　OTU
Blonde, Dolores J　1941–
　A client follow-up study of The Family Service Bureau of Windsor, by
　Dolores J. Blonde, Anne Murphy. Windsor, Ontario: 1975.
　vii, ix, 130 leaves. charts, tables.
　M.S.W. thesis, University of Windsor (microfiche 29115).　　　　　　　　OWA
Boes, Lillian F
　The Ontario Charitable Institutions Act and regulations as they affected
　Children's Institutions in 1949-1950. [Toronto] 1950.
　vi, 188 leaves. tables.
　M.S.W. thesis, University of Toronto.　　　　　　　　OTU
Bogue, Daniel Bernard, 1945–
　A socio-economic and attitudinal profile of general welfare assistance clients
　in Essex county, Ontario, by Daniel B. Bogue, Joanne Helper, Mara
　Pavelsons, Arthur J. Pope, Resela Shum, Joyce B. Timpson. [Windsor,
　Ontario] 1970.
　ix, 243 leaves. diagrs., tables.
　M.S.W. thesis, University of Windsor.　　　　　　　　OWA
Campbell, Sylvia Frances, 1917–
　The role of counselling in manpower policy: an exploratory study of selected
　Canada Manpower Centres in Ontario. [Toronto] c1976.
　v, 128 leaves. charts.
　M.A. thesis, University of Toronto.　　　　　　　　OTU
Carlin, William Francis.
　Flood control and the Thamesville area. London, Ontario: 1973.
　ix, 85 leaves. illus., graphs, map, tables.
　B.A. thesis, The University of Western Ontario.　　　　　　　　OLU
Cassano, Rosemary.
　Changing trends in the institutional care of the aged: a study of the
　institutional arrangements for the aged in the Metropolitan Toronto area
　with special reference to social policy development. [Toronto] 1965.
　iv, 118 leaves. tables.
　M.S.W. thesis, University of Toronto.　　　　　　　　OTU
Cresswell, Eric Graydon, 1938–
　The Canadian conservation movement and education in Ontario:
　1880–1914. [Toronto] c1972.
　106 leaves.
　M.A. thesis, University of Toronto.　　　　　　　　OTU

Davenport, Gwen.
  From Neighbourhood Workers' Association District Association to Social
  Planning Area Council – a study in change. [Toronto] 1962.
  92 leaves.
  M.S.W. research report, University of Toronto.   OTU
Dawe, Jane-Alice Kathleen.
  The impact of social change on the development of welfare services in
  Ontario, 1891–1921: "a historical study of the transition from institutional to
  foster care for children in Ontario, 1891–1921." [Toronto] 1966.
  iii, 185 leaves.
  M.S.W. thesis, University of Toronto.   OTU
Day, John Chadwick, 1936–
  The water balance of the Upper Thames watershed. London, Ontario: 1964.
  xi, 78 leaves. illus., tables, maps.
  M.Sc. thesis, The University of Western Ontario.   OLU
Eleta, Graciela Fermina.
  A study of the organization, adminstration and experience of the Home Care
  Program for Metropolitan Toronto. [Toronto] 1969.
  viii, 159 leaves. charts, tables (part fold.).
  M.Sc. thesis, University of Toronto.   OTU
Fields, Betty Penn.
  A study of the resident homemaker service offered by the Visiting
  Homemakers Association of Toronto. [Toronto] 1952.
  v, 215 leaves.
  M.S.W. thesis, University of Toronto.   OTU
Fiser, Vladimir.
  Development of services for the juvenile delinquent in Ontario, 1891–1921.
  [Toronto] 1966 [c1974]
  v, 233 leaves.
  M.S.W. thesis, University of Toronto (microfilm 21388).   OTU
Giles, Harvey A
  Counseling services for young people: a study of the Counseling Services for
  young people provided by some agencies in the area of Metropolitan
  Toronto. [Toronto] 1948.
  ii, 231 leaves.
  M.S.W. thesis, University of Toronto.   OTU
Gladstone, Arthur Leslie, 1948–
  An adminstrative analysis of the effects of the introduction of industrial
  therapy in Ontario Psychiatric hospitals, 1958–1974. [Toronto] 1976.
  iii, 267 leaves.
  M.Sc. thesis, University of Toronto.   OTU
Griffith, Joanne Lucy.
  An analysis of community action and legislation in the Ontario human
  rights field. [Toronto] 1964.
  vi, 164 leaves. tables.
  M.S.W. thesis, University of Toronto.   OTU

Hawthorne, Kevin.
   A method for conservation area identification: a case study of the Catfish
   Creek watershed. London, Ontario: 1974.
   vii, 55 leaves. maps, plans, tables.
   B.A. thesis, The University of Western Ontario.   OLU
Hunsberger, Wilson A
   A history of the Ontario county House of Refuge and industrial farm,
   Whitby, Ontario (now known as The Ontario County Home): the change in
   function of a County Home for the Aged (1903–1950). [Toronto] 1951.
   vi, 127 leaves. map, forms.
   M.S.W. thesis, University of Toronto.   OTU
Hutchison, Helen Lorraine Isobel, 1912–
   A study of the Napanee River Improvement Company (An analysis of the
   background, formation, functioning and decline of the Company, its
   significance in relationship to the economic development and conservation of
   the Napanee River valley and its watershed). [Toronto] c1974.
   viii, 179 leaves. illus., photos., facsims., map.
   M.Museol. thesis, University of Toronto.   OTU
Jain, Nilima P
   Aspects of juvenile justice in Toronto. Toronto: 1974.
   ix, 143 leaves. tables.
   LL.M. thesis, York University (microfilm 21548).   OTY
James, Helen Denison.
   The Scarborough branch of the Children's Aid Society of Metropolitan
   Toronto, 1958–1966; a descriptive study of the effects of decentralization on
   a Metropolitan Child Welfare agency in respect to the adminstration of
   services at headquarters and the provision of services by one branch.
   [Toronto] 1967.
   v, 112 leaves. tables, charts, map.
   M.S.W. thesis, University of Toronto.   OTU
Johnson, Leonard Naismith, 1915–
   The development of the Upper Thames River Conservation Authority.
   London, Ontario: 1964.
   ix, 99 leaves. graph, maps (part fold.).
   M.A. thesis, The University of Western Ontario.   OLU
Jolliffe, Russell.
   The history of the Children's Aid Society of Toronto, 1891–1947. [Toronto]
   1952.
   vi, 93 leaves. tables, graphs.
   M.S.W. thesis, University of Toronto (microfiche 31246).   OTU
Kenny, Wilma Loreen Gossage.
   The impact of social change in the organization of welfare services in
   Ontario, 1891–1921; adult correctional institutions in Ontario, 1891–1921.
   [Toronto] 1966.
   vi, 114 leaves.
   M.S.W. thesis, University of Toronto.   OTU

Kronis, Murray, 1935–
   Dental health policy in Ontario: perspectives of selected professional leaders
   and politicians. [Toronto] 1976.
   x, 134 leaves.
   M.Sc. Dent. thesis, University of Toronto.   OTU
Latimer, Elspeth Anne, 1920–
   Methods of child care as reflected in the infants' homes of Toronto,
   1875–1920. [Toronto] 1953.
   76 leaves.
   M.S.W. research report, University of Toronto.   OTU
Law, John Thomas, 1917–
   Present and future roles of hospital boards of trustees in Ontario. [Toronto]
   1974.
   vii, 126 leaves. tables.
   M.Sc. thesis, University of Toronto.   OTU
Law, Maureen Margaret, 1940–
   Measuring the impact of organized public health services upon a rural
   population. Part I – The Household Interview Survey. [Toronto] 1970.
   xv, 216, 45 leaves. tables, figs., maps,
   M.Sc. thesis, University of Toronto.   OTU
Leckie, Judith Margaret.
   Change process in a voluntary health organization. [Toronto] 1968.
   v, 113 leaves. tables.
   M.S.W. thesis, University of Toronto.   OTU
Lin, Jean, 1941–
   Older people in Kingsville, Ontario: a study of their arrangements, health
   and social relations, by Jean Lin, Phyllis Neilson and Clayton Purcell.
   Windsor, Ontario: 1972.
   xii, 203 [i.e. 202] leaves. illus., maps.
   M.S.W. thesis, University of Windsor (microfilm 14751).   Can
Little, Anna Lou.
   Fair accommodation practices in Ontario: a study of the education
   programme of the Ontario Human Rights Commission: an appraisal,
   1962–1964. [Toronto] 1964 [c1974]
   vii, 138 leaves. tables.
   M.S.W. thesis, University of Toronto (microfilm 20587).   OTU
McCuaig, James Donald.
   Administrative problems of the conservation authorities and the Rideau
   Valley Conservation Authority. Ottawa: 1972.
   I v. (various pagings). illus., maps.
   B.A. research essay, Carleton University.   OOCC
McFarlane, Malcolm Charles.
   Changes in services to recent immigrants by agencies in Metropolitan
   Toronto with emphasis on flexibility in adjusting staff and program to
   immigrant needs. [Toronto] 1967.
   v, 95 leaves. tables.
   M.S.W. thesis, University of Toronto.   OTU

MacGregor, James Robert.
  Charges in services to recent immigrants by selected agencies and institutions
  in Metropolitan Toronto... [Toronto] 1967.
  v, 54 leaves. tables.
  M.S.W. thesis, University of Toronto.   OTU
McKenzie, Betty Ann (Makar).
  The impact of social change on the organization of welfare services in
  Ontario 1891–1921; care of the poor in Toronto. [Toronto] 1966 [c1975]
  iv, 71 leaves.
  M.S.W. thesis, University of Toronto (microfilm 22340).   OTU
Marten, Garth, 1942–
  A study of service delivery in a low income area from the perspective of the
  residents. Windsor, Ontario: 1972.
  viii, 89 leaves.
  M.S.W. thesis, University of Windsor (microfilm 14760).   Can
Maunder, Barbara.
  Flood damage reduction in the Humber valley. [Toronto] 1969.
  29 [2] leaves. illus., maps.
  B.A. research paper, University of Toronto.   OTU
Memon, Pyarali Addulla.
  Conservation authorities as an institutional approach to water resource
  management in southern Ontario: a case study of the Grand River
  Conservation Authority. Waterloo, Ontario: 1970.
  181 leaves. diagrs., maps (part col.), tables.
  M.A. thesis, University of Waterloo.   OWTU
Morrison, Terrence Robert, 1943–
  The child and urban social reform in late nineteenth century Ontario.
  [Toronto] c1971.
  iv, 534 leaves. tables.
  Ph.D. thesis, University of Toronto (microfilm 27928).   OTU
Munro, Donald Richard.
  The care of the dependent poor in Ontario, 1891–1921: a study of the
  impact of social change on the organization of welfare services in Ontario for
  the dependent poor, especially the unemployed, the aged, and the mother
  raising children by herself, between 1891–1921. [Toronto] 1966.
  v, 171 leaves.
  M.S.W. thesis, University of Toronto (microfiche 31294).   OTU
Myers, Marion Patricia.
  Social policy in the Ontario mental health services 1948–1960 and the After
  Care Department of the Ontario Hospital, London. [Toronto] 1966.
  v, 157 leaves. illus., tables, graph, maps.
  M.S.W. thesis, University of Toronto.   OTU
Nichols, M   Doreen.
  The adoption practices of the Children's Aid society of Toronto in 1949. A
  study of the philosophy and practices of the Adoption Department of the

Children's Aid Society of Toronto for the year 1949, as these applied to the adoptive parent and the child to be adopted. [Toronto] 1950.
iv, 133 leaves. tables, charts.
M.S.W. thesis, University of Toronto.   OTU
Nicholson, Norman Leon.
A geographic study of the watershed of the Ausable River, Ontario. [London, Ontario: 1947]
vii, 165 leaves. photos, tables, maps (part fold.).
M.Sc. thesis, The University of Western Ontario.   OLU
O'Brien, Michael Terence.
Foster parent's responsibilities: a comparison of the views of the Catholic Children's Aid Society, Toronto, and the foster parents serving the Society. [Toronto] 1950.
iv, 75 leaves. tables.
M.S.W. thesis, University of Toronto.   OTU
O'Connor, Catherine J   M
The history of the Catholic Children's Aid Society of Toronto with specific reference to the changing functions of the Board of Directors from 1894 to 1945. [Toronto] 1949.
iv, 104 leaves.
M.S.W. thesis, University of Toronto.   OTU
Phetteplace, Helen Margaret.
The role of the volunteer in institutional arrangements for the aged in Metropolitan Toronto, with special reference to social policy development. [Toronto] 1965.
viii, 147 leaves. tables, charts.
M.S.W. thesis, University of Toronto.   OTU
Pollock, Shelia Joy, 1926–
Social policy for mental health in Ontario 1930–1967. [Toronto] c1974.
iv, 431 leaves. illus., map.
D.S.W. thesis, University of Toronto (microfilm 27949).   OTU
— A study of the impact of social change on development in the philosophy of child welfare in Ontario between 1891–1921. [Toronto] 1966.
viii, 139 leaves. tables.
M.S.W. thesis, University of Toronto.   OTU
Pope, Frances Louise.
The impact of social change on the organization of welfare services 1891–1921; social policy considerations in the movement towards workmen's compensation. [Toronto] 1966, c1974.
127 leaves.
M.S.W. thesis, University of Toronto (microfilm 19728).   OTU
Potts, Harold W
The lower Big Creek watershed. Hamilton, Ontario: 1950.
114 leaves. illus., maps (part fold.).
B.A. thesis, McMaster University.   OHM

Price, Gifford C
    A history of the Ontario Hospital, Toronto. [Toronto] 1950.
    vii, 141 leaves. photo.
    M.S.W. thesis, University of Toronto.   OTU
Prueter, Herbert John.
    Care and education of crippled children in Ontario. [Toronto] 1936.
    179 [1] leaves. map.
    D.Paed. thesis, University of Toronto.   OTU
Ramsey, Dean P
    The development of child welfare legislation in Ontario: a history of child
    welfare legislation in Ontario with particular reference to the Children's
    Protection Act, the Adoption Act and the Children of Unmarried Parents
    Act and subsequent amendments to these acts. [Toronto] 1949.
    v, 113 leaves.
    M.S.W. thesis, University of Toronto (microfiche 31315).   OTU
Risk, Margaret McNeill, 1935–
    The origin and development of public health nursing in Toronto from 1890
    to 1918. [Toronto] c1973.
    103 leaves.
    M.Sc.N. thesis, University of Toronto.   OTU
Rixen, Jean Ellen.
    Terra Cotta conservation area: a study of recreational planning. Toronto:
    1975.
    85 leaves. illus.
    B.A. research paper, University of Toronto.   OTU
Robinson, Mona.
    A study of re-opened protection cases in the Children's Aid and Infants'
    Homes of Toronto in 1953. [Toronto] 1957.
    iv, 65 leaves.
    M.S.W. research report, University of Toronto.   OTU
Rowat, James A
    River valley preservation: a case study of the lower Bayfield River valley.
    [Toronto] 1976.
    ii, 63 [2] iii leaves. map.
    B.A. thesis, University of Toronto.   OTU
Setter, William Keith, 1917–
    The geographic bases of the Kettle Creek watershed as a planning unit in
    regional development. London, Ontario: 1951.
    xv, 187 leaves. graphs (part col.), photos, maps (part fold.).
    M.Sc. thesis, The University of Western Ontario.   OLU
Sohn, Herbert Alvin, 1929–
    Human rights legislation in Ontario: a study of social action. [Toronto]
    c1975.
    xii, 406 leaves.
    D.S.W. thesis, University of Toronto (accepted 1976).   OTU

Spasoff, Robert Allen, 1942–
  Utilization and costs of medical care in the out-patient department of a
  teaching hospital. [Toronto] 1971.
  ix, 164 leaves. tables, figs., forms, map.
  M.Sc. thesis, University of Toronto.   OTU
Splane, Richard Beverley, 1916–
  The administration the Children of Unmarried Parents Act of the province
  of Ontario. [Toronto] 1951.
  v, 141 leaves.
  M.S.W. thesis, University of Toronto.   OTU
— The development of social welfare in Ontario, 1791–1893: the role of the
  province. Toronto: 1961.
  2 v. [ix, 461 leaves] tables.
  D.S.W. thesis, University of Toronto.   OTU
Tan, Kok Chiang, 1937–
  The river valley conservation authorities in southwestern Ontario. London,
  Ontario: 1962.
  xvi, 206 leaves. graphs, photos, tables, maps.
  M.A. thesis, The University of Western Ontario.   OLU
Wismer, John Dyment.
  Public assistance in Ontario, 1950–61 ... [Toronto] 1964.
  vii, 129 leaves. tables, graphs.
  M.S.W. thesis, University of Toronto.   OTU
Wood, David Melville.
  An investigation of the objectives of the conservation authorities of Ontario.
  [Waterloo, Ontario] 1972.
  156 leaves. maps, tables.
  M.A. thesis, University of Waterloo.   OWTU
Woogh, Carolyn May, 1947–
  A study of services in Frontenac county for children with emotional and
  behavioural problems: need, demand, provision and utilization. Kingston,
  Ontario: c1973.
  xi, 185 leaves. tables, figs., map.
  M.Sc. thesis, Queen's University (microfilm 16516).   OKQ
Wright, Edward Allan, 1943–
  Attitudes towards multiple use of conservation authority agreement forests: a
  three case evaluation. London, Ontario: 1972.
  xiii, 204 leaves. illus., maps.
  M.A. thesis, The University of Western Ontario (microfilm 12018).   OLU

SPORTS AND RECREATION

Monographs and Pamphlets

Argonaut Rowing Club.
Historical sketch of the Argonaut Rowing Club, 1878–1911. Toronto [Scott Printers, Limited] 1911.
36 p. ports. OTAR

Batten, Jack.
The inside story of Conn Smythe's hockey dynasty: a fascinating history of the Toronto Maple Leaf Hockey Club. Toronto: Pagurian Press; distributed in Canada by General Publishing Co., Don Mills, Ontario [c1969]
viii, 190 p. illus., ports. OTU

— The Leafs in autumn. Toronto: Macmillan of Canada [1975]
143 p. illus., ports. OONL

Bull, William Perkins, 1870–1948.
From rattlesnake hunt to hockey; the history of sports in Canada and of sportsmen of Peel, 1798 to 1934. Toronto: Perkins Bull Foundation [1934]
xxvii, 564 p. illus. (part col.), plates, port., map. OTU

Cahill, Leo.
Goodbye Argos, by Leo Cahill and Scott Young. [Toronto: McClelland & Stewart Limited, c1973]
226 p. illus., ports. OLU

Canadian Outdoor Recreation Research Committee.
The economic impact of parks. A report produced by the Canadian Outdoor Recreation Research Committee for the Federal Provincial Parks Conference. [Toronto: Ontario Research Council on Leisure, c1975]
1 v. (various pagings). diagrs., table. OLU

Capital District Recreation Planning Survey, Ottawa.
[Report. Ottawa: 1951]
viii, 168 leaves. maps, plans. OTU

Centennial sports review, Hamilton, Canada. Sports over the century, 1867–1967. [Ivan Miller, editor, Hamilton, Ontario: Published by Al Macfarlane Enterprises on behalf of the Centennial Sports Committee, 1967?]
184 p. illus., ports. OTU

Crone, Bertha F   M
Belleville Exhibition Park investigative report. [Guelph, Ontario] Centre for Resources Development, University of Guelph, 1970.
iii, 36 [14] leaves. tables. (Guelph, Ontario. Centre for Resources Development. Publication no. 15). OTU

Dunbar, Nancy J   (comp.).
Images of sport in early Canada. Images du sport dans le Canada d'autrefois. Introduction by Hugh MacLennan. Montreal: McGill–Queen's University Press, 1976.
95 p. chiefly illus. OTU

Edwards, Charles Austin McNally, 1917–
    Taylor Statton: a biography. With a foreword by J. Alex. Edmison. Toronto:
    The Ryerson Press [c1960]
    xiii, 161 p.
    "A pioneer in camping and recreation for youth" in Ontario.   OTU
Fischler, Stan.
    Go Leafs go! The Toronto hockey story. Photography by Dan Baliotti.
    Scarborough, Ontario: Prentice–Hall of Canada, Ltd. [c1971]
    140 p. illus., ports.   OONL
— Make way for the Leafs: Toronto's comeback. Scarborough, Ontario:
    Prentice–Hall of Canada, Ltd., [1974?]
    128 p. illus.   OONL
Frayne, Trent.
    The mad men of hockey. [Toronto] McClelland & Stewart Limited [c1974]
    191 p. illus.   OONL
— The Queen's Plate: the first hundred years. [Toronto] McClelland and
    Stewart Limited [c1959]
    168 p. illus., tables.   OTU
Hamilton, Ontario. Planning Department.
    Proposals on recreation for the city of Hamilton, 1971. Hamilton, Ontario
    [1969]
    v leaves. 83 p. illus., col. maps (part fold.), plans.   OONL
Hewitt, Foster, 1903–
    Hockey night in Canada: the Maple Leafs' story. [Rev.] Toronto: The
    Ryerson Press [1968]
    ix, 244 p. illus.   OTU
Imlack, Punch, 1919–
    Hockey is a battle: Punch Imlack's own story, with Scott Young. Toronto:
    Macmillan of Canada, 1969.
    203 p. illus., ports.   OTU
Jackson, John Nicolas, 1925–
    Recreational development along the Lake Erie shoreline; a study of
    contrasts and conflicts along the shoreline of Lake Erie in the Niagara
    region. Research commissioned by the Niagara Regional Development
    Council. n.p. [1967]
    241 p. illus., fold maps.   OTMCL
Lennox, Muriel, 1942–
    E.P. Taylor: a horseman and his horses. Toronto: Burns & MacEachern
    [c1976]
    192 p. illus., ports.   OTU
Lewington, Peter.
    The Armbro story: the Armstrongs of Ontario, their standardbred horses,
    super highways, hackneys and holsteins. Toronto: Burns & MacEachern
    [c1974]
    xiv, 204 p. [25] leaves of plates, illus.   OTU

Lindsay, W   Ford.
90 years of curling in Oshawa, 1882–1972. [Oshawa, Ontario] Oshawa
Curling Club [1972]
20 p.   OTAR
Litteljohn, Bruce M   (ed.).
Why wilderness. A report on mismanagement in Lake Superior provincial
park. Edited for the Algonquin Wildlands League by Bruce M. Litteljohn
and Douglas H. Pimlott. Toronto: New Press, 1971.
108 p. illus., maps.   OTAR OTU
Loranger, Philip J
Cowboy on ice: the Howie Young story. [Winnipeg: Gateway Publishing,
c1975]
169 p. illus., ports.   OONL
Luftspring, Sammy, 1916–
Call me Sammy with Brian Swarbrick. [Foreword by Gordon Sinclair]
Scarborough, Ontario: Prentice–Hall of Canada Ltd. [c1975]
195 p. illus.
"A well-known and loved Toronto personality."   OTU
MacCabe, Eddie.
Profile of a pro: the Russ Jackson story. Scarborough, Ontario:
Prentice–Hall of Canada Ltd. [c1969]
192 p. illus., ports.   OTU
Marshall, Herbert, 1887–
History of the Ottawa Ski Club. [Ottawa? 1973]
155 p. [18] leaves of plates. illus., maps, ports.   OTU
Metropolitan Toronto. Parks Department.
Metropolitan Toronto parks; a compendium, 1967. [Compiled for the
information of the members of the Parks and Recreation Committee by
T.W. Thompson. Toronto] 1967.
72 leaves. illus., maps, tables.   OTUSA
Nielsen, Robert F
Garney Henley: a gentleman and a tiger. Hamilton, Ontario: Potlatch
publishers, 1972.
173 p. photos.   OONL
Nowell, Iris.
Cross-country skiing in Toronto and southern Ontario. [Toronto: Toronto
Life, 1974]
63 p. illus., map.   OONL
Obodiac, Stan, 1922–   (ed.).
The Leafs: the first fifty years. [Toronto] McClelland and Stewart Limited
[c1976]
287 p. illus., ports (part col.).   OOA
O'Brian, Andy, 1910–
Daredevils of Niagara. Toronto: The Ryerson Press [c1964]
xvii, 134 p. illus., map, ports.   OTU

Ontario. Ministerial Inquiry into Violence in Amateur Hockey.
    Under the Public Inquiries Act, 1971 and Under the Athletics Control Act,
    R.S.O. 1970, chapter 35 Investigation and inquiry into violence in amateur
    hockey. [Toronto. Ministry of Government Services, 1974]
    40 p.
    Commissioner: W.R. McMurty.   OTU
— [Report. Toronto] Ministry of Community and Social Services [1974]
    51 p. port.   OTAR
— Proceedings, May 27–June 5, 1974.
    5 v. [i.e. 1256 typewritten pages]$e   OTAR
Ontario. Physical Fitness Study Committee.
    Report. [Toronto] 1961.
    iv, 137 p. chart.
    Chairman: Harry S. Price.   OTU
Ontario. Quetico Provincial Park. Advisory Committee.
    Report. [Toronto: Ministry of Natural Resources, 1972]
    10 p. maps. (part fold.).
    Chairman: S.G. Hancock.   OTU
— Public hearings and briefs. 1971.
    4 v.   OTU
Ontario. Task Force on Off-Track Betting.
    Report. [Toronto: 1972]
    2 v. illus., maps, tables.
    Chairman: A.R. Dick.
    Contents: v. 1, Report; v. 2, Appendices.   OTAR OTUL
— Submissions.
    39 v.   OTAR
Ontario Agricultural College and Experimental Farm. Department of
    Agricultural Economics.
    Fish and wildlife base of recreational resources. Co-operating agencies:
    Department of Agricultural Economics, Ontario Agricultural College [et al.]
    Guelph, Ontario: 1963.
    iv, 20 p. tables. (Background studies for resource development in the Tweed
    forest district, Ontario. Study no. 6).   OTU
Ontario Athletic Commission.
    Report, findings and recommendations. [Toronto: 1935]
    16 typewritten leaves.
    Commissioner: Chester S. Walters.   OTAR
Parkes, Agnes Elsie Marie.
    The development of women's athletics of the University of Toronto.
    [Toronto] Women's Athletic Association, University of Toronto, 1961.
    59 p. illus., ports.   OTU
Pearson, Norman, 1928–
    Planning for the North Georgian Bay recreational reserve, by Norman
    Pearson, consultant to the Minister of Lands and Forests of the province of
    Ontario. [Toronto?] 1965.
    79 p. fold. maps.   OTU

— The great get-away: the quest for outdoor recreation. [Guelph, Ontario]
    University of Guelph, Centre for Resources Development, 1968.
    9 leaves. (Publication no. 26).   OTU
Podmore, Percy St. Michael.
    A sporting paradise; with stories of adventure in America and the back-
    woods of Muskoka. Illustrated with drawings by Harrington Bird and from
    photographs. London: Hutchison, 1904.
    xii, 273 p. illus.   OTU
Proctor, Frank, 1870–
    Fox hunting in Canada and some men who made it. Toronto: Macmillan
    and Company, 1929.
    373 p. illus., ports.
    Title page missing.
    London Hunt and Country Club.   OL
Proctor, Redfern, Bousfield & Bacon.
    City of London parks and recreation study. Prepared for the Public Utilities
    Commission of the City of London. Toronto: 1964.
    ii, 85, 22, 4 leaves. diagrs., maps.   OTUSA
Project Planning Associates, Ltd., Toronto.
    Recreation and community development on the Canadian Shield portion of
    southern Ontario. [Toronto? 1970]
    2 v. illus., maps. (ARDA project no. 25068).
    Contents: v. 1, Concepts of a model recreation community; v. 2, The district
    of Muskoka and the town of Bala.   OTU
Reed, Thomas Arthur, 1871–1958 (comp.).
    The Blue and White; a record of fifty years of athletic endeavour at the
    University of Toronto. Toronto: University of Toronto Press, 1944.
    xiii, 319 p. illus. (part col.), ports.   OTU
St. Catharines, Ontario. Planning Area Board.
    Report on parks and recreational needs. [St. Catharines, Ontario: 1965?]
    1 v. (unpaged). maps (part fold.), tables.   OTUSA
Social Planning Council of Hamilton and District.
    Hamilton recreation resources survey, 1960. [Hamilton, Ontario: 1960?]
    100 p. fold. map, diagrs., tables.   OTU
Stevenson, John A
    Curling in Ontario 1846–1946. Toronto: Ontario Curling Association, 1950.
    xii, 272 p. front. (port.), illus., ports.   OTAR
Sudbury, Ontario. Planning Board.
    Nepahwin Lake study: a report on beach oriented recreational needs of
    neighbourhoods 2 and 3 which compose the community of Lockerky East.
    [Sudbury, Ontario] 1966.
    29 leaves. maps (part fold.), tables.   OONL
Sullivan, John Allan, 1893?–
    Red sails on the Great Lakes. Toronto: Macmillan Company of Canada
    Limited, 1955.
    ix, 189 p.   OTAR

Toronto. City Planning Board.
    Natural parklands in the city of Toronto. [Toronto] 1960.
    30 p. illus., fold. maps (part col.).   OTU
Toronto Golf Club.
    Fiftieth anniversary, 1876–1926. [Toronto: 1926?]
    [14] p. illus., ports.   OTU
Toronto's Island park neighbourhoods. [Toronto] n.p. [1973]
    1 v. (various pagings). illus., plan, tables.   OTUSA
Tourism Outdoor Recreation Planning Study Committee.
    Ontario recreation survey: survey documents. Toronto: The Committee,
    1973.
    [125] p. illus., map.   OTU

Background study to Tourism Outdoor Recreation Planning Study Committee
Kates, Peat, Marwick & Co.
    Tourism and recreation in Ontario: concepts of a systems model framework.
    Prepared for the Committee on Tourism and Outdoor Recreation Plan,
    province of Ontario. [Toronto] 1970.
    1 v. (various pagings). graphs.   OTU

Watson, Beriah André.
    The sportsman's paradise: or, The lake lands of Canada ... with illustrations
    by Daniel C. and Harry Beard. Philadelphia: J.B. Lippincott Company,
    1888.
    xii, 290 p. front., illus.   OTU
Way, Ronald L
    Ontario's Niagara parks, a history. [Fort Erie, Ontario] The Niagara Parks
    Commission, 1946.
    xvii, 349 p. illus. (part col.), col. fold. maps.   OTU
— 2d ed. [Fort Erie, Ontario] The Niagara Parks Commission, 1960.
    xviii, 299 p. illus. (part col.), fold. col. maps.   OTU
Welfare Council of Toronto and District.
    The recreation survey of Metropolitan Toronto; an inventory of facilities
    and programs in relation to population data. [Toronto] 1956.
    xxviii, 490 [4] p. maps, tables.   OTU
Williamson, C   Hillier.
    Omemee: Mississauga camp site to Ontario village. Peterborough, Ontario:
    Printed by A.D. Newson Co., Ltd., 1968.
    xii, 336 p. illus., ports., map.   OTU
Wright, J   R
    Guidelines to recreation resource goals. [Guelph, Ontario] Centre for
    Resources Development, University of Guelph, 1971.
    35 leaves.   OTU

— Planning for urban recreational open space: towards community-specific standards, by J.R. Wright, W.M. Braithwaite and R.R. Forster; research assistants, P.E. Niece and W.B. Sargant. [Guelph, Ontario]: Centre for Resources Development, University of Guelph, 1976.

ix, 143 p.   OTUSA

Young, Scott, 1918–

The Leafs I knew. [Toronto] The Ryerson Press [c1966]

204 p.   OTU

Periodical Articles

Baseball history. Western Ontario Historical Notes 8: 112, 1950.

Batten, Jack.

Toronto greets the Lions. Canadian Forum 44: 99, 1964.

Boggs, G   David.

The administration of a Great Lakes recreational resource by an agricultural municipality: a case study of Bosanquet township. Ontario Geography 1: 45–54, 1967.

Bond, James R

Queen Victoria Niagara Falls Park. Welland County Historical Society. Papers and Records 3: 9–16, 1927.

Carruthers, C

New Woodbine Race track, Etobicoke township, Ontario. Royal Architectural Institute of Canada. Journal 34: 459–468, 1965.

Cosentino, Frank.

Ned Hanlan – Canada's premier oarsman: a case study in 19th century professionalism. Ontario History 66: 241–250, 1974.

Fisher, D   M

Major Conn Smythe. Canadian Forum 29: 276–277, 1950.

Fraleck, E   B

Algonquin Park. Canadian Magazine of Politics, Science, Art and Literature 2: 294–296, 1894.

Gibson, Thomas W

Algonquin National Park. Canadian Magazine of Politics, Science, Art and Literature 3: 542–555, 1894.

Gray, Maxim T

The Niagara Parks Commission. Ontario History 49: 61–62, 1957.

Griffin, Justus A

Gather and keep. Wentworth Historical Society. Journal and Transactions 3: 5–8, 1902.

Acquisition of Dundurn Park by city of Hamilton.

Guillet, Edwin C

Old-time curling. York Pioneer and Historical Society. Annual Report 16–25, 1968.

Hallman, D   E
    Tourism and outdoor recreation in northwestern Ontario: an overview.
    Lakehead University Review 6: 52–72, 1973.
Hanley, Robert.
    A century of sport. Wentworth Bygones 9: 62–66, 1971.
Helleiner, F   M
    The Trent – Severn recreational corridor. Canadian Geographical Journal
    93(no. 3): 14–19, 1976.
Hunt, W
    Cricket in Canada: its progress, prospects and prestige. Ontario Agricultural
    College Review 23: 514–520, 1911.
Kummer, O   A
    Idylwild. Waterloo Historical Society. Annual Volume 58: 30–32, 1970.
Leitch, Adelaide.
    Wilderness park – Lake Superior. Canadian Geographical Journal 55:
    42–45, 1957.
Litteljohn, Bruce M
    Quetico country: wilderness highway to wilderness recreation. Canadian
    Geographical Journal 71: 40–55, 78–91, 1965.
Lutton, William.
    A place of quiet breathing. Canadian Magazine of Politics, Science, Art and
    Literature 45: 111–116, 1915.
    Muskoka area.
McKelvey, J   A
    A story of recent football at Queen's. Queen's Quarterly 35: 288–296, 1928.
Mallory, Enid Swerdfeger.
    [The Bruce Trail]. Canadian Geographical Journal 71: 192–201, 1965.
— Hiker's paradise: Ontario's Bruce Trail. Canadian Geographical Journal
    87: 11–19, 1973.
— The provincial parks of Ontario. Canadian Geographical Journal 75: 78–93,
    1967.
Mastics, A   A
    Canada's cup races. Inland Seas 27: 87–97, 1971.
Moyse, Les.
    Stokes Bay tourist and fishing centre. Bruce County Historical Society.
    Yearbook 31–34, 1969.
Newlands, T   J
    The history and operation of Hamilton's parks. Wentworth Bygones 9: 9–15,
    1971.
Parkinson, Matthew.
    Lake Timagami, a northern Ontario playground. Canadian Magazine of
    Politics, Science, Art and Literature 43: 167–172, 1914.
Pequegnat, C   D
    The Waterloo county Hall of Fame. Waterloo Historical Society. Annual
    Volume 60: 88–89, 1972.

Pickett, L   E
    Tug boat racing on Lake Ontario. Inland Seas 19: 305–307, 1963.
Roxborough, Henry.
    The beginnings of organized sport in Canada. Canada: an historical
    magazine 2(no. 3): 30–43, 1975.
Seagram, Joseph Emm, (1841–1919). Waterloo Historical Society. Annual
    Volume 64: 18–22, 1976.
Sifton, Clifford.
    Toronto hunt 1843–1931; Toronto and North York hunt 1931–1974. York
    Pioneer, 70–74, 1975.
Smith, J   Harry.
    September in Algonquin Park. Canadian Magazine of Politics, Science, Art
    and Literature 37: 27–32, 1911.
Squirrel, W   J
    A short history of the development of athletics at the College. Ontario
    Agricultural College Review 21: 171–177, 1909.
Tilt, C   R
    Provincial parks in Ontario. Canadian Geographical Journal 58: 36–55,
    1959.
Warner, Clarence M
    Some early amusements of the county. Lennox and Addington Historical
    Society. Papers and Records 1: 61–70, 1909.
Way, Ronald.
    The work of the Niagara Parks Commission. Royal Architectural Institute of
    Canada. Journal 20: 207–218, 1943.
Weiler, E   J
    Sports in Mildmay. Bruce County Historical Society. Yearbook 22, 1971.
Wolfe, Roy I
    The summer resorts of Ontario in the nineteenth century. Ontario History
    54: 149–160, 1962.
— Underdone Ontario. Canadian Forum 32: 105–106, 1952.
Yeigh, Frank.
    The Queen Victoria Niagara Falls Park. Canadian Magazine of Politics,
    Science, Art and Literature 39: 541–547, 1912.

Theses
Addison, William Stanley.
    A descriptive analysis of outdoor recreation in York county. Waterloo,
    Ontario: 1969.
    viii, 175 leaves. graphs, maps.
    M.A. thesis, University of Waterloo (microfiche 18117).   OWTU
Alexander, John David, 1944–
    Popularity of recreation sites in the Metropolitan Toronto and region
    conservation authority. London, Ontario: 1972.
    x,128 leaves. tables, figures, maps.
    M.A. thesis, The University of Western Ontario (accepted 1973) (microfilm
    14928).   OLU

Allard, Raymond Joseph, 1944–
  The effect of faculty sharing agreemments on the availability of arenas and
  gymnasia for physical education and recreation programs in selected
  southwestern Ontario cities. London, Ontario: 1976.
  xi, 107 leaves.
  M.A. thesis, The University of Western Ontario (microfilm 28162).   Can
Anderson, Duncan Mackey,1929–
  Public outdoor recreational land use with special reference to the river valley
  lands of the London, Ontario day-trip recreational zone. London, Ontario:
  1962.
  x, 201 leaves. illus., tables, plates, maps (part fold.).
  M.Sc. thesis, The University of Western Ontario.   OLU
Barrett, Frank Alexandeı, 1935–
  The recreation potential of the Niagara Escarpment. [Toronto] 1958.
  viii, 45 leaves. illus., maps (part fold.).
  B.A. thesis, University of Toronto.   OTU
Bilodeau, Gerald Claude.
  An analysis of the use of private aircraft for recreational purposes in Ontario.
  Toronto: 1971.
  xi, 114 leaves. illus., maps.
  M.A. thesis, York University (microfilm 10632).   OTY
Bird, Larry, 1945–
  Student support for the intercollegiate athletics programmes at the
  University of Western Ontario. London, Ontario: 1975.
  xvi, 139 leaves. tables.
  M.A. thesis, The University of Western Ontario (microfilm 24491).   OLU
Booth, Peter J   1950–
  An alternative approach for evaluation and planning urban public
  recreation facilities. London, Ontario: 1975.
  xiii, 198 leaves. graphs, tables, maps.
  M.A. thesis, The University of Western Ontario (microfilm 24497).
  London, Ontario is the urban area investigated.   OLU
Bourke, Kathleen, 1940–
  Lake Simcoe: explanation and pattern of recreational use. [Toronto] 1963.
  vi, 72 leaves. illus., maps (part fold., part col.).
  B.A. thesis, University of Toronto.   OTU
Bradford, John Douglas, 1934–
  Lambton county shorelines recreational access and ownership. London,
  Ontario: 1968.
  xi, 171 leaves. fig., tables, maps.
  M.A. thesis, The University of Western Ontario (microfilm 2172).   OLU
Brown, Ronald F
  The natural outdoor recreation resources of Muskoka; an approach to the

inventory and evaluation of outdoor recreation resources. Waterloo,
Ontario: 1968 [c1971]
vii, 156 leaves. illus., maps.
M.A. thesis, University of Waterloo (microfilm 7862).   OWTU
Buszynski, Mario, 1949–
A study to determine the capacity of Otter Lake to withstand recreational
development. [Toronto] 1973.
xiii, 128 illus., maps (part fold.).
B.A. thesis, University of Toronto.   OTU
Byles, A   Jack.
A survey concerning the employment of volunteer leaders in program by
recreative agencies in the Greater Toronto area. [Toronto] 1948.
v, 134 leaves.
M.S.W. thesis, University of Toronto.   OTU
Carscadden, Mark D
The Bruce Trail: its users – its use. Toronto: 1976.
x, 168 leaves. illus., maps.
M.A. thesis, York University (microfiche 30903).   OTY
Chowdhary, Radhakrishna L   1933–
An economic analysis of providing campsites in provincial parks. [Toronto:
1972]
xiv, 219 leaves. tables, figs., col. folder bound.
M.Sc.F. thesis, University of Toronto.   OTU
Coomber, Nicholas Hutton.
Characteristics of recreational day tripping in the Ottawa – Hull area.
Ottawa: 1971.
x, 224 leaves. illus., maps, tables.
M.A. thesis, Carleton University.   OOCC
Cornell, Sylvia J
A case study in park planning. [Toronto] 1970.
iv, 76 leaves. col. illus., maps.
B.A. thesis, University of Toronto.   OTU
Cox, Kenneth Wayne.
Preferred rural recreational landscapes in the counties of Waterloo South –
Wellington. [Waterloo, Ontario] 1973.
xiii, 172 leaves. diagrs., tables.
M.A. thesis, University of Waterloo (microfilm 27772).   OWTU
Delalis, Aristotle Jason, 1948–
Conditions of sewage disposal and their implications for selected recreational
lake districts of southern Ontario. [Toronto] 1973.
127 [11] 4 [16] leaves. figs., maps (part col., part fold., 1 in pocket).
B.A. thesis, University of Toronto.   OTU
— The impact of environmental constraints on outdoor recreation decision
making. [Toronto] 1976.
xiv, 243 leaves. illus., tables, maps.
M.Sc.F. thesis, University of Toronto.   OTU

Dempsey, William A
>   Relationship between governmental officials and citizens in municipal
>   recreation. The development of the recreation programme in the village of
>   Forest Hill. [Toronto] 1949.
>   iv, 104 leaves. fold. map.
>   M.S.W. thesis, University of Toronto.   OTU

Dinning, Michael, 1949–
>   The role of the government of Canada and the province of Ontario in the
>   implementation of The Fitness and Amateur Sport Act, 1961–1974. London,
>   Ontario: 1974.
>   xiii, 185 leaves. illus.
>   M.A. thesis, The University of Western Ontario (microfilm 20486).   OLU

[Dobson, Murray R   ]
>   Recreational planning in the Humber watershed. [Toronto: 1948]
>   [103] leaves. illus., maps (part col., part fold.).
>   B.A. thesis, University of Toronto.   OTU

Doerr, William Henry.
>   A study of the differential functioning of area planning councils with special
>   reference to the participation of public recreation personnel. [Toronto] 1963.
>   iv, 55 leaves. [2] p. tables.
>   M.S.W. thesis, University of Toronto.   OTU

Dufty, Gene M
>   Supervision and training of staff in camping: a study of the provisions for
>   supervision and training of staff in 1948 in thirty-three member camps of the
>   Ontario Camping Association. [Toronto] 1948.
>   x, 128 leaves. charts.
>   N.S.W. thesis, University of Toronto.   OTU

Edginton, Christopher.
>   A study of the relationships between management style and propensity for
>   risk-taking among leisure services personnel. Iowa City, Iowa: 1975.
>   150 p.
>   Ph.D. thesis, University of Iowa (microfilm 76-13,379).   DA

Eggett, David C
>   The Metropolitan Toronto Stadium Question? Analysis and discussion.
>   [Toronto: 1975]
>   i, 40 leaves. illus.
>   B.A. research paper, University of Toronto.   OTU

Fieguth, Wolfgang Wilfred, 1925–
>   The recreational land system of North Simcoe county, with special reference
>   to the authentic past as a recreational resource. London, Ontario: 1966.
>   ix, 157 leaves. illus., graphs, tables, maps.
>   M.A. thesis, The University of Western Ontario.   OLU

French, Harry Lionel.
>   A regional approach to planning outdoor recreational open space and its
>   application to Prince Edward county. [Guelph, Ontario] 1974.
>   vii, 173 leaves. fold. maps, tables.
>   M.Sc. thesis, The University of Guelph (microfilm 20909).   OGU

French, James Morgan Lewis, 1944–
    The demand for golf facilities as a function of income in southwestern
    Ontario. London, Ontario: 1968.
    xi, 128 p. tables, maps (part fold.).
    M.A. thesis, The University of Western Ontario (microfilm 2975).   OLU
Garland, John James, 1949–
    A study of the intramural sport programs in selected colleges of applied arts
    and technology in the province of Ontario, 1975–1976. London, Ontario:
    1976.
    xi, 138 leaves. tables.
    M.A. thesis, The University of Western Ontario (microfilm 28227).   OLU
Graham, Harold Colin.
    The rehabilitation of pits and quarries for multiple use recreation sites.
    [Toronto] 1976.
    163 leaves. illus.
    B.A. thesis, University of Toronto.   OTU
Gregory, Catherine Jane, 1948–
    Superstitions among male and female intercollegiate athletes and non-
    athletes of the University of Western Ontario, 1971-1972. London, Ontario:
    1973.
    xii, 181 leaves. tables.
    M.A. thesis, The University of Western Ontario (microfilm 14950).   OLU
Griffith, Charles Arthur.
    A study of municipal recreation personnel in Ontario with implications for
    continuing education. Bloomington, Indiana: 1969.
    229 p.
    Re.D. thesis, Indiana University (microfilm 70-01699).   DA
Hancock, Anne Eloise.
    Recreational land use on Trout Lake, Nipissing county. Ottawa: 1969.
    vii, 53 leaves. illus., maps.
    B.A. research essay, Carleton University.   OOCC
Hargrave, Mark Richard.
    Recreation on the shore of Lake Erie in Welland and Haldimand counties,
    Ontario. [Toronto] 1959.
    v, 69 leaves. illus., maps (part col., part fold.).
    B.A. thesis, University of Toronto.   OTU
Helleiner, Frederick Maria, 1933–
    A geographical interpretation of recreational waterways, with special
    reference to the Trent – Severn waterway. London, Ontario: 1972.
    xiii, 190 leaves. graphs, tables, maps (part fold.).
    Ph.D. thesis, The University of Western Ontario (microfilm 12887).   OLU
Helmsley, A   F
    Algonquin provincial park: a geographic study. [Toronto] 1949.
    i, 74 leaves. illus., maps (part fold., part col.).
    B.A. thesis, University of Toronto.   OTU

Innis, William Campbell, 1946–
    An analysis of organizational conflict and change in the Ontario – Quebec
    Athletic Association. Windsor, Ontario: 1973.
    xi, 132 leaves. charts, tables.
    M.P.E. thesis, University of Windsor (microfilm 19909).   OWA
Jarvis, John D
    A study of outdoor swimming facilities provided by Metropolitan Toronto.
    [Toronto] 1971.
    ii, 62 leaves. illus., maps (part fold.).
    B.A. thesis, University of Toronto.   OTU
Jones, John Russell.
    A geographical assessment of recreational facilities in the conservation areas
    of the Humber watershed. [Toronto: 1966]
    iv, 41 leaves. illus., maps.
    B.A. thesis, University of Toronto.   OTU
Joseph, Jacob R
    Probability models of outdoor recreation in Ontario. Waterloo, Ontario:
    1972.
    112 leaves.
    Ph.D. thesis, University of Waterloo (microfilm 10918).   Can
Kennedy, Margaret F
    Recreation for the aged. [Toronto] 1952.
    iv, 115 leaves. tables.
    M.S.W. research report, University of Toronto.   OTU
Laurendeau, W   Edward, 1947–
    Sport and Canadian culture in the border cities 1867 to 1929. Windsor,
    Ontario: 1971.
    iii, 108 leaves.
    M.P.H.E. thesis, University of Windsor.   OWA
Liddle, David Brian.
    The role of aircraft in recreational resource development. [Toronto] 1967.
    iii, 94 leaves. illus., maps.
    B.A. thesis, University of Toronto.   OTU
Lucas, Robert Charles.
    The Quetico – Superior area: recreational use in relation to capacity. St.
    Paul, Minnesota [1962]
    390 p.
    Ph.D. thesis, University of Minnesota (microfilm 63-04317).   DA
MacDonald, Wayne Peter, 1948–
    The perceived responsibility, authority and delegation of athletic
    administrators in Ontario universities. Windsor, Ontario: 1975.
    x, 96 leaves. graphs, tables.
    M.P.E. thesis, University of Windsor.   OWA
MacNeil, Ian Kenneth.
    Urban-oriented provincial parks and the Ontario park system. [Guelph,
    Ontario] 1974.
    v, 110 leaves. diagr., map.
    M.Sc. thesis, The University of Guelph (microfilm 20134).   OGU

Mancktelow, Anthony R   E
  Toronto Island Park: A study of park utilization. [Toronto] 1971.
  vi, 76 leaves. illus., maps
  B.A. thesis, University of Toronto.   OTU
Markle, Brian Rodney, 1939–
  A perception study of Canada's national parks system. London, Ontario:
  1975.
  xiii, 242 leaves. graphs, maps, tables.
  M.A. thesis, The University of Western Ontario.   OLU
Morrow, Leslie Donald, 1949–
  An historical study of the development of the intramural sports program at
  the University of Western Ontario 1878–1972. London, Ontario: 1972.
  xiv, 289 leaves. photos, tables.
  M.A. thesis, The University of Western Ontario (microfilm 12005).   OLU
Munro, Neil William Peter.
  An island oriented recreation resource analysis and planning approach as
  applied to the Thousand Islands area of Ontario. Ottawa: 1969 [i.e. 1970]
  viii, 163 leaves. graphs, fold. maps.
  M.A. thesis, Carleton University.   OOCC
Myles, Jack S
  The organization and administration of industrial recreation in Toronto.
  [Toronto] 1951.
  vii, 175 leaves. charts, map (fold.).
  M.S.W. thesis, University of Toronto.   OTU
Norquay, Margaret Madelaine (Dillon).
  A study of a community recreation council as an agent of social change.
  Toronto: 1950.
  393 leaves.
  M.A. thesis, University of Toronto.
  No copy located.
Pearce, David Ross, 1946–
  An analysis of the Ontario provincial park classification system, case study:
  Parry Sound, Ontario. London, Ontario: 1975.
  x, 145 leaves. maps, tables.
  M.A. thesis, The University of Western Ontario (microfilm 24636).   OLU
Phillips, Susan E
  Recreational preferences in lake planning: a survey of cottages and campers
  at Six Mile Lake, Muskoka, Ontario. [Toronto: 1975]
  136 leaves. map.
  M.A. research paper, University of Toronto.   OTU
Pincombe, Paul Glenn, 1942–
  Analysis of the recreational activities of urban adults: case study, London,
  Ontario. London, Ontario: 1969 [c1970]
  xv, 199 leaves. illus., maps.
  M.A. thesis, The University of Western Ontario (accepted 1970) (microfilm
  5779).   OLU

Pitters-Caswell, Marian Irene, 1952–
    Women's participation in sporting activities as an indicator of femininity
    and cultural evolution in Toronto, 1910 to 1920. Windsor, Ontario: 1975.
    194 leaves. graphs, tables.
    M.H.K. thesis, University of Windsor (microfilm 29223).   OWA
Purcell, John W   1946–
    English sport and Canadian culture in Toronto 1867–1911. Windsor,
    Ontario: 1974.
    vii, 102 leaves. graphs.
    M.P.E. thesis, University of Windsor (microfilm 23938).   OWA
Roberts, Gregory Alan.
    Classification of the recreation landscape of southern Ontario: a comparison
    of the techniques of factor analysis and analysis of extremes. Toronto: 1972.
    xi, 163 leaves. illus., maps.
    M.A. thesis, York University (microfilm 14065).   OTY
Romsa, Gerald Henry.
    The Kawarthas: a recreational study. [Waterloo, Ontario] 1967.
    xi, 118 leaves. graphs, maps, tables.
    M.A. thesis, University of Waterloo.   OWTU
Sargant, William Bell.
    Some relationships between recreation patterns and types of dwelling units.
    [Guelph, Ontario] 1974.
    viii, 192 leaves. tables.
    M.Sc. thesis, The University of Guelph (microfilm 20145).   OGU
Short, George Douglas, 1941–
    Sport and economic growth in the Windsor area 1919 to 1939. Windsor,
    Ontario: 1972.
    ix, 108 leaves. graphs.
    M.P.E. thesis, University of Windsor (accepted 1973) (microfilm 14785).
                                                                            OWA
Shulman, Rhona Francine, 1950–
    An investigation of the present state of recreational programming for
    children with specific learning disabilities in the city of Toronto. [Toronto:
    1975?]
    ii, 75, 4, 3, 3, 3 leaves. tables.
    M.A. thesis, University of Toronto.   OTU
Skrien, Terje, 1945–
    Physical activity and injury (sports injuries at the University of Toronto,
    1951–68). [Toronto] 1970.
    v, 278 leaves. tables (1 fold.).
    M.Sc. thesis, University of Toronto.   OTU
Smith, Ronald G   W
    Cottaging: an outdoor recreation resource study. [Waterloo, Ontario] 1974.
    ix, 335 leaves. tables, maps.
    M.A. thesis, University of Waterloo (microfilm 27775).   OWTU

Sproule, William James, 1948–
   Some transportation aspects of a sports stadium. [Toronto] 1973.
   [iv] 84 [21] leaves. graphs, maps, tables.
   M.Eng. thesis, University of Toronto.   OTU
Sullivan, Gary Vernon, 1943–
   Urban recreation: an overview; a case study of London, Ontario. London,
   Ontario: 1968 [c1969]
   x, 160 leaves. illus.
   M.A. thesis, The University of Western Ontario (accepted 1969) (microfilm
   3788).   OLU
Taylor, James Addison.
   The natural and cultural relationships of tourist outfitter's camps in
   northern Ontario. Urbana, Illinois [1962]
   188 p.
   Ph.D. thesis, University of Illinois (microfilm 62-06242).   DA
Thorsen, Sally Anne.
   Planning for regional outdoor recreation in its legislative and administrative
   aspects in the greater Metropolitan Toronto area . [Toronto] 1965.
   168, xxi leaves. diagrs., maps.
   M.Sc.(Pl.) thesis, University of Toronto.   OTU
Watson, Geoffrey G
   Sport and games in Ontario private schools: 1830–1930. Edmonton,
   Alberta: 1970.
   209 p. tables.
   M.A. thesis, University of Alberta.   AEU
Williams, Peter Wilder.
   A case study of industrial recreation in Kitchener – Waterloo and its role in
   urban recreational planning. [Waterloo, Ontario] 1971.
   xiii, 178 leaves. graphs, maps, tables.
   M.A. thesis, University of Waterloo.   OWTU
Wuorinen, Richard Frederick.
   The development of the parkland system in Middlesex county, Ontario.
   London, Ontario: 1976.
   viii, 85 leaves. graphs, maps, tables.
   B.A. thesis, The University of Western Ontario.   OLU